Y0-ARS-024

Business Executive's Handbook

Business Executive's Handbook

Edited by

STANLEY M. BROWN

Associate Editors

LILLIAN DORIS
EDITH J. FRIEDMAN
JOHN D. SMYERS
BERTRAND R. CANFIELD

Revised by

LILLIAN DORIS

SECOND EDITION
Revised and Enlarged

New York · 1942
PRENTICE · HALL · INC ·

First printing ....November 1936
Second printing ....January 1937
Third printing ......October 1937
Fourth printing ....February 1938
Fifth printing ....August 1939
Sixth printing ......January 1941
Seventh printing ......April 1941

SECOND EDITION
Revised and Enlarged

Eighth printing ....March 1942

PRINTED IN THE
UNITED STATES OF AMERICA

Preface to Revised Edition

In the revision of this book, a net addition of over three hundred pages has been made. Two new sections, one on Sales Management and one on Office Management, have been added. Throughout, in addition to such changes as time itself made necessary, there has been an amplification of the material to further the original object of saving the business man time and trouble by giving him reliable information in the most concise form.

The additions made to such sections as "How to Write Business Letters," "Purchasing," and "Credits and Collections" have been in the nature of ideas, practices, and procedures that successful business organizations have actually used and found profitable. The handbook thus becomes also a source book of profitable business ideas.

This revision was undertaken at a time when most of industry was passing through a transition from peacetime production to wartime activity. In spite of the burden that this change placed upon business executives, they were as ready as ever to give generously of their time in order to pass on to others details of methods, practices, and ideas that may prove beneficial to industry generally. We are deeply grateful for this wholehearted help.

PRENTICE-HALL, INC.

Preface to First Edition

The *Business Executive's Handbook* has been designed to provide, within the covers of one handy volume, direct and practical answers to the business man's questions and problems.

The information contained in the Handbook will be found to be specific and to the point. Forms, tables, short cuts, listings of facts, outlines of procedure—these will save the business man time, trouble, and expense. Whether the problem to be dealt with relates to Credits, Purchasing, Selling, Advertising, Insurance, Direct-Mail—to mention only a few of the subjects included—the Handbook supplies reliable information in the most concise form.

For assistance and advice in the preparation of the book, grateful acknowledgment is made to the hundreds of business men throughout the country who contributed very generously of their time and experience.

PRENTICE-HALL, INC.

Contents

(A detailed table of contents will be found at the beginning of each section.)

Business Executive's Handbook

SECTION I

Business Mathematics

1. HOW TO CALCULATE SIMPLE INTEREST

2. PARTIAL PAYMENTS ON DEBTS —RULES FOR COMPUTING INTEREST

3. HOW TO CALCULATE BANK DISCOUNT

4. SAVINGS THROUGH CASH DISCOUNT

5. HOW TO COMPUTE TRADE DISCOUNTS

6. HOW TO COMPUTE AVERAGES

7. HOW TO FIND THE AVERAGE DATE OF AN ACCOUNT

13. SHORT CUTS IN BUSINESS MATHEMATICS

Addition

Subtraction

Multiplication

Division

Fractions

14. EXPEDITING CALCULATIONS WITH PREPARED TABLES

15. VERIFICATION OF COMPUTATIONS BY CHECK NUMBERS

16. TABLES OF WEIGHTS, MEASURES, AND VALUES

17. MISCELLANEOUS HANDY TABLES

SECTION I

Business Mathematics

1. HOW TO CALCULATE SIMPLE INTEREST

What interest is.—Interest is money paid for the use of money. In interest calculations three factors are involved: (1) principal; (2) time; (3) rate.

The principal is the sum of money upon which the interest is paid—the sum loaned, borrowed, or invested.

The time is the number of periods for which the interest is paid. One year is generally considered as the unit period of time.

The rate is the percentage per period of the principal that is paid as interest. The rate is usually expressed as a certain percentage per year.

There are two kinds of interest:

1. Simple interest.
2. Compound interest.

If the interest is calculated on the original principal only, it is called simple interest. If, however, at the end of the first period of time, the interest for that period is added to the principal and the interest for the second period calculated on this sum, and this process is continued for the given number of periods, the interest is said to be compounded, and the total interest thus realized is called compound interest.

Legal and contract rates of interest in the states of the United States.—The rate of interest that may be charged is governed by state statute. The table on page 6 shows the legal and the contract rate in the various states of the United States. The legal rate is the rate of interest charged in the absence of express contract between the parties. The contract rate is the highest rate upon which parties may agree.

LEGAL AND CONTRACT RATES OF INTEREST IN THE STATES OF THE UNITED STATES

State	*Legal Rate, Per Cent*	*Contract Rate, Per Cent*	*State*	*Legal Rate, Per Cent*	*Contract Rate, Per Cent*
Alabama	6	8	Nebraska	6	9
Arizona	6	8	Nevada	7	12
Arkansas	6	10	New Hampshire	6	No limit
California	7	10	New Jersey	6	6
Colorado	6	No limit	New Mexico	6	10
Connecticut	6	12	New York	6	6
Delaware	6	6	North Carolina	6	6
District of Columbia	6	8	North Dakota	4	7
Florida	8	10	Ohio	6	8
Georgia	7	8	Oklahoma	6	10
Idaho	6	8	Oregon	6	10
Illinois	5	7	Pennsylvania	6	6
Indiana	6	8	Rhode Island	6	30
Iowa	5	7	South Carolina	6	7
Kansas	6	10	South Dakota	6	8
Kentucky	6	6	Tennessee	6	6
Louisiana	5	8	Texas	6	10
Maine	6	No limit	Utah	6	10
Maryland	6	6	Vermont	6	6
Massachusetts	6	No limit	Virginia	6	6
Michigan	5	7	Washington	6	12
Minnesota	6	8	West Virginia	6	6
Mississippi	6	8	Wisconsin	6	10
Missouri	6	8	Wyoming	7	10
Montana	6	10			

Note.—Rates are subject to change by state statute.

How to calculate the due date of an obligation.—The date of maturity of a loan or other obligation is determined by the wording of the obligation. For example, if, in a transaction on September 5, a debtor agrees to repay a loan in *four months,* the money is due on January 5. If, on the other hand, another obligation contracted on September 5 is by agreement to run 120 days, the repayment is due on January 3. In this case the exact number of days is counted in determining the due date because the time was stated in days.

How to calculate the time between dates.—There are two methods of calculating the time between dates:

1. Ordinary method.
2. Exact method.

Ordinary method.—In the ordinary method (sometimes called the "bond method") the year is considered as having 12 months of 30 days each, or 360 days. The time between dates is then calculated by subtraction, as illustrated in the following example.

EXAMPLE

Find the time between June 15, 1941, and August 3, 1942.

Solution

Years	*Months*	*Days*
1942	8	3
1941	6	15
1	1	18

The time between June 15, 1941, and August 3, 1942, is therefore 1 year, 1 month, 18 days, or 408 days ($360 + 30 + 18 = 408$).

The ordinary or bond method of calculating the time between dates is not commonly used except in interest computations involving long periods of time (usually a period greater than 1 year), and in the calculation of interest on bonds (other than United States Government and some municipal bonds). Where the period of time is short, businessmen and bankers generally use the exact method.

Exact method.—In the exact method of calculating the time between dates, the actual number of days in each month is counted. The first day (the day on which the obligation is incurred)is excluded, and the last day (the day on which the obligation terminates) is included.

EXAMPLE

A loan made April 17 is repaid June 26. For how many days should the interest be calculated?

Solution

Exclude the first day, April 17; include the last day, June 26. Then:

Number of days remaining in April	13
Number of days in May	31
Number of days in June to be counted	26
Total number of days	70

The interest should therefore be calculated for 70 days.

Where the exact number of days between dates is counted, it is the general practice of businessmen and bankers to exclude the first day and include the last day, as in the above example. However, in certain sections of the United States (and also in France, Holland, and some other foreign countries), it is customary to include both the first and the last days. If this procedure were followed in the above example, interest would be due for 71 days instead of for 70.

Short method of finding the exact number of days between dates.—The table below may be used as a short cut in finding the exact number of days between dates. The exact number of days between the corresponding dates of any two months is indicated on the line of the month of the beginning date, under the month of the later date. Thus, from any day in January to the same day in August, there are 212 days. In the table this figure is found opposite January, in the column marked *Aug.*

EXACT NUMBER OF DAYS BETWEEN DATES

From Any Day Of	To the Same Day of the Next											
	Jan.	*Feb.*	*Mar.*	*Apr.*	*May*	*June*	*July*	*Aug.*	*Sept.*	*Oct.*	*Nov.*	*Dec.*
January....	365	31	59	90	120	151	181	212	243	273	304	334
February...	334	365	28	59	89	120	150	181	212	242	273	303
March......	306	337	365	31	61	92	122	153	184	214	245	275
April.......	275	306	334	365	30	61	91	122	153	183	214	244
May.......	245	276	304	335	365	31	61	92	123	153	184	214
June.......	214	245	273	304	334	365	30	61	92	122	153	183
July........	184	215	243	274	304	335	365	31	62	92	123	153
August.....	153	184	212	243	273	304	334	365	31	61	92	122
September..	122	153	181	212	242	273	303	334	365	30	61	91
October....	92	123	151	182	212	243	273	304	335	365	31	61
November..	61	92	120	151	181	212	242	273	304	334	365	30
December ..	31	62	90	121	151	182	212	243	274	304	335	365

The following examples show how the table is used to measure the exact number of days between any two different dates.

EXAMPLE 1

A loan made June 10 is repaid August 17. For how many days should the interest be calculated?

Solution

From the table, June 10 to August 10	61 days
Add, August 10 to August 17	7 days
Number of days	68 days

EXAMPLE 2

A loan made October 16 is repaid March 13. For how many days should the interest be calculated?

Solution

From the table, October 16 to March 16	151 days
Deduct, March 13 to March 16	3 days
Number of days	148 days

Whenever February 29 of a leap year is included in the period for which the exact number of days is being calculated from the table, add 1 to the result obtained.

Ordinary and exact simple interest.—Ordinary interest is simple interest computed on the basis of 360 days to the year. Exact or accurate interest is simple interest computed on the basis of 365 days to the year.

Although ordinary interest is greater than exact interest, owing to the discrepancy of 5 days, the difference is not material except where a large principal and an extended period of time are involved. For example, ordinary simple interest on $500.00 for 90 days at 6% is only 10 cents more than exact simple interest. Since calculations are much easier on the basis of 360 days to the year than of 365, business houses and commercial banks generally compute simple interest on the basis of 360 days to the year, even where the exact number of days for which interest is due is counted.

EXAMPLE 1

Find the simple interest on \$2,000.00 from November 16, 1941, to April 8, 1942, at 6%.

Solution

In this case the interest period is short. The usual procedure would therefore be:

(1) Find the exact number of days between the dates.

(2) Compute the interest for this exact number of days on the basis of 360 days to the year.

From the table, the exact number of days between November 16, 1941, and April 8, 1942, is found to be 143. Then:

$$\text{Interest} = \frac{2000}{1} \times \frac{143}{360} \times \frac{6}{100}$$
$$= \$47.67$$

EXAMPLE 2

Find the simple interest on \$2,000.00 from December 16, 1941, to February 10, 1943, at 6%.

Solution

In this case the interest period is long. The usual procedure would therefore be:

(1) Find the number of days between the dates by assuming 30 days in each month.

(2) Using this number of days, compute the interest on the basis of 360 days to the year.

Years	*Months*	*Days*
1943	2	10
1941	12	16
1	1	24

At 30 days to each month, 1 year, 1 month, 24 days is 414 days. Then:

$$\text{Interest} = \frac{2000}{1} \times \frac{414}{360} \times \frac{6}{100}$$
$$= \$138.00$$

How to use short methods of calculating ordinary interest at 6%: *Sixty-day method.*—At 6% per year:

Interest on	$1.00	for	360	days	is $.06
"	"	"	60	"	.01 (1/6 of $.06)
"	"	"	6	"	.001 (1/10 of $.01)

It is evident that interest on $1.00 for 6 days at 6% may be computed by moving the decimal point in the principal three places to the left. If this is true of $1.00, it is true of any principal, and a general rule may be stated as follows: Given any principal, to find the interest at 6%:

For	6 days,	point off	three	places	to the left
	60 "	"	two	"	"
	600 "	"	one	place	"
	6,000 "	the interest is the same as the principal			

Thus:

Interest on	$1,280.00	for	6 days	at 6% is $	1.28
"	"	"	60 "	"	12.80
"	"	"	600 "	"	128.00
"	"	"	6,000 "	"	1,280.00

In calculating the interest at 6% on any principal for any number of days, the time, stated in days, may be separated into parts that are multiples or fractions of 6, 60, 600, or 6,000, and the computations are greatly simplified.

EXAMPLE 1

Find the ordinary interest on $760.00 for 15 days at 6%.

Solution

Interest for 60 days = $7.60
" " 15 " = $7.60 ÷ 4
= $1.90

Explanation.—Pointing off two places in the principal gives the interest for 60 days. Fifteen days is ¼ of 60 days. Hence divide the interest for 60 days by 4.

EXAMPLE 2

Find the ordinary interest on $842.60 for 124 days at 6%.

Solution

Interest for	60	days	=	$ 8.4260
" "	60	"	=	8.4260
" "	4	"	=	.5617
" "	124	"	=	$17.4137, or $17.41

Explanation.—Sixty days plus 60 days plus 4 days equals 124 days. The interest for the 4 days is found by pointing off three places in the principal (which gives the interest for 6 days) and then multiplying this figure by $\frac{2}{3}$, since 4 days is $\frac{2}{3}$ of 6 days.

EXAMPLE 3

Find the ordinary interest on $754.90 for 137 days at 6%.

Solution

Interest for	60	days	=	$ 7.5490
" "	60	"	=	7.5490
" "	12	"	=	1.5098
" "	5	"	=	.6290
" "	137	"	=	$17.2368, or $17.24

Explanation.—Pointing off two decimal places gives the interest for 60 days. Double this to find the interest for 120 days. Twelve days is $\frac{1}{5}$ of 60 days; therefore, the interest for 12 days is $\frac{1}{5}$ of 60-days' interest, or $1.5098. Five days is $\frac{1}{12}$ of 60 days, and the interest is $\frac{1}{12}$ of $7.5490, or $0.629. The sum, $17.24, is the interest for 137 days.

One-day or product method.—The one-day or product method is convenient where the number of days for which ordinary interest is being calculated cannot be readily divided into fractions or multiples of 6, 60, 600, or 6,000. To find the ordinary interest on any principal at 6% by this method:

1. Point off three decimal places in the principal; this gives the interest for 6 days.
2. Multiply the figure found in (1) by the number of days for which the interest is being calculated; this gives the interest for 6 times the number of days required.
3. Divide the result by 6.

EXAMPLE

Find the ordinary interest on $137.65 for 77 days at 6%.

Solution

$.13765, interest for 6 days
77
.96355
9.6355
$10.59905, interest for 6 × 77 days
$10.59905 ÷ 6 = $1.7665, or $1.77, interest for 77 days

Interchange of principal and number of days.—Where the principal is a factor or multiple of 6, the calculation of ordinary interest at 6% can be shortened by interchanging the principal and the number of days. Thus, finding 6% interest on $120.00 for 187 days is the same as finding 6% interest on $187.00 for 120 days. Six per cent interest on $187.00 for 60 days is $1.87, obtained by moving the decimal point two places to the left. Six per cent interest on $187.00 for 120 days is twice $1.87, or $3.74. The interest on $120.00 for 187 days at 6% is, therefore, $3.74.

How to use a short method of calculating ordinary interest at a rate other than 6%.—To find the ordinary interest at a rate other than 6%:

1. First find the interest at 6% by one of the methods described in the preceding pages.
2. Adjust the result by adding to or subtracting from the interest computed at 6%, the fractional part thereof that the specified rate is greater or less than the 6% rate.

For 3%, decrease the interest by ½ of the amount computed at 6%
4%, " " " ⅓ " " " "
4½%, " " " ¼ " " " "
5%, " " " ⅙ " " " "
5½%, " " " 1/12 " " " "
7%, increase the interest by ⅙ " " " "
7½%, " " " ¼ " " " "
8%, " " " ⅓ " " " "
8½%, " " " 5/12 " " " "
9%, " " " ½ " " " "

EXAMPLE

Find the ordinary interest on \$380.00 for 90 days at $4\frac{1}{2}\%$.

Solution

(1) First calculate the interest at 6%.

Interest	for	60	days	= \$3.80
"	"	30	"	= 1.90
"	"	90	"	= \$5.70

(2) The interest at 6% is \$5.70. To find the interest at $4\frac{1}{2}\%$, deduct $\frac{1}{4}$ of \$5.70. \$5.70 ÷ 4 = \$1.43. \$5.70 — \$1.43 = \$4.27, the interest on \$380.00 for 90 days at $4\frac{1}{2}\%$.

The cancellation method.—The cancellation method may be used to advantage in many interest calculations, especially in those having odd or fractional rates.

EXAMPLE

Find the ordinary interest on \$345.75 for 90 days at $4\frac{1}{2}\%$.

Solution

$$\frac{345.75 \times \overset{3}{\cancel{90}} \times .09}{\underset{4}{\cancel{12}} \times \cancel{30} \times 2} = \frac{31.1175}{8}$$
$$= \$3.889, \text{ or } \$3.89$$

Divisors for rates of interest.—Find the interest by multiplying the principal by the number of days and dividing by the divisor shown in the table for the rate of interest to be applied. When the principal contains cents, point off four places from the right of the result. When the principal contains only dollars, point off two places. The use of the divisor saves one operation. Thus, instead of multiplying the product of the principal times the number of days by .06, and dividing by 360, to determine interest at 6%, the product mentioned is divided immediately by 60, the divisor for 6%.

EXAMPLE

Find the interest on \$625.24 for 39 days at 4%.

Solution

Multiply the principal by the days: $625.24 × 39 = $2438436. Then divide the product by the general divisor for 4%, and point off four places. 2438436 ÷ 90 = $2.71.

DIVISORS FOR RATES OF INTEREST

For			
For 2%,	divide	by	180
$2\frac{1}{2}$%,	"	"	144
3%,	"	"	120
$3\frac{1}{2}$%,	"	"	102.86
4%,	"	"	90
5%,	"	"	72
6%,	"	"	60
7%,	"	"	51.43
8%,	"	"	45
9%,	"	"	40
10%,	"	"	36
12%,	"	"	30
15%,	"	"	24

How to use a short method of calculating exact interest.—The simplest method of calculating exact interest (that is, interest on the basis of 365 days to the year) is the following:

1. Calculate the ordinary (360-day) interest by one of the short methods described in the preceding pages.
2. Adjust the result to exact interest by deducting from the ordinary interest $\frac{1}{73}$ of itself (because the difference of 5 days is $\frac{1}{73}$ of 365).

EXAMPLE

Find the exact interest on $60,000.00 for 56 days at 6%.

Solution

(1) The ordinary interest is found to be $560.00.
(2) To find the exact interest, deduct from $560.00 $\frac{1}{73}$ of $560.00, or $7.67. The exact interest on $60,000.00 for 56 days at 6% is, then, $560.00 — $7.67, or $552.33.

Exact interest table.—The table on page 16 gives the interest on $100 (computed on the basis of 365 days to the year) for 1 day to 100 days at various rates of interest. From the table the interest accruing for other sums and for any other number of days can be easily calculated.

EXAMPLE

Compute the interest on $920 for 22 days at 4%.

Solution

Interest on $100 for 20 days at 4% (from table) ..	.219179
" " " " 2 " at 4% (from table) ..	.021918
" " " " 22 "	.241
Multiply by 9.2 ($920 is 9.2 times $100)	9.2
	482
	2169
Interest on $920 for 22 days at 4%	$2.2172, or $2.22

(*Note:* On sums of less than $1,000, the last three digits can be dropped [being careful to increase the last remaining digit by 1 where the digits dropped are more than one-half—thus: .021918 became .022]).

EXACT INTEREST TABLE

Interest on $100 at Various Rates for Various Periods of Time

Days	2%	3%	4%	5%	6%
1	.005479	.008220	.010959	.013699	.016438
2	.010959	.016439	.021918	.027397	.032877
3	.016438	.024658	.032877	.041096	.049315
4	.021918	.032877	.043836	.054795	.065753
5	.027397	.041096	.054795	.068493	.082192
6	.032877	.049315	.065754	.082192	.098630
7	.038356	.057534	.076712	.095890	.115068
8	.043836	.065753	.087671	.109589	.131507
9	.049315	.073973	.098630	.123288	.147945
10	.054795	.082192	.109589	.136986	.164384
20	.109589	.164384	.219179	.273973	.328767
30	.164384	.246576	.328768	.410959	.493151
40	.219178	.328768	.438357	.547945	.657534
50	.273973	.410959	.547946	.684932	.821918
60	.328767	.493151	.657536	.821918	.986301
70	.383562	.575342	.767125	.958904	1.150685
80	.438356	.657534	.876714	1.095890	1.315068
90	.493151	.739726	.986304	1.232877	1.479452
100	.547945	.821918	1.095893	1.369863	1.643836

Use of interest tables.—Where calculations in simple interest have to be made very frequently, much time can be saved by the use of a book of interest tables, from which the desired information is obtainable at a glance. In Figure 1 is reproduced a section of one page from the "Delbridge 6% Interest Computer," published by the Delbridge Company, 206 Walnut Street, St. Louis, Missouri. In this volume one page is devoted to each day in the year, and the principal on which interest is computed—on the basis of 360 days to the year—ranges from \$0.01 to \$200,000.00. Similar tables are available showing simple interest on the basis of 365 days to the year. The same company also publishes volumes of interest tables for rates other than 6% and various small-size books of interest tables.

		9 MONTHS AND 17 DAYS.						6 % Interest; on basis of 360 days to a year. 287									
1¢	\$0 00	1	05	101	4 83	201	9 61	301	14 40	401	19 18	501	23 96	601	28 75	701	33 58
2¢	00	2	10	102	4 88	202	9 66	302	14 45	402	19 23	502	24 01	602	28 80	702	33 58
3¢	00	3	14	103	4 93	203	9 71	303	14 49	403	19 28	503	24 06	603	28 84	703	33 68
4¢	00	4	19	104	4 97	204	9 76	304	14 54	404	19 32	504	24 11	604	28 89	704	33 67
5¢	00	5	24	105	5 02	205	9 81	305	14 59	405	19 37	505	24 16	605	28 94	705	33 72
6¢	00	6	29	106	5 07	206	9 85	306	14 64	406	19 42	506	24 20	606	28 99	706	33 77
7¢	00	7	33	107	5 12	207	9 90	307	14 68	407	19 47	507	24 25	607	29 03	707	33 82
8¢	00	8	38	108	5 17	208	9 95	308	14 73	408	19 52	508	24 30	608	29 08	708	33 87
9¢	00	9	43	109	5 21	209	10 00	309	14 78	409	19 56	509	24 35	609	29 13	709	33 91
10¢	00	10	48	110	5 26	210	10 04	310	14 83	410	19 61	510	24 39	610	29 18	710	33 96
11¢	01	11	53	111	5 31	211	10 09	311	14 88	411	19 66	511	24 44	611	29 23	711	34 01
12¢	01	12	57	112	5 36	212	10 14	312	14 92	412	19 71	512	24 49	612	29 27	712	34 06
13¢	01	13	62	113	5 41	213	10 19	313	14 97	413	19 76	513	24 54	613	29 32	713	34 11
14¢	01	14	67	114	5 45	214	10 24	314	15 02	414	19 80	514	24 59	614	29 37	714	34 15
15¢	01	15	72	115	5 50	215	10 28	315	15 07	415	19 85	515	24 63	615	29 42	715	34 20
16¢	01	16	77	116	5 55	216	10 33	316	15 12	416	19 90	516	24 68	616	29 47	716	34 25
17¢	01	17	81	117	5 60	217	10 38	317	15 16	417	19 95	517	24 73	617	29 51	717	34 30
18¢	01	18	86	118	5 64	218	10 43	318	15 21	418	19 99	518	24 78	618	29 56	718	34 34
19¢	01	19	91	119	5 69	219	10 48	319	15 26	419	20 04	519	24 83	619	29 61	719	34 39
20¢	01	20	96	120	5 74	220	10 52	320	15 31	420	20 09	520	24 87	620	29 66	720	34 44
21¢	01	21	1 00	121	5 79	221	10 57	321	15 35	421	20 14	521	24 92	621	29 70	721	34 49
22¢	01	22	1 05	122	5 84	222	10 62	322	15 40	422	20 19	522	24 97	622	29 75	722	34 54
23¢	01	23	1 10	123	5 88	223	10 67	323	15 45	423	20 23	523	25 02	623	29 80	723	34 58
24¢	01	24	1 15	124	5 93	224	10 71	324	15 50	424	20 28	524	25 06	624	29 85	724	34 63
25¢	01	25	1 20	125	5 98	225	10 76	325	15 55	425	20 33	525	25 11	625	29 90	725	34 68
26¢	01	26	1 24	126	6 03	226	10 81	326	15 59	426	20 38	526	25 16	626	29 94	726	34 73
27¢	01	27	1 29	127	6 07	227	10 86	327	15 64	427	20 42	527	25 21	627	29 99	727	34 77
28¢	01	28	1 34	128	6 12	228	10 91	328	15 69	428	20 47	528	25 26	628	30 04	728	34 82
29¢	01	29	1 39	129	6 17	229	10 95	329	15 74	429	20 52	529	25 30	629	30 09	729	34 87
30¢	01	30	1 43	130	6 22	230	11 00	330	15 78	430	20 57	530	25 35	630	30 13	730	34 92
31¢	01	31	1 48	131	6 27	231	11 05	331	15 83	431	20 62	531	25 40	631	30 18	731	34 97
32¢	02	32	1 53	132	6 31	232	11 10	332	15 88	432	20 66	532	25 45	632	30 23	732	35 01
33¢	02	33	1 58	133	6 36	233	11 15	333	15 93	433	20 71	533	25 50	633	30 28	733	35 06
34¢	02	34	1 63	134	6 41	234	11 19	334	15 98	434	20 76	534	25 54	634	30 33	734	35 11
35¢	02	35	1 67	135	6 46	235	11 24	335	16 02	435	20 81	535	25 59	635	30 37	735	35 16
36¢	02	36	1 72	136	6 51	236	11 29	336	16 07	436	20 86	536	25 64	636	30 42	736	35 21
37¢	02	37	1 77	137	6 55	237	11 34	337	16 12	437	20 90	537	25 69	637	30 47	737	35 25
38¢	02	38	1 82	138	6 60	238	11 38	338	16 17	438	20 95	538	25 73	638	30 52	738	35 30
39¢	02	39	1 87	139	6 65	239	11 43	339	16 22	439	21 00	539	25 78	639	30 57	739	35 35
40¢	02	40	1 91	140	6 70	240	11 48	340	16 26	440	21 05	540	25 83	640	30 61	740	35 40
41¢	02	41	1 96	141	6 74	241	11 53	341	16 31	441	21 09	541	25 88	641	30 66	741	35 44
42¢	02	42	2 01	142	6 79	242	11 58	342	16 36	442	21 14	542	25 93	642	30 71	742	35 49
43¢	02	43	2 06	143	6 84	243	11 62	343	16 41	443	21 19	543	25 97	643	30 76	743	35 54
44¢	02	44	2 10	144	6 89	244	11 67	344	16 45	444	21 24	544	26 02	644	30 80	744	35 59

Figure 1.—Page from the Delbridge 6% Interest Computer.

In the excerpt from one page of the "Delbridge 6% Interest Computer," the numbers in boldface type represent principal, while the numbers in lightface represent the corresponding interest for 287 days at 6%. The following example illustrates the use of these tables.

EXAMPLE

Find the ordinary interest on $328.36 for 287 days at 6%.

Solution

The amount in the table, opposite the boldface number 328, is $15.69. The amount opposite 36¢ is $0.02. The sum of the two amounts, $15.69 and $0.02, or $15.71, is the ordinary interest on $328.36 for 287 days at 6%.

Periodic interest.—Periodic interest is simple interest on the principal, plus simple interest on each installment of interest that is not paid when due.

EXAMPLE

Find the periodic interest on a loan of $5,000.00 for 1 year and 6 months at 6%, interest due quarterly; no interest paid until the maturity of the loan.

Solution

Simple interest on $5,000.00 for 3 months			$ 75.00
Multiply by (number of quarterly periods)			6
Total simple interest			$450.00
First quarterly interest is unpaid	15	months	
Last " " " "	0	"	
Average	$7\frac{1}{2}$	"	
Multiply by (number of periods)	6		
Total	45	"	
Interest on $75 for 45 months			16.88
Total periodic interest			$466.88

2. PARTIAL PAYMENTS ON DEBTS—RULES FOR COMPUTING INTEREST

Adapted from Curtis and Cooper, "Mathematics of Accounting" New York: Prentice-Hall, Inc.

A debtor who owes a large amount may by agreement make equal or unequal payments on the principal at regular or irregular intervals.

The creditor should have interest on the loan, and it is only fair that each payment made should draw interest in favor of the debtor.

There are two methods of applying these payments of principal and interest to the reduction of the debt. The method adopted by the Supreme Court of the United States is termed the "United States Rule"; the other method, which is widely used by businessmen, is termed the "Merchants' Rule."

United States Rule.—The United States Rule is now a law in most states, having been made so either by statute or by court decision. The procedure under the United States Rule is as follows:

1. Payments must be applied against accrued interest before any deductions can be made from the principal.
2. Payments that do not equal the accrued interest leave the principal undiminished until other payments are made which are sufficient to cover all accrued interest.
3. Any excess remaining after the payments exceed the accrued interest is applied on the principal.

EXAMPLE

An interest-bearing note for $1,800.00 dated March 1, 1941, had the following indorsements:

September 27, 1941	$500.00
March 15, 1942	25.00
June 1, 1942	700.00

How much was due September 1, 1942?

Solution

	Yr. Mo. Da.	*Yrs.*	*Mos.*	*Days*
Date of note	1941—3— 1			
First payment, $500.00	1941—9—27		6	26
Second payment, $25.00	1942—3—15		5	18
Third payment, $700.00	1942—6— 1		2	16
Settlement	1942—9— 1		3	0
		1	6	0

Explanation.—The time is found by successive subtractions of the first date from the second, the second from the third, and so on. The sum of the different times is equal to the time between the date of the note and the date of settlement.

Face of note, March 1, 1941		$1,800.00
Interest on $1,800.00 at 6% from March 1 to September 27, 6 months and 26 days		61.80
Amount due September 27, 1941		$1,861.80
Deduct payment		500.00
Balance due September 27, 1941		$1,361.80
Interest on $1,361.80 at 6% from September 27 to March 15, 5 months and 18 days, $38.13. As this interest is larger in amount than the payment made at March 15, the interest is not added, and the payment is not deducted.		
Interest on $1,361.80 at 6% from September 27 to June 1, 1942, 8 months and 4 days		55.38
Amount due June 1, 1942		$1,417.18
Deduct sum of payments: March 15	$ 25.00	
June 1	700.00	725.00
Balance due June 1, 1942		$ 692.18
Interest on $692.18 at 6% from June 1 to September 1, 1942, 3 months		10.38
Balance due September 1, 1942		$ 702.56

Merchants' Rule.—The procedure under the Merchants' Rule is as follows:

1. The principal draws interest from the date of the loan until the date of final settlement, and such interest is added to the principal.
2. Each payment draws interest from the date of the payment until the date of final settlement.
3. The balance due is the principal plus interest, minus the payments plus interest.

Where the debt runs for more than one year, the principal draws interest from the date of the loan until the end of the first year (one year from the date on which the loan was made). Each payment draws interest from the date of payment until the end of the first year. The balance due at the end of the first year is the principal plus interest for one year, minus the payments plus the interest from the dates on which the payments were made until the end of the first year. The balance due at the end of the second, third, and subsequent years is calculated in a similar manner.

EXAMPLE

For purposes of comparison, the same problem will be used here as was used to illustrate the United States Rule.

Solution

Face of note, March 1, 1941		$1,800.00
Interest, 1 year at 6% to March 1, 1942		108.00
		$1,908.00
Deduct:		
First payment, September 27, 1941	$500.00	
Interest at 6% to March 1, 1942, 5 months and 4 days	12.83	512.83
Balance due at beginning of second year		$1,395.17
Interest on $1,395.17 at 6%, March 1 to September 1, 1942, 6 months		41.86
		$1,437.03
Deduct:		
Second payment, March 15, 1942	$ 25.00	
Interest at 6% from March 15 to September 1, 1942, 5 months and 16 days	.69	
Third payment, June 1, 1942	700.00	
Interest at 6% from June 1 to September 1, 1942, 3 months	10.50	736.19
Balance due		$ 700.84

United States Rule and Merchants' Rule compared.—In the examples given in the preceding pages, the difference between the balance as computed by the United States Rule and the balance as computed by the Merchants' Rule is only $1.72, but a much greater difference will occur when the time is long and the amount large.

It is usual to compute the balance due on obligations of one year or less by the Merchants' Rule; the balance due on obligations of more than one year is generally computed by the United States Rule.

3. HOW TO CALCULATE BANK DISCOUNT

What bank discount is.—Bank discount is the interest charge made by a bank for converting commercial paper into cash before maturity. Bank discount is computed as simple interest on the amount due at maturity on a note or draft and is deducted in advance. The amount received from the bank—amount due at maturity less the discount and the collection charge—is called the proceeds. The number of days from the date the note is discounted to the date of maturity is called the "term of discount."

How the number of days is counted in bank discount.—In bank discount the time is the period from the date of discount to the date of maturity of the instrument. It is the common practice of commercial banks in the United States to charge discount for the actual or exact number of days in the discount period, and to compute the discount on the basis of 360 days to the year. Thus, if a note due May 6 is discounted March 6, the bank counts the actual number of days between these dates, 61, and computes the discount on the basis of 360 days to the year. For the method of calculating the exact number of days between dates, and a useful table, see page 8; for the method of calculating the date of maturity of an obligation, see page 6.

How to calculate the bank discount and proceeds on non-interest-bearing paper.—The procedure is as follows:

1. The amount due at maturity on non-interest-bearing paper is the amount stated on the face of the instrument.
2. Using the discount rate, compute the bank discount on the face.
3. Compute the collection charge on the face.
4. Deduct from the face the sum of the bank discount and the collection charge; the result is the proceeds.

EXAMPLE

Compute the bank discount and proceeds on a $500.00 non-interest-bearing note, dated June 5, due in 60 days, and discounted June 18 at 6%; collection charge, $\frac{1}{10}$%.

Solution

Sixty days from June 5 is August 4, the due date of the note. The exact number of days from June 18, the date of discount, to August 4, the due date, is 47.

Value of note at maturity		$500.00
Bank discount: 6% on $500.00 for 47 days	$3.92	
Collection charge: $\frac{1}{10}$% on $500.00	.50	
Total charges		4.42
Proceeds		$495.58

How to calculate the bank discount and proceeds on interest-bearing paper.—The procedure is as follows:

1. Compute the value of the instrument at maturity; the value of an interest-bearing instrument is its face plus the interest for the full time of the note.
2. Compute the interest on the value at maturity for the discount period, using the discount rate; the result is the bank discount.
3. Compute the collection charge on the value at maturity.
4. Deduct from the value at maturity the sum of the bank discount and the collection charge; the result is the proceeds.

EXAMPLE

Compute the bank discount and proceeds on a note for $500.00 dated June 5, due in 60 days, and bearing 5% interest; the note is discounted June 18 at 6%, and the collection charge is $\frac{1}{10}$%.

Solution

Sixty days from June 5 is August 4, the due date of the note. The exact number of days from June 18, the date of discount, to August 4, the due date, is 47.

Face value of note		$500.00
Interest at 5% for 60 days		4.17
Value of note at maturity		$504.17
Bank discount: 6% on $504.17 for 47 days	$3.95	
Collection charge: $\frac{1}{10}$% on $504.17	.50	
Total charges		4.45
Proceeds		$499.72

4. SAVINGS THROUGH CASH DISCOUNT

Cash discount explained.—Cash discount is the allowance made by the seller of goods to the buyer on condition that the invoice is paid within a specified time. Assume that goods are sold on terms of "2/10, net 30." This means that if the goods purchased are paid for in cash within ten days from the date of the invoice, the purchaser may subtract 2% from the amount of the invoice. This deduction is called the "cash discount." The goods are supposed, at any rate, to be paid for within 30 days of the date of the invoice. In practice, the debt is usually not paid until 30 days after the first of the month succeeding the month in which the goods are bought. Thus the purchaser gets 2% discount for paying 20 days earlier than the date on which he could be compelled to pay. The discount, therefore, is practically at the rate of 2% for 20 days, or 36% per year.

The following table shows the ordinary discount rates and their equivalent interest rates figured on an annual basis:

CASH DISCOUNT TABLE

½%	10	days	net	30	days	= 9%	per	annum
1%	"	"	"	"	"	= 18%	"	"
1½%	"	"	"	"	"	= 27%	"	"
2%	"	"	"	"	"	= 36%	"	"
2%	"	"	"	60	"	= 14%	"	"
2%	30	"	"	"	"	= 24%	"	"
2%	"	"	"	4	mos.	= 8%	"	"
2%	40	"	"	60	days	= 36%	"	"
2%	70	"	"	90	"	= 36%	"	"
3%	10	"	"	30	"	= 54%	"	"
3%	"	"	"	4	mos.	= 10%	"	"
3%	30	"	"	60	days	= 36%	"	"
4%	10	"	"	"	"	= 29%	"	"
4%	"	"	"	4	mos.	= 13%	"	"
5%	"	"	"	30	days	= 90%	"	"
5%	"	"	"	60	"	= 36%	"	"
5%	"	"	"	4	mos.	= 16%	"	"
6%	"	"	"	60	days	= 43%	"	"
6%	"	"	"	4	mos.	= 20%	"	"
7%	"	"	"	"	"	= 23%	"	"
8%	"	"	"	"	"	= 26%	"	"

5. HOW TO COMPUTE TRADE DISCOUNTS

Uses of trade discounts.—Trade discounts are commonly used as a means of adjusting list or catalogue prices to changed market conditions. Manufacturers and jobbers who deal in merchandise that is more or less standardized issue catalogues describing the goods; the prices quoted in the catalogues are the list prices. As the market prices fluctuate, discounts from the list prices are given, these discounts being issued to customers on separate discount sheets to obviate the necessity of frequent reprinting of the catalogues. Successive discounts from the list prices enable the seller to keep in touch with a declining market. If the market turns upward, the seller can raise his prices step by step as desired by canceling successively the discounts previously offered. The seller can allow different discounts to different classes of customers, without naming separate prices, by giving his customers different discount sheets. Trade discounts are also a means of partly concealing the real prices; the catalogue alone, without the appropriate discount sheet, tells nothing as to the real prices of the merchandise.

Chain discounts.—Several discounts from the one list price are often given; for example, goods may be priced at $500.00 less discounts of 20%, 10%, and 5%. These are known as "chain discounts," and the several discounts are referred to as a "series of discounts."

How chain discounts are computed.—Each discount is deducted from the balance remaining after the deduction of the preceding discount.

EXAMPLE

Goods are priced at $500.00 less discounts of 20%, 10%, and 5%. Find the net price.

Solution

List price	$500.00
20% of $500.00	100.00
	$400.00
10% of $400.00	40.00
	$360.00
5% of $360.00	18.00
Net price	$342.00

Hence the net price is $342.00, and the amount of the discount is $158.00.

Several discounts are *not* equal to the sum of the discounts. Thus, in the above example, the sum of the discounts 20%, 10%, and 5% is 35%; 35% of $500.00 is $175.00. The correct discount is $158.00.

How to find the single trade discount equivalent to a series.— Where only two discounts are involved:

1. Add the discounts.
2. Multiply the discounts.
3. Subtract (2) from (1); the result is the single discount equivalent to the two discounts.

EXAMPLE

Find the single trade discount equivalent to discounts of 20% and 10%.

Solution

20% + 10%	30%
20% × 10%	2%
30% − 2%	28%

Hence the single trade discount equivalent to discounts of 20% and 10% is 28%.

An extension of the above method can be used where it is desired to find the single trade discount equivalent to three or more discounts.

EXAMPLE

Find the single trade discount equivalent to discounts of 30%, 10%, and 5%.

Solution

First find the single discount equivalent to the first two discounts— 30% and 10%.

30% + 10%	40%
30% × 10%	3%
40% − 3%	37%

Thus the single discount equivalent to discounts of 30% and 10% is 37%. Now find the single discount equivalent to discounts of 37% and 5%.

37% + 5%	42%
37% × 5%	1.85%
42% − 1.85%	40.15%

The single discount equivalent to discounts of 30%, 10%, and 5% is, then, 40.15%.

A second method is:

1. Subtract each single discount from 100%.
2. Find the product of the remainders.
3. Subtract the product from 100%; the remainder is the single discount equivalent to the series.

EXAMPLE

Find the single discount equivalent to the series 30%, 10%, and 5%.

Solution

100%	100%	100%
30%	10%	5%
70%	90%	95%

$.70 \times .90 \times .95 = .5985$, or 59.85%

$100\% - 59.85\% = 40.15\%$, the single discount

A third method is:

1. Subtract the first discount from 100%.
2. Multiply the remainder by the second discount, and deduct the product.
3. Multiply this remainder by the third discount, and deduct the product.
4. Subtract this remainder from 100%; the result is the single discount.

EXAMPLE

Find the single discount equivalent to the series 20%, 10%, and $8\frac{1}{3}$%.

Solution

$100\% - 20\%$	80%
$80\% \times 10\%$	8%
$80\% - 8\%$	72%
$72\% \times 8\frac{1}{3}\%$	6%
$72\% - 6\%$	66%
$100\% - 66\%$	34%

The single discount equivalent to the series 20%, 10%, and $8\frac{1}{3}$% is, therefore, 34%.

DECIMAL EQUIVALENTS OF CHAIN DISCOUNTS

Secondary Discount	Primary Discount														
	5	7½	10	12½	15	16⅔	20	22½	25	27½	30	32½	33⅓	35	37½
2	.93100	.90650	.88200	.85750	.83300	.81667	.78400	.75950	.73500	.71050	.68600	.66150	.65333	.63100	.61250
2½	.92625	.90188	.8775	.85313	.82875	.8125	.78	.75562	.73125	.70688	.6825	.65813	.65	.63375	.60938
5	.9025	.87875	.855	.83125	.8075	.79166	.76	.73625	.7125	.68875	.665	.64125	.63333	.6175	.59375
5 2½	.87994	.85678	.83363	.81047	.78731	.77187	.741	.71784	.69469	.67153	.64838	.62522	.6175	.60206	.57891
5 5	.85738	.83481	.81225	.78969	.76713	.75208	.722	.69943	.67688	.65431	.63175	.60919	.60167	.58663	.56406
5 5 2½	.83594	.81394	.79194	.76994	.74795	.73328	.70395	.68195	.65995	.63795	.61596	.59396	.58663	.57196	.54996
7½	.87875	.85563	.8325	.80938	.78625	.77083	.74	.71688	.69375	.67063	.6475	.62438	.61667	.60125	.57813
7½ 2½	.85678	.83423	.81169	.78914	.76659	.75156	.7215	.69895	.67641	.65386	.63131	.60877	.60125	.58622	.56367
7½ 5	.83481	.81284	.79088	.76891	.74694	.73229	.703	.68103	.65906	.6371	.61513	.59316	.58583	.57119	.54922
10	.855	.8325	.81	.7875	.765	.75	.72	.6975	.675	.6525	.63	.6075	.60	.585	.5625
10 2½	.83363	.81169	.78975	.76781	.74588	.73125	.702	.68006	.65813	.63619	.61425	.59231	.585	.57038	.54844
10 5	.81225	.79088	.7695	.74811	.72675	.7125	.684	.66263	.64125	.61988	.5985	.57713	.57	.55575	.53438
10 5 2½	.79194	.77111	.75026	.72941	.70858	.69469	.6669	.64606	.62522	.60438	.58354	.5627	.55575	.54186	.52102
10 7½	.79088	.77006	.74925	.72844	.70763	.69375	.666	.64519	.62438	.60356	.58275	.56194	.555	.54113	.52031
10 7½ 5	.75134	.73156	.71179	.69202	.67225	.65906	.6327	.61293	.59316	.57338	.55361	.53384	.52725	.51407	.49429
10 10	.7695	.74925	.729	.70875	.6885	.675	.648	.62775	.6075	.58725	.567	.54675	.54	.5265	.50625
10 10 2½	.75026	.73052	.71078	.69103	.67129	.65812	.6318	.61206	.59231	.57257	.55283	.53308	.5265	.51334	.49359
10 10 5	.73103	.71179	.69255	.67331	.65408	.64124	.6156	.59636	.57713	.55789	.53865	.51941	.513	.50018	.48094
10 10 5 2½	.71276	.694	.67524	.65648	.63772	.62519	.60021	.58145	.5627	.54394	.52518	.50643	.50018	.48767	.46891
10 10 10	.69255	.67433	.6561	.63788	.61965	.6075	.5832	.56498	.54675	.52853	.5103	.49208	.486	.47385	.45563
12½	.83125	.80938	.7875	.76563	.74375	.72923	.70	.67813	.65625	.63438	.6125	.59063	.58334	.56875	.54688
12½ 2½	.81047	.78915	.76781	.74649	.72516	.711	.6825	.66118	.63984	.61852	.59719	.57587	.56876	.55453	.53321
12½ 5	.78969	.76891	.74813	.72735	.70656	.69277	.665	.64422	.62344	.60266	.58188	.5611	.55417	.54031	.51954
12½ 7½	.76891	.74868	.72844	.70821	.68797	.67454	.6475	.62727	.60703	.5868	.5666	.54633	.53904	.52609	.50586
12½ 10	.74813	.72844	.70875	.68907	.66938	.65631	.63	.61032	.59063	.57094	.55125	.53157	.52448	.51188	.49219
12½ 10 5	.71072	.69202	.67331	.65462	.63591	.6235	.5985	.5798	.5611	.54239	.52369	.50499	.49826	.48629	.46758
12½ 10 5 2½	.69295	.67472	.65648	.63826	.62001	.60791	.58354	.56531	.54707	.52883	.51060	.49237	.48580	.47413	.45589
12½ 10 7½	.69202	.67381	.65559	.63739	.61918	.60709	.58275	.56455	.54633	.52812	.50991	.49170	.48514	.47349	.45528
12½ 10 10	.67332	.6556	.63788	.62016	.60244	.59068	.567	.54929	.53157	.51385	.49613	.47841	.47203	.46069	.44297
15	.8075	.78625	.765	.74375	.7225	.70833	.68	.65875	.6375	.61625	.595	.57375	.56667	.5525	.53125
15 2½	.78732	.76660	.74588	.72516	.70444	.69062	.663	.64229	.62157	.60084	.58013	.55941	.55251	.53869	.51797
20	.76	.74	.72	.70	.68	.66667	.64	.62	.60	.58	.56	.54	.53333	.52	.50

Secondary Discount	Primary Discount														
	40	42½	45	47½	50	52½	55	57½	60	62½	65	66⅔	70	72½	75
2	.58800	.56350	.53900	.51450	.4900	.46550	.44100	.41650	.39200	.36750	.34300	.32667	.29400	.26950	.24500
2½	.585	.56063	.53625	.51188	.4875	.46313	.43875	.41438	.39	.36563	.34125	.325	.2925	.26813	.24375
5	.57	.54625	.5225	.49875	.475	.45125	.4275	.40375	.38	.35625	.3325	.31667	.285	.26125	.2375
5 2½	.55575	.53259	.50944	.48628	.46313	.43997	.41681	.39366	.3705	.34374	.32419	.30875	.27788	.25472	.23156
5 5	.5415	.51894	.49638	.47381	.45125	.42869	.40613	.38356	.361	.33844	.31588	.30083	.27075	.24819	.22563
5 5 2½	.52796	.50596	.48397	.46194	.43997	.41797	.39597	.37397	.35198	.32998	.30798	.29331	.26398	.24198	.21998
7½	.555	.53188	.50875	.48563	.4625	.43938	.41625	.39313	.37	.34688	.32375	.30833	.2775	.25438	.23125
7½ 2½	.54113	.51858	.49603	.47348	.45094	.42839	.40584	.3833	.36075	.3382	.31566	.30063	.27056	.24802	.22547
7½ 5	.52725	.50529	.48331	.46135	.43938	.41741	.39544	.37347	.3515	.32954	.30756	.29292	.26363	.24166	.21969
10	.54	.5175	.495	.4725	.45	.4275	.405	.3825	.36	.3375	.315	.30	.27	.2475	.225
10 2½	.5265	.50456	.48263	.46069	.43875	.41681	.39488	.37294	.351	.32906	.30713	.2925	.26325	.24131	.21938
10 5	.513	.49163	.47025	.44888	.4275	.40613	.38475	.36338	.342	.32063	.29925	.285	.2565	.23513	.21375
10 5 2½	.50018	.47933	.45849	.43765	.41681	.39597	.37513	.35429	.33345	.31261	.29177	.27788	.25009	.22925	.20841
10 7½	.4995	.47869	.45788	.43706	.41625	.39544	.37463	.35381	.333	.31219	.29138	.2775	.24975	.22894	.20183
10 7½ 5	.47453	.45476	.43499	.41521	.39544	.37567	.3559	.33612	.31635	.29658	.27681	.26363	.23726	.21749	.19772
10 10	.486	.46575	.4455	.42525	.405	.38475	.3645	.34425	.324	.30375	.2835	.27	.243	.22275	.2025
10 10 2½	.47385	.45411	.43436	.41462	.39488	.37514	.35539	.33564	.3159	.29616	.27641	.26325	.23693	.21718	.19744
10 10 5	.4617	.44246	.42323	.40399	.38475	.36551	.34628	.32704	.3078	.28856	.26933	.2565	.23085	.21161	.19238
10 10 5 2½	.45016	.4314	.41264	.39389	.37513	.35637	.33762	.31886	.3001	.28135	.26259	.25009	.22508	.20632	.18757
10 10 10	.4374	.41918	.40095	.38273	.3645	.34628	.32805	.30983	.2916	.27338	.25515	.243	.2187	.20048	.18225
12½	.525	.50313	.48125	.45938	.4375	.41663	.39375	.37188	.35	.32813	.30625	.29138	.2625	.24063	.21875
12½ 2½	.51188	.49055	.46922	.4479	.42656	.40622	.38391	.36258	.34125	.31993	.29859	.2841	.25594	.23462	.21328
12½ 5	.49875	.47797	.45719	.43641	.41563	.3958	.37406	.35329	.3325	.31172	.29094	.27681	.24938	.2286	.20781
12½ 7½	.48563	.4654	.44516	.42493	.40469	.38538	.36422	.34399	.32375	.30352	.28328	.26953	.24281	.22258	.20234
12½ 10	.4725	.45282	.43313	.41344	.39375	.37497	.35438	.33469	.315	.29532	.27563	.26224	.23625	.21657	.19688
12½ 10 5	.44888	.43018	.41147	.39277	.37406	.35622	.33666	.31796	.29925	.28055	.26185	.24913	.22444	.20574	.18704
12½ 10 5 2½	.43766	.41943	.40118	.38295	.36471	.34732	.32824	.31001	.29177	.27354	.2553	.2429	.21883	.2006	.18236
12½ 10 7½	.43706	.41886	.40065	.38243	.36422	.34685	.32780	.30959	.29138	.27317	.25496	.24257	.21853	.20033	.18211
12½ 10 10	.42525	.40754	.38982	.37210	.35438	.33747	.31894	.30122	.2835	.26579	.24807	.23602	.21263	.19491	.17719
15	.51	.48875	.4675	.44625	.425	.40375	.3825	.36125	.34	.31875	.2975	.28333	.255	.23375	.2125
15 2½	.49725	.47653	.45582	.43510	.4144	.39366	.3730	.35222	.3315	.31097	.29007	.27625	.24863	.22791	.20719
20	.48	.46	.44	.42	.40	.38	.36	.34	.32	.30	.28	.26667	.24	.22	.20

Note.—Reproduced by courtesy of Lefax, Inc., Philadelphia, Pa., from "Business Data Sheet No. 5–167."

How to calculate the net price.—The procedure is as follows:

1. Reduce the trade discount series to a single discount, by one of the methods described in the preceding pages.

2. Multiply the list price by this single discount; this gives the amount of the discount.

3. Deduct the amount of the discount from the list price; the result is the net price.

EXAMPLE

Find the net price of a gas pump listed at $3,500.00, with discounts of 20%, 12½%, 5%, and 2%.

Solution

100%	100%	100%	100%
20%	12½%	5%	2%
80%	87½%	95%	98%

.80 × .875 × .95 × .98 = .6517, or 65.17%
100% — 65.17% = 34.83%, the single discount
$3,500.00 × 34.83% = $1,219.05, amount of discount
$3,500.00 — $1,219.05 = $2,280.95, the net price

Table of decimal equivalents of chain discounts.—The table on pages 28–29 will be found useful in chain discount computations. Its use is illustrated below.

EXAMPLE

Find the net price of an article listed at $300.00, with discounts of 15%, 10%, and 5%.

Solution

The primary discount is 15%. In the 15% column, on the line for secondary discounts of 10% and 5%, the decimal .72675 is given. Multiply this decimal by the list price. $300.00 × .72675 = $218.03, the net price.

6. HOW TO COMPUTE AVERAGES

Adapted from Curtis and Cooper, "Mathematics of Accounting" New York: Prentice-Hall, Inc.

Simple average.—The simple average of a group of items is obtained by adding the items to be averaged and dividing the sum by the number of items added.

EXAMPLE

From the following statistics, find the average rate per kilowatt hour for electrical energy:

New England States	2.88¢
South Atlantic States	2.77¢
Atlantic States	2.19¢
North Central States	1.88¢
Pacific Northwest	1.81¢

Solution

$$2.88 + 2.77 + 2.19 + 1.88 + 1.81 = 11.53$$
$$11.53 \div 5 = 2.306$$

Explanation.—The number of items to be added is 5, and the sum is 11.53¢. 11.53 divided by 5 = 2.306, or 2.306¢, the average rate per kilowatt hour.

A not uncommon error in business computations is the use of a simple average where a weighted average is required to give the correct result (for explanation of weighted average, see page 34).

Moving average.—A moving average is a series of simple averages of statistics applicable to groups of an equal number of time units, each successive group excluding the first time unit of the preceding group and including the unit immediately following those of the preceding group. For example, a yearly moving average, by months, may begin with an initial group including the data applicable to the twelve months of 1942. The next group would omit the data applicable to January, 1942, and include the data applicable to the remaining eleven months of 1942 and those applicable to the month of January, 1943.

EXAMPLE

The labor costs in a certain manufacturing plant for the first six months of 1942 were as follows:

January	$3,363.17
February	3,644.15
March	4,472.90
April	3,209.20
May	3,415.40
June	4,152.05

The labor costs for the next two months were:

July	$3,824.06
August	4,015.25

What has been the average labor cost for each six months since January 1, 1942?

Solution

The labor cost for the period from January 1 to June 30 is the sum of the labor costs for each of the six months, or $22,256.87. The average for the period is $22,256.87 ÷ 6, or $3,709.48.

The average for the period from February 1 to July 31 is computed as follows:

Total: January 1 to June 30	$22,256.87
Deduct: January labor cost	3,363.17
	$18,893.70
Add: July labor cost	3,824.06
	$22,717.76

$22,717.76 ÷ 6 = $3,786.29

The average for the period from March 1 to August 31 is calculated in the same manner:

Total: February 1 to July 31	$22,717.76
Deduct: February labor cost	3,644.15
	$19,073.61
Add: August labor cost	4,015.25
	$23,088.86

$23,088.86 ÷ 6 = $3,848.14

Comparison of these averages, \$3,709.48, \$3,786.29, and \$3,848.14, shows an increase for each period.

In permanent records, these averages should be tabulated.

1942	*Labor Cost*	*Moving Average*	*Increase or Decrease*†
January–June	\$22,256.87	\$3,709.48	\$.......
February–July	22,717.76	3,786.29	76.81
March–August	23,088.86	3,848.14	61.85

† Indicate decreases by means of daggers.

Further comparisons, based on the figures of prior periods, may be made in succeeding years. A column may be annexed to show the increase or decrease of the average of each six-month period compared with the simple average for the preceding year. Another column may be used to show the increase or decrease in the moving average for the current six-month period compared with the moving average for the same period of the preceding year.

Progressive average.—The method of progressive average is cumulative. The results of the lastest period are added to the total previously computed, and the amount is divided by the previous divisor plus 1.

EXAMPLE

Department A sales were: January, \$5,364.00; February, \$4,872.00; March, \$5,024.00. Department B sales were: January, \$2,561.00; February, \$2,325.00; March, \$2,753.00. Find the progressive monthly averages.

Solution

SALES RECORD

Dept.	*Jan.*	*Feb.*	*Total*	*Aver.*	*March*	*Total*	*Aver.*	*April*
A	5,364	4,872	10,236	5,118	5,024	15,260	5,087	
B	2,561	2,325	4,886	2,443	2,753	7,639	2,546	*etc.*

Explanation.—Department A sales for January and February total \$10,236.00. \$10,236.00 ÷ 2 = \$5,118.00, the average for the two months. \$10,236.00 + \$5,024.00 = \$15,260.00, the total sales for the three months. \$15,260.00 ÷ 3 = \$5,087.00, the average for the three months. The record for the year would be completed in this manner.

The totals and averages of Department B are computed in the same manner.

Periodic average.—Periodic average is simple average applied for several periods to statistics applicable to the same unit of time. It may be used to show a variation in expenses, earnings, sales, and so forth.

EXAMPLE

EXPENSES

Month	*1942*	*1941*	*1940*	*1939*	*Total*	*Average*
January	$478.60	$392.85	$429.65	$356.00	$1,657.10	$414.28
February	462.37	529.83	531.33	535.35	2,058.88	514.72
March	347.92	629.89	432.45	567.89	1,978.15	494.54

Explanation.—The expenses for January for the four years are totaled; the total, $1,657.10, divided by 4, the number of years shown, equals $414.28, the average monthly expense for January. The other averages are calculated in the same manner.

Weighted average.—A weighted average should be used where the items entering into the group to be averaged differ from each other in value. The following example illustrates the average-price method of pricing requisitions in cost accounting.

EXAMPLE

A stock record shows the following receipts:

4,800 lbs. @ 20¢
3,000 lbs. @ 18¢
4,000 lbs. @ 21¢

What is the average price per pound for the month?

Solution

4,800 lbs. @ 20¢	=	$ 960.00
3,000 lbs. @ 18¢	=	540.00
4,000 lbs. @ 21¢	=	840.00
11,800 lbs.	=	$2,340.00

2,340 ÷ 11,800 = 19.83, or 19.83¢ per pound, average price

A simple average of the three prices paid during the month could be found by adding, 20¢ + 18¢ + 21¢ = 59¢, and dividing by 3,

59¢ ÷ 3 = 19.67¢. This, however, is not the correct average price per pound for the month. If the three prices are to be averaged, each price must be weighted according to the number of pounds bought at that price.

In the averaging of percentages, a simple average is sometimes used where a weighted average is required to give the correct result.

EXAMPLE

A manufactured product is composed of four ingredients, the ratios and costs per pound being as follows:

Material	*Pounds*	*Price per Pound*
A	1	$1.50
B	3	.75
C	4	1.25
D	2	2.00

It was found in the second year that, owing to price fluctuations, the raw material costs had increased as follows:

Material	*Per Cent*
A	50
B	100
C	10
D	25

What was the average percentage of increase in the cost of raw material composing the finished product?

Solution

Material	*Pounds*	*Cost per lb.*	*Total Cost*	*Percentage Price Increase*	*Increased Cost*
A	1	$1.50	$ 1.50	50	$ .75
B	3	.75	2.25	100	2.25
C	4	1.25	5.00	10	.50
D	2	2.00	4.00	25	1.00
			$12.75		$4.50

4.50 ÷ 12.75 = 35.29%, the weighted average percentage

A simple average of the four percentages could be found by adding, 50% + 100% + 10% + 25% = 185%, and dividing by 4,

185% ÷ 4 = 46.25%. This, however, is not the correct average percentage of increase in the cost of raw materials composing the finished product. Each of the percentages must be weighted according to the number of pounds of that material in the product. When this is done, as illustrated above, the correct average percentage of increase in cost is found to be 35.29%.

7. HOW TO FIND THE AVERAGE DATE OF AN ACCOUNT

Adapted from Finney, "Principles of Accounting"
New York: Prentice-Hall, Inc.

Average or equated date.—The average or equated date of an account is the date on which the balance of the account can be paid without loss of interest to either party. The average date may be desired for several purposes, among which are:

1. To determine the date on which settlement is to be made.
2. To determine the date that should be given to an interest-bearing note issued in settlement of the account.
3. To determine the amount of interest to be added to the balance of the account in making settlement. For instance, if the balance of the account is $500.00, the average date June 5, and the settlement date July 16, interest should be paid on $500.00 for 41 days.

George Smith has the following account with William Dawson:

WILLIAM DAWSON

June	1	Terms 30 days	100.00	
"	11	Terms 30 days	100.00	

One bill is due on July 1, the other on July 11. The average date is July 6, because the payment of the first $100.00 five days after it is due is exactly offset by the payment of the second $100.00 five days before it is due.

This account might be settled by the payment of $200.00 on July 6. If it is paid on July 16, interest on $200.00 for 10 days should be included in the payment. If an interest-bearing note is given on July 16, it should be dated July 6, or interest from July 6 to July 16 should be included in its face.

How to find the average date of a one-sided account.—When an account contains debits only or credits only, the procedure in determining the average date is as follows:

1. Assume that all items in the account are paid at a date prior to the maturity of any item in the account. This assumed date is called the focal date. (Any date can be used as the focal date, but the most convenient focal date is the last day of the month preceding the first date on which any item is due.)
2. Determine the number of months and the number of days between the focal date and the maturity of each item.
3. Multiply each item in the account by the number of months and by the number of days between the focal date and the maturity date of the item.
4. Add the products of months, and reduce to a basis of days by multiplying by 30.
5. Add the products of days, including those obtained by reducing months to days.
6. Divide this total number of days by the balance of the account.
7. Reduce the days, determined in step (6), to months and days on the basis of 30 days to the month. Count forward from the focal date this number of months and days; the result is the average date of the account.

EXAMPLE

Find the average date of the following account.

JAMES WHITE

Aug.	3	Terms cash	600.00	
"	12	Terms 2/10; n/30	500.00	
Sept.	7	Terms 2/10; n/30	400.00	

Solution

The focal date is July 31, the last day of the month preceding the first date on which any item is due.

			Time from Focal Date		Products	
Date	*Debits*	*Date Due*	*Months*	*Days*	*Months*	*Days*
Aug. 3	600.00	Aug. 3	0	3	0	1,800.00
Aug. 12	500.00	Sept. 11	1	11	500.00	5,500.00
Sept. 7	400.00	Oct. 7	2	7	800.00	2,800.00
					30 × 1,300.00 =	39,000.00
	1,500.00					49,100.00

$49{,}100 \div 1{,}500 = 32\frac{10}{15}$, or 33 days, or 1 month and 3 days

The average date is 1 month and 3 days forward from July 31, or September 3.

Dates used in averaging.—The dates to be used in the averaging should be the dates on which the items have a cash value equal to their face.

1. Sales on cash terms take the date of sale.
2. Sales on credit terms take the date on which the credit term expires.
3. Returns and allowances take the date that applies to the invoice on which the return or allowance is being made.
4. An interest-bearing note takes the date of the note, because the note is worth face value on that date.
5. A non-interest-bearing note takes the date of maturity, because it is not worth face value until maturity.

How to find the average date of a compound account.—When an account contains both debits and credits, the process of determining the average date is called compound average. Compound averaging is performed as follows:

Steps (1), (2), (3), (4), and (5) are taken as in the averaging of a one-sided account, for both debits and credits.

6. Compute the balance of the account.
7. Determine the difference between the sum of the debit products and the sum of the credit products.

8. Divide this difference by the balance of the account, and reduce the quotient to months and days.

9. If the balance of the account and the balance of the products are both debits or both credits, the average date is forward from the focal date. If either is a debit and the other a credit, the average date is backward from the focal date.

Two examples of compound averaging are given below. In the first the average date is forward from the focal date; in the second, backward from the focal date.

EXAMPLE 1

Find the average date of the following compound account:

D. L. BURTON

May	7 Terms cash	750.00	June	2 Int.-bearing note 1 month	1,500.00
"	19 2/30; n/30	1,200.00	"	10 Cash	100.00

Solution

The focal date is April 30, the last day of the month preceding the first date on which any item is due.

			Time from Focal Date		Products	
Date	*Amount*	*Date in Average*	*Months*	*Days*	*Months*	*Days*
Debits:						
May 7	750.00	May 7	0	7	0	5,250.00
May 19	1,200.00	June 18	1	18	1,200	21,600.00
					30 × 1,200 =	36,000.00
	1,950.00					62,850.00
Credits:						
June 2	1,500.00	June 2	1	2	1,500	3,500.00
June 10	100.00	June 10	1	10	100	1,000.00
					30 × 1,600 =	48,000.00
	1,600.00					52,000.00
Balances	350.00					10,850.00

10,850 ÷ 350 = 31, or 1 month and 1 day

Since the balance of the account and the balance of the products are both debits, the average date is 1 month and 1 day forward from April 30, or June 1.

EXAMPLE

For purposes of this example, assume the same account, except that the note does not bear interest.

Solution

Date	Amount	Date in Average	Time from Focal Date: Months	Time from Focal Date: Days	Products: Months	Products: Days
Debits (Totals as above):						
	1,950.00					62,850.00
Credits:						
June 2	1,500.00	July 2	2	2	3,000	3,000.00
June 10	100.00	June 10	1	10	100	1,000.00
					30 × 3,100 =	93,000.00
	1,600.00					97,000.00
Balances Dr.	350.00				Cr.	34,150.00

$$34{,}150 \div 350 = 97\tfrac{20}{35}, \text{ or } 98, \text{ or 3 months and 8 days}$$

In this case the balance of the account is a debit, while the balance of the products is a credit. The average date is therefore 3 months and 8 days backward from the focal date, or January 22 (still considering 30 days to the month).

How can the average date of an account be prior to any date in the account? In the first example the $1,500.00 note bore interest, and the average date of the account was June 1; the $350.00 balance in the account bore interest from that date. In the second example the $1,500.00 note, due in one month, bore no interest; as an offset, the $350.00 balance of the account should bear interest for approximately 4⅓ additional months, or from January 22.

8. HOW TO COMPUTE MARKUP AND SELLING PRICE

Difference between figuring percentage of profit on cost price and on selling price.—The difference between figuring the percentage of profit on the cost price and on the selling price is indicated in the following examples.

EXAMPLE 1

The cost price of an article is \$3.00. The selling price is to be computed as cost plus 25%. What is the selling price?

Solution

$$\frac{3}{1} \times \frac{25}{100} = \$0.75$$

$$\$3.00 + \$0.75 = \$3.75, \text{ the selling price}$$

EXAMPLE 2

The cost price of an article is \$3.00. The selling price is to be computed so that a profit of 25% will be made on the selling price. What is the selling price?

Solution

$$\begin{aligned} \text{Let } 100\% &= \text{selling price} \\ 25\% &= \text{margin} \\ 75\% &= \text{cost price, or } \$3.00 \\ 100\% &= \frac{300}{75}, \text{ or } \$4.00, \text{ the selling price} \end{aligned}$$

From these two examples it is apparent that a merchant who sold this \$3.00 article for \$3.75, with the idea of making a profit of 25%, would be acting on an illusion. He would have to sell the \$3.00 article for \$4.00 in order to make a profit of 25%, because the cost is only a part of the selling price. Actually, a margin of 25% on the cost price is equivalent to a margin of only 20% on the selling price; this can be shown from the figures used in Example 1, above:

$$\text{Cost price} = \$3.00$$
$$\text{Addition to cost price} = .75$$
$$\text{Selling price} = 3.75$$
$$\text{Percentage profit on selling price} = \frac{0.75}{3.75} \times \frac{100}{1} = 20\%$$

The table below shows the percentage that has to be added to the cost in order to make a given percentage on the selling price.

PROFIT PERCENTAGE TABLE

Add to Cost (%)	*To Make on Selling Price* (%)	*Add to Cost* (%)	*To Make on Selling Price* (%)
5	$4\frac{3}{4}$	31.58	24
$7\frac{1}{2}$	7	$33\frac{1}{3}$	25
10.00	9	35.00	26
11.11	10	$37\frac{1}{2}$	$27\frac{1}{4}$
12.36	11	40.00	$28\frac{1}{2}$
$12\frac{1}{2}$	$11\frac{1}{8}$	42.86	30
13.63	12	45.00	31
14.94	13	47.00	32
16.28	14	50.00	$33\frac{1}{3}$
16.43	$14\frac{1}{4}$	53.85	35
17.65	15	55.00	$35\frac{1}{2}$
19.05	16	60.00	$37\frac{1}{2}$
20.00	$16\frac{2}{3}$	65.00	$39\frac{1}{2}$
20.49	17	$66\frac{2}{3}$	40
21.96	18	70.00	41
23.46	19	75.00	$42\frac{3}{4}$
25.00	20	80.00	$44\frac{1}{2}$
26.58	21	85.00	46
28.21	22	90.00	$47\frac{1}{2}$
29.88	23	100.00	50

How to calculate the markup and the selling price when cost of doing business and percentage of profit are based on selling price.—Markup is that component which is added to cost in order to arrive at a selling price. The table on page 44 shows the markup percentage on cost necessary to meet the total percentage deductions from selling price.

EXAMPLE

What should be the markup and the selling price of an article if the cost price is \$15.00, the discount is 2% of the selling price, the commission allowed salesmen is 5% of the selling price, the overhead cost of doing business is 15% of the selling price, and the profit desired on the selling price is 7%?

Solution

The "total deductions from selling price" equal 29% (2% + 5% + 15% + 7%). In the table on page 44, the figure opposite 29% is 40.8451%. To find the markup, multiply the cost price, \$15.00 by 40.8451; the result is \$6.13. The selling price is \$15.00 plus \$6.13, or \$21.13.

To find the markup without the use of the table, the procedure would be as follows:

1. Let 100% represent the selling price.
2. Deduct from 100% the sum of the percentage deductions from selling price.
3. Divide the total deductions from the selling price by the figure found in (2).

$$100\% = \text{selling price}$$
$$100\% - (2\% + 5\% + 15\% + 7\%) = 71\%$$
$$29\% \div 71\% = 40.8451\%$$

To find the selling price without the use of the table, the procedure would be as follows:

1. Let 100% represent the selling price.
2. Deduct from 100% the total deductions from the selling price and the percentage of net profit desired.
3. Divide the cost price by the figure found in (2).

Solution

$$100\% = \text{selling price}$$
$$100\% - (2\% + 5\% + 15\% + 7\%) = 71$$
$$\$15.00 \div 71\% = \frac{15}{1} \times \frac{100}{71} = \$21.13, \text{ the selling price}$$

MARKUP TABLE

Total Deductions from Selling Price	*Markup Percentage on Cost*	*Total Deductions from Selling Price*	*Markup Percentage on Cost*
1%	1.0101%	26%	35.1351%
2	2.0408	27	36.9863
3	3.0928	28	38.8889
4	4.1667	29	40.8451
5	5.2632	30	42.8571
6	6.383	31	44.9275
7	7.5269	32	47.0588
8	8.6957	33	49.2537
9	9.8901	34	51.5151
10	11.1111	35	53.8461
11	12.3595	36	56.25
12	13.6364	37	58.7301
13	14.9425	38	61.2903
14	16.2791	39	63.9344
15	17.647	40	66.6667
16	19.0476	41	69.4915
17	20.4819	42	72.4138
18	21.9512	43	75.4386
19	23.4568	44	78.5714
20	25.	45	81.8181
21	26.5823	46	85.1851
22	28.2051	47	88.6792
23	29.8701	48	92.3076
24	31.5789	49	96.0784
25	33.3333	50	100.

9. HOW TO CALCULATE COMPOUND INTEREST

Adapted from Moore, "Handbook of Financial Mathematics"
New York: Prentice-Hall, Inc.

How to calculate the compound amount.—The compound amount of any sum is the amount to which that sum accumulates in a specified time and at a specified rate of compound interest. Thus the compound amount is the original investment, or principal, plus the compound interest. The compound amount minus the original principal is the compound interest.

Table of compound amount of 1.—The table on pages 48–51 shows the compound amount of 1 ($1, £1, 1 peso, or any other monetary unit) for different numbers of periods and at different rates of interest per period. In calculating, by the use of the table, the amount to which any sum accumulates at compound interest, the procedure is as follows:

1. Find in the table the compound amount of 1 for the given number of periods and at the given rate of interest per period.
2. Multiply this figure by the original principal.

How to calculate the number of periods and the rate of interest per period.—The rate of interest is usually expressed as a certain percent per year. The interest at this stated percent per year may, however, be compounded more often than once a year; as, semiannually, quarterly, monthly.

If the interest is compounded annually:

1. The number of periods is the number of years.
2. The rate of interest per period is the stated rate.

If the interest is compounded more often than once a year:

1. The number of periods is the number of years multiplied by the times per year that the interest is compounded. Thus, if the number of years is 5 and the interest is compounded quarterly, the number of periods is $5 \times 4 = 20$. If the number of years is 3 years and 6 months and the interest is compounded semiannually, the number of periods is $3\frac{1}{2} \times 2 = 7$.
2. The rate of interest per period is the stated rate divided by the times per year that the interest is compounded. Thus, if the stated rate is 4% per year compounded quarterly, the rate of interest per period is $4\% \div 4 = 1\%$.

EXAMPLE 1

What will $1,000.00 amount to in 10 years at 4% per year compounded annually?

Solution

Since the interest is compounded annually, the number of periods is the number of years, 10, and the rate of interest per period is the stated rate, 4%. Then:

(1) In the table on page 50 the figure given in the 4% column opposite 10 is 1.48024428. This is the amount to which $1.00 will accumulate in 10 years at 4% per year compounded annually.

(2) To find what $1,000.00 will amount to, multiply 1.48024428 by 1,000. The result is $1,480.24.

EXAMPLE 2

What will $1,000.00 amount to in 10 years at 4% per year compounded quarterly?

Solution

Since the interest is compounded more often than once a year, the number of periods is the number of years multiplied by the times per year that the interest is compounded; $10 \times 4 = 40$. The rate of interest per period is the stated rate divided by the times per year that the interest is compounded; $4\% \div 4 = 1\%$. Then:

(1) In the table on page 48 the figure given in the 1% column opposite 40 is 1.48886373. This is the amount to which $1.00 will accumulate in 10 years at 4% per year compounded quarterly.

(2) To find what $1,000.00 will amount to, multiply 1.48886373 by 1,000. The result is $1,488.86.

Formula for compound amount.—The compound amount may also be calculated by the use of the formula

$$P(1+i)^n,$$

where

$P =$ original principal
$i =$ rate of interest per period
$n =$ number of periods

How to calculate the compound present value.—The compound present value (or present worth) of a sum of money due at a fixed future date is that sum which, at compound interest, will increase in the given time to the sum due. Thus, if $10,000.00 is due 4 years hence, and money is worth 4% per year compounded semiannually, the compound present value is that principal which, placed at interest now at 4% per year compounded semiannually, will accumulate in 4 years to $10,000.00.

Table of compound present value of 1.—The table on pages 52–55 shows the compound present value of 1 ($1, £1, 1 peso, or any other monetary unit) for different numbers of periods and at different rates of interest per period. In calculating, by the use of the table, the compound present value of any sum, the procedure is as follows:

1. Find in the table the compound present value of 1 for the given number of periods and at the given rate of interest per period.
2. Multiply this figure by the sum whose present value is to be ascertained.

For method of determining number of periods and rate of interest per period, see page 45, "How to calculate the number of periods and the rate of interest per period."

EXAMPLE

The Maryland Finance Company signs an agreement to sell a piece of real estate 2 years and 3 months hence for $33,500.00. If money is worth 4% per year compounded quarterly, what is the present value of the contract?

Solution

Since the interest is compounded quarterly, the number of periods is $2\frac{1}{4} \times 4 = 9$. The rate of interest per period is $4\% \div 4 = 1\%$. Then:

(1) In the table on page 52 the figure given in the 1% column opposite 9 is 0.91433982. This is the compound present value of $1.00 for 2 years and 3 months at 4% per year compounded quarterly.

(2) To find the compound present value of $33,500.00, multiply 0.91433982 by 33,500. The result, $30,630.38, is the present value of the contract.

Formula for compound present value.—The compound present value may also be calculated by the use of the formula

$$P\left(\frac{1}{(1+i)^n}\right)$$

where

P = sum whose present value is to be ascertained
i = rate of interest per period
n = number of periods

COMPOUND AMOUNT OF 1

	½%	⅝%	¾%	⅞%	1%	1⅛%
1	1.0050 0000	1.0062 5000	1.0075 0000	1.0087 5000	1.0100 0000	1.0112 5000
2	1.0100 2500	1.0125 3906	1.0150 5625	1.0175 7656	1.0201 0000	1.0226 2656
3	1.0150 7513	1.0188 6743	1.0226 6917	1.0264 8036	1.0303 0100	1.0341 3111
4	1.0201 5050	1.0252 3535	1.0303 3919	1.0354 6206	1.0406 0401	1.0457 6509
5	1.0252 5125	1.0316 4307	1.0380 6673	1.0445 2235	1.0510 1005	1.0575 2994
6	1.0303 7751	1.0380 9084	1.0458 5224	1.0536 6192	1.0615 2015	1.0694 2716
7	1.0355 2940	1.0445 7891	1.0536 9613	1.0628 8147	1.0721 3535	1.0814 5821
8	1.0407 0704	1.0511 0753	1.0615 9885	1.0721 8168	1.0828 5671	1.0936 2462
9	1.0459 1058	1.0576 7695	1.0695 6084	1.0815 6327	1.0936 8527	1.1059 2789
10	1.0511 4013	1.0642 8743	1.0775 8255	1.0910 2695	1.1046 2213	1 1183 6958
11	1.0563 9583	1.0709 3923	1.0856 6441	1.1005 7343	1.1156 6835	1.1309 5124
12	1.0616 7781	1.0776 3260	1.0938 0690	1.1102 0345	1.1268 2503	1.1436 7444
13	1.0669 8620	1.0843 6780	1.1020 1045	1.1199 1773	1.1380 9328	1.1565 4078
14	1.0723 2113	1.0911 4510	1.1102 7553	1.1297 1701	1.1494 7421	1.1695 5186
15	1.0776 8274	1.0979 6476	1.1186 0259	1.1396 0203	1.1609 6896	1.1827 0932
16	1.0830 7115	1.1048 2704	1.1269 9211	1.1495 7355	1.1725 7864	1.1960 1480
17	1.0884 8651	1.1117 3221	1.1354 4455	1.1596 3232	1.1843 0443	1.2094 6997
18	1.0939 2894	1.1186 8053	1.1439 6039	1.1697 7910	1.1961 4748	1.2230 7650
19	1.0993 9858	1.1256 7229	1.1525 4009	1.1800 1467	1.2081 0895	1.2368 3611
20	1.1048 9558	1.1327 0774	1.1611 8414	1.1903 3980	1.2201 9004	1.2507 5052
21	1.1104 2006	1.1397 8716	1.1698 9302	1.2007 5527	1.2323 9194	1.2648 2146
22	1.1159 7216	1.1469 1083	1.1786 6722	1.2112 6188	1.2447 1586	1.2790 5071
23	1.1215 5202	1.1540 7902	1.1875 0723	1.2218 6042	1.2571 6302	1.2934 4003
24	1.1271 5978	1.1612 9202	1.1964 1353	1.2325 5170	1.2697 3465	1.3079 9123
25	1.1327 9558	1 1685 5009	1.2053 8663	1.2433 3653	1.2824 3200	1.3227 0613
26	1.1384 5955	1.1758 5353	1.2144 2703	1.2542 1572	1.2952 5631	1.3375 8657
27	1.1441 5185	1.1832 0262	1.2235 3523	1.2651 9011	1.3082 0888	1.3526 3442
28	1.1498 7261	1.1905 9763	1.2327 1175	1.2762 6052	1.3212 9097	1.3678 5156
29	1.1556 2197	1.1980 3887	1.2419 5709	1.2874 2780	1.3345 0388	1.3832 3989
30	1.1614 0008	1.2055 2661	1.2512 7176	1.2986 9280	1.3478 4892	1.3988 0134
31	1.1672 0708	1.2130 6115	1.2606 5630	1.3100 5636	1.3613 2740	1.4145 3785
32	1.1730 4312	1.2206 4278	1.2701 1122	1.3215 1935	1.3749 4068	1.4304 5140
33	1.1789 0833	1.2282 7180	1.2796 3706	1.3330 8265	1.3886 9009	1.4465 4398
34	1.1848 0288	1.2359 4850	1.2892 3434	1.3447 4712	1.4025 7699	1.4628 1760
35	1.1907 2689	1.2436 7318	1.2989 0359	1.3565 1366	1.4166 0276	1.4792 7430
36	1.1966 8052	1.2514 4614	1.3086 4537	1.3683 8315	1.4307 6878	1.4959 1613
37	1.2026 6393	1.2592 6767	1.3184 6021	1.3803 5650	1.4450 7647	1.5127 4519
38	1.2086 7725	1.2671 3810	1.3283 4866	1.3924 3462	1.4595 2724	1.5297 6357
39	1.2147 2063	1.2750 5771	1.3383 1128	1.4046 1843	1.4741 2251	1.5469 7341
40	1.2207 9424	1.2830 2682	1.3483 4861	1.4169 0884	1.4888 6373	1.5643 7687
41	1.2268 9821	1.2910 4574	1.3584 6123	1.4293 0679	1.5037 5237	1.5819 7611
42	1.2330 3270	1.2991 1477	1.3686 4969	1.4418 1322	1.5187 8989	1.5997 7334
43	1.2391 9786	1.3072 3424	1.3789 1456	1.4544 2909	1.5339 7779	1.6177 7079
44	1.2453 9385	1.3154 0446	1.3892 5642	1.4671 5534	1.5493 1757	1.6359 7071
45	1.2516 2082	1.3236 2573	1.3996 7584	1.4799 9295	1.5648 1075	1.6543 7538
46	1.2578 7892	1.3318 9839	1.4101 7341	1.4929 4289	1.5804 5885	1.6729 8710
47	1.2641 6832	1.3402 2276	1.4207 4971	1.5060 0614	1.5962 6344	1.6918 0821
48	1.2704 8916	1.3485 9915	1.4314 0533	1.5191 8370	1.6122 2608	1.7108 4105
49	1.2768 4161	1.3570 2790	1.4421 4087	1.5324 7655	1.6283 4834	1.7300 8801
50	1.2832 2581	1.3655 0932	1.4529 5693	1.5458 8572	1.6446 3182	1.7495 5150
51	1.2896 4194	1.3740 4375	1.4638 5411	1.5594 1222	1.6610 7814	1.7692 3395
52	1.2960 9015	1.3826 3153	1.4748 3301	1.5730 5708	1.6776 8892	1.7891 3784
53	1.3025 7060	1.3912 7297	1.4858 9426	1.5868 2133	1.6944 6581	1.8092 6564
54	1.3090 8346	1.3999 6843	1.4970 3847	1.6007 0602	1.7114 1047	1.8296 1988
55	1.3156 2887	1.4087 1823	1.5082 6626	1.6147 1219	1.7285 2457	1.8502 0310
56	1.3222 0702	1.4175 2272	1.5195 7825	1.6288 4093	1.7458 0982	1.8710 1788
57	1.3288 1805	1.4263 8224	1.5309 7509	1.6430 9328	1.7632 6792	1.8920 6684
58	1.3354 6214	1.4352 9713	1.5424 5740	1.6574 7035	1.7809 0060	1.9133 5259
59	1.3421 3946	1.4442 6773	1.5540 2583	1.6719 7322	1.7987 0960	1.9348 7780
60	1.3488 5015	1.4532 9441	1.5656 8103	1.6866 0298	1.8166 9670	1.9566 4518

From J. W. Glover, "Tables of Applied Math. in Finance, Insurance, Statistics"

COMPOUND AMOUNT OF 1 (*Cont.*)

	1¼%	1⅜%	1½%	1¾%	2%	2¼%
1	1.0125 0000	1.0137 5000	1.0150 0000	1.0175 0000	1.0200 0000	1.0225 0000
2	1.0251 5625	1.0276 8906	1.0302 2500	1.0353 0625	1.0404 0000	1.0455 0625
3	1.0379 7070	1.0418 1979	1.0456 7838	1.0534 2411	1.0612 0800	1.0690 3014
4	1.0509 4534	1.0561 4481	1.0613 6355	1.0718 5903	1.0824 3216	1.0930 8332
5	1.0640 8215	1.0706 6680	1.0772 8400	1.0906 1656	1.1040 8080	1.1176 7769
6	1.0773 8318	1.0853 8847	1.0934 4326	1.1097 0235	1.1261 6242	1.1428 2544
7	1.0908 5047	1.1003 1256	1.1098 4491	1.1291 2215	1.1486 8567	1.1685 3901
8	1.1044 8610	1.1154 4186	1.1264 9259	1.1488 8178	1.1716 5938	1.1948 3114
9	1.1182 9218	1.1307 7918	1.1433 8998	1.1689 8721	1.1950 9257	1.2217 1484
10	1.1322 7083	1.1463 2740	1.1605 4083	1.1894 4449	1.2189 9442	1.2492 0343
11	1.1464 2422	1.1620 8940	1.1779 4894	1.2102 5977	1.2433 7431	1.2773 1050
12	1.1607 5452	1.1780 6813	1.1956 1817	1.2314 3931	1.2682 4179	1.3060 4999
13	1.1752 6395	1.1942 6656	1.2135 5244	1.2529 8950	1.2936 0663	1.3354 3611
14	1.1899 5475	1.2106 8773	1.2317 5573	1.2749 1682	1.3194 7876	1.3654 8343
15	1.2048 2918	1.2273 3469	1.2502 3207	1.2972 2786	1.3458 6834	1.3962 0680
16	1.2198 8955	1.2442 1054	1.2689 8555	1.3199 2935	1.3727 8571	1.4276 2146
17	1.2351 3817	1.2613 1843	1.2880 2033	1.3430 2811	1.4002 4142	1.4597 4294
18	1.2505 7739	1.2786 6156	1.3073 4064	1.3665 3111	1.4282 4625	1.4925 8716
19	1.2662 0961	1.2962 4316	1.3269 5075	1.3904 4540	1.4568 1117	1.5261 7037
20	1.2820 3723	1.3140 6650	1.3468 5501	1.4147 7820	1.4859 4740	1.5605 0920
21	1.2980 6270	1.3321 3492	1.3670 5783	1.4395 3681	1.5156 6634	1.5956 2066
22	1.3142 8848	1.3504 5177	1.3875 6370	1.4647 2871	1.5459 7967	1.6315 2212
23	1.3307 1709	1.3690 2048	1.4083 7715	1.4903 6146	1.5768 9926	1.6682 3137
24	1.3473 5105	1.3878 4451	1.4295 0281	1.5164 4279	1.6084 3725	1.7057 6658
25	1.3641 9294	1.4069 2738	1.4509 4535	1.5429 8054	1.6406 0599	1.7441 4632
26	1.3812 4535	1.4262 7263	1.4727 0953	1.5699 8269	1.6734 1811	1.7833 8962
27	1.3985 1092	1.4458 8388	1.4948 0018	1.5974 5739	1.7068 8648	1.8235 1588
28	1.4159 9230	1.4657 6478	1.5172 2218	1.6254 1290	1.7410 2421	1.8645 4499
29	1.4336 9221	1.4859 1905	1.5399 8051	1.6538 5762	1.7758 4469	1.9064 9725
30	1.4516 1336	1.5063 5043	1.5630 8022	1.6828 0013	1.8113 6158	1.9493 9344
31	1.4697 5853	1.5270 6275	1.5865 2642	1.7122 4913	1.8475 8882	1.9932 5479
32	1.4881 3051	1.5480 5986	1.6103 2432	1.7422 1349	1.8845 4059	2.0381 0303
33	1.5067 3214	1.5693 4569	1.6344 7918	1.7727 0223	1.9222 3140	2.0839 6034
34	1.5255 6629	1.5909 2419	1.6589 9637	1.8037 2452	1.9606 7603	2.1308 4945
35	1.5446 3587	1.6127 9940	1.6838 8132	1.8352 8970	1.9998 8955	2.1787 9356
36	1.5639 4382	1.6349 7539	1.7091 3954	1.8674 0727	2.0398 8734	2.2278 1642
37	1.5834 9312	1.6574 5630	1.7347 7663	1.9000 8689	2.0806 8509	2.2779 4229
38	1.6032 8678	1.6802 4633	1.7607 9828	1.9333 3841	2.1222 9879	2.3291 9599
39	1.6233 2787	1.7033 4971	1.7872 1025	1.9671 7184	2.1647 4477	2.3816 0290
40	1.6436 1946	1.7267 7077	1.8140 1841	2.0015 9734	2.2080 3966	2.4351 8897
41	1.6641 6471	1.7505 1387	1.8412 2868	2.0366 2530	2.2522 0046	2.4899 8072
42	1.6849 6677	1.7745 8343	1.8688 4712	2.0722 6624	2.2972 4447	2.5460 0528
43	1.7060 2885	1.7989 8396	1.8968 7982	2.1085 3090	2.3431 8936	2.6032 9040
44	1.7273 5421	1.8237 1999	1.9253 3302	2.1454 3019	2.3900 5314	2.6618 6444
45	1.7489 4614	1.8487 9614	1.9542 1301	2.1829 7522	2.4378 5421	2.7217 5639
46	1.7708 0797	1.8742 1708	1.9835 2621	2.2211 7728	2.4866 1129	2.7829 9590
47	1.7929 4306	1.8999 8757	2.0132 7910	2.2600 4789	2.5363 4351	2.8456 1331
48	1.8153 5485	1.9261 1240	2.0434 7829	2.2995 9872	2.5870 7039	2.9096 3961
49	1.8380 4679	1.9525 9644	2.0741 3046	2.3398 4170	2.6388 1179	2.9751 0650
50	1.8610 2237	1.9794 4464	2.1052 4242	2.3807 8893	2.6915 8803	3.0420 4640
51	1.8842 8515	2.0066 6201	2.1368 2106	2.4224 5274	2.7454 1979	3.1104 9244
52	1.9078 3872	2.0342 5361	2.1688 7337	2.4648 4566	2.8003 2819	3.1804 7852
53	1.9316 8670	2.0622 2460	2.2014 0647	2.5079 8046	2.8563 3475	3.2520 3929
54	1.9558 3279	2.0905 8019	2.2344 2757	2.5518 7012	2.9134 6144	3.3252 1017
55	1.9802 8070	2.1193 2566	2.2679 4398	2.5965 2785	2.9717 3067	3.4000 2740
56	2.0050 3420	2.1484 6639	2.3019 6314	2.6419 6708	3.0311 6529	3.4765 2802
57	2.0300 9713	2.1780 0780	2.3364 9259	2.6882 0151	3.0917 8859	3.5547 4990
58	2.0554 7335	2.2079 5541	2.3715 3998	2.7352 4503	3.1536 2436	3.6347 3177
59	2.0811 6676	2.2383 1480	2.4071 1308	2.7831 1182	3.2166 9685	3.7165 1324
60	2.1071 8135	2.2690 9163	2.4432 1978	2.8318 1628	3.2810 3079	3.8001 3479

COMPOUND AMOUNT OF 1 (*Cont.*)

	2½%	2¾%	3%	3½%	4%	4½%
1	1.0250 0000	1.0275 0000	1.0300 0000	1.0350 0000	1.0400 0000	1.0450 0000
2	1.0506 2500	1.0557 5625	1.0609 0000	1.0712 2500	1.0816 0000	1.0920 2500
3	1.0768 9063	1.0847 8955	1.0927 2700	1.1087 1788	1.1248 6400	1.1411 6613
4	1.1038 1289	1.1146 2126	1.1255 0881	1.1475 2300	1.1698 5856	1.1925 1860
5	1.1314 0821	1.1452 7334	1.1592 7407	1.1876 8631	1.2166 5290	1.2461 8194
6	1.1596 9342	1.1767 6836	1.1940 5230	1.2292 5533	1.2653 1902	1.3022 6012
7	1.1886 8575	1.2091 2949	1.2298 7387	1.2722 7926	1.3159 3178	1.3608 6183
8	1.2184 0290	1.2423 8055	1.2667 7008	1.3168 0904	1.3685 6905	1.4221 0061
9	1.2488 6297	1.2765 4602	1.3047 7318	1.3628 9735	1.4233 1181	1.4860 9514
10	1.2800 8454	1.3116 5103	1.3439 1638	1.4105 9876	1.4802 4428	1.5529 6942
11	1.3120 8666	1.3477 2144	1.3842 3387	1.4599 6972	1.5394 5406	1.6228 5305
12	1.3448 8882	1.3847 8378	1.4257 6089	1.5110 6866	1.6010 3222	1.6958 8143
13	1.3785 1104	1.4228 6533	1.4685 3371	1.5639 5606	1.6650 7351	1.7721 9610
14	1.4129 7382	1.4619 9413	1.5125 8972	1.6186 9452	1.7316 7645	1.8519 4492
15	1.4482 9817	1.5021 9896	1.5579 6742	1.6753 4883	1.8009 4351	1.9352 8244
16	1.4845 0562	1.5435 0944	1.6047 0644	1.7339 8604	1.8729 8125	2.0223 7015
17	1.5216 1826	1.5859 5595	1.6528 4763	1.7946 7555	1.9479 0050	2.1133 7681
18	1.5596 5872	1.6295 6973	1.7024 3306	1.8574 8920	2.0258 1652	2.2084 7877
19	1.5986 5019	1.6743 8290	1.7535 0605	1.9225 0132	2.1068 4918	2.3078 6031
20	1.6386 1644	1.7204 2843	1.8061 1123	1.9897 8886	2.1911 2314	2.4117 1402
21	1.6795 8185	1.7677 4021	1.8602 9457	2.0594 3147	2.2787 6807	2.5202 4116
22	1.7215 7140	1.8163 5307	1.9161 0341	2.1315 1158	2.3699 1879	2.6336 5201
23	1.7646 1068	1.8663 0278	1.9735 8651	2.2061 1448	2.4647 1554	2.7521 6635
24	1.8087 2595	1.9176 2610	2.0327 9411	2.2833 2849	2.5633 0416	2.8760 1383
25	1.8539 4410	1.9703 6082	2.0937 7793	2.3632 4498	2.6658 3633	3.0054 3446
26	1.9002 9270	2.0245 4575	2.1565 9127	2.4459 5856	2.7724 6978	3.1406 7901
27	1.9478 0002	2.0802 2075	2.2212 8901	2.5315 6711	2.8833 6858	3.2820 0956
28	1.9964 9502	2.1374 2682	2.2879 2768	2.6201 7196	2.9987 0332	3.4296 9999
29	2.0464 0739	2.1962 0606	2.3565 6551	2.7118 7798	3.1186 5145	3.5840 3649
30	2.0975 6758	2.2566 0173	2.4272 6247	2.8067 9370	3.2433 9751	3.7453 1813
31	2.1500 0677	2.3186 5828	2.5000 8035	2.9050 3148	3.3731 3341	3.9138 5745
32	2.2037 5694	2.3824 2138	2.5750 8276	3.0067 0759	3.5080 5875	4.0899 8104
33	2.2588 5086	2.4479 3797	2.6523 3524	3.1119 4235	3.6483 8110	4.2740 3018
34	2.3153 2213	2.5152 5626	2.7319 0530	3.2208 6033	3.7943 1634	4.4663 6154
35	2.3732 0519	2.5844 2581	2.8138 6245	3.3335 9045	3.9460 8899	4.6673 4781
36	2.4325 3532	2.6554 9752	2.8982 7833	3.4502 6611	4.1039 3255	4.8773 7846
37	2.4933 4870	2.7285 2370	2.9852 2668	3.5710 2543	4.2680 8986	5.0968 6049
38	2.5556 8242	2.8035 5810	3.0747 8348	3.6960 1132	4.4388 1345	5.3262 1921
39	2.6195 7448	2.8806 5595	3.1670 2698	3.8253 7171	4.6163 6599	5.5658 9908
40	2.6850 6384	2.9598 7399	3.2620 3779	3.9592 5972	4.8010 2063	5.8163 6454
41	2.7521 9043	3.0412 7052	3.3598 9893	4.0978 3381	4.9930 6145	6.0781 0094
42	2.8209 9520	3.1249 0546	3.4606 9589	4.2412 5799	5.1927 8391	6.3516 1548
43	2.8915 2008	3.2108 4036	3.5645 1677	4.3897 0202	5.4004 9527	6.6374 3818
44	2.9638 0808	3.2991 3847	3.6714 5227	4.5433 4160	5.6165 1508	6.9361 2290
45	3.0379 0328	3.3898 6478	3.7815 9584	4.7023 5855	5.8411 7568	7.2482 4843
46	3.1138 5086	3.4830 8606	3.8950 4372	4.8669 4110	6.0748 2271	7.5744 1961
47	3.1916 9713	3.5788 7093	4.0118 9503	5.0372 8404	6.3178 1562	7.9152 6849
48	3.2714 8956	3.6772 8988	4.1322 5188	5.2135 8898	6.5705 2824	8.2714 5557
49	3.3532 7680	3.7784 1535	4.2562 1944	5.3960 6459	6.8333 4937	8.6436 7107
50	3.4371 0872	3.8823 2177	4.3839 0602	5.5849 2686	7.1066 8335	9.0326 3627
51	3.5230 3644	3.9890 8562	4.5154 2320	5.7803 9930	7.3909 5068	9.4391 0490
52	3.6111 1235	4.0987 8547	4.6508 8590	5.9827 1327	7.6865 8871	9.8638 6463
53	3.7013 9016	4.2115 0208	4.7904 1247	6.1921 0824	7.9940 5226	10.3077 3853
54	3.7939 2491	4.3273 1838	4.9341 2485	6.4088 3202	8.3138 1435	10.7715 8677
55	3.8887 7303	4.4463 1964	5.0821 4859	6.6331 4114	8.6463 6692	11.2563 0817
56	3.9859 9236	4.5685 9343	5.2346 1305	6.8653 0108	8.9922 2160	11.7628 4204
57	4.0856 4217	4.6942 2975	5.3916 5144	7.1055 8662	9.3519 1046	12.2921 6993
58	4.1877 8322	4.8233 2107	5.5534 0098	7.3542 8215	9.7259 8688	12.8453 1758
59	4.2924 7780	4.9559 6239	5.7200 0301	7.6116 8203	10.1150 2635	13.4233 5687
60	4.3997 8975	5.0922 5136	5.8916 0310	7.8780 9090	10.5196 2741	14.0274 0793

COMPOUND AMOUNT OF 1 (*Cont.*)

	5%	5½%	6%	6½%	7%	8%
1	1.0500 0000	1.0550 0000	1.0600 0000	1.0650 0000	1.0700 0000	1.0800 0000
2	1.1025 0000	1.1130 2500	1.1236 0000	1.1342 2500	1.1449 0000	1.1664 0000
3	1.1576 2500	1.1742 4138	1.1910 1600	1.2079 4963	1.2250 4300	1.2597 1200
4	1.2155 0625	1.2388 2465	1.2624 7696	1.2864 6635	1.3107 9601	1.3604 8896
5	1.2762 8156	1.3069 6001	1.3382 2558	1.3700 8666	1.4025 5173	1.4693 2808
6	1.3400 9564	1.3788 4281	1.4185 1911	1.4591 4230	1.5007 3035	1.5868 7432
7	1.4071 0042	1.4546 7916	1.5036 3026	1.5539 8655	1.6057 8148	1.7138 2427
8	1.4774 5544	1.5346 8651	1.5938 4807	1.6549 9567	1.7181 8618	1.8509 3021
9	1.5513 2822	1.6190 9427	1.6894 7896	1.7625 7039	1.8384 5921	1.9990 0463
10	1.6288 9463	1.7081 4446	1.7908 4770	1.8771 3747	1.9671 5136	2.1589 2500
11	1.7103 3936	1.8020 9240	1.8982 9856	1.9991 5140	2.1048 5195	2.3316 3900
12	1.7958 5633	1.9012 0749	2.0121 9647	2.1290 9624	2.2521 9159	2.5181 7012
13	1.8856 4914	2.0057 7390	2.1329 2826	2.2674 8750	2.4098 4500	2.7196 2373
14	1.9799 3160	2.1160 9146	2.2609 0396	2.4148 7418	2.5785 3415	2.9371 9362
15	2.0789 2818	2.2324 7649	2.3965 5819	2.5718 4101	2.7590 3154	3.1721 6911
16	2.1828 7459	2.3552 6270	2.5403 5168	2.7390 1067	2.9521 6375	3.4259 4264
17	2.2920 1832	2.4848 0215	2.6927 7279	2.9170 4637	3.1588 1521	3.7000 1805
18	2.4066 1923	2.6214 6627	2.8543 3915	3.1066 5438	3.3799 3228	3.9960 1950
19	2.5269 5020	2.7656 4691	3.0255 9950	3.3085 8691	3.6165 2754	4.3157 0106
20	2.6532 9771	2.9177 5749	3.2071 3547	3.5236 4506	3.8696 8446	4.6609 5714
21	2.7859 6259	3.0782 3415	3.3995 6360	3.7526 8199	4.1405 6237	5.0338 3372
22	2.9252 6072	3.2475 3703	3.6035 3742	3.9966 0632	4.4304 0174	5.4365 4041
23	3.0715 2376	3.4261 5157	3.8197 4966	4.2563 8573	4.7405 2986	5.8714 6365
24	3.2250 9994	3.6145 8990	4.0489 3464	4.5330 5081	5.0723 6695	6.3411 8074
25	3.3863 5494	3.8133 9235	4.2918 7072	4.8276 9911	5.4274 3264	6.8484 7520
26	3.5556 7269	4.0231 2893	4.5493 8296	5.1414 9955	5.8073 5292	7.3963 5321
27	3.7334 5632	4.2444 0102	4.8223 4594	5.4756 9702	6.2138 6763	7.9880 6147
28	3.9201 2914	4.4778 4307	5.1116 8670	5.8316 1733	6.6488 3836	8.6271 0639
29	4.1161 3560	4.7241 2444	5.4183 8790	6.2106 7245	7.1142 5705	9.3172 7490
30	4.3219 4238	4.9839 5129	5.7434 9117	6.6143 6616	7.6122 5504	10.0626 5689
31	4.5380 3949	5.2580 6861	6.0881 0064	7.0442 9996	8.1451 1290	10.8676 6944
32	4.7649 4147	5.5472 6238	6.4533 8668	7.5021 7946	8.7152 7080	11.7370 8300
33	5.0031 8854	5.8523 6181	6.8405 8988	7.9898 2113	9.3253 3975	12.6760 4964
34	5.2533 4797	6.1742 4171	7.2510 2528	8.5091 5950	9.9781 1354	13.6901 3361
35	5.5160 1537	6.5138 2501	7.6860 8679	9.0622 5487	10.6765 8148	14.7853 4429
36	5.7918 1614	6.8720 8538	8.1472 5200	9.6513 0143	11.4239 4219	15.9681 7184
37	6.0814 0694	7.2500 5008	8.6360 8712	10.2786 3603	12.2236 1814	17.2456 2558
38	6.3854 7729	7.6488 0283	9.1542 5235	10.9467 4737	13.0792 7141	18.6252 7563
39	6.7047 5115	8.0694 8699	9.7035 0749	11.6582 8595	13.9948 2041	20.1152 9768
40	7.0399 8871	8.5133 0877	10.2857 1794	12.4160 7453	14.9744 5784	21.7245 2150
41	7.3919 8815	8.9815 4076	10.9028 6101	13.2231 1938	16.0226 6989	23.4624 8322
42	7.7615 8756	9.4755 2550	11.5570 3267	14.0826 2214	17.1442 5678	25.3394 8187
43	8.1496 6693	9.9966 7940	12.2504 5463	14.9979 9258	18.3443 5475	27.3666 4042
44	8.5571 5028	10.5464 9677	12.9854 8191	15.9728 6209	19.6284 5959	29.5559 7166
45	8.9850 0779	11.1265 5409	13.7646 1083	17.0110 9813	21.0024 5176	31.9204 4939
46	9.4342 5818	11.7385 1456	14.5904 8748	18.1168 1951	22.4726 2338	34.4740 8534
47	9.9059 7109	12.3841 3287	15.4659 1673	19.2944 1278	24.0457 0702	37.2320 1217
48	10.4012 6965	13.0652 6017	16.3938 7173	20.5485 4961	25.7289 0651	40.2105 7314
49	10.9213 3313	13.7838 4948	17.3775 0403	21.8842 0533	27.5299 2997	43.4274 1899
50	11.4673 9979	14.5419 6120	18.4201 5427	23.3066 7868	29.4570 2506	46.9016 1251
51	12.0407 6978	15.3417 6907	19.5253 6353	24.8216 1279	31.5190 1682	50.6537 4151
52	12.6428 0826	16.1855 6637	20.6968 8534	26.4350 1762	33.7253 4799	54.7060 4084
53	13.2749 4868	17.0757 7252	21.9386 9846	28.1532 9377	36.0861 2235	59.0825 2410
54	13.9386 9611	18.0149 4001	23.2550 2037	29.9832 5786	38.6121 5092	63.8091 2603
55	14.6356 3092	19.0057 6171	24.6503 2159	31.9321 6963	41.3150 0148	68.9138 5611
56	15.3674 1246	20.0510 7860	26.1293 4089	34.0077 6065	44.2070 5159	74.4269 6460
57	16.1357 8309	21.1538 8793	27.6971 0134	36.2182 6509	47.3015 4520	80.3811 2177
58	16.9425 7224	22.3173 5176	29.3589 2742	38.5724 5233	50.6126 5336	86.8116 1151
59	17.7897 0085	23.5448 0611	31.1204 6307	41.0796 6173	54.1555 3910	93.7565 4043
60	18.6791 8589	24.8397 7045	32.9876 9085	43.7498 3974	57.9464 2683	101.2570 6367

COMPOUND PRESENT VALUE OF 1

	½%	⅝%	¾%	⅞%	1%	1⅛%
1	0.9950 2488	0.9937 8882	0.9925 5583	0.9913 2590	0.9900 9901	0.9888 7515
2	0.9900 7450	0.9876 1622	0.9851 6708	0.9827 2704	0.9802 9605	0.9778 7407
3	0.9851 4876	0.9814 8196	0.9778 3333	0.9742 0276	0.9705 9015	0.9669 9537
4	0.9802 4752	0.9753 8580	0.9705 5417	0.9657 5243	0.9609 8034	0.9562 3770
5	0.9753 7067	0.9693 2750	0.9633 2920	0.9573 7539	0.9514 6569	0.9455 9970
6	0.9705 1808	0.9633 0683	0.9561 5802	0.9490 7102	0.9420 4524	0,9350 8005
7	0.9656 8963	0.9573 2356	0.9490 4022	0.9408 3868	0.9327 1805	0.9246 7743
8	0.9608 8520	0.9513 7745	0.941 7540	0.9326 7775	0.9234 8322	0.9143 9054
9	0.9561 0468	0.9454 6827	0.9349 6318	0.9245 8761	0.9143 3982	0.9042 1808
10	0.9513 4794	0.9395 9580	0.9280 0315	0.9165 6765.	0.9052 8695	0.8941 5881
11	0.9466 1489	0.9337 5980	0.9210 9494	0.9086 1724	0.8963 2372	0.8842 1142
12	0.9419 0534	0.9279 6005	0.9142 3815	0.9007 3581	0.8874 4923	0.8743 7470
13	0.9372 1924	0.9221 9632	0.9074 3241	0.8929 2273	0.8786 6260	0.8646 4742
14	0.9325 5646	0.9164 6840	0.9006 7733	0.8851 7743	0.8699 6297	0.8550 2835
15	0.9279 1688	0.9107 7604	0.8939 7254	0.8774 9931	0.8613 4947	0.8455 1629
16	0.9233 0037	0.9051 1905	0.8873 1766	0.8698 8779	0.8528 2126	0.8361 1005
17	0.9187 0684	0.8994 9719	0.8807 1231	0.8623 4230	0.8443 7749	0.8268 0846
18	0.9141 3616	0.8939 1025	0.8741 5614	0.8548 6225	0.8360 1731	0.8176 1034
19	0.9095 8822	0.8883 5802	0.8676 4878	0.8474 4709	0.8277 3992	0.8085 1455
20	0.9050 6290	0.8828 4027	0.8611 8985	0.8400 9624	0.8195 4447	0.7995 1995
21	0.9005 6010	0.8773 5679	0.8547 7901	0.8328 0917	0.8114 3017	0.7906 2542
22	0.8960 7971	0.8719 0736	0.8484 1589	0.8255 8530	0.8033 9621	0.7818 2983
23	0.8916 2160	0.8664 9179	0.8421 0014	0.8184 2409	0.7954 4179	0.7731 3210
24	0.8871 8567	0.8611 0985	0.8358 3140	0.8113 2499	0.7875 6613	0.7645 3112
25	0.8827 7181	0.8557 6135	0.8296 0933	0.8042 8748	0.7797 6844	0.7560 2583
26	0.8783 7991	0.8504 4606	0.8234 3358	0.7973 1101	0.7720 4796	0.7476 1516
27	0.8740 0986	0.8451 6378	0.8173 0380	0.7903 9505	0.7644 0392	0.7392 9806
28	0.8696 6155	0.8399 1432	0.8112 1966	0.7835 3908	0.7568 3557	0.7310 7348
29	0.8653 3488	0.8346 9746	0.8051 8080	0.7767 4258	0.7493 4215	0.7229 4040
30	0.8610 2973	0.8295 1300	0.7991 8690	0.7700 0504	0.7419 2292	0.7148 9780
31	0.8567 4600	0.8243 6075	0.7932 3762	0.7633 2594	0.7345 7715	0.7069 4467
32	0.8524 8358	0.8192 4050	0.7873 3262	0.7567 0477	0.7273 0411	0.6990 8002
33	0.8482 4237	0.8141 5205	0.7814 7158	0.7501 4104	0.7201 0307	0.6913 0287
34	0.8440 2226	0.8090 9520	0.7756 5418	0.7436 3424	0.7129 7334	0.6836 1223
35	0,8398 2314	0.8040 6976	0.7698 8008	0.7371 8388	0.7059 1420	0.6760 0715
36	0.8356 4492	0.7990 7554	0.7641 4896	0.7307 8947	0.6989 2495	0.6684 8667
37	0.8314 8748	0.7941 1234	0.7584 6051	0.7244 5053	0.6920 0490	0.6610 4986
38	0.8273 5073	0.7891 7997	0.7528 1440	0.7181 6657	0.6851 5337	0.6536 9578
39	0.8232 3455	0.7842 7823	0.7472 1032	0.7119 3712	0.6783 6967	0.6464 2352
40	0.8191 3886	0.7794 0693	0.7416 4796	0.7057 6171	0.6716 5314	0.6392 3216
41	0.8150 6354	0.7745 6590	0.7361 2701	0.6996 3986	0.6650 0311	0.6321 2080
42	0.8110 0850	0.7697 5493	0.7306 4716	0.6935 7111	0.6584 1892	0.6250 8855
43	0.8069 7363	0.7649 7384	0.7252 0809	0.6875 5500	0.6518 9992	0.6181 3454
44	0.8029 5884	0.7602 2245	0.7198 0952	0.6815 9108	0.6454 4546	0.6112 5789
45	0.7989 6402	0.7555 0057	0.7144 5114	0.6756 7889	0.6390 5492	0.6044 5774
46	0.7949 8907	0.7508 0802	0.7091 3264	0.6698 1798	0.6327 2764	0.5977 3324
47	0.7910 3390	0.7461 4462	0.7038 5374	0.6640 0792	0.6264 6301	0.5910 8355
48	0.7870 9841	0.7415 1018	0.6986 1414	0.6582 4824	0.6202 6041	0.5845 0784
49	0.7831 8250	0.7369 0453	0.6934 1353	0.6525 3853	0.6141 1921	0.5780 0528
50	0.7792 8607	0.7323 2748	0.6882 5165	0.6468 7835	0.6080 3882	0.5715 7506
51	0.7754 0902	0.7277 7886	0.6831 2819	0.6412 6726	0.6020 1864	0.5652 1637
52	0.7715 5127	0.7232 5849	0.6780 4286	0.6357 0484	0.5960 5806	0.5589 2843
53	0.7677 1270	0.7187 6620	0.6729 9540	0.6301 9067	0.5901 5649	0.5527 1044
54	0.7638 9324	0.7143 0182	0.6679 8551	0.6247 2433	0.5843 1336	0.5465 6162
55	0.7600 9277	0.7098 6516	0.6630 1291	0.6193 0541	0.5785 2808	0.5404 8120
56	0.7563 1122	0.7054 5606	0.6580 7733	0.6139 3349	0.5728 0008	0.5344 6843
57	0.7525 4847	0.7010 7434	0.6531 7849	0.6086 0817	0.5671 2879	0.5285 2256
58	0.7488 0445	0.6967 1985	0.6483 1612	0.6033 2904	0.5615 1365	0.5226 4282
59	0.7450 7906	0.6923 9239	0.6434 8995	0.5980 9571	0.5559 5411	0.5168 2850
60	0.7413 7220	0.6880 9182	0.6386 9970	0.5929 0776	0.5504 4962	0.5110 7887

From J. W. Glover, "Tables of Applied Math. in Finance, Insurance, Statistics"

COMPOUND PRESENT VALUE OF 1 (*Cont.*)

	1¼%	1⅜%	1½%	1¾%	2%	2¼%
1	0.9876 5432	0.9864 3650	0.9852 2167	0.9828 0098	0.9803 9216	0.9779 9511
2	0.9754 6106	0.9730 5696	0.9706 6175	0.9658 9777	0.9611 6878	0.9564 7444
3	0.9634 1833	0.9598 5890	0.9563 1699	0.9492 8528	0.9423 2233	0.9354 2732
4	0.9515 2428	0.9468 3986	0.9421 8423	0.9329 5851	0.9238 4543	0.9148 4335
5	0.9397 7706	0.9339 9739	0.9282 6033	0.9169 1254	0.9057 3081	0.8947 1232
6	0.9281 7488	0.9213 2912	0.9145 4219	0.9011 4254	0.8879 7138	0.8750 2427
7	0.9167 1593	0.9088 3267	0.9010 2679	0.8856 4378	0.8705 6018	0.8557 6946
8	0.9053 9845	0.8965 0571	0.8877 1112	0.8704 1157	0.8534 9037	0.8369 3835
9	0.8942 2069	0.8843 4596	0.8745 9224	0.8554 4135	0.8367 5527	0.8185 2161
10	0.8831 8093	0.8723 5113	0.8616 6723	0.8407 2860	0.8203 4830	0.8005 1013
11	0.8722 7746	0.8605 1899	0.8489 3323	0.8262 6889	0.8042 6304	0.7828 9499
12	0.8615 0860	0.8488 4734	0.8363 8742	0.8120 5788	0.7884 9318	0.7656 6748
13	0.8508 7269	0.8373 3400	0.8240 2702	0.7980 9128	0.7730 3253	0.7488 1905
14	0.8403 6809	0.8259 7682	0.8118 4928	0.7843 6490	0.7578 7502	0.7323 4137
15	0.8299 9318	0.8147 7368	0.7998 5150	0.7708 7459	0.7430 1473	0.7162 2628
16	0.8197 4635	0.8037 2250	0.7880 3104	0.7576 1631	0.7284 4581	0.7004 6580
17	0.8096 2602	0.7928 2120	0.7763 8526	0.7445 8605	0.7141 6256	0.6850 5212
18	0.7996 3064	0.7820 6777	0.7649 1159	0.7317 7990	0.7001 5937	0.6699 7763
19	0.7897 5866	0.7714 6020	0.7536 0747	0.7191 9401	0.6864 3076	0.6552 3484
20	0.7800 0855	0.7609 9649	0.7424 7042	0.7068 2458	0.6729 7133	0.6408 1647
21	0.7703 7881	0.7506 7472	0.7314 9795	0.6946 6789	0.6597 7582	0.6267 1538
22	0.7608 6796	0.7404 9294	0.7206 8763	0.6827 2028	0.6468 3904	0.6129 2457
23	0.7514 7453	0.7304 4926	0.7100 3708	0.6709 7817	0.6341 5592	0.5994 3724
24	0.7421 9707	0.7205 4181	0.6995 4392	0.6594 3800	0.6217 2149	0.5862 4668
25	0.7330 3414	0.7107 6874	0.6892 0583	0.6480 9632	0.6095 3087	0.5733 4639
26	0.7239 8434	0.7011 2823	0.6790 2052	0.6369 4970	0.5975 7928	0.5607 2997
27	0.7150 4626	0.6916 1847	0.6689 8574	0.6259 9479	0.5858 6204	0.5483 9117
28	0.7062 1853	0.6822 3771	0.6590 9925	0.6152 2829	0.5743 7455	0.5363 2388
29	0.6974 9978	0.6729 8417	0.6493 5887	0.6046 4697	0.5631 1231	0.5245 2213
30	0.6888 8867	0.6638 5615	0.6397 6243	0.5942 4764	0.5520 7089	0.5129 8008
31	0.6803 8387	0.6548 5194	0.6303 0781	0.5840 2716	0.5412 4597	0.5016 9201
32	0.6719 8407	0.6459 6985	0.6209 9292	0.5739 8247	0.5306 3330	0.4906 5233
33	0.6636 8797	0.6372 0824	0.6118 1568	0.5641 1053	0.5202 2873	0.4798 5558
34	0.6554 9429	0.6285 6546	0.6027 7407	0.5544 0839	0.5100 2817	0.4692 9641
35	0.6474 0177	0.6200 3991	0.5938 6608	0.5448 7311	0.5000 2761	0.4589 6960
36	0.6394 0916	0.6116 3000	0.5850 8974	0.5355 0183	0.4902 2315	0.4488 7002
37	0.6315 1522	0.6033 3416	0.5764 4309	0.5262 9172	0.4806 1093	0.4389 9268
38	0.6237 1873	0.5951 5083	0.5679 2423	0.5172 4002	0.4711 8719	0.4293 3270
39	0.6160 1850	0.5870 7850	0.5595 3126	0.5083 4400	0.4619 4822	0.4198 8528
40	0.6084 1334	0.5791 1566	0.5512 6232	0.4996 0098	0.4528 9042	0.4106 4575
41	0.6009 0206	0.5712 6083	0.5431 1559	0.4910 0834	0.4440 1021	0.4016 0954
42	0.5934 8352	0.5635 1253	0.5350 8925	0.4825 6348	0.4353 0413	0.3927 7216
43	0.5861 5656	0.5558 6933	0.5271 8153	0.4742 6386	0.4267 6875	0.3841 2925
44	0.5789 2006	0.5483 2979	0.5193 9067	0.4661 0699	0.4184 0074	0.3756 7653
45	0.5717 7290	0.5408 9252	0.5117 1494	0.4580 9040	0.4101 9680	0.3674 0981
46	0.5647 1397	0.5335 5612	0.5041 5265	0.4502 1170	0.4021 5373	0.3593 2500
47	0.5577 4219	0.5263 1923	0.4967 0212	0.4424 6850	0.3942 6836	0.3514 1809
48	0.5508 5649	0.5191 8050	0.4893 6170	0.4348 5848	0.3865 3761	0.3436 8518
49	0.5440 5579	0.5121 3860	0.4821 2975	0.4273 7934	0.3789 5844	0.3361 2242
50	0.5373 3905	0.5051 9220	0.4750 0468	0.4200 2883	0.3715 2788	0.3287 2608
51	0.5307 0524	0.4983 4003	0.4679 8491	0.4128 0475	0.3642 4302	0.3214 9250
52	0.5241 5332	0.4915 8079	0.4610 6887	0.4057 0492	0.3571 0100	0.3144 1810
53	0.5176 8229	0.4849 1323	0.4542 5505	0.3987 2719	0.3500 9902	0.3074 9936
54	0.5112 9115	0.4783 3611	0.4475 4192	0.3918 6947	0.3432 3433	0.3007 3287
55	0.5049 7892	0.4718 4820	0.4409 2800	0.3851 2970	0.3365 0425	0.2941 1528
56	0.4987 4461	0.4654 4829	0.4344 1182	0.3785 0585	0.3299 0613	0.2876 4330
57	0.4925 8727	0.4591 3518	0.4279 9194	0.3719 9592	0.3234 3738	0.2813 1374
58	0.4865 0594	0.4529 0770	0.4216 6694	0.3655 9796	0.3170 9547	0.2751 2347
59	0.4804 9970	0.4467 6468	0.4154 3541	0.3593 1003	0.3108 7791	0.2690 6940
60	0.4745 6760	0.4407 0499	0.4092 9597	0.3531 3025	0.3047 8227	0.2631 4856

COMPOUND PRESENT VALUE OF 1 (*Cont.*)

	2½%	2¾%	3%	3½%	4%	4½%
1	0.9756 0976	0.9732 3601	0.9708 7379	0.9661 8357	0.9615 3846	0.9569 3780
2	0.9518 1440	0.9471 8833	0.9425 9591	0.9335 1070	0.9245 5621	0.9157 2995
3	0.9285 9941	0.9218 3779	0.9151 4166	0.9019 4271	0.8889 9636	0.8762 9660
4	0.9059 5064	0.8971 6573	0.8884 8705	0.8714 4223	0.8548 0419	0.8385 6134
5	0.8838 5429	0.8731 5400	0.8626 0878	0.8419 7317	0.8219 2711	0.8024 5105
6	0.8622 9687	0.8497 8491	0.8374 8426	0.8135 0064	0,7903 1453	0.7678 9574
7	0.8412 6524	0.8270 4128	0.8130 9151	0.7859 9096	0.7599 1781	0.7348 2846
8	0.8207 4657	0.8049 0635	0.7894 0923	0.7594 1156	0.7306 9021	0.7031 8513
9	0.8007 2836	0.7833 6385	0.7664 1673	0.7337 3097	0.7025 8674	0.6729 0443
10	0.7811 9840	0.7623 9791	0.7440 9391	0.7089 1881	0.6755 6417	0.6439 2768
11	0.7621 4478	0.7419 9310	0.7224 2128	0.6849 4571	0.6495 8093	0.6161 9874
12	0.7435 5589	0.7221 3440	0.7013 7988	0.6617 8330	0.6245 9705	0.5896 6386
13	0.7254 2038	0.7028 0720	0.6809 5134	0.6394 0415	0.6005 7409	0.5642 7164
14	0.7077 2720	0.6839 9728	0.6611 1781	0.6177 8179	0.5774 7508	0.5399 7286
15	0.6904 6556	0.6656 9078	0.6418 6195	0.5968 9062	0.5552 6450	0.5167 2044
16	0.6736 2493	0.6478 7424	0.6231 6694	0.5767 0591	0.5339 0818	0.4944 6932
17	0.6571 9506	0.6305 3454	0.6050 1645	0.5572 0378	0.5133 7325	0.4731 7639
18	0.6411 6591	0.6136 5892	0.5873 9461	0.5383 6114	0.4936 2812	0.4528 0037
19	0.6255 2772	0.5972 3496	0.5702 8603	0.5201 5569	0.4746 4242	0.4333 0179
20	0.6102 7094	0.5812 5057	0.5536 7575	0.5025 6588	0.4563 8695	0.4146 4286
21	0.5953 8629	0.5656 9398	0.5375 4928	0.4855 7090	0.4388 3360	0.3967 8743
22	0.5808 6467	0.5505 5375	0.5218 9250	0.4691 5063	0.4219 5539	0.3797 0089
23	0.5666 9724	0.5358 1874	0.5066 9175	0.4532 8563	0.4057 2633	0.3633 5013
24	0.5528 7535	0.5214 7809	0.4919 3374	0.4379 5713	0.3901 2147	0.3477 0347
25	0.5393 9059	0.5075 2126	0.4776 0557	0.4231 4699	0.3751 1680	0.3327 3060
26	0.5262 3472	0.4939 3796	0.4636 9473	0.4088 3767	0.3606 8923	0.3184 0248
27	0.5133 9973	0.4807 1821	0.4501 8906	0.3950 1224	0.3468 1657	0.3046 9137
28	0.5008 7778	0.4678 5227	0.4370 7675	0.3816 5434	0.3334 7747	0.2915 7069
29	0.4886 6125	0.4553 3068	0.4243 4636	0.3687 4815	0.3206 5141	0.2790 1502
30	0.4767 4269	0.4431 4421	0.4119 8676	0.3562 7841	0.3083 1867	0.2670 0002
31	0.4651 1481	0.4312 8391	0.3999 8715	0.3442 3035	0.2964 6026	0.2555 0241
32	0.4537 7055	0.4197 4103	0.3883 3703	0.3325 8971	0.2850 5794	0.2444 9991
33	0.4427 0298	0.4085 0708	0.3770 2625	0.3213 4271	0.2740 9417	0.2339 7121
34	0.4319 0534	0.3975 7380	0.3660 4490	0.3104 7605	0.2635 5209	0.2238 9589
35	0.4213 7107	0.3869 3314	0.3553 8340	0.2999 7686	0.2534 1547	0.2142 5444
36	0.4110 9372	0.3765 7727	0.3450 3243	0.2898 3272	0.2436 6872	0.2050 2817
37	0.4010 6705	0.3664 9856	0.3349 8294	0.2800 3161	0.2342 9685	0.1961 9921
38	0.3912 8492	0.3566 8959	0.3252 2615	0.2705 6194	0.2252 8543	0.1877 5044
39	0.3817 4139	0.3471 4316	0.3157 5355	0.2614 1250	0.2166 2061	0.1796 6549
40	0.3724 3062	0.3378 5222	0.3065 5684	0.2525 7247	0.2082 8904	0.1719 2870
41	0.3633 4695	0.3288 0995	0.2976 2800	0.2440 3137	0.2002 7793	0.1645 2507
42	0.3544 8483	0.3200 0968	0.2889 5922	0.2357 7910	0.1925 7493	0.1574 4026
43	0.3458 3886	0.3114 4495	0.2805 4294	0.2278 0590	0.1851 6820	0.1506 6054
44	0.3374 0376	0.3031 0944	0.2723 7178	0.2201 0231	0.1780 4635	0.1441 7276
45	0.3291 7440	0.2949 9702	0.2644 3862	0.2126 5924	0.1711 9841	0.1379 6437
46	0.3211 4576	0.2871 0172	0.2567 3653	0.2054 6787	0.1646 1386	0.1320 2332
47	0.3133 1294	0.2794 1773	0.2492 5876	0.1985 1968	0.1582 8256	0.1263 3810
48	0.3056 7116	0.2719 3940	0.2419 9880	0.1918 0645	0.1521 9476	0.1208 9771
49	0.2982 1576	0.2646 6122	0.2349 5029	0.1853 2024	0.1463 4112	0.1156 9158
50	0.2909 4221	0.2575 7783	0.2281 0708	0.1790 5337	0.1407 1262	0.1107 0965
51	0.2838 4606	0.2506 8402	0.2214 6318	0.1729 9843	0.1353 0059	0.1059 4225
52	0.2769 2298	0.2439 7471	0.2150 1280	0.1671 4824	0.1300 9672	0.1013 8014
53	0.2701 6876	0.2374 4497	0.2087 5029	0.1614 9589	0.1250 9300	0.0970 1449
54	0.2635 7928	0.2310 9000	0.2026 7019	0.1560 3467	0.1202 8173	0.0928 3683
55	0.2571 5052	0.2249 0511	0.1967 6717	0.1507 5814	0.1156 5551	0.0888 3907
56	0.2508 7855	0.2188 8575	0.1910 3609	0.1456 6004	0.1112 0722	0.0850 1347
57	0.2447 5956	0.2130 2749	0.1854 7193	0.1407 3433	0.1069 3002	0.0813 5260
58	0.2387 8982	0.2073 2603	0.1800 6984	0.1359 7520	0.1028 1733	0.0778 4938
59	0.2329 6568	0.2017 7716	0.1748 2508	0.1313 7701	0.0988 6282	0.0744 9701
60	0.2272 8359	0.1963 7679	0.1697 3309	0.1269 3431	0.0950 6040	0.0712 8901

COMPOUND PRESENT VALUE OF 1 (*Cont.*)

	5%	5½%	6%	6½%	7%	8%
1	0.9523 8095	0.9478 6730	0.9433 9623	0.9389 6714	0.9345 7944	0.9259 2593
2	0.9070 2948	0.8984 5242	0.8899 9644	0.8816 5928	0.8734 3873	0.8573 3882
3	0.8638 3760	0.8516 1366	0.8396 1928	0.8278 4909	0.8162 9788	0.7938 3224
4	0.8227 0247	0.8072 1674	0.7920 9366	0.7773 2309	0.7628 9521	0.7350 2985
5	0.7835 2617	0.7651 3435	0.7472 5817	0.7298 8084	0.7129 8618	0.6805 8320
6	0.7462 1540	0.7252 4583	0.7049 6054	0.6853 3412	0.6663 4222	0.6301 6963
7	0.7106 8133	0.6874 3681	0.6650 5711	0.6435 0621	0.6227 4974	0.5834 9040
8	0.6768 3936	0.6515 9887	0.6274 1237	0.6042 3119	0.5820 0910	0.5402 6888
9	0.6446 0892	0.6176 2926	0.5918 9846	0.5673 5323	0.5439 3374	0.5002 4897
10	0.6139 1325	0.5854 3058	0.5583 9478	0.5327 2604	0.5083 4929	0.4631 9349
11	0.5846 7929	0.5549 1050	0.5267 8753	0.5002 1224	0.4750 9280	0.4288 8286
12	0.5568 3742	0.5259 8152	0.4969 6936	0.4696 8285	0.4440 1196	0.3971 1376
13	0.5303 2135	0.4985 6068	0.4688 3902	0.4410 1676	0.4149 6445	0.3676 9792
14	0.5050 6795	0.4725 6937	0.4423 0096	0.4141 0025	0.3878 1724	0.3404 6104
15	0.4810 1710	0.4479 3305	0.4172 6506	0.3888 2652	0.3624 4602	0.3152 4170
16	0.4581 1152	0.4245 8109	0.3936 4628	0.3650 9533	0.3387 3460	0.2918 9047
17	0.4362 9669	0.4024 4653	0.3713 6442	0.3428 1251	0.3165 7439	0.2702 6895
18	0.4155 2065	0.3814 6590	0.3503 4379	0.3218 8969	0.2958 6392	0.2502 4903
19	0.3957 3396	0.3615 7906	0.3305 1301	0.3022 4384	0.2765 0832	0.2317 1206
20	0.3768 8948	0.3427 2896	0.3118 0473	0.2837 9703	0.2584 1900	0.2145 4821
21	0.3589 4236	0.3248 6158	0.2941 5540	0.2664 7608	0.2415 1309	0.1986 5575
22	0.3418 4987	0.3079 2567	0.2775 0510	0.2502 1228	0.2257 1317	0.1839 4051
23	0.3255 7131	0.2918 7267	0.2617 9726	0.2349 4111	0.2109 4688	0.1703 1528
24	0.3100 6791	0.2766 5656	0.2469 7855	0.2206 0198	0.1971 4662	0.1576 9934
25	0.2953 0277	0.2622 3370	0.2329 9863	0.2071 3801	0.1842 4918	0.1460 1790
26	0.2812 4073	0.2485 6275	0.2198 1003	0.1944 9579	0.1721 9549	0.1352 0176
27	0.2678 4832	0.2356 0450	0.2073 6795	0.1826 2515	0.1609 3037	0.1251 8682
28	0.2550 9364	0.2233 2181	0.1956 3014	0.1714 7902	0.1504 0221	0.1159 1372
29	0.2429 4632	0.2116 7944	0.1845 5674	0.1610 1316	0.1405 6282	0.1073 2752
30	0.2313 7745	0.2006 4402	0.1741 1013	0.1511 8607	0.1313 6712	0.0993 7733
31	0.2203 5947	0.1901 8390	0.1642 5484	0.1419 5875	0.1227 7301	0.0920 1605
32	0.2098 6617	0.1802 6910	0.1549 5740	0.1332 9460	0.1147 4113	0.0852 0005
33	0.1998 7254	0.1708 7119	0.1461 8622	0.1251 5925	0.1072 3470	0.0788 8893
34	0.1903 5480	0.1619 6321	0.1379 1153	0.1175 2042	0.1002 1934	0.0730 4531
35	0.1812 9029	0.1535 1963	0.1301 0522	0.1103 4781	0.0936 6294	0.0676 3454
36	0.1726 5741	0.1455 1624	0.1227 4077	0.1036 1297	0.0875 3546	0.0626 2458
37	0.1644 3563	0.1379 3008	0.1157 9318	0.0972 8917	0.0818 0884	0.0579 8572
38	0.1566 0536	0.1307 3941	0.1092 3885	0.0913 5134	0.0764 5686	0.0536 9048
39	0.1491 4797	0.1239 2362	0.1030 5552	0.0857 7590	0.0714 5501	0.0497 1341
40	0.1420 4568	0.1174 6314	0.0972 2219	0.0805 4075	0.0667 8038	0.0460 3093
41	0.1352 8160	0.1113 3947	0.0917 1905	0.0756 2512	0.0624 1157	0.0426 2123
42	0.1288 3962	0.1055 3504	0.0865 2740	0.0710 0950	0.0583 2857	0.0394 6411
43	0.1227 0440	0.1000 3322	0.0816 2962	0.0666 7559	0.0545 1268	0.0365 4084
44	0.1168 6133	0.0948 1822	0.0770 0908	0.0626 0619	0.0509 4643	0.0338 3411
45	0.1112 9651	0.0898 7509	0.0726 5007	0.0587 8515	0.0476 1349	0.0313 2788
46	0.1059 9668	0.0851 8965	0.0685 3781	0.0551 9733	0.0444 9859	0.0290 0730
47	0.1009 4921	0.0807 4849	0.0646 5831	0.0518 2848	0.0415 8747	0.0268 5861
48	0.0961 4211	0.0765 3885	0.0609 9840	0.0486 6524	0.0388 6679	0.0248 6908
49	0.0915 6391	0.0725 4867	0.0575 4566	0.0456 9506	0.0363 2410	0.0230 2693
50	0.0872 0373	0.0687 6652	0.0542 8836	0.0429 0616	0.0339 4776	0.0213 2123
51	0.0830 5117	0.0651 8153	0.0512 1544	0.0402 8747	0.0317 2688	0.0197 4188
52	0.0790 9635	0.0617 8344	0.0483 1645	0.0378 2861	0.0296 5129	0.0182 7952
53	0.0753 2986	0.0585 6250	0.0455 8156	0.0355 1982	0.0277 1148	0.0169 2548
54	0.0717 4272	0.0555 0948	0.0430 0147	0.0333 5195	0.0258 9858	0.0156 7174
55	0.0683 2640	0.0526 1562	0.0405 6742	0.0313 1638	0.0242 0428	0.0145 1087
56	0.0650 7276	0.0498 7263	0.0382 7115	0.0294 0505	0.0226 2083	0.0134 3599
57	0.0619 7406	0.0472 7263	0.0361 0486	0.0276 1038	0.0211 4096	0.0124 4073
58	0.0590 2291	0.0448 0818	0.0340 6119	0.0259 2524	0.0197 5791	0.0115 1920
59	0.0562 1230	0.0424 7221	0.0321 3320	0.0243 4295	0.0184 6533	0.0106 6592
60	0.0535 3552	0.0402 5802	0.0303 1434	0.0228 5723	0.0172 5732	0.0098 7585

How to calculate the compound present value of an interest-bearing debt.—To find the compound present value of a debt bearing compound interest, two steps are necessary:

1. Calculate the compound amount of the debt; that is, the face plus the compound interest to maturity.

2. Calculate the compound present value of the result found in 1.

EXAMPLE

The Brockton Machine Tool Company is put into a receiver's hands. Among the assets is a 5-year obligation of $9,500.00 bearing interest at $5\frac{1}{2}\%$ per year compounded annually. What is the present value of the asset if money is worth 6% per year compounded annually?

Solution

(1) Calculation of compound amount: The number of periods is 5. The rate of interest per period is $5\frac{1}{2}\%$. The table on page 51 shows the compound amount of 1 for 5 periods at $5\frac{1}{2}\%$ per period to be 1.30696001. Hence the compound amount of $9,500.00 is $1.30696001 \times 9{,}500 = \$12{,}416.12$.

(2) Calculation of compound present value: The number of periods is 5. The rate of interest per period is 6%. The table on page 55 shows the compound present value of 1 for 5 periods at 6% per period to be 0.74725817. Hence the compound present value of $12,416.12 (the result found in the preceding step) is $0.74725817 \times 12{,}416.12 = \$9{,}278.05$. Thus the receiver of the Brockton Machine Tool Company holds an asset whose present value is $9,278.05.

How to calculate the compound discount.—The compound discount on a sum due in the future is the difference between that sum and its compound present value.

EXAMPLE

What is the compound discount, at 6% per year compounded annually, on a loan of $8,200.00 due in 7 years?

Solution

(1) The table on page 55 shows the compound present value of 1 for 7 periods at 6% to be 0.66505711. The compound present value of $8,200.00 is, therefore, $0.66505711 \times 8{,}200 = \$5{,}453.47$.

(2) The compound discount is the difference between the sum due and its compound present value, or $\$8{,}200.00 - \$5{,}453.47 = \$2{,}746.53$.

10. HOW TO COMPUTE ANNUITIES

Adapted from Moore, "Handbook of Financial Mathematics" New York: Prentice-Hall, Inc.

What an annuity is.—An annuity is a series of equal payments made or due at equal intervals of time. Examples of annuities are: bond coupons, regular preferred stock dividends, periodic contributions to sinking funds and depreciation funds, insurance premiums, periodic payments to beneficiaries by insurance companies, income from trust funds, rent on land or buildings, and installment payments. Although the word annuity suggests annual payments, it applies to any series of equal payments made at equal intervals of time, whether the payments be made annually, semiannually, quarterly, monthly, or otherwise.

Ordinary annuities and annuities due.—Annuities are of two principal types:

1. Ordinary annuities.
2. Annuities due.

An ordinary annuity is one in which the payments are made at the end of each period; payments to sinking funds and to depreciation funds are usually made at the end of each period. An annuity due

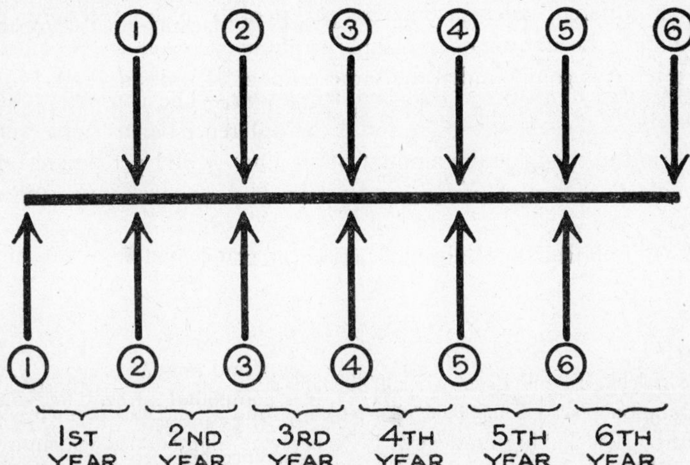

Figure 2.—Comparison of an Ordinary Annuity with an Annuity Due.

is one in which the payments are made at the beginning of each period; insurance premiums and rent payments on land or buildings are usually made at the beginning of each period.

It is necessary to distinguish between these two classes of annuities because the method of computation used in connection with ordinary annuities is slightly different from that used in connection with annuities due. The distinction can best be visualized by means of a diagram. As an example, take two annuities payable at annual intervals for a term of 6 years. In Figure 2, the arrows in the upper half (pointing downward) indicate the time of the six payments in an ordinary annuity; the arrows in the lower half (pointing upward) indicate the time of the payments in an annuity due. It is important to note that the straight line in the center of the diagram indicates the length of the term, and that this length is the same for both these annuities.

How to calculate the amount of an ordinary annuity.—The amount of an annuity is the sum of the invested rents (periodic payments) and the compound interest thereon to the end of the term of the annuity.

Table of amount of annuity of 1 per period.—The table on pages 66–69 shows the amount of an annuity of 1 per period ($1, £1, 1 peso, or any other monetary unit) for different numbers of periods and at different rates of interest per period. The procedure in calculating the amount of an ordinary annuity is as follows, provided the interest is compounded the same number of times a year as the rent payments are made (which is generally the case):

1. Find in the table the amount of an annuity of 1 per period for the given number of periods and at the given rate of interest per period.
2. Multiply this figure by the periodic rent.

EXAMPLE

To redeem a bond issue of $2,000,000.00 in 20 years, the Eastport Oil Corporation placed $30,000,00 in a sinking fund at the end of each six months. The sinking fund earned 5% per year compounded semiannually. What was the amount in the fund at the end of 10 years?

Solution

Since the payments are made at the end of each six months, the number of periods is $10 \times 2 = 20$. The rate of interest per period is $5\% \div 2 = 2\frac{1}{2}\%$. Then:

(1) In the table on page 68 the figure given in the $2\frac{1}{2}\%$ column opposite 20 is 25.54465761. This is the amount of an annuity of 1 for 20 periods at $2\frac{1}{2}\%$ per period.

(2) To find the amount of an annuity of $30,000.00, multiply 25.54465761 by 30,000. The result, $766,339.73, is the amount in the sinking fund at the end of 10 years, if payments of $30,000.00 are made at the end of each six months and interest at 5% per year is compounded semiannually.

Formula for amount of an ordinary annuity.—The amount of an ordinary annuity may also be calculated by the use of the formula

$$R\left[\frac{(1+i)^n - 1}{i}\right]$$

where

$R =$ periodic rent
$i =$ rate of interest per period
$n =$ number of periods

How to calculate the amount of an annuity due.—In an annuity due the periodic rent payments are made at the beginning of each period, while in an ordinary annuity the periodic rent payments are made at the end of each period.

In the diagram on page 57, it is seen that the ordinary annuity of six rents earns no interest after the date of the sixth payment; the annuity due of six rents earns interest for one full period after the date of the sixth payment. Consequently, the amount of the annuity due of six rents is equal to:

1. The amount of the ordinary annuity of six rents; *plus*
2. Interest on the amount of the ordinary annuity of six rents for one period.

This is equivalent to saying that the amount of the annuity due of six rents is equal to:

1. The amount of an ordinary annuity of seven rents; *minus*
2. One rent.

The procedure in calculating the amount of an annuity due is, therefore, as follows:

1. Calculate the amount of an ordinary annuity for one more than the given number of periods.

2. Deduct from the figure found in (1), one periodic rent; the result is the amount of the annuity due.

EXAMPLE

At the beginning of each six-month period, the Donahue Construction Company places $40,000.00 in a depreciation fund for its machinery. To what amount will the fund have accumulated at the end of 7 years, if interest at 5% per year compounded semiannually is earned?

Solution

Since the payments are made semiannually, the given number of periods is $7 \times 2 = 14$. The rate of interest per period is $5\% \div 2 = 2\frac{1}{2}\%$. Then:

(1) Adding 1 to the given number of periods makes the number of periods 15. In the table on page 68 the figure in the $2\frac{1}{2}\%$ column opposite 15 is 17.93192666. This is the amount of an annuity of 1 for 15 periods at $2\frac{1}{2}\%$ per period. To find the amount of an annuity of $40,000.00, multiply 17.93192666 by 40,000. $17.93192666 \times 40{,}000 =$ $717,277.07.

(2) Deducting one rent, $40,000.00, from $717,277.07 gives $717,277.07 — $40,000.00 = $677,277.07. This is the amount to which the depreciation fund will have accumulated at the end of 7 years, if payments of $40,000.00 are made at the beginning of each six-month period and interest at 5% per year compounded semiannually is earned.

Formula for amount of an annuity due.—The amount of an annuity due may also be calculated by the use of the formula

$$R\left[\frac{(1+i)^{n+1}-1}{i}-1\right]$$

where

$R =$ periodic rent
$i =$ rate of interest per period
$n =$ number of periods

How to calculate the present value of an ordinary annuity.— The present value (or present worth) of an annuity is that sum which, invested at compound interest, will provide for the withdrawal of a stated number of equal rents at equal intervals of time.

The interest earning increases the investment, and the rent withdrawals decrease it. The withdrawal of the last rent should exhaust the investment.

If the rents are withdrawn at the end of each period, the annuity is an ordinary annuity. If the rents are withdrawn at the beginning of each period, the annuity is an annuity due.

The present value of an annuity is also sometimes referred to as the "cash equivalent" of the annuity.

Table of present value of annuity of 1 per period.—The table on pages 70–73 shows the present value of an annuity of 1 per period ($1, £1, 1 peso, or any other monetary unit) for different numbers of periods and at different rates of interest per period. The procedure in calculating the present value of an ordinary annuity is as follows, provided the interest is compounded the same number of times a year as the rent withdrawals are made (which is generally the case):

1. Find in the table the present value of an annuity of 1 for the given number of periods and at the given rate of interest per period.
2. Multiply this figure by the periodic rent.

EXAMPLE

Under the terms of a contract the Dubois Celluloid Novelty Company is obligated to make payments of $2,500.00 at the end of each quarter for 8 years. To provide for these payments the Dubois Company decides to set up a fund out of which the quarterly payments will be made. What amount must be invested in the fund, if interest at 5% per year compounded quarterly is earned?

Solution

Since the payments are to be made quarterly, the number of periods is $8 \times 4 = 32$. The rate of interest per period is $5\% \div 4 = 1\frac{1}{4}\%$. Then:

(1) In the table on page 71 the figure in the $1\frac{1}{4}\%$ column opposite 32 is 26.24127418. This is the present value of an annuity of 1 for 32 periods at $1\frac{1}{4}\%$ per period.

(2) To find the present value of an annuity of $2,500.00, multiply 26.24127418 by 2,500. $26.24127418 \times 2{,}500 = \$65{,}603.19$. This is the amount which must be invested in the fund, at 5% per year compounded quarterly, to provide for payments of $2,500.00 at the end of each quarter for 8 years.

Formula for present value of an ordinary annuity.—The present value of an ordinary annuity may also be calculated by the use of the formula

$$R\left[\frac{1-\frac{1}{(1+i)^n}}{i}\right]$$

where

$R =$ periodic rent
$i =$ rate of interest per period
$n =$ number of periods

How to calculate the present value of an annuity due.—In an annuity due the periodic rents are due at the beginning of each period, while in an ordinary annuity the periodic rents are due at the end of each period.

Referring to the diagram on page 57, if the present value of the ordinary annuity of six rents is to be calculated, it is apparent that, since the first rent is due at the end of the first period, this first rent will be subject to discount; in the annuity due of six rents, however, the first rent is due at the beginning of the first period, and hence this first rent will not be subject to discount. Consequently, the present value of the annuity due of six rents is equal to:

1. The present value of the ordinary annuity of six rents; *minus*
2. The discount on one rent (the first).

This is equivalent to saying that the present value of the annuity due of six rents is equal to:

1. The present value of an ordinary annuity of five rents; *plus*
2. One rent (that is, the first rent, which is not subject to discount).

The procedure in calculating the present value of an annuity due is, therefore, as follows:

1. Calculate the present value of an ordinary annuity for one less than the given number of periods.

2. Add to the figure found in 1, one periodic rent; the result is the present value of the annuity due.

EXAMPLE

A building is leased for 15 years at an annual rental of $7,000.00, payable in installments of $1,750.00 at the beginning of each quarter.

What is the cash value of the lease if money is worth 4% per year compounded quarterly?

Solution

Since the payments are due quarterly, the number of periods is 15 × 4 = 60. The rate of interest per period is 4% ÷ 4 = 1%. Then:

(1) Deducting 1 from the given number of periods makes the number of periods 59. In the table on page 70 the figure in the 1% column opposite 59 is 44.40458879. This is the present value of an annuity of 1 for 59 periods at 1% per period. To find the present value of an annuity of $1,750.00, multiply 44.40458879 by 1,750. 44.40458879 × 1,750 = $77.708.03.

(2) Adding one periodic rent, $1,750.00, gives $77,708.03 + $1,750.00 = $79,458.03.

The cash value of the lease is, therefore, $79,458.03.

Formula for present value of an annuity due.—The present value of an annuity due may also be calculated by the use of the formula

$$R\left[\frac{1-\frac{1}{(1+i)^{n-1}}}{i}+1\right]$$

where

R = periodic rent
i = rate of interest per period
n = number of periods

Deferred annuities.—A deferred annuity is an annuity in which a number of periods are to elapse before the periodic payments or rents are to begin. Since, when the payments do begin, they may occur either at the end or at the beginning of each period, there are two kinds of deferred annuities:

1. Deferred ordinary annuities.
2. Deferred annuities due.

A deferred ordinary annuity is a deferred annuity in which the payments are to be made at the end of each period after the interval of deferment has expired. A deferred annuity due is a deferred annuity in which the payments are to be made at the beginning of each period after the interval of deferment has expired.

How to calculate the amount of a deferred annuity.—The amount of a deferred annuity is the same as the amount of an annuity that is not deferred. No interest is earned during the deferment interval, because no payments have been made during this interval. Therefore, if it is desired to find the amount of a deferred ordinary annuity, the procedure described on page 58, "How to calculate the amount of an ordinary annuity," may be followed without modification; if it is desired to find the amount of a deferred annuity due, the procedure described on page 59, "How to calculate the amount of an annuity due," may be followed. The deferment interval is disregarded in the calculation of the amount of a deferred annuity.

How to calculate the present value of a deferred ordinary annuity.—The present value of a deferred annuity is the value of the annuity as of the beginning of the interval of deferment. Hence the present value of a deferred annuity is not the same as the present value of an annuity that is not deferred.

The procedure in calculating the present value of a deferred ordinary annuity is as follows:

1. Eliminate the number of periods in the interval of deferment, and calculate the present value, at the given rate of interest per period, of an ordinary annuity for a number of periods corresponding to the number of rents.

2. Multiply the figure found in 1 by the present value of 1, at the given rate of interest per period, for the number of deferred periods; the result is the present value of the deferred ordinary annuity.

EXAMPLE

The Broadfield Bituminous Company has a mine estimated to yield $75,000.00 net per year for 16 years, but it is not deemed advisable to start production until 3 years from now. What is the present value of the output, if money is worth $5\frac{1}{2}\%$ per year compounded annually?

Solution

(1) The number of periods corresponding to the number of rents is 16; the rate of interest per period is $5\frac{1}{2}\%$. In the table on page 73, the present value of an ordinary annuity of 1 for 16 periods at $5\frac{1}{2}\%$ is found to be 10.46216203. The present value of an annuity of $75,000.00 is, therefore, $10.46216203 \times 75{,}000 = \$784{,}662.15225$.

(2) The number of periods in the interval of deferment is 3; the rate

of interest per period is $5\frac{1}{2}\%$. In the table on page 55, the present value of 1 for 3 periods at $5\frac{1}{2}\%$ is shown to be 0.85161366. Then, \$784,662.15225 × 0.85161366 = \$668,229.01.

Thus the present value of the output of the mine is \$668,229.01.

How to calculate the present value of a deferred annuity due. —The procedure in calculating the present value of a deferred annuity due is as follows:

1. Eliminate the number of periods in the interval of deferment, and calculate the present value, at the given rate of interest per period, of an annuity due for a number of periods corresponding to the number of rents.

2. Multiply the figure found in 1 by the present value of 1, at the given rate of interest per period, for the number of deferred periods; the result is the present value of the deferred annuity due.

EXAMPLE

The Thorndike Engineering Corporation is at present devoting its entire resources to subway construction, but expects to complete this work by the end of 3 years. At that time it will be able to undertake some survey work in the Andes which, it is estimated, will take 6 years, and for which work the company will receive a fee of \$150,000.00 a year, payable in advance. If money is worth 5% per year compounded annually, what is the present value of this contract?

Solution

(1) The first step is to calculate the present value of an annuity due of \$150,000.00 for 6 periods at 5% per period. This is equivalent to finding the present value of an ordinary annuity of \$150,000.00 for 5 periods at 5% per period, and adding one rent (for method of calculating present value of an annuity due, see page 62). In the table on page 73, the present value of an ordinary annuity of 1 for 5 periods at 5% is found to be 4.32947667. The present value of an ordinary annuity of \$150,-000.00 is, therefore, 4.32947667 × 150,000 = \$649,421.50. Adding one rent gives \$649,421.50 + \$150,000.00 = \$799,421.50. This is the present value of an annuity due of \$150,000.00 for 6 periods at 5%.

(2) The number of periods in the interval of deferment is 3; the rate of interest per period is 5%. In the table on page 55, the present value of 1 for 3 periods at 5% is shown to be 0.86383760. Then, \$799,421.50 × 0.86383760 = \$690,570.35.

Thus the present value of the contract is \$690,570.35.

AMOUNT OF ANNUITY OF 1

	½%	⅝%	¾%	⅞%	1%	1⅛%
1	1.0000 0000	1.0000 0000	1.0000 0000	1.0000 0000	1.0000 0000	1.0000 0000
2	2.0050 0000	2.0062 5000	2.0075 0000	2.0087 5000	2.0100 0000	2.0112 5000
3	3.0150 2500	3.1087 8906	3.0225 5625	3.0263 2656	3.0301 0000	3.0338 7656
4	4.0301 0013	4.0376 5649	4.0452 2542	4.0528 0692	4.0604 0100	4.0680 0767
5	5.0502 5063	5.0628 9185	5.0755 6461	5.0882 6898	5.1010 0501	5.1137 7276
6	6.0755 0188	6.0945 3492	6.1136 3135	6.1327 9133	6.1520 1506	6.1713 0270
7	7.1058 7939	7.1326 2576	7.1594 8358	7.1864 5326	7.2135 3521	7.2407 2986
8	8.1414 0879	8.1772 0468	8.2131 7971	8.2493 3472	8.2856 7056	8.3221 8807
9	9.1821 1583	9.2283 1220	9.2747 7856	9.3215 1640	9.3685 2727	9.4158 1269
10	10.2280 2641	10.2859 8916	10.3443 3940	10.4030 7967	10.4622 1254	10.5217 4058
11	11.2791 6654	11.3502 7659	11.4219 2194	11.4941 0662	11.5668 3467	11.6401 1016
12	12.3355 6237	12.4212 1582	12.5075 8636	12.5946 8005	12.6825 0301	12.7710 6140
13	13.3972 4018	13.4988 4842	13.6013 9325	13.7048 8350	13.8093 2804	13.9147 3584
14	14.4642 2639	14.5832 1622	14.7034 0370	14.8248 0123	14.9474 2132	15.0712 7662
15	15.5365 4752	15.6743 6132	15.8136 7923	15.9545 1824	16.0968 9554	16.2408 2848
16	16.6142 3026	16.7723 2608	16.9322 8183	17.0941 2028	17.2578 6449	17.4235 3780
17	17.6973 0141	17.8771 5312	18.0592 7394	18.2436 9383	18.4304 4314	18.6195 5260
18	18.7857 8791	18.9888 8532	19.1947 1849	19.4033 2615	19.6147 4757	19.8290 2257
19	19.8797 1685	20.1075 6586	20.3386 7888	20.5731 0526	20.8108 9504	21.0520 9907
20	20.9791 1544	21.2332 3814	21.4912 1897	21.7531 1993	22.0190 0399	22.2889 3519
21	22.0840 1101	22.3659 4588	22.6524 0312	22.9434 5973	23.2391 9403	23.5396 8571
22	23.1944 3107	23.5057 3304	23.8222 9614	24.1442 1500	24.4715 8598	24.8045 0717
23	24.3104 0322	24.6526 4387	25.0009 6336	25.3554 7688	25.7163 0183	26.0835 5788
24	25.4319 5524	25.8067 2290	26.1884 7059	26.5773 3730	26.9734 6485	27.3769 9790
25	26.5591 1502	26.9680 1492	27.3848 8412	27.8098 8900	28.2431 9950	28.6849 8913
26	27.6919 1059	28.1365 6501	28.5902 7075	29.0532 2553	29.5256 3150	30.0076 9526
27	28.8303 7015	29.3124 1854	29.8046 9778	30.3074 4126	30.8208 8781	31.3452 8183
28	29.9745 2200	30.4956 2116	31.0282 3301	31.5726 3137	32.1290 9669	32.6979 1625
29	31.1243 9461	31.6862 1879	32.2609 4476	32.8488 9189	33.4503 8766	34.0657 6781
30	32.2800 1658	32.8842 5766	33.5029 0184	34.1363 1970	34.7848 9153	35.4490 0769
31	33.4414 1666	34.0897 8427	34.7541 7361	35.4350 1249	36.1327 4045	36.8478 0903
32	34.6086 2375	35.3028 4542	36.0148 2991	36.7450 6885	37.4940 6785	38.2623 4688
33	35.7816 6686	36.5234 8820	37.2849 4113	38.0665 8820	38.8690 0853	39.6927 9829
34	36.9605 7520	37.7517 6000	38.5645 7819	39.3996 7085	40.2576 9862	41.1393 4227
35	38.1453 7807	38.9877 0850	39.8538 1253	40.7444 1797	41.6602 7560	42.6021 5987
36	39.3361 0496	40.2313 8168	41.1527 1612	42.1009 3163	43.0768 7836	44.0814 3417
37	40.5327 8549	41.4828 2782	42.4613 6149	43.4693 1478	44.5076 4714	45.5773 5030
38	41.7354 4942	42.7420 9549	43.7798 2170	44.8496 7128	45.9527 2361	47.0900 9549
39	42.9441 2666	44.0092 3359	45.1081 7037	46.2421 0591	47.4122 5085	48.6198 5906
40	44.1588 4730	45.2842 9130	46.4464 8164	47.6467 2433	48.8863 7336	50.1668 3248
41	45.3796 4153	46.5673 1812	47.7948 3026	49.0636 3317	50.3752 3709	51.7312 0934
42	46.6065 3974	47.8583 6386	49.1532 9148	50.4929 3996	51.8789 8946	53.3131 8545
43	47.8395 7244	49.1574 7863	50.5219 4117	51.9347 5319	53.3977 7936	54.9129 5879
44	49.0787 7030	50.4647 1287	51.9008 5573	53.3891 8228	54.9317 5715	56.5307 2957
45	50.3241 6415	51.7801 1733	53.2901 1215	54.8563 3762	56.4810 7472	58.1667 0028
46	51.5757 8497	53.1037 4306	54.6897 8799	56.3363 3058	58.0458 8547	59.8210 7566
47	52.8336 6390	54.4356 4146	56.0999 6140	57.8292 7347	59.6263 4432	61.4940 6276
48	54.0978 3222	55.7758 6421	57.5207 1111	59.3352 7961	61.2226 0777	63.1858 7097
49	55.3683 2138	57.1244 6337	58.9521 1644	60.8544 6331	62.8348 3385	64.8967 1201
50	56.6451 6299	58.4814 9126	60.3942 5732	62.3869 3986	64.4631 8218	66.6268 0002
51	57.9283 8880	59.8470 0058	61.8472 1424	63.9328 2559	66.1078 1401	68.3763 5152
52	59.2180 3075	61.2210 4434	63.3110 6835	65.4922 3781	67.7688 9215	70.1455 8548
53	60.5141 2090	62.6036 7586	64.7859 0136	67.0652 9489	69.4465 8107	71.9347 2332
54	61.8166 9150	63.9949 4884	66.2717 9562	68.6521 1622	71.1410 4688	73.7439 8895
55	63.1257 7496	65.3949 1727	67.7688 3409	70.2528 2224	72.8524 5735	75.5736 0883
56	64.4414 0384	66.8036 3550	69.2771 0035	71.8675 3443	74.5809 8192	77.4238 1193
57	65.7636 1086	68.2211 5822	70.7966 7860	73.4963 7536	76.3267 9174	79.2948 2981
58	67.0924 2891	69.6475 4046	72.3276 5369	75.1394 6864	78.0900 5966	81.1868 9665
59	68.4278 9105	71.0828 3759	73.8701 1109	76.7969 3900	79.8709 6025	83.1002 4923
60	69.7700 3051	72.5271 0532	75.4241 3693	78.4689 1221	81.6696 6986	85.0351 2704

From J. W. Glover, "Tables of Applied Math. in Finance, Insurance, Statistics"

AMOUNT OF ANNUITY OF 1 (*Cont.*)

	1¼%	1⅜%	1½%	1¾%	2%	2¼%
1	1.0000 0000	1.0000 0000	1.0000 0000	1.0000 0000	1.0000 0000	1.0000 0000
2	2.0125 0000	2.0137 5000	2.0150 0000	2.0175 0000	2.0200 0000	2.0225 0000
3	3.0376 5625	3.0414 3906	3.0452 2500	3.0528 0625	3.0604 0000	3.0680 0625
4	4.0756 2695	4.0832 5885	4.0909 0338	4.1062 3036	4.1216 0800	4.1370 3639
5	5.1265 7229	5.1394 0366	5.1522 6693	5.1780 8938	5.2040 4016	5.2301 1971
6	6.1906 5444	6.2100 7046	6.2295 5093	6.2687 0596	6.3081 2096	6 3477 9740
7	7.2680 3762	7.2954 5893	7.3229 9419	7.3784 0831	7.4342 8338	7.4906 2284
8	8.3588 8809	8.3957 7149	8.4328 3911	8.5075 3045	8.5829 6905	8.6591 6186
9	9.4633 7420	9.5112 1335	9.5593 3169	9.6564 1224	9.7546 2843	9.8539 9300
10	10.5816 6637	10.6419 9253	10.7027 2167	10.8253 9945	10.9497 2100	11.0757 0784
11	11.7139 3720	11.7883 1993	11.8632 6249	12.0148 4394	12.1687 1542	12.3249 1127
12	12.8603 6142	12.9504 0933	13.0412 1143	13.2251 0371	13.4120 8973	13.6022 2177
13	14.0211 1594	14.1284 7745	14.2368 2960	14.4565 4303	14.6803 3152	14.9082 7176
14	15.1963 7988	15.3227 4402	15.4503 8205	15.7095 3253	15.9739 3815	16.2437 0788
15	16.3863 3463	16.5334 3175	16.6821 3778	16.9844 4935	17.2934 1692	17.6091 9130
16	17.5911 6382	17.7607 6644	17.9323 6984	18.2816 7721	18.6392 8525	19.0053 9811
17	18.8110 5336	19.0049 7697	19.2013 5539	19.6016 0656	20.0120 7096	20.4330 1957
18	20.0461 9153	20.2662 9541	20.4893 7572	20.9446 3468	21.4123 1238	21.8927 6251
19	21.2967 6893	21.5449 5697	21.7967 1636	22.3111 6578	22.8405 5863	23.3853 4966
20	22.5629 7854	22.8412 0013	23.1236 6710	23.7016 1119	24.2973 6980	24.9115 2003
21	23.8450 1577	24.1552 6663	24.4705 2211	25.1163 8938	25.7833 1719	26.4720 2923
22	25.1430 7847	25.4874 0155	25.8375 7994	26.5559 2620	27.2989 8354	28.0676 4989
23	26.4573 6695	26.8378 5332	27.2251 4364	28.0206 5490	28.8449 6321	29.6991 7201
24	27.7880 8403	28.2068 7380	28.6335 2080	29.5110 1637	30.4218 6247	31.3674 0338
25	29.1354 3508	29.5947 1832	30.0630 2361	31.0274 5915	32.0302 9972	33.0731 6996
26	30.4996 2802	31.0016 4569	31.5139 6896	32.5704 3969	33.6709 0572	34.8173 1628
27	31.8808 7337	32.4279 1832	32.9866 7850	34.1404 2238	35.3443 2383	36.6007 0590
28	33.2793 8429	33.8738 0220	34.4814 7867	35.7378 7977	37.0512 1031	38.4242 2178
29	34.6953 7659	35.3395 6698	35.9987 0085	37.3632 9267	38.7922 3451	40.2887 6677
30	36.1290 6880	36.8254 8602	37.5386 8137	39.0171 5029	40.5680 7921	42.1952 6402
31	37.5806 8216	38.3318 3646	39.1017 6159	40.6999 5042	42.3794 4079	44.1446 5746
32	39.0504 4069	39.8588 9921	40.6882 8801	42.4121 9955	44.2270 2961	46.1379 1226
33	40.5385 7120	41.4069 5907	42.2986 1233	44.1544 1305	46.1115 7020	48.1760 1528
34	42.0453 0334	42.9763 0476	43.9330 9152	45.9271 1527	48.0338 0160	50.2599 7563
35	43.5708 6963	44.5672 2895	45.5920 8789	47.7308 3979	49.9944 7763	52.3908 2508
36	45.1155 0550	46.1800 2835	47.2759 6921	49.5661 2949	51.9943 6719	54.5696 1864
37	46.6794 4932	47.8150 0374	48.9851 0874	51.4335 3675	54.0342 5453	56.7974 3506
38	48.2926 4243	49.4724 6004	50.7198 8538	53.3336 2365	56.1149 3962	59.0753 7735
39	49.8862 2921	51.1527 0636	52.4806 8366	55.2669 6206	58.2372 3841	61.4045 7334
40	51.4895 5708	52.8560 5608	54.2678 9391	57.2341 3390	60.4019 8318	63.7861 7624
41	53.1331 7654	54.5828 2685	56.0819 1232	59.2357 3124	62.6100 2284	66.2213 6521
42	54.7973 4125	56.3333 4072	57.9231 4100	61.2723 5654	64.8622 2330	68.7113 4592
43	56.4823 0801	58.1079 2415	59.7919 8812	63.3446 2278	67.1594 6777	71.2573 5121
44	58.1883 3687	59.9069 0811	61.6888 6794	65.4531 5367	69.5026 5712	73.8606 4161
45	59.9156 9108	61.7306 2810	63.6142 0096	67.5985 8386	71.8927 1027	76.5225 0605
46	61.6646 3721	63.5794 2423	65.5684 1398	69.7815 5908	74.3305 6447	79.2442 6243
47	63.4354 4518	65.4536 4131	67.5519 4018	72.0027 3637	76.8171 7576	82.0272 5834
48	65.2283 8824	67.3536 2888	69.5652 1929	74.2627 8425	79.3535 1927	84.8728 7165
49	67.0437 4310	69.2797 4128	71.6086 9758	76.5623 8298	81.9405 8966	87.7825 1126
50	68.8817 8989	71.2323 3772	73.6828 2804	78.9022 2468	84.5794 0145	90.7576 1776
51	70.7428 1226	73.2117 8237	75.7880 7046	81.2830 1361	87.2709 8948	93.7996 6416
52	72.6270 9741	75.2184 4437	77.9248 9152	83.7054 6635	90.0164 0927	96.9101 5661
53	74.5349 3613	77.2526 9798	80.0937 6489	86.1703 1201	92.8167 3746	100.0906 3513
54	76.4666 2283	79.3149 2258	82.2951 7136	88.6782 9247	95.6730 7221	103.3426 7442
55	78.4224 5562	81.4055 0277	84.5295 9893	91.2301 6259	98.5865 3365	106.6678 8460
56	80.4027 3631	83.5248 2843	86.7975 4292	93.8266 9043	101.5582 6432	110.0679 1200
57	82.4077 7052	85.6732 9482	89.0995 0606	96.4686 5752	104.5894 2961	113.5444 4002
58	84.4378 6765	87.8513 0262	91.4359 9865	99.1568 5902	107.6812 1820	117.0991 8992
59	86.4933 4099	90.0592 5804	93.8075 3863	101.8921 0405	110.8348 4257	120.7339 2169
60	88.5745 0776	92.2975 7283	96.2146 5171	104.6752 1588	114.0515 3942	124.4504 3493

AMOUNT OF ANNUITY OF 1 (*Cont.*)

	2½%	2¾%	3%	3½%	4%	4½%
1	1.0000 0000	1.0000 0000	1.0000 0000	1.0000 0000	1.0000 0000	1.0000 0000
2	2.0250 0000	2.0275 0000	2.0300 0000	2.0350 0000	2.0400 0000	2.0450 0000
3	3.0756 2500	3.0832 5625	3.0909 0000	3.1062 2500	3.1216 0000	3.1370 2500
4	4.1525 1563	4.1680 4580	4.1836 2700	4.2149 4288	4.2464 6400	4.2781 9113
5	5.2563 2852	5.2826 6706	5.3091 3581	5.3624 6588	5.4163 2256	5.4707 0973
6	6.3877 3673	6.4279 4040	6.4684 0988	6.5501 5218	6.6329 7546	6.7168 9166
7	7.5474 3015	7.6047 0876	7.6624 6218	7.7794 0751	7.8982 9448	8.0191 5179
8	8.7361 1590	8.8138 3825	8.8923 3605	9.0516 8677	9.2142 2626	9.3800 1362
9	9.9545 1880	10.0562 1880	10.1591 0613	10.3684 9581	10.5827 9531	10.8021 1423
10	11.2033 8177	11.3327 6482	11.4638 7931	11.7313 9316	12.0061 0712	12.2882 0937
11	12.4834 6631	12.6444 1585	12.8077 9569	13.1419 9192	13.4863 5141	13.8411 7879
12	13.7955 5297	13.9921 3729	14.1920 2956	14.6019 6164	15.0258 0546	15.4640 3184
13	15.1404 4179	15.3769 2107	15.6177 9045	16.1130 3030	16.6268 3768	17.1599 1327
14	16.5189 5284	16.7997 8639	17.0863 2416	17.6769 8636	18.2919 1119	18.9321 0937
15	17.9319 2666	18.2617 8052	18.5989 1389	19.2956 8088	20.0235 8764	20.7840 5429
16	19.3802 2483	19.7639 7948	20.1568 8130	20.9710 2971	21.8245 3114	22.7193 3673
17	20.8647 3045	21.3074 8892	21.7615 8774	22.7050 1575	23.6975 1239	24.7417 0689
18	22.3863 4871	22.8934 4487	23.4144 3537	24.4996 9130	25.6454 1288	26.8550 8370
19	23.9460 0743	24.5230 1460	25.1168 6844	26.3571 8050	27.6712 2940	29.0635 6246
20	25.5446 5761	26.1973 9750	26.8703 7449	28.2796 8181	29.7780 7858	31.3714 2277
21	27.1832 7405	27.9178 2593	28.6764 8572	30.2694 7068	31.9692 0172	33.7831 3680
22	28.8628 5590	29.6855 6615	30.5367 8030	32.3289 0215	34.2479 6979	36.3033 7795
23	30.5844 2730	31.5019 1921	32.4528 8370	34.4604 1373	36.6178 8858	38.9370 2996
24	32.3490 3798	33.3682 2199	34.4264 7022	36.6665 2821	39.0826 0412	41.6891 9631
25	34.1577 6393	35.2858 4810	36.4592 6432	38.9498 5669	41.6459 0829	44.5652 1015
26	36.0117 0803	37.2562 0892	38.5530 4225	41.3131 0168	44.3117 4462	47.5706 4460
27	37.9120 0073	39.2807 5467	40.7096 3352	43.7590 6024	47.0842 1440	50.7113 2361
28	39.8598 0075	41.3609 7542	42.9309 2252	46.2906 2734	49.9675 8298	53.9933 3317
29	41.8562 9577	43.4984 0224	45.2188 5020	48.9107 9930	52.9662 8630	57.4230 3316
30	43.9027 0316	45.6946 0830	47.5754 1571	51.6226 7728	56.0849 3775	61.0070 6966
31	46.0002 7074	47.9512 1003	50.0026 7818	54.4294 7098	59.3283 3526	64.7523 8779
32	48.1502 7751	50.2698 6831	52.5027 5852	57.3345 0247	62.7014 6867	68.6662 4524
33	50.3540 3445	52.6522 8969	55.0778 4128	60.3412 1005	66.2095 2742	72.7562 2628
34	52.6128 8531	55.1002 2765	57.7301 7652	63.4531 5240	69.8579 0851	77.0302 5646
35	54.9282 0744	57.6154 8391	60.4620 8181	66.6740 1274	73.6522 2486	81.4966 1800
36	57.3014 1263	60.1999 0972	63.2759 4427	70.0076 0318	77.5983 1385	86.1639 6581
37	59.7339 4794	62.8554 0724	66.1742 2259	73.4578 6930	81.7022 4640	91.0413 4427
38	62.2272 9664	65.5839 3094	69.1594 4927	77.0288 9472	85.9703 3626	96.1382 0476
39	64.7829 7906	68.3874 8904	72.2342 3275	80.7249 0604	90.4091 4971	101.4644 2398
40	67.4025 5354	71.2681 4499	75.4012 5973	84.5502 7775	95.0255 1570	107.0303 2306
41	70.0876 1737	74.2280 1898	78.6632 9753	88.5095 3747	99.8265 3633	112.8466 8760
42	72.8398 0781	77.2692 8950	82.0231 9645	92.6073 7128	104.8195 9778	118.9247 8854
43	75.6608 0300	80.3941 9496	85.4838 9234	96.8486 2928	110.0123 8169	125.2764 0402
44	78.5523 2308	83.6050 3532	89.0484 0911	101.2383 3130	115.4128 7696	131.9138 4220
45	81.5161 3116	86.9041 7379	92.7198 6139	105.7816 7290	121.0293 9204	138.8499 6510
46	84.5540 3443	90.2940 3857	96.5014 5723	110.4840 3145	126.8705 6772	146.0982 1353
47	87.6678 8530	93.7771 2463	100.3965 0095	115.3509 7255	132.9453 9043	153.6726 3314
48	90.8595 8243	97.3559 9556	104.4083 9598	120.3882 5659	139.2632 0604	161.5879 0163
49	94.1310 7199	101.0332 8544	108.5406 4785	125.6018 4557	145.8337 3429	169.8593 5720
50	97.4843 4879	104.8117 0079	112.7968 6729	130.9979 1016	152.6670 8366	178.5030 2828
51	100.9214 5751	108.6940 2256	117.1807 7331	136.5828 3702	159.7737 6700	187.5356 6455
52	104.4444 9395	112.6831 0818	121.6961 9651	142.3632 3631	167.1647 1768	196.9747 6946
53	108.0556 0629	116.7818 9365	126.3470 8240	148.3459 4958	174.8513 0639	206.8386 3408
54	111.7569 9645	120.9933 9573	131.1374 9488	154.5380 5782	182.8453 5865	217.1463 7262
55	115.5509 2136	125.3207 1411	136.0716 1972	160.9468 8984	191.1591 7299	227.9179 5938
56	119.4396 9440	129.7670 3375	141.1537 6831	167.5800 3099	199.8055 3991	239.1742 6756
57	123.4256 8676	134.3356 2718	146.3883 8136	174.4453 3207	208.7977 6151	250.9371 0960
58	127.5113 2893	139.0298 5692	151.7800 3280	181.5509 1869	218.1496 7197	263.2292 7953
59	131.6991 1215	143.8531 7799	157.3334 3379	188.9052 0085	227.8756 5885	276.0745 9711
60	135.9915 8995	148.8091 4038	163.0534 3680	196.5168 8288	237.9906 8520	289.4979 5398

AMOUNT OF ANNUITY OF 1 (*Cont.*)

	5%	5½%	6%	6½%	7%	8%
1	1.0000 0000	1.0000 0000	1.0000 0000	1.0000 0000	1.0000 0000	1.0000 0000
2	2.0500 0000	2.0550 0000	2.0600 0000	2.0650 0000	2.0700 0000	2.0800 0000
3	3.1525 0000	3.1680 2500	3.1836 0000	3.1992 2500	3.2149 0000	3.2464 0000
4	4.3101 2500	4.3422 6638	4.3746 1600	4.4071 7463	4.4399 4300	4.5061 1200
5	5.5256 3125	5.5810 9103	5.6370 9296	5.6936 4098	5.7507 3901	5.8666 0096
6	6.8019 1281	6.8880 5103	6.9753 1854	7.0637 2764	7.1532 9074	7.3359 2904
7	8.1420 0845	8.2668 9384	8.3938 3765	8.5228 6994	8.6540 2109	8.9228 0336
8	9.5491 0888	9.7215 7300	9.8974 6791	10.0768 5648	10.2598 0257	10.6366 2763
9	11.0265 6432	11.2562 5951	11.4913 1598	11.7318 5215	11.9779 8875	12.4875 5784
10	12.5778 9254	12.8753 5379	13.1807 9494	13.4944 2254	13.8164 4796	14.4865 6247
11	14.2067 8716	14.5834 9825	14.9716 4264	15.3715 6001	15.7835 9932	16.6454 8746
12	15.9171 2652	16.3855 9065	16.8699 4120	17.3707 1141	17.8884 5127	18.9771 2646
13	17.7129 8285	18.2867 9814	18.8821 3767	19.4998 0765	20.1406 4286	21.4952 9658
14	19.5986 3199	20.2925 7203	21.0150 6593	21.7672 9515	22.5504 8786	24.2149 2030
15	21.5785 6359	22.4086 6350	23.2759 6988	24.1821 6933	25.1290 2201	27.1521 1393
16	23.6574 9177	24.6411 3999	25.6725 2808	26.7540 1034	27.8880 5355	30.3242 8304
17	25.8403 6636	26.9964 0269	28.2128 7976	29.4930 2101	30.8402 1730	33.7502 2569
18	28.1323 8467	29.4812 0483	30.9056 5255	32.4100 6738	33.9990 3251	37.4502 4374
19	30.5390 0391	32.1026 7110	33.7599 9170	35.5167 2176	37.3789 6479	41.4462 6324
20	33.0659 5410	34.8683 1801	36.7855 9120	38.8253 0867	40.9954 9232	45.7619 6430
21	35.7192 5181	37.7860 7550	39.9927 2668	42.3489 5373	44.8651 7678	50.4229 2144
22	38.5052 1440	40.8643 0965	43.3922 9028	46.1016 3573	49.0057 3916	55.4567 5516
23	41.4304 7512	44.1118 4669	46.9958 2769	50.0982 4205	53.4361 4090	60.8932 9557
24	44.5019 9887	47.5379 9825	50.8155 7735	54.3546 2778	58.1766 7076	66.7647 5922
25	47.7270 9882	51.1525 8816	54.8645 1200	58.8876 7859	63.2490 3772	73.1059 3995
26	51.1134 5376	54.9659 8051	59.1563 8272	63.7153 7769	68.6764 7036	79.9544 1515
27	54.6691 2645	58.9891 0943	63.7057 6568	68.8568 7725	74.4838 2328	87.3507 6836
28	58.4025 8277	63.2335 1045	68.5281 1162	74.3325 7427	80.6976 9091	95.3388 2983
29	62.3227 1191	67.7113 5353	73.6397 9832	80.1641 9159	87.3465 2927	103.9659 3622
30	66.4388 4750	72.4354 7797	79.0581 8622	86.3748 6405	94.4607 8632	113.2832 1111
31	70.7607 8988	77.4194 2926	84.8016 7739	92.9892 3021	102.0730 4137	123.3458 6800
32	75.2988 2937	82.6774 9787	90.8897 7803	100.0335 3017	110.2181 5426	134.2135 3744
33	80.0637 7084	88.2247 6025	97.3431 6471	107.5357 0963	118.9334 2506	145.9506 2044
34	85.0669 5938	94.0771 2207	104.1837 5460	115.5255 3076	128.2587 6481	158.6266 7007
35	90.3203 0735	100.2513 6378	111.4347 7987	124.0346 9026	138.2368 7835	172.3168 0368
36	95.8363 2272	106.7651 8879	119.1208 6666	133.0969 4513	148.9134 5984	187.1021 4797
37	101.6281 3886	113.6372 7417	127.2681 1866	142.7482 4656	160.3374 0202	203.0703 1981
38	107.7095 4580	120.8873 2425	135.9042 0578	153.0268 8259	172.5610 2017	220.3159 4540
39	114.0950 2309	128.5361 2708	145.0584 5813	163.9736 2995	185.6402 9158	238.9412 2103
40	120.7997 7424	136.6056 1407	154.7619 6562	175.6319 1590	199.6351 1199	259.0565 1871
41	127.8397 6295	145.1189 2285	165.0476 8356	188.0479 9044	214.6095 6983	280.7810 4021
42	135.2317 5110	154.1004 6360	175.9505 4457	201.2711 0981	230.6322 3972	304.2435 2342
43	142.9933 3866	163.5759 8910	187.5075 7724	215.3537 3195	247.7764 9650	329.5830 0530
44	151.1430 0559	173.5726 6850	199.7580 3188	230.3517 2453	266.1208 5125	356.9496 4572
45	159.7001 5587	184.1191 6527	212.7435 1379	246.3245 8662	285.7493 1084	386.5056 1738
46	168.6851 6366	195.2457 1936	226.5081 2462	263.3356 8475	306.7517 6260	418.4260 6677
47	178.1194 2185	206.9842 3392	241.0986 1210	281.4525 0426	329.2243 8598	452.9001 5211
48	188.0253 9294	219.3683 6679	256.5645 2882	300.7469 1704	353.2700 9300	490.1321 6428
49	198.4266 6259	232.4336 2696	272.9584 0055	321.2954 6665	378.9989 9951	530.3427 3742
50	209.3479 9572	246.2174 7645	290.3359 0458	343.1796 7198	406.5289 2947	573.7701 5642
51	220.8153 9550	260.7594 3765	308.7560 5886	366.4863 5066	435.9859 5454	620.6717 6893
52	232.8561 6528	276.1012 0672	328.2814 2239	391.3079 6345	467.5049 7135	671.3255 1044
53	245.4989 7354	292.2867 7309	348.9783 0773	417.7429 8108	501.2303 1935	726.0315 5128
54	258.7739 2222	309.3625 4561	370.9170 0620	445.8962 7485	537.3164 4170	785.1140 7538
55	272.7126 1833	327.3774 8562	394.1720 2657	475.8795 3271	575.9285 9262	848.9232 0141
56	287.3482 4924	346.3832 4733	418.8223 4816	507.8117 0234	617.2435 9410	917.8370 5752
57	302.7156 6171	366.4343 2593	444.9516 8905	541.8194 6299	661.4506 4569	992.2640 2213
58	318.8514 4479	387.5882 1386	472.6487 9040	578.0377 2808	708.7521 9089	1072.6451 4390
59	335.7940 1703	409.9055 6562	502.0077 1782	616.6101 8041	759.3648 4425	1159.4567 5541
60	353.5837 1788	433.4503 7173	533.1281 8089	657.6898 4214	813.5203 8335	1253.2132 9584

PRESENT VALUE OF ANNUITY OF 1

	½%	⅝%	¾%	⅞%	1%	1⅛%
1	0.9950 2488	0.9937 8882	0.9925 5583	0.9913 2590	0.9900 9901	0.9888 7515
2	1.9850 9938	1.9814 0504	1.9777 2291	1.9740 5294	1.9703 9506	1.9667 4923
3	2.9702 4814	2.9628 8699	2.9555 5624	2.9482 5570	2.9409 8521	2.9337 4460
4	3.9504 9566	3.9382 7279	3.9261 1041	3.9140 0813	3.9019 6555	3.8899 8230
5	4.9258 6633	4.9076 0029	4.8894 3961	4.8713 8352	4.8534 3124	4.8355 8200
6	5.8963 8441	5.8709 0712	5.8455 9763	5.8204 5454	5.7954 7647	5.7706 6205
7	6.8620 7404	6.8282 3068	6.7946 3785	6.7612 9323	6.7281 9453	6.6953 3948
8	7.8229 5924	7.7796 0813	7.7366 1325	7.6939 7098	7.6516 7775	7.6097 3002
9	8.7790 6392	8.7250 7640	8.6715 7642	8.6185 5859	8.5660 1758	8.5139 4810
10	9.7304 1186	9.6646 7220	9.5995 7958	9.5351 2624	9.4713 0453	9.4081 0690
11	10.6770 2673	10.5984 3200	10.5206 7452	10.4437 4348	10.3676 2825	10.2923 1832
12	11.6189 3207	11.5263 9205	11.4349 1267	11.3444 7929	11.2550 7747	11.1666 9302
13	12.5561 5131	12.4485 8837	12.3423 4508	12.2374 0202	12.1337 4007	12.0313 4044
14	13.4887 0777	13.3650 5676	13.2430 2242	13.1225 7945	13.0037 0304	12.8863 6880
15	14.4166 2465	14.2758 3281	14.1369 9495	14.0000 7876	13.8650 5252	13.7318 8509
16	15.3399 2502	15.1809 5186	15.0243 1261	14.8699 6656	14.7178 7378	14.5679 9514
17	16.2586 3186	16.0804 4905	15.9050 2492	15.7323 0885	15.5622 5127	15.3948 0360
18	17.1727 6802	16.9743 5931	16.7791 8107	16.5871 7111	16.3982 6858	16.2124 1395
19	18.0823 5624	17.8627 1733	17.6468 2984	17.4346 1820	17.2260 0850	17.0209 2850
20	18.9874 1915	18.7455 5759	18.5080 1969	18.2747 1445	18.0455 5297	17.8204 4845
21	19.8879 7925	19.6229 1438	19.3627 9870	19.1075 2361	18.8569 8313	18.6110 7387
22	20.7840 5896	20.4948 2174	20.2112 1459	19.9331 0891	19.6603 7934	19.3929 0371
23	21.6756 8055	21.3613 1353	21.0533 1473	20.7515 3300	20.4558 2113	20.1660 3580
24	22.5628 6622	22.2224 2338	21.8891 4614	21.5628 5799	21.2433 8726	20.9305 6693
25	23.4456 3803	23.0781 8473	22.7187 5547	22.3671 4547	22.0231 5570	21.6865 9276
26	24.3240 1794	23.9286 3079	23.5421 8905	23.1644 5647	22.7952 0366	22.4342 0792
27	25.1980 2780	24.7737 9457	24.3594 9286	23.9548 5152	23.5596 0759	23.1735 0598
28	26.0676 8936	25.6137 0889	25.1707 1251	24.7383 9060	24.3164 4316	23.9045 7946
29	26.9330 2423	26.4484 0635	25.9758 9331	25.5151 3319	25.0657 8530	24.6275 1986
30	27.7940 5397	27.2779 1935	26.7750 8021	26.2851 3823	25.8077 0822	25.3424 1766
31	28.6507 9997	28.1022 8010	27.5683 1783	27.0484 6417	26.5422 8537	26.0493 6233
32	29.5032 8355	28.9215 2060	28.3556 5045	27.8051 6894	27.2695 8947	26.7484 4236
33	30.3515 2592	29.7356 7265	29.1371 2203	28.5553 0998	27.9896 9255	27.4397 4522
34	31.1955 4818	30.5447 6785	29.9127 7621	29.2989 4422	28.7026 6589	28.1233 5745
35	32.0353 7132	31.3488 3761	30.6826 5629	30.0361 2809	29.4085 8009	28.7993 6460
36	32.8710 1624	32.1479 1315	31.4468 0525	30.7669 1757	30.1075 0504	29.4678 5127
37	33.7025 0372	32.9420 2550	32.2052 6576	31.4913 6810	30.7995 0994	30.1289 0114
38	34.5298 5445	33.7312 0546	32.9580 8016	32.2095 3467	31.4846 6330	30.7825 9692
39	35.3530 8900	34.5154 8369	33.7052 9048	32.9214 7179	32.1630 3298	31.4290 2044
40	36.1722 2786	35.2948 9062	34.4469 3844	33.6272 3350	32.8346 8611	32.0682 5260
41	36.9872 9141	36.0694 5652	35.1830 6545	34.3268 7335	33.4996 8922	32.7903 7340
42	37.7982 9991	36.8392 1145	35.9137 1260	35.0204 4446	34.1581 0814	33.3254 6195
43	38.6052 7354	37.6041 8529	36.6389 2070	35.7079 9947	34.8100 0806	33.9435 9649
44	39.4082 3238	38.3644 0774	37.3587 3022	36.3895 9055	35.4554 5352	34.5548 5438
45	40.2071 9640	39.1199 0831	38.0731 8136	37.0652 6944	36.0945 0844	35.1593 1212
46	41.0021 8547	39.8707 1634	38.7823 1401	37.7350 8743	36.7272 3608	35.7570 4536
47	41.7932 1937	40.6168 6096	39.4861 6774	38.3990 9535	37.3536 9909	36.3481 2891
48	42.5803 1778	41.3583 7114	40.1847 8189	39.0573 4359	37.9739 5949	36.9326 3674
49	43.3635 0028	42.0952 7566	40.8781 9542	39.7098 8212	38.5880 7871	37.5106 4202
50	44.1427 8635	42.8276 0314	41.5664 4707	40.3567 6047	39.1961 1753	38.0822 1708
51	44.9181 9537	43.5553 8201	42.2495 7525	40.9980 2772	39.7981 3617	38.6474 3345
52	45.6897 4664	44.2786 4050	42.9276 1812	41.6337 3256	40.3941 9423	39.2063 6188
53	46.4574 5934	44.9974 0671	43.6006 1351	42.2639 2324	40.9843 5072	39.7590 7232
54	47.2213 5258	45.7117 0853	44.2685 9902	42.8886 4757	41.5686 6408	40.3056 3394
55	47.9814 4535	46.4215 7370	44.9316 1193	43.5079 5298	42.1471 9216	40.8461 1514
56	48.7377 5657	47.1270 2976	45.5896 8926	44.1218 8647	42.7199 9224	41.3805 8358
57	49.4903 0505	47.8281 0410	46.2428 6776	44.7304 9465	43.2871 2102	41.9091 0613
58	50.2391 0950	48.5248 2396	46.8911 8388	45.3338 2369	43.8486 3468	42.4317 4896
59	50.9841 8855	49.2172 1636	47.5346 7382	45.9319 1939	44.4045 8879	42.9485 7746
60	51.7255 6075	49.9053 0818	48.1733 7352	46.5248 2716	44.9550 3841	43.4596 5633

From J. W. Glover, "Tables of Applied Math. in Finance, Insurance, Statistics"

PRESENT VALUE OF ANNUITY OF 1 (*Cont.*)

	1¼%	1⅜%	1½%	1¾%	2%	2¼%
1	0.9876 5432	0.9864 3650	0.9852 2167	0.9828 0098	0.9803 9216	0.9779 9511
2	1.9631 1538	1.9594 9346	1.9558 8342	1.9486 9875	1.9415 6094	1.9344 6955
3	2.9265 3371	2.9193 5237	2.9122 0042	2.8979 8403	2.8838 8327	2.8698 9687
4	3.8780 5798	3.8661 9222	3.8543 8465	3.8309 4254	3.8077 2870	3.7847 4021
5	4.8178 3504	4.8001 8962	4.7826 4497	4.7478 5508	4.7134 5951	4.6794 5253
6	5.7460 0992	5.7215 1874	5.6971 8717	5.6489 9762	5.6014 3089	5.5544 7680
7	6.6627 2585	6.6303 5140	6.5982 1396	6.5346 4139	6.4719 9107	6.4102 4626
8	7.5681 2429	7.5268 5712	7.4859 2508	7.4050 5297	7.3254 8144	7.2471 8461
9	8.4623 4498	8.4112 0308	8.3605 1732	8.2604 9432	8.1622 3671	8.0657 0622
10	9.3455 2591	9.2835 5421	9.2221 8455	9.1012 2291	8.9825 8501	8.8662 1635
11	10.2178 0337	10.1440 7320	10.0711 1779	9.9274 9181	9.7868 4805	9.6491 1134
12	11.0793 1197	10.9929 2054	10.9075 0521	10.7395 4969	10.5753 4122	10.4147 7882
13	11.9301 8466	11.8302 5454	11.7315 3222	11.5376 4097	11.3483 7375	11.1635 9787
14	12.7705 5275	12.6562 3136	12.5433 8150	12.3220 0587	12.1062 4877	11.8959 3924
15	13.6005 4592	13.4710 0504	13.3432 3301	13.0928 8046	12.8492 6350	12.6121 6551
16	14.4202 9227	14.2747 2754	14.1312 6405	13.8504 9677	13.5777 0931	13.3126 3131
17	15.2299 1829	15.0675 4874	14.9076 4931	14.5950 8282	14.2918 7188	13.9976 8343
18	16.0295 4893	15.8496 1651	15.6725 6089	15.3268 6272	14.9920 3125	14.6676 6106
19	16.8193 0759	16.6210 7671	16.4261 6837	16.0460 5673	15.6784 6201	15.3228 9590
20	17.5993 1613	17.3820 7320	17.1686 3879	16.7528 8130	16.3514 3334	15.9637 1237
21	18.3696 9495	18.1327 4792	17.9001 3673	17.4475 4919	17.0112 0916	16.5904 2775
22	19.1305 6291	18.8732 4086	18.6208 2437	18.1302 6948	17.6580 4820	17.2033 5232
23	19.8820 3744	19.6036 9012	19.3308 6145	18.8012 4764	18.2922 0412	17.8027 8955
24	20.6242 3451	20.3242 3193	20.0304 0537	19.4606 8565	18.9139 2560	18.3890 3624
25	21.3572 6865	21.0350 0067	20.7196 1120	20.1087 8196	19.5234 5647	18.9623 8263
26	22.0812 5299	21.7361 2890	21.3986 3172	20.7457 3166	20.1210 3576	19.5231 1260
27	22.7962 9925	22.4277 4737	22.0676 1746	21.3717 2644	20.7068 9780	20.0715 0376
28	23.5025 1778	23.1099 8508	22.7267 1671	21.9869 5474	21.2812 7236	20.6078 2764
29	24.2000 1756	23.7829 6925	23.3760 7558	22.5916 0171	21.8443 8466	21.1323 4977
30	24.8889 0623	24.4468 2540	24.0158 3801	23.1858 4934	22.3964 5555	21.6453 2985
31	25.5692 9010	25.1016 7734	24.6461 4582	23.7698 7650	22.9377 0152	22.1470 2186
32	26.2412 7418	25.7476 4719	25.2671 3874	24.3438 5897	23.4683 3482	22.6376 7419
33	26.9049 6215	26.3848 5543	25.8789 5442	24.9079 6951	23.9885 6355	23.1175 2977
34	27.5604 5644	27.0134 2089	26.4817 2849	25.4623 7789	24.4985 9172	23.5868 2618
35	28.2078 5822	27.6334 6080	27.0755 9458	26.0072 5100	24.9986 1933	24.0457 9577
36	28.8472 6737	28.2450 9080	27.6606 8431	26.5427 5283	25.4888 4248	24.4946 6579
37	29.4787 8259	28.8484 2496	28.2371 2740	27.0690 4455	25.9694 5341	24.9336 5848
38	30.1025 0133	29.4435 7579	28.8050 5163	27.5862 8457	26.4406 4060	25.3629 9118
39	30.7185 1983	30.0306 5430	29.3645 8288	28.0946 2857	26.9025 8883	25.7828 7646
40	31.3269 3316	30.6097 6996	29.9158 4520	28.5942 2955	27.3554 7924	26.1935 2221
41	31.9278 3522	31.1810 3079	30.4589 6079	29.0852 3789	27.7994 8945	26.5951 3174
42	32.5213 1874	31.7445 4332	30.9940 5004	29.5678 0135	28.2347 9358	26.9879 0390
53	33.1074 7530	32.3004 1264	31.5212 3157	30.0420 6522	28.6615 6233	27.3720 3316
44	33.6863 9536	32.8487 4243	32.0406 2223	30.5081 7221	29.0799 6307	27.7477 0969
45	34.2581 6825	33.3896 3495	32.5523 3718	30.9662 6261	29.4901 5987	28.1151 1950
46	34.8228 8222	33.9231 9108	33.0564 8983	31.4164 7431	29.8923 1360	28.4744 4450
47	35.3806 2442	34.4495 1031	33.5531 9195	31.8589 4281	30.2865 8196	28.8258 6259
48	35.9314 8091	34.9686 9081	34.0425 5365	32.2938 0129	30.6731 1957	29.1695 4777
49	36.4755 3670	35.4808 2941	34.5246 8339	32.7211 8063	31.0520 7801	29.5056 7019
50	37.0128 7574	35.9860 2161	34.9996 8807	33.1412 0946	31.4236 0589	29.8343 9627
51	37.5435 8099	36.4843 6164	35.4676 7298	33.5540 1421	31.7878 4892	30.1558 8877
52	38.0677 3431	36.9759 4243	35.9287 4185	33.9597 1913	32.1449 4992	30.4703 0687
53	38.5854 1660	37.4608 5566	36.3829 9690	34.3584 4633	32.4950 4894	30.7778 0623
54	39.0967 0776	37.9391 9178	36.8305 3882	34.7503 1579	32.8382 8327	31.0785 3910
55	39.6016 8667	38.4110 3998	37.2714 6681	35.1354 4550	33.1747 8752	31.3726 5438
56	40.1004 3128	38.8764 8826	37.7058 7863	35.5139 5135	33.5046 9365	31.6602 9768
57	40.5930 1855	39.3356 2344	38.1338 7058	35.8859 4727	33.8281 3103	31.9416 1142
58	41.0795 2449	39.7885 3114	38.5555 3751	36.2515 4523	34.1452 2650	32.2167 3489
59	41.5600 2419	40.2352 9582	38.9709 7292	36.6108 5526	34.4561 0441	32.4858 0429
60	42.0345 9179	40.6760 0081	39.3802 6889	36.9639 8552	34.7608 8668	32.7489 5285

PRESENT VALUE OF ANNUITY OF 1 (*Cont.*)

	2½%	2¾%	3%	3½%	4%	4½%
1	0.9756 0976	0.9732 3601	0.9708 7379	0.9661 8357	0.9615 3846	0.9569 3780
2	1.9274 2415	1.9204 2434	1.9134 6970	1.8996 9428	1.8860 9467	1.8726 6775
3	2.8560 2356	2.8422 6213	2.8286 1135	2.8016 3698	2.7750 9103	2.7489 6435
4	3.7619 7421	3.7394 2787	3.7170 9840	3.6730 7921	3.6298 9522	3.5875 2570
5	4.6458 2850	4.6125 8186	4.5797 0719	4.5150 5238	4.4518 2233	4.3899 7674
6	5.5081 2536	5.4623 6678	5.4171 9144	5.3285 5302	5.2421 3686	5.1578 7248
7	6.3493 9060	6.2894 0806	6.2302 8296	6.1145 4398	6.0020 5467	5.8927 0094
8	7.1701 3717	7.0943 1441	7.0196 9219	6.8739 5554	6.7327 4487	6.5958 8607
9	7.9708 6553	7.8776 7826	7.7861 0892	7.6076 8651	7.4353 3161	7.2687 9050
10	8.7520 6393	8.6400 7616	8.5302 0284	8.3166 0532	8.1108 9578	7.9127 1818
11	9.5142 0871	9.3820 6926	9.2526 2411	9.0015 5104	8.7604 7671	8.5289 1692
12	10.2577 6460	10.1042 0366	9.9540 0399	9.6633 3433	9.3850 7376	9.1185 8078
13	10.9831 8497	10.8070 1086	10.6349 5533	10.3027 3849	9.9856 4785	9.6828 5242
14	11.6909 1217	11.4910 0814	11.2960 7314	10.9205 2028	10.5631 2293	10.2228 2528
15	12.3813 7773	12.1566 9892	11.9379 3509	11.5174 1090	11.1183 8743	10.7395 4573
16	13.0550 0266	12.8045 7315	12.5611 0203	12.0941 1681	11.6522 9561	11.2340 1505
17	13.7121 9772	13.4351 0769	13.1661 1847	12.6513 2059	12.1656 6885	11.7071 9143
18	14.3533 6363	14.0487 6661	13.7535 1308	13.1896 8173	12.6592 9697	12.1599 9180
19	14.9788 9134	14.6460 0157	14.3237 9911	13.7098 3742	13.1339 3940	12.5932 9359
20	15.5891 6229	15.2272 5213	14.8774 7486	14.2124 0330	13.5903 2634	13.0079 3645
21	16.1845 4857	15.7929 4612	15.4150 2414	14.6979 7420	14.0291 5995	13.4047 2388
22	16.7654 1324	16,3434 9987	15.9369 1664	15.1671 2484	14.4511 1533	13.7844 2476
23	17.3321 1048	16.8793 1861	16.4436 0839	15.6204 1047	14.8568 4167	14.1477 7489
24	17.8849 8583	17.4007 9670	16.9355 4212	16.0583 6760	15.2469 6314	14.4954 7837
25	18.4243 7642	17.9083 1795	17.4131 4769	16.4815 1459	15.6220 7994	14.8282 0896
26	18.9506 1114	18.4022 5592	17.8768 4242	16.8903 5226	15.9827 6918	15.1466 1145
27	19.4640 1087	18.8829 7413	18.3270 3147	17.2853 6451	16.3295 8575	15.4513 0282
28	19.9648 8866	19.3508 2640	18.7641 0823	17.6670 1885	16.6630 6322	15.7428 7351
29	20.4535 4991	19.8061 5708	19.1884 5459	18.0357 6700	16.9837 1463	16.0218 8853
30	20.9302 9259	20.2493 0130	19.6004 4135	18.3920 4541	17.2920 3330	16.2888 8854
31	21.3954 0741	20.6805 8520	20.0004 2849	18.7362 7576	17.5884 9356	16.5443 9095
32	21.8491 7796	21.1003 2623	20.3887 6553	19.0688 6547	17.8735 5150	16.7888 9086
33	22.2918 8094	21.5088 3332	20.7657 9178	19.3902 0818	18.1476 4567	17.0228 6207
34	22.7237 8628	21.9064 0712	21.1318 3668	19.7006 8423	18.4111 9776	17.2467 5796
35	23.1451 5734	22.2933 4026	21.4872 2007	20.0006 6110	18.6646 1323	17.4610 1240
36	23.5562 5107	22.6699 1753	21.8322 5250	20.2904 9381	18.9082 8195	17.6660 4058
37	23.9573 1812	23.0364 1609	22.1672 3544	20.5705 2542	19.1425 7880	17.8622 3979
38	24.3486 0304	23.3931 0568	22.4924 6159	20.8410 8736	19.3678 6423	18.0499 9023
39	24.7303 4443	23.7402 4884	22.8082 1513	21.1024 9987	19.5844 8484	18.2296 5572
40	25.1027 7505	24.0781 0106	23.1147 7197	21.3550 7234	19.7927 7388	18.4015 8442
41	25.4661 2200	24.4069 1101	23.4123 9997	21.5991 0371	19.9930 5181	18.5661 0949
42	25.8206 0683	24.7269 2069	23.7013 5920	21.8348 8281	20.1856 2674	18.7235 4975
43	26.1664 4569	25.0383 6563	23.9819 0213	22.0626 8870	20.3707 9494	18.8742 1029
44	26.5038 4945	25.3414 7507	24.2542 7392	22.2827 9102	20.5488 4129	19.0183 8305
45	26.8330 2386	25.6364 7209	24.5187 1254	22.4954 5026	20.7200 3970	19.1563 4742
46	27.1541 6962	25.9235 7381	24.7754 4907	22.7009 1813	20.8846 5356	19.2883 7074
47	27.4674 8255	26.2029 9154	25.0247 0783	22.8994 3780	21.0429 3612	19.4147 0884
48	27.7731 5371	26.4749 3094	25.2667 0664	23.0912 4425	21.1951 3088	19.5356 0654
49	28.0713 6947	26.7395 9215	25.5016 5693	23.2765 6450	21.3414 7200	19.6512 9813
50	28.3623 1168	26.9971 6998	25.7297 6401	23.4556 1787	21.4821 8462	19.7620 0778
51	28.6461 5774	27.2478 5400	25.9512 2719	23.6286 1630	21.6174 8521	19.8679 5003
52	28.9230 8072	27.4918 2871	26.1662 3999	23.7957 6454	21.7475 8193	19.9693 3017
53	29.1932 4948	27.7292 7368	26.3749 9028	23.9572 6043	21.8726 7493	20.0663 4466
54	29.4568 2876	27.9603 6368	26.5776 6047	24.1132 9510	21.9929 5667	20.1591 8149
55	29.7139 7928	28.1852 6879	26.7744 2764	24.2640 5323	22.1086 1218	20.2480 2057
56	29.9648 5784	28.4041 5454	26.9654 6373	24.4097 1327	22.2189 1940	20.3330 3404
57	30.2096 1740	28.6171 8203	27.1509 3566	24.5504 4760	22.3267 4943	20.4143 8664
58	30.4484 0722	28.8245 0806	27.3310 0549	24.6864 2281	22.4295 6676	20.4922 3602
59	30.6813 7290	29.0262 8522	27.5058 3058	24.8177 9981	22.5284 2957	20.5667 3303
60	30.9086 5649	29.2226 6201	27.6755 6367	24.9447 3412	22.6234 8997	20.6380 2204

PRESENT VALUE OF ANNUITY OF 1 (*Cont.*)

	5%	5½%	6%	6½%	7%	8%
1	0.9523 8095	0.9478 6730	0.9433 9623	0.9389 6714	0.9345 7944	0.9259 2593
2	1.8594 1043	1.8463 1971	1.8333 9267	1.8206 2642	1.8080 1817	1.7832 6475
3	2.7232 4803	2.6979 3338	2.6730 1195	2.6484 7551	2.6243 1604	2.5770 9699
4	3.5459 5050	3.5051 5012	3.4651 0561	3.4257 9860	3.3872 1126	3.3121 2684
5	4.3294 7667	4.2702 8448	4.2123 6379	4.1556 7944	4.1001 9744	3.9927 1004
6	5.0756 9206	4.9955 3031	4.9173 2433	4.8410 1356	4.7665 3966	4.6228 7966
7	5.7863 7340	5.6829 6712	5.5823 8144	5.4845 1977	5.3892 8940	5.2063 7006
8	6.4632 1276	6.3345 6599	6.2097 9381	6.0887 5096	5.9712 9851	5.7466 3894
9	7.1078 2168	6.9521 9525	6.8016 9227	6.6561 0419	6.5152 3225	6.2468 8791
10	7.7217 3493	7.5376 2583	7.3600 8705	7.1888 3022	7.0235 8154	6.7100 8140
11	8.3064 1422	8.0925 3633	7.8868 7458	7.6890 4246	7.4986 7434	7.1389 6426
12	8.8632 5164	8.6185 1785	8.3838 4394	8.1587 2532	7.9426 8630	7.5360 7802
13	9.3935 7299	9.1170 7853	8.8526 8296	8.5997 4208	8.3576 5074	7.9037 7594
14	9.8986 4094	9.5896 4790	9.2949 8393	9.0138 4233	8.7454 6799	8.2442 3698
15	10.3796 5804	10.0375 8094	9.7122 4899	9.4026 6885	9.1079 1401	8.5594 7869
16	10.8377 6956	10.4621 6203	10.1058 9527	9.7677 6418	9.4466 4860	8.8513 6916
17	11.2740 6625	10.8646 0856	10.4772 5969	10.1105 7670	9.7632 2299	9.1216 3811
18	11.6895 8690	11.2460 7447	10.8276 0348	10.4324 6638	10.0590 8691	9.3718 8714
19	12.0853 2086	11.6076 5352	11.1581 1649	10.7347 1022	10.3355 9524	9.6035 9920
20	12.4622 1034	11.9503 8249	11.4699 2122	11.0185 0725	10.5940 1425	9.8181 4741
21	12.8211 5271	12.2752 4406	11.7640 7662	11.2849 8333	10.8355 2733	10.0168 0316
22	13.1630 0258	12.5831 6973	12.0415 8172	11.5351 9562	11.0612 4050	10.2007 4366
23	13.4885 7388	12.8750 4240	12.3033 7898	11.7701 3673	11.2721 8738	10.3710 5895
24	13.7986 4179	13.1516 9895	12.5503 5753	11.9907 3871	11.4693 3400	10.5287 5828
25	14.0939 4457	13.4139 3266	12.7833 5616	12.1978 7672	11.6535 8318	10.6747 7619
26	14.3751 8530	13.6624 9541	13.0031 6619	12.3923 7251	11.8257 7867	10.8099 7795
27	14.6430 3362	13.8980 9991	13.2105 3414	12.5749 9766	11.9867 0904	10.9351 6477
28	14.8981 2726	14.1214 2172	13.4061 6428	12.7464 7668	12.1371 1125	11.0510 7849
29	15.1410 7358	14.3331 0116	13.5907 2102	12.9074 8984	12.2776 7407	11.1584 0601
30	15.3724 5103	14.5337 4517	13.7648 3115	13.0586 7591	12.4090 4118	11.2577 8334
31	15.5928 1050	14.7239 2907	13.9290 8599	13.2006 3465	12.5318 1419	11.3497 9939
32	15.8026 7667	14.9041 9817	14.0840 4339	13.3339 2925	12.6465 5532	11.4349 9944
33	16.0025 4921	15.0750 6936	14.2302 2961	13.4590 8850	12.7537 9002	11.5138 8837
34	16.1929 0401	15.2370 3257	14.3681 4114	13.5766 0892	12.8540 0936	11.5869 3367
35	16.3741 9429	15.3905 5220	14.4982 4636	13.6869 5673	12.9476 7230	11.6545 6822
36	16.5468 5171	15.5360 6843	14.6209 8713	13.7905 6970	13.0352 0776	11.7171 9279
37	16.7112 8734	15.6739 9851	14.7367 8031	13.8878 5887	13.1170 1660	11.7751 7851
38	16.8678 9271	15.8047 3793	14.8460 1916	13.9792 1021	13.1934 7345	11.8288 6899
39	17.0170 4067	15.9286 6154	14.9490 7468	14.0649 8611	13.2649 2846	11.8785 8240
40	17.1590 8635	16.0461 2469	15.0462 9687	14.1455 2687	13.3317 0884	11.9246 1333
41	17.2943 6796	16.1574 6416	15.1380 1592	14.2211 5199	13.3941 2041	11.9672 3457
42	17.4232 0758	16.2629 9920	15.2245 4332	14.2921 6149	13.4524 4898	12.0066 9867
43	17.5459 1198	16.3630 3242	15.3061 7294	14.3588 3708	13.5069 6167	12.0432 3951
44	17.6627 7331	16.4578 5063	15.3831 8202	14.4214 4327	13.5579 0810	12.0770 7362
45	17.7740 6982	16.5477 2572	15.4558 3209	14.4802 2842	13.6055 2159	12.1084 0150
46	17.8800 6650	16.6329 1537	15.5243 6990	14.5354 2575	13.6500 2018	12.1374 0880
47	17.9810 1571	16.7136 6386	15.5890 2821	14.5872 5422	13.6916 0764	12.1642 6741
48	18.0771 5782	16.7902 0271	15.6500 2661	14.6359 1946	13.7304 7443	12.1891 3649
49	18.1687 2173	16.8627 5139	15.7075 7227	14.6816 1451	13.7667 9853	12.2121 6341
50	18.2559 2546	16.9315 1790	15.7618 6064	14.7245 2067	13.8007 4629	12.2334 8464
51	18.3389 7663	16.9966 9943	15.8130 7607	14.7648 0814	13.8324 7317	12.2532 2652
52	18.4180 7298	17.0584 8287	15.8613 9252	14.8026 3675	13.8621 2446	12.2715 0604
53	18.4934 0284	17.1170 4538	15.9069 7408	14.8381 5658	13.8898 3594	12.2884 3152
54	18.5651 4556	17.1725 5486	15.9499 7554	14.8715 0852	13.9157 3453	12.3041 0326
55	18.6334 7196	17.2251 7048	15.9905 4297	14.9028 2490	13.9399 3881	12.3186 1413
56	18.6985 4473	17.2750 4311	16.0288 1412	14.9322 2996	13.9625 5964	12.3320 5012
57	18.7605 1879	17.3223 1575	16.0649 1898	14.9598 4033	13.9837 0059	12.3444 9085
58	18.8195 4170	17.3671 2393	16.0989 8017	14.9857 6557	14.0034 5850	12.3560 1005
59	18.8757 5400	17.4095 9614	16.1311 1337	15.0101 0852	14.0219 2383	12.3666 7597
60	18.9292 8952	17.4498 5416	16.1614 2771	15.0329 6574	14.0391 8115	12.3765 5182

ANNUITY WHICH AMOUNTS TO 1

	½%	⅝%	¾%	⅞%	1%	1⅛%
1	1.0000 0000	1.0000 0000	1.0000 0000	1.0000 0000	1.0000 0000	1.0000 0000
2	0.4987 5312	0.4984 4237	0.4981 3200	0.4978 2203	0.4975 1244	0.4972 0323
3	0.3316 7221	0.3312 5865	0.3308 4579	0.3304 3361	0.3300 2211	0.3296 1130
4	0.2481 3279	0.2476 6842	0.2472 0501	0.2467 4257	0.2462 8109	0.2458 2058
5	0.1980 0997	0.1975 1558	0.1970 2242	0.1965 3049	0.1960 3980	0.1955 5034
6	0.1645 9546	0.1640 8143	0.1635 6891	0.1630 5789	0.1625 4837	0.1620 4034
7	0.1407 2854	0.1402 0082	0.1396 7488	0.1391 5070	0.1386 2828	0.1381 0762
8	0.1228 2886	0.1222 9118	0.1217 5552	0.1212 2190	0.1206 9029	0.1201 6071
9	0.1089 0736	0.1083 6218	0.1078 1929	0.1072 7868	0.1067 4036	0.1062 0432
10	0.0977 7057	0.0972 1962	0.0966 7123	0.0961 2538	0.0955 8208	0.0950 4131
11	0.0886 5903	0.0881 0358	0.0875 5094	0.0870 0111	0.0864 5408	0.0859 0984
12	0.0810 6643	0.0805 0742	0.0799 5148	0.0793 9860	0.0788 4879	0.0783 0203
13	0.0746 4224	0.0740 8039	0.0735 2188	0.0729 6669	0.0724 1482	0.0718 6626
14	0.0691 3609	0.0685 7198	0.0680 1146	0.0674 5453	0.0669 0117	0.0663 5138
15	0.0643 6436	0.0637 9845	0.0632 3639	0.0626 7817	0.0621 2378	0.0615 7321
16	0.0601 8937	0.0596 2202	0.0590 5879	0.0584 9965	0.0579 4460	0.0573 9363
17	0.0565 0579	0.0559 3732	0.0553 7321	0.0548 1346	0.0542 5806	0.0537 0698
18	0.0532 3173	0.0526 6239	0.0520 9766	0.0515 3756	0.0509 8205	0.0504 3113
19	0.0503 0253	0.0497 3252	0.0491 6740	0.0486 0715	0.0480 5175	0.0475 0120
20	0.0476 6645	0.0470 9597	0.0465 3063	0.0459 7042	0.0454 1531	0.0448 6531
21	0.0452 8163	0.0447 1083	0.0441 4543	0.0435 8541	0.0430 3075	0.0424 8145
22	0.0431 1380	0.0425 4281	0.0419 7748	0.0414 1779	0.0408 6372	0.0403 1525
23	0.0411 3465	0.0405 6360	0.0399 9846	0.0394 3921	0.0388 8584	0.0383 3833
24	0.0393 2061	0.0387 4959	0.0381 8474	0.0376 2604	0.0370 7347	0.0365 2701
25	0.0376 5186	0.0370 8096	0.0365 1650	0.0359 5843	0.0354 0675	0.0348 6144
26	0.0361 1163	0.0355 4094	0.0349 7693	0.0344 1959	0.0338 6888	0.0333 2479
27	0.0346 8565	0.0341 1523	0.0335 5176	0.0329 9520	0.0324 4553	0.0319 0273
28	0.0333 6167	0.0327 9159	0.0322 2871	0.0316 7300	0.0311 2444	0.0305 8299
29	0.0321 2914	0.0315 5946	0.0309 9723	0.0304 4243	0.0298 9502	0.0293 5498
30	0.0309 7892	0.0304 0969	0.0298 4816	0.0292 9434	0.0287 4811	0.0282 0953
31	0.0299 0304	0.0293 3430	0.0287 7352	0.0282 2068	0.0276 7573	0.0271 3866
32	0.0288 9453	0.0283 2633	0.0277 6634	0.0272 1454	0.0266 7089	0.0261 3535
33	0.0279 4727	0.0273 7964	0.0268 2048	0.0262 6976	0.0257 2744	0.0251 9349
34	0.0270 5586	0.0264 8883	0.0259 3053	0.0253 8092	0.0248 3997	0.0243 0763
35	0.0262 1550	0.0256 4911	0.0250 9170	0.0245 4324	0.0240 0368	0.0234 7299
36	0.0254 2194	0.0248 5622	0.0242 9973	0.0237 5244	0.0232 1431	0.0226 8529
37	0.0246 7139	0.0241 0636	0.0235 5082	0.0230 0473	0.0224 6805	0.0219 4072
38	0.0239 6045	0.0233 9614	0.0228 4157	0.0222 9671	0.0217 6150	0.0212 3589
39	0.0232 8607	0.0227 2250	0.0221 6893	0.0216 2531	0.0210 9160	0.0205 6773
40	0.0226 4552	0.0220 8271	0.0215 3016	0.0209 8780	0.0204 5560	0.0199 3349
41	0.0220 3631	0.0214 7429	0.0209 2276	0.0203 8169	0.0198 5102	0.0193 3069
42	0.0214 5622	0.0208 9499	0.0203 4452	0.0198 0475	0.0192 7563	0.0187 5709
43	0.0209 0320	0.0203 4278	0.0197 9338	0.0192 5493	0.0187 2737	0.0182 1064
44	0.0203 7541	0.0198 1583	0.0192 6751	0.0187 3039	0.0182 0441	0.0176 8949
45	0.0198 7117	0.0193 1243	0.0187 6521	0.0182 2943	0.0177 0505	0.0171 9197
46	0.0193 8894	0.0188 3106	0.0182 8495	0.0177 5053	0.0172 2775	0.0167 1652
47	0.0189 2733	0.0183 7032	0.0178 2532	0.0172 9228	0.0167 7111	0.0162 6173
48	0.0184 8503	0.0179 2890	0.0173 8504	0.0168 5338	0.0163 3384	0.0158 2632
49	0.0180 6087	0.0175 0563	0.0169 6292	0.0164 3265	0.0159 1474	0.0154 0910
50	0.0176 5376	0.0170 9943	0.0165 5787	0.0160 2900	0.0155 1273	0.0150 0898
51	0.0172 6269	0.0167 0928	0.0161 6888	0.0156 4142	0.0151 2680	0.0146 2494
52	0.0168 8675	0.0163 3425	0.0157 9503	0.0152 6899	0.0147 5603	0.0142 5606
53	0.0165 2507	0.0159 7350	0.0154 3546	0.0149 1084	0.0143 9956	0.0139 0149
54	0.0161 7686	0.0156 2623	0.0150 8938	0.0145 6619	0.0140 5658	0.0135 6043
55	0.0158 4139	0.0152 9171	0.0147 5605	0.0142 3430	0.0137 2637	0.0132 3213
56	0.0155 1797	0.0149 6925	0.0144 3478	0.0139 1449	0.0134 0824	0.0129 1592
57	0.0152 0598	0.0146 5821	0.0141 2496	0.0136 0611	0.0131 0156	0.0126 1116
58	0.0149 0481	0.0143 5801	0.0138 2597	0.0133 0858	0.0128 0573	0.0123 1726
59	0.0146 1392	0.0140 6809	0.0135 3727	0.0130 2135	0.0125 2020	0.0120 3366
60	0.0143 3280	0.0137 8795	0.0132 5836	0.0127 4390	0.0122 4445	0.0117 5985

From J. W. Glover, "Tables of Applied Math. in Finance, Insurance, Statistics"

ANNUITY WHICH AMOUNTS TO 1 (*Cont.*)

	1¼%	1⅜%	1½%	1¾%	2%	2¼%
1	1.0000 0000	1.0000 0000	1.0000 0000	1.0000 0000	1.0000 0000	1.0000 0000
2	0.4968 9441	0.4965 8597	0.4962 7792	0.4956 6295	0.4950 4950	0.4944 3758
3	0.3292 0117	0.3287 9173	0.3283 8296	0.3275 6746	0.3267 5467	0.3259 4458
4	0.2453 6102	0.2449 0243	0.2444 4478	0.2435 3237	0.2426 2375	0.2417 1893
5	0.1950 6211	0.1945 7510	0.1940 8932	0.1931 2142	0.1921 5839	0.1912 0021
6	0.1615 3381	0.1610 2877	0.1605 2521	0.1595 2256	0.1585 2581	0.1575 3496
7	0.1375 8872	0.1370 7157	0.1365 5616	0.1355 3059	0.1345 1196	0.1335 0025
8	0.1196 3314	0.1191 0758	0.1185 8402	0.1175 4292	0.1165 0980	0.1154 8462
9	0.1056 7055	0.1051 3906	0.1046 0982	0.1035 5813	0.1025 1544	0.1014 8170
10	0.0945 0307	0.0939 6737	0.0934 3418	0.0923 7534	0.0913 2653	0.0902 8768
11	0.0853 6839	0.0848 2973	0.0842 9384	0.0832 3038	0.0821 7794	0.0811 3649
12	0.0777 5831	0.0772 1764	0.0766 7999	0.0756 1377	0.0745 5960	0.0735 1740
13	0.0713 2100	0.0707 7903	0.0702 4036	0.0691 7283	0.0681 1835	0.0670 7686
14	0.0658 0515	0.0652 6246	0.0647 2332	0.0636 5562	0.0626 0197	0.0615 6230
15	0.0610 2646	0.0604 8351	0.0599 4436	0.0588 7739	0.0578 2547	0.0567 8852
16	0.0568 4672	0.0563 0388	0.0557 6508	0.0546 9958	0.0536 5013	0.0526 1663
17	0.0531 6023	0.0526 1780	0.0520 7966	0.0510 1623	0.0499 6984	0.0489 4039
18	0.0498 8479	0.0493 4301	0.0488 0578	0.0477 4492	0.0467 0210	0.0456 7720
19	0.0469 5548	0.0464 1457	0.0458 7847	0.0448 2061	0.0437 8177	0.0427 6182
20	0.0443 2039	0.0437 8054	0.0432 4574	0.0421 9122	0.0411 5672	0.0401 4207
21	0.0419 3748	0.0413 9884	0.0408 6550	0.0398 1464	0.0387 8477	0.0377 7572
22	0.0397 7238	0.0392 3507	0.0387 0331	0.0376 5638	0.0366 3140	0.0356 2821
23	0.0377 9666	0.0372 6080	0.0367 3075	0.0356 8796	0.0346 6810	0.0336 7097
24	0.0359 8665	0.0354 5235	0.0349 2410	0.0338 8565	0.0328 7110	0.0318 8023
25	0.0343 2247	0.0337 8981	0.0332 6345	0.0322 2952	0.0312 2044	0.0302 3599
26	0.0327 8729	0.0322 5635	0.0317 3196	0.0307 0269	0.0296 9923	0.0287 2134
27	0.0313 6677	0.0308 3763	0.0303 1527	0.0292 9079	0.0282 9309	0.0273 2188
28	0.0300 4863	0.0295 2134	0.0290 0108	0.0279 8151	0.0269 8967	0.0260 2525
29	0.0288 2228	0.0282 9689	0.0277 7878	0.0267 6424	0.0257 7836	0.0248 2081
30	0.0276 7854	0.0261 5511	0.0266 3919	0.0256 2975	0.0246 4992	0.0236 9934
31	0.0266 0942	0.0260 8798	0.0255 7430	0.0245 7005	0.0235 9635	0.0226 5280
32	0.0256 0791	0.0250 8850	0.0245 7710	0.0235 7812	0.0226 1061	0.0216 7415
33	0.0246 6786	0.0241 5053	0.0236 4144	0.0226 4779	0.0216 8653	0.0207 5722
34	0.0237 8387	0.0232 6864	0.0227 6189	0.0217 7363	0.0208 1867	0.0198 9655
35	0.0229 5111	0.0224 3801	0.0219 3363	0.0209 5082	0.0200 0221	0.0190 8731
36	0.0221 6533	0.0216 5438	0.0211 5240	0.0201 7507	0.0192 3285	0.0183 2522
37	0.0214 2270	0.0209 1394	0.0204 1437	0.0194 4257	0.0185 0678	0.0176 0643
38	0.0207 1983	0.0202 1327	0.0197 1613	0.0187 4990	0.0178 2057	0.0169 2753
39	0.0200 5365	0.0195 4931	0.0190 5463	0.0180 9399	0.0171 7114	0.0162 8543
40	0.0194 2141	0.0189 1931	0.0184 2710	0.0174 7209	0.0165 5575	0.0156 7738
41	0.0188 2063	0.0183 2078	0.0178 3106	0.0168 8170	0.0159 7188	0.0151 0087
42	0.0182 4906	0.0177 5148	0.0172 6426	0.0163 2057	0.0154 1729	0.0145 5364
43	0.0177 0466	0.0172 0936	0.0167 2465	0.0157 8666	0.0148 8993	0.0140 3364
44	0.0171 8557	0.0166 9257	0.0162 1038	0.0152 7810	0.0143 8794	0.0135 3901
45	0.0166 9012	0.0161 9941	0.0157 1976	0.0147 9321	0.0139 0962	0.0130 6805
46	0.0162 1675	0.0157 2836	0.0152 5125	0.0143 3043	0.0134 5342	0.0126 1921
47	0.0157 6406	0.0152 7799	0.0148 0342	0.0138 8836	0.0130 1792	0.0121 9107
48	0.0153 3075	0.0148 4701	0.0143 7500	0.0134 6569	0.0126 0184	0.0117 8233
49	0.0149 1563	0.0144 3424	0.0139 6478	0.0130 6124	0.0122 0396	0.0113 9179
50	0.0145 1763	0.0140 3857	0.0135 7168	0.0126 7391	0.0118 2321	0.0110 1836
51	0.0141 3571	0.0136 5900	0.0131 9469	0.0123 0269	0.0114 5856	0.0106 6102
52	0.0137 6897	0.0132 9461	0.0128 3287	0.0119 4665	0.0111 0909	0.0103 1884
53	0.0134 1653	0.0128 4453	0.0124 8537	0.0116 0492	0.0107 7392	0.0099 9094
54	0.0130 7760	0.0126 0797	0.0121 5138	0.0112 7672	0.0104 5226	0.0096 7654
55	0.0127 5145	0.0122 8418	0.0118 3018	0.0109 6129	0.0101 4337	0.0093 7489
56	0.0124 3739	0.0119 7249	0.0115 2106	0.0106 5795	0.0098 4656	0.0090 8530
57	0.0121 3478	0.0116 7225	0.0112 2341	0.0103 6606	0.0095 6120	0.0088 0712
58	0.0118 4303	0.0113 8287	0.0109 3661	0.0100 8503	0.0092 8667	0.0085 3977
59	0.0115 6158	0.0111 0380	0.0106 6012	0.0098 1430	0.0090 2243	0.0082 8268
60	0.0112 8993	0.0108 3452	0.0103 9343	0.0095 5336	0.0087 6797	0.0080 3533

ANNUITY WHICH AMOUNTS TO 1 (*Cont.*)

	2½%	2¾%	3%	3½%	4%	4½%
1	1.0000 0000	1.0000 0000	1.0000 0000	1.0000 0000	1.0000 0000	1.0000 0000
2	0.4938 2716	0.4932 1825	0.4926 1084	0.4914 0049	0.4901 9608	0.4889 9756
3	0.3251 3717	0.3243 3243	0.3235 3036	0.3219 3418	0.3203 4854	0.3187 7336
4	0.2408 1788	0.2399 2059	0.2390 2705	0.2372 5114	0.2354 9005	0.2337 4365
5	0.1902 4686	0.1892 9832	0.1883 5457	0.1864 8137	0.1846 2711	0.1827 9164
6	0.1565 4997	0.1555 7083	0.1545 9750	0.1526 6821	0.1507 6190	0.1488 7839
7	0.1324 9543	0.1314 9747	0.1305 0635	0.1285 4449	0.1266 0961	0.1247 0147
8	0.1144 6735	0.1134 5795	0.1124 5639	0.1104 7665	0.1085 2783	0.1066 0965
9	0.1004 5689	0.0994 4095	0.0984 3386	0.0964 4601	0.0944 9299	0.0925 7447
10	0.0892 5876	0.0882 3972	0.0872 3051	0.0852 4137	0.0832 9094	0.0813 7882
11	0.0801 0596	0.0790 8629	0.0780 7745	0.0760 9197	0.0741 4904	0.0722 4818
12	0.0724 8713	0.0714 6871	0.0704 6209	0.0684 8395	0.0665 5217	0.0646 6619
13	0.0660 4827	0.0650 3252	0.0640 2954	0.0620 6157	0.0601 4373	0.0582 7535
14	0.0605 3653	0.0595 2457	0.0585 2634	0.0565 7073	0.0546 6897	0.0528 2032
15	0.0557 6646	0.0547 5917	0.0537 6658	0.0518 2507	0.0499 4110	0.0481 1381
16	0.0515 9899	0.0505 9710	0.0496 1085	0.0476 8483	0.0458 2000	0.0440 1537
17	0.0479 2777	0.0469 3186	0.0459 5253	0.0440 4313	0.0421 9852	0.0404 1758
18	0.0446 7008	0.0436 8063	0.0427 0870	0.0408 1684	0.0389 9333	0.0372 3690
19	0.0417 6062	0.0407 7802	0.0398 1388	0.0379 4033	0.0361 3862	0.0344 0734
20	0.0391 4713	0.0381 7173	0.0372 1571	0.0353 6108	0.0335 8175	0.0318 7614
21	0.0367 8733	0.0358 1941	0.0348 7178	0.0330 3659	0.0312 8011	0.0296 0057
22	0.0346 4661	0.0336 8640	0.0327 4739	0.0399 3207	0.0291 9881	0.0275 4565
23	0.0326 9638	0.0317 4410	0.0308 1390	0.0290 1880	0.0273 0906	0.0256 8249
24	0.0309 1282	0.0299 6863	0.0290 4742	0.0272 7283	0.0255 8683	0.0239 8703
25	0.0292 7592	0.0283 3997	0.0274 2787	0.0256 7404	0.0240 1196	0.0224 3903
26	0.0277 6875	0.0268 4116	0.0259 3829	0.0242 0540	0.0225 6738	0.0210 2137
27	0.0263 7687	0.0254 5776	0.0245 6421	0.0228 5241	0.0212 3854	0.0197 1946
28	0.0250 8793	0.0241 7738	0.0232 9323	0.0216 0265	0.0200 1298	0.0185 2081
29	0.0238 9127	0.0229 8935	0.0221 1467	0.0204 4538	0.0188 7993	0.0174 1461
30	0.0227 7764	0.0218 8442	0.0210 1926	0.0193 7133	0.0178 3010	0.0163 9154
31	0.0217 3900	0.0208 5453	0.0199 9893	0.0183 7240	0.0168 5535	0.0154 4345
32	0.0207 6831	0.0198 9263	0.0190 4662	0.0174 4150	0.0159 4859	0.0145 6320
33	0.0198 5938	0.0189 9253	0.0181 5612	0.0165 7242	0.0151 0357	0.0137 4453
34	0.0190 0675	0.0181 4875	0.0173 2196	0.0157 5966	0.0143 1477	0.0129 8191
35	0.0182 0558	0.0173 5645	0.0165 3929	0.0149 9835	0.0135 7732	0.0122 7045
36	0.0174 5158	0.0166 1132	0.0158 0379	0.0142 8416	0.0128 8688	0.0116 0578
37	0.0167 4090	0.0159 0953	0.0151 1162	0.0136 1325	0.0122 3957	0.0109 8402
38	0.0160 7012	0.0152 4764	0.0144 5934	0.0129 8214	0.0116 3192	0.0104 0169
39	0.0154 3615	0.0146 2256	0.0138 4385	0.0123 8775	0.0110 6083	0.0098 5567
40	0.0148 3623	0.0140 3151	0.0132 6238	0.0118 2728	0.0105 2349	0.0093 4315
41	0.0142 6786	0.0134 7200	0.0127 1241	0.0112 9822	0.0100 1738	0.0088 6158
42	0.0137 2876	0.0129 4175	0.0121 9167	0.0107 9828	0.0095 4020	0.0084 0868
43	0.0132 1688	0.0124 3871	0.0116 9811	0.0103 2539	0.0090 8989	0.0079 8235
44	0.0127 3037	0.0119 6100	0.0112 2985	0.0098 7768	0.0086 6454	0.0075 8071
45	0.0122 6752	0.0115 0693	0.0107 8518	0.0094 5343	0.0082 6246	0.0072 0202
46	0.0118 2676	0.0110 7493	0.0103 6254	0.0090 5108	0.0078 8205	0.0068 4471
47	0.0114 0669	0.0106 6358	0.0099 6051	0.0086 6919	0.0075 2189	0.0065 0734
48	0.0110 0599	0.0102 7158	0.0095 7777	0.0083 0646	0.0071 8065	0.0061 8858
49	0.0106 2348	0.0098 9773	0.0092 1314	0.0079 6167	0.0068 5712	0.0058 8722
50	0.0102 5806	0.0095 4092	0.0088 6550	0.0076 3371	0.0065 5020	0.0056 0215
51	0.0099 0870	0.0092 0014	0.0085 3382	0.0073 2156	0.0062 5885	0.0053 3232
52	0.0095 7446	0.0088 7444	0.0082 1718	0.0070 2429	0.0059 8212	0.0050 7679
53	0.0092 5449	0.0085 6297	0.0079 1471	0.0067 4100	0.0057 1915	0.0048 3469
54	0.0089 4799	0.0082 6491	0.0076 2558	0.0064 7090	0.0054 6910	0.0046 0519
55	0.0086 5419	0.0079 7953	0.0073 4907	0.0062 1323	0.0052 3124	0.0043 8754
56	0.0083 7243	0.0077 0612	0.0070 8447	0.0059 6730	0.0050 0487	0.0041 8105
57	0.0081 0204	0.0074 4404	0.0068 3114	0.0057 3245	0.0047 8932	0.0039 8506
58	0.0078 4244	0.0071 9270	0.0065 8848	0.0055 0810	0.0045 8401	0.0037 9897
59	0.0075 9307	0.0069 5153	0.0063 5593	0.0052 9366	0.0043 8836	0.0036 2221
60	0.0073 5340	0.0067 2002	0.0061 3296	0.0050 8862	0.0042 0185	0.0034 5426

ANNUITY WHICH AMOUNTS TO 1 (*Cont.*)

	5%	5½%	6%	6½%	7%	8%
1	1.0000 0000	1.0000 0000	1.0000 0000	1.0000 0000	1.0000 0000	1.0000 0000
2	0.4878 0488	0.4866 1800	0.4854 3689	0.4842 6150	0.4830 9179	0.4807 6923
3	0.3172 0856	0.3156 5407	0.3141 0981	0.3125 7570	0.3110 5166	0.3080 3351
4	0.2320 1183	0.2302 9449	0.2285 9149	0.2269 0274	0.2252 2812	0.2219 2080
5	0.1809 7480	0.1791 7644	0.1773 9640	0.1756 3454	0.1738 9069	0.1704 5645
6	0.1470 1747	0.1451 7895	0.1433 6263	0.1415 6831	0.1397 9580	0.1363 1539
7	0.1228 1982	0.1209 6442	0.1191 3502	0.1173 3137	0.1155 5322	0.1120 7240
8	0.1047 2181	0.1028 6401	0.1010 3594	0.0992 3730	0.0974 6776	0.0940 1476
9	0.0906 9008	0.0888 3946	0.0870 2224	0.0852 3803	0.0834 8647	0.0800 7971
10	0.0795 0458	0.0776 6777	0.0758 6796	0.0741 0469	0.0723 7750	0.0690 2949
11	0.0703 8889	0.0685 7065	0.0667 9294	0.0650 5521	0.0633 5690	0.0600 7634
12	0.0628 2541	0.0610 2923	0.0592 7703	0.0575 6817	0.0559 0199	0.0526 9502
13	0.0564 5577	0.0546 8426	0.0529 6011	0.0512 8256	0.0496 5085	0.0465 2181
14	0.0510 2397	0.0492 7912	0.0475 8491	0.0459 4048	0.0443 4494	0.0412 9685
15	0.0463 4229	0.0446 2560	0.0429 6276	0.0413 5278	0.0397 9462	0.0368 2954
16	0.0422 6991	0.0405 8254	0.0389 5214	0.0373 7757	0.0358 5765	0.0329 7687
17	0.0386 9914	0.0370 4197	0.0354 4480	0.0339 0633	0.0324 2519	0.0296 2943
18	0.0355 4622	0.0339 1992	0.0323 5654	0.0308 5461	0.0294 1260	0.0267 0210
19	0.0327 4501	0.0311 5006	0.0296 2086	0.0281 5575	0.0267 5301	0.0241 2763
20	0.0302 4259	0.0286 7933	0.0271 8456	0.0257 5640	0.0243 9293	0.0218 5221
21	0.0279 9611	0.0264 6478	0.0250 0455	0.0236 1333	0.0222 8900	0.0198 3225
22	0.0259 7051	0.0244 7123	0.0230 4557	0.0216 9120	0.0204 0577	0.0180 3207
23	0.0241 3682	0.0226 6965	0.0212 7848	0.0199 6078	0.0187 1393	0.0164 2217
24	0.0224 7090	0.0210 3580	0.0196 7900	0.0183 9770	0.0171 8902	0.0149 7796
25	0.0209 5246	0.0195 4935	0.0182 2672	0.0169 8148	0.0158 1052	0.0136 7878
26	0.0195 6432	0.0181 9307	0.0169 0435	0.0156 9480	0.0145 6103	0.0125 0713
27	0.0182 9186	0.0169 5228	0.0156 9717	0.0145 2288	0.0134 2573	0.0114 4809
28	0.0171 2253	0.0158 1440	0.0145 9255	0.0134 5305	0.0123 9193	0.0104 8891
29	0.0160 4551	0.0147 6857	0.0135 7961	0.0124 7440	0.0114 4865	0.0096 1854
30	0.0150 5144	0.0138 0539	0.0126 4891	0.0115 7744	0.0105 8640	0.0088 2743
31	0.0141 3212	0.0129 1665	0.0117 9222	0.0107 5393	0.0097 9691	0.0081 0728
32	0.0132 8042	0.0120 9519	0.0110 0234	0.0099 9665	0.0090 7292	0.0074 5081
33	0.0124 9004	0.0113 3469	0.0102 7293	0.0092 9924	0.0084 0807	0.0068 5163
34	0.0117 5545	0.0106 2958	0.0095 9843	0.0086 5610	0.0077 9674	0.0063 0411
35	0.0110 7171	0.0099 7493	0.0089 7386	0.0080 6226	0.0072 3396	0.0058 0326
36	0.0104 3446	0.0093 6635	0.0083 9483	0.0075 1332	0.0067 1531	0.0053 4467
37	0.0098 3979	0.0087 9993	0.0078 5743	0.0070 0534	0.0062 3685	0.0049 2440
38	0.0092 8423	0.0082 7217	0.0073 5812	0.0065 3480	0.0057 9505	0.0045 3894
39	0.0087 6462	0.0077 7991	0.0068 9377	0.0060 9854	0.0053 8676	0.0041 8513
40	0.0082 7816	0.0073 2034	0.0064 6154	0.0056 9373	0.0050 0914	0.0038 6016
41	0.0078 2229	0.0068 9090	0.0060 5886	0.0053 1779	0.0046 5962	0.0035 6149
42	0.0073 9471	0.0064 8927	0.0056 8342	0.0049 6842	0.0043 3591	0.0032 8684
43	0.0069 9333	0.0061 1337	0.0053 3312	0.0046 4352	0.0040 3590	0.0030 3414
44	0.0066 1625	0.0057 6128	0.0050 0606	0.0043 4119	0.0037 5769	0.0028 0152
45	0.0062 6173	0.0054 3127	0.0047 0050	0.0040 5968	0.0034 9957	0.0025 8728
46	0.0059 2820	0.0051 2175	0.0044 1485	0.0037 9743	0.0032 5996	0.0023 8991
47	0.0056 1421	0.0048 3129	0.0041 4768	0.0035 5300	0.0030 3744	0.0022 0799
48	0.0053 1843	0.0045 5854	0.0038 9766	0.0033 2506	0.0028 3070	0.0020 4027
49	0.0050 3965	0.0043 0230	0.0036 6356	0.0031 1240	0.0026 3853	0.0018 8557
50	0.0047 7674	0.0040 6145	0.0034 4429	0.0029 1393	0.0024 5985	0.0017 4286
51	0.0045 2867	0.0038 3495	0.0032 3880	0.0027 2861	0.0022 9365	0.0016 1116
52	0.0042 9450	0.0036 2185	0.0030 4617	0.0025 5553	0.0021 3901	0.0014 8959
53	0.0040 7334	0.0034 2130	0.0028 6551	0.0023 9382	0.0019 9509	0.0013 7735
54	0.0038 6438	0.0032 3245	0.0026 9602	0.0022 4267	0.0018 6110	0.0012 7370
55	0.0036 6686	0.0030 5458	0.0025 3696	0.0021 0137	0.0017 3633	0.0011 7796
56	0.0034 8010	0.0028 8698	0.0023 8765	0.0019 6923	0.0016 2011	0.0010 8952
57	0.0033 0343	0.0027 2900	0.0022 4744	0.0018 4563	0.0015 1183	0.0010 0780
58	0.0031 3626	0.0025 8006	0.0021 1574	0.0017 2999	0.0014 1093	0.0009 3227
59	0.0029 7802	0.0024 3959	0.0019 9200	0.0016 2177	0.0013 1689	0.0008 6247
60	0.0028 2818	0.0023 0707	0.0018 7572	0.0015 2047	0.0012 2923	0.0007 9795

ANNUITY WHICH 1 WILL BUY

	½%	⅝%	¾%	⅞%	1%	1⅛%
1	1.0050 0000	1.0062 5000	1.0075 0000	1.0087 5000	1.0100 0000	1.0112 5000
2	0.5037 5312	0.5046 9237	0.5056 3200	0.5065 7203	0.5075 1244	0.5084 5323
3	0.3366 7221	0.3375 0865	0.3383 4579	0.3391 8361	0.3400 2211	0.3408 6130
4	0.2531 3279	0.2539 1842	0.2547 0501	0.2554 9257	0.2562 8109	0.2570 7058
5	0.2030 0997	0.2037 6558	0.2045 2242	0.2052 8049	0.2060 3980	0.2068 0034
6	0.1695 9546	0.1703 3143	0.1710 6891	0.1718 0789	0.1725 4837	0.1732 9034
7	0.1457 2854	0.1464 5082	0.1471 7488	0.1479 0070	0.1486 2828	0.1493 5762
8	0.1278 2886	0.1285 4118	0.1292 5552	0.1299 7190	0.1306 9029	0.1314 1071
9	0.1139 0736	0.1146 1218	0.1153 1929	0.1160 2868	0.1167 4037	0.1174 5432
10	0.1027 7057	0.1034 6963	0.1041 7123	0.1048 7538	0.1055 8208	0.1062 9131
11	0.0936 5903	0.0943 5358	0.0950 5094	0.0957 5111	0.0964 5408	0.0971 5984
12	0.0860 6643	0.0867 5742	0.0874 5148	0.0881 4860	0.0888 4879	0.0895 5203
13	0.0796 4224	0.0803 3039	0.0810 2188	0.0817 1669	0.0824 1482	0.0831 1626
14	0.0741 3609	0.0748 2198	0.0755 1146	0.0762 0453	0.0769 0117	0.0776 0138
15	0.0693 6436	0.0700 4845	0.0707 3639	0.0714 2817	0.0721 2378	0.0728 2321
16	0.0651 8937	0.0658 7202	0.0665 5879	0.0672 4965	0.0679 4460	0.0686 4363
17	0.0615 0579	0.0621 8732	0.0628 7321	0.0635 6346	0.0642 5806	0.0649 5698
18	0.0582 3173	0.0589 1239	0.0595 9766	0.0602 8756	0.0609 8205	0.0616 8113
19	0.0553 0253	0.0559 8252	0.0566 6740	0.0573 5715	0.0580 5175	0.0587 5120
20	0.0526 6645	0.0533 4597	0.0540 3063	0.0547 2042	0.0554 1532	0.0561 1531
21	0.0502 8163	0.0509 6083	0.0516 4543	0.0523 3541	0.0530 3075	0.0537 3145
22	0.0481 1380	0.0487 9281	0.0494 7748	0.0501 6779	0.0508 6371	0.0515 6525
23	0.0461 3465	0.0468 1360	0.0474 9846	0.0481 8921	0.0488 8584	0.0495 8833
24	0.0443 2061	0.0449 9959	0.0456 8474	0.0463 7604	0.0470 7347	0.0477 7701
25	0.0426 5186	0.0433 3096	0.0440 1650	0.0447 0843	0.0454 0675	0.0461 1144
26	0.0411 1163	0.0417 9094	0.0424 7693	0.0431 6959	0.0438 6888	0.0445 7479
27	0.0396 8565	0.0403 6523	0.0410 5176	0.0417 4520	0.0424 4553	0.0431 5273
28	0.0383 6167	0.0390 4159	0.0397 2871	0.0404 2300	0.0411 2444	0.0418 3299
29	0.0371 2914	0.0378 0946	0.0384 9723	0.0391 9243	0.0398 9502	0.0406 0498
30	0.0359 7892	0.0366 5969	0.0373 4816	0.0380 4431	0.0387 4811	0.0394 5953
31	0.0349 0304	0.0355 8430	0.0362 7352	0.0369 7068	0.0376 7573	0.0383 8866
32	0.0338 9453	0.0345 7633	0.0352 6634	0.0359 6454	0.0366 7089	0.0373 8535
33	0.0329 4727	0.0336 2964	0.0343 2048	0.0350 1976	0.0357 2744	0.0364 4349
34	0.0320 5586	0.0327 3883	0.0334 3053	0.0341 3092	0.0348 3997	0.0355 5763
35	0.0312 1550	0.0318 9911	0.0325 9170	0.0332 9324	0.0340 0368	0.0347 2299
36	0.0304 2194	0.0311 0622	0.0317 9973	0.0325 0244	0.0332 1431	0.0339 3529
37	0.0296 7139	0.0303 5636	0.0310 5082	0.0317 5473	0.0324 6805	0.0331 9072
38	0.0289 6045	0.0296 4614	0.0303 4157	0.0310 4671	0.0317 6150	0.0324 8589
39	0.0282 8607	0.0289 7250	0.0296 6893	0.0303 7531	0.0310 9160	0.0318 1773
40	0.0276 4552	0.0283 3271	0.0290 3016	0.0297 3780	0.0304 5560	0.0311 8349
41	0.0270 3631	0.0277 2429	0.0284 2276	0.0291 3169	0.0298 5102	0.0305 8069
42	0.0264 5622	0.0271 4499	0.0278 4452	0.0285 5475	0.0292 7563	0.0300 0709
43	0.0259 0320	0.0265 9278	0.0272 9338	0.0280 0493	0.0287 2737	0.0294 6064
44	0.0253 7541	0.0260 6583	0.0267 6751	0.0274 8039	0.0282 0441	0.0289 3949
45	0.0248 7117	0.0255 6243	0.0262 6521	0.0269 7943	0.0277 0505	0.0284 4197
46	0.0243 8894	0.0250 8106	0.0257 8495	0.0265 0053	0.0272 2775	0.0279 6652
47	0.0239 2733	0.0246 2032	0.0253 2532	0.0260 4228	0.0267 7111	0.0275 1173
48	0.0234 8503	0.0241 7890	0.0248 8504	0.0256 0338	0.0263 3384	0.0270 7632
49	0.0230 6087	0.0237 5563	0.0244 6292	0.0251 8265	0.0259 1474	0.0266 5910
50	0.0226 5376	0.0233 4943	0.0240 5787	0.0247 7900	0.0255 1273	0.0262 5898
51	0.0222 6269	0.0229 5928	0.0236 6888	0.0243 9142	0.0251 2680	0.0258 7494
52	0.0218 8675	0.0225 8425	0.0232 9503	0.0240 1899	0.0247 5603	0.0255 0606
53	0.0215 2507	0.0222 2350	0.0229 3546	0.0236 6084	0.0243 9956	0.0251 5149
54	0.0211 7686	0.0218 7623	0.0225 8938	0.0233 1619	0.0240 5658	0.0248 1043
55	0.0208 4139	0.0215 4171	0.0222 5605	0.0229 8430	0.0237 2637	0.0244 8213
56	0.0205 1797	0.0212 1925	0.0219 3478	0.0226 6449	0.0234 0823	0.0241 6592
57	0.0202 0598	0.0209 0821	0.0216 2496	0.0223 5611	0.0231 0156	0.0238 6116
58	0.0199 0481	0.0206 0801	0.0213 2597	0.0220 5858	0.0228 0573	0.0235 6726
59	0.0196 1392	0.0203 1809	0.0210 3727	0.0217 7135	0.0225 2020	0.0232 8366
60	0.0193 3280	0.0200 3795	0.0207 5836	0.0214 9390	0.0222 4445	0.0230 0985

From J. W. Glover, "Tables of Applied Math. in Finance, Insurance, Statistics"

ANNUITY WHICH 1 WILL BUY (*Cont.*)

	1¼%	1⅜%	1½%	1¾%	2%	2¼%
1	1.0125 0000	1.0137 5000	1.0150 0000	1.0175 0000	1.0200 0000	1.0225 0000
2	0.5093 9441	0.5103 3597	0.5112 7792	0.5131 6295	0.5150 4950	0.5169 3758
3	0.3417 0117	0.3425 4173	0.3433 8296	0.3450 6746	0.3467 5467	0.3484 4458
4	0.2578 6102	0.2586 5243	0.2594 4478	0.2610 3237	0.2626 2375	0.2642 1893
5	0.2075 6211	0.2083 2510	0.2090 8932	0.2106 2142	0.2121 5839	0.2137 0021
6	0.1740 3381	0.1747 7877	0.1755 2521	0.1770 2256	0.1785 2581	0.1800 3496
7	0.1500 8872	0.1508 2157	0.1515 5616	0.1530 3059	0.1545 1196	0.1560 0025
8	0.1321 3314	0.1328 5758	0.1335 8402	0.1350 4292	0.1365 0980	0.1379 8462
9	0.1181 7055	0.1188 8906	0.1196 0982	0.1210 5813	0.1225 1544	0.1239 8170
10	0.1070 0307	0.1077 1737	0.1084 3418	0.1098 7534	0.1113 2653	0.1127 8768
11	0.0978 6839	0.0985 7973	0.0992 9384	0.1007 3038	0.1021 7794	0.1036 3649
12	0.0902 5831	0.0909 6764	0.0916 7999	0.0931 1377	0.0945 5960	0.0960 1740
13	0.0838 2100	0.0845 2903	0.0852 4036	0.0866 7283	0.0881 1835	0.0895 7686
14	0.0783 0515	0.0790 1246	0.0797 2332	0.0811 5562	0.0826 0197	0.0840 6230
15	0.0735 2646	0.0742 3351	0.0749 4436	0.0763 7739	0.0778 2547	0.0792 8852
16	0.0693 4672	0.0700 5388	0.0707 6508	0.0721 9958	0.0736 5013	0.0751 1663
17	0.0656 6023	0.0663 6780	0.0670 7966	0.0685 1623	0.0699 6984	0.0714 4039
18	0.0623 8479	0.0630 9301	0.0638 0578	0.0652 4492	0.0667 0210	0.0681 7720
19	0.0594 5548	0.0601 6457	0.0608 7847	0.0623 2061	0.0637 8177	0.0652 6182
20	0.0568 2039	0.0575 3054	0.0582 4574	0.0596 9122	0.0611 5672	0.0626 4207
21	0.0544 3748	0.0551 4884	0.0558 6550	0.0573 1464	0.0587 8477	0.0602 7572
22	0.0522 7238	0.0529 8507	0.0537 0331	0.0551 5638	0.0566 3140	0.0581 2821
23	0.0502 9666	0.0510 1080	0.0517 3075	0.0531 8796	0.0546 6810	0.0561 7097
24	0.0484 8665	0.0492 0235	0.0499 2410	0.0513 8565	0.0528 7110	0.0543 8023
25	0.0468 2247	0.0475 3981	0.0482 6345	0.0497 2952	0.0512 2044	0.0527 3599
26	0.0452 8729	0.0460 0635	0.0467 3196	0.0482 0269	0.0496 9923	0.0512 2134
27	0.0438 6677	0.0445 8763	0.0453 1527	0.0467 9079	0.0482 9309	0.0498 2188
28	0.0425 4863	0.0432 7134	0.0440 0108	0.0454 8151	0.0469 8967	0.0485 2525
29	0.0413 2228	0.0420 4689	0.0427 7878	0.0442 6424	0 0457 7836	0.0473 2081
30	0.0401 7854	0.0409 0511	0.0416 3919	0.0431 2975	0.0446 4992	0.0461 9934
31	0.0391 0942	0.0398 3798	0.0405 7430	0.0420 7005	0.0435 9635	0.0451 5280
32	0.0381 0791	0.0388 3850	0.0395 7710	0.0410 7812	0.0426 1061	0.0441 7415
33	0.0371 6786	0.0379 0053	0.0386 4144	0.0401 4779	0.0416 8653	0.0432 5722
34	0.0362 8387	0.0370 1864	0.0377 6189	0.0392 7363	0.0408 1867	0.0423 9655
35	0.0354 5111	0.0361 8801	0.0369 3363	0.0384 5082	0.0400 0221	0.0415 8731
36	0.0346 6533	0.0354 0438	0.0361 5240	0.0376 7507	0.0392 3285	0.0408 2522
37	0.0339 2270	0.0346 6394	0.0354 1437	0.0369 4257	0.0385 0678	0.0401 0643
38	0.0332 1983	0.0339 6327	0.0347 1613	0.0362 4990	0.0378 2057	0.0394 2753
39	0.0325 5365	0.0332 9931	0.0340 5463	0.0355 9399	0.0371 7114	0.0387 8543
40	0.0319 2141	0.0326 6931	0.0334 2710	0.0349 7209	0.0365 5575	0.0381 7738
41	0.0313 2063	0.0320 7078	0.0328 3106	0.0343 8170	0.0359 7188	0.0376 0087
42	0.0307 4906	0.0315 0148	0.0322 6426	0.0338 2057	0.0354 1729	0.0370 5364
43	0.0302 0466	0.0309 5936	0.0317 2465	0.0332 8666	0.0348 8993	0.0365 3364
44	0.0296 8557	9.0304 4257	0.0312 1038	0.0327 7810	0.0343 8794	0.0360 3901
45	0.0291 9012	0.0299 4941	0.0307 1976	0.0322 9321	0.0339 0962	0.0355 6805
46	0.0287 1675	0.0294 7836	0.0302 5125	0.0318 3043	0.0334 5342	0.0351 1921
47	0.0282 6406	0.0290 2799	0.0298 0342	0.0313 8836	0.0330 1792	0.0346 9107
48	0.0278 3075	0.0285 9701	0.0293 7500	0.0309 6569	0.0326 0184	0.0342 8233
49	0.0274 1563	0.0281 8424	0.0289 6478	0.0305 6124	0.0322 0396	0.0338 9179
50	0.0270 1763	0.0277 8857	0.0285 7168	0.0301 7391	0.0318 2321	0.0335 1836
51	0.0266 3571	0.0274 0900	0.0281 9469	0.0298 0269	0.0314 5856	0.0331 6102
52	0.0262 6897	0.0270 4461	0.0278 3287	0.0294 4665	0.0311 0909	0.0328 1884
53	0.0259 1653	0.0266 9453	0.0274 8537	0.0291 0492	0.0307 7392	0.0324 9094
54	0.0255 7760	0.0263 5797	0.0271 5138	0.0287 7672	0.0304 5226	0.0321 7654
55	0.0252 5145	0.0260 3418	0.0268 3018	0.0284 6129	0.0301 4337	0.0318 7489
56	0.0249 3739	0.0257 2249	0.0265 2106	0.0281 5795	0.0298 4656	0.0315 8530
57	0.0246 3478	0.0254 2225	0.0262 2341	0.0278 6606	0.0295 6120	0.0313 0712
58	0.0243 4303	0.0251 3287	0.0259 3661	0.0275 8503	0.0292 8667	0.0310 3977
59	0.0240 6158	0.0248 5380	0.0256 6012	0.0273 1430	0.0290 2243	0.0307 8268
60	0.0237 8993	0.0245 8452	0.0253 9343	0.0270 5336	0.0287 6797	0.0305 3533

ANNUITY WHICH 1 WILL BUY (*Cont.*)

	2½%	2¾%	3%	3½%	4%	4½%
1	1.0250 0000	1.0275 0000	1.0300 0000	1.0350 0000	1.0400 0000	1.0450 0000
2	0.5188 2716	0.5207 1825	0.5226 1084	0.5264 0049	0.5301 9608	0.5339 9756
3	0.3501 3717	0.3518 3243	0.3535 3036	0.3569 3418	0.3603 4854	0.3637 7336
4	0.2658 1788	0.2674 2059	0.2690 2705	0.2722 5114	0.2754 9005	0.2787 4365
5	0.2152 4686	0.2167 9832	0.2183 5457	0.2214 8137	0.2246 2711	0.2277 9164
6	0.1815 4997	0.1830 7083	0.1845 9750	0.1876 6821	0.1907 6190	0.1938 7839
7	0.1574 9543	0.1589 9747	0.1605 0635	0.1635 4449	0.1666 0961	0.1697 0147
8	0.1394 6735	0.1409 5795	0.1424 5639	0.1454 7665	0.1485 2783	0.1516 0965
9	0.1254 5689	0.1269 4095	0.1284 3386	0.1314 4601	0.1344 9299	0.1375 7447
10	0.1142 5876	0.1157 3972	0.1172 3051	0.1202 4137	0.1232 9094	0.1263 7882
11	0.1051 0596	0.1065 8629	0.1080 7745	0.1110 9197	0.1141 4904	0.1172 4818
12	0.0974 8713	0.0989 6871	0.1004 6209	0.1034 8395	0.1065 5217	0.1096 6619
13	0.0910 4827	0.0925 3252	0.0940 2954	0.0970 6157	0.1001 4373	0.1032 7535
14	0.0855 3653	0.0870 2457	0.0885 2634	0.0915 7073	0.0946 6897	0.0978 2032
15	0.0807 6646	0.0822 5917	0.0837 6658	0.0868 2507	0.0899 4110	0.0931 1381
16	0.0765 9899	0.0780 9710	0.0796 1085	0.0826 8483	0.0858 2000	0.0890 1537
17	0.0729 2777	0.0744 3186	0.0759 5253	0.0790 4313	0.0821 9852	0.0854 1758
18	0.0696 7008	0.0711 8063	0.0727 0870	0.0758 1684	0.0789 9333	0.0822 3690
19	0.0667 6062	0.0682 7802	0.0698 1388	0.0729 4033	0.0761 3862	0.0794 0734
20	0.0641 4713	0.0656 7173	0.0672 1571	0.0703 6108	0.0735 8175	0.0768 7614
21	0.0617 8733	0.0633 1941	0.0648 7178	0.0680 3659	0.0712 8011	0.0746 0057
22	0.0596 4661	0.0611 8640	0.0627 4739	0.0659 3207	0.0691 9881	0.0725 4565
23	0.0576 9638	0.0592 4410	0.0608 1390	0.0640 1880	0.0673 0906	0.0706 8249
24	0.0559 1282	0.0574 6863	0.0590 4742	0.0622 7283	0.0655 8683	0.0689 8703
25	0.0542 7592	0.0558 3997	0.0574 2787	0.0606 7404	0.0640 1196	0.0674 3903
26	0.0527 6875	0.0543 4116	0.0559 3829	0.0592 0540	0.0625 6738	0.0660 2137
27	0.0513 7687	0.0529 5776	0.0545 6421	0.0578 5241	0.0612 3854	0.0647 1946
28	0.0500 8793	0.0516 7738	0.0532 9323	0.0566 0265	0.0600 1298	0.0635 2081
29	0.0488 9127	0.0504 8935	0.0521 1467	0.0554 4538	0.0588 7993	0.0624 1461
30	0.0477 7764	0.0493 8442	0.0510 1926	0.0543 7133	0.0578 3010	0.0613 9154
31	0.0467 3900	0.0483 5453	0.0499 9893	0.0533 7240	0.0568 5535	0.0604 4345
32	0.0457 6831	0.0473 9263	0.0490 4662	0.0524 4150	0.0559 4859	0.0595 6320
33	0.0448 5938	0.0464 9253	0.0481 5612	0.0515 7242	0.0551 0357	0.0587 4453
34	0.0440 0675	0.0456 4875	0.0473 2196	0.0507 5966	0.0543 1477	0.0579 8191
35	0.0432 0558	0.0448 5645	0.0465 3929	0.0499 9835	0.0535 7732	0.0572 7045
36	0.0424 5158	0.0441 1132	0.0458 0379	0.0492 8416	0.0528 8688	0.0566 0578
37	0.0417 4090	0.0434 0953	0.0451 1162	0.0486 1325	0.0522 3957	0.0559 8402
38	0.0410 7012	0.0427 4764	0.0444 5934	0.0479 8214	0.0516 3192	0.0554 0169
39	0.0404 3615	0.0421 2256	0.0438 4385	0.0473 8775	0.0510 6083	0.0548 5567
40	0.0398 3623	0.0415 3151	0.0432 6238	0.0468 2728	0.0505 2349	0.0543 4315
41	0.0392 6786	0.0409 7200	0.0427 1241	0.0462 9822	0.0500 1738	0.0538 6158
42	0.0387 2876	0.0404 4175	0.0421 9167	0.0457 9828	0.0495 4020	0.0534 0868
43	0.0382 1688	0.0399 3871	0.0416 9811	0.0453 2539	0.0490 8989	0.0529 8235
44	0.0377 3037	0.0394 6100	0.0412 2985	0.0448 7768	0.0486 6454	0.0525 8071
45	0.0372 6752	0.0390 0693	0.0407 8518	0.0444 5343	0.0482 6246	0.0522 0202
46	0.0368 2676	0.0385 7493	0.0403 6254	0.0440 5108	0.0478 8205	0.0518 4471
47	0.0364 0669	0.0381 6358	0.0399 6051	0.0436 6919	0.0475 2189	0.0515 0734
48	0.0360 0599	0.0377 7158	0.0395 7777	0.0433 0646	0.0471 8065	0.0511 8858
49	0.0356 2348	0.0373 9773	0.0392 1314	0.0429 6167	0.0468 5712	0.0508 8722
50	0.0352 5806	0.0370 4092	0.0388 6550	0.0426 3371	0.0465 5020	0.0506 0215
51	0.0349 0870	0.0367 0014	0.0385 3382	0.0423 2156	0.0462 5885	0.0503 3232
52	0.0345 7446	0.0363 7444	0.0382 1718	0.0420 2429	0.0459 8212	0.0500 7679
53	0.0342 5449	0.0360 6297	0.0379 1471	0.0417 4100	0.0457 1915	0.0498 3469
54	0.0339 4799	0.0357 6491	0.0376 2558	0.0414 7090	0.0454 6910	0.0496 0519
55	0.0336 5419	0.0354 7953	0.0373 4907	0.0412 1323	0.0452 3124	0.0493 8754
56	0.0333 7243	0.0352 0612	0.0370 8447	0.0409 6730	0.0450 0487	0.0491 8105
57	0.0331 0204	0.0349 4404	0.0368 3114	0.0407 3245	0.0447 8932	0.0489 8506
58	0.0328 4244	0.0346 9270	0.0365 8848	0.0405 0810	0.0445 8401	0.0487 9897
59	0.0325 9307	0.0344 5153	0.0363 5593	0.0402 9366	0.0443 8836	0.0486 2221
60	0.0323 5340	0.0342 2002	0.0361 3296	0.0400 8862	0.0442 0185	0.0484 5426

ANNUITY WHICH 1 WILL BUY (*Cont.*)

	5%	5½%	6%	6½%	7%	8%
1	1.0500 0000	1.0550 0000	1.0600 0000	1.0650 0000	1.0700 0000	1.0800 0000
2	0.5378 0488	0.5416 1800	0.5454 3689	0.5492 6150	0.5530 9179	0.5607 6923
3	0.3672 0856	0.3706 5407	0.3741 0981	0.3775 7570	0.3810 5166	0.3880 3351
4	0.2820 1183	0.2852 9449	0.2885 9149	0.2919 0274	0.2952 2812	0.3019 2080
5	0.2309 7480	0.2341 7644	0.2373 9640	0.2406 3454	0.2438 9069	0.2504 5645
6	0.1970 1747	0.2001 7895	0.2033 6263	0.2065 6831	0.2097 9580	0.2163 1539
7	0.1728 1982	0.1759 6442	0.1791 3502	0.1823 3137	0.1855 5322	0.1920 7240
8	0.1547 2181	0.1578 6401	0.1610 3594	0.1642 3730	0.1674 6776	0.1740 1476
9	0.1406 9008	0.1438 3946	0.1470 2224	0.1502 3803	0.1534 8647	0.1600 7971
10	0.1295 0458	0.1326 6777	0.1358 6796	0.1391 0469	0.1423 7750	0.1490 2949
11	0.1203 8889	0.1235 7065	0.1267 9294	0.1300 5521	0.1333 5690	0.1400 7634
12	0.1128 2541	0.1160 2923	0.1192 7703	0.1225 6817	0.1259 0199	0.1326 9502
13	0.1064 5577	0.1096 8426	0.1129 6011	0.1162 8256	0.1196 5085	0.1265 2181
14	0.1010 2397	0.1042 7912	0.1075 8491	0.1109 4048	0.1143 4494	0.1212 9685
15	0.0963 4229	0.0996 2560	0.1029 6276	0.1063 5278	0.1097 9462	0.1168 2954
16	0.0922 6991	0.0955 8254	0.0989 5214	0.1023 7757	0.1058 5765	0.1129 7687
17	0.0886 9914	0.0920 4197	0.0954 4480	0.0989 0633	0.1024 2519	0.1096 2943
18	0.0855 4622	0.0889 1992	0.0923 5654	0.0958 5461	0.0994 1260	0.1067 0210
19	0.0827 4501	0.0861 5006	0.0896 2086	0.0931 5575	0.0967 5301	0.1041 2763
20	0.0802 4259	0.0836 7933	0.0871 8456	0.0907 5640	0.0943 9293	0.1018 5221
21	0.0779 9611	0.0814 6478	0.0850 0455	0.0886 1333	0.0922 8900	0.0998 3225
22	0.0759 7051	0.0794 7123	0.0830 4557	0.0866 9120	0.0904 0577	0.0980 3207
23	0.0741 3682	0.0776 6965	0.0812 7848	0.0849 6078	0.0887 1393	0.0964 2217
24	0.0724 7090	0.0760 3580	0.0796 7900	0.0833 9770	0.0871 8902	0.0949 7796
25	0.0709 5246	0.0745 4935	0.0782 2672	0.0819 8148	0.0858 1052	0.0936 7878
26	0.0695 6432	0.0731 9307	0.0769 0435	0.0806 9480	0.0845 6103	0.0925 0713
27	0.0682 9186	0.0719 5228	0.0756 9717	0.0795 2288	0.0834 2573	0.0914 4809
28	0.0671 2253	0.0708 1440	0.0745 9255	0.0784 5305	0.0823 9193	0.0904 8891
29	0.0660 4551	0.0697 6857	0.0735 7961	0.0774 7440	0.0814 4865	0.0896 1854
30	0.0650 5144	0.0688 0539	0.0726 4891	0.0765 7744	0.0805 8640	0.0888 2743
31	0.0641 3212	0.0679 1665	0.0717 9222	0.0757 5393	0.0797 9691	0.0881 0728
32	0.0632 8042	0.0670 9519	0.0710 0234	0.0749 9665	0.0790 7292	0.0874 5081
33	0.0624 9004	0.0663 3469	0.0702 7293	0.0742 9924	0.0784 0807	0.0868 5163
34	0.0617 5545	0.0656 2958	0.0695 9843	0.0736 5610	0.0777 9674	0.0863 0411
35	0.0610 7171	0.0649 7493	0.0689 7386	0.0730 6226	0.0772 3396	0.0858 0326
36	0.0604 3446	0.0643 6635	0.0683 9483	0.0725 1332	0.0767 1531	0.0853 4467
37	0.0598 3979	0.0637 9993	0.0678 5743	0.0720 0534	0.0762 3685	0.0849 2440
38	0.0592 8423	0.0632 7217	0.0673 5812	0.0715 3480	0.0757 9505	0.0845 3894
39	0.0587 6462	0.0627 7991	0.0668 9377	0.0710 9854	0.0753 8676	0.0841 8513
40	0.0582 7816	0.0623 2034	0.0664 6154	0.0706 9373	0.0750 0914	0.0838 6016
41	0.0578 2229	0.0618 9090	0.0660 5886	0.0703 1779	0.0746 5962	0.0835 6149
42	0.0573 9471	0.0614 8927	0.0656 8342	0.0699 6842	0.0743 3591	0.0832 8684
43	0.0569 9333	0.0611 1337	0.0653 3312	0.0696 4352	0.0740 3590	0.0830 3414
44	0.0566 1625	0.0607 6128	0.0650 0606	0.0693 4119	0.0737 5769	0.0828 0152
45	0.0562 6173	0.0604 3127	0.0647 0050	0.0690 5968	0.0734 9957	0.0825 8728
46	0.0559 2820	0.0601 2175	0.0644 1485	0.0687 9743	0.0732 5996	0.0823 8991
47	0.0556 1421	0.0598 3129	0.0641 4768	0.0685 5300	0.0730 3744	0.0822 0799
48	0.0553 1843	0.0595 5854	0.0638 9766	0.0683 2506	0.0728 3070	0.0820 4027
49	0.0550 3965	0.0593 0230	0.0636 6356	0.0681 1240	0.0726 3853	0.0818 8557
50	0.0547 7674	0.0590 6145	0.0634 4429	0.0679 1393	0.0724 5985	0.0817 4286
51	0.0545 2867	0.0588 3495	0.0632 3880	0.0677 2861	0.0722 9365	0.0816 1116
52	0.0542 9450	0.0586 2186	0.0630 4617	0.0675 5553	0.0721 3901	0.0814 8959
53	0.0540 7334	0.0584 2130	0.0628 6551	0.0673 9382	0.0719 9509	0.0813 7735
54	0.0538 6438	0.0582 3245	0.0626 9602	0.0672 4267	0.0718 6110	0.0812 7370
55	0.0536 6686	0.0580 5458	0.0625 3696	0.0671 0137	0.0717 3633	0.0811 7796
56	0.0534 8010	0.0578 8698	0.0623 8765	0.0669 6923	0.0716 2011	0.0810 8952
57	0.0533 0343	0.0577 2900	0.0622 4744	0.0668 4563	0.0715 1183	0.0810 0780
58	0.0531 3626	0.0575 8006	0.0621 1574	0.0667 2999	0.0714 1093	0.0809 3227
59	0.0529 7802	0.0574 3959	0.0619 9200	0.0666 2177	0.0713 1689	0.0808 6247
60	0.0528 2818	0.0573 0707	0.0618 7572	0.0665 2047	0.0712 2923	0.0807 9795

11. SINKING FUNDS AND AMORTIZATION

Adapted from Moore, "Handbook of Financial Mathematics"
New York: Prentice-Hall, Inc.

Sinking-fund computations.—Sinking funds are created to provide money for payment of long-term obligations when they fall due. Thus a sinking fund may be established to retire an issue of bonds when the issue matures, to meet a mortgage, to replace worn-out assets, to provide money for old-age pensions. Periodic payments are made to the fund; these periodic payments are invested and accumulated until the maturity of the debt; at maturity the principal of the debt is then paid off in one lump sum.

Difference between sinking-fund method and amortization method.—The following are the essential points of difference between the sinking-fund method and the amortization method of providing for the payment of an obligation:

1. Under the sinking-fund method, the principal of the debt remains constant until maturity, at which time it is paid in one lump sum. Under the amortization method, however, the periodic payments are not accumulated in a fund but are paid to the creditors; the principal is thus progressively reduced.

2. The sinking-fund method makes no provision for payment of interest on the debt. For example, if a sinking fund is created to retire an issue of bonds at maturity, the sinking fund will not pay the coupons as they fall due; the money for that purpose will have to be provided for independently of the sinking fund. In an amortization, on the other hand, each periodic payment pays off, in addition to a portion of the principal itself, the current interest upon the principal. Thus, if an issue of bonds is being amortized, each periodic payment redeems a certain number of the bonds and also pays the coupons on the outstanding bonds.

Table of annuity which, at compound interest, amounts to 1.— The table on pages 66–69 shows the annuity which amounts to 1 ($1, £1, 1 peso, or any other monetary unit) in different numbers of periods and at different rates of interest per period. This table, which is sometimes called the "Sinking Fund Table," is designed to answer the question "What sum should be invested at the end of each of a given number of periods so that the sum total with all interest accumulations will amount to 1 at the end of that given number of periods?" The procedure in calculating the periodic contribution required to be made to a sinking fund is as follows, provided the interest is compounded the same number of times a year as the periodic payments are made (which is generally the case):

1. Find in the table on pages 74–77 the annuity that amounts to 1 in the given number of periods and at the given rate of interest per period.

2. Multiply the figure found in 1 by the total amount to be accumulated in the sinking fund; the result is the periodic contribution required to be made to the fund.

EXAMPLE

The Manitoba Paper and Pulp Corporation wishes to provide a sinking fund to retire a bond issue of $2,225,000.00, maturing in 10 years. What semiannual payment must be made into the sinking fund, if the fund earns 4% per year compounded semiannually?

Solution

Since the payments into the sinking fund are to be made semiannually, the number of periods is $10 \times 2 = 20$. The rate of interest per period is $4\% \div 2 = 2\%$. Then:

(1) In the table on page 75, the annuity that will amount to 1 in 20 periods at 2% is shown to be 0.04115672.

(2) Multiplying the figure found in (1) by the total amount to be accumulated in the sinking fund gives $0.04115672 \times \$2,225,000.00 =$ $91,573.70.

Thus the Manitoba Corporation must pay $91,573.70 into the sinking fund at the end of each 6 months for 10 years. At the end of the 10 years the amount in the sinking fund will be the amount required to retire the bond issue; namely, $2,225,000.00.

Schedule of sinking-fund payments.—The schedule for the Manitoba Corporation's sinking fund is given on page 84. The items in column *B* represent the semiannual payments into the sinking fund. The total in the sinking fund at the end of each half year is shown in column *E*. A half-year's interest on each item in column *E* is shown, *one line lower down,* in column *C*. Each semiannual payment in column *B* plus the interest item in column *C* gives the total added to the fund at the end of that half year, and these totals form the items in column *D*.

SCHEDULE OF SINKING-FUND PAYMENTS, MANITOBA PAPER AND PULP CORPORATION

A	B	C	D	E
Date	*Semiannual Installment*	*Interest on Fund*	*Total Added to Fund*	*Total in Fund*
End of each half year:				
1st	$91,573.70	$........	$91,573.70	$ 91,573.70
2nd	91,573.70	1,831.47	93,405.17	184,978.87
3rd	91,573.70	3,699.58	95,273.28	280,252.15
4th	91,573.70	5,605.04	97,178.74	377,430.89
5th	91,573.70	7,548.62	99,122.32	476,553.21
6th	91,573.70	9,531.06	101,104.76	577,657.97
7th	91,573.70	11,553.16	103,126.86	680,784.83
8th	91,573.70	13,615.70	105,189.40	785,974.23
9th	91,573.70	15,719.48	107,293.18	893,267.41
10th	91,573.70	17,865.35	109,439.05	1,002,706.46
11th	91,573.70	20,054.13	111,627.83	1,114,334.29
12th	91,573.70	22,286.69	113,860.39	1,228,194.68
13th	91,573.70	24,563.89	116,137.59	1,344,332.27
14th	91,573.70	26,886.65	118,460.35	1,462,792.62
15th	91,573.70	29,255.85	120,829.55	1,583,622.17
16th	91,573.70	31,672.44	123,246.14	1,706,868.31
17th	91,573.70	34,137.37	125,711.07	1,832,579.38
18th	91,573.70	36,651.59	128,225.29	1,960,804.67
19th	91,573.70	39,216.09	130,789.79	2,091,594.46
20th	91,573.70	41,831.89	133,405.59	2,225,000.05*
	$1,831,474.00	$393,526.05	$2,225,000.05	

* Discrepancy of 5 cents. Schedules of sinking funds or amortizations can seldom be set up with absolute accuracy, even if tables with many decimal places are used. There is usually a small discrepancy which, in accounting practice, is adjusted by "doctoring" one or more of the items in the final entries in the schedule.

Formula for sinking-fund contribution.—The periodic contribution required to be made to a sinking fund may also be calculated by the use of the formula

$$\frac{P}{\frac{(1+i)^n - 1}{i}}.$$

where

$P =$ total amount to be accumulated in sinking fund
$i =$ rate of interest per period
$n =$ number of periods

Amortization.—The word "amortization" is derived from the Latin word for "death." This etymology gives an idea of the meaning of the term as applied to finance. Amortization is the process of gradually extinguishing a debt bearing compound interest, by means of a series of periodic payments to the creditor. The method of amortization most in favor is that which calls for *equal* periodic payments to be made at *equal* intervals of time. In an amortization each payment includes interest on the outstanding debt and a repayment of part of the principal.

Table of annuity that 1 will buy.—The table on pages 78–81 shows the annuity that 1 will buy ($1, £1, 1 peso, or any other monetary unit) for different numbers of periods and at different rates of interest per period. The procedure in calculating the periodic amortization payment required to be made in order to extinguish a debt in a given time is as follows, provided the interest is compounded the same number of times a year as the payments are made (which is generally the case).

1. Find in the table on pages 78–81 the annuity that 1 will buy for the given number of periods and at the given rate of interest per period.
2. Multiply the figure found in 1 by the amount of the debt.

EXAMPLE

On March 1, 1941, the Reynolds Whitmark Corporation borrows $700,000.00 at 5% per year compounded quarterly, agreeing to amortize the debt in 5 years by means of equal quarterly payments, the first payment to be made June 1, 1941. What will be the size of each quarterly amortization payment?

Solution

Since the payments are to be made quarterly, the number of periods is $5 \times 4 = 20$. The rate of interest per period is $5\% \div 4 = 1\frac{1}{4}\%$. Then:

(1) In the table on page 79, the annuity which 1 will buy for 20 periods at $1\frac{1}{4}\%$ is shown to be 0.05682039.

(2) Multiplying the figure found in (1) by the amount of the debt gives 0.05682039 × 700,000 = $39,774.27.

Thus the Reynolds Whitmark Corporation will amortize its debt by making quarterly payments of $39,774.27.

Schedule of amortization payments.—The schedule for the Reynolds Whitmark Corporation's $700,000.00 indebtedness is given below. The first item in column *E,* or the principal outstanding

SCHEDULE OF AMORTIZATION PAYMENTS,
REYNOLDS WHITMARK CORPORATION

A	B	C	D	E
Date	*Quarterly Installment*	*Interest on Outstanding Principal at 5% per Annum, Payable Quarterly*	*Amortization of the Principal of the Debt*	*Total Outstanding Principal of the Debt*
March 1, 1941				$700,000.00
June 1, 1941	$39,774.27	$8,750.00	$31,024.27	668,975.73
Sept. 1, 1941	39,774.27	8,362.20	31,412.07	637,563.66
Dec. 1, 1941	39,774.27	7,969.55	31,804.72	605,758.94
March 1, 1942	39,774.27	7,571.99	32,202.28	573,556.66
June 1, 1942	39,774.27	7,169.46	32,604.81	540,951.85
Sept. 1, 1942	39,774.27	6,761.90	33,012.37	507,939.48
Dec. 1, 1942	39,774.27	6,349.24	33,425.03	474,514.45
March 1, 1943	39,774.27	5,931.43	33,842.84	440,671.61
June 1, 1943	39,774.27	5,508.40	34,265.87	406,405.74
Sept. 1, 1943	39,774.27	5,080.07	34,694.20	371,711.54
Dec. 1, 1943	39,774.27	4,646.39	35,127.88	336,583.66
March 1, 1944	39,774.27	4,207.30	35,566.97	301,016.69
June 1, 1944	39,774.27	3,762.71	36,011.56	265,005.13
Sept. 1, 1944	39,774.27	3,312.56	36,461.71	228,543.42
Dec. 1, 1944	39,774.27	2,856.79	36,917.48	191,625.94
March 1, 1945	39,774.27	2,395.32	37,378.95	154,246.99
June 1, 1945	39,774.27	1,928.09	37,846.18	116,400.81
Sept. 1, 1945	39,774.27	1,455.01	38,319.26	78,081.55
Dec. 1, 1945	39,774.27	976.02	38,798.25	39,283.30
March 1, 1946	39,774.27	491.04	39,283.23	0.07*
	$795,485.40	$95,485.47	$699,999.93	

* Discrepancy of 7 cents; see footnote to schedule on page 84.

on March 1, 1941, is equal to the principal of the debt, $700,000.00. The first item in column *B* is the quarterly amortization payment due on June 1, 1941. This payment consists of two portions. The first portion, in column *C*, is the interest on the outstanding principal, found in column *E, as of the preceding date.* Thus the first item in column *C* is seen to be $1\frac{1}{4}\%$ of the first item in column *E*. Similarly, every item in column *C* is equal to $1\frac{1}{4}\%$ of the item in column *E* as of the date immediately preceding. The interest item in column *C* is now subtracted from the quarterly amortization payment item in column *B*, and the result, found in column *D*, is used toward the repayment of the principal of the debt. Thus, on June 1, 1941, a payment of $39,774.27 is made. Of this payment, $8,750.00 is interest on the debt, while the remaining $31,024.27 is a repayment of principal. Since $31,024.27 of the principal has been repaid, the outstanding principal on June 1, 1941, is $700,000.00—$31,024.27, or $668,975.73, which is found on the same line in column *E*. It should be noted that the total of all the items in column *D* is equal to the principal of the debt, $700,000.00.

Amortization of bonded debt.—It is frequently desirable for a corporation to amortize a bonded debt by redeeming a number of the bonds from time to time. Where the corporation redeems the bonds at equal intervals of time, it may wish to make approximately the same payment at each interval. Part of every payment will meet the current interest on the debt, and the balance will redeem a number of the bonds. The periodic amortization payment, as calculated by the table on pages 78–81, cannot, in such cases, be used directly, since the bonds are generally in denominations of $1,000.00 or some other round number, while the amortization payment calculated by the table on pages 78–81 is usually a figure carried out to the nearest cent. Thus if, for example, a payment of $18,431.76 is to be applied to the reduction of the principal, it is plain that with this amount not more than $18,000.00 worth of $1,000.00 bonds can be redeemed. Therefore, the procedure in cases of this kind is to use the mathematical amortization payment as a basis for arbitrarily fixing each payment so as to leave, after the deduction of interest, a sum (for redeeming a number of the bonds) that will make the total paid for amortization and interest approximate the mathematical payment. The payments are adjusted to make them as nearly equal as possible.

EXAMPLE

The Campbell Realty Corporation decides to amortize a bonded debt of \$850,000.00 in denominations of \$1,000.00 by redeeming a number of the bonds at par on each semiannual interest date, beginning July 1, 1941, for 4 years. Interest is payable on January 1 and July 1, at $4\frac{1}{2}\%$ per annum. Construct an amortization schedule.

Solution

It is first necessary to calculate the mathematical amortization payment, which will then be used as the basis for the construction of the schedule.

Since the payments are to be made semiannually, the number of periods is $4 \times 2 = 8$. The rate of interest per period is $4\frac{1}{2}\% \div 2 = 2\frac{1}{4}\%$. Then:

(1) In the table on page 79, the annuity which 1 will buy for 8 periods at $2\frac{1}{4}\%$ is shown to be 0.13798462.

(2) Multiplying the figure found in (1) by the amount of the debt gives $0.13798462 \times 850{,}000 = \$117{,}286.93$.

Thus \$117,286.93 is the mathematical amortization payment made each half year.

The amortization schedule is reproduced on page 89. The method of its construction was as follows: On July 1, 1941, the interest due on the \$850,000.00 worth of bonds outstanding is $2\frac{1}{4}\% \times \$850{,}000.00$, or \$19,125.00. Deducting this from the mathematical amortization payment of \$117,286.93 leaves a balance of \$98,161.93 to be used in redeeming bonds and thus repaying the principal of the loan. Since the bonds are of \$1,000.00 denomination, only 98 bonds can be redeemed. Hence \$98,000.00 is used for reducing the outstanding indebtedness, and the first amortization payment is \$117,125.00 instead of \$117,286.93. In some cases the actual amortization payment is larger than the mathematical payment, while in other cases it is smaller, but where the bonds are of \$1,000.00 denomination, the actual payment should never deviate by more than \$500.00 from the mathematical payment.

The reason that the columns are arranged differently in this schedule is that, whereas in the schedule on page 86 the periodic amortization payment was definitely known, and the amount of principal repaid was computed from it, here the amortization payment is a varying quantity, not widely apart from the mathematically determined quantity, \$117,-286.93, depending upon what the current interest is found to be. The procedure in constructing the schedule was first to compute the current interest, and then to determine the number of bonds to be redeemed which would make the total payment come *nearest* to $117,286.93. The two were then added, and the total periodic payment was thus obtained.

SCHEDULE OF AMORTIZATION PAYMENTS, CAMPBELL REALTY CORPORATION

A	B	C	D	E
Date	*Interest at $2\frac{1}{4}\%$ per Period*	*Principal Repaid by Bond Purchases*	*Total Amortization Payment*	*Principal Outstanding*
Jan. 1, 1941	....	....	....	$850,000.00
July 1, 1941	$19,125.00	$ 98,000.00	$117,125.00	752,000.00
Jan. 1, 1942	16,920.00	100,000.00	116,920.00	652,000.00
July 1, 1942	14,670.00	103,000.00	117,670.00	549,000.00
Jan. 1, 1943	12,352.50	105,000.00	117,352.50	444,000.00
July 1, 1943	9,990.00	107,000.00	116,990.00	337,000.00
Jan. 1, 1944	7,582.50	110,000.00	117,582.50	227,000.00
July 1, 1944	5,107.50	112,000.00	117,107.50	115,000.00
Jan. 1, 1945	2,587.50	115,000.00	117,587.50	0.00
	$88,335.00	$850,000.00	$938,335.00	

Formula for amortization payment.—The periodic amortization payment required to be made to extinguish an indebtedness in a given time may also be calculated by the use of the formula

$$\frac{P}{\dfrac{1-\dfrac{1}{(1+i)^n}}{i}}$$

where

$P =$ total amount of the debt
$i =$ rate of interest per period
$n =$ number of periods

12. DEPRECIATION METHODS

Adapted from Finney, "Principles of Accounting," and Curtis and Cooper, "Mathematics of Accounting" New York: Prentice-Hall, Inc.

Factors to be taken into account in calculating depreciation. —The factors that must be taken into consideration in estimating depreciation are:

1. Cost, which includes installation and other incidental expenditures.

2. Scrap or residual value, which is the estimated value that may be recovered from the asset after it is taken out of service. This scrap value should be net after estimated costs of dismantling are deducted.

3. Estimated life. This will, of course, be affected by the policy concerning repairs, and this policy should be taken into consideration in estimating the life.

These factors determine the total depreciation to be provided and the estimated life over which the total depreciation is to be spread. The portion of the total depreciation to be charged to each period of the total life depends upon the depreciation method used.

Straight-line method of depreciation.—This is the simplest and most common method. It results in spreading the total depreciation equally over all periods of life. The procedure under the straight-line method is as follows:

1. Find the difference between the cost and the scrap value.
2. Divide the figure found in 1 by the number of periods that the asset is expected to be of service. The result is the depreciation charge per period.

EXAMPLE

What will be the depreciation charge and the asset valuation at the end of each year for an asset costing $1,000.00, and having an estimated life of 10 years and an estimate scrap value of $100.00?

Formula

Cost — Scrap = Depreciation
Depreciation ÷ Number of years = Annual charge

Arithmetical Substitution

$1,000.00 — $100.00 = $900.00
$900.00 ÷ 10 = $90.00

TABLE OF DEPRECIATION

Years	*Periodic Depreciation Charge*	*Accumulated Depreciation Reserve*	*Asset Value*
			$1,000.00
1	$90.00	$ 90.00	910.00
2	90.00	180.00	820.00
3	90.00	270.00	730.00
4	90.00	360.00	640.00
5	90.00	450.00	550.00
6	90.00	540.00	460.00
7	90.00	630.00	370.00
8	90.00	720.00	280.00
9	90.00	810.00	190.00
10	90.00	900.00	100.00

Working-hours method of depreciation.—This method recognizes the fact that property, particularly machinery, depreciates more rapidly if it is run full time or overtime than if it is run part time. Not only is the wear and tear greater, but there is less opportunity for making repairs. Moreover, the full-time and overtime years get more benefit from the asset than do the part-time years. The procedure under the working-hours method is as follows:

1. Find the difference between the cost and the scrap value.
2. Divide the figure found in 1 by the total number of hours that the asset is expected to be of service; this gives the depreciation charge per hour.
3. Multiply the figure found in 2 by the number of working hours per period. The result is the depreciation charge per period.

EXAMPLE

A machine costing $7,400.00 will have a scrap value of $200.00. Machines of this class have a working-hour average life of 24,000 hours. What will be the depreciation charge and the asset valuation at the end of each year, if the machine is run as follows:

First year	2,000 hours	Sixth year	2,000 hours
Second year	2,000 "	Seventh year	3,000 "
Third year	1,800 "	Eighth year	3,000 "
Fourth year	2,600 "	Ninth year	3,000 "
Fifth year	2,800 "	Tenth year	1,800 "

Formula

Cost — Scrap = Depreciation
Depreciation ÷ Total number of hours = Charge per hour

Arithmetical Substitution

$7,400.00 — $200.00 = $7,200.00
$7,200.00 ÷ 24,000 = $0.30

TABLE OF DEPRECIATION

Years	*Number of Hours*	*Periodic Depreciation Charge*	*Accumulated Depreciation Reserve*	*Asset Value*
				$7,400.00
1	2,000	$600.00	$ 600.00	6,800.00
2	2,000	600.00	1,200.00	6,200.00
3	1,800	540.00	1,740.00	5,660.00
4	2,600	780.00	2,520.00	4,880.00
5	2,800	840.00	3,360.00	4,040.00
6	2,000	600.00	3,960.00	3,440.00
7	3,000	900.00	4,860.00	2,540.00
8	3,000	900.00	5,760.00	1,640.00
9	3,000	900.00	6,660.00	740.00
10	1,800	540.00	7,200.00	200.00

Unit-production method of depreciation.—This method is similar to the working-hours method in that it distributes the depreciation among the periods in proportion to the use made of the asset during each period. The estimated life is stated in units of product which can be produced by the asset before it is worn out, and the rate of depreciation is a rate per unit of product. The procedure under the unit-production method is as follows:

1. Find the difference between the cost and the scrap value.
2. Divide the figure found in 1 by the total number of units of product that it is expected the asset will produce during its life; this gives the depreciation charge per unit of product.
3. Multiply the figure found in 2 by the number of units produced per period. The result is the depreciation charge per period.

EXAMPLE

A certain one-purpose machine that costs $1,000.00, and has no scrap value, has been installed in a factory. A machine of this class produces

10,000 units of product during its life. Assuming that the annual production is as given below, set up a table showing the depreciation to be written off each year.

First year..........	1,000 units	Fifth year........	1,000 units
Second year....	2,000 "	Sixth year........	1,200 "
Third year......	1,800 "	Seventh year....	1,200 "
Fourth year......	1,000 "	Eighth year......	800 "

Formula

Cost — Scrap = Depreciation

Depreciation ÷ Total number of units = Charge per unit

Arithmetical Substitution

$1,000.00 — $0.00 = $1,000.00

$1,000.00 ÷ 10,000 = $0.10

TABLE OF DEPRECIATION

Years	*Units Produced*	*Periodic Depreciation Charge*	*Accumulated Depreciation Reserve*	*Asset Value*
				$1,000.00
1....................	1,000	$100.00	$ 100.00	900.00
2....................	2,000	200.00	300.00	700.00
3....................	1,800	180.00	480.00	520.00
4....................	1,000	100.00	580.00	420.00
5....................	1,000	100.00	680.00	320.00
6....................	1,200	120.00	800.00	200.00
7....................	1,200	120.00	920.00	80.00
8....................	800	80.00	1,000.00	0.00

Reducing-charge methods of depreciation.—Although actual depreciation is usually small during the early periods of life, and large during the later periods, it is sometimes contended that theoretical depreciation should be provided in an opposite manner; that is, by making large charges during the early periods and small charges during the later periods. This procedure is advocated on the theory that the cost of the use of an asset is composed of two elements—repairs and depreciation—and that the sum of these two charges should be a fairly uniform amount year by year. Since repairs tend to increase with the age of the asset, it is contended that the depreciation charge should decrease, in order that the increasing repair charges and the decreasing depreciation charges will tend to equalize each other and produce a uniform total charge.

This method is excellent theory, but the plan of making decreasing depreciation charges assumes that repairs will increase in the same proportion that depreciation decreases. Perhaps they will, but it is likely to be a matter of luck. If it is desirable to equalize the total repair and depreciation charges, it would seem better to create two reserves: one for depreciation on the straight-line method, and another for repairs. By estimating the total repair charges to be made during the life of the asset, and by providing a reserve for repairs by equal periodical charges, an equality is maintained as between periods. Such a plan is subject to the objection that it may be difficult to estimate accurately the total future repair cost, but with statistics showing past experience it should be no more difficult to do this than to estimate depreciation.

Three methods of providing a diminishing depreciation charge are:

1. Fixed-percentage-of-diminishing-value method.
2. Sum-of-digits method.
3. Diminishing-rates-on-cost method.

Fixed-percentage-of-diminishing-value method.—The difficulty encountered in this method is that of finding the rate percent to be used in the calculation of the charge. The procedure is as follows:

1. Divide the scrap value by the cost.
2. Extract the root, corresponding to the number of periods of depreciation to be taken on the life of the asset, of the figure found in 1.
3. Deduct from 1 the result obtained in 2, to find the rate percent to be used.
4. Multiply the net asset or the carrying value of the asset at the beginning of each period by the rate found in 3, to obtain the depreciation charge for each period.

EXAMPLE

What will be the depreciation charges for an asset valued at $1,000.00, with a scrap value of $100.00, which is to be written off in 10 years by the fixed-percentage-of-diminishing-value method?

The following are the formula and solution for the calculation of the rate:

Formula

$$1 - \sqrt[n]{\frac{\text{Scrap value}}{\text{Cost value}}} = r$$

Arithmetical Substitution

$$1 - \sqrt[10]{\frac{100}{1{,}000}} = 20.5672\%$$

Solution, Part 1

$$100 \div 1{,}000 = .1$$
$$\log .1 = \bar{1}.000000$$
$$\text{Changed, } \bar{1}.000000 = 9.000000 - 10$$
$$9.000000 - 10 \div 10 = .900000 - 1$$
$$\text{Changed} = \bar{1}.900000$$
$$\text{The antilog of } \bar{1}.900000 = .794328$$
$$1 - .794328 = .205672, \text{ or } 20.567\%$$

Solution, Part 2

$1,000.00 × 20.567% = $205.67, first depreciation charge
$1,000.00 — $205.67 = $794.33, new asset value
$794.33 × 20.567% = $163.37, second depreciation charge

This process is continued for each of the 10 years.

TABLE OF DEPRECIATION
(Rate, 20.567%)

Year	*Periodic Depreciation Charge*	*Accumulated Depreciation Reserve*	*Asset Value*
			$1,000.00
1	$205.67	$205.67	794.33
2	163.37	369.04	630.96
3	129.77	498.81	501.19
4	103.08	601.89	398.11
5	81.88	683.77	316.23
6	65.04	748.81	251.19
7	51.66	800.47	199.53
8	41.04	841.51	158.49
9	32.60	874.11	125.89
10	25.89	900.00	100.00

It should be clearly understood that the rate to be used in the fixed-percentage-of-diminishing-value method cannot be computed by dividing 100% by the years of life. If this were done in the above example, a rate of 10% would be obtained. Since the correct rate is 20.567%, it is evident that the use of a 10% rate would leave a large balance undepreciated at the end of 10 years.

Sum-of-digits method.—The procedure under this method is as follows:

1. Find the sum of the digits, or numbers representing the periods of useful life of the asset. Use this sum as the denominator of certain fractions.
2. Use the same digits or numbers in inverse order as the numerators of these fractions.
3. Compute the periodic depreciation by multiplying the total depreciation by the fractions obtained in 1 and 2.

EXAMPLE

An asset is valued at $1,000.00, and has a scrap value of $100.00. What should be the depreciation charges if the asset is to be written down in 9 years by the sum-of-digits method?

Solution

TABLE OF DEPRECIATION

Year	*Fractional Part*	*Periodic Depreciation Charge*	*Accumulated Depreciation Reserve*	*Asset Value*
				$1,000.00
1	9/45	$180.00	$180.00	820.00
2	8/45	160.00	340.00	660.00
3	7/45	140.00	480.00	520.00
4	6/45	120.00	600.00	400.00
5	5/45	100.00	700.00	300.00
6	4/45	80.00	780.00	220.00
7	3/45	60.00	840.00	160.00
8	2/45	40.00	880.00	120.00
9	1/45	20.00	900.00	100.00
45	45/45	$900.00		

The denominator of the fractions used in the second column is found by adding the first column. The numerators are the same numbers taken in inverse order.

Diminishing-rates-on-cost method.—The procedure under this method is as follows:

1. Choose a depreciation rate for each year. No formula is used in determining the rates, which are chosen arbitrarily and diminish from year to year.

2. Multiply the cost by the rate chosen for the year. The result is the depreciation charge.

EXAMPLE

What will be the depreciation charge each year on an asset the cost of which is $6,000.00, scrap value $400.00, and estimated life 8 years?

Solution

DEPRECIATION TABLE

Year	*Rate*	*Periodic Depreciation Charge*	*Accumulated Depreciation Reserve*	*Asset Value*
				$6,000.00
1.	$15\frac{2}{3}$%	$ 940.00	$ 940.00	5,060.00
2.	$14\frac{2}{3}$	880.00	1,820.00	4,180.00
3.	13	780.00	2,600.00	3,400.00
4.	12	720.00	3,320.00	2,680.00
5.	11	660.00	3,980.00	2,020.00
6.	10	600.00	4,580.00	1,420.00
7.	9	540.00	5,120.00	880.00
8.	8	480.00	5,600.00	400.00
	$93\frac{1}{3}$%	$5,600.00		

Annuity method of depreciation.—The theory applied in this method is that the depreciation charge should include, in addition to the amount credited to the reserve, interest on the carrying value of the asset.

The investment in property is regarded, first, as the amount of scrap value that draws interest, and second, as an investment in an annuity to be reduced by equal periodic amounts. The interest on the scrap value plus the equal periodic reduction of the investment is the charge to depreciation, offset by a credit to interest computed on the diminishing value of the property, and a credit to the reserve account for the balance. This charge to depreciation is the same each period during the life of the property. The theory of an investment in an annuity is that the annuity is to be reduced by equal periodic payments, and as the credits to interest will decrease, the credits to the reserve must correspondingly increase.

The procedure under the annuity method is as follows:

1. Find the difference between the cost and the scrap value.

2. Divide the figure found in 1 by the present value of an annuity of 1.

3. Calculate the interest on the scrap value for one period at the given rate percentage.

4. Determine the sum of 2 and 3. The result is the periodic charge to depreciation.

EXAMPLE

Calculate by the annuity method the annual charge to depreciation for an asset valued at \$1,000.00, with a scrap value of \$100.00, which is to be written off in 10 years on a 6% basis.

Formula

$$\left[\frac{\text{Cost} - \text{Scrap}}{\dfrac{1 - \dfrac{1}{(1+i)^n}}{i}}\right] + (\text{Scrap} \times i) = \text{Periodic charge}$$

Arithmetical Substitution

$$\left[\frac{1{,}000 - 100}{\dfrac{1 - \dfrac{1}{(1.06)^{10}}}{.06}}\right] + (100 \times .06) = \$128.28$$

Solution

(1) The difference between the cost and the scrap value is \$1,000.00 — \$100.00 = \$900.00.

(2) The present value of an annuity of 1 for 10 years at 6% is 7.36008705 (from the table on page 73). Then, \$900.00 ÷ 7.36008705 = \$122.28.

(3) The interest on the scrap value for one period is \$100.00 × .06 = \$6.00.

(4) The sum of (2) and (3) is \$122.28 + \$6.00 = \$128.28. This is the periodic charge to depreciation.

In the above example, the \$900.00 represents the present value of the sum to be spread over the life of the asset, and the \$100.00 represents the scrap value. In the following tables, the fifth column always contains the carrying value of the annuity, plus $100.00. The two tables are given to show the similarity between an annuity in which an investment was made and equal annual rents withdrawn, and the annuity method of depreciation.

TABLE OF REDUCTION OF AN ANNUITY

End of Period	*Rents Withdrawn*	*Credits to Interest*	*Amortization of Investment*	*Present Value of Annuity, Plus $100*
				$1,000.00
1	$ 128.28	$ 60.00	$ 68.28	931.72
2	128.28	55.90	72.38	859.34
3	128.28	51.56	76.72	782.62
4	128.28	46.96	81.32	701.50
5	128.28	42.08	86.20	615.10
6	128.28	36.91	91.37	523.73
7	128.28	31.42	96.86	426.87
8	128.28	25.61	102.67	324.20
9	128.28	19.45	108.83	215.37
10	128.29	12.92	115.37	100.00
	$1,282.81	$382.81	$900.00	

TABLE OF REDUCTION OF THE VALUE OF AN ASSET

End of Period	*Depreciation Charge*	*Credits to Interest*	*Credits to Reserve*	*Value of Asset*
				$1,000.00
1	$ 128.28	$ 60.00	$ 68.28	931.72
2	128.28	55.90	72.38	859.34
3	128.28	51.56	76.72	782.62
4	128.28	46.96	81.32	701.50
5	128.28	42.08	86.20	615.10
6	128.28	36.91	91.37	523.73
7	128.28	31.42	96.86	426.87
8	128.28	25.61	102.67	324.20
9	128.28	19.45	108.83	215.37
10	128.29	12.92	115.37	100.00
	$1,282.81	$382.81	$900.00	

Two objections may be raised to the annuity method. First, it results in the addition of interest to the cost of production, a procedure of more than doubtful propriety. Second, it throws the interest charge into operations under the name of depreciation. Even if interest were a proper element of cost, it would seem that the charge should be clearly stated as interest and should not be confused with depreciation.

Sinking-fund method of depreciation.—The theory of the sinking-fund method is that the money set aside in a fund should draw interest, this interest to be added to the fund at the end of each year. The total accumulation of the fund should be equal to the depreciation charged during the life of the asset. While in theory a fund equal to the total accumulation is set aside, usually in practice no such fund exists.

The procedure under the sinking-fund method is as follows:

1. Find the amount of the total depreciation of the asset by deducting the scrap value from the cost.
2. Divide the figure found in 1 by the amount of an ordinary annuity of 1 at the sinking-fund interest rate, for the number of periods of the life of the asset. This will give the periodic sum to be placed in the sinking fund.
3. To the periodic sum found in 2, add a sum equal to the interest on the sinking fund for the period. This gives the periodic charge to depreciation and the credit to reserve for depreciation.

EXAMPLE

An asset costs $1,000.00, and has a scrap value of $100.00 at the end of 10 years. Determine the periodic depreciation charge by the sinking-fund method, on a 6% interest basis.

Formula

$$\frac{\text{Cost} - \text{Scrap}}{\dfrac{(1+i)^n - 1}{i}} = \text{Periodic deposit in sinking fund}$$

Arithmetical Substitution

$$\frac{1{,}000 - 100}{\dfrac{(1.06)^{10} - 1}{.06}} = \$68.28$$

Solution

(1) The difference between the cost and the scrap value is $1,000.00 — $100.00 = $900.00.

(2) The amount of an ordinary annuity of 1 for 10 years at 6% is 13.18079494 (from the table on page 69). Then, $900.00 ÷ 13.18079494 = $68.28.

The formula and solution just shown give only the first periodic charge to depreciation. Each periodic charge is an amount equal to the sum of the first periodic payment and the interest on the accumulated depreciation reserve. Table B, below, shows the periodic charges to depreciation and the credits to the reserve account for each of the 10 years.

It is not necessary to accumulate a sinking fund in order to use the sinking-fund method of depreciation. The depreciation entries are independent of the fund entries. If a sinking fund were accumulated for the above example, the entries would be as shown in Table A.

TABLE A.—ENTRIES TO THE SINKING FUND

Year	*Debit to Sinking Fund*	*Credit to Cash*	*Credit to Interest*	*Accumulation of Fund*
1	$ 68.28	$ 68.28	$........	$ 68.28
2	72.38	68.28	4.10	140.66
3	76.72	68.28	8.44	217.38
4	81.32	68.28	13.04	298.70
5	86.20	68.28	17.92	384.90
6	91.37	68.28	23.09	476.27
7	96.86	68.28	28.58	573.13
8	102.67	68.28	34.39	675.80
9	108.83	68.28	40.55	784.63
10	115.37	68.29	47.08	900.00
	$900.00	$682.81	$217.19	

TABLE B.—DEPRECIATION ENTRIES BY THE SINKING-FUND METHOD OF DEPRECIATION

End of Year	*Depreciation Charge and Reserve Credit*	*Accumulated Depreciation Reserve*	*Asset Value*
			$1,000.00
1	$ 68.28	$ 68.28	931.72
2	72.38	140.66	859.34
3	76.72	217.38	782.62
4	81.32	298.70	701.30
5	86.20	384.90	615.10
6	91.37	476.27	523.73
7	96.86	573.13	426.87
8	102.67	675.80	324.20
9	108.83	784.63	215.37
10	115.37	900.00	100.00

The sinking-fund method is sometimes used by public utilities in order to determine what amount must be taken out of income to provide a fund for the replacement of the assets. Having determined this amount, the utility is allowed to charge a rate for its service sufficient to provide for depreciation as well as for the other expenses. The cash provided by the income is put into the fund, and the charges to depreciation are made in accordance with the accumulation of the fund. Thus, as the investment in, or carrying value of, the fixed assets is diminished, the fund is increased, and the capital is kept intact.

Appraisal method of depreciation.—This method consists merely of estimating the value of the asset at the end of each period and writing off as depreciation the difference between the balance of the asset account and the appraised value. The appraisal method is likely to result in burdening some periods with heavy charges and relieving other periods, for if the depreciation charges correspond with actual depreciation, the charges will be light during the early years and heavy during the later ones. On the other hand, the burden may be reversed by charging the early periods with large amounts, on the theory that the property loses value rapidly in the early part of its life, because its value is quickly reduced to a second-hand basis. This practice improperly introduces the element of realizable values, when only going-concern values should be considered.

When the appraisal method is used, care should be taken to ignore upward or downward fluctuations in market value.

Composite-life method of depreciation.—The composite life of a plant as a whole, sometimes called the average or mean life, may be computed as in the following illustration:

Asset	*Cost*	*Residual Value*	*Total Depreciation*	*Estimated Life*	*Annual Depreciation (Straight-Line)*
A	$20,000.00	$5,000.00	$15,000.00	20 years	$ 750.00
B	12,000.00	2,000.00	10,000.00	10 years	1,000.00
C	8,000.00	2,000.00	6,000.00	8 years	750.00
D	500.00	100.00	400.00	2 years	200.00
			$31,400.00		$2,700.00

$31,400.00 ÷ $2,700.00 = $11\frac{17}{27}$, the composite, or average, life.

This computation indicates that \$31,400.00 depreciation should be provided to cover one exhaustion of the plant as a whole. On the straight-line method, \$2,700.00 depreciation will be provided annually. At this rate it will take $11\frac{17}{27}$ years to provide \$31,400.00 depreciation. Hence $11\frac{17}{27}$ years is the composite life of the plant.

Federal income tax; deduction for depreciation.—In computing the Federal income tax, a reasonable allowance is made for the exhaustion, wear, and tear of property used in the trade or business. While the straight-line method is generally used, the income-tax regulations provide that the deduction need not necessarily be at a uniform rate. According to an early ruling, any recognized trade practice is permissible, provided it results in an annual charge over the useful life of the property according to some reasonably consistent plan. The unit-production method, the diminishing-value method, and the sinking-fund method are specifically mentioned in a pamphlet, issued by the Treasury Department in 1928, known as "Depreciation Studies of the Bureau of Internal Revenue."

It should be remembered, however, that the depreciation deduction under the Federal income tax law is highly technical and hedged about by numerous rules and regulations. For example, the basis upon which depreciation is computed is the same as that for com-

TABLE SHOWING DEPRECIATION RATE FOR VARIOUS ASSETS

(Page from a table contained in the pamphlet "Depreciation Studies," issued by the Bureau of Internal Revenue and reprinted in the *Prentice-Hall Federal Tax Service.*)

Motor and Other Vehicles	*Probable Useful Life (Yrs.)*	*Depreciation Rate (%)*	*Motor and Other Vehicles*	*Probable Useful Life (Yrs.)*	*Depreciation Rate (%)*
Automobiles	4	25	Trucks:		
Buses, motor:			Electric	10	10
Under \$5,000	5	20	Gas:		
\$5,000 to \$7,500	6	$16\frac{2}{3}$	Under \$1,000	3	$33\frac{1}{3}$
Over \$7,500	7	14	\$1,000 to \$1,500	4	25
Horse-drawn vehicles	8	$12\frac{1}{2}$	\$1,500 to \$2,500	5	20
Tractors	6	$16\frac{2}{3}$	Over \$2,500	6	$16\frac{2}{3}$
Trailers	6	$16\frac{2}{3}$			

Office Equipment	Probable Useful Life (Yrs.)	Depreciation Rate (%)	Office Equipment	Probable Useful Life (Yrs.)	Depreciation Rate (%)
Adding machines	10	10	Fans, electric	10	10
Addressographs	10	10	Folding and sealing machines	10	10
Billing machines	8	$12\frac{1}{2}$	Helmets, rescue	6	$16\frac{2}{3}$
Binders, loose-leaf	20	5	Hospital equipment	15	$6\frac{2}{3}$
Blue-printing machines	15	$6\frac{2}{3}$	Lamps, desk and floor	10	10
Bookkeeping machines	6	$16\frac{2}{3}$	Linoleum	8	$12\frac{1}{2}$
Cabinets and files	15	$6\frac{2}{3}$	Lockers	20	5
Calculators	6	$16\frac{2}{3}$	Lunchroom equipment	15	$6\frac{2}{3}$
Call system and annunciators	14	7	Mimeograph machines	10	10
Cases:			Mirrors	20	5
Book	20	5	Money machines	10	10
Display	20	5	Multigraph machines	10	10
Chairs:			Numbering machines	10	10
Bentwood	5	20	Photostat machines	16	$6\frac{1}{4}$
Heavy	16	$6\frac{1}{4}$	Pneumatic-tube systems	20	5
Check perforators	10	10	Racks and stands	15	$6\frac{2}{3}$
Check writers	8	$12\frac{1}{2}$	Rugs, carpets, and mats	6	$16\frac{2}{3}$
Cleaners, electric vacuum	6	$16\frac{2}{3}$	Safes and vaults	40	$2\frac{1}{2}$
Clocks:			Scales, counter and mail	10	10
Time	15	$6\frac{2}{3}$	Settees	13	$7\frac{1}{2}$
Time-stamping	10	10	Shades, window	10	10
Wall	20	5	Signs	10	10
Comptometers	10	10	Tables	15	$6\frac{2}{3}$
Coolers, water	10	10	Transophones, electric	6	$16\frac{2}{3}$
Desks	15	$6\frac{2}{3}$	Typewriters	6	$16\frac{2}{3}$
Dictaphones and dictographs	6	$16\frac{2}{3}$	Wardrobes	20	5

puting the gain from a sale, which may be entirely different from book value. For a thorough and complete discussion of the subject, the *Prentice-Hall Federal Tax Service* should be consulted.

The rate of depreciation, under the Federal income tax law, depends in every instance upon the estimated useful life of the property. In a report issued by the Bureau of Internal Revenue in January, 1931, the probable useful life of several hundred items is set forth. Since that date, the courts and Board of Tax Appeals have handed down numerous decisions approving a certain rate for various assets. While the rates given in the Bureau's table and in the decisions of the courts and Board of Tax Appeals are entitled to great weight, they may not be used arbitrarily, but are a useful guide or starting-point from which the correct rate may be determined. The question in every case is one of fact to be determined in the light of the experience of the property under consideration and all other pertinent evidence. The Bureau's table, together with a table prepared from the court and Board decisions, appears in the *Prentice-Hall Federal Tax Service*. The Service, therefore, reveals at a glance all the rates that have received official approval. A page from the Bureau's table is illustrated on pages 103–104. A page from the table compiled from court and Board decisions is illustrated below.

ANOTHER TABLE SHOWING DEPRECIATION RATE FOR VARIOUS ASSETS

(Page from a table in the *Prentice-Hall Federal Tax Service,* compiled from decisions of the courts and the Board of Tax Appeals.)

Asset	*Useful Life (Yrs.)*	*Rate (%)*	*Authority*
Plumbing	33⅓	3	Union Co., 14 B.T.A. 1310
	20	5	Lord & Bushnell Co., 7 B.T.A. 86
Plank roads	10	10	Lord & Bushnell Co., 7 B.T.A. 86
Plows	5	20	Louis Titus, 2 B.T.A. 754
Power plants	20	5	Art. Metal Const. Co., 4 B.T.A. 493
			Chicago Ry. Equipment Co., B.T.A. 471
	15	6⅔	Frost Manufacturing Co., 13 B.T.A. 802
	14$\frac{2}{7}$	7	Lassen Lumber & Box Co., 6 B.T.A. 241
	10	10	Atlas Tack Co., 9 B.T.A. 1322
Power transmission lines	15$\frac{5}{13}$	6½	Quito Electric Light & Power Co., 10 B.T.A. 538
	10	10	Lord & Bushnell Co., 7 B.T.A. 86
Rafting gear	2	50	J. S. Hoskins Lumber Co., 3 B.T.A. 846
Railroads	25	4	Great Northern Railway Co., 30 B.T.A. 691
	6⅔	15	Fort Orange Paper Co., 1 B.T.A. 1230
	3	33⅓	Lytle Const. Co., 21 B.T.A. 1423†
. bridges and trestles	10	10	Richmond Belt Railway Co., 13 B.T.A. 1291
. grading	33⅓	3	Richmond Belt Railway Co., 13 B.T.A. 1291
. rails	20	5	Richmond Belt Railway Co., 13 B.T.A. 1291
. ties	8	12½	Richmond Belt Railway Co., 13 B.T.A. 1291
Raisin Stemmers	10	10	Lloyd H. Wilbur, 5 B.T.A. 597
Refrigerators	5	20	Strauss Market, Inc., 2 B.T.A. 1264
Refrigerator cars	20	5	American Refrigerator Transit Co., 31 B.T.A. 465 (No. 96) (nonacquiescence, C.B. June 1935, p. 23)
Scales	10	10	Hickory Spinning Co., 2 B.T.A. 439
			Lord & Bushnell Co., 7 B.T.A. 86

Asset	Useful Life (Yrs.)	Rate (%)	Authority
	4	25	David T. Long, 17 B.T.A. 584
Scows	30	3⅓	Morris & Cummings Dredging Co., 10 B.T.A. 351
	20	5	Bartley Scow Co., 1 B.T.A. 1165
Sewing machines	10	10	Pinkus Happ, 7 B.T.A. 865
Signs	20	5	Cooperative Publishing Co., 5 B.T.A. 340
	10	10	Lord & Bushnell Co., 7 B.T.A. 86
	6⅔	15	When Clothing Co., 1 B.T.A. 973
Smoke stack	4	25	Magdalen Doerfler, Beneficiary, 13 B.T.A. 921
Sprinkler systems	40	2½	Oliver Finnie Co., 2 B.T.A. 134
	20	5	H. Sheldon Mfg. Co., 13 B.T.A. 1299
	10	10	Atlas Plywood Co., 17 B.T.A. 156
	16	6¼	Long Island Drug Co., 35 B.T.A. 328
	15	6⅔	Elberta Crate & Box Co. (Memo B.T.A., 3-3-40)
Steam shovels	5	20	Parker Gravel Co., Inc., 21 B.T.A. 51
	3	33⅓	Nichols Contracting Co., 15 B.T.A. 102
Steamships, freight	33⅓	3	Kinsman Transit Co., 1 B.T.A. 552**
			Valley Steamship Co., 1 B.T.A. 1107**
. Great Lakes	33⅓	3	A.R.R. 27, C.B. June 1920, p. 139
. lumber trade	20	5	A.R.R. 279, C.B. Dec. 1920, p. 168
. ocean-going	20	5	A.R.R. 4822, C.B. June 1924, p. 159
	12	8⅓	Seas Shipping Co., Inc., 16 B.T.A. 841, (nonacquiescence, C.B. June 1930, p. 75)
	28$\frac{4}{7}$	3½	American So. African Line, 30 B.T.A. 753*
	25	4	American So. African Line, 30 B.T.A. 753*

* Includes obsolescence allowance.

† Construction work only.

** Great Lakes.

13. SHORT CUTS IN BUSINESS MATHEMATICS

Adapted from Curtis and Cooper, "Mathematics of Accounting"
New York: Prentice-Hall, Inc.

Addition

Addition of columns.—Add each column separately, setting the sums one place to the left each time. After the last column has been added, add the individual sums in regular order—that is, from right to left. (See Example 1.)

To check, repeat the process beginning at the left.

or

Add each column separately, and, as each sum is set one place to the left, add the number carried from the column at the right. The answer is the total of the last column and the outer figures. (See Example 2.) The second method saves a little time but is not checked as in Example 1.

Example 1	*Example 2*
4572	4572
3986	3986
2173	2173
5911	5911
2765	2765
4937	4937
24	24
32	34
40	43
20	24
24344	

Savings accomplished.—

1. Time required to readd a column of figures for the purpose of picking up the carrying figure is saved.

2. Saves time in checking for errors. For example, if, in the final summary of additions, there is an error of $100.00, the hundreds' columns of the subtotals may be verified quickly without the necessity of readding all the columns.

Subtraction

Subtraction by addition.—Instead of subtracting in the usual way, add to the subtrahend the number required to make the subtrahend equal to the minuend.

Thus, in the following example, instead of thinking 7 from 16 is 9, think $7+9=16$. Write the 9. Add 1, the digit carried over, to the 8, making 9. $9+8=17$. Write 8 and add 1, the digit carried over, to 1, making 2. $2+0=2$. Write 0. $3+5=8$. Write 5. Answer: 5,089.

EXAMPLE

Minuend	8276
Subtrahend	3187
Difference	5089

Purpose.—The common error in subtraction caused by overlooking the fact that borrowing from the next higher order has taken place is avoided by changing the process of subtraction to that of addition.

Balancing an account.—In most cases inspection will tell which side of the account is the greater in amount. Add the larger side, and put the same footing on the smaller side, leaving space for the balance; then add from the top downward, supplying the figures necessary to make the column total equal to the footing previously placed there.

EXAMPLE

Debits		*Credits*
$ 1,956.18		$ 134.26
3,452.75		258.19
289.34		764.83
5,726.31		2,375.94
	Balance,	7,891.36
$11,424.58		$11,424.58

Explanation.—The balance, $7,891.36, was found as follows: Inspection showed the debit side to be the larger in amount. It was therefore added, and the footing of the account, $11,424.58, was placed under both debit and credit columns. The first order of the credits—that is, the cents—adds to 22. Insert 6 to make 28. With 2, the digit carried over, the second order, the dimes, adds to 22. Insert 3 to make 25. The third order, the dollars, with the digit carried over, adds to 23. Insert 1 to make 24. The fourth order, the tens of dollars, with the digit carried over, adds to 23. Insert 9 to make 32. The fifth order, the hundreds of dollars, with the digit carried over, adds to 16. Insert 8 to make 24. The sixth order, the thousands of dollars, with the digit carried over, adds to 4. Insert 7 to make 11.

Multiplication

TABLE OF SHORT CUTS IN MULTIPLICATION

To multiply by				To multiply by			
$1\frac{1}{4}$	add 0	and divide by	8	25	add 00	and divide by	4
$1\frac{2}{3}$	" 0	" " "	6	$31\frac{1}{4}$	" 00	" " "	32
$2\frac{1}{2}$	" 0	" " "	4	$33\frac{1}{3}$	" 00	" " "	3
$3\frac{1}{3}$	" 0	" " "	3	50	" 00	" " "	2
5	" 0	" " "	2	$66\frac{2}{3}$	" 000	" " "	15
$6\frac{1}{4}$	" 00	" " "	16	$83\frac{1}{3}$	" 000	" " "	12
$6\frac{2}{3}$	" 00	" " "	15	125	" 000	" " "	8
$8\frac{1}{3}$	" 00	" " "	12	$166\frac{2}{3}$	" 000	" " "	6
$12\frac{1}{2}$	" 00	" " "	8	250	" 000	" " "	4
$14\frac{2}{7}$	" 00	" " "	7	$333\frac{1}{3}$	" 000	" " "	3
$16\frac{2}{3}$	" 00	" " "	6				

Using factors as a short cut in multiplication.—When factors of the multiplier are used, there are only two multiplications, whereas in the ordinary method there is an addition as well.

EXAMPLE

Multiply 439 by 24.

Solution

Ordinary Method	*Shorter Method*
439	439 $24 = 6 \times 4$
24	6
1756	2634
878	4
10536	10536

Multiplication by 11.—Put down the units' digit (right-hand figure) as the units' digit of the product. Then add the tens' digit (second figure) to the units' digit and put down the sum. If it is over 10, put down the right-hand figure and carry 1. Then add the hundreds' digit (third figure) to the tens' digit, adding the 1 if there was a carry-over. If it is over 10, put down the right-hand figure and carry 1, as before. Continue in the same way with each digit to the left. Then put down the first figure and carry 1 if there is a carry-over.

EXAMPLE

Multiply 5,846 by 11.

Solution

Put down 6, the units' digit. Add 4 and 6, put down 0, and carry 1. Add 8 and 4 and 1 carried over, and put down 3 and carry 1. Add 5 and 8 and 1 carried over, and put down 4 and carry 1. Put down 5 plus 1 carried over, 6. The answer is 64306.

Multiplication by 15.—Annex a cipher to the multiplicand, and increase the result by one half of the multiplicand.

EXAMPLE

Multiply 8,435 by 15.

Solution

```
 84350
 42175
------
126525
```

Multiplication by 75.—Annex two ciphers, then divide by 4, and subtract this quotient from the product.

EXAMPLE

Multiply 4,728 by 75.

Solution

```
472800
118200
------
354600
```

Multiplication of numbers ending with ciphers.—Multiply the significant figures and annex as many ciphers as there are final ciphers in both the multiplier and the multiplicand.

EXAMPLE

Multiply 756,000 by 4,200.

Solution

```
  756
   42
-----
31752
```

Annex five ciphers. Answer: 3,175,200,000.

Multiplication by 9, 99, 999, etc.—Multiply by 10, 100, or 1,000, etc., and subtract the original number from the result.

EXAMPLE

Multiply 8,356 by 99.

Solution

$$\begin{array}{lr} & 835{,}600 \\ & -\ 8{,}356 \\ \hline \text{Answer:} & 827{,}244 \end{array}$$

Multiplication by numbers near 100, as 98, 97, 96, etc., and by numbers near 1,000, as 997, 996, etc.—This method is of value in finding the net proceeds of some amount less 2%, 3%, etc., and also in many other situations.

Multiply the number by 100 (or 1,000) and subtract the product of the multiplicand and the difference between 100 (or 1,000) and the exact multiplier.

EXAMPLE

Multiply 3,247 by 97.

Solution

Multiply the number by 100, and subtract 3 times the number.

$$\begin{array}{r} 324{,}700 = 3{,}247 \times 100 \\ 9{,}741 = 3{,}247 \times 3 \\ \hline 314{,}959 = 3{,}247 \times 97 \end{array}$$

Multiplication of two numbers, each near 100, 1,000, etc.—Products of numbers in this class may be calculated mentally.

EXAMPLE 1

Multiply 96 by 98.

Explanation.—Step 1. Multiply the complements of the two numbers, and, if the product occupies units' place only, prefix a cipher. Result, 08.

Step 2. Subtract the complement of one number from the other number, and write the result at the left of the result in Step 1. The complement of either number subtracted from the other number leaves the same remainder; as, 96 — 2 or 98 — 4 each equal 94. Answer: 9,408.

Solution

	Complement
96	4
98	2
9408	

EXAMPLE 2

Multiply 996 by 988.

Solution

	Complement
996	4
988	12
984,048	

Explanation.—When numbers near 1,000 are multiplied, ciphers are prefixed to the product of the complements, so that the product occupies three places.

Multiplying by numbers a little larger than 100, as 101, 102, etc.—Annex two ciphers to the multiplicand, and to this add the product of the multiplicand and the units' figure of the multiplier. Annex three ciphers for multipliers over 1,000.

EXAMPLE

Multiply 3,475 by 104.

Solution

347,500	
13,900	(4 × 3,475)
361,400	

Multiplication of two numbers, each a little more than 100. To the sum of the numbers (omitting one digit in the hundreds' column), annex two ciphers, and add the product of the supplements (excess over 100).

EXAMPLE

Multiply 112 by 113.

Solution

```
  112
  113
12500  (sum of numbers, with one digit in the hundreds' column omitted)
  156  (product of supplements, 12 × 13)
12656
```

Explanation.—In instances similar to the foregoing, a knowledge of the multiplication tables to 20 × 20 makes mental results possible, and is invaluable in inventory and other extensions.

Mental multiplication by a single method.—Instead of using the various methods of rapid multiplication for different multipliers explained in the preceding pages, it is possible to use one method for all two- and three-digit multipliers. The following explanation is adapted from *Mental Multiplication, How to Figure Mentally,* by Charles Lipkin, C.P.A.

Mental multiplication with two-digit multipliers.—The multiplying is done downward. In multiplying by the units' digit of the multiplier, put the answer down, but only in one digit, and carry the rest. Thus, in multiplying 6 by 7, answer 42, put down 2 and carry 4. In multiplying by any other digit of the multiplier except the units' digit, do not put the answer down, but carry, except at the end.

EXAMPLES

```
                                          439
                                         × 11
9 × 11 = 99, carry 9 ......................  9
9 + 3 × 11 = 42, carry 4 ................   29
4 + 4 × 11 = 48 ........................  4829

                                          439
                                         × 75
9 × 75 = 675, carry 67 ..................    5
67 — 3 × 75 = 292, carry 29 .........       25
29 — 4 × 75 = 329 ......................  32925
```

In the above examples knowledge of the multiplication tables was assumed. Assuming now that no multiplication table is known above 9×9, the process is as follows: Multiply downward as above. Set down the partial product's *units'* digit when multiplying by the *units'* figure of the multiplier; always carry the *entire* partial product when multiplying by the *tens'* figure of the two-digit multiplier.

EXAMPLES

	439
	$\times$ 11
$9 \times 1 =$	9
$9 \times 1 = 9$, carry 9	
$9 + 3 \times 1 = 12$, carry 1	29
$1 + 3 \times 1 = 4$, carry 4	
$4 + 4 \times 1 = 8$	829
$4 \times 1 = 4$	4829

	439
	$\times$ 75
$9 \times 5 = 45$, carry 4	5
$4 + 9 \times 7 = 67$, carry 67	
$67 + 3 \times 5 = 82$, carry 8	25
$8 + 3 \times 7 = 29$, carry 29	
$29 + 4 \times 5 = 49$, carry 4	925
$4 + 4 \times 7 = 32$	32925

Mental multiplication with three-digit multipliers.—In multiplying by a number of three digits, consider such multiplier as consisting of *two* figures: a *tens'* figure of *one* digit (the hundreds' digit of the multiplier), and a *units'* figure of *two* digits (the tens' and units' digits of the multiplier); thus, 119 is seen as 1 19, 223 as 2 23, etc.

EXAMPLES

	439
	$\times$ 119
$9 \times 19 = 171$, carry 17	1
$17 + 3 \times 19 + 90$ (9 of 439×10) $= 164$, carry 16	41
$16 + 4 \times 19 + 30$ (3 of 439×10) $= 122$, carry 12	241
$12 + 40$ (4 of 439×10) $= 52$	52241

	439
	× 327
9 × 27 = 243, carry 24	3
24 — 3 × 27 — 270 (9 of 439 × 30) = 375, carry 37	53
37 — 4 × 27 — 90 (3 of 439 × 30) = 235, carry 23	553
23 — 120 (4 of 439 × 30) = 143	143553

How to abbreviate decimal multiplication when a given number of decimal places is required.—It is a waste of time to carry out decimal multiplication to a denomination smaller than that in which the data are expressed; often it is unnecessary to carry it beyond the third or fourth decimal.

EXAMPLE

Multiply 4.7892 by 3.1765, and obtain the answer correct to four decimal places.

Solution

4.7892		= multiplicand
56713		= multiplier reversed
14.3676		= 4.7892 × 3.
.4789	2	= 4.789~~2~~ × .1
.3325	4 ~~4~~	= 4.78~~92~~ × .07
. 287	3 ~~5~~ ~~2~~	= 4.7~~892~~ × .006
. 23	9 ~~4~~ ~~6~~ ~~0~~	= 4.~~7892~~ × .0005
15.2128	~~0~~ ~~3~~ ~~8~~ ~~0~~	

Explanation.—The multiplier, 3.1765, is written in the reverse order, 56713, the units' digit being placed under the lowest order of the multiplicand that is desired in the product—ten thousandths. Multiply by each digit of the reversed multiplier, beginning with that digit of the multiplicand which stands directly above the digit of the multiplier used, taking care to include the digit carried over from the multiplication of the one (or two) rejected digits at the right.

Multiplication by use of a table of multiples.—It is not uncommon to have to use the same number many times in making calculations, especially in cost accounting. A saving of time and increased accuracy in the work are achieved if a table of multiples of the number is constructed. Suppose that you have to perform a number of multiplications in which 326,834 is one of the factors. A table of multiples may be constructed with an adding machine by locking the repeat key. Subtotal after each pull of the handle. The subtotals should check with the product column shown below. If the table is prepared by repeated additions, and not with an adding machine, the 10th product should be computed, as it will verify all, unless there are compensating errors in the work.

TABLE OF MULTIPLES

Multiplier		*Product*
1		326,834
2 (326,834 + 326,834)	....	653,668
3 (653,668 + 326,834)	....	980,502
4 (980,502 + 326,834)	....	1,307,336
5 (1,307,336 + 326,834)	....	1,634,170
6 (1,634,170 + 326,834)	....	1,961,004
7 (1,961,004 + 326,834)	....	2,287,838
8 (2,287,838 + 326,834)	....	2,614,672
9 (2,614,672 + 326,834)	....	2,941,506

Verification

10 (2,941,506 + 326,834)	....	3,268,340

EXAMPLE

Multiply 326,834 by 5,249.

Solution

2941506 = 9 times 326,834
1307336 = 4 times 326,834
653668 = 2 times 326,834
1634170 = 5 times 326,834

1715551666 = product

HANDY MULTIPLICATION AND DIVISION TABLE

1	2	3	4	5	6	7	8	9	10	11	12	13	14	15	16	17	18	19	20	21	22	23	24	25	
2	**4**	6	8	10	12	14	16	18	20	22	24	26	28	30	32	34	36	38	40	42	44	46	48	50	**2**
3	6	**9**	12	15	18	21	24	27	30	33	36	39	42	45	48	51	54	57	60	63	66	69	72	75	**3**
4	8	12	**16**	20	24	28	32	36	40	44	48	52	56	60	64	68	72	76	80	84	88	92	96	100	**4**
5	10	15	20	**25**	30	35	40	45	50	55	60	65	70	75	80	85	90	95	100	105	110	115	120	125	**5**
6	12	18	24	30	**36**	42	48	54	60	66	72	78	84	90	96	102	108	114	120	126	132	138	144	150	**6**
7	14	21	28	35	42	**49**	56	63	70	77	84	91	98	105	112	119	126	133	140	147	154	161	168	175	**7**
8	16	24	32	40	48	56	**64**	72	80	88	96	104	112	120	128	136	144	152	160	168	176	184	192	200	**8**
9	18	27	36	45	54	63	72	**81**	90	99	108	117	126	135	144	153	162	171	180	189	198	207	216	225	**9**
10	20	30	40	50	60	70	80	90	**100**	110	120	130	140	150	160	170	180	190	200	210	220	230	240	250	**10**
11	22	33	44	55	66	77	88	99	110	**121**	132	143	154	165	176	187	198	209	220	231	242	253	264	275	**11**
12	24	36	48	60	72	84	96	108	120	132	**144**	156	168	180	192	204	216	228	240	252	264	276	288	300	**12**
13	26	39	52	65	78	91	104	117	130	143	156	**169**	182	195	208	221	234	247	260	273	286	299	312	325	**13**
14	28	42	56	70	84	98	112	126	140	154	168	182	**196**	210	224	238	252	266	280	294	308	322	336	350	**14**
15	30	45	60	75	90	105	120	135	150	165	180	195	210	**225**	240	255	270	285	300	315	330	345	360	375	**15**
16	32	48	64	80	96	112	128	144	160	176	192	208	224	240	**256**	272	288	304	320	336	352	368	384	400	**16**
17	34	51	68	85	102	119	136	153	170	187	204	221	238	255	272	**289**	306	323	340	357	374	391	408	425	**17**
18	36	54	72	90	108	126	144	162	180	198	216	234	252	270	288	306	**324**	342	360	378	396	414	432	450	**18**
19	38	57	76	95	114	133	152	171	190	209	228	247	266	285	304	323	342	**361**	380	399	418	437	456	475	**19**
20	40	60	80	100	120	140	160	180	200	220	240	260	280	300	320	340	360	380	**400**	420	440	460	480	500	**20**
21	42	63	84	105	126	147	168	189	210	231	252	273	294	315	336	357	378	399	420	**441**	462	483	504	525	**21**
22	44	66	88	110	132	154	176	198	220	242	264	286	308	330	352	374	396	418	440	462	**484**	506	528	550	**22**
23	46	69	92	115	138	161	184	207	230	253	276	299	322	345	368	391	414	437	460	483	506	**529**	552	575	**23**
24	48	72	96	120	144	168	192	216	240	264	288	312	336	360	384	408	432	456	480	504	528	552	**576**	600	**24**
25	50	75	100	125	150	175	200	225	250	275	300	325	350	375	400	425	450	475	500	525	550	575	600	**625**	**25**
	2	**3**	**4**	**5**	**6**	**7**	**8**	**9**	**10**	**11**	**12**	**13**	**14**	**15**	**16**	**17**	**18**	**19**	**20**	**21**	**22**	**23**	**24**	**25**	

Multiplication.—A number in the top line multiplied by a number in the column at the extreme left produces the number shown where the top line and the side line meet. *Example:* 17 × 14 = 238.

Division.—A number in the table divided by the number at the top of that column produces the number shown in the column at the extreme left. Also, a number in the table divided by the number in the column at the extreme left produces the number shown at the top of that column. *Example:* 266 ÷ 14 = 19.

Division

TABLE OF SHORT CUTS IN DIVISION

To divide by				
$1\frac{1}{4}$	multiply by	8	and divide by	10
$1\frac{2}{3}$	"	6	" "	10
$2\frac{1}{2}$	"	4	" "	10
$3\frac{1}{3}$	"	3	" "	10
$3\frac{3}{4}$	"	8	" "	30
$6\frac{1}{4}$	"	16	" "	100
$7\frac{1}{2}$	"	4	" "	30
$8\frac{1}{3}$	"	12	" "	100
$9\frac{1}{11}$	"	11	" "	100
$11\frac{1}{9}$	"	9	" "	100
$12\frac{1}{2}$	"	8	" "	100
$14\frac{2}{7}$	"	7	" "	100
$16\frac{2}{3}$	"	6	" "	100
25	"	4	" "	100
$31\frac{1}{4}$	"	16	" "	500
$33\frac{1}{3}$	"	3	" "	100
75	"	4	" "	300
125	"	8	" "	1,000
175	"	4	" "	700
275	"	4	" "	1,100
375	"	8	" "	3,000
625	"	8	" "	5,000
875	"	8	" "	7,000

Division by use of a table of multiples.—If a number of divisions are to be made with the same divisor, it is advantageous to set up a table of multiples of the divisor.

EXAMPLE

Assume that 328 is to be used a number of times as a divisor, and that one of the dividends is 587,954.

TABLE OF MULTIPLES

Multiplier	*Product*
1	328
2	656
3	984
4	1,312
5	1,640
6	1,968
7	2,296
8	2,624
9	2,952

Explanation.—Inspection shows the first digit in the quotient to be 1. The second partial dividend is 2,599. The table of multiples shows the largest product contained therein to be 2,296, opposite 7. The third partial dividend is 3,035, and the table of multiples shows the largest product contained therein to be 2,952, opposite 9. The fourth partial dividend is 834, and the largest product contained therein is 656, opposite 2. The remainder is 178. The fraction $\frac{178}{328}$ may be reduced to $\frac{89}{164}$, or it may be changed to a decimal.

Solution

```
328)587954(1792 89/164
    328
    2599
    2296
     3035
     2952
      834        178   89
      656        --- = ---
      178        328   164
```

Division in this manner is rapid, as no time is lost through selection of a quotient so large that when the product is found it exceeds the dividend, necessitating another trial.

Reciprocals in division.—The reciprocal of any number is found by dividing 1 by the number. The reciprocal of 5 is $1 \div 5$, or .2, and the reciprocal of 25 is $1 \div 25$, or .04.

The quotient in a division may be found by multiplying the dividend by the reciprocal of the divisor. Hence, in instances in which it is necessary to find what percent each item is of the total of the items, the use of the reciprocal of the divisor will save time and provide a check on these computations.

Procedure: To find what percent each item is of the total of the items:

1. Divide 1 by the total of the items to obtain the reciprocal of the total.

2. Using the result obtained in 1 as a fixed multiplier, multiply each of the individual items, and the respective results obtained will be the percentages that the individual items are of the total sum.

EXAMPLE

Find the percentage that each department's monthly expense is of the total monthly expense.

Department	*Expense*
A	$ 600.00
B	500.00
C	1,200.00
D	700.00
E	1,000.00
Total	$4,000.00

Solution

Divide 1 by 4,000 to obtain the reciprocal, .00025. Multiply the expense of each department by this reciprocal, and the product will be the percentage that the department's expense is of the total expense.

Department	*Expense*		*Reciprocal*		*Per Cent*
A	$ 600.00	×	.00025	=	15 %
B	500.00	×	.00025	=	12½%
C	1,200.00	×	.00025	=	30 %
D	700.00	×	.00025	=	17½%
E	1,000.00	×	.00025	=	25 %
Total	$4,000.00				100 %

The foregoing method of calculating the rate percentage has a great many applications.

Division of decimals.—Division of decimals may often be abbreviated, especially when the divisor is given to a greater number of decimal places than are contained in the dividend, and when only three or four decimals are essential in the quotient.

EXAMPLE

Divide 4.39876 by 2.4871934, and obtain the quotient correct to three decimal places.

Solution

Ordinary Method	*Abbreviated Method*
2.4871934)4.398 7600 (1.768	2.487 1934)4.398 7(1.768
2 487 1934	2 487 2
1 911 56660	1 911 5
1 741 03538	1 741 0
170 531220	170 5
149 231604	149 2
21 2996160	21 3
19 8975472	19 9
1 4020688	1 4

Explanation.—Observation of the ordinary method shows that the third decimal place in the quotient is not affected by the digit in the third decimal place in the divisor (except through the digits carried).

Since the units' digit of the divisor is contained in the units' digit of the dividend, the first digit in the quotient is in the units' place, and, as three decimal places are required, the quotient will contain four digits. Therefore, the last four digits of the divisor will not affect the quotient, except through the digits carried over.

The first four digits of the divisor, 2.487, are contained once in 4.398. Multiplication of that part of the divisor used, by the quotient digit (including the digit carried over from the one or two following digits—in this case considering the 9 as a unit and adding it to the 1, making 2) gives 24872, and this result deducted from the previous dividend leaves 1911 5 for the new dividend.

Cancel the right-hand digit, 7, of the divisor, and divide 1911 by 248, obtaining the quotient 7. Multiplying the divisor by 7 (and including the carrying digit) gives 1741 0, and subtracting leaves a new dividend of 170 5.

Cancel another digit, 8, of the divisor, and divide by 24. This is contained 6 times in 170. The product (including the digit carried over) is 149 2, and this product subtracted leaves a new dividend of 21 3.

Cancel another digit, 4, of the divisor. Divide 21 by 2, using the carried digit; the result is 8. The new product is 19 9, and this product subtracted from 21 3 leaves a remainder of 1 4.

Fractions

Kinds of fractions.—There are two ways of writing fractions: $\frac{3}{4}$ is a common fraction; .75, or 0.75, is a decimal fraction.

A proper fraction is a fraction that has a numerator smaller than its denominator; for example, $\frac{3}{4}$.

An improper fraction is a fraction that has a numerator greater than its denominator; for example, $\frac{4}{3}$

A mixed number is a whole number and a fraction; for example, $23\frac{2}{5}$.

Multiplication of any two mixed numbers ending in ½.—

1. *When the sum of the whole numbers is an even number.*—To the product of the whole numbers, add one half of their sum, and annex $\frac{1}{4}$.

EXAMPLE

Multiply $24\frac{1}{2}$ by $8\frac{1}{2}$.

Solution

$24\frac{1}{2}$	
$8\frac{1}{2}$	
192	(8×24)
16	($\frac{1}{2}$ of the sum of 24 and 8)
$208\frac{1}{4}$	($\frac{1}{4}$ annexed)

2. *When the sum of the whole numbers is an odd number.*—To the product of the whole numbers, add one half of their sum, less 1, and annex $\frac{3}{4}$.

EXAMPLE

Multiply $15\frac{1}{2}$ by $6\frac{1}{2}$.

Solution

$15\frac{1}{2}$	
$6\frac{1}{2}$	
90	(6×15)
10	($\frac{1}{2}$ of $15 + 6 - 1$)
$100\frac{3}{4}$	($\frac{3}{4}$ annexed)

Multiplication of a mixed number by a mixed number.—

EXAMPLE

Multiply $524\frac{1}{2}$ by $27\frac{1}{3}$.

Solution

$$
\begin{array}{rcl}
524\frac{1}{2} & & \\
\underline{27\frac{1}{3}} & & \\
14148 & 6 & = \text{common denominator of fractions} \\
174\frac{2}{3} & 4 & \\
13\frac{1}{2} & 3 & \left.\right\} = \text{numerators of changed fractions} \\
\frac{1}{6} & 1 & \\
\hline
14336\frac{1}{3} & \frac{8}{6} & = 1\frac{1}{3}
\end{array}
$$

Explanation.—Multiply 524 by 27, obtaining the first part of the answer, 14,148. Next, take $\frac{1}{3}$ of 524, obtaining $174\frac{2}{3}$. Then take $\frac{1}{2}$ of 27, obtaining $13\frac{1}{2}$. Finally, take $\frac{1}{3}$ of $\frac{1}{2}$, obtaining $\frac{1}{6}$. Add the four partial products, and the complete product is $14,336\frac{1}{3}$.

How to use aliquot parts.—An aliquot part of any number is a part which will be contained in that number without leaving a remainder. Thus, 5, 10, 20, and 50 are aliquot parts of 100; that is, $5 = \frac{1}{20}$ of 100, $10 = \frac{1}{10}$ of 100, etc.

As a means of saving time in multiplication and in division, it is convenient to know the decimal equivalent of a common fraction, or, conversely, to know the common fraction equivalent to a decimal fraction. The table on page 124 will be useful in this connection.

Multiplication by aliquot parts.—

EXAMPLE

Find $16\frac{2}{3}\%$ of \$475.34.

Solution

$$
\begin{array}{r}
6\overline{)\$475.34} \\
\hline
\$79.22
\end{array}
$$

Explanation.—Since $.16\frac{2}{3}$ equals $\frac{1}{6}$, find $\frac{1}{6}$ of \$475.34.

EXAMPLE

Find the cost of 256 units at $37\frac{1}{2}$¢ each.

ALIQUOT PARTS OF 1

(Decimal Equivalents of Common Fractions)

Common Fraction	*Decimal Equivalent*	*Common Fraction*	*Decimal Equivalent*
$\frac{1}{2}$	.50	$\frac{11}{12}$	$.91\frac{2}{3}$
$\frac{1}{3}$	$.33\frac{1}{3}$	$\frac{1}{16}$	$.06\frac{1}{4}$
$\frac{2}{3}$	$.66\frac{2}{3}$	$\frac{3}{16}$	$.18\frac{3}{4}$
$\frac{1}{4}$	.25	$\frac{5}{16}$	$.31\frac{1}{4}$
$\frac{3}{4}$	.75	$\frac{7}{16}$	$.43\frac{3}{4}$
$\frac{1}{5}$	.20	$\frac{9}{16}$	$.56\frac{1}{4}$
$\frac{2}{5}$	.40	$\frac{11}{16}$	$.68\frac{3}{4}$
$\frac{3}{5}$	.60	$\frac{15}{16}$	$.93\frac{3}{4}$
$\frac{4}{5}$	.80	$\frac{1}{24}$	$.04\frac{1}{6}$
$\frac{1}{6}$	$.16\frac{2}{3}$	$\frac{5}{24}$	$.20\frac{5}{6}$
$\frac{5}{6}$	$.83\frac{1}{3}$	$\frac{7}{24}$	$.29\frac{1}{6}$
$\frac{1}{7}$	$.14\frac{2}{7}$	$\frac{9}{24}$	$.37\frac{1}{2}$
$\frac{2}{7}$	$.28\frac{4}{7}$	$\frac{11}{24}$	$.45\frac{5}{6}$
$\frac{3}{7}$	$.42\frac{6}{7}$	$\frac{13}{24}$	$.54\frac{1}{6}$
$\frac{4}{7}$	$.57\frac{1}{7}$	$\frac{17}{24}$	$.70\frac{5}{6}$
$\frac{5}{7}$	$.71\frac{3}{7}$	$\frac{19}{24}$	$.79\frac{1}{6}$
$\frac{6}{7}$	$.85\frac{5}{7}$	$\frac{23}{24}$	$.95\frac{5}{6}$
$\frac{1}{8}$	$.12\frac{1}{2}$	$\frac{1}{32}$	$.03\frac{1}{8}$
$\frac{3}{8}$	$.37\frac{1}{2}$	$\frac{3}{32}$	$.09\frac{3}{8}$
$\frac{5}{8}$	$.62\frac{1}{2}$	$\frac{5}{32}$	$.15\frac{5}{8}$
$\frac{7}{8}$	$.87\frac{1}{2}$	$\frac{7}{32}$	$.21\frac{7}{8}$
$\frac{1}{9}$	$.11\frac{1}{9}$	$\frac{9}{32}$	$.28\frac{1}{8}$
$\frac{2}{9}$	$.22\frac{2}{9}$	$\frac{11}{32}$	$.34\frac{3}{8}$
$\frac{4}{9}$	$.44\frac{4}{9}$	$\frac{13}{32}$	$.40\frac{5}{8}$
$\frac{5}{9}$	$.55\frac{5}{9}$	$\frac{15}{32}$	$.46\frac{7}{8}$
$\frac{7}{9}$	$.77\frac{7}{9}$	$\frac{17}{32}$	$.53\frac{1}{8}$
$\frac{8}{9}$	$.88\frac{8}{9}$	$\frac{19}{32}$	$.59\frac{3}{8}$
$\frac{1}{10}$	.10	$\frac{21}{32}$	$.65\frac{5}{8}$
$\frac{3}{10}$	.30	$\frac{23}{32}$	$.71\frac{7}{8}$
$\frac{7}{10}$	.70	$\frac{25}{32}$	$.78\frac{1}{8}$
$\frac{9}{10}$	.90	$\frac{27}{32}$	$.84\frac{3}{8}$
$\frac{1}{12}$	$.08\frac{1}{3}$	$\frac{29}{32}$	$.90\frac{5}{8}$
$\frac{5}{12}$	$.41\frac{2}{3}$	$\frac{31}{32}$	$.96\frac{7}{8}$
$\frac{7}{12}$	$.58\frac{1}{3}$		

Note.—The fractions in the above table can be extended as decimals as far as the work demands.

Solution

$$256 \times \frac{3}{8} \times \$1 = \$96$$

Explanation.—$37\frac{1}{2}$¢ is $\frac{3}{8}$ of \$1. Therefore, $256 \times \frac{3}{8} \times \$1 = \$96$.

Division by aliquot parts.—It is difficult to divide a number by a mixed number. If the divisor is an aliquot part, the quotient may be found by multiplication, as follows:

EXAMPLE

Divide 4,875 by $16\frac{2}{3}$.

Solution

$$\begin{array}{r} 48.75 \\ 6 \\ \hline 292.50 \end{array}$$

Explanation.—Since $16\frac{2}{3}$ is $\frac{1}{6}$ of 100, divide 4,875 by $\frac{1}{6}$ of 100, or $\frac{100}{6}$. This is the same as multiplying by $\frac{6}{100}$. Therefore, divide by 100 by pointing off two decimal places from the right, and multiply the result by 6. The answer is 292.50, or $292\frac{1}{2}$.

EXAMPLE

The production cost of 1,250 units is \$3,170. Find the cost per unit.

Solution

$$\begin{array}{r} .3170 \\ 8 \\ \hline \$2.5360 \end{array}$$

Explanation.—1,250 is $\frac{1}{8}$ of 10,000. Divide \$3,170 by 10,000 by pointing off 4 decimal places from the right; then multiply the result by 8. The cost per unit is found to be \$2.536.

14. EXPEDITING CALCULATIONS WITH PREPARED TABLES

Specially prepared tables.—Companies that have to make frequent calculations of various types can have special tables prepared to insure accuracy and speed, or they can purchase prepared tables that meet their needs. Two examples of such tables are given on pages 127 and 128.

Prorating of insurance premiums expedited by charts.—Prorating of insurance premiums, which occurs through changes in car coverages during the policy period, has been expedited for the State Farm Insurance Companies, Illinois, by the use of calculators prepared by Meilicke Systems, Inc., Chicago, Illinois.

The calculators consist of 180 cards, one for each day of a six-month period. Each card, which is $8 \times 5\frac{1}{4}$ inches, carries the pro-rata unearned premium for a particular period for the amounts of $1 to $15, with 5-cent divisions. For instance, suppose the unearned premium is wanted on a policy that has run 4 months 6 days. The card for this period is examined, and the unearned premium under $12 is noted. Reference to the card reproduced in Fig. 3 shows that it is $3.60. If the premium were $12.20, the unearned premium would be $3.66. The earned premium is easily found by subtracting the unearned premium from the full premium.

The cards are kept on a small metal container for easy handling. The cost of these calculators is about 7% of the cost of electrically operating calculating machines. This cost included making 54,000 necessary calculations, for which the accuracy was guaranteed by Meilicke Systems, Inc.

The user of this system points out these additional advantages: (1) the life of the calculators will be at least as long as the average calculating machine; (2) no maintenance is required; (3) calculators are conveniently kept on the desk of the individuals using them, and occupy less space than the average calculating machine.

Freight-rate calculator with prefigured totals improves calculation efficiency.—Freight-rate calculation efficiency increased 50%, auditing efficiency 200%, and labor cost decreased 75% in a trucking company after it had purchased two sets of prefigured freight-charge computations. Each set consists of loose-leaf sheets in a binder, each sheet consisting of two banks of figures, the upper bank showing totals in units from 1 to 100, and the lower bank totals in hundreds from 100 to 10,000. A supplementary row at the bottom shows totals in steps of 10,000 up to 70,000 (see Fig. 4, page 128, which shows these calculations for a multiplier of 68). The freight-rate calculator gives immediate and accurate totals with no mental dis-

4 MO. **6**

			1		2		3		4		5		6		7		8		9		10		11		12		13		14
			30		60		90		120		150		180		210		240		270		300		330		360		390		420
5	02	*5*	32	*5*	62	*5*	92	*5*	122	*5*	152	*5*	182	*5*	212	*5*	242	*5*	272	*5*	302	*5*	332	*5*	362	*5*	392	*5*	422
10	03	*10*	33	*10*	63	*10*	93	*10*	123	*10*	153	*10*	183	*10*	213	*10*	243	*10*	273	*10*	303	*10*	333	*10*	363	*10*	393	*10*	423
15	05	*15*	35	*15*	65	*15*	95	*15*	125	*15*	155	*15*	185	*15*	215	*15*	245	*15*	275	*15*	305	*15*	335	*15*	365	*15*	395	*15*	425
20	06	*20*	36	*20*	66	*20*	96	*20*	126	*20*	156	*20*	186	*20*	216	*20*	246	*20*	276	*20*	306	*20*	336	*20*	366	*20*	396	*20*	426
25	08	*25*	38	*25*	68	*25*	98	*25*	128	*25*	158	*25*	188	*25*	218	*25*	248	*25*	278	*25*	308	*25*	338	*25*	368	*25*	398	*25*	428
30	09	*30*	39	*30*	69	*30*	99	*30*	129	*30*	159	*30*	189	*30*	219	*30*	249	*30*	279	*30*	309	*30*	339	*30*	369	*30*	399	*30*	429
35	11	*35*	41	*35*	71	*35*	101	*35*	131	*35*	161	*35*	191	*35*	221	*35*	251	*35*	281	*35*	311	*35*	341	*35*	371	*35*	401	*35*	431
40	12	*40*	42	*40*	72	*40*	102	*40*	132	*40*	162	*40*	192	*40*	222	*40*	252	*40*	282	*40*	312	*40*	342	*40*	372	*40*	402	*40*	432
45	14	*45*	44	*45*	74	*45*	104	*45*	134	*45*	164	*45*	194	*45*	224	*45*	254	*45*	284	*45*	314	*45*	344	*45*	374	*45*	404	*45*	434
50	15	*50*	45	*50*	75	*50*	105	*50*	135	*50*	165	*50*	195	*50*	225	*50*	255	*50*	285	*50*	315	*50*	345	*50*	375	*50*	405	*50*	435
55	17	*55*	47	*55*	77	*55*	107	*55*	137	*55*	167	*55*	197	*55*	227	*55*	257	*55*	287	*55*	317	*55*	347	*55*	377	*55*	407	*55*	437
60	18	*60*	48	*60*	78	*60*	108	*60*	138	*60*	168	*60*	198	*60*	228	*60*	258	*60*	288	*60*	318	*60*	348	*60*	378	*60*	408	*60*	438
65	20	*65*	50	*65*	80	*65*	110	*65*	140	*65*	170	*65*	200	*65*	230	*65*	260	*65*	290	*65*	320	*65*	350	*65*	380	*65*	410	*65*	440
70	21	*70*	51	*70*	81	*70*	111	*70*	141	*70*	171	*70*	201	*70*	231	*70*	261	*70*	291	*70*	321	*70*	351	*70*	381	*70*	411	*70*	441
75	23	*75*	53	*75*	83	*75*	113	*75*	143	*75*	173	*75*	203	*75*	233	*75*	263	*75*	293	*75*	323	*75*	353	*75*	383	*75*	413	*75*	443
80	24	*80*	54	*80*	84	*80*	114	*80*	144	*80*	174	*80*	204	*80*	234	*80*	264	*80*	294	*80*	324	*80*	354	*80*	384	*80*	414	*80*	444
85	26	*85*	56	*85*	86	*85*	116	*85*	146	*85*	176	*85*	206	*85*	236	*85*	266	*85*	296	*85*	326	*85*	356	*85*	386	*85*	416	*85*	446
90	27	*90*	57	*90*	87	*90*	117	*90*	147	*90*	177	*90*	207	*90*	237	*90*	267	*90*	297	*90*	327	*90*	357	*90*	387	*90*	417	*90*	447
95	29	*95*	59	*95*	89	*95*	119	*95*	149	*95*	179	*95*	209	*95*	239	*95*	269	*95*	299	*95*	329	*95*	359	*95*	389	*95*	419	*95*	449
																												1500	450

MEILICKE SYSTEMS, Inc.
3466 N. Clark St., Chicago, Ill.
Pat. Aug. 10, 1915—Feb. 19, 1929

Figure 3.—Calculator for Pro-rating Insurance Premiums.

[actual size 8″ × 5¼″]

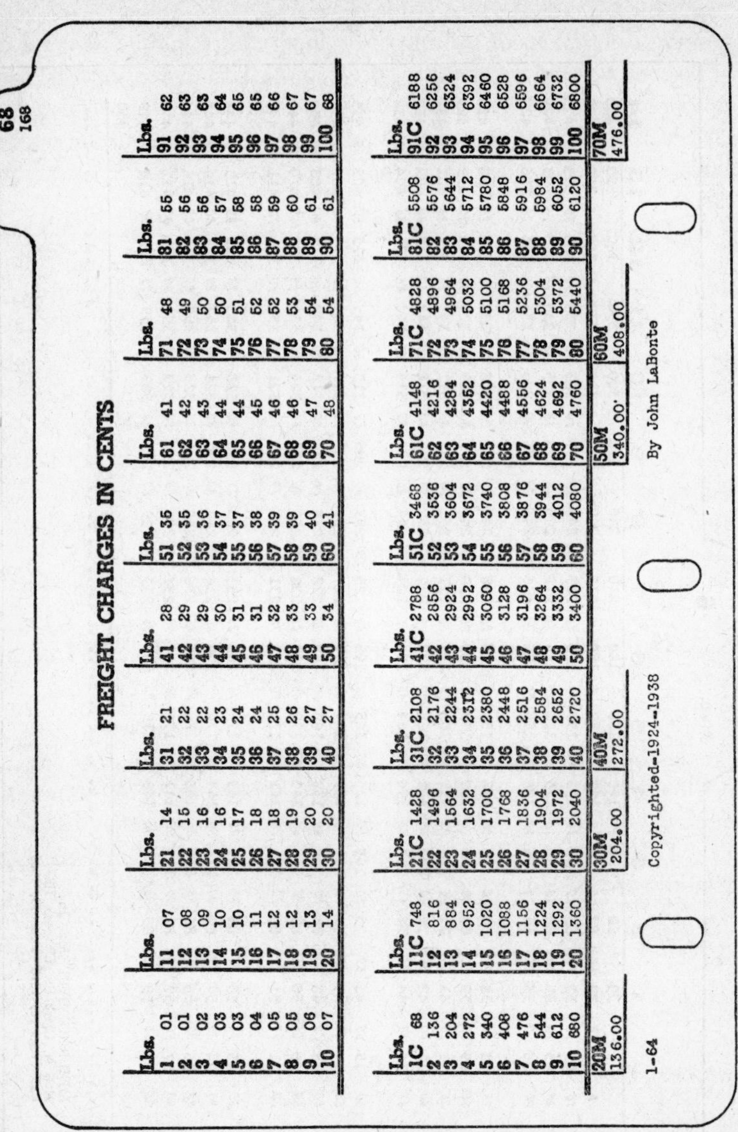

68
168

FREIGHT CHARGES IN CENTS

Lbs.		Lbs.		Lbs.		Lbs.		Lbs.		Lbs.		Lbs.		Lbs.		Lbs.		Lbs.	
1	01	11	07	21	14	31	21	41	28	51	35	61	41	71	48	81	55	91	62
2	01	12	08	22	15	32	22	42	29	52	35	62	42	72	49	82	56	92	63
3	02	13	09	23	16	33	22	43	29	53	36	63	43	73	50	83	56	93	63
4	03	14	10	24	16	34	23	44	30	54	37	64	44	74	50	84	57	94	64
5	03	15	10	25	17	35	24	45	31	55	37	65	44	75	51	85	58	95	65
6	04	16	11	26	18	36	24	46	31	56	38	66	45	76	52	86	58	96	65
7	05	17	12	27	18	37	25	47	32	57	39	67	46	77	52	87	59	97	66
8	05	18	12	28	19	38	26	48	33	58	39	68	46	78	53	88	60	98	67
9	06	19	13	29	20	39	27	49	33	59	40	69	47	79	54	89	61	99	67
10	07	20	14	30	20	40	27	50	34	60	41	70	48	80	54	90	61	100	68

Lbs.		Lbs.		Lbs.		Lbs.		Lbs.		Lbs.		Lbs.		Lbs.		Lbs.		Lbs.	
1C	68	11C	748	21C	1428	31C	2108	41C	2788	51C	3468	61C	4148	71C	4828	81C	5508	91C	6188
2	136	12	816	22	1496	32	2176	42	2856	52	3536	62	4216	72	4896	82	5576	92	6256
3	204	13	884	23	1564	33	2244	43	2924	53	3604	63	4284	73	4964	83	5644	93	6324
4	272	14	952	24	1632	34	2312	44	2992	54	3672	64	4352	74	5032	84	5712	94	6392
5	340	15	1020	25	1700	35	2380	45	3060	55	3740	65	4420	75	5100	85	5780	95	6460
6	408	16	1088	26	1768	36	2448	46	3128	56	3808	66	4488	76	5168	86	5848	96	6528
7	476	17	1156	27	1836	37	2516	47	3196	57	3876	67	4556	77	5236	87	5916	97	6596
8	544	18	1224	28	1904	38	2584	48	3264	58	3944	68	4624	78	5304	88	5984	98	6664
9	612	19	1292	29	1972	39	2652	49	3332	59	4012	69	4692	79	5372	89	6052	99	6732
10	680	20	1360	30	2040	40	2720	50	3400	60	4080	70	4760	80	5440	90	6120	100	6800

20M	30M	40M	50M	60M	70M
136.00	204.00	272.00	340.00	408.00	476.00

1-64 Copyrighted-1924-1938 By John LaBonte

Figure 4.—Freight Rate Calculator.

(68 refers to multiplier on the side shown, and 168 refers to the multiplier on the reverse side.)

position of fractions or shifting of decimals and is simple to operate.

To compute the freight charges for an LCL shipment of 3280 lbs. at 68 cents per 100 lbs., first refer to the figure opposite 32 in the lower bank ($21.76) and then to the figure opposite 80 in the upper bank ($.54), the total being the freight charge ($22.30) for the shipment.

Another use of the calculator is in the determination of freight-charge proration between two or more carriers, as in a joint haul. Thus, "A" Line gets 37% of the rate and "B" Line 63%. Reference to the lower bank would show that "A" gets 25.16 cents of each 68 cents, and "B" 42.84 cents, or a total of 68 cents for the through rate.

The calculator can also be used for computing payroll earnings. Thus, an employee works 39¾ (39.75) hours at 68 cents per hour. Reference to 39 in the lower bank gives $26.52 as his pay for 39 hours' work, and reference to 75 in the upper bank gives 51 cents as his pay for ¾ hours, making his total paycheck $27.03.

Other applications include inventory and billing extensions.

15. VERIFICATION OF COMPUTATIONS BY CHECK NUMBERS

Adapted from Curtis and Cooper, "Mathematics of Accounting" New York: Prentice-Hall, Inc.

Check numbers obtained by casting out 9's.—A common method of verifying arithmetical computations is by casting out the 9's. This is the simplest of all methods of verification and may be used to good advantage in many cases.

Verification of addition by casting out 9's.—

EXAMPLE

8342	8
8967	3
8378	8
9276	6
8431	7
43394—5	32—5

Explanation.—The sum of the digits of 8,342 is 17 (8 + 3 + 4 + 2). Cast out 9 and set down 8. If a number contains a 9, skip it in adding the digits; thus, in 8,967, 8 + 6 + 7 equals 21. Cast out the nines and set down the excess, 3. Find the check number of each line in the same way. Add the check numbers, and cast the nines out of their sum. Find the check number of the sum of the column being verified. The final check number in each case is 5.

Verification of subtraction by casting out 9's.—

EXAMPLE

7856	8
2138	5
5718	3

Explanation.—7,856 checks 8, and 2,138 checks 5. $8 - 5 = 3$, and 5,718 checks 3.

Verification of multiplication by casting out 9's.—

EXAMPLE

482	5
376	7
181232—8	35—8

Explanation.—482 checks 5, and 376 checks 7. $7 \times 5 = 35$. 35 checks 8, and the product, 181,232, also checks 8.

Verification of division by casting out 9's.—Division may be verified by multiplication; that is, the product of the quotient and the divisor should equal the dividend. Apply the same principle in verifying with check numbers.

EXAMPLE

```
13)76492(5884
   65
   114
   104
    109
    104
      52
      52
```

Explanation.—76,492 checks 1. 13 checks 4. 5,884 checks 7. $4 \times 7 = 28$, and 28 checks 1, which is also the check number of the dividend.

Verification of division where there is a remainder by casting out 9's.—The check number of the remainder added to the product of the check number of the quotient and the check number of the divisor should equal the check number of the dividend.

EXAMPLE

```
32)75892(2371
   64
   118
    96
    292
    224
     52
     32
```

Explanation.—Step 1: The remainder, 20, checks 2. The quotient, 2,371, checks 4. The divisor, 32, checks 5. $2 + (4 \times 5) = 22$, and 22 checks 4.

Step 2: The dividend, 75,892, checks 4.

Step 1 and Step 2 should produce the same check number.

Check figure "11" verifies posting as made.—The check figure "11" for inventory and cost-record posting verifies every posting immediately. Somewhat like the method of casting out 9's, it can be used for arithmetic processes other than posting.

EXAMPLE

Check the following addition:

951.63	2
615.38	4
2,397.43	9
3,964.44	4

Explanation.—Starting with the last digit to the right, add the alternate (odd) figures. Then add the in-between (even) figures. If the former sum is less than the latter, add sufficient multiples of 11 to make it larger. Then subtract the sum of the evens from the sum of the odds.

If the remainder is 11 or over, subtract the largest multiple of 11 less than the remainder. The result is the check figure. Thus, in 951.63, $3 + 1 + 9 = 13$, and $6 + 5 = 11$. $13 - 11 = 2$, the check figure.

In 615.38, $8 + 5 + 6 = 19$, and $3 + 1 = 4$. $19 - 4 = 15$. Since 15 is larger than 11, 11 is subtracted to give the check figure 4.

In 2,397.43, $3 + 7 + 3 = 13$, and $4 + 9 + 2 = 15$. Here 11 must be added to 13 (giving 24) in order to make the odds larger than the evens, and $24 - 15 = 9$.

The total is similarly checked, and the sum of the check figures less the largest possible multiple of 11 gives the check figure for the column total.

This check figure will catch the common error of transposition of adjacent figures, such as posting 2,317.43 as 2,317.34, which the figure 9 will not catch. The check figure 11, however, will not catch the transposition of alternate figures, such as posting 2,317.43 as 2,713.43. Multiplication, division, and subtraction can be verified with the check figure 11 in a manner similar to that described for the check figure 9.

Another method of using check figures in posting.—To use the check figure 11 or other check figures in proving the accuracy of postings from one source to another, determine the check figure for the entry in the ledger (or other record to which the posting is being made), and place that check figure in the check column for the entry in the journal (or other source of the posting), without computing the check figure for the journal entry. If you fail to balance out, determine the check figures for the original data (in this case, the journal entries) and compare with the check figures entered from the ledger sheets. For example, $43,668.94 is posted from journal to ledger as $43,686.94. The check figure for the ledger amount (using the method described in the preceding paragraph) is 0, and is entered opposite $43,668.94 in the check column of the journal. When the figures do not balance out, the journal entry check figures are determined, whereupon the check figure for $43,668.94 is found to be 4, while a 0 appears in the check column, thus indicating the source of error.

This method is more rapid than that of determining both check figures in the beginning.

16. TABLES OF WEIGHTS, MEASURES, AND VALUES

LONG MEASURE

United States Standard

12 inches	1 foot
3 feet	1 yard
5½ yards, or 16½ feet	1 rod
320 rods, or 5,280 feet	1 mile
1,760 yards	1 mile
40 rods	1 furlong
8 furlongs	1 statute mile
3 miles	1 league

Metric System

10 millimeters	1 centimeter
10 centimeters	1 decimeter
10 decimeters	1 meter
10 meters	1 dekameter
10 dekameters	1 hektometer
10 hektometers	1 kilometer
10 kilometers	1 myriameter

Comparisons of Long Measures

1 inch	25.4001 millimeters	1 centimeter	.3937 inch
1 foot	.304801 meter	1 meter	39.37 inches
1 yard	.914402 meter	1 meter	3.28083 feet
1 rod	5.029 meters	1 meter	1.093611 yards
1 mile	1.60935 kilometers	1 kilometer	.62137 mile

SQUARE MEASURE

United States Standard

144 square inches	1 square foot
9 square feet	1 square yard
30¼ square yards	1 square rod
272¼ square feet	1 square rod
40 square rods	1 rood
4 roods	1 acre
160 square rods	1 acre

640 acres	1 square mile
43,560 square feet	1 acre
4,840 square yards	1 acre

Metric System

100 square millimeters	1 square centimeter
100 square centimeters	1 square decimeter
100 square decimeters	1 square meter
100 square meters	1 square dekameter
100 square dekameters	1 square hektometer
100 square hektometers	1 square kilometer
100 square kilometers	1 square myriameter

Comparisons of Square Measures

1 square inch	6.452 square centimeters
1 square foot	.0929 square meter
1 square yard	.8361 square meter
1 square rod	25.293 square meters
1 acre	.40467 hectare
1 square mile	2.59 square kilometers
1 square millimeter	.00155 square inch
1 square centimeter	.155 square inch
1 square meter	10.764 square feet
1 square meter	1.196 square yards
1 square kilometer	.3861 square mile
1 square kilometer	247.11 acres
1 square dekameter, or 1 are	1,076.41 square feet
100 ares = 1 hectare	2.4711 acres

SOLID OR CUBIC MEASURE (VOLUME)

United States Standard

1,728 cubic inches	1 cubic foot
27 cubic feet	1 cubic yard
128 cubic feet	1 cord of wood
$24\frac{3}{4}$ cubic feet	1 perch of stone
2,150.42 cubic inches	1 standard bushel
231 cubic inches	1 standard gallon
40 cubic feet	1 ton (shipping)

Metric System

1,000 cubic millimeters	1 cubic centimeter
1,000 cubic centimeters	1 cubic decimeter
1,000 cubic decimeters	1 cubic meter
1,000 cubic meters	1 cubic dekameter
1,000 cubic dekameters	1 cubic hektometer
1,000 cubic hektometers	1 cubic kilometer
1,000 cubic kilometers	1 cubic myriameter

Comparisons of Solid or Cubic Measures (Volume)

1 cubic inch	16.3872 cubic centimeters
1 cubic foot	.02832 cubic meter
1 cubic yard	.7646 cubic meter
1 cubic centimeter	.061 cubic inch
1 cubic meter	35.314 cubic feet
1 cubic meter	1.3079 cubic yards
1 cubic decimeter = 1 liter	61.023 cubic inches
1 liter	1.05671 liquid quarts
1 liter	.9081 dry quart
1 hectoliter or decistere	3.5314 cubic feet or 2.8375 bushels
1 stere, kiloliter, or cubic meter	1.3079 cubic yards or 28.37 bushels

LIQUID MEASURE (CAPACITY)

United States Standard

4 gills	1 pint
2 pints	1 quart
4 quarts	1 gallon
31½ gallons	1 barrel
2 barrels	1 hogshead
1 gallon	231 cubic inches
7.4805 gallons	1 cubic foot
16 fluid ounces	1 pint
1 fluid ounce	1.805 cubic inches
1 fluid ounce	29.59 cubic centimeters

Metric System

10 milliliters	1 centiliter
10 centiliters	1 deciliter
10 deciliters	1 liter

10 liters	1 dekaliter
10 dekaliters	1 hektoliter
10 hektoliters	1 kiloliter
10 kiloliters	1 myrialiter

DRY MEASURE

United States Standard

2 pints	1 quart
8 quarts	1 peck
4 pecks	1 bushel
2,150.42 cubic inches	1 bushel
1.2445 cubic feet	1 bushel

Metric System

In the metric system the same table is used for both Liquid Measure and Dry Measure.

Comparisons of Liquid and Dry Measures

1 liquid quart	.94636 liter
1 liquid gallon	3.78543 liters
1 dry quart	1.1012 liters
1 peck	8.80982 liters
1 bushel	.35239 hektoliter
1 milliliter	.03381 liquid ounce, or .2705 apothecaries' dram
1 liter = 1 cubic decimeter	61.023 cubic inches .03531 cubic foot .2642 gallon 2.202 pounds of water at 62° F.
28.317 liters	1 cubic foot
3.785 liters	1 gallon

AVOIRDUPOIS MEASURE (WEIGHT)

(Used for weighing all ordinary substances except precious metals, jewels, and drugs)

United States Standard

$27\frac{11}{32}$ grains	1 dram
16 drams	1 ounce

16 ounces	1 pound
25 pounds	1 quarter
4 quarters	1 hundredweight
100 pounds	1 hundredweight
20 hundredweight	1 ton
2,000 pounds	1 short ton
2,240 pounds	1 long ton

Metric System

10 milligrams	1 centigram
10 centigrams	1 decigram
10 decigrams	1 gram
10 grams	1 dekagram
10 dekagrams	1 hektogram
10 hektograms	1 kilogram
10 kilograms	1 myriagram
1,000 kilograms	1 metric ton

TROY MEASURE (WEIGHT)

(Used for weighing gold, silver, and jewels)

24 grains	1 pennyweight
20 pennyweights	1 ounce
12 ounces	1 pound

Comparison of Avoirdupois and Troy Measures

1 pound troy	5,760 grains
1 pound avoirdupois	7,000 grains
1 ounce troy	437½ grains
1 ounce avoirdupois	480 grains
1 karat, or carat	3.2 troy grains
24 karats	pure gold

Comparison of Avoirdupois and Troy Measures with Metric Weights

1 grain	.0648 gram	1 gram	15,4324 grains .03527 ounce (avoir.) .03215 ounce (troy)
1 ounce (avoir.)	28.3495 grams		
1 ounce (troy) ..	31.10348 grams		
1 pound (avoir.)	.45359 kilogram	1 kilogram ..	2.20462 pounds (avoir.) 2.67923 pounds (troy)
1 pound (troy) ..	.37324 kilogram		
		1 tonne, or metric ton..	.9842 ton of 2,240 pounds, or 19.68 hundred-weight 1.1023 tons of 2,000 pounds

1,000 kilograms ..	2,204.6 pounds
1.016 metric tons, or 1,016 kilograms	1 ton of 2,240 pounds
.9072 metric ton....	1 ton of 2,000 pounds

APOTHECARIES' MEASURE (WEIGHT)

(Used for weighing drugs)

20 grains	1 scruple
3 scruples	1 dram
8 drams	1 ounce
12 ounces	1 pound

APOTHECARIES' FLUID MEASURE (CAPACITY)

60 minims	1 fluid dram
8 fluid drams	1 fluid ounce
16 fluid ounces	1 pint
8 pints	1 gallon

Comparisons (Approximate Liquid Measure)

Apothecaries'	*Common*	*Metric*
1 minim	1 to 2 drops	0.06 cu. cm.
60 minims, or		
1 fluid dram	1 teaspoonful	3.75 cu. cm.
2 fluid drams	1 dessertspoonful	7.50 cu. cm.
4 fluid drams	1 tablespoonful	15.00 cu. cm.
8 fluid drams	1 fluid ounce	28.39 cu. cm.
2 fluid ounces	1 wineglassful	59.20 cu. cm.
4 fluid ounces	1 teacupful	118.40 cu. cm.
16 fluid ounces	1 pint	473.11 cu. cm.

Note: Drops are not accurate measures, but for practical purposes it may be considered that one minim equals one drop of watery liquids and fixed oils, but two drops of volatile oils and alcoholic liquids, such as tinctures and fluid extracts.

SURVEYORS' LONG MEASURE

7.92 inches	1 link
25 links	1 rod
4 rods, or 100 links	1 chain
80 chains	1 mile

SURVEYORS' SQUARE MEASURE

625 square links	1 square rod
16 square rods	1 square chain
10 square chains	1 acre
640 acres	1 square mile
36 square miles	1 township

MARINERS' MEASURE

6 feet	1 fathom
120 fathoms	1 cable's length
7½ cable lengths	1 mile
5,280 feet	1 statute mile
6,080 feet	1 nautical mile, or British Admiralty knot
$50.71\frac{11}{15}$ feet	1 knot
120 knots, or	
$1.152\frac{2}{3}$ statute miles	1 nautical or geographical mile

3 geographical miles	1 league
60 geographical miles, or 69.16 statute miles	1 degree of longitude on the equator, or 1 degree of meridian
360 degrees	1 circumference

Note: A knot is properly $\frac{1}{120}$ of a marine mile, but current usage makes it equivalent to a marine mile. Hence, when the speed of vessels at sea is being measured, a knot is equal to a nautical mile, or 6,086.08 feet, or 2,028.69 yards.

CIRCULAR OR ANGULAR MEASURE

60 seconds (60″)	1 minute (1′)
60 minutes (60′)	1 degree (1°)
30 degrees	1 sign
90 degrees	1 right angle or quadrant
360 degrees	1 circumference

Note: One degree at the equator is approximately 60 nautical miles.

COUNTING

12 units or things	1 dozen
12 dozen, or 144 units	1 gross
12 gross	1 great gross
20 units	1 score

UNITED STATES MONEY

10 mills	1 cent
10 cents	1 dime
10 dimes	1 dollar
10 dollars	1 eagle

PAPER MEASURE

24 sheets	1 quire
20 quires	1 ream
2 reams	1 bundle
5 bundles	1 bale

Note: Although a ream contains 480 sheets, 500 sheets are usually sold as a ream.

UNITED STATES AND BRITISH WEIGHTS AND MEASURES COMPARED

1 British Imperial bushel	1.03205 United States (Winchester) bushels
1 United States bushel	.96895 British Imperial bushel
1 British quart	1.03205 United States dry quarts
1 United States dry quart	.96895 British quart
1 British quart (or gallon)	1.20094 United States liquid quarts (or gallons)
1 United States liquid quart (or gallon)	.83268 British quart (or gallon)

METRIC SYSTEM EXPLAINED

(For metric tables of weights and measures see page 133ff.)

The fundamental units of the metric system are the meter—the unit of length, and the kilogram—the unit of mass.

The liter is defined as the volume of a kilogram of water at the temperature of its maximum density, 4° centigrade. All other units are the decimal subdivisions or multiples of these. These three units are simply related. For example, for all practical purposes 1 cubic decimeter equals 1 liter and 1 liter of water weighs 1 kilogram.

The metric tables are formed by combining the words "meter," "gram," and "liter" with the six numerical prefixes, as in the following:

Prefixes *Meaning*		*Units*
milli- = *one-thousandth*	.001	
centi- = *one-hundredth*	.01	"meter" *for length*
deci- = *one-tenth*	.1	"gram" *for weight or mass*
..........*Unit* = *one*	1.	
deka- = *ten*	10	"liter" *for capacity.*
hecto- = *one hundred*	100	
kilo- = *one thousand*	1000	

FOREIGN WEIGHTS AND MEASURES

Denominations	Where Used	American Equivalents
Almude	Portugal	4,422 gals.
Ardeb	Egypt	5.6188 bu.
Are	Metric	0.02471 acre.
Arratel or libra	Portugal	1.0119 lbs.
Arroba	Argentine Republic	25.32 lbs.
"	Brazil	32.38 lbs.
"	Cuba	25.36 lbs.
"	Paraguay	25.32 lbs.
"	Venezuela	25.40 lbs.
" (liquid)	Cuba, Spain, and Venezuela	4.263 gals.
Arshine	Russia	28 in.
" (sq.)	"	5.44 sq. ft.
Artel	Morocco	1.12 lbs.
Baril	Argentine Republic	20.077 gals.
	and Mexico	20.0787 gals.
Barrel	Malta (customs)	11.2 gals.
Berkovets	Russia	361.128 lbs.
Bongkal	Fed. Malay States	832 grains.
Bouw	Sumatra	7,096.5 sq. metrs.
Bu	Japan	0.12 inch.
Bushel	British Empire	1.03205 U. S. bu.
Caffiso	Malta	5.40 gals.
Candy	India (Bombay)	569 lbs.
"	India (Madras)	500 lbs.
Cantar	Egypt	99.05 lbs.
"	Morocco	112 lbs.
"	Turkey	124.45 lbs.
Cantaro	Malta	175 lbs.
Carat, metric	World	3.086 grains.
Catty	China	$1.333\frac{2}{3}$ lbs.
"	Japan	1.32 lbs.
"	Java, Malacca	1.36 lbs.
"	Siam	$2\frac{1}{3}$ lbs.
" (stand.)	Siam	1.32 lbs.
"	Sumatra	2.12 lbs.
Centaro	Central America	4.2631 gals.
Centner	Brunswick	117.5 lbs.
"	Bremen	127.5 lbs.
"	Denmark, Norway	110.23 lbs.
"	Prussia	113.44 lbs.
"	Sweden	93.7 lbs.
"	Double or metric	220.46 lbs.
Chetvert	Russia	5.957 bu.

Denominations	Where Used	American Equivalents
Ch'ih	China	12.60 inches.
" (metric)	China	1 meter.
Cho	Japan	2.451 acres.
Comb	England	4.1282 bu.
Coyan	Siam	2,645.5 lbs.
Cuadra	Argentine Republic	4.2 acres.
"	Paraguay	94.70 yds.
" (sq.)	Paraguay	1.85 acres.
"	Uruguay	1.82 acres.
Cubic meter	Metric	35.3 cu. ft.
Cwt. (hundredweight)	British	112 lbs.
Dessiatine	Russia	2.6997 acres.
Drachma (new)	Greece	15.43 gr., or 1 grm.
Fanega (dry)	Ecuador, Salvador	1.5745 bu.
"	Chile	2.75268 bu.
"	Guatemala, Spain	1.53 bu.
"	Mexico	2.57716 bu.
" (double)	Uruguay	7.776 bu.
" (single)	Uruguay	3.888 bu.
"	Venezuela	3.334 bu.
" (liquid)	Spain	16 gals.
Feddan	Egypt	1.04 acres.
Frail (raisins)	Spain	50 lbs.
Frasco	Argentine Republic	2.5098 liq. qts.
"	Mexico	2.5 liq. qts.
Frasila	Zanzibar	35 lbs.
Fuder	Luxemburg	264.18 gals.
Funt	Russia	0.9028 lb.
Gallon	British Empire	1.20094 U. S. gal.
Garnice	Poland	1.0567 gal.
Gram	Metric	15.432 grains.
Hectare	"	2.471 acres.
Hectoliter: Dry	"	2.838 bu.
" Liquid	"	26.418 gals.
Jarib	Persia (New)	2.471 acres.
Joch	Austria	1.422 acres.
"	Hungary	1.067 acres.
Ken	Japan	5.97 feet.
Kilogram (kilo)	Metric	2.2046 lbs.
Kilometer	"	0.62137 mile
Klafter	Austria	2.074 yds.
Koku	Japan	5.119 bu.
Kwamme	Japan	8.2673 lbs.
Last	Belgium, Holland	85.134 bu.

Denominations	Where Used	American Equivalents
Last	England	82.56 bu.
Last	Germany	2 metric tons. (4,409 + lbs.)
"	Prussia	112.29 bu.
"	Scotland, Ireland	82.564 bu.
League (land)	Paraguay	4,633 acres.
Li	China	1,890 ft.
Libra (lb.)	Argentine Republic	1.0128 lbs.
"	Central America	1.014 lbs.
"	Chile	1.014 lbs.
"	Cuba	1.0143 lbs.
"	Mexico	1.01467 lbs.
"	Peru	1.0143 lbs.
"	Uruguay	1.0143 lbs.
"	Venezuela	1.0143 lbs.
Litre	Metric	1.0567 liq. qts.
"	Metric	0.90810 dry qts.
Livre (lb.)	Greece	1.1 lbs.
"	Guiana (Dutch)	1.089 lbs.
Load (timber)	England	50 cu. ft.
Lumber (std.)	in Europe	165 cu. ft., or 1,980 ft. b. m.
Manzana	Nicaragua	1.742 acres.
"	Costa Rica, Salvador	1.727 acres.
Marc	Bolivia	0.507 lb.
Maund	India	$82\frac{2}{7}$ lbs.
Metre	Metric	39.37 inches.
Mil	Denmark	4.68 miles.
" (geographic)	Denmark	4.61 miles.
Milla	Nicaragua	1.1594 miles.
"	Honduras	1.1493 miles.
Mina (old)	Greece	2.202 lbs.
Morgen	Prussia	0.63 acre.
Oke	Egypt	2.8052 lbs.
" (Ocque)	Greece	2.82 lbs.
"	Turkey	2.828 lbs.
Pic	Egypt	22.83 inches.
Picul	Borneo and Celebes	135.64 lbs.
"	China	$133\frac{1}{3}$ lbs.
"	Java	136.16 lbs.
"	Philippine Islands	139.44 lbs.
Pie	Argentine Republic	0.94708 foot.
"	Spain	0.91416 foot.
Pik	Turkey	27.9 inches.
Pood	Russia	36.113 lbs.

Denominations	Where Used	American Equivalents
Pund (lb.)	Denmark	1.102 lbs.
Quart	British Empire	1.20094 liq. qt.
"	" "	1.03205 dry qt.
Quarter	Great Britain	8.256 bu.
Quintal	Argentine Republic	101.28 lbs.
"	Brazil	129.54 lbs.
"	Castile, Peru	101.43 lbs.
"	Chile	101.41 lbs.
"	Mexico	101.47 lbs.
"	Metric	220.46 lbs.
Rottle	Palestine (south)	6.35 lbs.
Sack (flour)	England	280 lbs.
Sagene	Russia	7 feet.
Salm	Malta	8.2 bu.
Se	Japan	0.02451 acre.
Seer	India	2 2-35 lbs.
Shaku	Japan	11.9303 inches.
Sho	"	1.91 liq. quarts.
Skalpund	Sweden	0.937 lbs.
Stone	British	14 lbs.
Sun	Japan	1.193 inches.
Tael (Kuping)	China	575.64 grs. (troy)
Tan	Japan	0.25 acre.
Tchetvert	Russia	5.96 bu.
To	Japan	2.05 pecks.
Ton	Space measure	40 cu. ft.
Tonde (cereals)	Denmark	3.9480 bu.
Tonde Land	"	1.36 acres.
Tonne	France	2204.62 lbs.
Tsubo	Japan	35.58 sq. ft.
Tsun	China	1.26 inches.
Tunna (wheat)	Sweden	4.5 bu.
Tunnland	"	1.22 acres.
Vara	Argentine Republic	34.0944 inches.
"	Costa Rica, Salvador	32.913 inches.
"	Guatemala	32.909 inches.
"	Honduras	32.953 inches.
"	Nicaragua	33.057 inches.
"	Chile and Peru	32.913 inches.
"	Cuba	33.386 inches.
"	Mexico	32.992 inches.
Vedro	Russia	2.707 gals.
Verst	"	0.663 mile.
Vloka	Poland	41.50 acres.
Wey	Scotland and Ireland	41.282 bu.

The *metric carat* of 200 milligrams is now very generally in use. The word also is used to denote the proportion of alloy in a metal. Thus, pure gold is 24 carats fine.

APPROXIMATE WEIGHT OF PETROLEUM AND PRODUCTS

In the United States petroleum and its products are measured by bulk, not weight. Whether or not handled in containers, the quantities are customarily reduced to the equivalent of barrels of 42 United States gallons (barrel thus equals 158.984 liters). In many foreign countries these commodities are measured by weight. The specific gravity of the different grades of crude petroleum and of the finished products varies materially. On the basis of approximate averages the Department of Commerce, in converting foreign-weight statistics to gallons or barrels of 42 gallons, uses the factors shown in the following table:

	Weight of U. S. Gallon		Weight of Barrel of 42 Gallons	
	Pounds	*Kilograms*	*Pounds*	*Kilograms*
Crude petroleum	7.3	3.311	306.6	139.07
Lubricating oils	7.0	3.175	294.0	133.36
Illuminating oils (kerosene)	6.6	2.994	277.2	125.74
Gasoline and related products (motor spirit, benzine, etc.)	6.1	2.767	256.2	116.21
Fuel and gas oils	7.7	3.493	323.4	146.69

17. MISCELLANEOUS HANDY TABLES

PRORATION OF TAXES

(Compiled by Walter C. Clark, for the San Francisco Real Estate Yearbook)

The following table is for computing the pro rata of taxes for six months. For example, you are prorating taxes as of October 22, so there is to be charged against the seller of the property 3 months and 22 days. Refer to the table, and you will find 3 months .50, and 22 days .1221, making a total of .6221, which is the amount to be charged against the seller, per $1.00 of taxes.

MONTHS

1	.1666	4	.6666
2	.3333	5	.8333
3	.50	6	1.000

DAYS

1	.0055	16	.0888
2	.0111	17	.0944
3	.0166	18	.0999
4	.0222	19	.1055
5	.0277	20	.1111
6	.0333	21	.1166
7	.0388	22	.1221
8	.0444	23	.1277
9	.05	24	.1333
10	.0555	25	.1389
11	.0611	26	.1444
12	.0666	27	.15
13	.0722	28	.1555
14	.0777	29	.1611
15	.0833	30	.1666

RENTAL READY RECKONER
(Cushman & Wakefield, Inc., New York)

Rent per Year	*Rent per Month*	*Rent per Day* (30 *days*)	*Rent per Day* (31 *days*)	*Rent per Year*	*Rent per Month*	*Rent per Day* (30 *days*)	*Rent per Day* (31 *days*)
$1	$.09	....	....	1,025	85.42	2.847	2.756
2	.17	....	....	1,050	87.50	2.917	2.823
3	.25	....	....	1,075	89.59	2.986	2.890
4	.34	....	....	1,100	91.67	3.056	2.958
5	.42	....	....	1,125	93.75	3.125	3.025
6	.50	....	....	1,150	95.84	3.195	3.092
7	.59	....	....	1,175	97.92	3.264	3.159
8	.67	....	....	1,200	100	3.334	3.226
9	.75	....	....	1,225	102.09	3.403	3.293
10	.84	.028	.027	1,250	104.17	3.472	3.36
20	1.67	.056	.054	1,275	106.25	3.541	3.428
25	2.09	.070	.068	1,300	108.34	3.611	3.495
30	2.50	.084	.081	1,325	110.42	3.681	3.562
40	3.34	.111	.108	1,350	112.50	3.75	3.629
50	4.17	.139	.134	1,375	114.59	3.82	3.697
60	5	.166	.161	1,400	116.67	3.889	3.764
70	5.84	.195	.189	1,425	118.75	3.958	3.831
75	6.25	.208	.202	1,450	120.84	4.028	3.898
80	6.67	.222	.215	1,475	122.92	4.098	3.965
90	7.50	.25	.242	1,500	125	4.167	4.033
100	8.34	.278	.269	1,525	127.09	4.236	4.10
125	10.42	.347	.336	1,550	129.17	4.306	4.167
150	12.50	.417	.403	1,575	131.25	4.375	4.234
175	14.59	.486	.470	1,600	133.34	4.445	4.301
200	16.67	.556	.538	1,625	135.42	4.514	4.369
225	18.75	.625	.605	1,650	137.50	4.584	4.436
250	20.84	.695	.672	1,675	139.59	4.653	4.503
275	22.92	.764	.740	1,700	141.67	4.723	4.570
300	25	.834	.807	1,725	143.75	4.792	4.638
325	27.09	.903	.874	1,750	145.84	4.861	4.705
350	29.17	.972	.941	1,775	147.92	4.931	4.772
375	31.25	1.042	1.009	1,800	150	5	4.84
400	33.34	1.112	1.076	1,825	152.09	5.07	4.906
425	35.42	1.181	1.143	1,850	154.17	5.139	4.973
450	37.50	1.25	1.21	1,875	156.25	5.209	5.04
475	39.59	1.32	1.277	1,900	158.34	5.278	5.108
500	41.67	1.389	1.344	1,925	160.42	5.347	5.175
525	43.75	1.458	1.412	1,950	162.50	5.417	5.242
550	45.84	1.528	1.479	1,975	164.59	5.487	5.31
575	47.92	1.598	1.546	2,000	166.67	5.56	5.377
600	50	1.667	1.613	3,000	250	8.334	8.065
625	52.09	1.737	1.68	4,000	333.34	11.111	10.753
650	54.17	1.806	1.748	5,000	416.67	13.889	13.441
675	56.25	1.875	1.815	6,000	500	16.667	16.13
700	58.34	1.945	1.882	7,000	583.34	19.445	18.818
725	60.42	2.01	1.950	8,000	666.67	22.223	21.506
750	62.50	2.084	2.017	9,000	750	25	24.194
775	64.59	2.153	2.084	10,000	833.34	27.778	26.882
800	66.67	2.223	2.151	11,000	916.67	30.556	29.57
825	68.75	2.292	2.218	12,000	1,000	33.34	32.259
850	70.84	2.361	2.286	13,000	1,083.34	36.111	34.947
875	72.92	2.431	2.352	14,000	1,166.67	38.889	37.635
900	75	2.50	2.420	15,000	1,250	41.667	40.323
925	77.09	2.57	2.487	16,000	1,333.34	44.445	43.011
950	79.17	2.639	2.554	17,000	1,416.67	47.223	45.699
975	81.25	2.708	2.621	18,000	1,500	50	48.388
1,000	83.34	2.778	2.689	19,000	1,583.34	52.778	51.076

MONTHLY, SEMIANNUAL, AND ANNUAL PAYMENTS TO PRINCIPAL AND INTEREST PER $1,000 AT VARYING RATES OF INTEREST

The following table shows the amount that must be repaid to principal and interest per thousand dollars (where payments are made monthly, semiannually, or annually) on loan terms from five to twenty-five years and at interest rates varying from 5% to 3½%. Suppose you borrow $5,000 at 4% interest, interest and principal to be paid monthly over a term of 10 years, at which time the loan will be completely amortized. How much will you have to pay per month? Consulting the table, you see that the loan will cost $10.13 per thousand. Your total cost will be five times this amount, or $50.65.

Amortization Period in Years	For Loans Amortized Monthly						For Loans Amortized Semiannually					For Loans Amortized Annually				
	No. of Payments	*At 5% Interest*	*At 4½% Interest*	*At 4¼% Interest*	*At 4% Interest*	*At 3½% Interest*	*No. of Payments*	*At 5% Interest*	*At 4½% Interest*	*At 4% Interest*	*At 3½% Interest*	*No. of Payments*	*At 5% Interest*	*At 4½% Interest*	*At 4% Interest*	*At 3½% Interest*
5	60	18.88	18.65	18.53	18.42	18.20	10	114.26	112.79	111.33	109.88	5	230.98	227.80	224.63	221.49
8	96	12.66	12.43	12.31	12.19	11.96										
10	120	10.61	10.37	10.25	10.13	9.89	20	64.15	62.65	61.16	59.70	10	129.51	126.38	123.30	120.25
12	144	9.25	9.01	8.88	8.76	8.52										
15	180	7.91	7.65	7.53	7.40	7.15	30	47.78	46.20	44.65	43.13	15	96.35	93.12	89.95	86.83
17	204	7.29	7.03	6.90	6.77	6.52										
19	228	6.81	6.54	....	6.27	6.02	38	41.08	39.43	37.83	36.25	19	82.75	79.41	76.14	72.95
20	240	6.60	6.33	6.20	6.06	5.80	40	39.84	38.18	36.56	34.98	20	80.25	76.88	73.59	70.37
24	288	5.97	5.69	....	5.41	5.14	48	36.01	34.29	32.61	30.97	24	72.48	68.99	65.59	62.28
25	300	5.85	5.56	5.42	5.28	5.01	50	35.26	33.52	31.83	30.18	25	70.90	67.44	64.02	60.68

TIME IN WHICH MONEY DOUBLES ITSELF AT INTEREST

Rate per cent	*Simple Interest*		*Compound Interest*	
2	50 years		35 years	1 day
$2\frac{1}{2}$	40 "		28 "	26 days
3	33 "	4 months	23 "	164 "
$3\frac{1}{2}$	28 "	208 days	20 "	54 "
4	25 "		17 "	246 "
$4\frac{1}{2}$	22 "	81 days	15 "	273 "
5	20 "		14 "	75 "
6	16 "	8 months	11 "	327 "
7	14 "	104 days	10 "	89 "
8	12 "	6 months	9 "	2 "
9	11 "	40 days	8 "	16 "
10	10 "		7 "	100 "

TABLE SHOWING PRICE OF FRACTIONAL PART OF A DOZEN

The following table shows the cost of any fractional part of a dozen ranging from 50 cents to $5.00, in steps of 5 cents each. With proper placement of ciphers and decimals, the table can range from $5.00 to $50.00 per dozen, or from 5 cents to 50 cents per dozen. Fractions have been dropped, and the nearest even cent prices are given.

COST OF ANY FRACTIONAL PART OF A DOZEN

Cost Per Doz.	NUMBER OF ARTICLES 1	2	3	4	5	6	7	8	9	10	11	12
50	4	8	13	17	21	25	29	33	38	42	46	50
55	5	9	14	18	23	28	32	37	41	46	50	55
60	5	10	15	20	25	30	35	40	45	50	55	60
65	5	11	16	22	27	33	38	43	49	54	60	65
70	6	12	18	23	29	35	41	47	53	58	64	70
75	6	13	19	25	31	38	44	50	56	63	69	75
80	7	13	20	27	33	40	47	53	60	67	73	80
85	7	14	21	28	35	43	50	57	64	71	78	85
90	8	15	23	30	38	45	53	60	68	75	83	90
95	8	16	24	32	40	48	55	63	71	79	87	95

COMPARISON OF CENTIGRADE AND FAHRENHEIT TEMPERATURES

To convert from ° F to ° C, subtract 32 from ° F and divide by 1.8.
To convert from ° C to ° F, multiply ° C by 1.8 and add 32.
Water freezes at 0°C and 32°F. Water boils (at sea level) at 100° C and 212° F.

C	F	C	F	C	F	C	F
−40	−40	8	46.4	56	132.8	104	219.2
−39	−38.2	9	48.2	57	134.6	105	221.
−38	−36.4	10	50.	58	136.4	106	222.8
−37	−34.6	11	51.8	59	138.2	107	224.6
−36	−32.8	12	53.6	60	140.	108	226.4
−35	−31.	13	55.4	61	141.8	109	228.2
−34	−29.2	14	57.2	62	143.6	110	230.
−33	−27.4	15	59.	63	145.4	111	231.8
−32	−25.6	16	60.8	64	147.2	112	233.6
−31	−23.8	17	62.6	65	149.	113	235.4
−30	−22.	18	64.4	66	150.8	114	237.2
−29	−20.2	19	66.2	67	152.6	115	239.
−28	−18.4	20	68.	68	154.4	116	240.8
−27	−16.6	21	69.8	69	156.2	117	242.6
−26	−14.8	22	71.6	70	158.	118	244.4
−25	−13	23	73.4	71	159.8	119	246.2
−24	−11.2	24	75.2	72	161.6	120	248.
−23	− 9.4	25	77.	73	163.4	121	249.8
−22	− 7.6	26	78.8	74	165.2	122	251.6
−21	− 5.8	27	80.6	75	167.	123	253.4
−20	− 4.	28	82.4	76	168.8	124	255.2
−19	− 2.2	29	84.2	77	170.6	125	257.
−18	− 0.4	30	86.	78	172.4	126	258.8
−17	+ 1.4	31	87.8	79	174.2	127	260.6
−16	3.2	32	89.6	80	176.	128	262.4
−15	5.	33	91.4	81	177.8	129	264.2
−14	6.8	34	93.2	82	179.6	130	266.
−13	8.6	35	95.	83	181.4	131	267.
−12	10.4	36	96.8	84	183.2	132	269.6
−11	12.2	37	98.6	85	185.	133	271.4
−10	14.	38	100.4	86	186.8	134	273.2
− 9	15.8	39	102.2	87	188.6	135	275.
− 8	17.6	40	104.	88	190.4	136	276.8
− 7	19.4	41	105.8	89	192.2	137	278.6
− 6	21.2	42	107.6	90	194.	138	280.4
− 5	23.	43	109.4	91	195.8	139	282.2
− 4	24.8	44	111.2	92	197.6	140	284.
− 3	26.6	45	113.	93	199.4	141	285.8
− 2	28.4	46	114.8	94	201.2	142	287.6
− 1	30.2	47	116.6	95	203.	143	289.4
0	32.	48	118.4	96	204.8	144	291.2
+ 1	33.8	49	120.2	97	206.6	145	293.
2	35.6	50	122.	98	208.4	146	294.8
3	37.4	51	123.8	99	210.2	147	296.6
4	39.2	52	125.6	100	212.	148	298.4
5	41.	53	127.4	101	213.8	149	300.2
6	42.8	54	129.2	102	215.6		
7	44.6	55	131.	103	217.4		

COST OF ANY FRACTIONAL PART OF A DOZEN

Cost Per Doz.	Number of Articles											
	1	2	3	4	5	6	7	8	9	10	11	12
100	8	17	25	33	42	50	58	67	75	83	92	100
105	9	18	26	35	44	53	61	70	79	88	96	105
110	9	18	28	37	46	55	64	73	83	92	101	110
115	10	19	29	38	48	58	67	77	86	96	105	115
120	10	20	30	40	50	60	70	80	90	100	110	120
125	10	21	31	42	52	63	73	83	94	104	115	125
130	11	22	33	43	54	65	76	87	98	108	119	130
135	11	23	34	45	56	68	79	90	101	113	124	135
140	12	23	35	47	58	70	82	93	105	117	128	140
145	12	24	36	48	60	73	85	97	109	121	133	145
150	13	25	38	50	63	75	88	100	113	125	138	150
155	13	26	39	52	65	78	90	103	116	129	142	155
160	13	27	40	53	67	80	93	107	120	133	147	160
165	14	28	41	55	69	83	96	110	124	138	151	165
170	14	28	42	57	71	85	99	113	127	142	156	170
175	15	29	44	58	73	88	102	117	131	146	160	175
180	15	30	45	60	75	90	105	120	135	150	165	180
185	15	31	46	62	77	93	108	123	139	154	170	185
190	16	32	48	63	79	95	111	127	143	158	174	190
195	16	33	49	65	81	98	114	130	146	163	179	195
200	17	33	50	67	83	100	117	133	150	167	183	200
205	17	34	51	68	85	103	120	137	154	171	188	205
210	18	35	53	70	88	105	123	140	158	175	193	210
215	18	36	54	72	90	108	125	143	161	179	197	215
220	18	37	55	73	92	110	128	147	165	183	202	220
225	19	38	56	75	94	113	131	150	169	188	206	225
230	19	38	58	77	96	115	134	153	173	192	211	230
235	20	39	59	78	98	118	137	157	176	196	215	235
240	20	40	60	80	100	120	140	160	180	200	220	240
245	20	41	61	82	102	123	143	163	184	204	225	245
250	21	42	63	83	104	125	146	167	188	208	229	250
255	21	43	64	85	106	128	149	170	191	213	234	255
260	22	43	65	87	108	130	152	173	195	217	238	260
265	22	44	66	88	110	133	155	177	199	221	243	265
270	23	45	68	90	113	135	158	180	201	225	248	270

COST OF ANY FRACTIONAL PART OF A DOZEN

Cost Per Doz.	1	2	3	4	5	6	7	8	9	10	11	12
	Number of Articles											
275	23	46	69	92	115	138	160	183	206	229	252	275
280	23	47	70	93	117	140	163	187	210	233	257	280
285	24	48	71	95	119	143	166	190	214	238	261	285
290	24	48	73	97	121	145	169	193	218	242	266	290
295	25	49	74	98	123	148	172	197	221	246	270	295
300	25	50	75	100	125	150	175	200	225	250	275	300
305	25	51	76	102	127	153	178	203	229	254	280	305
310	26	52	78	103	129	155	181	207	233	258	284	310
315	26	53	78	105	131	158	184	210	236	263	289	315
320	27	53	80	107	133	160	187	213	240	267	293	320
325	27	54	81	108	135	163	190	217	244	271	298	325
330	28	55	83	110	138	165	193	220	248	275	303	330
335	28	56	84	112	140	168	195	223	251	279	307	335
340	28	57	85	113	142	170	198	227	255	283	312	340
345	29	58	86	115	144	173	201	230	259	288	316	345
350	29	58	88	117	146	175	204	233	263	292	321	350
355	30	60	89	118	148	178	207	237	266	296	325	355
360	30	60	90	120	150	180	210	240	270	300	330	360
365	30	61	91	122	152	183	213	243	274	304	335	365
370	31	62	93	123	154	185	216	247	278	308	339	370
375	31	63	94	125	156	188	219	250	281	313	344	375
380	32	63	95	127	158	190	222	253	285	317	348	380
385	32	64	96	128	160	193	225	257	289	321	353	385
390	33	65	98	130	163	195	228	260	293	325	358	390
395	33	66	99	132	165	198	230	263	296	329	362	395
400	33	67	100	133	167	200	233	267	300	333	367	400
405	34	68	101	135	169	203	236	270	304	338	371	405
410	34	68	103	137	171	205	239	273	308	342	376	410
415	35	69	104	138	173	208	242	277	311	346	380	415
420	35	70	105	140	175	210	245	280	315	350	385	420
425	35	71	106	142	177	213	248	283	319	354	390	425
430	36	72	108	143	179	215	251	287	323	358	394	430
435	36	73	109	145	181	218	254	290	326	363	399	435
440	37	73	110	147	183	220	257	293	330	367	403	440
445	37	74	111	148	185	223	260	297	334	371	408	445

COST OF ANY FRACTIONAL PART OF A DOZEN

Cost Per Doz.	Number of Articles 1	2	3	4	5	6	7	8	9	10	11	12
450	38	75	113	150	188	225	263	300	338	375	413	450
455	38	76	114	152	190	227	265	303	341	379	417	455
460	38	77	115	153	192	230	268	307	345	383	422	460
465	39	78	116	155	194	233	271	310	349	388	426	465
470	39	78	118	157	196	235	274	313	353	392	431	470
475	40	79	119	158	198	238	277	317	356	396	435	475
480	40	80	120	160	200	240	280	320	360	400	440	480
485	40	81	121	162	202	243	283	323	364	404	445	485
490	41	82	123	163	204	245	286	327	368	408	449	490
500	42	83	125	167	208	250	292	333	375	417	458	500

MATHEMATICAL SIGNS AND SYMBOLS

$+$ ...... Plus, the sign of addition.

$-$ ...... Minus, the sign of subtraction.

$\times$ ...... The sign of multiplication.

$\div$ ...... The sign of division.

$:$ ...... Is to
$::$ ...... As
$:$ ...... Is to
— The signs of proportion. Thus $3 : 6 :: 4 : 8$.

$\because$ ...... Because.

$\therefore$ ...... Therefore.

$=$ ...... Equals, the sign of equality.

$>$ ...... Greater than.

$<$ ...... Less than.

$\sqrt{\ }$ ...... Square Root.

$\sqrt[3]{\ }$ ...... Cube Root. $\sqrt[4]{\ }$ Fourth Root. $\sqrt[5]{\ }$ Fifth Root, etc.

( ) [ ] { } .. Indicate that the figures enclosed are to be taken together. Thus $10 \times (7 + 4)$; $8 - [9 \div 3]$; $30\left\{\frac{7+3}{4-2}\right\}$.

° ′ ″ ...... Degrees, minutes, seconds. Thus 25° 15′ 10″ represents 25 degrees, 15 minutes, 10 seconds.

′ ″ ...... Feet, inches. Thus 9′ 10″ = 9 feet 10 inches.

∞ ...... Infinity.

$\perp$ ...... Perpendicular to.

$\parallel$ ...... Parallel to.

...... Number; numbered.

° ...... Degree.

○ ...... Circle.

$\angle$ ...... Angle.

∟ ...... Right-angle.

□ ...... Square.

▭ ...... Rectangle.

Δ ...... Triangle.

0 ...... The cipher, zero.

% ...... Per cent.

‰ ...... Per thousand.

℈ Scruple.
ʒ Drachm.
℥ Ounce.
— Apothecaries' weight.

ANNUAL, MONTHLY, WEEKLY, AND DAILY SALARIES

ANNUAL	MONTHLY	WEEKLY*	DAILY†
	12 mo. to yr.	*52 weeks to yr.*	*6 days to week*
$1000.00	$ 83.33	$19.23	$3.20
1040.00	86.67	20.00	3.33
1080.00	90.00	20.77	3.45
1092.00	91.00	21.00	3.50
1100.00	91.67	21.15	3.52
1144.00	95.33	22.00	3.67
1196.00	99.67	23.00	3.83
1200.00	100.00	23.08	3.85
1248.00	104.00	24.00	4.00
1300.00	108.33	25.00	4.17
1320.00	110.00	25.38	4.23
1352.00	112.67	26.00	4.33
1380.00	115.00	26.54	4.42
1400.00	116.67	26.92	4.49
1404.00	117.00	27.00	4.50
1440.00	120.00	27.69	4.61
1456.00	121.33	28.00	4.67
1500.00	125.00	28.85	4.81
1508.00	125.67	29.00	4.83
1560.00	130.00	30.00	5.00
1600.00	133.33	30.77	5.13
1612.00	134.33	31.00	5.17
1620.00	135.00	31.15	5.19
1664.00	138.67	32.00	5.33
1680.00	140.00	32.31	5.38
1700.00	141.67	32.68	5.45
1716.00	143.00	33.00	5.50
1740.00	145.00	33.46	5.57
1768.00	147.33	34.00	5.67
1800.00	150.00	34.61	5.77
1820.00	151.67	35.00	5.83
1860.00	155.00	35.77	5.96
1872.00	156.00	36.00	6.00
1900.00	158.33	36.54	6.09
1920.00	160.00	36.92	6.15
1924.00	160.33	37.00	6.17
1976.00	164.67	38.00	6.33
1980.00	165.00	38.08	6.35
2000.00	166.67	38.46	6.41
2028.00	169.00	39.00	6.50
2040.00	170.00	39.23	6.54
2080.00	173.33	40.00	6.67
2100.00	175.00	40.38	6.73
2132.00	177.67	41.00	6.83
2160.00	180.00	41.54	6.92
2184.00	182.00	42.00	7.00
2200.00	183.33	42.31	7.05
2220.00	185.00	42.69	7.11
2236.00	186.33	43.00	7.17
2280.00	190.00	43.85	7.31
2288.00	190.67	44.00	7.33
2300.00	191.67	44.23	7.37
$ 2340.00	$195.00	$ 45.00	$ 7.50
2392.00	199.33	46.00	7.67
2400.00	200.00	46.15	7.69
2444.00	203.67	47.00	7.83
2496.00	208.00	48.00	8.00
2500.00	208.33	48.08	8.01
2520.00	210.00	48.46	8.08
2548.00	212.33	49.00	8.17
2600.00	216.67	50.00	8.33
2640.00	220.00	50.77	8.46
2700.00	225.00	51.92	8.65
2760.00	230.00	53.08	8.85
2800.00	233.33	53.85	8.97
2860.00	238.33	55.00	9.17
2880.00	240.00	55.38	9.23
2900.00	241.67	55.77	9.29
3000.00	250.00	57.69	9.61
3120.00	260.00	60.00	10.00
3240.00	270.00	62.31	10.38
3360.00	280.00	64.62	10.77
3380.00	281.67	65.00	10.83
3480.00	290.00	66.92	11.15
3500.00	291.67	67.31	11.22
3600.00	300.00	69.23	11.54
3640.00	303.33	70.00	11.67
3900.00	325.00	75.00	12.50
4160.00	346.67	80.00	13.33
4200.00	350.00	80.77	13.46
4420.00	368.33	85.00	14.17
4500.00	375.00	86.54	14.42
4680.00	390.00	90.00	15.00
4800.00	400.00	92.31	15.38
4940.00	411.67	95.00	15.83
5000.00	416.67	96.15	16.02
5100.00	425.00	98.08	16.35
5200.00	433.33	100.00	16.67
5400.00	450.00	103.85	17.31
5500.00	458.33	105.77	17.63
5700.00	475.00	109.62	18.27
6000.00	500.00	115.38	19.23
6300.00	525.00	121.15	20.19
6500.00	541.67	125.00	20.83
6600.00	550.00	126.92	21.15
6900.00	575.00	132.69	22.11
7000.00	583.33	134.62	22.44
7200.00	600.00	138.46	23.08
7500.00	625.00	144.23	24.04
8000.00	666.67	153.85	25.64
8500.00	708.33	163.46	27.24
9000.00	750.00	173.08	28.85
9500.00	791.67	182.69	30.45
10000.00	833.33	192.31	32.05

* Fifty-two weeks to the year instead of $52\frac{1}{6}$ weeks.

† Weekly rate on the basis of six days to the week.

SQUARES, SQUARE ROOTS, CUBES, AND CUBE ROOTS OF NUMBERS 1–100

No.	Sq.	Cube	Square Root	Cube Root	No.	Sq.	Cube	Square Root	Cube Root	No.	Sq.	Cube	Square Root	Cube Root
1	1.000	1.000	1.000	1.000	35	1225	42875	5.916	3.271	68	4624	314432	8.246	4.081
2	4	8	1.414	1.259	36	1296	46656	6.000	3.301	69	4761	328509	8.306	4.101
3	9	27	1.732	1.442	37	1369	50653	6.082	3.332	70	4900	343000	8.366	4.121
4	16	64	2.000	1.587	38	1444	54872	6.164	3.362	71	5041	357911	8.426	4.140
5	25	125	2.236	1.710	39	1521	59319	6.245	3.391	72	5184	373248	8.485	4.160
6	36	216	2.449	1.817	40	1600	64000	6.324	3.420	73	5329	389017	8.544	4.179
7	49	343	2.645	1.913	41	1681	68921	6.403	3.448	74	5476	405224	8.602	4.198
8	64	512	2.828	2.000	42	1764	74088	6.480	3.476	75	5625	421875	8.660	4.217
9	81	729	3.000	2.080	43	1849	79507	6.557	3.503	76	5776	438976	8.717	4.235
10	100	1000	3.162	2.154	44	1936	85184	6.633	3.530	77	5929	456533	8.775	4.254
11	121	1331	3.316	2.224	45	2025	91125	6.708	3.556	78	6084	474552	8.831	4.272
12	144	1728	3.464	2.289	46	2116	97336	6.782	3.583	79	6241	493039	8.888	4.290
13	169	2197	3.605	2.351	47	2209	103823	6.855	3.608	80	6400	512000	8.944	4.308
14	196	2744	3.741	2.410	48	2304	110592	6.928	3.634	81	6561	531441	9.000	4.326
15	225	3375	3.873	2.466	49	2401	117649	7.000	3.659	82	6724	551368	9.055	4.344
16	256	4096	4.000	2.519	50	2500	125000	7.071	3.684	83	6889	571787	9.110	4.362
17	289	4913	4.123	2.571	51	2601	132651	7.141	3.708	84	7056	592704	9.165	4.379
18	324	5832	4.242	2.620	52	2704	140608	7.211	3.732	85	7225	614125	9.219	4.396
19	361	6859	4.358	2.668	53	2809	148877	7.280	3.756	86	7396	636056	9.273	4.414
20	400	8000	4.472	2.714	54	2916	157464	7.348	3.779	87	7569	658303	9.327	4.431
21	441	9261	4.582	2.758	55	3025	166375	7.416	3.803	88	7744	681472	9.380	4.448
22	484	10648	4.690	2.802	56	3136	175616	7.483	3.825	89	7921	704969	9.434	4.464
23	529	12167	4.795	2.843	57	3249	185193	7.549	3.848	90	8100	729000	9.486	4.481
24	576	13824	4.899	2.884	58	3364	195112	7.615	3.870	91	8281	753571	9.539	4.497
25	625	15625	5.000	2.924	59	3481	205379	7.681	3.893	92	8464	778688	9.591	4.514
26	676	17576	5.099	2.962	60	3600	216000	7.746	3.914	93	8649	804357	9.643	4.530
27	729	19683	5.196	3.000	61	3721	226981	7.810	3.936	94	8836	830584	9.695	4.546
28	784	21952	5.291	3.036	62	3844	238328	7.874	3.957	95	9025	857375	9.746	4.562
29	841	24389	5.385	3.072	63	3969	250047	7.937	3.979	96	9216	884736	9.798	4.578
30	900	27000	5.477	3.107	64	4096	262144	8.000	4.000	97	9409	912673	9.848	4.594
31	961	29791	5.567	3.141	65	4225	274625	8.062	4.020	98	9604	941192	9.899	4.610
32	1024	32768	5.656	3.174	66	4356	287496	8.124	4.041	99	9801	970299	9.944	4.626
33	1089	35937	5.744	3.207	67	4489	300763	8.185	4.061	100	10000	1000000	10.000	4.641
34	1156	39304	5.831	3.239										

AMERICAN EXPERIENCE TABLE OF MORTALITY

Age	No. Living	Deaths Each Year	Death-Rate Per 1,000	Expect. of Life	Age	No. Living	Deaths Each Year	Death-Rate Per 1,000	Expect. of Life	Age	No. Living	Deaths Each Year	Death-Rate Per 1,000	Expect. of Life
10....	100.000	749	7.49	48.72	39....	78.862	756	9.59	28.90	68....	43.133	2.243	52.00	9.47
11....	99.251	746	7.52	48.08	40....	78.106	765	9.79	28.18	69....	40.890	2.321	56.76	8.97
12....	98.505	743	7.54	47.45	41....	77.341	774	10.01	27.45	70....	38.569	2.391	61.99	8.48
13....	97.762	740	7.57	46.80	42....	76.567	785	10.25	26.72	71....	36.178	2.448	67.66	8.00
14....	97.022	737	7.60	46.16	43....	75.782	797	10.52	26.00	72....	33.730	2.487	73.73	7.55
15....	96.285	735	7.63	45.50	44....	74.985	812	10.83	25.27	73....	31.243	2.505	80.18	7.11
16....	95.550	732	7.66	44.85	45....	74.173	828	11.16	24.54	74....	28.738	2.501	87.03	6.68
17....	94.818	729	7.69	44.19	46....	73.345	848	11.56	23.81	75....	26.237	2.476	94.37	6.27
18....	94.089	727	7.73	43.53	47....	72.497	870	12.00	23.08	76....	23.761	2.431	102.31	5.88
19....	93.362	725	7.76	42.87	48....	71.627	896	12.51	22.36	77....	21.330	2.369	111.06	5.49
20....	92.637	723	7.80	42.20	49....	70.731	927	13.11	21.63	78....	18.961	2.291	120.83	5.11
21....	91.914	722	7.85	41.53	50....	69.804	962	13.78	20.91	79....	16.670	2.196	131.73	4.74
22....	91.192	721	7.91	40.85	51....	68.842	1.001	14.54	20.20	80....	14.474	2.091	144.47	4.39
23....	90.471	720	7.96	40.17	52....	67.841	1.044	15.39	19.49	81....	12.383	1.964	158.60	4.05
24....	89.751	719	8.01	39.49	53....	66.797	1.091	16.33	18.79	82....	10.419	1.816	174.30	3.71
25....	89.032	718	8.06	38.81	54....	65.706	1.143	17.40	18.09	83....	8.603	1.648	191.56	3.39
26....	88.314	718	8.13	38.12	55....	64.563	1.199	18.57	17.40	84....	6.955	1.470	211.36	3.08
27....	87.596	718	8.20	37.43	56....	63.364	1.260	19.88	16.72	85....	5.485	1.292	235.55	2.77
28....	86.878	718	8.26	36.73	57....	62.104	1.325	21.33	16.05	86....	4.193	1.114	265.68	2.47
29....	86.160	719	8.34	36.03	58....	60.779	1.394	22.94	15.39	87....	3.079	933	303.02	2.18
30....	85.441	720	8.43	35.33	59....	59.385	1.468	24.72	14.74	88....	2.146	744	346.69	1.91
31....	84.721	721	8.51	34.63	60....	57.917	1.546	26.69	14.10	89....	1.402	555	395.86	1.66
32....	84.000	723	8.61	33.93	61....	56.371	1.628	28.88	13.47	90....	847	385	454.54	1.42
33....	83.277	726	8.72	33.21	62....	54.743	1.713	31.29	12.86	91....	462	246	532.47	1.19
34....	82.551	729	8.83	32.50	63....	53.030	1.800	33.94	12.26	92....	216	137	634.26	.98
35....	81.822	732	8.95	31.78	64....	51.230	1.889	36.87	11.67	93....	79	58	734.18	.80
36....	81.090	737	9.09	31.07	65....	49.341	1.980	40.13	11.10	94....	21	18	857.14	.64
37....	80.353	742	9.23	30.35	66....	47.361	2.070	43.71	10.54	95....	3	3	1000.00	.50
38....	79.611	749	9.41	29.62	67....	45.291	2.158	47.65	10.00					

READY-REFERENCE CALENDAR

For Ascertaining Any Day of the Week for Any Given Date within Two Hundred Years from the Introduction of the New Style, 1752 *to* 2000 *inclusive*

COMMON YEARS NEW STYLE, **1753** TO **1999.**										Jan. (31 d.)	Feb. (28 d.)	Mar. (31 d.)	April (30d.)	May (31 d.)	June (30d.)	July (31 d.)	Aug. (31 d.)	Sept. (30d.)	Oct. (31 d.)	Nov. (30d.)	Dec. (31 d.)
1761 1767 1778	1789 1795	1801 1807 1818	1829 1835 1846	1857 1863 1874	1885 1891	1903 1914 1925	1931 1942 1953	1959 1970 1981	1978 1998	4	7	7	3	5	1	3	6	2	4	7	2
1762 1773 1779	1790 1802	1813 1819 1830	1841 1847 1858	1869 1875 1886	1897 1909	1915 1926 1937	1943 1954 1965	1971 1982 1993	1999	5	1	1	4	6	2	4	7	3	5	1	3
1757 1763 1774	1785 1791	1803 1814 1825	1831 1842 1853	1859 1870 1881	1887 1898	1910 1921 1927	1938 1949 1955	1966 1977 1983	1994	6	2	2	5	7	3	5	1	4	6	2	4
1754 1765 1771	1782 1793 1799	.... 1805 1811	1822 1833 1839	1850 1861 1867	1878 1889 1895	.... 1901 1907	1918 1929 1935	1946 1957 1963	1974 1985 1991	2	5	5	1	3	6	1	4	7	2	5	7
1755 1766 1777	1783 1794	1800 1806 1817	1823 1834 1845	1851 1862 1873	1879 1890	1902 1913 1919	1930 1941 1947	1958 1969 1975	1986 1997	3	6	6	2	4	7	2	5	1	3	6	1
1758 1769 1775	1786 1797	1809 1815 1826	1837 1843 1854	1865 1871 1882	1893 1899	1905 1911 1922	1933 1939 1950	1961 1967 1978	1989 1995	7	3	3	6	1	4	6	2	5	7	3	5
1753 1759 1770	1781 1787 1798	1810 1821 1827	1838 1849 1855	1866 1877 1883	1894 1900	1906 1917 1923	1934 1945 1951	1962 1973 1979	1990	1	4	4	7	2	5	7	3	6	1	4	6
LEAP YEARS, NEW STYLE, **1756** TO **2000.**											*										
1764	**1792**	**1804**	**1832**	**1860**	**1888**	....	**1928**	**1956**	**1984**	**7**	**3**	**4**	**7**	**2**	**5**	**7**	**3**	**6**	**1**	**4**	**6**
1768	**1796**	**1808**	**1836**	**1864**	**1892**	**1904**	**1932**	**1960**	**1988**	**5**	**1**	**2**	**5**	**7**	**3**	**5**	**1**	**4**	**6**	**2**	**4**
1772	....	**1812**	**1840**	**1868**	**1896**	**1908**	**1936**	**1964**	**1992**	**3**	**6**	**7**	**3**	**5**	**1**	**3**	**6**	**2**	**4**	**7**	**2**
1776	....	**1816**	**1844**	**1872**	....	**1912**	**1940**	**1968**	**1996**	**1**	**4**	**5**	**1**	**3**	**6**	**1**	**4**	**7**	**2**	**5**	**7**
1780	....	**1820**	**1848**	**1876**	....	**1916**	**1944**	**1972**	**2000**	**6**	**2**	**3**	**6**	**1**	**4**	**6**	**2**	**5**	**7**	**3**	**5**
1756	**1784**	**1824**	**1852**	**1880**	....	**1920**	**1948**	**1976**	....	**4**	**7**	**1**	**4**	**6**	**2**	**4**	**7**	**3**	**5**	**1**	**3**
1760	**1788**	**1828**	**1856**	**1884**	....	**1924**	**1952**	**1980**	....	**2**	**5**	**6**	**2**	**4**	**7**	**2**	**5**	**1**	**3**	**6**	**1**

* In leap years February has 29 days.

1	2	3	4	5	6	7
1 Monday	1 Tuesday	1 Wednesday	1 Thursday	1 Friday	1 Saturday	1 SUNDAY
2 Tuesday	2 Wednesday	2 Thursday	2 Friday	2 Saturday	2 SUNDAY	2 Monday
3 Wednesday	3 Thursday	3 Friday	3 Saturday	3 SUNDAY	3 Monday	3 Tuesday
4 Thursday	4 Friday	4 Saturday	4 SUNDAY	4 Monday	4 Tuesday	4 Wednesday
5 Friday	5 Saturday	5 SUNDAY	5 Monday	5 Tuesday	5 Wednesday	5 Thursday
6 Saturday	6 SUNDAY	6 Monday	6 Tuesday	6 Wednesday	6 Thursday	6 Friday
7 SUNDAY	7 Monday	7 Tuesday	7 Wednesday	7 Thursday	7 Friday	7 Saturday
8 Monday	8 Tuesday	8 Wednesday	8 Thursday	8 Friday	8 Saturday	8 SUNDAY
9 Tuesday	9 Wednesday	9 Thursday	9 Friday	9 Saturday	9 SUNDAY	9 Monday
10 Wednesday	10 Thursday	10 Friday	10 Saturday	10 SUNDAY	10 Monday	10 Tuesday
11 Thursday	11 Friday	11 Saturday	11 SUNDAY	11 Monday	11 Tuesday	11 Wednesday
12 Friday	12 Saturday	12 SUNDAY	12 Monday	12 Tuesday	12 Wednesday	12 Thursday
13 Saturday	13 SUNDAY	13 Monday	13 Tuesday	13 Wednesday	13 Thursday	13 Friday
14 SUNDAY	14 Monday	14 Tuesday	14 Wednesday	14 Thursday	14 Friday	14 Saturday
15 Monday	15 Tuesday	15 Wednesday	15 Thursday	15 Friday	15 Saturday	15 SUNDAY
16 Tuesday	16 Wednesday	16 Thursday	16 Friday	16 Saturday	16 SUNDAY	16 Monday
17 Wednesday	17 Thursday	17 Friday	17 Saturday	17 SUNDAY	17 Monday	17 Tuesday
18 Thursday	18 Friday	18 Saturday	18 SUNDAY	18 Monday	18 Tuesday	18 Wednesday
19 Friday	19 Saturday	19 SUNDAY	19 Monday	19 Tuesday	19 Wednesday	19 Thursday
20 Saturday	20 SUNDAY	20 Monday	20 Tuesday	20 Wednesday	20 Thursday	20 Friday
21 SUNDAY	21 Monday	21 Tuesday	21 Wednesday	21 Thursday	21 Friday	21 Saturday
22 Monday	22 Tuesday	22 Wednesday	22 Thursday	22 Friday	22 Saturday	22 SUNDAY
23 Tuesday	23 Wednesday	23 Thursday	23 Friday	23 Saturday	23 SUNDAY	23 Monday
24 Wednesday	24 Thursday	24 Friday	24 Saturday	24 SUNDAY	24 Monday	24 Tuesday
25 Thursday	25 Friday	25 Saturday	25 SUNDAY	25 Monday	25 Tuesday	25 Wednesday
26 Friday	26 Saturday	26 SUNDAY	26 Monday	26 Tuesday	26 Wednesday	26 Thursday
27 Saturday	27 SUNDAY	27 Monday	27 Tuesday	27 Wednesday	27 Thursday	27 Friday
28 SUNDAY	28 Monday	28 Tuesday	28 Wednesday	28 Thursday	28 Friday	28 Saturday
29 Monday	29 Tuesday	29 Wednesday	29 Thursday	29 Friday	29 Saturday	29 SUNDAY
30 Tuesday	30 Wednesday	30 Thursday	30 Friday	30 Saturday	30 SUNDAY	30 Monday
31 Wednesday	31 Thursday	31 Friday	31 Saturday	31 SUNDAY	31 Monday	31 Tuesday

To ascertain what day of the week a particular date fell on, or will fall on, first find the year in the table on page 156. Then see what number is indicated for the particular month in the section in which the year appears. Locate the corresponding column number in the table on page 157. *Example.*—To know on what day of the week July 4, 1918, fell, look in the table of years for 1918, and in a parallel line under July is figure 1, which directs to column 1 in which it will be seen that July 4 fell on Thursday.

ROMAN NUMERALS

I	1	IX	9	XVII	17	LXX	70	D	500
II	2	X	10	XVIII	18	LXXX		DC	600
III	3	XI	11	XIX	19	or XXC	80	DCC	700
IV	4	XII	12	XX	20	XC	90	DCCC	800
V	5	XIII	13	XXX	30	C	100	CM	900
VI	6	XIV	14	XL	40	CC	200	M or	
VII	7	XV	15	L	50	CCC	300	cIc	1000
VIII	8	XVI	16	LX	60	CCCC	400	MM	2000

Note.—A dash line over a numeral multiplies the value by 1,000. Thus, $\overline{\text{X}} = 10{,}000$; $\overline{\text{L}} = 50{,}000$; $\overline{\text{C}} = 100{,}000$; $\overline{\text{D}} = 500{,}000$; $\overline{\text{M}} = 1{,}000{,}000$; $\overline{\text{CLIX}} = 159{,}000$; $\overline{\text{DLIX}} = 559{,}000$.

GENERAL RULES IN ROMAN NUMERALS

(1) Repeating a letter repeats its value: XX = 20; CCC = 300.

(2) A letter placed after one of greater value adds thereto: VIII = 8; DC = 600.

(3) A letter placed before one of greater value subtracts therefrom: IX = 9; CM = 900.

ARABIC NUMERALS

Trillions	Billions	Millions	Thousands	Hundreds
7,	256,	423,	896,	384

Note.—In the United States and France a billion is a thousand millions (1,000,000,000). In Britain and Germany a billion is a million millions (1,000,000,000,000).

CONTENTS—SECTION 2

Tested Business Letters

5. LETTERS THAT BUILD GOODWILL

Holding and Increasing Goodwill of Established Customers

Building Goodwill among New Patrons

Goodwill Through Acknowledgments

General Goodwill Letters

6. KEEPING GOODWILL IN ANSWERING COMPLAINTS

7. LEGAL ASPECTS OF BUSINESS LETTERS

Contracts by Correspondence

Libelous Letters

Letters as Evidence of Admission Against the Writer

8. LAYOUT OF THE LETTER

9. MECHANICS OF THE LETTER

10. SPECIAL FORMS OF ADDRESS, SALUTATION, AND COMPLIMENTARY CLOSE FOR PERSONS OF RANK

11. DICTIONARY OF CORRECT USAGE

SECTION 2

Tested Business Letters

Acknowledgment is made to P. T. Ward, "Modern Business English" (New York: Prentice-Hall, Inc.), J. C. McCloskey, "Handbook of Business Correspondence" (New York: Prentice-Hall, Inc.), and William H. Butterfield, "Goodwill Letters That Build Business" (New York: Prentice-Hall, Inc.) for permission to reproduce material from these books in this section.

1. A BETTER-LETTERS PROGRAM

Do your letters lose or win business for you?—Under the usual procedure in many business houses, only occasionally do the files give up their dead. The so-called routine correspondence of the sales, credit, adjustment, and other departments is handled by minor employees. The department head is as a rule too busy with his own work to read every letter that is mailed. Through ignorance or carelessness on the part of his subordinates, curt, vague, and poorly worded letters may be sent out, and the carbon copies may simply disappear into the files. The resultant loss of company prestige and customer goodwill (not to mention actual sales) goes unnoticed, since for every customer who will go to the trouble of criticizing the way in which his correspondence is handled, ten will remain silent and place their business elsewhere. Yet one tactless or sarcastic letter, written by a "clever" clerk in reply to a customer's complaint, may destroy the goodwill that has been built up through intensive effort by the sales department. Likewise, the superficial handling of an inquiry may drive away a prospective customer whose business would be worth thousands of dollars a year.

It is not sufficient that letters shall not lose your business; they should actually improve customer relations, build goodwill, and increase sales. How to make letters perform these positive functions is treated in other parts of this section.

A plan to improve letters.—To make letters perform the positive functions mentioned above, and to avoid their doing harm, a definite plan or program with regard to the company correspondence is desirable. Such a program may provide for two things:

1. Training of employees in the best methods of writing various types of business letters.
2. Supervision of the company correspondence, so that fewer letters will be mailed that are not up to the standard set.

In recent years many progressive companies have attacked the problem of improving their correspondence with a seriousness equal to that with which they train their salesmen. Some of these companies have established training schools for their employees; others have engaged expert correspondence supervisors whose duty it is to examine the company correspondence and act continuously in an advisory capacity. Programs such as these may entail considerable expense, and for this reason possibly only the larger companies could afford to support them. Some of the methods used by larger companies to "make every letter better" are described below. However, a very simple better-letters program, which involves neither expenses nor a formal course of study nor the employment of an expert, can readily be put into effect by any business house. One such program will be briefly described.

Choosing a correspondence adviser.—The first step in a better-letters program is to choose a member of the company to act as correspondence adviser. This individual may be the advertising manager, the sales manager, a vice-president, the secretary, or even the president. Whoever he is, he should have the following minimum qualifications for the work.

1. He should be one of the best letterwriters in the organization and have had considerable experience in writing various types of business letters—sales, credit, collection, adjustment, and others. Obviously, to nominate a person who cannot practice what he preaches, and whose letters are inferior to those of some of the people whom he is undertaking to advise, is to reduce the whole program to the level of an office joke.
2. The correspondence adviser must be a person of natural tact. Some members of the organization may resent the criticism implied

in the program, and the adviser must therefore be an individual who can overcome this resentment and place the program on a basis of cordiality and mutual helpfulness.

3. The correspondence adviser should have a flair for teaching and must be the type of person who can distinguish between essential and nonessential points. For example, the proper tone in letters is a question for the adviser to discuss at length; however, he need not debate controversial points of grammar.

After the correspondence adviser has been chosen, it is important that it be made clear to the members of the staff that he has the full support of the executives of the company, and that all employees will be expected to co-operate and to participate actively.

Telling the staff about the correspondence supervisor.—A memorandum signed by the president may be the most effective method of informing the staff of the appointment of a correspondence adviser and of securing its co-operation. The memorandum may take some such form as the following:

TO ALL MEMBERS OF THE STAFF

There are only two ways in which prospects and customers have any contact with us. The first is through a salesman; the second is by letter. For every call that a salesman makes, possibly three to ten letters are written. It is only natural, then, for us to consider how we can make our letters most effective.

I am going to ask everyone to co-operate in an effort to improve the content, tone, and appearance of the letters written for the company.

We are judged largely by our letters. If they are abrupt, discourteous, badly organized, poorly typed, hard to understand, they will detract from the company prestige rather than add to goodwill. In recent weeks I have seen carbon copies of a number of letters which did not convey the very best impression of our business.

Every letter on the company letterhead should be:

(1) Correct.
(2) Clear.
(3) Friendly.
(4) Courteous.

Every letter should build goodwill, especially in those cases in which we find it necessary to refuse a request, ask for payment of a bill, or adjust a complaint.

It will not be necessary for us to engage in an involved technical study of business correspondence in order to improve our letters. All that we need do is pay particular attention to a few fundamental principles of good letterwriting and make a sincere effort to apply these principles in every letter we write. To help you do this, I have appointed Mr. Clark as Correspondence Adviser. Mr. Clark will prepare, every two weeks, a bulletin called "Better-Letters Bulletin," copies of which will be sent to all members of the organization. These bulletins are intended as a medium of co-operation; I know that you will accept them in a spirit of friendliness and good feeling.

Please participate actively in this program to improve our correspondence. If you have any comments regarding these bulletins, if you have any ideas or suggestions for topics to be discussed, if you have any letter problem on which you would like assistance, be sure to communicate with Mr. Clark.

Preparing better-letters bulletins.—Before the correspondence adviser begins to issue bulletins, it is advisable for him to draw up a list of the topics that he intends to discuss. He should then confine himself, in each bulletin, to one particular topic. Moreover, a mere outline of general principles is of little value; the application of each principle must be illustrated by specific examples. Thus, if the topic treated in Bulletin No. 3 is "Opening and Closing the Letter," examples of how to open and close (and how not to) should be cited. Similarly, if Bulletin No. 5 deals with "Replying to Complaint and Claim Letters," it may be well for the adviser to take an actual complaint letter, prepare a reply to it, and then reproduce both letters in the bulletin, together with explanatory comments. Other means of increasing the practical value of the bulletins will readily suggest themselves.

Topics to be discussed in bulletins.—These topics will vary somewhat according to the nature of the company's business. However, the following list may be useful:

1. *Tone and spirit of the letter.*—It will probably be found that some members of the staff whose work involves frequent letter writing have a formal, dull, routine style; others may be curt; still others too garrulous. Getting a cordial feeling into the business letter, without becoming undignified, is something of an art, but one that can be acquired through training and practice. This, the

tone and spirit of the letter, is perhaps the most important of all the topics that should be dealt with in the bulletins. (For further discussion, see "Tone and Spirit of the Letter," page 176.)

2. *Every letter is a sales letter.*—This statement is true in the sense that any letter, regardless of the subject, can "sell" goodwill and a favorable impression of the company.

3. *Sales opportunities in letter writing.*—As an illustration of this point, suppose that a clerk in the collection department is writing a routine collection letter on a small past-due account. He knows that his company has recently added a new item to its line. In writing his collection letter there is an opportunity for the clerk to mention this new item and possibly to enclose a catalogue or other mailing piece. Similarly, a reply to a complaint might properly end with a brief reference to a special offer that the company is making to its customers for a limited period.

4. *Cutting correspondence costs.*—Under this heading suggestions may be made for greater efficiency in the handling of correspondence. For example, some of the company correspondents may be in the habit of dictating names, addresses, and salutations when replying to letters received. A more efficient method is to number each letter to which a reply is being dictated, and to begin the reply by dictating only the number; as, "Letter No. 6." The transcriber can then obtain the name and address by referring to the letter received. (For further suggestions, see the chart on page 174, "Are Your Letters Costing Too Much?")

5. *Opening and closing the letter.*—The opening and the closing sentences or paragraphs of the letter are pitfalls for many correspondents. (For further discussion, see "How to Open and Close the Letter," page 181.)

6. *Mechanics of the letter.*—A section on this subject will be of interest chiefly to the company secretaries and stenographers. To adopt a standard style for all letters has many advantages. (For illustrations of various types of letter styles, and also rules governing the form of the inside address, salutation, complimentary close, and so on, see "Mechanics of the Letter," page 258.)

7. *Correctness in grammar and usage.*—A periodic review of grammar, sentence structure, and punctuation, with particular attention to common errors, is useful and necessary even in the case of

experienced correspondents. (For rules governing correct usage, see "Dictionary of Correct Usage," page 288.)

8. *Special types of letters.*—Collection letters, sales letters, answers to inquiries, adjustment letters—each type of business letter gives rise to its own particular problems. After having covered letter writing in general, the correspondence adviser may take up each type separately.

Compiling a correspondence manual.—The bulletins may be mimeographed at very slight cost. It is convenient to have them run off on punched paper and to supply members of the staff with ring binders into which the bulletins may be inserted as they are received. Each correspondent will then have at all times on his desk an invaluable reference manual on all matters pertaining to letter writing. Furthermore, when a new employee is engaged, he should be given an up-to-date copy of the manual; this will acquaint him with the company's policy with regard to its correspondence and will also largely dispense with the need for continuous verbal training by the department head.

In addition to issuing bulletins of advice on topics such as those suggested above, the correspondence adviser may also distribute from time to time, for inclusion in the manual, mimeographed copies of actual letters, with comments. Suitable for use are particularly effective letters of all kinds, whether received by the company or written by members of the staff. To include copies of letters prepared by the staff will serve to dispel any idea that the better-letters program is a form of destructive, and not constructive, criticism. The program must permit praise to be given where praise is due.

Supervising current correspondence.—The mere issuance of bulletins, however, is likely to prove only partially effective. Provision should also be made for supervision of current correspondence, with the object of bringing to light those aspects of the company letters that could be improved, and also of showing the extent to which the bulletins are being utilized in everyday practice.

One method of supervision is to have a carbon copy of each letter sent through the house mail to the correspondence adviser. The latter can then rapidly glance through the correspondence, select those letters that are deficient in some respect, and return them to the writers with friendly comments and suggestions; letters that are particularly good may be chosen for inclusion in the manual, as previously suggested; letters that are satisfactory, and that call for neither criticism nor praise, may simply be destroyed.

If the volume of correspondence is heavy and the above procedure would consume too much of the adviser's time, a rotation system may be used. Thus, for a period of one month or longer, the sales department may be asked to send carbon copies to the adviser; the following month, the collection department; then the adjustment department; and so on.

Whatever means is used, it is important that the supervision be continuous. If the better-letters program is to produce enduring results, it must be permanent. The company correspondents need to be kept continually "on their toes," just as do the company salesmen.

Getting the staff to participate in the program.—If a better-letters program is put into effect, everything possible should be done to stimulate the active participation and co-operation of all members of the staff. Toward this end the tone of the bulletins should be friendly and informal; the attitude of the adviser one of encouragement rather than of criticism or blame. The adviser may inquire frankly whether or not the bulletins are proving helpful, what topics that he has failed to mention should be discussed, and what other members of the staff think of his ideas. Contributions and comments should be solicited, since the more people who participate, the greater the benefits are likely to be. In the final analysis, the object of a better-letters program is to lift the writing of letters out of the rut of routine into which it is apt to fall. Once interest and enthusiasm have been aroused, improvement in the company correspondence will follow. This improvement will result in increased prestige for the company, increased goodwill among customers, and, very probably, as a consequence of these, an advance of a step or two in sales.

Letter-writing class results in better letters.—A letter-writing class, under the direction of the advertising manager, was formed by Jantzen Knitting Mills. As a result of the instruction given, better public relations and better personnel relations were created, and, in addition, the company derived direct profits from increased sales through better selling letters. Here are two examples of the results of efforts to improve letters through the letter-writing class.

A factory executive decided to return a textile machine that he had purchased on trial. Keeping in mind some of the pointers made in a letter-writing class, the executive wrote the manufacturer explaining the firm's efforts to utilize the machine and its reasons for not being able to do so, and offering to prepay the transportation. The maker of the machine was warm in his appreciation of the consideration shown him. If the machine had been returned with a terse explanation such as "cannot use," which situation the manufacturer indicated was not an unusual one, the goodwill of the manufacturer would have been lost. The machine manufacturer and his family are potential users of the company's product.

One of the company's salesmen criticized a letter written to a retailer in his territory by one of the firm's new correspondents. As a result of the better-letters program, the subsequent correspondence of this man showed such marked improvement that the same salesman later could not give adequate praise.

Letter-writing program of a large company.—The program of the Gates Rubber Company, Denver, to improve company correspondence consists primarily of a systematic review by the correspondence supervisor of letters written by nearly one hundred correspondents, periodic checking by department heads, a letter-writing manual, and a monthly letter-writing contest.

The correspondence supervisor reads all letters written by new correspondents for the first two or three months and periodically reviews the correspondence of the remaining letter writers. To simplify the periodic review, the correspondents are divided into three groups. Carbon copies of the letters of the first group are sent to the supervisor the first week; of the second group, the second week; and of the third group, the third week. This system is repeated continuously, so that the supervisor always has a representative cross section of the letters written by all correspondents.

Any shortcomings that are discovered are called to the correspondent's attention, and any letters containing serious mistakes, such as misrepresentation of company policies or improper handling of people, are rewritten. The supervisor marks suggested corrections on the face of the letter and returns it to the correspondent for revision. Since the correspondent makes the revisions himself, he benefits from his mistakes by developing an ability to correct them. Relatively unimportant errors in phraseology, poor English, and the like, are simply called to the correspondent's attention for his future guidance, and the letters are not rewritten unless the flaws endanger the clarity or tone of the message.

The supervisor is always available to the correspondents for the discussion of letter-writing problems. By talking over certain difficulties, the correspondent and the supervisor can usually work out a satisfactory letter in a few minutes.

On one day of each week, extra copies are made of each letter and sent to the various department heads. In this way divisional executives check on the type of letters sent out by individuals under their supervision.

Frequently letter-writing bulletins are issued to correspondents. These have been collected and placed in a loose-leaf notebook that has proved invaluable to correspondents. The manual also includes exceptionally interesting articles on letter writing and excerpts from helpful books.

Monthly letter-writing contest stimulates good letter writing. —As indicated above, the better-letters program of the Gates Rubber Company includes a monthly letter-writing contest among correspondents, who are divided into four teams. A special problem, such as writing a goodwill letter, handling a certain situation, shortening a previously written letter, is assigned each month. Cash prizes are awarded for the best letters, and points are given for the winning ones and those receiving honorable mention. At the end of the year the team with the most points is given a banquet. Scoreboards showing the standing of the teams and charts showing the names of contest winners are displayed in prominent places.

In order that the same people may not win all the prizes all the time (and thus discourage competition), a "Top-Notchers Letter Club" has been formed. Membership is limited to those who have won a certain number of points in one contest year; members may not participate in the contests. They serve as coaches for the teams, act as judges, share in the prizes won by their teams, and attend all the banquets.

The judges are selected from the correspondents. The committee of judges always includes the correspondence supervisor and a member of the Top-Notchers Letter Club.

A "better-letters" pamphlet.—Some companies supply their employees with a printed pamphlet designed to improve the standard of letters that are sent out on the letterhead, and over the signature, of the company. Such a pamphlet is ordinarily not intended as a textbook of English, or of spelling, grammar, or punctuation. It deals chiefly with the basic principles of letter writing, and with the letter practices that the company has adopted.

The 36-page booklet of the Caterpillar Tractor Co., entitled "Better Letters—A discussion for all employees of Caterpillar Tractor Co. who dictate letters or who write them," is an example of this type of pamphlet. The first half is devoted to letter-writing principles. The second half deals with "Caterpillar" Standard Practices and gives instructions on the following: use of trade name, letter routing, dating memoranda, signature, interdepartmental letters, information as to distribution of the letter to others, letters to other companies, how to avoid waste in correspondence, letter files, export correspondence, letters of introduction, promptness of reply, and "Caterpillar" nomenclature.

New employees who dictate or write letters find the nomenclature section especially helpful. The following excerpt from this section shows how the instruction as to nomenclature is given:

Parts—it is preferred that "Caterpillar" parts be referred to as "parts" only—not "repair" parts.

Starting Engine—our Diesel engines are started by a starting engine. Call it by that name—not "starting motor"—not "auxiliary engine."

Water Cooling—in modern engine design and particularly in starting our Diesels, water serves to warm the engine and maintain correct temperature. The term "water-circulating system" is therefore preferred to "water cooling."

Letter-appraisal chart improves correspondence.—The letter-appraisal chart reproduced in Fig. 5 helped develop a high standard of correspondence in the Department of Agriculture under James F. Grady. Not only is the chart useful for self-criticism, but, if used in group conferences, it saves time by confining any discussion of the letter to specific reasons for its inadequacy.

LETTER APPRAISAL

This appraisal form is intended to assist you in revising your own letters or in indicating to others the specific weaknesses of the letters that are submitted to you for review.

Before appraising a letter, be sure to determine its exact purpose. What message is it expected to convey? What response is desired from the addressee?

Place a check mark in the column "Yes" or "No" opposite each question which applies to the letter you are appraising.

IS THE LETTER:	Yes	No
1. COMPLETE		
a. Does it give, in the most effective order, all information necessary to accomplish its purpose?		
b. Does it answer fully all the questions, asked or implied, in the incoming letter?		
2. CONCISE		
a. Does the letter include <u>only</u> the essential facts?		
b. Are the ideas expressed in the fewest words consistent with clearness, completeness, and courtesy; have irrelevant details and unnecessary repetition been eliminated?		
3. CLEAR		
a. Is the language adapted to the vocabulary of the addressee?		
b. Do the words exactly express the thought?		
c. Is the sentence structure clear?		
d. Are the paragraphs logical thought units, arranged to promote easy reading?		
4. CORRECT		
a. Is the accuracy of all factual information beyond question?		
b. Are all statements in strict conformity with policies?		
c. Is the letter free from: (1) grammatical errors, (2) spelling errors, (3) misleading punctuation?		
5. APPROPRIATE IN TONE		
a. Is the tone calculated to bring about the desired response?		
b. Is the tone calculated to build or protect good will?		
c. Does the entire letter evidence a desire to cooperate fully?		
d. Is it free from antagonistic words or phrases?		
6. NEAT AND WELL SET UP		
Will a favorable first impression be created by: (1) freedom from strike-overs and obvious erasures; (2) even typing; (3) position of letter on the page?		

HOW EFFECTIVE IS THE LETTER AS A WHOLE?

To what extent is the letter likely to accomplish its purpose, obtain the desired response, and build good will? In other words, how do you rate its <u>general effectiveness</u>? Underline the word which best expresses your rating:

A. OUTSTANDING B. GOOD C. PASSABLE D. UNSATISFACTORY

IN RATING ANOTHER'S LETTER

If the letter is "unsatisfactory," be sure to indicate the specific weaknesses which necessitate revision. Similarly, if the letter is only "passable," indicate clearly the weaknesses to which attention should be given in future letters.

Figure 5.—Letter Appraisal Chart.

ARE YOUR LETTERS COSTING TOO MUCH?

Cost Factor	*Average Cost*	*Possible Saving*	How Savings Can Be Made
DICTATOR'S TIME Based on a salary of $50 a week of 40 hours, and an average of 8 minutes for each letter written........	.166	.016	10% by inaugurating a campaign, under supervision of correspondence adviser, to eliminate long-windedness in letters; equipping executives with dictating machines, desk "companion" files, and form paragraph indexes. A study made by one large company indicated that equipping executives with dictating machines saved 13% of their time.
STENOGRAPHIC COST Based on a salary of $18 a week of 40 hours, and an average of 24 letters per day, including time taking dictation........................	.15	.05	$33\frac{1}{3}$% by centralizing stenographic and typing department; using transcribing and duplicating machines; modernizing typewriters; using efficiency desks and chairs; installing bonus plan. Under the bonus plan, operators are guaranteed a straight basic salary, regardless of the quantity of work produced. The quota set for each operator is 2,400 6-inch elite type lines per week, and a bonus is paid on all production over this quota, at the rate of $\frac{1}{2}$¢ per line (typewriters are equipped with devices which count the number of lines). One company which introduced the bonus plan reduced its cost per line from $.0106 to $.0064.
NON-PRODUCTIVE LABOR Time lost by dictator and stenographer due to waiting, illness, vacations, and other causes—10% of labor cost......................	.031	.004	13% by using labor-saving equipment (such as automatic typewriters or duplicating machines for form letters) to reduce number of employees needed, with corresponding reduction in non-productive time losses.

Cost Factor	*Average Cost*	*Possible Saving*	How Savings Can Be Made
Fixed Charges Depreciation, supervision, rent, light, interest, taxes, insurance, and similar overhead costs—40% of labor cost	.126	.037	30% by savings in floor space through centralization of correspondence departments; labor-saving equipment reduces employee's compensation insurance needs.
Materials Stationery, carbon papers, typewriter ribbons, pencils, and other supplies	.007	.001	15% by using better quality paper, but baronial and note sizes for short letters; gang printing of inter-office letterheads and enclosures with other forms on office printing equipment.
Mailing Cost Postage, gathering, sealing, stamping, and delivering to post office	.032	.006	20% by use of modern sealing and stamping machines, not only to save labor but to reduce losses due to pilfering of stamp box.
Filing Cost Clerk's time, depreciation on filing equipment, cost of filing supplies, etc.	.012	.001	15% by centralizing all files and filing operations; modernizing filing equipment and methods.
Total	.524	.115	

Courtesy of American Business, Chicago.

2. TONE AND SPIRIT OF THE LETTER

A "routine" letter rewritten.—A large shoe manufacturing company located in Boston, Massachusetts, received from a retailer in Johnstown, New York, a small initial order. The retailer's credit was checked, and the following letter written to the customer by a clerk in the credit department:

Dear Sir:

In response to your kind favor of March 12 beg to advise that we have opened a credit account in your name and are handling your order under our number 3467, which please note for future reference.

Hoping to receive your future orders, we remain,

Yours truly,

Before this letter was mailed, it came accidentally to the notice of as executive, who rewrote it as follows:

Dear Mr. Ferguson:

We appreciate very much your order of March 12, which will be shipped on the 17th by motor express. We are shipping this order to you on our most favorable credit terms, 2/10 net 30.

You can depend on us to co-operate with you at all times and to help you gain larger profits through the quick sale of our goods.

We are packing with your order our latest window display cards, and also a booklet of suggestions for using the cards. Within the next few days you will hear from our business promotion department, which is conducted exclusively for our customers. Please feel free to make use of this service at any time, without charge or obligation.

We welcome you as a customer, and hope that this order is only the first of many which will prove profitable to you.

Very truly yours,

The difference between the two letters is apparent. The first is written in stilted language—*your kind favor of March 12; beg to advise; hoping to receive your future orders, we remain.* In addition, the writer fails to show any real appreciation of the customer's order and likewise fails to attempt to win reorders by mentioning the window display cards and the services of the business promotion department. In contrast, the second letter is cordial. It is a "sales" letter. It cultivates the customer's goodwill by showing appreciation of his order and expressing an interest in his business. Furthermore, it is specific: the credit terms are stated so that there can be no subsequent misunderstanding, and the date and method of shipment are also given.

Avoid stilted phraseology.—The primary requisite of good business writing is the avoidance of stilted or formal phraseology. An examination of the morning mail will supply ample evidence of the fact that many correspondents appear to feel that there is a special language or style for business intercourse. The use of this special style involves the elimination of all friendly feeling from the letter and frequent repetition of such expressions as *same, kind favor, even date, the writer wishes to state, thanking you in advance,* and the like. In reality there is no special language of business correspondence. So-called "Business English" is merely everyday English adapted to the needs of business. It is adapted in the sense that it is improved in organization and clarity. There are, however, no rigid conventions with regard to it. If two businessmen were lunching together, one would not say to the other, "I am in receipt of your esteemed favor of March 5, and in reply beg to state . . ." Neither is it necessary or desirable that such language be used through the mails.

Among the expressions that are regarded as stilted, and hence are not good usage in business writing, are the following:

advise
and oblige
as per your instructions
at hand
attached please find
awaiting your further instructions
beg to state; advise; inform; acknowledge; etc.
contents duly noted
enclosed please find
esteemed favor
even date; recent date
for your information wish to state
hand you herewith
has come to hand
hoping to hear from you

in re
inst.; prox.; ult.
kind favor; order; etc.
oblige
our Mr. Clark
permit me to say
please be advised that
pursuant to
regarding your communication
same
thanking you in advance
the writer wishes to say
this letter is for the purpose of inquiring
trusting you will
up to this writing
we are; beg; remain; etc.
wish to say; advise; inform; acknowledge; etc.
would ask; state; advise; etc.

To illustrate the improvement that results when stilted phraseology is eliminated, take the following example of a business letter as originally written and then as rewritten:

(Stilted and Verbose)

Dear Sir:

Replying to your kind favor of the 15th inst. in which you inform us that the enameling sheets ordered by you have not come to hand, beg to advise we have checked up on this shipment and find same left our factory March 10 and should have reached you March 13. For your information wish to state that we are now tracing through the express company. If the shipment does not arrive by March 19, kindly wire us collect, and we will duplicate same.

Regretting the inconvenience caused you, we are,

Yours truly,

(Clear and Straightforward)

Dear Mr. Bradley:

Your letter of March 15 reached us this morning.

The shipment of enameling sheets left our factory on March 10, and should have been delivered to you not later than March 13. We have asked the express company to trace the shipment immediately.

If you do not receive the sheets by March 19, please wire us collect, and we will start another shipment at once.

We are very sorry that this delay occurred and assure you that we will do everything possible to expedite delivery.

Very truly yours,

It will be noted that the second letter contains exactly the same information as the first. The improvement in tone is brought about not by the addition of any new material but merely by the elimination of stilted phraseology.

Use short sentences and paragraphs.—Lack of clarity, the cardinal sin of business writing, results chiefly from the use of involved language and long sentences. The contents of a business letter should be apparent at a glance. To make the letter easy to read and to preclude misunderstanding, use simple words and short sentences, and paragraph wherever a new subject is introduced.

(Confused and Wordy)

Gentlemen:

Replying to your letter of October 15, with reference to our carload shipment of September 11, in which you received a five-gallon can of Collodion with a nail driven into the can through the wooden case, which resulted in contents leaking out and running down onto a couple of cases of 11 by 14 Duplitized X-Ray Film Super Speed in six-dozen packages, staining fifteen of the boxes; wish to advise that the cartons for the film were shipped to you by parcel post on October 27, which we hope you will receive without delay. We regret very much the accident of the nail being driven through the case, and have called it to the attention of the shippers of this material and asked them to be very careful on future shipments.

Very truly yours,

(Clear and Straightforward)

Gentlemen:

We regret very much the damage caused by the punctured can of Collodion, to which you referred in your letter of October 15. On October 27 we sent you by express another can of Collodion and new cartons to replace those which were damaged.

We have taken up the matter of the punctured can with our shipping department, and also with the carrier, and assure you that every effort will be made to insure the safe arrival of future shipments.

Very truly yours,

Methodical habits of dictation.—It is not uncommon to see a correspondent pick up a letter, glance at it, and immediately begin to dictate a reply before having formed, either in his own mind or on paper, an outline of what he intends to say. A letter written in this way can hardly be other than muddled. The writer probably starts with one thought, passes to a second, and then jumps back to the first before going on to the third. The person who receives the letter is confused, perhaps irritated. And it goes without saying that loss of business results, for a person who has written an inquiry and receives a muddled letter in reply will doubtless turn elsewhere for any purchase that he wishes to make.

Methodical habits of dictation consist of gathering all the necessary information and visualizing the letter as a whole before beginning to dictate the first paragraph. A simple procedure followed by many of the best correspondents in handling complaints, inquiries, and so forth, is to underscore the main points in the letter received and then to jot down rapidly at the foot of the page an outline of what the reply should contain. For example, suppose that a manufacturer of electric irons has received an order for a single iron from an individual; he is compelled to refuse the order because he sells only through retail dealers. The outline of the reply in this case might be as follows:

1. Thanks.
2. Sell only through dealers.
3. Returning check; visit or telephone dealer.
4. Name, address, and telephone number of dealer.
5. Guarantee.
6. Sales talk.

With this outline as a working basis, the correspondent would proceed to dictate the letter.

Dear Mrs. Robertson:

Thank you very much for your order of November 5 for one of our new ELECTRA electric irons.

We sincerely appreciate this evidence of your interest in the new ELECTRA and wish that we could fill your order. However, as manufacturers, we sell through retail dealers, and our arrangement with the dealers throughout the country does not permit our selling direct from the factory.

We regret, therefore, that we must return your check with the request that you either visit or telephone the ELECTRA dealer in your city, who will be glad to deliver the iron at the price advertised. In buying from the dealer you will have the advantage of choosing from a large stock and will avoid the annoyance of possible delay in shipment.

The name, address, and telephone number of the ELECTRA dealer in York is:

Polk Electrical Supply Company, 424 Main Street
Telephone: YORK 3200

Every ELECTRA is guaranteed by us, and also by the dealer, to be in perfect condition.

We hope that you will soon be numbered among the many thousands of women who have found that with the new ELECTRA ironing is no longer a drudgery. The ELECTRA is easy to handle. It saves 30% of the time needed when you use any other electric iron now on the market.

To bring an ELECTRA to your home, simply pick up the telephone and call:

YORK 3200

Sincerely yours,

The above letter is a logical, clear reply to the request received. Visualizing the letter as a whole and, if necessary, making an outline of it, is the work of a moment. It may be the means of saving the writer the embarrassment of realizing, when he is reading over the finished letter, that he has omitted an important point, or the further embarrassment of receiving from the customer a second letter saying that the reply is not clear.

How to open and close the letter.—The opening sentence or paragraph of the letter should generally go straight to the point, without any beating about the bush. The object is to gain the reader's attention immediately.

In writing a letter of reply it is unnecessary to give a restatement of the contents of the letter received. To state that the letter is in reply to one of such-and-such a date is sufficient. Participial openings, such as *Referring to your communication of, Answering your letter of, Replying to your letter of, In reply to yours of,* should be avoided. Some examples of poor and good openings follow; for further examples, see the specimen letters given in each of the later parts of this section.

(Poor Opening)

Dear Sir:

Replying to your letter of June 9 in which you request that we send you samples of our new WEAREVER fabrics, we are asking our agents in Cleveland, John Brown & Company, to supply you with the samples requested, and they will be pleased to assist you in carrying out any tests that you may wish to make.

(Better Opening)

Dear Sir:

Thank you very much for your request of June 9 for samples of our new WEAREVER fabrics.

We have asked our agents in Cleveland, John Brown & Company, to supply you with a full line of samples. They will be glad to assist you in carrying out any tests you may wish to make.

(Poor Opening)

Dear Sir:

In reply to yours of the 15th in which you state that you would be interested in receiving more complete information as to our STEADY-HEAT OIL BURNER, as you are considering installing a burner in your home, we are enclosing a booklet describing the advantages of the STEADY-HEAT which we think you will find of value and are also requesting our local representative in your community, Wallace & Company, to call upon you.

(Better Opening)

Dear Sir:

We are glad to respond to your letter of April 15, in which you request more complete information concerning the STEADY-HEAT OIL BURNER.

The enclosed booklet, "Better Heat with STEADY-HEAT," discusses the many advantages of the STEADY-HEAT BURNER. We have also asked our representative in your community, Wallace & Company, to call upon you at your convenience. Wallace & Company will be pleased to give you full information, without any obligation.

(POOR OPENING)

Dear Sir:

Answering your letter of April 5 in which you suggest that we take your 60-day note for our March invoice, we note what you say as to poor business conditions in Harrisburg at the present time due to the closing of several local plants, but regret that it is not a practice with us to take notes.

(BETTER OPENING)

Dear Sir:

We were very sorry to learn from your letter of April 5 that business conditions in Harrisburg have been poor in recent months. We can readily appreciate that under the circumstances you will be having difficulty in making collections.

Since it is not a practice with us to take notes, we are sorry that we cannot agree to your suggestion. However, we are always glad to co-operate with our customers in every possible way and . . . .

A comparison of the "poor" and the "better" openings in the above examples shows the greater effectiveness of a short, clear-cut opening paragraph. The purpose of this opening paragraph is merely to state the subject of the letter, and perhaps to express a word or two of thanks, appreciation, or regret; the subject is then developed in the succeeding paragraphs. The chief fault of the "poor" examples is that they attempt to state the subject and to develop it at one and the same time; openings such as these leave the reader mentally breathless.

The closing paragraph or sentence should add something to the letter; it need not be a meaningless formality. The better correspondents do not use participial closings such as the following:

Hoping to be favored with an early reply, we are,
Trusting that this will be satisfactory to you, we remain,
Trusting that you will let us hear from you if we can be of further service,
Thanking you for your order, we remain,
Assuring you of our desire to please you, we are,
Hoping to receive your future orders, we remain,

A more forceful and sincere way of closing the business letter is to use a complete sentence or a direct statement. Examples of this type of closing follow; for further examples of effective closings, see the specimen letters given in each of the later parts of this section.

We appreciate your interest and thank you for writing us.

We hope that this initial order is only the beginning of a long business relationship, which we shall try to make both pleasant and profitable to you.

We are looking forward to pleasant business relations.

We sincerely hope that we may find your name on our active list within the next thirty days.

Please do not hesitate to write us again if we can be of further service to you.

We are always eager to make every transaction satisfactory. Please do not hesitate to write us at any time.

We very much regret the delay, and assure you that your future orders will be handled promptly.

Adapt the letter to the reader.—Writing good business letters requires imagination. This is obviously true of sales letters but is also equally true of any other type. The most successful correspondents are those who are able to visualize the person to whom they are writing, to reconstruct his or her mode of living and habits of thought, and to adapt their letters to the reader. A letter suitable for a small retailer in a town in the Middle West would not make a favorable impression on a large retailer in New York; a letter that one would send to a New England farmer would not do for an attorney in Chicago; a straight-from-the-shoulder, man-to-man letter would be absolutely wrong for a middle-aged spinster.

The question of adapting the letter to the reader can, of course, be ignored. More often than not it is ignored. By taking a safe middle stand a correspondent can write in exactly the same tone and spirit to anyone with whom his company does business, without giving offense. There is, however, the reverse side of the medal. Letters written in such a way that they might be intended for anyone often have interest and appeal for no one in particular.

Every letter is a business opportunity. Even though the letter may not be a sales letter in the sense that it is an attempt actually to sell goods, it should be a sales letter in the sense that it "sells" goodwill and cements a cordial relationship. The question must, then, arise in the mind of the correspondent: "Considering the station in life, education, and other circumstances of this particular individual to whom I am about to write, what tone in my letter will be most likely to make for friendship between us—friendship that may, at a later date, result in sales?" If the letter is to a small retailer, the correspondent may decide that a human, friendly letter showing interest in the retailer's business and perhaps offering him advice would be most suitable. If the letter is to a large manufacturer, a concise, businesslike style might be most appropriate. If the letter is to a farmer, a neighborly, gossipy tone may meet with the best reception.

For most correspondents, of course, adaptation to the reader is greatly simplified by the fact that the majority of the people to whom the company writes letters are of one class or type. The problem then resolves itself into experimenting with letters of different tone until the most appropriate one is found. The selection is determinable largely from the nature of the replies received to the letters mailed. When experiments of this kind are being made, personal preference and prejudice must be set aside. The correspondent for a farm machinery company may be, personally, a man of culture with an interest in the arts. He himself may prefer the formal, well-written business letter. On the other hand, the farmers who buy the company's machinery may respond more readily to letters beginning, "I was mighty glad, Mr. Hansen, to see from your letter of August 15 that the drought situation in Kansas is now clearing up a bit," rather than, "We are pleased to note from your letter of August 15 that the drought situation in Kansas is now somewhat alleviated." The reader's psychology, and not the writer's, is the primary consideration.

Illustration of how to adapt the letter to the reader.—To illustrate how the business letter may be adapted to the reader, the following two letters are given. In both cases the situation is the same: the letters are replies to complaints, written by a correspondent in a large radio manufacturing company. In the first case, however, the complaint was received from a woman whose letter indicated that she was well educated and had perhaps had business experience; the second was written—in pencil, on ruled paper, and with frequent misspellings—by a farmer in Iowa. The correspondent's replies follow:

TO THE WOMAN

Dear Mrs. Ashton:

We were very sorry to learn from your letter of January 6 that the reception on your TRUETONE RADIO has not been entirely satisfactory.

As manufacturers of this radio we take pride in its reputation for reliable, quality performance. We therefore guarantee every TRUETONE against mechanical defect for a period of one year from the date of purchase.

If you will return the radio to us by parcel post insured or by express insured, we shall be glad to give it a thorough examination and to remedy whatever defect is causing the "fading" mentioned in your letter. The charge for this service will be only $1. This fee covers merely the handling and shipping costs; we make no charge for labor or for any new parts that may be necessary.

To protect the radio against possible damage in transit, please pack it in the original carton, if you still have this, and merely enclose $1. The radio will be returned to you within three days after we receive it.

We appreciate very much your writing us direct and assure you of our desire that you derive full satisfaction from ownership of your TRUETONE.

Very truly yours,

TO THE FARMER

Dear Mr. Petersen:

I was mighty sorry to see from your letter of January 6 that your TRUETONE RADIO has been acting up. As you say, it shouldn't do this, being only three months old.

What I wish you would do is pack it up and send it right back to me. Whatever is the matter with it, we'll fix it here in the factory. Every TRUETONE is guaranteed by us for one year from the day you buy it.

When you send the radio, pack it in the box that it was in when you bought it, and put a $1 bill in the box. This $1 is all that you will have to pay, no matter what is wrong with the radio. It covers just the cost of packing the radio and sending it back to you. We pay for the workman's time and for any new parts that have to be put in. That's fair enough, isn't it?

Mail the box by parcel post insured, and we'll send you back the radio three days after we get it.

We want you to know that we're glad you wrote us, and we'll see that your TRUETONE is fixed right.

Yours truly,

Possibly the foregoing letters are an extreme example of contrast in tone. They may, however, be taken as an illustration of the possibilities in adapting the letter to the reader. The woman would probably be favorably impressed by the courteous tone of the letter written to her; the farmer would doubtless be glad to receive, in reply to his complaint, a letter that he could understand. If the correspondent had written to both parties merely in a standardized tone, two opportunities for creating goodwill would have been lost.

In conclusion, a word of warning may not be out of place. Not all farmers misspell words; not all women are well educated. There is danger in generalizing as to which tone to adopt in addressing a particular class. The correspondent must therefore be guided by the character of the letter received from the person to whom he is writing.

3. MAKING SALES FROM INQUIRIES BY LETTER

(*Note:* "How to Write Sales Letters" begins at page 334.)

How to answer an inquiry.—The following are the chief points to keep in mind in replying to letters of inquiry:

1. Answer inquiries promptly—if possible, within twenty-four hours. To secure the inquirer's business or to make a sale, you must strike while the iron is hot. Should it be necessary to refuse the request, a prompt reply will create goodwill and may result in your name being favorably remembered by the inquirer for future reference. Your business reputation is built upon the small, day-to-day experiences of the people who have contact with you.

2. Every inquiry is a sales opportunity. Your reply should therefore be courteous, helpful, and should show a desire to serve. Because the inquirer's interest is likely to have waned rapidly in the interval before your reply reaches him, it is necessary for you to revive his interest by reselling him on your product or service. For this purpose, include sales talk in your reply.

3. Although the reply to an inquiry should be a selling letter, it should first answer specifically and clearly the question that was asked. Nothing is more irritating to an inquirer than to receive a reply which does not answer his question.

4. Most inquiries are incomplete and sketchy. At the time that he is writing, the inquirer probably knows very little about your product or service. You should therefore not restrict yourself to answering the one or two questions that it occurred to him to ask. Try to anticipate further questions, objections, and points that may not be clear.

5. Open by thanking the inquirer for his letter and for his interest in your goods. Close by assuring him that you will be glad to be of service to him and to supply him with any additional information that he may need.

The letter that accompanies a request for booklets.—You have secured the prospect's attention when you have succeeded in getting him to send in a request for booklets. The letter accompanying the booklet is an out-and-out sales letter. Notice how the following letter moves from the direct inquiry to sales material.

Dear Mr. Benson:

Thank you for your request for our new booklets, VARIADEX and TRIPLE CHECK AUTOMATIC. Your copies are being mailed today.

You will find these booklets unusually interesting in their description of Remington Rand's two new filing systems. VARIADEX and TRIPLE CHECK AUTOMATIC are scientifically designed to handle efficiently and economically the complex filing procedure in the modern business office.

You may be concerned with the problem of how to increase speed in file operation, how to eliminate wasteful errors in filing and finding, or how to handle peculiar lists or an unusual volume of correspondence. Whatever your problem, one of these two new filing systems will give you a practical solution.

After you have read these two booklets, you will be interested in seeing an actual demonstration in your office of the system you believe most suited to your purpose. If you wish, a Remington Rand representative will also make an analysis of your filing situation and will recommend the system that can give you the best possible service from your files.

A demonstration of either VARIADEX or TRIPLE CHECK AUTOMATIC will be given you, or an analysis of your files will be made for you, entirely without obligation. Please write or phone the Remington Rand office at 205 East 42 Street, Murrayhill 4-5000.

Very truly yours,

An answer to a request for more information.—Here is an example of an answer to a request for more information about a product. The inquirer asked no specific question; hence the letter is a general sales letter. If specific information were called for, this particular letter would not be satisfactory.

Dear Doctor Brown:

Your desire to know more about Anabolic Products is good news to us, and we look forward to welcoming you to our ever-growing family of doctors.

You will find no mystery about Anabolic Products—we have no "secret" ingredients—and you will find our literature entirely free from sensationalism. The rationale of Anabolic Supplemental Nutrition is far from difficult.

As a means of acquainting you with our products most in demand, I am enclosing a bulletin entitled, "Simplicity Itself." In every case, you will note that the complete ingredients are given—with Anabolic you know what you are using. May I suggest that you slip this bulletin under the blotter on your desk where it will be convenient for quick reference.

We feel justified in stressing the quality of Anabolic Products since our vegetables are grown in tested soil, fertilized by our own chemical fertilizers, and dehydrated by a method on which we hold exclusive rights and patents. Our glandular ingredients are the finest obtainable—never cold storage—and our vitamin concentrates are standardized by biological assay.

Your questions are invited, and your orders will be given every attention.

Cordially yours,
ANABOLIC FOODS, Inc.

Giving further information.—Some inquiries reveal doubt in the prospect's mind as to some feature of the product. The reply in such cases must convince the reader that the product meets his needs or desires. The following letter stresses quality to convince the reader that the particular product is superior to others:

Dear Mr. Benson:

It is quite true, just as you say, that sheet steel and ARMCO INGOT IRON look alike on the surface. Careful examination under the microscope, however, reveals a vast difference.

In general, when you select articles, you rely upon sight and touch to determine the quality. Take clothing, for instance: the "feel" of the cloth will tell whether the material is all wool as well as a yard wide. When you buy shoes, the "feel" again comes into play and discloses whether the leather is of coarse or fine texture.

With metals, however, sight and touch cannot reveal the true quality. The quality of metal is determined by the degree of scientific skill used in the elimination of impurities.

Here is a simple illustration that brings out the point: you have one defective apple in a barrel of prize winners, and what happens? You either throw out the decaying apple or lose all.

And so it is with sheet metal. The elements that produce decay, or rust, in ferrous metals are carbon, sulphur, phosphorus, manganese, silicon, and the gases—oxygen, hydrogen, and nitrogen. These detrimental elements must be entirely eliminated if possible. If not completely eliminated, they must be reduced to the smallest possible degree.

Here is where ARMCO INGOT IRON excels all other sheet metals. The impurities named are guaranteed not to exceed 16/100 of one per cent. No other sheet manufacturer can give you this guarantee.

It is the pure metal in ARMCO INGOT IRON that will make your roof last longer, because pure iron will resist rust.

Very truly yours,

Letters accompanying catalogues.—A request for a catalogue is a step toward a future sale. The tie-up between the enclosure and the letter should be made vital and stimulating. The following letters have a conversational tone that brings the reader close to the vendor:

Dear Mr. Donald:

We were glad to receive your inquiry. The enclosed catalogue of the SUPER ELTO for 19— will give you the information you want on our motor.

But catalogues are funny things—each year we labor intensely to compress between the two covers everything we think you might want to know about the ELTO—and everything we want you to know, as well. But a catalogue seems never to be more—than a catalogue.

It seems always to leave untold a lot of things you'd appreciate knowing.

As you read through it, you'll notice that we strongly emphasize a certain few points about the SUPER ELTO. Quarter-turn starting, as a particular example:

> The plain fact is, we know of nothing more important than this matter of easy starting—easy starting in the genuine, honest sense of the word. Before everything else—before every trip you make, through every year of its use, you must *start* your motor. And on *starting,* more than anything else, will depend your satisfaction and pleasure.

But even easy starting should not overshadow other ELTO qualities. For the ELTO has feature after feature far too sound and valuable to be subordinated.

Rudder steering, for instance. One of our users wrote us that "rudder steering *gives brains to the motor!*"

It does seem that way! It's twice as pleasant for the user when he can sit where he pleases, changing his course with a gentle tug on a vibrationless tiller line, letting that rudder do about nine tenths of his steering for him.

Then there is the Propello-Pump—the huge bearings—the Safety Cushion Drive and . . . .

But it's time to let the catalogue tell its own story. Only, as we pointed out before, a catalogue is just a catalogue. If you find a single question left unanswered, or want fuller information on any point, please write us. We'll answer as fully as we possibly can.

Cordially yours,

* * *

Dear Mr. Muirhead:

You made us feel mighty good when we received your request for our proposition, and we know that you are going to be glad that you wrote, for the rugs that we have for this year's selling are the finest in the field, and the best that we have ever produced.

The catalogue which we are sending you tells our story of weaves, patterns, and profit opportunities in an interesting way, while our prices, as shown on the attached list, are as good as you will find our rugs to be.

But don't forget, in considering the prices, that they are list prices. From these you secure a trade discount of 10-5% off. After deducting this percentage from the lists, you get net prices that are as low as can be secured anywhere. There are none better.

Then, too, we allow the full cost of your freight on all orders that weigh 100 pounds or more (except for Deltone and Tufted Rugs, which are f.o.b. the mill). This policy eliminates the bother of adding freight costs to your merchandise costs after arrival of the goods, which we know you will say is a big help.

Our representative, Mr. Peters, will visit with you within the next thirty days, but if you desire to order before he calls, just drop your specification in the mail box with the assurance that we will give it speedy attention.

With best good wishes,

Sincerely yours,

Answering a letter from a retailer.—Where a company distributes its product through a wholesale distributor, it must gently inform the retailer of this fact and at the same time keep in mind the possibility of the retailer becoming a dealer. The following letter covers this situation:

Dear Mr. Stephens:

Immediately upon receipt of your letter of November 8 asking about the CROSLEY LINE, we wrote our wholesale distributor, The Homer King Company, 711 Broadway, Tacoma, Washington, and asked them either to call on you or write you to explain our terms and discounts.

Inasmuch as we have placed wholesale distributors in most of the large centers so that your needs can be more promptly served, we do not sell direct to retailers.

Will you please fill in on the enclosed application blank your name, address, primary business, and the number of sets that you believe will sell in your community? If the wholesale distributor named above does not write you or call upon you within the next five days, please return the application blank direct to us.

We want you to know that we appreciate your interest in the CROSLEY LINE and that we hope your name can be included among the many dealers in your state who are finding CROSLEY their most profitable line.

Very truly yours,

Sending a representative with samples.—Sometimes a request is best answered by sending a representative. The following letter shows one large company's method of utilizing a sales possibility in its answer to a request for samples:

Dear Mr. Thompson:

Thank you for your request for samples of our REMCRAFT folder.

We have asked a representative of our branch office, which is listed below, to supply you with samples of REMCRAFT so that you may test them in your own office.

When he delivers these samples, our representative will welcome an opportunity to offer suggestions on any of your filing problems.

Very truly yours,

Letters refusing requests.—A letter of this type should be courteous, should explain clearly the reasons for the refusal, and should express regret. It may close with a sales talk about the product.

Dear Sir:

As requested in your letter of January 9, I am glad to send you a copy of the issue of January 2. Please accept it with our compliments.

I also wish to thank you for your kind words for our magazine, but since our publications are made especially for national advertisers and advertising agencies, we are prevented from accepting subscriptions outside this field.

In selecting our prospects for subscriptions, we are careful to pick out only those who are actually advertising in some form. Our experience has been that readers outside of our field find little of interest in the magazine, and discontinue as soon as their subscriptions are up.

We therefore seek only what we call "logical" subscribers.

I feel quite certain that you will understand our position, but I want you to know that your interest is very much appreciated.

Very sincerely yours,

* * *

Dear Miss Robson:

Because each woman's search for youth and beauty is an individual problem, it necessarily requires individual attention.

We therefore do not find the use of set formulas suitable for the requirements of our customers. We are sorry that we do not have any of the booklets you requested us to send you.

Why not see your nearest DOROTHY DALE representative for a personal analysis of your beauty problems, and be sure that you are using the course of treatment exactly suited to your type of beauty?

Very truly yours,

* * *

Dear Mr. Ward:

We appreciate very much your order of July 16, but regret that we are unable to accept it because of our established merchandising policy.

Our policy is to grant an exclusive agency for the sale of our products in towns that have a population of 25,000 or less.

This arrangement assures the retailer a very profitable trade. We already have an established agency in your city.

Although no change is contemplated at present, we take pleasure in keeping your name in our files, and assure you that we appreciate your interest in our products.

Very truly yours,

4. LETTERS TO REVIVE INACTIVE ACCOUNTS

Bringing inactive customers back to life.—A study [1] of why customers stop buying at a particular store shows that of every 100 whose accounts are inactive:

68 have drifted away because of store indifference toward them;
14 have stopped buying because of unadjusted grievances;
9 have transferred their patronage to a competitor who offers lower prices or better service;
5 have been influenced by friends to trade elsewhere;
3 have moved, taking their business to more convenient shopping centers, or have made other arrangements more convenient or economical;
1 is dead or unaccounted for.

This record shows that not every inactive account is a lost account. Remove indifference to customers by letters containing words of encouragement and showing individual attention, and many of the inactive accounts will show signs of life. A warm, personal tone is essential in letters to revive inactive accounts. The customer must be made to feel that he has been missed. If his absence is due to

---

[1] The findings of this survey, as tabulated above, are listed as authentic by Jules J. Paglin in "The Direct Mail Approach in the Retail Market," *The Reporter Study Course in Direct Mail Advertising* (Henry Hoke, Editor), and by Frieda E. Burger, of Namm Store, Brooklyn, New York, in "Reviving Inactive Accounts," *The Credit World,* February, 1937.

dissatisfaction, he must be won over by the expression of a sincere desire on the part of the store to remove the dissatisfaction.

In letters calling attention to the inactive status of the account, it is sometimes effective to mention some special event to stimulate interest. For example, the arrival of new merchandise, price reductions, and the like, may add pulling power to the letter.

A single letter may be effective to regain a substantial part of the inactive accounts. Frequently, however, a series of letters is used. Examples of both kinds are given below.

Series to persons who opened accounts and made no purchases.—The following three letters, used by Ovington's, New York, constitute an effective series to individuals who opened accounts and made no purchases on credit:

Dear Mr. Johnston:

We had the pleasure of opening an account for you some time ago. But you have not made use of it, and so we're sending along this note with the hope that you will do so soon—and often.

We'll be very grateful if you do.

Sincerely,

* * *

Dear Mr. Johnston:

We do not wish to appear persistent with reference to the charge account you opened with us, but we are concerned that you have not made use of it. May I inquire whether, by any chance, this has come about by some error on our part? I should be very glad to hear from you.

Sincerely,

* * *

Dear Mr. Johnston:

As indicated in a previous letter, it pleased us greatly when you opened a charge account with us. However, you have not used it, and we're wondering whether it is through any fault of ours. If so, we wish that you would frankly tell us.

And, of course, if you simply overlooked it, won't you accept this as a little reminder that we're anxious to serve you?

Sincerely,

Letters to old customers who have not been using their accounts.—When a desirable account has been inactive for several months, it may often be brought to life by one or more letters similar to the following:

Dear Mrs. Arnsman:

Your account has not been used for several months, and we are anxious to know the reason. Of course, you may have been away or not had an opportunity to visit the store. However, if your absence is due to any fault of ours, we wish you would give us this opportunity to make it right.

Every one of our Six Sales Floors is teeming with the newest and smartest apparel, things for the home and newest Spring merchandise, at prices which make this indeed a store of moderate price.

We want you to know that your charge account is at your disposal, and we hope you will soon take advantage of its convenience.

We appreciate your past patronage here, and want to do all we can to help you enjoy your visits here.

Very truly yours,

* * *

Dear Mrs. Schmuck:

For over 65 years we have enjoyed the patronage of the people of Quincy and many other places in this vicinity. As we grow older, we appreciate more and more the importance of keeping old friends.

We have found that you have not made any purchases through your charge account for some time, and, if it is due to any failure of ours, we wish that you would write us or tell us about it so that we may improve our service to you.

Foremost of all our assets, we place the goodwill and the friendship of our customers, and we sincerely hope that we may have the opportunity to serve you in the very near future.

Very sincerely,

* * *

Dear Mrs. Brown:

Your account has just been placed on my desk, showing that it has not been used for some time. Naturally I am concerned and wonder why you have not used it recently.

Sometimes something happens in our service that displeases a customer. We rarely hear of this in the credit department. Will you take just a minute of your time and tell us if we have failed somewhere along the line? We sincerely miss you as a valuable charge customer, and, now that Easter is so near, I hope to receive a report that you have used your account again.

Speaking of Easter. Have you seen the new Spring things ready for you in our Fashion Centers? This is a special invitation to call. You may use either your monthly charge or our convenient Budget Plan for your purchases. Our merchandise is moderately priced and styled in the usual Brock manner—of course.

I want to take this opportunity to thank you for the privilege of having served you in the past. I hope the Bookkeeping Department will advise me soon that your account is again active. This would please me very much.

Cordially yours,

Letters to find out why good customers have not purchased.—Where there is reason to believe that the customer has ceased purchasing because of some dissatisfaction, a letter such as the following may be used:

Dear Mr. Kirk:

If, one of these days, you should discover that a mighty good friend of yours had suddenly stopped visiting you without apparent cause, you would want to know why, wouldn't you? You can readily understand, then, our concern at not having heard from you for several months.

Although we have always done the very best we could to meet your requirements, being human, we may have fallen down in some particular. If this is so, won't you please let us know?

You can rest assured that, whatever the trouble was, we will make things right. We shall not feel that we are a success until your account bears evidence that you are again one of our regular customers.

Very truly yours,

* * *

Dear Mr. Beebe:

In checking through our sales records today, I noticed that you haven't given our salesman an order for merchandise for a considerable time.

Every day our stocks are being augmented with new items that will be of much interest to your customers and profitable for you to handle. I hope that it will be convenient for you to give our salesman an order the next time he calls.

We value your business highly, and it occurs to me that we, in some manner, have not served you properly. I would appreciate your using the enclosed envelope to tell me why our salesman has not been getting your business.

Sincerely yours,

Dear Mr. Jones:

Each year we have a sort of "housecleaning" of our office files, and I was surprised when I found that your name was not among our customers for the winter just past.

I wonder, Mr. Jones, if we have fallen down somewhere in our service to you in the past?

Naturally, we like to keep our customers. So if something has happened to cause you to buy elsewhere, we would like to know about it, and to do what we can to make things right.

Give us a ring, Mr. Jones, and let's talk it over.

Sincerely yours,[2]

* * *

Dear Mrs. Allaway:

Just a friendly note to tell you that we have missed you. . . . Your charge account has not been used for several months, and we are wondering why.

This is the time of year when a Forman charge account should serve its best purposes . . . a season of special opportunities!

You can tell by the calendar that winter is here . . . social festivities have begun . . . Thanksgiving and Christmas are coming apace! Your charge account fits this program like the proverbial glove!

It is yours to use . . . and it applies to this store and this season with special emphasis because Forman's devotes all its thought and energy to the things that make a woman's world!

We want you to have all the advantages that Forman's can offer in the way of fashion and value . . . we want to make your charge account serve you in the most practical and personal way!

So we cordially invite you!

And we invite you also, if our service in the past has been anything less than completely satisfactory, to tell us frankly. We like to know our shortcomings . . . so that we can correct them. No postage will be required when you use the enclosed envelope, and we'll appreciate hearing from you.

Sincerely yours,[3]

* * *

---

[2] Courtesy of Cabin Creek Consolidated Sales Co., Cincinnati, Ohio. Letter supplied to coal dealers.

[3] Courtesy of B. Forman Co., Rochester, New York (Mr. Leonard Berry, Director of Accounts).

Dear Mr. Smith:

Our records show that it has been some time since you last visited our service department. We are wondering whether the service you received was entirely satisfactory? Whether the work was well done; your car ready when promised? Did you receive courteous attention?

Our service manager is anxious to demonstrate to you what an efficient department he is operating; how he can save you money on your regular specials. He will tell you how we give fifteen dollars worth of oiling and greasing for ten dollars.

We will be pleased to call for and deliver your car at no additional charge.

We await an opportunity to be of service to you, and add your name to our growing list of satisfied customers.

Yours very truly,

* * *

Dear Mrs. Spellman:

The faint heart that ne'er won the fair lady of old wouldn't do a very thriving grocery business in this day and age.

For we realize it's not enough to supply clean, fresh, dependable foods at the right price. Besides that, a grocer must be willing to render the extra measure of service to make and keep friends. He must possess the courage to ask *why* when one whose friendship and business he values stops trading with him.

So we wish you would tell us with the same frankness: What has happened to break our past relationship? If it has been due to any fault of ours, we'd like to know about it and correct it immediately.

Just a few lines on the back of this letter will be enough. The enclosed postage-paid envelope is for your convenience.

With every assurance of our appreciation of this courtesy, let us leave the reminder that your account here is always good—that you will receive the best telephone-delivery service we can possibly render—and that we will be glad indeed to serve you again.

Hopefully yours,[4]

Stunt letters to revive inactive accounts.—The stunt letter has been used with considerable success in reviving inactive accounts. Here are several examples.

---

[4] Courtesy of Heiden's Mailing Bureau, Seattle, Washington (Mr. H. B. Heiden, Manager). Prepared for Laurel Grocery, Seattle, Washington.

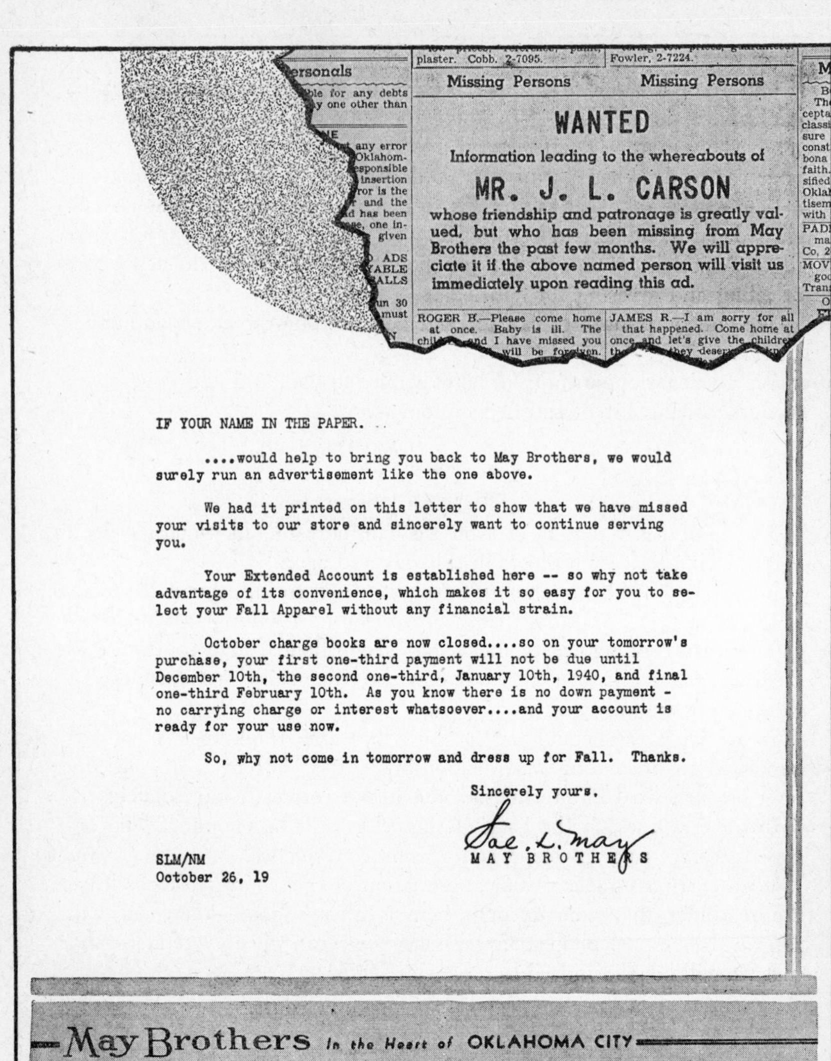

Missing Persons Missing Persons

WANTED

Information leading to the whereabouts of

MR. J. L. CARSON

whose friendship and patronage is greatly valued, but who has been missing from May Brothers the past few months. We will appreciate it if the above named person will visit us immediately upon reading this ad.

IF YOUR NAME IN THE PAPER. . .

....would help to bring you back to May Brothers, we would surely run an advertisement like the one above.

We had it printed on this letter to show that we have missed your visits to our store and sincerely want to continue serving you.

Your Extended Account is established here -- so why not take advantage of its convenience, which makes it so easy for you to select your Fall Apparel without any financial strain.

October charge books are now closed....so on your tomorrow's purchase, your first one-third payment will not be due until December 10th, the second one-third, January 10th, 1940, and final one-third February 10th. As you know there is no down payment - no carrying charge or interest whatsoever....and your account is ready for your use now.

So, why not come in tomorrow and dress up for Fall. Thanks.

Sincerely yours,

Sol. L. May

MAY BROTHERS

SLM/NM
October 26, 19

May Brothers In the Heart of OKLAHOMA CITY

Figure 6.—A Cleverly Personalized Stunt Letter to Inactive Patrons.

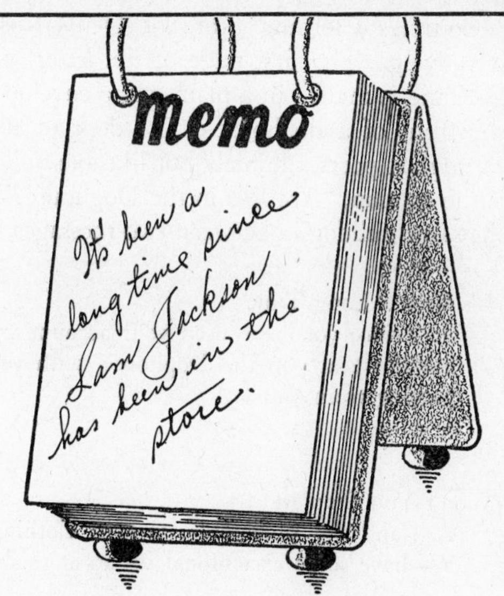

Mr. Sam Jackson
2419 Blaine Avenue
Oklahoma City, Okla.

Dear Mr. Jackson:

As I turned the page

of my memo pad

this morning ...

I was forcefully reminded that you have not given us the opportunity to serve you lately. When a good customer stops buying, it makes us feel that we have fallen down -- that somewhere our service or carefully selected clothing has not measured up to expectations.

We have tried to make our store a little different from most stores. Our business has been built on the confidence our customers have in us and our merchandise. We have tried to make our relationship with customers a little more personal and friendly.

Since you have not been in lately, you will be more delighted than ever before ... for right now all stocks are at the peak of completeness! You will enjoy seeing the new styles in straw hats, hot weather suitings, and seasonable furnishings.

Just to see you in the store again will make us feel good.

Expectantly yours,

Tom Baugh

TOM BAUGH - Men's Wear

TOM BAUGH • MEN'S WEAR • 117 NORTH ROBINSON PERRINE BUILDING OKLAHOMA CITY, OKLAHOMA

Figure 7.—A Cleverly Personalized Stunt Letter to Inactive Patrons.

Cottrell's Clothing Store of Denver used a "doghouse" letter effectively. The first page of the letter, which is of greeting-card size, and is mailed in a plain white envelope, hand-addressed, shows the front of a doghouse. The door of the house is cut out and through it peers a homely but likeable bulldog. Beneath the house is the caption, "Are We in the Doghouse?" The third page shows the same bulldog in between two messages, which read:

"It's Been a Long Time
. . . since you have used your account with us and we're wondering if we are 'in the Doghouse' with you. We would appreciate hearing from you."

and:

"Won't You Stop In
. . . and see our new styles in clothing, hats, and furnishings. We have some exceptional values at this time, too."

followed by the store's name and address.

Old customers return after receiving checkup letter.—Businesses selling a product or a service that has a limited life will increase sales by writing to customers about the time that renewal should be made. Such a follow-up shows desire to serve, efficiency, and progressiveness. Here is a letter that brings repeat business to the Haskin Optical Company, optometrists and manufacturing opticians of Miami, Florida.

As a vital service to my patients, careful records are kept of all examinations, the condition of the eyes, and the date when a checkup should be made.

This is to remind you that an examination of your eyes should be made at this time, as it has been over two years since they were examined.

To safeguard previous work and to insure future good vision and appearance, an appointment is desirable now.

Please telephone 2-5526.

Sincerely yours,

5. LETTERS THAT BUILD GOODWILL

Points that help make goodwill letters effective.—In the section on "Tone and Spirit of the Letter" some fundamental principles of good letter writing were given. In addition to applying these principles to the letter that aims specifically at creating goodwill, the letter writer should give attention to the following points:

1. Give the envelope an individual personality by individually typewriting the address.
2. Send the letter first class so that it arrives sealed.
3. Avoid metered mail, since this smacks of mass mailings and lithographed form letters.
4. Use a good-quality paper to give the letter importance.
5. Have the letter paper and envelope match.
6. Give the letter eye appeal. See the section on "Mechanics of the Letter."
7. Be certain that the details of the inside address are absolutely correct. Calling a person by an incorrect name, addressing him as "Mr." when he is a "Dr.," and errors in his address will annoy the reader and hurt the letter as an ambassador of goodwill.
8. Make the letter personal in the salutation by using the expression *Dear Mr. Jones,* instead of the impersonal *Dear Sir, Dear Madam,* and the like.
9. Make the letter radiate warmth, friendship, and sincerity.
10. In closing the letter, use terms that harmonize with a warm personal tone, such as *Very sincerely yours, Yours sincerely, Cordially yours,* and the like.
11. Wherever possible, have the goodwill letter signed by someone in authority. A letter signed by the President, Vice-president, General Manager, or other ranking officer will create more goodwill than one that is signed by a person holding a modest title or no title at all.

Holding and Increasing Goodwill of Established Customers

Old customers need attention.—More and more companies are coming to realize that they have been taking their regular patrons for granted and by so doing have been overlooking opportunities to retain the goodwill of steady customers. They go after the accounts that they have lost with letters to recapture goodwill, but, while the account is alive, neglect to write letters that will keep it from becoming inactive. Business affords many opportunities for writing to old customers with the purpose of building goodwill. Some of these opportunities and the letters that have been written for the purpose are given in this section.

Appreciation for patronage.—A few words thanking an old customer for his patronage can be written at any time. Such letters should be completely friendly and should express in simple, direct language that "rings" true the sincere appreciation of the sender. They should by no means include any sales talk. Here are some examples:

Dear Mr. Belden:

This is the kind of letter that I am most happy to write, because I am taking this means of thanking you for your constant choice of the Palmer House as your home in Chicago.

Your name ranks high among those of our loyal and distinguished "repeat" clientele who, year after year, give us definite proof that we are setting the pace of hotel leadership in Chicago. It is to friends like you that we owe the success of the Palmer House.

And so I wish to express my sincere appreciation of your patronage and to assure you that we shall continue to do everything within our power to maintain our present standards of service, cuisine, and furnishings.

Thank you again.

Very sincerely yours,[5]

Appreciation for meeting obligations promptly.—When a customer has met all his obligations under an installment purchase, a letter thanking him and inviting him to continue to use the credit facilities of the company will help build goodwill.

Dear Mr. Gould:

Your fully paid Accommodation Coupon Book account has just been placed upon my desk, and I am writing to thank you personally for the satisfactory manner in which you cared for this responsibility.

---

[5] Courtesy of Palmer House, Chicago, Illinois (Mr. Edward T. Lawless, General Manager).

We hope to enjoy the privilege of serving you again within the very near future. Our facilities of credit are always at your disposal.

Very truly yours,

A "thank you" for prompt payment.—An occasional word of gratitude for prompt payment will be appreciated and long remembered. A "thank-you" letter is one way of building goodwill. The following letter is an example:

Dear Mrs. Walters:

Time does have a way of passing, doesn't it? And we are apt to forget the part you and many others have contributed to our pleasant relations during the past year. It seems most of us are inclined to remember the less pleasant contacts we have experienced, and often overlook the happy ones.

As we close another year, we again recall that the dependable customer, who pays promptly, many times seems to go unnoticed. You have definitely placed yourself in this class, and if we did not send at least one letter expressing our sincere appreciation, we should doubtless appear ungrateful.

It has been a pleasure and privilege to have your account on our books, and your record sets a high standard for others to attain. We look forward to a mutually pleasant and profitable year during 19—.

Very sincerely yours,[6]

A "thank-you" letter for a large order.—This type of goodwill letter falls in the class of acknowledgment of orders and is treated along with other acknowledgments on page 220.

Thanking an old customer for a recommendation.—A customer who has recommended your company and brought you a new customer deserves a letter of appreciation. Since such letters are not common in business, they are appreciated and remembered. The following letter shows how simply such a message of gratitude can be expressed:

Dear Mr. Fleming:

This afternoon, when Mr. Walter Pearson purchased a new Standard portable typewriter, he told me that your recommendation had been an important factor in his decision.

---

[6] Courtesy of M. L. Parker Company, Davenport, Iowa.

I am very glad, Mr. Fleming, that your experience with your Standard portable has been like that of thousands of other Standard owners. The highest compliment you could pay our product was your recommendation of it to a friend.

Mr. Pearson will get a great deal of service and satisfaction from his new Standard, and I am confident he will thank you again and again for recommending this splendid machine. And I want to thank you, too, for your faith in our product and in our organization. We appreciate your friendship and shall always try our best to merit your confidence.

Cordially yours,

Seasonal greetings build goodwill.—The holiday season at the end of the year is an ideal opportunity to strengthen friendship through a letter of seasonal greeting. Like the letter of "thank you" for patronage, it should omit any sales message. The following letter is an example of a goodwill builder. Such a letter can be written on letterhead decorated in holiday style.

Friends:

Living in a world where war is raging and taking its toll of human lives, where fear, hatred, and covetousness may again plunge us into another world catastrophe, it is pleasant to pause in deep reverence at this beautiful season of the year to try and catch the spirit of the Christ, the Prince of Peace, and to tune in and listen to the angelic choir as it sings once more, "Peace on Earth, Good Will Toward Men."

And what, my friends, is more important than Good Will? Year in and year out, in periods of depression as well as prosperity, it is your Company and you who make our business possible. So, not in a sense of custom only, but also because of the happiness derived from the genuine appreciation of your friendship and Good Will do we pause at this happy Christmas Season to reflect on these pleasant associations.

Therefore, as you close your office door and depart for your fireside, there to gather with your loved ones, may you enjoy an old-fashioned Christmas, may the Star of Hope burn more brightly, may you have a year of happiness and prosperity, and may the promise of the Angel Choir be fulfilled, "Peace on Earth to Men of Good Will."

These are the wishes from the Officers and Personnel of the

STEEL CITY GAS COAL COMPANY [7]

---

[7] Courtesy of J. B. Sugden, Jr., President of Steel City Gas Coal Company.

Friendly service letters.—Goodwill is promoted by offering special, unexpected service to customers. Opportunities present themselves during the year for showing evidence of a desire to serve customers well, and a letter to them will be appreciated. For example, you may want to offer old cash customers a charge account; you may be ready to give the car a customer bought from you a free inspection; you may want to send customers a free useful gift. A friendly service letter is shown below.

Dear Mrs. Buchanan:

Shopping trips downtown, these hot summer days, are nothing less than hard work. The heat, the crowds, the trip down and home again —all these consume energy and tire one out.

We can't control either the weather or the crowds, but we *can* offer you a cool, comfortable place to rest and get your "second wind" in the heat of the day.

Next Monday, June 22, our new air-conditioned lounge will be ready for use. The lounge will occupy the entire north half of the fourth floor. It has been completely equipped with easy chairs, tables, reading lamps, ash stands, and all the other accessories that make for perfect comfort. The latest issues of all the leading magazines will be at your disposal. And most important of all at this time of year, the temperature will always be 72 degrees.

We invite you to make our new lounge your headquarters when you are spending the day downtown. It is an ideal place to meet friends, while away idle moments before an appointment, or "just plain rest." Simply take the elevator to the fourth floor and follow the green neon arrows.

Cordially yours,

Invitation to special events.—If you are planning a special event of some kind, invite your customers to attend. They will feel that you appreciate their patronage, and many will welcome the opportunity to attend your special functions. Thus, if your department store is having a special style show, invite old customers to it; if a series of lectures are to be given in the store, ask your customers to come; if it is a special demonstration that is to be given, let your customers know about it. Here is a personal invitation to attend a series of book reviews.

Dear Mrs. Chalmers:

We have good news for you! Beginning next Thursday afternoon, July 18, McIntire's will conduct a series of ten weekly book reviews of the latest outstanding contributions to fiction. You are cordially invited to attend, and an easy chair is being reserved for you.

The book to be reviewed next Thursday is John Jennings' new novel, *Next to Valour,* published by the same house that gave us *Gone With the Wind.* The reviewer will be a well-known Kansas Citian, Miss Elizabeth Larrimore, herself a novelist of established reputation.

This review, and all others in the series, will be given in our air-conditioned lounge on the third floor. All will begin at 2:30 P.M. On Thursday we shall announce the name of next week's reviewer and the title of the novel to be discussed.

We are sure you will enjoy this Thursday feature during the next ten weeks, for we have engaged only persons whose background and experience distinguish them as experts in the art of book reviewing.

Please plan to be with us next Thursday afternoon at 2:30.

Cordially yours,

Congratulations to old customers.—Especially in small communities is there opportunity to build goodwill by congratulating customers upon their accomplishments, or upon the success of those closely related to them. If you watch the local newspapers, you can easily find many opportunities for congratulations. Such events as advancement to a better position, election as the officer of a club or lodge, publication of an article or book, graduation of children from school, the purchase of a home—all are worth a friendly note of congratulation. Here is one such letter sent to a customer who had been appointed assistant manager of a hotel:

Dear Mr. Sanford:

Davison's wishes to congratulate you on your appointment as Assistant Manager of Hotel Georgian, which we find mentioned in today's press.

When we hear of the advancement of one of our young citizens, we are especially interested, because the young people of today are the leaders of tomorrow. The future of Atlanta depends upon the young people of today—and what Atlanta becomes in the future interests Davison's immensely, because we are a substantial part of it and are eager to see it progress.

In your new position we wish for you every success. Our relationship with you in the past has been a pleasure, and we hope it will continue through the years.

Cordially yours,[8]

Letters of sympathy to customers.—Friendly notes that sincerely offer sympathy to a customer who has suffered bereavement, accident, or other misfortune can be a welcome surprise. They can, however, be an intrusion if they are not simple and straightforward. The letter of condolence to a customer upon death of a near one should be very brief; it should not philosophize on the meaning of death or quote scripture or poetry. Here are a few examples:

Dear Mrs. Griffith:

I learned with deep regret of the recent passing of Mr. Griffith and wish to extend my sincere sympathy in your bereavement.

Very sincerely yours,

* * *

Dear Mr. Jurgens:

Upon my return to Topeka this morning, I was grieved to learn of the sudden passing of Mrs. Jurgens. You have my deepest sympathy. I only wish there were some small way in which I could lighten your burden of sorrow.

Sincerely,

* * *

Dear Mrs. DeWitt:

I have just read in this morning's paper that your home was damaged by fire last night. I know only too well how discouraging this experience is, for I have been through it myself.

If there is anything I can do to help you, such as providing packing boxes or storing household articles in our storeroom, please let me know. Any service I may be able to render will be a pleasure.

Sincerely yours,

Letters requesting suggestions and criticisms.—When you go to old customers for suggestions and criticisms, you usually expect to profit by the replies. This type of letter can at the same time be a goodwill builder because: first, it shows the customer that you

---

[8] Courtesy of Davison Paxon Co., Atlanta, Georgia.

value his opinion; and, second, it shows that you are trying to offer a better product or service. Letters that ask such a favor will bring better response if the following points are covered, although not necessarily in the order mentioned:

1. Present a concise statement of what is wanted.
2. Justify the request. If possible, demonstrate the advantage that will accrue to the individual or firm which is asked to supply the information.
3. Express appreciation.
4. Make it easy for the person to answer the inquiry. A self-addressed card or envelope, or a suitable blank on which the information may be given, can be included, if appropriate.

The following letter was made easy to answer by phrasing the questions so that only a check was required:

Dear Mr. (name):

We want to give you a better product. Will you help us?

We are now planning the revision of the Insurance Tax Service. As an old friend, we think that you can give us some mighty fine ideas on how it can be improved. We want this Service to give you in a practical, clear, and authoritative way all of the material that will help you plan estates and take advantage of the tax laws to sell more insurance. To achieve this purpose, we are asking you to become an assistant editor, so to speak. All you need do is to answer the few simple questions on the enclosed sheet and return it to us as soon as possible.

The new Insurance Tax Service will be off the press next April—rewritten and revised from cover to cover, with hundreds of new ideas to help you sell more insurance. Among the things we would like you to pass on are (1) whether the size of the Service should be increased; (2) whether or not we should enlarge the section on Business Insurance; and (3) whether or not you would like a new section on How to Use the Social Security Act to Sell More Insurance.

We want to help you make 19...... and 19...... banner years. But at the same time we do not want you to pay for material that is of no value to you. With your co-operation we can accomplish both of these aims. Will you, therefore, kindly check the enclosed questionnaire, and return it to us, now, before it slips your mind. It will take only a minute.

No postage is required. Just check the statements that you agree with and drop it in the mail.

Sincerely yours,

Here are other letters that merely ask for suggestions:

Dear Mr. DeLong:

As you know, we are doing everything possible to assure you of the very best of service at The Star. But something may have occurred to you—either a new service or an improvement in one which we already offer—that would make The Star more helpful to you.

If you have such a suggestion, we'd certainly appreciate your giving it to us. Won't you write it on the enclosed business reply card, which requires no postage, and drop it into the mail?

Thank you.

Sincerely yours,

* * *

Dear Mrs. Howell:

Our organization is greatly interested in serving you satisfactorily. May we have the pleasure of hearing how we can best meet your requirements, to enable us to be of service to you more frequently?

For your convenience a stamped, addressed envelope and a correspondence card are enclosed.

Very truly yours,

Acknowledging criticism or suggestion.—Every letter of criticism or suggestion should be promptly acknowledged with a friendly "thank you" for the writer's interest and help. The acknowledgment builds goodwill by showing appreciation and eagerness to improve the product and service. Here is one example of a letter acknowledging praise and one replying to a criticism:

Dear Mrs. Ridgeway:

Thank you for your very welcome note of October 2, included with the check in payment of your account.

We certainly appreciate your kind words of approval and encouragement. Naturally, we are very glad that you have found our delivery service so dependable, and we assure you that every effort will be made to maintain this standard.

If ever you think of any additional way in which we can serve you, please let us know.

Sincerely yours,

Dear Mrs. Sturgis:

Thank you for your helpful letter of June 10. We certainly appreciate a customer who stops to do us a good turn, and that is exactly what you have done.

You are quite right in your suggestion regarding our elevator service, and we are making every effort to remedy the situation as soon as possible. You may have noticed that four of the elevators have not been in operation during the past two weeks. These are being equipped with the newest and most efficient automatic floor regulators, which will practically double their speed. As soon as they are ready for operation, the remaining four elevators will be similarly equipped.

Within the next month these improvements will be completed, and we feel sure they will enable us to give our customers prompt and efficient elevator service.

Meanwhile, we know you will bear with us. We sincerely appreciate your interest and helpful co-operation, and we shall strive always to deserve it.

Cordially yours,

Letters of apology.—Goodwill can be retained through prompt and courteous handling of a customer's complaints. Patronage is most easily lost through failure to express regret and offer a reasonable adjustment to a customer who has reported a flaw in merchandise or service. This subject is so important that an entire section is devoted to it. See page 233.

Welcoming back the old patron.—When a customer has returned to the fold, a letter showing that you have missed him and are glad to see him back will please and flatter him. The opportunity to build goodwill in this way should not be missed. Such letters are usually short and to the point, as is the following one:

Dear Mr. Fuller:

It was good to see you drive in again yesterday, for we haven't had the pleasure of serving you lately.

I hope that you will stop often in the future and give us a chance to prove by our actions that we're sincerely glad to have you back.

Cordially yours,

Goodwill letters in times of emergency.—When emergencies such as the national defense effort, war, and the like, cause companies to refuse orders, to delay deliveries, to raise prices, or in other ways to make drastic changes in regular customer relations, letters may be used to preserve customer goodwill while the critical adjustments are being made. Several examples are given below.

In the first letter the company is telling its distributors of new policies governing prices, shipping, billing, deliveries, and so forth.

To Sylvania Distributors:

The unusual conditions under which the radio industry is operating and the uncertainties of the future call for a redefining of a number of our policies governing prices, shipping, billing, etc.

We do not think it necessary to review these conditions in any detail, since they are so well known to you. By the same token, it is idle to even attempt to prognosticate what may be ahead of us.

Consistent with the part we are playing and may play in the National Defense Program, we will endeavor to furnish you radio tubes at a price based fairly on manufacturing costs, and delivered on the basis of the best service we are able to give.

We will continue to aggressively promote your business and our own in the renewal field. We sincerely trust that you will have the resolve and foresight to strengthen your position in the field of distribution at a time which bids fair to provide unusual opportunities in both present profits and long range growth and stability.

The following outline of policy has been set up to insure fair and equitable treatment of all of our customers:

1. All orders on hand, placed prior to June 1, for immediate shipment, will be billed at current prices (Distributors' Net Cost Prices, effective February 1, 1941).

2. All orders placed on and after June 1 will be accepted subject to the following conditions:

(a) Prices in effect on the date orders are received will apply on such portion as shipped within 30 days from date of receipt.

(b) In the event all or any portion of such orders are not shipped within 30 days from date of receipt, prices in effect as of date of shipment will apply.

(c) Any orders or parts thereof which remain unshipped by us after 30 days from date of receipt, may be cancelled by the customer. (Such cancellation would destroy any seniority which would otherwise be accorded.)

(d) Should a revision in prices become necessary, such revision will take effect upon announcement.

May we with all sincerity thank you for the satisfactory relations we have had in the past and solicit both your goodwill and your business in a future period where mutual understanding and cooperation will be well near a necessity.

Very truly yours,[9]

[9] Courtesy of Hygrade Sylvania Corporation, New York.

UNTIL WE HEAR FROM YOU!

Because our 1941 catalog was printed in January of this year and since that time nearly all prices have advanced we have found it necessary to change our prices at this time. We dislike holding your order, but under the circumstances, we feel it necessary to advise you of these changes before completing your order. Will you please check the information below, complete the instructions to us and then mail it back to us in the first mail today. Many thanks for your order.

YOU ORDERED:

Item No.	New Price	DESCRIPTION

NEW TOTAL ______

AS SENT IN ______

DIFFERENCE ______

R-U-S-H

TEAR OFF AND MAIL RIGHT NOW!

NAME ______

STORE NAME ______

CITY ______

STATE ______

Tell us what you want us to do

______

Return At Once To — **ASH-BRADFORD, Inc.** *South Bend, Indiana*

Figure 8.—Goodwill Letter in Time of Emergency.

When a direct-mail firm was unable to publish a supplementary catalogue because of constantly advancing prices on its products it met the situation with the letter reproduced on page 214 (Figure 8). Printed in dubonnet ink, it was mailed as a "reply with a smile" to customers who had already ordered items on which prices had advanced above the prices listed in the latest regular company catalogue.

The third letter was sent to buyers who had entered orders for "Ebonettes," synthetic rubber gloves made of neoprene, which was listed on the Government's priorities critical list. The letter treats a most critical subject, the inability to fill a customer's order, yet it communicates this fact realistically and at the same time stimulates the recipient's admiration as a means of preserving goodwill.

Gentlemen:

We're Sorry!

While your order .... for Ebonettes is appreciated, we sincerely regret that it cannot be entered immediately for shipment.

Neoprene from which Ebonettes are made, has been placed under government priority. Our share has been reduced to almost nothing. The defense program is taking most of the available supply.

In these times we all wish to do our part by cooperating fully. We are confident of your support.

Your order is being held by us in rotation by date with others. If and when we obtain neoprene so that your order can be filled, we will write you immediately for instructions so that you can alter the order or cancel if you wish.

Frankly, there is no chance, that we see now, that your order will be shipped within the next few weeks and this time may lengthen out to a much greater period.

We're truly sorry. Your support has helped a lot to put Ebonettes over with a 120% increase in sales in 1940 and already a 41% jump this year over last.

Ebonettes are down—but not out. You'll be hearing from us again.

Sincerely yours,[10]

Building Goodwill Among New Patrons

Letters to new customers.—The new patron is forming an opinion of your firm the moment he enters your place of business and

[10] Courtesy of Pioneer Rubber Co., Willard, Ohio.

makes his first purchase. If he is satisfied with his purchase and with your service, he may return; but if you give him something beyond this minimum, which he has a right to expect, he will be more likely to remember your firm favorably and keep coming back. A friendly "thank-you" letter, a courteous expression of your interest in his satisfaction, or a cordial letter inviting him to come back will help build goodwill and increase his trade.

Appreciation to new charge customers.—The opening of a charge account creates an opportunity for writing a goodwill letter. Such letters usually thank the customer, welcome him as a user of account facilities, express desire to serve, and may explain the credit policy of the firm. The following letter has proved to be a goodwill builder:

Dear Mrs. Ormsby:

It was a genuine pleasure to open a charge account for you. Thank you most cordially for this expression of confidence and goodwill.

This is the beginning of what we feel sure will be a lasting friendship, and we want you to be perfectly satisfied in every respect with our merchandise and service.

You can do us no greater favor than to speak frankly if any detail does not "measure up" at any time, so we may make amends immediately.

For our part, we will exert every effort toward making your dealings here so thoroughly pleasant and satisfactory that you'll always look back upon the opening of this account as the beginning of a most worthwhile association.

Sincerely yours,

Letters of appreciation for initial purchase.—Letters of thanks to new customers, written after initial purchases, add a personal touch that often results in bringing the customer back more quickly. The examples below build goodwill by a friendly expression of appreciation.

Thank you, Mr. Hollingsworth . . .

. . . for selecting Freeman's for your purchase yesterday.

We hope you will come back often and give us the chance to prove by our service how much we appreciate your patronage. We'll certainly do our best to give you satisfaction plus.

Cordially yours,

Dear Mrs. Nicholson:

It is a pleasure to welcome you as a customer of the Home Laundry and to thank you sincerely for the opportunity to serve you.

As I take a very real and personal interest in your satisfaction, I should greatly appreciate your letting me know—by mail or telephone—how you liked our handling of your first laundry.

More than that, I want you to know that my interest does not stop with the first bundle. If at any time our workmanship or service should not merit your enthusiastic approval, I should consider it a favor if you would call me at once.

We are ready and eager to serve you in every way possible.

Cordially yours,[11]

Another example of acknowledging the order of a new customer with a view to building goodwill is given on page 222.

Offering the credit privilege.—An offer to reliable cash customers to use the charge-account privilege not only builds goodwill but, when accepted, frequently results in greater sales to the patron. Such letters should show the advantages of the charge privilege, explain the credit-payment policy, and emphasize the desire to serve. The following letters have a strong service keynote, and are cordial and convincing. Other examples will be found in "How to Write Credit Letters," pages 1028 et seq.

Dear Mr. Chandler:

When we cashed a check for you the other day, it occurred to us that you might enjoy a convenient service which makes cash payment unnecessary—a charge account.

The charge privilege eliminates the need of paying individually for each purchase and makes it convenient for you to order by telephone. It also provides you with an itemized statement of each month's purchases and brings to you all our announcements of special events arranged for charge customers.

It will be a pleasure to extend our credit service to you, and we're sure you will find an account a real convenience and time saver. Won't you fill out the enclosed credit card and return it to us in the postage-free envelope?

Your account will be ready twenty-four hours after we hear from you. It will place all our service facilities at your convenience.

Cordially yours,

---

[11] Courtesy of Home Laundry, Washington, D. C. (Mr. Joseph E. Coe, Manager).

Dear Miss McClellan:

The Auerbach Company has selected your name from a very limited and preferred credit list and is happy to extend to you an invitation to open a charge account.

All that is necessary is simply to sign and return the enclosed card or call at the Department of Accounts whenever convenient and leave your signature so that we may make up a Charga-plate, the most modern convenience in shopping. This affords you protection, quicker service, and eliminates any possibility of error.

You simply ask to have the merchandise charged—there is no waiting for change or other delay; it is easy to purchase at any time, whether you are prepared with the cash or not. A charge account also makes it easier to order by telephone or mail.

An itemized statement is mailed each month, and, by charging, you eliminate the nuisance of sales tax tokens by having the tax included in the bill at the end of the month.

We offer you service and values which will merit your frequent visits to the store, and we sincerely hope that you will enjoy the convenience of a charge account here.

Very cordially yours,[12]

Checking up on customer satisfaction.—A message to a customer some time after he has made a purchase, inquiring as to whether or not he is satisfied with the product or service, will show that you have the customer's interest at heart, that you are dependable, and that you wish to fulfill your service guaranty. Such letters are bound to result in increased respect, confidence, and goodwill on the part of your patrons. Here is how some companies have written to their customers along these lines:

Just checking up, Mr. Kimball,

. . . because we want to be absolutely sure that you are receiving complete satisfaction from the new tuxedo you bought here recently. We shall not be content to mark the transaction "closed" until you are satisfied one hundred per cent.

So, if the alteration of any detail would give you more pleasure in wearing your new "tux," please let us attend to it for you.

This store is founded upon quality merchandise and efficient service. Our complete lines of leading brands are your guaranty of top-quality

---

[12] Courtesy of Auerbach Company, Salt Lake City, Utah (Miss Dorothy Ashby, Credit Manager).

goods when you come here to buy wearing apparel. And we want our service to measure up to the same high standard.

So please help us see to it that you are always completely satisfied.

Sincerely yours,

* * *

Dear Mr. Turner:

It is a pleasure to welcome you to the family of owners of the new Chevrolet, and it is a double pleasure because we at Hammond Jones Company had the privilege of delivering it to you.

Your new Chevrolet is built to give you thousands of miles of dependable, economical, and trouble-free motoring, but just as you have insurance on your property, so the insurance of that service will be found in regular visits to our Service Department.

We are quite proud of our reputation as an outstanding Chevrolet Service Department—a reputation that has been built on skilled workmanship and confidence.

Be sure to take advantage of the free inspection and adjustment service which you receive at 500 miles. The purpose of this free service is not only to protect your car, but also to enable our Service Manager to meet you and advise you about the attention your car should receive. I am sure you will find everyone in his department efficient and eager to give you the best of attention.

And if I can ever be of service to you, I hope you will call on me.

Cordially yours,[13]

* * *

Dear Mr. Jones:

We wish to thank you for your recent coal order. And we hope you found the coal satisfactory—and that our men took good care of you in the delivery.

We select our coal with care and try to train our men so that our deliveries are made promptly and with courtesy.

If your order was not handled perfectly, we want to know about it —for we are here for just one purpose—to please you.

And we hope you will like us well enough to remember our phone number the next time you get chilly!

Warmly yours,[14]

---

[13] Courtesy of Hammond Jones, Inc., Lakeland, Florida (Mr. Hammond Jones, President). Prepared by Grizzard Advertising, Atlanta, Georgia.

[14] Courtesy of Cabin Creek Consolidated Sales Co., Cincinnati, Ohio.

Inviting the use of other departments.—A letter to patrons who have confined their purchases to one or two departments, inviting them to visit others, will make better friends and better customers. Such a letter should appear as a friendly suggestion rather than as a sales solicitation letter. The following examples graciously offer to be of service to such customers:

Dear Mr. Sheldon:

I want to send you a personal word of appreciation for opening your account with this bank. All our facilities are at your disposal, and I hope you will utilize the services of any department which can help to make your banking a pleasure.

Our trust, title, bond, investment, and safe deposit department are all equipped to render efficient service. Moreover, any of our officers will welcome a visit from you at any time his counsel may be of assistance.

When you opened an account here, this became your bank. Please let us serve you in any way which will add to your convenience.

Cordially yours,

* * *

Dear Mrs. Reynolds:

Because it is a pleasure to serve you—and we are eager to do it completely and well—we'd like to make a suggestion.

All next week, March 12–17, our Kitchen Karnival will be in full swing. This is an annual feature of our Household Department in the Basement. There will be special displays and demonstrations of the newest time- and effort-saving devices in kitchenwear. In addition, our entire stock of up-to-the-minute kitchen utensils will be on sale at a 10 per cent price reduction.

We are sure you will find a visit to our Houshold Department next week both interesting and profitable, so we cordially invite you to come in.

Sincerely yours,

Goodwill Through Acknowledgments

Acknowledging the order.—Orders can be acknowledged through personal letters or through routine form letters. The latter, if used, should be confined to the usual order. In the following situations acknowledgment by personal letter is essential for the maintenance of goodwill:

1. Large orders from old customers.
2. First orders from new customers.
3. Orders that are not clear.
4. Delays in shipment.
5. Goods out of stock.

Promptness in acknowledging orders is absolutely necessary, for delay will break down goodwill.

How to acknowledge a large order.—Goodwill may be retained by writing a special letter to an old customer who has placed a large order. Such a letter will accomplish its purpose if it is definite, cheerful, and persuasive. Divide the letter as follows to get a good structure:

1. Thank the customer.
2. Restate the order.
3. Tell how the order is being handled and shipped.
4. Include a paragraph or two of sales talk, concentrating upon the sales points of the goods and the possibilities for profit.

The following letter carries out the usual plan of a good letter acknowledging a large order from an old customer:

Dear Mr. Calton:

Thank you for your generous order of March 12, which we take as an indication of your increased business in our goods.

Item	Price	Amount
3 doz. Frocks of Fashion, No. 208, Size 36	$39.00	$117.00
2 doz. Ultra Smart, No. 214, Size 34	35.00	70.00
4 doz. Utility, No. 126, Size 38	19.00	76.00
6 doz. French Inspiration, No. 38, Size 34	49.50	297.00
Total		$560.00

These gowns are being shipped today by American Railway Express and should reach you on Thursday in time for your week-end trade.

Your customers will find in these smart models just the quality and design most in vogue among women who pride themselves on their dress. As in the past, we are supplying the unusual, the different, the uncommon modes, at lowest prices. To sell our gowns is to convince your fashionable trade that you have initiative, and that you are the one who first features new styles for those who look for inspiration and individuality in dress.

The styles that we are sending you are authentic, original, and appropriate.

The most critical buyers will immediately recognize the quality and style of these gowns.

We assure you of our personal attention and of our steadfast desire to please you.

Sincerely yours,

Getting the goodwill of a new customer.—Here is a workable outline for constructing the letter to a new customer with a view to building goodwill:

1. Show appreciation of the order and welcome the customer.
2. Restate the order.
3. State how the order is being handled and shipped.
4. Include one or two paragraphs of sales material creating confidence in the house, its goods, and its service.
5. Stress interest in the customer's needs and convince him that the firm means to serve him.

The following opening and closing paragraphs make the preceding letter suitable for a new customer:

Dear Sir:

Thank you for your order of March 17. I wish to welcome you into our large family of satisfied customers and to assure you that we shall do everything in our power to make the sale of our gowns profitable to you. We take a genuine interest in the increased profits of our dealers.

* * *

Your interests are our interests. Quality, style, and price make our gowns easy to sell to a discriminating trade. You are situated so that we can supply you unfailingly and immediately. Gowns shipped you today reach you tomorrow morning. This service means that you can carry a representative stock in your store, depending upon us to replenish your stock within twenty-four hours after you have made sales. The result, for you, is a small investment with large profits, made possible by our highly organized and always dependable service.

Sincerely yours,

How to perfect incomplete orders.—Occasionally an order is received that lacks essential information. The letter sent to the customer for additional information should be developed as follows:

1. Acknowledge the order with thanks.
2. Ask for the additional information without letting the customer feel that he is at fault.
3. Present the request as a desire to give prompt and efficient service.

A letter such as the following will bring the necessary information that was missing in the order.

Dear Sir:

Thank you for your order of October 10.

The size that you desire was omitted from your order for M-289, suede gloves.

Please send us this necessary information, which will enable us to fill the order exactly as you want it. As soon as we hear from you, we will release the order for immediate shipment.

Very truly yours,

Acknowledgment when shipment is delayed.—If the order has been delayed, a letter must be written that will keep the customer satisfied. Here are suggestions for the contents of such a letter:

1. Explain what has been done with the order.
2. Express regret.
3. Offer an adjustment.

Gentlemen:

Your order No. 245 was billed out this morning over the Southern Pacific Railroad. I am very sorry that there was a delay, but this was unavoidable because of a shortage of the quality of coal we know your trade requires.

Ever since the recent labor troubles, we have had a little difficulty in keeping supplied with this grade. We could, however, have made prompt shipment of an inferior grade, but as I know that your customers demand the best, I waited until I had coal of the quality I usually ship you.

I hope this supply reaches you before your present stock is exhausted.

Very truly yours,

Acknowledgment when goods are out of stock.—The letter explaining that goods are out of stock will retain goodwill if it includes:

1. An acknowledgment with thanks and an expression of regret that the order cannot be filled.
2. An explanation that the predicament is unusual and will not recur.
3. A substitution, if past experience with the customer warrants this procedure.
4. A request for permission to substitute some other item, with a sales talk to induce acceptance.
5. An offer to be of assistance if no substitution can be made.

Some of the above suggestions are carried out in the following letter:

Dear Madam:

Thank you for your order of November 10.

We are sending you today, by parcel post insured, the ten yards of poplin that you ordered.

Because we realize your immediate need for this material, we have taken the liberty of sending the poplin in two lengths, 8½ yards and 3 yards, as this is all we have in stock. The new supply will not be available until November 18.

We are certain that you will like this poplin, which is of the best quality, and for which we are glad to accept your check in full payment as for ten yards.

Sincerely yours,

How to handle an order that cannot be filled because of policy.—When an order cannot be filled, the letter of explanation to the customer will build goodwill and leave the way open for future business if it is constructed as follows:

1. Express appreciation for the order.
2. Courteously explain the reasons.
3. If pertinent, show the customer that the refusal is in his own interests.

The letter on page 180 refuses the order in a straightforward, businesslike way. It uses the opportunity to sell the product at the same time.

How to acknowledge remittances.—The routine acknowledgment of remittances may be covered by a courteous form letter, unless other factors make a special letter advisable. The following forms are among many that can be used:

Gentlemen:

Thank you for your check in payment of your May account.

We wish to express our appreciation of the satisfactory manner in which you have made your payments.

Very truly yours,

* * *

Gentlemen:

We have received your remittance of $, for which we thank you. The amount will be placed to your credit.

Very truly yours,

* * *

Gentlemen:

Thank you for your check for $, which we have placed to your credit. The unpaid balance is now $.

Very truly yours,

Building goodwill through acknowledgments of inquiries.—Answers to inquiries about the company's products are really sales letters. These were discussed on pages 187 et seq.

In the following paragraphs we are concerned with acknowledgments of inquiries not directly related to sales. Every company receives requests at times for information, help, data to be used in research, and the like. The answer affords an opportunity to build goodwill. Below are some suggestions for letters complying with requests and refusing requests.

Retaining goodwill while refusing requests. In a letter refusing to grant a request, the following procedure will guard against alienating goodwill:

1. Be courteous and concise.
2. Refuse the request, state the reason, and express regret.
3. Close with sales material, if pertinent.
4. Offer other assistance, if possible.

Here is a letter that refuses information and at the same time creates goodwill.

Dear Mr. Smith:

Mr. Jones has just turned over to me your letter of February 3, as I am in charge of the correspondence activities of the firm.

Yes, we believe that the people in our organization have written some unusually good letters. Nothing would give me greater pleasure than to select a portfolio of these and send them to you, but unfortunately I am not permitted to do so. It has always been against the policy of the firm to send out our letters for publicity purposes.

If Mr. Sullivan were in town I might try a little salesmanship on him and see if he wouldn't be willing to make an exception in this case. However, he is in Hawaii, and I would not have time to contact him before you will need the letters.

So, under the circumstances, there is nothing that we can do to help you in the preparation of your manuscript—except give you our best wishes that it will be completely successful. There is much need for missionary work in the field of business letter writing, and anyone who is undertaking something of this kind deserves the heartiest commendation.

Very truly yours,

Getting the maximum goodwill from complying with requests.—The person who receives the material requested will naturally feel kindly disposed toward the company granting it. However, more is gained in goodwill if a letter accompanies the material. Such a letter should cover the following:

1. Cheerfully grant the favor.
2. Offer further assistance.
3. Close with sales material, if pertinent.

Here is a letter that obtains the maximum goodwill.

Dear Mr. Smith:

I consider it a pleasure to be able to assist any way I can in furnishing material for your new manuscript on better business letters.

The letter I mailed to our agents and salesmen last December, a copy of which is enclosed, was intended to stimulate their business-building efforts, and, at the same time, bring to their attention the importance of good public relations. The response to this letter was all that could be expected.

I hope that you will be able to use this in your book.

If I can be of further assistance, please consider me at your service.

Cordially yours,

How to acknowledge letters that praise.—Voluntary letters from customers expressing satisfaction with a product may form excellent testimonials for future advertising and sales letters. Such letters require a cheerful, gracious acknowledgment, with a request for permission to quote the comments of the customer in advertising matter.

The acknowledgment may also be used to sell the satisfied customer another product, provided the customer has a real or potential need for the article offered.

The following letter, asking permission to quote the customer's comments, brought the requested "O.K." and an order for the product offered.

Dear Miss Bell:

Thank you for your letter of the 21st, received today, enclosing remittance of $3.56 to cover our invoice for *The Private Secretary's Manual,* and containing your gratifying comment on the material in the book.

If we may have permission to quote your comment, along with that of other alert secretaries, in some of our advertising matter, will you please return this letter to me with your "O.K." and initials opposite this paragraph.

In the hope of returning the favor, I would like to make a suggestion that I think would be in line with your ideas of what constitutes a good secretary.

We have just published a book—*Successful Salesmanship*—that contains at least a score of particularly good ideas and "ammunition" for the sales manager of a company like John Morris & Co. A brief description of the book is attached.

Since we will gladly send the book on five days' approval, my suggestion is that you return the attached card—which is all ready to sign and mail—and let me send you *Successful Salesmanship* with the distinct understanding that if the Sales Manager, after seeing the book, isn't perfectly willing to O.K. our memo invoice for the price of the book—only $5—then you need only mail it back to us. That will end the matter.

A stamped, addressed envelope is enclosed for the return of this letter with your "O.K." opposite the second paragraph giving permission to quote your comment on the Secretary's Manual.

Yours very truly,

Letters received in absence of addressee.—A letter received in the absence of the addressee should be immediately acknowledged by the secretary or assistant of the addressee if it cannot be answered with authority by someone else. The purpose is to build goodwill through courtesy.

Dear Sir:

In the absence of Mr. Van der Beek, I wish to acknowledge your letter of July 25, which is being held for his attention on his return early next week.

Very truly yours,
(signed) Mary Fitts
Secretary to Mr. Van der Beek.

* * *

Dear Sir:

Your letter of August 14 arrived the day after Mr. Tauber left on a three-week selling trip. Since it does not appear to require an immediate reply, I will hold it for his attention on his return.

Very truly yours,
(signed) Joan McGregor
Secretary to Mr. Tauber.

General Goodwill Letters

A letter to disappointed applicants.—If applicants for positions are future prospects for the company's product, a letter to those who are not successful in obtaining employment will help to build goodwill. The following letter of the L. E. Waterman Company suggests the type of letter suitable under such circumstances:

Dear Mr. Morgan:

Thank you, Mr. Morgan, for the interest you display in Waterman's, evidenced by your application for a position on our sales staff.

We regret that our response must be disappointing, as there is no opening at the present time, nor do we anticipate any in the near future. However, we are retaining your application in our files, should we have the occasion to engage a man of your qualifications.

We shall be glad to call on you if the opportunity arises. And meanwhile, we wish you very early success in attaining a position that will be both profitable and pleasant.

Very truly yours,

Goodwill through letters of introduction.—Letters of introduction must state the name of the person being introduced, the reason for the introduction, and sufficient personal or business details to make the introduction appear appropriate.

When written for delivery by the person being introduced, the letter is left unsealed, and it is properly assumed that it has been read before being presented.

The tone of the letter of introduction depends upon how well the writer knows the principals and the reasons for writing it. Although the letter may actually be conferring a favor on the addressee by bringing him in contact with a person who will be valuable to him, it is usually written in the spirit of asking a favor. For example:

Mr. Harry W. Overbeck,
Winchendon Knitting Mills,
Ware, Massachusetts.

Dear Mr. Overbeck:

This letter will be handed to you by my friend of long standing, Horace Bowes, a well-known writer of articles on business.

Mr. Bowes is engaged in the preparation of a book in which he hopes to outline the development of the textile industry during the last half-century. He believes that through a talk with you he could obtain both information and inspiration that would be valuable to him in this work.

Since you are *the* authority on your particular phase of the industry, he has asked for an introduction to you. I shall appreciate any courtesies you may show him, and I know he will.

Sincerely yours,

The following letter is less formal than that above because it is based on a first-name acquaintanceship:

Dear Harry:

When we had lunch together, I mentioned Jack Hunt, who was doing some big things for one of our lines. Since that time he has decided that he ought to be handling something that will give him a bigger opportunity.

I don't know whether you're interested in getting additional sales right now or not. Maybe you're too far behind in production as it is.

But seriously, talk to this fellow, won't you? Jack Hunt is a good egg.

The next lunch is on me.

Sincerely,

The business-pleasure introduction.—Sometimes a letter of introduction is written for a business acquaintance who is traveling for pleasure. For example:

My dear McKenna:

John Henry Mainwaring, my good friend and the company's valued client, is on his way to the Pacific Coast. He is accompanied by Mrs. Mainwaring, which means that it is a pleasure trip.

I told him that if his route led through Toledo, he should not fail to look you up, and he said he wouldn't. So if he presents this letter, he has!

Don't let him get away without seeing the factory. And ask him if he'd like to have any checks cashed. Take it from me, they'll be good.

I shall appreciate any courtesies you may show him.

Sincerely,

Introduction on cards.—Often an introduction written on a personal or business card adequately fulfills the purpose if there is no necessity for formality or detailed information. Such introductions might read:

Introducing Mr. Samuel A. Leffingwell.
(signed) George D. Twelvetrees.

To introduce Ned Gannon. Treat him right.
(signed) Jack Halliburton.

This is George Rand, the man I spoke to you about.
(signed) H. F. Jones.

Goodwill through thank-you letters.—Thank-you letters help to build goodwill. Opportunities are constantly arising in which they can be used in business. The letters may be short and should not be forced. The following examples illustrate circumstances in which they are useful:

Gentlemen:

Thank you for allowing us the 2% cash discount on our bill after the ten days had elapsed. Basing our belief on your invariable fairness through all our dealings, we felt sure you would make this allowance when you understood the circumstances.

Sincerely yours,

* * *

Dear Mr. Fordyce:

I want to express to you my personal appreciation of your courtesy to our salesman, John Titus, when you learned of the disquieting news he had received from home. We are glad to report that his mother passed the crisis and is now resting comfortably.

The help you gave Mr. Titus made us all feel good.

Sincerely yours,

Goodwill through sympathy.—A simple but effective way to gain the goodwill of employees is to show concern about them when they are absent because of illness. Here are two illustrative letters:

Dear Mr. Saunders:

I am no doctor, but I know I can help you. Here is how:

Your regular salary check will be sent each week to Mrs. Saunders as long as you are incapacitated. This will relieve your mind of financial worries.

Your work at the office will not get behind, as your good friends here have offered to absorb your duties while you are away. You don't have to worry about your work.

Your job will be waiting for you when you are ready to go on with it—but no sooner.

That leaves you with practically nothing to do except get better.

The boys at the office send you their best.

Sincerely,

* * *

Dear Miss Owens:

I was very sorry to hear of the accident that has laid you up in the hospital. I am told that it was not serious, but I know that it must be painful, and my sympathies are all with you.

My correspondence is being handled by the three other young women, but, without wishing to appear too critical, I feel as if I were working with my right hand tied behind my back.

We shall all be glad to see you when you are well enough to return.

Sincerely,

Goodwill through congratulations.—One of the best ways of fostering goodwill in business is to take advantage of opportunities to send congratulatory letters. Such letters presuppose a certain degree of personal relationship. The tone of the letter is governed by the closeness of the relationship. Several examples given below show opportunities for building goodwill in this way.

Mr. Harvey S. Wing,
Boston Store,
Ottumwa, Iowa.

Dear Mr. Wing:

As one department store man to another, I wish to pay homage to your genius for dramatizing your window displays. The way you have worked out the selling idea for party gowns in your southeast window is masterly.

Congratulations!

Sincerely,

* * *

Mr. Howard M. Gurney, President,
Wickwire Hosiery Company,
New York City.

Dear Mr. Gurney:

I have just read in today's paper of your election as Mayor of Billings Center, and I hasten to congratulate both you and the community you represent. I am sure that you will bring to your job the same ability that has made your business such a success.

Sincerely yours,

* * *

Mr. Samuel S. Dakin,
Hotel St. Anthony,
San Antonio, Texas.

Dear Sam:

When a salesman breaks his own record for the size of an order, it may or may not be something for the sales manager to talk about, but—

When a salesman breaks all the records in his company—*that's news!*

You know perfectly well that I am talking about the Wales Company order.

Great work, boy.

Sincerely,

* * *

Mr. A. J. Wortman,
Cooperative Credit Association,
New York City.

Dear Mr. Wortman:

Your talk on "Collection Methods" at yesterday's Rotary Club meeting was instructive and interesting to everyone present. I congratulate you on your command of the subject and the manner in which you presented it.

Sincerely yours,

6. KEEPING GOODWILL IN ANSWERING COMPLAINTS

How to reply to complaint letters.—The following are the chief points to keep in mind in replying to letters of complaint.

1. Answer the complaint or claim letter promptly—if possible, within twenty-four hours. Delay is liable to aggravate the customer's dissatisfaction. If a decision as to whether or not an adjustment should be made cannot be reached immediately, write a brief letter of acknowledgment, expressing regret for the cause of the complaint or claim and assuring the customer that an investigation is being made and that prompt action will be taken.

2. The adjustment letter is a sales letter; it should sell service and satisfaction. The object is to settle the difficulty in a manner satisfactory to both parties, to retain the customer, and to build goodwill.

3. The adjustment letter should assume that the customer is honest in his complaint or claim. Do not try to put the customer in the wrong.

4. Adapt the adjustment letter to the reader and show sincere appreciation of his point of view. Write the letter in a spirit of service and fair treatment.

5. Thank the customer for his letter, and for the opportunity that it gives you to explain your policies or to remedy defects in your goods or service. Take the view that the customer is benefiting you by his criticism. Do not express surprise at the customer's dissatisfaction or tell him that his is the only complaint you have received.

6. Emphasize the positive, constructive side of the adjustment problem. Do not revive the unpleasant aspects by restating the complaint or claim. Do not use offensive words and phrases, such as *you assert, you state, you say, you claim, your claim, your complaint, we cannot understand, we are at a loss, our records show.*

7. If the customer is in the right, explain the cause of the error on your part clearly, concisely, and completely. Express regret, but do not be effusive in apologies.

8. If the customer's letter is sarcastic, angry, or abusive, do not assume that this gives you license to reply in the same tone. Never show irritation, however much the circumstances may seem to justify it. If the customer is in the wrong, do not try to be funny or clever at his expense.

9. If the complaint or claim is the result of a misunderstanding on the part of the customer, do not suggest that he is ignorant or careless. Write a pleasant, friendly letter of explanation; do not adopt a superior tone.

10. Convince the customer of the justness of your decision.

Workable outline for an adjustment letter.—The following is a practical outline for the adjustment letter:

1. Get on common ground with the claimant by thanking him for his letter or by expressing regret for the inconvenience caused him. Search out some point on which you can agree with the customer, even though this point be merely an expression of sympathy. An opening of this kind disarms the reader and puts him in a receptive mood.

2. Explain the facts in connection with the claim. However, do

not restate the claim in full. Show that you have given the customer's letter careful consideration.

3. State cheerfully the adjustment action that you propose to take.
4. Close by expressing appreciation and a desire to co-operate.

Example of poor adjustment letter.—The following letter illustrates the tone that should *not* be used in replying to complaint and claim letters:

Dear Sir:

We were very much surprised to receive your letter of January 27, in which you assert that the ECONOMY OIL BURNER recently installed in your home is not everything that we advertise our burner to be.

If the difficulty of which you complain were caused by faulty design or manufacture, it would certainly seem that we would get complaints from other people. Yours, however, is the only complaint that we have received, and in the past few months we have sold through our agents more than fifty burners in your state alone.

From what you say about the performance you have been getting, we believe that it is not the fault of the burner that the results are not all you had hoped for. The burner must have been poorly installed.

We advise you to get in touch with whoever installed your ECONOMY for you, and have it put right. We definitely do not advertise anything that is not true.

Very truly yours,

This same letter, rewritten in a better tone, might read as follows:

Dear Mr. Ferguson:

We appreciate very much your writing us direct with regard to the ECONOMY OIL BURNER that you recently purchased. The performance of every ECONOMY is guaranteed by us, and we welcome any opportunity to show that we are always ready to stand behind our guaranty.

We have mailed a copy of your letter of January 27 to our agents, John Brown & Company, who installed the burner for you. We have also instructed John Brown & Company to give the burner a thorough examination—to check the installation in every particular. In the event that any parts are found to be defective, they will be replaced at our expense. It will not be necessary for you to communicate with John Brown & Company; they will call at your home within the next few days.

Since I am anxious to number you among the many enthusiastic users of the ECONOMY, I wish that you would write me personally in, say, two weeks' time, and let me know whether the burner is operating to your entire satisfaction.

Very truly yours,

Letters granting adjustments and acknowledging error.—A prompt, complete adjustment is in order when investigation shows that the goods were defective, that there was a delay in shipment, that a mistake was made in filling the order, or that some other error for which the seller is to blame occurred. A frank acknowledgment of the error should be written, and the customer assured that precautions have been taken to avoid similar trouble in the future. The seller should not try to defend himself or offer a lengthy explanation. Such an explanation will merely serve to develop in painful detail the shortcomings of the house. A brief, frank, cheerful letter is most effective.

Gentlemen:

Thank you for writing us on November 10 regarding the platinum setting that you ordered on October 29.

By immediately checking back, we found that a mistake had been made when your order was transcribed in our order department.

We are very sorry that you and your customer have been inconvenienced, but we are at the same time grateful to you for helping us place the blame and prevent similar mistakes in the future.

Although we have never, in the case of expensive settings such as yours, promised delivery in less than two weeks, I am personally taking care of your order and am having it handled so that you will receive the setting not later than Saturday morning.

Please be assured of our desire to co-operate with you, as we have in the past.

Very truly yours,

* * *

Dear Mr. Mitchell:

We are glad you notified us promptly that some of your sheets were damaged in transit.

No doubt the error was made by one of the inspectors in the shipping department. We try to use every safeguard to prevent such an occurrence, but, try as we do, there will be a slip once in a great while.

Whenever an error is brought to our attention, we are glad to make things right as quickly as possible.

We have entered a replace order for the fifty sheets. These will be sent not later than Monday of next week.

We are very sorry that you have been inconvenienced, and in the future we shall do everything in our power to see that your shipments reach you in perfect condition.

Very truly yours,

* * *

Dear Mr. Gardner:

We were very sorry to learn from your letter of May 3 of the inconvenience caused you by the error in your last shipment. Despite the constant and diligent supervision that we give to filling orders correctly, it seems that once in a great while a mistake is made.

We are sending you today, by express, the case of canned peaches that you ordered.

With regard to the case of pears sent you in error, we should be obliged if you would hold this in the meantime. Mr. Stark, of our sales department, will visit you on Wednesday of next week. If you are not able to use the pears in your own trade, possibly Mr. Stark can dispose of them to another customer and save the cost of returning them to us.

We appreciate your writing us promptly concerning the error, and assure you that every care will be taken in filling your future orders.

Very truly yours,

How to handle complaints about service.—When a customer complains about the service that he has been receiving, the letter of reply is most effective if it bears the signature of a vice-president or other officer of the company. The signature of an officer has a conciliatory effect, in that it impresses the customer with the fact that his complaint has received serious attention. The letter may apologize for the difficulty, sympathize with the customer, and assure him that his business is appreciated and that his unfortunate experience has been unusual. It may close with the suggestion that the customer give the company further opportunity to prove the quality of its service, and that in the future his orders be directed to the personal attention of the writer.

Dear Mr. Lewis:

I very much appreciate your frank letter of August 4.

It was so specific as to details that I was able to take immediate action toward correcting a situation that obviously had no reason to exist.

I assure you of my regret at your inconvenience. May I suggest that you communicate with me whenever you find our service not up to the standard of your experiences before this incident.

Sincerely yours,

Vice-President

* * *

Dear Mr. Wright:

Your frank letter of May 2 was referred to me, and, despite your request that no appology be made, I am writing you this letter, which, however, is to be a letter of thanks rather than an apology.

Once in a while I read a report in which one of our customers has (as in this instance) a real, honest-to-goodness reason for thinking that Graham & Company do not know how to fill an order correctly. I question whether, if I were you, I should have written as considerately as you did. I sometimes wonder, when such a report comes to me, why some of our customers don't take their business elsewhere without letting us know their grievance. That is why Graham & Company should thank you for telling us where we have fallen down in connection with your business.

Your order was filled on April 23. During that period we received more than double our usual amount of business. With the great increase in volume of orders, coupled with our desire to make immediate shipment of every order, and with a percentage of comparatively inexperienced employees, the ordinarily careful supervision and inspection of orders were probably relaxed. The management of a business such as ours, therefore, has to depend to some extent on the letters that come from customers; and it is for this reason that I welcome yours.

We want an opportunity to prove to you that Graham & Company can and do handle orders correctly; and since you have had so much misfortune in connection with your orders, I am going to ask that, in the event you do decide to give us an opportunity to prove that your recent experience is not typical, you send your next few orders to me personally, so that I may have them checked and satisfy myself that you are not going to be caused further inconvenience.

I am doing this because I am sure you are convinced that in buying from us you do save money, and that your sole reason for discontinuing your dealings with us is that we have made mistakes in recent orders.

Very truly yours,

Vice-President

Handling complaints where carrier is at fault.—If the carrier is to blame for delay in delivery, the letter should state the date and method of shipment and tell the customer that the goods are being traced at once. It may also ask the customer to write or wire collect if delivery is not made by a certain date, in which event a duplicate shipment will be forwarded.

The seller is usually not legally responsible for damage to goods that he delivered safely into the hands of the carrier, for it is the buyer's responsibility to seek redress from the carrier. However, as a service and a goodwill gesture, many companies make an immediate adjustment to the customer and then take upon themselves the filing of a claim with the carrier, with or without the aid of the customer, as the situation demands. If the goods have been badly damaged, a duplicate shipment is forwarded immediately. If the damage is slight, the goods may be offered to the customer at a discount.

Dear Mr. Hayes:

Your letter of May 3 reached us this morning.

The shipment of furniture that you ordered on April 18 left our factory on April 23, N.Y.N.H. & H. freight, car #238967, and should certainly have been delivered to you not later than April 26. We have asked the railroad to trace the shipment immediately.

If the furniture does not reach you by May 7, please wire us collect, and we will forward a duplicate shipment at once, by express.

We very much regret the delay and hope that it will not cause you serious inconvenience.

Very truly yours,

* * *

Dear Mr. Davidson:

We were very sorry to learn from your letter of March 12 that the mahogany desk which you ordered as a birthday gift for your son arrived so badly damaged that you cannot accept it.

As the Chicago, Milwaukee and St. Paul Railroad gave us a receipt acknowledging that the desk was received by them perfectly crated, it must have been damaged in transit. Although our responsibility ends when the railroad has accepted the desk, we know how much you are interested in this handsome and useful gift for your son. We are, therefore, sending you today, by prepaid express, another desk exactly like the one you ordered. It should reach you promptly.

If you will please telephone the express company to make a special delivery immediately upon the arrival of the desk at their receiving station, you should have the desk not later than the day of your son's birthday.

Please leave the damaged desk in the hands of the railroad. We shall enter a claim with them so that you will not be troubled further.

We appreciate your writing us promptly and hope that your son will be pleased with the gift that you have chosen for him.

Sincerely yours,

* * *

Dear Mr. Kenney:

We were very sorry to learn from your letter of September 6 that the case of canned tomatoes included with your last order reached you in damaged condition.

As we received from the shipper a receipt showing that the goods as handed over to him were properly crated, the case must have become wet and the labels soiled in transit. Although our responsibility ended when we delivered the goods into the hands of the carrier, we realize that you would have a good deal of difficulty in proving a claim, since the shipment was signed for before the damage was discovered. Under the circumstances we will be glad to co-operate with you, and suggest that you accept the tomatoes at a 20% discount.

While it is true that the labels are badly soiled and torn, the contents of the cans will still be in perfect condition, and no doubt you could readily dispose of the tomatoes by placing them on special sale. The 20% discount will enable you to do this without suffering any loss. It will also save you the trouble of repacking the goods and trucking them to the freight station.

If this suggestion is agreeable to you, please let us know, and we will credit your account with the 20% discount. We appreciate your writing us promptly and are asking the carrier to be more careful in handling your future shipments.

Very truly yours,

Handling the customer who is at fault.—If the customer is in the wrong, but his claim is a small one or his business is valuable, it may be better to grant the claim than run the risk of causing offense. The expense in such cases may be regarded as an investment in advertising and goodwill. A reasonably liberal adjustment policy may make many friends.

Any letter covering this type of situation must be carefully written.

The tone must be firm, or the customer may think the company an "easy mark." The fact that an exception is being made must be clearly indicated, and yet not in such a way that the customer will be irritated or humiliated by being made to feel that the adjustment is granted reluctantly or that he is receiving something to which he is not entitled. The object is, on the one hand, to sell service and satisfaction; on the other, to avoid setting up a dangerous precedent.

Dear Mr. Lewis:

Thank you for your letter of September 6. We were very sorry to learn that you have been having trouble with one of the stabilators on your STANDARD car.

A careful examination of the stabilator, as returned to us by your service station in Lynbrook, leads us to believe that the spring did not break because of defective materials or poor workmanship. The adjusting nut appears to have been turned three notches tighter than is necessary on a STANDARD. Each turn of the nut winds the stabilator spring tighter; and, when the spring is too tight, there is excessive strain during the recovery of the car springs after the car has passed a hole or obstruction in the road.

Our guaranty covers only defects in materials and workmanship. However, in view of the fact that you have driven your STANDARD less than three months, we are glad to make an exception and to put a new spring in the stabilator without charge.

We are today sending the stabilator to your service station in Lynbrook. It will take the service man less than fifteen minutes to attach it.

The enclosed booklet, "The Stabilators on Your STANDARD," may be of interest. We hope that you will derive full satisfaction from the easy-riding qualities that these stabilators give to thousands of STANDARD cars.

Very truly yours,

* * *

Dear Mrs. Davies:

We wish to thank you for writing us with regard to your purchase of July 14, and also for returning the shoes for our inspection.

We have examined the shoes, and certainly agree that they are in poor condition, considering the fact that they have been used for only three weeks. However, there seems to have been a misunderstanding between us. The shoes that you purchased were advertised, at a special price, as suitable for indoor wear. Shoes of this type are not strong enough to be worn for tennis.

Although the shoes cannot, of course, be repaired, we wish you to be fully satisfied with every purchase that you make here. Accordingly, we are sending you a shoe that is made of durable canvas and is also unusually light in weight. Many prominent tennis players wear this model, which we now have on sale at the remarkably low price of $2.50.

If you wish to keep the shoes that we are sending, we will be glad to credit you with the full cost of the original pair, $1.50, and to add the balance, $1.00, to your charge account. We are doing this in appreciation of your patronage, and in the hope that you will continue to be one of our valued customers.

Very truly yours,

Letters refusing adjustments.—If the claim or complaint is clearly unreasonable or unjust, the letter refusing an adjustment should state the facts in frank, straightforward style. Although the seller must, of course, absolve himself of blame or responsibility, he should be careful to avoid using a tone that seems to accuse the customer. A sincere statement of facts, together with an appeal to the customer's sense of fairness, is most effective. The facts speak for themselves in convincing the customer of the justness of the decision, and the writer's sincerity wins his respect and goodwill. Letters refusing adjustments may properly be long, since the explanation must be complete.

Dear Mr. Jackson:

The return of merchandise shipped as ordered has become a costly problem, and, insofar as the goods mentioned in your letter of October 3 are concerned, we are asking your co-operation.

These goods were delivered to you some months ago in exact conformity with your order. If they did not please you or were not precisely what you had expected, we feel that in all fairness to us they should have been returned promptly.

Oftentimes, when delay in returning goods occurs, the styles are sold out, and delayed returns then become odd lots for which we have no outlet except at a sacrifice. This is true of the merchandise that you list in your letter.

It is quite embarrassing to us, as I am sure you understand, to offer you any credit less than one hundred cents on the dollar. On the other hand, however, I know that you would not expect us to assume an unwarranted loss.

We are willing to take back the goods and issue credit to you for whatever we can get for them. However, it would undoubtedly be better for you to move the goods through your own store at reduced prices. This, I am sure, would entail a smaller loss.

We leave the decision in your hands.

Cordially yours,

* * *

Dear Mr. Adams:

When a customer writes us for the privilege of returning boots for exchange or credit, the first thought that comes to him is that we have customers scattered all over the United States, and that we can use this returned merchandise by placing it with others.

Naturally, it's embarrassing to us to decline an accommodation, which in itself appears to be only a small item, but, when you consider that over a period of time such requests run into the thousands, you can appreciate that it would be necessary for us to set up a department requiring additional help and resulting in added expense. This expense cannot readily be added into the cost of the goods, because that would be unfair to those customers who carry large stocks and who do not ask for such privileges. They, therefore, should not be penalized with such costs.

It has been estimated that the cost of handling returned goods ranges from slightly over 50¢ per pair in the case of shoes, lace boots, and cowboy boots to slightly over $1.00 in the case of riding and field boots. This last figure is greater because usually these boots must again be placed on the forms and retreed.

All of us realize that a properly balanced stock is the only satisfactory method of fitting a customer. To attempt to fit a customer with a pair of boots, judging from the size of his or her foot, is almost impossible, due to the variation in the types of lasts, etc. There are times when you feel you cannot afford the risk of keeping a special size in stock, if the boots do not fit, and it is then that you think of an exchange or return.

In our fifty-odd years of dealing with merchants, we have found most of them to be fair. The trouble, if any, has been that we have not always understood each other's problems. In this case, if you are willing to reimburse us for the extra handling cost, plus postage both ways, and if the bottoms have not been scratched or soiled, the deal is made. Is this satisfactory?

Yours very truly,

P. S. Write your reply on the back of this letter and drop it into the mail.

Gentlemen:

Thank you for your letter of May 4 regarding the shipment of furniture delivered to you on April 28. We were very glad to hear from you, especially since you are one of our new customers, and your letter gives us the opportunity to explain our policies.

We regret that we cannot refund the freight charges paid by you, in the amount of $18.35. It has always been our policy to ship f.o.b. Chicago, the home of our factory. By doing this we can give you our merchandise at the lowest possible figure, which just covers the cost of production plus a small competitive profit.

Many firms ship their goods f.o.b. the city in which the retail store is located. However, since someone must pay the freight, and the seller cannot afford to do so, the charges are added to the cost of the merchandise. We do not believe that this policy is fair. What it really means is that the total freight charges are divided among all the customers of the house, regardless of the fact that some are located only a few miles away from the factory while others are in Maine or California.

We endeavor to bring you the high quality of EASYREST FURNITURE at the lowest possible price. We hope that the merchandise recently delivered to you is entirely satisfactory and that we will have many business dealings in the future.

Very truly yours,

* * *

Gentlemen:

The charge of $7.50 for the halftone cut we made for you, to which you refer in your letter of August 3, covers only the actual cost of manufacture.

Your impression that the charge is too high is understandable, for the cost of making such cuts varies greatly. Not only the fineness and clearness of the reproduction, but also the quality of the printing paper, affect materially the labor charge involved in any particular cut.

Our engravers are employees of long standing, who know thoroughly the quality of paper and the type of presses we use. Consequently they are able to do their work with a minimum loss of time and can produce precisely the results required.

After taking these factors into consideration, you will, we are sure, willingly remit the full amount of our statement. You have our assurance that the charge is regular and in accordance with our established rates.

Very truly yours,

* * *

Dear Mr. Hopkins:

We wish that it were possible to grant your request of December 10. Were we to do so, however, we should be compelled in all fairness to do likewise for the several thousand people who purchased STANDARD cars this summer and fall. It would be exceedingly difficult to know where to draw the line.

Styles change in automobiles just as they do in furniture and clothes and hats, and it is impossible to make an adjustment as a result of such changes. For instance, a man would not think of going to his local hat dealer with a hat that he had purchased a month previously to ask that he be given a rebate merely because a new style had just come out.

Your local dealer did not act in bad faith, because no dealer definitely knows just when a model will be changed. When you purchased your STANDARD, you made your selection on the basis of value and assured satisfaction. Only the most modern production methods and our large resources enabled us to manufacture that model to sell at that price.

It is not our policy to stand still. Whenever we find any improvements that have been thoroughly tested, they are embodied at once. Hence, the STANDARD that will come out of the factory six months from now will doubtless have some improvements which are not yet in production. For the same reason the car that we will be building a year hence will differ still further.

You can readily see, therefore, that it is never going to be possible to have the latest model, or perhaps we should say the ultimate model, because our engineers and designers are constantly striving to bring out a better and better automobile.

It may interest you to know that I personally purchased a new STANDARD only eight weeks ago, although by waiting I could have had one of the new models at a saving. We are confident that the car that we manufacture has no superior, and we are sure that you will more and more appreciate your own STANDARD as time goes on.

Very truly yours,

Handling the customer where nothing is really wrong.—In many cases a complaint will be made that shows the user of the product needs further education in its use. A proper handling of the situation will save expense, build goodwill, and satisfy the customer.

In the fountain pen industry, for example, the greatest common complaint is so-called "leaking." In almost all cases, the pen itself is absolutely perfect, but its use has been imperfect. To ask people to send their pens in immediately would involve handling expense to the company and a service fee to customers. Furthermore, the impression would be created that the pen is faulty—something to be avoided if the pen is perfect.

The L. E. Waterman Company found the following letter an excellent solution to the problem:

Dear Mrs. Seale:

We're glad you wrote and gave us the opportunity to make any necessary adjustment to your Waterman's gift pen so that it gives you the writing satisfaction millions of other Waterman's users experience.

Rather than inconvenience you immediately by asking you to send your pen to us, may we make this suggestion. Many instances of leaking are caused by improper filling of the pen. When the pen is almost empty, the great amount of air in the barrel will expand and force a few drops of ink out.

Make certain that these "almost empty periods" are kept few and far between, by making certain that your pen is completely full when you fill it. Keep the entire nib under ink for the count of ten, after you snap the filling lever back into place. Give your pen a good big drink of Waterman's ink.

Then, at the first sign of ink flowing heavier again, refill—and you should have no repetition of the trouble. But if these simple instructions do not help, if something is actually wrong with your pen, by all means send it to us at our main office in Newark. We'll be glad to give it our thorough and complete attention.

Very truly yours,

Handling the satisfied customer who asks too much.—In many lines of business the owner of a product that has given satisfaction over a period of years will offer the product back to the company in exchange for a new one on the assumption that the company will value the testimonial and possibly use the old product as a relic. The L. E. Waterman Company, for example, receives many letters from people with old fountain pens who offer them in exchange for new ones. To make the exchange would be unprofitable; to refuse the offer might create ill will. The following letter solves the problem by showing why the offer cannot be accepted and interposing a fair and mutually profitable trade-in for those who do want a new pen:

Dear Mr. Swanton:

Thank you for the very kind offer of your fountain pen and a letter of testimonial regarding it.

We have never offered to exchange 30-year-old Waterman's for new ones, Mr. Swanton, for a very good reason. Strange as it seems, there are far too many Waterman's pens, 30 years and older, still in active service. Then, too, the sentimental and curiosity value of pens that age still performing perfectly deters owners from returning them.

As we have many of these old veterans in our display cases now, we're certain your pen would be of far greater service working for you, than merely reclining on display for us. Should it need some minor adjustment to restore it to perfect working order, we'd be glad to look it over for you.

Or, if you'd prefer to trade in your old Waterman's for a new one, we'd accept it as one-third payment for any new pen retailing at up to $5.00, in accordance with our special trade-in plan for the convenience of Waterman's patrons.

Thank you again, Mr. Swanton, for your courtesy and consideration, and, if we can be of service to you, please don't hesitate to get in touch with us.

Very truly yours,

7. LEGAL ASPECTS OF BUSINESS LETTERS

Business letters and the law.—The law cannot prevent a person from writing anything he pleases, but it can and often does make him responsible for his statements. A letter may involve a person in a contractual obligation; it may subject him to liability for injury to the reputation of another person; it may be used in a lawsuit as evidence of an admission against the writer's interests. The lawbooks are filled with cases in which a letter, thoughtlessly written, has cost the writer endless embarrassment and thousands of dollars. A proper understanding of the legal consequences of a written statement, a moment's consideration of the contents or phraseology of the letter, might have avoided the litigation entirely or changed its outcome.

The dangers of careless letter writing are further increased by the fact that the law may hold a person responsible, not only for the letters which he himself writes, but for those written by his agents and employees. An agent may, by correspondence, bind his principal to contracts entered into within the scope of his authority. A principal, or employer, is responsible for libelous letters written by his agent or employee, not only where the agent or employee was carrying out express directions or acting pursuant to express authority, but also where he was acting in the usual course of his employment. Admissions of an agent made in letters within the scope of his authority are allowed as evidence against his principal. A person is, of course, always liable for letters written by his agent or employee where he ratifies them expressly or by his conduct acquiesces therein.

Contracts by Correspondence

What a contract is.—A contract has been defined as an agreement by which two parties mutually promise and engage, or one of them promises or engages to the other, to give some particular thing or to do or abstain from doing some particular act. The contract is created by a proposal or offer by one of the parties and an acceptance thereof by the other. It may be oral or written, express or implied. The following elements are necessary to make the contract valid and enforceable:

1. The parties must be competent to contract. A person under 21 years of age is an infant according to law and is not competent to contract; an insane person cannot enter into a contract, although he may be held liable for necessaries supplied to him.
2. There must be an agreement between the parties—that is, a clear and definite offer on one side, and an unconditional and unqualified acceptance of the offer on the other.
3. The agreement must be supported by a consideration—that is, something of value in the eyes of the law, in the way of price or compensation that may be a benefit to the party promising or a loss to the person to whom the promise is made.
4. The subject matter of the contract must be legal. Gambling and usurious contracts, for example, are illegal.

A letter may constitute a contract.—A letter containing a proposal, signed by the person making the proposal, may constitute an offer, and a reply acquiescing in the proposal, signed by the person to whom the offer was addressed or by his duly authorized agent, may constitute an acceptance. The two letters together may result in a valid and enforceable contract. To establish a contract by correspondence, the offer must be clear and definite, and the acceptance must be without conditions or qualifications. An acceptance upon terms varying from those offered is a rejection of the offer and puts an end to the negotiations unless the party who made the original offer renews it or properly assents to the modification suggested. This does not mean that all the terms of the agreement must appear in a single letter or even in two letters. The complete contract may be gathered from a series of letters between the parties, determining step by step the various terms of the contract. It must, however, be clear from the correspondence that the minds of the parties have met with respect to the material elements of the contract. A circular and price list announcing goods for sale at specified prices is generally considered simply as an invitation for an offer and not an offer itself. The final determination of whether or not it is an offer depends upon the intent of the parties as gathered from the correspondence between them.

May oral statements contradict the terms of a contract evidenced by letters?—Where letters contain a definite and complete contract, the law will not permit oral evidence to show what the contract between the parties was. This protection against variation or contradiction is furnished by the so-called "parol evidence rule." The parol evidence rule is a general rule of law which holds that, in the absence of fraud or mistake, extrinsic evidence is not admissible upon a trial to show that the real agreement of the parties was different from that expressed in a writing; nor where a writing is free from ambiguity is parol evidence admissible to explain its meaning. If a series of letters does not contain all the terms of the contract, either in the proposition made or in its acceptance, parol evidence may be allowed to prove the exact terms of the contract.

Letters as memoranda satisfying the statute of frauds.—The term "statute of frauds" is used to describe the laws in the various states requiring certain contracts and transfers of property to be evidenced by a writing signed by the party who is to be charged therewith, or by his duly authorized agent. The following agreements, among others, are subject to the statute of frauds:

1. An agreement to answer for the debt, default, or miscarriage of another person.

2. Agreements not to be performed within one year from the making thereof.

3. Transfers and contracts for the transfer of real property and interests therein.

4. Contracts for the sale of goods, wares, or merchandise, for the price of $50 or more, except where a part of the goods is accepted and received by the buyer or where he gives something in part payment.

No particular form of instrument or language is required for the written memorandum. Any document, written either to evidence the contract or for any other purpose, is sufficient if it states all the essential elements of the contract with reasonable certainty and is signed by the party to be charged or by his agent. A letter may be a sufficient writing to satisfy the statute of frauds, and several letters may be considered together in supplying the essential elements of such a memorandum as will satisfy the statute. The writing need not be addressed to the other party to the contract; a letter to the writer's agent may constitute an adequate memorandum of the contract.

Libelous Letters

What libel is.—A libel has been defined as a false and malicious publication that tends to injure the reputation of a living person or the memory of a deceased person, and to expose him to public hatred, contempt, or ridicule. A corporation is a person in this sense, as well as an individual, and a publication that injures the corporation's credit, property, or business is actionable. The libel may be in the form of a writing such as a letter, a printing such as a newspaper, or it may be by signs and pictures. The statutes in some states define a libel, and in such cases the statute governs in determining whether or not a publication constitutes a libel. In Missouri, for example, a libel is defined by law as "the malicious defamation of a person made public by any printing, writing, sign, picture, representation, or effigy, tending to provoke him to wrath or expose him to public hatred, contempt, or ridicule, or to deprive him of the benefits of public confidence and social intercourse, or any malicious defamation made public as aforesaid, designed to blacken and vilify the memory of one who is dead, and tending to scandalize or provoke his surviving relatives and friends." The fact that a statement which is libelous is proved to be true generally frees the person who made the defamation from civil liability therefor.

A libelous letter must be communicated to a third party in order to be actionable.—In order that a suit may be maintained for a defamatory writing, it must have been read by someone other than the person defamed. A letter containing a libel that is addressed to the person libeled and is not read by anyone else is generally not actionable. The reader may be a copyist who reproduces a longhand draft. He may be a stenographer who takes the libelous writing by dictation and examines and transcribes the notes, although some courts have taken the view that publication to a stenographer is privileged and does not subject the writer to liability unless impelled by actual malice. A private letter between officers of a corporation in the course of a company's business, which is not communicated to others, has been held not to be published, and the corporation has been deemed immune from liability for any damages resulting therefrom. Similarly, a letter written and mailed by one agent of a corporation within the scope of his employment to another agent of the same corporation does not amount to a publication of such a nature as to constitute a libel against the corporation.

Must pecuniary loss be shown in a suit for libel?—The law divides written words charged to be libelous into three classes:

1. Words libelous *per se.*
2. Words libelous *per quod.*
3. Words that cannot possibly bear a defamatory meaning.

The first class includes those words which are injurious upon their face and without the aid of extrinsic proof. The law presumes damage from the mere publication of the libel, and hence calls it libel *per se*—that is, "by itself." To be libelous *per se,* the words must be susceptible of but one meaning and must be of such a nature that the court can presume that they tend to disgrace and degrade a person, to injure him in his business or profession, or to hold him up to public hatred or ridicule and cause him to be shunned and avoided. The second class of libelous words, libel *per quod* (meaning "by which"), includes those words which are reasonably susceptible of a defamatory meaning as well as an innocent one, and may be defamatory by reason of their imputation or of extrinsic facts; such words require proof of pecuniary loss. Words that fall into the third class, and cannot possibly bear a defamatory meaning, cannot be made the basis of an action for libel.

Examples of communications that are libelous.—The following kinds of statements have been held in court cases to inflict an injury on a person's business, and to be actionable without proof of pecuniary loss:

1. Imputing insolvency or bankruptcy, or suggesting that a person is in pecuniary difficulties.
2. Imputing to a merchant or tradesman want of credit or responsibility.
3. Charging a merchant with falsifying his scales and selling merchandise to customers by false weight.
4. Charging one with receiving stolen goods.
5. Imputing want of knowledge, skill, or capacity to conduct business; but disparaging the merchandise of another person or the quality of his products, without imputing fraud, is not actionable without proof of pecuniary loss.
6. Imputing to an officer or employee dereliction of duty or lack of due qualification; but a letter to the employer of a person not engaged in a vocation requiring credit, to the effect that the employee refuses to pay his debts, sent for the purpose of obtaining the employer's help in effecting collection, is not actionable without proof of pecuniary loss.

Libelous letters may be privileged.—Under certain circumstances communications that ordinarily would be defamatory are deemed by the law to be justified or "privileged." This means that no civil liability for their publication attaches, unless it is proved that the communication was made maliciously. Such privilege occurs where the communication is made by one person in pursuance of a duty—political, judicial, social, or personal—in a matter where his interest is concerned, to another person having a corresponding duty or interest. The court determines in the first instance whether the occasion exists that justifies the publication of the defamatory statement in the absence of malice, and the person suing must then show the existence of actual or express malice in order to sustain his action. Malice, in this case, does not necessarily imply hatred, ill will, anger, wrath, or vindictiveness; it may mean no more than the antithesis of good faith.

When is the privilege lost?—Whether or not a communication is privileged depends, not only upon the occasion which calls for the publication, but also upon the character of the communication. If, for example, the defamatory statement goes beyond the plain necessities of the situation, and uses excessive language, the privilege is lost, and the nature of the communication furnishes evidence of express malice. If a communication is privileged, the privilege covers all incidents of the transmission of the communication in accordance with the usual course of business. For example, the communication may be dictated to a stenographer for transmission without loss of the privilege. There is considerable authority for the view that communications between employer and employee are privileged where the communication relates to matters pertaining to the employment and is made in good faith.

Examples of libelous letters that are privileged.—The following letters have been held to be privileged:

1. A letter written in answer to a request for information concerning a former employee.

2. A communication from a mercantile agency to a person having an interest in the particular matter, but not in a report issued for general circulation among its subscribers. A false publication that a person is a criminal, voluntarily made by a credit bureau to subscribers and others, is not privileged.

3. A letter written by a steamship company in the ordinary course of its business to the seller of merchandise to ascertain what it should do with merchandise left in its hands, in which it was stated that the purchaser had filed a petition in bankruptcy.

4. A letter written by an attorney for one creditor to another creditor, stating that the debtor was insolvent, and requesting authorization to represent the creditor in bankruptcy proceedings.

5. An answer by a businessman to a confidential inquiry as to the financial standing of some individual, firm, or corporation, where the answer is fairly and honestly made, and the writer has reasonable and probable cause to believe his statements to be true.

6. A letter from the cashier of a bank to a stockholder regarding the financial standing of a surety on an official bond to the bank.

7. An answer to a request for information concerning the trustworthiness of another who has applied for credit.

Letters as Evidence of Admission Against the Writer

What is an admission that can be used as evidence against the firm?—In order that a letter may be offered in evidence as an admission against the interest of the firm or person writing, the letter itself must contain an admission of some fact. A letter containing merely an innuendo from which one must conjecture what the writer was referring to cannot be used as evidence of an admission against his interest. A letter containing an admission against interest, to be allowed as evidence against the writer, need not have been written to the person who is offering it as evidence. It may be written to one who is not a party to the suit. For example, a letter written to a third person telling such person to deal with a designated individual, the writer's agent, and stating that any deal made with him would be satisfactory, was held in a court action to be competent proof of the agent's authority. An anonymous threatening letter, written to frighten a litigant into abandoning a pending suit, was deemed to be in the nature of an admission that a valid cause of action existed and that the writer had no defense thereto. A letter to a third party in which the writer stated that he had entered into a contract with the plaintiff was held admissible in an action on the contract.

When a letter containing an offer of compromise may be admissible as evidence of liability.—The law favors the settlement of disputed claims without litigation, and to encourage such settlements the general rule has been laid down that an offer of settlement which has been rejected cannot be used as evidence of the existence or of the amount of liability. This fact is true whether the offer of compromise is made before or after suit has been begun. Letters containing offers of compromise are, however, generally admitted in evidence under the following circumstances:

1. Where an offer of settlement is not rejected but is accepted and agreed upon and thereafter repudiated by the person making

the offer; evidence of the offer is allowed in an action on the claim.

2. Where an admission against interest of particular facts, material to the issue before the court, accompanies an offer of compromise but is independent of it, the admission may be received as evidence tending to establish the facts stated, unless:

(*a*) The admission is so integrated that the offer of compromise is inseparable from it.

(*b*) It appears that the admission against interest is made as a concession to induce a compromise.

(*c*) The admission is stated to be made without prejudice.

3. Where a letter making an offer to pay a certain amount is written and received before any controversy is pending as to the amount due, the letter is admissible to show the amount due. Similarly, a letter seeking to determine differences of opinion as to title to property, written long before suit is brought involving title to the property, is not considered an offer of compromise and is allowed to be introduced as evidence.

May letters be used as evidence against the recipient?—A person to whom a letter is addressed is ordinarily not required to make any reply, and failure to answer the letter is no evidence of the truth of the facts stated therein. The reason for this general rule is that a person cannot make evidence for himself by his own "self-serving" declarations as to the character of his dealings or as to the liability of the person to whom the statement is addressed; a letter from one party to the other is incompetent to prove the statements therein in favor of the writer. There are, however, exceptions to the general rule. When a letter is written making such a claim as in common experience would naturally be denied by the addressee, or where it is his duty to reply, the letter and the failure to reply may be admitted in evidence. Whether or not an unanswered letter is proof of an admission depends upon the circumstances of each case. Want of facility in writing, habitual delay in correspondence, or press of business, may tend to lead to the conclusion that silence is not acquiescence.

A letter may extend or revive an outlawed debt.—Statutes have been enacted in the various states limiting to a fixed period the time within which suit may be brought on certain causes of action. In

New York, for example, an action on a contract, express or implied, other than a judgment or a sealed instrument, is barred unless commenced within six years after accrual of the cause of action—that is, within six years after the contract has been breached and a right to sue thereon has arisen. These statutes, commonly known as "statutes of limitations," are the outgrowth of a legal fiction resting upon the theory that after a long lapse of time during which a claimant has made no assertion of his rights, the obligation is presumed to have been paid or discharged. The presumption may, however, be waived by the debtor in any one of the following ways:

1. By an admission or acknowledgment of the existence of the debt, from which a promise to pay may be implied; no express promise to pay is required, but a mere acknowledgment of a debt is not sufficient unless the acknowledgment is one from which a promise to pay is clearly inferable.
2. By an unconditional promise to pay the debt.
3. By a conditional promise to pay the debt, provided the condition has been performed.

The acknowledgment or promise may be made either before or after the entire statutory period has expired. If it is made before the expiration of the limited period, the old debt is vitalized for another statutory period, dating from the time of the acknowledgment or promise; if it is made after the statutory period has run, a new cause of action arises. In some states the statutes specifically require that an acknowledgment of indebtedness or promise to pay shall be in writing, signed by the party to be charged therewith, and in such cases signed letters or other signed documents are sufficient to satisfy the requirements. The letter or other document must, however, identify the debt explicitly and certainly; where there are several debts, a general acknowledgment of them is insufficient. Similarly, an acknowledgment is not sufficient if it leaves the amount of the debt in dispute. In some states the statutes requiring acknowledgments or promises to be in writing have been held to apply only to those acknowledgments or promises made after the statutory period of limitations has fully expired.

8. LAYOUT OF THE LETTER

Stationery and letterhead.—Rightly or wrongly, people judge many things by appearances. An old-fashioned letterhead, poorly designed and reproduced on cheap stationery, must inevitably make an unfavorable impression. The appearance of the business letter—the design of the letterhead, the quality of the stationery, and the neatness and correctness of the typing—has a real sales value; it forms in the mind of the reader a subconscious picture of the character of the firm whose name appears at the top of the sheet.

Most business houses use bond stock for their letter paper; ledger, parchment, and many book papers are also suitable. In bond stock the weight most commonly used is twenty-pound, although twenty-four or twenty-eight pound is sometimes employed. Bond stock of less than twenty-pound weight is not desirable.

The standard size of letter paper for commercial use is $8\frac{1}{2} \times 11$ inches; other sizes preferred by some firms are $5\frac{1}{2} \times 8\frac{1}{2}$ inches and $7\frac{1}{4} \times 10\frac{1}{2}$ inches. Many houses use stationery of note-paper size for business letters addressed to women. The size of the letter paper used for sales letters varies greatly.

The design of the letterhead should reflect the character of the firm. In general, simplicity and compactness are desirable. The best procedure is to have a specialist submit designs from which a choice can be made. A number of companies produce letterheads exclusively. Artists, printers, engravers, and lithographers also do excellent work in designing individual letterheads.

The most usual methods of reproduction are letterpress (printing), lithography, offset, engraving, embossing, die-stamping, and plateless engraving. Each of these methods has its advantages; selection may be made on the basis of taste and expense.

Examples of effective letterheads.—A number of effective letterheads, representative of various lines of business, are reproduced on pages 260–261.

Setup of the letter.—The competent secretary or stenographer gives careful attention to the mechanical setup of the letter—the arrangement on the page, the width of the margins, and the position of the date, the inside address, the salutation, and the complimentary close. Modern business practice has established certain conventions of good usage and correctness in respect to such matters; observance of these conventions reflects good taste.

A number of styles of letter setup are illustrated on pages 262–264.

9. MECHANICS OF THE LETTER

Date line.—The following are the rules governing the date line.

1. Type the date line not less than two spaces below the letterhead, and as much lower as necessary for centering the letter on the page. The end of the date line should mark the right-hand margin of the letter. Sometimes, however, the date is typed in the center of the page, about two spaces below the last line of the letterhead; it may also be placed on the same line as the address in the letterhead, immediately to the right.

2. Do not use *d, nd, rd, st,* or *th* following the day of the month.

Wrong:	*Right:*
March 5th, 19—	March 5, 19—
May 2nd, 19—	May 2, 19—
June 23rd, 19—	June 23, 19—
July 21st, 19—	July 21, 19—

3. Do not abbreviate the date.

Wrong:	*Right:*
9-15-41	September 15, 1941
9/15/41	
9'15'41	

4. Except in very formal letters, do not spell out the day of the month or the year.

Wrong:	June fifth, Nineteen hundred and forty-one
Right:	June 5, 1941

Inside address.—The following are the rules governing the inside address.

1. The inside address contains the name of the individual or company to whom the letter is written, and the street, city, and state address. It may be typed in either the block or the indented style. With the block style, open punctuation is most usual; with the indented form, closed punctuation is used.

Block form with open punctuation:

Mr. Arthur F. Gardner
302 Church Street
Chicago, Illinois

Indented form with closed punctuation:

Mr. Arthur F. Gardner,
  302 Church Street,
    Chicago, Illinois.

2. Begin the inside address at the left-hand margin of the letter.

Mr. Arthur F. Gardner
302 Church Street
Chicago, Illinois

Dear Mr. Gardner:

We very much appreciate your having forwarded us . . . .

3. Type the inside address not less than two spaces below the date line; the exact number of spaces depends upon the length of the letter. The inside address should correspond exactly with the envelope address and should not extend beyond the middle of the page.

March 23, 19—

Mr. F. H. Brownell, President
Garrison Machinery Company
Newark, New Jersey

My dear Mr. Brownell:

4. In official letters or personal letters, the inside address may be placed in the lower left-hand corner of the page, even with the left-hand margin and two spaces below the level of the signature. When this style is followed, the letter begins with the salutation.

Respectfully yours,

Edward F. Baker

Mr. Arthur F. Gardner
302 Church Street
Chicago, Illinois

Printed in Black and Blue, on Franconia Bond.

Engraved in Black and Red, on Crane's Japanese Linen Bond.

Engraved in Black, on Howard Bond.

Printed in Black and Orange.

Figure 9.—Examples of Effective Letterheads.

Lithographed in Grey, on Howard Bond.

THE HUSSEY MANUFACTURING COMPANY

IRONWORKERS SINCE EIGHTEEN THIRTY-FIVE

STRUCTURAL STEEL AND ORNAMENTAL IRON

PHONE 39-2 · NORTH BERWICK, ME.

Printed in Blue and Red, on Rockledge Bond.

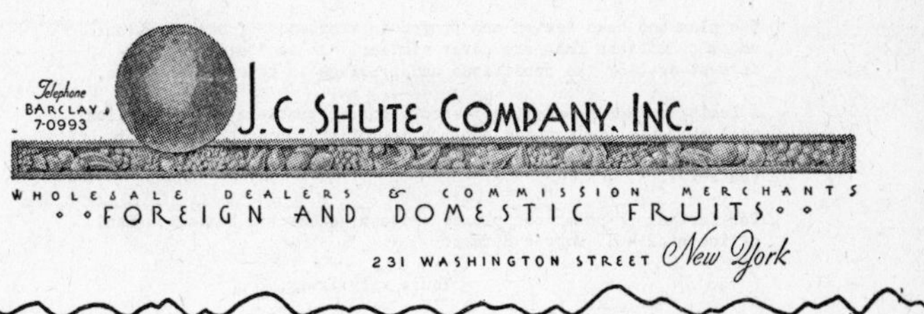

Designed and engraved by Nahm Photogravure Co., N. Y. C.

Engraved on Adirondack Bond

Printed in Black, on Arrowhead Bond.

Figure 10.—Examples of Effective Letterheads.

REMINGTON RAND BUSINESS SERVICE INC.

BUFFALO, N.Y.

November 14, 19--

Mr. Kenneth Fairfield
Johnson Hardware Company
205 E. Sixteenth Street
Chicago, Illinois

Dear Mr. Fairfield:

Thank you for your request for our new book "Let's Take Stock." Your copy is being mailed today.

The Remington Rand visible stock control plan described in this book provides a method whereby you can have, always and instantly in usable form, the facts you need for practical, profitable control of inventories.

Wide usage proves this plan productive of faster turnover, lower investment, and increased profits. Doubling of turnover has not been unusual where this plan has been installed.

The plan has been tested and proved in thousands of organizations under conditions that are never similar. It is "tailor-made"-- to meet exactly the conditions and problems in your own business.

A Remington Rand analysis of stock control problems in your office will show you the precise application of the plan that will most effectively increase profits through efficient control of your inventories.

For further information, please write or phone the Remington Rand office at 214 W. Monroe Street.

Yours very truly,

REMINGTON RAND BUSINESS SERVICE INC.

F. J. Hastings

Advertising Department

FJHastings:EB

REMINGTON *Typewriters and Accounting Machines* — LIBRARY BUREAU *Filing Systems and Indexing Service*
RAND — KARDEX *and* INDEX VISIBLE *Visible Records* — SAFE-CABINET *Record Protection Devices*
POWERS *Tabulating Machine* — DALTON *Adding and Bookkeeping Machines* — KALAMAZOO *and* BAKER VAWTER *Loose Leaf*

J. C. McCloskey, "Handbook of Business Correspondence"

Figure 11.—Block Form of Letter Setup, with Open Punctuation.

INTERTYPE CORPORATION

EXECUTIVE OFFICES • THREE HUNDRED SIXTY FURMAN STREET • BROOKLYN, NEW YORK

NEW YORK, CHICAGO, NEW ORLEANS, SAN FRANCISCO LOS ANGELES AND BOSTON LONDON, BERLIN

November 5, 19—

Mr. Walter A. Post
987 Wilson Street
Emporia, Kansas

Dear Mr. Post:

This letter is written in the form known as the "semi-block" or the "modified block" form.

In this particular letter the paper guide on the typewriter is set so that when the paper is inserted and the marginal stop set at 20, the margin at the left will be two inches wide.

The first line of each paragraph of the body is indented five spaces from the left margin, but each succeeding line begins even with the left margin. To accomplish this, set the marginal stop at 20 and the tabulator stop at 25. The lines of the body are single spaced, with double spacing between the paragraphs.

The first line of the inside address begins at the left margin. The following lines and the salutation begin on the margin established by the first line of the inside address.

Very truly yours,

INTERTYPE CORPORATION

B. W. Jones

B. W. Jones, Manager

BWJ:IN

J. C. McCloskey, "Handbook of Business Correspondence"

Figure 12.—Semi-block Form of Letter Setup, with Open Punctuation.

The WILSON H. LEE COMPANY
MAILADVERTISING
497 ASYLUM STREET, HARTFORD, CONN.
Telephone 2-9074

October 4, 19--.

Mr. R. A. White,
324 Oak Street,
Athens, Ohio.

Dear Mr. White:

This letter is written in the form known as the "indented form," with closed punctuation.

In this particular letter the paper guide on the typewriter is set so that when the paper is inserted and the marginal stop set at 20, the margin at the left will be two inches wide.

The first line of each paragraph of the body is indented five spaces from the left margin, but each succeeding line begins even with the left margin. To accomplish this, set the marginal stop at 20 and the tabulator stop at 25. The lines of the body are single spaced, with double spacing between the paragraphs.

The first line of the inside address begins at the left margin, while each succeeding line begins four spaces to the right of the preceding line.

Very truly yours,

WILSON H. LEE COMPANY

J. L. Knoll

J. L. Knoll, Manager

JLK:BM

J. C. McCloskey, "Handbook of Business Correspondence"

Figure 13.—Indented Form of Letter Setup, with Closed Punctuation.

5. The inside address should correspond exactly with the official title of the company addressed. If *Company, Co., The, Inc.,* or *&* is part of the company's official name, use this form.

The Third National Bank	National Machinery Co., Inc.
F. K. Mayer Company	Thomas White & Co.

6. Do not place a word or a sign preceding the street number.

Wrong:

Mr. L. K. Hamilton	Mr. L. K. Hamilton
#45 South Street	No. 45 South Street
Dayton, Ohio	Dayton, Ohio

Right:

Mr. L. K. Hamilton
45 South Street
Dayton, Ohio

7. Spell out the numeric names of streets and avenues if they are composed of single numbers; express them in figures if they are compounds.

Right:	*Right:*
Sixth Avenue	63rd Street *or* 63 Street
Fifth Street	71st Street *or* 71 Street
Sixtieth Street	122nd Street *or* 122 Street

8. In the inside address and the envelope address, the name of the state may be abbreviated. The following are the approved forms of abbreviations for the states, territories, and possessions:

Alabama	Ala.	Florida	Fla.
Arizona	Ariz.	Georgia	Ga.
Arkansas	Ark.	Hawaii	T. H.
California	Calif.	Illinois	Ill.
Canal Zone	C. Z.	Indiana	Ind.
Colorado	Colo.	Kansas	Kans.
Connecticut	Conn.	Kentucky	Ky.
Delaware	Del.	Louisiana	La.
District of Columbia	D. C.	Maryland	Md.

Massachusetts	Mass.	Oregon	Oreg.
Michigan	Mich.	Pennsylvania	Pa.
Minnesota	Minn.	Philippine Islands	P. I.
Mississippi	Miss.	Puerto Rico	P. R.
Missouri	Mo.	Rhode Island	R. I.
Montana	Mont.	South Carolina	S. C.
Nebraska	Nebr.	South Dakota	S. Dak.
Nevada	Nev.	Tennessee	Tenn.
New Hampshire	N. H.	Texas	Tex.
New Jersey	N. J.	Vermont	Vt.
New Mexico	N. Mex.	Virginia	Va.
New York	N. Y.	Washington	Wash.
North Carolina	N. C.	West Virginia	W. Va.
North Dakota	N. Dak.	Wisconsin	Wis.
Oklahoma	Okla.	Wyoming	Wyo.

Do not abbreviate the following:

Alaska	Iowa	Samoa
Guam	Maine	Utah
Idaho	Ohio	Virgin Islands

9a. In addressing an individual in a firm, corporation, or other group, place the individual's name on the first line, and the company name on the next line. If a person's business title is short, place it on the first line; if it is long, place it on the second line. The city and state may be placed either on the same line or on separate lines.

Mr. James E. Lambert, President
Lambert & Woolf Company
1035 Tower Street
Cleveland, Ohio

Mr. C. M. Higgins, Secretary
Southern Hardware Company
265 Bennett Avenue
Norfolk, Virginia

Mr. J. A. Hovey
Collector of Internal Revenue
Customs House
Albany, New York

Western Oil Company
263 Fourth Avenue
Indianapolis
Indiana

Mr. Henry F. Daley
Manufacturing Department
Hibbard Publishing Company
156 Claremont Avenue
Toledo, Ohio

Mr. George F. Moore
Advertising Manager
Price & Patterson
234 Broad Street
Chicago, Illinois

b. Do not abbreviate titles such as *President, Secretary, Treasurer, Superintendent,* and *Sales Manager.* Such titles are commonly preceded by *Mr.* (or *Miss* or *Mrs.*).

Mr. James E. Lambert, President
Lambert & Woolf Company
1035 Tower Street
Cleveland, Ohio

Mr. C. M. Higgins, Secretary
Southern Hardware Company
265 Bennett Avenue
Norfolk, Virginia

10*a.* To bring the letter (addressed to a firm, corporation, or other group) to the attention of an individual, use the following form, with the name of the individual on the same line as the salutation, and as least five spaces from the end of the salutation.

Monroe Knitting Mills
784 Wadsworth Avenue
Los Angeles, California

Gentlemen: <u>Attention of Mr. J. F. Montgomery</u>

b. If a subject line is required in addition to the *Attention* line, type it on the same line as the salutation, or place it two spaces below the salutation. If an *Attention* line is not used, the subject line should be placed halfway between the last line of the inside address and the salutation.

Monroe Knitting Mills
784 Wadsworth Avenue
Los Angeles, California

Attention of Mr. J. F. Montgomery

Gentlemen: <u>Order No. 78345</u>

Monroe Knitting Mills
784 Wadsworth Avenue
Los Angeles, California

Attention of Mr. J. F. Montgomery

Gentlemen:

<u>EXPRESS SHIPMENTS</u>

Monroe Knitting Mills
784 Wadsworth Avenue
Los Angeles, California

MORGAN CONSTRUCTION COMPANY ESTIMATE

Gentlemen:

c. Place filing numbers in the center of the page, on the same line as the salutation.

Laidlaw Printing Company, Inc.
32 Broadway
New York, New York

Gentlemen: Our File No. 456

11*a*. Initials indicating degrees and other honors may be placed after the name of the person addressed. Use only the initials of the highest degree; more than one degree may be used, however, if the degrees are in different fields.

Wrong: Professor Arthur T. Haughton, A.B., A.M., Ph.D.
Right: Arthur T. Haughton, Ph.D.
Right: Frederick H. March, A.M., LL.B.

b. It is incorrect to use both *Doctor* and *Ph.D., M.D.,* or any other doctoral degree.

Wrong: Dr. Philip Martin, Ph.D.
Right: Dr. Philip Martin
Right: Philip Martin, Ph.D.

Wrong: Dr. Ernest Jones, M.D.
Right: Dr. Ernest Jones
Right: Ernest Jones, M.D.

c. It is discourteous to abbreviate *Doctor* or *Professor* if the last name only is used.

Wrong: Dr. Martin
Right: Doctor Martin

Wrong: Prof. Clark
Right: Professor Clark

12. If the last name only is used, the word *Reverend* should be followed by *Mr*. (or *Dr*. if the clergyman is a D.D.). *Reverend* is commonly abbreviated unless preceded by *The*.

Wrong:	Rev. Waite	*Right:*	Rev. Mr. Waite
Wrong:	Reverend Waite	*Right:*	Rev. Dr. Waite

Right: Rev. William Waite
Right: The Reverend Mr. Waite
Right: The Reverend Doctor Waite
Right: The Reverend William Waite

13. The rule stated for *Reverend* applies also to *Honorable.*

Wrong:	Hon. Root	*Right:*	Hon. Elihu Root
Wrong:	Honorable Root	*Right:*	The Honorable Elihu Root
Right:	Hon. Mr. Root	*Right:*	The Honorable Mr. Root

14. The title *Esquire,* usually shortened to *Esq.,* should be used after the names of chief clerks and chiefs of bureaus of the executive departments, mayors of cities (when the name is used before the title, as James Brown, Esq., Mayor of ....), American diplomatic officers below the grade of minister, American consular officers, the clerk of the U. S. Supreme Court, and officers of the court. It may also be used for any gentleman, except when addressed with his wife.

Where a title is used before the name, the *Esq.* must never appear.

Wrong: Dr. C. A. Carlton, Esq.
Wrong: Mr. L. A. Jones, Esq.
Right: C. A. Carlton, Esq., M.D.
Right: L. A. Jones, Esq.

15. *Messrs.* may be used in addressing a firm of men, or men and women, when the names denote individuals. Do not use *Messrs.* as a form of address for corporations or other business organizations that bear impersonal names.

Wrong: Messrs. American Manufacturing Company
Right: American Manufacturing Company
Wrong: Messrs. New York Central Railroad
Right: New York Central Railroad
Right: Messrs. Marvin, Tobin and Smart
Right: Messrs. James Marshall & Sons
Right: Messrs. Frederick and Noyes

16. In addressing a firm composed of women, either married or unmarried, use *Mesdames* or *Mmes.*

Mesdames Roberts and Smith
Mmes. Neale and Sanford

17. It is customary to address a married woman by her husband's given name and initials.

Mrs. Henry F. Walters

18. A widow continues to use her husband's name socially, but in legal and financial matters she is addressed by her own given name.

Mrs. Hilda F. Walters

19. A divorced woman usually retains the legal and social right to use her husband's full name, but, if she prefers, she may use her maiden surname and her husband's surname.

Mrs. John Smith
or
Mrs. Jones Smith

She does not call herself Mrs. Mary Jones unless she wishes to give the impression that she was the guilty one in the divorce.

If she has legally resumed her maiden name, she may be addressed as Miss Mary Jones.

Salutation.—The following are the rules governing the salutation.

1. Type the salutation two spaces below the inside address, and level with the left-hand margin.

Mr. Charles H. Johnson
Lowell Manufacturing Company
Lowell, Massachusetts

Dear Mr. Johnson:

2. Use a colon following the salutation. Do not use a semicolon or a dash; a comma should be used only in friendly letters.

My dear Mr. Jensen:

3. Capitalize the first word of the salutation. Do not capitalize *dear* except when it is used as the first word of the salutation.

Dear Sir:
My dear Sir:
My dear Mr. Jensen:
Madam:
My dear Madam:
My dear Miss Davis:

4. The following are the most commonly used salutations.

Official:

Sir:
Sirs:
Gentlemen:
Madam:
Mesdames:

Very formal:

Sir:
My dear Sir:
Madam:
My dear Madam:

Formal:

Dear Sir:
Dear Madam: (used in addressing either a married or an unmarried woman)
Gentlemen: (used in addressing two or more men, a firm, corporation, post office box, committee, or a firm composed of both men and women)
Mesdames: (used in addressing two or more women or a firm composed entirely of women)

Implying personal acquaintance or previous correspondence:

Dear Mr. Marvin:
My dear Mr. Marvin:
Dear Mrs. Marvin:
My dear Mrs. Marvin:
Dear Miss Marvin:
My dear Miss Marvin:

Informal or friendly:

Dear Marvin:
My dear Marvin:
Dear Walter:

5. *Dear Sirs* is not commonly used in this country, except by conservative business houses, banks, and lawyers.

6. Do not use *Messrs.* or *Miss* as a salutation.

Wrong:

Messrs. Foster and Clark:
Dear Miss:

Right:

Gentlemen:
Dear Madam:

7. Never abbreviate titles in salutations, except *Mr., Mrs.,* and *Dr.*

Wrong:	*Right:*
D'r. Sir:	Dear Sir:
D'r. S'r:	Dear Sir:
Gents.:	Gentlemen:
Mmes.:	Mesdames:

8. It is incorrect to use only a person's name as a salutation.

Wrong: Mr. James Curtis:
Right: Dear Mr. Curtis:

9. If the letter is addressed to a company, and the inside address does not contain the name of an individual, make the salutation plural. If the first line of the inside address bears the name of an individual, make the salutation singular.

Mr. William F. Cutting, President
James Whitcomb Company
325 Pine Street
York, Pennsylvania

Dear Sir:

James Whitcomb Company
325 Pine Street
York, Pennsylvania

Gentlemen:

Complimentary close.—The following are the rules governing the complimentary close.

1. Type the complimentary close two spaces below the last line of the letter. It should begin slightly to the right of the center of the page, and should not extend beyond the right-hand margin.

We enclose a stamped, addressed envelope for your convenience.

Yours very truly,

2. Capitalize only the first word of the complimentary close.

Yours very truly,
Very truly yours,

3. A comma should follow the last word of the complimentary close.

Yours very truly,

4. The following are the complimentary closes most commonly used.

Closes for letters addressed to high officials:

Very respectfully yours,
Yours very respectfully,
Respectfully yours,
Yours respectfully,
Respectfully,
Yours very truly,
Very truly yours,

Closes for ordinary business letters:

Yours very truly,
Very truly yours,

Personal and friendly closes:

Sincerely,
Yours sincerely,
Sincerely yours,
Most sincerely,
Very sincerely,
Cordially,
Yours cordially,
Cordially yours,

5. The complimentary close should correspond to the salutation in the degree of formality or familiarity.

Salutations	*Closes*
My dear Sir: *or* My dear Madam:	Yours very truly, Very truly yours,
Dear Sir: *or* Dear Madam:	Yours very truly, Very truly yours,
Gentlemen: *or* Mesdames:	Yours very truly, Very truly yours,
Dear Mr. Richmond: *or* Dear Mrs. Richmond: *or* Dear Miss Richmond:	Very truly yours, Yours very truly, Sincerely yours, Yours very sincerely,
Sir: *or* Madam:	Respectfully yours, Yours respectfully, Very respectfully yours,
Dear Bill:	Cordially,

Signature.—The following are the rules governing the signature.

1. In business letters the signature ordinarily consists of the name of the writer of the letter, his title, and the name of the firm.

Very truly yours,
PIERSON RADIATOR COMPANY

R. J. Pierson, President

2. Type the firm name two spaces below the complimentary close, the writer's name four spaces below the firm name, and the writer's title either on the same line as his name or on the next line. No part of the signature should extend beyond the right-hand margin of the letter.

Very truly yours,
HOWARD PRODUCE COMPANY

George F. Anson, President

Very truly yours,
JAMES STEWART & COMPANY

John B. Hutchinson
Advertising Manager

3. An unmarried woman signs her full name, preceded by *Miss* in parentheses. However, *Miss* may be omitted, it being assumed that the writer of the letter is unmarried if *Mrs.* does not appear before her name. It is unnecessary for business women to use either *Miss* or *Mrs.* when signing letters for the company that they represent. It is also not uncommon for business women to use merely their initials, instead of given and middle names; some companies favor this method, because they feel that the recipient of the letter may be prejudiced if he knows that the letter was written by a woman.

Yours very truly,

(Miss) Anne P. Shipman
Anne P. Shipman
A. P. Shipman

4. The title *Mrs.* is correctly used only with the name of the husband. In common business practice, however, a married woman uses her own given name preceded by *Mrs.* in parentheses, or she may write her married name in parentheses below her signature. (See also "3," above.)

Very truly yours,

(Mrs.) Katherine F. Noyes

Very truly yours,

Katherine F. Noyes
(Mrs. Gerald A. Noyes)

5. A widow continues to use the full given name of her husband socially, but in legal and financial matters she signs her own given name in the same manner as a married woman. (See "18" on page 270 and "3" and "4" above.)

6. Socially a divorcée uses her husband's full name, but, if she prefers, she may use her maiden surname and her husband's surname, unless she legally resumes her maiden name. In legal and financial matters she signs in the same manner as a married woman, unless her name has legally been changed. (See "19" on page 270 and "3" and "4" above.)

7. No titles (except *Mrs.* or *Miss*) should precede the signature.

8. Type the initials of the dictator (or his initials and surname) and the initials of the transcriber flush with the left-hand margin of the letter, either on a line with the last line of the signature or one or two spaces below. The initials of the dictator should be placed first.

(*a*)

J. E. Nugent/HAE   Advertising Manager

(*b*)

JTDay:FR   Superintendent

(*c*)

Secretary and Treasurer

JLP/FR

(*d*)

George F. Anson, President

GFA/NB

9. A reference to enclosures should be placed flush with the left-hand margin of the letter, one space below the dictator's and transcriber's initials.

(*a*)

CJB/MB
Encl.

(*b*)

CJB/MB
2 encls.

Heading for second page.—If the letter runs over onto a second page, the latter should be a plain sheet, without a letterhead, but of the same size and quality as the first. The heading should contain the number of the page, the name of the addressee, and the date. Three spaces should be left between the heading and the body of the letter.

2.

Mr. F. J. Barlow September 15, 19—

10. SPECIAL FORMS OF ADDRESS, SALUTATION, AND COMPLIMENTARY CLOSE FOR PERSONS OF RANK

A

Abbot

Envelope and inside address: The Right Reverend Abbot Bernard, O.S.B. (or other initials of the order).
Salutation: Right Reverend and dear Abbot; *or* Dear Father Abbot.
Complimentary close: Respectfully yours; *or* Very truly yours.

Alderman

Envelope and inside address: Alderman James Clark.
Salutation: Dear Sir.
Complimentary close: Very truly yours.

Ambassador

Envelope and inside address: His Excellency, the Ambassador of Great Britain; *or* His Excellency, George Beveridge, Ambassador of Great Britain.
Salutation: Sir; *or* Your Excellency; *or* My dear (*or* Dear) Mr. Ambassador.
Complimentary close: I have the honor to remain, Sir, Your obedient servant; *or* I have the honor to remain, Very truly yours; *or* Respectfully yours; *or* Faithfully yours; *or* Very truly yours.

Archbishop

Envelope and inside address: The Most Reverend Archbishop of Baltimore; *or* The Most Reverend William Carroll, Archbishop of

Baltimore; *or* The Most Reverend Archbishop Carroll.
Salutation: Most Reverend Sir; *or* Most Reverend Archbishop.
Complimentary close: Most respectfully yours; *or* Respectfully yours.

Archdeacon

Envelope and inside address: The Venerable the Archdeacon of Boston; *or* The Venerable William Carroll, Archdeacon of Boston.
Salutation: Venerable Sir.
Complimentary close: Most respectfully yours; *or* Respectfully yours.

Army Officers

Envelope and inside address: Major General James S. Adams, U.S.A., Commanding General, Second Corps Area; Colonel Charles F. Grant, Commanding Officer, 165th Field Artillery; First Lieutenant William Stewart, 205th Infantry.
Salutation: My dear General Adams; My dear Colonel Grant; My dear Lieutenant Stewart (*or* My dear Mr. Stewart).
Complimentary close: Respectfully yours; *or* Very truly yours.

Assemblyman

Envelope and inside address: The Honorable James Clark, Member of Assembly; *or* Assemblyman James Clark.
Salutation: Sir; *or* Dear Sir; *or* My dear (*or* Dear) Mr. Clark.
Complimentary close: Respectfully yours; *or* Very truly yours.

Assistant Secretary (Assistant to a Cabinet Officer)

Envelope and inside address: The Assistant Secretary of the Department of Commerce; *or* The Honorable William Foster, Assistant Secretary of Commerce.
Salutation: Sir; *or* Dear Sir; *or* My dear (*or* Dear) Mr. Foster. [Never Mr. Secretary.]
Complimentary close: Respectfully yours; *or* Very truly yours.

Associate Justice of the Supreme Court

Envelope and inside address: The Honorable William H. Black, Associate Justice of the Supreme Court; *or* The Honorable William H. Black, Justice, Supreme Court of the United States.
Salutation: Sir; *or* Dear Sir; *or* My dear (*or* Dear) Mr. Justice; *or* My dear (*or* Dear) Mr. Justice Black.
Complimentary close: I have the honor to remain, Very truly yours; *or* Most respectfully yours; *or* Respectfully yours.

Attorney General

See *Cabinet Officer*.

B

Bishop (Methodist)

Envelope and inside address: The Reverend Bishop Richard Steele.
Salutation: Dear Sir; *or* My dear (*or* Dear) Bishop Steele.
Complimentary close: Respectfully yours; *or* Very truly yours.

Bishop (Protestant Episcopal)

Envelope and inside address: The Right Reverend Arthur White, Bishop of Baltimore.
Salutation: Right Reverend and Dear Sir; *or* My dear (*or* Dear) Bishop White.
Complimentary close: I have the honor to remain, Very truly yours; *or* Most respectfully yours; *or* Respectfully yours.

Bishop (Roman Catholic)

Envelope and inside address: The Most Reverend Arthur White, Bishop of Baltimore; *or* The Most Reverend Bishop White.
Salutation: Your Excellency; *or* My dear (*or* Dear) Bishop.
Complimentary close: Most respectfully yours; *or* Respectfully yours.

C

Cabinet Officer

Envelope and inside address: The Honorable the Secretary of Agriculture (*or* War, State, etc.); The Honorable the Secretary of the Treasury; The Honorable the Postmaster General; *or* The Honorable James Black, Secretary of Agriculture (*or* War, State, etc.).
Salutation: Sir; *or* Dear Sir; *or* My dear Mr. Secretary; My dear Mr. Postmaster General; My dear Mr. Attorney General.
Complimentary close: I have the honor to remain, Very truly yours; *or* Most respectfully yours; *or* Respectfully yours.

Canon

Envelope and inside address: The Very Reverend Canon Arthur White; *or* The Very Reverend Arthur Canon White.
Salutation: Very Reverend Canon; *or* My dear (*or* Dear) Canon White.
Complimentary close: Respectfully yours; *or* Very truly yours.

Cardinal

Envelope and inside address: His Eminence Cardinal White; *or* His Eminence Arthur, Cardinal White.
Salutation: Your Eminence.
Complimentary close: I have the honor to remain, Most respectfully yours; *or* Most respectfully yours; *or* Respectfully yours.

Cardinal (if also an Archbishop)

Envelope and inside address: His Eminence the Cardinal Archbishop of Baltimore; *or* His Eminence Cardinal White, Archbishop of Baltimore.
Salutation: Your Eminence.
Complimentary close: I have the honor to remain, Most respectfully yours; *or* Most respectfully yours; *or* Respectfully yours.

Chargé d'Affaires

Envelope and inside address: The Chargé d'Affaires of Great Britain; *or* Mr. Arthur Beveridge, Chargé d'Affaires.
Salutation: Sir; *or* Dear Sir; *or* My dear Mr. Beveridge.
Complimentary close: I have the honor to remain, Very truly yours; *or* Respectfully yours; *or* Very truly yours.

Chief Justice of the United States

Envelope and inside address: The Chief Justice of the United States; *or* The Honorable Charles F. Grant, Chief Justice of the Supreme Court of the United States.
Salutation: Sir; *or* My dear (*or* Dear) Mr. Chief Justice; *or* My dear (*or* Dear) Mr. Justice Grant.
Complimentary close: I have the honor to remain, Very truly yours; *or* Most respectfully yours; *or* Respectfully yours.

Clergyman

Envelope and inside address: The Reverend Arthur White; *or,* if a Doctor of Divinity, The Rev. Dr. Arthur White.
Salutation: Dear Sir; *or* My dear Mr. (*or* Dr.) White; *or* Dear Mr. (*or* Dr.) White.
Complimentary close: Respectfully yours; *or* Very truly yours.

Clerk of the Senate or of the House

Envelope and inside address: The Honorable William Saunders, Clerk of the Senate (*or,* of the House).
Salutation: Sir; *or* Dear Sir; *or* My dear Mr. Saunders.
Complimentary close: Respectfully yours; *or* Very truly yours.

Colonel

See *Army Officers.*

Commissioner of a Bureau

Envelope and inside address: The Honorable Arthur Robinson, Commissioner of the Bureau of Education.
Salutation: Sir; *or* Dear Sir; *or* My dear Mr. Robinson.
Complimentary close: Respectfully yours; *or* Very truly yours.

Comptroller of the Currency

Envelope and inside address: The Honorable James Evans, Comptroller of the Currency.
Salutation: Sir; *or* Dear Sir; *or* My dear Mr. Evans.
Complimentary close: Respectfully yours; *or* Very truly yours.

Congressman

Envelope and inside address: The Honorable James J. Martin, House of Representatives, Washington, D. C.; *or* The Honorable James J. Martin, Representative in Congress, Springfield, Mass.
Salutation: Sir; *or* Dear Sir; *or* My dear Congressman Martin; *or* My dear Mr. Martin.
Complimentary close: Respectfully yours; *or* Very truly yours.

Consul

Envelope and inside address: To the American Consul at London; *or* Mr. James Everett, American Consul at London. (In addressing a Consul in South or Central America, substitute "United States" for "American" in the forms given above.)
Salutation: Sir; *or* Dear Sir; *or* My dear Mr. Everett.
Complimentary close: I have the honor to remain, Very truly yours; *or* Respectfully yours; *or* Very truly yours.

D

Dean (Ecclesiastical)

Envelope and inside address: The Very Reverend the Dean of St. Thomas's; *or* The Very Reverend Dean Arthur White.

Salutation: Sir; *or* Very Reverend Sir; *or,* in Roman Catholic Church, Very Reverend Father.

Complimentary close: Respectfully yours; *or* Very truly yours.

Dean of a College or Graduate School

Envelope and inside address: Dean Frederick Adams.

Salutation: Dear Sir; *or* My dear Dean Adams.

Complimentary close: Respectfully yours; *or* Very truly yours.

Diplomat

See *Ambassador; Chargé d'Affaires; Minister* (*Diplomatic*). For diplomats of lower rank, use common forms, unless the individual has a military, naval, or hereditary title.

E

Envoy

Same as *Minister* (*Diplomatic*).

G

Governor

Envelope and inside address: His Excellency, The Governor of Massachusetts; *or* His Excellency William Cox; *or* The Honorable the Governor of Massachusetts; *or* The Honorable William Cox, Governor of Massachusetts.

Salutation: Your Excellency; *or* Sir; *or* Dear Sir; *or* My dear Governor Cox.

Complimentary close: I have the honor to remain, Very truly yours; *or* Most respectfully yours; *or* Respectfully yours; *or* Very truly yours.

J

Judge

Envelope and inside address: The Honorable William Black, United States District Judge (*or,* Chief Judge of the Court of Appeals, etc.).

Salutation: Sir; *or* Dear Sir; *or* My dear Judge Black.
Complimentary close: Most respectfully yours; *or* Respectfully yours; *or* Very truly yours.
See also *Chief Justice; Associate Justice.*

Justice

See *Chief Justice; Associate Justice; Judge.*

L

Lawyer

Envelope and inside address: Mr. Arthur Wilson, Attorney at Law.
Salutation: Dear Sir; *or* My dear (*or* Dear) Mr. Wilson.
Complimentary close: Very truly yours.

Lieutenant Governor

Envelope and inside address: The Honorable Frederick Layden, Lieutenant Governor of Massachusetts.
Salutation: Sir; *or* Dear Sir; *or* My dear (*or* Dear) Mr. Layden.
Complimentary close: I have the honor to remain, Very truly yours; *or* Most respectfully yours; *or* Respectfully yours; *or* Very truly yours.

M

Mayor

Envelope and inside address: The Mayor of the City of Boston; *or* The Honorable Frederick Smith, Mayor of the City of Boston.
Salutation: Sir; *or* Dear Sir; *or* My dear Mr. Mayor; *or* My dear (*or* Dear) Mayor Smith.
Complimentary close: Respectfully yours; *or* Very truly yours.

Military Officers

See *Army Officers.*

Minister (Diplomatic)

Envelope and inside address: The Swedish Minister, The Swedish Legation, Washington, D. C.; *or* His Excellency, The Swedish Minister. For American Minister resident in Europe or Asia, use the form: His Excellency, The American Minister, Stockholm, Sweden; *or* His Excellency (*or* The Honorable) Charles F. Phillips, American Minister, Stockholm, Sweden. For American Minister resident in Central or South America, substitute "United States" for "American" in preceding forms.

Salutation: Your Excellency; *or* Sir; *or* My dear Mr. Minister.

Complimentary close: I have the honor to remain, Very truly yours; *or* Most respectfully yours; *or* Respectfully yours; *or* Very truly yours.

Minister of Religion

See *Clergyman; Priest; Rabbi.*

Monk

See *Priest.*

Monsignor

Envelope and inside address: The Right Reverend Monsignor Arthur White.

Salutation: Right Reverend Sir.

Complimentary close: Most respectfully yours; *or* Respectfully yours.

Mother Superior of a Sisterhood

Envelope and inside address: The Reverend Mother Superior, Convent of Belwood; *or* Reverend Mother Angelina, O.S.D. (or other initials of the order); *or* Mother Angelina, Superior, Convent of Belwood.

Salutation: Reverend Mother; *or* Dear Madam; *or* My dear (*or* Dear) Reverend Mother.

Complimentary close: Most respectfully yours; *or* Respectfully yours; *or* Very truly yours.

N

Naval Officers

Envelope and inside address: Captain Arthur Jones, U.S.N.; Lieutenant Commander James G. Wyckoff, U.S.N.; Ensign Henry Robertson, U.S.N.

Salutation: Dear Sir; *or* My dear Captain Jones; My dear Commander Wyckoff (not My dear Lieutenant Commander Wyckoff); Dear Mr. Robertson (not Dear Ensign Robertson).

Complimentary close: Respectfully yours; *or* Very truly yours.

Nun

See *Sister of a Religious Order.*

P

Pope

Envelope and inside address: His Holiness Pope Pius XII.
Salutation: Most Holy Father; *or* Your Holiness.
Complimentary close: Most respectfully yours.

Postmaster General

See *Cabinet Officer.*

President of a College or University

Envelope and inside address: James Arthur Brown, LL.D. (use only initials of highest degree, unless degrees are in different fields), President, Southeastern University; *or* President James Arthur Brown, Southeastern University. If a clergyman, Reverend James Arthur Brown, President, Southeastern University.
Salutation: Dear Sir; *or* My dear President Brown.
Complimentary close: Respectfully yours; *or* Very truly yours; *or* Very sincerely yours.

President of State Senate

Envelope and inside address: The Honorable Henry L. Bacon, President of the Senate of Kansas.
Salutation: Sir.
Complimentary close: Respectfully yours; *or* Very truly yours.

President of the Senate of the United States

Envelope and inside address: The Honorable the President of the Senate of the United States; *or* The Honorable Henry L. Bacon, President of the Senate, Washington, D. C.
Salutation: Sir.
Complimentary close: Most respectfully yours; *or* Respectfully yours; *or* Very truly yours.

President of the United States

Envelope and inside address: The President of the United States, Washington, D. C.; *or* The President, The White House, Washington, D. C.
Salutation: Sir; *or* My dear (*or* Dear) Mr. President.

Complimentary close: I have the honor to remain, Sir, Your most obedient servant; *or* I have the honor to remain, Most respectfully yours; *or* I am, dear Mr. President, Faithfully yours.

Priest (Roman Catholic Church)

REGULAR (except as noted below)

Envelope and inside address: The Reverend Father James Francis, O.S.M. (or other initials of the order).
Salutation: Reverend Father; *or* Dear Father Francis.
Complimentary close: Respectfully yours; *or* Very truly yours.

BENEDICTINE, CISTERCIAN, or CANON REGULAR

Envelope and inside address: The Very Reverend Dom James Francis, C.R.L. (or other initials of the order).
Salutation: Reverend Father; *or* Dear Father Francis.
Complimentary close: Respectfully yours; *or* Very truly yours.

CARTHUSIAN

Envelope and inside address: The Venerable Father James Francis, O. Cart.
Salutation: Venerable Father; *or* Dear Father Francis.
Complimentary close: Respectfully yours; *or* Very truly yours.

SECULAR

Envelope and inside address: The Reverend James Francis (followed by initials of degree).
Salutation: Reverend Sir; *or* Dear Sir; *or* My dear (*or* Dear) Father Francis.
Complimentary close: Respectfully yours; *or* Very truly yours.

R

Rabbi

Envelope and inside address: Rabbi Jacob Solomon; *or* The Reverend Jacob Solomon.
Salutation: Reverend Sir; *or* Dear Sir; *or* My dear (*or* Dear) Rabbi Solomon.
Complimentary close: Respectfully yours; *or* Very truly yours.

Representative

See *Congressman.*

S

Secretary of War, Agriculture, Commerce, etc.

See *Cabinet Officer.*

Senator (United States or State)

Envelope and inside address: Senator James K. Grant; *or* The Honorable James K. Grant, United States Senate, Washington, D. C.
Salutation: Sir; *or* Dear Sir; *or* My dear (*or* Dear) Senator Grant.
Complimentary close: I have the honor to remain, Very truly yours; *or* Respectfully yours; *or* Very truly yours.

Sister of a Religious Order

Envelope and inside address: The Reverend Sister Mary Louise; *or* Sister Mary Louise (followed by initials of the order).
Salutation: My dear (*or* Dear) Sister; *or* My dear (*or* Dear) Sister Mary Louise.
Complimentary close: Respectfully yours; *or* Very truly yours.

Speaker of the House of Representatives

Envelope and inside address: The Honorable the Speaker of the House of Representatives; *or* The Honorable Charles F. Smith, Speaker of the House of Representatives.
Salutation: Sir; *or* My dear (*or* Dear) Mr. Speaker.
Complimentary close: I have the honor to remain, Very truly yours; *or* Most respectfully yours; *or* Very truly yours.

U

Undersecretary of State

Envelope and inside address: The Undersecretary of State; *or* The Honorable Richard F. Durant, Undersecretary of State.
Salutation: Sir; *or* Dear Sir; *or* My dear Mr. Durant.
Complimentary close: Respectfully yours; *or* Very truly yours.

V

Vice-Consul

Similar to *Consul.*

Vice-President of the United States

Envelope and inside address: The Vice-President, Washington, D. C.; *or* The Honorable Charles G. Grant, Vice-President of the United States.

Salutation: Sir; *or* My dear (*or* Dear) Mr. Vice-President.

Complimentary close: I have the honor to remain, Sir, Your most obedient servant; *or* I have the honor to remain, Most respectfully yours; *or* I am, dear Mr. Vice-President, Very truly yours.

11. DICTIONARY OF CORRECT USAGE

A

accept, except. ACCEPT means to receive with approval, reply to affirmatively, agree to; EXCEPT means to exclude, make an exception to. *This order will be* ACCEPTED ON [agreed to on] *our usual terms. This order will be* EXCEPTED FROM [made an exception to] *our usual terms.*

addicted to, subject to. ADDICTED TO means devoted to persistently, as to a bad habit or indulgence; SUBJECT TO means prone to, conditional upon. *Jones is* ADDICTED TO *alcohol. Jones is* SUBJECT TO [prone to] *colds. This arrangement is* SUBJECT TO [conditional upon] *approval by Mr. Jones.*

affect, effect. These two verbs are totally different in meaning. AFFECT means to have an influence upon, produce an effect upon, effect a change in, concern; EFFECT means to cause, bring about, produce, result in, have as a result. *Passage of this bill would have* AFFECTED [influenced or concerned] *the entire country. Passage of this bill can be* EFFECTED [brought about] *only through the co-operation of both parties.* Note the difference in meaning between the following sentences: *The change of climate may* AFFECT [alter for better or for worse the prospects of] *his recovery. The change of climate may* EFFECT [bring about] *his recovery.* The word AFFECT can never be used as a noun; EFFECT used as a noun, means result. *The* EFFECT [result; not, AFFECT] *of a sarcastic business letter is to antagonize the customer.*

all right. This expression should always be written as two words. There is no such word as ALRIGHT; the forms ALLRIGHT and ALL-RIGHT are also incorrect. *Are you* ALL RIGHT? *It will be* ALL RIGHT *to ship the goods on the tenth.*

all-round. Informal but permissible. There is, however, no such word as ALL-AROUND. *Jones is a good* ALL-ROUND [not, ALL-AROUND] *salesman.*

almost. See **most.**

already, all ready. ALREADY means beforehand, by or before a particular time; ALL READY means prepared, wholly ready. *I* ALREADY *have all the goods I need. I have the goods* ALL READY [prepared] *for shipment.*

altogether, all together. ALTOGETHER means wholly, completely, entirely; ALL TOGETHER means gathered, assembled. *The story is* ALTOGETHER [entirely] *false. We were* ALL TOGETHER [assembled] *in the room.*

among. See **between.**

an. The use of AN before such words as history, historical, humble, is now regarded as unnecessary; A is the preferred usage, in both written and spoken English [A *history;* A *historical work;* A *humble workman*]. Use A before all consonants except silent *h* [A *history;* but, AN *hour*]. Also, use A before words beginning with the sound of *y* or *w* [A *unit;* A *eulogy;* A *one*].

anyone, any one. Should be written as one word when used to mean anybody. *If we send* ANYONE [anybody], *it should be Jones.* Write as two words when the meaning is one particular person or thing from among a number. *If we send* ANY ONE *of the salesmen, it should be Jones.*

any place, every place, no place, some place. Commonly misused for ANYWHERE, EVERYWHERE, NOWHERE, SOMEWHERE. *Are you going* ANYWHERE [not, ANY PLACE] *this afternoon? I have looked* EVERYWHERE [not, EVERY PLACE] *for the missing bill. I have* NOWHERE [not, NO PLACE] *to go this afternoon. The book must be* SOMEWHERE [not, SOME PLACE] *in the room.*

anywheres, nowheres. Incorrect; use ANYWHERE, NOWHERE. *I can't find the letter* ANYWHERE [not, ANYWHERES] *in the files. The letter was* NOWHERE [not, NOWHERES] *to be found.*

apt, liable. These two words are frequently confused. APT usually means having an unfortunate tendency to; LIABLE usually means exposed to a risk. Correct: *We have found that when we ship by parcel post delays are* APT [have an unfortunate tendency] *to occur.* Correct: *This shipment is* LIABLE *to be* [exposed to the risk of being] *delayed if we ship by parcel post.* Correct: *Businessmen are* APT [have an unfortunate tendency] *to dictate letters carelessly.* Correct: *A businessman who dictates letters carelessly is* LIABLE *to lose* [exposed to the danger of losing] *his customers.* Where the sense is simple probability, use LIKELY. *The goods are* LIKELY *to* [probably will] *arrive on the tenth.*

as . . . as, so . . . as. Use AS . . . AS in affirmative statements; in negative statements and in questions implying a negative answer, good usage requires the use of so . . . AS. Affirmative statement: *This window display is* AS *attractive* AS *the last one.* Negative statement: *This window display is not* so *attractive* AS *the last one.* Question implying a negative answer: *Could any businessman be* so *foolish* AS *to ship such an order?*

as, like. Use AS when a verb follows. *Do* AS *I do. Write this exactly* AS *I dictated it. He tried,* AS *any businessman would* [try], *to get a lower price. It looks* AS THOUGH *Smith is going to visit us.* When no verb follows, use LIKE. *His dictation is* LIKE *mine.*

as, whether. Do not use AS in place of WHETHER or THAT. *I am not sure* WHETHER [not, AS] *I can ship the goods on that date.*

at about. Omit the AT. *Jones arrived this morning* ABOUT [not, AT ABOUT] *ten o'clock.*

aught. Means "anything," but in this sense is now obsolete. The name of the symbol 0 is NAUGHT, not AUGHT.

B

back of. Preferable to use BEHIND. *His store is just off Clinton Street,* BEHIND [not, IN BACK OF] *the post office.*

beside, besides. BESIDE means by the side of, close to; BESIDES means additionally, in addition to. *The letter is on my desk,* BESIDE [alongside; not, BESIDES] *the telephone.* BESIDES [in addition to; not, BESIDE] *these two bills, there are several others that should be paid before the fifteenth. We have these two bills, and several others* BESIDES [in addition; not, BESIDE].

between, among. Use BETWEEN where only two persons or things are referred to; use AMONG where more than two are referred to. *On this point there was a difference of opinion* AMONG [not, BETWEEN] *the directors. On this point there was a difference of opinion* BETWEEN [not, AMONG] *Jones and Smith.*

biweekly, bimonthly. BIWEEKLY means once every two weeks; BIMONTHLY means once every two months. SEMIWEEKLY means twice a week; SEMIMONTHLY means twice a month. All four expressions are confusing and should be avoided. It is clearer to use ONCE EVERY TWO WEEKS, ONCE EVERY TWO MONTHS, TWICE A WEEK, TWICE A MONTH.

but that, but what. The most common error here is the use of BUT THAT or BUT WHAT after "doubt." Wrong: *There is no doubt* BUT WHAT [or, BUT THAT] *the shipment will reach you promptly.* Correct: *There is no doubt* THAT *the shipment will reach you promptly.*

C

can, may. CAN denotes ability or power; MAY denotes permission. CAN *you* [will you be able to] *make payment next month?* MAY *we* [will you give us permission to] *ship your order by freight?* CAN *I* [is it possible for me to] *go to Alaska by plane?* MAY *I* [do I have your permission to] *go to Alaska by plane?*

compare to, compare with. If the meaning is merely to suggest a similarity, or state that a similarity exists, use TO. If the meaning is to estimate the degree of similarity, or state the details of a similarity, use WITH. *The speaker compared the British law* WITH *the American* [here the meaning is that the speaker made a detailed comparison]. *The speaker compared the new law* TO *a plague* [here the meaning is that the speaker merely suggested a similarity]. In many cases either TO or WITH may be used. *Compared* TO [or, WITH] *him, I am a genius.* After an intransitive verb, only WITH can be used. *Round steak cannot compare* WITH *filet mignon.*

contemplate. Should not be followed by ON, OVER, or any other preposition. *I am* CONTEMPLATING [not, CONTEMPLATING ON, CONTEMPLATING ON MAKING, or CONTEMPLATING OVER] *a trip through the Middle West.*

contemptible, contemptuous. CONTEMPTIBLE means despicable, deserving of being despised; CONTEMPTUOUS means scornful. *He played a* CONTEMPTIBLE [despicable] *trick on Jones. His comments on the new sales plan were very* CONTEMPTUOUS [scornful].

continual, continuous. CONTINUAL means occurring in close succession, frequently repeated; CONTINUOUS means without stopping, without interruption. CONTINUAL [frequent] *breakdowns in the factory delayed delivery of the goods. The machinery has been in* CONTINUOUS *operation* [has not been stopped] *for sixty hours. He is* CONTINUALLY [frequently] *asking for special favors. He drove* CONTINUOUSLY [without stopping] *for six hours.*

could of. See **of.**

credible, credulous, creditable. CREDIBLE means believable; CREDULOUS means easily imposed upon, believing too easily; CREDITABLE means praiseworthy. *The price quoted seems hardly* CREDIBLE [believable]. *He is too* CREDULOUS [easily imposed upon] *to make a good purchasing agent. His record as a salesman was highly* CREDITABLE [praiseworthy].

D

data. The word DATA is plural; the singular form, now seldom used, is DATUM. *We have proved that* THESE [not, THIS] *data* ARE [not, IS] *reliable.*

different from. This is the correct form, DIFFERENT THAN being invariably wrong. *My sales plan is* DIFFERENT FROM [not, DIFFERENT THAN] *the one that you suggested.*

differ from, differ with. DIFFER used in the sense of being different, exhibiting a difference, is followed by FROM, not WITH; in the sense of having a difference of opinion, expressing dissent, disputing, it is usually followed by WITH. *My sales campaign* DIFFERS FROM [is unlike] *yours in three ways. I* DIFFER WITH [disagree with] *you as to the value of your sales campaign.*

disinterested, uninterested. DISINTERESTED means unselfish, impartial, without thought of personal gain; UNINTERESTED means not interested, not enthusiastic. *A magistrate must perform his duties in a* DISINTERESTED *manner* [impartial manner, without thought of personal gain]. *He seems* UNINTERESTED *in his work* [lacking in interest or enthusiasm].

E

each other, one another. No differentiation need be made. The rule that EACH OTHER should be used when only two things are referred to, and that ONE ANOTHER should be used when more than two are referred to, is no longer generally accepted. Hence all the following forms are correct: *Smith and I see* ONE ANOTHER *quite often. Smith and I see* EACH OTHER *quite often. It will be interesting for the four of us to see* ONE ANOTHER *again after so many years. It will be interesting for the four of us to see* EACH OTHER *again after so many years.* The possessive of EACH OTHER is EACH OTHER'S, not EACH OTHERS'; the possessive of ONE ANOTHER is ONE ANOTHER'S, not ONE ANOTHERS'. *They tore* EACH OTHER'S [not, EACH OTHERS'] *clothes. They tore* ONE ANOTHER'S [not, ONE ANOTHERS'] *clothes.*

effect. See **affect.**

either. Correct when used to designate one of two persons or things; not correct when used to designate one of three or more. Correct: EITHER *of the two men will be suitable.* Wrong: EITHER *of the four men will be suitable.* Correct: ANY [or, ANY ONE] *of the four men will be suitable.* EITHER should be followed by a singular verb. *If*

EITHER *Jones or Smith* IS [not, ARE] *going to Chicago, tell* HIM [not, THEM] *to see Brown.*

else. A common error is to combine ELSE with BUT. Wrong: *It was nothing* ELSE BUT *selfishness on his part.* Correct: *It was nothing* BUT *selfishness on his part.* Correct: *There was no one* BUT [not, ELSE BUT] *him in the room.* For the possessive form, use SOMEBODY ELSE'S [not, SOMEBODY'S ELSE]. *He took* SOMEBODY ELSE'S [not, SOMEBODY'S ELSE] *hat.* Similarly: EVERYONE ELSE'S, ANYONE ELSE'S, NO ONE ELSE'S, etc. *I took mine, but he took* EVERYONE ELSE'S [not, EVERYONE'S ELSE].

everybody. Write as one word.

everyone, every one. Write as one word when the meaning is everybody. EVERYONE [everybody] *in the department should attend the weekly sales meetings.* Write as two words when the meaning is each one of a group of persons or things. EVERY ONE [each one] *of the department heads must be present at this meeting. All of the salesmen have done well;* EVERY ONE [each one] *of them deserves a prize.*

every place. See **any place.**

except. See **accept.**

F

farther, further. No differentiation need be made. Most writers prefer FURTHER. *I will walk one mile, and no* FURTHER. *The speaker was asked to cite some* FURTHER *examples.*

firstly. When SECONDLY, THIRDLY, etc., follow, begin with FIRSTLY, not FIRST. The choice between FIRSTLY, SECONDLY, THIRDLY, etc., and FIRST, SECOND, THIRD, etc., is a matter of personal preference.

former. Correct when used to designate the first of two persons or things; incorrect when used to designate the first of three or more. Correct: *Smith and Jones were at the convention; the* FORMER *gave a very interesting talk.* Wrong: *Smith, Jones, and Brown were at the convention; the* FORMER *gave a very interesting talk.* Correct: *Smith, Jones, and Brown were at the convention; the* FIRST-NAMED *gave a very interesting talk.* However, this construction is awkward; where three or more are mentioned, it is best to repeat the word referred to. Thus: *Smith, Jones, and Brown were at the convention;* SMITH *gave a very interesting talk.*

G

guarantee, guaranty. For the verb, always use GUARANTEE. *We* GUARANTEE [not, GUARANTY] *that the goods will be satisfactory.* For the noun, business convention has established a specialized use of GUARANTY, which is illustrated in such expressions as *contract of* GUARANTY, *act of* GUARANTY. However, GUARANTEE is never wrong, even in these connections, and hence a safe rule to follow is: When in doubt, use GUARANTEE.

H

had better, had best. Both good usage. Correct: *You* HAD BETTER *not stay in Chicago more than two weeks.* Correct: *It* HAD BEST *be done at once.*

had have, had of. Often incorrectly used in place of HAD. Wrong: *If he* HAD OF [or, HAD HAVE] *tried, he could have done it.* Correct: *If he* HAD *tried, he could have done it.*

had ought, hadn't ought. See **ought.**

hardly. This word itself carries a negative idea, and hence should not be followed or preceded by NOT. Wrong: *I* COULDN'T HARDLY *get the table through the door.* Correct: *I* COULD HARDLY *get the table through the door.*

help. Should not be followed by BUT when used in the sense of avoid. Wrong: *I can't* HELP BUT *feel that he really meant to do it.* Correct: *I can't* HELP FEELING *that he really meant to do it.*

Honorable. See page 269.

hopes. Sometimes incorrectly used in place of HOPE. Wrong: *We have no* HOPES *of ever receiving payment.* Correct: *We have no* HOPE *of ever receiving payment.*

I

if. Often misused in place of WHETHER. Wrong: *I am not sure* IF *I can ship the goods on that date.* Correct: *I am not sure* WHETHER *I can ship the goods on that date.*

imply, infer. IMPLY is used to denote something suggested, assumed, insinuated, or vaguely expressed. *Your letter* IMPLIES *that I have tried to evade payment of the bill.* INFER means to draw from, deduce from, gather from, or conclude from. *I* INFER *from your letter that you cannot grant an extension of time.*

in back of. See **back of.**

inferior, superior. Should always be followed by TO, not THAN. *It is* INFERIOR *from every point of view* TO [not, THAN] *the material previously used.*

ingenious, ingenuous. INGENIOUS means clever, skillful; INGENUOUS means frank, innocent, trusting. *His suggestion is a very* INGENIOUS [clever] *solution of the problem. You would think that a young man of 22 would not be so* INGENUOUS [trusting, easily imposed upon].

irregardless. There is no such word; the correct form is REGARDLESS. Misuse is perhaps caused by confusion with the word IRRESPECTIVE, which is somewhat similar in meaning and is correct. *We should acknowledge all orders,* REGARDLESS [not, IRREGARDLESS] *of the amount involved.*

kind, sort. Write THIS KIND, THAT KIND, not THESE KINDS, THOSE KINDS. Similarly, write THIS SORT, THAT SORT, not THESE SORTS, THOSE SORTS. Wrong: *I don't like* THESE KINDS *of pencils.* Correct: *I don't like* THIS KIND *of pencil.* Wrong: *I don't like* THOSE SORTS *of pencils.* Correct: *I don't like* THAT SORT *of pencil.*

kind of, sort of. These expressions should not be followed by A or AN. *What* KIND OF [not, KIND OF A] *place is it? It's the* SORT OF [not, SORT OF AN] *account that has to be carefully watched.*

L

latter, last. The word LATTER may be used to designate the second of two persons or things previously mentioned, but should not be used where more than two have been mentioned. Correct: *We are now conducting a special sale of suits and overcoats; the* LATTER *are particularly good value.* But: *We are now conducting a special sale of hats, suits, and overcoats; the* LAST [or, LAST-NAMED; not, LATTER] *are particularly good value.* In most cases, as here, the construction with LAST is awkward and may prove ambiguous; it is usually best to repeat the word referred to. Thus: *We are now conducting a special sale of hats, suits, and overcoats; the* OVERCOATS *are particularly good value.*

lay, lie. LAY means to put or set down, place, deposit; LIE means to rest, be in a certain position or location. *He likes to* LIE [not, LAY] *down after lunch. The letters are* LYING [not, LAYING] *on your table. He let the pen* LIE [not, LAY] *where it had fallen.* LAY [not, LIE] *the letters on the table.*

learn, teach. Do not use LEARN in the sense of TEACH. *The experience will* TEACH [not, LEARN] *him a lesson. Several years ago I* TAUGHT [not, LEARNED] *him how to check a credit.*

leave go, leave go of. Use LET GO. LET IT GO [not, LEAVE IT GO] *in the meantime. If you* LET GO [not, LEAVE GO OF] *the rope, you'll fall.*

less. Apply the word LESS only to things that are measured by amount, and not by size, quality, or number. Correct: *He bought* LESS [a smaller amount of] *butter this month than last.* But: *The staff in the New York office is* SMALLER [not, LESS] *than that in the Chicago office.* FEWER [not, LESS] *industrial accidents occurred this year than last.*

liable. See **apt.**
like. See **as, like** and **such as, like.**
likely. See **apt.**
loan, lend. Many authorities object to any use of LOAN as a verb. It is best to use the word only in connection with formal business transactions—as, for example, the placing of a loan by a bank. For general purposes use LEND. *Will you* LEND [not, LOAN] *me ten dollars? He* LENT [not, LOANED] *me ten dollars.* But: *The bank* LOANED *the money at six per cent.*

M

may. See **can.**
may of. See **of.**
Messrs. See page 269.
might of. See **of.**
most, almost. Do not use MOST in place of ALMOST. Apart from the fact that MOST is not good usage, in many constructions it changes the meaning. Thus, *I am* MOST *ready to go* [meaning, I am very willing to go] is totally different from, *I am* ALMOST *ready to go.*
must of. See **of.**

N

naught. See **aught.**
nobody. Always write as one word.
no one. Always write as two words.
no place. See **any place.**
nowheres. See **anywheres.**

O

of. COULD OF, SHOULD OF, WOULD OF, MUST OF, MAY OF, MIGHT OF are all incorrect; use COULD HAVE, SHOULD HAVE, WOULD HAVE, MUST HAVE, MAY HAVE, MIGHT HAVE. *I* COULD HAVE *made a larger profit. I* SHOULD HAVE *made a larger profit. I* WOULD HAVE *made a larger profit. I* MUST HAVE *made a mistake. I* MAY HAVE *made a mistake. I* MIGHT HAVE *made a mistake.*
off, from. Do not use OFF in place of FROM. *I bought it* FROM [not, OFF] *Jones.*
off of. Incorrect; omit the OF. *I will give you ten per cent* OFF [not, OFF OF] *the list price.*
one another. See **each other.**

oneself, one's self. The one-word form is preferred. *It is dangerous to cut* ONESELF. However, if emphasis is desired, ONE'S SELF may be used. *It is wise to know* ONE'S SELF.

only. The meaning that the sentence is intended to convey determines the position of the word ONLY. (1) ONLY *the teacher spoke to John.* (2) *The teacher* ONLY *spoke to John.* (3) *The teacher spoke* ONLY *to John,* or, *The teacher spoke to John* ONLY. Each of these three sentences conveys a different meaning. The first states that the teacher, and no one else, spoke to John; the second that the teacher did nothing beyond merely speaking to John; the third that the teacher addressed John to the exclusion of everyone else. No hard and fast rule can be given. The writer must consider carefully the exact meaning that he wishes to convey, and place the ONLY accordingly. As a final resort, if there is danger of ambiguity or misunderstanding, the construction should be changed to eliminate the ONLY entirely.

only that. Do not use ONLY THAT in place of EXCEPT THAT. *Your pen is the same as mine,* EXCEPT THAT [not, ONLY THAT] *the nib is different.*

ought. Do not combine OUGHT with HAD. *I* OUGHT [not, HAD OUGHT] *to have waited for the shipment.*

over with. Omit the WITH. *Our annual fall sale is now* OVER [not, OVER WITH].

P

pair, set. These are the singular, not the plural, forms. Wrong: *Send five* PAIR *of stockings and three* SET *of dishes.* Correct: *Send five* PAIRS *of stockings and three* SETS *of dishes.*

practicable, practical. PRACTICABLE means feasible, capable of being put into practice; PRACTICAL means useful or successful in actual practice. PRACTICAL may be used with reference to either persons or things. *Jones is a* PRACTICAL *man* [a "doer" rather than a theorist]. *No* PRACTICAL *solution could be found* [no solution that would work]. Note, however, that PRACTICABLE cannot be used with reference to persons, but only with reference to things. Thus, *Jones is a* PRACTICABLE *man* [a man "capable of being put into practice"] is meaningless. The following sentences illustrate the change in meaning that results when one word is substituted for the other: *The scheme is* PRACTICABLE [it can be carried out]. *The scheme is* PRACTICAL [it will be successful when carried out].

prescribe, proscribe. PRESCRIBE means to lay down definite rules or directions, to dictate, direct, order the use of. PROSCRIBE means to prohibit, condemn. *The sales manager* PRESCRIBED *regular selling hours* *for the salesmen. The doctor* PRESCRIBED *cod-liver oil. The president* PROSCRIBED [prohibited] *smoking during office hours.*

principal, principle. A handy rule to keep in mind when using either of these words is: The word PRINCIPLE is a noun only, and cannot be used as an adjective. Therefore, whenever the form is an adjective, it is always spelled PRINCIPAL. *The New England states have been our* PRINCIPAL *source of business during the past five years.* PRINCIPLE means a fundamental or general truth, a rule. PRINCIPAL, which in the noun form has a variety of meanings, is used in all other cases. *We have always acted on the* PRINCIPLE [fundamental truth] *that honesty is the best policy. The loan, including* PRINCIPAL *and interest, amounted to $158.63. An agent may, by correspondence, bind his* PRINCIPAL *to contracts entered into within the scope of his authority.*

proven. Not good usage; use PROVED. *It was* PROVED [not, PROVEN] *that the carrier was to blame.*

providing. Not good usage in place of PROVIDED. It is preferable not to use THAT after PROVIDED. *I will give you the order,* PROVIDED [not, PROVIDING] *you agree to make delivery not later than the tenth.*

R

reason. Do not complete a sentence beginning in some such way as THE REASON IS with: (1) a BECAUSE clause; (2) a BECAUSE OF phrase; (3) a DUE TO phrase; or (4) an ON ACCOUNT OF phrase. Complete the sentence with a THAT clause. Wrong: *The reason the goods were delayed was* BECAUSE *an error was made in the shipping department.* Wrong: *The reason the goods were delayed was* BECAUSE OF *an error in the shipping department.* Wrong: *The reason the goods were delayed was* DUE TO *an error in the shipping department.* Wrong: *The reason the goods were delayed was* ON ACCOUNT OF *an error in the shipping department.* Correct: *The reason the goods were delayed was* THAT *an error was made in the shipping department.*

regard. Do not use REGARDS in place of REGARD in the expressions IN REGARD TO, WITH REGARD TO. Correct: *With* REGARD [not, REGARDS] *to our past-due accounts, the situation is still unchanged.*

Reverend. See page 268.

S

same. Not good business usage. Poor: *We will repair the spring and ship* SAME *to you on Wednesday of next week.* Correct: *We will repair the spring and ship* IT *to you on Wednesday of next week.*

semiweekly, semimonthly. See **biweekly.**
set. See **pair.**
should of. See **of.**
size. Never use SIZE as an adjective; use SIZED. *The different* SIZED [not, SIZE] *screws should be kept separate.*
so . . . as. See **as . . . as.**
someone. Write as one word. *We will have to appoint* SOMEONE *to take charge of the job.*
some place. See **any place.**
sort. See **kind.**
sort of. See **kind of.**
such as, like. LIKE is commonly misused in place of SUCH AS, where the meaning is for example. *In his factory are a number of useful machines,* SUCH AS [not, LIKE] *cutters and stampers, which are very seldom idle.*
superior. See **inferior.**

T

teach. See **learn.**
this here, these here, that there, those there. Incorrect; use merely THIS, THESE, THAT, THOSE. *Shipment of* THIS [not, THIS HERE] *order was supposed to have been made last week.*

W

wait on. Do not use in place of WAIT FOR. *We have been* WAITING FOR [not, WAITING ON] the goods to arrive for three days.
ways. Do not use in place of WAY. *He was a little* WAY [not, WAYS] *ahead. This year's sales are quite a* BIT [not, WAYS] *ahead of last year's,* or, *This year's sales are* CONSIDERABLY *ahead of last year's.*
where. Sometimes misused in place of THAT. *I see in this morning's paper* THAT [not, WHERE] *the Ames Corporation has declared a fifty-cent dividend.*
whether. See **as, whether.**
would of. See **of.**

CONTENTS—SECTION 3

Selling By Direct Mail

1. HOW TO SELL BY DIRECT MAIL

2. HOW TO GET AND BUILD MAILING LISTS

3. HOW TO WRITE SALES LETTERS

SECTION 3

Selling by Direct Mail

1. HOW TO SELL BY DIRECT MAIL

What products can be sold by mail.—Sooner or later in the life of most business concerns, the question arises as to the advisability of using the mails for direct sales—that is, for soliciting actual orders as distinguished from using the mail to influence a sale that will be closed later by a salesman. If a product can be sold at all, it can be sold by mail. However, this fact is of academic interest only, inasmuch as businessmen are primarily interested in profitable methods of selling their products.

Judging by the type of product that has been sold profitably by mail, without the aid of a salesman, it can be concluded that products or services with the following characteristics are suitable for profitable mail-order sales:

1. The product or service has a high degree of uniqueness in that it is totally different from others or stands alone in some respect. Thus a product that could easily be picked up at any corner store would be difficult to sell by mail; whereas a proposition such as the Book-of-the-Month Club plan of selling books would, because of its high degree of uniqueness, make a good mail-order proposition. It does not follow, however, that everyday products cannot be sold by mail. The tremendous success of the Green Brothers, of Denver, Colorado, in selling quality food products by mail shows that a product which is ordinarily purchasable at any store can, through uniqueness of quality, combined with uniqueness of packaging, be profitably sold by mail.

2. The sales appeal is not so limited that lists of prospects to be solicited by mail cannot be compiled.

3. The product or service has a definite price and can be sold on open account, cash with order, by free trial, or on approval.

4. The product or service to be sold lends itself to easy description.

5. The price is not too low to absorb the cost of the mail-order campaign and delivery. Products that cost the customer less than $2 or $3 generally are not suitable for mail-order sale.

6. The price is not so high that the prospect will refuse to make the expenditure without seeing what he is getting. Thus, houses, high-priced cars, certain machinery, and the like, are not suitable mail-order items.

Cost of direct mail.—It is, of course, impossible to give an exact figure as to the cost of selling by mail. If a generalization can be made, it might be said that the cost of selling is about 25 to 35 per cent. There have been cases in which the sales cost has been as low as 2 per cent. On the other hand, certain items, even today, are profitably sold at a cost of 50 per cent. In cases such as the latter, the products are generally *ideas,* as opposed to *merchandise.* If you can absorb a sales cost of 25 to 35 per cent, you have a chance of selling profitably by direct mail, assuming that your product has approximately normal manufacturing costs and overhead.

There is one important exception to this rule, exemplified by the firms selling seeds by mail. These organizations make their profit on *repeat sales,* and so are able to pay heavily for their first sale. To cite one example, W. Atlee Burpee considers an approximate cost of 30 cents per inquiry from magazine advertising, which is followed up by mail, a good investment even though no money is made on a customer during the first year. Repeat orders provide a substantial profit beyond the cost of the first sale. If yours is a product that will give you a steady repeat business, you probably can afford a higher sales cost than the normal 25 to 35 per cent.

Steps in planning direct-mail selling.—Each of the following steps must be considered in planning the direct-mail campaign:

1. Know and use the facts concerning the market for the product or service.

2. Select the lists.

3. Plan the advertising budget to be spent on direct mail.

4. Time the direct advertising to the individual marketing problem.

5. Select the basic theme for the promotional activity.
6. Decide upon the form of piece that will best present the message.
7. Prepare the advertising piece.
8. Test the proposed mailing and, if results warrant continuation, proceed with the entire mailing.

Each of these items is discussed below.

Know and use facts.—In some phases of selling and advertising it is exceedingly important that the merchandiser discover the character of individuals and groups composing the market before a campaign is undertaken. In the field of direct-mail selling, however, a detailed investigation in advance is not absolutely essential. The reason for this difference is the fact that, at a comparatively low cost, a test mailing can be made, and the profitability of the venture proved. Similarly, while other types of marketing may require a thorough analysis of competitors' activities to discover strong and weak points in their products, in direct-mail selling the advertiser's general knowledge of his competitors' product is ordinarily sufficient to help him develop a distinctive basic selling idea for his product. His direct-mail tests will tell him whether the selling idea he has chosen to talk about in his letter is the correct one.

Once direct-mail selling has proved a profitable method of distributing a company's product, very little special study in the form of market surveys is necessary, provided, of course, that there is an alertness to the ever-changing moods and habits of buyers, and that testing is made a prerequisite of every large mailing.

Select the lists.—The choice of lists is the most important factor in direct mail. The most expertly conceived and elaborately prepared direct-mail compaign will fail if the lists are not good, while even a poorly executed campaign may bring results if the lists are excellent.

The subject of the mailing list is too important for brief treatment. It is therefore given separate treatment, beginning at page 325.

Plan the advertising budget for direct mail.—The usual methods of budgeting expenditures for space and other advertising are discussed on page 434. In the direct-mail field the only sound approach to the question of how much to spend on advertising is, first, to have a thorough knowledge of the costs, and, second, to test constantly. The mail-order seller must have known facts regarding the results of his advertising. He buys, with a given advertisement or series of advertisements, a certain number of direct sales or direct sales leads. Thus there is a direct relation between the cost and the results obtained. While this cost is not constant, the advertiser can, over a period of time, find upper and lower limits between which he may expect to find his selling cost. He will then appropriate for advertising an amount set by multiplying the number of sales he believes necessary by the cost per sale—usually taking the upper figure.

Time the direct-mail advertising.—Proper timing of the promotion effort is essential to obtaining the best results from direct-mail advertising. Such factors as seasonal variations of the particular business, customers' buying habits, and the like, must be considered. Notice how the intensive campaign of the Southern States Iron Roofing Co., described on page 381, was planned to reach the prospects at the most favorable time. It is interesting to observe that, in the original tests made before the most favorable buying period, the letter that was selected to be used in this campaign pulled 11 per cent inquiries. When it was mailed to the entire list four months later, at the most favorable time, the response was 14 per cent.

Aside from timing in relation to individual marketing problems, timing in relation to general marketing problems must be considered. Experience has proved that mailings should not be undertaken in times of national crisis, such as a stock crash or a declaration of war, when the public is absorbed in a presidential election, before a holiday, at the end of the month, and immediately before or after important income tax payment dates.

Select the basic theme for the promotional activity.—Some appeal must be selected to form the major theme of the advertisement. To arrive at the appeal, or theme, it is necessary to study: (1) the product itself, (2) the ways in which it has or can be used, and (3) the users of the product. From the following examples of themes that have been used in successful direct-mail campaigns, it is evident that, in arriving at the theme, the creators of the advertising matter in each case had analyzed carefully each of the three basic sources and had selected one that had a basic appeal and was capable of effective copy and art treatment.

Purpose	*Theme and Execution*
Selling wire fences	Your local dealer can give you a good tip. Acting on knowledge gained from a survey of the agricultural market, to the effect that farmers rely upon the advice of local dealers, Republic Steel Corporation built a campaign around the theme of taking a tip from a dealer. The direct-mail piece was a four-page broadside, carrying on the address side a photograph of the local dealer, with a caption, "Take a tip from (and the name of the dealer)." The first spread was a letter to the prospect signed by the dealer; the inside contained illustrations covering features of the product and a build-up for the dealer. The free offer of a booklet was used to bring the prospect to the dealer's store.
Selling advertising space in low-priced popular magazines	The magazines appeal to the average woman and therefore are a good advertising medium. A booklet, prepared by Fawcett Publications, Inc., told the story of "Myrtle," the average woman. The booklet, when folded, resembled a woman's handbag.
Selling accounting machines	Leading companies are using National machines. The National Cash Register Company used this testimonial theme, carrying the heading "Does it with Nationals." A series of folders, each one playing up the name of a well-known company that does its work with National machines, was sent to businessmen.
Selling fire insurance	The company is an old, established one whose prestige and reputation assure excellent service. Three letters offering a booklet entitled "You're in Good Company" were prepared by the Merrimack Mutual Fire Insurance Company and distributed to prospects by its agents.

Decide upon the form of advertising.—In deciding upon the form that the direct-mail advertising will take to express the theme selected and carry the message effectively, the advertiser has a number of types upon which to draw. Broadly classified, they are: (1) letters, (2) cards, (3) leaflets, (4) folders, (5) broadsides, (6) booklets, (7) brochures, (8) catalogues, (9) house organs, and (10) novelties.

Each form presents its particular problem of mailing, as well as of the reply form to be used with it. The various forms are discussed briefly below.

The sales letter.—Letters, of course, are the most common direct-mail medium because they come closest to personal selling. If the purpose of the mailing is to get immediate orders or inquiries, letters are generally used. The subject of "How to Write Sales Letters" is treated fully in a separate section, beginning at page 334.

In the preparation of letters for large-quantity distribution, one of the following processes may be used: (1) multigraph, (2) multilith, (3) super-process, (4) printing, or (5) automatic typewriter.

Multigraphing.—Multigraphing is one of the common forms of producing letters for direct mail. In this process the letters are set in type similar to that used by a typewriter, and placed on a circular drum. The drum rotates and prints through a ribbon. The final effect is much like typewriting. From 2,500 to 5,000 copies can be produced per hour. Facsimile typewritten letters may be personalized on a typewriter, by the use of a matching ribbon, or may be filled in on the addressing machine. See also page 846.

Multilith—offset printing.—The photo-offset process has come into prominence in recent years as a method of preparing direct-mail letters. For a description of this process, see page 845. From 3,000 to 5,000 reproductions can be made per hour. Fill-ins can be made as in the case of multigraphing.

Super-process—flat-bed process.—The super-process, or flat-bed process, is produced on a flat-bed press through a ribbon with typewriter type. It produces a personalized letter at from one-third to one-half less cost than the automatic typewriter (Hooven or Autotypist), and at from 10 per cent to 20 per cent more cost than by multigraph. The type simulates typewriter type exactly. Certain of the characters are deliberately uneven, and the periods punch through the paper exactly as with the typewriter. The fill-in is done on a typewriter having the same type and ribbon as the letter.

While automatic typewriting requires first-class postage, multigraph, multilith, and flat-bed letters may be mailed at the third-class letter rates. See page 934.

Printing.—Some firms selling by direct mail have their letters printed. This method has the advantage of lower cost, inasmuch as the letterhead may be printed at the same time as the body of the letter. In the long run, a considerable saving may be effected, but it is generally agreed that for best results the processed letter (multigraph, multilith, super-process) is advisable.

Automatic typewriter.—The Hooven or Autotypist method uses automatic typewriters. For a description of the process, see page 845. Letters produced in this way are original typewritten letters with perfect fill-ins. The process is much slower and more costly than any of the other methods of duplication mentioned. As indicated above, such letters must be mailed at the first-class letter rate.

Personalizing the direct-mail sales letter.—The object of personalizing sales letters is not to delude the reader into believing that the letter was produced solely for him, but rather to get the attention of the reader. These methods have been used successfully to personalize sales letters:

1. Fill-in of salutation on the typewriter or by stencils.
2. Insertion of the reader's name in the body of the letter. This step has been done perfectly by letter-service organizations, in processed letters.
3. Brush-scripting of the name of the prospect at the top of the letter, as in the illustration on page 404.

Four-page letters.—The direct-mail advertiser who wishes to send a long message, without at the same time using enclosures such as folders, leaflets, circulars, and the like, may find the four-page letter suitable for the purpose.

The first page is usually devoted to the letter, which is no different from the single-sheet letter except that there must be some tie-up between the letter and the inside pages. The copy and illustrations on the inside pages of the four-page letter generally contain the material that is to convince the reader and arouse in him the desire to do what the advertiser wants him to do. The fourth page of the letter may be blank, may be of the same nature as the second and third page, or may form the address section of a self-mailer. For organizations engaging in a considerable amount of institutional advertising—real estate companies, for example—the fourth page may be used for institutional advertising; that is, to keep the name of the advertiser before the public, to make known the qualities of the firm and the service offered by it, and the like.

Post cards and mailing cards.—The penny post card, carrying a message that is flashed to the prospect, has proved a useful medium, especially for retailers. Penny cards have been used extensively by local merchants to announce weekly sales and specials, seasonal items, new departments or services, and to keep the name of the firm before its customers. The wholesaler has also used penny post cards for somewhat similar purposes. Mailing cards have also been used to introduce more elaborate mailing pieces and to vary a campaign composed of more detailed selling messages. Copy and illustrations can be handled effectively even by smaller advertisers if they are equipped with proper machines for card reproduction. To be effective, solid type should be avoided on penny cards. Simple illustrations that catch the eye, headlines that tie in with the copy, and short sentences help to get the card read.

For postal information as to government cards and private mailing cards, see pages 945 and 946.

Leaflets.—Any small-sized sheet, printed on one or both sides, and folded, is a leaflet. When used in direct-mail advertising, it must be designed to fit the size of the envelope into which it is to go. Because the leaflet is small, it must overcome the disadvantage of size by excellence of copy, good typography, and attractive layout. The leaflet, if used to supplement a letter, should support the sales message. Thus, a leaflet designed to supplement a letter offering the sale of stores and a garage was made up as follows: page 1, an attractive heading and indication of the nature of the property; page 2, a map showing the exact location of the property; page 3, text showing the details of location, the reasons why the location is desirable, and other information as to size, construction, heating, rents obtainable, and the prospect for increase in value; and page 4, institutional copy.

The leaflet is used frequently in direct-mail advertising for announcements of special events. It is particularly suitable in selling an inexpensive item, since its cost is not great. Furthermore, it can be inserted easily in an envelope.

Folders.—A folder is larger than a leaflet, printed usually on heavier stock, and folded more than once. Because of the variety of sizes that the folder may take, it can be used separately or as an envelope enclosure to supplement a letter. A complete story may be told in a folder. The reader should be able to open the folder naturally and follow the illustrations and copy without trouble. Three thoughts should be kept in mind in deciding upon the size of the folder and the arrangement of its folds: (1) keep the idea simple; (2) select a size that cuts economically from a standard-size sheet; and (3) consider the envelope into which it is to go.

Broadsides.—An enlarged folder, about 19 × 25 inches in size or larger, is often called a "broadside." Usually it is designed as a self-mailing piece; that is, it is prepared for mailing with a portion of the first or last page given over to the address. In such cases it is held together at the open fold by a seal, or a postage stamp. In designing self-mailing folders or broadsides, care must be used to see that the two sides of the folder—that is, the address side and the back or front, as the case may be—are kept absolutely distinct to avoid confusion.

The broadside is used to give a smashing impression of a single idea or to tell a lengthy story in picture or type. Because of the variety of folds that are possible, and the combination of color and illustration that may be used, the broadside possesses a high degree of adaptability and variability. To carry out its purpose of a smashing impression, its text must be concise, its illustrations simple, and its copy not crowded. The broadside, nevertheless, must tell a complete sales story. It usually does this by catching the prospect's attention at the outside with an illustration and a tie-in phrase or single word, both of which lead the prospect to break the seal and look inside or to open the folder. The interest must be maintained with each step of the unfolding process.

It is necessary to keep in mind that the broadside must be suitable for the mailbag. If, when folded, the broadside is larger than the general run of mail, it may be delivered torn, folded again in half, or curled up. The following sizes are best suited for mailing: $9\frac{1}{2} \times 6\frac{1}{4}$ inches, or $9\frac{1}{2} \times 4\frac{1}{6}$ inches, folded from a sheet 19×25 inches or 25×38 inches; or $8 \times 5\frac{1}{2}$ inches, folded from a sheet 22×32 inches.

Booklets.—A booklet is a small book whose pages are in multiples of four to permit binding as a book by stitching, stapling, or glue. The term, however, has been applied to a multitude of different kinds of advertising pieces from a small bound insert to a large handbook. The booklet is used to elaborate and impress a point that requires considerable space for its presentation. It tells a complete story of the product or service.

Booklets have been used for the following purposes:

1. As an aid to salesmen.
2. To create inquiries.
3. To answer inquiries.
4. To instruct customers on the use of a product.
5. For trade and consumer sales promotion.
6. To promote group interests.
7. General propaganda.

The size, kind of paper, quality of cover, and extent to which color and illustration will be employed vary with the purpose of the booklet and the amount of money available for its production. The person planning the booklet should keep in mind that too large a booklet may be wasteful; one that is too small may not offer enough information; one with too much copy may discourage the reader; and one with too many pictures may be interesting but, because of lack of copy, not persuasive enough, to bring results.

Brochures.—Beautiful, de luxe booklets, prepared at considerable cost, are generally termed *brochures*. They are commonly used whenever it is necessary to make an impression on the reader. Business houses, advertising agencies, investment dealers, and others use them as a sort of window-dressing device.

Catalogues.—Catalogues that are designed to sell products to wholesalers, retailers, or consumers make buying possible without a personal inspection of the goods. Along with the description of the merchandise, there are usually an illustration and text presentation of the benefits of the product, data on various methods of using the product, and convincing copy on consumer satisfaction that the product offers through its quality, construction, and the like. Thus the catalogue not only lists, describes, and illustrates the merchandise offered, but does a selling job as well. The catalogue may or may not show the price. Frequently prices are offered in a separate listing. To meet the problem of changes in items, prices, and other data that are included in the catalogue, some firms prefer to prepare less elaborate catalogues and issue them more frequently.

If the company has a diversified line of products, it may handle the catalogue problem in one of the following ways:

1. Issue a wide range of separate catalogues.
2. Issue departmentalized or sectionalized catalogues.
3. Provide loose-leaf catalogues with supplements showing changes.
4. Prepare a portfolio consisting of a folder or envelope in which loose sheets are conveniently filed.

Where catalogues are prepared at infrequent intervals, bulletins are generally issued from time to time to keep the catalogue up to date.

The catalogue may serve to aid the company's salesmen, develop inquiries and convert them into sales, sell special groups or interests, and sell the consumer direct.

House organs.—A house organ is a publication issued periodically by a firm for the purpose of maintaining contacts, creating goodwill, and establishing a favorable attitude toward the organization so that the reader will give preference to the firm when he is in need of its product or service. It is not designed to obtain direct, immediate action.

House organs fall into four main types:

1. Sales department house organs. These are prepared essentially for the salesmen. Information and ideas for increasing sales are passed on to the sales force through the house organ.
2. Dealer house organs. These aim at developing goodwill among dealers and maintaining communication between the manufacturer and the dealer.
3. Buyer house organs. These are designed to create a favorable attitude toward the house and to increase the use of its products.

4. Employee house organs. These are prepared to promote goodwill within the organization.

Dealer house organs and buyer house organs offer the advertiser an opportunity to aid the sale of goods by building goodwill among sales outlets and by passing on to the buyer information that will help keep him satisfied with his purchase and content to repeat or replace it in the future.

Novelties.—In the field of direct advertising, novel forms are constantly being introduced. The pop-up, animated cards, and models are only a few of the novelties that have been used.

The most common advertising novelties are the blotter and the calendar. Wherever possible, the advertising blotter should carry a message that will be remembered. Timely features increase the value of the blotter, for they give the advertiser an added excuse for mailing his sales message to his prospect. A calendar is often used, most commonly a one-month calendar plate, printed as part of the advertisement. As an envelope stuffer, a blotter travels "postage free," because the stamp that carries a letter or bill is usually sufficient for the blotter as well.

Calendar advertising is institutional advertising, and its purpose is to make the advertiser's name familiar to buyers. Proper presentation of calendars is highly important, because the manner of giving often determines whether the calendar will be hung in a prominent position or stowed away out of sight.

Reply forms.—The selection of a reply form must be made in all cases where the objective of the mailing is to obtain orders or inquiries, or ascertain in some measure the success of the mailing. Here is a list of the ways in which the reply can be facilitated:

1. Enclose a separate business reply card.
2. Attach the business reply card to the booklet, folder, or mailing piece with a seal, or by means of slits like a picture in a photograph album.
3. Provide for a tear-off reply card on the letterhead, folder, or other mailing piece.
4. Use a business reply envelope.
5. Provide a card, coupon, blank, or order form to be returned in the business reply envelope.

6. Use a combination letter and return envelope, especially for letters requesting a remittance with order. For an illustration, see page 402. Usually the combination letter and envelope is a patented device in which the letter and envelope are one piece, with the place at which the envelope is to be torn off indicated by markings.

The return card must tell the entire story of its purpose so that, if it becomes separated from the enclosure, it will be clearly understood. It should be attractive and simple, with plenty of room for signature and address.

The envelope.—Without losing sight of the postal regulations with regard to envelopes (see page 943), it is possible to make the envelope help in the selling job. A few examples will illustrate how this can be done. Nunn-Busch Shoe Company of Milwaukee used a cellophane envelope to enclose a four-color-process promotion broadside. While permitting full visibility of the enclosure, the envelope added to the general appearance and interest value of the broadside. Special permission to use this type of envelope had to be secured from Washington, D. C.

The National Sportsman, Inc., Boston publisher of sporting magazines, tested a plain envelope against one in which the entire back of the envelope was covered with an attractive photograph of a lake-and-woods scene printed in cool green. The pictured envelope pulled 3.386 per cent cash orders for subscriptions, while the plain envelope brought 2.976 per cent. The larger returns more than paid for the cost of the envelopes.

The Book-of-the-Month Club found that on a mailing to teachers the response was doubled, and on a mailing to golfers the response was almost trebled, by writing the prospect's name in brush script across the outside of the envelope.

Some advertisers have made third-class mail pay well by making type talk on the envelope. With an interesting flash or message on the envelope, they attract the attention of the reader and arouse his curiosity as to the contents of the envelope. Others have used a mailing with an outside window envelope to increase results. The enclosure, of course, contains the name of the person to whom it is addressed, and this fill-in, showing through the window, is what attracts the attention of the recipient. The letter, of course, must hold the attention once it has been attracted.

Where successive mailings are to be made, attention must be paid to varying the style of the envelope in order to give each mailing distinction, and to prevent prospects from recognizing the sender of the material before he opens the envelope. Variety can be achieved by changing the color, shape, style, arrangement of name and return address, or by using a different flash or message.

Letterheads.—If successive letters are to be sent to the same list, variety in the use of letterheads is as essential as variety in the use of envelopes. Changes in color, style, and size of the letterhead increase the likelihood that the copy will be read. Many firms experienced in direct-mail advertising find that occasionally it is worth while to dispense with the letterhead entirely; instead, they place the company name and address at the bottom of the letter, starting the letter with the selling message, with a flash, or with an illustration that ties up with the message.

Preparing the advertising piece.—After the form that the advertising piece will take has been selected, the actual preparation is begun. The steps in putting together the direct-mail advertisement vary, of course, with the working processes of the individual, and with the facilities available in the advertising department. The usual steps are:

1. Make a trial dummy of the booklet, leaflet, or whatever form the advertisement is to take, mapping out the illustrations and indicating the headlines. In this step consideration should be given to the size of the mailing piece, its mailing weight, and the cost of mailing. For economy, the size of the sheet used should be standard or of a size that will cut from a standard sheet without waste. For information as to mailing methods and costs, see the "Postal Guide" at pages 925 et seq. For information as to paper stocks, see page 524.
2. Determine the size and face of type that will be used and the kind of illustration. See discussion under "Printing and Typography," on page 496.
3. Select the paper stock suitable for the job.
4. Have the illustrations made.
5. Write the copy to fit the space.
6. Have plates made of the illustrations, if necessary, and type set for the copy.

7. Make a paste-up dummy, and submit both to the printer for final revised proof.

8. Correct the page proofs and O.K. for printing.

This sketchy outline of the procedure for getting together the direct-mail advertisement makes the process appear considerably simpler than it is. The self-question chart on direct advertising, given below, gives a clearer idea of the many points that must receive attention in the preparation of direct-mail advertising.

SELF-QUESTION CHART ON DIRECT ADVERTISING [1]

What factors determine the selection of this medium?
- What is the main purpose of the advertising effort?
- Can direct advertising best accomplish this purpose?

What factors determine the form of the piece?
- How much material must be presented?
- Are illustrations and type matter relatively equal in sales importance? Is message mainly attention-getting, or mainly informative?
- What kind of illustration best fits the purpose?
- What kind of art work do the illustrative needs suggest?
- What general form of piece will best present the message? (Leaflet, stuffer, package insert, blotter, calendar, circular, illustrated letter, booklet, book, catalogue, broadside?)

What factors determine production?
- What kind of engraving and printing do illustrations require? (Letterpress, lithography, gravure, collotype, etc.) Is color a major factor?
- What kind of paper does reproduction require? Is mailing weight important?
- Is length of run suitable for economical use of printing process chosen?
- What sheet or page size will cut to advantage from standard-size stock?
- Will this cut of stock provide press sheets of proper size?
- Will stock fold the required number of times without cracking?
- Has grain direction been checked with direction of main folds?
- Has number of folds been checked against weight of stock?
- Is stock heavy enough to require scoring?
- If piece is to be machine-folded, has dummy been checked with printer or binder to avoid waste of paper in imposition, and to allow possible economies in binding?
- Is stock available in duplicate lots if needed?
- Is piece a self-mailer? If not, will it fit standard-size envelope?
- If a self-mailer, is sufficient space left for address?
- Has complete dummy, including envelope, if any, been checked for mailing weight? (Allow for ink, stamps, stickers, etc.)

Layout and general factors
- If folder, circular, or broadside, have folds been planned to open consecutively with progress of message, and without obliging reader to turn piece in his hands as he reads?

---

[1] Excerpt from a larger chart in *The Technique of Advertising Production,* by Thomas Blaine Stanley, Prentice-Hall, Inc., New York, 1940.

Does the effort to achieve novelty and interest sacrifice legibility or ease of reading in any way? (Monotony in type treatment, and in size and shape of illustrations should be avoided, but not at the expense of a clear presentation of the message.)

Has care been taken to harmonize line and halftone illustrations appearing on the same page? (Tint blocks under line cuts, or line borders around halftones will help to pull the two together. As a rule, the halftones should dominate such a combination showing.)

Is it possible to use a folding scheme in which one piece of display does double duty (*i.e.,* is seen on both of two spreads as they are opened consecutively? Watch stock envelope size when planning unusual folds, and remember that grain of paper should run with major folds.

Is each pair of facing pages or set of facing areas designed as a unit?

If color is used, has piece been planned for maximum effect? Does color as planned accomplish more than merely attract attention?

Has proposed color treatment been considered from the point of view of appropriate suggestion (of qualities such as warmth, coolness, purity, etc.)?

Do important cost or time factors tend to change any decision suggested above?

Testing direct-mail advertising.—The key to success in direct-mail advertising is careful testing and careful checking of results of tests. By means of experience with small mailings, it is possible to determine in advance whether the complete mailing will be successful, and to eliminate guesswork. So important is this step in direct-mail advertising that some large companies have set up a direct-mail laboratory for the purpose of testing and recording results of each proposed mailing. As a part of 750,000 letters mailed by McGraw-Hill Publishing Co., which mails about 6,000,000 pieces a year to increase circulation of its magazines, 146 different tests, each test involving 1,500 letters, were made. In most cases copy for each of its publications was tested to determine future mailings, but many other variables were tested and retested.

What shall be tested.—An exhaustive list of tests that have been made by direct-mail advertisers cannot be presented because the number of variables that can be tested is countless. The following list, however, gives a clear picture of the kind of test frequently made.

Results of individual tests are not given here, because what is found to be true for one product might not be applicable to another, and what resulted at one time might not result at another. Companies which test constantly find that many of the results do not hold for all of the company's products. For this reason constant testing and retesting are essential.

LIST OF COMMON TESTS OF DIRECT-MAIL ADVERTISING

Proposition

Type of proposition
Unit of sale most suitable
Selling price
Terms of payment
Shall a premium be offered?

Mailing List

Responsiveness of different types of lists
Areas that can be circularized profitably

Timing

Frequent *vs.* infrequent mailings
Interval between mailings
Time of year, month, or day in which to mail to particular groups or localities

Type of Mailing Piece

Letters, broadsides, booklets, folders tested against each other
Various combinations of mailing pieces
A cheaper mailing piece *vs.* a more expensive one
Printed announcements *vs.* Government post cards

Letters

Different appeals
Automatic typewritten letters *vs.* processed letters
Personalized *vs.* nonpersonalized
Letters with fill-in *vs.* those without fill-in
Multigraphed fill-in *vs.* automatic typewritten
Two-page *vs.* both sides on one letterhead
One color *vs.* two colors
Style and size of letterheads
Engraved stationery and high-grade stock *vs.* less expensive grades

Enclosures

Number of enclosures
Types of enclosures
Inclusion of a "pass-along" card for a friend
One-color *vs.* two-color enclosures
Methods of affixing enclosures
Addition of card for another product

Envelopes

Color of envelope
Flash on the envelope
Hand-addressed *vs.* type-addressed *vs.* stencil-addressed
Style and size of envelope
Window envelopes *vs.* addressed envelopes
Testimonials on back of envelope

Stamps

Metered postal indica *vs.* precanceled stamps
Commemorative *vs.* ordinary stamps
Stamped *vs.* metered postage
First-class *vs.* third-class postage

Reply Forms

Business reply cards *vs.* business reply envelopes
Business reply card *vs.* plain reply card
One-color *vs.* two-color reply card
Filled-in reply card *vs.* plain reply card
Air-mail business reply envelope *vs.* regular business reply envelope
Unstamped business reply card *vs.* stamped reply card *vs.* stamped, addressed envelope
Color of reply form
Tab on reply card
Order form as part of mailing piece *vs.* separate card order form

How large a test shall be made.—No hard-and-fast rules can be set as to how large a mailing should be used to test the list, the mailing piece, or any other variable. A good deal depends upon the type of list, the price of the product, the purpose of the test, and the quota necessary to make the mailing profitable. In figuring how much to mail on any test, it is advisable to think, not in terms of number of pieces mailed, but in terms of the quota set. Thus, if a mailing of 1,000 letters required a quota of 5 orders to prove it profitable, it would be unwise to make two tests of 1,000 each to determine which of two letters pulled better, because the results from the two tests would not be sufficiently different to warrant drawing any positive conclusion. If one mailing brought 7 orders and the other 5 orders, it is entirely possible that the extra 2 orders could be attributed to special cases that did not at all represent the rest of the list. If the test were increased in size, say to 5,000, and one letter brought 35 orders and the other 20 orders, there would be no doubt as to which was the better letter.

In some lines, especially if the product is low in price, a fair test of a 10,000 list is 1,000, provided the 1,000 names are geographically representative.

Testing the variables.—Only one variable should be tested at a time, and care should be taken to eliminate all extraneous factors that might influence the returns. It would be fatal to the value of the test to change any detail of the mailing other than the item that is to be tested. Of course, several tests can be made at the same time, covering different variables. Thus, simultaneously with the test as to appeal, another split mailing can be made to test the reply form. The mailings testing the appeal would be identical with each other except for the appeal; the mailings testing the reply form would be identical with each other except for the reply form.

If several lists are to be used in a mailing, more than one list should be used in testing a variable. The size of the list will, of course, influence the number of different tests that will be made. On a mailing list of 1,000, for example, it is hardly likely that more than one variable can be tested.

In order to be able to check results from comparative tests, the reply form must be so keyed that, when returns come in, they can be credited to the proper mailing. The most common method of keying is to use different key numbers on the reply cards, each representing a unit of the mailing, or different colored reply cards.

Mechanics of the test.—If a specific test is being made to determine whether or not the campaign, complete in all its details, will bring a sufficient number of returns to indicate success of the entire mailing, the procedure is very simple. A certain percentage of the list to be used is circularized, and the returns are checked and tabulated.

If a comparative test is to be made to determine the relative value of one method or detail against another of the same general type, the procedure is more complicated. For instance, let us suppose that two entirely different folders, one elaborate and the other inexpensive, have been written, and that it is necessary to determine which will prove more profitable. Here is the procedure that is followed:

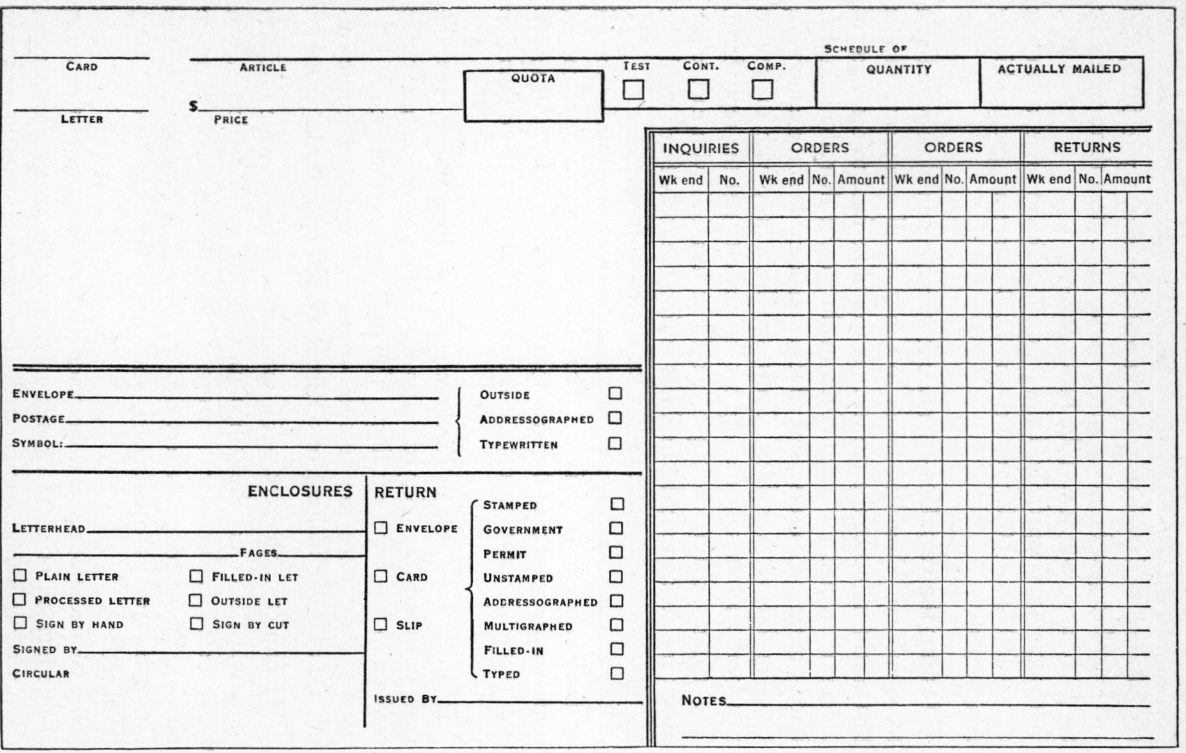

CARD ______ ARTICLE ______ QUOTA ______

LETTER ______ $ ______ PRICE

SCHEDULE OF

TEST	CONT.	COMP.	QUANTITY	ACTUALLY MAILED
☐	☐	☐		

INQUIRIES		ORDERS			ORDERS			RETURNS		
Wk end	No.	Wk end	No.	Amount	Wk end	No.	Amount	Wk end	No.	Amount

NOTES ______

ENVELOPE ______
POSTAGE ______
SYMBOL: ______

- OUTSIDE ☐
- ADDRESSOGRAPHED ☐
- TYPEWRITTEN ☐

ENCLOSURES

LETTERHEAD ______

______ FAGES ______

- ☐ PLAIN LETTER
- ☐ PROCESSED LETTER
- ☐ SIGN BY HAND
- ☐ FILLED-IN LET
- ☐ OUTSIDE LET
- ☐ SIGN BY CUT

SIGNED BY ______

CIRCULAR

RETURN

- ☐ ENVELOPE
- ☐ CARD
- ☐ SLIP

- STAMPED ☐
- GOVERNMENT ☐
- PERMIT ☐
- UNSTAMPED ☐
- ADDRESSOGRAPHED ☐
- MULTIGRAPHED ☐
- FILLED-IN ☐
- TYPED ☐

ISSUED BY ______

Figure 14.—Advertising Department Mail Order Record.

1. Determine a quota for each piece on the basis of the number of returns that must be received to make the mailing profitable.
2. Address all the envelopes to be used in both tests.
3. Alternate these envelopes into two groups.
4. Stuff, stamp, and seal each group, one with the first mailing, the other with the alternate.
5. Deliver both to the post office at the same time.

In this way all extraneous factors have been eliminated. Letters go out on the same day to the same territory, to the same quality names. Of course, they are keyed differently to make it possible to credit the correct mailing.

Recording results of direct-mail tests.—A record of each mailing should be kept not only as a guide to the results of the particular test but for future use. Fig. 14 is an example of a record used to enter the results of test mailings, as well as the results of complete mailings after tests have been made.

Over the word "Card" is inserted the key number used on the test. Over the word "Letter" is inserted the key number of the letter used. The objectives of the mailing are noted in the large white space. To compare the results of a test, the cards bearing the key numbers of the particular test are examined. The company using these cards files them according to articles advertised, in numerical order according to key number.

2. HOW TO GET AND BUILD MAILING LISTS

Where to get the list of prospects.—The sources of prospect lists are too numerous for complete enumeration. The most important include:

1. Customers of the firm.
2. Names rented from other firms.
3. Names exchanged with other firms.
4. Names supplied by list brokers.
5. Directories.
6. Rating books.
7. Membership lists from organizations.
8. Public records.

9. Lists built through space or radio advertising.
10. Names supplied by satisfied customers and prospects.
11. Salesmen's reports.
12. Press clippings.
13. Special list-building plans.

The firm's own customers' list as a mailing list source.—One of the most profitable sources for a good mailing list is the company's own records. Active customers, inactive customers, cash customers, C.O.D. purchasers may all be good prospects for further sales. In a department store, for example, a direct-mail piece on hosiery can be sent to buyers of women's shoes. To use another example, a firm selling roofing material and paint uses its list of satisfied buyers of roofing material as prospects for paint sales.

Names rented from other firms.—Most firms selling by mail are glad to rent their lists of prospects or customers to noncompeting firms. For example, many magazines will be glad to rent the names of their expired subscribers. Book publishers will often rent the names of those who have not recently purchased. Direct-mail sellers of general merchandise often allow noncompeting firms to mail to their names.

In most cases, owners of lists do not allow addressed envelopes to be returned to the rentor, but deliver them directly to the post office when addressed. The usual procedure in this case is:

1. The rentor agrees with the list owner to test a certain number of names, usually 1,000 or 2,000, at a normal renting rate of between $10 and $15 per thousand.
2. The rentor delivers this number of stuffed, sealed envelopes for addressing and mailing. An additional charge of perhaps $1 a thousand is added for stamping.
3. The list owner addresses the envelopes, stamps and sorts, if necessary, and delivers them to the post office. Post-office receipts give proof of mailing.
4. If the test is successful, the procedure is continued for the full mailing.

A large percentage of direct-mail sellers rely heavily on the lists of others to bring them their business. Lists of buyers of any one item are usually good direct-mail prospects for other items and are well worth the rental charge involved.

Names exchanged with other firms.—Exchanges of lists are generally made between noncompetitive firms whose lists are more or less similar from the standpoint of type of prospect. For example, a book publisher might exchange lists with a publisher of a magazine, or with a publisher of an entirely different type of book. The procedure is similar to that outlined in the preceding paragraph, except that in place of a rental fee for the list, each firm addresses from its own list an equivalent amount of mailing matter delivered by the other for addressing. As in the case of rented lists, tests are usually made before large lists are exchanged.

Names supplied by list brokers.—The function of the list broker is to dig up names of prospects for anyone interested in using the mails for advertising. List brokers are found in every important city. They sometimes operate in connection with firms offering letter services, such as multigraphing, processing, addressing, and mailing. The broker may arrange for the rental of lists from other firms, as described on page 326.

To obtain best results in dealing with a list broker, the most successful plan is to call him in and explain the entire plan of sales. He will know what good prospect lists are available and how much they will cost. Where a directory might serve the purpose, the broker will usually mention it, even though he makes no money on these mailings.

Brokers work on a percentage basis, usually 20 per cent. Each broker has a few lists which he handles on an exclusive basis—that is, other brokers cannot handle except through him—and many other lists which are open to all brokers.

The advantage of working with a broker is that he has accumulated a great deal of information about various lists and can recommend those which have the best chance of bringing back a profit. He will know which lists are doing well for other houses, and which are not. He may discourage the use of a particular list and suggest new lists about which the mailer might not otherwise know. Experienced direct mailers avail themselves of the services of brokers constantly; new firms in direct mail would do well to lean heavily on the judgment of the better known brokers.

Directories.—Hundreds of directories are published each year, many of which can be profitably utilized by firms selling by mail. The great advantage of these directories, of course, is that they are comparatively inexpensive. For instance, a list of all the banks in the country, together with all the important executives of those banks, can be had for about $15. A list of lawyers, containing the names and addresses of perhaps 160,000 attorneys, can be had for about $25. Obviously, if such lists can be used, they are much cheaper to obtain than rented lists.

The objection to the use of such directories is that, because of frequent usage, the names are not so responsive as are those on rented lists. Hence, it is necessary to analyze these directory lists carefully and to select the names that seem most logical. For example, it is possible to secure at a low price a book containing the names of many thousand corporation directors; but few direct-mail firms can mail profitably to the entire list. As an illustration, it might happen that directors who are treasurers of corporations would be better prospects than those who are presidents; or that directors who are secretaries might buy more willingly than those who are treasurers. Where lists are large enough, it is worth while to study them to determine whether or not there is some logical breakdown that would make at least part of the list pay.

The most common directories are trade directories, telephone directories, street directories, city directories, and blue books.

Rating books as a source of names.—The credit-rating books published by Dun and Bradstreet and by the special or trade agencies that are confined to a single industry constitute a good source for names. These books generally give the firm name, line of business, special credit conditions, and ratings—that is, estimated financial worth and pay ratings.

Membership lists from organizations.—Membership lists of clubs, social organizations, lodges, trade associations, professional groups, labor unions, and other organizations make good mailing lists for some types of propositions. The roster of membership is usually obtained from the secretary or president upon tactful request and satisfactory explanation of the use to which it is to be put. Sometimes some inducement must be offered for the use of the list.

A list of trade and commercial associations with the names and addresses of the secretaries is published annually by the United States Department of Commerce.

Using public records for mailing lists.—Public records frequently make excellent mailing lists. These are obtainable from national sources and county, state, and municipal records. Thus, voting and tax lists, marriage licenses, building permits, automobile licenses, and the like, supply valuable names. Inquiry at the place in which the public record is filed should be made to determine whether the names may be copied from the source, or whether a list can be secured upon application. Sometimes a nominal fee is charged for the list.

Lists built through space or radio advertising.—Some direct-mail firms obtain most efficient results from leads obtained from space advertising or through radio advertising. To build a list rapidly, the most successful procedure is to offer a premium, such as a booklet, an article of merchandise, or some other item.

The greatest advantage of building a list through advertising is that it is an exclusive list; no one other than the advertiser has access to it. It is also a selective list. The disadvantage is that such lists are expensive to build.

It is not unusual, for instance, for a list of names compiled from magazine advertising to cost 50 cents a name. Obviously, business obtained from these names must be substantially greater than that obtained from rented or directory lists before there will be any profit on the investment.

To eliminate curiosity seekers from the list a small charge may be made for the premium offered. For further discussion of the handling of coupons in advertisements, see page 463.

Names supplied by satisfied customers and prospects.—Customers and other prospects may be willing to supply names of friends, relatives, or acquaintances who might be interested in the proposition. The following practices have been found useful in building mailing lists with the aid of satisfied customers:

1. Send letters to all customers at one time asking them to suggest names of friends who might be interested in the product or service. Supply a form for listing the names.

2. Send a letter, or a series of letters, to each new customer within a reasonable period after he has made his first purchase, and in the letter, or in one of the series, ask for a list of names.

3. Offer a premium in return for the favor of submitting names. If salesmen are used, they can deliver the premium.

4. Ask for a list of names and offer a substantial reward if actual sales are made to any of the prospects. For example, a profit-sharing plan was used by a fuel- and oil-burner dealer to get prospects' names from customers. Each customer for whom a job had been installed received an impressive folder, the cover of which resembled a bond. Upon opening the document, the customer found ten perforated coupons with ruled lines for the names and addresses of suggested prospects. If a sale were made, within three months, to one of the names filed, the customer was given five dollars.

5. If distribution is through a dealer, wholesaler, or jobber, and names of customers are sought, enclose a return post card in the package, and offer a premium if the card is returned by the customer.

Building a list through salesmen.—Various methods have been used to secure the co-operation of the sales force in building up a list of names that are good mail-order prospects. Among these are:

1. Have salesmen send in daily, weekly, or monthly reports of prospects upon whom they have called.

2. Supply salesmen with report forms, cards, or other equipment that simplifies the process of noting names of prospects.

3. Require salesmen to submit certain information about the prospect in addition to his name and address, to permit proper classification of the prospect.

4. Place a limit on the number of names to be submitted. This tactic assures a better grade of names.

5. Set up rules that must be met before names can be considered acceptable prospects.

6. Offer incentives to arouse interest in suggesting live-prospect names.

7. Educate salesmen in the importance of mailing-list work, and show them by means of booklets, sales meetings, and bulletins how to gather names of prospects.

Lists built through clippings.—The list that is compiled by making press clippings of direct leads for sales is likely to be up to date and correct. For example, clippings of marriages may form the basis of circularization for furniture sales, and news items of fires may create a list of prospects for fireproof roofing. The clippings can be secured at a low cost from firms offering newspaper-clipping services. Careful instruction should be given as to the clippings desired and the areas to be covered.

Special list-building plans.—Any number of miscellaneous ways can be mentioned for collecting names of prospects. For example, retail stores frequently undertake to build their lists through special services. The personal shopping bureau may keep a list of names of shoppers assisted; a special boys' broadcast as a store-promotion stunt may yield the names of all persons attending the broadcast and furnish an excellent list of propects for junior clothing. One department store builds a mailing list by having a birthday registration book in the children's department. An inexpensive present is sent to each child on its birthday. This prompts customers to register their children and to notify the store of changed addresses.

Contests are a common method of building mailing lists. Employee contests with prizes offered for the person submitting the largest number of names resulting in sales have helped to build good lists. Contests in which the public participates is another popular method, for the names and addresses of those who take part in the contest can thus be secured.

Checking names before adding to list.—Some companies enhance the quality of their mailing lists and thus increase the percentage of returns from each mailing by checking all names before adding them to the list. The trouble and expense of this preliminary check are considered worth while if frequent and expensive mailings are made from the list. The checking is usually done by the sales or credit department.

How to keep mailing lists.—Any organization that has invested time and money in building up mailing lists will want to keep a careful file of them. Since lists may be kept in the form of cards, a directory, a book, a printed list taken from a book, typewritten sheets, or in the form in which it is received from various sources, some system must be devised for locating the lists as they are needed. File boxes, drawers, and bookcases are generally used for housing the lists. In addition, a card record is made up for each individual list, indexed by field, subject, or title. A record of the number of times the list is used may be made directly on the index card.

The list of prospects, if made on 3 × 5 inch cards or stencils, should be grouped geographically by city or town and state, in alphabetical order. The names in each group should also be alphabetical, preferably with the last name first. This arrangement facilitates the weeding out of "undeliverables."

A number of concerns using stencils report that if a list is to be used ten to twelve times a year, it is more economical to have a stencil made for each name, to be used in addressing, than to have the list addressed by typewriter or by hand each time.

Increasing the effectiveness of the mailing list.—If the mailing lists are broken down after use to segregate the names of those who have responded from those who have remained inactive, the effectiveness of the lists is increased.

Lists of individuals must be watched for errors in the spelling of names, incorrect addresses, wrong titles, and other mistakes. Corrections should be made, and names of persons who have moved and left no address or who have died should be removed. Lists of firm names must be watched for similar errors. Changes in names of buyers, managers, presidents, secretaries, and other officers must be noted, and the names of bankrupt firms must be removed.

Keeping a list up to date requires not only constant vigilance to insure that the details are accurate but also breakdown of the list into special classifications that suit the purposes of the firm. Such classifications may be: (1) sources of the list; (2) type of list; (3) frequency of purchase; (4) profession of prospect; (5) volume of purchases; and the like.

Care must be exercised in deciding whether names should be removed entirely from the mailing list into an inactive list because no response has been received after repeated mailings. Such factors as the profit on a sale, repeat possibilities, and any other items showing how much can be spent on mailing to a prospect before it becomes unprofitable to do so must guide the firm in segregating inactive names from his lists.

Occasional checking of mailing lists by salesmen and dealers in particular territories may help to keep the list correct. An established procedure in the organization for getting information from various company departments to the mailing department, as to changes in names, addresses, and closings of accounts, will facilitate keeping the list correct.

The checkup mailing.—The mailing list should be cleaned out at regular intervals to remove the names of persons not receiving the mail. To accomplish this step the statement "Return Postage Guaranteed" is included on the envelope under the sender's return address, in the upper left-hand corner of the envelope. All envelopes carrying this statement which cannot be delivered are returned to the sender (unless the Form 3547 statement is used), with the reasons for nondelivery.

When a list is several years old, it is usually worth while to obtain forwarding addresses of prospects. To secure such addresses, there can be printed or rubberstamped on the lower left-hand portion of the envelope or wrapper used to send third- or fourth-class mail: "If addressee has removed and new address is known, notify sender on Form 3547, postage for which is guaranteed." The post office will destroy the mail not delivered but will send a card with the new address. The card costs 2 cents. See also page 955.

Other ways of cleaning out a list.—Various other methods can be used for bringing a mailing list up to date. One way is to make a free offer in a letter that is sent to the entire list. This method was used, for example, by a printer who sent a mailing piece in the form of a French folder, on the back of which was an inspirational poem. Beneath the verse was a notice to the effect that copies of the poem printed on good stock and suitable for framing would be supplied to the reader without charge. Over 50 per cent of the firms on the mailing list responded to this offer.

It is sometimes profitable to clean out the entire list by frankly asking the prospect to make corrections and to indicate any suggestions he has with regard to his listing. *Parents' Magazine* checked its mailing list with a frank, inexpensive mailing piece sent to a list of 9,300 space buyers. The mailing piece consisted of a large envelope enclosing a Reply-O Form (see page 403) monarch-size letter. Three words, "Keep It Clean," comprised the only copy that appeared on the envelope, other than the third-class indicia, the return postage guaranty, and the return address. The letter repeated the envelope copy on the letterhead with the question mark "Keep It Clean?" and then said:

We're trying to—our complimentary mailing list, that is. So—you will be a good fellow—and slide the card—out of the pocket—on the back of this sheet—and let us know—whether you've moved—died—changed your name—gotten a better job—or anything else—that may have happened to you—that makes our present stencil—incorrect . . .

This plan brought 46.1 per cent returns.

3. HOW TO WRITE SALES LETTERS

The uninvited guest.—What is the person whose name is on your mailing list likely to be doing at the time your sales letter reaches him? The executive may be dictating a letter, figuring out estimates, interviewing a salesman, or talking over the telephone. The retailer may be serving a customer, taking stock, considering a new proposition, making up his books, or planning a sale. The housewife may be preparing breakfast, washing dishes or clothes, sweeping, cleaning carpets, or hanging pictures. Each of these and the many other persons you are seeking to address may be doing one or another of a thousand things at the moment your sales letter is delivered. You have no way of knowing what their activities are, what their thoughts are; but you may be certain that they are doing and thinking something. No one is just waiting for your letter to arrive.

What this means for the sales letter writer is largely a matter of viewpoint. To one the situation may seem to be bristling with obstacles, like a barbed-wire section of No Man's Land. To another it may be alive with opportunities.

No one is just waiting for your letter to arrive. But the opportunities in the situation arise from the fact that everyone is waiting for something—waiting in the sense of working toward, aiming at, or hoping for it. To the executive it may be a method of reducing costs; to the retailer a means of increasing sales; to the housewife a new way of lessening the drudgery of her daily routine. Then, into the mind of the name on your mailing list, preoccupied as it is with such problems, hopes, ambitions, and fears, walks the uninvited guest—your sales letter.

No uninvited guest is at once welcomed with open arms. He has to make his way in the face of indifference and suspicion. So also does your sales letter.

The reader is constantly thinking of himself, is mulling over in his conscious or subconscious mind ways and means of achieving certain things that mean a great deal to him. If the sales letter tries merely to distract his attention by clamoring about itself and about what it wants, there is a conflict of which the reader can readily rid himself by simply reaching toward the wastebasket. If, however, the letter talks about the reader—tells the executive that it can show him a method of reducing his costs, or the retailer a means of increasing his sales, or the housewife a new way of lessening the drudgery of her work—the *me* interest is stirred, and the reader is prepared to "listen."

What is it that makes a letter sell? The letter wants and asks the reader to do something—to "mail the enclosed card today," to "ride in the new Standard," to "examine this book for five days without obligation." The reader, however, already has his own wants. He is not interested in what you are wanting and asking him to do. He is not interested, that is, until you show him that what you are wanting and asking him to do is so closely connected with what he himself wants, that by doing as you ask he will be taking a step nearer one of his own hopes and desires or a step further away from an old fear or anxiety. In a word, the letter that sells is the letter that succeeds in tying up what it has to offer with the reader's wants.

Know your reader; know your product.—To tie up what you have to offer with the reader's wants, study your reader and study your product—imaginatively. By putting yourself in the reader's place, find out what his interests are. Then study your product to discover how it can be made to tie up with those interests. Above all, cultivate the habit of visualizing clearly and simply. Eliminate from your mind the preconceived notions as to human nature and the technical knowledge of your product that prevent you from seeing the wood for the trees.

The ingredients of the successful sales letter.—For the successful sales letter there can be no formula. Sales letter writing places a premium upon originality—upon keeping one step ahead of the times. What pulls today because it is new, is old tomorrow and has to be thrown into the discard. If, however, a formula were to be stated, the ingredients of the successful sales letter might be listed as follows:

1. *The opening*—which gains the reader's attention by tying in with his thoughts and emotions concerning himself, thus exciting his curiosity and tempting him to read further.
2. *The explanation or description*—which pictures for the reader the main features of your product or service.
3. *The motive*—which creates in the reader the *want* for what you are selling by describing what your product or service will do for him; how it will contribute to his pleasure, comfort, security, or gain.
4. *The evidence*—which establishes in the reader's mind conviction as to the truth of your statements and the value of your product to him.
5. *The penalty or inducement*—which gets the reader to act at once.
6. *The close*—which tells the reader exactly what to do, how to do it, and makes action easy.

These are the essential ingredients. The method of their combination, however, varies when different hands do the mixing.

Getting the reader's interest in the opening.—The opening must flag the reader's attention. It can do this best by speaking to him of himself—his problems, hopes, ambitions, and fears. Then, his interest excited, the reader is led into a description of the product or service offered and is made to want it and to act in order to get it, *for what it will do for him*. Notice how the following openings tie up with the particular reader's wants.

TO AN EXECUTIVE

Dear Mr. Simpson:

Do you ship by Parcel Post?

If you do, you can't afford to miss knowing about a new and very efficient method of handling C.O.D. and insured shipments. It will speed up your shipments—and cut your labor and error costs by 30%.

This remarkable and simple system is fully described and illustrated in a little booklet entitled, "If You Ship by Parcel Post." . . . .

TO A RETAILER

Dear Mr. Beckman:

Do the companies that furnish you with the fountain pens you now sell ever think about your turnover problems?

For example, how often does their advertising demand that you handle a new color?

Here's Sheaffer's way—our new Grey Pearl, one of the most beautiful colors we've ever introduced, was announced to our dealers nearly four months ago. Shipment of this color wasn't promised until October, and we won't begin to advertise it until June of next year.

What does it mean?

It means that Sheaffer dealers are given an opportunity to move out the oldest color in their stock to prepare for the new color, which will be shown to customers

only when the dealers are ready for it.

The selfish way is suddenly to flood the country with advertising . . . .

TO A DOCTOR

Dear Doctor Blake:

Doctor, what shall I do for my cold?

At this season of the year your patients ask you that troublesome question many times.

The local symptoms of colds in the head are quickly relieved by the use of EfeDroN Hart Nasal Jelly.

EfeDroN promptly relieves the nasal congestion by contracting capillaries, reducing turbinates, and diminishing hyperemia. It quickly opens the nasal air passages . . . .

TO A YOUNG MAN

Dear Mr. Williams:

Step into your employer's office tomorrow and demand a 100 per cent increase in your salary. Will you get it?

Could you step out to some other firm and get a job paying twice your present salary? Probably not, or you would do it, of course.

Yet this is exactly what LaSalle-trained men are doing every day . . . .

TO A WHITE-COLLAR WORKER

Dear Mr. Burnett:

On pay day—does your money go around? Or does it fail to stop all the gaps made by last month's bills?

Just yesterday we helped a family solve a problem that threatened to cause the head of the house to lose his job. It was the same old story—pay reduced, and unexpected extra expenses had thrown the family budget out of gear. Creditors were pressing. Bills had to be paid to save his credit—and to save his job.

This problem was solved through our Personal Loan Department..........

TO A MOTHER

Dear Mrs. Ferguson:

After baby's food and baby's clothes, the most important thing you have to decide upon is the little cart baby is going to ride in—is going to be seen in—is going to be admired in.

Never a child came into the world but was worthy of as good a cart..........

TO A FARMER

Dear Mr. Jensen:

You're interested in better hay? You want to increase the value of your hay crop, and at the same time put up that crop with less expense?

The John Deere Way of Making Hay will do both these things. The method is built around the John Deere-Dain System Rake. Do not confuse this rake with the common side-delivery rake. It is different, because it has—

curved teeth
inclined front frame
wheels of adjustable width

—all of which are absolutely necessary to make a light, fluffy windrow. It is a left-hand rake..........

Whether you are selling a fountain pen or an automobile, a lipstick or a piece of real estate, the principle is the same. Discover what the reader is most interested in, and play to that interest as a baseball pitcher pitches to the batter's weakness. Forget yourself, and tell the reader what your product or service *will do for him.*

Tell a story to get interest.—One of the fundamental interests of all human nature is the interest in a story. The most sophisticated person can be attracted by an anecdote or a short narrative. The story should have a close application to the subject and purpose of the letter and, of course, should be very skillfully written.

Example of story beginning.—The following paragraphs illustrate a story opening that immediately enlists the interest of the reader. The letter begins with a narrative that is full of warm human interest. In the very first sentence it begins to sell fish. The first paragraph leads the reader on to the next. Notice how its third paragraph starts with a query, often an effective device for waking up the reader when the letter comes to a point where the indifferent reader is likely to doze. Paragraph four introduces the offer in a pleasantly offhand manner: "You won't mind, will you, if I ship some of my fish direct to your home?" The clauses, "It won't cost you anything unless . . ." and "Try the fish at my expense, and judge for yourself whether . . ." are effective in the direct-mail selling of many products.

Dear Friend:

Way back in 1623, a small group of Pilgrims gathered in their small fish huts to name this fishing port Gloucester. They were a hardy lot of folks, living mostly on game and salt water fish. They built small boats and braved the treacherous waters off Gloucester to get fish for their families. In those times women folks helped too—for every hand meant more food for the cold winter months to come.

I remember, as a small boy, my father telling me about being lashed to the mainmast in a stiff blow, when his father's schooner was half buried in the plunging sea. It was a hard life. But still, Gloucester boys follow it year after year. It's in our blood. It's our way of Livin'. Nature has located us close to the richest waters there are.

Have you ever wondered why Gloucester is one of the greatest fishing ports in the world? You see, we have many varieties of delicious fish landed here daily. More good fish come right in here to Gloucester than any other port in the world. That's why you can never say you've tasted fish at its perfect prime unless you get it direct from Gloucester.

So you won't mind, will you, if I ship some of my fish direct to your home? It won't cost you anything, unless you feel like keeping it. All I ask is that you try the fish at my expense, and judge for yourself whether it isn't exactly what you have always wanted.

This letter of the Frank E. Davis Fish Company contained five more paragraphs and an enclosure.

Using news as an attention-getter.—News in a sales letter will usually supply the attention value necessary to enlist and carry the reader's interest, but it should always lead to and tie up with the selling message. Here are two letters that make good use of the news opening.

Dear Sir:

Last week the XYZ Company checked over its stock of our ice-cream cans, and sent us 500 cans for re-tinning. They feel that putting their cans in condition now will save them money next spring and summer. They know that in the busy season, no one has time to wait for a can to be re-tinned—it is quicker and easier to order a new one.

Of course, you know we make more money by selling you new cans than by re-tinning your old ones. But we want to be selling you cans a good many years, and we know that if we can save you money on your annual expenditure for cans, you are going to think mighty well of us and of our cans.

Now, won't you please go over your stock and send us every one of our cans you have that needs re-tinning? You know our charge for this re-tinning is only one-fourth the price of a new can.

And if you don't use our cans, you may feel that our low re-tinning charge is another good reason for using our cans next year.

Dear Sir:

We all sympathize with our neighbor, Mr. J. P. Jones, whose home burned to the ground last Thursday.

And we all hope we shall never have a similar disaster affect our own homes. There is one sure way to eliminate this ever-present menace of Fire. That's to be certain the roof, where most residential fires start, is of fire-resistant material.

Flintkote Mineral Surfaced Shingles give you this fire resistance. Every package carries the approved label of the Fire Underwriters' Laboratory. Insurance companies recognize, in most communities, the fire-safety of Flintkote Mineral Surfaced Roofs by giving lower insurance rates.

Let us talk with you about your home. Give us a ring today . . . we shall be pleased to call at your convenience.

Cordially yours,

Stunt letters to get attention.—Stunts are used in letter writing to get attention. They have been used in sales letters, promotion letters, and collection letters principally. If the stunt meets the following tests, the letter may be effective:

1. Is it in good taste? You can't risk offending the reader.
2. Does it tie up with the subject of the letter?
3. Is it original? You don't want the reader to say "old stuff" and stop there.
4. Does its cleverness distract from the message? A stunt may be so clever that the reader forgets about what he is being asked to do.

Example of stunt letter that meets the tests.—The following letter gets right down to brass tacks with its stunt. The two brass-headed paper staples inserted on the first line cannot offend anyone, and cannot hurt anyone. The stunt is original in its approach and is not so clever that the reader forgets what the writer wants.

Mr. Tag Buyer:

Getting down to brass tacks . . . . [Here the two brass heads appeared] . . . . it's your tag business we're after.

Will you meet us half way and let us show you what we can offer on your tag requirements?

It won't take but a few minutes of time to take samples of your tags, mark on them the quantities that you buy, drop them in the postage prepaid envelope attached—and mail.

Will you do it? You can bet the favor will be most welcome and that prices and samples will reach you by return mail.

Thanks a lot.

Yours very truly,

WURZBURG BROTHERS

We are ready to supply all sizes of good tags . . . plain . . . printed . . . numbered . . . perforated . . . scored . . . all weight stocks . . . metal eyelets . . . plain eyelets . . . with deadlocks, wires or strings . . . in gangs . . . in fact almost any type of tag you want.

A stunt opening that worked.—The stunt used in the following letter not only attracted attention but tied up immediately with the quality of the product that was offered. The letter, sent to 300 carefully selected prospects, brought 40 replies and resulted in sales of 56 units.

You can really
treat 'em rough!

(Here was attached a pearl)

(Here was a drawing of a hammer, poised ready to strike the pearl)

HoTaY Pearls will take an awful beating. Even hammering doesn't faze them. Not that you are likely to hammer your necklace, but this shows you that they are all that I claim.

HoTaY Pearls are not the ordinary simulated pearls. Their beauty is inherent. They are to all intents unbreakable. They will not scale or crack. They will wear and wear and WEAR and retain their original luster.

I'll send you postpaid a graduated necklace 18 inches long with a non-tarnish safety clasp of white metal in an attractive box for only $3.00. These are identical with those I formerly sold at $10.00 and up.

This chance comes to you just when you are beginning to think of the perplexing Christmas problem. Then there are birthdays to remember all through the year—graduation presents for next spring or maybe a really different and breath-taking bridge prize.

This 18 inch graduated necklace will nestle alluringly at your throat. It is the season's most popular length. The beads are perfectly matched and evenly graduated to the size knowing buyers are choosing. At only $3.00 it is a real bargain.

Those who bought HoTaY Pearls years ago still prize and praise them and ask for more. Those in the business have valued them at much more than the price I charge.

I haven't a great many, so it's best to act without delay. Mail the convenient card TODAY, so that you'll not be disappointed.

Very truly yours,
J. D. Oakley

Story opening combined with stunt.—A mail advertising agency reported unusually good results from the following letter, which combines a story opening with a stunt. An opened oyster was faintly imprinted at the top of the sheet. Half an imitation pearl was tipped in at the correct spot in the outline of the oyster. The regular letterhead form appeared at the bottom of the sheet, while the statement "You Have to Open Oysters to Get Pearls" headed the top of the sheet. The pearl, of course, provided the lead for the story that follows.

Mr. Jones:

In the South Sea Islands deep-chested natives dive time after time, bringing up great handsful of oysters in the hope that some of them may contain pearls.

There is no way of telling which oysters *do* bear pearls, and the oysters themselves are strangely reticent about the whole matter. A diver may work for hours without acquiring more than the basis for a stew. But the law of averages dictates that every so often he *will* find a pearl . . . and the more oysters he brings up the more pearls he will find.

Your business, like ours, is based on that old law of averages.

Your oysters are your prospects; your pearls, the orders you sell. Not all of those prospects can be sold, but the law of averages says that if you call on enough of them . . . tell enough of them your story . . . keep the mailman placing your literature on their desks . . . you will get the orders you need to keep growing and prospering. And if you concentrate on a list of *known* prospects, you are bound to increase the number of orders you get from the calls you make.

Before you start your Fall selling, it will pay you to scrutinize your lists of prospects carefully . . . make sure that you have enough "oysters" to keep the pearls rolling in during the months ahead. If your lists are old or incomplete, we can supply you with new ones that are up-to-the-minute in the information they contain and double-checked for accuracy.

Our list service covers more than 8,000 local and national markets. A copy of our 1940 list catalog, giving estimated counts and prices of these markets, is yours for the asking. It doesn't cost you a penny to call AT 4457, or to drop the enclosed card in the mail, but it may pave the way to more sales and more profitable sales in the future. Call us, or use the postage-free card, today.

Yours very truly,
BURGESS-BECKWITH, INC.

Gadgets and stunts.—A broadcasting company has made effective use of gadgets attached to colored cards to call attention to the selling message on the cards. For example, a red card measuring $7\frac{1}{2}'' \times 5''$ has a tiny hatchet slipped into an opening on the card, with the following heading and message:

WHY NOT BURY THE HATCHET?

Are you at war with that vicious monster, Increasing Selling Costs? If so, there's probably nothing you'd like better than to bury the hatchet.

Retailers, wholesalers, service organizations—large and small alike—have found that KSO-KRNT advertising keeps their selling costs down and sales up. Call 3-2111 today and ask a KSO-KRNT representative to show you "case histories" of Des Moines advertisers who are selling more economically on KSO or KRNT.

Iowa Broadcasting Company
Craig Lawrence
Commercial Manager

Tests to apply to an opening.—Don't be satisfied with an opening until you have tested it with the following questions:

1. Is it timorous? An opening that is lacking in vitality or is hackneyed will not impress the reader. Avoid such weak expressions as, "It gives us pleasure to inform you"; "You will be interested to know that"; "I am offering something that may interest you."

2. Is it negative? An opening that contains an unpleasant suggestion or an apology does not attract the reader. For example, avoid suggesting trouble, or that you are taking the reader's valuable time. Of course, if the principal purpose of the article is to protect the reader from trouble or disagreeable experience, the negative suggestion may be effective.

3. Is it relevant? If the opening is not relevant, no matter how interesting and clever it is, it will fail in its purpose of holding the reader's attention. The opening must tie up with the sales message of the letter.

4. Is it indirect and vague? A colorless generalization cannot excite the curiosity of the reader and make him feel inclined to read further. If the opening seems vague, make it direct and specific and notice how it gains strength. For example, compare the following openings:

Vague: It does not cost much to run an Electrolux.

Specific: A few pennies a day—25 to 70 cents a week—that is all it costs to run an Electrolux.

5. Is it too smart? Mere smartness will deprive the letter of character and may offend the reader. The following is effective as an attention-getter, but so is stepping on a person's toes.

I hope I am wrong
in addressing you as
Dear Ostrich:
But you should not avoid facing facts, etc.

Create desire for the product.—After favorable attention has been obtained, the next step is to create a desire in the reader for the product that is offered. To achieve this end, the reader should be told what your product or service will do for him. The central selling point should be selected and fitted to a need or desire of the prospect. The prospect must be made aware of that need or desire by appeal to his intellect or his emotions. *Appeal to emotions* is the more important of the two in a sales letter. Fundamentally, people act on the rather simple notion of desiring to have pleasant things and to avoid unpleasant things. This does not mean that the writer of a sales letter can afford to neglect to give facts and logical arguments that will convince the reader of the superiority of the product in satisfying his needs. It merely means that in the appeal to reason the importance of emotional appeal should not be overlooked.

A letter that disguises the appeal to reason.—As an illustration of the above principle, take the case of an automobile agency trying to interest a banker in the purchase of a low-priced car. A low-priced car? A banker? Impossible, you may say, to make any contact with an individual of this class—a man whose everyday experience teaches him to think slowly and cautiously and to act only after careful check and double-check—impossible to make contact with this man by any means other than mere cold logic and reasoning. But consider how persuasively the emotional appeal is put forward in the following letter:

Dear Mr. Spencer:

At a meeting of bankers at the Missouri Athletic Club last month, there was only one bank president who did not own a Ford.

He asked the others,

"Why do you fellows ride around in Fords when you can afford the best?"

One answer was,

"I made my money through sound investments and careful management, and there is more value dollar for dollar in a Ford than in any other car made."

Another answer was,

"In the first place, my investment is very small. I can afford to let my car stand on the street in all kinds of weather, can park it in a small space, and then at the end of the year can trade it in and get greater value in proportion than with any other car I ever owned."

We offer the best investment in the automotive world.

Come in and see us. Our showrooms are attractively arranged for your comfort. You are under no obligation to buy.

Sincerely yours,

This letter is a skillful sales message, for two reasons. First, it opens by speaking to the banker of himself and his own interests—"At a meeting of bankers . . ."—and thus stimulates him to read further. Second, although at first glance it may appear to be an appeal to reason, on closer analysis it shows itself to be really an emotional appeal cleverly disguised. It addresses itself to the emotion to which, above all others, a banker would probably be most susceptible—the desire to make even his minor purchases sound and dividend-paying investments. Furthermore, it conveys its message the more effectively by refraining from arguments regarding body style, gasoline consumption, easy-riding qualities, etc., etc., and, instead, merely quoting the opinions of those to whom a banker would be most willing to listen—his own colleagues. If the emotional appeal can be used to sell a low-priced automobile to a banker, it can be adapted even more readily to other products and to other classes of people.

What emotions can you appeal to?—The emotional appeals are numerous, but basically they simmer down to these six: love, duty, pride, gain, self-indulgence, and self-preservation or fear. These are also the primary buying motives.

In a sales letter, the more motives you can appeal to, the more effective may be your sales letter. Thus, if you are attempting to interest a married man in the purchase of insurance, you can appeal to some or all of the following emotions: (1) his *love* for his wife and family; (2) his sense of *duty* in providing for his dependents; (3) his *pride* in meeting his responsibilities; (4) his sense of *gain* in purchasing a form of insurance that is an investment as well as a protection; and (5) his *fear* either that his dependents will be left destitute in the event of his death or that he will be without a source of income in his old age.

Determining which emotion to appeal to.—Determining which emotion or emotions to stir is, once again, a matter of knowing your reader, knowing your product, and tying a Gordian knot between the two. If you are selling a business magazine to an executive, you may stress gain (the magazine will prove a valuable source of new ideas), and/or fear (by not subscribing the executive may miss something and, as a result, may fall behind in the competitive race).

In selling to a retailer you may choose to play up to his pride in the quality of the merchandise that he sells; his sense of gain if price is a feature of your product; or his fear that, if he fails to stock your goods, he may lose business to those of his competitors who do.

In selling furniture to a housewife you may aim to stir her pride in her home; cosmetics, her personal pride or vanity; a luxury, her self-indulgence; a baby carriage, her love for her child.

If you are to make your reader *want* your product for what it will do for him and *act* in order to get it (and not merely eye it from afar with mild approval), it is to the appropriate emotion or buying motive in him that your sales letter must be addressed. After you have stirred in the reader the feeling of wanting what you have to offer, it is a relatively easy matter to prove to him that he should have it.

The following sales letters, each of proved effectiveness in its particular field, illustrate how in actual practice the emotional appeal has been used in the selling of different types of goods and services to various classes of people.

"Make-and-save-money" appeal—specimen letter.—The most powerful sales letters are those that offer the recipient the probability of making money, or of saving it. The following letter is in the "make-and-save-money" class:

Dear Sir:

If we offered you one hundred dollars a month, would you accept it? Besides saving you that much money monthly, the following offer simplifies the buying and cutting of your trimmings.

To make pockets for the normal monthly output of one thousand dozen suits requires one thousand ninety-one yards of "Indian Head" or "Fruit of the Loom" muslin, the price of either of which is eighteen cents a yard. The thousand dozen pockets cost you—not including the cost of laying out and cutting—$196.38.

We can supply you with seven by eight pockets (the standard size), at ten cents a dozen, or one hundred dollars for the thousand dozen—a genuine saving to you of about one hundred dollars a month.

In addition to this saving, you have the benefit of another service. In order to get the advantageous price of eighteen cents a yard on the muslin, you have to buy at least a case of it. From us you can buy just as much as you need. Our large stock and quick delivery enable you to receive your goods just a few hours after the order reaches us.

The pockets are neatly wrapped in packages of fifty dozen, each of which contains ten folds of five dozen. This arrangement enables you to give your contractor just the number he needs. Our cutting machine not only insures neat and clean cutting, but also makes the pockets perfect in size and shape.

You cannot afford to neglect this opportunity. The more quickly you act, the sooner your saving begins.

We shall gladly send you a fifty-dozen package on approval if you mail the enclosed card immediately.

Yours truly,

Durability is a strong appeal.—If durability of your product is the selling point that will stimulate the buyer, the following letter may be adapted.

Dear Mr. Bascom:

Getting 58 years of average service out of a McCormick-Deering Ball-Bearing separator in about 4 years is unusual—but read the letter from Anton J. Johnson, Manager, Macomb Dairy Company, Macomb, Illinois.

> "Our No. 6 McCormick-Deering cream separator, purchased from you in December, 19—, is still in daily service. A conservative estimate of the amount of milk put through this separator in four years is 425,000 gallons. At 60 degrees Fahrenheit our butterfat loss is less than 1/100 of 1 per cent. The remarkable thing, however, is that without special attention this separator has never been out of service a single day in four years. If this separator ever wears out (which seems doubtful) we certainly would put in another McCormick-Deering."

With an average production of 5,188 pounds of milk per cow, per year, it would take 12 cows a total of 58 years to produce 425,000 gallons of milk. In other words, Mr. Johnson's McCormick-Deering cream separator has done in four years the work that would be required in 58 years on a 12-cow dairy farm. Space does not permit us to list all the many desirable features of this cream separator, but the enclosed folder includes practical information that will be of special interest.

Farming today and in the future holds the greatest promise for the man who takes advantage of every possible means of lowering his production costs. The McCormick-Deering line of farm operating equipment offers many opportunities for reducing crop production costs. In addition, it presents possibilities for making the difficult farm tasks easier and speeding up the seasonal operations that frequently have an influence on crop yield and quality, thus bringing proportionately greater returns from both equipment and labor.

There is no expense involved in becoming posted on what is latest and best in equipment. You can do this at "Farm Machine Headquarters" —the above-named McCormick-Deering dealer's store. You and your family are always welcome. You can secure practical information and see the machines best adapted to your needs. Make it a point to come in and get better acquainted and look over the facilities available for McCormick-Deering service.

Very truly yours,

A letter appealing to love, self-preservation, maternal instinct, and thrift.—The following letter deals with opening a bank account for baby:

Dear Baby:

We have just learned of your arrival in our city and want to congratulate you—and mother and daddy and everybody—on the happy event.

For a little while you will not bother your head about the big world outside. You'll just delight in mother's smile, and learn to wiggle your toes and with great frequency ask as best you can with a limited vocabulary, "When do I eat?"

But it is not far, my dear, from the cradle to college, from swaddling clothes to wedding gown; today's babe is tomorrow's bride. Now, mother will stand watch over you while a doting dad fights life's battles the harder on your account. But after a while you, too, will be grown up—a beautiful American girl, ready to step into a home of your own.

Wouldn't it be a fine thing for you to begin to build a bank account now? Then, by the time you are big, it, too, will have grown until you will have enough money to do any number of things—to pay your way through college—to buy that lovely trousseau—to buy for yourself the many, many pretty things that mother, perhaps, longed for.

We like the plan so well that we have already placed a dollar in a brand-new bank account for you. If daddy or mother will put a dollar with the one we have given you and will add another each month, your bank account will grow so fast that by the time you are a grown-up lady you'll have a lot of money.

Tell daddy or mother to come in soon and sign a signature card so that they can take care of your account for you until you are big enough to come to the bank yourself.

Affectionately yours,

A letter appealing to desire for knowledge and self-esteem.— A magazine for the general public is offered in the following letter:

Dear Mr. Owens:

If you think the world is larger than your parish, this letter has reached the right man.

If you would keep up with the newest plays in Paris, the literary gossip of London, the talk of the Continent. . . .

If you want to know the difference between rumor and fact about Russia and Germany, the truth about France and England. . . .

If you care for news from China and Japan, from India and the Argentine. . . .

If, in short, you want to talk intelligently or to listen with discretion. . . .

Then, here is the magazine for you.

From every large city in every civilized country the leading newspapers and magazines come to the offices of the *LIVING AGE.* There the editors select, translate, and reprint the finest material they can find—political articles, short stories, poems, and book reviews.

With the *LIVING AGE* on your table, you will keep up to the mark on foreign affairs every week in the year.

Here we wish to make only one point more—that it is of an extremely practical nature.

At the bottom of this page there is a coupon. It quotes you the generous rate of *Three Months for One Dollar*—the regular price is *Six Dollars* a year. Fill out and send it to us with your remittance, and you will find yourself looking at the world with a more understanding, a more interested eye.

Sincerely yours,

A letter appealing to beauty, exclusiveness, pleasure, and pride.—

A SAGA IN WOOL *

A short time ago, in one of the locked rooms of the Metropolitan Museum, I saw a rug, and I want to tell you about it.

It was an old rug, of a motif that predates Christianity; an example of a handicraft born before history and which lives on, owing nothing to modern science or invention.

This rug had been cast over a group of chairs, obscuring them under its negligent folds.

Within the room there was a stillness, faintly accented by the staccato voice of a distant Elevated. Outside, just beyond the huge expanse of plate-glass window, a gusty wind had arisen and was chasing rubbish up and down the street.

I straddled a chair, folded my arms on its back, and stared at the rug. It was at one and the same time the most subdued and the most vivid object I had ever beheld. The longer I looked, the more did I wish to look. Here was the immortal germ of artistic creation, woven by mortal and unknowing hands—the sole perpetuation of a vision, dreamed long ago and far away.

I gave myself up unconsciously to a long journey. I saw a blistered hillside; against it the sunbaked wall of a flat-roofed hut; and against the wall, beneath a crude scaffold, a rude loom. Below, a rough roller; above it, a dull cotton warp, golden brown by reason of the dazzling glare, and suggesting a foundation as basic as the earth itself. High up, the balls of yarn, a rare gaudy blob here and there, but most of them soft as the blossoms in a rose garden.

Most fascinating of all to my gaze, however, were the thin-fingered hands that plied against the cumbersome skeleton.

I saw no bodies, only hands. I saw these hands change from youth to old age; one moment smooth with the oil of youth, and next wrinkled and dry in old age—changing hands, but always the same rug, making light of a lifetime though itself not yet completely born.

With the passing of a decade, the weft shot from left to right; another ten years of brown-fingered painting of still music on a harp, and back went the weft, locking beauty in its cage. And always, just beneath the level of the hands, the pattern developed resplendently, until finally this vibrant, enduring fabric—with its strange power of remaining unsullied, of smiling across the centuries—was completed.

---

* Reproduced by permission of Mr. Jules Livingston, of the Livingston Company, Binghamton, N. Y.

Pressed by lips, knees, and feet, long since decayed; familiar of shrine and prayer, of castle and orgy; background for the changing web of soiled humanity; victim of the mart, bought and sold, sold and bought—and yet retaining within itself that indestructible essence of purity which dwells forever within the trampled soul of beauty.

How many rugs of this kind are there in existence today? Not very many to be sure—that is, if one demands AGE as well as enduring beauty. But there ARE hundreds of masterpieces today possessing all the subtle charm, romance, beauty, and that indefinable something we in the Oriental Rug business call "soul."

Yes, we have them right here in Binghamton.

If you demand something MORE than just so many square feet of floor covering, come over to Clinton Street and see these creations of the weavers' art. Look at them. Look through them and see the artist's soul caught up in a web of wool.

You will not be importuned to buy, but should you perchance be interested in possessing one or more of them for your very own, you will find the prices most reasonable.

We consider it a pleasure to display these treasures, and we hope you will come.

Sincerely yours,

Seasonal appeal—specimen letter.—Sales letters can often be advantageously based on a seasonal appeal—spring, summer, fall, winter, and most of the holidays. Here is a before-Christmas resultful letter that was sent to silver-fox ranchers:

Mr. E. S. Carson
McCammon, Idaho.

The Mrs. expects something.

You know how the fair sex are on Christmas. So give her, with all your love. . . .

A beautiful silver-fox scarf. One of your own fox skins can be transformed into a lovely neckpiece. That's a gift that continues to give pleasure for many years.

Such a gift bears eloquent evidence that you still care. Pays an appreciative tribute to heaven's best gift to any man—a good wife.

Let us convert one of your fox skins into an Elliott custom scarf. In style, workmanship and wear, an Elliott custom scarf has every refinement of a Fifth Avenue creation.

How much does it cost? You'll be pleased when you hear it—only $14. Surely that's cheap for the smile in her eyes on Christmas morn when she says: "It's perfectly gorgeous—you *are* a dear!

Obey that good impulse. Send on one of your best pelts immediately. It's the human thing to do.

Yours—for a real Christmas for her,

Exclusiveness appeal helps sell quality product.—What made the following letter that was sent to 140 grocers bring 12 per cent returns—17 orders within 2 days, with more orders following? First, attention is gained by placing the recipient in an exclusive group. Second, the benefit for the buyer is clearly shown. Third, confidence in the product is established by the guaranty. Fourth, protection of the buyer is offered in refusing to sell to price cutters. Fifth, action is stimulated in the closing and facilitated by an enclosed reply card. Note also the short paragraphs that make the letter easy to read.

We understand you are among the "400" of the highest class establishments in the United States serving a clientele that appreciates the *superlative* in foods.

Being not only up to the minute but ahead of it, you have heard of of Those Green Bros. Denver Pascal Celery, The World's Finest—unequalled anywhere at any price—Nutty, Crisp, Sweet, Delicious, Waxy white.

When you buy our Pascal celery—three of us have a treat coming, you, your customer, and ourselves. Your high class trade will be delighted to know that they can get our *Pascal, The National Delicacy* from you regularly.

You take no chances. We guarantee perfect delivery by fast railway express.

Our Pascal is so popular that many thousands of individuals in every state in the Union have ordered it as Thanksgiving, Christmas and good-will gifts—costing $1.70 per DeLuxe Box of 12 stalks. Our celery has a National reputation; you can reap the benefits, charging a price that will show you from 50% to 75% profit, and your customers will want it. You get the benefit of our wholesale price, because we can eliminate the cost of the individual DeLuxe Gift Box and "fixings."

We don't sell to price cutters. Please read the enclosed circular. Our price to you, delivered to your door—

Pascalettes (celery hearts), 4 to 6 stalks to bunch, per bunch ....

Country Club Brand, 12 stalks to bunch, per bunch ....

Shouldn't you start *right now* by writing an initial order on the enclosed postpaid card? Then, after you receive the trial shipment, place a standing order to arrive certain days of EVERY WEEK.

As Go Getters and "Profit Makers," do it now.

Ac-celery-atingly yours,

THOSE GREEN BROTHERS

Appeal to reader's vanity useful in subscription letter.—Attention-getting approaches are particularly effective when tied in closely with the subject matter of the letter. In the following example, a medical publisher appeals directly to personal vanity and professional pride. The ingenious first sentences impel further reading.

Dear Doctor:

Will you sit on a jury?

As a dermatologist, you naturally are a good judge of literature on the venereal infections. Will you examine the AMERICAN JOURNAL OF SYPHILIS, GONORRHEA AND VENEREAL DISEASES and give us your opinion of its worth to the average dermatologist?

Your examination of the Journal may help us solve a perplexing problem—how to find those dermatologists who want to keep themselves fully informed on venereology—and it may reveal to you an unsuspected source of great assistance in meeting some of your difficulties.

We don't know the answer to our difficulty—but we suspect it is simply to acquaint the non-subscribing dermatologists with the Journal. We, therefore, are considering sending the Journal on a free trial basis to a representative group—a jury—of them. And we should like you to be one of that jury!

Here's what we propose: To send the Journal to you for three months at our expense. We won't ask you to pay a penny for it—not even for postage! Our only request will be that you read it and analyze its worth to you.

We should desire you to judge the Journal as a juror—and bring in your verdict in the same manner! If your decision is that you cannot use the Journal—simply write us a note requesting us to stop sending it—if you like it and want us to continue it, you need do nothing further. We will then enter a subscription for you for a full year—we will not count the three months—and we will bill you at the regular rate of $7.50.

You can't lose—you will be doing us a favor—and you may gain immeasurably! Accept our invitation, on the form below, today!

Cordially yours,

Yes, I will serve on the jury! I will consider the Journal on your offer. At the expiration of the trial period, enter my subscription for one year at $7.50 unless I request service of the Journal discontinued.

Dr. ....

DS-55 Street & Number City & State

Convince the reader that your product meets his needs or desires.—You have secured the reader's attention with a good beginning and have made him aware of his need or desire for the product. Your next job is to convince him that your statements are true and that the product meets his needs or desires.

The methods by which you can carry conviction are illustrated in the following pages. These methods are:

1. *Guaranty of the product.* To be convincing, a guaranty must be expressed in simple language and with few, if any, reservations.
2. *Trial use or free examination.* This is an old stand-by and will always be one of the most effective forms of evidence. It appeals to the reader's common sense—seeing is believing—and to his cautious desire to avoid taking any risks or spending any money until he has had the opportunity to "show himself." Readers of sales letters have, in fact, become so accustomed to being offered free trial or examination of certain articles—books, for example—that in many cases they will not respond to a letter which does not contain such an offer.
3. *Samples.* The sample method is convenient for a wide variety of products—soap, tooth paste, perfume, hair tonic, shaving cream, cosmetics, breakfast foods, coffee, milk chocolate, wall plaster and wallpaper, paints and varnishes, beaver board, and so forth.
4. *Tests.* Tests as a form of evidence may be of two kinds: (a) tests that you, the seller, have made; and (b) tests that the reader can conduct himself.
5. *Facts and figures.* Facts and figures must be specific and must be presented in a form that will enable the reader readily to grasp their significance. For the general public, dramatization and graphic description are the best media; the reader can then visualize the data as a part of the story.
6. *Testimonials.* The reader is more likely to accept statements from a third person than from you. While it is true that in these

days many people have come to feel, as far as testimonials are concerned, that "the devil can cite Scripture for his purpose," nevertheless there probably never will be a time when a letter with testimonials will not be stronger than one without. Outwardly the reader may scoff, but inwardly he is impressed in spite of himself. For this reason it is usually advisable to include testimonials either in the body of the letter or in the enclosures.

Example of letter carrying conviction.—Almost every paragraph of the following letter selling a cockroach powder carries a conviction that is contagious.

Dear Mr. Ashton:

Every cockroach on your premises
is there with your full permission.

I will undertake to prove this to you—if you will give two minutes to the reading of this letter.

I will rid your premises of every last trace of roaches without one penny of your money being produced. I mean every syllable of that statement. I can't make it too strong. So, I am going to repeat it and emphasize it.

Tell me how many floors or rooms you have, and what size they are.

I'll send you enough of MURRAY'S ROACH DOOM to exterminate every roach. And they'll stay exterminated for one year by Shrewsbury clock—one year.

Now let me tell you what MURRAY'S ROACH DOOM is.

It's a powder that isn't poisonous. It is practically odorless.

It is distributed, first, by means of the Murray powder "Gun," which a ten-year-old child can use. Get it where the roaches are. Then the fun begins.

Roaches can't keep away from this powder. They love it. But the minute they touch it they actually go crazy. They race through every nook and cranny of their hiding places. They carry it with them. They distribute it where no human agency could reach. The young roaches, which very rarely appear in public, come in contact with it, and they're gone.

The strength of MURRAY'S ROACH DOOM doesn't abate for one year. As the eggs, which are deposited in the runway, hatch out, the young encounter the powder. And they're gone.

And I prove all these things to you by standing behind my 24-year guarantee of "No riddance—no pay."

You send me no money until the roaches are gone.

I'm even enclosing a Special Trial Offer slip which lets you in on a special price when you do remit—because you will......it never misses.

If you can name any fairer offer than that I'll gladly sign it—but, remember, you're responsible for the presence of roaches on your premises after this.

Very sincerely yours,

Trial offer brings in accounts.—The following letter, sent to several manufacturers of men's shirts, was directly responsible for three excellent accounts that buy several thousand dollars' worth of the firm's pins a year. The letter carries conviction through its offer to send a quantity of the pins, without charge, to the prospect.

Mr. Anthony Jones, please

Why have so many firms like yours switched to De Long Shirt Pins?

Because they have found, most of them by testing the pins before adopting them, that De Long Shirt Pins are the best kind for their purpose.

Would you care to test these distinctive pins? It's easy to do so—and it costs you nothing. Simply tell us which of the accompanying sizes is best suited to your needs and we'll send you a pound gratis. Ask one of your star operators to put them to a thorough test.

She'll like them because, thanks to their extra large, slightly dome-shaped, smooth heads, they won't irritate her fingers. Operators can pin garments with them hour after hour without suffering finger irritation.

As they have strong, smooth, needle-sharp points, De Long Shirt Pins glide smoothly through thick fabrics, and they don't make ugly marks on fine fabrics like silk.

Made of solid brass wire, *they never rust.* You'll agree that such pins are preferable to quick-rusting steel or adamantine pins which, by making unsightly rust spots on garments, cause no end of headaches, customer dissatisfaction and unnecessary expense.

Why not put De Long Shirt Pins to a rigorous test? Remember—it costs you nothing. Just tell us which size you desire and we'll send you a pound—about 4500 pins—without charge.

If you agree, as so many others do, that they are the best pins for your purpose, we'll gladly quote prices—prices which we're confident will please you.

May we hear from you in the enclosed no-postage-required envelope?

DE LONG COMPANY

Swatches attached to letter.—Swatches attached to sales letters provide tangible evidence of the quality of the product that the letter aims to sell. Here is a letter that carries a suggestive inducement in the last sentence and an action-motivating postscript.

Dear Mrs. Bruce.

They're here! We mean our new Quadriga cloth prints in dozens of most attractive designs and color combinations. Of course we don't need to tell you that the name Quadriga stands for high quality in prints just as the name Packard does for cars or sterling for silverware.

This nationally known print is the first piece goods line to be endorsed by the American Institute of Laundering. And remember, Quadriga is the 80-square print with a special needleized finish for easy sewing.

We are enclosing a few sample swatches to show you just how lovely the new Spring designs are. Vivid new florals in multi-colors, clever juvenile patterns, new geometrics and the always popular polka dots and plaids. 36-inches wide; guaranteed color fast. Priced only 19 cents a yard.

Don't they make you eager to start making dresses, a smock or a housecoat?

Very truly yours,

P.S. Mail orders filled on any of these prints. Designate first and second choice. We will pay postage on mail orders.

The letter is the proof.—A letter-service concern sold its direct-mail service through the sales letter that is reproduced in Fig. 15. The attractive appearance, the perfect matching of the fill-ins, and the clever use of testimonials—all were proof of the quality of the service the concern was prepared to offer.

Suggestions for expressing a guaranty.—Tested letters have shown that the following guaranties are convincing:

(1) AND HERE'S OUR GUARANTEE:

If, after you've read the first issue, you don't think the magazine is the most exciting, entertaining and VALUABLE you ever saw—or if you don't think you're getting back HUNDREDS OF DOLLARS worth of value for the one dollar you are spending—just drop us a line. WE'LL LET YOU KEEP THE COPY WE SENT YOU WITHOUT CHARGE. AND WE'LL CANCEL THE BILL ALTOGETHER—

April 2, 1940
Ahrend's 48th Year

Dear Mr. Harmon:

You are the man who ultimately decides every important move made in your organization. That is why we have addressed this letter to you. When your firm prepares a mail advertising campaign, you O. K. the plans ... you, as President, have the final word.

Isn't it a mighty pleasant feeling when your judgment proves to be correct, and at last you write "it worked" across a letter that pulled business for you? Hundreds of letters <u>that worked</u> are in our files .. Ahrend Process letters that brought in extra business even where it was believed no extra business existed. Each Ahrend letter succeeds because it closely resembles an individually dictated letter ... carrying a personal message from you to your customer.

To show his appreciation of the Ahrend Process, one of our friendly clients recently sent us a clipping from THE REPORTER, of an article by the Sales Manager of a firm which mails six million letters annually. He asked us to note especially these facts:

> "As a result of these tests, we have come to the conclusion that as a general rule the multigraphed filled-in letter fools no one.
>
> "The super process letter costs less than half as much as the Hooven letter and may be mailed under third class postage. We are finding today that the super process letter produces about as well as the Hooven letter and at a lower cost."

You are reading an Ahrend Process letter, Mr. Harmon. Have you noticed that your name appears twice? This is one of the Ahrend "matching" processes that help to individualize the letters you send. Ahrend services range from copy and art work, if desired, to addressing and mailing.

Let us adapt our forty-eight years of experience to the preparation of your campaign. Simply return the post paid card.

Cordially yours,

D. H. Ahrend

DHA:BB

Figure 15.—The Letter Is the Proof.

(On the original the black border was a royal blue. "It worked" appeared in red.)

OR, IF YOU'VE ALREADY SENT US YOUR DOLLAR, WE'LL SEND IT BACK TO YOU AT ONCE—NO QUESTIONS ASKED!

Repeated as follows in a P.S.

MONEY BACK GUARANTEE. We'll send your dollar back at once and you can keep the issue we sent, if you are not 100% satisfied with YOUR LIFE.

(2) All SHEAFFER pens are guaranteed for life, and the SHEAFFER LIFETIME is guaranteed unconditionally against everything except loss, for the life of the owner.

(3) In fairness to yourself—check the above questions before you buy. Only FRIGIDAIRE answers all of them in the way you want them answered. And only FRIGIDAIRE is backed by a three-year General Motors guarantee.

(4) The moment this booklet reaches you, turn to the back cover and read carefully the remarkable PAPEC guarantee, which has been printed for years and which no other cutter has been able to meet.

How to offer trial use or free examination.—When you have reached that part of the sales letter in which you are ready to offer the product for trial or for free examination, compare your paragraphs with the following for strength, directness, and tone.

(1) I am enclosing a postage paid card, marked for my attention. As soon as you return it, I will arrange to have a machine delivered to you so you can try it, and if you don't believe it will save you time and money, I will take it back—NO OBLIGATION ON YOUR PART AT ALL. Just use the card. Put it in the mail tonight with your name and date you want to try the machine.

(2) The book costs $4. And remember, after you have looked it over you are free to return it within five days—if you can part with it! Under these conditions, since you risk nothing, isn't it just good business to at least *see* the book, and then decide? The enclosed card brings it to you.

(3) The enclosed card requires not even a stamp to bring you a LONGWEAR GLADSTONE BAG, postpaid and free of charge. Compare it with any fine bag. Keep it for a week. Take it on a trip. Then. . . .

If you are convinced that there are more miles of travel-satisfaction per dollar in the LONGWEAR than in any other bag you've ever seen, mail your check for $14.85. Otherwise, return the bag at my expense.

(4) Simply fill out the enclosed FREE EXAMINATION CARD.

Mail it (no postage necessary), and I'll ship you one of these beautiful Bathroom Showers for you to look at and examine and use. Then, at the end of five days, if you don't think it's worth $12.95 instead of the $7.95 I am asking for it. . . . if you feel that you can part with it . . . return it at my expense. But if you like it—and I know you will—just keep it and send me only $7.95.

How to make the reader ask for a sample.—Is your offer of a sample inviting? That is the test after you have written the paragraph. The following paragraphs show by example how to make the offer of a sample irresistible:

(1) We want you to try HEINZ RICE FLAKES at our expense. So we'll send you a generous free trial package—enough for three delicious servings—free. Just fill in your name and address on the enclosed card, and drop it in the mail—no postage required.

(2) Let us send you samples of these sturdy, laboratory-proved COLUMBIAN CLASP envelopes for your heavier-than-letter mail. Just fill in and return the enclosed card—no stamp required—and the samples will come to you by return mail.

(3) This sample of INGRAM'S SHAVING CREAM brings you seven of the *coolest* shaves you've ever had in your life!

INGRAM'S is the first shaving cream primarily planned to take the nicking sting out of the morning shave and to leave a clear cheek and a cool skin when the job is finished. Its three special ingredients cool and soothe your face the moment you put on the lather.

You'll find that INGRAM lather is luxurious and extra-heavy—and that it lies close to the bristles and retains its moisture and thus keeps the skin surface wet. You can shave closer, or more often, without discomfort.

A week from today, after you've enjoyed seven cool INGRAM shaves, get the economical regular size of INGRAM'S—more than enough for 100 shaves. It's waiting for you at the nearest drug store now.

Examples of paragraphs asking the reader to make a test.—The directions given to the reader for making the test must be simple, clear, and explicit to insure favorable results. The following illustrations are suggestive of ways to express the invitation to try the test:

(1) Try this dissolving test. Put one of the new curly IVORY FLAKES in your hand. Pour a teaspoonful of warm water over it.

Then another. Notice how the flake melts away first at the curly edges—then completely! In the wash basin, one swish dissolves the new IVORY FLAKES instantly, even in lukewarm water—they can't flatten down on the fabric. No danger of soap spots.

(2) Here is the way to put SUNBRITE double-action to a real test. Cut an onion with a knife. Wash the knife in soapsuds. Then cut a lemon. The knife *looks* clean! But the onion odor still persists. Now sprinkle the knife with SUNBRITE CLEANSER. Rub, rinse, and dry. Not a trace of onion remains. That's the way double-action SUNBRITE ALWAYS WORKS.

(3) Will you try this experiment?

Ask your jeweler to show you a perfect deep-sea pearl. Put the enclosed DELTAH manufactured pearl alongside it. Then try to tell them apart!

The jeweler can do it—with the aid of his magnifying glass. But neither you nor any other person not an expert in precious stones can distinguish the natural from the manufactured pearl.

In luster, in weight, in iridescence, in color, the little pearl we are sending you will measure up to all the requirements of the genuine deep-sea pearl. Step on it! It will stand the weight of an ordinary-size man. Boil it in hot water! It will come out lustrous, with the soft opalescence that only a pearl can give. Weigh it! You will find it heavy, firm, indistinguishable in any way from the natural pearl, except to the expert with his magnifying glass.

An example of effective use of a test to convince.—If the seller has tested his product and wishes the reader to know about that test, the description of the test must be interesting as well as convincing. Notice how in the following example the narrative form of telling about the test keeps the reader interested and at the same time brings out the merit of the product:

Behind the footlights of Boston's Jordan Hall, four famed performers awaited the curtain...... four famous radio sets, hidden by a silken screen......ready for the tone-test.

And just beyond the orchestra pit—what an audience! Fifty-four members of the noted New England Conservatory of Music. *Teachers* of music—connoisseurs of tone—ready to listen.

The master of ceremonies was talking, "Each set will perform anonymously. Not by name, but by number. And to insure fairness, five senior classmen from the Massachusetts Institute of Technology will handle the sets."

Half an hour later a GENERAL ELECTRIC RADIO—known only as "Number 3"—had sung its way to a new tone triumph! Pitted against three *higher-priced* sets, it won the *best tone* vote of Boston's best-trained ears. Won *three times* as many votes as all the other radios combined....41 out of 54 votes!

In some instances it may be better to present the material showing the tests made by the manufacturer in an illustrated enclosure.

Examples of facts and figures to convince the reader.—To be convincing, the facts and figures must be verifiable. Notice how the following examples present verifiable facts:

(1) Fabrication economies possible with EVERDUR not only absorbed the difference in the cost between the two metals, but, in addition, provided an average saving in the cost of the finished bolts of 14.75 per cent for a thousand pieces.

(2) For with one motion, Addressograph does the work of 50 to 100 motions—10 to 50 times faster—and absolutely without error.

(3) Detroit's large department stores just recently made 672 sales from 2 small advertisements in the *Free Press*. One advertisement of 143 lines, single column, featuring a $1.95 dress, produced 511 customers. The other advertisement of 165 lines, single column, featuring a suit at $16.50, produced 161 customers. Here is a high rate of production . . . low cost of selling . . . $3,652.95 worth of sales from 308 lines.

Good selling knows neither seasons nor "situations." Here is proof . . . outstanding . . . that business is being done in Detroit . . . that *Free Press* readers have the dollars and are spending them with those advertisers who make a bid for their business.

How to write the testimonial paragraphs.—If testimonials are to be mentioned in the letter, they must be brief. The following short paragraphs can be adapted easily to any product:

(1) Over in Springfield, Ohio, the Armstrong Manufacturing Company has been making tubs and pails for 15 years. They used to make them from galvanized steel, but last year they changed to ARMCO INGOT IRON.

Why? Let Mr. Armstrong tell you in his own words:

> "We now use ARMCO INGOT IRON GALVANIZED SHEETS after having given them a thorough test to determine the workability and welding qualities of the metal. The iron

> forms easily, and the coating does not peel. Our loss, caused by the poor working qualities of steel, has decreased 10% since we changed to ARMCO. In addition, our tubs and pails find a more ready market, because ARMCO is so well and favorably known."

You, too, will find that the use of ARMCO will reduce your costs and at the same time increase your sales.

(2) The other day someone asked Judge Ben Lindsay, of Juvenile Court fame, if he wouldn't name his favorite O. Henry story.

> "My favorite O. Henry story," said the judge, "is *all of them.* No writer ever had greater knowledge of human nature, and the charm of his stories makes it possible to read them over and over again."

Have you got your set yet? Almost everybody else in this country seems to have. More than four million volumes of these inimitable stories have been sold to American readers in the past few years.

Getting the reader to "act now."—In the opening of your sales letter you have excited the reader's interest. With this interest as a basis you have proceeded to build up, by imaginative word-pictures or vital language, a description of what your product or service will do for the reader. You have cited facts and figures, tests, testimonials, or some other form of evidence. The reader now wants your product; and he is convinced of its value to him. But how are you to overcome his natural human tendency to procrastinate—to put off until "tomorrow" what you want him to do today?

The answer is, by imposing a penalty upon delay. Hold out an inducement to immediate action—perhaps a premium of some sort. Or, impress upon the reader the fact that circumstances over which you have no control have compelled you to limit the quantity of the goods that you are selling or the period over which you can sell them at their present price.

This idea has been applied in a great variety of ways to different types of goods and services. In the sale of books there is the "free volume as a premium," the "damaged book sale," the low price that can be given only for a short period because of "rapidly rising production costs." In the sale of magazines there is the "special introductory offer for new subscribers." In the sale of insurance there is the offer of a premium in the shape of a diary, a fountain pen, a wallet, and so forth, only a limited number of which are available for distribution. In the sale of jewelry and other merchandise, the "gift certificate that is worth $5 to you if you buy before March 1" has proved effective, as has the "special birthday-dividend check which can be cashed with us only if it is mailed on or before midnight October 31."

These are only a few examples from among many, but they serve to illustrate the point. To interest the reader, to make him want your goods, to convince him of their worth—these are essentials of sales letter writing. In themselves, however, they are not sufficient to induce the reader to "act and act now." To get him to do this you have to stir in him a definite fear of the consequences of delay on his part. Moreover, you have to give him a reasonable and specific explanation of the facts of the situation, so that he will know in his own mind that you are not bluffing but mean exactly what you say—that if he fails to act at once, he will miss an opportunity that may never return.

Make it easy for the reader to "act now."—Again, getting immediate action depends a good deal upon your ingenuity in *making action easy*. This may involve temporarily catering to the reader's weakness for putting things off. You need not try to get him to decide upon your main proposition immediately—he would probably balk at that. Besides, you can afford to bide your time. Instead, lead him off on the right foot by merely asking him to take the first and minor step—to mail your card for further particulars, for a free trial or examination of the goods, for a sample, for a salesman's call. Then, after he has taken this first step, it should not be difficult to keep him from turning back. Be sure, however, that you make plain exactly what you want him to do. Leave as little as possible to his own decision or volition. Do not offer him a choice of alternatives. Make the action to be taken clear, simple, and "without obligation."

Example of "limited-time" offer to get immediate action.—The entire letter reproduced below stimulates the reader to action. It contains an inducement to immediate action and shows how easy it is to obtain the product offered. Furthermore, its tone is adapted to people who are likely to want to understand accounting.

Dear Sir:

May we send you, with our compliments, HOW TO UNDERSTAND ACCOUNTING, by H. C. Greer?

Will you accept with our compliments, in return for doing us a small favor, a copy of H. C. Greer's HOW TO UNDERSTAND ACCOUNTING—a new, 250-page book which every man in business ought to have?

The favor is simple, and may in itself be highly profitable to you. Briefly, we want you to make a test for us.

In the COMPLETE ACCOUNTING COURSE described in the enclosed circular, we have something which we do not hesitate to call one of the outstanding developments of the day in accounting training. So marked are its advantages that we feel that, if once the material can be placed in the right hands, further urging on our part will be unnecessary.

This course has been developed by Northwestern University and is now used. . . .

And now here is the courtesy we would like you to render: Will you look through this course, go over some of the lectures, putting the material to any test you desire, and see if this isn't just the training you want to make the plans you have made for your business future come true?

If you will do this, we will include with your course, without charge, a copy of HOW TO UNDERSTAND ACCOUNTING. But whether or not you keep the course, *this book is yours in return for your courtesy.*

Just fill in and mail the attached reply card, and both the COMPLETE ACCOUNTING COURSE and the book HOW TO UNDERSTAND ACCOUNTING will come to you immediately. Then, after you have examined the course, if for any reason whatever you decide that it isn't exactly the thing to help you get ahead, merely send it back at our expense—and keep the book HOW TO UNDERSTAND ACCOUNTING.

But we must have your reply at once. THIS OFFER IS GOOD FOR A LIMITED TIME ONLY. So fill in and mail the reply card *now.*

Very truly yours,

Immediate action urged because low price is experimental.—Here is a letter that overcomes the reader's tendency to put off action by showing him that it is to his advantage to act now. The device used is to fix a new low price and to try it out for a month. The reductions in prices are explained by the seller's desire to make more sales.

Dear Sir:

I want to introduce to you, as an experienced traveler, a Gladstone Bag so handsome that you will be proud to carry it into the most exclusive hotel lobby.

I want to send you this fine bag entirely at my own expense—and you're to be under no obligation whatever.

I want to give you just a hint about the many features of this Gladstone that will appeal to you—and tell you how I can make a very low price this month to a selected group of men.

My LONGWEAR Gladstone Bag is genuine. . . .

You'll Like the Bag—You'll Marvel at My Low Price

I've studied the luggage business for a long time. I've actually sold a *half million* of my bags. And, as the largest distributor of luggage in the world, I can afford to sell for less.

Just a short time ago I sold my genuine Cowhide Gladstones for $19.85 each—and *that* was a bargain! Thousands of discriminating travelers bought them, many saying the bags were worth $30. I dropped the price to $17.50—and sold *more* bags—then to $16.50.

There's one further tumble—$14.85—and that I can justify only if it will boost my sales way up. I think it will—but I'm going to find out this month by trying this price to a selected group of men. So $14.85 is my price to you *if you act promptly.*

Buy or not—but at least *see* this great bag free!

The enclosed card requires not even a stamp to bring you a LONGWEAR Gladstone Bag, postpaid and free of charge. Compare it with *any* fine bag. Keep it a week. Take it on a trip. Then. . . .

If you are convinced that there are more miles of travel-satisfaction in the LONGWEAR than in *any* other bag you've ever seen, mail your check for my low price. Otherwise, return the bag *at my expense.*

But remember, this is an experiment to see if the $14.85 price will sell more bags. So, if you're thinking of getting a bag—even a little bit—you'll want to hurry your card along.

Cordially yours,

Examples of closings that stimulate action.—The examples of complete letters given in this section contain suggestions for strong closings that make action easy. Below are several more examples taken from letters that have worked.

(1) Don't let the heating plant dominate your home life. Find out now—before another day has passed—how little it really costs to enjoy Oil-O-Matic heat without work or worry. Telephone today for a FREE Heating Survey. This will prove an accurate estimate of how

much Oil-O-Matic heating will cost in your home. Installed in your present heating plant in but a few hours' time. Act now while present prices are in effect.

(2) This offer expires on December 1. If you are not prepared to order at once on the inclosed order blank, send me the attached post card, and I shall reserve a set for you for ten days.

(3) Five cents a week is the average cost to you for an intelligent view of Public Affairs if you take advantage of our special introductory offer of $1.00 for twenty issues. This offer is good for ten days. Write your name and address on the enclosed postage paid card and mail it now. We will bill you later.

(4) RIGHT NOW, not later, is the time for you to begin to watch sub-surface Washington developments, so that you may know what is in prospect, and be prepared to shift your plans and operations as the necessity arises. Use the enclosed order card to start the Letters coming to you AT ONCE.

(5) BUT LET ME WARN YOU .... this offer is such a sensational bargain that it has never been offered to anyone before. We will never offer it to anyone again, and it is only open for a limited time. You can cash this special birthday-dividend check with us only if it is mailed on or before midnight, October 31, 19...

....so don't delay. All you have to do now is to pick up your pen and endorse the check on the back. Then mail it today in the postage paid envelope. NOTHING ELSE. We'll do the rest.

How to write to special classes of buyers.—A sales letter to a special class of buyers is constructed in the same way as any other sales letter. That is, it must attract favorable attention, create desire, carry conviction, and stimulate to action. The fundamental appeals mentioned on page 346 apply to sales letters to a special class of buyers as strongly as they do to sales letters generally. However, the structure, substance, and appeals must be adjusted to the class of buyers. In the following paragraphs selected letters are presented that are addressed to particular classes of buyers. These letters have proved successful because they recognize the habits, tastes, desires, and needs of the class in question.

Hints that help sell dealers by mail.—A sales letter must take into account the following characteristics of this group of buyers:

(1) The dealer's principal concern is to make profits and turn the product over quickly.

(2) He is attracted by offers of help and service. The assistance may be in the form of aids in advertising, form letters that can be sent to his prospects, aids in window displays, offers of more customers, selling tools, instruction manuals for sales clerks, and the like.

(3) The dealer wants convincing proof that the product will sell readily and that sales will be profitable. Offers of samples, trial orders, and enclosures of folders and booklets help to get the order.

(4) The dealer, as a businessman, requires a short letter, written in crisp, colloquial language, and one that is attractive, colorful, and businesslike.

A sales letter to dealers that stresses the profit possibilities.—The following letter to clothing dealers stresses the money-making appeal and strongly urges the dealer to inspect the line with no obligations to buy:

Dear Mr. Smith:

If yours is the problem of getting more customers into your store, we know that we can interest you.

We are after more business and want part of yours by deserving it.

Frankly, the "Club Clothes" line is a profit-maker and in its price ranges it is second to none, for it compares on every point of fabric, tailoring, and style with the more costly nationally advertised makes. Repeat orders prove our profit claims, and today over 1,400 shrewd, progressive retailers throughout the country favor and feature "Club Clothes."

Why not let us prove what we say? Let us send you, for your examination, a set of suits which we wholesale at $19.50 to retail at $30, or a group at $22 retailing at $35.

The mere effort of returning the post card will bring these suits to you without the slightest obligation. Look them over carefully, giving them the most critical inspection, and we feel certain that you will quickly see the turnover and profit possibilities of the line.

Drop the card in the mail today.

Very truly yours,

What to remember in writing to executives.—In writing to executives it is necessary to keep in mind the following characteristics of this group:

1. An executive is usually busy. However, this does not mean, as many people believe, that letters to executives must be limited to less

than a page in length. A number of companies, including successful mail-order houses, have used letters as long as seven pages, with good results. Of course, the long letter must use devices for making the letter physically easy to read that may not be necessary in a short one. Such devices as frequent and interesting captions, different colored inks, illustrations, examples, and tabulations help to break up the letter.

2. He is on the lookout for ideas and products that will increase profits, promote efficiency, cut costs, and build goodwill. He must be shown with convincing evidence that the product has merit and that the price is fair. Facts, figures, and testimonials are effective.

3. He reads quickly. Present the letter in language that is easy to read. Clarity and language that appeal to the imagination are much more important than superficial dignity and restraint in the letter.

Successful letters to executives.—The two letters reproduced below together brought the TelAutograph Corporation over 36 per cent response, much of which can be attributed to the high degree of personalization, proper attention to the mechanics of fill-in matter, prompt follow-up, and attention to the interests of executives. The first letter drew a 25 per cent response—for the most part requests for the folders offered via an enclosed requisition form. The first line of the fourth paragraph was filled in with the reader's name and reference to his specific products, such as "Mr. Jones, other manufacturers of equipment such as yours have." . . . The second letter was sent out three weeks later to those who did not reply to the first. This follow-up letter drew a 15 per cent response. Enclosure of the requisition form, printed on a different color paper, enabled the sender to distinguish replies to the follow-up letter from belated replies to the first letter.

ORIGINAL MAILING PIECE

We have just completed a job for you. We are now ready to submit in folder form the results of our experience in working with basic systems and procedures of a sizeable cross section of manufacturing companies. We invite you to accept copies without charge and without feeling obligated in any way.

These folders will prove valuable to you as a check on your own plant's operations. They offer you a means of comparing your own systems with those of other plants. You'll find much helpful information in them that may enable you to cut corners in time and cost.

Our facts are based on actual in-the-plant surveys made by specially trained engineers—aided in many companies by executives like yourself. They represent our experience in a cross section of plants, both small and large, differing widely in physical layouts, nature of products and in volume of business.

Mr. Jones, other manufacturers of equipment such as yours have basically similar procedures. Of course, they vary in terminology and in scope for different types of business and for different plant sizes —simple in small plants and complex in large ones.

We present six basic systems: SALES ORDER . . . PRODUCTION PLANNING AND SCHEDULING . . . INSPECTION AND QUALITY CONTROL . . . WAREHOUSING AND SHIPPING . . . JOB COST ANALYSIS . . . OFFICE RECORDS-CREDITS-AND-CASHIERING. Each of these systems is discussed fully in an easy-to-read, graphically illustrated four-page folder. Three such folders are now ready to be placed in your hands:

SALES ORDER—Answers such questions as: What is the crucial test of an efficient sales order procedure? What are other companies doing to keep their hard-won customers from slipping through their fingers—by insuring fast, errorless service on orders . . . avoiding slip-ups on delivery promises . . . handling unexpected delays and order changes easily and quickly.

PRODUCTION PLANNING AND SCHEDULING—Gives you a quick picture of a typical planning and scheduling system. Tells how companies have developed systems that enable them to plan production on quick-turnover basis . . . how they get action on schedule changes instantly . . . stop production on not-so-urgent stock items . . . make way for rush orders . . . and keep inventories at a minimum. Discusses management's problem of correlating the responsibilities of the production and sales departments.

INSPECTION AND QUALITY CONTROL—Shows what other companies are doing to reduce their scrap losses, lower salvaging costs, hold down "off-standard" products, or "seconds," and eliminate production hold-ups due to late reports from laboratories. Cites specific examples in six different types of industries.

Experiences summarized in folder form, analyzing the last three of the six procedures, are now "in work." These will be available to you in a short time. All have this single purpose—to help executives like yourself compare their present mode of operation with systems now in use in other companies.

Since we are sending these folders without charge or obligation, it occurs to us that you may want copies sent to several of your department heads or systems men—in addition to your own copies. Please feel free to requisition as many as you need.

To avoid unnecessary delays in getting them to you, we are enclosing a convenient requisition form. Please check which of the folders you desire for yourself, and which ones we should send to other men in your company. Slip this form into the stamped envelope attached and drop it into your out-going mail.

Cordially yours,
W. F. Vieh
President

FOLLOW-UP LETTER

A short time ago I wrote you in regard to several new folders we've prepared for free distribution to the management of a cross section of manufacturing companies. As mentioned in my previous letter, these folders summarize our company's experience during many years past in working with basic manufacturing systems and procedures.

I firmly believe that you'll find these folders, as described in the leaflet enclosed, of great value. Each one presents a system common to your plant, to ours, and to the majority of all plants.

These folders not only offer you a means of comparing your own operating procedures with those in other plants, but included in each folder is a considerable amount of helpful information designed to help you cut corners in time and cost in your operations.

Since I wrote you, we've received requests from many hundreds of executives like yourself, manifesting great interest in our presentation of systems. We've supplied these men with copies, as well as their various department heads and systems men.

May I repeat my invitation to you to obtain copies of these folders. They will be sent you without charge or obligation. We want you to feel perfectly free to request as many copies as you need—for yourself and for other men in your company responsible for basic operations.

A requisition form and stamped addressed envelope are enclosed for your convenience in requesting copies. Please check which of the folders you desire and which ones we should send to other men in your company. It'll be a pleasure to see that they're sent without delay.

Very truly yours,
W. F. Vieh
President

Hints on writing to men consumers.—In writing to a businessman concerning an article or service for use in his business, the hints given in the preceding paragraphs on writing to executives should be considered. In writing to men consumers about an article or service for personal or domestic use, the following points should be remembered:

1. Men look upon expenditures as investments. A purchase of a home is an investment in comfort and security; a purchase of a radio is an investment in wholesome recreation; a purchase of good clothes is an investment in appearance.
2. They want to be shown why the product offered should be given preference. Therefore the reason-why appeal should be used.
3. They respond to the following appeals: ambition and desire for success, power, responsibility, recognition or honor, and greater income.

A good letter to men consumers.—

Dear Mr. Smith:

When you build your home, it will pay you to remember that cheap materials are not necessarily economical materials. Low first cost seldom buys durability, but often leads to expensive upkeep or replacement.

This is particularly true when metals that rust are used for service where water and moisture are encountered. Anaconda metals cannot rust and are by far the most economical to use. Copper sheet metal work, brass pipe plumbing, copper or Everdur hot water tanks, bronze screens, and solid brass or bronze hardware pay for their slightly higher first cost many times over by the repair and replacement expense they save.

The attached sheet points out those instances in which economy dictates the use of rust-proof metals. For further information, send the enclosed card for the booklet described at the left.

Very truly yours,

THE AMERICAN BRASS COMPANY

What to stress in letters to women.—In writing sales letters to women in the home, the following summary of the characteristics of this class of buyers will aid in helping the letter writer strike the correct tone and appeal:

1. Women respond to descriptions that envision satisfaction from the use of the article. Sell them "dreams of leisure hours, of rest, and of happy, contented homes, and simplified housework," says Marion Hertha Clarke.

2. They are not impressed by technical descriptions of the construction of the product.

3. They want to receive good value for their money. They are practical as well as visionary.

4. They are influenced by the physical make-up of the copy. It should be attractive and personal. Social stationery may be more effective than the usual business sheet.

5. The dominant appeals are: mother love, instinct for the beautiful, thrift, and the instinct to save labor.

Other helpful hints in preparing direct mail for women are contained in the following summary of a survey made by Miss Helen Slator, Director of the Consumer Division of Francis H. Leggett & Co., New York: *

(1) Women are fundamentally curious. They do not throw direct mail away. They want to find out what is in it.

(2) The morning mail seems to get the best reaction from most women. Women are more relaxed after getting the family off to work or to school, and can read the morning mail with fewer interruptions.

(3) Each woman who reads direct mail wants to know that *she is important.* Make her think you are talking to her as an individual.

(4) Women like "gilding the lily." They like to have appeals "dressed up."

(5) Women are confused by complex ideas. Make your presentations simple. Avoid wild colors, trick folds, die-cuts.

(6) Women like an unselfish approach to a sales explanation. That is, women want to know what the product will do for them, not why the manufacturer wants to sell it.

(7) Women are fundamentally honest and can understand or see through dishonesty or "white lies" better than men. So make your direct mail truthful.

(8) Women object to the words that men ad-writers put into hypothetical conversations.

Example of sales letter to women.—The following letter was sent out by a firm of New York resident buyers:

---

* The Reporter of Direct Mail Advertising, Oct. 1940, p. 8.

My dear Mrs. Babthorne:

Have you ever had some friend in the dress business take you around to a manufacturer's, and let you pick the exact model you wanted, at the wholesale price?

Remember what a bargain it was—how far below the regular retail store figure it was priced?

Well, that is the service we offer you on all your dresses and coats. We do not take you to one manufacturer. We bring the best from the stocks of a hundred manufacturers here, for you to choose from, at wholesale prices.

Now, here is the point. As resident buyers for a number of out-of-town stores, we are making the rounds of the manufacturers every day. You know yourself what bargains you can pick up even in the stores just by shopping around. Imagine, then, what we can do when we are daily shopping among the manufacturers themselves. Whenever they bring out some "Special," or whenever they have only a few of a style left, or whenever they finish copying their designer's model gowns, we get them.

At such a time the manufacturers, who cannot afford to bother with such small lots, are willing to let us have them at our own price. The result is that we can offer you many of the season's loveliest and most distinctive models, in all sizes, in the most fashionable colors and materials, at actually less than their regular wholesale prices.

Come and see for yourself. It costs nothing to be shown. And if you can save half on all your dresses, you wish to know it. Be sure to look here before you buy your next dress.

Sincerely yours,

How to write to business women.—The habits and needs of the business woman are different in some respects from those of women in the home. A letter to business women should take into account the following characteristics:

1. The business woman is in the habit of receiving business letters. The letter should therefore be businesslike in appearance. Ordinary business letterheads may be more suitable than social stationery.
2. She has learned how to be efficient and practical and looks for efficiency and practicality in the products offered her.
3. She remains ever the woman, and therefore the appeals mentioned on page 374 apply.

A good letter to business women.—The following letter, which was written on a business letterhead, appeals to the business woman's desire to appear energetic and pleasant and to her need to be comfortable. It also takes into account her taste for attractive clothes.

My dear Miss Jones:

Wouldn't you say that of the three or four top requisites for any woman's business success the one about second on the list is:

"Boundless energy and a pleasant face, free from nervous frowns." Wrong, uncomfortable shoes can affect everything from her posture to the expression in her face as well as the state of mind and nerves at the end of her busy day.

Some women seem to swing along so buoyantly—yet are always in the lead with the newest, daintiest, most frivolous new shoe fashions. They know that glorious extra support doesn't have to mean extra weight in shoes—when they walk on weightless Rhythm Treads.

You can prove all this for yourself in less time than it takes to put on your lipstick. Visit Stern Brothers third floor Shoe Salon—they have the exclusive on Rhythm Steps for New York City. Try on any of their gorgeous new spring Rhythm Step styles—then take three steps. You'll notice the difference quickly, we think—for so many women have.

Now is the ideal time to make this 3 Step Test. Stern's glorious new array of Rhythm Step styles is so complete you can easily find the perfect footwear companions to the newest fashions in your wardrobe—and with that extra comfort too, which is so important to the business girl.

We promise you—there's a real walking thrill waiting for you—in the newest, smartest Rhythm Step shoes.

Cordially yours,

How to write a sales letter to farmers.—Before you can write effectively to farmers, you must know the general characteristics of this class of buyers and adapt your letter to their traits. Whatever the product, the following characteristics of the reader cannot be lost sight of:

1. The farmer is concerned with utility and must have complete facts. He cannot be sold with generalizations; he is quick to detect insincere statements. Price, quality, and service are important considerations.

2. He has more time, except during the planting and harvesting seasons, than city dwellers to spend on his mail. Therefore letters can be two pages long and can contain numerous enclosures.

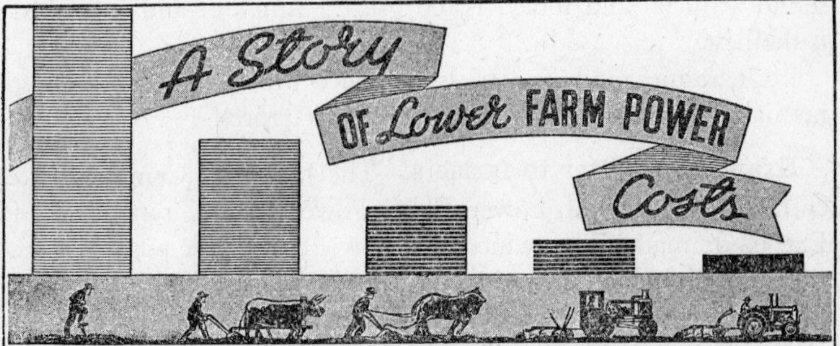

The cost of farm power was vastly reduced when man tossed aside crude hand tools and pulled heavier and bigger capacity implements with animals. Then came the tractor with a further reduction in power costs.

PRESENT day improvements in tractors are almost as striking in reduction of power costs as the change from hand tools to animals. For example -- a new Case tractor as compared with one of fifteen to twenty years ago of equal power costs half as much, weighs half as much, costs less than half as much to operate, is vastly easier to operate, and travels many times faster. All this means a great reduction in power costs and a greater opportunity for profit from the farm business.

Your problem today is a matter of selecting the right tractor and using it to best advantage. I hope, therefore, for your own best interests that you will read carefully the booklet enclosed. Written largely by present Case users, it gives

FORTY REASONS WHY CASE POWER IS THE LOWEST COST FARM POWER.

Inquire about the performance of Case tractors near you. Ask about fuels burned and the amount consumed, ask about wearing qualities, repairs, and other upkeep expense, ask about ease of starting and steering under load; ask about the resale value of used Case tractors, and you'll be surprised After four to five years of hard use Case tractors are selling for two-thirds the original purchase price. People are just beginning to learn of the performance and long life built into them.

Detailed catalogs tell just why Case tractors burn a variety of fuels from gasoline to furnace oil economically, require but little upkeep expense, reduce farm power costs and are the choice of discriminating buyers. These catalogs can be secured free of charge and without obligation. The enclosed card is for your convenience Merely sign and drop in your mail box.

Yours for a larger farm income
thru lower power costs,
J. I. CASE COMPANY,

Branch Manager

CASE

J. I. CASE COMPANY
444-454 N. Front Street
COLUMBUS, OHIO

Figure 16.—A Letter That Dramatizes Reduction in Farm Power Costs.

3. He is not impressed with fancy language. Nor is it necessary to try to use the farmer's language. The risk of making the letter sound artificial and forced is too great. Simple, standard English is the best.

4. Guaranties and free trials convince the farmer, as do testimonials, carefully substantiated facts, and figures.

Example of letter to farmers.—The J. I. Case Company letter entitled "A Story of Lower Farm Power Costs," reproduced in Fig. 16, dramatizes the reduction in power costs made possible by the tractor. The letter was printed on buff paper. Requests for catalogues showed that the letter was effective.

The letters used by the Southern State Roofing Co. in its direct-mail campaign, described on pages 381–399, are excellent examples of letters to farmers. They illustrate perfectly the four principles of writing to farmers, listed above.

Making a letter to professional people effective.—Among the professionals are lawyers, doctors, dentists, teachers, ministers, musicians, artists, actors, writers, and architects. They have in common the following characteristics that must be considered in writing sales letters to them:

1. Professionals are accustomed to weighing evidence and arriving at conclusions independently. The letter should therefore be phrased in a manner that seems to allow full independence of decision.

2. They are accustomed to dealing with individuals and being treated with great respect. The letter, to receive attention, must appear absolutely individual. Care must therefore be taken in making fill-ins match. The tone of the letter should be dignified and seldom familiar. The language should be conventionally correct.

3. The letter should be confined to one page in length. Enclosures can be used to convey the evidence.

4. Professionals possess an instinct for orderliness and beauty. The appeal to this quality may be used if combined with substantiated facts. If the article or service offered is designed to satisfy professional needs, the professional appeal can be used; if intended for personal needs, the appeal is the same as that of letters addressed to educated and cultured people in general.

A letter using the professional appeal.—Here we have a letter to architects reminding them of a certain product and the readiness of the company to be of service. The letter is really a sales-promotion letter. Notice its dignity, briefness, and tone.

Dear Sir:

Many architects are already familiar with the Westinghouse Magnalux lighting unit from experience. However, because it is such a popular unit and because it has so many fine points, I am reminding you about it by means of the enclosed descriptive sheet.

But, as you know, differing requirements of application, style, and price call for different units to meet those conditions. Westinghouse has a wide variety of lighting units to meet every sort of need.

The services of lighting specialists, who devote their full time to application and layout, are available to you for whatever assistance you may feel they can give you on your lighting jobs—at no cost or obligation, of course.

Whenever you want complete information on our units, or want the help of a lighting specialist, let me know. I'll see that you get it.

Yours very truly,

Follow-up letters break down sales resistance.—When a sale depends upon the cumulative effect of repeated arguments and appeals, or the presentation of new ones, follow-up letters help to increase orders. By a repetition of appeals and a variety of arguments, a series of sales letters tends to break down sales resistance and build up the desire to buy. This is a task that a single sales letter might not be able to accomplish.

Three types of follow-up letters are used: (1) the campaign series, (2) the wear-out series, (3) the continuous series.

How to determine length of campaign series.—A campaign series must be planned in advance. Six major factors help to determine the number of letters and enclosures, the length of each letter, and the time interval between letters. They are:

1. *The cost of the campaign.* Printing, paper, and mailing costs must be predetermined.
2. *The article or service to be sold.* If the price is high or the article is new, a long series might be required to develop confidence or wear down resistance.

3. *The price of the article or service.* The higher the price, the greater the sales resistance. This in turn influences the number of letters necessary in a series.

4. *Margin of profit.* It is important to know in advance if the margin of profit justifies the campaign.

5. *The type of prospect.* The prospect's age, intelligence, education, wealth, occupation, gullibility, or skepticism help to determine the number of units and the length of the series.

6. *Ultimate purpose of the campaign.* If the purpose is to introduce a new product, the series should be long enough to educate the prospect and create desire. If the purpose is to prepare for a salesman's call, a few one-page letters might arouse sufficient interest and curiosity to accomplish this purpose. If the purpose is to stimulate inquiries, then each letter should be written with this aim in view.

In a follow-up campaign, each letter is definitely related to the others in the series. Taken in its entirety, a series should perform the same functions as are found in a single sales letter—namely, attract attention, create interest and desire, stimulate conviction, and induce action. Letter No. 3 in a series, for instance, presupposes letters No. 1 and No. 2, and paves the way for subsequent letters.

Test mailing list with wear-out series.—The wear-out series is used principally to test the effectiveness of a mailing list. The length and number of letters in a series are not planned in advance, and subsequent letters are not sent out until returns from the previous mailing have been checked—and then only to those prospects who did not respond. Although all letters are prepared to sell the same product or service, each letter is separate and distinct from preceding or following letters.

Use continuous follow-up series to keep product or service before public.—The continuous follow-up series is sent out at intervals year after year and is intended to keep a product or service before the buying public. This system does not restrict itself to the sale of one article or service; each unit is distinct from others in the series. A department store used the following series in which most of the mailing pieces were in the form of printed circulars:

January........Announcement of after-Christmas sales and reductions in all departments.

February......Announcement of fashion show and sale of famous-make shoes.
March ....Three printed folders showing spring merchandise for Easter wear.
April ....Letter announcing new credit plan for customers.
May ....Sale of women's spring coats and men's suits.
June ....Folders for bridal gowns and trousseaus; folder of summer camp equipment.
July ....Announcement of special purchases in misses' dresses for weekend of July 4.
August ....Folders on August furniture sales and household furnishings.
September....Announcement of back-to-school sales and fall millinery.
October.........Letter advertising wraps and evening gowns for the social season.
November....Announcement and booklets of Christmas sales throughout the store.
December ....Special letter to persons who have bought books, announcing a book-of-the-month club, and soliciting membership.

Example of intensive campaign follow-up.—The following campaign letters used by Southern States Iron Roofing Co. illustrate a campaign by a company that has found direct mail the most effective medium for reaching its rather scattered market. The campaign was planned to cover the first half of a year. Its purpose was simple: to secure orders for steel roofing from farm owners. It had a secondary purpose of establishing a favorable impression for the company and its products in the mind of the Southern farmer, whether or not he bought immediately. The campaign consisted of two parts: (1) A mailing to a large list for inquiries (this was a one-shot effort); and (2) a concentrated follow-up of the inquiries from this big mailing.

For the first part, the company used two lists, one of farm owners and the other of former buyers. The list of farm property owners was compiled from the tax records of individual counties. The list to which the campaign was directed consisted of 479,232 farm owners throughout an eleven-state territory. The list of former buyers consisted of 26,921 names. Inquiries from either list received practically the same set of follow-up letters. The schedule of mailing was as follows:

Quantity	*Title*	*Date*
506,153	(1) Original mailing for inquiry	January 7 to 21
71,757	(2) Answer to inquiry	As inquiries were received
72,321	(3) 1st follow-up	February 12
75,841	(4) 2nd follow-up	March 15
77,126	(5) 3rd follow-up	April 17

The third follow-up letter contained a card on which the inquirer could request further information about a "Summer Special" combination offer on roofing and paint. The middle of April generally marks the end of the company's good season as farmers swing into their summer work. Rather than mail to the complete list of inquirers all through the summer, the list was cut down materially by asking for the second inquiry; then only those who showed their interest were sent the second set of follow-up letters. The following schedule was used for those who responded to the third follow-up:

Quantity	*Title*	*Date*
3,721	(6) Answer to inquiry	As cards were received
3,853	(7) 1st follow-up to that	May 13
3,919	(8) 2nd follow-up to that	June 5

The series of eight letters are reproduced with an explanatory comment preceding each letter.

LETTER 1

(Soliciting inquiries for "Roofing Book." Enclosure: Card)

For the 4:32 mail train

Will you accept a
valuable Book FREE?

In a few days I am going to send you an interesting Book that shows how to SAVE MONEY on Roofing. I'll tell you more about this in just a minute—but first, listen to an interesting story.

T. C. Kormat needed a Roof. He got one from a small Roofing Company (which has since gone out of business).

Ed Wilson also needed a Roof. He ordered an EVERWEAR Roof direct from the Sourthern States Iron Roofing Company.

Less than five years later Kormat had to do the whole job over again because the Roof he bought didn't last.

But Ed Wilson, who ordered the Genuine EVERWEAR Roof, still has it on his building. It looks just as good as it did when he put it on 18 years ago. Ed Wilson made a mighty wise deal when he got that EVERWEAR Roof.

By now you are probably wondering who I am and how I happened to write to you. My name is Charlie Foster. I am General Manager of the Southern States Iron Roofing Company, one of the oldest and best known Steel Roofing Manufacturers in the country. We manufacture Genuine EVERWEAR Roofing. I'm not bragging when I say that but I will admit that I'm mighty proud of the Roofing we make.

For over a quarter of a century now we've been making Zinc Galvanized Steel Roofs for all types of buildings—Steel Roofs *that have to be good* because they have the fine character and reputation of this Company built right into them——Steel Roofs that have covered more than a half million buildings in the South and SAVED MONEY for the owners.

Of course, I don't know whether you need any Roofing right now for any of your buildings or not, but I do want you to know more about EVERWEAR so that you can SAVE MONEY when you do need to cover some of your buildings.

EVERWEAR Roofing is made of PRIME, Full-weight, Grade "A" Steel, heavily coated on both sides with Galvanizing that is 98 and 44 1/100% Pure Zinc. And Zinc, as you know, is the best metallic coating for the rust-proofing of Steel. Therefore, EVERWEAR gives you long-lasting, water-tight Roofs for your home, barns, and other buildings—Roofs that SAVE YOU MONEY in the long run. It is Fire-proof, Lightning-proof, Rust-resisting. That's the kind of Roofing you want on your buildings, isn't it?

I'd like to go on and on—telling you more about EVERWEAR Guaranteed Roofing but this letter just isn't big enough. That's why I want to send you the Book I told you about in the first part of this letter. It tells you the whole story about Genuine EVERWEAR Roofing.

This book contains much valuable Roofing information. It shows pictures and descriptions of the many styles of Genuine EVERWEAR Roofing. Also letters from folks who have SAVED MONEY by using it on their buildings. The Book shows how you, too, can SAVE MONEY by ordering DIRECT-FROM-THE-FACTORY——and keeping all the extra profits right in your own pocket.

It shows the same kinds of Roofing that Mr. Phillips, Mr. Merdith, and Mr. Brantley have on their buildings. And,—

Mr. Phillips ordered his EVERWEAR Roofing TEN YEARS ago.

Mr. Merdith got his FIFTEEN YEARS ago. Mr. Brantley put on his first EVERWEAR Roof about TWENTY YEARS ago. And they all say, *"It's fine Roofing, it hasn't leaked a drop."*

These folks are just a few of the many thousands who have SAVED MONEY and have gotten better Roofs by using EVERWEAR. Let me prove that we can do the same for you. You be the judge as to whether or not you think EVERWEAR Roofing can save you money and also give you a better Roof. Just read our Book—see our LOW PRICES for this high grade Roofing—and then decide for yourself.

I've got your Roofing Book all packed up—ready to go. But I want to make sure that it's going to reach you PERSONALLY.

Therefore, to make absolutely sure that I've got your address right—and that you will get this Book without delay—just fill out the enclosed card and drop it in the mail. No postage is necessary—I take care of that when your card gets here.

Sincerely yours,

Charlie Foster

CF:AFT

P.S. When you order Roofing from us we pay all the Freight Charges.

LETTER 2

(Anwers to inquiries. Built around the "Roofing Book" (catalogue) that the prospect wrote for. On the envelope the company emphasizes that this is something the prospect has asked for. The letter plays up interesting points in the catalogue and tries to sell the prospect on the company and its roofing. A special effort is made to persuade the prospect to write about his roofing problems or to ask for quotations. Correspondence is invited by enclosing a "letter sheet" on which the prospect can write about his roofing needs. The mailing carries all the information necessary for ordering: specifications of roofing, prices, order blank, reply envelope.)

Serving the Roofing Needs
of the South for 26 Years

From the
ROOFING HEADQUARTERS
of the South!

. . . . Here's the Roofing Book you asked for.

When you have looked this over, you will see why 569,700 wise property owners have ordered EVERWEAR Galvanized "PRIME" Steel Roofing from us during the past twenty-six years. Some of your very own neighbors probably have EVERWEAR Roofing on their homes or other buildings; and they can tell you better than I can what satisfactory roofing it is.

But, I'm not going to take up your time, telling you why over half-a-million well-informed property owners think EVERWEAR Roofing is so good. You are much more interested in what EVERWEAR Roofing will do for you when it's on your own buildings——how strong and tough it is—how it will keep out rain and moisture—how it is fireproof—lightning-proof—will not curl, crack, or dry out, and how it will increase the value of your property.

You're interested in the low price and the fact that you don't have to paint this roofing every year to make it last. These are the things you are interested in—so that's what I want to tell you about:

—EVERWEAR ROOFING IS PRICED VERY LOW. Our roofing is priced low because we manufacture it in large quantities, and sell it direct to you. Look at the low prices in the Roofing Book I am sending you. You don't have to add any freight to these prices. *We pay all the freight charges right to you.*

—LASTS MUCH LONGER than ordinary roofing. When you put Genuine EVERWEAR Roofing on your home or other buildings you KNOW IT is there to stay for many, many years. Because it is made of "PRIME" steel, galvanized on both sides with a heavy coating that is 98 and 44/100% pure zinc. And zinc is one of the most rust-resisting metals known. This is why genuine EVERWEAR Roofing will last so much longer than ordinary light-weight galvanized roofing. In fact your EVERWEAR Roof should last as long as the building you put it on.

—EVERWEAR Steel Roofing is GUARANTEED. Every sheet of galvanized steel used in making Genuine EVERWEAR Roofing is marked "PRIME" before it leaves the steel mill. We insist that every sheet be marked "PRIME" so that we can guarantee the roofing to you. You may examine your roofing before accepting it. If you find that it is not as represented by us, or if you are not satisfied with it in every way, just send it right back to us, and we will pay the freight both ways. And of course, we will return all your money to you. You will not be out of pocket a single penny.

You Get These Patented End-Lock Cleats . . . FREE
(U.S. Patent Office Number 1880318)

You'll find the patented End-Lock Cleats, which we give you FREE with your order for Lock-Tight, Improved 5 V-Crimp, and Seal-Tight Roofing, are fully described in your EVERWEAR Roofing Book. Property owners find these patented cleats very valuable for holding down the end of the sheets where they lap.

There is a special EVERWEAR Galvanized Steel Roofing and Siding for every purpose. When looking through your Book, notice that you can now get DRAIN-type roofing as low as corrugated. See the safety drain in the Seal-Tight sheets. And see the tall sharp V-Crimps and wide gutter space in the Improved EVERWEAR 5 V-Crimp Roofing. And, above all, be sure to read—and study—the page on Genuine EVERWEAR Lock-Tight Roofing.

Notice how the side edges "lock-tight" together and form a water-tight seam, and how all the nail-heads are covered with the solid sheet of steel. Having all the nail-heads covered, this way, saves you a lot of time and trouble—and money, too. The sun can't draw out the nails. You won't have to go up on your roof every few years "to tighten the nails."

Now just in case you want to hear what some of the property owners who use our roofing have to say about it, here are just a few of their letters:

> "I'm well pleased with my roofing. My fire insurance agent changed (lowered) the rate, without my saying anything about it. I hope to send you another order this year."
>
> C. H. Arendall,
> Adamsville, Tenn.
>
> "Your (EVERWEAR) Roof is the best I know of. Every sheet cut square made to fit. I got my first roofing from you 7 years ago, it still looks like new; and 4 years ago I got some more. My father uses your Lock-tight and he's well pleased with it."
>
> Erwin L. Carmley,
> Brewton, Ala.
>
> "I received the roofing OK, in good condition. I saved at least $27 on my order. When I need some more roofing I'm going to order from you.
>
> B. T. Meetze,
> Lexington, S. C.

These good folks and a half-a-million others are enjoying the money-saving and trouble-free service of EVERWEAR Roofing and Siding. You, too, can save money and end your roofing troubles by ordering your roofing direct from our factory.

It is very easy to order from us at our low, freight-paid prices. Read how easy it is on page 16 of our Roofing Book. Ordering by mail from us is just as simple as driving up to our factory and picking out what you want. Here's all you do. . . .

. . . . Just look through the EVERWEAR Roofing Book and select the kind of roofing you want. Then measure your building (see page 16 of the book), fill out the order blank for what you want, and mail it to us in the enclosed envelope that needs no stamp.

Or, if you don't want to bother with figuring how much roofing you'll need, just put the measurements of your building on the enclosed Correspondence Sheet and send us these measurements. We'll give you, absolutely FREE, an estimate of just what your roofing will cost.

Send your order or the measurements of your building. Get the roofing and siding that you've been wanting. Don't let your buildings deteriorate. Don't put up with leaks and unsafe roofs. Protect your home, your family and property during storms of all kinds. And don't delay. There's nothing to be gained by waiting, as the freight-paid prices of EVERWEAR Roofing are now very low.

Sincerely yours,
Charlie Foster

CF:AFV

P.S. Guaranteed EVERWEAR Galvanized Steel Shingles come in 7 different styles and 4 beautiful colors. Write for FREE Shingle Book showing styles and colors.

LETTER 3

(First follow-up. A price hook with a time limit features this letter. It also contains all the essential information for ordering. Letterhead showed someone speaking into a microphone, and carried this message: Flash! Here are more roofing savings for property owners who act now. New . . . Lower Prices on EVERWEAR Roofing. Company's name and address were at the bottom of the letterhead.)

This Offer Good Until March 2

February 12, 19. .

"Now I can save you still
more money on your roofing. . . ."

EVERWEAR Roofing is already priced so low that only once in a blue moon am I able to write you a letter like this. However, this is an emergency, so we must tell you that . . .

. . . . for a limited time we are slashing prices on
all styles of EVERWEAR Roofing and Shingles.

This reduction will be in effect from February 12 to March 2. During that time you can get any quantity of genuine EVERWEAR Roofing and Siding at 16¢ a square below our regular prices. Steel shingles are 20¢ a square lower. The price list I am enclosing gives you the new, reduced prices, which may save you as much as several dollars on your order. Compare the reduced prices on this list with the prices in the Roofing Book we sent you not long ago, and see just what you save.

This offer applies only to orders mailed before Midnight, March 2. You would be wise to send your order at once to get the advantage of these low prices.

The Facts Behind This Unusual Offer

You may wonder what emergency would cause us to cut the already-low price of EVERWEAR Roofing. Well, the emergency was caused by the long cold spell throughout the Southern States during January. Remember those freezing days? You did not feel much like working outside and neither did the other property owners who ordinarily would have bought and applied roofing in January. They put off ordering until the end of the cold spell.

That left us in a "hole" because most of the steel we had planned to make into roofing and ship during January is still sitting in our factories. That would be all right except for the fact that 'way last fall we placed orders for 153 carloads of steel to be delivered now. The steel mills are starting to ship these orders, and we have no room to pile the steel.

When I called the managers together the other day, they said, "Charlie, we either have to rent additional warehouse space or sell a lot of roofing in a hurry. We must make room for the big lots of steel that are coming in now. The railroad is already starting to run the cars on our sidings."

Well, rather than pay out rent for storage space, we decided to pass this money along to our customers by temporarily reducing our prices. Naturally we would rather let you pocket an extra saving than let the storage man pocket rent money. Either way costs us money, but the first way saves for you, so of course that is what we want to do.

Why This Offer Must End March 2

Although we would like to continue this price reduction after March 2, it must end on that date. All possible space in our factories has to be cleared by then to make room for the shipments from the steel mills. This chance to save extra dollars on the roofing you need will not last long, so why not order today.

The price list I have enclosed gives all prices and other information necessary for ordering. Once you have figured out how much roofing or shingles you need, you can sit down in an easy chair and fill out the order form. We even pay the postage on the enclosed reply envelope.

SEND NO MONEY—unless you want to

We are glad to ship your roofing without a penny's deposit. When it arrives at the freight station, you may examine it to make sure it is just as good as we say it is. If you think it is not, just tell the freight agent to ship it right back at our expense. It will not cost you a penny. If you like it—and I believe you will—you can keep it and just pay the freight agent the reduced price that appears on the price list I'm sending with this letter. You don't have to pay him for the freight because we pay that.

We are not asking you to buy anything you don't see first. EVERWEAR Roofing must satisfy you, or you do not have to accept it. It is just like having our store right in your town, except that we offer you anything in our complete stock at direct-from-factory prices rather than high local prices.

Take advantage now of these "February Sale" bargains. Prices may not be as low as this again for a long time. Make out your order and mail it today.

Hurriedly,

Charlie Foster
General Manager

P.S.—Even if you do not want your roofing or shingles shipped yet, you still can take advantage of these low prices. Fill out your order and send it NOW—no deposit necessary. Add a note saying that you do not want the roofing to reach you until . . . (and fill in the date). We allow you to reserve roofing for shipment at "February Sale" prices as far ahead as March 31. The only requirement is that you mail your order by Midnight, March 2, and that shipment is made not later than March 31, 19. . .

LETTER 4

(Second follow-up. This was the most effective single piece used in the campaign. The certificate was filled in with the prospect's name. The two-page letter was run on the front and back of the letterhead. The envelope flash, the cover of the folder, and the first paragraph of the letter all emphasized the idea of the certificate and its value. The mailing contains all necessary information for ordering.)

This offer good
only until April 13, 19—

Now—save 50¢ a square on
guaranteed EVERWEAR Lock-Tight Roofing . . .

Your name on the enclosed certificate makes it possible for you to save as much as $8.00 or $10.00 on your next roof . . . IF YOU ACT NOW.

> Until April 13, this certificate entitles you to a special allowance of 50¢ a square on EVERWEAR Lock-Tight Roofing . . . the roofing that covers every nail head with a solid sheet of steel. Until that same date, it also entitles you to an allowance of 24¢ a square on EVERWEAR Seal-Tight Roofing.

This special offer is being made only to a selected group of property owners—to just 7 out of every 100 Southern Farm owners. We make it at this time not because we expect to make money on any roofing we sell at such a reduction but because experience has proved that one new EVERWEAR Lock-Tight Roof leads to another . . . particularly when the first one is used by one of the respected and well-known members of a community.

For example, when you put a Lock-Tight Roof on your house, folks are bound to notice it and ask your opinion of it. They may even come by to examine the heavy "PRIME" sheets and the sturdy locks that snap the sheets together. And we are so confident that you are going to be satisfied with your Lock-Tight Roof and give it a boost with many of your neighbors, that we are glad even to lose money to get you to send in your order for Lock-Tight Roofing at this time

Of course, whether we lose money is our worry; most important to you is the fact that by using your certificate and ordering now you can get premium Lock-Tight Roofing for only 39¢ more per square than 5 V-Crimp . . . as little as $3.90 more on an order for ten squares.

Extra Saving with Lock-Tight Roofing, Too

That 50¢ a square you save by ordering Lock-Tight Roofing now is just the beginning of your savings, for Lock-Tight is built to give you more years of fire-proof, leak-proof protection than any other sheet roofing.

You know from experience that most roofing troubles start right around the nail hole. A tiny drop of water leaks in; the decking beneath rots; the nail pulls loose; . . . and pretty soon this all adds up to trouble and expense for you. Well, Sir, Lock-Tight Roofing rules out all this trouble right from the start because on a Lock-Tight Roof *every nail head is covered with a solid sheet of steel.* This keeps the nail head bone-dry even in a driving rain.

Lock-Tight gives you extra protection at the three other vital spots on a roof—as the folder I am enclosing explains. This extra protection naturally adds years of life to each Lock-Tight Roof. When you divide the cost of roofing by the number of years you can expect it to last, you will almost certainly find that Lock-Tight is far less expensive than any other roofing.

Remember that the price of Lock-Tight even before this 50¢ special reduction was already the rock-bottom factor price, freight-paid to you. The additional reduction means that this is an opportunity that comes only once in ten years—an opportunity you should not pass up if you plan to buy roofing this year.

FREE Roofing Estimate Service

Without charge or obligation to you, we are glad to estimate just how much roofing you need and tell you in advance what it will cost, right to the penny. In order to get this free service, all you have to do is fill in the dimensions of your roof on the back of the sheet I have enclosed for you to use in writing me. I'll have one of our roofing experts figure your entire job and rush the figures right back to you.

How to Get Your Discount

Because we are not making this offer to everyone, we have registered the certificate in your name. It must be used only by you, and before April 13, 19.., in order to get this discount.

The folder that I am enclosing gives you the regular and also the reduced prices that you may have by using this certificate. It also gives you the facts about various styles of EVERWEAR Roofing. Select your roofing from it, and then use the enclosed order blank to mail your order before the deadline, April 13. Be sure to enclose your price reduction certificate with your order so that we will know you are entitled to the special discount.

I'll count on hearing from you in the next few days.

Expectantly,
Charlie Foster

CF:AKX

P.S.—In case you need some corrugated galvanized steel and have misplaced your Roofing Book, you can also figure the corrugated price by using the 5 V-Crimp price given in the enclosed folder. Subtract 7¢ from the 5-V price for 1¼ inch corrugated; subtract 12¢ from the 5-V price for 2½-inch corrugated.

LETTER 5

(Third follow-up. This letter asks for a second inquiry. The purpose was to cut down the mailing list drastically, since, by the middle of April, Southern farmers are exceedingly busy with their crops. The letter and card enclosed offer a substantial saving, but by experience the company knows that any farmer who takes times at this busy season of the year to fill out an inquiry card is a "hot" prospect and deserves concentrated attention for the next month or so. The letter also provides a way of bringing the company's paint line, which sells later in the spring, to the attention of prospects.)

Rush message—Mail at once

Read how this "Summer Special"
slashes 40¢ a square off price
of your EVERWEAR Roofing . . .

You certainly will not want to miss an opportunity like this, so mail the enclosed card at once for complete details of the "Summer Special" by which you save 40¢ a square on EVERWEAR Steel Roofing and Shingles—a saving that amounts to about 10% on most styles.

Here, in brief, is the plan that enables you to make such a saving:

> For every gallon of "Southern States" Guaranteed Paint that you buy, we allow you a reduction of 40¢ on the price of one square of roofing—any style or weight.

Take Time Now to Order—and Save Plenty

Since you probably will need paint and roofing before long, you naturally would be wise to buy them both at the best possible price. For that reason, this "Summer Sale" reduction (which lasts only to June 30) is your opportunity. You can make a saving by placing your order for roofing and paint at once—a saving that more than repays the small time and effort required for this. Even if you do not plan to use them at once, you can afford to order at this money-saving price and store them until you are ready to use.

Are We Foolish to Make Such an Offer?

We might seem foolish to some folks when we make a reduction now on roofing that probably will be bought anyway at full prices in the fall—but we do not think we are. You see, if people do not complete their roofing in early spring, they ordinarily put it off until fall, even though leaks threaten to ruin much of their property. They lose, of course, but so do we because our business falls off during the summer and we are faced with the necessity of either letting some of our loyal workers go—which we certainly don't intend to do—or carrying more men on our pay roll than we actually need in the slack season.

By making you an offer so attractive that it would be worth acting upon even in the middle of spring planting, we hope to keep our factories humming and our men at work. Will you help us by figuring your paint and roofing needs for the next six months and ordering at today's low prices? You will be helping yourself too, because every gallon of paint ordered means 40¢ saving on a square of EVERWEAR Roofing or Shingles.

New Free Book Tells How to Cut Property Upkeep Cost

Now, I know that up to date I have not told you about our line of "Southern States" Paint—so rather than just say that its quality is as high as our roofing in every way, I am going to send you a new book (coming from the printer in the next day or two) that is packed with facts about "Southern States" Paint.

From this book you can find out for yourself about the unusual spreading and lasting qualities of our paint. In addition it has many suggestions for lengthening the life of your buildings and farm equipment. Likewise it has money-saving ideas for the practical painter: how to make paint go further and cover better, how to prepare a surface for painting, how to make brushes last longer, what paint to use for each surface, etc.

As I said, I have a copy of this book for you, but first I would like to be sure you want it. Will you put your OK on the enclosed card and return it to me? The book will reach you within a few days then.

The same card will bring you the complete story about our amazing "Summer Special," together with a new roofing price list showing the regular prices on EVERWEAR Guaranteed Steel Roofing—prices that are 16¢ a square lower than they were in January. Thus the card brings you all the information you need for taking advantage of our "Summer Special."

Don't Miss This—Mail Your Card *Today*

Mailing a little card that requires no postage is a pretty easy way to save 40¢ a square on your roofing—why not sign that card right this minute while you have it in hand. There is no obligation, and it can save you plenty.

Expectantly,
Charlie Foster
General Manager

CF:ALM

P.S.—I know you will be interested in the recent results of 153 laboratory tests on our roofing at Pittsburgh Testing Laboratory, Pittsburgh, Pa. Scientists found that the weight of the protective zinc coating on EVERWEAR Sheets averaged 32% heavier than United States Government requirements for standard roofing. Because even a small increase in the weight of the zinc coating substantially lengthens the life of the roofing, EVERWEAR Roofing may last 64% longer than sheets which would pass Government standards as "good" roofing . . . and that is something to consider in buying your next roofing!

LETTER 6

(Answer to inquiry—second series. The letter makes a combination offer of roofing and paint. The letterhead was varied to emphasize paint.)

For the 4:32 mail train

How to save 40¢ a square
on steel roofing . . .

Enclosed with this letter is the paint book I promised to send you, together with a roofing price sheet and full information about our special "Summer Sale" offer. This unusual offer enables you to save 40¢ a square on roofing if you purchase your paint needs at the same time. I am mighty glad to be able to make such a money-saving offer to you, because my business grows only if I can save money for Southern property owners who are building or repairing.

Briefly, the offer is this: For each gallon of paint that you purchase you are entitled to one square of roofing at a 40¢ reduction from our already-low, freight-paid prices. The enclosed folder gives you the details.

Understand, please, that the roofing and paint on which this special offer is made are our full-quality, first-line products—the same ones that we sell every day at full price. We make such a reduction only because we want to encourage you to buy your roofing and paint now, rather than waiting until fall. That way—although we may lose money

—we can keep our factories busy and our men at their places throughout the summer, which is usually our dull season.

Figure What You Save

These prices make it worth while for you to buy now, even if you have to store your paint and roofing for a while before you have time to use them. The money you save more than repays the slight inconvenience. For example, on an order for 14 squares of roofing you save $5.60 if you buy paint at the same time. That's worth saving!

If you have absolutely no use for paint at this time, there is certain to be one or more of your neighbors who can use paint. By combining your roofing order with a neighbor's paint order you can still take advantage of this reduction.

To make it easy to order, we have prepared a combination roofing-and-paint order form and enclosed it with this letter. It has a blank for ordering paint and a blank for ordering roofing. These are on opposite pages, facing each other. Just fill in each one, and then for each gallon of paint ordered, deduct 40¢ from the price of a square of roofing.

We are always glad to hear from our friends like yourself, so be sure to write us if there is any way we can help you select the proper roofing or paint.

Cordially yours,
Charlie Foster
General Manager

CF:ALT

P.S.—Our Estimate service is FREE. Just send us the measurements of your building and we will figure, without charge or obligation, the paint and roofing you need and the total price.

LETTER 7

(First follow-up. Second series. Again it was necessary for the mailing to carry prices on both paint and roofing and a combination order blank. The letter and "?" folder were built around new laboratory tests that established the high quality of EVERWEAR Roofing.)

Spring Bargain Season
19. .

Here is what thrifty buyers
do when they want to be sure
of getting their money's worth . . .

They ask: "How does this product you are offering me compare with the requirements of the United States Government's Bureau of Standards?"

Through the years they have come to know that "Bureau of Standards requirements" spell quality, whether they are buying sewing machines or bath tubs, motor oil or steel roofing. The Bureau is Uncle Sam's checking laboratory. It sets up certain standards of performance and excellence that all products purchased by the Government must meet. Because the Government is so careful in its purchases, practical farmers and other businessmen figure that when they demand the same standards as the Government, they are sure to get full value and satisfactory merchandise.

Facts about Government Standards for Galvanized Roofing

The U. S. Bureau of Standards rates galvanized steel roofing by the thickness of its protective coating of zinc galvanizing; the thicker the coating, they have learned, the longer a sheet will last. Moreover, a small increase in the weight of the coating means a much greater increase in the life of the roofing.

In view of these facts, I know you will be interested in tests we had made recently on EVERWEAR Roofing sheets by an independent steel laboratory, the Pittsburgh Testing Laboratory, in Pittsburgh, Pa. They made a total of 153 tests, and found that EVERWEAR's zinc coating averaged 32% heavier than U. S. Government standards for "good" roofing.

What This Means to You

This means that you can buy—at regular prices—a roofing that is 32% better than Government standards. And because just a small increase in the weight of the zinc coating adds greatly to the life of the roofing—roofing experts indicate that such roofing with 32% heavier coating should last 64% or more longer than roofing that just meets Government standards.

Therefore, though you pay no more for the heavier-coated EVERWEAR Roofing it should give you 64% more trouble-free storm-proof service.

You can sit at home in your easy chair and order EVERWEAR Roofing by mail, direct-from-the-factory. The enclosed order blank shows you how to figure the roofing you need; and the price sheet shows you the details of each kind of roofing as well as the low, factory prices at which you can purchase now.

Our estimate service is free, if you would like to have us figure your roofing needs for you. Just send the dimensions of your roof to our experts and tell them what style of EVERWEAR Roofing you want. They figure just how much you need and tell you to the penny the freight-paid price on it.

Extra Saving on EVERWEAR Now

Right now our Summer Special on EVERWEAR Roofing and "Southern States" Paint gives you an opportunity to get this heavier-coated roofing at an unusual saving . . .

For every gallon of "Southern States" Paint or Varnish
that you buy, you are entitled to a reduction of 40¢
on one square of EVERWEAR Roofing.

Figure what this means to you: for example, on an order for only ten gallons of paint and ten squares of roofing, you save $4.00—a remarkable saving on paint and roofing that are already offered at bargain prices.

The enclosed combination order blank has space for ordering paint and roofing together, and it also gives you more detailed information about this "Summer Special." The price sheets on paint and roofing give you the information you need in choosing these products.

You need not send cash or check with your order. Order now, while the order blank and envelope are at hand. Then pay your freight agent only after you have examined and approved your paint and roofing.

This offer is good for a limited time only, so better act at once.

Cordially,
Charlie Foster
General Manager

CF:AMD

P.S.—If you have no need for both paint and roofing at this time, please do not hesitate to order just the one product you do need. The enclosed price sheets give the correct prices to use in ordering either paint or roofing by themselves, and you may use the enclosed order blank to return your order for fast service.

LETTER 8

(Second follow-up. Second series. In this letter roofing is ignored completely, and a paint special is concentrated upon. This is the last letter of the follow-up campaign.)

Next week I am sending you
a full gallon of paint FREE
to try at my expense . . .

Will you fill in (on the slip I am enclosing) the grade and color of house paint that you want? Then I can send you by return freight a full gallon of "Southern States" paint absolutely free.

The idea is that you agree to take this free gallon of paint and try it on your home or outbuilding—you to be the sole judge of whether it is the best paint you ever bought at its price. The only requirement is that, at the time I send you the free gallon, you place a tentative order for at least five more gallons of the same grade paint. By the time you have used up that first trial gallon, I feel you will agree with thousands of other Southern property owners that "Southern States" is the most paint for the money on the market today. If you don't, then just return the remaining five gallons to us at our expense . . . and without obligation to you in any way.

How can you lose on this offer?

We give you the first gallon free so that you can find out about our paint without risking one penny of your own. The decision is entirely up to you. If you say, "No, I don't like your paint," we take back the remaining five gallons and instantly refund any freight or money you have paid. If you do like the paint—and we believe you will—the first extra gallon is still yours FREE, and you can finish your painting with the remaining five gallons . . . and pay us just the low, freight-paid price on them.

By taking advantage of this offer, you get six gallons of paint at our usual price for five. For example, if you order "Southern States" First-Quality House Paint, we would send you one gallon free and then five at the regular price of $2.40 per gallon: a total of only $12 for six gallons or at the amazingly low price of $2 per gallon for what is practically the finest house paint made—a paint that few local dealers can begin to equal at less than $3.50 a gallon.

You don't have to take our word for how good our paints are: we are giving you the opportunity to try them without risking a cent. You may choose a free trial gallon of any of these four grades:

"Southern States" First-Quality House Paint	$2.40 per gal.
"Economy" House Paint	1.65 per gal.
Mildew-Resisting Paste Paint	3.34 per gal.
Barn & Roof Paint	1.40 per gal.

You will find these listed on the enclosed price sheet, together with a complete description and all colors. You may order several different colors if you want, rather than have all six gallons one color.

You won't have to bother about thinner either. You always get a gallon of turpentine FREE with every five gallons of "Southern States" paint. The turpentine will be sent right along with your paint.

How to get your free trial gallon—*Be sure to read this.*

You may give us the information about the trial gallon you want in the space provided on the pink request slip. Then attach this slip to a tentative order (on the regular paint order blank) for five gallons more to be shipped at the same time that we send the test gallon. You can either send payment for the five gallons with your order, or else we are glad to ship them to you C. O. D. In either case, at any time after you have tested the first gallon and decide that you do not want to keep the other five, your money is subject to instant refund.

Since we pay the freight on all orders for five gallons or more, there will be no freight charges for you to pay.

This opportunity to test "Southern States" paint at our expense is good only until June 30, so fill out the request and mail it today. The paint is all ready to ship to you. All I need is your "OK."

Expectantly,
CF:AML Charlie Foster

P.S.—Whether you keep or return the five gallons, the one FREE gallon is yours without obligation. There are no "strings" to our offer.

Where to mention price in a sales letter.—The traditional treatment of price in a sales letter is to have it follow the sales talk. However, the price can appear in any part of the letter if it is handled properly. In the letter on page 402 it is referred to in the first paragraph; in the letter on page 342 it is mentioned in the third paragraph; in the letter on page 350 it appears at the end.

Hints for proper handling of price.—The following hints for proper handling of price have been offered by experienced sales letter writers:

1. Don't appear to apologize for the price. Avoid getting into the frame of mind where you think your price is high, and you will avoid unconsciously apologizing for the price.

2. Don't use such expressions as "and the price is amazingly little," or, "the price is only $350," to minimize the price.

3. Give the price the appearance of being small by presenting it in understandable terms of how little it is for the value received, as,

for example, the price per day if the item is a service for a year; the cost per year if the product has a long life, and the like. The advertising salesmen of the *Saturday Evening Post* make the $8,000 page rate appear small by quoting it at $3 a page to reach 1,000 readers.

4. Quote the price clearly; don't make it necessary for the reader to figure out how much the product will cost; don't leave room for misunderstanding.

5. When the selling appeal is based exclusively on the greatly reduced or lower-than-average price, state convincingly why the reduction has been made; otherwise the prospect will doubt the quality of the product. In the letter on page ...... the manufacturer shows clearly how he saves the buyer $100 a month. Other reasons might be given for low price, such as a statement that the seller eliminates the profit taken by distributors and dealers by selling directly to the consumer, or by selling only for cash.

Devices that make sales letters work.—A good sales letter can be made a better sales letter if it is combined with a device for getting attention and action. In the following paragraphs examples are given of devices that have given sales letters a special pulling power.

Extra-size letter.—The following letter took the form of a self-mailing folder measuring $13\frac{1}{2} \times 21\frac{1}{2}$ inches when open. It was folded in half from left to right and then three times to measure $4\frac{1}{2} \times 10$ inches when folded for mailing. An attractive illustration on the address side suggested that the reader open the folder. When the folder was opened, there appeared these words in a design that suggested speed: "There's a big letter for you inside." Then appeared the following letter in enormous typewriter type, on an enlarged J. I. Case Company letterhead. The number of cards received and the number of farmers who visited Case dealers to see the mower and other hay tools were evidence that the mailing piece was effective.

Hay Time Is
No Play Time

When it's time to make hay there's no time to waste with machinery that breaks down or gives trouble in the field. Maybe there's corn to be laid by, grain harvest coming on, perhaps something else—but there's always something to make haying a rush season job.

And it's no time to make your horses pull a hard-running mower.

After the long, hard grind of spring work they are in no shape to worry along under a load of neck weight and side draft. It's hot, sultry weather, and you need to keep them in good condition for harvest.

Maybe you can afford hours of wasted labor—possibly your horses can stand the risk of sore necks—but nobody can afford to take chances on a hay crop. Don't blame the weather entirely for sun-bleach, rain-damage, leaf-loss, and the other things that make the difference between hay worth a good price on the market or in your own mangers, and the other kind—at which both buyers and "bossies" turn up their noses.

With exceedingly few exceptions you can beat the weather and escape most of these losses if you use a modern method of hay making and have machinery you can depend on to get every job done right on time. For the cutting operation you can't beat the Case Hi-Lift Oil Bath Mower described in the enclosed folder. The difference in quality and value of hay on only ten acres might easily pay for it in a single year. But this is a mower that will give you years of good service. It is light-running and has easy adjustments for maintaining a clean cut and minimizing the replacement of working parts.

Don't wait until the last minute—see this great mower now at your Case dealer.

At the same time get full information on Case sulky and side delivery rakes as well as the new Case combination cylinder and push bar hay loader with tight bottom—the loader that has the best features of both types, and saves a lot of loose leaves. Learn all about the pick-up method of baling hay or straw that puts it in the bale with less labor than to put it in a stack. Just check the enclosed card, sign and drop it in the mail.

Very truly yours,

Devices to facilitate action by the reader.—The fact that it contains a device to make it easy for the reader to act is one of the reasons for the success of the letter reproduced on page 402. An application is attached to the letter; the need for an envelope is eliminated; and the directions for forwarding are simple. Notice the following about the letter:

(1) Its handling of price. "We have just put a NEW accident policy on the market that COSTS ONLY ONE CENT A DAY!"

(2) The tie-up with the benefit to the prospect.

(3) The convincing figures to prove that the policy meets the reader's needs. "More than A QUARTER MILLION people have already bought Postal accident policies."

N M EBY PRESIDENT
E O KUNAU, VICE PRESIDENT
L WIEBELER TREASURER

Policy Holders from Coast to Coast
ESTABLISHED 1927

J W WALKER VICE PRESIDENT
M H GREGORY SECRETARY
A B MAHON ASST TREASURER

POSTAL LIFE INSURANCE & CASUALTY COMPANY

4727 WYANDOTTE STREET
KANSAS CITY, MO.

Dear Friend:

We have just put a NEW accident policy on the market that COSTS ONLY ONE CENT A DAY!

This policy will pay you up to $100.00 a month for a period of TWENTY-FOUR MONTHS if you are disabled.

It has a special HOSPITAL BENEFIT which pays in addition as much as $50.00 a month for TWO MONTHS for hospital care in accidental injury.

It pays up to $1,000.00 to your beneficiary if you are killed! And it covers accidents such as happen every day--accidents due to riding in or driving automobiles, house trailers, trucks, taxicabs or buses (including school or chartered buses); being struck by vehicles on any public street, road or highway; accidents while operating or riding in trains, street cars, elevators, mail, express or baggage cars; accidents while riding as a fare-paying passenger on a regularly scheduled airplane.

It also covers being injured or killed by lightning, tornadoes, hurricanes; by the collapse of the outer walls of a building or the burning of any church, theater, library, school or public building and numerous other accidents. This new policy covers farm implement, wagon, and tractor accidents--being kicked by a horse or mule, or gored by a bull or cow--and accidents while riding a bicycle.

As an emergency benefit, the company will pay all expenses up to $100.00 of putting you in touch with friends or relatives if you are injured

A medical benefit of $20.00 is provided in case of minor injuries--this benefit alone is nearly six times the amount of the yearly premium.

Think of all this protection for only $3.65 a year! You do not have to be killed to secure the indemnity, but if you are killed, it pays for that too. So you have protection whether you live or die.

More than A QUARTER MILLION people have already bought Postal accident policies. Men, women and children are eligible. No medical examination is required, and it does not matter how many other policies you have.

Just fill in and return application today! Don't send any money. See the policy first and if you're satisfied, then just mail your check for $3.65.

The policy will be sent directly to you and no salesman will call.

Sincerely yours,

J. W. Walker
Vice President

JWW:A
27

REFERENCES. TRADERS GATE CITY NATIONAL BANK · PLAZA BANK OF COMMERCE · FIRST NATIONAL BANK

OVER ONE-HALF MILLION DOLLARS PAID IN CLAIMS

COPYRIGHT 1939

NO ENVELOPE NECESSARY
JUST—FOLD, SEAL AND MAIL

APPLICATION

This Policy Is Issued to Men, Women and Children. To Avoid Any Errors Please Print All Information.

Please send me one of your NEW, IMPROVED accident policies for FREE EXAMINATION, without obligation. If I decide to keep the policy I will send you a check for $3.65 to cover the first year's premium. I certify that I am in sound condition mentally and physically and that the following answers are true and correct.

Full Name ______________________
PRINT NAME IN FULL

Address ______________________
STREET NO. OR R. F. D.

____
CITY STATE

Sex ______ Age ______ Birth Date: Month ______ Day ______ Year ______

Occupation ______________________

Print below name, address and relation of person to whom you want insurance paid in case you are killed.

Beneficiary ______________________
NAME RELATIONSHIP

Address ______________________

If you want additional applications for friends or relatives, check here (______).

Figure 17.—A Sales Letter That Has Met All Tests.

(4) The evidence of confidence in what is offered. "Don't send any money. See the policy first and, if you're satisfied, then just mail your check for $3.65."

(5) The stimulation to one specific action at the close.

Reply-O-Letter makes it easy for the reader to act.—The Reply-O-Letter is a patented device used by the Reply-O-Products Corporation, New York, in the letter service that it supplies. The reply card is slipped into a pocket attached to the letter. The card serves as the inside address on the letter and makes it unnecessary for the person to whom it is addressed to write his name and address on the card. It also enables the sender to check the exact number of replies to a letter sent out with the reply card. Companies which have used the Reply-O-Letter have indicated that it has helped to increase the percentage of returns and has also cut operating costs by reducing the motions required to complete a campaign.

Personalization and showmanship important.—By catching the eye and persuading attention through personalization, the following letter (Fig. 18) produced excellent results for Mailings, Incorporated, a direct-mail service. The prospect's name was written across the top, brush-scripted in gold paint. An Aspirin tablet was attached on the left. Here was showmanship and personalization of a high order.

Form letter personalized by photos.—What better way to get "in step" with the reader at the outset than to let him come face to face with his own photograph? By using the pictures of hotel executives published in a trade journal, an Indiana furniture firm constructed a novel letter to be sent to the person photographed. A form letter on the subject of hotel chairs was prepared, and the picture of the executive was cut out and pasted at the top of the letterhead. Alongside the picture, the following copy was typewritten:

GOOD MORNING
You look to me like a man
who would appreciate
GOOD HOTEL CHAIRS

An additional copy of the hotel publication was secured, and a similar cutout was pasted on the envelope next to the name and address.

Does your D. M. give you a headache?

Here's relief:

No --- not Aspirin --- but experience!

Patent medicines, panaceas and poultices have their place --- but, they try to correct, they don't prevent.

If you're displeased with your Direct Mail results --- perhaps we can be the Doctor.

We can apply "preventative medicine" or give your direct mail a tonic stimulant. Experience in creating and producing millions of mailing pieces (5,000,000 for the Book-of-the-Month Club alone) has taught us what to do and what not to do.

Most doctors charge a fee for consultation. We run a Clinic --- diagnose your case and prescribe copy and ideas without charge.

If you should retain us for treatment, you will receive the skilled services of a Specialist at the modest fee of a General Practitioner.

There's a Prescription card enclosed that's already filled in with your name. It will bring a Specialist and Case Histories of remarkable cures.

Professionally yours,

Lewis Kleid

LEWIS KLEID, President

LK:G

Mailings incorporated 25 WEST 45th STREET • NEW YORK CITY

Figure 18.—Showmanship in a Personalized Sales Letter.

The envelope and letter succeeded in securing eye attention from the reader, and the envelope had a better chance of getting past the mail clerk and into the hands of the executive.

Novel presentation of testimonials.—Miniature testimonial letters were inserted in the sales letter of the Mutual Broadcasting System, reproduced below. The miniatures were kept in place by means of a pocket placed in back of the letterhead. The reproductions were graduated in length so that each letterhead would show. (See Fig. 19) The shortest measured 2½ inches; the longest, 3½ inches. A black arrow above the date pointed to the insertion. The letter merely calls attention to "what leading advertisers are actually doing about Mutual's new Volume Plan."

Tie-up with premium.—Using a rabbit's foot charm as a premium in a direct-mail campaign to sell accident policies required a letter that brought both the superstition and the premium to the attention of the prospect. A provocative opening question and a closing reference to the premium, in the Maryland Casualty Company letter reproduced below, shows a simple but effective tie-in. A common-sense appeal, supported by facts, is used.

My dear Mr. Hunt:

Would you trust to luck to protect you against accidents, Mr. Hunt? Even a good luck charm will not prevent them. It is an established ract that one person in twenty-seven will be seriously injured this year. You may be that one.

If you are, your income is more needed than ever. Your home expenses must go on and in addition there are hospital, doctors' and nurses' bills. Accident Insurance guarantees you a weekly income while you are disabled, plus payment of hospital, doctors' and nurses' bills up to the amount specified in the policy. You can relax from worry.

Invest in an accident policy. Then, if you are injured, you will be lucky. One of our agents, Mr. Robert L. Ward, Parker Building, Bridgeville, will call on you within a few days. Incidentally, he has a rabbit's foot charm for you.

Yours very truly,
Vice-President

Rabbit's Foot Accident

MUTUAL BROADCASTING SYSTEM

NEW YORK OFFICES ★ 1440 BROADWAY

Sept. 11, 1940

Mr. Robert Bruce
Prentice-Hall, Inc.
New York City

Dear Mr. Bruce:

Recently, in a booklet of school-pad proportions,* complete with pencil, we pointed out that Mutual's new Volume Plan stands ready to save you 20 - 30% of your network time cost.

Attached here, is a story of a different color -- a fact, not a forecast. A story of what leading advertisers are actually doing about Mutual's new Volume Plan.

It is the story of three of the latest clients to sign Mutual volume contracts.

And by the way, isn't this a three-fold answer to the armchair critics who confide, "Certainly it's a marvelous value, but can Mutual clear time?"

Sincerely,

Robert A. Schmid

Robert A. Schmid
Director of Advertising

RAS:LP

*If by any chance you failed to receive your copy of "Air-rithmetic", or would find another helpful, we would be glad to send one of our limited supply on its way.

Figure 19.—Novel Presentation of Testimonials.

How to get the most out of successful sales letters.—A letter that has brought results can be used again and again. It should not be discarded until it ceases to work.

A successful letter can even be repeated as a follow-up. Variations can be added to get attention. The following devices have been used successfully on repeat letters:

1. Reproduce the letter on a different colored paper with the word C O P Y in red ink across its face and a brief note in red ink in the upper right-hand corner. One firm added the following note:

> "91 Arizona employers accepted the offer made in my letter of July 5.
>
> "With the thought that the original may not have reached you, I am sending this duplicate.
>
> "I hope you, too, will want to take advantage of this special offer.
>
> D.A.L."

2. Use the same letter with a handwritten and initialed sentence at the top of the page, such as: "Did you overlook this letter mailed to you recently? D.A.L."

SECTION 4

Advertising

1. UNDERSTANDING THE FUNCTION OF ADVERTISING

2. ADVERTISING AGENCIES

3. FIXING THE ADVERTISING APPROPRIATION

4. ADVERTISING MEDIA

5. TESTING YOUR ADVERTISING

Pretesting by the Sales-Area Method

Pretesting by the Inquiries Method

Pretesting by the Consumer-Jury Method

6. HOW TO DESIGN AND REGISTER A TRADE-MARK

7. COPYRIGHT PROCEDURE

8. PRINTING AND TYPOGRAPHY

9. GLOSSARY OF ADVERTISING PROCEDURE

SECTION 4

Advertising*

I. UNDERSTANDING THE FUNCTION OF ADVERTISING

What is advertising?—Advertising is not necessarily what you see or hear. That advertisement in a national magazine or newspaper, that program you hear over the air—that is not "advertising"; that is merely a part of advertising.

Advertising is not a "thing apart." It is not divorced from the rest of business. In fact, it cannot be successful unless and until it is part and parcel of business.

There is only one way to obtain an accurate answer to the question, What is advertising? and that is, to study a list of the functions of a large advertising and sales-promotion department.

Functions of an advertising department.—If you could sit down with the executive in charge of such a department, in the offices of a company spending several million dollars annually in advertising, and ask him, What does your department do? here is how he would answer that question. "First," he would say, "with regard to strictly advertising functions, this is what we do:

ADVERTISING DUTIES

Preparation of the advertising budget
Supervision of the preparation and purchase of space in

Newspapers	Car cards
Magazines	Posters
Radio	Theater programs

* Acknowledgment is made to E. B. Weiss, Advertising Agency Consultant, for his assistance in revising this Section.

- Business papers
- Industrial publications
- Farm papers
- Religious papers
- Class journals
- Outdoor advertising
- Window displays
- Counter displays
- Novelties
- Booklets
- Directories

Supervision of the preparation of cards and labels
Preparation of catalogues
Preparation of package inserts
Preparation of motion pictures (including talking pictures when used for consumer advertising)
Preparation of consumer samples
Supervision of copy testing
Preparation of consumer house organs
Supervision of improvements of packages, labels, tags, display cartons
Supervision of trade-mark design
Purchase of paper, artwork, engravings, mats, electros, and other material used in advertising (except where agency does such detail and advertising department approves)
Preparation and maintenance of files of advertising material, scrapbooks of same, etc.
Analysis and study of competitive advertising
Wrapping and distributing advertising material
Contact with the advertising agency
Preparation and maintenance of mailing lists (which apply to advertising work as distinguished from mailing lists prepared and maintained by the sales-promotion department)
Purchase of office supplies and fixtures for advertising department (except where purchasing department does this)
Advertising accounting work (in addition to work carried on by regular accounting department)
Co-operation with engineering and/or production department in developments that will affect advertising
Sales-convention work to explain reasons for and values of advertising and to present advertising plans (as distinguished from more detailed convention work often carried on by the sales-promotion department)
Preparation of advertising exhibits for sales conventions
Development and preparation of advertising portfolios for salesmen (except where these are almost entirely made up of promotion-department material)
Preparation of advertising material directed at company's personnel

Sales-analysis work to determine where best to carry on special advertising effort
Analysis of dealer and distributor media advertising (sometimes in co-operation with sales-promotion department)
Individual dealer and distributor correspondence on advertising matters
Co-operation in preparing annual report (where company makes report something more than a balance sheet)
Co-operation with other departments on public-relations work
Choice and purchase of consumer premiums
Representing the company in associations or other organizations devoted to advertising
Supervision of our co-operation with testing bureaus where results of work are used for advertising purposes
Preparation of purchase and display signs on the factory or office building
Checking and maintaining record of advertising returns"

"Then," he would continue, "with respect to so-called 'sales-promotion functions,' which are part and parcel of advertising, this is what we do:

SALES PROMOTION DUTIES

Preparation of direct mail done by dealers and distributors
- Preparation and/or checking of lists for dealers or distributors
- Preparation of folders or pamphlets to accompany monthly statements sent out by dealers
- Preparation of folders or pamphlets for counter distribution
- Preparation of complete mail campaigns
- Preparation of new customer letters
- Preparation of lost customer letters

Planning and supervision of motion pictures (for dealer or distributor effect)
Preparation of permanent display stands (as opposed to perishable display material)
Preparation of dealer identification signs
Co-operation in the issuance of house magazines:
- A. Internal
  - 1. Sales
  - 2. Employee
- B. External
  - 1. Dealer

Purchase of paper, artwork, engravings, mats, electros, and other materials used in sales promotion

Preparation of dealer samples
Preparation and maintenance of files and scrapbooks, etc., of promotion material
Sales-promotion accounting work (in addition to work done by accounting department)
Purchase of office supplies and fixtures for sales-promotion department (except where purchasing department does this)
Maintenance of mailing lists (which apply to promotion work)
Preparation of sales-promotion budget
Exchange of experiences within far-flung parts of large organizations
Co-operation with engineering and/or production departments in developments that will affect promotion duties
Experimental sales work. This means actual selling in the field to test the effects of certain promotion plans
Handling of sales-training courses (under supervision of sales department) for
  Company salesmen
  Distributors' salesmen
Sales training in the field (where not done by representatives of sales department)
Co-operation with sales department in following through individual dealer inquiries
Sales correspondence (where not handled by sales department)
Keeping of sales records (where not handled by sales department)
Development of salesmen's portfolios (except where these are largely advertising)
Development of visual sales presentations
Preparation of sales bulletins (where this is not done by an assistant sales manager)
Preparation of salesmen's sample case (where not done by sales department)
Development of salesmen's display material
Working with sales department to prepare material for sales conventions (except advertising exhibits)
Salesmen and dealer training
  Programming of meetings instructing in product and how to sell
Informing salesmen of new equipment, new product, etc. (where not done by sales department)
Securing data by which sales quotas can be assigned
Special-analysis work of customer problems too complicated for individual salesmen to handle

Co-ordination of programs and itineraries of traveling representatives from home office to branches so there will be no overlapping or back-tracking of effort
Contacting of dealers in matters other than sales
Contacting of distributors in matters other than sales
Dealer and distributor adjustments (where not handled by sales department)
Planning distributor and dealer contests
Educational work among dealers' salespeople
Working with dealers on customer-control systems
Arrangement for distribution of films among dealers and distributors
Individual dealer and distributor correspondence dealing with promotional matters
Analysis of dealer and distributor direct-mail advertising
Liaison work for distributors and their dealers—as between licensees and dealers
Guidance of trade relations through
  Education
  Trade Associations
  Meetings
  Product Information
Preparation and supervision of product exhibits in trade meetings
Preparation and supervision of product exhibits in dealers' stores
Planning and supervision of demonstrations (except salesmen's demonstrations)
Helping dealer with his advertising budget
Sales research
Analysis to determine new product needs
Sales analysis to determine where best to carry out promotion effort
Analysis of accounts, new and lost, to determine promotion effort
Development of sales-facilitating services, such as time-payment plans
Maintenance of unit sales records for individual products
Corresponding with home-demonstration agents and home-economics teachers
Planning and supervision of exhibition of product in branch houses
Preparation of material for trade shows
Handling of trade-show space where sales department does not take over function
Contact with competitors
Study and analysis of competitive products from the standpoint of product improvement
Contact with trade associations whose members sell company's products"

"And then," he would conclude, "there are some functions that we are sometimes called upon to do which may not be strictly advertising or sales promotion—but nobody else is equipped to do these things, so we undertake to do them. They include:

BORDERLINE DUTIES

Production of direct-mail material (other than that used by dealers)
Creation and design of letterheads, billheads, shipping labels
Supervision of the preparation and distribution of traveling window displays
Preparation of instruction sheets and manuals to insure proper use of products
Preparation and supervision of factory outside display signs
Distribution of display material
Supervision of design and purchase of salesmen's automobiles where these are used for advertising purposes
Co-operation with window display services
Distribution of circulars and pamphlets to the consumer
Distribution of circulars and pamphlets to the trade
Supervision of premium distribution
Gathering of photographic evidence of use of product
Gathering of testimonial data
Supervision of printing plant, duplicating department
Institutional publicity
Gaining publicity for the firm for new products
Market research
Complete cataloguing of product
Clearing house for leads from distributors or dealers
Following through with dealers inquiries developing from advertising and promotion effort
Co-ordinating sales and advertising activities
Maintaining file of historical material of company's activities
Preparation of salesmen's catalogue
Preparation, supervision, and distribution of special exhibits for schools and colleges."

Who advertises.—No more than 700 companies in this country spend in excess of $50,000 annually in so-called commissionable advertising—that is, advertising in magazines, newspapers, radio, and farm papers. But there are over 8,000 advertisers listed in the advertising directory. The remaining 7,300 advertisers, therefore, are comparatively small advertisers. Consequently, when you think of advertising, it is well to think of it, not as practiced by the 700 large advertisers, but as practiced by the 7,300 smaller advertisers.

Think of a typical grocery store. What percentage of the items carried do you suppose are actually *demanded* by brand name by the majority of customers who make purchases? Ask yourself that question with regard to department stores. Picture the thousands of items stocked by a typical department store and then realize the tiny percentage *demanded* by brand name.

Copy, art, radio technique, media—all are of paramount importance. But they can rarely carry the entire burden of making the merchandise move into consumption. They should seldom be asked to carry that terrific load. Advertising should and must be merchandised if the utmost is to be squeezed out of the advertising investment.

Facts for smaller advertisers.—Let us look at the 95 per cent of advertisers whose total advertising appropriations run from perhaps $10,000 to $100,000 annually. These facts are revealed:

First, 95 per cent of our advertisers spend sufficient money for actual consumer advertising to cover the country only thinly. Second, with this thin coverage, those advertisers can usually hope to create, through their own advertising, only a sporadic consumer *demand*. Third, their advertising can, and should, create consumer *interest*. Fourth, their advertising can, and should, create a measurable degree of consumer acceptance.

Now, when we view the results of the consumer advertising of the large majority of our advertisers in this light, some further facts promptly become clear. These may be summarized as follows: First, consumer *interest* is a passive quality. It means little to the advertiser unless and until it is cultivated—developed. Second, consumer *acceptance* is also a passive quality. It, too, is of little importance as an asset unless and until it is cultivated—developed. Third, both consumer *interest* and consumer *acceptance* are actually consumer *demand* in the incipient stage. The breath of life must be pumped into them. They must be vitalized—energized.

Developing demand for an advertiser's product.—These additional facts are of importance to the advertiser on the question of developing demand for a product. First, consumer interest and consumer acceptance ripen most quickly into consumer demand in the retail store. The retailer is the modern magician who, practically with the wave of a wand, can turn the consumer interest and consumer acceptance developed by the manufacturer's advertising into consumer demand. Second, the retailer can also nurse along the actual consumer demand created by the manufacturer, play along with it, build it up. Third, the retailer has a consumer demand of his own. Very often his own consumer demand is stronger than the consumer demand possessed by most of the brands that he stocks. This is particularly true of department stores. The large department stores in many cities spend more money advertising specific items in their areas than do the manufacturers of these items. They have a powerful consumer demand. The retailer can take his consumer demand and turn it over to the manufacturer.

But will the retailer wave that magic wand over the manufacturer's consumer interest and consumer acceptance? Will the retailer nurse along the manufacturer's actual consumer demand? Will the retailer turn over his own consumer demand to the manufacturer? No, he will not, if he is ignored in the manufacturer's planning.

First and foremost, then, throw overboard the delusion that irresistible consumer demand is created by small consumer-advertising appropriations. Second, *merchandise the manufacturer's consumer advertising to and through the trade.*

The distributor, in the final analysis, holds the key to success in consumer advertising in so far as 95 per cent of the advertisers are concerned. If he is roused to enthusiasm about the manufacturer's advertising, if he is not merely told to tie up but is shown how to tie up, then the manufacturer gets the bonus on his advertising appropriation to which he is justly entitled.

Tools for merchandising the advertising.—Here is a list of the tools available to the advertising man who wants to do a thorough job of merchandising the advertising:

Related selling in retail stores
Case histories
Store histories demonstrations
Circularizing dealers' prospects
Bill inserts for stores
New shipping cartons for trade shipments
Direct-mail campaign to dealers
Advertising allowances
Profit-sharing plan for distributors

Helping dealer sell right product (like device for measuring gloves, etc.)
Bulletins for dealers on various subjects (telephone selling, collection letters, etc.)
Mailing lists of jobbers' salesmen and retail salespeople (home addresses)
Tags on merchandise (to help salespeople do more effective selling job)
Co-operative merchandising with a noncompetitive manufacturer
Securing interest of wives, mothers, etc. of dealers, salespeople, manufacturers' salesmen
Bringing back lost customers (both lost accounts to the manufacturer and lost customers to the dealer)
Store-wide promotions—promotions in more than one department—interdepartment merchandising
Plans for tying up with special events—new events, holidays, etc.
Finding changes in consumer habits (rug sizes have not kept pace with changes in room design)
Clinics for dealers and salespeople
Merchandising manual for retailer
Helping retailers sell outside the store
Deals—free deals, etc.
Premiums for dealers
Mat service
Promotion kits for dealers
Motion pictures for distributors
Counter catalogue
Manual for dealer and salespeople
House magazine for dealers
Dealer contest
Accounting system for retailers
Trade paper advertising
Handling inquiries received from the advertising
Reports from salesmen
Portfolio for manufacturers' salesmen
Bulletins for manufacturers' salesmen
Contest for manufacturers' salesmen
Quota system for distributors
Sales manual
Special merchandise arrangements
Giant blow-ups
Counter cabinets
Use of demonstrators
Window displays
Interior displays
Counter demonstration devices
Itinerant displays
Assortment packages
Improved method of packing
New convenience of the container
New use of the package
New size (larger or smaller) for container
New labels for container
New color scheme for container
New general design of container
New construction of container
Cross advertising on package
Double-use containers
Improved package design
Package inserts
Tested sales sentences
Clubs for salespeople
Correspondence course for salespeople
Instruction manual for salespeople
Manual for jobbers' salesmen

Special tables or sections for stores
Window display contest; interior display contests
Routing exclusive window displays from one dealer to another
General helps for salespeople
Jobbers' salesmen contests
Consumer contest
Promotional calendar
Style promotions
Special "weeks"
Anniversary promotions
Sampling
Guaranty
Installing department in stores
Exhibition and demonstration trucks and trailers
Model stock plans
Development of new uses
Quotas for jobbers' salesmen
Dealers' salesmen contests
Fashion show
Tests of brand pulling power
Factory showrooms (model store at factory, etc.)
Advertising novelties and specialties—calendars, etc.
Exclusive agency plan
Miniature models for demonstration purposes, etc.
Trial offers
Dramatic demonstration ideas for products
Trade-ins
Installment selling
Consignment selling
Exhibit at shows, fairs, etc.

Many of these tools may not fit into the tool chests of most advertising men. Nevertheless, each and every one is part and parcel of the big job of merchandising the advertising. It will pay any advertising man to check this list periodically and determine what he is not doing that he should do—and what he is doing that can be done better. It is in this kind of soil that advertising functions most effectively. It is when these things are done that we have fewer so-called advertising failures, for the simple reason that advertising is not being asked to carry an impossible load.

2. ADVERTISING AGENCIES

Choosing an advertising agency.—The choice of an advertising agency should be the subject of careful investigation and consideration. At the present time there are in the United States approximately 1,200 concerns that call themselves advertising agencies. However, although these concerns do business under the same general title, there is considerable variation in the nature of the services that they perform. The success of the advertising will depend to a large extent upon the success in choosing the agency best fitted to handle any particular advertising situation.

What points to investigate in choosing an advertising agency.—The best basis upon which an advertiser can select an advertising agency is *facts*—as to the agency's experience, its record of past success, and the like. In the following paragraphs are listed a number of specific points that may be investigated.

1. *Names of agency's chief executives.*—The success of an advertising agency, even more than that of most other businesses, depends upon the experience and ability of its chief executives. The advertiser should inquire who are the agency's chief executives and, particularly, what has been their sales, general business, and advertising experience. The advertiser himself suffers from the handicap of specialization in his chosen field. One of the reasons for placing advertising in the hands of an agency is to benefit from the agency's broad knowledge of selling methods and market conditions. Can the agency demonstrate, by pointing to what it has done for other clients, that it does possess a broad knowledge of modern selling methods and the vision to apply them effectively to a particular situation?

2. *Who will handle account.*—The advertiser may inquire beforehand who is to handle his account—that is, who in the agency is to plan the expenditure of his appropriation. Since the relation between an advertiser and his agency is an intimate one, much depends upon the personal factor. Is the individual in the agency who is to handle the account acceptable to the advertiser on grounds of personality, as well as on grounds of ability and experience?

3. *Number of accounts that agency handles.*—This factor is likely to bring up, in the advertiser's mind, the question of large versus small agencies. Some advertisers feel that if they select a large agency, or an agency that has several very large accounts, their own advertising will not receive proper attention if their appropriation is relatively small. On the other hand, the criticism is sometimes made that many of the smaller agencies are one-man businesses and cannot give adequate service. The question is one on which no general statement can be made. However, if the advertiser's appropriation is relatively small, and he is doubtful that his account should be given to a large agency, he can ask the agency to give him the names of

companies whose advertising it has handled on appropriations comparable to his, and can then get in touch with those companies to ascertain whether their experience with the agency has been satisfactory.

4. *Names of accounts now on agency's books.*—The advertiser may ask the agency to list the names of its leading accounts, and to state how long it has handled each account. Can the agency give evidence that it has originated merchandising plans for its clients, or has its work been chiefly the "placing" of advertising?

Also to be considered are the names of accounts that the agency has gained during the preceding, say, two years, and the names of accounts lost during that period. A high turnover of accounts is an unfavorable factor.

The advertiser may write to the companies whose names have been given, requesting a statement as to their experience with the agency.

5. *Agency's knowledge of advertiser's line of business.*—This is one point to which the advertiser is likely to give too much weight. Unless the advertiser's line is especially difficult, the question may not be important, and too much emphasis should not be placed on it. One of the objects of retaining an agency is to benefit from an outside, fresh viewpoint and insight.

6. *Completeness of recognition.*—Recognition means that the agency is granted commissions by the media in which the advertising is placed. There are various media associations that grant recognition to agencies:

A.N.P.A. American Newspaper Publishers' Association.
A.B.P. Associated Business Papers.
P.P.A. Periodical Publishers' Association.
A.P.A. Agricultural Publishers' Association.
N.O.A.B. National Outdoor Advertising Bureau.

Recognition from an association is generally honored by the members of the association. However, recognition by an association is not binding upon the members, and some media act independently of their association in investigating and recognizing agencies; for example, the Curtis Publishing Company grants its own recognition. Further, an agency that is not recognized by a national association may be recognized by a local association or by individual media. Some publications do not grant commissions to agencies, and hence do not recognize them; this is true of a number of trade papers, which feel that a general agency cannot serve the interests of clients in their specialized field, and maintain their own "service departments" to service the advertising in their publications.

The system of agency recognition arose from the necessity, on the part of advertising media, of having information as to the financial standing and integrity of agencies from whom the media were accepting advertising. Essentially, recognition means two things:

(*a*) That the agency has met certain requirements established by the media. In this sense recognition is a recommendation by the association to its members that the agency is a good credit risk, that it conducts its business on a legitimate basis, and that the media are warranted in accepting the agency's advertising.

(*b*) That the agency is active in the field in which it has obtained recognition. An agency cannot obtain recognition from an association merely by meeting the association's requirements as to financial strength, business methods, and so on. The agency must be actively engaged in placing advertising in, for example, business papers, or newspapers, or outdoor media, before the association representing the media in one of these fields will grant the agency recognition.

The chief requirements for recognition are the following:

(*a*) *Financial strength.*—Since the agency is often solely liable to the media for the payment of bills covering the advertising that it has placed for its clients, the associations naturally inquire carefully into the financial strength of an agency before granting recognition.

(*b*) *Constructive service to clients.*—Before recognition is granted, the agency must satisfy the associations that it has had adequate experience in the practice of advertising and that it is performing a constructive service for its clients.

(*c*) *Sound business methods.*—An agency may not make indirect or secret rebates to clients of a portion of the commissions allowed by the media.

From the advertiser's standpoint recognition is important because an agency that lacks recognition may have difficulty in securing credit from the media, and possibly the advertiser may be asked to guarantee payment. Moreover, the agency is likely to be prejudiced in favor of the media in the field in which it has obtained recognition.

7. *Method of compensation proposed.*—A number of methods of compensation, each of which has its advantages and disadvantages, are in common use. These are discussed on page 429.

Some agencies, a small percentage of the total number, solicit accounts on a price basis, offering special inducements and indirect rebates of various kinds. It is not wise to assume that because an agency makes a special inducement it is necessarily a weak agency. Some successful agencies make special compensation arrangements. But neither is it safe to conclude that a special financial arrangement is a "bargain." It may be just the opposite.

The seven points below are an outline of the scope of the investi-

1. List the names of your agency's chief executives.
   (*a*) State briefly the sales, general business, and advertising experience of the executives listed above.
   (*b*) Are the above executives active in the conduct of the agency's business?
2. Which member of your agency would handle our account?
3. How many accounts are you now handling?
4. Give the names of the accounts that you are now handling, State how long you have handled each.
   (*a*) Give such facts and figures as are not confidential to show how you have contributed to the sales of the companies whose accounts you have handled.
   (*b*) What merchandising plans have you originated for your clients?
   (*c*) List the names of accounts that you have gained during the past two years.
   (*d*) List the names of accounts that you have lost during the past two years.
5. Outline briefly your experience in and knowledge of our line of business.
6. By which associations are you recognized?
7. On what basis of compensation would you handle our account?

Points to Investigate in Choosing an Advertising Agency.

gation that an advertiser may make before he chooses an agency. It will be noted that one question which is *not* asked is how the agency will handle the advertising if it secures the advertiser's business. This is a question that advertisers frequently ask agencies, and sometimes, in response to it, agencies prepare advertising plans for the prospective client. In many cases they will prepare complete advertisements, with copy and illustrations. A few large agencies, however, will not do this. The large majority will if the account is worth while.

Scope of agency service.—Forty or fifty years ago advertising agencies were little more than brokerage or commission houses, selling space in media. However, these pioneer agencies early found that it was to their advantage to contribute to making the space that they sold productive for the advertiser, and accordingly they broadened their function to include the writing of the advertising. In the past fifteen years there have been further developments, until at the present time the term "advertising agency" no longer truly describes the services that an agency makes available to its clients. Agencies now commonly act as marketing counselors; in many cases they are practically partners in the business, in everything but name.

The chief services of the present-day agency may be briefly outlined as follows.

1. *Analysis of the product.*—The agency usually makes a thorough study and analysis of the product before any advertising is prepared. In other words, from the intermediate ground that it occupies between the advertiser on the one hand and the public on the other, the agency reviews the advertiser's proposition. What are the distinctive features of the product? In design, is it what the public wants? Would changes in design widen the appeal and increase sales? Is the packaging effective? Is the product priced right? How does it compare with competitive products? That this analysis of the product is worth while from the advertiser's standpoint has been demonstrated many times. Agencies have contributed suggestions on product design, packaging, pricing, and other problems, which have proved invaluable to their clients. For example, the agency handling the Bon Ami account recommended that Bon Ami be made up in a new package, which could be left in the bathroom. Similarly, a number of ideas suggested by another agency were in-

corporated in a model of the Buick car. Continuous advice on problems connected with the product itself is one of the newer features of agency service.

2. *Analysis of the market.*—This involves a study of the product's present and potential markets. What are the product's principal markets at the present time? Are there potential markets as yet untapped? Where are they? In which markets is competition most acute? How do consumers react to the product? Those who buy—why do they buy, and how often? Can new uses be found for the product that would result in more frequent buying? Those who do not buy—why do they not buy? Do they prefer competing products? If so, why—style, packaging, price? These are examples of questions which the advertising agency, because of its familiarity with selling methods and markets, is peculiarly fitted to answer from experience or to develop by research.

3. *Analysis of present sales structure.*—What is the advertiser's present sales and distribution setup? Is it producing results? Are relations with dealers satisfactory? Are selling costs in line? Possibly the advertiser should add new channels of distribution or eliminate some of those now in use? Questions such as these fall within the province of the advertising agency's work.

4. *Formulation of definite plan.*—On the basis of the facts obtained from its analysis of the product, the market, and the present sales structure, the agency will probably recommend a definite plan. It is worth noting, however, that this "definite plan" may or may *not* be that the client undertake an advertising campaign. Although any agency is likely to be prejudiced in favor of advertising as a means of developing a business, the right kind of agency will not advise a client to advertise unless it is satisfied that advertising will produce results. An agency cannot afford to be associated with a failure, since its reputation is built upon its record in increasing sales. It may be that modification of the product will be necessary before advertising is undertaken. Possibly the time is not propitious for an advertising campaign in the client's line of business. Consideration of all the factors involved may make it advisable for the client to spend only a small sum on advertising at the present moment, later gradually increasing his appropriation. The right kind of agency can be relied upon for a frank statement of the facts and for a reasonable appraisal of future prospects.

Advertising

Determining basic copy appeal	Production
Copy research	Traffic control
Copy testing	Advertising economies
Copy writing	Advertising checking
Copy supervision	Art policies
Space-buying policies	Radio

Merchandising the Advertising

Retail promotion program	Getting jobber co-operation
Dealer-help program	Getting jobber's salesman's co-operation
Window displays	Traveling among jobbers and jobbers' salesmen
Interior displays	Traveling among retailers
Counter merchandising units	Advertising portfolios
Education of salespeople	Contest for distributors
House magazine for dealer	Retail mats
House magazine for salespeople	Films—reprints of ads—etc.
Seasonal drives by retailer	

Tying up Advertising with Sales Organization

Sales portfolios	Distribution of jobber material through salesmen
Bulletins to salesmen	Advertising training for salesmen
Distribution of dealer material through salesmen	Checking advertising appeals with salesmen
Traveling with salesmen	Getting advertising information from sales force
Maintaining salesmen's interest and enthusiasm	Study of salesmen's reports
Sales conventions	Promotion ideas for salesmen to pass on to distributors
Sales manuals	
Contests for salesmen	
Advertising portfolios	

General Sales Promotion

Catalogue	Demonstration devices
Price lists	Flow of letters, bulletins, etc., to trade
Trade shows	Follow-up of advertising inquiries
Trade conventions	Special plans for local areas
Sampling	Special emergency plans
Premiums	

Merchandise

Styling and designing	Pricing
Size or quantity units	General study of merchandise
Development of special features	Market research
Trade names and trade-marks	New uses
Packages	New markets
Shipping cartons	

General Policies

Trade discounts	Organization of sales force
Public relations	Compensation of sales force
Employee relations	Distribution policies
Distribution channels	Manufacturing policies
Elimination of, or additions to, line	

Miscellaneous

Publicity	Work with stockholders

Functions Performed by Advertising Agencies.

If, however, the agency believes that an advertising campaign can successfully be inaugurated, the definite plan may comprise recommendations as to the market to which the campaign should be directed, the media to be used (newspapers, class magazines, trade publications, radio, outdoor, car cards, and the like), the features of the product that are to be emphasized, and the nature of the appeals that the advertising is to contain.

5. *Execution of plan.*—Execution of the plan includes:

(*a*) Writing, designing, and illustrating of advertisements, or other appropriate forms of the message.

(*b*) Contracting for the space or other means of advertising.

(*c*) Proper incorporation of the message in mechanical form, and forwarding of the message with instructions for the fulfillment of the contract.

(*d*) Preparation of catalogues, trade literature, dealer broadsides and portfolios, dealer displays, direct-mail literature, and so forth.

(*e*) Preparation of material for salesmen, such as sales kits.

(*f*) Checking and verifying of insertions, display, or other means used.

(*g*) Auditing, billing, and paying for the service, space, and preparation.

How to work with an advertising agency.—The function of the advertising agency may be said to be twofold:

1. To interpret the advertiser to the public.
2. To interpret the public to the advertiser.

For best success, the advertiser and his agency should work in close collaboration.

Two mistakes that advertisers frequently make in working with agencies are:

1. Having given their account to the agency and determined the appropriation, they sit back and expect the agency to do the rest. They adopt the attitude, "Here's what I want to spend; now you go ahead and get the results." This attitude is a handicap to the agency, which definitely needs the advertiser's co-operation. A free exchange of viewpoints, ideas, and experience is to the benefit of both parties concerned.

2. At the opposite extreme is the advertiser who handicaps his agency by undue interference, and particularly by trying to force onto the agency his own personal preferences and prejudices or those of other executives of the company (not to mention his wife).

It is often difficult for the advertiser to appreciate the agency's viewpoint. However, bringing a different, fresh viewpoint to the advertiser's business is one of the chief services that an agency can perform. Perhaps the best procedure is for the advertiser to give the agency a free hand in formulating its plans for the advertising; then, to examine these plans closely, question thoroughly, and require the agency to justify whatever appears doubtful—but give it the opportunity to so justify itself.

Some additional "don'ts" are:

1. Don't regard your advertising merely as a plaything; it is an expensive toy.

2. Don't place undue faith in advertising "company tradition," "company name," or "established reputation." What the public wants is a better article at a lower price.

3. Don't begin by telling your agency "exactly what kind of advertising I want." Give the agency an opportunity to determine what kind of advertising you need.

4. Don't be impatient if, after your advertising appears, results in accordance with your expectations are not immediately forthcoming. Although there have been cases of instantaneous success, as a rule it takes time to make an impression—time, and persistent advertising.

Three plans of agency compensation.*—The media bill the agency, and the agency, in turn, bills the advertiser. A recognized agency receives a commission from the various media in which the advertising is placed. The rate is fixed by the individual media, but it is usually 15 per cent of the card rate. In addition, an extra 2 per cent cash discount is often allowed on the net payment made by the agency (2 per cent on 85 per cent). Many publications, however, allow no extra discount for cash and require that the agency pay by a fixed date to obtain the agency commission.

---

* From Kleppner, *Advertising Procedure.* New York: Prentice-Hall, Inc.

The following are the three plans of agency compensation in most common use:

1. *Straight commission plan.*—Under the straight commission plan the agency accepts as payment for its services the commission granted by the media upon the client's advertising. The client merely pays the card rates.

EXAMPLE

For space costing $3,000 the publisher bills the agency	$3,000.00	
Less 15%	450.00	
Net	$2,550.00	
Discount for cash, 2% on net	51.00	
Agency pays publisher		$2,499.00
Agency bills client	$3,000.00	
Cash discount if client pays promptly	51.00	
Client pays agency		$2,949.00

In connection with the cash discount, it should be noted that the client receives only 2 per cent on the net (or 2 per cent on 85 per cent), and that he does not receive 2 per cent on the gross. It is held that the agency commission, like a professional service bill, is not subject to cash discount.

Art work, engraving, typographical setups, and so forth, are usually billed to the client at cost plus the usual 15 per cent for the agency's service.

EXAMPLE

Art work	$450.00	
Plates	180.00	
Typographical composition	45.00	
	$675.00	
Plus 15%	101.25	
Charge to client for mechanical costs		$776.25

The same arrangement is followed in the purchase of radio time; the agency receives a commission, ordinarily 15 per cent, from the broadcasting station on the cost of the time. The cost of talent and incidents of broadcasting is usually non-commissionable. The better agencies make a service charge, usually 15 per cent, on such items, as they do on art work and mechanics in publication advertising.

2. *Plus 15, less commissions plan.*—Another method used by a number of agencies is that of charging for their services a flat fee representing usually 15 per cent of the card rates (and of expenditures for art work or mechanical charges), crediting the client with whatever commissions and discounts they receive.

EXAMPLE

There is spent in		
Publication *A*	$10,000.00	
Publication *B*	20,000.00	
Publication *C*	2,000.00	
There is also spent		
Art work	500.00	
Type setup and plates	145.00	
Total expenditure	$32,645.00	
Agency fee for its services is 15%, or	4,896.75	
Assume that agency commissions on publications *A* and *B* were 13% each, and 2% for cash on net amount, and assume that publication *C* granted no commission to agencies; the total commission would be		$ 4,422.00
which would be credited to the advertiser. He would actually be debited	$37,541.75	
and credited	4,422.00	
leaving his total bill		$33,119.75

It will be noted that this plan does not result in a saving to the advertiser. In the example the total fee to the agency is $4,896.75, while the total of commissions and discounts is $4,422; $4,896.75 − $4,422 = $474.75. Of this, $96.75 represents the fee on art work and type setup and plates, leaving $378 as the amount that the advertiser has to pay in excess of what he would have had to pay under the straight-commission plan. In fact, the 15-per-cent-less-commissions plan cannot result in a saving to the advertiser, since, if the agency's fee amounted to less than the total of commissions and discounts, the plan would, in effect, be a concealed means of rebating and would therefore be illegitimate. The advantage to the advertiser in the 15-per-cent-less-commissions plan is that the danger that the agency will be biased toward the media from which it receives the largest commissions is removed. It is immaterial to the agency whether a certain piece of its client's advertising is placed in a publication that allows no commission to agencies, or in one that grants 15 per cent; the agency's fee is the same in either case. Accordingly, the 15-per-cent-less-commissions plan is suitable for use when the agency has to do considerable work among media where the amount of commissions varies, or some grant a commission and others do not. Another advantage is the comparative simplicity of its bookkeeping.

3. *Retainer plus commissions plan.*—The chief value of an agency to a client may consist of its research, its counsel, and its ideas, though little publication advertising is used. A "retainer-plus-commissions" plan has been introduced to provide for this situation and offers a method that is rapidly coming into wide acceptance. By this plan the agency is assured a definite income of, say, $15,000 for the year. Toward this amount the agency will credit whatever commissions it receives. The client pays a monthly retainer that is to make up for the difference between the income from commissions and the set fee. If the commissions exceed the fee, the client need pay no retainer, and the agency continues on its straight-commission basis.

EXAMPLE 1

Retainer fee set for the year	$15,000.00
Commissions from publications amount to	11,500.00
Client credited with this sum.	

EXAMPLE 2

Retainer fee set for the year	$15,000.00
Commissions from publications amount to	15,500.00
Client need pay no further retainer, but only the card-rate cost of the space used.	

The agency is not allowed to rebate its commissions, and accordingly cannot agree to a flat fee that represents less than the commissions from the media.

The retainer-plus-commissions plan provides a solution to the paradoxical situation whereby an agency serves one master but apparently receives its payment from another. The retainer plan, as its name implies, retains the agency to serve the client without preference toward any form of media. Further, there is no incentive to rush the client into advertising.

Agreement with the advertising agency.—While formal agreements hiring an agency to aid in selling and advertising a firm's products are entered into, the more usual practice is for the company employing the agency to address a letter to the agency stating the mutually agreed-upon terms. The following is a typical client contract form, prepared by the advertising agency:

Date

Agency name
Address

Gentlemen:
We hereby appoint you our advertising agency upon the following terms and conditions:

1. All our advertising is to be placed through you for a minimum period of one year beginning .... This agreement is subject to cancellation by either party during the term of this agreement by giving sixty days' written notice in advance.

2. You are to secure for us the best possible terms for all our magazine, newspaper, trade paper and all other advertising space, charging to our account the net card rates of the vendors.

3. We understand and agree that you will allow us the full amount of all cash discounts as allowed you, only provided your bills for advertising space are paid by us within the discount period specified on your bills.

4. You are to give advice and counsel and to prepare for us such material as is required for any and all advertising material ordered by us, making no additional charge for any such service or work performed by your organization in the preparation of such material except for all art work, drawings, engravings, photographic work, typesetting, printing and electrotyping, etc., which are to be charged at your cost. Bills for all this work are net. We agree to pay them when rendered.

5. Traveling expenses incurred by any of your representatives working in our interest and authorized by us, and shipping charges on plates

and other advertising material, are to be billed to us at their cost to you. We understand that you are not responsible for the return of cuts after their use in publications.

6. In consideration of all the above services, we agree to pay you a service fee of .... Dollars per annum; in addition to this service fee, we shall pay you .... Dollars for the *writing* of six issues of .... We agree to pay this total fee of .... Dollars in monthly installments of .... Dollars. You are to return to us all commissions earned on advertising during the term of this agreement up to the amount of the fee ....

Very truly yours,
COMPANY NAME

Treasurer

____

Director

____

We do hereby accept your foregoing offer and agree to perform and render the services therein contained upon the terms and conditions set forth therein.

AGENCY NAME

____

____
Title

3. FIXING THE ADVERTISING APPROPRIATION

Three methods in common use.—Three methods of determining the advertising appropriation are in common use:

1. Percentage-of-sales method.
2. Unit-of-sales method.
3. Market-survey method.

Each of these has its advantages and disadvantages for particular businesses. The first two recommend themselves to many advertisers by the fact that they are relatively easy to use. The third is less easy but more thorough; the market-survey method is being increasingly used.

Percentage-of-sales method.—This method consists of setting aside for advertising a fixed percentage of some figure related to sales volume. The figure may be:

1. Percentage of gross or net sales for a preceding period.
2. Percentage of average of gross or net sales for several periods in the past.
3. Percentage of estimated gross or net sales for a future period.
4. Percentage of average of gross or net sales for one or more periods in the past and estimated sales for one or more periods in the future.

The figure most generally taken by advertisers using the percentage-of-sales method is a percentage of estimated sales for a future period (a year, a half year, or a quarter). Many advertisers who formerly allocated to advertising a percentage of sales for a period in the past, or a percentage of average sales for several periods in the past, have changed their ground. Their reasoning is that past sales are not a good index to the amount that should be spent for future advertising. They are prepared to back up their analysis of the market for their product with an advertising expenditure in proportion to the sales volume that they aim to achieve.

Other advertisers, who wish to be more conservative and to offset any undue optimism as to the future, use a combination figure representing a percentage of average sales for a certain period in the past and estimated sales for a certain period in the future.

A variation of the percentage-of-sales method is to use a percentage of profits instead of a percentage of sales. The objection to this plan is that profits are dependent upon operating efficiency and many other factors, and the advertising appropriation should not be affected by these.

How the percentage is determined.—There is no formula for determining the percentage figure to be used in the percentage-of-sales method. The figure varies in different industries, and also with companies in the same industry, from 1 per cent to as high as 30 per cent of gross sales. In many cases the figure is based upon the average figure for the industry as a whole, or upon figures used by other companies in the same line. In the final analysis, the advertiser has to decide the percentage in the light of his individual circumstances. A company recently formed might feel that 25 per cent was not too high, while one that has been established for a number of years might spend 5 per cent. The matter is one of judgment for each particular business.

Advantages and disadvantages of percentage-of-sales method.— The chief advantages of the percentage-of-sales method are two:

1. It is easy to use.
2. It relates advertising expenditure to sales volume. That is, the amount spent for advertising is made dependent upon the volume of sales—usually upon the estimated volume of sales for a future period. To base advertising expenditure upon sales volume is, in general, a logical procedure.

As against the above, two important disadvantages of this method are:

1. Where, as is often the case, the percentage figure is based upon the figure for the industry as a whole or upon figures used by other companies in the same line, the method is liable to become one of just keeping up, proportionately to sales, with competitors' advertising. Competitors may be wasteful in spending money on advertising or may have overlooked opportunities that increased advertising would turn into sales. The advertiser has to be careful that he is not allowing himself to be led by the blind.
2. Although the percentage-of-sales method does relate advertising expenditure to sales volume, this relation is often approximate and indefinite. For example, assume that sales for the coming year are estimated at $1,000,000. It is decided to appropriate 5 per cent of this figure, or $50,000, for advertising. This amount appears and is considered "adequate." However, whether $50,000 is the amount actually required (neither too much nor too little) to enable advertising to play its part in the $1,000,000 sales program may not be known. In this respect the percentage-of-sales method does not compare favorably with the market-survey method, under which a reasonable sales objective for the given period is first decided; then the job that advertising is to do is determined; and finally an amount is appro-

priated for advertising that will be sufficient for advertising's part in the sales program.

Unit-of-sales method.—This method consists of allocating to advertising a fixed sum per unit of sales. Production costs are known; selling costs are known from past experience; an estimate of sales for a future period—say, one year—is made. A certain sum per unit of anticipated sales is then appropriated for advertising. Thus, an automobile manufacturer might estimate his sales for the coming year at 400,000 cars and set aside for advertising $5 per car. His total appropriation would then be $5 × 400,000, or $2,000,000.

Advantages and disadvantages of unit-of-sales method.—Some of the advantages of this method are:

1. If the sum per unit is not arrived at by guesswork, but is the sum which, judged by past experience, will be necessary to move each unit through the market, this method definitely relates advertising expenditure to sales volume, and is reliable and at the same time easy to use. It is particularly convenient for companies selling specialty goods, such as automobiles, refrigerators, oil burners, washing machines, and so forth.

2. The unit-of-sales method can readily be applied to co-operative advertising by a manufacturer and his dealers. The manufacturer allocates to advertising a fixed sum per unit of anticipated sales and also assesses the dealer a fixed sum. The dealer's assessment is commonly charged to the dealer on his invoice and is usually included in the list price to the dealer, not billed as a separate item. The majority of automobile manufacturers operate on this plan.

3. The unit-of-sales method has also been successfully used by co-operative associations of manufacturers, fruit growers, and so forth. For example, co-operative organizations of fruit growers have determined the advertising appropriation for the industry by assessing against each member a certain number of cents per case.

The chief limitation of the unit-of-sales method is the difficulty of applying it in many lines of business. For example, the method can hardly be used by a company selling style merchandise, or, in general, by a company selling in irregular markets.

Market-survey method.—This method is being increasingly favored. Stated in its simplest terms, it consists of determining, for a certain future period, the job that advertising is to do as a part of the sales program, and then appropriating whatever amount will be necessary to enable advertising to do that job. In fixing the advertising appropriation by the market-survey method, the advertiser asks himself three general questions:

1. What is the sales objective to be for the next six months, the next year, or longer?
2. What part is advertising to play in the plan to reach that objective; what is to be advertising's job?
3. How much money will advertising require to do its job?

Different companies follow different procedures in answering these three questions. Some depend chiefly upon information obtained from past experience, and from sales managers, salesmen, dealers, and similar sources. Other companies inquire exhaustively into market conditions and potentialities. The procedure in such cases may be briefly outlined as follows:

1. The total market is divided into merchandising and trading areas, or spheres of sales influence. The idea here is that division of the total market into sections facilitates analysis and, in the end, the direction of selling effort to those sections which the analysis shows have not been fully exploited or which are likely to prove most profitable.

2. With the trading areas determined and mapped, the next step is to make an analysis of each area. Factors entering into the analysis are:

(*a*) Past sales record of each area. This record should cover several years, so that the trend of sales in the area will be apparent.

(*b*) Buying power index for each area. This index should be made as simple as possible. The object should be to include only factors that will affect sales of the advertiser's own product. For example, a company selling an electric refrigerator would be interested chiefly in the number of wired homes, income tax returns, bank deposits, and similar data.

(*c*) Index figure indicating the relative cost of selling in each area. This figure can be obtained from past sales records. The object of including it is to avoid overspending in areas where the cost of selling is high.

3. On the basis of the past sales record, buying power index, and index of relative cost of selling, a sales quota for each area is set.

4. The advertising appropriation for each trading area is determined in the light of the facts obtained from the above analysis.

Advantages and disadvantages of market-survey method.—The chief point in favor of the market-survey method is that it represents an attempt to substitute for guesswork a method of determining the advertising appropriation which is founded on known facts. It defines the job that advertising is to do, and then allocates the amount necessary for that job. The market-survey method is, indeed, more than just a means of deciding how much to spend for advertising. It is a thorough review of the company's marketing and selling system, of which advertising is one part, and points the way to a planned program.

The chief objection to the market-survey method is the work and expense that it entails. Furthermore, unforeseen changes may upset the most careful calculations. Nevertheless, if applied with common sense, it will clarify advertising and selling policies to a marked degree.

What to charge to advertising costs.—After the advertising budget has been determined, the question of what is properly chargeable to advertising arises. The following list of items is recognized as properly chargeable to the advertising appropriation:

Space:

Cartons and labels (when used exclusively for advertising purposes, such as in window displays)

Package inserts (when used as advertising and not just as direction sheets)

(Paid advertising in all recognized mediums, including:)

Newspapers
Periodicals
Business papers
Technical journals
Farm papers
Religious papers
Class journals
Car cards
Catalogues
Posters
Theater programs
Outdoor advertising
Window displays
Counter displays
Store signs
Novelties
Booklets
Directories
Direct advertising

Slides
Export advertising
Dealer helps
Reprints of advertisements used in mail or for display
Radio
House magazines to dealers or consumers
Motion pictures (including talking pictures) when used for advertising
All other printed and lithographed material used directly for advertising purposes

Administration:

Salaries of advertising department executives and employees
Office supplies and fixtures used solely by advertising department
Commissions and fees to advertising agencies, special writers, or advisers
Expenses incurred by salesmen when on work for advertising department
Traveling expenses of department employees engaged in departmental business
(Note: In some companies these go into special "Administration" account)

Mechanical:

Artwork
Typography
Engraving
Mats
Electros
Photographs
Etc.

Miscellaneous:

Transportation of advertising material (to include postage and other carrying charges)
Fees to window display installation services
Other miscellaneous expenses connected with items on the above list

The guardian of the advertising budget must be on constant guard against the following improper advertising charges:

Free goods
Picnic and bazaar programs
Charitable, religious, and fraternal donations
Other expenses for "goodwill" purposes
Cartons
Labels
Instruction sheets
Packages
Press agentry
Stationery used outside advertising department
Price lists
Salesmen's calling cards
Motion pictures for sales use only

House magazines going to factory employees
Bonuses to trade
Special rebates
Salesmen's samples (including photographs used in lieu of samples)
Welfare activities among employees
Such recreational activities as baseball teams, etc.
Membership in trade associations
Entertaining customers or prospects
Annual reports
Showrooms
Demonstration stores
Sales convention expenses
Sales expenses at conventions
Cost of salesmen's automobiles
"Special editions" which approach advertisers on "goodwill" basis

Because advertising, like sales work, is, admittedly, far from being a scientific procedure, there are some advertising charges that may or may not be proper advertising expenses. Circumstances will indicate what the decision should be. These charges include:

Samples
Demonstrations
Fairs
Canvassing
Rent
Telephone and other overhead expenses, apportioned to advertising department
House magazines going to salesmen
Membership in associations or other organizations devoted to advertising
Testing bureaus
Advertising portfolios for salesmen
Contributions to special advertising funds of trade associations
Display signs on the factory or office building
Light
Heat
Depreciation of equipment used by advertising department
Advertising automobiles
Premiums
Salesmen's catalogues
Research and market investigations
Advertising allowances to trade for co-operative effort

4. ADVERTISING MEDIA

Principal media.—The principal media available for advertising by advertisers with merchandise to be sold to the general public include:

1. Newspapers.
2. Magazines.

3. Radio.
4. Farm papers.
5. Direct mail.

This group accounts for probably 75 per cent of the total sum spent in so-called consumer advertising. The less important advertising media include:

1. Outdoor advertising.
2. Car cards.
3. Premiums.
4. Advertising specialties.
5. Trade papers.

Selecting the right media.—One question frequently asked in connection with these media is: Which one is best? Only one answer can be made to that question—namely: It all depends.

No one medium is best for everybody. In fact, there is no one medium that is necessarily best for any specific advertiser. That is why we see some advertisers putting the lion's share of their budget into radio one year, into magazines the next year, and perhaps into newspapers the third year.

Undoubtedly, certain sets of circumstances exist that definitely indicate the advisability of using one or the other of these media to the exclusion of all the others. Other sets of circumstances occur that sometimes definitely point to a certain combination of these media. But, more often, two advertising experts might make radically different media suggestions to the same advertiser—and both might be right! Advertising is far from being a science. Until it does become a science—if it ever does—the selection of media will be most often a matter of opinion, backed up by experience; scientific selection of media is only rarely possible.

Suppose, therefore, we scan quickly the major values offered by each of the principal media, bearing in mind that none of these major values may be the exclusive property of any one of the media. For example, the magazines might be pointed to as the medium to use for broad national coverage. However, if that is done, the newspapers will promptly point out that some highly successful national campaigns have been run exclusively in newspapers, and, of course, the radio people will make the same assertion. Therefore, while we will endeavor to assign certain specific points of merit to each of the media, it must be remembered that, actually, there is no such sharp cleavage between them.

Magazines.—Magazines tend to classify themselves upon bases of frequency of issue, type of editorial content, sex of reader, economic status of reader, and so on. There are women's magazines, fiction magazines, weekly and monthly magazines, so-called class magazines like *Harper's,* and others. Magazines at one time were looked upon as *the* national advertising media. However, newspapers began to challenge that claim, and, of course, radio has certainly taken considerable advertising revenue away from magazines. In general, however, it may be said that magazines offer an excellent advertising "buy" to the company with a broad national distribution. The distribution phase is important because magazine circulation is apt to be scattered over the entire country, and, if distribution does not follow the advertising, there is considerable waste.

Magazines, as an advertising medium, did not show the same rebound from the depression low of 1933 as did newspapers. Radio is one reason for this development. Another reason is the demand on the part of advertisers for greater flexibility in the disbursement of their consumer advertising budget. However, while in general the magazines have not made robust progress in recent years, some individual magazines have scored notable advertising gains. The weekly and monthly periodicals continue to be a vitally important advertising medium. Actually hundreds of trade names that are household words today became part of our everyday language almost entirely through the power of magazine advertising.

The long life and leisurely reading enjoyed by most magazines is an exceptional advantage. Few magazines are purchased and discarded within a day. Although the length of life varies, an average might be a life of a week for the weekly magazines and a month for the monthly publications.

Newspapers.—No other nation has as many newspapers as the United States. Without a doubt, the newspapers represent the voice of the people. There is scarcely a home in the country that cannot be reached with some regularity through a newspaper—be it a daily, semiweekly, or weekly newspaper. Approximately 1,900 daily newspapers and over 10,000 weekly newspapers are published in the United States.

Newspapers carried national advertising almost before magazines came into existence. They are, today, the backbone of the majority of the advertising programs of manufacturers. The basic reason for this fact is that, actually, of our several hundred thousand manufacturers, only a comparative handful have national distribution—or sufficient national distribution to justify national magazine advertising. However, of manufacturers with sectional, or state, or even merely trading-area distribution, there is no end. These manufacturers usually find that newspapers enable them to buy circulation that matches their distribution—and circulation that outruns distribution is usually either complete waste or rather expensive circulation.

Of the 361 advertisers who spent over $100,000 in national advertising in 1940 in magazines, radio, and farm papers, over 200 were also large newspaper advertisers. In brief, newspapers constitute the most widely used media for manufacturers. They enable an advertiser to put his advertising pressure precisely where and when he feels it should be put. Schedules can be changed quickly—in 24 hours when necessary. They make it possible for an advertiser to start in a small way, and then expand as his sales expand. They enable an advertiser to run a campaign quickly in a territory that needs bolstering.

As advertising has become more and more a business policy planned with all of the timeliness and swiftness of action of a military campaign, newspapers have become more popular as an advertising medium. Successful advertising today demands elasticity, mobility, speed, and change of pace. Newspapers make all of this maneuvering feasible.

Radio.—At the end of 1940, there were 29,397,000 homes with radio sets. Of these, 11,000,000 had more than one set. In addition, some 8,000,000 automobiles had radios. The growth of radio as an advertising medium has been a veritable fairy tale. Like anything that has enjoyed a mushroom growth, radio has had millions in advertising money wasted on it; it has also created millions in sales for advertisers. Hundreds of advertisers exist whose entire business has been built by radio advertising. Some former magazine advertisers now put practically all of their consumer advertising appropriations into radio; the same is true of some newspaper advertisers. By and large, radio has created more advertising than it has siphoned off from other advertising media.

Purposes accomplished by radio advertising.—Advertisers have used radio successfully to accomplish the following purposes. In nearly all cases merchandising and promotional tie-ins have also been employed.

1. Introduce a new product.
2. Remedy seasonal drop of sales volume.
3. Establish product name in mind of the consumer.
4. Familiarize consumers with new and varied uses of a product.
5. Dramatize special features of a product or service.
6. Reach specific audiences—for example, children, housewives.
7. Build mailing lists.
8. Boost holiday "specials."
9. Educate the public to quality of product.
10. Promote public confidence in service or product.
11. Gain additional retail outlets.
12. Encourage retailers to push a product.
13. Build industrial morale.
14. Maintain top prices in a price-cutting market.
15. Force retailers to stock product despite small margin of profit.

Types of successful radio programs.—The following list cites the different types of radio programs that have met with success. In many cases a program may consist of combined elements such as a musical program combining music with dramatic skits, a news program interspersed with music and educational talks, or a studio contest combined with popular music.

Amusement Programs

Drama	*Music*	*Audience Participation*
Complete plays	Popular	Studio contests
Variety shows	Classical	Listener contests
Skits	Backgrounds	Games
Serial	Interludes	Personal experiences
		Quiz

"SERVICE" PROGRAMS

News	*Sports*	*Educational*	*Public Service*
News flashes	Game results	Music	Employment service
Commentators	Game descriptions	Literature	Safety program
	Sport comments	Interviews	Personal advice
		Talks	Political speeches
			Institutional
			Weather reports

Major values offered by radio.—Radio offers equal opportunities to the small and to the large advertiser. Through spot broadcasting, through programs having as many as a dozen different sponsors, advertisers with actually tiny budgets have "gone on the air" and put their message over. With the advent of frequency-modulation broadcasting, which will create thousands of small stations where there are now only hundreds of large ones, radio will become still more available to the small advertiser.

Spot broadcasting may be defined as local radio advertising, although there are advertisers who use as many as 300 or 400 stations simultaneously in a spot campaign. Because all such broadcasting originates from the studios of the stations selected, the use of electrical transcriptions, or recordings, has become an economic necessity in most of these programs. A program is selected, rehearsed, and recorded in some metropolitan center convenient to talent and production experts, and individual discs are shipped to the stations carrying the campaign. Special equipment "feeds" the record into the station's transmitter, and a local announcer takes care of the commercials. The whole procedure may be compared to the shipment of plates and mats to local newspaper offices for simultaneous insertion in a dealer-advertising campaign.

The wide use of electrical transcriptions in spot broadcasting does not mean that facilities for local live talent shows have been neglected. Many stations are prepared to work with their local clients in the production of programs, and the larger stations maintain very complete production units and talent staffs.

Radio is, essentially, entertainment. To that extent, it is very much of a gamble, just as is a show on Broadway or a Hollywood movie. However, smart radio advertisers are, more and more, buying proved and tested programs. This is as true of the small advertiser as it is of the large.

It is undoubtedly correct to say that advertising money can be squandered more easily in radio than in most advertising media. This statement is no reflection on radio. It simply implies that radio is still in the "infant" stage, and, like most infants, it is not too predictable.

Television is an offspring of radio. It is most assuredly on the way. To say that it will have profound effects on advertising is to say the obvious. The advertising student as well as the experienced advertising practitioner will want to follow television closely. It will open new advertising horizons, and close others.

Farm papers.—Few publications get a closer and more appreciative reading than the well-established farm paper. If ever a publication is read "like a bible," that publication is the successful farm paper. What is more, it is apt to be the "bible" for the entire farm family.

Farm papers divide naturally into two groups, national and state. National farm papers have a national circulation; state farm papers usually confine their circulation to a single state. The farm papers have survived every advertising vicissitude. At the bottom of the 1933 depression they stood up better than did most advertising media. They offer a highly valuable shortcut to the great farm market. Actually, they have as competing advertising media only the radio and the semiweekly and weekly newspaper. They always succeed in putting up a good fight against the rural newspaper. The radio, however, is becoming increasingly important as a competitor. More and more advertisers are finding it advisable to supplement their farm paper advertising with radio to strengthen certain sales territories.

Direct mail.—Direct mail is not always looked upon as a consumer-advertising medium. It is used to such a large extent, however, in conjunction with the other advertising media that it certainly warrants mention here. It must be remembered that the majority of advertisers, whether they use magazines, newspapers, radio, or farm papers, offer a booklet, a leaflet, a premium, or an advertising novelty. When these inquiries come to the advertiser, they become part of a direct-mail follow-up. Most advertising budgets make a fairly liberal allowance for consumer direct-mail work. For a complete discussion of direct-mail advertising, see pages 305 et seq.

Outdoor advertising.—The two principal forms of outdoor advertising are posters and paint. Posters are sold in the standard twenty-four sheet size and smaller three-sheet panels. Paint is standardized to some extent, but the size is flexible.

Posters are of two kinds, regular and special. The regular panels sell for $7.80 or $8.25 per month, and the specials, which are generally illuminated and in more choice locations, cost $30 or $35 per month.

Ordinarily, posters are available for a thirty-day period only and in quantities based upon a standard set showing for each city. The average set showing is the "one-half" or "representative" showing, which consists of a specified number of panels (regulars or regulars plus specials) that are theoretically necessary to cover completely the entire population of the town. Two representative showings in one month, called a full showing, are available for intensified coverage; or, one half of a representative showing, called a quarter showing, may be purchased for partial coverage.

Each plant operator has only a limited number of posters in each city, which will permit only a certain number of representative showings in any one month. Posters are ordinarily contracted for well in advance, and in most of the better areas the plant is completely sold out during the warmer months. It is usually advisable, therefore, to plan poster advertising well ahead of the time of appearance.

Outdoor advertising has a complete geographical selectivity. It may be used to cover a single city or state, or the entire country. It has considerable flexibility within a market and usually may be selected for specific application to the outlets of the advertiser. It offers full color and a dominating size, which is frequently of importance to smaller advertisers who may be out-advertised in number of impressions, but among posters, at least, cannot be out-advertised in the size of the individual panel or the colors appearing on that panel.

Painted bulletins are generally purchased on a twelve-month or a thirty-six-month contract. They may be selected individually, and the price of each is often subject to individual negotiations. The more expensive and elaborate painted bulletins are located within the city limits on heavy traffic boulevards. They are sometimes located at eye level or may be elevated and visible from a great distance. They cost from $50 to $500 per month and up. Highway bulletins situated out on the open road are more frequently sold at a standard price and are less expensive than boulevard locations, costing about $25 to $35 per month.

Car cards.—Car cards appearing in streetcars, subways, elevated trains, busses, and even taxicabs, are sold very much as are twenty-four sheet posters—by towns and on the basis of representative, or full and half, runs. For reminder advertising, and as part of an advertising campaign in which other media are used, they serve an excellent purpose.

Premiums.—While it may not be absolutely correct to classify premiums as an advertising medium, they are used in many instances as such. For this reason they bear discussion here.

Premiums are used for the following purposes:

1. To help introduce new products.
2. To help increase the unit of sale.
3. To help consumers use the product correctly.
4. To encourage more frequent use of the product.
5. To win the interest of children.
6. To check radio programs.
7. As prizes in contests.

Premiums are used for the following purposes:

1. In a package—as some of the cereal manufacturers do.
2. Through a coupon—as some of the soapmakers do.
3. As a combination sale—where a manufacturer offers his regular item and a premium in combination.
4. Through the consumer returning a stipulated number of box tops or bottle tops.

Premiums are of all types, ranging from seeds, miniature posters and stamps to coffee makers, lamps, silverware, and every other conceivable item.

Millions of dollars are spent annually in this country on premiums, and the premium business has grown as a result. Procter & Gamble distributed premiums valued at over $1,000,000 in the course of a single year.

Advertising specialties.—Sometimes there is difficulty in differentiating between an advertising specialty and a premium. In general, an advertising specialty is an article that is usually given without cost and always without condition of sale of other goods. It always bears the name of the company that gives it away. The simplest kind of advertising specialty is a pencil, with the name of the giver on it. Knives, watch fobs, desk calendars, desk weights, blotters, wall calendars—all of these are advertising specialties. Many of these specialties have an amazingly long life. They build a tremendous amount of goodwill and have a great advertising value.

Trade papers.—Trade papers are magazines or newspapers devoted editorially to business or the professions. A tremendous number of them are published. Since every industry has its own particular features, and the structure within each field is peculiar to it, trade papers are difficult to classify. They do, however, fall into two broad classifications: horizontal media and vertical media.

Horizontal media appeal to a common interest of many industries and, therefore, circulate among many industries. Broad examples in this class are *Nation's Business* and *Business Week,* which treat business generally and are of interest to everyone connected with business. Other more specific examples would be *Purchasing Agent, Printers' Ink, Advertising and Selling, Factory Superintendent,* and others.

Each of the vertical papers deal with a single industry or a single phase of one industry. Some examples of this group are *Petroleum News, Hotel Management,* and *American Druggist,* confined to one phase of a single industry.

Trade papers can also be generally classified into business papers and professional or technical papers. The former are concerned with phases of business that follow production—namely, transportation, distribution, advertising, selling, credit, auditing, and so forth. The professional or technical papers cover production problems addressed to engineers, chemists, and technicians, and are likely to be highly technical. In addition, there are many publications that appeal to the professions—medicine, engineering, architecture, and so forth, and the numerous phases and shades of interests within each profession.

5. TESTING YOUR ADVERTISING

Can an advertiser forecast the results of his advertising?—The great question which every advertiser asks himself is: How can I tell whether the money that I am about to spend on advertising will produce the hoped-for results? In general, there are two ways in which an advertiser can answer this question for himself:

1. In determining whether the advertising that he proposes to launch will produce results, he can rely on his own judgment, supplemented by the knowledge and accumulated experience of his advertising agency.
2. He can pretest his advertising. That is, he can experiment and test on a small scale before advertising on a large scale and can then base his large-scale advertising on the results that he obtains from his tests.

Advertiser's personal judgment not reliable.—With regard to the first of the above methods—the advertiser's relying on his personal judgment—it is a curious fact that, although ninety-nine out of a hundred businessmen will hesitate to pass on a question relating to finance or production, few will hesitate to state definitely that such-and-such is a good or a bad piece of advertising and will support their statements with arguments that seem to them entirely convincing. Yet the most positive opinions have been proved again and again, when checked by actual results, to be wrong, and very far wrong. If this seems an exaggeration, refer to the two advertisements reproduced in Figures 20 and 21. One of these advertisements produced a greater number of inquiries than the other. Which one was it? Even if you are successful in choosing the better of these two advertisements, perhaps the fact that one was *72 to 75 per cent* more productive than the other will cause you to question whether, after all, you can depend on yourself to judge advertising and be sure that you are right. And you must be sure that you are right before you begin to plan the expenditure of your own advertising appropriation.

PINEAPPLE MINUTE TAPIOCA, see p. 13, in Cook-Book

MASQUERADE PUDDINGS, see recipe below

GOLDEN APRICOT ARABESQUE, see recipe below

DESSERTS GAY, DESSERTS ENTRANCING!

So easy to serve... so wholesome for all... send now for whole bookful Free

ARE you willing to make a wonderfully economical discovery? Then study the recipes on this page. They introduce you to the secret of making dozens of dessert sensations — as saving of time and worry as they are of cost. For they show you how really delightful Minute Tapioca dishes can be — and once you try them, you will surely want *all* the suggestions in the cook-book, free to you.

Just see how a simple recipe can play fairy godmother to a cup of grated pineapple, setting it all a'twinkle with sparkling bits of tapioca, and crowning it with a snowy star of whipped cream. "Pineapple Minute Tapioca" is the name in the recipe book and the picture is above.

You see also the amber beauty of Golden Apricot Arabesque. So much more tempting than apricots alone—for there is the full flavor of the fruit blended with the more delicate tartness of apricot and tapioca in cream. Or Masquerade Puddings — sunset hued, with the cerise trickle of cherry sauce spreading over their golden goodness. What a picture!

And then, just to introduce a totally different possibility, there is Chocolate Soufflé, light as a cloud, fragrant and rich with chocolate. Each serving boasts its own cream rosette.

MASQUERADE PUDDINGS

CHERRY RED SAUCE

GOLDEN APRICOT ARABESQUE

CHOCOLATE SOUFFLÉ see p. 14, in Cook-Book

Of course you will notice in these recipes that Minute Tapioca requires no soaking and only brief cooking, for this product of General Foods Corporation comes in delicate gleaming granules, already partly cooked, especially easy to digest, and so inexpensive. What good news it is, then, to know that Minute Tapioca is so versatile, and so thoroughly wholesome for children.

FREE — dessert suggestions for 30 days to come — send for Cook-Book

The scores of delicious desserts are not the only treasures in the new Minute Tapioca Cook-Book. There are equally as many amazing recipes using Minute Tapioca as a "precision ingredient"—showing how to keep high omelets from tumbling, how to prevent berry pies from running over, how to give tender body and texture to croquettes and meat loaves which will not crumble, how to add new sparkle to soups. Get this useful book without delay — send the coupon on its way today.

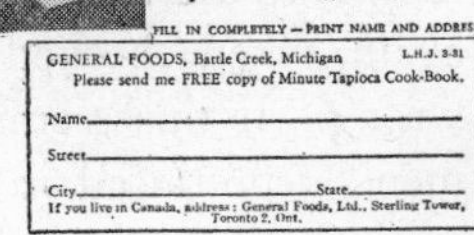

FILL IN COMPLETELY — PRINT NAME AND ADDRESS

GENERAL FOODS, Battle Creek, Michigan L.H.J. 3-31
Please send me FREE copy of Minute Tapioca Cook-Book.

Name__________

Street__________

City__________ State__________

If you live in Canada, address: General Foods, Ltd., Sterling Tower, Toronto 2, Ont.

© 1931, G. F. Corp.

From Kleppner, "Advertising Procedure." New York: Prentice-Hall, Inc.

Figure 20.—Is This a Better Advertisement Than Figure 21?

One of these advertisements produced 72 to 75 per cent more inquiries than the other. Can you guess which one? The answer, obtained through actual coupon responses, is at the bottom of page 454.

HOW TO MAKE GAY PARTY DESSERTS THAT ARE GOOD FOR CHILDREN TOO!

Write now for a "Cook's Tour with Minute Tapioca," a wonderful new cook-book, yours for the asking

1 Grapefruit Minute Tapioca, *recipe below* 2 Peanut Butterscotch, *recipe on page 7 of the new Cook-Book* 3 Celestine Lemon Tapioca, *recipe on page 12 of the new Cook-Book* 4 Creamy Apricot Pudding *recipe on page 9 of the new Cook-Book*

As the French know so well, the dessert triumph of a dinner party is not so much a matter of cost as it is a matter of knowing how.

There are literally dozens of dessert sensations that can be made easily and inexpensively with Minute Tapioca. And a recently-published cook-book that *tells you how* is *free* for the asking.

Here, for instance, you will find a recipe for Creamy Apricot Pudding, a soft orange cloud enriched with a deep topping of apricots. A success at any dinner — and *so easy* with Minute Tapioca.

Peanut Butterscotch — inexpensive, yet mellow and smooth as a continental mousse; this grand cook-book gives you the secret.

A piquant fluffed-up cream, delicately permeated with lemon flavor . . . Celestine Lemon Tapioca! And Grapefruit Minute Tapioca . . . glistening segments of grapefruit garnished with orange and a tiny chain of green mint cherries. What pictures!

Such gay, sparkling colors! Such subtle, haunting flavors! Such texture!

Minute Tapioca is wonderfully wholesome for children, and so easily digested. And what a relief and perhaps a surprise . . . to know that you can make desserts good enough to tempt the most blasé palate, yet safe for the small child. How much time and effort it saves you!

All these and many others just as irresistible, together with instructions for using Minute Tapioca as a "Precision Ingredient," are gathered together into one priceless book "A Cook's Tour with Minute Tapioca."

FREE NOW TO YOU—

The new Minute Tapioca Cook-Book

The best recipes we've tested to date are now given in the new Minute Tapioca Cook-Book. Half a hundred enchanting desserts . . . equally as many amazing recipes, using Minute Tapioca as "precision ingredient" . . . featuring *non-collapsible omelets, non-crumbling meat loaves, non-runny berry pies* . . . All made quickly, easily . . . since Minute Tapioca doesn't have to be soaked, and cooking it is only a matter of minutes . . . The sooner you send for a "Cook's Tour with Minute Tapioca" the better your family will like it! Put the stamp on the envelope today!

GRAPEFRUIT MINUTE TAPIOCA

⅓ cup Minute Tapioca; 1½ cups hot water; ¾ cup sugar; 1 cup grapefruit juice; 2 grapefruit, sections free from membrane; 1 orange, sections free from membrane.

Add Minute Tapioca to water, and cook in double boiler 15 minutes, or until tapioca is clear, stirring frequently. Add sugar and grapefruit juice. Pour over grapefruit sections. Chill. Serve in sherbet glasses. Garnish with sections of orange and bits of green mint cherries or jelly. Serves six.

All measurements are level.

FILL IN COMPLETELY — PRINT NAME AND ADDRESS

GENERAL FOODS TS-3-31
Battle Creek, Michigan

Please send me FREE copy of Minute Tapioca Cook-Book.

NAME ____________________

STREET ____________________

CITY __________ STATE __________

If you live in Canada, address General Foods, Ltd., Sterling Tower, Toronto 2, Ontario

From Kleppner, "Advertising Procedure"

Figure 21.—Is This a Better Advertisement Than Figure 20?

The more experience an advertiser has, the less likely he is to judge an advertisement by appearance alone. He tries to get some actual facts about its effectiveness, by means of a test, before spending a large amount of money.

Knowledge and experience of advertising agency not an infallible guide.—The advertising agency, because of its specialized knowledge and accumulated experience, is undoubtedly a better judge of effective advertising than the advertiser himself. However, tests have shown that advertising men are far from infallible. The most notable test on this point was that made by Kenneth M. Goode. Mr. Goode took eleven pairs of advertisements, each pair advertising the same product, and presented them in turn to the assembled members of fifteen advertising clubs in all sections of the country. All the advertisements had actually been used and records of results kept; in each pair there was one advertisement that had proved considerably more resultful than the other. The clubs participating in the test were:

- Baltimore
- Cedar Rapids
- Chicago (Advertising Post, American Legion)
- Cincinnati
- Des Moines
- Grand Rapids
- Hartford
- Lincoln
- Milwaukee (Women's)
- Newark
- New Haven
- Pittsburgh
- Richmond
- Toledo
- Washington

Copies of the eleven pairs of advertisements were distributed to each member of these clubs; the advertisements were discussed; and then a vote was taken to determine the majority opinion as to which was the more effective advertisement in each pair. The results are reported by Mr. Goode as follows (Kenneth M. Goode and Carroll Rheinstrom, *More Profits From Advertising*):

> Every man had his opinion. Few ever missed voting! And frequently when the voting results were compared with the facts, pandemonium reigned. As well it might! For out of the fifteen representative professional clubs, only three achieved as high as 72 per cent correctness! Four attained 63 per cent correctness! Six, the greatest number, were only 54 per cent right! One club was marked 45 per cent; and another, numbering among its members some of the best known advertising men in the country, was dismayed with a correctness of only 27 per cent!

Answer to Question on Pages 452, 453

Figure 21 proved 72 to 75% better than Figure 20.

The results of the tests are tabulated below:

Club	*Per Cent*
A	54
B	54
C	27
D	54
E	72
F	54
G	54
H	63
I	54
J	63
K	63
L	72
M	63
N	45
O	72

What pretesting aims to do.—The fact that tests have shown that advertisers and advertising men are not reliable judges as to which advertisements will produce results is not entirely surprising. Personal prejudices are one factor. Close contact with the product, and remoteness from the public, is perhaps another factor. Still a third is the "professional viewpoint," which causes an advertiser or advertising man to judge advertisements in accordance with standards other than the simple, practical standards of the consumer. Many other explanations of the unreliability of personal judgment could be found, but what is of chief importance is the fact that, whatever the explanation, personal judgment and experience cannot be depended upon to any great extent.

Pretesting attempts to eliminate mere opinion, prejudice, and theory in the planning of an advertising campaign. It aims to subject the ingredients of the campaign to tests on a small scale—tests conducted on the same public that is to read the final advertising and ultimately purchase the product—with the object of discovering which ingredients will have the desired effect and produce the desired results.

There are a number of methods of pretesting. These are described in the following pages.

Pretesting by the Sales-Area Method

What the sales-area method is.—The so-called sales-area test may be illustrated by the following hypothetical case. The product to be advertised is a toilet soap. Analysis of the product and of the market suggests that a number of different advertising appeals are possible. For example, one appeal might be the purity appeal; this particular soap has been shown by chemical analysis to be purer than any other soap in its price class. Another approach might be the beauty appeal; buy this soap to protect and beautify your complexion. A third appeal might be semihumorous. A fourth possibility might be an appeal to fear; a poor complexion is a social handicap. The advertiser himself may favor one type of advertising; his advertising manager another; his agency perhaps a third. The fundamental question is: Which of these various appeals is the best; which will produce the greatest public response and hence the greatest sales results? Before launching his advertising and spending his appropriation, the advertiser wishes to be able to answer this question with some degree of certainty. He decides to conduct a sales-area test.

Procedure in the sales-area test.—To conduct his sales-area test the advertiser proceeds as follows:

1. He selects sales areas in various sections of the country.
2. In each of these areas he chooses one or more cities to serve as "test" cities.
3. In the same areas he chooses one or more cities to serve as "control" cities.
4. In the control cities he continues to run the advertising that he has previously been using; or, in the event that he has not been advertising, he withholds his advertising from the control cities.
5. In the test cities he substitutes for the old advertising the new advertising that he proposes to use subsequently on a large scale.
6. A careful check is kept of sales in the control and test cities (the old *versus* the new advertising), and on the basis of the results obtained, the advertiser decides whether the new advertising will be successful.

To continue the hypothetical case mentioned above, assume that the advertiser wishes to test the purity appeal against the fear appeal. Assume, further, that he chooses a certain section as one of his sales areas; that City *A* and City *B* are to be the test cities in this area; and that City *X* is to be the control city in this area. Then, in City *A* the purity appeal is run; in City *B* the fear appeal is run; and in City *X* the previous campaign is continued. A careful tabulation of sales in the three cities is made.

Suppose that analysis of the results obtained from the test in this particular area reveals the following facts:

1. In City *X*, the control city, sales are slipping. This may suggest that the effect of the advertising campaign that is now being used is probably waning.
2. In City *A* the purity appeal stimulated an increase of 6.5 per cent in dollar sales.
3. In City *B* the fear appeal stimulated an increase of 16.5 per cent in dollar sales.

In this particular area, therefore, the fear appeal is considerably more effective than either the present campaign or the purity appeal. If results from tests in other sales areas were similar, the advertiser would undoubtedly choose the fear appeal in preference to the purity appeal as his next large-scale campaign, with reasonable assurance that he was making no mistake.

Safeguards to observe in sales-area testing.—From the above description of the procedure followed in pretesting by the sales-area method, it is apparent that there is danger of the results being distorted unless the greatest care is exercised. There are many variables that have to be taken into account; for example, the closing down of a large factory in either the control city or one of the test cities would probably affect the tests. If the results of a sales-area test are to be reliable, as many of the variables as possible must be controlled or eliminated. The following are a number of practical safeguards derived from the experience of companies that have used the sales-area test.

1. *Factors to consider in choosing sales areas.*—A single sales area, no matter how large, cannot be depended upon to give reliable results. Not less than three areas, but preferably five, should prob-

ably be used. Moreover, the sales areas chosen should, as far as possible, be typical of larger territories, and in the aggregate should be typical of the total territory in which the product is sold.

2. *Factors to consider in choosing test and control cities.*—The following are the most important factors:

(*a*) The test and control cities should be as nearly comparable as possible.

(*b*) Small cities are of little value for testing purposes; 30,000 population may be taken as the minimum.

(*c*) A growing, progressive city is more suitable than a city whose population is standing still or declining.

(*d*) Each of the cities should be an independent market; that is, the bulk of the purchasing by consumers should be done within the city itself, and not to any great extent in neighboring cities.

(*e*) Cities that have a number of different sources of income are preferable to cities depending to a great degree on a single industry. The purchasing power of a city that is dependent upon a single industry follows the curve of current conditions in that industry.

(*f*) The dealer setup in each city should be equal. Avoid cities in which one dealer, or a chain organization, dominates the market.

(*g*) As a final check, it is advisable to obtain first-hand information as to current business conditions in each of the cities under consideration. Cities in which abnormal conditions prevail (owing to closing down of a plant, strikes, and the like) can then be eliminated from the list.

3. *Check of sales for period preceding tests.*—In order that the effect of the advertising which is being tested can be accurately measured, it is necessary that sales in the test and control cities be checked for a period preceding the tests; sales during the testing period and during the period preceding the tests are then compared. How long should the preliminary checking period be? In deciding this it must be remembered that sales of the same product, in the same city, and without any material change in business conditions, fluctuate greatly from week to week. In some of the tests that have been conducted, the preliminary checking period has varied from two weeks to three months. Two weeks is entirely too short a period to take account of sales fluctuations. Four or six weeks would appear

to be the minimum, and a longer period is advisable if the expense involved is not prohibitive.

4. *How long should the test period be?*—The answer to this question depends to a certain extent upon the type of product that is being advertised. Some products are purchased frequently; others only at intervals. The advertising must be given time to produce results. Four or six weeks is the minimum for a product that is bought frequently. Hurrying the tests will produce misleading results. The longer the period in which the advertising is tested, the more likely it is that variables tending to distort the results will be eliminated.

5. *How should sales in the test and control cities be checked?*—Companies that have used the sales-area test have found it advisable actually to check the sales themselves, through weekly or semiweekly calls at the stores, rather than rely on the dealers to furnish reports. It is not necessary, however, to check sales in all the stores in the test and control cities. It is usually true that a percentage of the stores in any city do most of the business; small stores may safely be ignored for testing purposes.

6. *Should the sales check be of jobbing sales or retail sales?*—Sometimes a check of jobbing sales is used instead of a check of retail sales. There are advantages and disadvantages in this method. Some of the advantages are:

(*a*) A check of jobbing sales reduces to a minimum the expense involved in the collection of sales data.

(*b*) The advertising tests can be started immediately, without a preliminary checking period, since figures on past sales to jobbers are usually readily available. When retail sales are checked, it is necessary to delay the tests of the advertising while sales data for the preliminary checking period are being collected.

Some of the disadvantages of checking jobbing sales instead of retail sales are:

(*a*) It is necessary to use larger sales areas, and this increases the cost of the advertising during the test period.

(*b*) The test period has to be longer, because of the "lag" between retail sales and jobbing sales.

(*c*) Jobbing sales are a less direct check on the effects of the advertising than retail sales.

The majority of companies conducting sales-area tests favor a check of retail sales rather than jobbing sales.

7. *Sales conditions uniform in all test and control cities.*—It is important that sales conditions be kept as uniform as possible in all the test and control cities. During the testing period there should be no extra sales effort on the part of dealers, the sales force, or newspapers that perform merchandising services for the advertiser. If dealers and salesmen push sales with more than usual enthusiasm during the testing period, then the tests are not tests strictly of the advertising. When tests are being conducted, it is a good plan to keep the program confidential until it is under way, and then not to encourage dealers and salesmen to be unduly aggressive.

Advantages and disadvantages of sales-area method.—In comparison with other methods of pretesting, the sales-area method has a number of advantages, as well as certain disadvantages. The following are some of the disadvantages:

1. The sales-area method involves considerable expense. The check of sales during the preliminary checking period and during the testing period is expensive. So also is the actual running of the advertisements in the test cities for periods that may extend from four weeks to three months.

2. The sales-area method requires time. Taking into account the preliminary checking period and the testing period itself, dependable results can hardly be obtained in less than three months as a minimum. To lessen this difficulty, however, there is the possibility of running test campaigns concurrently with the regular campaign; that is, while a campaign is being run on a national scale, certain cities are segregated, and future campaigns are tested in those cities. This is the procedure followed by a number of companies using the sales-area test. Some of these companies have had as many as four or six campaigns under test at the same time that another campaign was being used nationally. The test campaign that proves to be most effective is then chosen as the next national campaign.

3. By its nature, the sales-area test can be applied only through local media—chiefly newspapers. It cannot be used in national magazines.

4. The practical problems involved in applying the principles of

the sales-area test may in some cases be hard to solve. There are numerous factors that may affect the results of the tests, and these factors are often not subject to the advertiser's control. The sales-area method of testing must therefore be applied with the utmost vigilance, and the results very carefully interpreted in the light of the total situation.

As against the above, the following are some of the advantages of the sales-area method:

1. The sales-area plan is the only method of pretesting that is a direct check upon sales. Under other methods the effect of the advertising upon sales is usually estimated by indirect means.
2. Although the sales-area method is expensive and takes time, if a large sum of money is to be spent on the final advertising campaign, the expenditure involved in pretesting is justifiable. A large advertiser who does not test merely because of the expense may be open to the criticism that he is penny wise and pound foolish.
3. If a sales-area test is planned and executed carefully, the results are dependable. The experience of advertisers who have used the sales-area test would appear to confirm this. Among these advertisers are the following: Pepsodent, Kolynos, Listerine, Ambrosia, Campbell's Soup, Fleischmann's Yeast.

Pretesting by the Inquiries Method

What the inquiries method is.—As its name suggests, the inquiries method is a system of testing advertisements by a count of the inquiries that different advertisements pull. The system is comparable to the methods used by mail-order advertisers. Mail-order advertisers generally "key" all their advertisements, usually through the use of key numbers on coupons; the key number is different on each advertisement. A record is kept of the number of inquiries pulled by each advertisement; the inquiries, when followed up, result in sales. Analysis of his records enables the mail-order advertiser to know, with regard to each advertisement that he runs, the following facts:

1. Number of inquiries that the advertisement pulled.
2. Number of these inquiries that were consummated as sales.
3. Cost per sale.

Through this system of coupons, inquiries, and tabulations of cost per sale, the mail-order advertiser obtains definite answers to his problems. For example, there may be doubt as to whether Publication *A* is better for advertising purposes than Publication *B*. The mail-order advertiser can run test advertisements in both publications (exactly the same advertisement being used in each); his results may show that the cost per sale in Publication *A* is 85 cents, while the cost per sale in Publication *B* is 57 cents; on the basis of these results the advertiser would choose Publication *B* for regular use. The inquiries system of testing so-called "general" advertising is an attempt to apply mail-order testing methods to general advertising, with a view to building up for the general advertiser as solid a foundation of facts and figures as that enjoyed by the mail-order advertiser.

Procedure in the inquiries test.—One of the chief differences between the sales-area method and the inquiries method is that the sales-area method tests the complete campaign (in a limited area), whereas the inquiries method is often used to test the various elements in the campaign, for the purpose of determining the most productive combination of those elements. Assume that an advertiser wishes to pretest by the inquiries method a campaign that he has formulated. His procedure is roughly as follows:

1. Certain media are chosen for purposes of the tests.
2. In the test media the advertiser runs his campaign and keeps a record of the inquiries produced. To stimulate inquiries, an offer —commonly in the form of a coupon—is placed on each advertisement.
3. The various elements in the campaign are tested, only one particular being changed at a time. For example, the advertising as first run may bear a certain type of headline. It is desired to test another type of headline. Then the advertisement is run again, with only the headline changed, under exactly similar conditions—in the same media, in the same size, in the same position, with the same offer, and so forth. A count of the inquiries produced indicates which is the more effective type of headline. The other elements that it is desired to test are changed one at a time; and, when the tests are concluded, the advertiser can tell from his count of inquiries which is the most productive combination of the various elements that his advertising is to contain.

The following are a few of the points that may be tested as described above, by a count of inquiries:

1. Which media are most effective? Within limits, a count of inquiries is a useful guide for the advertiser in his selection of media.
2. What size of space is most productive—full pages, half pages, quarter pages, or smaller?
3. Are preferred positions in publications worth the extra cost?
4. Is color worth the extra cost?
5. Of several different styles of copy, which is the most productive?
6. Is long copy better than short copy?
7. Which of a number of different headlines will pull best?
8. Are photographs better than illustrations?
9. What season of the year is best for advertising the product?

Two problems in the use of the inquiries method.—The general advertiser who uses the inquiries method of testing is brought face to face with a problem that does not confront the mail-order advertiser. This problem is: Is the volume of inquiries received from the advertising an accurate index to the volume of sales that the advertising produces? The mail-order advertiser can readily obtain the answer to this question; he follows up his inquiries and knows definitely the number of sales that result. The general advertiser does not follow up his inquiries (other than to send to each inquirer whatever he has offered), and apparently he is left in the dark as to:

1. Whether the people who inquire about his product subsequently go to a local store and buy it; or, are the inquirers mere coupon-clippers?
2. Whether the number of people who mail inquiries is an index to the number of people who do not inquire, but buy the product as a result of the advertising.

Are inquirers mere coupon-clippers? how to defeat coupon-clippers.—There is the danger that the inquirers may be mere coupon-clippers, and not serious prospects. However, there are a number of ways in which coupon-clippers may be defeated. Some of these are:

1. The offer may be made a "hidden" offer. That is, the offer may not be featured in a headline, nor need there be a coupon; the offer can be contained in the body of the copy, in the form of a simple statement that a booklet or sample will be mailed to those

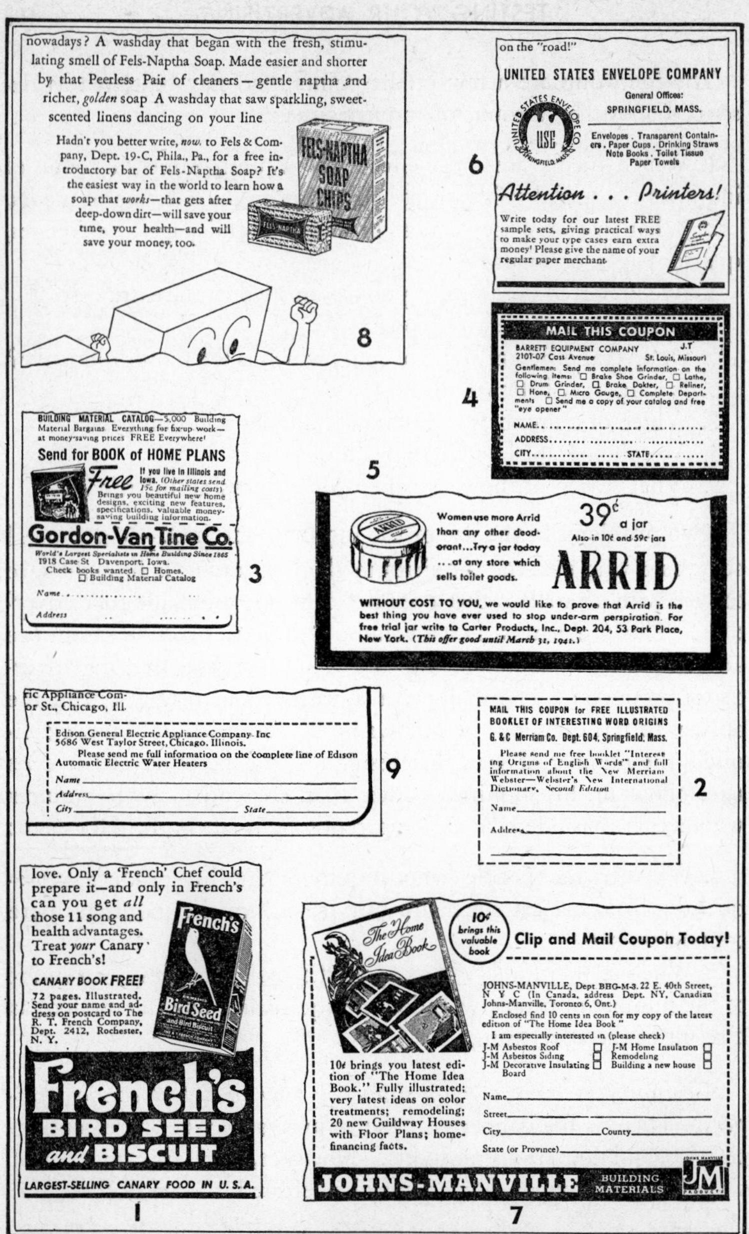

Figure 22.—Chart of Coupons and Special Offers.

who write to the advertiser. Only those who are sufficiently interested to read the body of the advertisement will find the offer and go to the trouble of writing a letter.

2. A small charge may be made for whatever is offered. A charge of 10 cents will usually eliminate inquiries from children, residents in rural communities, and others who make a practice of clipping coupons.

3. In some cases the offer can be made in such form that it will interest only those who are prospects for the advertised product. For example, if a manufacturer of pipe tobacco offered a free ash tray to inquirers, he would doubtless receive thousands of worthless inquiries —from women, cigarette and cigar smokers, and others. If, on the other hand, he offered a pipe reamer, the bulk of his inquiries would come from men who were pipe smokers and potential users of his product.

4. The offer may be conditioned upon the inquirer's mailing to the advertiser a carton or some other evidence of the fact that he has purchased the product.

By testing from time to time, there can also be determined the number of inquirers who subsequently become purchasers and the percentage of coupon-clippers among the inquirers. One method is to use anonymous follow-ups. These follow-ups consist of cards on which a number of products are listed, the name of the adver-

---

Explanation of Figure 22.

(1) Common form of offer of booklet, without coupon. Instructions simple. Product pictured.
(2) Common form of coupon for free booklet.
(3) Free offer; literature pictured. Small charge to cover mailing costs for distant residents secures interest only of those who are prospects.
(4) Common form of coupon where several products are sold and information on each is handled in separate literature. Enables classification of mailing list.
(5) Method of developing trial orders. Limitation of time of offer stirs reader to prompt action.
(6) Attention of certain class of prospects called to free offer of sample. Absence of coupon reduces number of non-prospect inquiries.
(7) Charge of 10 cents eliminates those who make practice of clipping coupons. Check list helps classify prospects.
(8) Hidden offer of a sample cuts down number of inquiries from coupon clippers. Inquiries show actual reading of ad. Expectation of automatic repeat sales makes offer possible.
(9) Simple effort to get inquiries.

tiser's product being among them; the people receiving the cards are asked merely to check off the products that they have recently purchased. The cards do not bear the name of the advertiser, but of a dummy "research bureau."

Is volume of inquiries an index to volume of sales?—A number of studies have been made of the reliability of inquiries as a criterion of sales. Dr. Daniel Starch conducted an "Analysis of Five Million Inquiries" produced by 3,500 advertisements of 163 advertisers over a period of 12 years. Doctor Starch's conclusion was that sales figures roughly parallel volume of inquiries. Other investigators have reached the same conclusion. However, fundamentally the answer to the question as to whether volume of inquiries is an index to volume of sales depends upon the manner in which the inquiries method is used. Carelessly applied, it may produce misleading results; adequately safeguarded, its dependability is correspondingly increased.

Safeguards to observe in testing by the inquiries method.—The following are the chief safeguards:

1. *Do not force inquiries.*—It would obviously be easy to obtain a very large number of inquiries if the offer were featured in the advertisement and dominated everything else. The offer should be simple and businesslike; also, if at all possible, the offer should be of such a nature that it will interest only those who are potential users of the advertised product.

2. *Test only one particular at a time.*—This is a fundamental principle of testing by the inquiries method. If it is desired to test the effectiveness of two different types of headlines, then everything other than the headlines must remain the same. If the value of preferred position in a publication is to be tested, the advertisement in the preferred position must be exactly the same as that in the non-preferred position. If two different offers are to be tested, then except for the change in the offers the advertisements must be alike to the minutest detail. The reason for the principle that only one particular should be tested at a time is apparent; if, for example, both headline and offer were changed, it would be difficult to determine which of the two changes produced the variation in results.

3. *Rely only on comparative count of inquiries.*—The number of inquiries obtained from a single advertisement has little meaning.

There must be some standard with which the results can be compared. This standard is the number of inquiries received from one or more other advertisements run under exactly similar conditions. If, for example, Advertisement *A* pulls 5,000 inquiries, this by itself has little significance. If, however, Advertisement *B* is run under exactly the same conditions and pulls 8,000 inquiries, it is reasonable to conclude that Advertisement *B* is a better sales instrument than Advertisement *A*; if, further, the only difference between the two is in the headlines, then the results indicate that the type of headline used in Advertisement *B* is more effective than that used in Advertisement *A*.

In addition to the three safeguards mentioned above, other safeguards will suggest themselves as necessary in particular cases. The inquiries method cannot be applied automatically or with mathematical precision. It needs the support of strong common sense. For example, an advertiser running copy in an expensive magazine, such as *Town & Country,* would doubtless receive poor returns if he used a coupon, for the reason that people would not wish to mutilate an expensive and beautifully printed magazine; if it was desired to key the advertisement, a hidden offer or a simple request that readers write to the advertiser would be more logical. Similarly, if an advertiser intends to use a coupon, it may be advisable for him not to place his adverisement on the back cover of certain serious magazines of which many readers keep files; readers would not wish to cut the back cover of a magazine of this type.

Pretesting by the Consumer-Jury Method

Procedure in the consumer-jury test.—In general, the consumer-jury test consists of submitting to a "jury of consumers" specimens of the advertising that it is proposed to use. The jury is asked to rank the various pieces of advertising in the order of their effectiveness. The advertising chosen by the majority is run in the campaign.

In practice, the methods followed by advertisers in applying the consumer-jury test differ considerably in detail. For example:

1. In some cases the advertising submitted to the jury is in final form; that is, the headlines and copy are set in type, the illustra-

tions made, and so forth, and what the jury sees are final proofs showing the advertisements as they would actually appear in publications. In other cases the advertising submitted to the jury is in rough-draft form, with the headlines and layout merely sketched in. The latter method is the more economical.

2. Occasionally, when the advertisements that are under test are given to the jury, the jury is required not to analyze them but merely to give an answer to some such question as: "Which of these advertisements would be most likely to make you want to buy the product?" On the other hand, some advertisers have required the jury to analyze the advertisements, and to rate them for attention value and appeal, or for attention value, headline, and text.

3. Some advertisers mail the advertisements to the members of the jury, the arrangement being that the members of the jury will receive a small gift in return for their services. Other advertisers prefer to send out investigators to interview the members of the jury and obtain their reactions at first hand.

Safeguards to observe in using the consumer-jury test.—The following are the chief safeguards:

1. The persons chosen for the jury should be typical prospects for the product. If, for example, the product to be advertised is a baby food, as far as possible the jury should be comprised of women who have babies.

2. The number of persons tested should be adequate. Tests on a small number may produce misleading results. A jury of two hundred persons may be regarded as a safe minimum.

Advantages and disadvantages of the consumer-jury test.—The criticism most frequently made of the consumer-jury test is that it requires the jury to express a conscious reaction to the advertisements, whereas under actual conditions the reaction of the consumer to the advertisements that he sees is largely subconscious. Critics of the consumer-jury test say that no one can tell, merely by looking at two or more advertisements, which would have the greatest effect upon him if read in a publication. There is also the difficulty of getting the jury to be strictly honest. For example, if two advertisements for the same product are submitted to a jury, and one features low price while the other features the established reputation of the manufacturer, doubtless quite a number of the jury will *vote* for the reputation appeal, whereas in "real life" it would be the price appeal that would stimulate them to *buy*.

Various means have been used to overcome the difficulties outlined above. One advertiser tested his advertisements by direct mail. The advertisements were set up in exactly the form in which they would appear in publications. Then the last few lines of each advertisement, in which the reader was urged to call at his local store and purchase the product, were removed; in their place was inserted a hidden free offer—a sample of the product would be sent to inquirers. The advertisements under test were mailed to a split list; included in each envelope was a card bearing only the advertiser's name and address and, on the reverse side, three blank lines on which the inquirer could write his name and address. The product was not mentioned on the cards, and no effort was made to direct attention to the free offer. A count of the inquiries received indicated which was the strongest advertisement.

Another advertiser, who was employing field investigators to test two different types of advertising, used a simple trick to obtain frank and unartificial responses from the people who were interviewed. An investigator would call on an individual, and say that he wished to obtain an opinion regarding a new kind of advertising that his company was thinking of using. Then, reaching into his briefcase, he would pretend that he could not find what he was looking for, but, drawing out two advertisements, would say: "Oh, incidentally, while I'm looking for the new advertising, would you mind taking a look at these two ads?" A moment later he would produce a new set of advertisements and discuss these with the person being interviewed. When the interview was concluded, the investigator would ask: "By the way, you remember the two advertisements that I showed you first? Can you describe them for me?" The advertisements first shown were, of course, the advertisements under test, and the individual's ability to describe one or the other more fully and completely indicated which had made the greater impression upon him.

Mention has been made of some of the disadvantages of the consumer-jury test. However, this method of testing also has important advantages. Chief among these is the fact that it involves no great expenditure of time and money, and that it is comparatively easy to use. An advertiser who cannot afford to test by the sales-area method or by the inquiries method will find the consumer-jury method of considerable value.

6. HOW TO DESIGN AND REGISTER A TRADE-MARK

Adapted from Kleppner, "Advertising Procedure." New York: Prentice-Hall, Inc.

The four "musts" of trade-mark law.—A trade-mark must:

1. Be physically affixed to a commercial article or to its container.
2. Identify only.
3. Not be deceptive.
4. Be eligible for appropriation by one person to the exclusion of others.

Trade-mark must be affixed to the product.—The mere use of a device in an advertisement, on a letterhead, or even in the architectural design of the factory, does not make it a trade-mark. The device must be stamped, pasted, printed, embossed, or otherwise attached to the specific piece of merchandise or to its package.

From the standpoint of advertising, it is not sufficient to get the trade-mark on the product. *The trade-mark must adhere to it until it reaches the consumer.* Wrappers bearing the trade-mark for oranges were often lost before the fruit reached the housewife. A better method was found in the use of small labels, which were pasted on the fruit, and a subsequent improvement resulted in a machine that actually stamped the trade-mark on each individual orange. *The trade-mark must be inexpensive to apply.* The expense of trade-marking may involve the device itself, the machines necessary to affix it, and, of most importance, the slowing up of production. Finally, the *trade-mark must not be injurious to the product.* Over $30,000 was spent in perfecting the machine that could stamp oranges of different sizes without mashing the fruit. It is quite evident that the advertising office is not the only department whose wishes are to be considered in the creation of the trade-mark.

Trade-mark must identify only.—In considering trade-marks it is necessary to distinguish between the identifying device and the goods themselves. The identifying device can be stamped, printed, pasted, embossed, or otherwise attached to the product itself. As long as its *sole* function is to identify the goods, it is a trade-mark. It must not be a quality of the article, or a description of it; nor must it affect the utility of the product, or be an ornamenal or useful feature of it. If it is, the idea loses its status as a trade-mark and is regarded as a simple manufacturing feature that others may use (unless it is patented).

A concern making golf balls offered as its trade-mark an unusual mesh on the ball. It was held, however, that a mesh on a golf ball is a feature of its construction which, by its design, affects wind resistance and rolling; hence it was more than an identifying device, and not eligible as a trade-mark. Tire manufacturers have tried to hold out the designs of their treads as their trade-marks, but have been unable to do so. Treads are necessary on tires to secure better traction and prevent skidding. Consequently it was held that the design was not merely an identifying device but part of the product, required in its performance, and not acceptable as a trade-mark. (Such ideas may, however, be protected under design patents.) Odd-shaped packages or bottles are frequently offered as trade-marks, but similarly are ruled out because the oddity referred to is merely a construction distinctiveness. The trade-mark must identify only.

Trade-mark must not be deceptive.—A trade-mark must not appear so similar to an existing trade-mark for that class of goods that the public may mistake it for another mark. The test of whether one trade-mark imitates another is not whether a careful examination of the two reveals the difference, but whether the public in its ordinary course of affairs would be misled by the trade-mark as a whole.

Imitation of another trade-mark in sound, structure, significance, or appearance is misleading, unfair, and foolhardy. As a rule, infringements are made only upon successful trade-marks. Some day the infringing trade-mark may, despite itself, be successful. How can it hope to protect itself against its own infringers? With so many different fields of thought and expression from which to choose, there is no excuse for creating a trade-mark that is even doubtfully akin to an existing mark in that field.

The rights to a trade-mark are furthermore not enforceable if the trade-mark indicates a quality that does not exist. The use of *Syrup of Figs* was questioned because the product contained no such ingredient, and not until its formula was changed to do so was the trade-mark held acceptable. The use of the words *United States Standard* was denied to a flour miller as tending to imply that the flour was of a Government-guaranteed quality, when, in fact, no such guaranty was offered. *Half-Spanish* for cigars which were not half Spanish was held deceptive.

Trade-mark must be eligible for exclusive use by one person.—The law frowns on a man's appropriating for his exclusive use a right that is the common property of others too. It is as though a man were to claim for his own private use a part of a public highway. So in trade-marks, men may try to claim as their own special identifying device an idea that others also have a right to use. Just how the law imposes its restrictions upon such practices will be shown in the discussion of specific forms of trade-marks.

Forms of trade-marks.—The law does not say what a trade-mark must look like; it merely says that the trade-mark must identify the product to which it is affixed and suggests that this may be done by "symbol, sign, word, or device." The forms of trade-marks in most frequent use may be grouped into these classifications:

(1) *Dictionary words* (English words found in the dictionary, used in an arbitrary, suggestive, or fanciful manner).—

Ivory Snow *(soap powder)*
Meadow Gold *(butter)*
Hickory *(belts)*
Old Gold *(cigarettes)*
Champion *(spark plugs)*
Caterpillar *(tractors)*

(2) *Coined or invented words.*—

Kelvinator *(refrigerator)*
Spam *(meat)*
Kodak *(camera)*
Kleenex *(tissue)*
Nylon *(fabric)*
Duco *(paint)*
Teel *(dentifrice)*
Philco *(radio)*

(3) *Foreign words.*—

Bon Ami *(soap)*
La Favorita *(cigar)*

(4) *Personal names (actual).*—

Elizabeth Arden *(cosmetics)*
Chrysler *(automobiles)*
Dr. Lyons *(tooth powder)*
Macgregor *(golf clubs)*
Fleischmann *(yeast)*
Firestone *(tires)*

(5) *Personal names (historical or mythological).*—

Chesterfield *(cigarettes)*
Prince Albert *(tobacco)*
Robert Burns *(cigars)*
Lincoln *(car)*
Venus *(pencils)*
Hercules *(explosives)*

(6) *Geographical names.*—

Paris *(garters)*
Waterbury *(clocks)*
Kalamazoo *(parchment)*
Ohio *(electric cleaner)*

(7) *Initials and numbers.*—

B. V. D. *(underwear and swimming suits)*
A. C. *(spark plugs)*
4711 *(perfume)*
7-21 *(cigars)*
U. S. *(tires)*

(8) *Portraits, designs, symbols.*—Usually used in connection with one of the foregoing.

(9) *Novel uses of color and other physical devices.*

A single trade-mark may embody several of these classifications, as is done when a picture and a word are combined, or when a symbol and a syllable are used together.

Dictionary words—must not be descriptive.—The law excludes for trade-mark purposes words that are *descriptive*. For trade-mark purposes a term is held descriptive if it defines the nature, quality, structure, or use *of the goods under consideration*. Comparative adjectives such as *fine, high-class, grade A,* and *excellent* clearly have reference to the character of the goods. They are ineligible as trade-marks. Other examples of marks that have been held descriptive are:

Malted Milk
Computing Scale
Safe-t-Seal Envelopes
Fig Nuts Cereal
Instantaneous Tapioca
U-Put-On Rubber Heels
Vacuum Cup Tires
Keep Kold Packing Boxes

However, a term might be acceptable *if it is not ordinarily applied* to the particular type of article under consideration, although it is a familiar term when used in a different sense. The law holds such usage to be "suggestive" rather than "descriptive," and suggestive words are permitted. "Ivory" was held descriptive when applied to a toilet goods set, but merely "suggestive" when applied to soap. On the same principle "Elastic-seam" was held descriptive of hosiery, but "Elastic" was acceptable for bookcases, because the public did not generally refer to bookcases in that manner. "Army" towels was held descriptive, as leading people to believe that the towels were the kind used by the army. "Navy" candy, on the other hand, was held not descriptive, as people do not or would not presume that the navy, officially or unofficially, eats candy of some special composition or brand.

A study of acceptable words reveals that the courts themselves have laid down no set rules on the question of descriptiveness. When the validity of a trade-mark depends upon an interpretation of what is and what is not descriptive, and when claims of its legal eligibility are based upon the precedent of trade-marks that are even more descriptive, all experiences indicate that it is best to leave trouble alone and create another idea.

Coined or invented words.—Regarding coined words (such as *Fab, Probak, Ansco*), one of the best forms of trade-mark to protect, the courts have held: "When a person forms a new word to designate an article made by him, which has never been used before, he may obtain such a right to that name as to entitle him to the sole use of it as against others who attempt to use it for the sale of similar articles." However, the misspelling or hyphenating of a word (*Yung-felo* instead of *Young Fellow*) gives it no rights that a phonetic pronunciation or correct spelling of the word would not have, and does not make a word that otherwise would be regarded as descriptive into one that is non-descriptive.

Foreign words.—A foreign word has no rights that an English translation of that word would not enjoy. *Le Bon* was held ineligible for use as a trade-mark for baking powder because its English translation is *good,* and *good* is regarded as a descriptive term.

Geographical names.—Because new geographical names are now difficult to protect, the names of geographical places *do not* provide

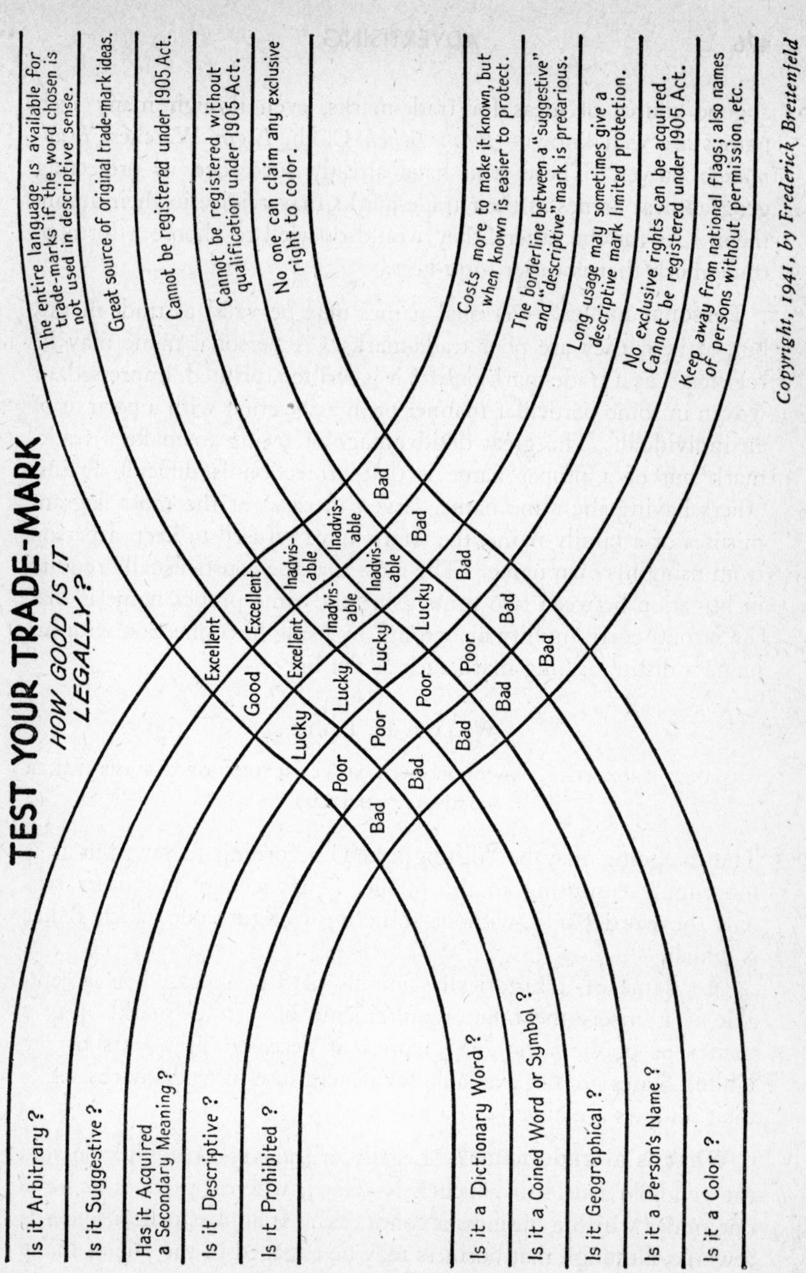

TEST YOUR TRADE-MARK

HOW GOOD IS IT LEGALLY?

Is it Arbitrary?

Is it Suggestive?

Has it Acquired a Secondary Meaning?

Is it Descriptive?

Is it Prohibited?

Is it a Dictionary Word?

Is it a Coined Word or Symbol?

Is it Geographical?

Is it a Person's Name?

Is it a Color?

Excellent

Good Excellent

Lucky Excellent Inadvisable

Poor Lucky Inadvisable Inadvisable

Bad Poor Lucky Inadvisable Bad

Bad Poor Lucky Bad

Bad Poor Bad

Bad Bad

Bad

The entire language is available for trade-marks if the word chosen is not used in descriptive sense.

Great source of original trade-mark ideas.

Cannot be registered under 1905 Act.

Cannot be registered without qualification under 1905 Act.

No one can claim any exclusive right to color.

Costs more to make it known, but when known is easier to protect.

The borderline between a "suggestive" and "descriptive" mark is precarious.

Long usage may sometimes give a descriptive mark limited protection.

No exclusive rights can be acquired. Cannot be registered under 1905 Act.

Keep away from national flags; also names of persons without permission, etc.

Figure 23.—Test Your Trade-Mark.

a good source of ideas for trade-marks, even though many such names are well known—*Palm Beach* Cloth, *Elgin* Watches, *Kalamazoo* Stoves. Those who have already succeeded in protecting geographical names as their trade-marks may rejoice in their attainment. As for the others, they would do well to choose a form of trade-mark that is easier to protect.

Personal names.—Personal names may be valid as trade-marks, but, at best, they are poor trade-marks. A personal name may be registered as a trade-mark only if it is written, printed, impressed, or woven in some particular manner or in association with a portrait of an individual. The great disadvantage of trying to make a trade-mark out of a proper name is that protection is difficult against others having the same name. Even in cases of the most flagrant misuses of a family name, the courts have refused to keep a person from using his own name. The most that the courts usually require in litigation between two firms using the same proper name is that the second party "nullify his wrong" by using in connection with his name a distinguishing mark such as the line:

WILLIAM H. BAKER

(DISTINCT FROM THE OLD CHOCOLATE MANUFACTORY OF WALTER BAKER COMPANY, LIMITED)

The foregoing may be "distinguished" according to law, but it is thoroughly confusing to the public. The average purchaser sees only the word *Baker,* without bothering to figure out which Baker is which.

The name of a historically famous person, deceased, is acceptable if it meets the other requirements of a trade-mark. (As a matter of public policy, the names of deceased presidents of the United States are not available for general use in trade-marks while their widows are alive.)

What is a trade name?—Legally, a *trade-mark* applies only to the vendible article to which it is affixed, whereas a *trade name* is one under which a business is conducted. It applies to a business as a whole, although that business may be engaged in the sale of many articles. Words like *Ivory* (soap), *Old Dutch Cleanser,* and *Gargoyle* (oil) are trade-marks, but *Procter & Gamble, Cudahy Packing*

Company, and *Vacuum Oil Company* are trade names. Trade names can be protected on grounds of unfair competition, but do not enjoy the form of protection accorded to trade-marks. Words used for trade-mark purposes are often called trade names. Although this practice is common, it is incorrect, unsound, and extremely confusing. Words used for trade-marks clearly come under the category of trade-marks, and not of trade names.

Advertisers often prefix their trade name to the trade-mark to improve their protection against infringement. We thus read of *Eastman* Kodak, *DuPont* Cellophane, *Vicks* Vapo-Rub, *General Electric* Hotpoint.

Initials and numbers.—Initials and numbers sometimes have a significance in a trade just as words do. In such instances they are regarded as being descriptive and are subject to the same limitations as words used for trade-mark purposes. From the advertising viewpoint, initials and numbers are the most difficult to establish as trade-marks, since they are the hardest for people to remember, and the easiest to imitate.

Portraits, designs, symbols.—A portrait of a person is legally acceptable as a trade-mark. Anyone may use the portrait of a deceased person (provided it is not already being used on a similar product). Portraits of living people may be used only with their consent. From the advertising standpoint, portraits are not highly effective as trade-marks. Most portraits look very much alike when reduced to the small size that may be required for trade-mark purposes. They are not easily reproduced. The style of picture they represent may go out of fashion soon. The whiskers of the Smith Brothers may have helped make their portraits a valuable trade-mark (as has the fortune spent in the advertising of them), but other successful examples are few.

A trade-mark must not include the flag or any insignia of the United States, or of any state or municipipility, or of any foreign country. It must not be the insignia of the Red Cross or of any organization that has adopted and publicly used an emblem. (The only exception to this is the right of firms who used a red cross on their products prior to the incorporation of the American National Red Cross in 1904.) The trade-mark must not be immoral, scandalous, or against public policy.

Color and other devices.—Appearance of goods is not a valid trade-mark, nor is its style of wrapping or its color. The law does not wish to give a monopoly of a color to any one person, since the number of colors is limited. A match company was unable to protect the color of its match heads as a trade-mark, a soap manufacturer the color of his soap, a bottle maker the color of his bottles, and a tire manufacturer the color of his tires. It is a well-settled rule that there can be no trade-mark in the mere form, size, or color of the package containing a product. But color may constitute a valid trade-mark when impressed in a particular design. From the advertising viewpoint, the use of color has many drawbacks, chief of which is the fact that it may be hard to show the trade-mark in publication advertisements.

How to create a trade-mark.—A trade-mark needs to be distinctive so that it may overcome confusion with competing articles, help the reader recollect the advertised brand when he thinks of buying the product, and assist him to recall previous advertisements whenever he sees the trade-mark.

The use of a word for a trade-mark generally gives its owner the right to alternative ways of saying the same thing—the use of a picture or the use of a symbol. The picture and the words are one and the same trade-mark. They may be used separately, together, or interchangeably. (We have, for example, the word *gargoyle* and a picture of a gargoyle.) It is well to have a trade-mark word that can be shown in pictorial form also, as it helps the public to remember the trade-mark and to recollect the word whenever they see the pictorial version of the trade-mark.

The trade-mark should be simple. It should require no explanation. If a design is used, it should have one distinguishing feature easy to remember and to put into words.

If a picture is adopted, it should be one that will not soon become obsolete. No element that the normal progress of time and custom may make obsolete should be introduced in a new trade-mark. If pictures of people are to be used, beware of the changes that take place in the style of hairdressing and of clothing.

In the designing of a trade-mark, cognizance must also be taken of the method whereby it is to be reproduced. Automobiles usually carry their trade-marks on their radiators and on the hubs of their wheels. Simple, open-faced designs are here particularly necessary. For jewelry, a trade-mark even more simple is required to permit of reduction in size. For most package goods, a trade-mark with its width three-fifths its height will be found adaptable to the container and to advertisements alike.

The use of broadcasting influences the choice of a trade-mark. A word that can be dramatized, or a name that suggests a radio personality, is preferable to a colorless combination of words or numbers or syllables or designs.

Copy demands of a trade-mark word.—The suitability of a word for use as a trade-mark can well be decided by good copy sense. The word should be as adaptable as some of the patented reading lamps, which can be hung, clamped, or stuck anywhere and still give forth their light.

The following qualifications help a trade-mark in its work. A single trade-mark may not embody all of these virtues, but it may at least strive to achieve them. Words chosen for trade-mark purposes should be:

1. *Simple and crisp.*—Such words are typified by *Lux, Zonite, Mazda, Fab, Vapex, Force.*

2. *Easy to say and to spell.*—What is the average reader to do with names such as *Hexylresorcinol, Houdailles, Hyomei, Telekathoras, Glycothymoline, Sempre Giovine?* Advertisers of products with such names may find it necessary to run an explanatory line spelling the name phonetically. This is one of the two ways out of the difficulty. The other way is to change the name before the product is advertised. Trade-marks must be easy for people to recognize when they hear them over the radio, and easy to spell. Lehn & Fink, makers of Pebeco, have received mail calling their product *Pebigle, Pedalgo, Pebsico, Publico.*

3. *Pronounceable in one way only.*—Is *Olivilo* to be pronounced "Ah-leev-eye-lo," or "Olive-eelo"; *Pall Mall,* "Pawl Mawl" or "Pell Mell"; *Michelin,* "Mish-elin," or "Mike-elin"? The public's pronunciation may be corrected by a simple expedient, such as was used by the Standard Oil Company. Their name, *Socony,* was mispronounced "sock-ohnee" and "soak-ohnee." The desired pronunciation was So-co′-ny, which they impressed by printing their name SoCOny and So*co*ny.

4. *Distinctive.*—A great fault of many new trade-marks is their commonness. One issue of *Hendrick's Commercial Register* listed 95 *National's,* 122 *Champion's,* 134 *Star's,* 142 *Ideal's,* 149 *Universal's,* and 184 *Standard's.* What claim to individuality could any new trade-mark make if it consisted of, or included, one of those terms?

5. *Suggestive of the product.*—The trade-mark must not literally describe the product, but it can suggest the nature of the article, as does each of the following: *Super Suds, Sheetrock* Wall-board, *Palmolive* Soap, *Sealdsweet* Fruits, *Mulsified* Shampoo. In contrast, *Electrolux* is a poor name for a *gas* refrigerator being sold in competition with *electric* refrigerators.

Protecting a trade-mark.—A most important point of American trade-mark law is that the first person to use a trade-mark is its owner *for that class of goods.* He is its owner whether or not he goes through any legal steps to record his ownership. As long as he can prove that he used the trade-mark before anyone else, for that class of goods, he is given the sole rights to it in that field—provided, also, that he does not abandon the mark once he begins using it.

The fact that a man is the first user of a trade-mark for a certain product does not automatically give him an exclusive right to that trade-mark for all products. The law limits his claim to products of the "descriptive class" to which he applies it. *Packard* as a trade-mark is owned by one firm for automobiles, and by another for pianos. *Cadillac* is a trade-name for a car owned by one company. An entirely different concern secured the right to use *Cadillac* on vacuum cleaners. *Beech-nut Bacon* and *Beech-nut Cigarettes* are each owned by different organizations, as are *Krumbles Cornflakes* and *Golden Crumbles* (candy).

What, then, is meant by products of "the same descriptive class"? Generally, two products are held to be in the same descriptive class if the public might be led to believe that both were produced or sold by the same house. The legal test is based on a liberal interpretation of these questions:

1. Would the public confuse one product with the other? (Two brands of cheese, for example.)

2. Might the public be confused as to the origin of the goods because they are both sold over the same counter? (As in the case of canned peaches and canned berries.)

3. Is there a reasonable possibility that the firm making one product may, in the natural course of events, expand its activities to include the second type of product? (As in the case of phonographs and radio receiving sets.)

In the light of the foregoing, the following list showing products which have and products which have not been held to be in the same descriptive class may be interesting:

Same Descriptive Class

Tea, Coffee .... Peanut Butter, Relish
Shirts, Hats, Caps .... Pajamas
Collars .... Collar Buttons
Cake Scouring Soap .... Scouring Powder
Pancake Syrup .... Pancake Flour

Not Same Descriptive Class

Textile Fabrics .... Lubricating Oils
Animal Feed .... Human Food
Wardrobe Bags .... Overshoes
Cigars, Tobacco .... Soft Drinks

Although a trade-mark applies to only one class of goods at a time, a man can protect his trade-mark on as many different classes of goods as he makes and sells, provided he is the first to use the trade-mark in each of the respective classes.

Procedure for registering a trade-mark.—Application for registration of a trade-mark should be made to the Patent Office, Washington, D. C. (Trade-marks may also be registered in individual states.) Ownership of a trade-mark arises from its use; hence it must be used *before* it can be registered. A new trade-mark may be registered for a term of 20 years, with the privilege of renewal for an equal term. *The services of an attorney should be secured in any contemplated trade-mark action before the proposed trade-mark is used in any way whatsoever; certainly before any money is spent in printing or packaging.*

Every article whose trade-mark is registered should bear the notice: "Registered U. S. Patent Office," or "Reg. U. S. Pat. Off.," or a similar phrase. When the article itself cannot bear the trade-mark, the notice may be placed on its container with the trade-mark.

When the phrase "Trade-Mark Registered" appears under a device in an advertisement, it does not necessarily follow that the entire device has been appropriated as a trade-mark, for only one element within it may be so regarded. A design containing a word, or the distinctive style in which the word is lettered, may be registered as a trade-mark even though the word itself is not eligible for registration. This element may be: a word, but not the ornamental border in which it appears, and vice versa, or a word without the descriptive term accompanying it; or else it may be a style of lettering, but not the word alone. When a device such as this is offered for registration, a "disclaimer" listing the parts to be excluded accompanies the application. This precaution is not necessary, however, when the entire mark is distinctive.

What registration of a trade-mark means.—Registration of a trade-mark is not obligatory, for a trade-mark rightfully belongs to the first person who has used it for the class of products in question; registration merely provides greater convenience in proving prior usage, but does not prevent another from proving the mark to be his, even though he did not record it. Neither does registration automatically protect the owner from litigation. Once the trade-mark has been registered, the Patent Office is empowered to refuse the registration of infringing ideas, but the owner himself has to bring suit actually to restrain the use by another who has unlawfully appropriated his trade-mark.

Federal registration gives a trade-mark these advantages:

1. It provides a record that others can consult before using a trade-mark to make sure they are not infringing upon an existing trade-mark.

2. The filing date of the application for registration is accepted as prima facie evidence of the trade-mark's use and ownership on that date, and thus helps avoid dispute and expense. (With an unregistered mark one must show prior use by means of old records, containers, witnesses, or advertisements, often difficult to produce.)

3. It gives Federal courts jurisdiction in infringement actions.

4. Domestic registration is necessary before a trade-mark can be registered in certain foreign countries.

5. The owner of a registered trade-mark can secure an automatic

embargo at the customs of any foreign goods entering this country that infringe on that trade-mark.

6. The award of damages for infringement is not limited to actual injury but may in the discretion of the court be increased to three times the amount of actual damages.

The "ten-year clause."—A large number of trade-marks were already in existence when the present law went into effect in 1905. To protect these, a "ten-year clause" was introduced which provided that any trade-mark in actual and exclusive use for ten years prior to the passage of the Act would be accorded the protection of the law, even though that trade-mark might have been disqualified under the more stern requirements of the new law. These old trade-marks form many of the present exceptions to the current law. In creating a new trade-mark, the actual intention of the law, and not the confusing precedents of the trade-marks that may have existed when the law went into effect, should serve as the basis of understanding.

The Canadian trade-mark law.—The Canadian law differs essentially from that of the United States law in the following respects: (1) The first one to use a trade-mark becomes its owner, *provided that he applies for registration within six months;* in the United States, registration is entirely optional. (2) The Canadian act divides marks into "word marks" and "design marks"; each is considered separately and must be registered separately. In the United States they are considered together and can be registered at one time. (3) A trade-mark cannot consist of a corporation or personal name, although a trade-mark may be registered if it is the chief part of the corporate name of the applicant. For example, *Coca-Cola* might be registered by the Coca-Cola Company.

Trade-marks in other countries.—The owner of any trade-marked product which shows signs of developing into national prominence will find it most advisable to protect that trade-mark properly in all foreign countries in which he may some day do business. If he does not do so at the outset, he may find an unpleasant surprise awaiting him when he tries to do it later. Most other countries, particularly those in Latin America, have an entirely different concept of property rights in trade-marks. The owner of the trade-mark is the man who *registers it first,* regardless of whether he originated the trade-mark or has even used it. As a result, a great practice of piracy of American trade-marks has developed in certain foreign countries. An unscrupulous resident in one of those countries, aware of the pitfalls of the trade-mark law, will calmly and deliberately register the trade-marks of whichever companies he decides to trade on (he will watch American magazines for new advertisers in order to register their marks). If those companies have not protected themselves by registration, they will find their hands tied in doing business there. They may be compelled to buy back their trade-mark from the usurper on whatever terms he sees fit to make.

Such experiences have been very costly for American advertisers and emphasize the importance of securing full legal protection before going too far in the advertising.

7. COPYRIGHT PROCEDURE

Outline of copyright procedure.—Copyright procedure is relatively simple. The three requirements to be met are:

1. The work to be copyrighted should bear the copyright notice.

2. Application for registration of copyright should be made to the Register of Copyrights, Library of Congress, Washington, D. C., on a form supplied by the Register of Copyrights. A different form is used for each class of copyrightable material; to obtain the proper application form for the class of material that it is desired to copyright, write to the Register of Copyrights. When the application for registration of copyright is filed, it should be accompanied by the stipulated fee, which in most cases is $2.

3. A number of copies of the work should be deposited with the Register of Copyrights, at the time the application is made. The number of copies required to be deposited is usually two, although in some cases only one copy is required.

Classification of copyrightable material.—Under the United States Copyright Law, copyrightable material is classified as:

1. Books, including composite and cyclopedic works, directories, gazetteers, and other compilations. The term "book" includes pamphlets, leaflets, or single pages.

2. Periodicals, including newspapers.
3. Lectures, sermons, addresses, prepared for oral delivery.
4. Dramatic or dramatico-musical compositions.
5. Musical compositions.
6. Maps.
7. Works of art; models or designs for works of art.
8. Reproductions of a work of art.
9. Drawings or plastic works of a scientific or technical character.
10. Photographs.
11. Prints and pictorial illustrations, including prints or labels used for articles of merchandise.
12. Motion-picture photoplays.
13. Motion pictures other than photoplays.

Regulations governing works reproduced in copies for sale or public distribution.—The following are the regulations governing this type of copyrightable material:

1. *Publish work with copyright notice.*—In connection with the copyright notice, the following rules should be observed:

(*a*) *Form of copyright notice.*—The usual form of copyright notice, and that recommended by the Copyright Office, is:

COPYRIGHT, 19—, BY
PRENTICE-HALL, INC.

While the above form is sufficient to satisy the requirements of the Copyright Office, it is often advisable to add, underneath the copyright notice, a statement such as the following:

ALL RIGHTS RESERVED. NO PART OF THIS WORK MAY BE REPRODUCED IN ANY FORM, BY MIMEOGRAPH OR ANY OTHER MEANS, WITHOUT PERMISSION IN WRITING FROM THE COPYRIGHT PROPRIETOR.

A statement such as that given above is a specific warning to the public, which is generally not aware of the necessity for obtaining written permission to use copyrighted material.

(*b*) *Special form of copyright notice permitted in certain cases.*—In the case of works (6)-(11), specified in the classification list above, the copyright notice may consist of the symbol ©, accompanied by the initials, monogram, mark, or symbol of the copyright proprietor. However, the name of the copyright proprietor must appear on some accessible part of the copies.

(*c*) *Place where copyright notice should appear.*—In a book or other printed publication, the copyright notice should be placed on the title page or on the back of the title page. In a periodical the notice should appear either on the title page or on the first page of text of each separate number, or under the title heading. In a musical work the copyright notice should be placed either on the title page or on the first page of music.

(*d*) *Use of fictitious name in copyright notice prohibited.*—The name of the copyright owner given in the notice should be the true, legal name of the person, firm, or corporation owning the copyright, and no other. The use of a fictitious or assumed name, or the name of any person other than the copyright proprietor, may result in loss of the copyright protection.

2. *Deposit copies of the work with Register of Copyrights.*—In connection with the deposit of copies, the following information will be useful:

(*a*) *Number of copies to be deposited.*—Immediately after publication, two copies of the work should be sent to the Register of Copyrights, Library of Congress, Washington, D. C. However, if the work is by an author who is a citizen or subject of a foreign state or nation, and if it has been published in a language other than English, only one copy is required to be deposited with the Register of Copyrights. In the case of a contribution to a periodical, one complete copy of the periodical containing the contribution should be deposited. There is little difficulty in connection with the deposit of copies, since the form of application for each different class of copyrightable material states the number of copies required to be deposited.

(*b*) *Affidavit required in certain cases.*—In some cases the application for copyright is required to be accompanied by an affidavit. A different form of application is used for each class of copyrightable material; if an affidavit is necessary, provision is made for it in the application form.

(*c*) *Free mailing privilege.*—The copies of works sent to be registered for copyright may be mailed to the Copyright Office free, if directly delivered for that purpose to the postmaster. The Copyright Office does not furnish franking labels, and the copies cannot be mailed by deposit in a street mail box; they must be taken to the post office and delivered to the postal authorities; a receipt may be obtained upon request.

Regulations governing works not reproduced in copies for sale or public distribution.—Copyright may be secured on certain classes of works, copies of which are not reproduced for sale:

1. *Lectures and oral addresses, dramatic or musical compositions.* —One complete manuscript or typewritten copy of the work should be deposited with the Register of Copyrights.
2. *Photographs.*—In the case of photographs not intended for general circulation, one photographic print should be deposited.
3. *Works of art.*—This includes paintings, drawings, sculpture, models or designs, and drawings or plastic works of a scientific or technical character. One photograph or other identifying reproduction of the work should be deposited.
4. *Motion-picture photoplays.*—A title and description, together with one print taken from each scene of every act, should be deposited.
5. *Motion pictures other than photoplays.*—A title and description, together with not less than two prints taken from different sections of a complete motion picture, should be deposited.

In the case of each of the works listed above, not reproduced in copies for sale, a second deposit of printed copies for registration and the payment of a second fee must be made upon publication.

Term of copyright in the United States.—The original term of copyright in the United States is 28 years. Within one year prior to the expiration of the original term, the copyright may be renewed for an additional 28 years. The total of 56 years (original term plus renewal term) is the longest possible period for which a work can be copyrighted in the United States.

Copyright fees.—The following are the fees required by the Register of Copyrights:

For registration of unpublished works	$1.00
For registration of copyright for all published works, including certificate	2.00

For registration of a published photograph, with certificate	$2.00
For registration of a published photograph, without certificate..	1.00
For every additional or duplicate certificate of registration	1.00
For registration of renewal of copyright	1.00
For recording assignments or licenses, or making and certifying copies of same: for each Copyright Office record-book page or additional fraction of a page over one-half page	2.00
For recording notice of user or acquiescence: for each notice of not more than five titles	1.00
For comparing copy of an assignment with record of such document in the Copyright Office and certifying the same under seal	2.00
For recording transfer of proprietorship of copyrighted articles: for each title or other article (this is in addition to the fee prescribed for recording the assignment)	.10
For search of Copyright Office records, indexes, or deposits: for each hour of time consumed	1.00
For registering a claim of copyright in any print or label not a trade-mark	6.00

Remittances should be made by money order or bank draft, payable to the Register of Copyrights, Library of Congress, Washington, D. C. Checks may not be accepted by the Register in payment of copyright fees.

Copyright on a new edition of a copyrighted work.—If a work which has previously been copyrighted is reissued with changes or revisions, application should be made, on a special form available from the Register of Copyrights, for copyright protection on the new material contained in the work. A mere reprinting of a work previously copyrighted needs no additional protection and cannot be recopyrighted, but if substantial changes have been made, these changes should be protected by filing of the application form and payment of the required fee. The special application form for a reissued work requires the applicant to state specifically what the new material is on which copyright is desired.

Copyright on an unpublished manuscript.—Copyright may be obtained on a manuscript or typewritten copy of a dramatic composition or a lecture, sermon, or address prepared for oral delivery. However, text matter in general is classified under the broad category of "book," and is not copyrightable until *after* it has been printed and *published* with the copyright notice. Hence, the answer to the question "Can a manuscript be copyrighted before publication?" is "No—unless the manuscript is a dramatic composition or a lecture, sermon, or address prepared for oral delivery." Prior to publication literary manuscripts are protected under the common law without the need for observing any formalities, provided authorship and date of creation are established.

Quotations from a copyrighted work.—The utmost caution should be observed in the quotation or use of copyrighted material in a new work. It is not generally understood that quotation from or use of material from a copyrighted work can be made only upon written permission of the copyright owner. Suit for damages, and enforced withdrawal of the infringing work from circulation, may be the penalty for infringement of copyright. A working rule applied by some publishers is to require the author of a manuscript to obtain written permission in every case where the total number of words quoted from another work exceeds 50. Two exceptions to this rule are poetry, for which permission to quote should be obtained regardless of the number of words used, and publications of the Government and other official bodies, reasonable quotations from which can be made without permission. In all cases where quotations are made, the following information should be cited:

1. Name of the author.
2. Title of the work from which the quotation is made.
3. Name of the publisher, and the city of publication.
4. Date of publication.

Copyright in Great Britain.—The term of a British copyright (except in the case of photographs and sound records) is the life of the author, plus 50 years from the date of his death. In the event that the work is that of joint authors, the copyright is in force for the life of the one who dies first and either another 50 years or the life of the one who dies last, whichever period is the longer. The term of copyright for photographs and sound records is 50 years from the date on which the original negative or the original plate was made.

Registration of copyright is not required in Great Britain. The British Copyright Act provides that copyright shall subsist:

1. In the case of a published work, if it was first published within such parts of the British Dominions to which the Act applies.

2. In the case of an unpublished work, if the author was, at the

HOW TO PROTECT IDEAS LEGALLY IN THE UNITED STATES

Idea	Special Method of Protection	Requirements for this Protection	Duration	Remarks
	Regarding the Product and the Business			
1. Product (construction or composition)	Patent from Patent Office, Washington, D. C.	Must be a new invention of an art, machine, manufacture, composition of matter, or else a new and useful improvement in one.	17 years, not renewable.	The idea becomes public property when patent expires.
2. Product (appearance)	Design Patent from Patent Office.	Must be new, ornamental, and original.	3½, 7, or 14 years at option when patent is issued. Not renewable.	1. Idea becomes public property when patent expires. 2. Refers to design or appearance, not to construction or composition of product.
3. Trade-Mark	Registration with Patent Office. (Can be registered also in individual states.)	1. Must be physically affixed to a product or its container. 2. Must point distinctly to origin of product. 3. Must not be descriptive. 4. Must not be misleading. 5. Must not be like another for its class of goods.	20 years. Renewable for similar periods upon expiration.	1. A word may be a trade-mark. 2. The first one to begin continuous use of a trade-mark is its owner whether or not he registers it. 3. Registration is chiefly an aid in establishing who used the trade-mark first. 4. The phrase "Reg. U. S. Pat. Off." should appear with trade-marks so registered.
4. Trade Name (name which applies to a business as a whole, and	First user can restrain infringer in court on grounds of unfair competition.	Owner of name must show that another is leading people to believe that they are purchasing from the original user	As long as name is used.	A trade-mark is not a trade name. "Wheaties" is a trade-mark; "General Mills" is a trade name.

From Kleppner "Advertising Procedure." New York: Prentice-Hall, Inc.

not to an individual product)		when, in fact, they are buying from the infringer.		
5. PERSONAL NAME	See Trade-Mark			1. Poor trade-mark. 2. Can't be registered as trade-mark unless written or printed in unique fashion, or unless associated with a portrait. Signature will do. 3. Can't adopt name of living person without consent. 4. Name of deceased famous persons may be adopted and registered, except name of deceased President during life of his widow.
6. PACKAGE CONSTRUCTION	Patent.	See requirements for patenting Product (No. 1 above).		
7. PACKAGE DESIGN	1. Design patent. 2. Registration as trade-mark (sometimes possible). 3. Infringers can be restrained in court on grounds of unfair competition.	See requirements under Product (appearance) (No. 2 above). See Trade Name (No. 4 above).		1. If a design of the package meets all the requirements of a trade-mark, it may be registered as a trade-mark. 2. If people, deceived by purposeful similarity in appearance between two products, buy the infringer's product thinking they are buying the original, this provides basis for court

HOW TO PROTECT IDEAS LEGALLY IN THE UNITED STATES—*Continued*

Idea	Special Method of Protection	Requirements for this Protection	Duration	Remarks
				action . . . whether or not package design has been patented or registered.
8. Package Insert (leaflet wrapped with product, but not attached to it)	Copyright.	See Copyright, at end of table.		Write to Register of Copyrights for application form A-1.
9. Label	Copyright.	1. Must be an artistic or intellectual creation. 2. Must be attached to product or its container. 3. Must be descriptive of product. 4. For other requirements see Copyright, at end of table.	28 years, renewable once.	1. A label differs from a trade-mark in that it must be descriptive, whereas a trade-mark must not be descriptive. 2. Must be attached to product.
10. Title of Periodical (as "The Saturday Evening Post")	Registration (as a trade-mark).	Title of the periodical is really its identifying device and is regarded as its trade-mark. See Trade-Mark (No. 3).	20 years, renewable for similar periods.	
11. Title of Single Book (as novel or text book)	No special form of protection. Might be protected in court on grounds of unfair competition.			

	Regarding the Advertisement			
12. Publication Advertisements (as a whole)	Copyright.	See Copyright, at end of table.		Write to Register of Copyrights for application form A-5, if no illustration in advertisement. If it contains illustration, form KK.
13. Car Cards	Copyright.	See Copyright, at end of table.		Write to Register of Copyrights for application form KK.
14. Outdoor Posters	"	"		
15. Direct Mail (subject matter)	"	"		Write to Register of Copyrights for application form A-1.
16. Direct Mail (special construction)	Patent.	See patent requirements under Product No. 1 above.	17 years, not renewable.	
17. Radio Program	Copyright.	See Copyright, at end of table.		Write to Register of Copyrights for the following application forms: radio talk ....form C dramatic performance ....form D-2 dramatic performance with music............form D-4
18. Title of Radio Program	See Title of Single Book (No. 11 above).			
19. Slogan	A slogan as such cannot be copyrighted or registered.			

HOW TO PROTECT IDEAS LEGALLY IN THE UNITED STATES—*Concluded*

Idea	Special Method of Protection	Requirements for this Protection	Duration	Remarks
20. Illustrations	Copyright.	See Copyright, at end of table.		Write to Register of Copyrights for application form KK.
21. Copy	Copyright.	"		Write to Register of Copyrights for application form A-1.
22. Radio (commercial)	Copyright.	"		Write to Register of Copyrights for application form C.
23. Merchandising idea, selling plan, advertising idea	No special way to protect such ideas in the abstract.			If the idea is sufficiently concrete, it may provide the basis of a contract with someone to pay for it *if it is original.*
24. Physical material and forms for use in such plans as above	Copyright possible.	See Copyright, at end of table.		
	Patent possible.	See requirements for patenting under No. 1 above.		
25. Color	An advertiser cannot reserve the exclusive right to use a particular color, but he may register as his trademark an arbitrary combination of colors used with his label.			An advertiser may restrain another from imitating the color scheme, package design or label arrangement so as to be mistaken for his, on the ground of unfair competition.

COPYRIGHT

Requirements for This Protection:

1. Must be an artistic or intellectual creation.

2. Must bear copyright notice *when first* published and before application is made, as follows:
   Copyright 19—, by ———
   In case of maps, pictorial illustrations, etc., if the copyright notice might deface the subject matter, the notice may be abbreviated as follows provided that the full name appears elsewhere:
   © 19——, [initials]

3. Copyright notice must appear on title page, or back of title page, in case of booklet.

Duration:
28 years, renewable once.

Remarks:
Write to Register of Copyrights, Library of Congress, Washington, D. C., for appropriate application form.

FOR FURTHER INFORMATION

Regarding trade-marks and patents, write to Patent Office, Washington, D. C.

Regarding copyrights, write to Register of Copyrights, Washington, D. C.

From Kleppner "Advertising Procedure." New York: Prentice-Hall, Inc.

date of the making of the work, a British subject or a resident within the British Dominions.

If a work is published in Great Britain, the only formal requirement that has to be met is delivery of a copy of the work, within one month after publication, to the Library of the British Museum and, on demand (with some exceptions) to the Bodleian Library at Oxford, the University Public Library at Cambridge, the Library of the Faculty of Advocates at Edinburgh, the Library of Trinity College, Dublin, and the Welsh National University Library at Aberystwyth.

It should be noted that the absence of a copyright notice in a work published in Great Britain does not mean that the work is not copyrighted. The copyright notice is not required under the British Copyright Act.

Copyright on prints and labels.—Prints and labels may be copyrighted for 28 years, with the privilege of renewal for an additional 28 years. Prints and labels are copyrighted with the Register of Copyrights.

To be copyrightable, a print or a label must name, or picture, or be descriptive of, some particular article or class of articles. In addition, before the application for copyright is made, the print or label must be published with the copyright notice. If a print or label is first published without the copyright notice, it cannot subsequently be copyrighted.

A label must be attached to the goods that it represents; as, for example, by being pasted onto the container. A print cannot be attached to the goods, but must be used to advertise them; advertisements such as those appearing in magazines and streetcar cards are prints.

A label differs from a trade-mark in that it must be descriptive of its goods. The copyright on a label covers all the matter appearing thereon, rather than some special part or detail. However, it should be noted that copyrighting a label is not a substitute for registration of a trade-mark. The trade-mark may appear on the label, but it is not protected by virtue of the label's copyright.

8. PRINTING AND TYPOGRAPHY

Printing processes.—Of the three types of printing processes, (1) letterpress, (2) intaglio, and (3) lithography, the first two are most commonly used for advertising purposes.

Letterpress covers all types of printing from raised surfaces in which the type or design stands out in relief and comes in direct contact with the paper. In the intaglio process the printing surface is depressed, or etched, thus producing a raised impression on the paper. A common use of the intaglio process is in the printing of "engraved" visiting cards. Rotogravure is a form of intaglio printing in which the plate etching is done by a photochemical process.

Lithographic printing, sometimes called planographic printing, is printing from a plane surface, one which is neither intaglio nor relief. This type of process has three broad classifications: direct lithography, offset lithography, and photo-offset lithography. In direct lithography, the printing plate or surface comes in direct contact with the paper. In offset, or indirect, lithography, the printing plate or surface transfers its impression to an intermediary rubber roller, which in turn prints on the paper. Photo offset is merely an elaboration of this latter method, employing a photographic negative in preparing the printing plate.

Because of the increased use of photo offset in recent years in the advertising field, the advantages and uses of this method are described more fully below.

Advantages of photo offset.—The following advantages of the photo-offset process show why this method of printing has replaced letterpress work to a considerable extent in the advertising field:

1. Saves typesetting costs. Photo offset permits high-speed quantity reproduction of copy without the typesetting costs incurred by letterpress printing. For example, a single page of copy may be photographed many times on one plate, permitting speed-up of printing, whereas in letterpress printing, a separate typesetting job would be required for each extra printing plate of the page.

On reruns where a few slight changes in copy are necessary, photo offset is particularly effective and inexpensive. In letterpress printing, the lines requiring minor changes would have to be reset. Furthermore, it would be necessary to have the original plates available. If the rerun is offset, the changes are typeset and pasted on or over the original copy, which is then rephotographed. This advantage is particularly important in the rerunning of catalogues or bulletins where price changes have been made.

2. Saves storage space. Photo-offset plates do not require much storage room. It is standard practice among lithographers to keep plates for one year, particularly if these plates have half tones. Negatives are kept indefinitely.

3. Saves engraving costs. In the photo-offset process, screening is necessary only for half tones. Black-and-white drawings or illustrations are pasted on the copy page and photographed, without necessitating the extra time and expense of making engravings or line cuts.

4. Permits use of fancy-finish papers. Rippled, pebble stock, and

other fancy-finish papers that are impractical in letterpress printing because the type impression does not fill in the paper crevices can be offset with perfect results. The rubber blanket of the offset press fills in the paper crevices and leaves a clean-cut type impression.

5. Permits enlargement or reduction of all sorts of copy, including type. Photo offset permits effects that could not be obtained without exorbitant expense by other printing processes. Copy can be reduced to miniature size and still be legible. An advertising agency reverses this process for an eye-catching sales letter. The typewritten letter is "blown up" to giant size and sent to prospects.

6. Permits tone and shade control of half tones. The offset process permits a control of printing shade and tone that is not possible in letterpress. Such control is particularly effective in the offset printing of half tones.

Uses of photo offset.—The photo-offset process has become popular principally because of its expense-saving features and its adaptability to the forms of advertising used by large and small concerns. Broadsides, testimonials, letters, labels, package inserts, post cards, folders, and other types of mailing pieces have been printed effectively and cheaply by photo offset. By this process magazine and newspaper advertisements can be reproduced in direct-mail pieces such as folders and broadsides. Bulletins for salesmen, distributors, or consumers can be turned out in quantity inexpensively by this method.

Preparation of copy for photo offset.—The one point to bear in mind when preparing copy that is to be photo offset is to lay it out *exactly* as it is to appear in the finished piece. If the copy is composed of previously printed illustrations and printed type matter (proofs or clipped pages), the copy can be mounted in exact proportion and printed in its original size or reduced or enlarged. If the illustrations are in varying colors or require reduction or enlargement, separate negatives will be required. In such a case the layout should indicate the exact size and position of the illustrations.

If typewritten copy is to be photographed, clean copy from a black ribbon will serve. However, it may be advisable to use a special carbon-paper ribbon in an electric typewriter, which provides an evenness in the weight of each stroke. If the copy is written in this manner on a sheet of paper backed up by a sheet of carbon paper, with the carbon side facing the back side of the sheet, the copy will have the greater density desirable for photographing.

How to plan a printing job.—The businessman whose printing requirements are too small or too occasional to necessitate the employment of an advertising manager or an agency to handle the work will save time, money, and energy if he outlines the problem of buying printing as follows:

1. Determines what the printed job is to accomplish.
2. Determines the form it is to take.
3. Prepares the copy and art work.

Step number one is the crystallization of the idea that a piece of printing is to fulfill a definite need, accomplish a definite purpose, or do a certain job better than anything else can do it. At this stage only the rough idea of the finished job is known.

Step number two requires an expert knowledge of printing—its possibilities and its limitations—or expert advice. This is the stage at which the format is decided; the stage at which the type, illustrations, colors, size, shape, paper, binding, and other details are settled. All this work should be done with the co-operation of the printer. A mistake too often made by the inexperienced is that of neglecting to call in the printer until after much of the work is done. Only the buyer who is thoroughly familiar with printing—who knows the printer's processes and tools—can eliminate this consultation with the printer or defer it until a later time.

The third and final step is the preparation of the copy and art work. This should always be the last step. The specifications of the finished job are now known, and the copy can be written to fit the allotted space, and the proper illustrations correctly made. To write the copy before knowing where it is to go often means rewriting, padding, or cutting, or changing the layout, to the detriment of the job in general. If the illustrations are prematurely made, they may fit haphazardly into the final plan, or new illustrations or alterations in the old ones may be necessary.

The new printing buyer who has never before dealt with printers may wonder about the choice of a printer to do the work. For the first job, the best choice is a printer of sound reputation for good work and service to the customer. Succeeding jobs may be taken to the same printer if he proves satisfactory, or the buyer may take his work to several printers and obtain competitive bids. He should be sure that where prices vary, the results will be the same. Giving business to a printer whose chief virtue is low prices is a questionable economy, since cheap printing is usually money wasted; good printing is not necessarily expensive printing, but poor printing is expensive at any price.

How type is set.—The buyer of printing, and particularly the occasional buyer, ordinarily need not concern himself with the technical aspects of printing; such, for example, as the way in which the type is set in the printer's plant, the kind of machines used and the method of their operation, and so forth. However, the following very brief statement of how type is set may assist the new printing buyer to understand the printer's end of the work and some of the terms that he may use when talking to the customer.

Type used in printed matter is principally of two kinds:

1. Foundry type.
2. Machine type.

Foundry type is set by hand, in single letters, and is redistributed after the job is printed, to be used again. Display faces are commonly set in foundry type; for example, the headlines in advertisements, set in large type, are commonly foundry type. The body matter in expensive advertising pieces is also sometimes set in foundry type. Hand setting, it is usually considered, has finer points than machine setting; it is, however, considerably more expensive.

Machine type is cast by a machine and is re-melted after the job is done. Machine type is of two kinds:

1. Single types.
2. Slugs.

The monotype casts and sets single letters that are very similar to foundry type. Monotype is generally used in advertising pieces, where the columns of body matter are of irregular widths.

The linotype (or the intertype, a machine almost identical to the linotype) casts a line of type at a time, on a single slug. Linotype is generally used for extensive pieces of copy; a booklet, for example, would ordinarily be set on the linotype.

The monotype and the linotype are both operated from keyboards, roughly similar to the keyboard on a typewriter.

Another machine, the typograph, is sometimes used. This machine, which may be used to set display faces, is not operated from a keyboard, but is manually operated.

How type is measured.—Type matter has its own peculiar system of measurement. Until recent times type sizes were known by names. Now a standard system, known as the point system, is used. There are approximately 72 points to the inch, and all type sizes are given in points. Sizes from 72 point down to 4 point are available; some of the more commonly used sizes are illustrated in Figure 24a. Figure 24b shows the basic resemblance in the various members of a type "family."

Although the size of the type itself is indicated in points, the dimensions of the space which the type is to occupy (the length of the lines and the depth of the space) are not indicated in points but in picas. The pica * (or pica em, as it is sometimes called) is $\frac{1}{6}$ of an inch, or 12 points. For example, this book is set 24 × 41 picas; that is, the pages are 24 picas wide and 41 picas deep. Since a pica is one-sixth of an inch, a page 24 × 41 picas is 4 inches wide and $6\frac{5}{6}$ inches deep.

In newspaper advertising still a third term, the agate line, is used. The agate line always means 1/14 of an inch deep and one column wide. There are 14 agate lines in every inch of space, measured from the top of the page to the bottom, regardless of the number of printed lines actually set up within that space.

To summarize: there are 72 points to the inch, 6 picas to the inch, 14 agate lines to the inch.

Use of leading.—By leading is meant space between the lines of type. If type is set without any space between the lines, it is said to be set solid. For the sake of appearance and legibility, it is generally advisable to insert space between the lines. The printer does this by inserting so-called leads, which are thin strips of metal separating the lines of type. Leading is specified in points. Figure 25 is an illustration of the difference in appearance and legibility between a para-

* Pronounced pī'cá.

THE SIZE of

48 point

THE SIZE of ty

42 point

THE SIZE of type

36 point

THE SIZE of type

30 point

THE SIZE of type

24 point

THE SIZE of type

18 point

THE SIZE of type

14 point

THE SIZE of type

12 point

THE SIZE of type

10 point

THE SIZE of type

8 point

Figure 24a.—Common Type Sizes (Caslon Old Style).

From Kleppner, "Advertising Procedure." New York: Prentice-Hall, Inc.

A FAMILY OF TYPE

Caslon Old Style

A FAMILY OF TYPE

Caslon Old Style italic

A FAMILY OF TYPE

Caslon Bold

A FAMILY OF TYPE

Caslon Bold italic

A FAMILY OF TYPE

Caslon Condensed

A FAMILY OF TYPE

Caslon Shaded

a family of type

Caslon Old Style

a family of type

Caslon Old Style italic

a family of type

Caslon Bold

a family of type

Caslon Bold italic

a family of type

Caslon Condensed

a family of type

Caslon Shaded

Figure 24b.—A "Family" of Type.

From Kleppner, "Advertising Procedure." New York: Prentice-Hall, Inc.

graph set solid and a paragraph of the same type leaded 2 points (the type used is Granjon, the face in which this book is set. For further comparison, the body type of this book is leaded one point).

Set solid:

The citizen is inevitably nation-conscious nowadays, inevitably conscious too of the reaction of foreign and international events upon his purse and his larder, his home and his employment. Man is more and more identified with his country and its fortunes. Is there then a philosophy of international life in which patriotism—this identification of the man with his country—has its part? For that surely is the new patriotism which we must seek. I believe there is.

Leaded 2 points:

The citizen is inevitably nation-conscious nowadays, inevitably conscious too of the reaction of foreign and international events upon his purse and his larder, his home and his employment. Man is more and more identified with his country and its fortunes. Is there then a philosophy of international life in which patriotism—this identification of the man with his country—has its part? For that surely is the new patriotism which we must seek. I believe there is.

Figure 25.—A Piece of Copy Set Solid, and the Same Piece of Copy Leaded 2 Points.

The amount of lead that should be used depends upon a number of factors, such as the type face in which the copy is to be set, the size of type to be used, and the length of the lines. In general, small faces need less lead than large ones; light faces need less lead than heavy ones; and short lines need less lead than long ones. On the following page are given two tables that will be useful in this connection; the first shows column widths for easy reading, and the second the amount of lead that it is advisable to use with various sizes of body types.

COLUMN WIDTHS FOR EASY READING

Size of Type	*Column Width, in Picas*
6	8 to 10
7	8 " 12
8	9 " 13
9	10 " 14
10	13 " 16
11	13 " 18
12	14 " 21
14	18 " 24
18	20 " 34

AMOUNT OF LEAD TO USE BETWEEN LINES OF BODY TYPE FOR EASY READING

Size of Type	*Minimum Lead*	*Maximum Lead*
6	Solid	1 Pt.
7	Solid	1 "
8	Solid	2 "
9	1 Pt.	2 "
10	1 "	4 "
11	1 "	4 "
12	2 "	6 "
14	3 "	8 "
18	4 "	8 "

Choosing a type face.—A glance into a printer's specimen book of types will often surprise and discourage one who is a novice in the preparation of printed material. The number and variety of type faces seems endless, and the novice is at a loss to know which type to choose for his particular work. To dispel some of the mystery associated with type faces and their uses, on the following pages some of the better known faces are illustrated and their characteristics briefly described. Each face is illustrated in two sizes: 24 point, and 12 point leaded 2.

This type is CASLON

THIS PARAGRAPH IS SET IN CASLON. An old proverb of typography is, "When in doubt, use Caslon." Caslon is warm and sympathetic, yet impersonal. It is one of the most serviceable of all types, one of the most easily read, and one of the most widely used. There are a number of varieties of Caslon; this is Caslon Old Style. *Caslon Old Style italic is illustrated by this sentence.*

This type is KENNERLEY

THIS PARAGRAPH IS SET IN KENNERLEY. Kennerley, like the Caslon Old Style face illustrated above, combines beauty of form with a high degree of legibility. And legibility is, of course, the primary consideration in the choice of a type face. Printed matter has but one function: it is meant to be read. *Kennerley italic is illustrated by this sentence.*

This type is GARAMOND

THIS PARAGRAPH IS SET IN GARAMOND. Garamond is one of the most useful and beautiful of type faces, and is one of the faces most frequently used by advertisers. Its grace and beauty make it suitable for use where the beauty of the product itself is one of the points featured in the advertisement. *Garamond italic also has a good appearance; the italic is illustrated by this sentence.*

This type is CLOISTER

THIS PARAGRAPH IS SET IN CLOISTER. As will be seen from this paragraph, Cloister sets a slightly darker page than either Caslon or Garamond. Cloister is a good type for the body matter of advertisements, and it also gives excellent results when used for display; its appearance in display may be judged from the line set in 24 point. *Cloister italic is illustrated by this sentence.*

This type is BODONI

THIS PARAGRAPH IS SET IN BODONI. The types previously illustrated — Caslon, Kennerley, Garamond, and Cloister — are all so-called Old Style faces. Bodoni is a so-called Modern face. Old Style types can be distinguished by their slanting serifs (serifs are the little bars or finishing strokes at the tops and bottoms of letters) and by their slight contrast between light and heavy strokes. Modern type faces have greater contrast between light and heavy strokes, and have precise but graceful lines. Bodoni comes in a number of varieties; this is Bodoni Book. The headline is set in Bodoni Bold. *Bodoni italic is illustrated by this sentence.*

This type is CENTURY

THIS PARAGRAPH IS SET IN CENTURY. Century, like Bodoni, is a Modern type face. It is not an especially good looking face, particularly in the larger sizes, but its legibility in the smaller sizes is to be recommended. Where it is necessary to fit a large message into a comparatively small space, Century is a good choice. *Century italic is illustrated by this sentence.*

This type is SCOTCH

THIS PARAGRAPH IS SET IN SCOTCH ROMAN. Scotch Roman may be considered a Modern face, although it has certain of the characteristics of Old Style faces. While it is not especially beautiful, Scotch Roman is a very legible, useful face for both display and text purposes. Its appearance in display may be judged from the line set in 24 point. *Scotch Roman italic is illustrated by this sentence.*

This type is FUTURA

THIS PARAGRAPH IS SET IN FUTURA. Futura is an example of a so-called Sans Serif face. Sans Serif faces have straight lines, with no contrast between light and heavy strokes, and they have no serifs. Sans Serif faces are popular because they strike a modern note. Futura may be used as either a body or a display type. However, although it is a good looking type, it is not very easily read, and hence should not be used except where only a few lines have to be set. Futura comes in a number of weights; this is Futura Medium. *Futura italic is illustrated by this sentence.*

This type is KABEL

THIS PARAGRAPH IS SET IN KABEL. Kabel, like the Futura type illustrated above, is a Sans Serif face. It has the modern styling of a streamlined automobile. As in the case of other Sans Serif faces, Kabel should be used sparingly. Kabel comes in a number of weights; this is Kabel light. *Kabel italic is illustrated by this sentence.*

This type is GIRDER

THIS PARAGRAPH IS SET IN GIRDER. Girder is an example of a so-called Square Serif face. Square Serif faces have simple, square serifs of the same weight as the type lines. Square Serif faces, like Sans Serif faces, create a modern atmosphere. Girder comes in a number of weights; this is Girder light.

The type faces illustrated in the preceding pages are only a few of the almost innumerable varieties available. However, the business-man who is not an expert in typography will do well to restrict his choice to one or other of the faces shown; he can then be reasonably sure that the results obtained will be satisfactory. Only the expert should attempt the striking or unusual.

The types shown are illustrated in only two sizes, but it should not be forgotten that a wide range of sizes is available (as illustrated in Figure 24a). Also, type of the same face and size can be set in capitals, in capitals and small capitals, in italic, and so on. Some of these variations are illustrated on the next page.

THIS LINE IS SET IN CAPITALS (OR CAPS)

THIS LINE IS SET IN CAPS AND SMALL CAPS

THIS LINE IS SET IN SMALL CAPS

This Line is Set in Caps and Lower Case

this line is set in lower case

This line is set in italic

This line is set in boldface

Capitals are well suited to short headlines, but not to lines of body type. THIS SENTENCE IS AN ILLUSTRATION OF THE DIFFICULTY FOUND IN READING PRINTED MATTER THAT IS SET COMPLETELY IN CAPS; THE LINES OF TYPE ARE TOO EVEN, AND THERE IS TOO LITTLE TO CATCH THE EYE. In contrast, it is at once apparent that this sentence, set in lower case, is much easier to read.

Caps and small caps are suitable chiefly for subheadings; they are not sufficiently striking to serve as headlines. Italic type is graceful, but it, too, is not easily read; it is best to use italic sparingly. Boldface may be used for headlines or, when emphasis is desired, for short paragraphs of text matter or even for complete advertisements.

Preparing copy for the printer.—In the printing business the material that the printer is to set in type is referred to as the "copy." The copy sent to the printer should be carefully prepared. If the copy is "dirty"—if, for example, part is typewritten and part handwritten, or if the copy is interlined with changes, or if, in general, it is difficult to follow—the printer will take this into account in figuring his price for the job. Clean, neat copy, therefore, results in a saving to the customer.

All copy should be typewritten. Be sure, also, that your copy is correct. The printer makes a separate charge for all changes made on the proofs. Hence it pays to spend time in revising the copy before it is sent to the printer, rather than to rewrite it on the proofs.

Detailed specifications should always accompany the copy. The printer will want to know the dimensions (width and depth), the type face to be used, the type size, the leading, and any other details that may be required in a particular case. It often pays to prepare

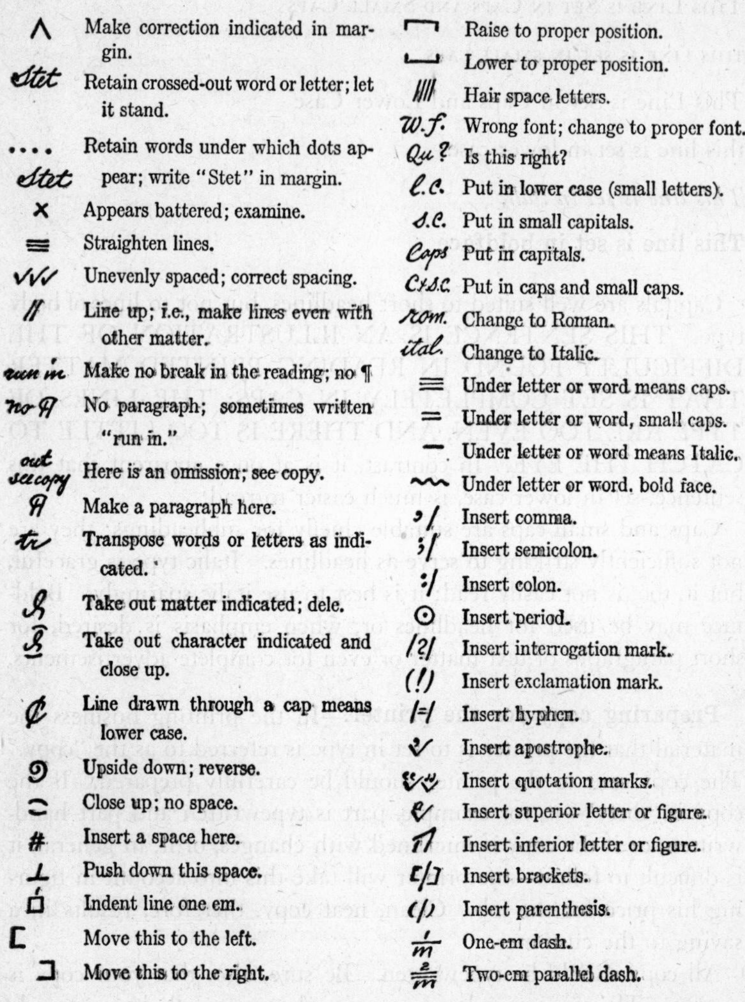

Make correction indicated in margin.
Stet
Retain crossed-out word or letter; let it stand.
Retain words under which dots appear; write "Stet" in margin.
Stet
Appears battered; examine.
Straighten lines.
Unevenly spaced; correct spacing.
Line up; i.e., make lines even with other matter.
run in
Make no break in the reading; no ¶
no ¶
No paragraph; sometimes written "run in."
out see copy
Here is an omission; see copy.
Make a paragraph here.
tr
Transpose words or letters as indicated.
Take out matter indicated; dele.
Take out character indicated and close up.
Line drawn through a cap means lower case.
Upside down; reverse.
Close up; no space.
Insert a space here.
Push down this space.
Indent line one em.
Move this to the left.
Move this to the right.
Raise to proper position.
Lower to proper position.
Hair space letters.
w.f.
Wrong font; change to proper font.
Qu?
Is this right?
l.c.
Put in lower case (small letters).
s.c.
Put in small capitals.
Caps
Put in capitals.
C+s.c.
Put in caps and small caps.
rom.
Change to Roman.
ital.
Change to Italic.
Under letter or word means caps.
Under letter or word, small caps.
Under letter or word means Italic.
Under letter or word, bold face.
Insert comma.
Insert semicolon.
Insert colon.
Insert period.
Insert interrogation mark.
Insert exclamation mark.
Insert hyphen.
Insert apostrophe.
Insert quotation marks.
Insert superior letter or figure.
Insert inferior letter or figure.
Insert brackets.
Insert parenthesis.
One-em dash.
Two-em parallel dash.

Figure 26.—Proofreader's Marks.

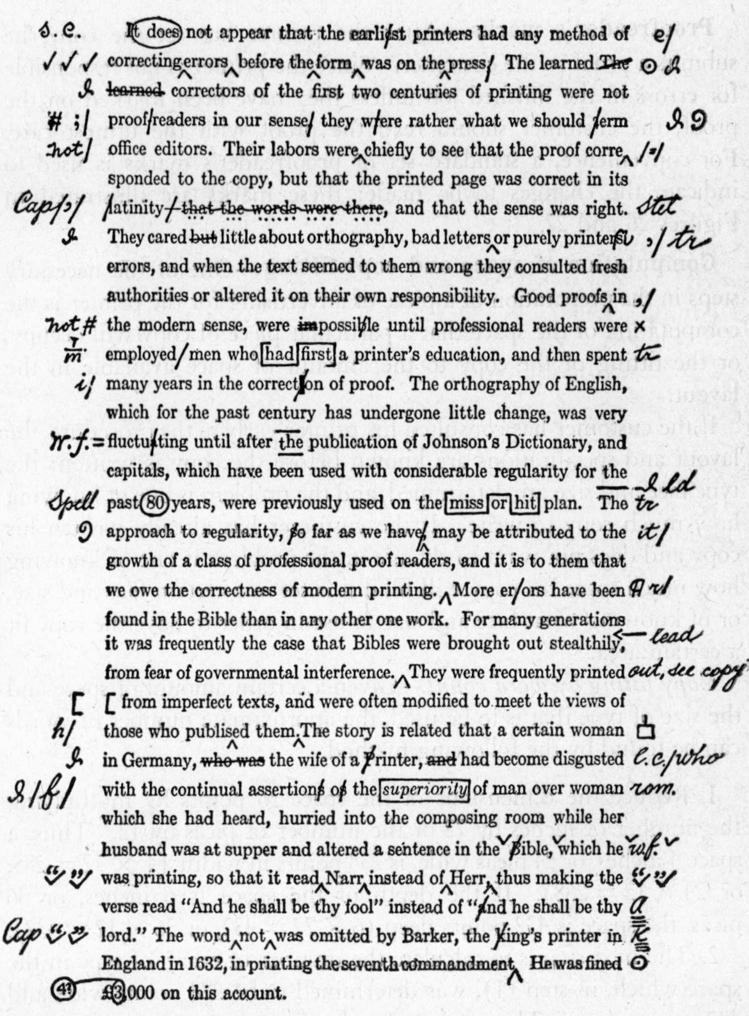

It does not appear that the earliest printers had any method of correcting errors before the form was on the press The learned The learned correctors of the first two centuries of printing were not proofreaders in our sense they were rather what we should term office editors. Their labors were chiefly to see that the proof corre sponded to the copy, but that the printed page was correct in its latinity that the words were there, and that the sense was right. They cared but little about orthography, bad letters or purely printers errors, and when the text seemed to them wrong they consulted fresh authorities or altered it on their own responsibility. Good proofs in the modern sense, were impossible until professional readers were employed men who had first a printer's education, and then spent many years in the correction of proof. The orthography of English, which for the past century has undergone little change, was very fluctuating until after the publication of Johnson's Dictionary, and capitals, which have been used with considerable regularity for the past 80 years, were previously used on the miss or hit plan. The approach to regularity, so far as we have may be attributed to the growth of a class of professional proof readers, and it is to them that we owe the correctness of modern printing. More errors have been found in the Bible than in any other one work. For many generations it was frequently the case that Bibles were brought out stealthily, from fear of governmental interference. They were frequently printed from imperfect texts, and were often modified to meet the views of those who publised them. The story is related that a certain woman in Germany, who was the wife of a Printer, and had become disgusted with the continual assertions of the *superiorily* of man over woman which she had heard, hurried into the composing room while her husband was at supper and altered a sentence in the Bible, which he was printing, so that it read Narr instead of Herr, thus making the verse read "And he shall be thy fool" instead of "and he shall be thy lord." The word not was omitted by Barker, the king's printer in England in 1632, in printing the seventh commandment He was fined £3,000 on this account.

Figure 27.—A Piece of Corrected Proof.

a layout, or sketch, for the printer; the layout will indicate exactly how the customer wants the finished job to appear.

Proofreader's marks.—After the printer has set the copy, he submits a proof to the customer. Since the printer is not responsible for errors in the finished job unless they have been marked on the proof, the customer should read the proof with the utmost care. For convenience, a standard set of proofreader's marks is used to indicate the changes to be made; these marks are illustrated in Figures 26 and 27.

Computation of space and copy-fitting.—One of the necessary steps in the preparation of a piece of advertising for the printer is the computation of the space that a particular piece of copy will occupy, or the fitting of the copy to the amount of space available in the layout.

If the customer has consulted his printer early in the procedure, the layout and specifications are known before the copy is written; the type face and size are determined, and the problem is one of knowing how much copy to write. If the customer has already written his copy and does not want to change it, the problem is one of knowing how much space the copy will fill if it is set in a certain face and size, or of knowing what face and size to use in order to have the copy fit a certain area.

Copy fitting by word count.—Given a certain amount of space and the size of type that is to be used, the approximate number of words can be found by the following method.

1. Reduce the dimensions of the space to points by multiplying the number of inches by 72 or the number of picas by 12. Thus, a space 4 inches, or 24 picas wide, is 288 points in width ($4 \times 72 = 288$, or $24 \times 12 = 288$). If the depth of the space is 6 inches, or 36 picas, the space is 432 points deep ($6 \times 72 = 432$, or $36 \times 12 = 432$).

2. The next step is to calculate the number of ems * of type in the space which, in step (1), was determined to be 288 points wide and 432 points deep. This is done by dividing the number of ems in the width by the size of the type in points, dividing the number of ems in the depth by the size of the type in points, and then multiplying the two figures obtained; the result is the number of ems of type in the space. Thus:

* The *em* is approximately the space occupied by the capital M in the type used.

If the type to be used is 10 point:

$$288 \div 10 = 28.8, \text{ length}$$
$$432 \div 10 = 43.2, \text{ depth}$$
$$28.8 \times 43.2 = 1244.16, \text{ ems of type}$$

If the type to be used is 11 point:

$$288 \div 11 = 26.1, \text{ length}$$
$$432 \div 11 = 39.2, \text{ depth}$$
$$26.1 \times 39.2 = 1023.12, \text{ ems of type}$$

If the type to be used is 12 point:

$$288 \div 12 = 24, \text{ length}$$
$$432 \div 12 = 36, \text{ depth}$$
$$24 \times 36 = 864, \text{ ems of type}$$

If the type to be used is 14 point:

$$288 \div 14 = 20.5, \text{ length}$$
$$432 \div 14 = 30.8, \text{ depth}$$
$$20.5 \times 30.8 = 631.40, \text{ ems of type}$$

3. For convenient figuring, the average word is taken to be 3 ems in length. To complete the computation and find the number of words that will fill the given space, divide the number of ems in the space by 3:

In 10 point,	$1244.16 \div 3 = 414.72$	words will fill the space
11 "	$1023.12 \div 3 = 341$	" " " " "
12 "	$864 \div 3 = 288$	" " " " "
14 "	$631.4 \div 3 = 210.4$	" " " " "

The above computations are for type that is set *solid*—that is, without any extra space between the lines of type. When type is leaded, the space computation must take the leading into consideration. The leading has the effect of increasing the depth of the lines of type, but does not increase the width. Thus, if the type to be used is 12 point, and it is to be leaded 2 points, for the width the 12 point computation is used, but for the depth the type is considered to be 14 points. For example, assume that a space 4 inches (or 24 picas) wide, and 6 inches (or 36 picas) deep, is to be set in 12 point type leaded 2 points; then the number of words in the space is calculated as follows.

$$4 \text{ inches (or 24 picas)} = 288 \text{ points}$$
$$288 \div 12 = 24, \text{ width}$$
$$6 \text{ inches (or 36 picas)} = 432 \text{ points}$$
$$432 \div 14 = 30.8, \text{ depth}$$
$$24 \times 30.8 = 739.2, \text{ ems of type}$$
$$739.2 \div 3 = 246.4, \text{ words in space}$$

For the convenience of their customers, many printers prepare tables showing the number of words of type per square inch. Such a table is illustrated below. The figures are, of course, only approximate, and apply to the average type face.

NUMBER OF WORDS OF TYPE PER SQUARE INCH

Size of Type	*Set Solid*	*Leaded Two Points*
5	69	49
$5\frac{1}{2}$	55	45
6	48	37
7	36	27
8	30	23
9	25	20
10	20	15
11	15	12
12	12	11
14	10	9

To illustrate the use of the table, assume that a space 4 inches by 6 inches is to be set in 12 point type, solid. In this space there are $4 \times 6 = 24$ square inches. According to the table, there are 12 words to the square inch in 12 point type set solid; then the number of words that will fit the space is $24 \times 12 = 288$. According to the table, there are 11 words to the square inch in 12 point type leaded 2 points; hence, if the space 4 inches by 6 inches were to be set in 12 point type leaded 2 points, there would be $24 \times 11 = 264$ words.

Some printers go further, and, when preparing tables for the use of their customers, take into consideration the fact that the number of words per square inch varies with different type faces. The table given on page 517 is a portion of a table used by one printer to show the number of words per square inch for some of the more commonly used type faces.

NUMBER OF WORDS PER SQUARE INCH FOR VARIOUS TYPES

	6 Point	*8 Point*	*10 Point*	*12 Point*	*14 Point*
Bodoni	52	29	19	15	11
Bodoni Bold	48	26	17	13	10
Bookman	43	27	17	12	9
Caslon No. 471	53	36	23	15	11
Caslon No. 540	58	32	21	14	10
Cloister Old Style	53	32	22	15	13
Cloister Bold	45	30	20	14	11
Futura Light	—	32	22	15	12
Futura Medium	—	31	19	14	12
Futura Bold	—	28	17	11	8
Garamond Old Style	50	32	21	16	12
Garamond Bold	44	28	18	14	10

Copy fitting by character count.—Word-count methods of copy fitting are not always accurate enough for careful work. Where exactness is necessary, the character-count method is preferable. As an illustration of the character-count method, assume that a space 3 inches by 4 inches is to be set in 11 point Caslon No. 540, leaded 1 point. How many lines of typewritten copy will be required to fill the space? The calculation is made as follows:

1. The printer will supply the customer with specimens of type faces, and, after the face to be used has been chosen, the customer can determine the average number of characters to an inch by counting the characters per inch in the specimen of the type chosen. The number of characters per linear inch for 11 point Caslon No. 540 is found to be 15; the number of characters in a line 3 inches long is, therefore, $15 \times 3 = 45$.

2. The next step is to find the number of lines in the depth. Since the type is 11 point leaded 1, there will be 24 lines in the space 3 inches by 4 inches ($6 \times 4 = 24$).

3. The number of characters in the space 3 inches by 4 inches is

now found by multiplying the number of characters per line by the number of lines; $45 \times 24 = 1080$.

4. A typewriter with pica type types 10 characters to an inch; a typewriter with elite type types 12 characters to an inch. Suppose that the typewriter has elite type, and that it is set to type lines 5 inches in length. Then the number of typewriter characters per line is $12 \times 5 = 60$.

5. The number of characters of 11 point Caslon No. 540 leaded 1 in the space 3 inches by 4 inches was found to be 1080. The number of typewriter characters per line was found to be 60. The number of typewriter lines, each 5 inches in length, which will be required to fill the space 3 inches by 4 inches is found by dividing 1080 by 60 ($1080 \div 60 = 18$). Hence the copywriter should write 18 lines of copy, 5 inches in length, to fill the space on the layout.

Many printers provide their customers with character-count tables, showing the number of characters per linear inch for various type faces. The following is a portion of a table of this kind.

CHARACTERS PER LINEAR INCH

	Size of Type				
Type Face	*10*	*11*	*12*	*14*	*18*
Bodoni	16	15	14	13	10
Caslon No. 540	16	15	13	10	9
Scotch Roman	17	16	13	11	8
Century	14	13	12	11	10
Cloister	20	18	17	16	12
Garamond	18	17	16	14	11

Always use the tables provided by the printer who is to do the work. If your printer has no such tables, reliable tables can be obtained from the Mergenthaler Linotype Company, Brooklyn, New York; the Intertype Corporation, Brooklyn, New York, or the Lanston Monotype Machine Company, Philadelphia, Pennsylvania.

Illustrations.—Illustrations are of two kinds: half tones and line cuts. The half tone is used to reproduce photographs and drawings that have gradations in tone between black and white. The half tone breaks the illustration into small dots, known as the screen, which by their comparative size render all the intermediate tones. Half tones can be made in many screens—that is, with various numbers of dots to a given area. The finer the screen, the more dots, and the truer the reproduction. Before you have your half tones made, it is wise to consult your engraver. He will advise you what screen to use in order to obtain the best possible results on your paper; the proper screen to use is determined by the paper on which the job is to be printed.

Line cuts reproduce only black lines. They are used for simple illustrations that have no intermediate shadings. However, a semblance of shades or tones can be introduced into line cuts by mechanical processes, such as the Ben Day, which adds patterns of dots or cross-hatchings to indicate the various gradations.

There are many variations of line cuts and half tones, each suited to certain kinds of jobs; nearly all are adaptable to color work. It is also possible to make combination plates—half tones and line cuts together. A number of different types of illustrations are shown in Figures 28–35, pages 520–523.

Paper.—The small or occasional buyer of printing will seldom be confronted with the necessity of buying paper. The printer can recommend the proper paper to use and can secure it for the customer. Paper may be roughly divided into three classifications:

1. Writing.
2. Book.
3. Cover.

The chart on pages 524–527 summarizes much useful information with regard to each of these three types of paper (this chart is reproduced from Kleppner, *Advertising Procedure*. New York: Prentice-Hall, Inc.).

Jobs are usually printed on large sheets, which are cut to the proper size after printing. Since paper comes in standard sizes, most of which are kept in stock by large paper houses, certain sizes for the finished job are more economical than others, as there is less waste in the cutting. Here, again, the advice of the printer is valuable. The tables on page 528 give recommended paper sizes for booklets and catalogues and recommended paper sizes for unstitched circulars.

Figure 28.

Figure 29.

Figure 30.

Figure 31.

Figure 28: Line Plate.—The line plate (or line cut, as it is frequently called) is the simplest form of photoengraving. Note that there are no gradations of tone between black and white; shading can be suggested only by lines of various weights and by areas of solid black. A line plate cannot be made from a photograph, a painting, or a wash drawing; it can be made only from a drawing that consists of lines and of areas of solid black. The drawing from which this line plate was made was a pen-and-ink sketch. A line plate is the least expensive form of photoengraving and can be printed on even the roughest papers with good results.

Figure 29: Line Plate With Ben Day.—The Ben Day process, named after the man who perfected it, adds life and sparkle to a line plate, and gives it some of the gradations of shading found in a half tone. Ben Day is available in various "screens"; a pattern book may be obtained from your engraver. In the line plate shown in Figure 29, five screens have been used; close study of the picture will reveal where the different screens were "laid on." Ben Day is a hand operation, and hence is expensive. Compare the line plate with Ben Day with the line plate illustrated in Figure 28 and with the square-finish half tone illustrated in Figure 30.

Figure 30: Square-Finish Half Tone.—There are various kinds of half tones. The simplest is the so-called square-finish half tone. The term "square finish" does not refer to the shape of the picture or to the shape of the plate, for a picture which is oval or circular may be reproduced as a square-finish half tone. The term refers to any half tone on which the screen covers the entire area. A square-finish half tone is the least expensive type. Comparison of Figure 30 with Figure 28 shows the obvious difference between a half tone and a line plate. The half tone has subtle gradations of shading between the black and white areas.

Figure 31: Half Tone Showing Screens.—The term "screen" refers to the fact that when the picture is being photographed, a screen is placed in the camera in front of the plate. Screens are known by numbers; those most commonly used are 55, 60, 65, 85, 100, 110, 120, 133, 150. In Figure 31 three screens are illustrated; namely, 85, 55, and 110. The fineness of the screen affects the fidelity of the results obtained. The proper screen to use depends upon the quality of the paper on which the half tone is to be printed. Smooth-finish paper can "take" a fine-screened half tone; the coarser grades of paper require coarse-screened half tones.

Figure 32.

Figure 33.

Figure 34.

Figure 35.

Figure 32: Vignette Half Tone.—The so-called vignette half tone, illustrated in Figure 32, shows the object against a background that fades away with soft, cloudlike effect. Vignette half tones can be used very effectively in advertisements or advertising literature, but paper of good quality, and first-class presswork, are required. On paper of the coarser grades, a vignette half tone tends to smudge rather than fade. Thus, a vignette half tone can seldom be employed in a newspaper; it can be used, however, in a magazine that is printed on good paper stock. A vignette half tone costs approximately 50% more than a square-finish half tone.

Figure 33: Silhouette Half Tone.—In the square-finish half tone illustrated in Figure 30, the screen covers the entire area of the picture. There are times, however, when a screen over the background is not desired. When all that is wanted is the object, a silhouette half tone (sometimes called an outline-finish half tone) may be ordered. In Figure 33, everything but the subject is cut away, and hence the background is pure white. A silhouette half tone has more character than a square-finish half tone; the objects silhouetted stand out clearly on the page. A silhouette half tone costs about 50% more than a square-finish half tone.

Figure 34: Highlight Half Tone.—A highlight half tone (also sometimes called a drop-out half tone) is one in which certain areas of the picture are highlighted or cut away. In the highlight half tone illustrated in Figure 34, the area around the fish is highlighted; so also is the fisherman's white shirt and a part of the sky in the background. When the half tone is made, the white areas in the original illustration are covered by the screen; the screen covering the areas that are to be highlighted is then tooled out by hand, and the areas so tooled are pure white. A highlight half tone is approximately three times as expensive as a square-finish half tone.

Figure 35: Surprint.—It may be desired to combine a half tone and a line plate in a single engraving. This can be done in either of two ways. In a surprint, the line plate material (Fishing in Canada) is made to appear superimposed upon the half tone picture. In a so-called combination plate (see Figures 20 and 21) the line plate and the half tone adjoin each other. These figures could have been made square half tones, but the screen would then have covered the entire area, and the printed material would have been less legible. There is a slight extra charge for a surprint; a combination plate costs about twice as much as a square-finish half tone.

COMPARISON CHART OF PAPER STOCKS

including only the better known writing, book, and cover papers

Paper	Specification	Description	Photo-Engraving Recommended	Comments
WRITING	Flat Writing.	This is the paper used in the making of inexpensive school writing tablets and notebooks. Better grades of it are used in correspondence stationery.	A. Line plates.	I. Not used extensively for advertising purposes. II. As the quality of a Flat Writing stock becomes better, it moves into the class of Bonds.
	Bonds.	Most letters received in the business office are on this stock. Its grades vary from that in which wood pulp and sulphite are used, to the better qualities made of linen rags. The weight in most common use is 20 lbs.	A. Line plates. B. 100-screen half tones. C. Highlight half tones.	I. Bonds provide a large variety of tints. II. Some come in finishes such as "crash," simulating the cloth; also glazed. Most bonds come in a plain unglazed finish. III. Engraving plates for use on bonds should be etched deep.
	Ledger.	A very high-class sheet of writing paper, used mostly for documents and accounting work. Has a tough, sturdy body, and a surface finish which has been plated (compressed between sheets of metal). Is heavier, as a class, than bonds; also more expensive. In its lighter weights it is also used for executive stationery.	A. Line plates. B. 100-screen half tones.	I. Comes mostly in white and buff.

Paper	Specification	Description	Photo-Engraving Recommended	Comments
BOOK	Newsstock.	Received its name from its use for newspapers. The least expensive of book papers and sometimes considered as a class by itself. Has a thin, porous body and a rough surface.	A. Line plates. B. 65-screen halftones, tooled well. C. Quarter tones.	I. Comes mostly in white (which varies in its tones). II. Qualities vary. Finish does not have to be specified.
	Antique.	A book paper whose body is of higher quality and heavier weight than that of news, but which likewise has a rough, uneven surface.	A. Line plates only.	I. Limited range of colors. II. Has a number of different finishes, as *eggshell*, *antique wove*, *antique laid*.
(*Cont.*)	Machine Finish. (M. F.)	The least expensive of the book papers which can take half tones dependably well. Represents an additional process through which antique paper goes. The stock is "sized," or submersed in chemicals, which fill up the pores, making the paper less absorbent. It is then "calendered" or ironed, the surface obtaining the smooth finish which permits the use of half tone. Sometimes known as "S. & C." (Sized and Calendered.)	A. 120-screen halftones.	I. Moderate range of colors. II. A very utilitarian paper. Permits reproduction of wash drawings and photographs. Creases well. Especially good for booklets and catalogues to be issued in quantity.

(*Cont.*)

COMPARISON CHART OF PAPER STOCKS (*Cont.*)

including only the better known writing, book, and cover papers

Paper	Specification	Description	Photo-Engraving Recommended	Comments
BOOK (*Cont.*)	English Finish.	A grade smoother than Machine Finish, but not as high as the one next described. For most purposes in which a halftone is to be used, this offers a serviceable, attractive stock.	A. 120-screen halftones.	I. Moderate range of colors. II. Folds well. Can withstand fingering and usage. Good for leaflets and booklets, house organs, and moderately high-class catalogues.
	Sized and Super Calendered ("S.&S.C.").	This is a machine-finished paper which has been "sized," like Machine Finish and English Finish, but which has been given an additional ironing. The surface is consequently glossy.	A. 133-screen halftones.	I. Moderate range of colors. II. Folds well. Suited for uses similar to those of English Finish, when a more attractive effect is sought.
	Enamel Coated ("Coated").	The smoothest of book papers. This is a machine-finish paper which has been given a coating of clay and glue, then passed through the calender rolls at high speed. The result is a hard surface, dull, or glossy. Is brittle. Does not fold well. Otherwise shows reproductions to very best advantage.	A. 133, 150-screen halftones. Can take vignette finish.	I. Most expensive of the book papers. Looks good. Good for extra fine work. Cannot stand much fingering and usage.

PAPER	SPECIFICATION	DESCRIPTION	PHOTO-ENGRAVING RECOMMENDED	COMMENTS
COVER	Antique.	Refers to the rough-surfaced finish. Antique cover is usually rougher than antique book.	I. Line plates.	I. Broad range of finishes, including *ripple linen*, *crash*, and many fancy-finish patterns. II. Good for folders, and for booklet covers.
	Plated.	The surface has been pressed, as in ledgers.	I. 120-screen halftones.	I. Good for booklet covers.
	Enamel Coated ("Coated").	A cover stock which has been given a treatment similar to book cover stock.	I. 133, 150, 175-screen halftones.	I. The acme of cover stocks in appearance.

From Kleppner, "Advertising Procedure." New York: Prentice-Hall, Inc.

RECOMMENDED PAPER SIZES FOR BOOKLETS AND CATALOGUES

This Page Size	In the Following Number of Pages	Cuts Economically Out of These Sheet Sizes
3×6	4, 8, 16, 24, 48	25×38—38×50
4×9	4, 6, 8, 16, 24, 48	25×38—38×50
$4\frac{1}{2} \times 6$	4, 8, 16, 32, 64	25×38—38×50
$6 \times 9\frac{1}{8}$	4, 8, 16, 32	25×38—38×50
$9\frac{1}{4} \times 12\frac{1}{8}$	4, 8, 16, 32	25×38—38×50
$3\frac{1}{2} \times 6\frac{3}{8}$	4, 8, 16, 24, 48	$30\frac{1}{2} \times 41$—41×61
$5 \times 7\frac{1}{4}$	4, 8, 16, 32, 64	$30\frac{1}{2} \times 41$—41×61
$7\frac{3}{8} \times 9\frac{7}{8}$	4, 8, 16, 32	$30\frac{1}{2} \times 41$—41×61
$10 \times 14\frac{7}{8}$	4, 8, 16	$30\frac{1}{2} \times 41$—41×61
$3\frac{3}{4} \times 5\frac{1}{8}$	4, 8, 16, 32, 64	32×44—44×64
$3\frac{3}{4} \times 6\frac{7}{8}$	4, 8, 16, 24, 48	32×44—44×64
$5\frac{1}{4} \times 7\frac{5}{8}$	4, 8, 16, 32, 64	32×44—44×64
$7\frac{1}{2} \times 10\frac{5}{8}$	4, 8, 16, 32	32×44—44×64
$10\frac{3}{4} \times 15\frac{5}{8}$	4, 8, 16	32×44—44×64

RECOMMENDED PAPER SIZES FOR UNSTITCHED CIRCULARS

This Page Size	In the Following Number of Pages	Cuts Economically Out of These Sheet Sizes
$3\frac{1}{8} \times 6\frac{1}{4}$	4, 6, 8, 12, 16, 24	25×38—38×50
$4\frac{1}{8} \times 9\frac{1}{2}$	4, 6, 12, 16, 24	25×38—38×50
$4\frac{3}{4} \times 6\frac{1}{4}$	4, 8, 16, 32	25×38—38×50
$6\frac{1}{4} \times 9\frac{1}{2}$	4, 8, 16, 32	25×38—38×50
$9\frac{1}{2} \times 12\frac{1}{2}$	4, 8, 16, 32	25×38—38×50
$3\frac{3}{4} \times 6\frac{3}{4}$	4, 6, 8, 12, 16, 24	$30\frac{1}{2} \times 41$—41×61
$5\frac{1}{8} \times 7\frac{5}{8}$	4, 8, 16, 32	$30\frac{1}{2} \times 41$—41×61
$7\frac{5}{8} \times 10\frac{1}{4}$	4, 8, 16, 32	$30\frac{1}{2} \times 41$—41×61
$10\frac{1}{4} \times 15\frac{1}{4}$	4, 8, 16	$30\frac{1}{2} \times 41$—41×61
$4 \times 5\frac{1}{2}$	4, 8, 16	32×44—44×64
$4 \times 7\frac{1}{4}$	4, 8, 16, 24	32×44—44×64
$5\frac{1}{2} \times 8$	4, 8, 16, 32	32×44—44×64
8×11	4, 8, 16, 32	32×44—44×64
11×16	4, 8, 16	32×44—44×64

9. GLOSSARY OF ADVERTISING PROCEDURE

From Kleppner, "Advertising Procedure." New York: Prentice-Hall, Inc.

Following is a list of the advertising terms most frequently used whose applied meaning may not be self-evident. The definitions either have been drawn from authoritative sources, or else are based upon general acceptance. In many instances the glossary does not confine itself to a definition of a term, but indicates the practices connected with it as well.

A.A.A.A. (The 4 A's). American Association of Advertising Agencies. An organization of leading advertising agencies.

A.B.C. Audit Bureau of Circulations. The organization sponsored by publishers, agencies, and advertisers for the securing of accurate circulation statements.

A.B.P. Associated Business Papers, an organization of trade papers.

Account executive. That member of an advertising agency staff who directs the handling of a client's advertising. He serves as the liaison man between the agency and the advertiser—one of the highest positions in an agency. Known also as *contact man.*

Ad lib (radio). To extemporize lines not written in the script, or in music to play parts not in the score, entirely at the announcer's or musician's discretion. Music or lines so delivered.

Advertising agency. A professional organization rendering advertising service to two or more clients.

A.F.A. Advertising Federation of America, the senior organization consisting of member divisions representing different advertising activities.

Agate line. A unit measurement of publication advertising space, one column wide and one fourteenth of an inch deep. Although the column width may vary in different publications, there are always fourteen agate lines to the column inch.

Aided-recall method. A method used in testing memory of advertisements. Some clue, such as the campaign theme, is given that may assist in recalling the brand name.

Allocation. The assignment of frequency and power made by the Federal Communications Commission to a broadcasting station.

A.N.A. Association of National Advertisers.

Announcements (radio). Brief commercial statements usually varying from 20 to 150 words, interspersed between programs on the air.

Announcer. The member of a radio station or network system staff assigned the duty of introducing and describing program features to the radio audience.

A.N.P.A. American Newspaper Publishers' Association.

Antique-finish paper. Book or cover paper that has a rough, uneven surface. It can reproduce illustrations from line plates but not from half tones.

Applause mail. Letters of comment or appreciation received by radio station or sponsors from the listening audience; fan mail.

A.S.C.A.P. American Society of Composers, Authors, and Publishers. A group that protects the copyright rights of its members and collects royalties in their behalf.

Association test. A method of measuring the degree to which people are familiar with brand names. A commodity is mentioned and respondents are asked to tell which brand name comes to mind first.

Audition. A trial of artists or musicians under actual broadcasting conditions.

Author's corrections. Alterations or changes made in proofs, not due to the printer's errors and chargeable to whoever is paying for composition—advertiser or publisher, as the case may be. Unnecessary expense for this item can be reduced by careful editing of copy before it is sent to the printer.

Background (radio). A sound effect, musical or otherwise, designed for use behind dialogue or other program elements.

Backing up. A term used by printers to indicate that one side of a sheet has been printed and its reverse side is now being printed.

Balloons. A visualizing device with the words of a person in the picture so written as to appear coming right from his mouth. Borrowed from the newspaper comic pages.

Basic network. The minimum grouping of stations for which an advertiser must contract in order to use the facilities of a network.

Basic weight. The weight of a ream of paper if cut to the standard or basic size for that class of paper. The basic sizes are: writing papers, 17×22; book papers, 25×38; cover stocks, 20×26.

Bearers. Excess metal left on an engraving to protect and strengthen it during the process of electrotyping. Also, strips of metal placed at the sides of a type form for protection during electrotyping.

Ben Day process. The process invented by Benjamin Day whereby an engraver can produce mechanically a great variety of shaded tints and mottled effects in line plates.

Bite (engraving). The etching action of acid on metal. A good deep bite gives a sharper engraving reproduction than does a shallow bite (usually caused by hurrying a plate through production).

Bleeding. Printed matter trimmed so that the type or plates run over the edges of a sheet.

Blow-up. An enlargement of an advertisement big enough for a window or for other display purposes.

Blue print. A quick, low-price photographic print, in white on dark blue background. It can be made and delivered several hours before the completion of the plate, enabling the advertiser to prepare type layout while the engraving is still being made.

Body type. The type commonly used for reading matter, as distinguished from *display* type, which is that used in the headlines of advertisements. Usually type 14 points in size, or smaller.

Boiler plate. Pages in stereotype supplied by news agencies or other syndicates to country weeklies to cut their costs of composition. Also called "patent insides." These pages often include news and advertisements. Boiler plate originally meant any thin metal sheet.

Boldface type. A type that stands out strongly and prominently.

Bond paper. The writing paper most frequently used in commercial correspondence, originally a durable quality used for printing bonds and other securities. The weight in most extensive use for letterheads is 20 lb. (17×22–20).

Book paper. A paper used in printing books, as well as for lightweight leaflets and folders, distinguished from *writing papers* and *cover stocks.* Basic size, 25×38.

Box-top offers. An invitation to the consumer to get a gift or premium by sending in the label or box top from a package of the product (with or without an additional sum). Popular over the radio.

Breaking for color; separating for color. When an advertisement in two or more colors is to be printed from type, it will first be set up in its entirety. The printer will then separate the type to appear in one color from that to appear in the other colors; this is said to be *breaking for color.*

Bridge (radio). Music or sound effects used by the director in dramatic shows to indicate scene transitions.

Broadcasting. The distribution of sound programs by means of radiotelephone transmission for the purpose of public entertainment and education.

Broadcast spectrum. That part of the range of frequencies of electromagnetic waves assigned to broadcasting stations, ranging in the United States from 550 to 1600 kilocycles.

Bulldog edition. That edition of a morning paper that is printed early the preceding evening and sent to out-of-town readers on the night trains. If an advertiser does not get his copy in early, he misses this edition.

Burnishing (engraving). The mechanical act of making the dark areas in a half tone appear still darker. It is accomplished by smoothing over the dots in a half tone with a tool that causes those dots to spread and fill up the areas between them.

Buying space. Buying the right to insert an advertisement in a given medium, such as a periodical, a program, or an outdoor sign.

C. (1) Column; (2) capital letter.

C.A.B. rating (Co-operative Analysis of Broadcasting rating). Figures showing the comparative popularity of certain sponsored radio programs, based on answers to telephone inquiries in thirty-three major cities; made for a group of radio advertisers by Crossley, Inc., research organization. Also called *Crossley rating.*

Calendered paper. A paper with a smooth, burnished surface, secured by passing the paper between heavy rolls, called calenders.

Call letters. The combination of letters assigned by the Federal Communications Commission to a broadcasting or other radio station, which serves as its official designation and establishes its identity, as WJZ, WOR, KGN.

Caps. (1) Capital letters. The large, or upper case letters, SUCH AS THESE, as compared to lower case letters. (2) Paper covers for protecting the edges of a book while it is being covered and finished.

Caption. The heading of a chapter, section, or page. Also the descriptive matter accompanying an illustration.

Casting off. Estimating the amount of space a piece of copy will occupy when set in type of a given size.

Center spread. The space occupied by an advertisement on the two facing center pages of a publication. The two pages will always be a continuous sheet, so that printing is better and reading is easier than on other kinds of double-page spreads. Often it is possible to print such an advertisement without losing the space usually taken up by the center margins, or gutters.

Chains (radio). A regularly established system of broadcasting stations interconnected by high-grade wire telephone circuits over which program features are distributed for simultaneous broadcasting through the associated stations.

Checking copy. A copy of a publication sent to an advertiser or to his agency so that he may see that his advertisement appears as specified.

Class A (Class B) rates (radio). Rates for radio time varying with the hour of the day that the time is used. The most costly time (usually between 6 P.M. and 11 P.M.) is quoted at Class A rates; the next most costly, at Class B; and so on. Each chain and station has its own allocation of classes.

Clear-channel station (radio). A station that is allowed the maximum power and is given a channel on the frequency band all to itself, with possibly one or two sectional or local stations far removed from it, so as not to interfere. (See *Local-channel station; Regional-channel station.*)

Closing date; closing hour. (1) The day or hour, respectively, when all copy and plates must be in the publisher's hands if the advertisement is to appear in a given issue. The closing time is specified by the publisher. If proof is to be seen, all material has to be in when *first forms close.* (2) (Radio) The last hour or day that a program or announcement may be submitted for approval to a station or network management to be included in the station's schedule.

Clubbing offer. An arrangement whereby subscriptions to two or more different publications are offered at a reduced combination price. Considered in judging the character of the circulation of a publication.

Coarse-screen half tone. A half tone with a comparatively low, or coarse, screen; usually 60, 65, or 85 lines to the inch.

Coated paper. A paper to which a coating has been applied, giving it a smooth, hard finish, suitable for the reproduction of fine half tones.

Coaxial cable (television). A special metallic cable used for transmitting the visible part of a telecast.

Coined word. An original and arbitrary combination of syllables forming a word for which the advertiser prescribes the meaning. Extensively used for trade-marks, as *Kodak, Moxie, Mazda.*

Column-inch. A unit of measure in a periodical one inch deep and one column wide, whatever the width of the column.

Combination plate. The joining of half tone and line plate in one engraving.

Combination rate. (1) A special space rate for two papers, such as a morning paper and an evening paper, owned by the same publisher. Applies also to any other special rate granted in connection with two or more periodicals. A *forced* combination is the rate for two or more papers in which space cannot be bought separately—there is no rate but the combination rate. (2) The rate paid for a combination photoengraving plate.

Comic strip. A series of cartoon or caricature drawings.

Commercial program (radio). A sponsored program from whch radio broadcasting stations derive revenue on the basis of the time consumed in broadcasting it.

Competitive stage. The advertising stage that a product reaches when its general usefulness is recognized but its individual superiority over similar brands has to be established in order that it shall secure the preference. (Compare *Pioneering stage; Retentive stage.* See *Spiral.*)

Composition. Typesetting.

Consumer advertising. Advertising directed by a producer to those people who will personally use his product.

Continuity (radio). A written script including spoken lines and cues for musical numbers used by artists and directors in rehearsing and presenting radio features.

Contract year. The period of time, in space-contracts, running for one year beginning with the insertion of the first advertisement under that contract. It is usually specified that the first advertisement shall appear within thirty days of the signing of the contract.

Conversion table. Table showing what the equivalent weight of paper stock of a given size would be if the sheet were cut to another size.

Copy. (1) The text of an advertisement. (2) Matter for a compositor to set. (3) Illustrations for an engraver to reproduce. (4) Any material to be used in the production of a publication.

Copy approach. The method of opening the text of an advertisement.

Copyholder. An assistant who reads copy aloud to the proofreader who reads and corrects the proof itself.

Copyright. Legal protection afforded an original intellectual effort. Application blank is procurable from the Copyright Office, Library of Congress, Washington, D. C.

Copy writer. A person who writes the text of advertisements.

Cover. The front cover of a publication is known as the *first cover;* the inside of the front cover is the *second cover;* the inside of the back cover is the *third cover;* the outside of the back cover is the *fourth cover.* Extra rates are charged for cover positions.

Coverage map (radio). A map showing the territory that a radio station regularly reaches. Usually divided into primary coverage and secondary coverage for both daytime and nighttime.

Cover stock. A paper made of heavy, strong fiber, used for folders and for booklet covers. Some cover stocks run into the low weights of paper known as *book paper,* but most cover stocks are heavier. Basic size is 20″×26″.

Crash finish. A surface design on paper simulating the appearance of rough cloth.

Cream plan. The tactics of directing the advertising to the most potential class of buyers first, then to the next best market, and so on, "taking the cream off first." Used in selling specialties. (Compare *Zone plan; National plan.*)

Cropping. An illustration is cropped when part of its foreground, background, or sides is trimmed off to enable the reproduction to fit into a specific space. Cropping is done either to eliminate nonessential background in an illustration or to change the proportions of the illustration to the desired size.

Crossley rating. See *C.A.B. rating.*

Cue (radio). (1) The closing words of an actor's speech and a signal for another actor to enter. (2) A sound, musical or otherwise, or a manual signal calling for action or proceeding. (3) A phrase designating the transfer of the point of program origin; or, as in the case of network identification, a line such as, "This is the Columbia Broadcasting System," "This is the National Broadcasting Company," "This is the Mutual Broadcasting System," as a signal to radio and telephone operators for the switching of channels.

Cue sheet. An orderly tabulation of radio program routine containing all cues.

Cut (engraving). The commonly used term meaning a photoengraving, electrotype, or stereotype. Derived from its use in the term *woodcut.* Also known as *block* (English).

Cut (radio). (1) To stop transmission or any part of the program abruptly, either by stopping performers or by use of an electrical switch on the control board. (2) The deletion of program material to fit a prescribed period of time.

Cut-out. A window or store counter sign with a design literally cut out of it.

Cylinder press. A press with a rotating cylinder under which a flat bed containing type or plates slides forward and backward. Used for large-quantity work, or for advertisements of large size.

Dead metal. Excess metal left on an engraved plate for protection during electrotyping. Such metal portions are sometimes called bearers.

Dealer imprint. The name and address of the dealer, printed or pasted on an advertisement of a national advertiser. In the planning of direct mail, space is frequently left for the dealer imprint.

Decalcomania. A transparent gelatinous film bearing an advertisement, which may be gummed onto the dealer's window. Also known as *transparency*.

Deckle-edge. The untrimmed ragged edge of a sheet of paper.

Definition (radio). Clean-cut transmission and reception, making possible the complete identification of the various musical units in an orchestra, in chorus and sounds from the effects table.

Delete. "Omit." Used in proofreading.

Depth of columns. The dimension of a column space measured from top of the page to the bottom, in agate lines, or in inches.

Die-cut. An odd-shaped paper or cardboard for a direct-mail piece or for display purposes, cut with a special knife-edge die.

Differential. The difference between the retail or local rate and the foreign or national rate in newspaper advertising.

Direct advertising. Any form of advertising reproduced in quantity by or for the advertiser and issued by him or under his direction directly to definite and specific prospects by means of the mails, canvassers, salesmen, dealers, or otherwise—as through letters, leaflets, folders, or booklets.

Direct half tone. A superior type of half tone made by photographing an object itself instead of a picture of it.

Direct-mail advertising. That form of direct advertising sent through the mails.

Display. Attention-attracting quality. (1) *Display type* is sizes larger than 14 point. Italics, boldface, and sometimes capitals are used for display; so are hand-drawn letters and script. (2) *Display advertisements* are set in different type sizes and styles, with varying line widths, various leading between lines, considerable white space, and sometimes illustrations. Newspaper space rates distinguish between *display* and *undisplay*, the latter being set in one size type. *Display* space in newspapers usually is not sold in units of less than 14 column lines; there is no such minimum requirement for undisplay classified advertisements. A *display order* from a department store to a newspaper requires the newspaper to set up an advertisement according to layout and instructions furnished and to supply the store with proofs; sometimes called a *wait order*, since it does not authorize insertion of the advertisement. (3) *Window display, interior display,* and *counter display* are different methods of advertising by showing the actual goods to be promoted. *Open* display puts the goods where they can be actually handled and examined by the customer; *closed* display has the goods in cases and under glass. (See *Traveling display.*)

Double-decker. Outdoor advertising stands erected one above another.

Double-leaded. See *Leading.*

Double-page spread. The space occupied by an advertisement on two facing pages. Called a *center* spread if the two pages are in the center of a publication.

Double truck. Same as *double-page spread.*

Drop-out half tone. See *Highlight.*

Dry-brush drawing. A drawing, made with a brush using ink or paint extra thick and dry.

Dubbing. The playing on a transcription of music or other subjects from another transcription. Rules of the musical unions severely oppose this practice.

Dummy. (1) Blank sheets of paper cut and folded to the size of a proposed leaflet, folder, booklet, or book, to indicate weight, shape, size, and general appearance. On the pages of the dummy the layouts can be drawn. Useful in designing direct-mail advertisements. A dummy may also be made from the proof furnished by the printer. (2) An empty package or carton, used for display purposes.

Duplicate plates. Photoengravings made from the same negative as an original plate.

Ears of newspaper. The boxes or announcements appearing at the top of the front page, alongside the name of the paper, in the upper right- and left-hand corners. Sold for advertising space by some papers.

E.D. Run advertisement every day.

E.F. English-finish paper.

Electrical transcription. A recorded program consisting of an entertainment or educational feature especially rendered for radio broadcasting and not made available in record or disc form to the general public.

Electric spectaculars. Outdoor advertisements in which electric lights are used to form the words and design. Not to be confused with illuminated *posters* or illuminated *painted bulletins.* Space on electric spectaculars is sold by the individual stand.

Electrotype. A metal plate that is a facsimile of another plate and made by the electrotype process. When several identical plates of a reproduction are required, one original can be made, and electrotypes can be made from that. Electrotypes cost less than original plates. They are made from a wax mold unless otherwise specified; a lead mold is more costly. Sometimes faced with steel for long runs.

Em. The square of a body of any given type face, the letter *M* being as wide as it is high. Usually short for *pica em.*

Enameled paper; enamel-coated stock. A book or cover paper that can take the highest screen half tone. It is covered with a coating of china clay and a binder, then ironed under high-speed rollers. This gives it a hard, smooth finish too brittle to fold well. Made also in dull and semidull finish.

English finish (E.F.). A hard, even, and unpolished finish applied to book papers.

Equivalent weight of paper. The weight of a given paper stock in terms of its basic weight.

Extended covers. A cover that is slightly wider and longer than the pages of a paper-bound booklet or catalogue; one that extends or hangs over the inside pages. Also called *overhang* and *overlap.* (See *Trimmed flush.*)

Face. The printing surface of type or a plate.

Facing text matter. The position of an advertisement in a periodical so that it is opposite reading matter.

Facsimile broadcasting. The sending by radio of a reproduction of picture, printed, or written matter.

Fading (radio). The variation in the intensity of a radio signal received over a great distance, arising from transmission conditions beyond the control of the transmitter, such as those due to changes in the sky wave reflecting layer (Kennelly-Heaviside layer) or to the shifting in phase of the ground and sky waves, usually observed only at night.

Fading area (radio). The area in which a broadcasting station suffers from the widest variations in fading, usually extending from fifty to seventy-five miles beyond the transmitter to points three or four hundred miles distant.

Family of type. Fonts of type faces related in design, as Caslon Bold, Caslon Old Style, Caslon Bold Italics, Caslon Old Style Italics.

F.C.C. Federal Communications Commission, the Federal authority empowered to license radio stations and to assign wave lengths to stations "in the public interest."

Field intensity contour map. A

map upon which field intensities delivered by a broadcasting station are plotted, with points receiving equal levels of significant values joined by a continuous line.

Field intensity measurement. The measurement of a signal delivered at a point of reception by a radio transmitter in units of voltage per meter of effective antenna height, usually in terms of microvolts or millivolts per meter. Developed by E. A. Felix.

15 and 2. The terms on which advertising agents secure space from the publishers: 15 per cent commission from publishers on the gross amount of space used, plus 2 per cent on the net for cash payment.

Fill-in. (1) The salutation and any other data which are inserted in the individual letters after they have been printed. (2) The blurring of an illustration due to the closeness of the lines or dots in the plate or to heavy inking.

Film transmission (television). The transmission of the sound and picture of motion picture film by means of television.

Flat proofs. Ordinary rough proofs, or *stone* proofs, taken of type when it is on the compositor's workbench, in contrast to *press proofs,* which are made after the type has been carefully adjusted to take the best possible impression.

Flat rate. A uniform charge for space in a medium, without regard to the amount of space used or the frequency of insertion. When *flat rates* do not prevail, *time discounts* or *quantity discounts* are offered.

F.M. (radio). Frequency modulation, a circuit designed by Major E. H. Armstrong. The practical effect is to do away with static and man-made noises, also to permit a large number of stations to use a wave length.

Following, next to, reading matter. The specification of a position for an advertisement to appear in a publication. Also known as *full position.* This is a *preferred position,* which usually costs more than *run-of-paper* position.

Follow style. When it is desired to have a piece of copy set up in accordance with a previous advertisement or proof, it is necessary for the advertiser merely to send that specimen to the printer, with the copy marked *follow style.* Saves work of making a new layout.

Font. An assortment of type in one size and face. Includes numerals and punctuation marks.

Font, wrong. See *Wrong font.*

Foreign advertising. (1) Newspaper advertising paid for directly or indirectly by a manufacturer or national distributor (usually nonresident), as contrasted with *local advertising,* which is paid for by the local retailer, at a lower rate. Also known as *national advertising.* (2) Advertising in another country.

Foreign-language advertising. Domestic advertising printed in a language other than English.

Form. (1) Pages of type locked into place in a strong, rectangular iron frame known as a *chase.* Usually holds 1, 2, 4, 8, 16, 32, or 64 pages (hence it is uneconomical to print booklets with 10, 12, 20, 26, or 50 pages). (2) The general style of a book, as opposed to its subject.

Format. The size, shape, style, and so forth, of a book or publication.

Forms close. The date on which all copy and plates for a periodical advertisement must be in.

Foundry proofs. The proofs of a typographical set-up just before the material is sent to the foundry for electrotyping; identified by the heavy funeral-black border (the foundry rules).

Four-color process. The photoengraving process whereby color illustrations are reproduced by means of a set of plates, one of which prints all the yellows, another the blues, a third the reds, the fourth the blacks (sequence variable). The plates are referred to as *process plates.*

Free lance. An independent artist or copy writer. Takes individual assignments from different accounts, but is not in the employ of, or associated with, any of them otherwise.

Frequency (radio). The number of alternations per second that a transmitter radiates. The frequency of broadcasting stations is defined in kilocycles or *thousands* of alternations per second.

Full position. A special preferred position of an advertisement in a newspaper. Either (1) the advertisement both follows a column, or columns, of the news reading matter, and is completely flanked by reading matter as well, or else (2) the advertisement is at the top of the page and alongside reading matter.

Full showing. In car cards, a full showing means one card in each car of a line, or of the city, in which space is bought.

Galley proofs. Proofs on sheets usually twenty to twenty-two inches long, printed from type as it stands in the *galley trays* before that type is separated into pages.

Ghosted view. An illustration showing an X-ray view of a subject.

Give-aways. Premiums that are given away.

Grain of paper. The direction in which most of the fibers lie. Paper folds easily with the grain. Grain should run with bending edge.

Ground wave. That component of the radiation from a radio antenna system which is distributed through the conducting earth and, therefore, not subject to the variations due to changes in transmission conditions in the upper atmosphere.

Group discount (radio). A special discount in station rates when specified groups of stations are used simultaneously by an advertiser.

Half showing. One half of a full showing.

Half tone. A photoengraving plate, photographed through a glass screen (in the camera) which serves to break up the reproduction of the subject into dots; makes possible the printing of half tone values, as of photographs. Screens vary from 45 to 300 lines to the inch. The most common are 120- and 133-line screens for use in magazines; 65- to 85-line screens for use in newspapers.

Hand composition. Type set up by hand, as distinguished from type set up by machine. (Compare *Linotype composition; Monotype composition.*)

Hand lettering. Any lettering that is drawn by hand (such as that in a name plate), as distinguished from type regularly set.

Hand tooling. Handwork on an engraving or plate to improve its reproducing qualities. Charged for by the hour. Hand tooling is necessary if it is desired to have pure whites appear in a half tone unless that plate is a *highlight half tone.*

Head-on position. An outdoor advertising stand that directly faces traffic on a highway.

Highlight half tone (drop-out). A half tone plate in which the white areas are "dropped out" *in the making of the plate.* An ordinary half tone has a fine screen over the white areas, which may cause trouble in printing on papers like newsstock.

''Hour'' (radio). A scheduled radio feature. At first applied only to 60-minute programs, but now loosely applied to shorter periods.

House organ. A publication issued periodically by a firm for the furtherance of its own interests, inviting attention on the strength of its editorial content. Also known as *company magazine* and *company newspaper*.

Iconoscope. The special television camera that picks up the image to be sent.

Inch. The unit of advertising measurement, a space one inch deep and one column wide. See *Column-inch*.

Individual location. The location of an outdoor advertisement in which there is but a single panel, and not several adjacent ones.

Initial letter. The first letter in a piece of copy, set in a size of type larger than that of the rest of the copy. Useful in getting the eye started on the message.

Insertion order. Instructions from an advertiser authorizing a publisher to print an advertisement of specified size on a given date at an agreed rate; accompanied or followed by the copy for the advertisement.

Inserts. (1) In letters or packages, an enclosure usually in the form of a little slip bearing an advertisement. (2) In periodicals, a page printed by the advertiser, or for him, and forwarded to the publisher, who binds it up in the publication. Usually in colors and on heavier stock (if publisher permits). Charged for at preferred space rates.

Intaglio printing. Printing from a depressed surface, such as from the copper plate or steel plate which produces *engraved* calling cards and announcements. *Rotogravure* is a form of intaglio printing. Compare *Letterpress printing* and *Lithographic printing*.

Interference (radio). The reception of an undesired program or extraneous electrical noise simultaneously with a desired program.

Island position. Position in a newspaper entirely surrounded by reading matter. Not generally procurable.

Job press. A press that takes sizes up to 25×38 inches. Best known types are the *Gordon* and the *Universal*.

Job ticket. A sheet or an envelope that accompanies a printing job through the various departments, bearing all the instructions and all records showing the progress of the work.

Justification of type. Arranging type so that it appears in even-length lines, with its letters properly spaced.

Keep standing. Instructions to printer to hold type after it has been used on a job, for further instructions. Where it may be necessary to hold type for any length of time, it is better to have an electrotype of the setup made.

Kennelly-Heaviside layer. A canopy or layer which forms at night in the upper atmosphere, against which radio signals are reflected back to earth. Television waves penetrate the Kennelly-Heaviside layer and do not reflect back.

Keying an advertisement. Giving an advertisement a code number or letter so that when people respond, the source of the inquiry can be traced. May be a variation in the address, or a letter or number printed in the corner of a return coupon.

Laid paper. Paper showing a regular water-marked pattern, usually of parallel lines.

Layout. A working drawing showing how an advertisement is to look. A *printer's layout* is a set of instructions accompanying a piece of copy showing how it is to be set up.

L.C. Lower-case letters.

Leaders. A line of dots or dashes used to guide the eye across the page, thus:

....

Leading (pronounced *ledding*). The insertion of metal strips (known as *leads*) between lines of type, causing greater space to appear between these lines. The usual size is 2 points. Leaded type requires more room than type that is not leaded but set *solid*.

Ledger papers. A high-grade writing paper of tough body and smooth, plated surface. Used for accounting work and for documents.

Letterpress printing. Printing from a raised or relief surface, like a rubber stamp. Most advertisements are printed by the letterpress method. Exceptions are *lithography* (and *offset*); *intaglio* (and *rotogravure*).

Limited time station (radio). A station that is assigned a channel for broadcasting for specified time only, sharing its channel with other stations at different times.

Linage. The total number of lines of space occupied by one advertisement or a series of advertisements.

Line. A unit for measuring space, 1/14th of a column-inch.

Line drawing. A drawing in which the lines are solid, undiluted. Made with brush, pen, pencil, or crayon. Such shading as occurs is produced by variations in size and spacing of lines, not by tone.

Line plate. A photoengraving made from a drawing composed of solid lines or masses, which can print on any quality stock. Less expensive than half tones but cannot be used to reproduce photographs, wash drawings, or similar illustrations.

Linotype composition. Mechanical typesetting by molding a line of type at a time. The linotype machine is operated by a keyboard resembling that of a typewriter. (Compare *Hand composition; Monotype composition.*)

Lithographic printing. The process of printing from a flat surface, usually a stone, on which the design has been drawn. Invented in 1796 by Alois Senefelder of Munich. Used for color work of large quantities, such as labels and package inserts. (See *Offset printing*. Compare *Intaglio printing* and *Letterpress printing.*)

Live. A broadcast by actual musicians and speakers, in contrast to a transcribed or recorded broadcast.

Local advertising. Newspaper advertising paid for by the local retailer at a *local* or lower rate than that charged the *national advertiser.*

Local-channel station (radio). A station that is allowed just enough power to be heard near its point of transmission and is assigned a channel on the air wave set aside for local-channel stations. (Compare *Regional-channel station; Clear-channel station.*)

Locking up. Tightening up the type matter put into a chase preparatory to going to press.

Log (radio). A record of every minute of broadcasting, including all errors. An accurate journal required by law.

Logotype. (1) Two letters cast on one block of type, such as fi, ct, ff. (2) The name plate of an advertiser.

Lower case (l.c.). The small letters in the alphabet, such as those in which this is printed, COMPARED WITH UPPER CASE OR CAPITAL LETTERS. Note that the difference lies in the formation of the letters. The term is derived from the lower case of the printer's type cabinet in which the type was formerly kept.

Machine-finish (M.F.) paper. The cheapest of book papers that take half tones well. A paper which has had its pores filled ("sized") but which is not ironed. Thus it possesses a moderately smooth surface. Smoother than *antique,* but not so smooth as *English-finish* or *sized and super-calendered paper.*

Mail-order advertising. That method of selling whereby the complete sales transaction is negotiated through advertising and the mails, and without the aid of a salesman. Not to be confused with *direct-mail advertising.*

Make-ready. The process of adjusting the form of type or the plates for the press to insure good printing. A preliminary proof of the form on the press is inspected for those letters or plates which appear lighter than the rest of the material. *Overlays* and *underlays* of paper are inserted under the printing surfaces to secure the uniform pressure necessary to obtain even effects. The skill and care in this work represent one of the hidden elements that serve to make a good printing job.

Make-up of a page. The general appearance of a page; the arrangement in which the editorial matter and advertising material are to appear.

Marketing. Those business activities that aid the movement of goods and services from production to consumption.

Matrix; "mat." (1) A mold of paper pulp, or similar substance, made by pressing a sheet of it into the type setup or engraving plate. Molten lead is poured into it, forming a replica of the original plate known as a *stereotype*. (2) The brass molds used in the linotype.

Matter. Composed type, often referred to as: (1) *dead matter*—of no further use; (2) *leaded matter*—having extra spacing between lines; (3) *live matter*—to be used again; (4) *solid matter*—lines set close to each other; (5) *standing matter*—held for future use.

M.C. (radio). Master of Ceremonies.

Medium. (1) The vehicle that carries the advertisement, as newspaper, magazine, letter, car card, and so on. (2) The tool and method used by an artist in drawing illustrations, as pen and ink, pencil, wash, or crayon.

Megacycle (radio). 1,000 kilocycles. For example, 50,000 kilocycles = 50 megacycles.

M.F. Machine-finish paper.

Microphone. An instrument for converting sound-wave impulses into corresponding electrical impulses, used in broadcasting for "picking up" programs from studios and other points.

Milline rate. A unit for measuring the rate of advertising space in relation to circulation; the cost of having one agate line appear before one million readers. Calculated thus:

$$\text{Milline rate} = \frac{\text{Actual line rate} \times 1{,}000{,}000}{\text{Circulation}}$$

Modern type. See *Old style type.*

Modulation. The process of combining or impressing the sound, program, or audio-frequency energy upon the carrier of a broadcasting station.

Monotype composition. Type set by a machine in which the individual letters are separately molded and automatically assembled into lines, as distinguished from *hand composition* and *linotype composition.*

Month preceding. *First month preceding* publication means that the closing date falls on the given day during the month which immediately precedes the publication date of a periodical. If the rate card says closing date is the 5th of the first month preceding, it means that the forms for the March issue, for instance, would close February 5th. *Second month preceding* would mean that forms close January 5th; *third month preceding,* December 5th.

Mortise. The section of an engraving plate sawed out to make room for type or another plate. When a border is engraved, the inside or white area will be mortised.

National advertising. (1) The advertising of any trade-marked product that potentially could be sold by dealers throughout the nation. (2) The advertising of a manufacturer or producer in contrast to that of a retailer.

National plan. The tactics, used in advertising campaigns, of trying to get all the business that can be secured from all over the country at one time. When rightfully used, it is the outgrowth of numerous *zone plans.* Compare also the *Cream plan.*

Natural fold. That method of folding a direct advertisement whereby the continuity of the copy is preserved as the advertisement is opened.

Neon. A luminous-tube sign by which vivid effects are secured.

Network (radio). A permanent setup of wire telephone lines interconnecting broadcasting stations for the purpose of distributing radio programs for simultaneous broadcasting by such stations.

Next to reading matter (n.r.). The location of an advertisement immediately adjacent to editorial or news matter in a publication.

Nickeltype. A nickel-faced electrotype, more durable than one of copper.

N.R. Next to reading matter.

Offset. (1) The method of lithographic printing whereby the impression is transferred not directly to the paper, but to a rubber blanket and then to the sheet. Gives a softer effect than direct lithography. Makes possible the use of rough-surfaced stock in the reproduction of lithographic illustration. (2) The blotting of a wet or freshly printed sheet against an accompanying sheet. Can be prevented by slip-sheeting. Antique paper absorbs the ink and prevents offsetting.

Old style type (o.s.). Originally the face of Roman type with slight difference in weight between its different strokes, as contrasted with *modern type,* which has sharp contrast and accents in its strokes. Its serifs, for the most part, are oblique; modern serifs are usually horizontal or vertical. Also refers to the Old Style member of a family of types, usually the lighter face.

One-time rate. The rate paid by an advertiser who uses less space than that necessary to earn a time or rate discount, when such discounts are offered. Same as *transient rate.*

One-way screen. A half tone with the screen in one direction only; it does not have the cross-screen which gives the dot effect. Good for odd effects. Makes tooling difficult.

On speculation. An offer to create an idea which, if used, is paid for, but if not used, is not to be paid for.

Order-of-merit method. Testing a piece of copy or an illustration, advertisement, trade-mark, design, or package, giving first place to the one with the highest vote.

Origination point (radio). The actual studio or other point at which artists perform, used especially in connection with features that are extensively distributed to numerous broadcasting stations through networks.

O.S. Old style type.

Overlapping circulation. The extent to which two or more media duplicate one another in reaching the same prospect. Sometimes this is a desirable feature, providing an immediate cumulative effect.

Overrun. The number of pieces of matter printed in excess of the specified quantity. According to the trade custom, an advertiser agrees to accept an overrun of no more than 10 per cent at pro rata cost.

P.; pp. Page; pages.

Page proof. A proof of type matter and plates arranged by pages, as they are finally to appear. Usually is made ("pulled") after *galley proof* has been shown and corrections are made.

Participation show (radio). A show usually created and conducted by a station, appealing to a specific type of audience, in which a number of advertisers can have their products featured or mentioned.

Pica; pica-em. The unit for measuring width in printing. There are 6 picas to the inch. Derived from *pica,* the name of the 12-pt. type ($\frac{1}{6}''$ high), and the letter M of that series, whose width likewise is $\frac{1}{6}''$. A page of type 25 picas wide is $4\frac{1}{6}$ inches wide ($25 \div 6 = 4\frac{1}{6}$).

Picture resolution (television). The clarity with which the image appears on the television screen.

Pied type. A type setup that has become disarranged.

Pioneering stage. The advertising stage of a product in which the need for such product is not recognized and has to be established, or when the need has been established, but the success of a commodity in filling those requirements has to be evidenced. See *Competitive stage; Retentive stage; Spiral.*

Plated stock. Paper with a high gloss and a hard, smooth surface, secured by being pressed between polished metal sheets.

Playback. The playing of a recording for audition purposes.

Point; pt. (1) The unit of measurement of type, $\frac{1}{72}$ inch in depth. Type is specified by its point size, as 8 pt., 12 pt., 24 pt., 48 pt. (2) The unit for measuring thickness of paper, one-thousandth of an inch.

Poster panel. A standard surface on which outdoor posters are placed. The posting surface is of sheet metal. An ornamental molding of standard green forms the frame. The standard poster panel is 12 feet high by 25 feet in length (outside dimensions).

Poster plant. The organization that provides the actual outdoor advertising service.

Poster showing. The unit of sale for poster service. The number of panels in a showing varies from city to city.

P.P.A. Periodical Publishers' Association.

Preferred position. When an advertiser wants to make sure that his advertisement appears in a given position in a periodical, he may be able to obtain that space by paying a higher, preferred-position rate for it. Otherwise the advertisement appears in *run-of-paper* position—that is, wherever the publisher chooses to place it. Certain pages are preferred in publication advertising, just as are the positions on a page.

Primary service area (radio). The area to which a broadcasting station delivers a high level of signal of unfailing steadiness and of sufficient volume completely to override the existing noise levels both day and night at all seasons of the year. The limits of the primary service area as determined by field-intensity measurements are usually considered to be the 5-millivolt-per-meter contour.

***Printers' Ink* Model Statute.** The act, directed at fraudulent advertising, prepared and sponsored by *Printers' Ink*, the popular advertising journal.

Private brand. When a wholesaler or retailer buys a product and has it labeled and sold under his own trademark, it is referred to as a "private brand"—in contrast to the nationally advertised brand that the wholesaler or retailer might also be selling.

Process plates. Photoengraving plates for printing two, three, or four colors, one over the other, to produce the final desired effect.

Process printing. Letterpress color printing in which one color is printed over the other by means of a set of process plates.

Producer (radio). (1) One who originates and brings a program or presentation. (2) The individual or the broadcasting company offering a program for observation or consideration, or bringing a performance before the public.

Production (radio). The building, organization, and presentation of a radio program.

Production department. (1) The department of an advertising agency responsible for the mechanical production of an advertisement, dealing with printers and engravers. In some agencies it includes the copy and art departments. (2) The department responsible for the proper broadcasting of a radio program.

Production director (radio). Individual in charge of a radio studio program.

Program following (radio). The program that follows a given program. Important in deciding upon the desirability of the station and hour.

Program opposite (radio). The radio programs that are running over other stations at the same time as the given program, broadcasting to the same territory. The competition for the radio audience that a program experiences.

Program preceding (radio). The program that is on directly before a given program. A good "program preceding" enhances the desirability of the time on the air.

Progressive proofs. A set of photoengraving proofs in color, in which the yellow plate is printed on one sheet and the red on another. The yellow and red are then combined. Next the blue is printed and a yellow-red-blue combination made. Then the black alone is printed, and finally all colors are combined (sequence varies). Used by the printer in matching up his inks when printing color plates.

Proof. (1) An inked impression of composed type or of a plate taken for the purpose of inspection or for filing. (2) In engraving and etching, an impression taken to show the condition of the illustration at any stage of the work. Taking a proof is known as *pulling a proof.*

Proof for files. When a corrected proof of an advertisement is returned to the periodical too late to secure a revised proof for final O. K., the corrected proof is marked *"O K with C"* (approved, with corrections), and proof for files is requested. The advertiser will then receive copies of the final advertisement for his records or for future use in preparing other advertisements.

Publisher's statement. The statement of circulation issued by a periodical publisher.

Quads. Blank pieces of metal used by the printer to fill out lines where the amount of type does not do so.

Quarter showing. One fourth of a *full showing.*

Quarter tones, or double-process half tones. A development of the half tone plate for use in reproducing illustrations on newspaper and other rough stock. Made in a coarse screen by a process which retains more detail than the ordinary coarse-screen half tone.

Railroad showing. An outdoor advertisement conspicuously placed so that it can be seen by passengers on trains.

Rate book. A compilation of the rates charged by periodicals for advertising space.

Rate card. A card giving the space rates of a publication, and additional data on mechanical requirements and closing dates.

Rate-holder. The minimum-sized advertisement which must appear during a given period if an advertiser is to secure a certain time or quantity discount. Takes its name from the fact that it holds a lower rate for an advertiser.

Reading notices. Advertisements in newspapers set up in a type similar to that of the editorial matter. Must be followed by "Adv." Charged for at rates higher than those for regular ads. Many publications will not accept reading notices.

Ream. In the publishing and advertising world, 500 sheets of paper (not 480). Thousand-sheet counts have been introduced.

Rebroadcast. A radio program repeated at a later hour to reach the parts of the country in a different time belt. Rebroadcasts may be either live or transcribed.

Recognized agency. An advertising agency recognized as such by the various publishers or their associations and granted a commission for the space it sells to advertisers. The commission is usually 15 per cent on the gross with 2 per cent on the net for cash, expressed *"15 and 2."*

Recorded program. Any radio program consisting of phonograph records or electrical transcriptions and not depending upon the presence of artists in the studio at the time of the actual broadcast.

Reducing glass. The opposite of a magnifying glass. Used in looking at illustrations to judge how they will appear when reproduced in smaller size.

Regional-channel station (radio). A station that is allowed more power than a local station but less than a clear-channel station. It is assigned a place on the frequency band set aside for regional channel stations. (See *Local channel* and *Clear channel.*)

Register. Perfect correspondence in printing. Facing pages register or are in register when top lines are even. In color printing, register means correct superimposition of each plate so that the colors mix properly.

Registering trade-mark. In the United States, the act of recording a trade-mark with the Commissioner of Patents.

Release (on a photograph). A statement by a person photographed authorizing the advertiser to use that photograph. In the case of minors, the guardian's release is necessary.

Relief printing. Printing in which the design reproduced is raised slightly above the surrounding, nonprinting areas. Letterpress is a form of relief printing. (Compare *Intaglio printing* and *Lithography.*)

Remote control. The operation of broadcasting a program from a point removed from the regular studios of the station.

Retentive stage. The third stage of a product, reached when its general usefulness is everywhere known, its individual qualities thoroughly appreciated, and when it is satisfied to retain its patronage merely on the strength of its past reputation. (See *Pioneering stage; Competitive stage; Spiral.*)

Retouching. The process of correcting or improving art work, especially photographs.

Reversed plate. (1) A line-plate engraving in which whites come out black, and vice versa. (2) An engraving in which right and left, as they appear in the illustration, are transposed.

Ripple-finish. Paper having a regularly uneven surface.

Roman type. (1) Originally, type of the Italian and Roman school of design, as distinguished from the blackface Old English style of type. Old style and modern are the two branches of the Roman family. (2) Type faces that are not italics are called roman.

ROP. Run-of-paper position; any location in publication convenient to publisher.

Rotation. Repeating a series of advertisements by beginning again with No. 1 after all have been run.

Rotogravure. The method of *intaglio printing* in which the advertisement is chemically etched out of a copper roller. (In photoengraving, the area not to appear in an illustration is etched away.) Useful in large runs of pictorial effects.

Rough (noun). The first pencil draft of an illustration executed in crude style. An artist submits a rough of an illustration to the advertiser for O. K. before proceeding, in order to insure correctness of the general conception and composition.

Routing out. Tooling out dead metal on an engraving plate.

R.P.M. Revolutions per minute, speed at which a radio transcription or phonograph record is played. Most transcriptions run $33\frac{1}{3}$ r.p.m.; most phonograph records, 78 r.p.m.

Run of paper. See *ROP.*

Saddle stitching. Binding a booklet

by stitching it with wire through the center. The stitching passes through the fold in the center pages and backbone of the booklet. Enables the booklet to lie flat. When booklet is too thick to permit this method, *side stitching* is used.

Sales promotion department. The department acting as a liaison between the sales department and the advertising department. Concerns itself with investigating for new markets, following up inquiries resulting from advertisements, and following up salesmen's visits with proper letters and literature.

S. and S.C. Sized and super-calendered paper.

S.C. (1) Single column. (2) Small caps.

Scale rate. In photoengraving, the standard cost rate.

Scaling down. Reducing illustrations to the size they are to have in the advertisement.

Script show (radio). A serial program, usually 15 minutes, on the air three or five times a week at the same hour and station.

Secondary service area (radio). The area beyond the primary service area where a broadcasting station delivers a steady signal of sufficient intensity to be a regular program service of loudspeaker volume by both day and night and at all seasons of the year. The limit of the secondary service area, as determined by field intensity measurements, is usually considered to be the 500-micro-volt-per-meter contour.

Segue (radio). The transition from one musical number to another without a break or announcements; originally Italian, meaning "it follows."

Self-mailer. A direct-mail advertisement folder, booklet, or book that requires no envelope for mailing.

Shallow half tone. An inferior half tone in which the dots have not been deeply etched and in which consequently the detail of the illustration is lost. When half tones have been overdeveloped, they may have their dots undermined.

Sheet. The old unit of a poster size, 26 × 39 inches. The standard-size poster is called a 24-sheet.

Short rate. When an advertiser signs a contract to use a certain amount of space in a given time and thereby secure a lower rate, and subsequently fails to use the specified amount of that space, he must pay for the space he did use at the higher rate for the lesser amount. The actual difference in dollars and cents is called the *short rate.*

Shoulder of type. The space between the upper or lower extremes of a type letter and the edge of the body on which it is mounted. The shoulder does not print. The type size, as given in points, includes the shoulder, thus accounting for the fact that a 36-point type letter, for example, does not appear exactly ½″ in size.

Side stitching. The method of wire-stitching from one side of a booklet to the other. Wiring can be seen on front cover and on back. Used in thick booklet work. Pages do not lie flat. See *Saddle stitching.*

Signature. (1) The name of an advertiser. (2) A sheet folded ready for stitching in a book, usually sixteen pages, but with thin paper thirty-two pages; a mark, letter, or number is placed at the bottom of the first page of every group of sixteen or thirty-two pages to serve as a guide in folding.

Signature (radio). The musical number or sound effect that regularly identifies a program.

Silhouette half tone. One in which all background is eliminated, the product alone appearing. Also known as *Outline half tone.*

Sized and super-calendered paper (s. and s.c.). Machine-finish book paper that has been given extra ironings to insure a smooth surface. Takes half tones very well.

Sized paper. Paper that has received a chemical bath to make it less porous. Paper sized once and ironed (calendered) is known as *machine-finish.* If it is again ironed, it becomes *sized and super-calendered (s. and s.c.).*

Sky wave. That component of the radiation from a radio antenna system which is at an angle above the horizontal and most of which reaches the listener only by reflection from the Kennelly-Heaviside layer.

Slip-sheeting. To prevent the sheets of a printing job from offsetting or smudging as they come from the press, a sheet of paper (usually tissue or a cheap porous stock) is placed between them.

Sniping. The mounting of an outdoor advertisement wherever space and opportunity permit, as against rocks, barrels, fences, and the like.

Sound effects (radio). Various devices or recordings used to produce lifelike imitations of sound, such as walking up stairs, ocean waves, phone bells, auto horns.

Space discount. A discount given by a publisher for the amount of linage that an advertiser uses. Compare with *Time discount.*

Space schedule. A schedule showing the media in which an advertisement is to appear, the dates on which it is to appear, its exact size, and the cost.

Special representative. An individual or organization that represents a certain publisher in selling space outside the city of publication. The same special representative may serve two or more publishers of different cities. Also known as *foreign representative.*

Spiral. A graphic representation of the advertising evolution through which a product passes in its acceptance by the public. The stages are the *pioneering,* the *competitive,* and the *retentive.*

Split channel (radio). Two or more network sections working simultaneously with different programs.

Sponsor. The firm or individual that pays for talent and broadcasting station time for a radio feature; the advertiser on the air.

Spot broadcast (radio). A program issued directly from a station in behalf of a national advertiser, in contrast to a *network* broadcast, which is broadcast over a series of connected stations, or a *local* broadcast, which is a program sent out by a local advertiser over a station in his city.

Square-finish half tone. A half tone in which the background has been left in, but trimmed by the engraver to a definite shape, usually rectangular. Can also be trimmed to an oval or circle.

Stage. See *Spiral.*

Staggered schedule. A schedule of space to be used in two or more periodicals, arranged so that the insertions alternate.

Station announcement. The announcement made to identify a radio transmitter.

Station director (radio). The executive in complete charge of the operation and management of a broadcasting station.

Station representative (radio). The sales representative of a radio station. One may represent a number of stations.

Steel-die embossing. Printing from steel dies engraved by the *intaglio process,* the sharp, raised outlines being produced by stamping over a counter die. Used for monograms, crests, stationery, and similar social and business purposes. When part of the detail is to be brought out in contour, the die is countersunk.

Steeltype. A trade name sometimes applied to an electrotype faced with nickel.

Stereotype. A plate cast by pouring molten metal into a matrix. One of the least expensive forms of duplicate plates. Lacks the strength and sharpness of detail of an electrotype. Newspapers are printed from stereotypes.

Should not be used in magazine advertisements.

Stet. A proofreader's term—"Let it stand as it is; disregard change specified." A dotted line is placed underneath the letter or words to which the instructions apply.

Stock cuts. Photoengraving plates of standard or conventional illustrations, sold by the piece.

Stone proof. See *Flat proof.*

Studio (radio). A room especially adapted by suitable acoustic treatment and by the installation of microphones and associated equipment, signaling lights, and other essentials to the presentation and picking up of sound programs for broadcasting purposes.

Style manual. A compilation of typographical rules to be followed in a publication, codifying the method of treating spelling, abbreviations, and other questions of uniformity in editing.

Substance No. (Usually followed by a figure, as *Substance No. 16, Substance No. 20, Substance No. 24.*) In specifying paper stock, the equivalent weight of a given paper in the standard size.

Surprint. (1) A photoengraving in which a line-plate effect appears over the face of a half tone, or vice versa. (2) To place printing over the face of an advertisement already printed.

Sustaining program. Entertainment or educational feature performed at the expense of a broadcasting station or network.

T. Time, such as 1-t, 5-t. Refers to the frequency with which an advertisement is to appear.

T.A.B. Traffic Audit Bureau.

Tail piece. A small typographical ornament or illustration placed at the end of a piece of copy.

T.C. Top of column.

Tear sheet. Copies of advertisements torn or "stripped" from newspapers, for distribution to interested individuals.

Telecast (radio). A sound and pictorial image that has been sent by television.

Television (radio). The method of broadcasting both sound and pictorial effects.

Test. A method of trying out an idea on a small scale before proceeding with it on a larger scale.

T.F. (1) Till-forbid. (2) To fill. (3) Copy is to follow.

Till-forbid; run T.F. Instructions to publisher meaning: "Continue running this advertisement until instructions are issued to the contrary."

Time discount. A discount given to an advertiser for the frequency or regularity with which he inserts his advertisements in a publication. Compare *Quantity discount.*

Tint block. Usually a solid piece of zinc, used to print a light shade of ink for a background.

Tip in. To paste a leaf, or leaves, on a page or on a mount. Half tones are often printed on a smooth stock which will be pasted into place in a book printed on a stock that will not take half tones.

To fill (T.F.). Instructions to printer meaning: "Set this copy in the size necessary to fill the specified space indicated in the layout."

Tr. Transpose type as indicated.

Trade advertising. Advertising directed by a manufacturer or distributor to the retail merchants through whom the product is sold.

Trade-mark. Any device that identifies the origin of a product, telling who made it or who sold it. (A word can be a trade-mark.) Not to be confused with *trade name.*

Trade name. A name that applies to a business as a whole and not to an individual product.

Traffic Audit Bureau (T.A.B.). An organization designed to investigate how many people pass and may see a given outdoor sign.

Traffic department. The department

in an advertising agency responsible for the prompt execution of the work in the respective departments and for turning over the complete material for shipment to the forwarding department on schedule time. When one person handles this work, he is popularly known as the *Accelerator*.

Transcription. See *Electric transcription*.

Transcription program library (radio). A collection of transcription records from which the advertiser may draw. Stations subscribe to various transcription libraries; hence, the advertiser need merely find out to which library a station subscribes and specify which numbers from the library service he wishes.

Transient rate. Same as *one-time rate* in buying space.

Transparency. Same as *decalcomania*.

Traveling display. An elaborate exhibit prepared by a manufacturer of a product and loaned by him to each of several dealers in rotation. Usually based on the product and prepared in such a way as to be of educational or dramatizing value.

Trimmed flush. A booklet or book trimmed after the cover is on, the cover thus being cut flush with the leaves. Compare with *Extended covers*.

25 × 38—80. Read *twenty-five, thirty-eight, eighty*. The method of expressing paper weight, meaning that a ream of paper 25×38 inches in size weighs 80 lbs. Similarly, 25×38—60, 25×38—70, 25×38—120, 17×22—16, 17×22—24, 20×26—80, 38×50—140.

Type face. The design of a type letter. Type faces are usually named after men, as, Caslon, Della Robbia, Jensen, Goudy. In machine composition, the faces are known also by numbers.

Type page. The area of a page that type can occupy; the total area of a page less the margins.

Up. Number of times a cut or page is duplicated in a form; one page two "up" is a two-page form; four pages two "up" is an eight-page form.

Vignette. A half tone in which the edges shade off gradually to very light gray. In some instances only part of the half tone may be finished in vignette.

Visual show (radio). A radio program that is also being presented before a studio audience.

Wait order. Instructions to a periodical to set up an advertisement and hold it in readiness to run upon the issuance of the subsequent insertion order.

Wash drawing. A brush-work illustration, usually made with diluted India ink or water color so that, in addition to its black and white, it has varying shades of gray, like a photograph. Half tones, not line plates, are made from wash drawings. Wash drawings are extensively used to picture merchandise, as they can emphasize details better than photographs.

Wax engraving. The process of coating a plate with wax upon which the design is drawn, photographed, or impressed. The wax is then cut through to the metal base. Used in making maps.

Wax-mold electrotype. An electrotype made from an impression taken in a sheet of wax. Compare *Lead-mold process*.

Wedge ladder. A graphic representation of that method of action whereby each step is planned to lead directly to the next and so on to the conclusion. In copy, refers to coherence; in campaigns, refers to method of using media in such a way that all dovetail in accordance with a complete plan.

W.F. See *Wrong font*.

Window envelope. A mailing envelope with a transparent panel in front, permitting the address on the enclosure to serve as a mailing address as well.

Wire circuits. A metallic conducting path connecting for communication purposes two or more points, such as broadcast transmitter, broadcasting studios, and remote sources of programs.

Woodcuts. Wooden printing blocks upon which the design is carved by hand. These preceded the use of metal for type plates.

Wove paper. Paper having a very faint, clothlike appearance when held to the light.

Writing paper. Paper made to accommodate pen-and-ink writing, varying from *flat writing paper,* such as that used in cheap memorandum pads, through *bonds* of various grades to *ledger paper.* Basic size is 17×22 inches.

Wrong font (w.f.). Letter from one series mixed with those from another series, or font. See if you can pick out the wrong font in this sentence.

Zinc etching. A photoengraving in zinc. Term is usually applied to line plates.

Zone plan. The tactics, used in advertising campaigns, of concentrating on a certain limited geographical area rather than trying to cover the entire country at once, as in the *national plan,* or picking the choice prospects from different parts of the country at the same time, as in the *cream plan.* Valuable for effective use of limited appropriations devoted to advertising a product in common use, such as soap, dentifrices, cigarettes, and shoes.

SECTION 5

Sales Management

1. DETERMINING SALES TERRITORIES

2. SALES QUOTAS

3. RECRUITING AND SELECTING SALESMEN

4. EQUIPPING SALESMEN

5. TRAINING SALESMEN

6. METHODS OF COMPENSATING SALESMEN

SECTION 5

Sales Management

1. DETERMINING SALES TERRITORIES

What is a sales territory?—A sales territory is the geographical area in which a salesman's activities are conducted. Most wholesale salesmen are confined to the territory to which they are assigned, whereas salesmen selling direct to consumers are often not restricted to definite territories but are permitted to sell wherever they wish. Frequently no territories are assigned to commission salesmen or to those engaged in the introduction of new products when the market is undeveloped or when the goods are highly competitive specialties or intangibles.

Certain functional types of salesmen, such as missionary salesmen engaged in sales promotional work, or specialty salesmen concentrating on the introduction of a new item or on reviving the sale of an inactive product, are usually not assigned a territory of their own but are transferred from territory to territory as the need for their specialized service demands.

Occasionally salesmen are assigned to a definite territory but given freedom to operate wherever they wish, subject to certain restrictions. In such cases a salesman is generally held responsible for production in his assigned territory, receives credit for all sales in his territory, and has referred to him all inquiries that originate in his territory. However, sales may be made to prospects or customers outside of a salesman's assigned territory through a mutual understanding with all salesmen in the organization to the effect that compensation for sales made outside of an assigned territory shall be divided with the salesmen in whose territory the sale is made. Commission salesmen "split" their commissions on such extraterritorial sales. Salesmen who are paid a bonus receive corresponding adjustments in quota.

Definite territories may be assigned to wholesale distributors and retail dealers as well as individual salesmen, and similar protection plans are devised to give the distributors protection within their territories. Both the Ford Motor Company and the Chevrolet Division of General Motors Corporation employ exclusive, retail-dealer, territory policies. Moreover, there appears to be a trend toward the establishment of definite territorial assignments for both salesmen and wholesale and retail outlets.

Why establish sales territories?—Sales territories are established for the following reasons:

1. To fix definite responsibility on salesmen for desired performance.
2. To save a salesman's time.
3. To insure maximum service to customers.
4. To make comparisons between the performance of salesmen in various territories.
5. To avoid conflicts between salesmen and overlapping of sales efforts.
6. To equalize more nearly the opportunities for all salesmen.
7. To adapt the personality of the salesman to the prevailing type of buyer in a territory.
8. To facilitate control and operation of salesmen by the management.
9. To effect reductions in traveling expenses.
10. To avoid aimless travel and backtracking by salesmen.
11. To insure a salesman ample sales opportunities.
12. To prevent a salesman from having more work than he can do efficiently.
13. To insure adequate coverage of the potential market.
14. To meet competition more effectively.

Why salesmen are not restricted to territories.—Salesmen are not restricted to territories for the following reasons:

1. Sales territories are difficult to establish fairly.
2. Salesmen operate more effectively when they are not restricted to a definite area.

3. Salesmen prefer to operate where they can get the best results, irrespective of territory.

4. Territory reductions arouse resentment on the part of salesmen and create dissatisfaction.

5. The security of territorial protection is not conducive to maximum activity on the part of the salesman.

Establishing basic sales territories.—The first step in a scientific determination of sales territory is to establish basic sales territories by considering the market potential and the number of salesmen to be involved in the distribution of the product under consideration. Such basic territories insure each salesman in the organization equal opportunities from the standpoint of potential sales.

Use of indexes.—To determine the potential for each territory, a market index or indexes relating to the product or service being sold is first selected. Other factors to be considered in selecting a market index are: the price of the product; whether it is a luxury or a necessity; and whether it is an industrial or individual consumption item. For such lines as refrigerators, washing machines, ranges, and other products where industry sales figures are available by states, the industry figures may form the base of the index. In addition to the current sales index, other indexes measuring potential consumption should be selected. In the case of products for individual consumption, the factors of population, buying power, standards of living, and distributive outlets should be considered and indexes relating to these factors employed.

The consumption factor of population may be expressed by the following specific indexes: foreign-born population, colored population, literate population, native whites, families, rural population, urban population, adult population, dwellings, and so forth.

The basic consumption factor of buying power may be expressed by any one or several of the following indexes: income tax returns, value of farm crops, value of livestock, individual bank deposits, check transactions, per capita wholesale and retail sales, automobile ownership, and so forth.

The factor of standards of living may be expressed by the following indexes: telephones, wired homes, radio ownership, life insurance sales, magazine circulation, and so on.

Indexes of distributive outlets include: number of wholesalers and retailers.

These market indexes may be weighted according to their relative importance in respect to the potential of the market being measured.

Applying indexes in determination of sales territory.—The second step in applying a market index or indexes in the determination of a sales territory is to convert the index figures, which may be available in county, city, state, or trading-area units, to a percentage of United States total. For example, a manufacturer of agricultural implements selects the market index "rural population" as one basis for determining sales territories. Consulting the latest Government census, he finds that the three Pacific-Coast states have the following percentage of the national total rural population: Washington, 1.29 per cent; Oregon, .87 per cent; and California, 2.87 per cent. Other index factors may be combined with that of "rural population" to obtain a combined average, and each factor may be readily weighted according to its relative importance.

Allotment of potential market to salesmen.—The third step in establishing a basic sales territory is to consider the number of salesmen involved and to allot an equal percentage of the total potential market to each salesman. The national market is thereby divided into as many potentially equal sales territories as there are salesmen available to develop them.

For example, the national manufacturer of agricultural implements mentioned previously employs twenty salesmen and wishes to divide the national market into twenty approximately equal potential sales territories. Approximately 5 per cent of the national potential should be included in each man's basic territory. Taking the index of "rural population" and starting on the Pacific Coast, we find that Washington, Oregon, and California combined have a total of 5.03 per cent of the United States figure, which is approximately equivalent to 1/20 of the total national rural population and affords a basic potential sales territory for one salesman. The other nineteen salesmen in the organization would similarly be allotted territories on the basis of this index of potential, and by this method the sales territories can be equitably allotted according to the potentiality of the market.

The number of salesmen involved will determine the size of the geographical units on which the territories should be based. In organizations with a limited number of salesmen, the state unit may be the minimum unit for basic territory establishment. In larger sales organizations, cultivating the country more intensively, the county unit may serve as a basis. Salesmen of consumer goods sold through wholesale and retail outlets may have territories established on the "trading-area"-unit basis.

Adjusted sales territories.—After sales territories based on market potential and number of salesmen employed have been established, it is necessary to adjust these basic territories to conform to local conditions, taking into consideration transportation facilities, competition, existing demand, extent of sales development, cost of coverage, method of distribution, economic conditions, type of product, ability of the salesman assigned to the area, and other factors affecting the ability of the company to attain its share of the potential volume of sales in the area. Basic sales territories in practically all cases must be adjusted to take into consideration these factors.

Adjustment to method of travel.—Basic sales territories established on market potential and number of salesmen in the organization must be reshaped to conform to the transportation lines and method of travel used by the salesmen in covering the areas. When a salesman travels by automobile, the territory may conform to highway lines. When railroads are used, a territory must necessarily be shaped by the prevailing lines of railroads. A careful study should be made of all train, trolley, air, bus, boat, and automobile highways in shaping the sales territory for most economical and efficient coverage.

Adjustment to competition.—The amount and character of competition are important factors to be considered in expanding or contracting a basic sales territory. If competition is localized and intense within a basic sales territory, the size of the area may be restricted to permit more frequent coverage and to meet existing competition more effectively. When competition is limited, the basic territory may be expanded, since frequent coverage to meet competition is not necessary.

If, on the other hand, competition is so firmly entrenched in a sales territory that there is little likelihood that a salesman can secure a profitable volume, the basic area may be expanded to enable the salesman to obtain a profitable volume, or the salesman may be withdrawn from the territory, and it may be turned over to a broker or sold direct by mail.

Adjustment to existing demand.—The existing demand for a product or service has a direct bearing on the adjustments that must be made in the size of a basic territory. If a strong demand exists for an item, selling progress is slow, and the basic sales territory may be restricted to insure thorough coverage. If, however, a new product is being introduced for which there is little existing demand, the basic territory may be expanded to enable the salesman to secure a profitable volume of sales.

Adjustment for extent of sales development.—If the policy of a company favors intensive distribution, basic sales territories will be restricted to permit thorough coverage. If, on the other hand, a policy of broad, national distribution is pursued, expanded, basic territories must result.

Adjustment for profitable operation.—The size of a sales territory must be regulated by the cost of travel in relation to the sales volume that may be secured therein. If, for example, the maximum ratio of direct selling expense to expected sales is 3 per cent, and anticipated sales are $100,000, the cost of covering the area must not exceed $3,000. Accordingly, the basic territory must be adjusted in area to permit coverage for this figure.

Adjustment for method of distribution.—If a product is sold through wholesale outlets exclusively, the basic territory may be larger than would be the case if the product were sold direct to the consumer. Salesmen calling on retail grocers should have smaller territories than men calling on retail hardware outlets.

Adjustment for type of product.—Basic territories for salesmen of repeat essentials may be relatively small in comparison with those of salesmen of novelties or luxuries.

Adjustment for ability of salesmen.—The basic territory of an able salesman may be expanded, while the territory of a mediocre salesman may have to be contracted. A new and inexperienced salesman may require a more limited area than a more experienced man.

Adjustment for individual factors.—The basic territories of salesmen with family responsibilities may be so arranged as to enable these men to live at home. Other salesmen who prefer continuous travel may be assigned to larger areas where more travel is involved. Some salesmen are more successful with intensive cultivation of their territories, and these men should be assigned restricted areas.

All of these factors should be taken into consideration in expanding or contracting basic sales territories so that each territory may be adjusted in area to afford maximum sales and profits.

Sources of sales-territory data.—In determining basic sales territories and adjusting them to the various factors affecting the sales potential of an individual concern, there is a wealth of information available. Valuable information is published by the U. S. Census Bureau, the U. S. Bureau of Foreign and Domestic Commerce, and other Government bureaus, as well as various trade associations, state governments, colleges and universities, and commercial organizations. The principal sources are "Consumer Market Handbook" and "Industrial Market Data Book of the United States," published by the Bureau of Foreign and Domestic Commerce of the U. S. Department of Commerce. In addition, "Consumer Use of Selected Goods and Services by Income Classes," published by the same Government bureau, is an excellent source of territory information. The census of distribution made by the U. S. Census Bureau in 1940 is the most recent source of market data available for the establishment of sales territories.

In addition to these sources, the following publications provide excellent territory information: "Survey of Buying Power," Sales Management, Incorporated, New York City; "Trading Area System of Sales Control," Hearst Magazines, Inc., New York City; "Sales Opportunities," Curtis Publishing Company, Philadelphia; "National Market and Crowell Circulation," The Crowell Publishing Company, New York City; "Market Exploration Maps" and "Families and How They Live," Printers' Ink Publications, New York City; "Industrial Market Data Book," Industrial Marketing, Chicago.

Allocating sales territories.—A sales territory may be allocated along political lines as state, county, township, city, or ward; or by transportation lines or buying habits that take no cognizance of political boundaries. Salesmen of consumer goods distributed through wholesale and retail outlets should have territories allocated by trading-area lines rather than by political boundaries. The same is true of wholesale and retail distributors of consumer goods. A salesman of industrial goods, insurance, securities, and other products or services not distributed through retail or wholesale outlets may have territories allocated by county lines.

Reallocating sales territories.—Sales territories must be examined at least annually and adjustments made in the size of the area to meet shifting demand, competition, and economic conditions affecting the potential of the area; to equalize the opportunities of all salesmen; and to secure a fair ratio of expense to the sales volume.

There is an urgent need in many sales organizations for consolidating or reducing the area of sales territories and for insuring thorough cultivation at a savings in time and expense. Restricted territories result in better service to customers, more frequent contacts, more new prospects, lower freight costs, and greater sales volume and profits than larger territories. When the factual evidence of market potential and sales volume is compared in a sales territory, both management and salesmen are usually quick to concede that the area can be reduced with a saving in expense and an increase in efficiency and profit.

2. SALES QUOTAS

What is a sales quota?—A sales quota answers the question "What sales should I expect to secure?" From the management standpoint, it is the proportional part or share of the total sales volume that may be expected from a given market. In other words, it is a goal of sales accomplishment, a task, objective, or standard that a sales organization strives to attain.

There are four distinct types of sales quotas, the most common of which is the estimated volume of sales that a company expects to secure within a definite period of time. As sales volume is one of the most important as well as the most conveniently computed factors of sales accomplishment, a majority of quotas are of this type. The estimate may be expressed in terms of dollars and cents or in units such as pounds, cases, gallons, and so forth.

The growing interest in profitable sales is contributing to an increasing use of "profit quotas," which are established to estimate the profit expectancy from a given territory. Profit quotas may be expressed in percentages of gross profit sought from the sale of single items or groups of items in given markets.

The necessity of curtailing sales expense has resulted in the establishment of "expense quotas" in some sales organizations. The maximum expense that may be expected from operations in a given market is established, and expenses are controlled by this standard. A large industrial manufacturer established an expense quota of ½ of 1 per cent of total net sales in small, thickly settled territories and 4 per cent of total net sales in large, thinly settled territories.

To encourage performance of specific sales operations, "activity quotas" are established on "number of calls," "number of interviews," "number of prospects secured," "number of service calls," "number of new customers," and so forth, which may be expected from a given territory in a specified time. Quotas may be set for such activity as "hours spent in the field daily," "miles traveled by automobile," "miles walked," and so on.

Division of sales quotas.—Sales quotas are prepared for wholesale and retail salesmen, retail dealers, wholesale distributors, branches or sales divisions, as well as for individual products, groups of products, and types of customers.

The appliance and merchandise department of the General Electric Company establishes quotas by districts, by principal-product lines, and by distributors.

While quotas for salesmen are the most common, many organizations also establish quotas for retail dealers and wholesale distributors as the basis of evaluation of distributor and dealer activities.

Product quotas are established for individual products and principal-product lines in order to obtain better co-ordination of production and sales, to insure that each product or product line will receive its share of sales efforts, and to enable the distribution of advertising for each product more equitably.

To provide for seasonal variations and to set the incentive closer to the salesman or distributor, quotas are usually broken down into quarterly, monthly, or weekly periods. Variables in seasonal activity and territorial conditions can thus be reflected in these breakdowns.

Advantages of sales quotas.—Organizations using sales quotas find that they have the following advantages:

1. Permit measurement of sales ability.
2. Aid in co-ordinating production and sales.
3. Serve as a basis for sales compensation.
4. Set definite goal for accomplishment.
5. Enable comparisons between salesmen, distributors, retailers, branches, and so on.
6. Provide incentive.
7. Serve as the basis for sales budgets.
8. Enable the proper distribution of advertising, sales promotion effort, warehouse stocks, and manpower.
9. Increase the efficiency of the distributing system.

Weaknesses of sales quotas.—The limitations of sales quotas are as follows:

1. Arbitrary establishment without taking into consideration sufficient factors to insure an accurate estimate of expected sales volume.
2. Arbitrary increases in quotas at periodic intervals without sufficient consideration of the factors involved.
3. Complex statistical methods for establishing quotas that are not understood by the salesman and arouse suspicion as to their accuracy.
4. Time and expense involved in making necessary research to establish a quota accurately.
5. Inadequate rewards for attainment of quotas.
6. Failure to consider the human element, especially the particular ability of the salesman or the distributor, and to secure his co-operation.

Essentials of a good quota.—A good sales quota should have the following characteristics:

1. It should be attainable; that is, it should not be set so high that it is impossible of accomplishment. When a quota is set too

high, the salesman or the dealer either loses interest or forces his efforts and creates ill will.

2. Simplicity is fundamental to a good sales quota. Complicated methods of determining a quota not only involve time and expense but create misunderstanding and arouse suspicion on the part of salesmen and dealers who are not clear as to the method used in arriving at the quota.

3. Taking into consideration the views of salesmen and distributors and permitting them to participate in the establishment of a quota insure that their co-operation in attaining the goal set will be secured.

4. Flexibility is an important consideration in adjusting a quota according to variable seasonal and economic conditions. It is a mistake to establish a quota and disregard those influences which are constantly affecting the possibility of attainment. Accordingly, some sales organizations make monthly or quarterly adjustments in quotas to keep them in line with changing conditions.

5. Incentives should be provided for stimulating the salesmen to meet their quotas. While it might be said that no special incentive should be necessary, the actual purpose of the quota is to encourage greater effort, and without an incentive it may fail of its purpose. That is why many firms offer salaried and commission men cash bonuses for making their quotas, and why some companies pay higher rates of commission to those making their quotas and still higher rates to those exceeding their quotas.

Bases for sales quotas.—Several factors must be taken into consideration in establishing a fair sales-volume quota: (a) past sales; (b) market potential; (c) estimates of salesmen and distributors; (d) manufacturing output; (e) advertising and sales promotion effort; (f) selling cost; (g) product improvements; (h) prices; (i) business conditions; (j) competition; and (k) particular ability of the salesmen or distributors. All of these factors must be weighted and considered carefully in arriving at a fair sales-volume quota. Each factor is discussed briefly below.

1. *Past sales.*—The initial basis for a sales-volume quota is past sales performance. The past year's sales, as well as an average for several years preceding, should be considered in establishing a trend of sales. Sales alone, however, are not a measure of the sales po-

tential of a salesman or a dealer in most cases. Sales volume should not be used exclusively as a basis for a quota. However, sales volume in past years is a definite and important factor in establishing the quota formula and provides a conservative basis for quota estimates.

2. *Market potential.*—No sound sales-volume quota can be established without a knowledge of the potential market. The market potential is most conveniently measured by selecting one or more market indexes. Some sales organizations use as many as nineteen separate factors in measuring market potential. However, for the sake of economy and to avoid complication, a simple index is recommended.

As in the establishment of sales territories, the market indexes of people and homes, purchasing power, standards of living, and distributive outlets may be used with varying weights according to the type of commodity under consideration.

The index of people and homes may be expressed by one or more of the following: population, total families, dwellings, literate native white population, colored population, and so on.

The standards-of-living index may be expressed by: automobile registrations, telephones, electric domestic customers, radio ownership, and so forth.

The buying-power index may be expressed by: bank deposits, income tax returns, check transactions, per capita sales, and so on.

The distributive-outlet index may be expressed by number of retail and wholesale outlets.

In establishing sales quotas for industrial products, the following market indexes may be used: value of manufactured products, number of manufacturers, number of industrial power consumers, and so forth.

An example of the use of market indexes in establishing sales quotas is the method employed by the appliance and merchandise department of the General Electric Company, as described in *Advertising and Selling* magazine. The General Electric index of purchasing power for electric refrigerators is compiled by states and counties by:

(a) Tabulating refrigerator sales for a period of years, converted into percentage of the national total.

(b) Selecting the most typical percentage for each state, allowing for trend.
(c) Establishing the relationship of sales by states to the industry sales percentage.
(d) Adjusting the state index by a climatic factor that is necessary to bring the index into line with actual sales.
(e) Applying the climatic adjustment factor to county figures.
(f) Using the adjusted county index to break down the industry state-sales percentage; index would be used without this step for those products whose sales are not reported by states.
(g) Regrouping final county index figures according to distributor's territory.

This index is considered, along with past sales performance, in preparing distributors' quotas, with the index given a weighting of one to two thirds.

The average annual sales of distributors are also converted to a percentage of the United States total and compared with the index.

National advertisers frequently use the combined circulation figures of the magazines in which their advertising appears as an index of market potential.

A large automobile tire manufacturer uses automobile registration figures as an index in establishing sales-volume quotas; a manufacturer of domestic sheeting uses department-store sales volume as an index in establishing quotas.

3. *Estimates of distributors and salesmen.*—The psychological value of asking salesmen or distributors for estimates of future sales volume is constructive, since they will accept quotas more readily when they have a part in their determination. The value of these estimates is dependent largely on the type of salesman and the product being sold. Intelligent salesmen or high-grade distributors frequently can make very accurate estimates of future sales volume.

4. *Manufacturing output.*—This factor should also be considered in establishing a sales-volume quota, and the point of profitable production should be kept in mind in determining the quota figure.

5. *Advertising and sales-promotion effort.*—The extent of advertising and sales-promotion effort has a direct bearing on the at-

tainment of a sales-volume quota, and the amount to be invested in advertising should be compared with previous investments in determining the quota figure. An increase in advertising and sales-promotion effort should be paralleled by an increase in the sales-quota figure.

6. *Selling cost.*—The cost of selling a given volume should be considered in establishing a sales-volume quota. To absorb the expense of salesman's compensation and travel as well as promotion, a territory must produce a certain volume of business. Accordingly, the profitable minimum volume of sales that must be secured to cover costs is a factor in determining a volume quota.

7. *Product improvements.*—This factor has a definite bearing on sales-volume quotas. The introduction of a new product or an improvement in an old product should make it possible for a salesman or a distributor to attain a greater volume of sales, and the quota must be adjusted upward accordingly.

8. *Prices.*—"Price policy" is an important factor in the establishment of sales quotas. A sharp reduction in price, for example, may result in a salesman's or a distributor's obtaining a considerably greater volume of sales with no additional effort. In a period of rising prices, however, sales may be curtailed, and quotas should be reduced.

9. *Business conditions.*—Economic conditions have an important bearing on the sales-quota figure. In periods of improved business, quotas may be higher, whereas in periods of depression, economic conditions call for a reduction in quota figures.

10. *Competition.*—The character and strength of competition have a bearing on the establishment of sales quotas. The amount of the potential sales available is reduced in proportion to the strength of competition. Accordingly, the competitive situation in each area must be carefully examined.

11. *Sales ability.*—The ability, attitude, and experience of the salesman are important factors in determining whether or not he can attain the quota figure. The human factor cannot be overlooked in determining sales quotas. If a salesman does not have the ability to attain the potential determined by market analysis and consideration of other factors, the quota figure must be reduced to come within reach of his ability.

Securing acceptance of quotas by salesmen.—A sales-volume quota is of little value unless salesmen, dealers, or distributors concerned are convinced of the fairness of the quota and accept it as a reasonable expectation of sales, possible of attainment. Accordingly, those concerned in attaining the quota should be consulted in its preparation. In one large electrical-equipment sales organization individual salesmen are required to estimate their sales volume; these estimates are checked by branch managers, who in turn forward them to district managers; the latter forward their sales estimates for their respective territories to the home office, where the total of these field estimates are combined to form a national quota. In each step of the process, the factors of past sales, selling costs, product improvement, business conditions, competition, advertising and sales promotion effort, and the ability of the salesman are considered.

After the sales or distributing organization is convinced of the fairness of the quota, the quota objectives should be kept before them by frequent reports on quota performance and personal conferences. Charts or graphs illustrating the progress of each distributor, dealer, or salesman in the attainment of quotas are effective aids in insuring quota performance.

3. RECRUITING AND SELECTING SALESMEN

The recruiting problem.—Recruiting is a continuous problem in most sales organizations because of resignations, retirements, disabilities, replacements, transfers, and deaths. In the sale of luxuries, specialties, and intangibles, recruiting is more difficult than in staple lines, and few salesmen volunteer for work in these fields. Accordingly, it is necessary for management to "sell the job" to men who can qualify for selling life insurance, securities, home appliances, and similar luxury or intangible lines. On the other hand, many small sectional or local sales organizations distributing staple or industrial products have low personnel turnover and no recruiting problem.

In large as well as small organizations distributing all types of products, a periodic review of sales personnel is desirable. Personnel requirements should be anticipated, and necessary changes planned at least a year in advance.

A large manufacturer of electrical apparatus requires each of its sales departments annually to budget its probable requirements for salesmen for the ensuing year by quarters. In this way the company is able to recruit and select competent men and train them properly for the openings that may develop. Instead of waiting until a demand for salesmen suddenly presents itself before seeking men to fill the opening, good management plans in advance for future personnel.

The recruiting process.—The process of recruiting salesmen is analogous to selling. The sales manager must locate prospective salesmen; he must learn as much as possible about their personal history and circumstances; he must present his proposal to them, convince them of the opportunities in the sales work, and then follow up to make sure that everything is done to help the recruit succeed in his new work.

Determining type of salesman wanted.—The first step in the recruiting process is to arrive at a definite understanding as to the type of man best qualified to perform the sales job. Obviously, the type of salesman will vary widely with the type of product or service to be sold, class of buyer, demand for the product, and nature of the sales job.

The method of determining the type of salesman qualified to perform a specific sales job is to prepare a job analysis describing the duties to be performed by the salesman, together with the difficulties likely to be encountered in the work. Such a duty and difficulty analysis discloses the specific requirements of the job, together with personal characteristics necessary to perform the duties and surmount the difficulties. A list of duties and difficulties may be readily prepared by consulting sales supervisors, salesmen, and drawing on the experience of the management. Opposite the duties and difficulties may be listed the obvious personal qualities needed, such as technical ability, college education, appearance, tact, initiative, analytical ability, age, nationality, physique, and so on.

The apparatus salesmen of a large electrical-equipment manufacturer must possess the following personal qualities to perform the duties and meet the difficulties in their specific work: (1) technical ability and general intelligence; (2) business sense; (3) energy or willingness to work; (4) personality; (5) appearance; (6) leadership or ability to organize, supervise, and inspire others; (7) character and loyalty.

In addition to such personal traits, other factors, including age, education, marital status, previous experience, membership in organizations, and savings, should also be considered, since these relate to the duties to be performed and the difficulties to be encountered in the specific sales job.

Analysis of the personal qualifications and characteristics of the present salesmen in a sales organization will serve to reveal the personal characteristics desirable for selling a specific product or service. For example, if the successful salesmen in an organization at the period when they were inducted into the business were under thirty years of age, college graduates, single, and without previous selling experience, it might be assumed that these characteristics were desirable for men who were to be engaged for selling the product in question.

Likewise, a study of the characteristics of successful salesmen of competitors in the same industry might also reveal traits identified with success in selling that type of product. An analysis of the membership of the life insurance "Million-Dollar Round Table," composed of million-dollar producers, revealed that 32 per cent of the group were formerly salesmen, 29 per cent business executives, and 21 per cent professional men. This study shows that over 80 per cent of the successful salesmen in this group came from three sources.

Establishing standard personal qualifications.—By studying the duties and difficulties of a specific sales job, the type of product or service to be sold, the class of buyer, and by analyzing the characteristics of present salesmen in the organization as well as successful salesmen in the business as a whole, a standard of personal qualifications may be readily established and used as a basis for future selection. Many sales managers have a general conception of the type of man desired, but few have reduced to writing the exact qualifications necessary for success in selling a specific product or service.

When several functional types of salesmen are employed in an organization, separate standard characteristics should be established for each type. A junior salesman may require certain personal characteristics not demanded by the work of a missionary salesman. An export salesman may need far more knowledge, experience, and education than a domestic senior salesman. A sales engineer may need considerable technical education and mechanical aptitudes.

Sources of salesmen.—When the type of salesman wanted has been determined, and standard qualifications for the sales job have been established, the sources from which such men may be selected are next explored.

The sources of present successful salesmen in the organization should first be considered. Analysis of the employment records of salesmen currently connected with the organization will reveal those sources from which the outstanding salesmen have been obtained in the past.

Likewise, analysis of the major sources from which salesmen for the entire industry are obtained will indicate likely sources of recruits. Through trade associations, industry magazines, by exchange of information with co-operative competitors, the most likely sources of salesmen can be identified. A recent study made by the Life Insurance Sales Research Bureau for the life insurance business revealed that there are four major sources of prospective agents:

1. From those personally known to the sales manager.
2. From centers of influence or nominators. Recruits secured through these two sources averaged $11,500 production in their first month under contract.
3. From the present agency force.
4. Through direct mail and advertising.

Recruits from group 3 averaged $7,500 production during their first month, while recruits from group 4 averaged only $1,500. As compared with the average length of time needed to complete negotiations with recruits from sources 3 and 4, approximately six times as long is required to induct into the business recruits from sources 1 and 2. This type of industry experience is invaluable to a sales manager in determining the most likely sources of salesmen for his organization.

Other sources of salesmen.—Following is a summary of the possible sources of prospective salesmen.

1. *Company training schools.*—A growing number of companies, large as well as small, are using training schools as a source of salesmen. Selected groups of young men are trained for a year or more in various departments of an organization, during which time their work is carefully observed and rated. At the completion of the training, a decision is made as to the acceptability of the trainee for sales work.

A progressive manufacturer of drug specialties recruits annually twenty-five selected college graduates; they are paid $75 a month, plus expenses of $50 a month, while they are in training. The candidates spend four weeks in the New York office of the company, followed by fourteen months of sales experience in the field. At the end of that time, men who have proved their ability as salesmen are retained by the company, while those who are not selected are given a graduation present of $300, and an effort is made to place them in other organizations. During the training period, company officials lecture to the trainees on such subjects as business organization and practices, current business problems, principles of salesmanship, food and drug legislation, fair trade, export advertising and merchandising, sales promotion, and similar subjects.

2. *Hiring from within.*—The current trend is toward the employment of salesmen from within an organization before any search is made outside. Men recruited from the office or factory are familiar with company policies and products and are loyal. Moreover, the management has had an opportunity to observe them closely and judge their abilities. A meat-packing company with 3,000 employees follows a firm policy of exhausting all possibilities among plant employees before looking elsewhere for salesmen.

3. *Through present salesmen.*—New salesmen may be recommended by experienced, successful men now representing the company. In their dealings with customers, salesmen have an opportunity to become acquainted with promising sales material. Wholesale salesmen have an opportunity to observe salespeople in retail stores, many of whom are possible candidates for wholesale-selling work. Through his acquaintance with such retail salespeople, a manufacturer's salesman is in a position to observe their industry, courtesy, and other qualifications.

The sales manager of a large paint manufacturer says: "We get good leads on new men from our own good salesmen. Poor salesmen, on the other hand, rarely produce good sales candidates."

4. *Through present customers.*—Customers who are favorably disposed toward a product and organization are frequently in a position to recommend likely salesmen. Nominating letters may be sent to selected lists of customers asking them for names of prospective salesmen. Life insurance agency managers and other specialty sales executives send out a continuous series of nominating letters to policyholders and customers. Purchasing agents who have frequent contact with salesmen are usually qualified to recommend candidates for sales positions.

5. *Advertising.*—Periodical advertising in the classified and display sections of daily newspapers and business magazines is a commonly used source of salesmen. However, exaggeration and misrepresentation by advertisers have in large part discredited classified advertising as a source of salesmen. Direct-mail advertising to selected occupational groups and recommended prospects is often an effective source. Advertising in business magazines is selective in coverage and normally produces a higher-grade candidate than newspaper advertising.

6. *Schools and colleges.*—The alumni placement services of colleges, particularly those offering business administration courses, provide a source of experienced salesmen with academic training. Men who are completing their college work are being sought intensively by many progressive sales organizations operating training schools. One large floor-covering organization that recruits annually twenty-five men for sales-training classes has interviewed 2,000 candidates at forty-three universities.

7. *Hiring from competitors.*—Fewer sales organizations are hiring from competitors than in the past. It is difficult to transfer a salesman successfully from one company to another in the same competitive field. Men hired from competitors are frequently independent in attitude, difficult to control, and demanding.

8. *Voluntary applicants.*—Occasionally, voluntary applicants provide a favorable but limited source of candidates. Naturally, in periods of depression, the volume of voluntary applicants increases. This source must be considered supplementary rather than basic.

9. *Employment agencies.*—While some employment agencies list salesmen, they are usually more concerned with placing clerical

workers and are little interested in placing salesmen on commission. The specialized sales employment agencies, however, recommend higher type sales personnel. These agencies are more familiar with the qualifications demanded in salesmen and are a more reliable source of sales material.

Selecting salesmen.—When a candidate for sales work has been discovered in one of the sources previously described, the next and more difficult problem is to determine his fitness for the sales work under consideration. The process of measuring or testing sales applicants is receiving more attention today than ever before. Effective manpower is the fundamental of every successful sales force. High turnover of salesmen and the expense of recruiting, selection, and training emphasize the importance of a sound selection system.

Process of selection.—The process of selection requires two basic steps. The first step is to establish the personal qualifications required for the sales job. These qualifications may be determined as discussed previously by a job analysis; consultation of the personal-history records of present successful and unsuccessful salesmen in the organization; and consideration of the type of product, class of trade, prevailing demand, and price. These factors will determine the specific personal qualifications required in an applicant as indicated by his age, education, number of dependents, previous experience, health, previous income, and other considerations. A standard of qualifications for each of these personal-history factors should be established before applicants are selected.

When the personal requirements for a specific sales job have been determined, the next step is to follow a system for discovering whether or not an applicant has the necessary qualifications to succeed in the sales job. Several devices are commonly used for comparing the qualifications of candidates for sales work with the standard qualifications established. These devices may be compared to a yardstick or tape in making linear measurements. These devices, each of which is discussed below, are:

1. Application forms.
2. Letters of reference from previous employers.
3. Personal interviews.

J U D G M E N T ** C H A R T

Interviewed by............ Name..........................

Date....................

* * * * * * * * * * * *

The prospective salesman should be judged on the qualities set out below. First, in reaching a judgment on a quality, mark, in the blank space following each of the questions, an "N" indicating negative and a "Y" indicating affirmative, or with a "?" if you are undecided. These questions, while not an exclusive list of points involved in each quality, will give you an indication of the elements to be considered in evaluating that particular quality. Then, indicate your opinion on each quality by making a check (✓) on the line, just where you think it ought to be. For example, if, in item 1, you think the prospective salesman is a little lower than "good", but not quite low enough to be recorded as "Fair" put the check mark on the line somewhere between 75 and 50.

oooooooooooooooooooooooooooo

Excellent Good Fair Poor

APPEARANCE 100________75________50________25________
Facial expression pleasing?___Erect carriage?___Clothes neat?___Hands and nails clean?___Physique impressive?___Inspires confidence?___Awkward?___ Sits erect in chair?___

MANNER 100________75________50________25________
Courteous?___Smoked uninvited?___Friendly?___Agreeable?___Polite?___ Over-familiar?___Breezy?___Grouchy?___Optimistic?___Rough?___Enthusiastic?___ Objective minded?___Tactful?___

PHYSICAL CONDITION- 100________75________50________25________
Would be willing to have exam by our doctor?___Nervous?___Eyes bright?___ Skin clear?___Exercises?___Recent serious ailments or conditions?___

VOICE-LANGUAGE 100________75________50________25________
Any foreign accent?___Sectional accent?___Speech peculiarities?___Talks too loud-too low?___Enunciates clearly?___Mumbles words?___Good vocabulary?___ Mistakes in grammar?___

DETERMINATION-COURAGE- 100________75________50________25________
Any athletic record?___Likes tough job?___Strong reaction to adverse comment on his selling ability?___Insists on consideration for job?___Confident he could sell product?___Easily discouraged about opportunity?___Annoyed by interruption?___

LOYALTY-COOPERATIVENESS- 100________75________50________25________
Mentions former employers favorably?___Complains of former superior?___ Complains of "raw deal"?___Would accept suggestions?___

HONESTY-RELIABILITY- 100________75________50________25________
Willing to be bonded?___Looks you in the eye?___Hesitant about any of past record?___Any discrepancies in experiences?___Previous positions of responsibility?___Boastful?___Sincere?___

IMAGINATION-RESOURCEFULNESS- 100________75________50________25________
Sells himself effectively?___Started and carried through any projects?___ Full of ideas?___Good Sales talk about previous items sold?___Good talk on hypothetical sales problem?___ Has checked company and products?___

INTELLIGENCE 100________75________50________25________
Good scholastic record?___Quick reaction to explanation of our Products?___ Slow in giving answers?___Open-minded?___Tolerant?___

KNOWLEDGE OF CURRENT AFFAIRS- 100________75________50________25________
Interested in political & economic problems?___Understands functions of Congress and Courts?___Reads something besides newspapers?___Familiar with names in public affairs?___

INDUSTRY 100________75________50________25________
Easy going attitude?___Hard worker in previous job?___Ambitious?___Worked while in school?___

METHODICAL 100________75________50________25________
Jumps at conclusions?___Kept records in former job?___Keeps personal record?___ Good attitude towards daily reports?___Explains ideas clearly?___Thrifty?___ Even tempered?___

PARTICIPATION IN INTERVIEW- 100________75________50________25________
Talked too much?___Organized answers to questions?___Volunteers information?___ Merely answers questions?___

REMARKS ----

Figure 36.—Judgment Chart. (See page 580)

4. Intelligence and aptitude tests.
5. Physical examinations.
6. Field observations.

Application forms.—When an applicant applies for sales work, he is usually given an application blank calling for information relative to his age, education, previous experience, dependents, previous income, number of previous employers, and other factors considered significant by the employer in respect to the personal qualifications necessary to perform the sales work successfully.

In a number of companies the information supplied by the applicant on the application form is scored by giving a numerical value to each personal-history factor listed on the form. Critical scores obtained from actual production records of present salesmen in the organization are used to evaluate the personal-history score of the applicant. By starting with a statement of facts, undesirable applicants are quickly eliminated, and time of interviewers is conserved. A permanent record is provided for future reference.

A form of application suitable for employment of salesmen is illustrated on pages 576–577. (Figs. 37a-b.)

Letters of reference.—A letter of reference or form is frequently sent to previous employers of a sales applicant to verify questions of fact regarding dates of previous employment and amount of income received. An example of such a form is the four-page folder reproduced on pages 578–580. (Figures 38a-b-c-d.) Aside from questions of fact, little worth-while information is ordinarily obtained when the opinion of the previous employer is sought on questions of the applicant's habits, industry, conduct, and ability.

Personal interviews.—Applicants for sales work are universally required to be interviewed by one or more sales executives for the purpose of determining whether the candidate's qualifications fit him for the sales job and to enable the employer to present the job to the applicant. While many experienced sales executives pride themselves on their ability to select salesmen solely by personal interview, personal judgment has been proved to be an ineffective method of evaluating an applicant's likelihood of success in the sales organization. Opinions of interviewers are usually subjective, col-

NY 626-48282-10M-3-30

....
(Name of Company)

APPLICATION FOR POSITION

(Must be in applicant's own Handwriting)

City.................................... Date....................

Name..
(First Name) (Middle Name) (Last Name)

Present address ....
(Street and Number) (City) (State) (Telephone)

Permanent address...
(Street and Number) (City) (State) (Telephone)

Do you live with parents.................. Board.................. Rent or own home.................. Rent per month..................

Age.............. Height.............. Weight.............. Present condition of health..............

Physical defects..

How much time have you lost through illness in last two years......................

Married or single.................. Number of children.................. Other dependents..................

Nationality or lineage (English, Scotch, Irish, Hebrew, etc.)......................

Religion.................. Lodges or fraternal orders..................

Name of Person to be notified in case of Emergency:

....
(Name) (Street and Number) (City) (State) (Telephone)

From what grade of schools did you graduate and when..............................

Other educational work..

....

Name and address of present or last employer (state which)........................

.... How long there.................. Salary..................

Nature of duties with above...

....

Name and address of last three employers, length of time with each and reason for leaving:

....

....

....

Character references..
(Name) (Street & Number) (City) (State)

....
(Name) (Street & Number) (City) (State)

....
(Name) (Street & Number) (City) (State)

Starting salary expected.................. Signature..................

(OVER)

Figure 37a.—Application for Position.

THESE ADDITIONAL QUESTIONS ARE TO BE ANSWERED BY APPLICANTS FOR A POSITION ON SALES FORCE
(Salesman, Distributor, Demonstrator, etc.)

Do you own real estate: .... Value .... Incumbrance ....

Do you own stock or bonds: .... Value .... Incumbrance ....

Do you own a car: .... Make ....

Do you carry liability Insurance: .... Amount ....

Have you any loans or debts: .... How much past due: ....

Particulars of same: ....

Have you any other income besides what you will receive from us: .... Amount $ ....

What insurance do you carry: Life $ .... Health $ .... Accident $ ....

Have you ever been employed by us before: .... In what capacity and where: ....

Have you any relatives in our employ: ....

Name of personal acquaintances in our employ: ....

In what territories have you had more than six month's experience: ....

....

With what territories are you most familiar: ....

What territory do you prefer: ....

What classes of trade have you sold: ....

What experience have you had in our line: ....

Have you ever been bonded, and for what amount: ....

Has bond ever been refused: ....

Can you give a surety bond (at our expense): ....

Does last or any previous employer claim any unpaid balance against you: ....

Applicant hereby consents to immediate dismissal if at any time hereafter

(a) *Applicant's bond be cancelled by Surety for any reason.*

(b) *It becomes apparent that applicant has made false, evasive, or incomplete answer in application for Surety bond, to any questions therein, and more particularly to the following: "18—Have you ever been discharged from any position? Give particulars"; "19—Have you ever been in arrears or default in your present, or any previous employment? Give full particulars"; "20—Do you owe any present or past Employer anything? If so, to whom, how much, on what account, how secured and when due."*

....

Signature of Applicant.

APPLICANTS FOR SALES FORCE POSITIONS MUST FURNISH POST CARD SIZE BUST PHOTOGRAPH

Figure 37b.—Application for Position—Reverse Side.

Dear Sir:

Mr. is being considered as a sales representative of this Agency. Your opinion of his fitness for our business will assist us in deciding whether or not he is likely to succeed as a life insurance salesman.

For your convenience we have arranged page 3 so that you can indicate your opinion by entering a few check marks.

We want to be fair to Mr. as well as to our Agency and Company. It would be unjust to him and disadvantageous to us to appoint him if he is not suited to our business. In order that his qualifications may be properly appraised, we hope you will give page 3 your prompt and thoughtful attention.

Yours very truly,

Figure 38a.—First page of four-page reference letter.

WE REQUIRE
OF THOSE WHO REPRESENT US:

1. A record of success in previous work
2. A record of industry
3. Happy home life
4. Self-reliance
5. Physical energy—endurance
6. Demonstrated ability to manage own affairs
7. Ambition to get ahead
8. Mental alertness
9. Eagerness to render social service
10. Loyalty

Probably no one life insurance salesman could possess all these qualifications. He should, however, possess a goodly number of them. Many of the others may be cultivated.

Figure 38b.—Page 2 of four-page reference letter.

Your answer to each question may be indicated by a cross (X) placed in the proper brackets. If the applicant has not been in your employ, please answer only questions 5 to 9 inclusive.

---

1. Mr. .... states that he

   was in your employ as ....

   Does this correspond with your record? Yes ( ) No ( )

2. He states that he left because ....

   ....

   Is this an adequate statement? Yes ( ) No ( )

3. Were you personally acquainted with him and his work? Yes ( ) No ( )

4. Was he always honest in financial dealings? Yes ( ) No ( )

	Exceptional	Very Good	Satisfactory	Poor	Very Poor
5. How do you rate his *personal habits* and *conduct*?	( )	( )	( )	( )	( )
6. How do you rate his *industry*?	( )	( )	( )	( )	( )
7. How do you rate his *determination* in spite of difficulties?	( )	( )	( )	( )	( )
8. How do you rate his fitness for a *selling position?*	( )	( )	( )	( )	( )
9. How do you rate his ability to direct his own work?....	( )	( )	( )	( )	( )

---

10. Would you be willing to re-employ him? Yes ( ) No ( )

We shall appreciate any additional information that may assist us in judging the applicant's fitness for the position.

Signature ....

Figure 38c.—Page 3 of four-page reference letter.

Please give any further information which you feel might affect the applicant's success as an insurance salesman. This information will be held in strict confidence.

Figure 38d.—Page 4 of four-page reference letter.

ored by personal experiences, and often unreliable. Nevertheless, with all their limitations, personal interviews remain one of the fundamental methods of ascertaining the intangible personal characteristics of an applicant which reveal his fitness for sales work.

In an effort to make personal interviews more valid, an interview judgment-rating form, on which interviewers check their impressions, provides a guide for each interviewer, prevents hasty opinions, and enables comparison of the views of several interviewers. A form of judgment chart is given in Fig. 36, on page 574. Some sales executives prefer to interview an applicant in his own home, at a club, or in an informal social setting. In a large electrical-equipment manufacturing organization, selected applicants are taken in groups of ten to attend a luncheon with the general sales executives, where each candidate is required to give a short talk about himself and tell specifically why he is interested in becoming a salesman for the company. After the luncheon, the sales executives carefully rate each of the applicants and decide which ones may be qualified for sales work.

Intelligence and aptitude tests.—No single selection device has aroused more interest in recent years than aptitude and intelligence tests. While a few of these tests have demonstrated their value in certain organizations, a majority, even though widely used, are in the experimental stage, and little evidence has been produced to reveal their value in the selection of salesmen. Many sales executives are vainly seeking for general aptitude tests which will enable them to predict the future sales success of a candidate for sales work. So far, no such test has been devised. A number of good intelligence tests have been developed to test mental alertness, personality, social sense, and the like, but these tests are in no sense a measure of proficiency in selling.

The appliance and merchandise department of a large electrical-equipment manufacturer uses the following intelligence and aptitude tests in selecting salesmen: Army, Alpha and Beta Tests; the Inglis Vocabulary Test; the McQuarrie Test for Mechanical Ability; The Vocational Interest Blank for Men by E. K. Strong, Jr.; and the Personality Inventory by R. G. Bernreuter. This company is developing a procedure to help establish the reliability of these tests.

A test of selling aptitudes for a specific sales job must take into consideration the duties and difficulties involved in the specific work, and some companies are developing their own aptitude tests along these lines.

Many sales managers are experimenting with different types of tests and making comparisons between the scores that new salesmen receive at the time they are employed and their subsequent success as measured by sales volume, new accounts, and so forth. These tests are also being evaluated by personal ratings of the salesmen's record, made by his supervisor and other sales executives. Tests are of little value until the meaning of the test scores in terms of probability of success in selling is determined.

Physical examinations.—Good health has such a direct bearing on the personal appearance, mental attitude, and industry of a salesman that physical examinations are universally given by all progressive companies in qualifying candidates for sales work. In some types of selling, unusual demands on the physical fitness of a salesman call for rigid physical qualifications.

Observation on the job.—When candidates for sales work are given preliminary training in the field, an opportunity is afforded to observe their qualifications on the job before they are contracted. Ratings by sales supervisors and trainers are used in determining a candidate's fitness.

Summary of selection methods.—A sound selection procedure includes several of the selection devices previously described. Each method of selection should be tested in the light of experience by comparing the performance of the salesman selected with the ratings and evaluations made by employing sales executives at the time of his selection. Continuous experimentation with various selection devices is necessary to insure an effective selection system.

4. EQUIPPING SALESMEN

Need for sales equipment.—An increasing number of sales organizations are aiding salesmen to improve their effectiveness by providing them with tested selling tools to save the salesmen's time; gain the attention of the buyer; make multiple selling appeals to the sight, touch, taste, and hearing of the buyer; keep salesman and prospect on a direct line of thought; avoid interruptions and distractions during sales presentations; provide salesmen with an abundance of selling points; enable salesmen to tell a complete story; increase the salesman's confidence; dramatize the sales presentation; and save the buyer's time.

Qualities of good sales equipment.—Well-planned salesmen's equipment should meet the five following requirements:

1. It should be related to the product or service being offered. Trick attention-getters not relevant to the salesman's presentation simply serve to distract the prospect and confuse the presentation.
2. Equipment should be designed to permit a prospect to participate in its use, thereby experiencing for himself the advantages illustrated by the equipment, and, at the same time, satisfying the human instinct to touch and handle the novel and ingenious.
3. Equipment should be light in weight and not bulky to permit easy handling and encourage use by the salesmen. Much interesting and convincing equipment is not used because of its large size and heavy weight.
4. Attractiveness in appearance and design is fundamental to good sales equipment. The quality of the product or service being offered by the salesman is reflected in the appearance of the sales equipment.
5. Novelty in conception to attract attention and arouse interest is characteristic of good sales equipment.

Types of selling equipment.—The type of selling equipment required by a salesman depends upon the nature of the product, type of prospect or customer, method of travel, number of salesmen employed, and custom in the trade. Salesmen of technical products are equipped with engineering data, mechanical-performance figures, cost information, blueprints, illustrations of installations, and facts for technically trained buyers. Consumer-goods salesmen, on the other hand, carry equipment to illustrate design, beauty, appearance, ease of operation, comfort, and similar consumer appeals.

The objective of salesmen's equipment is to provide the average salesman with information and devices to enable him to tell a better sales story, to add printed weight to his statements, and to create a more lasting impression of the product or service on prospects.

The most important types of salesmen's equipment are:

1. Samples of the product being sold by the salesman.
2. Various types of miniature models, including working models, nonoperating models, cross-section models, and toy models.
3. Portfolios, including loose-leaf, pyramid-easel, accordion-fold, and zipper, in standard $8\frac{1}{2} \times 11$ inch and miniature sizes.
4. Motion-picture projectors and sound and silent motion pictures in 16-mm. width.
5. Sound and silent slide films and projectors.
6. Demonstrating devices.
7. Charts and diagrams.
8. Advertising materials, including booklets, folders, broadsides, proofs of publication advertisements, business cards.
9. Sales and sample cases.
10. Sales manuals.
11. Service and engineering manuals, catalogues, price lists, and policy books.
12. Automotive trailers.

Applications of selling equipment.—The various types of selling equipment mentioned above have been applied to aiding salesmen in: locating prospects; securing interviews; staging interviews; opening interviews; and demonstrating, presenting, and closing sales. In addition, this equipment is used in training salesmen and facilitating the operation and control of salesmen in the field. Examples of the use of various types of sales equipment in locating prospects and making presentations follow.

Equipment to locate prospects.—A large manufacturer of oil-burner and domestic-stoker equipment equips dealer salesmen with sound-slide films and sound-slide projectors featuring the benefits of the product. The films are shown by the salesmen to their friends, neighbors, and acquaintances, who are asked for the names of any of their friends who might enjoy seeing the pictures. As a result of these showings, live prospects are uncovered. In one two-week period one salesman made sixty-one showings, uncovered eighteen prospects, and closed five sales for an average return of $2.20 per showing.

Equipment to secure interviews.—Salesmen may be provided with special equipment to enable them to secure interviews with prospects. One automobile manufacturer supplied retail salesmen with miniature models of passenger cars, suitable as paperweights or toys for children. Salesmen offered these models to prospects in return for an opportunity to present the features of the car. The Fuller Brush Company has for a long time been offering through its salesmen gift brushes as inducements to prospects to grant interviews to salesmen. Other novelty equipment, including memorandum books, ash trays, mechanical pencils, and business cards, are furnished salesmen to aid them in securing interviews.

Staging interviews.—Salesmen who are confronted with the problem of finding a suitable place to conduct interviews and demonstrations with prospects are equipped with automobile sales trailers fitted up as salesrooms, which are driven to a consumer's home or a dealer's place of business. Faced with the difficulty of getting the prospect to come to the showroom, salesmen with trailers overcome this problem by bringing the showroom to the prospect. The advantages of sales trailers are: (1) interruptions are prevented; (2) the novelty of a trailer presentation is impressive; (3) a full line of samples and sales equipment is available; (4) longer and more complete presentations are possible; and (5) actual demonstrations with the product are possible. On the other hand, trailers are difficult to park and operate in congested areas, while the initial investment and cost of operation are high. The Standard Oil Company of New Jersey uses an air-conditioned trailer equipped with motion-picture projector, radio, and lounge chairs in selling to retail dealers. The General Electric Supply Company in Detroit operates a trailer carrying a complete line of washing machines, dishwashers, radios, vacuum cleaners, lamps, and other electrical appliances in selling to prospective dealers.

Opening interviews.—Salesmen are provided with various types of equipment to use in opening sales interviews. Portable, record-playing radios were used by salesmen of George A. Hormel and Company, meat packers, to play to retail merchants a five-minute recording of the company's radio broadcast. The American Optical Company aided salesmen in opening interviews by providing them with a small paper box bearing the question, "Would you swap one of yours for this"? When the prospect opened the box, he found a glass eye. Salesmen of General Mills were equipped with badges reading, "One out of every three, what?" to aid them in opening a presentation on flour-coupon redemption for premiums. A string attached to the badge enabled a salesman to disclose the reverse side, which read: "One out of three coupons is now redeemed for beautiful gifts."

Demonstrating equipment.—Many companies equip their salesmen with unique demonstrating devices to enable them to present outstanding features of their products in dramatic and novel ways. The White Motor Company has equipped salesmen with miniature models of their "White Horse Truck" with removable power unit to demonstrate how easily power units can be removed from the trucks. Frigidaire Division of General Motors Sales Corporation supplies retail salesmen with cross-section models of the "meter-miser" for demonstrating purposes. The appliance and merchandise department of the General Electric Company equips salesmen with a cross-section model of the automatic electric water heater to use in demonstrating this appliance.

Presentation equipment.—To aid salesmen in making more effective sales presentations, various types of equipment have been devised. The most common type is a presentation portfolio in which sales points are arranged in logical order and illustrated with charts, photographs, or cartoons, accompanied by brief explanations. Included in presentation portfolios are: testimonial letters, illustrations of product installations, names of users, clippings, diagrams of construction features, and advertising, all or a part of which may be referred to by a salesman in making his presentation. A fine example of this type of portfolio is the 1941 showroom visualizer produced by the Westinghouse Electric and Manufacturing

Company, Appliance Division, for Westinghouse electric refrigerators.

Advertising portfolios containing proofs of advertisements, schedules of insertion, circulation coverage, and testimonials of effectiveness are also supplied to salesmen to aid them in presenting their advertising story.

Sound motion-picture and slide-film projectors and films are standard sales equipment in many organizations for selling both consumers and dealers. Typical consumer sales presentation films are "White Magic," Swift and Company; "House That Ann Built," Johns-Manville Sales Corporation; "Ford Rouge Plant," Ford Motor Company.

Charts and diagrams are effective sales tools. The Appliance and Merchandise Department of General Electric Company has devised a large chart, or "visualizer," mounted on the back of the G. E. Electric Range, featuring principal selling points with novel demonstrating devices attached for use by retail salesmen in making range presentations.

Closing equipment.—While much of the previously described sales equipment contributes to closing a sale, special equipment for this purpose has been designed in a number of companies. A large stationery-supply house has equipped its salesmen with novelty order books, 2 × 2 inches in size, as a suggestion to customers and a reminder to salesmen that the mission of the salesman is to secure orders. The Chevrolet Division, General Motors Sales Corporation, equipped retail salesmen with a "closing stone," a gilt pocket piece, to remind them to ask for an order.

Training equipment.—Equipment for training manufacturers', distributers', and dealers' salesmen consists of sales manuals, policy books, catalogues, specification sheets, engineering and service manuals, sound and silent motion pictures, and slide films. Some of this equipment is carried regularly by a salesman for ready reference as a source of answers to objections and technical information.

Many manufacturers train dealer salesmen with sound slide films and records issued periodically throughout the year. The Appliance and Merchandise Department of the General Electric Company furnishes the following equipment to retail dealers: twelve slide films and records, sound slide-film projector, film and record-carrying case, and twelve dozen film pamphlets. The dealer shares

CP 15714*

DAILY SUMMARY CONTROL

REVISED 11-1-38
FORM S 1-611-A

POST DAILY TOTALS FROM DAILY CALL REPORT — DAILY RECORD — USE SUNDAY LINE FOR WEEKLY TOTALS

A	1	2	3	4	5	6	7	8	9	10	11	12	13	14	15	16	17	18	19	20	21	22	23	24	25	26	27	28	29
	DAILY CALL REPORT							INSPECTION SLIPS				5 x 3 PROSPECT SLIPS																	
				NO. DIFF. RECORD FORMS SOLD		SALES THIS MONTH		NO. INSPECTIONS MADE				PROSPECTS																	
												NUMBER DEVELOPED CURRENT MONTH									DISPOSITION—CUR. MO.					TOTAL EST. VALUE ON HAND			
DAY	NO. CALLS	NO. ORDERS	NO. NEW ACC'TS SOLD	STOCK	SPEC	DAY	TO DATE	SAL.	STO.	LED.	FIL.	FIL.	LED	SAL	STO PUR	FUR.	SER.	REC. AS	MISC	TOTAL	SOLD	LOST	DROP.	TOTAL	TOTAL ON HAND	EST. VALUE DEV.	EST. VALUE DIS.	TOTAL EST. VALUE	% SOLD TO NO. ON HAND
FOR-WARD																													
1																													
2																													
3																													
4																													
5																													
6																													
7																													
8																													
9																													
10																													
11																													
12																													
13																													
14																													
15																													
16																													
17																													
18																													
19																													
20																													
21																													
22																													
23																													
24																													
25																													
26																													
27																													
28																													
29																													
30																													
31																													
T																													

MONTHLY RECORD

B	30	31	32	33	34	35	36	37	38	39	40	41	42	43
	THIS INFORMATION FROM SALES RECORD													
							NO. OF ACCOUNTS SYSTEMS PRODUCTS SOLD TO THIS YEAR				NO. OF INSTALLATIONS SOLD TO THIS YEAR			
MONTH	TOTAL NAMES IN FILE	NO. CALLED ON THIS MONTH	NO. NOT CALLED ON IN 6 MONTHS	% TO TOTAL NAMES IN FILE	NO. SOLD THIS MONTH	NO. SOLD THIS YEAR	VIS.	VER.	L. L	S. C	SALES	STOCK	LEDGER	FILING
T														

REMARKS

SALESMAN OFFICE MONTH

Figure 39.—Daily Summary Control.

A daily summary report of individual salesman's activities, showing amount and type of activity as well as results.

N. Y. 631-51871-50M-6-30.

This list must be mailed to your District and Territory Sales Manager not later than Saturday P. M. giving routing for the following week

Salesman's Advance Route List

Name ______________________________

Permanent Address ______________________________

For the week ending Saturday, ______________, 19___, and Sunday following.

	CITY	STATE	Name Hotel or Care General Delivery
Sunday			
Monday			
Tuesday			
Wednesday			
Thursday			
Friday			
Saturday			
Sunday			
FOLLOWING WEEK			
Monday			
Tuesday			

Figure 40.—Route List.

A simple form of planning sheet giving a salesman's itinerary for the next succeeding period.

Form 42

	TO BE FILLED IN BY BRANCH	
	AMOUNT	TOTALS
SALARY		
EXPENSE		
LESS E. B. A.		
STOCK		
NET AMT PAID	CHECK NO.	

Salesman's Weekly Report

BRANCH

WEEK ENDING __________ 19 ___

NAME __________ HDQTRS. __________

CLASS __________

TERRITORY __________

NUMBER OF DAYS WORKED	NUMBER OF CALLS	NUMBER OF ORDERS

ENTER DATES BELOW	RAILROAD AND INTERURBAN FROM	TO	R. R. FARE	AUTO EXPENSE	TOWN AND NAME OF HOTEL	HOTEL EXPENSE	SLEEPER	OTHER EXPENSE	TOTAL EXPENSE
SUN					B D S L				
MON					B D S L				
TUES					B D S L				
WED					B D S L				
THURS					B D S L				
FRI					B D S L				
SAT					B D S L				
TIME CARD RECEIVED	TOTALS								
SAMPLE REPORT RECEIVED						TOTAL EXPENSE FOR WEEK (EXCEPT SALARY)			

EXTS. O. K. _____ APPROVED _____ (TERRITORY MGR) APPROVED _____ APPROVED _____ PAY _____ (OVER)

Printed in U. S. A.

Figure 41a.—Salesman's Weekly Expense Report.

A weekly report giving details of expenditures.

Report of Expenses

INSTRUCTIONS

Expense accounts must be mailed at end of each week. The week's expenses will commence with breakfast Sunday and end with lodging Saturday, making the full week.

Under the head "R. R. & Interurban" enter names of towns to and from which each trip is made and amount of fare.

Railroad fares incurred on your own account or on trips outside of your own territory are not chargeable in the expense account.

Foot each of the five columns, show the TOTAL expense on the BOTTOM RIGHT hand line.

Each charge must be itemized, stating what it is for, and only such charges as are deemed reasonable and necessary will be allowed.

We do not pay for chair car or other transportation extras, except straight sleeping car rate for night trips.

All auto livery or sample charges must be accompanied by a receipt.

Automobiles, livery are not to be used as a convenience and are to be employed only when it will enable you to accomplish in one day that which without auto would require two or more days.

Salary or expenses will not be paid when salesmen are not working because of illness or other reasons.

No allowance will be made for incidental expenses unless previously arranged.

We do not honor drafts or send money by telegraph.

We pay legitimate traveling expenses necessarily incurred in the transaction of our business (such as hotel bills—for lodging and meals only—railroad fares and postage) at exactly the prices paid by our salesmen. We do not pay laundry, barber or any personal expense. Any overcharge or manipulation of expense items is dishonest and will not be tolerated.

Charge only such hotel bills as are incurred when working territory outside of your home city or "headquarters town," as hotel expenses incurred while you are at home or in "headquarters town" are not chargeable to us.

The above instructions must be strictly observed and daily and weekly reports agree exactly or expense accounts will be subject to deduction.

Checks will not be mailed until new time card and all reports are received.

Totals on reverse side of this sheet represent actual expense incurred.

Signature

Where shall we send check?

Town ---

Care of ---

Figure 41b.—Reverse Side of Salesman's Weekly Expense Report.

with the manufacturer in the cost of this training equipment. Similar training equipment is provided by other large manufacturers.

Operating equipment.—To facilitate the operation and control of salesmen in the field, a variety of forms are provided for reporting on calls, interviews, sales, lost orders, missionary work, adjustments, credits, and traveling expenses. Order books, price lists, and specification forms are included in a salesman's equipment. A few examples of typical sales reports are illustrated on pages 587–590, in Figures 39, 40, 41a and 41b.

Equipment cases and kits.—For convenience in carrying and protection, all of the aforementioned equipment is packed in sample cases or sales kits. The sales kits should be designed to insure the safety of their contents; to be readily accessible; to display the product to its best advantage; and to provide for convenient arrangement. A sales kit should be shaped for ease in handling and storage; light in weight to encourage its use; of good external appearance to create a favorable impression on prospects and customers; and so arranged internally as to permit individual items to be shown without unpacking.

Sales kits may be made to order to suit the requirements of an individual organization, or standard cases may be purchased that fit the equipment needs of many concerns. A periodic review of salesmen's cases to insure their good appearance and completeness is desirable. A few examples of sales kits are illustrated on page 592.

Getting salesmen to use equipment.—Some salesmen feel that sales equipment arouses resistance of prospects, is not needed in many interviews, is undignified to carry, and wastes energy. For these reasons, much helpful sales equipment is not used by salesmen, and the management is confronted with the problem of selling its value to the salesmen themselves.

To overcome these objections, first, the equipment should be well designed, convenient to carry, light in weight, attractive in appearance, novel in conception, and kept up to date. Second, new equipment should be tested by one or two salesmen in a small area to discover its weaknesses and correct them before the equipment is given to the entire sales force. Third, after the equipment has been tested, it should be sold to the sales organization at sales meet-

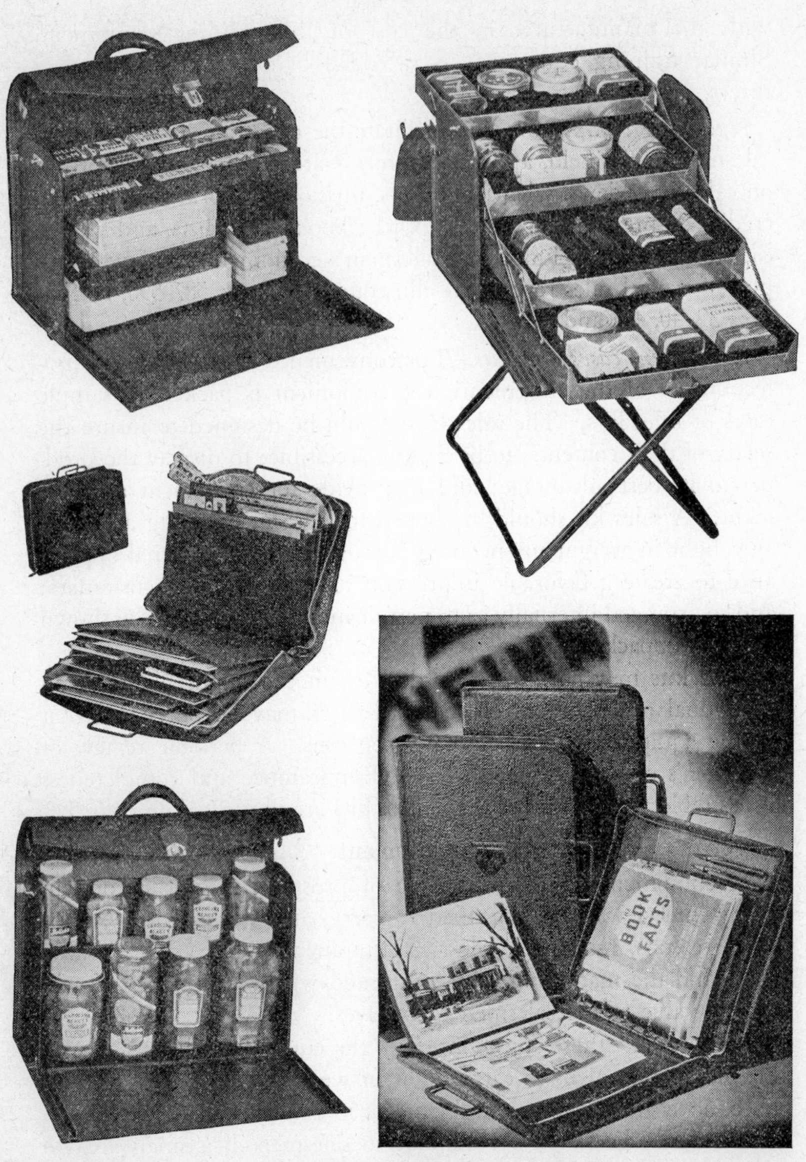

Figure 42.—Types of Sales Kits.

ings to arouse mass enthusiasm. Definite examples of the use of the equipment in the field should be discussed, the proper use demonstrated, and results of effective use cited. Fourth, some concerns charge salesmen for equipment to insure that it will be properly handled and used. This charge may be rebated after a certain volume of merchandise has been sold or when the equipment is retired. Fifth, by following through on equipment to prospects, some companies insure that it will be used. Manning, Maxwell and Moore get salesmen to use presentation equipment by writing prospects that a salesman will call and use the equipment in his presentation. Salesmen are given a copy of the letter to prospects as a reminder to use the equipment in their presentations.

5. TRAINING SALESMEN

Why train salesmen?—Economic instability, growing competition, government regulation, saturated markets, spreading specialization, and declining profit margins are creating a greater need for trained salesmen and emphasizing management's responsibility for developing sales personnel. Heretofore sales training has been considered a "fair-weather" activity, a luxury to be indulged in during periods of prosperity only, to be treated as an unnecessary overhead expense, and to be eliminated in periods of depression. Effective man power is the major problem of sales management, and sound training is a fundamental step in insuring sales effectiveness.

A constructive sales-training program makes possible the following accomplishments:

1. Increases sales.
2. Reduces selling costs.
3. Attracts a high type of salesman to the organization.
4. Results in better service to customers.
5. Safeguards the company's investment in new salesmen.
6. Reduces the number of salesmen by developing the ability of the individual.
7. Meets increasing competition and growing sales resistance.
8. Reduces the turnover of salesmen by making them more productive.

9. Shortens the time necessary to place a new salesman on a profitable producing basis.

10. Simplifies supervision and control of salesmen.

11. Insures satisfaction of customers through proper representation of product or service.

12. Stimulates salesmen through exchange of selling methods.

13. Provides sales-executive material.

Comparison of the work of trained with untrained salesmen shows average increases in sales by trained salesmen of 10 to 15 per cent.

Who should be trained?—The problem of sales training from a manufacturer's standpoint involves five classes of personnel: (1) apprentices; (2) new senior salesmen; (3) old senior salesmen; (4) sales supervisors; and (5) field sales-management executives, including branch managers, division managers, and district managers.

Training apprentices.—Both large and small sales organizations are establishing training courses for young men starting out in business. From these training groups men with selling aptitude are selected for sales work. Typical of such programs is the Student Engineers' Course of the Apparatus Division of the General Electric Company, from which men are selected for the Sales Engineers' Course. Men completing this course go into the General Office Sales Department and from there into field sales work.

The Armstrong Cork Company offers a similar apprentice program in which sixty-two men have been trained in the Building Material Division in the last five years. Twenty-five college graduates are recruited annually and trained for a period of approximately nine months in company history, organization, manufacturing facilities, and financial position; following this, in the engineering, research, production, advertising, credit, traffic, legal, accounting, and claims departments. This training is supplemented by required outside reading and actual field experience in retail stores.

The Vick Chemical Company operates a similar sales-apprentice school in the Vick School of Applied Merchandising.

Training senior salesmen.—Training a senior salesman who has been with an organization for some time is the most difficult sales-training problem. Many older men are not receptive to new ideas, consider that they know all that should be known about their work, are set in their ways, are too proud to admit lack of knowledge, and resent sales training as a childish activity. However, senior salesmen require periodic retraining as their information becomes outdated and as new products and policies create new selling problems. Training for senior salesmen, however, must be removed from the academic and must be "sugar-coated" with practical material.

Training new senior salesmen.—Irrespective of previous sales experience, salesmen who are beginning work with a sales organization require training to acquaint them with new products, policies, selling problems, difficulties, and duties. Salesmen who are new in an organization are receptive to sales training, and practically all companies give some degree of training to salesmen of this type.

Training sales supervisors.—In larger sales organizations the burden of field sales training falls on the sales supervisor in charge of a group of six to ten men in the field. For this reason, special courses have been established in a number of companies to train supervisors in the best method of training salesmen under their supervision. Since retraining or continuation training is usually a responsibility of supervisors, the training of these men is very important. Supervisors become part of the sales-training staff in many organizations and should be instructed in the best techniques for carrying on field training.

Training field sales-management executives.—In smaller organizations, branch managers are responsible for field supervision of salesmen in their territories and function as field trainers of salesmen for continuation and retraining of senior salesmen in the field. Some companies conduct special sales-training courses for branch managers, district managers, and division managers to train them in developing the men in their charge.

Training wholesale and retail dealers and their sales managers.—Manufacturers distributing through wholesale and retail outlets also assume responsibility for training wholesale and retail dealers and their sales managers. The objective of a dealers' training program is to train the dealer so that he will be able to train his own salesmen. The Oldsmobile Division of General Motors Sales Corporation trains retail automobile sales managers with a series of six manuals and sound slide films entitled "Sales Managing Your Sales Force," "Assigning the Salesman Work," "Checking Salesmen's Work," "Lining Up Live Leads," "Building Up Your Sales Force," and "Training Salesmen."

The Johns-Manville Sales Corporation holds management institutes for retail lumber and building-supply dealers and their sales managers, who are trained to give a course in consumer selling to their employee salesmen. The Appliance Department of General Electric Company has organized a retail sales-managers' club for the purpose of training retail appliance sales managers in developing their own salesmen. Retail sales managers are sent bulletins covering all phases of handling salesmen, sales policies, and methods.

Training wholesale and retail salesmen.—A limited number of sales organizations attempt to train wholesale and retail salesmen employed by dealers and distributors. Because of the large number of salesmen of this class, many of these training programs consist of correspondence courses. The Nash-Kelvinator National Salesman's Institute offers Kelvinator retail refrigerator salesmen a course of eleven lessons dealing with specialty selling. The Appliance Department of the General Electric Company trains 14,000 salesmen for dealers with a sound slide-film service, monthly bulletin service, moving-picture sound films, catalogues, manuals, and wall charts. Retail salesmen and their managers are members of the General Electric Retail Development League with local chapters that meet and discuss selling problems.

Subject matter of training.—The subject matter of a sales-training program depends upon the duties of the salesmen and the difficulties encountered in selling the specific product or service. A job analysis should be made to determine the duties of the salesmen and indicate the information that they must receive through training to enable them to perform these duties efficiently. In addition, a difficulty analysis should be made of the obstacles encountered by the salesmen in carrying out their work. The usual weaknesses of salesmen are in personality, knowledge, working system, and selling technique. A training course should present material to aid a salesman in correcting these difficulties.

The choice of subject matter depends upon the duties and difficulties of the salesmen to be trained and usually includes information on:

1. The product.
2. The market.
3. The company history and organization.
4. Advertising and sales promotion.
5. Policies on credit, service, adjustments, prices, and delivery.
6. Duties of salesmen.
7. Difficulties, and how to meet them.
8. Sales methods, involving locating prospects, planning presentations, conducting interviews, demonstrating, answering objections, and closing.
9. Systematizing, time control, and work organization.
10. Servicing customers.
11. Sales equipment.
12. Sales territories.

Tools for sales training.—After subject matter has been obtained based on the duty and difficulty analysis of the work of the salesmen, this material must be arranged in convenient form to impart to the salesmen. Training information is presented in the form of sales manuals, motion-picture films, slide films, charts, problems, bulletins, house organs, playlets, and dialogues.

The sales manual is the basic training tool. It is usually a loose-leaf, $8\frac{1}{2} \times 11$ inch binder, containing all of the essential information presented in the sales-training course. The material in the manual may be issued to salesmen serially and inserted in the loose-leaf binder as the course develops. Sometimes pocket-sized manuals or handbooks, each dealing with a specific subject in the training course, are printed and distributed to salesmen for study.

Sound slide films and records are the basis of many manufacturers' sales-training programs for their own salesmen as well as for the salesmen of distributors and dealers. The Charles P. Cochrane Company uses two technicolor sound slide films, "Craftsmanship" and "Sale-ing Orders," to train retail rug salesmen. Oldsmobile

Division, General Motors Sales Corporation, uses a series of sound slide films in training retail automobile salesmen.

Sound motion pictures are being used in increasing numbers in training manufacturers' as well as distributers' and retailers' salesmen. The Dictaphone Sales Corporation uses a film called "Two Salesmen in Search of an Order" in training its salesmen. General Mills, Incorporated, is showing a sound motion picture entitled "Turnover" to retail food dealers.

Phonographic recordings of salesmen's presentations for analysis and discussion are being made by progressive sales organizations as a part of their training program. The Appliance Division of the Westinghouse Electric and Manufacturing Company made more than 18,000 of these recordings of retail salesmen's presentations.

Supplementing these basic sales-training tools are charts to visualize sales points, the sales process, and organization for group instruction. Other supplementary tools are problems or cases taken from field sales experience of the salesmen being trained to serve as a basis for group discussions. Bulletins, house organs, outlines, and dramatizations also have a part in the sales-training program.

Sales-training meetings.—Sales-training meetings should be planned in advance, and consideration should be given to the following important features:

1. The subject of a sales-training meeting should be timely and significant, not a discussion of petty grievances and routine matters, but the solution of the principal selling problems encountered in the field. The introduction of a new product, the inauguration of a new feature, a new sales policy, a tested method of meeting competition, a better way of overcoming common objections, a more effective use of time—all these are important subjects to be considered at a training meeting. Each meeting should concern itself with only one subject to insure thorough treatment. Salesmen may be invited to suggest a subject, or the management may select the subject.

2. Treatment of the subject should next be planned in detail. A sound slide film or motion picture featuring the subject may be shown to the group. One of the salesmen may be called upon for a brief discussion of the topic. A question-and-answer treatment

may be used, or a demonstration by two salesmen, one posing as a prospect, may be arranged. An outside speaker or a customer may be invited to talk. A dramatic sketch may be staged by sales-office employees. A problem may be distributed in advance of the meeting for group discussion.

3. An outline and timetable of the program of the meeting is next prepared to provide a proper time for announcements, presentations, intermission for refreshments, and a closing summary. A training meeting should start and stop on time, and move briskly according to schedule, but not too rapidly for the group to absorb the material presented.

4. Build up the meeting by creating anticipation with preliminary announcements to the salesmen. Urge the men to come prepared to make suggestions or participate in discussion of the subject of the meeting.

5. Control the meeting by adhering closely to the time schedule, keeping discussion on the subject, silencing the talkative member of the group, avoiding criticism, sidetracking embarrassing complaints, encouraging participation of all, and avoiding competition with the speaker by excluding distracting charts, papers, and samples.

6. Provide for the comfort of those attending with plenty of light, fresh air, and ventilation. A "no-smoking" rule creates a better atmosphere.

Types of sales training.—Sales training may be classified according to method as individual, group or conference, field or job, and correspondence. The most common method of sales training is by group conferences at which lectures, round-table discussions, playlets, or dialogues are presented. This type of training is the least expensive, quickest, and most effective way of getting across information on the product; product applications; company policies on credits, collections and adjustments; advertising and sales promotion; company history and organization; routine duties; and sales techniques. Successful group training depends upon adequate preparation by the trainer and trainees, a favorable time and a comfortable place for the meeting, control of participants in the discussion, participation by the trainees, and, in conclusion, summarization of the information developed at the meeting.

Group training alone, however, is inadequate to develop salesmen. It is lacking in realism, is impersonal, and gives little opportunity to acquire skills vital to a salesman's effectiveness.

Individual training is the most important type of sales training because it takes into account the strength and weakness of an individual salesman and gives the trainer an opportunity to adjust his instruction to the individual need for knowledge or skill in selling. Since this type of training is expensive and slow, it is often neglected in the training process. Through individual conferences following field observation of a salesman's methods, a trainer can point out the specific difficulties of a salesman and advise him how to improve his technique.

Field training or coaching on the job is a form of individual instruction. Selling is a complicated skill that cannot be learned from books and may only be acquired slowly by field experience. Field sales experience without supervision or correction, however, often serves merely to fix imperfection. Accordingly, field coaching or training on the job is necessary to point out a salesman's strength and weakness. A tried field-training formula is the "D. O. C. method," or demonstration, observation, and correction by the trainer. By repeating this formula for several days with a skilled trainer, a salesman learns by actually doing much faster than he would by reading, listening, or watching in group conferences. While information may be acquired and the acquisition of selling skill speeded up by individual study, lectures, and group conferences, coaching on the job is vital to a sound training program.

Sales training by correspondence is a common and inexpensive method of developing salesmen. It provides information but gives no opportunity to develop skill, establish correct work habits, and improve methods by actually doing the job under proper supervision.

Where to conduct training.—Group or conference training may be conducted at the home office, branches, or at hotels in selected cities throughout the sales territory. Home-office training is generally practiced by small organizations training a limited number of salesmen, as well as by manufacturers of technical products that can be discussed most effectively at the home office or factory.

Individual or field training is conducted in the salesman's territory in combination with group training in the branch office. Companies with large sales organizations often use this type of training, thus saving the expense of bringing the salesmen into the home office for training, and making it possible for the salesmen to become producers at the earliest possible time.

After a salesman has received preliminary training in a branch office and in the field, he may be brought into the home office for advanced training in the product, product applications, and company policies.

Sources of training material.—The primary source of sales-training material is found in the duties of salesmen and the difficulties encountered by them in the field. Training material coming from this source is looked upon by the salesmen as practical, and it has a realistic value not found in "desk-made" training courses. While the time and expense involved in duty and difficulty analysis are considerable, this is an unparalleled source of training data.

Trade associations have developed sales-training material that can be adapted to the use of individual sales organizations in their field. The Merchandising Institute of the National Retail Lumber Dealers' Association offers a sales-training program to lumber and building-material dealers; Anthracite Industries, Incorporated, conducts a merchandising school and has collected sales-training material for coal dealers; and The New England Gas Association has developed a sales-development program for improving the efficiency of gas-appliance salesmen.

Textbooks in salesmanship are a source of excellent ideas that may be incorporated in a sales organization's training program. *Salesmanship, Practices and Problems,* by B. R. Canfield (McGraw-Hill, 1940), describes the twenty principal problems encountered by salesmen of various types of goods and services and suggests successful methods of solving these problems. These methods may be applied in training salesmen of any type of product or service.

6. METHODS OF COMPENSATING SALESMEN

Aims of a compensation plan.—A successful compensation plan for salesmen is one that secures the highest volume of sales, pushes the sale of the most profitable items, offers the salesmen an incentive to work harder, and at the same time permits sales to be made at a cost that returns a good profit to the employer. A plan that attains these ends necessarily recognizes the needs and problems of the salesmen. The objectives of a successful plan are as follows:

For the Company

(1) Stimulate salesmen to increase sales.
(2) Encourage loyalty to the firm.
(3) Promote co-operation of salesmen with each other and with the firm.
(4) Discourage overselling.
(5) Encourage salesmen to push high-profit items.
(6) Eliminate requests for special consideration and favors.
(7) Provide reasonable profit over sales expense.
(8) Provide control over salesmen's activities.

For the Salesman

(1) Increase their earnings in proportion to their sales accomplishments.
(2) Afford a reasonable payment for services.
(3) Pay for time spent in missionary work.
(4) Provide living wage during training.
(5) Promote pride in company.
(6) Provide security.
(7) Provide for retirement.
(8) Provide for seasonal slumps.
(9) Compare favorably to wage scales in similar lines.

Factors in the choice of a plan.—The factors that determine the choice of a compensation plan are:

1. The cash resources of the company.

2. The speed with which business can be closed in the field. The compensation plan for salesmen who are required to do considerable missionary work will be different from that in a field where little creative selling is required of the salesmen because of an established demand for the product created by advertising.

3. The policies of competitors.

4. The type of product. A product that requires extraordinary sales ability may call for a different plan of compensation from one that can be sold by men of average ability. Certain products, for instance, require specialized or technical knowledge on the part of salesmen, such as in the case of machinery parts, and so forth; others, such as staple products, require merely good selling ability. Both fields should be compensated accordingly.

5. The market for the product. Products sold in a narrow mar-

ket, such as those appealing to limited groups of customers, require one type of compensation plan, while products sold to broad classes of customers may call for an altogether different plan.

6. The method of distribution. If the product is sold to dealers, distributors, wholesalers, and others who in turn sell to consumers, sales are frequently made automatically. The compensation plan will take this factor into account. On the other hand, if creative selling is called for, as in the case of products sold directly by the manufacturer to the consumer, another type of compensation might apply.

7. The advertising policies of the company. Well-advertised products may require very little creative selling on the part of the salesman, while products that are not well known may call for a greater degree of sales ability. The compensation plan should take care of the salesman who has to spend part of his time creating a demand for the product.

8. The ability of the salesman. Obviously, certain selling jobs call for greater ability than others. Salesmen of outstanding ability who are accustomed to earning large salaries and enjoying a high standard of living prefer compensation plans that offer payment in direct proportion to the volume of sales made. On the other hand, some salesmen who have not proved themselves good earners may not be content to accept employment on a commission basis.

9. The variety of products making up the line. A man selling a variety of products may more easily maintain or increase his wage level than a man selling one product. This factor may affect the type of compensation.

10. Price of product and margin of profit. High-priced items are often more difficult to sell than low-priced items, and the salesman should be compensated accordingly. Also, the margin of profit dictated by such factors as cost, demand, established trade practices, and so on, may enter into the determination of the method of compensation.

Testing the compensation plan.—To inaugurate a compensation plan and put it into operation are not enough. The plan should be tested from time to time to detect hidden weaknesses, and steps should be taken to eliminate them. The following questions will help employers test the compensation plan:

1. Are the aims of the plan and their relative weight clearly defined? The plan should bring out the relative importance of increasing sales, getting new business, promoting goodwill, doing missionary work, reducing sales expense, selling specific items, and so on.

2. Is the relationship of compensation costs to profits fair?

3. Do the results show the plan to be successful? The conclusive test is the results obtained. Records must be maintained that will disclose whether the salesmen are doing missionary work, whether they are developing new accounts, whether they are pushing only certain items, and whether they are doing all parts of their selling job.

4. Are most of the salesmen satisfied with the plan? It is wise to consider the opinions of the salesmen in regard to the compensation plan, for in consulting the salesmen an opportunity is offered to promote loyalty and enthusiasm toward the company, as well as to disclose weaknesses in the compensation plan.

5. Is the plan flexible? The plan should be sufficiently flexible to provide for additional compensation for men with unusual ability.

Types of plans.—The two basic plans for compensating salesmen are (1) salary, and (2) commission. The type and size of the company and individual trade and market problems make it expedient in many cases to use a variation or combination of these plans. Some of these plans will be discussed later.

Salary compensation.—Under this plan a certain sum is paid to the salesmen each week regardless of the amount of sales made. The salary method of compensation is usually employed when considerable missionary work is required, when the efforts of several salesmen are necessary to complete a sale, or when it is desired to help salesmen maintain a living wage during training periods and seasonal slumps. Firms engaging in the type of business that has little yearly sales fluctuation and can therefore forecast their sales volume fairly accurately often pay salesmen on a flat-salary basis. Sales executives are usually paid a straight salary. The advantages and disadvantages of the salary plan to the company and to the salesman are as follows:

ADVANTAGES

For the Company

(1) Bookkeeping is simplified.
(2) A fixed cash responsibility is undertaken.
(3) Better control of men is obtained.
(4) Men are easily recruited.
(5) Overselling of customers is prevented.
(6) Salesmen's time can be arranged for nonselling activities.
(7) Loyalty of salesmen to the company is promoted.
(8) Co-operation among salesmen is encouraged.
(9) The transfer of salesmen from one territory.

For the Salesman

(1) Personal security is afforded.
(2) Home office control develops desirable habits of work.
(3) Income can be budgeted.
(4) Compensates for missionary work that may not result immediately in sales.
(5) Management takes risk for time invested in selling.
(6) Wage level during training periods and seasonal slumps is maintained.
(7) Changes in business conditions are not immediately reflected in lower salaries.

DISADVANTAGES

For the Company

(1) It does not set a definite ratio of cost to sales.
(2) Incentives for greater sales efforts are lacking.
(3) A lower type of sales personnel is attracted.
(4) It is difficult to adjust to declining business activity.
(5) Salesmen demand periodical increases.
(6) Responsibility is on the management to make a good selection of men.
(7) Salaries must be paid to salesmen before they prove their ability.

For the Salesman

(1) Incentives are limited.
(2) Income is limited.
(3) Improvement in business is not immediately reflected in high earnings.
(4) Does not reward superior sales efforts.

Commission compensation.—A commission is a percentage payment on sales. Compensation of salesmen working on a straight commission therefore fluctuates in direct relation to their sales accomplishments. Thus commission compensation may be considered the most direct form of payment for sales effort.

The commission plan is usually applied to the sale of specialties of fairly high price that have a broad market, such as automobiles, life insurance, office equipment, and so on. It is also commonly used in house-to-house or direct-to-the-customer selling, or where a high level of selling ability is required. The advantages and disadvantages of this plan, to company and salesmen, are as follows:

Advantages

For the Company

(1) The company with limited capital can obtain a selling staff.
(2) The plan immediately reflects the salesman's ability.
(3) The ratio of costs to sales is known immediately.
(4) More aggressive salesmen are attracted.
(5) The plan provides the incentive of higher earnings for greater sales effort.

For the Salesman

(1) Larger income is possible, and the incentive is greater.
(2) Greater independence is afforded.
(3) Co-operation with other salesmen is unnecessary.
(4) Sales efforts do not help to pay other salesmen who produce less.
(5) During periods of business prosperity earnings are rapidly increased.

Disadvantages

For the Company

(1) More bookkeeping is involved.
(2) The control of men is weakened.
(3) The employment problem is greater because many men prefer straight salaries.
(4) The morale of the salesmen may be impaired if their earnings decline during business slumps.

For the Salesman

(1) Irregularity of income lessens security.
(2) Little assistance is offered by the home office.
(3) During business depressions income falls rapidly.

(5) Customers are exposed to overselling.
(6) Missionary work is discouraged.
(7) Salesmen are inclined to concentrate on live prospects, to neglect profitable items that are hard to sell, and to spend little time in originating new business.
(8) Co-operation with other salesmen is reduced.

When prices are unstable, the straight-salary plan and the straight-commission plan are usually unsatisfactory. For example, commission rates may prove too high for the changing price level, and employers may find themselves burdened with excessive selling expenses. On the other hand, salesmen earning a straight salary during a period of rising prices may find their earnings out of line with the earnings of salesmen on a commission basis. Frequently companies change their methods of payment to meet changing conditions.

Variations of the commission compensation plan.—The straight-commission plan discussed in the preceding paragraphs makes no allowances for such factors as volume, difference in salability of items, differences of profitability of items to the company, or other factors. The following variations of the straight-commission plan make allowances for such differences:

1. Commission rate varying for individual items. In order to stimulate salesmen to push profitable items that are hard to sell, a higher rate of commission is given as an incentive. Items that are easy to sell and have a wide demand carry a lower rate of commission.

2. Sliding scale of commissions. Salesmen are paid a certain percentage up to a certain volume of business, after which the rate is increased or decreased progressively as sales grow in volume.

3. Group commissions. Various products are classified into groups, and rates of commission are set up for each group.

Drawing account.—This plan is actually a variation of the straight-commission plan and consists of an advance loan on a salesman's anticipated commission paid at regular intervals like a salary. The amount of the drawing account is generally determined by the expected sales based upon experience. For example, a company may give a salesman 10 per cent commission and $40 per week drawing account, based on the experience that a salesman selling that particular product will earn at least $40 per week commission. If a new product upon which no sales data exist is being sold, the amount of the drawing account is determined upon the company's anticipated sales based upon market research.

If the salesman has exceptional ability, his commission compensation will produce earnings over the drawing account, and these earnings will go to his credit. If, for any reason, the commission earnings fall below the drawings in any set period, this deficit is regarded as the salesman's indebtedness to the company. Such overdrafts are generally handled in the following ways:

1. A deduction is made from commission earnings in periods when such earnings are higher than normal.
2. A limit is placed on the total amount of overdrafts, and the salesmen are allowed to "pay back" a small percentage weekly. When the limit is reached, the drawing account is discontinued until the indebtedness has been paid in full.
3. The amount of the drawing account is reduced until the overdraft has been cleared.
4. Excess commission is set up as a reserve against overdrafts. The balance is paid to salesmen at the end of the year.
5. Salesmen are requested to sign one-year notes for overdrafts over a specified amount.
6. Overdrafts are written off at the end of the year so that salesmen may not feel too discouraged by accumulation of debts.
7. The overdraft accumulation is split 50-50 with the salesmen at the end of the year.

In all cases salesmen who consistently run up overdrafts must be carefully watched. With some salesmen the situation indicates that the commission or compensation plan needs adjustment. With others, the situation indicates poor planning or poor salesmanship and may necessitate replacement of the men. The advantages and disadvantages of drawing accounts are as follows:

Advantages

For the Company

(1) Exercises some control over the salesmen.
(2) Adds to incentives of the commission plan.
(3) Keeps salesmen satisfied during training periods and seasonal slumps.
(4) Provides an incentive to keep sales up to normal expectancy.
(5) Attracts more salesmen, thus permitting the company to have a wider selection of new men.

For the Salesman

(1) Assures a steady income despite slump periods.
(2) Permits budgeting.
(3) Indicates company interest and co-operation.

Disadvantages

For the Company

(1) Salesmen may leave with a deficit.
(2) Collection of overdrafts may cause ill feeling between management and salesmen.
(3) Involves considerable bookkeeping.
(4) Overdrafts cause mental handicap which interferes with the salesmen's production.
(5) May involve heavy losses, particularly when conditions bring sales below normal expectancy.
(6) Discourages missionary work, and may influence salesmen to earn no more than the minimum.

For the Salesman

(1) Puts salesmen in debt to the company.
(2) Requires a set volume of sales.
(3) Makes salesmen depend on the company's own estimation of possible sales.

The bonus plan.—A bonus is a special reward for effort resulting in increased sales or reduced expenses beyond a set goal or quota. The bonus is usually arranged on a percentage basis, although in some cases it may consist of a flat-cash award. It is always used in conjunction with some other form of compensation.

To illustrate the operation of a simple bonus plan, a company paying 10 per cent commission to its salesmen sets a monthly quota of $5,000 sales, and offers a 5 per cent bonus for sales exceeding this quota. A salesman bringing in orders totaling $7,000 for the month would obtain $700 commission plus 5 per cent of the $2,000 overage, or $100.

In the sale of low-priced items, staple merchandise, and consumer goods where the co-operative effort of salesmen is not a factor in the success of a sale, it is customary to give individual bonuses based upon the performances of the individual salesmen. In such cases the quotas are often based upon past performances of the individual salesmen or upon the sales expectancy in the particular territories covered by the salesmen. One advantage of the individual bonus is that the salesman is actually competing with himself and therefore does not feel that less energetic salesmen may reap the rewards of his labors.

Where teamwork of salesmen is an important merchandising factor, such as in the sale of high-priced items, machinery and industrial goods, and particularly where the sales force is divided into districts under the control of district sales managers, group bonuses are generally paid. While group bonuses do stimulate cooperativeness of salesmen, they often permit the lazy or inefficient salesman to benefit by the labors of the more active members of his group.

Described below are several common types of bonus plans in which either the quota arrangement or the method of applying the bonus has been adapted to meet specific needs.

1. The bonus based upon a quota of sales. A quota based upon previous sales volumes for a particular period is established, and a bonus is offered for certain percentages obtained over this quota. For example, if a company's sales for a previous year totaled $100,000, it might offer a 2 per cent bonus for a 10 per cent increase of the sales volume, a 5 per cent bonus for a 20 per cent increase, and so on.

2. The bonus based upon a quota of individual product sales. Where it is desired to push special items such as high-priced or slow-moving merchandise, a sales quota for the specific item is established, and a bonus is offered on sales exceeding this quota.

3. The bonus based on lower selling-cost quota. Where it is desired to reduce traveling expenses, a quota based upon previous sales experiences is established, and a bonus is offered for reducing expenses below this quota. One disadvantage of this plan is that it tends to reduce sales activity.

4. The profit-sharing bonus. This plan offers as a bonus a percentage of the company's yearly profits. To avoid misunderstandings with the salesmen, this plan should clarify the basis for arriving at profits. Generally, such a plan is complicated to operate and often causes salesmen dissatisfaction in lean years, when profits are small, and company dissatisfaction when earnings are high.

5. The bonus based on sales activities. Where it is desired to stimulate missionary work, a bonus may be offered for interviewing a certain number of prospects, arranging a certain number of store displays, and so forth. In such a plan the bonus is often a flat-cash award.

6. The sliding-scale bonus. There are two common forms of sliding-scale bonuses. One plan is the establishment of a flat reward for attaining a quota and the offering of a bonus equal to the percentage attained of that quota. For example, if a bonus of $500 is offered for attaining a $10,000 sales quota, and a salesman succeeds only in selling $5,000 within the quota period, he would receive 50 per cent of the award, or $250. Another plan increases the bonus according to a fixed scale. For instance, a company may offer 5 per cent of the first $5,000 sales, 7 per cent of the second $5,000, and 10 per cent on anything over this amount.

The advantages and disadvantages of bonus plans are as follows:

Advantages

For the Company

(1) Offers an additional incentive for better co-operation of salesmen.

(2) Is sufficiently flexible to serve specific needs, such as the

For the Salesman

(1) Permits increase in income in addition to the regular compensation plan.

(2) Indicates co-operation and interest of the management.

pushing of special items, reducing costs, and so on.
(3) Can be adjusted to suit conditions without interfering with the regular method of compensation.
(4) Creates a more satisfied group of salesmen by giving an opportunity to save, thus reducing turnover of the sales organization.
(5) Builds morale.

(3) Rewards unusual sales efforts.

DISADVANTAGES

For the Company

(1) May encourage salesmen (in the case of group bonuses) to be lazy.
(2) Causes disputes over quota arrangements.
(3) May involve excessive selling expense when prices are going up.

For the Salesman

(1) If quotas are unfair, salesmen must pay for the management's mistake.
(2) May be used as an excuse for reduction of regular compensation.
(3) May stress the sale of hard-to-sell items.
(4) Too sporadic, and often requires long periods of waiting before payment is made.

The point system.—The point system is a flexible means of measuring payment to salesmen for the performance of specific selling tasks, and for penalizing them for things the company does not want done. In its simplest form the plan consists of evaluating by points the sale of each of a number of products sold by a company, assigning the lowest number of points (usually 1 point) to the product easiest to sell, and then grading the other products and points accordingly. The point might represent a single item, a quantity such as a ton or case, or dollar sales. The points are given dollar values, and salesmen are paid on the basis of the number of points accumulated by each salesman.

The point system may also be used in evaluating specific jobs, such as interviewing new prospects, reducing expenses, increasing the number of daily calls, and so on. Points may be deducted for the neglect of these duties or for certain acts such as causing complaints from customers, and the like. In determining the number of points to be assigned to each duty, it is customary to assign the lowest number of points to the work with the least resistance, such as the turning in of daily reports.

Compensation may be based entirely upon the point system or upon a point system in conjunction with a salary. In the latter case the amount paid over salary would be based upon the number of points accumulated. One method of operating this plan is to give each salesman a point handicap based upon his salary, the lowest salaried man having the lowest handicap. For example, a man receiving $25 per week may be required to reach a mark of 1,000 points, thereafter receiving the dollar value of the points. A $50-per-week man would be required to reach a mark of 2,000 points, and so on.

Some companies change the point value of product sales according to the months in which sales are easier or harder, thus leveling the compensation of salesmen over slump periods.

The advantages and disadvantages of the point system are as follows:

ADVANTAGES

For the Company

(1) Gives strict control over salesmen's activities.
(2) Can be adapted to any selling situation.
(3) Provides an incentive to perform difficult or onerous selling tasks.
(4) Provides an accurate measure of sales ability.

For the Salesman

(1) Provides a direct reward for a good selling job.
(2) Provides for seasonal slumps.

DISADVANTAGES

For the Company

(1) May require excessive amount of record keeping.

For the Salesman

(1) Overemphasis on missionary work.

(2) Salesmen dispute point values or penalty scores.	(2) Overemphasis on hard-to-sell items.
	(3) Must accept company's evaluation of points and penalties.

Use of the point system in a sliding-scale bonus plan.—The sliding-scale principle explained on page 608 can be used effectively with the point system in stimulating salesmen to make greater efforts than seems justified by the flat-bonus plan. For example, a large midwestern food company paying salesmen salary plus expenses plus a flat bonus based on points found that salesmen were satisfied to reach a certain income level and did not have sufficient incentive to make greater sales efforts beyond that level. By giving scaled values to the points, the company gave the salesmen an opportunity to work into new brackets of business that offered bigger rates of compensation.

In the flat-bonus plan the point quota was established by the dollar cost of each man to the company. When the salesman reached the number of points equal to his salary and expenses, he went on bonus and was paid at the rate of 50 cents flat per point sold. Thus, a man being paid $200 salary and $150 expenses was set a quota of 350 points. If he earned 400 points, he would receive as an income $350 salary and expenses, plus $25 for the 50 extra points.

In the accelerated bonus plan, instead of starting this man on a 350-point basic starting point and paying him a flat 50 cents per point, the following scale of bonus payments was applied:

300 points to 340 points	25 cents per point basis
350 points to 399 points	50 cents per point basis
400 points to 449 points	75 cents per point basis
450 points and up	$1 per point basis

Thus, if a salesman earned 400 points, he would receive $350 salary and expenses plus a bonus of $37.50 (representing 50 points at 25 cents per point or $12.50 plus 50 points at 50 cents or $25).

Variations and combinations of basic compensation plans.—Many combinations and variations of the basic compensation plans described above have been used effectively in meeting the specific needs of companies. In fact, some companies employ several types of compensation plans within the organization. The choice of the proper plan depends upon such factors as the type and size of the company, the type of product, sales objectives, personnel, and so forth. A few of these combinations will be discussed in detail; others listed are self-explanatory.

1. Salary and commission. Firms paying a flat salary plus a commission on all sales over a certain amount are able to exercise more control over their men than if they paid on the straight-commission basis. Moreover, they can make the plan more attractive to salesmen than the straight-salary plan. This plan assists salesmen during slump seasons and encourages them to do missionary work. One firm using this plan paid new salesmen a low salary plus a flat one third of the regular salesmen's commission, thus inducing the salesmen to go on the more desirable straight-commission basis.

Sometimes the commission is based on all sales made by a particular group of people. This plan is especially suitable where salespeople's efforts overlap, and where co-operation is desirable.

2. Salary, expenses, and commission. This is a slight variation of the above plan and is particularly useful where traveling expenses are a considerable item. The percentage commission paid in this plan is usually relatively small.

3. Salary plus commission plus bonus. This plan is often applied where large territories are to be covered. The salary is usually based upon the expense of covering the territory. Bonus is paid above a specified weekly or monthly minimum sales volume. The sliding-scale bonus is sometimes used in this plan.

4. Salary and bonus. Flat salary plus bonus over quota.

5. Salary, expenses, bonus on sales over quota.

6. Salary and percentage of gross profits.

7. Commission and bonus.

8. Commission and drawing account. As previously described, the amount of the weekly drawing account is stipulated and deducted from commission earnings.

9. Commission plus traveling expense.

10. Commission with sliding-scale drawing account. The amount of the drawing account is raised or lowered according to commission earnings within set periods.

11. Percentage of gross profits.

SECTION 6

Sales Contracts and Forms

1. ESSENTIALS OF A CONTRACT

2. CONTRACTS FOR SALE OF MERCHANDISE

3. MISCELLANEOUS CLAUSES IN SALES CONTRACTS

4. CONTRACTS APPOINTING AGENTS FOR SALE OF MERCHANDISE

5. MISCELLANEOUS CLAUSES IN AGENCY AGREEMENTS

6. CONTRACTS EMPLOYING SALESMEN

7. MISCELLANEOUS CLAUSES IN CONTRACTS EMPLOYING SALESMEN

8. FOREIGN TRADE DEFINITIONS

SECTION 6

Sales Contracts and Forms

1. ESSENTIALS OF A CONTRACT

What a contract is.—We are apt to think of a contract as a formal document, solemnly entered into with strict observance of legal requirements. As a matter of fact, contracts are made every minute of the day—orally, by letter, or by other informal agreement—and these contracts are just as binding upon the parties involved as if they covered many printed pages and were duly signed and executed before a notary. A man boards a streetcar on the way to his office; he has entered into a contract with the transit company. His wife phones the day's food order; she has made a contract with her grocer. A businessman writes for an additional ream of his letterheads; he has contracted with his stationer. What are the elements that make each of these acts contracts? A contract has been defined as an agreement between two or more parties to do or not to do a particular thing, which is enforceable at law. In order to be enforceable at law, an agreement must have the following elements:

1. *Offer and acceptance.*—An agreement arises from an offer or proposal to do or to refrain from doing a certain thing, and from an acceptance of that same proposal. The offer must be clear and definite; it must be communicated in its exact terms to the party to whom the offer is made, either directly or by some definite act; and it must be accepted unconditionally by the person to whom it is made. If the person to whom an offer is made proposes modifications, those modifications must be accepted by the offeror before an agreement can result. In other words, in the figurative language frequently used by the courts, there must be a "meeting of

the minds" of the parties as to the terms of the agreement. However, an assent to the modifications may be inferred from the fact that the parties thereafter proceeded to carry on the transaction under the conditional acceptance.

2. *Competency of parties.*—The parties to the agreement must be legally competent to enter into a contract. The question of competency arises most frequently with respect to infants, insane persons, and drunkards.

An infant—that is, a person under 21 years of age—is not absolutely incapable of entering into a binding contract. Contracts made by persons under the legal age are not void, but they may generally be avoided or disaffirmed by the infant. In the case of contracts which have not yet been completely carried out—that is, executory contracts—the infant is not bound unless he affirms after coming of age, either by words, by sale of the property, by retaining it after a reasonable time has elapsed, and so forth; failure to affirm implies disaffirmance. In the case of contracts which have been completely carried out—that is, executed contracts—an infant may disaffirm either during infancy or within a reasonable time after he attains his majority; failure to disaffirm within a reasonable time implies affirmance. It is the general rule that an infant may disaffirm even if he cannot return the goods which he has received. Contracts by an infant for articles that are reasonably necessary to his existence, such as food, clothing, shelter, medical care, education, and the like, may be binding upon him in the same manner as if he were an adult.

Like infants, insane persons are not absolutely incapable of making contracts. Their contracts are voidable, not void, and they may be held liable for necessaries.

A person who is so drunk that he is deprived of his reason and does not understand the nature of his acts is in the same position as a mental incompetent, and his contracts may be disaffirmed by him if third persons are not injured thereby, and provided he disaffirms immediately upon restoration of his faculties.

3. *Legality of subject matter.*—An agreement that calls for the performance of an act forbidden by law or inimical to the interests of society is unenforceable. Gambling agreements, for example, are generally held to be illegal. In some states any contract entered into on a Sunday is illegal.

Federal and State laws may make illegal contracts that restrain trade, fix prices, or result in unfair trade practices. For example, under the Federal Robinson-Patman Act a contract that discriminates in price between competing customers of the same seller in the sale of commodities of like grade and quality is invalid, if the effect of the discrimination is to lessen competition or create a monopoly. The Act does permit allowances for differences in the cost of manufacture, sale, or delivery resulting from the different methods or quantities in which such commodities are sold or delivered to the purchasers. For further discussion of anti-price discrimination contracts, see page 698.

4. *Consideration.*—Consideration has been defined as something of benefit to the person making a promise, or something of detriment to the person to whom a promise is made. It is the price, motive, or matter inducing the contract and may consist of:

(*a*) Doing some act that one is not obligated to perform.

(*b*) Refraining from doing something that one would otherwise be free to do.

(*c*) Giving some money or property.

(*d*) Giving a promise.

The value of the consideration given to support a promise is generally immaterial.

2. CONTRACTS FOR SALE OF MERCHANDISE

What a sale is.—A sale is an agreement whereby the seller transfers property in goods to the buyer, for a consideration called the price. To be enforceable, a sale must have all the elements necessary to the validity of a contract—namely:

1. Offer and acceptance.
2. Competency of parties.
3. Legality of subject matter.
4. Consideration.

A sale must be distinguished from a bailment and from a consignment. A bailment is a transfer merely of possession of goods under an agreement to return the same goods at some future time. Under a consignment goods are sent by the owner to a commission merchant, to be sold by the latter to third persons, without any transfer of title in the merchandise delivered to the consignee.

Contract of sale and contract to sell.—A contract *of* sale should be distinguished from a contract *to* sell goods. In a contract to sell, the seller does not make an immediate transfer of property, but merely agrees to make a transfer at some future time. Under a contract of sale, in the absence of contrary intention, title to the goods sold passes immediately from the seller to the buyer, and the buyer assumes the risk of loss; in a contract to sell, title remains in the seller, and the seller carries the risk of loss, in the absence of contrary agreement, until the time fixed for the sale. The Uniform Sales Act* has formulated certain rules for ascertaining the intention of the parties as to when title is to pass. Goods that are in existence and are owned or possessed by the seller may be the subject of a sale or a contract to sell; goods that are to be subsequently manufactured or acquired by the seller and are to come into existence before the time fixed for delivery (called "future goods") may be the subject of a contract to sell, but not of a contract of sale.

When a sales contract must be in writing; statute of frauds.—The general rule, as embodied in the Uniform Sales Act, is that "a contract to sell or a sale may be made in writing (either with or without seal) or by word of mouth, or partly in writing and partly by word of mouth, or may be inferred from the conduct of the parties." However, under a provision of the Act (commonly known as the statute of frauds), a contract to sell or a sale of any goods of the value of $500 or upwards is not enforceable by action unless one of the three following alternatives has been complied with:

1. Some note or memorandum in writing of the contract or sale has been signed by the party to be charged or by his agent in his behalf;

---

* The Uniform Sales Act, which has been adopted in most of the states, is a codification of the law governing the sale of personal property. Prior to its enactment, a wide conflict of judicial opinion existed in the various jurisdictions with respect to the law governing the sale of merchandise, resulting in much confusion and uncertainty. This conflict has to a large extent been eliminated by the Act, although in some instances differences still exist owing to varying interpretations by the courts of some of the sections of the Act.

2. The buyer has accepted part of the goods and actually received them; or

3. The buyer has given something in earnest to bind the contract, or in part payment.

Where goods are to be manufactured by the seller especially for the buyer and are not suitable for sale to others in the ordinary course of the seller's business, the statute of frauds does not apply.

It should be noted that while the Uniform Sales Act fixed $500 as the amount that determines whether or not the statute of frauds applies, some other amount is fixed by statute in some states. Further, the amount is the price fixed in the sale, not the actual value of the merchandise sold. If several articles of merchandise have been sold at one time by one seller, the total purchase determines the amount, even though each article is separately priced.

The memorandum required by the statute of frauds is not necessarily the contract. The contract may be oral; as long as there is some memorandum of it, the statute is satisfied. The memorandum may merely indicate briefly the chief provisions of the contract and may consist of an entry in a book, on a bill head, or in a series of letters.

Essential provisions of sales contracts.—The provisions that may be included in a contract between seller and buyer for the sale of merchandise vary widely with the nature of the business and the individual desires and needs of the parties to the contract. It may be said, however, that such contracts generally include express provisions with respect to the following:

1. *Introduction.*—This includes the date and place of making the contract and the names and addresses of both seller and buyer.

2. *Description of merchandise.*—The quantity, nature, or quality of the goods should be clearly described, to prevent misunderstanding. Where the quantity is indicated by weight, it should be stated whether the weight is gross or net, and it should be indicated whether allowance is made for shrinkage or for wear and tear. The extent of the details in the description will depend upon how widely the article is known in the trade. Standard products that are extensively advertised may not need detailed description. In sales by sample, the article may be described merely "as per sam-

ple." On the other hand, goods specially manufactured for the buyer should be fully described and accompanied by blueprint and specifications. In the case of specially marked goods, the exact drawing or facsimile of the markings should be furnished by the buyer.

3. *Warranties.*—A warranty is a promise of the seller as to the nature, quality, or durability of the merchandise sold. To prevent dispute as to quality, provision is sometimes made for inspection of the merchandise and the obtaining of an inspection certificate at the time of shipment. A warranty as to quality or special fitness may be made even in a sale by sample. In addition to the warranties expressed in the contract, the law implies certain warranties as to quality, fitness for the purpose for which the goods were sold, and so on.

4. *Shipping instructions.*—Definite shipping instructions should be given, including instructions as to packing, marking, routing, and time of shipment. To protect the seller in the event that the buyer does not specify the routing, the contract should contain a clause to the effect that, unless specified, routing is at seller's option. If no time of shipment is specified, a reasonable time is implied. As a protection to the seller, the contract may contain a clause limiting his liability in the event of unavoidable delay or impossibility of performance. It may also be provided that each shipment is to be deemed a separate contract and paid for whether or not the balance of an order is filled; this, however, is a disadvantage to the buyer and may be objected to by him.

5. *Time of payment and price.*—The contract should definitely state the time of payment. It should also indicate the price of the goods, and whether shipping costs and insurance are included therein. This information is generally covered by the use of certain symbols, such as the following:

c.i.f.—This symbol means "cost, insurance, freight," and indicates that the price includes not only the cost of the goods, but the expense of insuring them during transit and the freight charge for transportation.

c.a.f. or *c. & f.*—These symbols have the same meaning—namely, "cost and freight." The price includes the transportation costs, but not insurance costs.

c.i.f. & e.—This is the same as c.i.f., except that the seller must pay the cost of exchange in addition to insurance and freight.

c.i.f.c.i.—The seller must pay collection and interest charges in addition to insurance and freight.

freight prepaid—This means that the price includes not only the cost of the goods but also the freight charge to the named point, which will be allowed to the buyer. If the buyer takes the goods at the point of shipment, he is nevertheless entitled to the allowance of the freight charge to the named point.

f.o.b.—This means "free on board" or "freight on board." A price quoted f.o.b. includes not only the cost of the goods, but all charges, such as trucking, packing, lighterage charges, and so forth, necessary to put the goods on board the car or vessel. The seller delivers the goods to the carrier at the named point, free of charge to the buyer.

f.a.s.—This means "free alongside steamer," and is the same as f.o.b. except that the seller is required to pay merely the cost of putting the goods alongside the vessel by delivery on the dock, wharf, or lighter, and not on board.

basis.—A sale "basis a certain point" means that the price includes the cost of the goods, plus freight charges to the designated point; in other words, the seller pays the freight charges to that point.

If no price is specified, the buyer is liable for the reasonable value of the merchandise. Where the parties make a sale at a valuation—that is, a sale or contract to sell, providing that the price shall be subsequently fixed by a third party—the value fixed by the third party is binding in the absence of fraud or unfair dealing. The Uniform Sales Act provides that if the third person, without fault of the seller or buyer, fails to fix the price, the contract is thereby avoided; if he is prevented from fixing the price by the seller or buyer, the party not in default is given certain remedies as though the contract had been breached.

6. *Claims.*—The contract may provide for the payment of a certain sum as "liquidated damages" in the event of a breach of the contract; or it may provide for adjustment of disputes by arbitration.

7. *Law governing the contract.*—Where the parties reside in different states, or where the contract is executed in one state but is

to be performed in another, or where the contract is to be performed in various states, the contract may indicate the state, the laws of which shall govern the construction of the contract and the rights and liabilities of the parties.

Additional provisions that may be included in sales contracts are indicated in the forms given below and in the miscellaneous clauses beginning on page 662. For an explanation of the distinction between contracts of sale and contracts to sell, see page 626.

FORM NO. 1

Contract of sale of merchandise (general form).

Dated at ...., ..., ..., 19...., ...

.... Corporation, hereinafter called "Seller," hereby sells and agrees to furnish, and ...., with offices at ...., ..., hereinafter called "Buyer," hereby purchases and agrees to accept, in accordance with the terms and conditions hereinafter set forth, the following material during the period from ...., 19...., to ...., 19...., inclusive.

MATERIAL AND QUANTITY:

QUALITY:

SHIPMENT: Shipments of the material covered hereby shall be made from .... to Buyer at .... as destination. When the price under this contract is on a delivered-at-destination basis, the named destination shall be the point of delivery, and, where such price is on an f.o.b. basis, the delivery to carrier shall constitute delivery to Buyer.

PRICE: All prices are f.o.b. ....

Any tax or other Governmental charge upon the production, sale and/or shipment of the material(s) herein specified, imposed by Federal, State, or Municipal authorities and hereafter becoming effective within the life of this contract, shall be added to the price herein provided and shall be paid by Buyer.

The Seller may from time to time revise (up or down) the price stated in this contract upon giving Buyer ten (10) days' written notice of any such revision. Such revised price shall be paid on all material(s) shipped after such ten (10) days' period unless, in the case of an increase in price, the Buyer shall, within said period, give Seller written notice that it is unwilling to accept such increase. In the event Buyer shall give Seller such notice, then Seller shall have the right to terminate this contract by giving Buyer, within ten (10) days after receipt by Seller of Buyer's notice, written notice to that effect.

Terms:

Deliveries: Against Buyer's orders in approximately equal monthly quantities. Buyer to advise Seller, on or before 15th of each month, quantity to be delivered the following month. Seller reserves right to route shipments.

Containers: In suitable containers. Where goods require returnable carboys, drums, or other special containers, a charge equal to Seller's prevailing charge for each container at the time of shipment shall be made against Buyer as a deposit against the return of such container. This amount shall be paid Seller without discount when the invoice for the contents is paid. A corresponding amount shall be credited to Buyer as each container is returned to Seller in good condition, freight prepaid, at place of original shipment. Such container shall be used by Buyer only for reasonable storage of material originally shipped therein. Seller reserves the right of refusing to accept containers and make refunds therefor when the same were used for other purposes and/or retained longer than ninety (90) days from the date of original shipment. Title to such returnable containers shall remain in Seller and charge on account thereof shall not constitute a purchase thereof, but merely security for their due return.

General Conditions: 1. Each shipment shall be made at Buyer's risk and shall be considered, as regards deliveries and terms of settlement, a separate and independent contract, and Seller's weights taken at shipping point shall govern. In case any lot or parcel shall not be accepted and/or paid for in accordance herewith, then Seller may, without prejudice to other lawful remedy, defer shipments until settlement is made, terminate this contract, or treat such failure as a breach of the entire contract. If, in the judgment of Seller, the financial responsibility of Buyer shall at any time become impaired, Seller may decline to make shipments against this contract and/or any other contract in force with Buyer except upon receipt of satisfactory security for payment or of cash before shipment. Failure of Seller to exercise any right under this contract shall not be deemed a waiver thereof.

2. Seller reserves the right to discontinue deliveries hereunder of any material, the manufacture, sale, and/or use of which, in the opinion of

Seller, would infringe any United States or Canadian Letters Patent now or hereafter issued and under which Seller is not licensed.

3. Materials purchased under this contract are for consumption and use by Buyer, its controlled, affiliated, and/or subsidiary companies, and not for resale. In the event Buyer shall resell the material purchased under this contract, or any part thereof, Seller, at its option, without prejudice to any other lawful remedies, may terminate this contract.

4. Buyer assumes all risks and liability for results of use by Buyer of material delivered under this contract, including use by Buyer of such material in combination with other substances. Notice of any claims for defects in the quality of the material delivered hereunder shall be given within ten (10) days after arrival of said material. Failure to give such notice shall constitute a waiver by Buyer of all claims therefor.

5. If either party is prevented from carrying out the herein-contained provisions by reason of any war, revolution, strike, epidemic, fire, cyclone, flood, embargo, Providential, Governmental, or other cause, whether of the same or a different nature, existing or future, beyond the reasonable control of such party and interfering with the production, delivery, or receipt of material as herein contemplated, the party so interfered with, upon prompt written notice to the other party in advance of actual shipment, shall be excused from making or taking deliveries to the extent of such interference. Seller shall have the option of extending the term of this contract for a period equal to that of such interference, and deliveries so omitted shall be made during such extended period.

6. This contract is to be construed and the respective rights of Buyer and Seller are to be determined according to the laws of the State of New York. This document constitutes the full understanding between the parties hereto with reference to the subject matter hereof, and no statements or agreements, oral or written, made prior to or at the signing hereof, shall vary or modify the written terms hereof; and neither party shall claim any amendment, modification, or release from any provision hereof by mutual agreement, unless such agreement is in writing signed by the other party and specifically stating it is an amendment to this contract.

7. This contract is not assignable or transferable by either party, except to its successor or to the transferee of all or substantially all of its assets, and shall be binding upon and inure to the benefit of such successor or transferee.

.... *(Buyer)* .... Corporation *(Seller)*

By ....

.... *(Official Capacity)* By ....

FORM NO. 2

Contract to sell in form of letter of proposal and acceptance.

Est. No. .... Office Date: ....

.... Project: ....

Location: ....

Architect: ....

Gentlemen:

.... Corporation proposes to furnish you for the above-mentioned project, subject to the terms and conditions herein included, the materials scheduled herein, all in accordance with our standard specifications.

Schedule of Material: All prices are f.o.b. ....

Any tax or other Governmental charge upon the production, sale, and/or shipment of the material(s) herein specified, imposed by Federal, State, or Municipal authorities and hereafter becoming effective within the life of this contract, shall be added to the price(s) herein specified, and shall be paid by you.

Shipments: We reserve right to route shipments.

Terms: Net cash on or before the 15th of each month for all deliveries made during the preceding month, with privilege of two (2) per cent discount for payment in cash within ten (10) days of delivery.

General Conditions: 1. We assume no liability for damage to material after delivery, resulting from improper storage and/or handling by you and/or your agents and/or employees.

2. All prices named herein are based upon the present rates of railroad freight. Any increase or decrease in such freight rates effective at the time of shipment shall be added to or deducted from such prices.

In the event of your failure to permit us to complete shipment of the material covered by this contract within one (1) year from the date hereof, you shall reimburse us for the expense involved in handling and storing such material at our factory after that date, as well as for any excess of the then-prevailing selling price of our material over the contract price with respect to that portion of the material covered by this contract delivered after such date.

3. Each shipment shall be construed, as regards deliveries and terms of settlement, a separate and independent contract. In case any lot or parcel shall not be accepted and/or paid for in accordance herewith, then we may, without prejudice to other lawful remedy, defer further shipments until settlement is made, terminate this contract, or treat such failure as a breach of the entire contract. If, in our judgment, your financial responsibility shall at any time become impaired, we may decline to make shipments against this contract and/or any other contract in force with you, except upon receipt of satisfactory security for payment, or of cash before shipment. Our failure to exercise any right under this contract shall not be deemed a waiver thereof.

4. Notice of any claim for defect in the quality of the material delivered hereunder shall be given to us in writing within five (5) days of the date of delivery. Failure to give such notice within such time shall constitute a waiver by you of all claims therefor.

5. If we are prevented from carrying out the herein-contained provisions by reason of any war, revolution, strike, epidemic, fire, cyclone, flood, embargo, weather conditions, car shortage, Providential, Governmental, or other cause, whether of the same or of a different nature, existing or future, beyond our reasonable control, and interfering with the production or delivery of the material as herein contemplated, upon written notice to you, we shall be excused from making deliveries to the extent and for the duration of such interference.

6. Should any dispute or disagreement arise with relation to the matter of payment, allowance or loss, or the interpretation of any one or more of the clauses of this contract, which dispute or disagreement cannot be satisfactorily settled by mutual conference, then the matter shall be settled by arbitration pursuant to the Arbitration Law of the State of New York, by reference to a board of three arbitrators, one to be selected by each of us and the third by the two so selected. In case the selection of any arbitrator is not made within fifteen (15) days of the time either party notifies the other of the name of the arbitrator selected by the notifying party, then the arbitrator or arbitrators not

selected shall be appointed pursuant to the New York Arbitration Law. The submission of any dispute or disagreement to arbitration shall not in any way affect or limit our right to file and prosecute a lien under the applicable State law for any and all sums that we claim to be due and owing to us under this contract.

7. This contract is to be construed, and our respective rights are to be determined, according to the laws of the State of New York, and constitutes the full understanding between us with reference to the subject matter hereof, and no statement or agreement, oral or written, made prior to or at the signing hereof, shall vary or modify the written terms hereof. Neither of us shall claim any amendment, modification, or release from any provision hereof by mutual agreement unless such agreement is in writing, signed by the other and specifically stating it is an amendment to this contract.

8. This contract is not assignable or transferable by either party, except to its successors or to the transferee of all or substantially all of its assets, and shall be binding upon and inure to the benefit of such successor or transferee.

This proposal, including all conditions printed or typed on either side hereof, is subject to your prompt acceptance, and to approval by an executive officer of this corporation; and, when so accepted and approved, shall constitute, with the attached schedule, if any, a contract between us, hereinabove sometimes referred to as "this contract." Until so approved by us, prices are subject to change without notice.

Respectfully submitted,

.... Corporation

By ....

Accepted: ...., 19....

....

By ....

Approved: ...., 19....

.... Corporation

By ....

FORM NO. 3

Acceptance of order, subject to conditions.

[*Note.—It has been held by the courts that this is merely a counteroffer which, in turn, must be accepted or rejected.*]

.... MANUFACTURING COMPANY

Subject to Terms on Reverse Side

Their Order No.	Dated	Date Entered	As Our Order No.
7512	......................., 19....	......................., 19....	B 31333

Sold to

....

....

This is an acknowledgment of your order, as we have entered it, and it is accepted subject to the following terms and conditions, whether or not they are at variance with terms appearing on your purchase order.

[*Here follow terms and conditions, including additional ones.*]

On orders for special materials, the right is reserved to ship and bill ten (10) per cent more or less than the exact quantity specified.

The order is not subject to cancellation.

.... Manufacturing Company

....

FORM NO. 4

Contract specifying minimum and maximum requirements.

This Contract made and entered into this .... day of ...., 19...., by and between the .... Company, hereinafter styled "Seller," and ...., of ...., ..., hereinafter styled "Buyer," whereby the Seller agrees to sell to the Buyer, and the Buyer agrees to buy from the Seller, ... per cent of requirements, the minimum to be supplied by the Seller estimated at .... tons, and the maximum not to exceed .... tons, except at the Seller's option, the following article in the quantities and upon the terms and conditions hereinafter stated:

During the period from ...., 19...., to ...., 19...., inclusive.

Product	*Package*	*Price*	*Per*
....	....	....	....
....	....	....	....
....	....	....	....

Price is based for delivery ....

Terms: Net cash within thirty (30) days from date of invoice, or one (1) per cent cash discount for payment within ten days from date of invoice.

The price in this contract is based upon Seller's present costs. If costs are increased because of present or future Federal or State legislation, Governmental ordinances, rules, orders, or licenses, or because of increases in cost of labor, raw materials, fuel, or transportation, Seller may make corresponding increases in price on March 31, 19...., June 30, 19...., September 30, 19...., or December 31, 19...., provided twenty (20) days' written notice to Buyer of such increase is given. If Buyer is unwilling to accept any such increase in price as computed by Seller, and so notifies Seller in writing prior to date such increase becomes effective, either party may terminate this contract upon ten (10) days' written notice to the other.

.... *(Buyer)* .... Company *(Seller)*

By ....

Accepted and Countersigned at

By .... Company

By ....

District Sales Manager

FORM NO. 5

Agreement providing for billing discount subject to correction after determination of actual discount earned on annual volume upon expiration of contract.

Agreement dated the .... day of ...., 19...., between ...., hereinafter called the "Seller," and ...., hereinafter called the "Buyer,"

Witnesseth:

The Seller and the Buyer hereby mutually agree that all of the rights and privileges hereinafter conferred upon or secured to the "Buyer," by this agreement, may be exercised by the subsidiary and affiliated companies of the "Buyer" (as enumerated in the list hereto attached and marked Exhibit "A"), and that the term "Buyer," as employed in this agreement, shall be deemed to include all such subsidiary and affiliated companies.

The Seller agrees to sell and the Buyer agrees to purchase, at the price and upon and subject to the following terms and conditions, the following articles:

Description: Buyer's purchases of .... Company [*here insert products*] of all grades and sizes, as handled and merchandised by the Seller, in the total amount of $............... at Seller's list prices current at the time orders are placed.

Basic Terms: The Seller will show on all invoices covering orders placed under this agreement a billing discount of .... per cent from the current list prices applicable in territory served. Terms of payment shall be Net Cash Thirty Days, No Cash Discount Allowed.

Volume Discount: The billing discount of .... per cent, as provided for herein, contemplates annual purchases of $............ at Seller's list prices current at the time orders are placed. Within sixty (60) days after the termination of the fiscal period provided herein, the Seller will furnish the Buyer an itemized list of all withdrawals against this contract, and, if the total of said volume exceeds the amount provided for in the billing discount, volume discount will be granted in accordance with the regular terms of the Seller as covered in the schedule listed below. In a contrary manner, if the total withdrawals against this contract do not equal the amount required to earn the billing discount, the Seller shall bill, and the Buyer agrees to pay to the Seller the amount of the unearned discount, in accordance with the same schedule.

All extra discounts will be computed from list prices current at time of purchase. In a like manner, all billbacks on unearned discounts will be computed from list prices current at time of purchase.

The Seller agrees to accept any individual order on the basis of his published terms for One Order, Immediate Delivery Transactions, when the amount of any such order will earn a larger billing discount than provided for herein. Such orders shall be considered in determining total business for fiscal-year period, on the basis of the list prices thereof prevailing at the time order was placed, but shall not in themselves be subject to any further discount unless the discount on the total annual volume exceeds the amount of discount allowed at time of billing.

Annual Buying Volume Discount Schedule

$ 0.00 to 9,999.99	List
10,000.00 to 10,999.00	5%
11,000.00 to 11,999.00	6%
12,000.00 to 12,999.00	7%
13,000.00 to 13,999.00	8%
14,000.00 to 14,999.00	9%
15,000.00 to 15,999.00	10%
16,000.00 to 16,999.00	11%
17,000.00 to 17,999.00	12%
18,000.00 to 18,999.00	13%
19,000.00 to 19,999.00	14%
20,000.00 and over	15%

TERMINATION: This agreement terminates ....

Accepted by	Submitted in behalf of:
.... (*Buyer*)	.... (*Seller*)
By	By ....
Title	Title ....

SPECIAL INSTRUCTIONS

[Here follows blank space]

EXHIBIT A

(List of Subsidiary Companies and Buying Offices that may place orders under this contract)

Company Name	*City*	*Name of Buyer*

Output and requirements contracts.—An output contract is one by which a seller agrees to sell his entire output to a single buyer. A requirements contract is one by which a buyer undertakes to buy his entire requirements of a commodity from a single seller (see Form No. 6).

These two types of contracts are often considered together, for they are governed by the same legal principles. It was formerly the general view that such agreements were invalid for want of consideration; the promise to sell in the one case, and to buy in the other, was thought illusory, because the seller in the output contract might have no output, and the buyer in the requirements contract might refrain from having any requirements. However, the validity of output and requirements contracts is now generally recognized. The seller in the output contract has given up his right to sell at large. The buyer in the requirements contract has surrendered his right to buy from anyone else. Some conflict of opinion still exists, however, as to the obligations of the parties under such agreements. Is the seller in the output contract required to produce the same amount as he was producing when the contract was made? Is the buyer in the requirements contract obligated to have substantially the same requirements as when the contract was entered into? According to the view that is supported by the weight of authority, the answer in both cases is "No." Both seller and buyer are required only to act in good faith. The seller in the output contract has performed his undertaking even if he cuts down his manufactures or closes up his plant, provided he does so in good faith; there is no implied agreement in the output contract to continue in business. Similarly, the buyer in the requirements contract does not agree to continue to have requirements. If his requirements taper off or cease because of a change in his needs or because of a sale or discontinuance of his business effected in good faith, he is not in default under the terms of his contract.

The requirements contract has been the subject of considerable comment from a business standpoint, as well as from a legal point of view. Large selling organizations often induce purchasers to enter into requirements contracts for their psychological rather than their legal effect. They are not interested in having a legally drawn document upon which suit can ultimately be brought, but they do want the purchaser to feel morally and legally obligated to purchase exclusively from them. The purchaser may even do some of his buying elsewhere; the seller will not sue, because he is more interested in keeping a substantial part of the buyer's business for a continuous period than he is in recovering damages for breach of the letter of the agreement. The requirements contract often calls the purchaser a "dealer" (see Form No. 6), thus making him believe that it is his duty to push the seller's product as well as to use it exclusively.

FORM NO. 6

Agreement to sell all products required by dealer for resale at designated location.

THE STANDARD OIL COMPANY (OHIO)

DEALER'S CONTRACT

Atlas Tires, Batteries, and Accessories

THIS AGREEMENT, entered into ...., 19...., between The Standard Oil Company (Ohio), hereinafter called "Standard," and .... of ...., hereinafter called "Dealer":

WITNESSETH: That

1. [*Agreement for sale and purchase*] Standard hereby designates Dealer its authorized dealer, and hereby agrees to sell and deliver to Dealer at ...., Ohio, and Dealer agrees to purchase, receive, and pay for, upon the terms and conditions hereinafter stated, all of the following products required by Dealer for resale or use at the foregoing location: Atlas Casings and Tubes, Atlas Batteries, and miscellaneous accessories shown on the appended price schedule.

2. [*Promotion of sales by dealer*] Dealer agrees actively to engage in the sale and distribution of the foregoing products as an "Authorized Dealer" at the foregoing location and will buy from Standard and keep on hand at all times during the life of this agreement a reasonable stock of Atlas tires and casings, and Atlas batteries, and of the miscellaneous accessories shown on the appended price schedule, of such types and sizes and in such quantities as will adequately meet the demands of the trade at Dealer's station; and Dealer will use his best efforts to sell and promote the sale of such products thereat.

3. [*Prices*] Dealer will pay to Standard for all products delivered hereunder the price or prices set forth in Standard's Dealer's price list for such products, respectively, in force on date of shipment, it being understood and agreed that all such prices are subject to change from time to time at Standard's option and without notice. For payment by the tenth (10th) of the month following that in which deliveries are made by Standard to Dealer, two (2) per cent cash discount will be allowed. It is understood, however, that Standard may at its discretion decline to make deliveries except on a cash in advance or C. O. D. basis, whenever Dealer's financial responsibility in the opinion of Standard will not warrant the extension of credit.

Should Standard make any downward revision in its established prices to its authorized dealers on any types or sizes of Atlas casings and tubes or batteries prior to the expiration or termination of this agreement, Standard agrees to protect Dealer by passing to Dealer's account a merchandise credit equal to the difference between the prices at which the same were purchased and the new lower prices to which the Dealer would then be entitled, on all first-class products of such kinds, types, and sizes (excepting discontinued models) which, as shown by the date of invoice therefor, were purchased by Dealer from Standard within thirty (30) days prior to the date of such price revision. Any such credit issued by Standard shall be used by Dealer during the term of this agreement, and if not so used, will be canceled.

4. [*Exchanges of merchandise*] Until further notice Standard will permit Dealer to exchange portions of Dealer's stock of Atlas casings and tubes purchased within one hundred and twenty (120) days, for other sizes. Dealer will be required, however, to pay all transportation charges and two and one-half ($2\frac{1}{2}$) per cent of the then value of the goods returned, to compensate Standard for the expense of handling. Any merchandise returned or exchanged must be in salable condition, must be first-grade merchandise, and will be subject to Standard's inspection and rejection. Any such exchange shall be made on the basis of Standard's Dealer's prices in effect at the time of such exchange, and will be made only on condition that Dealer place an order at the time of such exchange, to offset the value of the goods returned.

5. [*Adjustments*] Dealer agrees to refer all claims for adjustment (replacements or repairs) with respect to Atlas tubes and casings and Atlas batteries to Standard, it being understood that this agreement does not confer on Dealer any authority to make adjustments on such merchandise on behalf of Standard, or any authority to warrant any products except Atlas casings and tubes and Atlas batteries. As to these, Dealer's authority shall be limited to such warranties as are set forth in

Standard's "Guaranty for Atlas Tires" and the manufacturer's standard warranty on such tires in effect on the date of resale by Dealer, and as set forth in Standard's "Atlas Battery Guaranty and Adjustment Policy" in effect on the date of resale by Dealer. Under such guaranties the Atlas casings and Atlas batteries sold thereunder may be presented for adjustment or service to any Atlas retailer, and Dealer in turn hereby agrees that he will accept for adjustment and service under such guaranties any Atlas tires or Atlas batteries that have been sold by any other Atlas retailer, but will refer all claims for adjustment thereon to Standard for its action, unless otherwise authorized by Standard.

6. [*Liability for delays or failure to deliver*] Standard shall not be liable for delays or failure to make delivery of goods ordered hereunder when such delay or failure is caused by fires, strikes, or any other cause (whether of the kind herein enumerated or otherwise) beyond the reasonable control of Standard.

[*Aid in handling merchandise; removal of signs on termination of agreement*] Standard will give Dealer such aid generally as Standard gives other contract dealers handling the merchandise described herein, in carrying out Standard's policy of distribution. Upon termination of this agreement, Dealer agrees, upon demand, to remove and return to Standard all signs furnished by Standard (it being understood that Standard owns all signs for the cost or maintenance of which it pays in whole or in part), and to remove all painted signs at his place of business or elsewhere, displaying the name Standard or Atlas or any of Standard's trade-marks or trade names. Upon failure of the Dealer to remove such signs, Standard shall have the right to enter Dealer's place of business and effect such removals. Dealer agrees to hold Standard harmless from any liability arising out of or connected with the erection, maintenance, or removal of any such signs.

7. [*Duration of agreement*] This agreement shall continue in force until ...., 19....; *provided, however,* that the same may be canceled by either party upon five (5) days' written notice to the other party. In the event of such cancellation, Standard shall have the right to refuse further orders and to cancel such portion of all unfilled orders as are in excess of five (5) days' average requirements of Dealer based upon shipments previously made to Dealer on orders given under this contract.

[*Binding effect of agreement*] This agreement shall be binding upon and inure to the benefit of the successors and assigns and/or the executors, administrators, and assigns of the respective parties; *provided, however,* it shall not be assignable by Dealer without the written consent of Standard.

[*Modification of agreement*] This agreement sets forth the entire agreement of the parties with respect to the subject matter embraced herein, and no modification or change shall be binding upon Standard unless in writing, signed by its President, one of its Vice-Presidents, or one of its Division Managers.

The Standard Oil Company (Ohio)

By ....

.... (*Dealer*)

....

TEAR OFF

Send one copy to Sales Accounting

Division Contract No. ....

Name of Dealer ....

Address .... City .... County ....

Division manager ....

Division ....

Salesman ....

Date contract effective .... Date contract expires ....

Credit limit ....

AMOUNT OF PURCHASES

Tires	*Tubes*	*Batteries*	*Accessories*
....	....	....	....

Sale of merchandise through brokers.—In some industries the term "broker" is used interchangeably with "selling agent" or "manufacturer's agent." In a stricter sense, however, a broker is not a selling agent or a manufacturer's agent, but a wholesale middleman whose function it is to bring together a buyer and a seller, and to assist them in consummating a sale. The broker acts for both parties to the sale, but he has no formal contract with either one; he is simply an intermediary. The contract between buyer and seller is generally evidenced by a broker's memorandum of sale, or by a standard form of contract, adopted by a trade association of which both buyer and seller are members, in the name of seller and buyer.

Conditional sales contracts.—Conditional sales contracts are used frequently in the sale of goods on the installment plan. Under these contracts the seller transfers possession of the goods to the buyer, but retains title thereto until the buyer has paid the entire purchase price and has fully performed his obligations under the contract. If the buyer fails to make the payments as they fall due, or otherwise defaults, the seller has the right to take back his goods. In most states laws have been passed requiring certain formalities in the execution of conditional sales contracts and compelling the seller to file or record the contract with some designated state official if he wishes to protect the reserved title to the goods as against third persons. Except in a few states that have adopted the Uniform Conditional Sales Act, these laws are not uniform, and they vary particularly with respect to the following:

1. *Signing of contract.*—In some states the signature of the buyer is sufficient; in others, the seller's signature is also required. Witnessing and acknowledgment of the signature may be necessary. Some states require a special affidavit of good faith to be attached.

2. *Copy to be filed or recorded.*—In some states the original instrument must be filed; in others, it is sufficient to file a copy. Some states require the contract to be spread on the record in full; this is known as "recording." In some states contracts for certain kinds of goods must be filed, while contracts for other goods require no filing.

3. *Time for filing or recording.*—In several states filing or recording within the period fixed by statute relates back to the date the contract was executed, giving the seller protection in his reserved title from the date the contract was entered into. In other states the seller is protected only against those who acquire rights in the property subsequent to the time of filing or recording.

4. *Period of effectiveness of record.*—In some jurisdictions provision is made limiting the effectiveness of the record to a period of years. Generally, renewal may be made by refiling the instrument prior to the expiration of the period.

5. *Place of filing or recording.*—Most states require the contract to be filed or recorded at the place where the buyer resides. In some states filing or recording is in a local office, such as the office of the town clerk; in others, in a county office. Strict compliance

with the governing statute is required to protect the seller in his reservation of title against third persons.

6. *Refiling upon removal of property.*—In some states, upon removal of the goods by the buyer to another county in the state, or upon removal from another state, the contract must be refiled within a certain time after the seller has received notice of the removal, otherwise the seller loses his reservation of title to the property as against creditors and purchasers.

7. *Risk of loss.*—In most states the risk of loss is placed on the buyer, since he is the person who has the use and enjoyment of the property. A few states, however, place the risk on the seller. The terms of the contract may, of course, determine who shall bear the risk of loss, regardless of statute.

8. *Recording satisfaction of the contract.*—Some of the statutes provide for entering a release or satisfaction when all the payments have been met.

Form of conditional sales contract.—The form of a conditional sales contract will vary slightly to conform to the statutory requirements of a particular state. Most conditional sales contracts, however, cover the following details (see Form No. 7):

1. Names and addresses of buyer and seller.
2. Description of merchandise purchased.
3. Reservation of title in seller.
4. Agreement of buyer to cover merchandise by insurance, to pay taxes and assessments, to make repairs, and so forth.
5. Provision for retaking by seller in event of defaults in payment of installments, upon removal or encumbrance of merchandise, upon insecurity of buyer, withdrawal of surety, and so on.
6. Assignability of contract.
7. Restriction against oral representations or agreements.

The conditional sales contract is generally accompanied by a promissory note, signed by the buyer, covering the price of the merchandise (see Form No. 9).

In some respects the conditional sales contract resembles a sale on consignment, a lease, and a bailment. In each of these, as in the conditional sale, possession of the property is given to another, but title is retained by the owner. The consignment sale (see Form No. 11) differs from the conditional sale in that the merchandise delivered to the consignee is intended for resale to a third person. A bailment, on the other hand, contemplates no sale whatever, but merely temporary surrender of possession and the performance of some service pertaining to the goods, after which they are to be returned to the owner. In a lease of goods (see Form No. 12), the owner merely grants possession to another for his use and enjoyment over a designated period on payment of a stipulated rental. Contracts that appear to involve consignments, leases, or bailments are generally construed by the courts as conditional sales agreements if the intent is to effect a sale. A seller cannot avoid the necessity of giving notice of his reserved title to the goods through filing or recording of the conditional sales contract by calling the contract a lease or bailment. Under the Uniform Conditional Sales Act, except in Pennsylvania, any contract for the bailment or lease of goods by which the bailee or lessee contracts to pay as compensation a sum substantially equivalent to the value of the goods, or by which it is agreed that the bailee or lessee is bound to become, or has the option of becoming, the owner of such goods upon full compliance with the terms of the contract is a conditional sale.

A conditional sales contract must also be distinguished from a chattel mortgage. In the chattel mortgage title is not reserved in the owner, but passes to the buyer upon the execution of the instrument. Upon failure to meet the obligations of the mortgage, the seller may regain title through foreclosure proceedings. A few states make no distinction between chattel mortgages and conditional sales, but consider all conditional sales as chattel mortgages, subject to the statutes applicable to such mortgages. Form No. 10 illustrates the typical chattel mortgage.

The C.O.D. sale, meaning "cash on delivery" or "collect on delivery," is not a conditional sale. Passing of title is not conditional in a C.O.D. sale, as it is in the conditional sale. It is merely payment which is made conditional on delivery, and, vice versa, delivery which is made conditional on payment. In the usual C.O.D. sale, title passes upon the making of the contract, and the risk of loss, which is normally an incident of title, falls on the buyer prior to delivery and payment, in the absence of a contrary intention.

FORM NO. 7

Conditional sale contract.

(1) PARTIES: Seller: .... Co., a .... corporation.

Buyer: ....

of ....
(City) (County) (State or Province)

(2) SUBJECT OF AGREEMENT: Seller agrees to sell, and buyer agrees to buy, machines under the conditions hereinafter set forth as follows:

Quantity	*Machine and Model*	*Serial No.*	*Price*
....	....	....	....
....	....	....	....
....	....	....	....

(3) TERMS: F. O. B. ...., ..., the unpaid price of each machine to be evidenced by a promissory note of even date herewith, payable on demand, which notes may be sold or discounted by the seller without waiver of any rights under this contract. Said notes are not payment but merely evidence of the said indebtedness to become due hereunder.

(4) POSSESSION OF PROPERTY: Buyer acknowledges receipt of machines and agrees not to mortgage or encumber same or remove same from the aforesaid state or province or to create or permit any liens or charges thereon, or to part with or to surrender possession of the same or any of the same except on bona fide sale thereof and payment of full purchase price to the seller herein. Buyer agrees to notify seller immediately in the event that machines or any of them are attached, replevined, or levied upon. If a petition in bankruptcy is filed by or against buyer, or if he becomes insolvent or makes an assignment for the benefit of creditors, or takes any action under any law, the operation of which would relieve him from his debts, then, at the option of seller, all of buyer's rights under this contract shall end, and seller shall be entitled to the immediate possession of said machines upon the surrender of buyer's obligations to pay the price thereof.

(5) RESERVATION OF TITLE: Both parties hereto agree that title to said machines shall remain in the seller until the full price thereof is paid, and all of the terms and conditions hereof have been fully complied

with. The parties hereto intend a contract of conditional sale and not a chattel mortgage in any sense of the word.

(6) Remedies on Default: Should buyer make any default in the matter of payments or otherwise, seller, at its option, may either:

(a) Without notice, declare the total amount of the price to be due and payable immediately; or

(b) Immediately repossess said machines, wherever found, with or without process of law (using all necessary force so to do, the buyer hereby waiving all action for trespass or damage thereby), and retain the same, and any and all payments previously made by buyer shall be retained by seller, buyer waiving and relinquishing all rights in any sums paid and in said machines, and seller shall be relieved from all obligations to transfer the same or any of the same; or

(c) Avail itself of the remedies for the enforcement of a seller's rights under a conditional sale agreement provided by the laws of the aforesaid state or province.

(7) Still Exhibit, etc.: Said machines shall be used only for a still exhibit, shall not be demonstrated or operated, except in necessary moving to or from railroad yards, or warehouse, to or from buyer's place of business, unless seller's written or telegraphic consent is first obtained. Buyer agrees to save seller harmless from all loss or damage of every kind to said machines or to the person or property of the buyer or of any third person, by reason of the use of any of said machines.

(8) No Reimbursement of Advances, etc.: Buyer shall not be entitled to any reimbursement on account of freight, insurance, warehousing, or storage charges, taxes, etc., said machines having been shipped at buyer's request upon the express understanding that said charges shall be paid and discharged by buyer without cost to seller. Buyer agrees to pay and discharge all taxes, liens, charges, and assessments that may be imposed on said machines in the aforesaid state or province.

(9) Attorney's Fees, Costs, etc.: If default is made in the payment of any purchase money note, or if seller shall engage an attorney to enforce collection, or to preserve or enforce its rights under this agreement, buyer agrees to reimburse seller for all reasonable legal expenses, attorney's fees, and court costs and expenses incurred by seller.

(10) Recaption: It is agreed and understood, but not in limitation of the above, that, in the event of the termination of the Agreement subsisting between the parties hereto, seller, at its option, shall, on demand, be entitled to redelivery of the possession of said machines.

(11) Any portion of this contract, including any of the provisions of paragraph 6 hereof, prohibited by law of any state or province, shall,

as to said state or province, be ineffective to the extent of such prohibition without invalidating the remaining provisions of the contract.

(12) INTERPRETATION: Both parties intend that the operation and construction of this contract shall be governed by the laws of the State of Illinois.

(13) This agreement is expressly made subject to all and singular the terms and provisions of the Agreement now subsisting between the parties hereto.

(14) ADDITIONAL CLAUSES:

(15) RECEIPT OF COPY: Buyer acknowledges receipt of a full, true, and correct copy of this agreement in ....
(State or Province)

Dated at ...., ..., this .... day of ...., 19.....

Seller: .... Co., a corporation

By ....

WITNESS FOR BUYER: Buyer: ....

.... By ....

AFFIDAVITS:

FORM NO. 8

Assignment to be used when conditional sale contract is assigned.

ASSIGNMENT

For valuable consideration, the receipt whereof is hereby acknowledged, the undersigned hereby sells, assigns, transfers, and sets over to .... Corporation, the within contract, and all right, title, and interest in and to the property therein described, and all rights and remedies under said contract, and grants authority either in assignee's own behalf or in undersigned's name to take all such proceedings, legal or otherwise, as undersigned might have taken, save for this assignment.

Dated ...., 19.... .... } Signature of Seller

Witness .... By ....
(Signature of Witness Other Than Seller)

FORM NO. 9

Note to accompany conditional sale contract.

$.............. ...., 19....
(City) (State) (Date)

For value received, undersigned promises to pay to the order of .... Corporation, the sum of $............... at the office of .... Corporation, ..., in (City) (State) .... monthly installments, the first .... installments to be for $............... each and the final installment to be for $..............., with interest after maturity on delinquent installments at the highest legal rate and attorney's fees of ten (10) per cent of the amount thereof if placed with an attorney for collection. The first installment is to become due and payable on the .... day of ...., 19.... and one installment on the .... day of each ensuing month thereafter until all installments are paid.

Default of any payment indicated thereon shall cause the entire balance to become immediately due and payable at the election of the holder hereof without notice. The makers and endorsers hereby severally waive presentment, demand, protest, and notice of protest and nonpayment.

....

By ....
(Owner, Officer, or Firm Member)

....
(Street Address of Maker)

FORM NO. 10

Chattel mortgage.

Know All Men by These Presents, that .... (Dealer) (hereinafter termed "Mortgagor"), for securing the payment of the indebtedness hereinafter mentioned and in consideration of the sum of One ($1.00) Dollar to Mortgagor duly paid by .... Corporation (hereinafter termed *"X"*), does hereby grant, bargain, sell, convey, and confirm unto said *X*, its successors and assigns, the following motor vehicle or vehicles:

Make	*Model*	*Serial Number*	*Motor Number*	*Amount*
			* TOTAL	

* Total must agree with amount of Note.

now located in Mortgagor's place of business at ...., complete with all standard catalogue attachments and equipment, said vehicle or vehicles and equipment hereinafter referred to collectively as "Chattel."

Said Chattel shall remain in the aforesaid place of business of the Mortgagor until the full satisfaction of this mortgage.

To Have and to Hold said Chattel unto *X*, its successors and assigns, forever. And the Mortgagor, for his or its executors, heirs, administrators, successors, and assigns, hereby covenants to and with *X*, its successors and assigns, that the Mortgagor is lawfully vested of title to and possessed of the said Chattel and any and all replacements thereof and additions thereto; that the same is free from all encumbrances, claims, and liens, and that Mortgagor, or its heirs, executors, administrators, successors, and assigns, whether by voluntary or involuntary act or by operation of law, will warrant and defend the same to *X*, its successors and assigns, against all claims and demands of all persons, firms, and corporations whomsoever and their respective heirs, successors, and assigns, whether by voluntary or involuntary act or by operation of law.

Provided, Nevertheless, that if the Mortgagor shall pay unto *X*, its successors and assigns, the sum of $.................... (this figure must correspond with total above), on the .... day of ...., 19...., evidenced by promissory note or acceptance of even date herewith, executed by Mortgagor to *X*, then this Mortgage shall be void, otherwise to remain in full force and effect.

And the Mortgagor, for himself or itself, and his or its heirs, executors, administrators, successors, and assigns, does covenant and agree to and with *X*, its successors and assigns, that, upon nonpayment of the debt hereby secured at the due date thereof, or in the event of the insolvency or suspension of the Mortgagor or the Mortgagor's cessation of business as a going concern, or in the event of a filing of a petition in bankruptcy by or against the Mortgagor, or in the event of the sequestration or attachment of any property in the possession of Mortgagor, or of the appointment of a receiver for the Mortgagor, or in the event of nonpayment of any other obligation of Mortgagor to *X*, or of any breach by Mortgagor of any of the terms of this instrument, or whenever *X* may deem the debt insecure, the debt herein described and all other debts due from the Mortgagor to *X* shall immediately become due and payable, and it shall be lawful for and the Mortgagor does hereby authorize and empower *X*, its successors and assigns, to enter with or without breaking any store, garage, warehouse, or other premises where said Chattel may be and to take and carry away the same and sell and dispose of the same at public or private sale, and the Mortgagor agrees to pay any deficiency remaining due after such sale, including the costs of repossession, storage, and sale, as well as fifteen (15) per cent of the unpaid balance as attorney's fees if any attorney is employed by *X* for such repossession or collection or for the enforcement of any of its rights hereunder. And until default be made in the payment of said sum of money, or until other default by Mortgagor, the Mortgagor shall remain and continue in the quiet and peaceable possession of said Chattel, but the Mortgagor (except upon written consent of *X* first obtained) shall neither sell, mortgage, rent, loan, nor transfer said Chattel nor permit the same to go out of his or its possession, nor secrete the same, nor use the same for any purpose other than exhibition purposes, until this mortgage has been satisfied. The Mortgagor further agrees to keep a separate account of all motor vehicles held by the Mortgagor under this or any like instrument and (if sold with the prior written consent of *X* for not less than the balance due under this mortgage, this mortgage shall be deemed satisfied) of the proceeds thereof when sold, to keep the proceeds of such sale duly earmarked and separate and apart from the Mortgagor's funds, to report any sale and remit the proceeds to *X* immediately after the same is made, and to furnish to it on demand a true and complete report for the preceding month. The Mortgagor will also permit *X*, or its duly accredited representative, to examine the books of the Mortgagor and the cars in its possession at all reasonable times during business hours.

The Mortgagor hereby irrevocably constitutes and appoints *X*, its officers, and the agents of *X* designated in writing by it, the true and lawful attorneys in fact of Mortgagor, from time to time to execute and deliver all such instruments as may be required to be executed by Mortgagor for any of the purposes of this mortgage or to carry out any of the covenants and agreements on the part of the Mortgagor herein contained, including the giving of such receipts and other instruments as may be required by any possessor or custodian of said Chattel in order that *X* may obtain possession thereof, and each such possessor or custodian is by these presents authorized to deliver possession of said Chattel to *X*, its said officers and agents, and to receive and accept any receipt therefor as binding upon Mortgagor; and no waiver of or change in the terms of this agreement or the said note shall be binding on *X* Corporation unless evidenced by a writing signed by an officer of said corporation.

The Mortgagor agrees, if required by law, to obtain certificates of title on Chattel covered by this mortgage, indicating a lien in favor of *X* for the amount of the debt hereby secured, and to make such application in connection therewith, or otherwise, as may be necessary to preserve or perfect the lien of *X* thereon.

X shall, during the entire time said Chattel is held hereunder, at its own expense keep the same insured against loss by fire and theft.

In Witness Whereof, the Mortgagor has executed this Chattel Mortgage the .... day of .... 19....

....

By .... (L. S.) } Signature of Dealer

Street Address .... City .... State ....

(Proper acknowledgment on reverse must be filled out)

....

$.................................. ....19....
(Total Amount of Note) (City) (State) (Date)

.... after date, I, we, or either of us, promise to pay to *X* Corpora-
(Maturity Date)

tion or order, ... Dollars, with interest from maturity at
(Total Amount of Note)

the highest lawful rate and, if allowed by law, fifteen (15) per cent of the principal and interest of this note as attorney's fees, if placed in the hands of an attorney for collection, and authority is given irrevocably to any attorney-at-law to appear for me in any court, and waive the issue and service of process and confess a judgment against me in favor of the holder hereof, for such amount as may appear to be unpaid hereon after maturity, together with costs and attorney's fees, and to release all errors and waive all right of appeal. Value received without relief under any exemption or insolvency law. The makers, endorsers, and guarantors hereby waive notice of nonpayment, protest, presentment and demand, and consent that without notice to and without releasing the liability of endorsers, the holder may elect any remedy and compound or release any rights against the maker.

Negotiable and payable at the office of ....

(Signature of Dealer)

X Corporation

By ....

This Note is secured by Chattel Mortgage.

FORM NO. 10A

Reverse side of Form No. 10.

ACKNOWLEDGMENT WHEN DEALER IS AN INDIVIDUAL

STATE OF ILLINIOS } ss.:
COUNTY OF ....

This Chattel Mortgage was acknowledged before me, by ...., this .... day of ...., 19.....

Witness my hand and official seal.

....
Notary Public

ACKNOWLEDGMENT WHEN DEALER IS A CORPORATION

STATE OF ILLINIOS } ss.:
COUNTY OF ....

This Chattel Mortgage was acknowledged before me, by ...., Mortgagor, by .... and
(Name of Corporation) (President or Vice-President)

.... personally known to me to be the .... Presi-
(Secretary)

dent and Secretary, respectively, of Mortgagor, pursuant to authorization of the Board of Directors of Mortgagor, this .... day of ...., 19.....

Witness my hand and official seal.

....
Notary Public

FORM NO. 11

Consignment contract.

This contract made this .... day of ...., 19...., between .... Company, a .... corporation, hereinafter known as "Consignor," and ...., hereinafter known as "Consignee," is to cover total consignment requirements of Consignee for the goods listed from time to time on riders referred to in paragraph 3 hereof, for a period of one year from date, such goods to be shipped by Consignor to Consignee and accepted by Consignee on a consignment basis for sale.

1. It is agreed that if, during the life of this contract, any .... should be shipped under the terms of this contract, Consignor guarantees only the standard quality of such .... and its adherence to published specifications of Consignor, if any. Recommendations of Consignor for use of the goods are based upon tests believed to be reliable, but Consignor makes no guaranty of the results to be obtained.

2. It is further agreed that Consignee assumes full responsibility and liability for compliance with Federal, State, and local regulations governing unloading, discharge, storage, handling, and use of the goods supplied by Consignor under this contract.

3. Remittances by Consignee to Consignor for consigned goods sold by Consignee shall be in accordance with the following prices:

See Rider Attached

4. Sale prices to be used by Consignee in selling the consigned goods under the provisions of this contract shall be furnished to Consignee from time to time.

5. Any tax or other Governmental charge upon the production, sale, or shipment of the goods consigned hereunder, now imposed by Federal, State, or local authorities or hereafter becoming effective within the period hereof, shall be added to the prices mentioned in section 3 hereof. Further, in the event of any increases in cost of labor, raw materials, fuel, or transportation, Consignor may make corresponding increases in the prices mentioned in section 3 hereof, and it is understood that consigned goods on hand at time of any change in such prices shall be subject to such change.

6. It is agreed that Consignee is to remain fully responsible to Consignor for the merchantable condition and quality of all consigned

goods in Consignee's hands, and that Consignee is also responsible to Consignor for the loss of any goods by theft, or otherwise, whether or not covered by insurance.

7. Consignee agrees to accept and sell said goods at Consignee's own cost and expense, including all local property taxes and ad valorem taxes and other State and local excise taxes, including sales taxes and use taxes, if any, imposed upon or in respect of the consigned goods or the sale thereof; and also agrees to report to Consignor once each week (last report each month to be made on the 21st inst. showing sales up to and including the 20th inst.) all sales of the consigned goods. Consigned goods sold by Consignee shall be invoiced to Consignee by Consignor once each month; said invoice to be issued on the basis of reports by Consignee of sales made up to and including the 20th inst., and Consignee shall remit to Consignor on the tenth of the month following the month in which such sales are made the total amount of such invoice covering said sales of consigned goods.

8. It is agreed that title to the consigned goods shall be and remain in Consignor until sold by Consignee in the general course of business, and that, in the event the above-described goods or any part thereof shall be sold upon open account, whether or not the indebtedness be evidenced by notes or other forms of written obligations, such open accounts, notes, or obligations shall be and remain the property of Consignor. Consignee further agrees to hold any and all such open accounts, notes, or obligations in trust for Consignor and to identify each and every such open account, note, or obligation by conspicuous notice upon the books of Consignee as the property of Consignor. Consignee further agrees that in the event any part of the above-described goods shall be sold for cash, the proceeds of each and every such sale shall be and remain the property of Consignor. Consignee further agrees to hold all proceeds of cash sales and all cash received in full or partial payment of any above-mentioned open account, note, or obligation, in trust for the use and benefit of Consignor until Consignee shall have remitted to Consignor the amount payable by Consignee to Consignor with respect to the sale or sales for which such open accounts, notes, obligations, or cash shall have been received as provided in paragraph 7 hereof.

9. Consignee agrees to comply at all times with Consignor's requirements in regard to the method of making reports, taking inventory, forwarding remittances, etc., and further agrees to release any or all of the above-mentioned consigned goods remaining unsold upon demand of Consignor, wholly free from any encumbrance or charge whatsoever, including taxes assessed and unpaid, and promptly to return same to

Consignor upon demand, Consignee paying all freight or express charges for return of same.

IN WITNESS WHEREOF, the parties have hereunto affixed their signatures on the day and year first above written.

.... Company

A .... Corporation

Consignor

....

Consignee

By ....

Accepted and countersigned at ...., ...

.... Company

By ....

A .... Corporation

By ....

FORM NO. 12

Lease agreement with option to purchase equipment leased.

LEASE AGREEMENT

This instrument of lease, WITNESSETH:

That the .... Company, a corporation, of ...., ..., the Lessor, in consideration of the rents and covenants hereinafter stipulated to be paid or performed by ....

(If a partnership, give name and address of each partner)

a ...., of ...., with principal place of busi-
(Corp.—Partnership—Individual)

ness located at ...., the Lessee, does hereby demise and lease unto said Lessee the following described personal property hereinafter referred to as equipment—to wit:

To have and to hold the same unto the said Lessee for and during a period of .... months, beginning on the day said equipment is shipped from the manufacturer's factory at ...., ..., or such other place as said equipment is located, yielding and paying therefor during the term aforesaid a monthly rental of $..............., payable in advance on the first day of each and every rental month, and the retention of said leased equipment for any period less than a month shall, for the purposes of payment of rental hereunder, be considered an entire month; that is to say, there shall be no holding of said leased equipment, so far as rental is concerned, for any period less than a full month, and rental months hereunder shall be for the period beginning on the day of shipment of said equipment from ...., ..., or such other place as said equipment is located, and the same day of each successive month thereafter for the full period of .... months.

Lessee shall have the option of extending the term of this lease for a further period of .... months, subject to all terms and conditions hereof, and the payment of rental for the extended term at the same monthly rate as provided to be paid monthly for the original term of this lease.

In addition to said rental herein provided to be paid by Lessee to Lessor, Lessee further agrees to pay, within five (5) days after receipt of invoice therefor, the freight on said leased equipment from its location at the time of the execution of this agreement to destination, and from said destination to ...., ..., the destination of said equipment to be the place where delivery of the same is made to Lessee herein pursuant to Lessee's instructions.

Lessor agrees to furnish one erector to supervise the assembling and starting of said equipment, which erector shall remain with Lessee a sufficient length of time to instruct Lessee's crew in the operation of said equipment, but said period of time shall in no event exceed fifteen (15) days.

Lessee agrees that, in the use of said equipment during the period of this lease, it is contemplated that it shall be used not to exceed eight (8) hours out of each day of twenty-four (24) hours, and should Lessee make use of said equipment in any one day of twenty-four (24) hours for more than eight (8) hours thereof, Lessee shall pay to Lessor an increase in rental in proportion thereto.

It is agreed that Lessee shall have the option at any time during the period of this lease to purchase said equipment at a price of $............... Lessor agrees that, upon the exercise of said option by Lessee for the purchase of said equipment, ninety (90) per cent of all rental payments hereunder that have been made will apply against said purchase price. Lessee agrees to pay balance due on said purchase price as follows:

Said option to purchase shall be exercised by Lessee in writing, which said exercise of said option shall be delivered to Lessor at its home office in ...., ...

Lessee shall not remove or in any manner alter any numbering, lettering, or insignia displayed on said equipment and shall see that said equipment is not subjected to careless or rough usage, and the same shall be kept in good repair and operating condition by Lessee.

Lessee shall indemnify Lessor against all loss, damage, expense, and penalty arising from any action on account of personal injury or damage to property occasioned by the operation, handling, or transportation of said leased equipment during the entire rental period.

The title to said equipment shall at all times vest in the Lessor unless transferred to Lessee through sale by written and duly executed bill of sale, and Lessee shall give to Lessor immediate notice in case said equipment is levied upon or from any cause becomes liable to seizure.

Lessee shall not sublet said leased equipment or assign or transfer any interest in this agreement without written consent of Lessor.

Lessee agrees to pay all expenses of unloading said equipment at destination and of loading said equipment for shipment back to Lessor in event of Lessee's not exercising his option of purchase herein contained, and to save Lessor harmless against any loss or damage to said property by fire, flood, explosion, theft, or otherwise from the time said equipment leaves the possession of Lessor until same is returned to the possession of Lessor, and including the time when said equipment is en route and in the custody of any common carrier or other transporter.

Lessee agrees to comply with all County, State, or Municipal laws governing the operation of said leased equipment and to reimburse Lessor for any taxes or assessments that may be levied against the same.

Lessee acknowledges the receipt of said leased equipment in good order and condition and agrees that no representations, agreement or warranty relating to this contract or to the equipment herein described has been made or is to be implied, except as stated herein, and further agrees that Lessor shall not be liable for consequential damages of any kind or nature from whatever cause arising.

Lessee agrees to pay or reimburse Lessor on return of the equipment to Lessor, for any breakage, shortage, or damage to said leased equipment beyond ordinary wear during the life of this agreement.

It is further understood and agreed that this agreement shall become effective only when and if it is accepted by Lessor at its home office in ...., ...

Upon failure of Lessee to make payment of any amount due hereunder within five (5) days after it shall have become due, or upon Lessee's failure to maintain and operate said equipment, or upon Lessee's violation of any provision of this agreement, Lessor may terminate the same upon written notice deposited in the mail and directed to Lessee's last-known place of residence, and take possession of said equipment, and for said purpose may enter upon the premises of Lessee without becoming liable for trespass and may thereafter recover all rental due, together with damages for injury to and all expense incurred in recovering and repossessing said equipment.

In Witness Whereof, the parties hereto have caused this instrument to be executed in duplicate originals, this .... day of ...., 19....

Lessor

By ....

....

Lessee

By ....

Attest:

....

.... } Witnesses as to
.... } ....Co.

.... } Witnesses as to
.... }

[*Here follows acknowledgment*]

3. MISCELLANEOUS CLAUSES IN SALES CONTRACTS

FORM NO. 13

Clause providing for passing of title on delivery.

Unless otherwise specified, the title to goods sold passes to the Buyer (subject to the right of stoppage in transitu):

(1) Upon delivery f.o.b. to carrier, consigned to Buyer, and thereafter goods are at Buyer's risk.

(2) Upon arrival of goods at destination and delivery to Buyer of bill of lading or of goods, in the case of goods to be delivered f.o.b. elsewhere than to carrier.

(3) Upon delivery of endorsed bill of lading or of goods, in the case of goods consigned to Seller's order.

(4) Upon the separation of the goods and holding subject to Buyer's order (the invoice to follow by due course of mail), in the case of goods to be held or if Buyer fails to give shipping instructions.

FORM NO. 14

Clause providing for delivery of merchandise in transit, upon receipt by seller.

It is understood that the merchandise sold by us to you under the terms of this contract is now in transit bound for New York, and to the best of our information and belief is due to arrive within two (2) to four (4) weeks from the date of this contract, and that the said merchandise is to be delivered to you when and if received by us.

FORM NO. 15

Clause providing for sale of merchandise on approval, and return if not satisfactory.

[*Note.—In a sale or return, title passes subject to the buyer s option to rescind and revest title. In the absence of provisions to the contrary, the exercise of the option rests in the pleasure of the buyer, but it will be effective only if accomplished within the time set and in the manner prescribed in the contract.*]

It is understood that the order for the material specified above is placed subject to sixty (60) days' trial, and that if the material is not satisfactory to the Purchaser, it may be returned by him within sixty (60) days from receipt thereof. No extension of said trial period shall be binding on the Seller unless authorized by it in writing. In the event that the material is not accepted, the Purchaser agrees to pack it properly and return it to the Seller, the Purchaser paying the Seller the cost of any and all damages to the said material by reason of fire, act of God, or any other agency, except damage due to reasonable wear and tear occurring between the time of receipt thereof by the Purchaser and the time said material is received again by the Seller at its plant in the City of ...., ...

FORM NO. 16

Clause providing for sale of merchandise on approval, and return if not satisfactory (an alternative form).

If said merchandise shall prove unsatisfactory to the Purchaser, he may return the same to the Seller within seven (7) days from the date hereof, and the Seller shall thereupon return on demand the consideration received therefor, whereupon this contract shall forthwith be canceled.

FORM NO. 17

Clause providing that agreement is not a sale but an agreement for future sale.

It is distinctly understood by and between the parties hereto that this agreement is not, and is not intended to be, a sale of the said instrument, but only an agreement for a future sale thereof, and that until the price of said instrument shall be fully paid as above provided for, and a bill of sale thereof duly executed and delivered by the said parties of the first part, the title to the said instrument shall continue to be and remain in them, the said parties of the first part, and not in the said party of the second part.

FORM NO. 18

Clause providing for acceptance of agreement within definite time.

This proposal, which will become a contract when signed by both parties as hereinafter specified, is made for acceptance within ....

days from date, after which time it may either be revised on request of the Purchaser or shall, at the option of the Contractor, become void.

FORM NO. 19

Clause relating to acceptance of orders.

All orders and sales contracts are subject to written approval and acceptance by an executive officer of The .... Corporation at ...., ..., and are not binding on The Corporation until and unless so approved. Unless otherwise therein specifically provided, orders so approved and accepted shall be for shipment within thirty days from date of order. The acceptance of orders constitutes a complete and binding contract which cannot be modified or cancelled without written consent of both parties, except that all orders are accepted subject to failure or delay in delivery caused by strikes, lockouts, or other labor disturbances, war, insurrection, riots, car shortages, accidents at the mill, embargo, fire, floods, storms, or other causes and circumstances beyond the control of The Corporation.

FORM NO. 20

Clause in sales order providing that time is of essence.

Time is of the essence of this order and, if delivery is not made in accordance with the time specified in this order, the Buyer may at its option either refuse to accept and pay for the material not delivered within the specified time or may accept the same, and such acceptance will not be construed as a waiver of the right of the purchaser to hold the Seller liable for such delay.

FORM NO. 21

Clause providing for proportionate reduction in deliveries upon reduction in production.

If Seller's normal production should be reduced, or shipment or delivery of rock interfered with, by reason of any of the causes provided for above, Seller may prorate its deliveries during the period of such interference, or such subnormal production, among the Purchasers with which it has outstanding contracts during such period and to plants of Seller, its subsidiaries and affiliates, proportionately to the amounts required to be delivered under such contracts, whether entered into before or after this contract and (in the case of amounts required for its own plants and those of its subsidiaries and affiliates) according to the average thirty (30) day consumption of Phosphate Rock in such plants during the next preceding six (6) full calendar months.

FORM NO. 22

Clause showing maximum and minimum quantity to be delivered monthly.

Seller shall not be required to deliver in any month more than the monthly quantity above specified, or if no monthly quantity is specified, more than the pro-rata amount of the maximum quantity provided for. In the event of failure of buyer to take stipulated or minimum pro-rata quantity in any month, such deliveries or parts thereof may, at seller's option, be cancelled or included in subsequent deliveries hereunder. Seller shall not be bound to tender delivery of any quantities of which buyer has not given shipping instructions.

FORM NO. 23

Clause relating to price decrease.

In the event of a price decrease, all unfilled orders on hand on the effective date of such price decrease, and accepted by The .... Corporation, will be invoiced at the new and lower prices, and shipments in transit will be invoiced at the revised prices, provided evidence is presented in the form of carrier's expense bill showing that shipments were actually in transit and had not been delivered when the price decrease became effective. Prices are not guaranteed against decline. Inventory adjustments will not be allowed.

FORM NO. 24

Clause providing for lowering of price upon proof of competitive offer.

Should the Buyer be able to give Seller written satisfactory evidence of a bona fide offer at a price lower than above, from other reliable source covering a similar article of equal strength and purity, under same terms and conditions as herein expressed, at any time during the life of this contract, Seller is to meet such lower price from month to month, or Buyer to be allowed to cover his requirements for such time at the lower price, subject to cancellation of corresponding quantity on contract.

FORM NO. 25

Clause relating to price increase.

In the event of a price increase, all unfilled orders on hand prior to the effective date of such increase, and accepted by The .... Corporation, including those in transit by mail or telegraph (postmark on envelope or filing time on telegram to govern), and calling for shipment at mill convenience within thirty (30) days (Sundays and holidays included) from the date of such orders, will be invoiced at the prices in effect prior to such price increase, provided the mill is able to ship such order within such thirty (30) day period; otherwise they will be invoiced at the advanced price or cancelled.

FORM NO. 26

Clause providing for revision of prices.

The Seller may from time to time after July 1, 19...., revise (up or down) the price stated in this contract, upon giving Buyer thirty (30) days' written notice of any such revision. Such revised price shall be paid on all material(s) shipped after such thirty (30) day period unless, in case of an increase in price, Buyer shall within said period give Seller written notice that it is unwilling to accept such revision. In the event Buyer shall give Seller such notice, then Seller shall have the right to terminate this contract by giving Buyer, within ten (10) days after receipt by Seller of Buyer's notice, written notice to that effect.

FORM NO. 27

Clause providing for periodical change in price on written notice.

The price in this contract is based upon Seller's present costs. If costs are increased because of present or future Federal or State legislation, Governmental ordinances, rules, orders, or licenses, or because of increases in cost of labor, raw materials, fuel, or transportation, Seller may make corresponding increases in price on March 31, June 30, September 30, or December 31, provided twenty (20) days' written notice to Buyer of such increase is given. If Buyer is unwilling to accept any such increase in price as computed by Seller, and so notifies Seller in writing prior to date such increase becomes effective, either party may terminate this contract upon ten (10) days' written notice to the other.

FORM NO. 28

Clause providing for changes and allowances for sacks used in packaging.

Cloth sacks bearing Seller brands, in which cement herein contracted for is packed, are the property of Seller and are for a period of ninety (90) days from the delivery by Seller of the said cement, leased by it to Buyer at a charge of ten (10¢) cents each, which charge is included in price of cement packed in cloth sacks, and which charge Buyer agrees to pay at the same time and on the same terms as payment for cement is made.

Buyer agrees, within ninety (90) days of delivery of the cement, to deliver to Seller, the owner, at its nearest plant, freight charges collect, as provided by railroad classifications and tariffs, properly bundled and so marked as to insure complete identification, the cloth sacks bearing Seller's brands, in which the said cement is packed, and Seller agrees to refund to Buyer ten (10¢) cents for each said cloth sack so delivered in good condition subject to its count and inspection, and to assume freight charges thereon. If for any reason freight charges (per railroad tariffs) are prepaid, they will be refunded by Seller upon presentation of Railroad Company's receipted freight bill or bill of lading.

For useless cloth sacks that have been wet, no refund will be made. Cloth sacks bearing other than Seller's brands will be held by Seller for thirty (30) days subject to Buyer's order.

In the event that any of the said empty cloth sacks bearing Seller's brands are sold or otherwise disposed of by Buyer to any person other than Seller, the owner, Buyer agrees to pay Seller, as liquidated damages, ten (10¢) cents for each cloth sack so sold or disposed of.

If, during the life of this contract, Seller shall change its present charge for the lease of cloth sacks, or the liquidated damages, or both, it is expressly agreed that the said amount or amounts in the preceding paragraphs shall be changed accordingly, and the gross price specified herein for cement packed in cloth sacks shall be changed in accordance with the change in charge for lease of cloth sacks.

Price on cement packed in paper bags includes the paper bags, which are not returnable. Shipments in paper bags are made at Buyer's risk of breakage and resultant loss of cement.

FORM NO. 29

Clause providing for additional payment if Sunday or holiday work is necessary.

Unless otherwise agreed, the equipment will be made and installed during the regular working hours of regular working days. If "overtime," holiday, or Sunday work is required, the Purchaser shall pay the difference or excess cost thereof over regular time, plus fifteen (15) per cent for supervision.

FORM NO. 30

Clause providing for forwarding of shipping documents.

It is understood and agreed that the Seller will send forward complete shipping documents, as specified on face of this order, within forty-eight (48) hours after the goods leave the Seller's works.

FORM NO. 31

Clause covering failure to furnish shipping instructions or specifications.

In the event the Purchaser fails to furnish complete specifications and instructions within the time specified in the contract, the Seller shall be entitled at its option to cancel such portion of the contract as may remain unexecuted, or to make shipments in accordance with the specifications and instructions that the Purchaser may have furnished for previous shipments on account of the same or a previous contract.

FORM NO. 32

Clause providing for storage and insurance.

Goods invoiced and held subject to Buyer's orders shall be at Buyer's risk, but covered by fire insurance effected by Sellers, in reputable companies.

FORM NO. 33

Clause providing for assumption by buyer of risk in use of merchandise.

Buyer assumes all risks and liability for results of use by Buyer of material delivered under this contract, including use by Buyer of such material in combination with other substances. Notice of any claims for defects in the quality of the material delivered hereunder shall be given within ten (10) days after arrival of said material. Failure to give such notice shall constitute a waiver by Buyer of all claims therefor.

FORM NO. 34

Clause restricting purchase to use and not resale.

Materials purchased under this contract are for consumption and use by Buyer, its controlled, affiliated, and/or subsidiary companies, and not for resale. In the event Buyer shall resell the material purchased under this contract, or any part thereof, Seller, at its option, without prejudice to any other lawful remedies, may terminate this contract.

FORM NO. 35

Clause restricting use because of war conditions.

In view of present world conditions, it is agreed that the goods covered by this contract are for buyer's consumption in the United States of America, and shall not be resold or exported.

FORM NO. 36

Clause covering price increase due to rise in freight rates, taxes or to government price-fixing.

The Seller, at its option, may cancel this agreement, if deliveries hereunder are interfered with by civil or military authorities, fires, strikes, accidents, or other causes beyond its control, either at its own works or those of its sources of supply, including shortage of crude oil or fuel, car shortage, and railroad embargoes or delays. In case of an advance in freight rates, the Seller shall have the right to cease further deliveries unless the Purchaser agrees to pay the additional rate of freight.

It is mutually understood and agreed that the purchase price herein specified shall be increased by the amount of any tax or charge that the Seller may, by any law, or by any order or action of civil or military authorities, be required to pay upon the subject matter of this contract, or on the transportation of same, or because of the sale covered by this contract; and the Seller may, at its option, terminate this contract unless the Purchaser shall pay such increase.

Seller may, from time to time, on thirty (30) days' written notice to Buyer, increase the contract prices provided for in the event of: (1) increases in costs, manufacturing or marketing, attributable to Federal and State laws and regulations; (2) increased taxes, State or Federal, or depreciation of the currency of the United States of America; and/or (3) a general advance by Seller in the price of such products to like purchasers; and/or to conform the prices of such products to any that may be fixed by Government action or within the range of those prescribed by Governmental action.

If any such increase is not acceptable to Buyer, Buyer shall immediately notify Seller, and, if prior to the effective date of such increase the parties cannot agree in respect thereof, Buyer may, on written notice given prior to such effective date, terminate this contract insofar as it applies to products in respect of which the parties cannot agree on the increased prices. Unless so terminated prior to such effective date, the increased prices shall govern thereafter, subject to further change as aforesaid. Between the time when any such notice is given and the effective date of change, Buyer shall not be permitted to purchase more than the average monthly quantities of such products purchased by Buyer hereunder prior to said notice.

FORM NO. 37

Clause providing for billing of taxes paid by seller.

Purchaser shall pay Seller amounts equivalent to any tax and/or duty (not included in the price or otherwise paid by Purchaser) now or hereafter imposed, directly or indirectly, by any domestic or foreign governmental authority or agency, and any increases in such tax or duty, on, in respect of, or measured by (1) this agreement, (2) the goods covered by this agreement or any material contained in such goods, and/or (3) the manufacture, sale, use, and/or other handling of said goods or material; and the Seller, upon payment of or liability for such tax or duty, shall bill Purchaser for, and the Purchaser shall pay the amount thereof.

FORM NO. 38

Clause excusing nondelivery in certain contingencies.

The Seller shall not be liable for any default or delay caused by any contingency beyond its control, or the control of its supplier or manufacturer, with whom it may contract to cover this sale, or the manufacturer who is to furnish these goods, preventing or interfering with Seller's making delivery, including war, restraints affecting shipping, or credit, strike, lockout, accident, nonarrival or delay of steamer or carrier, floods, droughts, short or reduced supply of raw material, or excessive cost thereof, or of production over contract basis, and any other contingency affecting Seller or such supplier or manufacturer. Seller may deliver ratably with reference to all its customers and also its contracts with suppliers or manufacturers.

FORM NO. 39

Clause providing for contingency of war embargo.

If, by reason of an embargo, the fuse parts and primer parts cannot be exported from the United States, or in the event of war terminating before all deliveries under contract are completed, the Buyer, at its option, may terminate the agreement; but in such event Buyer shall pay to Seller the unpaid purchase price of any fuse or primer parts then actually manufactured and accepted, and in addition thereto a sum sufficient to cover the actual net expenditures and outstanding obligations of Seller and its subsidiary companies made with respect to the portion of the orders undelivered at the time of such termination, including therein any net expenditures or obligations for plant, equipment, and material or services of skilled or other employees. To the extent, if any, that advance payments made under this contract may exceed the amount due Seller in case of such cancellation, such excess of advance payments shall be returned to Buyer.

For the purpose of this contract, the net expenditures shall be defined to mean any sum that the Seller shall have actually spent, and any obligation incurred after aggregating the salable or appraised value of any material or in the case of other expenditures and obligations such portion of the Seller's expenditures and obligations with respect to this contract as the unfulfilled portion of the orders at the time of cancellation bear to the total orders; it being understood that no expenditures shall be made in excess of the reasonable demands of this contract.

FORM NO. 40

Clause permitting suspension of deliveries in case of causes beyond the control of buyer or seller.

Deliveries may be suspended in case of war, riots, fire, explosion, flood, strike, lockout, injunction, inability to obtain fuel, power, raw materials, labor, containers, or transportation facilities, accident, breakage of machinery or apparatus, Governmental action, national defense requirements, or other causes beyond the control of either party, preventing the manufacture, shipment, or acceptance of a shipment of the article, or pending total or partial suspension of the manufacture of a product upon which the manufacture of the article of this contract is dependent. Any deliveries so suspended may, at the option of seller, be cancelled, or delivered at the same rate of delivery commencing after the period assigned to this contract, but seller shall in no way be liable for any loss caused by such postponement of delivery.

FORM NO. 41

Clause providing that agreement is subject to Governmental regulations.

This agreement is made subject to Governmental (foreign or domestic) regulations and restrictions on materials and labor entering into the manufacture of the products mentioned herein. And, if, under any Federal or State law, now or hereafter enacted, the Seller is required to pay a tax on sales or process stock, the price or prices to be paid by the Buyer shall be increased by the amount of such tax.

FORM NO. 42

Clause providing for rejections and claims.

The Buyer cannot reject the goods for delay in delivery unless he notifies the Seller within five (5) business days from receipt of bill of lading, or of invoice if goods are to be held. When contract calls for delivery in installments, the Buyer cannot cancel the contract for any default in any one or more installments not amounting to a substantial breach of contract, but may cancel or replace at Seller's expense any delivery that is delayed.

Buyer cannot reject goods for defects in quality or other like defaults (1) if he cuts or converts them, nor (2) unless he notifies Seller within ninety (90) days from receipt by him or at finishing works of goods not held, or within ninety (90) days after date of invoice if goods are invoiced and held; or (3) unless such defects amount to a substantial breach of contract.

Loss of right to reject does not deprive the Buyer of his right to claim damages, if any; but no recovery shall be had on any claim not made within one (1) year from receipt of goods or from date of invoice if goods are held.

FORM NO. 43

Clause in which seller agrees to defend patent infringement suits.

The Seller agrees that it shall, at its own expense, defend any suits that may be instituted by any party against the Purchaser for alleged infringement of any electrical or mechanical patents relating to the machinery furnished under this contract, provided the Purchaser shall have made all payments then due therefor and shall give to the Seller immediate notice in writing of the institution of such suits, and permitted the Seller, through its counsel, to defend the same, and shall give all needed information, assistance, and authority to enable the Seller so to do, and thereupon in case of final award of damages in such suit, the Seller will pay such award.

FORM NO. 44

Clause providing for effect of seller's nonfulfillment of contract.

That if the Seller shall fail, for reasons other than fires, strikes, breakdowns, labor difficulties, acts of carriers, or any causes beyond the control of the Seller, to make any shipment on or before the expiration of contract time of shipment when shipping instructions are received by the Seller at least fifteen (15) days before the expiration date of contract time of shipment, or shall fail, in case of an extension hereof, to make any shipment on or before the extended time of shipment when shipping instructions are received by the Seller at least fifteen (15) days before the expiration date of extended time of shipment, then the Buyer may, at its option, give written notice to the Seller that the Buyer elects to treat the Seller's failure to make shipment as a breach of this contract, and in case such notice is received by the Seller before actual shipment, the Seller shall be liable to the Buyer for breach of contract and shall pay to the Buyer on demand any loss to the Buyer represented by the difference between the contract price of the commodities to be shipped or delivered and the market price thereof at the time of Seller's breach (it being understood that the market price of said commodities at the time of Seller's breach is Seller's list price in effect at such time for said commodities delivered f.o.b. at the same point and with freight charges added at the same rate per cwt. as provided under the paragraph marked "Prices" on the front of this contract). In the event the Buyer does not elect to treat such failure on the part of the Seller as a breach of contract, by written notice received by the Seller at any time before shipment, this contract shall be extended so as to include the shipment and delivery when made; provided that the Buyer, however, shall be entitled to a credit of ten (10¢) cents per barrel on flour and fifty (50¢) cents per ton on feed for each thirty (30) day period of delay or fractional part thereof until shipment is made.

FORM NO. 45

Clause providing for effect of buyer's nonfulfillment of contract.

That if the Buyer shall fail to furnish, at least fifteen (15) days prior to the expiration of contract time of shipment, shipping instructions for shipment within contract time of shipment, or shall fail, in case of an extension hereof, to furnish, at least fifteen (15) days prior to the expiration of the extended time of shipment, shipping instructions for shipment within the extended time of shipment, or shall refuse to accept or pay for any shipment as specified herein, or fail to perform any of the other terms of this contract, then the Seller may, without notice to the Buyer (except in the case of a failure on the part of the Buyer to furnish shipping instructions at least fifteen (15) days prior to the expiration of contract time of shipment, and then in such case upon written notice that the Seller elects to hold the Buyer for breach of contract, mailed or telegraphed by the seller to the Buyer at the Buyer's address above given on or before the expiration date of contract time of shipment) either:

(1) Treat this contract as breached with the understanding that the Buyer shall pay to the Seller any prevailing difference, representing a loss to the Seller, between the contract price of the commodities specified in this contract and the market price thereof at the time of breach (it being understood that the market price of said commodities at the time of breach is Seller's list price in effect at such time for said commodities delivered f.o.b. at the same point and with freight charges added at the same rate per cwt. as provided under the paragraph marked "Prices" on the front of this contract), plus an entry charge of twenty-five (25¢) cents per barrel on flour and fifty (50¢) cents per ton on feed;

(2) Sell for the Buyer's account all commodities specified in this contract not previously accepted by the Buyer, and the Buyer shall pay to the Seller on demand all loss occurring from such sale together with any and all selling and other costs and expenses—it being understood that

such sale is to be made at the Seller's option at any time within sixty (60) days after such refusal or failure of the Buyer;

(3) Pursue such other remedies as the law may provide.

In case of the refusal or neglect by the Buyer to accept or pay for any shipment or delivery or to perform any of the terms of this contract or of any other contract with the Seller or in case the Buyer shall become insolvent or be adjudged bankrupt, thereupon the Seller may, at its option, declare this whole contract due, and treat such refusal or neglect by, or insolvency or bankruptcy of, the Buyer as a breach by Buyer of this entire contract as to all the commodities specified in this contract not accepted and paid for by the Buyer prior thereto, and in such event and with reference to the entire contract, the Seller shall be entitled immediately to avail itself of any of the rights and remedies in this contract specified.

FORM NO. 46

Clause providing for separability of shipments.

Each shipment or delivery shall constitute a separate sale, and the default in any shipment or delivery shall not vitiate the contract as to other shipments or deliveries.

FORM NO. 47

Clause restricting additional warranties or representations.

There are no representations, warranties, or conditions, express or implied, statutory or otherwise, except those herein contained, and no agreement collateral hereto shall be binding upon either party unless in writing hereupon or attached hereto, signed by the Purchaser and accepted by the Seller at its head office.

FORM NO. 48

Clause in which seller is not liable for failure to deliver because of Government priority regulations.

The Seller shall not be liable for failure or delay in delivery by reason of Governmental regulations, including the adoption of a preference or priority system for Government and other orders.

FORM NO. 49

Clause guaranteeing compliance with Federal Food, Drug and Cosmetic Act of June 25, 1939, and holding Seller harmless from liability for Buyer's misbranding.

Seller guarantees that none of the articles of food sold under this contract will be adulterated or misbranded within the meaning of the Federal Food, Drug and Cosmetic Act of June 25, 1939, and that such food will not be produced or shipped in violation of Section 404 or 301(d) of said Act; provided, however, that the Seller does not guarantee against such goods becoming adulterated or misbranded within the meaning of said Act after shipment, by reason of causes beyond Seller's control; and provided also that where goods are shipped under Buyer's labels, Seller's responsibility for misbranding shall be limited to that resulting from the failure of the product to conform to the label furnished by the Buyer. Buyer undertakes to save Seller harmless from any liability under said Act for any other type of misbranding arising out of the use of Buyer's labels, or for any liability under said Act for misbranding where Buyer insists upon the use of any label after Seller has questioned in writing the use of such label.

FORM NO. 50

Model guaranty form for use under Food, Drug and Cosmetic Act.*

To *(Name of person to whom guaranty is given)*
(Address) *Here type in your own name and address*

The undersigned (name of person giving guaranty) *type in here the name of the supplier* whose address is (address of person giving guaranty) *here type in the address of the supplier* hereby guarantees that no food, drug, device, or cosmetic constituting, or being part of, any shipment or other delivery now or hereafter made to you by the undersigned will, at the time of such shipment or delivery, be adulterated or misbranded within the meaning of the Federal Food, Drug and Cosmetic Act, or within the meaning of any applicable state or municipal law in which the definitions of adulteration and misbranding are substantially the same as those contained in the Federal Food, Drug and Cosmetic Act, as said Act and such laws are constituted and effective

* Form prepared by National Association of Chain Drug Stores.

at the time of such shipment or delivery, or will be an article which may not, under the provisions of section 404 or 505 of said Act, be introduced into interstate commerce.

This guaranty shall be a continuing guaranty and shall be binding upon the undersigned with respect to all foods, drugs, devices, and cosmetics shipped or delivered to you by the undersigned (including goods in transit), before the receipt by you of written notice of the revocation hereof.

....
(Signature of person giving guaranty)

Dated ....

Bills of sale.—A bill of sale is a writing evidencing the transfer of personal property from one person to another. The writing contains a direct statement of the transfer of title for a valuable consideration, describes the property transferred, and warrants that the seller owns the property, that it is free from encumbrances, and that he has the right to sell and transfer. A bill of sale is generally not necessary for the transfer of title to personal property, although it is always valuable evidence of the sale and of the identity of the merchandise sold. Some states do, however, require a bill of sale, duly acknowledged and recorded, upon the transfer of certain classes of property, such as motor vehicles, livestock, and so forth. An illustration of a bill of sale appears below in Form No. 51.

No. ....

FORM NO. 51

Bill of sale.

KNOW ALL MEN BY THESE PRESENTS, That the undersigned for valuable consideration does hereby grant, sell, transfer, and deliver unto .... (Grantee) the following described equipment:
(Purchaser)

....

....

To have and to hold all and singular the said goods and chattels to said Grantee, his successors and assigns. The undersigned covenants with said Grantee that undersigned is the lawful owner of said chattels; that they are free from all encumbrances; that undersigned has a good right to sell the same; that undersigned will warrant and defend same against the lawful claims and demands of all persons.

WITNESS, the hand and seal of the seller, this .... day of ...., 19.....

Witness .... (L.S.)
(Seller)

4. CONTRACTS APPOINTING AGENTS FOR SALE OF MERCHANDISE

Agency contracts in general.—A person who produces, manufactures, or otherwise owns or possesses goods for sale may, instead of selling direct to wholesalers, retailers, or consumers, desire to effect the sale and distribution of his merchandise through agents. These agents may be appointed orally, by letter, or under formal written contracts, which vary in their essential terms in the following respects:

1. *Payment of commissions.*—The usual agency arrangement is to ship the goods to the agent on consignment, to be sold by the agent at price schedules fixed by the manufacturer (see Form No. 52). The manufacturer retains title in the goods until they are actually sold. The agent is compensated by payment of commission at a rate fixed in the agency contract (see Form No. 53), or in some instances by payment of the difference between the value of the sales made through him and the manufacturer's list prices, less a discount (see Form No. 52). The agency agreement may specify the rate of commission and periods in which it is to be settled on direct sales and on business reaching the principal through other agents or from customers direct. Or it may provide that commissions shall be paid only on orders which have been accepted by principals, have been shipped and paid for, less any deductions made by customers, and that no order taken after the expiration of the agreement is to be subject to payment of commissions.

2. *Nature and quantity of product to be distributed.*—The lines that the agent is to sell should be clearly described. An agency

contract may fix the minimum amount of yearly sales that the agent is required to negotiate, or it may fix both the minimum and the maximum amount of his sales (see Form No. 53).

3. *Extent of territory.*—The agent may be limited in respect to the territory in which he is to operate (see Form No. 55), or he may be allowed, under the terms of the contract, to sell anywhere and everywhere (see Form No. 53). In some instances the manufacturer may find it advisable to grant to the agent the exclusive right to sell and distribute the product within a designated territory, under a so-called "exclusive agency agreement" (see Form No. 54).

4. *Duration of agency.*—The term of the agency may be unlimited (see Form No. 55) or it may be fixed (see Form No. 53). The contract also generally contains specific provisions for termination prior to expiration of the term under certain contingencies. If the agency covers seasonal goods, the seller should fix the date for termination so that he can cancel the agreement some time before a new season starts, thus avoiding cancellation in the middle of the selling season. It is not uncommon to provide that the manufacturer may cancel the agreement, upon written notice to the agent, in the event of:

(*a*) Insolvency, bankruptcy, or other financial difficulty of the agent.

(*b*) Failure of the agent to conduct the business of the agency in a manner satisfactory to the manufacturer.

(*c*) Failure of the agent to perform the terms and conditions of the agreement.

Some agency contracts provide for termination at any time either by the manufacturer or by the agent, upon the giving of a designated amount of notice of intention to do so, with the proviso that orders accepted prior thereto shall be filled (see Form No. 54).

5. *Restriction against representing others.*—Many agency agreements contain a clause providing that the representative shall not represent, or be directly or indirectly in any way interested in the business of competing lines without the principal's knowledge. The agent is also required to impose the same condition on any subagent whom he may appoint.

6. *Nontransferability of agency.*—The agreement may provide that it is "personal," and that it cannot be transmitted by the agent to any other party.

7. *Sales assistance by principal.*—The principal may be required to furnish advertising matter, information, and samples, free. He may also be allowed to send his own salesmen into the agent's territory to promote sales. The agent, however, is to receive commissions on sales in the territory as provided in the agreement.

8. *Restriction against involving principal in obligations.*—The agency agreement may include a provision forbidding the agent to involve the principal in any obligations beyond those fixed in the agreement, or to accept payments from customers for account of the principal, unless specially authorized by the principal.

9. *Disputes.*—The agreement may be made subject to arbitration.

FORM NO. 52

Agreement appointing agent to sell specific product for indefinite period; product to be shipped to agent on consignment and sold at price schedules fixed by manufacturer; no specific territory designated.

[*Parties*] .... Company, a .... corporation (hereinafter called the "Manufacturer"), through its .... Branch, with office at ...., hereby appoints ...., of .... (Street), ... (City), ... (State), having branches at No. ...., ... (Street), ... (City), ... (State), and No. ...., ... (Street), ... (City), ... (State) (hereinafter called the "Agent"), an Agent to sell, for it, ... [*here insert name of product*], at price schedules of the Manufacturer in effect at the date hereof (a copy of which has been delivered to, and receipt of which is hereby acknowledged by, the Agent) or any revised schedule that may become effective during the life of this contract, upon the terms and subject to the conditions herein set forth; and said Agent hereby accepts the appointment and agrees to comply with said terms and to perform all conditions hereof:

1. [*Term of agency*] The agency hereby created shall remain in force until terminated as herein provided.

2. [*Maintenance of stock*] The Manufacturer agrees to maintain on consignment in the custody of the Agent, to be disposed of as herein provided, a stock of .... All of the .... in such

consigned stock shall be and remain the property of the Manufacturer until the .... is sold, and the proceeds of all .... sold shall be held in trust for the benefit and for the account of the Manufacturer until fully accounted for as hereinafter provided. The sizes, types, and quantity of .... and the length of time it shall remain in stock are to be at all times determined by the Manufacturer; but the intent is to maintain the stock on an average basis of approximately the normal requirements of the Agent for a reasonable period. No liability of any nature is assumed or incurred by the Manufacturer in the performance of this contract because of its inability to supply .... required by the Agent, arising from circumstances beyond the Manufacturer's reasonable control.

[*Storage and transportation*] All .... shipped direct to the Agent, until it is sold or distributed in accordance with the Agent's authority hereunder, shall be stored, housed, and displayed for sale only in the Agent's regular place or places of business specified above, and in such manner as to afford ready inspection and identification by the Manufacturer, and any duly authorized representative of the Manufacturer shall have access at all times during business hours to the place or places in which said .... is stored. The Agent shall pay all expenses in the storage, cartage, transportation, handling, sale, and distribution of .... hereunder, and all expenses incident thereto and to the accounting therefor and to the collection of accounts created.

[*Taxes*] The Agent shall pay all taxes, excises, and charges, which are now, or may hereafter be, levied, imposed, or charged (whether by Federal, State, Municipal, or other public authority), with respect to .... sold by the Agent hereunder. The Agent shall make all reports required by the public authorities with respect to such sales of .... When authorized by the law imposing such tax, excise, or charge, the Agent may, at his option, increase the price of .... to the purchaser by an amount equal to such tax-excise or charge.

[*Accounts and records*] The Agent shall return to the Manufacturer at any time when directed by it all or any part of the said consigned stock that has not been sold. The Agent shall keep account books and records giving complete information covering all of his transactions in connection with the sale and distribution of the Manufacturer's ...., and such books, records, and copies of invoices shall be open at all times during business hours to the inspection of any duly authorized representative of the Manufacturer.

3. [*Price schedules*] The Agent is hereby authorized to sell from said stock to any dealer or consumer .... at the schedule of prices as provided.

The Agent has no authority to sell or transfer or in any way dispose of such ...., except as herein expressly provided. The Agent has no authority to accept orders for or commit the Manufacturer to the sale or delivery of .... in excess of the unsold stock at the time in his custody.

Schedules pertaining to prices, discounts, terms, and conditions of sale will be supplied Agents, each and all of which are subject to change by the Manufacturer from time to time. All sales and quotations shall be made only at such prices, upon such terms, and under such conditions as may be established by the Manufacturer from time to time, and the Agent shall at all times observe the Manufacturer's sales policy, as may be determined by said Manufacturer.

4. [*Reports*] The Agent shall render to the Manufacturer, not later than the second (2nd) day of every month, on forms provided by the Manufacturer, a complete itemized report or inventory of all of the Manufacturer's .... on hand at the close of business on the last day of the preceding calendar month, and shall render within fifteen (15) days after the termination of this appointment a similar report of all such .... on hand at the date of such termination.

5. [*Remittances*] The Agent shall remit to the Manufacturer, not later than the fifteenth (15th) day of each month, an amount equal to the total sales value of all .... sold by said Agent during the preceding calendar month, less the compensation allowed him as provided in Paragraph 7 below. At the time of rendering his inventory report, the Agent shall pay the Manufacturer for all .... lost, missing from, or damaged in the aforesaid stock in his custody.

6. [*Change in date for reports and remittances*] The Agent agrees that, upon notice from the Manufacturer, specifying dates other than those specified herein for forwarding reports and remittances, he will promptly thereafter forward said reports and remittances on such changed dates.

7. [*Compensation of agent*] As compensation for the performance of his obligations hereunder, the Agent shall be allowed the difference between (*a*) the total value of his sales and (*b*) the Manufacturer's list price less discount of .... per cent.

If all reports have been forwarded as required in this contract of appointment, and if remittance is made not later than the fifteenth (15th) day of each month covering in full for all .... sold during the preceding calendar month by this agent, whether or not all accounts for such sales may have been collected, such remittance shall be subject to two (2) per cent discount.

The Manufacturer reserves the right, at any time during the term of this appointment, to change any or all rates or bases of compensation of the Agent upon written notice, which revised rates or bases of compensation become effective upon issuance of said notice.

8. [*Right to terminate agency*] If the Agent shall be or become insolvent, or shall fail to make any report or remittance herein required to be made, or shall fail to conduct the business of the agency to the satisfaction of the Manufacturer, or shall fail to observe or perform any of the other provisions, terms, or conditions herein contained on the part of the Agent to be observed or performed, or if the Agent shall become involved in any financial difficulty that in the opinion of the Manufacturer may impair the Agent's ability properly to conduct the business of the agency, then and in any such case the Manufacturer may cancel and terminate the agency hereby created by notice in writing to the Agent. This agency appointment is personal in its character, and the Manufacturer reserves the right to cancel the agency in the event of the transfer of the Agent's business or the control thereof to parties other than those now in control. This appointment is not assignable by the Agent without the written consent of the Manufacturer.

Either party to this agreement, by written notice to the other, may at any time terminate the agency hereby created.

The termination of this agency for any reason shall be without prejudice to the rights of the Manufacturer against the Agent, and shall not relieve the Agent of any of his obligations and guaranties hereunder. Immediately upon any such termination, the Agent shall deliver to the Manufacturer all .... consigned hereunder that remains unsold, and shall fully perform all obligations of the Agent that then remain unfulfilled.

9. [*Signature of manufacturer*] This appointment shall not be binding on the Manufacturer until signed for the Manufacturer by its duly authorized representative. None of the terms of this appointment shall be deemed to have been waived by the Manufacturer unless such waiver is in writing, signed by said duly authorized representative.

10. This appointment applies only to .... [*specify product*].

ACCEPTED:

.... Company

......................, 19.... By ....

.... Agent

By ....

FORM NO. 53

Agreement appointing agent to distribute specific products for a designated period, in unlimited territory; minimum and maximum amount of purchases to be made during term of agency fixed; agent to assume financial responsibility for drafts on shipments to agent's customers.

Date ...., 19...

Agreement between .... Company, ..., New York, N. Y. (hereinafter called "Company"), and .... (hereinafter called "Distributor").

.... is hereby appointed Company's distributor for the purpose of selling and distributing the hereinafter-named products for the period between the date of this agreement and ...., 19.....

In consideration of the above agreement and in consideration of the compensation to be paid by Company to Distributor, as hereinafter set forth, Distributor agrees:

1. To purchase at prices hereinafter set forth and distribute the following specified minimum amounts of the indicated products of Company, and Distributor may order out, before the specified expiration date of this agreement, up to the following specified maximum amounts in tons of two thousand (2,000) pounds each. Upon mutual agreement, the maximum quantities may be increased without drawing a new agreement:

.... tons of .... tons of ....
.... " " .... " " ....

2. Actively to solicit business on the above-described products and to put forth during the term of this agreement sales efforts best calculated to produce a maximum sale of said products and to exercise at all times his or its influence to promote goodwill toward the Company and its products.

3. To accept, on sight draft order notify bill of lading basis, all shipments of the products covered by this agreement on bona fide orders submitted to Company by Distributor. All shipments made to Distributor's customers as hereinafter provided shall also be on sight draft order notify bill of lading basis.

4. To assume full financial responsibility for all drafts covering shipments made by Company to consignees other than Distributor in all

cases in which such shipments are requested by Distributor and made by Company, as hereinafter provided.

In consideration of the above agreements on the part of Distributor, Company agrees:

1. To make shipments against the minimum and up to the maximum tonnage called for by this agreement, either direct to Distributor or to Distributor's customer or customers upon Distributor's request.

2. To allow Distributor a commission of .... per ton on the prices hereinafter set forth.

3. To deduct all commissions from the face of drafts and invoices covering shipments made direct to Distributor.

4. To pay Distributor by check and as a separate item, during the month following the date of shipment, commission on all shipments made to Distributor's customer or customers at Distributor's request.

5. To co-operate fully with Distributor at all times and to render such assistance as Company deems necessary to obtain a maximum tonnage in Distributor's locality.

It is mutually understood that the prices on the products covered hereby for the season 19....–19.... shall be as follows:

.........................., $............... per ton ...., $............... per ton
.........................., $............... " " ...., $............... " "

The above prices shall be on a delivered basis for shipment in minimum carload lots. On shipments of less-than-minimum-carload lots, the difference between the existing carload and less-than-carload rates of freight between point of shipment and destination shall be added to the carload price for the products in question. Company reserves the right to readjust prices at any time during the season to conform to market conditions after due notification has been sent to Distributor. In the event that such readjustment is made, Distributor's commission shall remain the same.

Shipment: (Indicate amount and material).

Special Instructions:

The Company reserves the right to route shipments.

Any tax or other Governmental charge upon the production and/or sale and/or shipment of the materials hereby covered, imposed by the Federal, State, or Municipal authorities or any Governmental authority of any foreign country, and hereafter becoming effective within the life of this agreement, shall be added to the price hereinabove provided for the respective products, after the deduction of the commission, and shall be paid by Distributor.

Failure of Distributor to take, or of Company to make, any one or more deliveries when due, if occasioned by war, fire, flood, embargo, car shortage, accident, explosion, expropriation of plant or product in whole or in part by Federal or State authority or other cause, whether of the same or a different nature, beyond the control of the parties hereto, or by strike, lockout, or other labor trouble interfering with the production, transportation, or consumption of the goods herein described, or with the supply of raw material from which said goods are manufactured, shall not affect the remainder of this agreement or subject the party so failing to any liability to the other because thereof, but at Company's option the contract period shall be extended pro tanto, and the delivery so omitted shall be made during the period of such extension.

Each party shall have the right to terminate this agreement in its entirety at any time upon giving to the other thirty (30) days' written notice by registered mail of its intention so to do. Notwithstanding any such termination, any and all orders accepted by Company prior to the effective date thereof shall be filled by Company and accepted by Distributor in accordance with the terms hereinabove set forth.

ACCEPTED:	.... Company
....	.... *Representative*
By	APPROVED:
Address	....
Date	*Director of Sales*

Exclusive agency contracts.—An exclusive agency contract is an agreement by which a manufacturer gives to a distributor, dealer, or agent the exclusive right to sell the manufacturer's products in a designated territory, the agent, in turn, agreeing to push sales in that territory but not to sell outside of it. The validity of such contracts has now been generally established by the decisions of the courts. While the exclusive agency is always based on a definite understanding, the agreement need not be a formal one. It may be oral; it may be embodied in a letter; or it may be incorporated in a formal written document. The formal contract usually contains provisions with respect to the following:

1. *Selling rights.*—The exclusive agency contract must give the agent a market that is wholly or partly his, exclusively. The manufacturer may give to the agent either:

(*a*) Full exclusive sales rights, agreeing not to sell the article or line to any other jobber in the territory, or to any other dealer in the local market.

(*b*) Limited exclusive sales rights, agreeing not to appoint more than a certain number of agents, or not to sell the article or line to other dealers within a certain radius of the dealer's place of business.

Metropolitan agents are sometimes given joint exclusive rights; that is, the agents in the city are limited in number, but they may sell anywhere in the city. The manufacturer may reserve the right to sell direct to special customers, such as the United States Government, State, County, and Municipal bodies, and to certain classes of trade, such as consumers who purchase for use and not for resale.

2. *Territory.*—The boundaries within which the agent is to have exclusive operation are clearly fixed in the agreement. This territory is generally large enough to induce the agent to push the product. The solicitation of business outside of the fixed territory is prohibited. The agent is specifically enjoined from soliciting business in territory belonging to other agents or assigned to branch offices of the manufacturer.

3. *Minimum quota of purchases.*—Some exclusive agency contracts fix a minimum amount that the agent is required to sell within a year in order to retain his exclusive agency. The quota may be based on the population in the territory, on the amount sold by competitors in the same territory, and so forth, and depends largely on the manufacturer's judgment and past experience. The total amount that the agent is to buy during the year may also be fixed in the exclusive agency contract.

4. *Maintenance of stock.*—The agent generally agrees to maintain a stock of the manufacturer's product which will adequately represent the line that he is to sell. Generally the amount of stock is a fixed percentage of the quantity that the agent is required to dispose of within a fixed period.

5. *Purchase price from manufacturer.*—Some manufacturers sell goods to their agents on a consignment basis; others make outright sales to the agents. The agency contract may include a price schedule, fixing the price from the manufacturer to the agent according to the quantity of the product purchased, or it may indi-

cate that the price is determined by a schedule of discounts issued by the manufacturer.

6. *Resale price by agent.*—In the case of trade-marked, copyrighted, or otherwise identified products, the exclusive agency contract may include a schedule of prices at which the product is to be resold. In thus seeking to maintain the resale price, the manufacturer should be careful to consider the State and Federal antitrust laws as well as the laws permitting resale price maintenance. This subject is treated further on page 697.

7. *Agreement not to sell competing lines.*—Under some agency contracts the agent is required merely to push the product for which he is granted an exclusive agency. Under other contracts, however, the agent agrees to handle the manufacturer's products exclusively. The question has been presented to the courts as to whether such a provision violates the Clayton Act, Section 3 of which provides that it shall be unlawful for a person to make a contract for sale of goods on the agreement that the purchaser shall not deal in the goods of a competitor, where the effect is substantially to lessen competition or where it tends to create a monopoly. The rule is now fairly well established that an exclusive agency agreement does not necessarily restrain competition or tend to create a monopoly in violation of the antitrust laws. An agreement by the agent not to sell the product of some other manufacturer does not stifle competition, for other dealers may sell other products.

8. *Duration of agency.*—Many exclusive agency contracts do not definitely fix their duration. Where the period is fixed, it usually runs for the term of one year, with privilege on the part of the manufacturer to renew if the agency has proved satisfactory. Some contracts may provide for termination:

(*a*) Upon the expiration of a fixed period of time.
(*b*) By the manufacturer at will upon written notice to the agent.
(*c*) By the manufacturer upon a specified number of days' notice to the agent.
(*d*) Immediately by either party upon violation of the terms of the contract.

FORM NO. 54

Agreement appointing exclusive agent.

[*Note.—This form appeared in a study and report of exclusive agencies, made by the New York University Graduate School of Business Administration.*]

THIS AGREEMENT, entered into this .... day of ...., between the .... Motor Truck Company, an Ohio corporation, to be known hereinafter as the "Manufacturer," and ...., to be known hereinafter as the "Distributor," WITNESSETH:

THE PARTIES HERETO MUTUALLY AGREE AS FOLLOWS:

TERRITORY. The Manufacturer grants to the Distributor the exclusive right to sell .... Motor Trucks and repair parts for .... Motor Trucks in the following described territory:

SCHEDULE. (A) The Distributor agrees to purchase and accept from the Manufacturer, and the Manufacturer agrees to sell and deliver to the Distributor, f.o.b. the Manufacturer's factory, the .... Motor Trucks specified for delivery in the yearly schedule of purchases, which will be executed by the parties hereto, and which will refer to this agreement, and which, when so executed, shall be attached to and become a part of this agreement and constitute subparagraph (B) of this paragraph, entitled "Schedule."

(C) It is mutually understood and agreed that no shipments will be made by the Manufacturer to the Distributor except upon individual shipping orders of the Distributor, and that no orders for such .... Motor Trucks shall be binding upon the Manufacturer unless accepted in writing, but, when so accepted, such orders shall become a part of this agreement.

ORDERS. The Distributor agrees that he will furnish the Manufacturer with specific shipping orders at least sixty (60) days prior to the shipping dates, and further agrees that such shipping orders are not subject to cancellation after they have been accepted by the Manufacturer.

PRICES. The Manufacturer may, without notice and prior to the effective date thereof, make such changes in the list price or prices, discounts, and allowances on any or all .... Motor Trucks or .... Motor Truck repair parts as the

Manufacturer may deem advisable, provided that, in case of any change, the Manufacturer shall endeavor to give notice thereof to the Distributor in advance.

Terms of Payment. The Manufacturer will ship .... Motor Trucks to the Distributor with sight draft against bill of lading attached, and the Distributor shall pay such drafts with exchange upon presentation. Upon failure to do so, the Distributor agrees to pay interest thereon at the rate of six (6) per cent per annum from date of presentation, together with demurrage and storage charges caused by the failure of the Distributor to pay such drafts promptly. It is further agreed that, in the event the Distributor fails to pay such drafts within fifteen (15) days after the arrival of shipment at destination, the Manufacturer shall have the option to make such disposition of the shipment as it may see fit, reserving its rights to reimburse itself as provided in subparagraph "B" of the paragraph entitled "Deposits." The Manufacturer's responsibility due to shortage, loss, damage, or otherwise ceases upon delivery to the transportation company or to the nominee of the Distributor, but this delivery shall not constitute a passing of title from the Manufacturer to the Distributor until the trucks have been fully paid for by the Distributor.

Discounts. (A) The Distributor agrees, in the manner provided above, to pay the Manufacturer, for the .... Motor Trucks referred to above, an amount equal to the current list prices of such .... Motor Trucks as the same may be established by the Manufacturer, less such discounts and allowances as may be in effect at the time.

(B) All prices are f.o.b. the Manufacturer's factory.

Government Taxes. The Distributor agrees to repay to the Manufacturer, as far as he may be permitted by law, any sum or sums that the Manufacturer may be required to pay directly to the United States Government, or to any other duly constituted government, in the form of excise taxes upon .... Motor Trucks and .... Motor Truck repair parts sold by the Manufacturer to the Distributor. Said sums shall be added to the purchase price of such motor trucks and such motor truck repair parts and shall be payable by the Distributor at the same time and in the same manner as the purchase price.

Service. (A) The exclusive selling rights of .... Motor Trucks and .... Motor Truck repair parts in the territory as set forth above are granted to the Distributor in consideration that prompt and efficient service be given by the Distributor in connection with .... Motor Trucks in said territory, whether or not sold by him. In order to maintain this service, the Distributor agrees to carry an adequate stock of repair parts. In order to obtain the maximum amount of business in the territory mentioned above, the Distributor agrees to maintain and have maintained for demonstration and show purposes sufficient .... Motor Trucks of current manufacture to carry out properly the work of sales promotion throughout his entire territory.

(B) All .... Motor Trucks and .... Motor Truck repair parts carry the Manufacturer's standard warranty and shall be sold by the Distributor under said standard warranty.

(C) The Distributor agrees, in the event of his returning to the Manufactor for credit any .... Motor Truck repair parts, whether claimed by him to be defective, or otherwise, he will in any event return said parts, transportation charges prepaid, subject to examination and inspection by the Manufacturer. The decision of the Manufacturer as to what credit, if any, shall be extended the Distributor on such parts shall be final and conclusive.

(D) The Distributor agrees that, from amounts due by him to the Manufacturer, he will make no deduction on account of parts returned or allowances claimed until after receipt from the Manufacturer of credit memorandum therefor.

(E) To facilitate and expedite the adjustment of claims for shortages, the Distributor agrees to make claim within ten (10) days after receipt of shipment. The Manufacturer's responsibility due to shortage, loss, damage, or otherwise ceases upon delivery to the transportation company, or to the nominee of the Distributor, but this delivery shall not constitute a passing of title from the Manufacturer to the Distributor until the parts have been fully paid for by the Distributor.

(F) The Distributor further agrees that all .... Motor Truck repair parts returned by the Distributor to the Manufacturer shall be considered abandoned unless the Manufacturer shall receive from the Distributor, within ten (10) days after receipt of such parts, full instructions as to the disposition thereof, and the Manufacturer may make such disposition as it may choose of all such parts returned without such instructions within ten (10) days after receipt, and shall not be liable to the Distributor or any other person therefor.

(G) All claims for damages should be made by the Distributor direct to the transportation company.

(H) The Distributor's purchases of .... Motor Truck repair parts shall be billed to the Distributor and be paid by him at the current list price of such repair parts as may be established from time to time, less a discount of .... per cent, plus additional discount for cash in .... days. The Distributor hereby agrees that all accounts with the Manufacturer shall be settled promptly by him in accordance with the usual terms of the Manufacturer.

National Accounts. (A) The Distributor agrees that he will waive all interest and commission, except as hereinafter provided, in sales to and sales made by any and all Departments of the United States Government and of corporations and individuals whose use of trucks (in the judgment of the Manufacturer) is national in scope, the right to make such sales being reserved. The Manufacturer agrees, however, that in the making of such sales, wherein a .... Motor Truck sold to the United States Government or to any corporation or individual classed by the Manufacturer as national is used in the territory allotted to the Distributor, that a certain proportion of the discount shall be credited to the Distributor. The amount of this commission shall be decided by the Manufacturer and will be credited only to the Distributor's Account after the Distributor has reported to the Manufacturer the delivery of a new .... Motor Truck in the Distributor's territory; such report shall include description and specifications of vehicle, motor number, chassis number, and proof that the Distributor has been called upon to render service under the Manufacturer's standard warranty.

(B) The Distributor shall not negotiate with the United States Government, or any foreign government, or with any corporation or individual classed by the Manufacturer as national in scope, for the sale of any of the Manufacturer's products, except with the Manufacturer's written permission.

Advertising. (A) The Manufacturer agrees to furnish the Distributor from time to time its current Motor Truck catalogues and other regular Motor Truck literature without charge, except the transportation charges thereon, which the Distributor agrees to pay. The Distributor agrees to return to the Manufacturer upon demand all and any Motor Truck catalogues and Motor Truck literature that may have been furnished by the Manufacturer to the Distributor.

(B) The Distributor agrees to co-operate faithfully with the Manufacturer in all its advertising policies; to report weekly to the Manufacturer the sale of all .... Motor Trucks in his territory, giving chassis number, motor numbers, and purchaser's and user's names and addresses; and to advise the Manufacturer of all matters affecting its interests in connection with this agreement.

Dealers. (A) The Distributor agrees to appoint dealers at all points in his territory necessary to meet the Manufacturer's ideas of appropriate representation in all local communities. The Manufacturer will assist the Distributor in the appointment of such dealers, with the understanding that the Distributor will be held responsible for all acts of such dealers as hereinafter provided.

(B) In order to receive full benefits of advertising publicity and sales promotion, the Distributor shall use only forms provided by the Manufacturer for all agreements with dealers. The Distributors shall file with the Manufacturer copies of all agreements with dealers, and no agreements with dealers shall become effective until so filed with and accepted by the Manufacturer.

(C) The Manufacturer reserves the right, in the event the Distributor fails to establish dealers in such places throughout his territory as the Manufacturer shall designate, within a reasonable length of time, to withdraw such territory from this agreement.

(D) If the Distributor undertakes to sell or in any way to represent any line of trucks other than that of the Manufacturer, then the Manufacturer may forthwith and without notice terminate this agreement.

(E) If the Distributor shall sell any of the trucks of the Manufacturer to a purchaser located outside his territory, or for operating chiefly outside his territory, the Distributor agrees to pay to other Distributor or Distributors such amounts as may be held by the Manufacturer to be just and payable to such other Distributor or Distributors. This shall not apply to used trucks.

Deposits. (A) The Distributor agrees to deposit forthwith with the Manufacturer the sum of $............... as a guaranty for the performance of this agreement.

(B) The Manufacturer shall credit the Distributor's account with interest at the rate of six (6) per cent per annum payable yearly, on the Distributor's cash deposit, as the same may exist from time to time. At the conclusion of this agreement, the amount of the Distributor's deposit remaining, after all claims of the Manufacturer and claims of other .... Motor Truck Co. Distributors have been satisfied, shall be returned to the Distributor. The Distributor hereby authorizes the Manufacturer at any time to transfer from the Distributor's deposit account a sum sufficient to cover any amount that the Distributor may owe to the Manufacturer.

(C) In the event that any demands are made by the Manufacturer, the Distributor shall from time to time remit funds sufficient to restore and maintain his deposit to the original amount as set forth above.

(D) The Distributor further agrees to deposit with the Manufacturer a sum sufficient to defray transportation charges on .... Motor Trucks ordered by Distributor and the cost of any items of special equipment that may be specified on said .... Motor Trucks, such deposit to accompany the Distributor's shipping order. The Manufacturer hereby agrees to apply said deposit on the invoice price of the truck so ordered.

Relation of Distributor to Manufacturer. Upon the termination of this agreement, the Distributor shall discontinue entirely the use of the name .... or .... or .... in connection with any business of any character whatsoever or as part of any corporate name.

Transfer of Agreement. The Distributor agrees not to transfer, or assign, in any manner whatsoever, this agreement, or any part of it, or any of the rights or benefits accruing under it, without the written consent of the Manufacturer, and without such consent endorsed on this agreement, no assignee shall receive any rights under this agreement.

Provisions of Cancellation. (A) This agreement shall continue in force until cancelled, and is at all times subject to cancellation by either party upon thirty (30) days' written notice to the other party, which notice shall be given by registered mail, telegram, or cable, said notice taking effect the day upon which notice is sent, except, however, that if the Distributor violates, or fails, or neglects to perform any of his agreements hereunder, the Manufacturer may forthwith, at its election, treat this agreement as cancelled and terminated, and so notify the Distributor, which notice shall be given by registered mail, telegram, or cable, taking effect the day upon which the notice is sent. Upon cancellation of this agreement, there shall be a prompt settlement of all then-existing obligations arising under this agreement.

(B) The Manufacturer agrees, in the event of a cancellation of this agreement, that if any accepted orders for .... Motor Trucks or .... Motor Truck repair parts then on file by the Distributor with the Manufacturer are filled, the Distributor shall have the benefit of established discounts and allowances on such trucks and parts.

(C) In the event of cancellation of this agreement, the Manufacturer shall have an option, for thirty (30) days from the date notice of cancellation was sent or received, to purchase at the then-current prices, less a discount of fifty (50) per cent, any .... Motor Truck repair parts that may be owned by the Distributor.

(D) In the event of cancellation of this agreement, the Manufacturer shall have an option, for thirty (30) days from the date notice of cancellation was sent or received, to purchase at the then-current list price, less a discount of fifty (50) per cent, any .... Motor Trucks that may be owned by the Distributor.

Special Provisions. (A) No letter, telegram, or communication passing between the parties hereto shall become a part of or in any way modify or change this agreement, unless it is distinctly stated in such communication that it is to be attached as a rider to this agreement and bears the signed assent thereto of both parties hereto.

(B) The Manufacturer shall not be held liable for any loss or damage for failure to perform its part of this agreement on account of fire, strike, accident, war, insurrection, or any other cause beyond the control of the Manufacturer.

(C) This agreement supersedes and annuls all former agreements between the parties hereto or between the Distributor and any other party for the sale of the Manufacturer's products.

Executed and effective the day and year first above written.

....
Manufacturer

By ....

....
Distributor

By ....

FORM NO. 55

Contract appointing exclusive retail dealer for designated territory to sell company's products.

Articles of Agreement, made this .... day of ...., 19...., by and between The .... Company, of ...., ..., Party of the First Part, and ...., of ...., ..., Party of the Second Part.

Witnesseth, That the Party of the First Part, manufacturing .... Stock Office Equipment at ...., ..., hereby appoints Party of the Second Part its Exclusive Retail Dealer for the .... line of Office Equipment, consisting of .... for the territory of ....

In Addition to Granting This Exclusive Franchise, Party of the First Part agrees:

1. To turn over all orders and inquiries received from the territory involved to the Party of the Second Part, in accordance with the National Policy of the Party of the First Part.

2. To furnish catalogues and all current advertising matter in reasonable quantities, free of charge.

3. To allow the Party of the Second Part the Trade Discounts as shown in the Current Published Trade Discount Sheet for the various divisions of the .... line.

4. To allow the Party of the Second Part to ship orders into other exclusive territory, provided the purchasing power is located in the territory of the Party of the Second Part or in open territory.

5. That, upon its acceptance by the proper authority located at ...., ..., this contract will become effective.

6. To allow the Party of the Second Part the privilege to terminate this contract by giving the Party of the First Part thirty (30) days' written notice, or without previous notice, upon violation of any of the conditions set forth herein.

7. The Party of the First Part reserves the right to seek outlets through other dealers for .... products that the Party of the Second Part fails aggressively to sell.

In Consideration of the Grant of Its Exclusive Franchise and Other Agreements Made by the Party of the First Part, Party of the Second Part agrees:

1. [*Competing products*] To give the lines of merchandise made available on an exclusive basis by the Party of the First Part adequate floor and window display, and not to purchase, display, or offer for sale competing products, in any grades or styles, offered by other manufacturers.

2. [*Terms*] To pay bills for purchases made from the Party of the First Part on the basis of two (2) per cent cash discount if remittance is placed in the mail on or before midnight of the .... of the month following the date of the invoices, or on the basis of net payment on the 30th of the month following the date of invoices.

3. [*Restrictions on soliciting business*] Not to solicit business on .... products in territories assigned exclusively to other dealers, or in cities where Party of the First Part has branch stores or sales offices, it being understood that its branch stores stand in exactly the same relation to exclusive dealers as one exclusive dealer to another.

4. [*Sales by others in territory*] To allow Party of the First Part, or any of its agents or exclusive dealers, to solicit business and accept orders in the territory made a part of this agreement, provided the authority for purchase is located in some other territory.

5. [*Special cases*] To allow the Party of the First Part the privilege to develop and close, through its own representatives, any prospects that require special technical or expert service, apportioning the commission of Party of the Second Part according to the extra expense or special concessions involved. It is understood, however, that before projects of this class are closed, Party of the Second Part will be advised as to the terms of sale and amount of commission that will be received.

6. [*Cancellation of contract*] To allow the Party of the First Part the privilege to terminate this contract by giving the Party of the Second Part thirty (30) days' written notice, or without previous notice, upon violation of any of the conditions set forth herein.

7. [*Government orders*] To allow Party of the First Part, or any branch, or any duly appointed agent or dealer, to accept and execute without obligation or violation of the terms of this Contract orders from the United States Government.

8. [*Termination on sale or consolidation*] To allow the Party of the First Part the option to terminate this contract in the event that there is a sale or consolidation of the business of the Party of the Second Part.

9. [*Notice of changes*] That all of the products, terms, prices, discounts, and conditions specified herein may be changed or discontinued by notice in writing or publication by the Party of the First Part.

10. [*Return of merchandise*] That Party of the First Part will be given the option of taking back all saleable .... merchandise in the possession of the Party of the Second Part in the event of a violation or cancellation of this contract.

This Contract cancels all other previous agreements.

The .... Company,

Retail Dealer .... By ....

By .... Accepted ....

Resale price-maintenance agreements.—All but a few of the states have enacted laws, known as "Fair Trade Acts," that permit producers or distributors of standard articles sold under trade names to contract with distributors, wholesalers, or retailers not to offer such articles for sale to consumers below certain established prices. Third parties with notice are bound by the terms of such contracts regardless of whether or not they are parties to them. Contracts between manufacturers, wholesalers, or retailers (so-called horizontal contracts) are uniformly excluded from operation of such statutes. Under the laws of some states, the agreement may apparently establish a fixed price that can be neither increased nor reduced; in other states only minimum prices may be established. In practice, resale price-maintenance agreements usually set minimum prices. For a form of manufacturer-wholesaler fair-trade agreement, see Form No. 56; for a form of manufacturer-retailer fair-trade agreement, see Form No. 57. For a form of agreement which provides that the manufacturer supply the dealer with a schedule of maximum discounts allowable from retail list prices, and which permits the manufacturer to change the schedule upon prescribed written notice, see Form No. 58.

The Fair Trade Acts exempt resale price-maintenance agreements from the State antitrust laws, which are designed to prohibit agreements that tend to lessen free competition and to restrain trade. The Miller-Tydings amendment to the Sherman Antitrust Act legalizes resale price-maintenance contracts for branded or trademarked goods sold in interstate commerce and resold within the jurisdiction of any state where such contracts have been legalized with respect to intrastate sales.

Unfair practices acts.—Another group of State laws affecting sales is that prohibiting price discrimination and sales below cost, where the effect is to injure competitors or destroy competition. These acts are frequently referred to as unfair practices acts and fair or unfair sales acts. Some of the laws also prevent discrimination between distributors of commodities of like grade and quality and between purchasers in different communities.

The Federal Robinson-Patman Anti-Price Discrimination Act, passed in 1936, amends the Clayton Act to prohibit specific abuses concerning price discrimination that grew up under the Clayton Act. The statute outlaws price-discriminatory practices in the sale and resale of commodities in the United States, including false brokerage, pseudo-advertising, and other discriminating service allowances that were found unfairly to favor the large buyer as against the small and independent businessman. It is unlawful under the Act for a buyer engaged in interstate commerce knowingly to induce or receive a discrimination in price that is prohibited by the Act. The Act permits due allowances for differences in the cost of manufacture, sale, or delivery resulting from different measures or quantities in which the commodities are sold or delivered to the purchasers, but allows the Federal Trade Commission to fix quantity limits beyond which no discount will be allowed.

FORM NO. 56

Manufacturer-wholesaler contract form for use under state resale price-maintenance laws and Tydings-Miller amendment to section 1 of Sherman Act.*

[*Short Form for Use under Federal Tydings-Miller Law and State Fair Trade Laws Suitable for Use by Manufacturers in Any State to Stipulate Wholesale Selling Prices in States Having Fair Trade Laws.*]

MANUFACTURER-WHOLESALER CONTRACT

AGREEMENT, made in the City of ...., State of ...., by and between .... (hereinafter called the "Manufacturer"), and .... (hereinafter called the "Wholesaler");

WHEREAS, the Manufacturer is the producer or the distributor of various Commodities, and the Wholesaler is engaged in the sale of such Commodities at wholesale in various states that have enacted fair-trade acts, so called, and the Manufacturer and the Wholesaler desire to avail themselves of the provisions of such fair-trade acts and of the fair-trade acts of such other states as shall enact such statutes;

NOW, THEREFORE, in consideration of the premises and the mutual benefits and obligations accruing to and assumed by the parties hereto from and by the execution and delivery of this agreement, the parties hereto agree as follows:

1. The word "Commodities" as used in this agreement is hereby defined to mean commodities that bear, or the label or container of which

---

* Form suggested by National Wholesale Druggists' Association. Reproduced by special permission.

bears, the trade-mark, brand, or name of the Manufacturer and that are in free, fair, and open competition with commodities of the same general class produced or distributed by others.

The word "Products" as used in this agreement is hereby defined to mean the Commodities that are specified in Schedule A hereto attached as such schedule shall from time to time be constituted.

The word "state" as used in this agreement shall be construed so as to include in its meaning, as the context requires or permits, "territory," "the District of Columbia," and each dependency and insular possession of the United States of America in which the Sherman Anti-Trust Act, so called, shall at the time have force and effect, and the word "states" shall be construed accordingly.

2. The Wholesaler will not (except as specifically permitted by statute) directly or indirectly advertise, offer for sale, or sell any of the Products to any buyer in any state in which at the time a fair-trade act shall be in effect at less than the minimum wholesale selling price at that time stipulated therefor in such state by the Manufacturer.

3. The minimum wholesale selling prices stipulated by the Manufacturer for the Products in various states are those now or hereafter designated in Schedule A plus, in each sale, the amount of all sales and excise taxes applicable to such sale.

The Manufacturer, at any time and from time to time, by written notice given to the Wholesaler as hereinafter provided, may: (a) eliminate one or more Products from Schedule A; (b) add one or more Products to Schedule A and stipulate minimum wholesale selling prices therefor; and/or (c) change the minimum wholesale selling price of any one or more of the Products.

Each elimination from and each addition to Schedule A and each change in any minimum wholesale selling price, including each such change made pursuant to article 4 of this agreement, shall be effective at the opening of business on the date specified in the notice thereof, and such notice shall be mailed so that, in the ordinary course of the mails, it will be received by the Wholesaler before the date so specified.

4. In the event that, pursuant to any agreement similar to this one, the Manufacturer shall stipulate a minimum wholesale selling price for any of the Products in any given state which shall be different from the minimum wholesale selling price at the time stipulated for such Products in such state under this agreement, the Manufacturer will give prompt written notice of such fact to the Wholesaler, and such different mini-

mum wholesale selling price shall be effective under this agreement as provided in article 3 hereof.

5. (a) The offering or giving of any article of value in connection with the sale by the Wholesaler of any of the Products; or (b) the offering or making of any concession of any kind whatsoever (whether by the giving of coupons, trading stamps, or otherwise), in connection with any such sale; or (c) the sale or offering for sale of any of the Products by the Wholesaler in combination with any other merchandise, shall, unless specifically authorized by the Manufacturer, constitute a breach by the Wholesaler of article 2 of this agreement.

6. The Manufacturer in good faith will employ all appropriate means, which in the circumstances shall be reasonable, including legal proceedings if other means fail, to prevent, and to enforce the discontinuance of, any violation of said minimum wholesale selling-price stipulations by any competitor of the Wholesaler, whether the person so violating or threatening such violation is or is not a party to a fair-trade contract with the Manufacturer covering the Products involved in such violation or threatened violation.

7. In addition to any other legal remedy, the parties hereto may have the remedy of injunction to prevent or to enforce the discontinuance of any violation of this agreement.

8. This agreement may be terminated by either party hereto on ten (10) days' written notice to the other, but such termination by the Wholesaler shall not affect the rights or obligations of either of the parties hereto under any applicable fair-trade act, whether now or hereafter enacted, or by reason of any contract made pursuant to any such act.

9. Any notice given under any of the provisions of this agreement shall be well and sufficiently given by delivering the same personally to the party hereto to whom it shall be addressed or by mailing the same in a sealed postpaid envelope to such party at its address given below.

10. This agreement shall apply to sales of the Products, or any of them, only at such times as agreements of the character of this agreement shall be lawful as applied to interstate transactions, under any statute, law, or public policy now or hereafter in effect in any State, Territory, the District of Columbia, or any dependency or insular possession of the United States of America in which the Sherman Anti-Trust Act, so called, shall at the time have force and effect, in which such sale is to be made, or to which the Products in question are to be transported for sale, by the Wholesaler.

11. This agreement shall become effective on the .... day of ...., 19....

....

Manufacturer

....	....	....
(Street)	(City)	(State)

....

Wholesaler

....	....	....
(Street)	(City)	(State)

FORM NO. 57

Manufacturer—retailer contract form for use under state resale price-maintenance laws and Tydings-Miller Amendment to section 1 of Sherman Act.*

Agreement, made in the State of ...., by and between the undersigned, "Manufacturer," and the undersigned, "Retailer,"

Witnesseth:

Whereas, the "Commodities," shown on Schedule A hereto attached, as such Schedule shall be constituted from time to time, are, or may hereafter be, distributed under the trade-mark(s), brand(s), or name of "Manufacturer" in fair, free, and open competition with commodities of the same general class produced by others, and the parties hereto desire to avail themselves of the benefit of the Fair Trade Act of the State of Retailer's address as shown below;

Now, Therefor, in consideration of the premises and the mutual obligations herein assumed, the parties hereto agree as follows:

(1) "Retailer" will not (except as specifically permitted by said Fair Trade Act) directly or indirectly advertise, offer for sale, or sell any of such "Commodities" in said state at less than the minimum retail prices stipulated therefor by "Manufacturer."

(2) The minimum retail prices stipulated by "Manufacturer" for the "Commodities" in said state are those now or hereafter designated

---

* Form suggested by National Association of Retail Druggists. Reproduced by special permission.

in Schedule A, plus, in each sale, the amount of all sales and excise taxes applicable to such retail sale in said State.

(3) "Manufacturer," at any time and from time to time, upon ten (10) days' written notice to "Retailer," may eliminate "Commodities" from Schedule A, and/or may add to said Schedule, and stipulate minimum retail prices for, additional "Commodities," and may change the minimum retail price of any one or more of the "Commodities."

(4) (a) The offering or giving of any article of value in connection with the sale by "Retailer" of any of the "Commodities"; (b) the offering or making of any concession of any kind whatsoever (whether by the giving of coupons, trading stamps, or otherwise), in connection with any such sale; or (c) the sale or offering for sale of any of the "Commodities" by "Retailer" in combination with any other merchandise shall constitute a breach by "Retailer" of article 1 of this agreement.

(5) "Manufacturer" in good faith will employ all appropriate means, which in the circumstances shall be reasonable, including legal proceedings if such other means fail, to prevent, and to enforce the discontinuance of, any violation of said minimum retail-price stipulations by any competitor of "Retailer," whether the person violating or threatening such violation is or is not a party to a fair-trade contract with "Manufacturer" covering said "Commodities."

(6) "Retailer" will not, where statute or law permits such restriction, sell any of the "Commodities" except to consumers for use.

(7) In addition to any other legal remedy, the parties may have the remedy of injunction to prevent or to enforce the discontinuance of any violation of this agreement.

(8) This agreement may be terminated by either party on ten (10) days' written notice to the other, but termination by "Retailer" shall not affect the rights or obligations of either of the parties hereto under the Fair Trade Act of said State or by reason of any contract made pursuant thereto.

(9) Any notice given under any of the provisions of this agreement shall be well and sufficiently given by delivering the same personally to the party hereto to whom it shall be addressed, or by mailing the same in a sealed postpaid envelope addressed to such party at its address given below.

(10) This agreement shall become effective on the .... day of ...., 19....

In Witness Whereof, the parties hereto have executed this agreement on the .... day of ...., 19.....

....
Retailer *Manufacturer*

....
(Street) (City) (State) (Street) (City) (State)
(attach store label)

(To be printed at the foot of the contract after the signatures and addresses.)

Schedule A

(If more space needed, add additional page or pages.)

....

....

....

FORM NO. 58

Retailer fair-trade agreement between manufacturer and dealer.

Agreement, made by and between .... Company, a .... corporation, with principal business office at .... Street, ..., ... (hereinafter called "A"), and the undersigned (hereinafter called "the Dealer"),

Witnesseth:

Whereas certain products manufactured by "A" (hereinafter called "said 'A' products"), listed in the Schedule attached hereto and made a part hereof, are or may hereafter be distributed under the trade-marks, brands, or trade names owned by "A" in fair, free, and open competition with commodities or products of the same general class produced or distributed by others, and the parties hereto desire to avail themselves of the benefits of the Fair Trade Act of the state in which the Dealer's principal place of business is located as indicated at the foot of this agreement,

Therefor, in consideration of the mutual covenants herein contained and of sales of said "A" products hereafter made by "A" to the Dealer, and in further consideration of the execution of similar agreements by other dealers located in the same state, it is mutually agreed between the parties as follows:

1. [*Resale price fixed*] The Dealer will not, except as specifically permitted by said Fair Trade Act and except as herein specifically provided, either directly or through any subsidiary or allied company or otherwise, offer for sale or sell at retail (i.e., to consumers for use) any of said "A" products at less than "A"'s retail list price less the maximum discount set forth in said Schedule.

2. [*Notice of changes in price schedule*] "A" may at any time upon ten (10) days' written notice to the Dealer, mailed to the said principal place of business of the Dealer, change said Schedule by adding to or removing products therefrom and by increasing or decreasing the maximum discounts stated therein, with like effect after said ten (10) day period as though such changes had been originally included. It is further agreed that the retail list prices to which said discounts shall apply are those contained in "A"'s Condensed Price List as published from time to time, with such changes as have been made or may hereafter from time to time be made by "A" and confirmed in "A"'s published Trade Circulars.

3. [*Concessions restricted*] The Dealer will not offer or give any article of value, or offer or make any other concession or privilege in connection with the sale at retail by the Dealer of any of said "A" products, which has the practical result, in violation of the provisions or the intent of the Fair Trade Act of said state, of reducing the selling price of said product below the retail list price less the maximum discount stipulated in said Schedule.

4. [*Exceptions*] This agreement shall not apply to sales of any of said "A" products to the United States or any State or local government or to sales of any of said products for .... [*here include any other exceptions*].

5. [*Termination of agreement*] This agreement shall continue in effect until terminated by either party upon ten (10) days' written notice to the other, mailed to the latter's principal business office or place of business as set forth herein, provided, however, that in case of any such termination the Dealer shall not thereby be released from any obligation in respect of sales of said "A" products imposed upon him by the Fair Trade Act or any other statute of said state. This agreement shall not apply to any sales in any state that has no Fair Trade Act.

6. The facsimile signature of the Vice-President of "A" printed below shall be deemed to be sufficient execution of this agreement by "A." This agreement shall apply to all of said "A" products sold at retail by the Dealer on or after the date hereof.

IN WITNESS WHEREOF, the parties hereto have executed this agreement, this .... day of ...., 19....

"A" Company

By ....
Vice-President

....
(Firm Name of Dealer)

By ....
(Signature of Owner or Official)

....
(Title)

....

....
(Address in Full of Principal Place of Business of Dealer)

[*Here follows schedule of maximum discounts allowable from retail list prices*]

5. MISCELLANEOUS CLAUSES IN AGENCY AGREEMENTS

FORM NO. 59

Clause in which manufacturer grants right to sell complete products of manufacturer and subsidiaries.

The Manufacturer agrees that the Dealer, during the life of this agreement or of any continuation thereof, shall have the exclusive right to sell the complete products of the Manufacturer, as well as the complete products of all companies owned and controlled by the Manufacturer, now made or handled or hereafter to be made or handled by the Manufacturer or such companies, hereinafter referred to as "Products," for delivery in the following sales territory:

FORM NO. 60

Clause in which manufacturer agrees to protect exclusive sales rights granted.

The Manufacturer agrees to use the utmost good faith and care in selling its products to others, to protect the Agent in its exclusive sales rights, and to the end that none of said products shall be sold or delivered in said territory by anyone whomsoever, either directly or indirectly, except through the Agent or its business connections or representatives, except as hereinafter provided; but it is agreed that if, in spite of the foregoing, any of the Manufacturer's products are shipped to, sold, or delivered in said territory, either directly or indirectly, by or through any party other than the Agent herein (except as provided in the next paragraph of this article), the Manufacturer, as soon as aware of such fact, shall immediately notify the Agent in writing of such sales, giving full particulars thereof, and shall also immediately pay the Agent an amount equal to the discount from the Manufacturer's current domestic list prices on the products so sold or delivered, which said discounts are specifically set forth in Article V of this contract.

FORM NO. 61

Clause describing agency and definite territory.

Company appoints Agent its .... Agent, for the distribution and sale, in less than full carload or tank-car lots, to retail dealers and consumers, of .... in the following territory.

Agent accepts such appointment and agrees to devote Agent's entire business time and best efforts to the performance of Agent's duties in accordance with this agreement, and not to engage directly or indirectly in any occupation that might interfere with Agent's duties hereunder. Agent's rights are to be strictly limited to those set forth herein and are not to be deemed extended by any course of dealing or otherwise.

Agent shall not obligate Company in any way without the prior written approval of the Division Manager of the .... Division of Company (or any other Manager whom Company may designate). Agent shall do nothing detrimental to Company's best interests and shall use no improper or questionable methods. Agent shall exert the utmost diligence in caring for Company's property under Agent's control.

FORM NO. 62

Clause in which manufacturer agrees to execute all orders accepted.

The Manufacturer agrees to execute, strictly in accordance with the terms thereof, all orders received from the Dealer and accepted by the

Manufacturer up to the proportion of output hereinafter agreed upon. It is understood and agreed, however, that the Manufacturer shall not be liable for any damages due to failure to deliver goods within the time specified, where such failure is caused by strikes, fires, embargoes, requirements of the Government, acts of God or of the public enemy, or other conditions beyond the control of the Manufacturer. In case of such failure to deliver products within the time specified, the Agent may at its option cancel the order. The Manufacturer further agrees that it will not unreasonably fail or refuse to fill any orders submitted by the Agent under this contract.

FORM NO. 63

Clause designating term of agreement and conditions precedent.

If no conditions are provided for in this section, the term of this agreement shall be one (1) year from the date hereof. Otherwise the term shall be one (1) year from the date of the completion of the performance, to the reasonable satisfaction of Company, of the conditions set forth below. If said conditions shall not be performed as aforesaid within .... days from the date hereof, Company may cancel this agreement and any others between the parties. Unless either party shall give written notice not less than .... days prior to the above date of termination of an intention not to renew, said term shall be deemed renewed on the same terms and conditions for a further period of one (1) year, without the necessity of any further action, and shall be similarly renewed from year to year thereafter until written notice of intention not to renew shall be given by either party not less than .... days prior to the end of any yearly period.

The above-mentioned conditions precedent are as follows:

FORM NO. 64

Clause in which manufacturer agrees to refer to agent all inquiries for quotations and offers.

The Manufacturer agrees to refer to the Agent all inquiries and requests for quotations and all offers to purchase any of said products for use and delivery in the territory, and that it will not, except upon the Agent's consent and direction, knowingly sell or ship any of its products to anyone for use or delivery in said territory.

FORM NO. 65

Clause in which manufacturer agrees to quote lowest prices to agent.

The Manufacturer agrees that prices and terms to the Dealer will at all times be its lowest and best prices and terms and that it will not quote or sell to any other concern, agency, or individual at net prices lower or on terms more favorable than the prices and terms quoted to the Dealer.

FORM NO. 66

Clause in which manufacturer guarantees quality of products and agrees to replace defective products.

The Manufacturer guarantees that all products furnished by it will be of first-class material and workmanship, of its latest design, and in every respect as represented. The Manufacturer further agrees to replace at its own cost, including cost of transportation to point of delivery to Purchaser, any and all parts of said products that may prove defective in any respect, under ordinary usage, within one year from the date of delivery to Purchaser. The Manufacturer may require the return at its expense of any replaced products or parts thereof for its examination.

FORM NO. 67

Clause in which manufacturer makes warranty of quality (an alternative form).

The Manufacturer warrants each new compressor manufactured and sold by it, as well as such accessories and parts of its manufacture so sold, to be free from defects in material and workmanship under normal use and service; such warranty being limited to ninety (90) days from delivery of such compressor to the original Purchaser from the distributor, the extent of its obligation under this warranty being limited to making good at its factory any part or parts thereof which shall, within ninety (90) days after delivery to the original Purchaser, be returned to it with transportation charges prepaid and which its examination shall disclose to have been defective. This warranty is in lieu of all other warranties, expressed or implied, and of all other obligations or liabilities on its part, there being no implied warranty with respect to said articles, whether of suitability or otherwise, and the Manufacturer neither assumes, nor authorizes any person to assume for it, any other liability in connection with the sale of said compressors thereto.

This warranty shall not apply to any piece of equipment or accessory that shall have been repaired or altered outside of the Manufacturer's factory in any way, nor to any compressor or accessory that has been subject to misuse, negligence, or accident, nor for one loaded beyond its normal load capacity.

FORM NO. 68

Clause in which manufacturer agrees to supply agent with advertising matter.

The Manufacturer agrees to supply to the Agent, promptly upon the Agent's request, without charge and in reasonable quantities, all necessary blueprints, drawings and specifications, catalogues, circulars and descriptive matter printed in English, and all photographs, half tones, and electrotypes, and such other advertising material as the Manufacturer may from time to time issue for the use of its customers. The Agent agrees to issue such advertising matter in any and all foreign languages as, from time to time, it may deem necessary.

FORM NO. 69

Clause in which manufacturer agrees to protect agent in case of infringement of patent or selling right.

The Manufacturer agrees to protect the Agent against all damage, loss, and expense of every kind that it may sustain by reason of its possession, use, or sale of the Manufacturer's products, insofar as the same are based on any claim that the said products, or any part thereof, constitute an infringement of any patent or other selling rights of the territory.

FORM NO. 70

Clause reserving to manufacturer right to make direct sales.

The Manufacturer reserves the right to sell its products direct to any other manufacturer of equipment, and no commission shall be due the Distributor from the Manufacturer on any such sale. The Manufacturer shall not be held liable for commissions on any compressor shipped into the Distributor's territory by some other distributor or dealer not located in his territory.

FORM NO. 71

Clause reserving to manufacturer title to unpaid merchandise.

In case any property sold hereunder shall be delivered to the Distributor before it is fully paid for, the title to such property and to the proceeds thereof in case of resale, whether in cash, notes, or securities, shall remain in the Manufacturer until the full purchase price and any notes given therefor have been paid in cash, but nothing herein shall release the Distributor from payment, and after delivery to the Distributor, said property shall be held and used at his risk and expense in respect to loss or damage and taxes and charges of every kind.

FORM NO. 72

Clause in which agent agrees not to represent any other manufacturer except with respect to designated business.

The Agent accepts the appointment as Agent of the Manufacturer upon the terms and conditions of this agreement, and covenants and agrees that he will not represent or render any services in any capacity for any other person, firm, or corporation, either directly or indirectly, nor conduct nor engage nor have any interest in any other business that may be in competition with the Manufacturer, unless consent of the Manufacturer in writing be given therefor; *provided, however,* that the Agent may continue his present business with respect to:

FORM NO. 73

Clause in which agent agrees not to sell competing goods.

During the continuance of this agreement and as long as the Agent shall enjoy the exclusive sales rights herein provided for, the Agent shall not, in said territory, sell or solicit, or permit the sale or solicitation by its representatives, or orders for any products of competitive make of similar type and description, coming within the range of the sizes made by the Manufacturer, and which are covered by this agreement.

FORM NO. 74

Clause in which agent agrees to promote sales diligently in designated territory.

The Agent agrees to prosecute diligently the sale of said products for delivery in said territory through personal solicitation of its salesmen and by correspondence and will not, at any time during the continuation of this contract, sell or solicit orders for any products of any kind or description made by any other person that come in competition with the said products manufactured by the Manufacturer, which are covered by this agreement.

FORM NO. 75

Clause in which agent agrees to promote sales diligently (an alternative form).

Agent shall diligently canvass for purchasers, obtain and submit to the Company orders for goods he deals in, and exert his best efforts to promote the business of the Company, and shall not take orders for sale or be interested in the sale of other goods designed for similar purposes until he has exhausted all efforts and influences possible to sell the Company's goods, including timely request of the Company's branch manager in his territory by telegraph, telephone, or otherwise for assistance, and he shall not interfere with any person seeking to purchase through or negotiating with any other person authorized by the Company.

FORM NO. 76

Clause in which agent agrees to employ sufficient sales staff.

The Agent agrees to employ a sufficient number of efficient salesmen who will regularly visit the trade in all parts of the territory, or, by appointing subagencies in distant parts of the territory, reach that part of the trade through them, in a manner satisfactory to the Manufacturer.

FORM NO. 77

Clause in which agent agrees to employ salesman from manufacturer's sales staff.

The Agent agrees to and shall employ for a period of one (1) year, and at a salary to be agreed upon, one salesman thoroughly familiar with said products, which salesman shall be taken from the Manufacturer's sales organization or employed subject to its approval, and it is agreed that during the first six (6) months of such employment the Manufacturer shall pay the salary of such salesman, and the Agent shall pay his reasonable expenses, and after such six (6) months' period both salary and expenses of such salesman shall be paid by the Agent.

FORM NO. 78

Clause in which agent agrees to confine itself to designated territory.

As far as the Manufacturer's line of said products is concerned, the Agent agrees to confine itself strictly to the territory mentioned in Article II hereof, and not to solicit or accept orders for said products for shipment into any other territory except with the written consent of the Manufacturer, its dealer or agent, in such other territory.

FORM NO. 79

Clause in which agent guarantees payment of accounts.

The Agent agrees to guarantee, and the Agent does hereby guarantee to the Manufacturer, the payment of all accounts arising on sales made by the Agent of ...., within the credit period allowed to the purchaser for such payment, which shall not be longer than thirty (30) days after the end of the calendar month during which such sales were made.

FORM NO. 80

Clause in which agent agrees to examine goods on arrival.

The Agent agrees to examine all goods on arrival and notify the Manufacturer of all claims on account of shortage, defective or damaged goods or parts, within ten (10) days after receipt of goods, and, failing so to do, the Manufacturer is not to be held responsible therefor. The Manufacturer shall have a reasonable time in which to make good any shortage or defective or damaged goods or to furnish parts to replace defective parts for which it is responsible.

FORM NO. 81

Clause requiring agent to give public notice of manufacturer's ownership of consigned merchandise.

All .... shipped to the Agent on consignment shall be held by the Agent as bailee of the Manufacturer and shall remain the property of the Manufacturer until sold by the Agent; and if the laws of the State in which the .... is held by the Agent require a public record or a legal or published notice, or make any other requirement concerning property held by a consignee, bailee or factor, for the purpose of showing ownership of the Manufacturer in the consigned ...., the Agent agrees at his expense to comply fully with any and all such requirements and to furnish the Manufacturer with evidence of such compliance.

FORM NO. 82

Clause providing for proportion of manufacturer's output to be available for agent.

During the first year of this contract, the Manufacturer agrees to make available for the Agent at least ten (10) per cent of the Manufacturer's entire output for the year 19.... of each of the products covered by this agreement; during the second (2nd) year, at least twenty (20) per cent of the Manufacturer's entire output for the year 19.... of each of said products, and during the third (3rd) and each succeeding year, at least thirty (30) per cent of the Manufacturer's entire output of each of said products.

The Agent will use its best efforts to place with the Manufacturer in each year orders for the greatest possible proportion of the Manufacturer's output made available to it in the preceding paragraph, and agrees that, as far as practicable, said orders shall be reasonably distributed throughout the year; but nothing herein shall require the Agent to take in any year a greater proportion of said output than it shall find it necessary to take in the regular course of its business.

FORM NO. 83

Clause providing for compliance by agent with legal requirements for doing business and payment of taxes thereon.

The Agent shall conduct the business of the agency in accordance with and be responsible for the proper observance of all laws, rules, and regulations of the territory and shall pay all expenses, charges, taxes, fees, etc., which may pertain to, be levied upon, or arise out of his carrying on the business of this agency, including taxes that may be imposed upon his earnings or income by the laws of the United States, no part of which shall be borne by the Manufacturer. All business undertaken by the Agent shall at all times be subject to the laws, treaties, rules, and regulations of the United States of America.

FORM NO. 84

Clause providing for negotiation by agent only with persons of approved standing, and for approval of transactions by manufacturer.

The Agent shall negotiate transactions only with persons, firms, and corporations of approved financial standing. All contracts, sales, purchases, and orders, and all extensions of credit and all new accounts that may be proposed to be opened shall be subject to the approval of the Manufacturer, and must be confirmed by the Manufacturer in writing before the same shall become binding on the Manufacturer. Any instructions that may be given by the Manufacturer shall be complied with.

FORM NO. 85

Clause relating to selling prices to be quoted by agent to prospective customers.

It is agreed between the parties that the selling prices to be quoted by the Agent to the prospective customers shall include all charges on the merchandise after the same leaves the warehouse, such as freight, duties, landing charges, and all other charges. Such charges shall be paid by the Agent and, when invoices are collected, the Agent may reimburse himself for the same and shall remit the net balance to the Manufacturer. All orders taken are subject to approval by the Manufacturer.

FORM NO. 86

Clause granting manufacturer right to change prices.

Prices may be changed from time to time by the Manufacturer's giving written or telegraphic notice to the Agent at its New York office, and the Agent shall promptly notify its branches and subagencies of such price changes, but no increase in price shall be effective with respect to orders taken by the Agent or any of its branches or agencies on quotations made by the Agent or any of its said branches or subagencies prior to the time they shall have respectively received notice of such increase in prices, provided such orders are placed with the Manufacturer within sixty (60) days after the receipt by the Agent of notice of an increase in price. In case of a reduction in price, the reduced price shall apply to all orders for stock that have been placed with the Manufacturer but that have not been delivered by it to the Dealer at the time such reduction in price is made.

FORM NO. 87

Clause in which dealer agrees to sell to actual users only.

It is the desire of the Company that the Dealer sell .... Appliances only at retail to actual users of the appliances unless by special agreement with the Company, and that the Dealer will not sell or transfer .... Appliances to another dealer or any retailer or wholesaler without permission from the Company. If a transfer is made with approval of the Company, the serial numbers of the appliances transferred must be furnished immediately by the Dealer to the Company. If the Dealer makes sales contrary to the expressed desire of the Company as contained in this paragraph, the Company reserves the right to make no further sales to the Dealer. Furthermore, the Dealer agrees if called upon at any time to give the Company a full accounting of his sales, including the date of each sale, name and address of the purchaser, serial number of the appliance sold, and serial numbers of all appliances in stock or on demonstration.

FORM NO. 88

Clause providing for marking, packing, and boxing of products.

The Manufacturer shall securely pack and box for export all products ordered by the Agent in such manner as to afford safety and protection against weather, theft, and breakage, including rough handling in transit. The Manufacturer shall mark all boxes in accordance with the Agent's instructions and furnish the Agent with complete and correct packing lists, specifications of net and gross weights, measurements, and such other information and documents as may be required for export shipment.

FORM NO. 89

Clause relieving manufacturer from liability for failure to deliver merchandise because of force majeure.

Orders from the Agent, when accepted by the Manufacturer, shall be firm contracts, and the time for delivery specified therein shall be of the essence thereof. The Manufacturer shall not be liable, however, for any damages due to its failure to deliver the goods within the time specified, where such failure is caused by strikes, fires, embargoes, requirements of the Government, acts of God or of the public enemy, or other conditions beyond the control of the Manufacturer. In case the Manufacturer fails to make delivery in accordance with the terms of an order accepted by it, the Agent shall, at its option, be released from all obligations under such order.

FORM NO. 90

Clause providing for payment of cable charges on orders.

The Manufacturer shall pay all cable charges with respect to cable orders, offers, or inquiries with respect to which the Agent may be unable to secure reimbursement from the customers interested therein, but the Agent shall use his best efforts to cause the merchants for whose accounts such cables may have been sent to pay such cable charges. If the merchants shall not pay the cable charges, the expense of them shall be items of expense to be deducted in the determination of the commissions and net profits with respect to which the compensation of the Agent is to be calculated, as stated herein.

FORM NO. 91

Clause providing for charge of losses from bad accounts against agent's commissions.

It is agreed that any losses occurring because of bad accounts will be charged against the commissions of the Agent, and the Agent agrees that he will use his utmost efforts not to transact business with concerns of doubtful financial responsibility, and that if in any particular instances any financial or other risk is involved in the sale of merchandise, he will fully acquaint the Manufacturer with all the facts relating thereto at the time the order is placed.

FORM NO. 92

Clause providing for interchange of information between agent and manufacturer.

The Agent shall promptly transmit to the Manufacturer copies of all orders, contracts, proposals, inquiries, correspondence, telegrams, cablegrams, and other memoranda concerning the business of the agency, and shall transmit to the Manufacturer all available information pertinent to the successful promotion of its business in the territory. The Manufacturer shall promptly inform the Agent of matters relating to prospective business and, in its discretion, submit copies of correspondence between the Manufacturer and customer in the territory. The Agent shall keep himself informed and promptly advise the Manufacturer by mail, and when proper by cable, concerning the credit of customers and prospective customers, general market conditions, and the activity of the Manufacturer's competitors in the territory and the various parts thereof. Whenever requested by the Manufacturer, the Agent shall furnish special reports to the Manufacturer concerning the financial standing and general responsibility and repute of any person, firm, or corporation in the territory, from at least two banks in the territory, one of which shall be a branch or correspondent of the .... Bank of New York, and from such other sources of information as may be available to him, together with the Agent's personal opinion and the opinion of the trade.

FORM NO. 93

Clause providing for co-operation between manufacturer and agent in compiling a mailing list for the territory.

The Manufacturer and the Agent shall faithfully co-operate and assist each other in the furtherance and promotion of their mutual interests under the agency hereby created. The Manufacturer may use such means as it may deem expedient for promoting the sale of merchandise in the territory, including advertising and the mailing of printed matter to prospective customers in the territory, and the Agent shall co-operate with the Manufacturer in the prosecution of such methods and assist the Manufacturer in compiling a classified mailing list for the territory.

FORM NO. 94

Clause making agreement between manufacturer and agent subject to agreement with another agent.

The Manufacturer has entered into an agreement with the .... Company, Inc., relative to selling rights in the territory designated aforesaid, and this agreement is made subject to the terms, obligations, and conditions thereof.

FORM NO. 95

Clause providing for transactions undertaken prior to commencement of agency.

It is understood between the parties hereto that at the time of the execution of this contract, the Manufacturer has made quotations upon its products to certain prospective purchasers. It is agreed that within sixty (60) days from the date hereof, the Manufacturer, on its own account, may enter into contracts with said prospective purchasers for the sale or delivery of its products in said territory, and that upon such contracts the Agent shall be entitled to no commissions, provided said contracts be consummated as a result of quotations made during the sixty (60) days next preceding the date hereof. It is further agreed that the Manufacturer shall immediately furnish the Agent with a list of all such quotations, and that the Agent may at any time hereafter in its own name and on its own behalf solicit orders for said business and make contracts for the sale or delivery in said territory of the

Manufacturer's said products with any of said prospective purchasers or any other person or persons.

FORM NO. 96

Clause in which agent agrees to take out workmen's compensation insurance and assumes responsibility as employer under Unemployment Insurance and other Social Security Acts.

Agent shall at Agent's expense take out and keep in force a policy with a company and in form satisfactory to Company in respect of workmen's compensation and/or employer's liability insurance, covering all employees of the Agent as Agent hereunder, and Agent shall promptly furnish Company with a certificate of such insurance.

This provision shall not alter the relationship of Agent to Company, or have the effect of making any employees of Agent employees of Company, it being understood that Agent alone is responsible for the employment, control, and conduct of Agent's employees and for the injury of such employees in the course of their employment or otherwise, or to others through the acts or neglect of such employees. Agent assumes full responsibility as employer for Agent and all employees of Agent under Unemployment Insurance, Old Age Pension, and other so-called Social Security Acts, and agrees to pay all taxes and contributions under such acts required of the employer in respect of Agent and Agent's employees and to execute on Company's demand any further agreement to this effect.

Agent shall not employ anyone without prompt notice to any insurance company whose policy may be affected by such employment.

FORM NO. 97

Clause in which dealer gives manufacturer option to purchase products in stock at time of termination of dealer agreement.

The Dealer agrees, in the event of the termination of this franchise, to give the Company, for a period of thirty (30) days from date of termination, an option to purchase at a price not to exceed the current invoice price to the dealer, any or all new .... Appliances on hand, and an option to purchase any or all used and repossessed

.... Appliances on hand at a price not to exceed seventy-five (75) per cent of the current invoice price to the Dealer; not to sell or offer for sale any .... Appliances to anyone else during such option period without written permission of the Company, and, if requested by the Company, to assemble all .... Appliances Dealer owns at place of business mentioned in this franchise.

FORM NO. 98

Clause in which dealer agrees to discontinue use of manufacturer's name and material upon termination of contract.

The Dealer agrees immediately to discontinue and relinquish any and all uses of the name .... in the firm name, telephone directory, classified listings, on store fronts, on poster boards, newspapers and periodicals, on trucks, or in any manner whatsoever, upon the termination of this franchise. To consider all parts, catalogues, service manuals, and advertising material such as store signs, window displays, circulars, mats, electros, and all other material furnished by the Company as property of the Company, and to return it upon the termination of the agreement or at any other time when so requested by the Company.

6. CONTRACTS EMPLOYING SALESMEN

Essential provisions of employment contracts.—It is the practice in many business houses not to enter into formal contracts in employing salesmen. The contention is that the psychological effect of requiring the employee to sign a formidable-looking paper is bad, and that, so far as the company is concerned, its interests are not furthered by having a legal document in its possession. The company wants good salesmen, not good lawsuits. However, the formal written contract of employment that puts into black and white the arrangements agreed upon between employer and employee still has its staunch adherents. The various provisions that may be included in such contracts are, perhaps, endless, but the following may be listed as those items that it is most essential and most common to cover:

1. The product that the salesman is to sell.
2. The territory that he is to cover.

3. The obligation of the salesman to devote full time to his work.

4. Compensation; whether payment is to be a straight salary, or commissions, or a combination of salary and commissions; whether credit losses may be charged against commissions; whether the salesman is to have a drawing account against commissions, and whether he is to be paid traveling expenses; when commissions are payable.

5. Furnishing of and responsibility for samples.

6. The making of reports by the salesman.

7. Restrictions on the employee's power to bind the company by orders.

8. Furnishing by the salesman of a fidelity bond for faithful performance of his duties.

9. Restrictions on salesman's activities before and after termination of employment.

10. Duration of contract.

11. Termination of contract—by advance notice, by expiration of fixed period, and so forth.

FORM NO. 99

Agreement for employment of salesman in allotted territory, on commission basis; provision for drawing account and traveling expenses; restriction against representing others during period of employment.

Agreement, made this .... day of ...., 19...., in the City of ...., State of ...., between the ...., Inc., a corporation organized under the laws of the State of .... and having its principal office at No. .... Street, City of ...., State of ...., party of the first part, and ...., of the City of ...., State of ...., party of the second part, Witnesseth:

1. [*Nature and period of employment*] The party of the second part agrees to continue in the service of the party of the first part as a salesman of .... and other products manufactured by the party of the first part and of such articles as the party of the first part deems necessary to assist it in the distribution of its products, in .... [*here insert description of salesman's territory*], for a period of ....

years from ...., 19....; this contract of employment may, however, be sooner terminated by either party giving .... months written notice of termination thereof to the other party.

2. [*Obligations of employee*] The party of the second part agrees to devote all of his time, attention, and energies to the performance of his duties as such salesman, subject to the control of the party of the first part, to serve the party of the first part diligently and according to the best of his ability in all respects, to make every effort to get orders in all parts of the territory allotted to him as aforesaid, and to straighten out to the best of his ability any complaints that may arise in connection with such orders.

3. [*Restriction against representing others during period of employment*] The party of the second part agrees not to represent, either directly or indirectly, any other person, firm, corporation, or business during said period of employment, unless the consent of the party of the first part is obtained thereto.

4. [*Price of goods and acceptance of orders*] The party of the second part agrees to sell all goods at prices fixed by the party of the first part, which prices shall not materially differ from competitor's prices on similar goods. All orders taken by the party of the second part are subject to acceptance by the party of the first part.

5. [*Payment of commissions*] The party of the first part agrees to pay commissions to the party of the second part, as follows:

(*a*) .... cents per gross on orders for .... [*here insert commodity*] taken by the party of the second part.

(*b*) .... cents per gross on those orders for .... received from customers or others on whom the party of the second part has sent reports to the party of the first part, and called on in person at least once a year.

(*c*) .... cents per gross on orders from jobbers on whom the party of the second part has sent in reports to the party of the first part, and called on in person at least once a year.

(*d*) .... per cent of the selling price on all orders for .... from manufacturers of .... or others on whom the party of the second part has sent in reports to the party of the first part, and called on in person at least once a year.

(*e*) .... on all shipments from contracts taken by the party of the second part before the date of this agreement and paid for after ...., 19...., as follows:

.... per cent per gross on shipments of ....
.... per cent per gross on shipments of ....
.... cents per gross on shipments of .... to jobbers.

Commissions as hereinabove provided shall not become due or payable to the party of the second part until the goods ordered are paid for by the respective customers.

6. [*Drawing account and traveling expenses*] The party of the first part agrees to allow the party of the second part against commissions a drawing account of $.............. per week, to be paid to the party of the second part on Thursday of each and every week. Traveling expenses incurred by the party of the second part outside of the cities of ...., ..., and ...., shall be paid by the party of the first part to the party of the second part on Thursday of each and every week for the preceding week.

The party of the first part agrees to pay to the party of the second part, on demand, the amount of commissions in excess of $.............. due the party of the second part on ...., ..., ..., and .... of each and every year during the period of his employment under this contract.

7. [*Records and reports*] The party of the first part agrees to keep an accurate account of all orders taken by the party of the second part in, or otherwise received from, the territory allotted to him as aforesaid, and to render to the party of the second part a statement of such account on the first (1st) days of ...., ..., ..., and .... of each year during the period of his employment under this contract.

In Witness Whereof, the parties hereto have hereunto set their hands and affixed their seals the .... day of ...., 19.....

.... Corporation

By ....
President

FORM NO. 100

Employment contract with regional manager.

Regional Manager's Employment Contract

.... Branch

This Agreement, made and entered into this .... day of ....,
19...., by and between The .... Company, ...

.................., hereinafter known as the "Company," and ...., of ...., hereinafter known as "Regional Manager."

Witnesseth: 1. That the Company authorizes the said .... to act as Regional Manager for the period from the .... day of ...., 19...., to and including the 31st day of December, 19...., in the territory described below—to wit:

....

....

This territory to be known as Block ....

2. [*Commission on dealers' sales*] The Company agrees to pay the Regional Manager on or before February 10th, 19...., a commission on wholesale sales of new .... Appliances shipped and invoiced from .... or branch warehouse stocks, and sold to and paid for by Authorized .... Dealers in the above-described territory, during the life of this contract, as per the following rate schedule:

[*Product*]

Models 108 and 109 .... 3% of net invoice
Models N, 10, and 11 .... 5% of net invoice
Models E, J, 32, and 33 .... 7% of net invoice

[*Product*]

Model F-7A .... 5% of net invoice
Models F-9 and F-10 .... 7% of net invoice
The provisions of Paragraph No. 2 do not apply to direct sales of .... products by The .... Company to the United States Government or any agency thereof.

3. [*Payment of commissions*] The Company further agrees to pay the Regional Manager Two Hundred ($200.00) Dollars per month, One Hundred ($100.00) Dollars payable on the fifteenth (15th) and thirtieth (30th) of each month, providing his commission balance equals or exceeds that amount. The amount of the semimonthly check will be determined by the amount of the commission balance, providing the latter is less than One Hundred ($100.00) Dollars. It is further agreed that the Company will remit the full amount of the Regional Manager's credit balance, up to an average of Two Hundred ($200.00) Dollars per month, on either the fifteenth (15th) or thirtieth (30th) of any month that his credit balance will warrant such payment.

4. [*Commissions on repair parts*] The Company further agrees to pay the Regional Manager a commission of three (3) per cent of the net

billing price on all eligible repair parts and accessories shipped and invoiced from .... or branch warehouse and sold and paid for in the above-described territory, during the life of this contract, the commission to be credited monthly to the regular commission account of the Regional Manager. In the event that such sales equal a quota of $............... during each six-month period, beginning January 1st, and ending June 30th, and beginning July 1st, and ending December 31st, 19...., the Company agrees to pay as a bonus an additional two (2) per cent of the net billing price. This bonus will be credited semiannually, after the close of each six-month period mentioned above. Parts used in the service or repair departments at ...., or the branch will not be eligible for commission.

5. [*Reports*] It is mutually agreed that the Regional Manager will promptly submit any reports required by the Company on the proper form provided for that purpose, and in accordance with directions printed thereon.

6. [*Inventory on termination of contract*] The Regional Manager agrees that, in case this contract is cancelled, or upon termination hereof by lapse of time or otherwise, an inventory may be taken of all machines that his dealer or dealers have in stock, and all machines that have not been sold at retail, upon which wholesale commission has been allowed, may be charged back to the Regional Manager at the current rates of commission.

7. [*Restrictions against employment by manager*] The Regional Manager is not authorized to employ any individual in any capacity on behalf of the Company: if the Regional Manager employs individuals on his own account, such individuals shall not be deemed employees of the Company.

8. [*Transfers between dealers*] The Regional Manager agrees to report to the Company all transfers of machines from dealers outside the above-described territory to dealers within the above-described territory and not to hold the Company liable for payment of commission on such transfers.

9. [*Quotas*] It is mutually agreed that fair and reasonable quarterly quotas for the above-described territory shall be set by the Company.

10. [*Settlement of commissions*] The Company further agrees to effect a settlement of not to exceed seventy-five (75) per cent of the commission balance for the first six (6) months of the current year, not later than August 10th, 19...., and to effect a complete settlement of the

commission balance due the Regional Manager hereunder, not later than February 10th, 19.....

11. [*Final settlement on termination*] In case this contract is terminated by the Company or by the Regional Manager or by the mutual consent of both, final settlement of any balance due the Regional Manager may be held at the Company's discretion, until the 10th of the following February.

12. [*Traveling expenses*] The Company shall defray the legitimate traveling expense of the Regional Manager if the Regional Manager is called to the Factory on the Company's business or to any other point upon specific instruction from the Company.

13. [*Overdrafts*] It is further mutually agreed that any commission account overdraft that may have been created under a former contract shall constitute a liability of the Regional Manager to The .... Company and shall be deducted from commission earned under this contract.

14. [*Independence from dealers*] The Regional Manager affirms that he does not now have any interest, financial or otherwise, in any retail or wholesale dealership and agrees that he will not acquire any such interest during the life of this contract. The Regional Manager further agrees to furnish complete information on all matters in connection with his activities whenever requested to do so by the Company.

15. [*Restrictions against side lines*] The Regional Manager agrees not to sell any side line of goods that are not considered the product of the Company.

16. [*Cancellation*] This contract cancels, takes the place of, and supersedes any previous contract that may have been in force at any time between the Regional Manager and The .... Company. The Company reserves the right to cancel and terminate this agreement at any time without advance notice for incompetency, immorality, misconduct, failure to render reports as above specified, or for any reason deemed sufficient by the Company, in which event the amount of the previous semimonthly payments shall be considered full settlement for the Regional Manager's services. This contract may be cancelled and terminated at any time by either party, without cause, by giving fifteen days' notice in writing.

17. [*Surety bond*] The Regional Manager agrees to furnish The .... Company a Surety Company bond in the amount of One Thousand ($1,000.00) Dollars, guaranteeing the faithful per-

formance of his duties and full accounting for all funds and property of the Company coming into his hands. The premium on said bond will be paid by the Company.

18. This Agreement shall become effective only when and if accepted and approved by the Sales Department of the Company.

Regional Manager

By ....

Approved: ...., 19....

Regional Manager

The .... Company

The .... Company

....

By ....

Sales Department

Branch Manager

FORM NO. 101

Agreement terminating employment contract.

AGREEMENT, made this .... day of ...., 19.... in the City of ...., State of ...., between ...., Inc., a corporation organized and existing under the laws of the State of ...., party of the first part, and ...., of the City of ...., party of the second part, WITNESSETH:

WHEREAS, an agreement was entered into between the parties hereto on the .... day of ...., 19...., under which the party of the first part employed the party of the second part as a ...., for a period of .... years from the said .... day of ...., 19...., and

WHEREAS, the parties hereto are both desirous of terminating said contract forthwith,

NOW, THEREFORE, in consideration of the sum of One ($1.00) Dollar and other good and valuable consideration by each of the parties to the other in hand paid, the receipt whereof is hereby acknowledged, and other good and valuable consideration, it is mutually agreed as follows:

1. That the said agreement of employment entered into between the parties hereto on the .... day of ...., 19...., be and it is this day terminated and cancelled.

2. That each of the parties hereto does hereby release and forever discharge the other party from any and all obligations or liabilities arising out of or under the aforesaid contract.

In Witness Whereof, the party of the first part has hereunto signed its name, by its President, duly authorized, and has caused its corporate seal to be affixed thereto, attested by its Secretary, and the party of the second part has hereunto set his hand and seal the day and year first above written.

(Corporate Seal) ...., Inc.

By ....
President

Attest:

.... *Secretary*

In the presence of:

....

7. MISCELLANEOUS CLAUSES IN CONTRACTS EMPLOYING SALESMEN

FORM NO. 102

Clause providing for indefinite period of employment, subject to cancellation at any time.

.... has agreed and hereby does agree to continue in the service of the Company for an indefinite period, subject to cancellation by either party to this agreement by giving sixty (60) days' notice in writing.

FORM NO. 103

Clause giving employer right to reject or cancel orders.

The Employer may refuse or reject, either in whole or in part, any order received by the Salesman, or may cancel any such order, either in whole or in part, after the acceptance thereof, or consent to a cancellation of any order, either in whole or in part, either before or after the shipment of merchandise, or accept any and all returns of merchandise made by customers, or grant such allowances to any customers as the Employer shall deem proper.

FORM NO. 104

Clause providing for quarterly payment of commissions.

The Employer shall pay to the Salesman a commission equal to .... per cent of all net moneys received by the Employer for merchandise shipped upon any order or orders procured by the Salesman, and a like amount of commission upon any repeat orders that shall be shipped by the employer, durng the term of this agreement.

The commissions earned hereunder shall be payable to the Salesman quarterly, after deducting therefrom the amount of all traveling expenses and advances then due from the Salesman.

FORM NO. 105

Clause providing for payment of salesman's commissions in event of termination of employment.

In the event of the termination of employment of the said .... as aforementioned, the said .... is to receive commissions on all contracts obtained by him up to the date of the termination of the employment, when the goods covered by the contract have been delivered by the .... Corporation, and the .... Corporation has received payment therefor.

FORM NO. 106

Clause providing that salesman shall receive commission on orders from jobbers.

The Company agrees to pay .... cents per gross, unless otherwise agreed upon in writing, as commission on orders for .... taken by ...., and those orders received from customers or others on whom .... has sent reports and called on at least once a year.

The Company further agrees to pay .... a commission of .... cents per gross, unless otherwise agreed on in writing, on orders from jobbers on whom .... has sent in reports or called on at least once a year, except those jobbers whom .... and the Company agree do not come under the terms of this agreement.

FORM NO. 107

Clause providing that salesman's commissions are not payable until payment is received from purchaser; maintenance of accounts and furnishing of statements.

It is further agreed that commissions are not to become due .... until the goods are paid for by the customers, and the Company agrees to pay on demand whatever amount in excess of $.............. is due ...., on ...., ..., ..., and .... of each and every year; and the Company further agrees to keep an accurate account of all the business done by .... and to render him a statement of such account on the first (1st) days of ...., ..., ..., and .... of each year.

FORM NO. 108

Clause providing for commission statements and requiring notice from salesmen, within a fixed time, of errors and omissions.

The Company shall render to the Salesman a monthly commission statement on or about the tenth (10th) day of each calendar month. The Salesman shall notify the Company within twenty (20) days after receipt of such statement of any errors, omissions, or items not understood by him. In the event that the Salesman does not raise any question as to the correctness of the statement within the twenty (20) days specified, he agrees, as a part of the consideration of this contract, not to raise any question after twenty (20) days have elapsed. The books of the Company shall be final as to the amount, list, and invoice price of all sales and commission due the Salesman. The Salesman shall have the right to inspect the books of the Company at any reasonable time on matters within the scope of this contract during the term of his employment.

FORM NO. 109

Clause granting employer right to withhold payments of accrued commission on termination of agreement.

In the event of termination of employment for any reason, the Company reserves the right to withhold payment of any accrued commissions or compensation for a period of four (4) months as a reserve against cancellations, charge-backs, or any other debit item.

FORM NO. 110

Clause for payment of traveling expenses up to fixed weekly amount, and for payment of advances, part of which is to be forwarded to salesman's wife.

The Employers shall pay the traveling expenses incurred by the Salesman when he is traveling outside of the City of New York, under the terms and provisions hereof, to the extent of, but not exceeding, the sum of One Hundred ($100.00) Dollars in any one week.

In addition to the aforesaid traveling expenses, the Employer shall advance to the Salesman the sum of One Hundred ($100.00) Dollars on Saturday of each week, during the term of this agreement, when the Salesman shall not be traveling, under the terms and conditions hereof, outside of the City of New York; and, during each and every week in which the Salesman shall, under the terms and conditions hereof, travel outside of the City of New York, the Employer shall advance to the Salesman the sum of One Hundred Fifty ($150.00) Dollars on Saturday of each and every week, as follows:

1. Seventy-five ($75.00) Dollars thereof, by mailing a check therefor to the wife of the Salesman, at the residence of the Salesman; and
2. The balance thereof, by mailing a check therefor to the Salesman.
3. That the aforesaid traveling expenses and advances shall be charged to, and deducted from, the commissions of the Salesman; but if such expenses and advances shall exceed the commissions earned by the Salesman hereunder, the Salesman shall not be liable for any such excess.

FORM NO. 111

Clause prohibiting salesman from making collections, giving receipts, or accepting gifts without employer's consent.

That the Salesman shall not, without first obtaining the written consent of the Employer:

1. Collect, or attempt to collect, any moneys due or to become due to the Employer;
2. Execute or deliver any receipt in the name or for the account of the Employer; or

3. Accept any gift, commission, gratuity, compensation, or article of value from any person, firm, or corporation whom he may solicit for orders.

FORM NO. 112

Clause providing for a daily report of orders by employee.

That the Salesman shall, at the end of each day, mail or deliver to the Employer a list of all orders daily received by him, as well as a daily list of all persons, firms, and corporations whom he may have solicited for orders.

FORM NO. 113

Clause requiring employer to furnish samples to traveling salesman.

That, to enable the Salesman to discharge his duties hereunder, the Employer shall, at his own cost and expense, supply the Salesman with samples of the .... manufactured by the Employer; that such samples shall always continue to be the sole and exclusive property of the Employer; that such samples shall be returned to the Employer immediately upon the Employer's demand therefor, or, in the absence of a prior demand therefor, immediately at the end of the term of this agreement, however occurring; and such samples shall be returned to the Employer in as good condition as the same were in when first received by the Salesman, reasonable depreciation resulting from their proper use alone excepted.

FORM NO. 114

Clause providing restriction against diverting trade or engaging in competitive business during employment and within fixed period thereafter.

[*Note.—In a suit involving the clause given below, the court held that this restrictive covenant was valid and not contrary to public policy.*]

The said Employee agrees that he will not at any time while he is in the employ of the said Corporation, or within two (2) years after leaving its service, for himself, or any other person, persons, or company, call for and deliver laundered and unlaundered goods to any person or persons who shall have been customers of said Corporation, and who shall have been supplied by said Corporation during any time he may have been employed under this contract, nor will he in any way, directly or indirectly, solicit, divert, take away, or attempt to solicit, divert, or take away, any of the custom, business, or patronage of such customers within such two (2) years, and said Employee further agrees that he will not at any time while he is in the employ of the said Corporation, or within two (2) years after leaving its service, for himself or any other person, persons, or company, engage in the laundry business, or call for and deliver any laundered or unlaundered goods, either directly or indirectly, in that portion of the City of ...., known as Route ...., between .... Street and .... Avenue (said portion of the city containing the laundry route or territory especially intrusted by said Corporation to said Employee).

FORM NO. 115

Clause in which driver-salesman agrees not to engage in similar business within fixed territory for one year after termination of contract.

In consideration of the premises, Driver agrees not to engage in the ice business directly or indirectly within the territory covered by the route or routes of which he may have had charge while in the employ of Company or within five (5) squares of same for a term of one (1) year immediately after his employment shall have ceased, whatever the reason, either for his own account or as agent or employee of any person, persons, corporations, or other entity, by canvassing or soliciting trade, by selling or delivering ice, by establishing, or endeavoring to establish, or pretending to establish, an ice route, by selling or transferring or giving anyone any right he may claim to have acquired in an ice route, nor shall driver assist anyone in doing the foregoing acts or give any information regarding said route or routes.

This agreement is made for the protection of the goodwill and business that may have been or may hereafter be acquired upon said route or routes; and, too, in consideration of this agreement, Driver does here assign and convey to Company all interest in goodwill and business upon said route or routes either existing or hereafter to be acquired or claimed by him in any manner.

Any re-employment from time to time of Driver by Company is hereby mutually recognized and accepted as a renewal of and ancillary to this original contract, the same as if re-executed by each and both without the necessity of actually executing a new contract, the provisions as to time and restrictions dating from last employment.

FORM NO. 116

Clause providing for giving of note by salesman for drawings.

The Salesman shall be allowed to draw or borrow against his commission account the sum of $............... per week, provided that he gives to the Company his personal note, payable on demand, to be applied against his commission credit, and no commission shall be payable to such Salesman until the amount of any such notes outstanding has been deducted therefrom.

FORM NO. 117

Clause making salesmen responsible for mistakes.

The salesman shall be responsible for any expense or loss to the Company occasioned by a mistake on his part. The commission on any sales credited to the Salesman shall be cancelled and credited to the Company as liquidated damages where the Salesman has:

(a) Misrepresented the quality, use, or purpose of the Company's product;

(b) Violated any terms of this contract in connection with any sale;

(c) Made any promise or representation contrary to the policy or instructions of the Company or unauthorized by the Company in connection with any sale; or

(d) Caused or permitted to exist any variance between the original and duplicate copies of any order taken by him.

FORM NO. 118

Clause providing restriction against other employment after termination of contract.

[*Note.— An express negative covenant not to work for another will not as a rule be enforced by the courts, save where, by reason of the peculiar character of the service, a violation of the agreement will cause injury to the employer for which an action at law will afford no adequate remedy. In cases where the courts have enforced a negative covenant by an employee not to work for another, the element of trade secrets or unfair dealing has been controlling and important.*]

That, at the expiration of the one (1) year term herein provided for, or upon sooner termination of his employment by the Corporation, by his resignation, discharge by the said Corporation, or for any other reason, the said Employee will not engage in any capacity in the business of contracting, remodeling, or repairing bungalows, cottages, sheds, garages, or any other buildings or structures of any kind, nature, or description, or in the making or securing of any contracts pertaining to the same, either for himself or for any other person, persons, firm, firms, corporation, or corporations, in any territory within a radius of fifty (50) miles from the site of the present City Hall, in the City of ...., State of ...., for a period of one (1) year from the time he leaves the employment of the said Corporation.

FORM NO. 119

Clause providing restriction against engaging in similar business in designated territory for a fixed period after employment.

The Employee agrees that he will not, directly or indirectly, either as principal, agent, or servant, for the term of three (3) years after any termination of said employment, enter or engage in any branch of the .... business in the following territory, without the written consent and approval of said Employer:

FORM NO. 120

Clause providing restriction against another person's accompanying employee while he is traversing assigned routes.

The Employee agrees that he will not allow any person or persons to accompany him while traversing the routes to which he is assigned, without the express permission of said Employer.

FORM NO. 121

Clause providing restriction against employee's divulging information concerning customers, during employment and for fixed period thereafter.

The Employee agrees that he will keep secret and will not divulge to any person, firm, or corporation, except by express order of his Employer, the names, addresses, or any information concerning any customers of the said Employer, during said employment and for three (3) years thereafter.

FORM NO. 122

Clause providing restriction against publication of information obtained by employee during employment.

It is understood and agreed that the Employee will not, without written approval of the Company, publish or authorize anyone else to publish, either during his term of employment or subsequent thereto, any information regarding apparatus, processes, and formulae acquired in the course of his employment under this agreement.

FORM NO. 123

Clause providing restriction against disclosure by employee of information obtained during employment; restriction against removal of papers.

The Employee agrees not to disclose any information obtained by him while in the employ of the Company, to any third person without the consent of an officer of the Company, whether during or after his employment; and further agrees, upon leaving the employ of the Company, not to take with him without its consent any notes, drawings, blueprints, descriptions, letters, or other papers or reproductions of such information.

FORM NO. 124

Clause requiring salesman to turn over to the company inventions relating to product he is selling.

In consideration of the employment herein granted, and of the instructions to said sales representative in the structures and the use of the devices developed and sold by the Company, the passing considerations of which are hereby acknowledged, said sales representative agrees that any inventions or improvements and/or devices that he may make, conceive, or develop, relating to office equipment allied to the products sold by the Company, during the continuance of this agreement, will be promptly disclosed to the Company, and, without further compensation than covered under the terms of this agreement, he shall, at the request of the Company, assign such inventions or developments to the Company for its full use and behalf.

FORM NO. 125

Clause granting employer right to assign rights under contract to partnership or corporation.

If the Employer shall, during the term of this agreement, form a partnership that shall acquire the business now conducted by the Employer, or if the Employer shall sell his said business to any corporation, then, and in either of such events, the Employer shall have the right to assign all of his right, title, and interest in this contract to such partnership or corporation; *provided, however,* that such partnership or corporation shall assume, and agree to perform, from and after the date of such assignment, all of the terms, provisions, and conditions hereof, with the same force and effect as if such partnership or corporation had originally been the Employer hereunder.

8. FOREIGN TRADE DEFINITIONS

[*Note.—The following explanation of terms common in foreign trade, together with recommendations as to their use, was issued by the National Foreign Trade Council.*]

It is strongly recommended to manufacturers and exporters that wherever abbreviated forms of export quotations are employed, the forms herein defined be used, so far as possible, to the exclusion of other forms.

1. *When the price quoted applies only at inland shipping point, and the seller merely undertakes to load the goods on or in cars or lighters furnished by the railroad company serving the industry, or most conveniently located to the industry, without other designation as to routing, the proper term is:*

f.o.b. (named point)

Under this quotation:

A. Seller must: (1) place goods on or in cars or lighters; (2) secure railroad bill of lading; (3) be responsible for loss and/or damage until goods have been placed in or on cars or lighters at forwarding point, and clean bill of lading has been furnished by the railroad company.

B. Buyer must: (1) be responsible for loss and/or damage incurred thereafter; (2) pay all transportation charges including taxes, if any; (3) handle all subsequent movement of the goods.

2. *When the seller quotes a price including transportation charges to the port of exportation without assuming responsibility for the goods after obtaining a clean bill of lading at the point of origin, the proper term is:*

f.o.b. (named point) freight prepaid to (named point on the seaboard)

Under this quotation:

A. Seller must: (1) place goods on or in cars or lighters; (2) secure railroad bill of lading; (3) pay freight to named port; (4) be responsible for loss and/or damage until goods have been placed in or on cars or lighters at forwarding point, and clean bill of lading has been furnished by the railroad company.

B. Buyer must: (1) be responsible for loss and/or damage incurred thereafter; (2) handle all subsequent movement of the goods; (3) unload goods from cars; (4) transport goods to vessels; (5) pay all demurrage and/or storage charges; (6) arrange for storage in warehouse or on wharf where necessary.

3. *Where the seller wishes to quote a price, from which the buyer may deduct the cost of transportation to a given point on the seaboard, without the seller assuming responsibility for the goods after obtaining a clean bill of lading at point of origin, the proper term is:*

f.o.b. (named point) freight allowed to (named point on the seaboard)

Under this quotation:

A. Seller must: (1) place goods on or in cars or lighters; (2) secure railroad bill of lading; (3) be responsible for loss and/or damage until goods have been placed in or on cars or lighters at forwarding point, and clean bill of lading has been furnished by the railroad company.

B. Buyer must: (1) be responsible for loss and/or damage incurred thereafter; (2) pay all transportation charges (buyer is then entitled to deduct from the amount of the invoice the freight paid from primary point to named port); (3) handle all subsequent movement of the goods; (4) unload goods from cars; (5) transport goods to vessel; (6) pay all demurrage and/or storage charges; (7) arrange for storage in warehouse or on wharf where necessary.

4. *The seller may desire to quote a price covering the transportation of the goods to seaboard, assuming responsibility for loss and/or damage up to that point. In this case the proper term is:*

f.o.b. cars (named point on seaboard)

Under this quotation:

A. Seller must: (1) place goods on or in cars; (2) secure railroad bill of lading; (3) pay all freight charges from forwarding point to port on seaboard; (4) be responsible for loss and/or damage until goods have arrived in or on cars at the named port.

B. Buyer must: (1) be responsible for loss and/or damage incurred thereafter; (2) unload goods from cars; (3) handle all subsequent movement of the goods; (4) transport goods to vessel; (5) pay all demurrage and/or storage charges; (6) arrange for storage in warehouse or on wharf where necessary.

5. *It may be that the goods, on which a price is quoted covering the transportation of the goods to the seaboard, constitute less than a carload lot. In this case the proper term is:*

f.o.b. cars (named port) l.c.l.

Under this quotation:

A. Seller must: (1) deliver goods to the initial carrier; (2) secure railroad bill of lading; (3) pay all freight charges from forwarding point to port on seaboard; (4) be responsible for loss and/or damage until goods have arrived on cars at the named port.

B. Buyer must: (1) be responsible for loss and/or damage incurred thereafter; (2) handle all subsequent movement of the goods; (3) accept goods from the carrier; (4) transport goods to vessel; (5) pay all storage charges; (6) arrange for storage in warehouse or on wharf where necessary.

6. *Seller may quote a price which will include the expense of transportation of the goods by rail to the seaboard, including lighterage. In this case, the proper term is:*

f.o.b. cars (named port) lighterage free

Under this quotation:

A. Seller must: (1) place goods on or in cars; (2) secure railroad bill of lading; (3) pay all transportation charges to, including lighterage at, the port named; (4) be responsible for loss and/or damage until goods have arrived on cars at the port named.

B. Buyer must: (1) be responsible for loss and/or damage incurred thereafter; (2) handle all subsequent movement of the goods; (3) take out the insurance necessary to the safety of the goods after arrival on the cars; (4) pay the cost of hoisting goods into vessel where weight of goods is too great for ship's tackle; (5) pay all demurrage and other charges, except lighterage charges.

7. *The seller may desire to quote a price covering delivery of the goods alongside overseas vessel and within reach of its loading tackle. In this case, the proper term is:*

f.a.s. vessel (named port)

Under this quotation:

A. Seller must: (1) transport goods to seaboard; (2) store goods in warehouse or on wharf if necessary, unless buyer's obligation includes provision of shipping facilities; (3) place goods alongside vessel either in a lighter or on the wharf; (4) provide the usual dock or ship's receipt; (5) be responsible for loss and/or damage until goods have been delivered alongside the ship or on wharf.

B. Buyer must: (1) be responsible for loss and/or damage thereafter, and for insurance; (2) handle all subsequent movement of the goods; (3) pay cost of hoisting goods into vessel where weight of goods is too great for ship's tackle.

8. *The seller may desire to quote a price covering all expenses up to and including delivery of the goods upon the overseas vessel at a named port. In this case, the proper term is:*

f.o.b. vessel (named port)

Under this quotation:

A. Seller must: (1) meet all charges incurred in placing goods actually on board the vessel; (2) provide the usual dock or ship's receipt; (3) be responsible for all loss and/or damage until goods have been placed on board the vessel.

B. Buyer must: (1) be responsible for loss and/or damage thereafter; (2) handle all subsequent movement of the goods.

9. *The seller may be ready to go farther than the delivery of his goods upon the overseas vessel and be willing to pay transportation to a foreign port of delivery. In this case, the proper term is:*

c.&f. (named port)

Under this quotation:

A. Seller must: (1) make freight contract and pay transportation charges sufficient to carry goods to agreed destination; (2) deliver to buyer or his agent clean bills of lading to the agreed destination; (3) be responsible for loss and/or damage until goods have been delivered alongside the ship and clean ocean bill of lading obtained (seller is not responsible for delivery of goods at destination).

B. Buyer must: (1) be responsible for loss and/or damage thereafter and must take out all necessary insurance; (2) handle all subsequent movement of the goods; (3) take delivery and pay costs of discharge, lighterage, and landing at foreign port of destination in accordance with bill-of-lading clauses; (4) pay foreign customs duties and wharfage charges, if any.

10. *The seller may desire to quote a price covering the cost of the goods, the marine insurance on the goods, and all transportation charges to the foreign point of delivery. In this case, the proper term is:*

c.i.f. (named foreign port)

Under this quotation:

A. Seller must: (1) make freight contract to pay freight charges sufficient to carry goods to agreed destination; (2) take out and pay for necessary marine insurance; (3) deliver to buyer or his agent clean bills of lading to the agreed destination, and insurance policy and/or negotiable insurance certificate; (4) be responsible for loss and/or damage until goods have been delivered alongside the ship, and clean ocean bill of lading and insurance policy and/or negotiable insurance certificate have been delivered to the buyer, or his agent (seller is not responsible for the delivery of goods at destination, nor for payment by the underwriters of insurance claims); (5) provide war risk insurance where necessary for buyer's account.

B. Buyer must: (1) be responsible for loss and/or damage thereafter, and must make all claims to which he may be entitled under the insurance directly on the underwriters; (2) take delivery and pay costs of discharge, lighterage, and landing at foreign port of destination in accordance with bill-of-lading clauses; (3) pay foreign customs duties and wharfage charges, if any.

EXPLANATION OF ABBREVIATIONS

f.o.b. .... Free on board
f.a.s. .... Free along side
c.&f. .... Cost and freight
c.i.f. .... Cost, insurance, and freight
l.c.l. .... Less-than-carload lot

GENERAL RECOMMENDATIONS

In reaching the conclusions set forth in this statement, the Conference considered the fact that there are, in more or less common use by manufacturers in different parts of the United States, numerous variations of these abbreviations, practically all of which are employed to convey meanings substantially synonymous with those here defined. For instance, there are manufacturers who quote "f.o.b. cars," "f.o.b. works," "f.o.b. mill," or "f.o.b. factory," meaning that the seller and buyer have the same responsibilities as those set forth in Section 1. The Conference considered all those variations and determined to recommend the use of "f.o.b. (named point)"—as "f.o.b. Detroit," "f.o.b. Pittsburgh," etc. Of the considerable number of these abbreviations which are used in the United States, the Conference felt that the form "f.o.b. (named point)" is most widely used and understood, and therefore should be adopted as the standard of practice.

The chief purpose of the Conference is to simplify and standardize American practice, and to that end it urges manufacturers and exporters to cease the use of synonymous abbreviations and quote habitually in the terms here recommended, just as far as these terms will cover the price conditions which it is desired to arrange with the buyer.

Variations of the abbreviations recommended in other sections also are in more or less common use throughout the United States. The recommendations of the Conference set forth above apply to them with the same force as to those cited under Section 1.

Manufacturers and exporters are urged to bear in mind that the confusion and controversies which have arisen have sprung in part from the use of an excessive number of abbreviated forms with substantially similar meanings, as well as from the use of abbreviations in a sense different from their original meanings, or in an application not originally given them and different from the sense or application understood by foreign buyers.

SECTION 7

Purchasing Procedure

1. ORGANIZATION OF THE PURCHASING DEPARTMENT

2. BUYING THE RIGHT THING

3. BUYING THE RIGHT AMOUNT

4. BUYING AT THE RIGHT PLACE

5. BUYING AT THE RIGHT TIME

6. BUYING AT THE RIGHT PRICE

7. REQUISITIONS

8. PURCHASE ORDERS

9. RECEIVING AND INSPECTING INCOMING GOODS AND CHECKING INVOICES

10. STORES AND INVENTORY CONTROL

SECTION 7

Purchasing Procedure

1. ORGANIZATION OF THE PURCHASING DEPARTMENT

Purchasing agent's place in the business.—The importance of sound purchasing policies and the value of the purchasing agent's services to the business organization as a whole have been receiving increased attention in recent years. There was a tendency at one time to regard purchasing as a comparatively insignificant function, and to relegate the duties connected with it to anyone who was reasonably intelligent and a good trader. That this view of purchasing is not in accordance with the facts is apparent when it is considered that in many cases purchases of equipment, materials, and supplies represent from 30 to 65 per cent of the total operating expenses of a business. One authority, using data collected and published by the Bureau of the Census, calculated that in industry as a whole, 57 cents of the manufacturer's dollar is spent for materials, and 17 cents for labor; the remaining item of 26 cents covers overhead, interest, taxes, and profits. The same authority estimated that gross sales must be increased $10, on the basis of average profits, to compensate for every $1 of waste resulting from unsound purchasing.* In many respects the purchasing department is one of the most fundamentally important departments of a business. Errors in purchasing are costly; every dollar saved in purchasing is 100 per cent profit. Purchasing profits are net.

---

* Gushee, Edward T., and Boffey, L. F., *Scientific Purchasing*. New York: McGraw-Hill.

Purchasing agent's qualifications.—Briefly described, the purchasing agent's job is to buy the *right materials* at the *right time* in the *right quantities* and at the *right price.* When reduced to these fundamentals, the job seems simple enough, but, in translating the fundamentals into practice, the purchasing agent requires varied technical and commercial knowledge and experience, specialized training, and strong common sense. He must be familiar with market conditions and tendencies, in order that he may know where to go for what he wants, when to buy, and what price to pay. He must have a general technical knowledge of the materials used in his organization and of the processes through which they pass. He must know the requirements, routines, and methods of all the departments of the business. He acts as one of the materials experts of the organization, not only furnishing information on materials when asked to do so, but also volunteering suggestions. When supplies show signs of scarcity, he urges research for substitutes. When new types of materials, new equipment or tools, improved processes, possible substitutes, or changes of standards appear, the purchasing agent is in the most favorable position to obtain this information. These surveys comprise the creative side of his job and are his opportunity to make valuable contributions to the progress of the business.

Aims of the purchasing department.—The aim of the purchasing department is to organize for economic purchasing. A sound organization permits better planning, more clearly understood objectives, and lower cost of operation.

To determine whether the purchasing department is organized for economic purchasing, the following tests should be applied:

1. Are the functions and authority of the various units defined?
2. Is responsibility for action fixed?
3. Is the relationship of the various departments with the purchasing department established to assure the greatest co-operation among them?
4. Has an adequate personnel been provided? An over-worked purchasing officer who is burdened with detail cannot give attention to possibilities for economies in the broader fields of purchasing and procedure.

5. Is there adequate supervision by people of specialized ability and experience?

6. Is there flexibility within the department? Flexibility facilitates the introduction of cost-saving ideas, methods, and policies. Especially is flexibility essential where branch plants do their own purchasing.

7. Are the purchasing department records complete? Complete records and files of specifications, suppliers, prices paid and bid, deliveries, discounts, quantities, and markets prevent duplication of effort and assure continuity of service and quality.

8. Is company policy consistently followed by the purchasing department?

Policies controlling the purchasing department.—The purchasing department is concerned with two types of policies: (1) company policies that apply to all departments of the organization, and (2) purchasing policies.

The purchasing officer should be made directly responsible to an authority who is responsible for the profits and general policies of the company. In this way the purchasing department can be informed of general company policies. In most organizations, as is indicated by the charts in Figures 43 and 44, pages 754–755, the purchasing officer is responsible to an executive committee or an executive officer such as the president, vice-president, or general manager.

It is ordinarily inadvisable for the general management or any other department to impose purchasing policies *in toto* upon the purchasing department. Such policies, as distinct from general company policies, are best determined by the purchasing officer himself on minor matters, and in collaboration with a committee or other officials of the company on major matters. In some instances buying policies are best determined by the purchasing and production departments working together, where these departments are closely interrelated.

Relation of purchasing department to other departments.—While purchasing is the prerogative of the purchasing department and should not be usurped by any other department, it cannot be carried out economically or satisfactorily without the fullest cooperation of other departments. In certain matters, such as negotiating with suppliers, arranging details of handling transactions, and completing the transactions, the purchasing department can act independently. The type of co-operation with other departments that is desirable and the method of obtaining it are discussed in the following paragraphs.

1. *Production.*—In working with the production department, the purchasing department sees that materials, supplies, and equipment conform to the standards of quality and service that production requirements dictate. The purchasing agent should find new and cheaper sources of supply and be able to suggest substitute materials and alternative designs and methods that will reduce production costs. In making suggestions the purchasing agent should try to overcome any bias or prejudice on the part of the production department for certain kinds of goods. In some instances, however, because of special considerations of quality, the production department will furnish the purchasing department with rigid specifications in order to conform to the company policy regarding the quality of the manufactured product. In such cases price becomes secondary to quality.

2. *Financial.*—Much of the purchasing agent's value to the business depends upon his ability to take immediate advantage of attractive offerings. However, purchases must be arranged at times and in quantities that will be convenient from the standpoint of the disbursement of funds. Co-operation with the financial department is, therefore, essential. Such co-operation is usually confined to supplying the purchasing budget, advising on future commitments, and approving invoices.

3. *Credit.*—The relation of the purchasing agent to the credit manager is perhaps less obvious than his relation to the production manager and the treasurer, but co-operation between the two is of considerable value to both. The purchasing agent, through his wide contacts, obtains much confidential information that would be of great assistance to the credit manager, and vice versa. For example, if the purchasing agent is able to pay cash for a car of copper wire, and he learns through the credit manager that one of the dealers is short of funds, this information places him in a much stronger bargaining position. Similarly, if the purchasing agent knows that the buyer for another firm is plunging on the

commodity market, a warning to the credit manager to watch that firm's credit may be useful.

It is advisable to furnish the credit manager with a list of those firms with whom the purchasing department deals in order to have available the latest and most reliable reports of the financial condition of each firm. The firm's condition has a very important bearing on its ability to execute its commitments at the proper time, and in the quantities and quality specified.

4. *Sales.*—Purchasing policies and decisions are affected by sales forecasts.

Reciprocal buying, discussed on page 770, is also a matter calling for co-operation with the sales department. A purchasing agent should let the sales manager know when he is placing heavy orders with a firm that is a good prospect for the company's products. He should also introduce to the buyer of such a firm the idea of becoming a customer if this procedure is recommended by the management.

5. *Stores.*—The question often arises as to whether the stores department should be under the supervision of the purchasing agent or the production manager. While there are arguments on both sides, and while the best solution in any organization depends largely upon the personnel involved, it is usually better to place the stores department under the direction of the purchasing agent. If the stores function is under the production department, the purchasing agent, in requesting requisitions for stock purchases that he regards as advantageous, will often be embarrassed not only by delay of the requisition but also by being required to convince the production manager of the wisdom of the purchase. Further, the production manager may very easily hamper the purchasing agent by making eleventh-hour demands for materials that cannot readily be secured to advantage. The responsibility for maintaining inventories at figures neither too low from the standpoint of safety nor too high from the standpoint of investment rests with the purchasing agent. Where the stores department is under the production manager, confusion is likely to result from division of responsibility and authority.

6. *Accounting.*—In the section dealing with invoice checking and payment of invoices (see pages 802 et seq.), the close relationship between the purchasing and accounting departments is brought out.

7. *Legal.*—A company can avoid legal entanglements and save itself the costly expense of lawsuits by encouraging close co-operation between the purchasing officer and the legal department. Where no legal department is established, the purchasing officer should be permitted to consult the company's attorney freely. The purchasing agent must have the advice of counsel on such matters as drawing contracts, handling claims, complying with the provisions of new legislation, and the like.

8. *Management.*—The management should advise the purchasing agent in advance of any changes in company policy and of all proposed additions to plant and equipment. One way to obtain this co-operation easily is to have a member of the purchasing department sit in on all meetings of the production division and of the general management.

Centralization of purchasing in a single department.—Centralized purchasing is ordinarily essential to maximum efficiency and economy. In most industrial and commercial organizations the procedure in connection with the purchase of all materials, supplies, machines, tools, and services needed in the conduct of the business is placed in the hands of a single department, headed by the purchasing agent.

The more standard the product and the more uniform the operations, the more advisable and effective is centralized control of purchasing for all plants. Centralized purchasing of all supplies, equipment, and material is recommended where there is but a single plant and where there are several plants in close proximity making the same or a similar product.

Among the many advantages that have been found to result from centralization are the following:

1. Responsibility for all purchases is definitely fixed, and there is less confusion of authority.

2. Haphazard, hit-and-miss methods of buying can be eliminated, and a consistent buying policy can be established. This results in smoother operation for all departments, and also in economies.

3. Buying power of the various departments is aggregated, and lower prices can be obtained through quantity purchases.

4. Standardization of purchases is made easier, and the tend-

ency to purchase a wide variety of materials and supplies differing in no essential respect is minimized. Standardization of purchases is one of the best means of effecting economies.

5. Because all purchase records are under the supervision of one department, it is easier to control inventories and to eliminate unnecessary variety in the materials carried in stock.

6. Market analysis is encouraged, permitting purchasing at the right time, under the most favorable conditions.

7. Studies can be made to determine whether substitute materials can be used that will reduce manufacturing costs without impairing the quality of the product.

8. More accurate adaptation of purchases to needs can be accomplished. This results in a better product and reduces the losses due to waste, scrap, and excess materials.

9. Greater co-operation with other departments is obtained where a central purchasing department is established and its authority is recognized.

10. Central supervision over the disposal of surplus stock permits transfer between departments or plants.

Decentralization of the purchasing department.—Where products are extremely diverse and plants are widely scattered, centralized purchasing is usually impractical. In such cases, a complete purchasing office at each plant, directed by a local purchasing agent, is usually the solution. Although the policies and procedure followed by each local purchasing agent may be determined by the head purchasing officer, the local agent will do all his buying independently of the main office.

Partial centralization of the purchasing department.—Partial centralization rather than total centralization may be advisable where plants that make the same or similar products are widely scattered, and where plants that make diverse products are within the same shipping and shopping districts.

Partial centralization requires that local purchasing agents direct the buying of plant supplies. For major purchases they can draw against a common contract or arrangement made for all plants by the main purchasing agent. Plant purchasing agents should know local requirements and sources of materials. In case of emergency they should have the power to take decisive action.

All local purchasing agents should report to an administrative head, who should determine the broad policies and contract for all common needs. The local agents should meet at regular intervals to discuss procedure and to adopt the same standards and specifications.

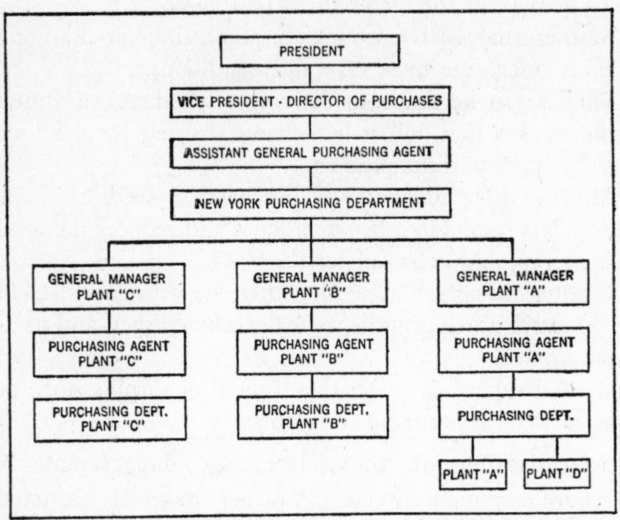

Figure 43.—Chart of Organization Which Is Partially Centralized.

Establishing centralization of the purchasing function.—The change from a decentralized purchasing system to a centralized system should be undertaken only after careful planning. Everything should be done to eliminate violent opposition from the plant executives, to avoid dissatisfaction among the personnel of the purchasing department, and to prevent any lack of co-operation between the factory and the purchasing departments that are being eliminated. The first suggestion, then, is to avoid abrupt changes, for such procedure usually brings with it the evils mentioned. To be sure, certain advantages of a quick change will be sacrificed and certain disadvantages of a slow change will have to be overcome, but, if experience is a guide, the gradual change is the better method.

Advantages of a rapid change.—

1. Centralization is achieved immediately and completely.
2. The initial cost of introducing the change is lower than if a gradual plan is used.

3. New purchasing policies can be put into effect more quickly.
4. Savings through centralization can begin immediately.
5. The advantage to supplier in calling at a centralized place is immediate.

Advantages of a gradual change.—

1. It is easier to introduce because there is less opposition to overcome. The gradual change permits an opportunity to convince the departments affected that there is merit in centralized purchasing.

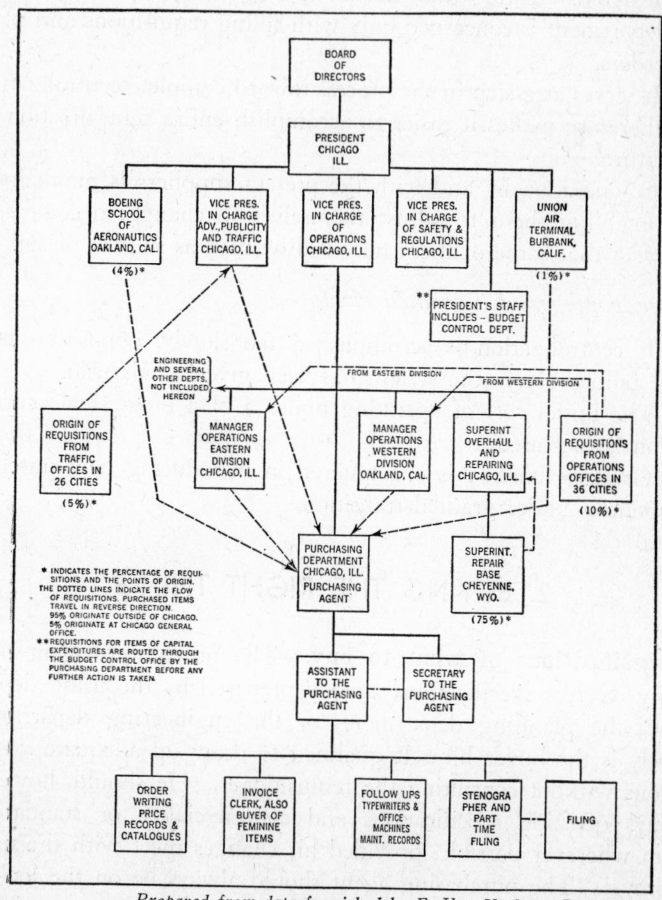

Prepared from data furnished by E. Van Vechten, Purchasing Agent, United Air Lines Transport Corporation

Figure 44.—Chart of Purchasing Organization Which Is Centralized.

2. It does not interfere with the efficiency of persons involved since it avoids, as far as possible, dissatisfaction among the personnel.

3. It does not sacrifice any existing close relationship between the factory and the established purchasing departments. Loss of the production department's co-operation might mean retarded development of new products and an indifference toward the practice of passing along to the centralized purchasing department new ideas concerning materials.

4. It avoids creating the impression that the centralized purchasing department is concerned only with filling requisitions and placing orders.

5. It serves as a step in the process toward complete centralization and therefore makes it easier to accomplish entire centralization in the future.

6. Co-operation by and with the present suppliers is maintained, thus enabling them to adjust themselves to changes necessary in the event that some of them may still be used as sources of supply.

Disadvantages of a gradual change.—

1. If centralization is accomplished too slowly, opposition may cause failure before the system has been given a fair trial.

2. The initial cost of operating under a plan of gradual centralization is increased.

3. Greater difficulty is encountered in introducing new purchasing policies under gradual transition.

2. BUYING THE RIGHT THING

Specifications of what to buy.—The purchasing agent ordinarily receives specifications already prepared by the using department, the planning department, or the engineering department. Rarely is the buyer himself qualified to draw up adequate specifications without consulting the requisitioner. He should, however, always question specifications and commercialize or standardize them wherever possible, provided his changes meet with the user's approval. The purchasing agent should always be on the lookout for alternative methods or materials that would lower cost without sacrificing quality. By pointing out the advantages of alternatives to the using departments, the buyer can help to promote their adoption.

Assurance of adequate specifications.—Adequate specifications reduce costs by insuring that goods meet the requirements of the producing departments. Rejection costs are lowered, and a better product results. The following practices will assure adequate specifications:

1. Leave no loophole of which an unscrupulous vendor can take advantage.
2. Accurately describe the exact requirement, physical or performance, which must be met; where variations are permitted, state the limits.
3. Allow flexibility to insure the widest competition and the use of latest developments in materials and methods.
4. Make meaning clear by using simple words.
5. Give detail in proportion to the value of the goods.
6. Adhere closely to, or allow room for, filling specifications with standard goods.
7. Describe the methods of inspection and testing that will determine acceptance or rejection of goods. A specification is worthless if it cannot be checked or verified with the product.
8. Stipulate any special packing or marking desired.
9. When more than one shipment is desired, state dates for each, as this information may be important to the stores department.

How to standardize specifications.—In purchasing, standardization is of the greatest importance. Standard materials should be purchased wherever practicable, and special features should be reduced to a minimum. Standardization may be achieved by simplifying inventory and by systematizing ordering.

Standardization by simplifying inventory.—Variety in stock is costly and should be reduced in every possible instance. Commercial and selective simplification should be adopted to determine what size or item of stock is the most important, practical, and adaptable to the use of all departments. Departments using similar, yet not identical, materials should use the same articles where differences are not fundamental. Such a practice will permit larger quantity purchases and the interchange of materials within the organization. Departments formerly requisitioning special equipment and goods will often accept standard goods to save time. Once used, standard goods are usually found to be as satisfactory as the more costly nonstandard product.

Standardization by systematizing ordering.—Standardization in ordering materials can be obtained to some degree by keeping a file of specifications for all items and by giving specifications consistent and standard nomenclature wherever possible.

Then, from the file, a general catalogue can be prepared of specifications for all items used by the company. The items carried in the stores department can be listed in a separate stores catalogue. These catalogues can then be distributed throughout the company to be used in ordering by the using departments.

In some lines vendors furnish catalogues setting forth full specifications under which their products are sold. The specifications selected as standards can be safely used as the purchaser's specifications unless, as in the case of steel equipment, a special unit is desired.

Value of standardized specifications.—The producer can save money and obtain other advantages by using standard materials wherever possible because:

1. Variety in inventory is reduced.
2. Lower prices are obtained. The purchaser benefits from the lower unit cost of continuous standard production.
3. Equitable competition is more readily secured. Buying special materials limits the number of manufacturers qualified as competitors. Purchasing identical materials from different sources increases the benefits of spreading sources.
4. Reordering is facilitated and less costly.
5. Delivery is quicker; this results in a smaller investment in inventory.
6. Constant measuring, testing, and checking become unnecessary once the standard goods are accepted as serviceable; occasional checks, however, are desirable.
7. Expense of ordering is less often disproportionate to the value of the goods.
8. Waste incurred by carelessly drawn specifications is avoided.

9. The trading reputation of the buyer is enhanced by full and precise specifications.

10. Production is stabilized.

Sources of information on standard specifications.—Practically every purchaser can make use of many widely known and published specifications familiar to both buyers and sellers. Most nationally recognized specifications are confined to raw and semimanufactured materials. The more commonly used specifications are the Commercial Standards established through the Division of Trade of the National Bureau of Standards. These industrial standards have been set up through the request and voluntary cooperation of producers, distributors, and consumers throughout the country.

The Government Printing Office, Washington, D. C., will send on request the following publications of the Bureau of Standards:

1. *The National Directory of Commodity Specifications.* This presents classified and alphabetical lists and brief descriptions of the standards and specifications of trade associations, technical societies, and organizations nationally representative of various branches of industry, plus those of the governmental agencies that represent the Federal Government as a whole.

2. The *Standards Year Book* and the *Industrial Standardization and Commercial Standards Monthly.*

3. An encyclopedia of specifications for different industries. Although some of the ten volumes of this encyclopedia are still in preparation, those on wood-using industries, nonmetallic minerals, metals, and metal products have been issued.

The Federal Standards Catalogue gives specifications used by several executive departments of the Federal Government and independent agencies. Published by the procurement division of the Treasury Department, it may be obtained from the Superintendent of Documents, Washington, D. C.

Many nongovernmental agencies have also established and published specifications. These are chiefly of a technical nature. Most widely used are those of the American Society of Testing Materials, known as A. S. T. M. specifications, the American Society of Mechanical Engineers, the Society of Automotive Engineers, the Underwriters' Laboratories, and the National Safety

Council. The American Standards Association, a member of the International Standards Association, acts as a clearing house for the development and adoption of national standards.

Buying standard goods on the certification or labelling plan.—Standard goods may also be bought on a certification plan. A list is compiled of manufacturers who will supply on contract materials that have nationally recognized specifications. These manufacturers then certify that the materials thus supplied comply with the testing requirements for the specifications and are so guaranteed. The Federal Bureau of Standards has compiled such a list which, while ordinarily limited in distribution to governmental and institutional buyers, may be obtained upon specific request.

A labelling plan is being developed by the Federal Bureau of Standards to substitute for the certification plan in certain instances. The noncontract or "over-the-counter" buyer will derive through it some of the benefits available to contract buyers under the certification plan. The buyer's confidence in the manufacturer's label, backed by the guaranty of a reliable inspecting agency, should obviate the need for testing commodities on delivery. Both of the above plans are suggested for the buyer whose company has inadequate facilities for testing materials. See page 805 for testing by college laboratories.

Ways to present nonstandard specifications.—When special requirements must be met, specifications for a special order must be presented to a manufacturer. The buyer can eliminate many of his difficulties by presenting specifications in one of the following ways:

1. *By brand.*—Purchase by brand is usually more expensive because of promotional costs. It is not recommended except in the following cases, and then should be used with caution:

(*a*) For ordinary supplies such as paper, ink, and so forth.

(*b*) Where continuous dependability of a certain quality is necessary.

(*c*) Where items or quantities are too small to justify the preparation of special specifications.

(*d*) For products manufactured by secret or patented process for which there is no satisfactory substitute.

(*e*) When testing cannot be assumed by the buyer, and reliance must be placed on the supplier's reputation and integrity.

2. *By market grade.*—Purchase on the basis of market grade is confined to certain primary materials such as wheat and cotton. Its value depends largely upon the following:

(*a*) The use to which it is put.
(*b*) The accuracy of the grading.
(*c*) The ability to inspect the material as to its grade before purchase.

3. *By chemical analysis.*—Definiteness and completeness of description in acceptable technical terms are necessary where requirements are exacting. Where specifications have been given by chemical analysis, make sure that laboratory tests are made in inspecting the goods. The material should also be supported by the manufacturer's chemical analysis.

4. *By materials and methods of manufacture.*—This method has proved the most satisfactory in purchasing certain chemicals, steel, automobile parts, and other products. It should, however, be used sparingly, with consideration for the following:

(*a*) Is the purchasing agent prepared for the tremendous responsibility that he must assume under this method?

(*b*) Is not the manufacturer, when informed of the use to which the goods are to be put, in a better position to judge the materials and methods?

5. *By blueprint or dimension sheet.*—This system assures clarity in requirements and comparative quotations. Since it is expensive, it is used primarily in the purchase of materials to be installed or erected, special equipment, tools, forgings, castings, and machine parts.

6. *By purpose or use.*—In some ways this is the simplest method for the buyer because it eliminates any need for exhaustive study and the preparation of detailed information. The buyer has only the responsibility of choosing a vendor who is absolutely reliable and an expert in his line. The vendor is given an opportunity to

use the latest developments in methods, but at the same time is made responsible for quality and service. This method is used for buying oils, special supplies, machinery, and equipment.

7. *By performance desired.*—The purchaser is concerned here only with the results of the product. The responsibility of service is placed with the vendor. The same buyer-seller considerations apply here as in buying for purpose or use.

8. *By sample.*—Presenting the vendor with a sample to be matched is a dubious method when the sample is not a standard manufactured article. It should be used only when no other method is available. The article may have been specially made originally, and matching may prove expensive, particularly if the raw material is not easily obtainable. The difficulties of exact duplication of special goods even when materials are available are often insurmountable. The uses to which the finished product is put should, whenever possible, be stated, in order to assist the vendor in properly preparing the samples from which the buyer can choose, or offering a substitute that might serve the purpose equally well. In such cases the substitute should be submitted to the using department for approval.

Precautions in using nonstandard specifications.—In using nonstandard specifications, the purchasing agent must be continually on guard against the following: (1) restricting competition; (2) discouraging research; (3) overlooking new developments in methods and materials; (4) passing by equally satisfactory and less expensive standard goods; and (5) additional expense of special requirements.

Sources of information in regard to the buyer's problems.—Information from outside the company on what to buy can be obtained from salesmen, catalogues distributed by vendors, and trade papers and journals. These sources of information will be further discussed on page 767.

Governmental bureaus and technical societies engaged in research are continually introducing new developments that may present the answer to many of the buyer's problems. The Bureau of Standards, the Bureau of Mines, and private technical groups co-operate in helping when the buyer's problems are brought to their attention. Activities of the governmental bureaus are published and may be obtained by having the buyer's name placed on a mailing list to receive notices of publications in his field of interest. A list of available documents may be had upon request to the Superintendent of Documents, Washington, D. C.

Specifications file.—The purchasing department may keep a file of the specifications for all the more important materials and equipment used in the business. This file will prove very useful when it becomes necessary to reorder, particularly in the case of rush orders for materials and breakdown orders for machinery parts. The specifications file should be revised from time to time, each specification being checked in the light of new developments; the purchasing and production departments may co-operate in this work.

The specifications file may be consolidated with other records, such as the vendor's record, price record, and former purchase record. The card shown in Figure 45, used by a drug company, combines the vendor's price record with information as to specifications. This combination card eliminates the necessity for a separate specification card in the purchasing department.

PW F-587A. 1M-6-39

COMMODITY CARD NO.

VENDOR	ORDER NO	DATE	SPECIFICATIONS	QUANTITY	PRICE	DELIVERED TO & ACCTG

Figure 45.—Price and Specification Record.

[Actual Size 5" x 8"]

3. BUYING THE RIGHT AMOUNT

Responsibility for determining the amount to buy.—For best results, the responsibility for determining the right amount to buy should be divided among several departments, with the purchasing department acting as a co-ordinating agency. This may be accomplished by having the sales and production departments regularly send the buyer a copy of their demand schedules, the planning department submit a weekly report, and the stores department record quantities on hand and estimates of the rate of their use. The management's policies as to investment in inventory should be known. To the purchasing department is left the delicate adjustment of timing supply to demand. By anticipating quantity requirements, a company protects its unit cost. Where a budget system is employed, the sales department should carefully note variations in its program so that the plans of the purchasing department can be adjusted accordingly.

Factors determining the amount to buy.—When the purchasing department is considering the amount to buy in relation to current inventory and stores, it should give attention to the following factors:

1. Quantity and value of stock on hand.
2. Time and extent of probable use of materials as based on production schedules.
3. Storage costs of carrying material in stock until it is used.
4. Deterioration and obsolescence possibilities.
5. Handling charges arising from inadequate storage facilities.
6. Cost of buying as proportionate to the value of goods.
7. Quantity price differentials or discounts allowed for goods.
8. Market conditions and price trends in relation to the period the quantity should cover.
9. Time required for delivery and replenishment of materials.

Ways to determine the basic amount to buy.—The most economical quantity to purchase is not always consistent with the most economical lot to produce. If the company turns out fairly standard products in substantially regular quantities, that quantity should be purchased which is most economical from the standpoint of discounts, storage facilities, and so on. When manufacturing is on special order, when warehouses and storerooms are not maintained, when style is important, or when no advantage accrues from quantity buying, buying should be from the standpoint of the most economical lot to produce. This method of purchasing will entail knowledge of exact production requirements whenever possible, but, in turn, will eliminate purchasing wastes by reducing inventory and keeping down obligations. Workable methods for determining the basic quantity to buy and ideas for applying them are given in the following paragraphs.

1. *Maximum-minimum system of buying.*—The maximum-minimum system is a method of determining how much and how little stock should be carried on hand at all times. The factors that control this—namely, market conditions, time of delivery, obsolescence, or spoilage—require constant consideration. The system is especially applicable where materials are standard.

The minimum quantity should be as low as possible, yet provide for a reserve stock from which withdrawals can be made in case of delayed delivery. The margin of safety depends upon the importance of the products, the rate of consumption, the availability of substitutes, and their price in the local market.

The maximum amount is the sum of the actual minimum plus the standard order. This is the point at which carrying costs and price risks on inventory balance the gains accruing from purchasing and storing in large quantities.

The standard order is the most economical amount to purchase and is determined by balancing the price concession for quantity purchases against the time required to receive the goods, the unit cost when ordered, the carrying charges, the rate of obsolescence, and price fluctuations.

The reorder point is that point at which stock is sufficiently in excess of the minimum to allow for the probable consumption of materials in the period between the placing of the order and the receiving of the materials. In determining the reorder point, the stores department should check with the using department on future demand, to determine how long the supply on hand will last. It must also make adjustments advised by the purchasing department to meet market conditions.

The maximum-minimum system resolves itself into a process of withdrawing stock, lowering inventory, and noting the amount remaining. When the reorder point is reached, the standard order is placed. By the time the new order arrives, stock is depleted to the minimum point. The new order is put in stock and the maximum regained. This system must not be mistaken for an automatic process. All four factors—minimum quantity, maximum quantity, standard order, and reorder point—need constant adjustment to changes in production schedules, storage facilities and charges, quantity discounts, and other things.

The ordering point is often based on a maximum and minimum

number of weeks' supply. The stock ledger clerk, at the time of posting withdrawals from stores, notes the elapsed time since the last order, the quantity remaining on hand, and the weekly rate of consumption. He thus determines the adequacy of the present supply for the probable requirements of the immediate future. When the balance available is reduced to a minimum number of weeks' supply, a replenishment order is placed to increase the stock to requirements for the maximum period.

2. *Time-coverage basis of buying.*—Where demand is subject to a wide fluctuation and where market-price trends have an important relation to sales, buying on a time-coverage basis is recommended. When the reorder point is reached, a decision is made to cover for a certain period on the basis of a review of the market trends and prospective demand. Such a review will usually coincide with the determination of the production rate for the period. Beyond this period the risk of change in demand or price could outweigh any possible profit that might be gained from quantity purchases. The advantages of using this system will depend upon the buyer's ability to forecast demand, the time required to replace stocks, the quantity price of goods, price trends, and the cost of carrying stocks. This system permits purchase at the reorder point for coverage in the face of advancing markets or increasing demand.

3. *Open-ended orders.*—Open-ended orders are used to transfer quantity risk from the buyer to the seller. Such an order may be just short of an actual quantity commitment; or it may be simply a provision "to cover requirements," with no mention of quantity. An open-ended order usually amounts to a definite commitment with the privilege of increasing quantity or cancelling a portion of the original commitment up to a specified time.

4. *Market-price basis.*—Purchase on a market-price basis alone may be used where price fluctuations are wide, as with raw materials. Actually this constitutes speculative market operations and should be practiced only when the quantity and timing of purchases are entirely dependent upon market outlook.

Purchasing budget to help determine right amount to buy.—Inventory, materials, and purchase budgets are invaluable in determining the right quantity to buy. The primary purpose of such budgets is to make certain that there will be a sufficient quantity of the necessary materials and supplies on hand at all times to meet the requirements of the production budget.

4. BUYING AT THE RIGHT PLACE

Knowledge of the sources of supply.—The purchasing agent will, as a rule, have little difficulty in finding sources of supply. Information of this nature is readily obtainable from salesmen, catalogues, and trade papers.

Salesmen as a source of information.—In general, it is to the advantage of the purchasing agent to interview as many of the visiting salesmen as time permits. Through talks with salesmen, the purchasing agent can obtain a great deal of useful data on the materials, equipment, and supplies in which he is interested. The purchasing agent should, however, adopt a definite policy with regard to the interviewing of salesmen and should not keep open house. Some companies specify certain days and hours when local salesmen will be interviewed, salesmen from out of town being admitted at any time. Other concerns request salesmen to conform to a schedule drawn up by the purchasing agent; thus, salesmen of products that the company buys in large quantities are asked to call once every two weeks or oftener, while salesmen of, for example, carbon paper and office supplies, are interviewed only every three or six months. It is often worth while, also, to keep a written record of the more important calls.

It is essential to develop dependable sources by winning the goodwill of salesmen. In cases of emergency, when orders already placed require modification or cancellation, the co-operation of the vendor is absolutely necessary. Mutual respect and co-operation assure continuous production. The purchaser thus knows that he can rely on the vendor for prompt delivery, ability to meet requirements of quality and service, and satisfactory adjustments for damages and spoilage, while the vendor feels that he can rely on the purchaser to give him due consideration in the placing of his order.

Catalogues as a source of information.—No purchasing department is without a large and miscellaneous assortment of catalogues. No catalogue should be dismissed by the purchasing agent without some attention. Nor should any catalogue pertaining to goods actually bought by the company be discarded. Catalogues are invaluable for cost analysis and as a permanent record and continual reminder of the existence of a potential source of supply. After catalogues have been read and routed through the interested departments, they should be indexed and filed. Incoming catalogues may be placed in a separate basket and examined by the purchasing agent at his leisure. He can indicate on the flyleaf the heading under which any catalogue that is not discarded should be filed.

How to organize a catalogue file.—Catalogues lose their value unless they are filed carefully. Variations in the sizes and binders make filing difficult, to be sure, but these drawbacks can be overcome. The following suggestions summarize the various methods used in successful organizations:

1. Use a vertical letter file where the accumulation is small and consists primarily of pamphlets. The file can be arranged by commodities or alphabetically by vendors. The letter file is not advisable, however, where catalogues are numerous or bound.
2. File catalogues alphabetically on open shelves of sectional bookcases. This method is useful where the collection consists of only a few hundred catalogues.
3. File catalogues on open shelves arranged numerically. All catalogues must be numbered with an automatic numbering machine as they are received. A finding list or index, which may be kept in a loose-leaf ledger or on cards, is then prepared, showing the number of the catalogue, the firm sending it, and the commodity. The index is arranged alphabetically by firms or by commodities to facilitate finding the desired catalogue.
4. File catalogues numerically by groups. This plan is suitable for a large file. All catalogues dealing with machinery, for example, are given numbers 1 to 100, while pamphlets dealing with the same matter are numbered P-1 to P-100. All pamphlets are then placed in a separate vertical letter file or in pamphlet boxes, which rest on the open shelves next to the bound volumes dealing with the same matter. An index, showing the firm name and the number of the catalogue, filed alphabetically by firm name, must be used in conjunction with this method. This system permits rapid reference to the desired materials and makes it unnecessary to cross-index the contents of the catalogue file by commodities.

Trade papers as a source of information.—The alert purchasing agent who makes it part of his duties to seek new materials and markets will find it well worth his while to subscribe to trade papers, which are a primary source of information on new products, processes, and markets. The purchasing agent should read at least two trade papers dealing with each of the items for which he makes the largest expenditures.

Choosing the right source of supplies.—Choosing the right source of supply is tantamount to obtaining a guaranty of quality and service for the product purchased. To become well acquainted with sources of supply, the purchasing agent should: (1) familiarize himself with the industry of which the source is a part, and (2) investigate the possible vendors.

1. *Investigate the source industry.*—In order for the buyer to have a mental picture of the industry of which the source is a part, he should investigate the following:

(*a*) Total production of the material.
(*b*) Approximate share of the total volume held by each supplier.
(*c*) Price policies of the industry. If there is a trade association, does it function adequately?
(*d*) Financial ratings of sources.
(*e*) Interownership of companies that outwardly appear to be competitors.
(*f*) Terms of payments and the extent of their uniformity among all producers.
(*g*) Efficiency of various companies and the recognized low-cost producers.
(*h*) Geographical location of the sources.

2. *Investigate the vendor.*—Knowledge of actual and potential sources entails, of course, general investigation of individual vendors, including those with whom the company has not previously done business. Get acquainted with the vendor by doing the following:

(*a*) Examine the vendor's capital rating and credit standing to determine his financial responsibility. Use such trade directories as

Dun and Bradstreet, Thomas' Register, and *MacRae's Blue Book* to make sure that his financial position is secure.

(*b*) Test the samples to make sure that the firm is capable of meeting specifications.

(*c*) Make a visit to the vendor's plant, become acquainted with his stock lists, and refer, when possible, to the buyer's own records of the vendor's past performance.

(*d*) Inquire into the seller's reputation for fulfilling delivery promises, as disclosed by his contacts with other purchasing agents —for example, members of the National Association of Purchasing Agents.

(*e*) Be familiar with the vendor's general and local transportation facilities.

Buying from middlemen.—Direct buying from the manufacturer is not invariably the cheapest way of purchasing. In fact, occasions exist where direct buying can actually increase purchasing costs. The following inquiries should help the buyer to decide whether to buy from the middleman instead of the manufacturer:

1. Is the local middleman of good standing?
2. Has he assembled in a single warehouse a greater variety of goods than a manufacturer could assemble in a branch warehouse?
3. Is his service prompt?
4. Is his price lower than the manufacturer's? It may be lower because of trade or other discounts or because he obviates the manufacturer's need for a costly sales and distributing force.
5. If his price is slightly higher than the manufacturer's, will the difference be less than the storage and depreciation costs for large quantities of goods stocked in the buyer's plant over extended periods?
6. What minimum will he supply below that obtainable from the manufacturer?

Buying from company's customers by practicing reciprocity. —The practice of buying from the company's customers originated in a sincere desire to increase goodwill. Reciprocity has now become a rather general practice in some organizations, particularly in manufacturing industries. Some managements still use it for the original purpose; some consider it essentially unsound in the long run and will not use it at all; others, such as those in the special-order business, cannot easily use it; and some use it entirely as a basis of soliciting orders. As a policy, reciprocity violates the essential principles of sound purchasing, especially if it involves a sacrifice of quality, service, or price. It is rarely defended by the enlightened purchasing agent. Nevertheless, the purchasing department is frequently under pressure from the management and the sales department to practice reciprocity, even if the price is a little higher or the quality slightly inferior.

Keeping competition alive.—Competition among sources must be maintained in order to secure advantages in price and quality. Poor judgment in distributing volume of business has often helped to create the monopolistic situation of which buyers complain. The common practice of signing long-term contracts, except where the source is highly localized and under the control of relatively few hands, should be discouraged, for it prevents taking full advantage of changes in process, new products, and new organizations.

The following suggestions may help the buyer to place orders in order to keep competition alive:

1. Keep a good record of sources of supply.
2. Adopt an open-market policy.
3. Spread the sources of supply.

Records of source of supply.—Records of sources of supply give warning of too great a concentration of purchases in one or two

Specifications..

Firm	Address	Terms and Delivery	Order No.	Date	Price	Quantity	Rejected

Figure 46a.—Vendor Price Record.

[Actual Size 4½" x 7"]

POSSIBLE SOURCES OF SUPPLY

FIRM	ADDRESS	REMARKS

Figure 46b.—Reverse Side of Vendor Price Record (Fig. 46a).

sources. This warning prompts a recheck of the competitive situation. Such records also simplify the relationship with salesmen by enabling the buyer to produce an accurate record of past dollar volume.

These records are frequently combined with price records and are filed alphabetically by the name of the commodity. Figures 46a and 46b illustrate the front of the record, showing the price record, and the back, showing the source of supply record.

Open-market policy.—Except where long-term contracts are advisable, it is best to leave a portion of the volume of purchases for open-market transaction. This policy aids in making comparisons between similar commodities.

The open-market policy, as practiced by the New York Central System, functions as follows. A list of bidders on all commodities to whom invitations for proposals are sent is prepared. When a bidder makes an application to be added to the list, his capacity and knowledge are carefully investigated. Bids on current materials are received quarterly. They are then tabulated, reviewed by the officer in charge, and placed on an accepted bid sheet. This sheet shows those vendors with whom orders are to be placed during a given period. The tabulations and accepted bid sheets are then filed in the requisitioning departments, where they are used as a guide by those making requisitions. As soon as a requisition is received, orders can be immediately placed with one of the accepted bidders. Quarterly revision of these bid sheets assures that open competition is maintained.

Spreading sources of supplies.—Maintaining more than one source of supply is a sound policy; it is sometimes worth adopting even at the sacrifice of some slight price advantage. Alternative sources insure the buying company continuous production, for no matter how dependable one vendor may be, circumstances beyond his control may interrupt his production. Spreading sources stimulate competition and thus increase the vendor's interest and alertness. Moreover, a company that has but a single source of supply may become the sole support of the supplier, a responsibility that few companies wish to assume. Hence, even though present service is adequate, quality is as specified, and price is satisfactory, the purchasing department should be always on the lookout for alternative sources.

On the other hand, care must be exercised not to spread sources to the extent that vendors will lose interest. A manufacturer who feels that no renewal orders will be forthcoming is likely to become indifferent to the quality and service he provides and lax about delivery dates. Furthermore, the buyer's credit opportunities are better if purchases are confined to fewer sources.

Methods of spreading purchases among sources.—The following are suggested methods of spreading purchases:

1. Divide purchases equally, permitting eligible bidders to share alike, or divide purchases in direct proportion to the vendor's total volume of business.
2. Divide purchases solely on the basis of vendor's qualifications.
3. Divide purchases unequally, giving the larger portion to a concern recognized as the principal source, and the smaller portion to another or several other sources. The latter should be made aware of their position as alternate sources and should recognize that they may some day become a permanent source.
4. Where certain items are used regularly and must always be on hand in definite quantities, develop at least one good reliable source, especially if the price does not fluctuate. If prices do fluctuate, a slight sacrifice in price may sometimes have to be made in order to insure dependability.
5. When goods are bought infrequently or are made up to order, shop around each time an order is to be placed and get quotations before placing the order. This is especially necessary if price fluctuates to any extent.
6. Split orders so as to maintain a balance between keeping several sources of supply available and ordering in sufficiently large quantities to command low prices.

5. BUYING AT THE RIGHT TIME

Importance of time factor.—The problem of when to buy is closely related to that of buying the right amount. Business conditions—locally, nationally, and internationally—may justify a liberal policy, with commitments made as quickly and as far ahead as the company's schedule permits; or, they may point to conservatism, with orders placed for quantities just sufficient to meet immediate needs. This, the time element, is a fundamental factor to be considered with reference to the general purchasing policies of the business. Unsystematic buying, without due regard to business conditions, may result in the virtual waste of large sums of money.

Market study.—The buyer must know market conditions and be able to judge probable market trends in order to time his buying properly. He should be familiar with, and must constantly review, the movement of prices, the business cycle, supply and demand, and the effect of Government regulations on commodities. For normal purposes he should be able to answer the following questions before making commitments:

1. What is the current phase of the business cycle?

2. Are current prices artificial; that is, does collusion exist among sellers?

3. Are labor problems or other local conditions adversely affecting the usual sources of supply?

4. Have new sources of supply recently become available?

5. What is the present state of the credit market?

Sources of market information.—Each purchasing agent knows the trade papers in his own and related fields and their value as a source of information. In addition to these publications, the following sources are useful in arriving at an opinion of the general business outlook.

1. Newspapers, including those that specialize in information pertinent to the problems of the businessman, such as the *New York Journal of Commerce,* the *Chicago Journal of Commerce,* and the *Wall Street Journal.*

2. Trade papers and business magazines covering the basic industries, such as *Iron Age, Electrical World, Railway Age,* and others.

3. Commercial services, such as the *Babson Economic Service, Brookmire Economic Service,* and the *Harvard Economic Review.*

4. Government publications, such as the *Survey of Current Business,* published by the Department of Commerce, the *Federal Re-*

serve Bulletin, and the monthly letters of business conditions, published by the regional Federal Reserve banks.

5. Independent studies of the market by the economics division of the organization. If there is no economics division within the purchasing department to attend to the preparation of these studies, the purchasing agent should prepare them himself from his own file of newspaper clippings, charts, graphs, statistics, and so forth. Graphs and charts can be conveniently kept in a large loose-leaf book.

Purchasing policies and the business cycle.—A definite program or policy of buying to cover a specified period should be outlined on the basis of a study of market conditions. The policy adopted must be flexible to allow for unforeseen contingencies. In general, the efficacy of the program will depend upon the consistency with which it is followed.

When business is declining, hand-to-mouth buying on the basis of averaging downward can be followed. In the depression phase of business substantial future commitments can be made, using the method of averaging downward on the market, with forward buying applied toward the close of the phase. In the revival phase, anticipation of requirements is justified, and forward buying should be followed as substantially as the policies of the business permit. In the prosperity phase, the monthly average, or hand-to-mouth, method should prevail. An explanation of the various policies is as follows:

1. *Buying on a monthly average.*—Under this method price is adjusted each month on the basis of market price at the date of adjustment. It is often expedient to adopt some date other than the first of the month for adjustment, as the market may be artificially stimulated on a date that is generally recognized in the trade as one on which commitments for the month are based. When raw materials that are subject to rapid fluctuations several times within a given month, such as nonferrous items, are bought on a monthly average, the buyer would do well to buy from that vendor who has based his quotation on the average cost of the materials for the month in question.

On the whole, buying on a monthly average is undesirable because the monthly average is affected by small-quantity transactions that tend to create fictitious prices in excess of those warranted by large-quantity purchases. Under certain circumstances this method of buying may be warranted. However, buying on a monthly average for several months ahead is not often justified.

2. *Buying to average downward in a falling market.*—Buying to average downward on the market involves contracting for a portion of known requirements at one point in a declining market. Consumption needs must be definite. Should the price again drop, further commitments are made. The process thus continues until requirements are fully covered. In this way the buyer can obtain a favorable average price on a declining market for the entire volume of requirements. In fact, the company's average price for this period can actually be below the average market price for the same period because of the uneven decline of prices. By buying at the lowest point of each technical price decline, this policy can be most successfully pursued.

3. *Forward buying.*—Forward buying enables the buyer to cover requirements as far ahead as seems desirable. Price is not always specified, but when it is, it is based on the values prevailing at the time the commitment is made. Carefully estimated requirements for a definite period should be compared with all available data on prices and production costs. Forward buying is usually done by placing long-term continuing contracts. In addition, small orders should be placed in the open market to check on new developments and price changes. Forward buying is suggested under the following circumstances:

(*a*) When prices are known to be near the cost of production, and a price rise seems imminent.

(*b*) To insure an available supply when satisfactory delivery is uncertain.

(*c*) For commodities marketed during a particular season only.

(*d*) For buying raw materials at a low price and transferring the saving to prices of the finished product. A strong competitive position is thus maintained.

4. *Hand-to-mouth buying.*—Hand-to-mouth buying means purchasing in limited quantities and for short periods of consumption. It may mean reducing inventories to avoid unnecessarily large investments in stocks, or buying less than safety requires in order to

profit from an anticipated fall in prices. Both procedures are risky. Neither must be carried to the point of interfering with continuous production.

Hand-to-mouth buying means foregoing the advantages of quantity purchases, such as quantity discounts and savings in ordering, freight, and handling costs. Furthermore, small lots command less of the supplier's attention. Overhead on storage space continues although the facilities go unused.

Hand-to-mouth buying does reduce the amount of capital tied up in inventories. To a certain extent it serves as a guard against price declines and permits a more accurate determination of purchasing requirements. Furthermore, it transfers the cost of inventory and storage, including obsolescence and deterioration, to the vendor. Its use is justified under the following circumstances:

(*a*) When prices are high or are definitely declining.
(*b*) When business conditions are unsettled.
(*c*) When requirements are uncertain or irregular.

Hedging.—Hedging transactions through use of the commodity exchanges and organized markets as a means of protection against price risks have very definite advantages and disadvantages. Hedging does not always provide complete protection. It requires much skill and experience on the part of the hedger. Moreover, the grading in the exchanges is not always sufficiently accurate for manufacturing purposes. Hedging is designed to protect only against unforeseen major price movements and should not be used to offset expected basic gains or losses. Nevertheless, buyers should understand the possibility of hedging against inventory or forward commitments, or against a falling market, as well as against forward sales.

Buying in a seller's market.—Buying in a seller's market does not always necessitate stocking up in advance and running the risk of obsolete inventory. It does require, however, that the buyer keep more closely in touch with suppliers and know the exact delivery possibilities, and that he be on guard against vendors overanxious to take advantage of a tight market. In buying in a seller's market, a buyer dealing in paper for printing and packing has found it wise to insist that price quotations be based on current raw-material prices, and not on prices two or three months in the future.

Speculation.—When the buyer makes price advantage the primary factor and the market outlook fundamental to quantity and timing, he is speculating and assuming more than normal risk. The ultimate answer to speculation is, of course, the comparative cost of gains or losses and their effect on the rest of the business. The buyer should seek the smallest possible portion of profits from speculative ventures. Trying to make profits by buying at a low price level in order to gain an advantage as prices rise distracts the buyer from his primary responsibility.

Some companies have found an answer to this problem. They recognize the potential advantages in speculation and approach speculative buying as a matter of major company policy, not as a policy that the buyer is free to pursue at his own discretion. Even when a speculative policy has been endorsed, it is not always the purchasing officer who is given the responsibility of effectuating the policy. In one company speculative transactions cannot be entered into without the specific approval of the president of the company. In another firm the only authority that may determine when to attempt to realize profits from price changes is a finance committee of which the general manager and purchasing agent are members.

6. BUYING AT THE RIGHT PRICE

Price as a factor in buying.—Price is ordinarily the last factor that the progressive purchasing agent considers after quality, service, and quantity have been determined. Naturally, he will want to buy as economically as possible in order to keep his company on an even competitive basis with others. Although the forces controlling the general trend of prices are far beyond the control of any one buyer, the purchaser must still buy suitable goods cheaply. To judge the best price, the buyer must have certain knowledge of market conditions, former transactions, and commodity data. The same methods of price determination cannot be used for all articles to be purchased.

Methods of judging prices.—Information on prices can be obtained more easily and the judging of comparative prices can be simplified if purchases are grouped according to the manner in which the commodities are sold. The following grouping is recommended: (a) goods subject to market-price movement, (b) goods available on quoted price only, and (c) goods sold on list and discount.

Goods subject to market-price movement.—Prices of goods subject to market movements can be judged on the basis of the following:

1. General business and economic conditions, including probable trends of major industries, wholesale commodity prices, interest rates, stock exchange quotations, foreign trade, and so forth. This information can be obtained by using library facilities, reading bank letters on business conditions, maintaining a statistical forecasting service in the purchasing department under the supervision of an economics division, and utilizing the services of commercial agencies such as those mentioned on page 774.
2. The exact status of the commodity in the market. From such publications as the *Survey of Current Business, The Annalist, McGill Commodity Service, Standard Economic Service,* the *Federal Reserve Bulletin,* and the *NAPA Bulletin,* data on the commodity position should be prepared in the form of charts, graphs, tables, and so forth.
3. A full record of the prices and conditions of past transactions.

Requesting bids.—A request for quotations may be sent to vendors in the following instances: (a) when goods are not available on any other basis; (b) when the goods have not theretofore been purchased by the company; (c) to renew long-term contracts; (d) to determine the reasonableness of a price under consideration; and (e) to check on prices currently paid or on inventory value. In the latter two cases make sure that the vendors know that no order is to be placed.

In judging prices of goods sold only on bid, it is important that a consistent policy of price determination be adopted. Many of the problems that arise in connection with bids can be handled easily if a definite policy is established and adhered to strictly.

Procedure for handling bids.—Make requests for bids clear, and, where specifications are furnished, have them conform to established standards and procedure if possible; such precautions will avoid misunderstandings that lead to a spread in quotations. Avoid delays by designating a definite date for replies. Adopt a firm policy of considering the original bid as the final one except in cases of misunderstood specifications. This is the fairest method of treating all suppliers alike. Moreover, it places stress on quality and service and secures competition in those factors as well as in price. When all vendors appreciate the circumstances and make their first quotation their lowest, the need for constant bargaining is obviated. Time and money are saved. Confidential treatment of the vendor's bid redounds to the buyer's advantage. A vendor who feels that he can trust a buyer's confidence will give him the benefit of his best price.

Buyers should avoid the practice of price cutting after bids are submitted. Vendors soon become aware of this practice and provide against it by bidding high enough to offset the anticipated cut. In such instances the danger is ever present that the purchaser will be penalized by high bids.

Analyzing bids for unit cost.—In analyzing bids, make an independent study of approximately what the costs should be. Refer to purchasing department price records, catalogues, and interviews with salesmen; or analyze and reduce costs to a unit basis, such as per pound, and so on.

Form of request for quotations.—The form of request for quotations used by The Atlantic Refining Company is reproduced in Figure 47 on page 781. The reverse side of the form contains terms and conditions similar to those generally included on the purchase order. See pages 795 et seq. for examples of clauses.

Price inquiries are usually sent to the vendor in duplicate. The original is to be returned to the buyer, and the duplicate is retained by the vendor making the bid.

Summary of response to requests for bids.—The form used by the Otis Elevator Company, shown in Figure 48, summarizes the bids submitted by the different vendors.

Ideas for keeping data on bids.—Data received in answer to requests for bids may be placed on the back of the purchase order, if: (1) the information is not too lengthy; or (2) the information is limited to price per unit. If other data are necessary for future reference, they may be kept simply in any of the following ways:

W-4102 11-38

THE ATLANTIC REFINING COMPANY
260 SOUTH BROAD STREET
PHILADELPHIA, PA.

PRICE INQUIRY
THIS IS NOT AN ORDER

DATE

REQ. No.

Please quote us your lowest price f.o.b.________________for materials specified below:
This price inquiry is submitted in duplicate, and TO RECEIVE CONSIDERATION, one copy of the inquiry must be in our hands not later than It must not be reassigned, if you cannot or do not care to quote please return to us.
If a purchase order is issued to you covering any or all of the material specified, it will be subject to the terms and conditions printed on the back hereof.
If you are unable to furnish material as described or specified, and desire to offer a substitute, give full details.
It is agreed that we have the privilege of accepting all or any part of the quotation.
YOUR QUOTATION MUST BE FILLED OUT ON THIS FORM AS REQUESTED OR BID WILL NOT BE CONSIDERED.

THE ATLANTIC REFINING COMPANY
J. S. PARKS, PURCHASING AGENT

BY________________
BUYER

QUANTITY	DESCRIPTION	PRICE EACH	DISCOUNT	NET

Wanted at destination on or before________________
Date you can ship________________
F. O. B.________________
Terms of Payment________________

Date________________ Signed________________

All communications must be addressed to J. S. PARKS, Purchasing Agent, 260 So. Broad Street, Philadelphia, Pa.

Figure 47.—Request for Quotations.
[Actual Size 8¼″ x 10¾″]

FORM Y 1263

COMPILATION OF COMPETITION

MATERIAL

QUANTITY DESCRIPTION

DATE
REQUESTED BY
FOR
COMPILED BY

VENDOR	PRICE	PER	F O B	TERMS	DEL Y	REMARKS

Figure 48.—Summary of Response to Request for Bids.
[Actual Size 11″ x 8″]

1. Separately by the name of the vendor.
2. Under the classification numbers of the materials requested.
3. In a quotations file under the name of the commodity, with the bid attached to, or the information written on, a summary of quotations form. The special folder in which current bids are accumulated may be transferred from the current file to the cumulative file

at the proper time by having the closing date signalled on the folder. This file also permits the buyer to show that he is not playing favorites among sellers. See page 781 for an example of a summary of quotations received form.

4. Place a copy of the request for bid in the file under the commodity or contract and list in the space provided the names of all vendors who have been invited to bid. When received, each bidder's information is noted opposite his name, and his bid is placed behind the request for bid. Bids are filed in the same order in which the names are shown on the request.

Price file.—The prices quoted should be checked against the purchasing agent's price file, which is a record of the prices paid for various materials over a period of time. If the prices quoted are higher than the prices last paid, as shown by the price file, and market conditions and other factors do not appear to warrant the increase, additional quotations may be obtained or negotiation with vendors undertaken.

The records in the price file are frequently combined with the source of supply records, discussed in a previous section. Figures 46A and B on page 771 illustrate the form of the price record.

Discounts.—In dealing with commodities sold on list and discount, as well as with many sold on quotation, the buyer should make special arrangements with regard to cash or trade discounts wherever possible. A file of discounts allowable on standard production, maintenance, and equipment items may be kept under the vendor's name and address, to be used in conjunction with the purchase record file. (See page 793 for a description of the purchase record file.) The file may be simplified by recording only those discounts that are an accepted policy of the vendor. An alternate method is to have the discount records kept in the bills payable division of the treasury department.

Cash discounts.—Cash discounts are offered to secure prompt settlement of an account. It is the buyer's duty to ascertain that cash discounts are granted equally to all buyers. He must make sure that he is not being denied postdating allowed others. If advantage is not being taken of cash discounts, the purchasing executive should bring to the attention of the proper officers the extent to which the firm is losing money by sacrificing discounts. It may also be necessary for the purchasing executive to inform the management of any need for expediting the receiving, inspecting, and acceptance of goods in order to take immediate advantage of such discounts.

Trade discounts.—Trade discounts are granted a distributor by a manufacturer to protect the channels through which his materials flow. By buying from the distributor instead of directly from the manufacturer, the buyer can usually share in these discounts. By taking advantage of these discounts, the purchaser is also furthering the well-being of a desirable and continuous source of supply.

Quantity discount.—Discounts offered the purchaser for buying in quantity vary with the quantity. Large orders lower marketing and production costs, a saving that can be passed back to the buyer in the form of lower prices. Because of a real justification for this form of discount, buyers should seek them wherever possible.

Cumulative discounts are granted on a basis of quantity purchases made at intervals over a period of time. They serve as an incentive to continued patronage. It is inadvisable to permit such discounts to lead to concentration of purchases with a single source. Cumulative discounts are an excellent solution for discounts on quantity purchases of perishable merchandise where deterioration would prevent storing large quantities or where substantial inventory or storage expenses are involved. Properly used, cumulative discounts should tend to avoid the danger of overstocking in order to secure advantages of quantity discounts.

Resale discount.—In some cases the purchasing agent is entitled to resale discounts. This type of discount applies to many articles that are in themselves finished appliances but are purchased to form part of another piece of equipment. For example, a builder of machinery who does not manufacture the motors for operating the machinery may obtain discounts on the motors if they are to be sold again with the machinery.

Terms f.o.b. destination.—The term "f.o.b. destination" should be used in shipping provisions whenever it can be arranged. The arrangement eliminates transportation consideration when comparing bids. Moreover, it places on the vendor the responsibility for all negotiations with the transportation company, including claims for damages.

Price guaranty.—A guaranty against a price rise or decline for a fixed period of time has definite advantages for the buyer. He will receive all his requirements within the designated period at a certain price regardless of change in the market price. Should prices rise, the buyer is entitled to the lower price prevailing when the contract was drawn. Should prices fall, he can purchase at the new and lower price. Thus the buyer is protected against loss, assured of prompt deliveries, and, because of the reduction in risk, is able to handle goods on a smaller margin of profit. The speculative responsibility is shifted to the producer, who is frequently able to offer lower prices because: (a) more and larger orders are secured; (b) seasonal fluctuations are avoided by securing advance orders; (c) goods can usually be shipped immediately upon completion, thus reducing warehouse expenses; and (d) cancellations because of a falling market are avoided. The practice also has the effect of tending to stabilize prices.

Price fixing on a sliding-scale basis.—By fixing prices on a sliding-scale basis both the buyer and seller are protected. Prices are based on the price of the principal raw material from which the goods are made. For example, prices may be adjusted every three months. This gives the buyer a slight advantage. On the rising market he can place an order at any time before the end of a quarter and have the price based on the average price of the raw material in the month preceding the quarter of the calendar year in which the order is placed. On the falling market he can delay placing an order until the first week of the following quarter, when prices will be based on more recent and lower raw material costs.

Economy in handling small orders.—Proper prices on items of small value upon which there is no market tendency to be observed and which do not justify maintenance of catalogues or the issuance of inquiries for quotations may be handled economically by any one of the following methods:

1. Sending out unpriced orders.
2. Indicating on the order the last price paid according to the purchase records.
3. Grouping the items under some contract arrangement or having a cost-plus basis with suppliers. The seller undertakes to supply materials when they are needed and to submit to periodical checking on the fairness of his prices.

4. Using local sources of supply, obtaining a price via the telephone, and placing the price on the purchase order as a part of the agreement.

5. Depending on the integrity of a carefully chosen supplier and omitting any detailed checking of price.

6. Leaving up to the supplier the price for a given class of items. "Spot-checking" his price by selecting a special item and carefully investigating the basis upon which it is being priced. This will be a clue to the supplier's general pricing policies.

7. REQUISITIONS

Authority to requisition.—A definite, comprehensible system of requisitioning, with fixed responsibility, is one of the essentials of economical procedure. The authority to requisition should be limited and recognized. Each requisition must be signed by the person authorized to make requisitions.

Time is saved if all requisitions originating with heads of using departments are sent directly to the storeroom instead of to the purchasing department, except where goods are not kept in stock. When the stock clerk or storekeeper is requisitioning to replenish stock, the requisition will naturally go directly to the purchasing agent.

The purchasing agent is generally able to recognize inadequate and misleading descriptions that need correction. Caution should be exercised, however, not to change a requisition arbitrarily without consulting the person making it. A sample should accompany the requisition for a special item wherever possible.

Economy in handling requisitions.—The following suggestions for cutting the time required to handle requisitions represent ideas that have proved effective in large and small organizations:

1. Require the use of a form in making requisitions. Never permit a requisition by telephone. Insist upon the required signature on the requisition form.

2. Establish uniformity in the use of terms. Proper nomenclature prevents costly misunderstandings.

3. Have requisitions made out in duplicate, at least. One copy should go to the stores department or the purchasing department,

and the other should be retained by the department making the requisition.

4. Insist upon having complete information on the requisition when it is presented.

Routing requisitions.—Several copies of a requisition are normally prepared. The forms may come in pads with carbons already inserted or to be inserted. Or, the forms may come bound in such a way that all the copies but one, which remains with the requisitioning department, are easily removed.

The routing of the requisition copies depends upon the procedure in the particular company. Often requisitions are issued in triplicate with two copies for the storekeeper. One is kept in the storeroom, and the other is sent to the stores record section. The storeroom copy is usually sent back to the stores record section to be matched with the first copy after the goods have been issued from stock. When the two copies of the requisition are matched, they are entered on the inventory record. An accumulation of unmatched requisitions in the stores record department indicates that the procedure is not being properly followed, and an investigation should be made.

The storeroom copy may be used as a delivery ticket, in which case it is returned with the goods to the requisitioner, who usually receipts it and forwards it to the storeroom.

When requisitions are sent directly to the purchasing department, the original and third copies are often sent to the purchasing agent. The original is subsequently returned to the requisitioner with a notation as to the promised delivery date. Where the tracing of the order is assumed jointly by the storekeeper and the purchasing department, a duplicate is placed in the storekeeper's tickler file by delivery date for follow-up.

Requisition forms.—The requisition form should provide space for the following items:

1. The date and a number.
2. The department in which the requisition originated or for which the goods are intended.
3. The account to which the purchase is to be charged.
4. The authorization.
5. Clear and complete specifications or descriptions.
6. A specified delivery date.

7. Purpose for which goods are intended.

8. The quantity desired and an indication of the period that the requisition is expected to cover.

9. The quantity of goods left, if the requisition is for materials kept in stock.

Purchase Requisition Date Req. No.

Please order the following:- Order No.

For Dept. Acct. Stk. or Job No.

QUANTITY	SIZE OR NO.	MATERIAL	PER	PRICE	

Mfr. or Party from whom previously purchased Signed: Tot.

Order from

F.O.B.
Terms
Routing
Del'y Req'd Our Plant

Figure 49.—Simple Form of Purchase Requisition.
[Actual Size $5\frac{1}{2}'' \times 7\frac{3}{4}''$]

Form 268 A-8-38 **Requisition on Storekeeper** № 15597

Date 19

Deliver to Charge Acct. No.

To be used for

Group	Floor	Mach. No.	Job No.
Bldg.	Dept.	Signed	

Figure 50.—Simple Requisition on the Stores Department.

Form A-570B 10 38

DUPLICATE—To be Retained

Purchase Requisition **No. A 1001**

_______________19___

Purchasing Department: Operating Department Requisition No.________

We herewith apply for the following:

Item No.	Quantity	Description Put Only Related Commodities on this Puchase Requisition	This space for use of Purchasing Department

Please specify MAKE, SIZE, CATALOG and MANUFACTURER'S NUMBER when necessary.
If you have quotations from local concerns for all or any of the items on this requisition list them on reverse side, giving full particulars.

Deliver to_______________ ___________________Refinery or Office

Date delivery desired_______________ Per___________________Superintendent or Manager

Figure 51a.—Purchase Requisition for Stores Not Carried in Stock.

10. Inventory classification and part number.
11. The storeroom to which the requisition is sent.

Figure 49 illustrates a simple form of purchase requisition suitable for most uses.

Requisition for stock on hand.—A simple requisition on the stores department, used by a sugar-refining company, is shown in Figure

COMPARISON OF QUOTATIONS

Material	Bidder's Name	Price	Terms	Freight	Net	Date Can Deliver	Reputation and Previous Service

Figure 51b.—Reverse Side of Purchase Requisition (Fig. 51a).

Form M-277 25 pads 2-39

Nº 10725

DATE________ INTERPLANT REQUISITION

ISSUED BY________ DEPT. ON________ DEPT. FINAL CHARGE________

Quantity	Gauge	Width	Length	Grade	DESCRIPTION OF MATERIAL WANTED	Weight	Price	Amount

Date wanted________ Special Instructions: Time________

Deliver to________

Door No.________

Signed________ Maker of Requisition

Signed________ Person Filling Order

Date Filled________

Send: 1st Copy (Pink)—Works Accounting
2nd Copy (Yellow)—Production Dept. When order is filled this copy forwarded to Works Accounting Dept.
3rd Copy (White)—File Copy for Dept. Issuing

Figure 52.—Interplant Requisition.

[Actual Size $8\frac{1}{2}'' \times 5''$]

50. This form authorizes the stores department to issue materials from stock on hand.

Requisition for stock not on hand.—When an operating department of a sugar-refining company requires stores not carried in stock, the form illustrated in Figure 51A is used. The form requires proper classification of commodities needed and also provides space for information furnished by the manufacturer. Loss of time through unnecessary correspondence is avoided by providing space for information gathered by the requisitioner. The form originates in a branch. The original is sent to the purchasing department; the duplicate is retained by the branch.

The form for comparison of quotations, reproduced in Figure 51B, is on the reverse side of the original requisition.

Interplant requisition.—Figure 52 illustrates a form used by a steel plant when materials are transferred from one department to another. The form shows the number of copies made and the use to which each is put. The forms are consecutively numbered, thus permitting an easy check on requisitions in transit. By including in the form such information as the time and date required, delays in delivery are avoided, and the requisition can be filled to fit in with the manufacturing schedules.

8. PURCHASE ORDERS

Items shown on the purchase-order form.—While order forms vary from company to company, the following items are found on practically all such forms:

1. Serial number. These are sometimes printed consecutively on the purchase-order form, especially when continuous forms are used. Often the numbers are filled in as the orders are drawn. Sometimes the purchase order is given the same number as the requisition, in which case the requisition should specify but one class of material.
2. Date of issue.
3. Name and address of supplier.
4. Quantity and description of items ordered.
5. Date delivery is required.
6. Shipping instructions.
7. Prices and discounts.
8. Terms of payment.
9. Identification marks for packages.
10. Specific billing instructions.
11. Any other conditions governing the transaction.

Form of purchase order.—A simple form of purchase order is illustrated in Figure 53. All information vital to the order is included. Six copies are made; each one indicates where it is to be routed.

The copies are routed as follows:

Original goes to the vendor.

Copy two is the receiving clerk's copy.

Copy three is the storekeeper's copy.

Copy four is the accounting department copy.

Copy five is for the department issuing requisition.

Copy six is for the purchasing department.

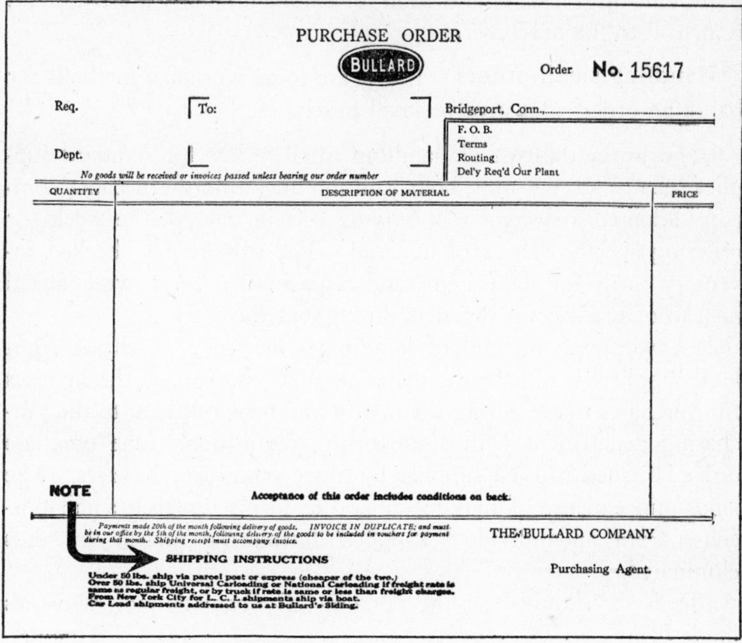

PURCHASE ORDER

BULLARD

Order **No. 15617**

Req.

To:

Dept.

Bridgeport, Conn.,

F. O. B.

Terms

Routing

Del'y Req'd Our Plant

No goods will be received or invoices passed unless bearing our order number

QUANTITY	DESCRIPTION OF MATERIAL	PRICE

NOTE

Acceptance of this order includes conditions on back.

Payments made 20th of the month following delivery of goods. INVOICE IN DUPLICATE; and must be in our office by the 5th of the month, following delivery of the goods to be included in vouchers for payment during that month. Shipping receipt must accompany invoice.

SHIPPING INSTRUCTIONS

**Under 50 lbs. ship via parcel post or express (cheaper of the two.)
Over 50 lbs. ship Universal Carloading or National Carloading if freight rate is same as regular freight, or by truck if rate is same or less than freight charges.
From New York City for L. C. L shipments ship via boat.
Car Load shipments addressed to us at Bullard's Siding.**

THE BULLARD COMPANY

Purchasing Agent.

Figure 53.—Simple Form of Purchase Order.

[Actual Size $8\frac{1}{2}'' \times 7''$]

The sixth copy is on lightweight cardboard to provide against wear and tear through frequent usage. The reverse side of this copy is used for a complete history of the order. The information is inserted under the following headings:

No. or Size	Date	Billed Quantity	Date	Received Quantity	Unit Price	Total	Bal. Due	Remarks

Acknowledgment of orders.—It is always best to have the vendor acknowledge the purchase order. Frequently an extra copy of the purchase order is sent to the vendor, to be returned to the purchasing department with the vendor's acknowledgment. Sometimes a card requesting acknowledgment is enclosed with the order and is to be returned by the vendor. Acknowledgment by letter or telegram is sometimes requested. Some companies have a perforated stub at the bottom of the vendor's copy of the order. The stub carries the order number. On it the vendor inserts information as to origin, date, and route of shipment, signs the stub, and returns it to the purchaser.

Handling small orders.—Below are some workable methods for handling orders that involve small purchases.

1. To lower the cost of handling small orders for standard supplies such as screws, nuts, bolts, and the like, a northern paper company adopted a system of specifying certain days of the week for ordering specific classes of material. The storekeeper checked inventory cards for these items and requisitioned for a week ahead instead of placing small orders throughout the week.

2. A workable method of handling emergency purchases from local suppliers is to have the materials supervisor collect the invoices for purchases made during the month and forward them to the purchasing department with a supporting requisition. One purchase order is issued to each supplier for these monthly purchases. The labor and expense of making out order forms for each small purchase from an individual supplier during the month are thus eliminated.

The order should bear the notation "Confirmation of deliveries made from ----------- -- to ----------- --19--." This prevents duplication of shipment by the supplier. If possible, the invoice numbers of the vendor should also be stated.

3. Emergency order forms can be used to take care of small emergency and miscellaneous local purchases of supplies not carried in the storeroom. Such forms eliminate the use of requisitions and go directly to the vendor. A book of emergency orders can be given to plant superintendents, branch managers, department heads, or others in authority who are charged with and held accountable for the book. These orders must have the same authorization as

requisitions. If this system is used, four copies of the emergency order are generally sufficient. They are routed as follows: original goes to the vendor; copy two is sent to the accounting department; copy three is sent to the purchasing department; and copy four is kept in the order book for reference.

Recurring orders.—Economy can be effected in the purchase of recurring items that show little change in price or style by estimating requirements for a definite period and contracting for this period. One large order in place of several small ones saves time in investigating bids and makes possible quantity discounts. The stock is retained by the vendor and shipped as directed upon receipt of "shipping instructions" from time to time during the contract period. This method is particularly applicable in the purchase of bulky items for which storage space is limited, such as stationery, office supplies, and certain maintenance materials.

Purchase-record file.—The purchasing department should have a purchase-record file of past purchases to serve as a guide for future transactions. The value of this file is that it can be consulted in regard to prices, quality, terms, vendor's dependability, and vendor's past record. The purchase record file should be so arranged as to make reference to it easy. Records may be filed by the name of the vendor or the name of the commodity.

A simple purchasing form filed by commodity is illustrated in Figure 54. The name of the commodity is entered on the line with "purchasing record." The card is the same on both sides.

306 500 10-38

PURCHASE RECORD

DATE	PRICE	UNIT	QUANTITY	F O B	VENDOR	TERMS	SHIP-MENT	REMARKS	

Figure 54.—Purchase Record to Be Filed by Commodities.

[Actual Size 5″ x 9″]

Follow-up of orders.—When delivery on time is extremely important, or when the vendor has specified no delivery date, it is advisable to follow up within a reasonable time after the date of the order. Often the purchasing department periodically informs the storekeeper or other frequent requisitioners of the length of time required to make delivery of various items after the receipt of the requisition in the purchasing department. The purchasing agent ordinarily follows up to get delivery within this time.

If the requisitioner requires an exceptionally early delivery, he should state the approximate delivery date on his requisition. The purchasing department will then embody this fact in the order and request a reply. The reply goes to the purchasing department, where the follow-up is actually done.

Where no special rush for delivery is requested, the most economical procedure is to wait until the receiving department notifies the buyer that the shipment has not arrived and then to get in touch with the vendor.

Responsibility for following up orders.—A means must be provided for following up orders to see that the material purchased is delivered on time and in acceptable condition. Without a systematic method for following up orders, unnecessary losses will be caused by delayed shipments and interrupted production.

The follow-up function should ordinarily rest with the purchasing department, especially if that department is responsible for checking deliveries. Within the department of a small company, the follow-up can be done by the telephone clerk. In a large organization special follow-up men or the buyers themselves usually have the responsibility. Men specializing in follow-up should be placed under the supervision of assistant buyers. These buyers can then be notified by the follow-up men of urgent cases and can bring additional pressure on the vendor through their personal contacts.

Systems for following up orders.—A systematically canvassed tickler file should be devised for reminding the purchasing department of outstanding orders. Several simple methods are suggested:

1. Make a note on an ordinary calendar pad of orders requiring attention.

2. Provide for a carbon copy of the purchase order to be sent to the follow-up clerk. These copies can be kept in a standard vertical file arranged numerically behind tabs, a tab being provided for each day of the month.

3. Place a detachable slip or section on one copy of the purchase order, on which the order number, date, and vendor's name can be

entered. File the slips by date; a new group of slips thus comes up each day for tracing.

4. Keep an open order file with the date for follow-up flagged. This can be done by having numbers 1 to 31 placed at the top or on the open side of the purchasing department's file copy of the purchase order. A colored tab, to designate the month, is placed at the date. Different colors can indicate consecutive months, the colors being repeated three or four times a year. A special colored tab can be placed on those orders that must be watched closely. The signal tabs for a given day then arrange themselves in a straight line throughout the order file; they can be instantly spotted and pulled out.

5. Have a series of thirty-one pigeonholes into which follow-up and acknowledgment cards, copies, or slips are placed.

6. Send an extra copy of the purchase order, dated ahead, to the regular follow-up division of the general filing department, which is regularly engaged in arranging follow-up correspondence. As this department has usually been organized by a filing expert, the return of the order on the proper date can be assured.

Conditions of purchase.—The conditions governing the purchase should be clearly stated, either on the face of the purchase order above the space for the purchasing agent's signature, or on the back, with a statement on the front to the effect that acceptance of the order means acceptance of the conditions on the reverse side. Conditions will necessarily vary with the type of purchases made, the market in which the buyer must deal, and other factors.

In the following paragraphs suggestions for conditional clauses are presented. All are in current use on purchase order forms of large, medium-sized, and small concerns throughout the county.

Clauses to Make Sure Vendor Includes Order Number.

Purchase order number and requisition number must appear on all invoices, packages, packing slips, shipping papers, and correspondence.

Purchase order number must be on invoice in duplicate, or same will be returned at once. Must be marked on every package. Must be marked on bill of lading. Must be marked on delivery slip; otherwise goods will be returned.

Our purchase order must appear on each and every shipment.

Clauses Relating to Invoice Instructions.

Furnish invoice in duplicate.

Render invoice in triplicate and mail original and duplicate copies to our branch office at point of destination and triplicate copy to our general office.

Render all invoices in triplicate. Mail separate invoice with bill of lading after each shipment.

Render invoice on our forms for each shipment, attaching original bill of lading or express receipt; show point of shipment and weight; car initials; number and routing if carload shipment; transportation charges prepaid or collect; and discount terms, which apply from date invoice is received.

Invoices must be made out in quadruplicate on our own invoice form and must be accompanied by original bills of lading and prepaid freight bills, express, or original signed delivery receipts.

Clauses Requiring Acknowledgment as a Condition of Purchase.

Order must be acknowledged promptly, advising delivery date, or your inability to meet delivery date requested.

Please acknowledge receipt of this order immediately.

Acknowledge receipt of this order on form attached giving shipping date. Do not say "as soon as possible."

Clauses Showing Vendor's Acceptance of Conditions.

Shipment of any part of this order constitutes acceptance of all conditions without reservation.

By accepting this order, you assent to all provisions contained hereon and to the conditions on the reverse side of this form.

Clauses Relating to Changes in the Terms of Purchase by the Seller.

This order contains the entire agreement of the parties and no modification thereof will be binding upon us, unless in a writing dated subsequently and signed by vendor, and agreed to by us.

All changes in specifications, shipment, routing, or other conditions of this contract shall be taken up with the purchaser by letter, and no change will be valid until an additional order in writing is given by the purchasing agent. Vendor shall not negotiate such changes directly with purchaser's ultimate customer without giving purchaser due notice and an opportunity to have a representative present at such negotiation. Changes resulting from such negotiation will not be valid until an additional order in writing is given by purchasing agent.

Clauses Relating to Special Package Markings.

Enclose with each shipment packing slips showing contents, part number or description, and order number.

Memorandum of content shall be enclosed in each box or package.

All packages must be plainly marked with name of consignor.

When material or packages are received improperly marked, and we are put to extra expense to deliver such materials or packages to the proper plant, we will charge to your account the extra expense incurred.

Shipments must include packing slips, and, in case of carload shipments, place packing slip on inside of car near door. Do not put material for two or more factories in the same box or package.

Clauses Relating to Charges for Packing and Cartage.

No charge will be allowed for boxing, packing, or cartage.

No charge will be allowed for packing, boxing, or carting unless agreed upon in writing at the time of purchase, but damage to any material not packed to insure proper protection to same will be charged to vendor.

Clauses Relating to Routing and Shipping.

All materials must be forwarded by the particular route named unless purchased f.o.b. destination. Purchaser does not consider any shipment completed until it has bill of lading or express receipt in its possession.

All shipments are to be made as noted on the face of this order, and notices sent to consignee. Ship via parcel post, express, rail, or lowest licensed truck rate: lowest rate must apply; otherwise we reserve the right to charge you back with the difference.

Bills of lading must be forwarded on day of shipment and show through routing, freight rate, and car number.

Clauses Reserving the Right to Cancellation.

Buyer reserves the right to cancel this order or any portion of same if delivery is not made when and as specified, time being of the essence of this order, and charge seller for any loss entailed.

Purchaser reserves the right to cancel all or any part of this order upon which deliveries have been delayed beyond thirty days, either after date of order or specified delivery date.

If you do not make shipment within the time agreed upon, or should none be specified, within five days of receipt of shipping order, or if any material is not entirely satisfactory to use for the purposes for which it is required, we may cancel this order and return the unsatisfactory material at your expense. Should it be necessary for us to do so, we may obtain material or equipment from other sources, in which case you are to reimburse us to the extent of any additional cost we may incur by reason of advanced prices or otherwise.

Clauses Relating to Quality and Quantity.

Shipment must equal exact quantity ordered, unless otherwise agreed.

All materials furnished must be of the best of their respective kinds.

All materials furnished must be as specified. It is our privilege to return at seller's expense: (a) merchandise received after date, or dates, specified; (b) merchandise shipped in excess of this order; (c) merchandise not according to sample or specifications; (d) merchandise that is not as represented.

Clauses Relating to Rejected Materials.

Transportation charges accruing from delivery of defective or incorrect material are chargeable to supplier.

Defective goods will be returned at your expense.

Defective goods will be promptly returned at your expense and credit taken on vouchers. No goods returned as defective shall be replaced without our formal replace order. All goods shall be subject to our inspection and rejection at our factories.

Payment for goods when due shall not constitute an acceptance thereof, but same shall be subject to our inspection; and, if said goods are not in accordance with blueprints, specifications, or samples furnished or are defective in material or workmanship, we may reject all or any part of said goods and hold such rejected goods at your risk. In case of failure to make replacement in sufficient time to meet our requirements, it is understood that we may replace the same elsewhere, and you agree to reimburse us for any excess expense incurred thereby, or we may deduct the same from any sum due or to become due from us to you. No material rejected by us can be returned or replaced by you without a replacement order from us covering same.

Clauses Allowing Inspection.

All materials furnished must be as specified and will be subject to the buyer's inspection and approval after delivery.

Sample of work must be submitted for O.K. on all manufacturing orders.

All goods ordered are subject to the approval of our inspector.

Goods are subject to our inspection and count notwithstanding prior payment to obtain cash discount.

Clauses Covering Buyer's Acceptance.

Acceptance of and responsibility for material shipped on this order begins only upon delivery in good condition by the carrier to the purchaser.

Acceptance of the merchandise by us after inspection shall not release or discharge you from liability in damages or other legal remedy for breach of any promise or warranty, express or implied, with respect to the merchandise ordered hereunder.

Clauses Relating to Price Change.

Order must not be filled at an advance in price over the last quotation on file in buyer's office without obtaining buyer's written permission.

Merchandise on this order is guaranteed against decline, and price will be as low as any other sales made during life of this contract.

If you cannot execute this order at prices last quoted or better, we must be advised.

Clauses Relating to Payment.

Payment will be figured from date of receipt at purchaser's office of invoices with bills of lading or express receipt attached.

Invoices not subject to cash discount will be paid, after necessary approval, on the 25th of the month following that in which the invoice is dated.

Payment shall be made on the 20th of the month following shipment, less customary discount, unless otherwise specially arranged for and stated on this order; or, in the event that merchandise has not been received, purchaser reserves the right to withhold payment until merchandise has been received and checked and does not waive the right to deduct the cash discount.

Unless otherwise agreed, we deduct cash discount from date of arrival of goods; also freight to destination.

All purchases subject to a discount of 2%—15th of the month following. Invoices not in the hands of the purchasing department three days before the end of the month will be considered as having been received the first of the following month and will be subject to discount as above indicated.

Clauses Relating to Honoring of Drafts.

Drafts will not be honored under any circumstances.

No drafts drawn by seller for purchases made by buyer will be honored unless by written agreement.

Clauses Relating to Conditions Beyond Control of Vendor or Vendee.

Neither party shall be liable for failure of performance due to strikes, fires, accident, or other causes beyond its control, and affecting its operation.

Fires, accidents, or strikes, in the plants of either party, or causes beyond the control of the parties, rendering buyer unable to receive or seller to deliver, or cessation of operation of buyer's plant for which order is destined, may, at the option of either party, render this contract inoperative during the continuance thereof.

Clauses Protecting the Buyer Against Patent Infringement.

The seller agrees to protect and save harmless the purchaser from all costs, expenses, or damages arising out of alleged infringements.

This order is given upon the condition that we are protected by vendor against all liability, loss, or expense, by reason of any patent or trade-mark litigation now existing, or hereafter instituted, arising out of any alleged infringement of patent or trade-mark, on the merchandise hereby ordered, on any part thereof.

By accepting this order, seller agrees to defend, protect, and save harmless purchaser against all suits at law, or in equity, and from all damages, claims, and demands for actual or alleged infringement of any United States or foreign patent, and to defend or assist in the defense of any suit or action that may be brought against purchaser by reason of any alleged infringement because of this purchase, sale, or use of the article or articles covered by this order.

Clauses Requiring That Vendor Comply with State and Federal Law.

It is agreed by the parties hereto that this order, and the acceptance thereof, shall be deemed a contract made in ___________ and governed by the laws thereof.

All articles furnished on this order must have been produced and sold in compliance with all Federal, State, and other laws.

It is understood and is an essential term and condition of this order, and by filling the same you represent, that all goods shipped or delivered by you hereunder have been produced in compliance with all of the terms and provisions of the Fair Labor Standards Act of 1938, and with all regulations or orders of the Administration issued under Section 14 thereof.

Seller agrees to and does hereby accept full and exclusive liability for the payment of any and all contributions or taxes for unemployment insurance, or old age retirement benefits, pensions, or annuities now or hereafter imposed by the Government of the United States, and any State or political subdivision thereof, with respect to all persons at any time employed by, or on the payroll of the seller, or performing any work for or on his behalf or in connection with or arising out of his business, in performance of this purchase order, whether the same be measured by the wages, salaries, or other remuneration paid to or earned by such persons, or the number of such persons, or otherwise.

9. RECEIVING AND INSPECTING INCOMING GOODS AND CHECKING INVOICES

Responsibility of the receiving department.—The receiving department should report on incoming goods. For purposes of economy, and especially if the purchasing department controls stores, the receiving division is often placed under the supervision of the purchasing department. Where the storehouses are at a distance from the plant at which buying is done, an independent receiving department or one under the stores department is preferable. Or, the receiving department may be independent of both the purchasing and stores department, with control established through either the plant superintendent or the chief accounting executive.

Except where more than one plant exists, most firms find it practical to centralize receiving. A small manufacturing concern has materials shipped directly to the purchasing department. The purchasing department of a chemical company has no control of receiving but requires a copy of the purchase order as notification of receipt of material. A large public utility receives most of its material at a general storehouse, where it is counted and checked. The rest of the supplies are sent by the vendor directly to the branch, where the superintendent or foreman checks receipt. All receiving reports go to the purchasing department.

Receiving memorandum.—In many firms a copy of the purchase order, minus the quantities ordered, is used as a receiving ticket. The receiving department checks the material and inserts a record of the count on this copy of the purchase order and routes it to the inspection department with the merchandise. The inspection department notes on the form any defections or rejections and sends the form with the material to the storeroom. In one company, the receiving ticket is then routed to the cost-accounting department, where notations of the receipt of the goods are made on the stores ledger. The receipt copy of the purchase order is then filed permanently in the stores department.

If the receiving department is not provided with a copy of the purchase order, or any other indication of what material to expect, the receiving department's report on incoming goods on a "receiving slip" or a "report of materials notice" constitutes an independent check. Usually, however, it is better for the receiving department to know what goods to expect and to check the material received against a copy of the purchase order or a memo invoice from the vendor.

Reporting receipt of goods on receiving slip.—When a copy of the purchase order is not sent to the receiving clerk for use in checking the receipt of goods, a separate "materials received" form should be used. Some companies prefer to use such a receiving slip in addition to a receiving copy of the purchase order. Thus, the R.C.A. Manufacturing Company uses the form of receiving sheet shown in Figure 55 and also sends a "receiving copy" of the purchase order to the receiving department. Seven copies are made of the receiving sheet, for the following purposes:

Copy No. 1 for purchasing
Copy No. 2 for accounting division
Copy No. 3 for receiving
Copy No. 4 for expeditor
Copy No. 5 for division receiving material
Copy No. 6 for inspection copy of material
Copy No. 7 for inspection file copy

RECEIVING SHEET

R. C. A. MANUFACTURING COMPANY, INC.
CAMDEN, N. J.
COPY NO. 1 FOR PURCHASING

FORM 10617
REC SHEET
219557

DISPOSITION OF MDSE | SHIPPER'S NAME | VIA AND CAR NO. | DATE REC. | INVOICE NOS.

CHARGE TO ACCOUNT | CHARGES PAID

PURCHASE ORDER NUMBERS	REQ NOS.	QUANTITY	ARTICLE-SIZE KIND	PART NUMBER	FIN.	UNIT COST	AMOUNT

Figure 55.—Receiving Sheet.

[Actual Size 8″ x 5″]

Items included in the receiving report form.—Receiving report forms frequently contain such items as the following, in addition to those shown in the form illustrated in Figure 55:

Weight—gross, tare, net
Quantity provisionally accepted
Quantity rejected
Inventory classification or symbol
A transportation record showing:
- Pro. No.
- Weight
- Frt. or Exp. chgs.
- Prepaid or collect
- No. of pkgs.
- Condition

Received by
Counted by
Checked by
Our count — Their count
Our weight — Their weight
Material charge distribution
Container record, showing number, kind, and description

Distribution of the receiving report copies.—The materials received report is usually prepared with sufficient copies to permit distribution of the report to various departments. In some companies three copies are sufficient; in others, more are necessary. Copies usually go to the purchasing department to be checked against the invoice; to the traffic division; to the accounting division; and to the storeroom. Of the copies sent to the stores division, one may be retained there and the other returned to the receiving department for the latter's protection.

The purchasing department should check the receiving department's report against the invoice and against the purchase order, where the receiving department has made an independent check of the goods. Where the checking is done in the accounting department, the purchasing department generally receives no copy of the materials received report.

Inspection of goods.—In conjunction with the receiving of goods, proper inspection is necessary to make sure that materials received are satisfactory. Where the cost of checking is out of proportion to the value of the goods, inspection is usually omitted. For example, small, minor items of inconsiderable cost can, as a rule, be accepted without inspection. Inspection can also be omitted when the manufacturer's certified report of tests and measurements can be relied upon for accuracy. It is, however, safer in such cases to supplement the certified report with a limited number of check tests and a somewhat curtailed inspection.

Responsibility for inspection.—The receiving clerk should always make a rough check of quality and quantity. More detailed inspection should be assumed by an inspection division, whenever possible.

In many small companies and in companies where a separate inspection division is not required, the receiving department inspects incoming shipments. The receiving clerk, in such cases, must be competent to inspect. In larger companies the responsibility for inspection is usually delegated to the engineering department, the purchasing department, an independent department, or a combination of several departments.

Where to inspect goods.—Incoming materials should be inspected at the purchaser's premises whenever possible. If the finished goods purchased are costly to build or move, they should be inspected at the plant of the supplier. If they are manufactured by a highly technical process, they should be inspected while in production at the vendor's plant. This kind of inspection is best done by a representative or employee of the purchaser. In extremely technical cases, however, an outside expert may have to be called upon to make the inspection.

When neither the manufacturer nor the purchaser possesses adequate facilities for inspecting, college testing laboratories may be used. A list of college research laboratories ready to test various kinds of commodities can be found in the Bureau of Standard's "Directory of Commercial Testing and College Research Laboratories," *Miscellaneous Publication No. 90.*

Methods of inspection.—The method of inspecting depends upon the nature and value of the goods. The following methods are in general use:

REPORT ON

MARKINGS

PURCHASED FROM

ADDRESS

ORDER NO. PRICE

SPECIFICATION

PRESENT SUPPLIER

PRESENT SPECIFICATION

SYMBOL

PRESENT COST

REASON FOR TEST

REPORT

APPROVED	DIS-APPROVED

AS 51 MADE IN U. S. A.

Figure 56.—Inspection Form.
[Actual Size 5″ x 7¾″]

1. Examine each article separately and thoroughly. Goods with a poor quality record should be examined this way. For example, major equipment and fabricating parts, which have been found to require careful checking, may be examined in this way.

2. Examine by markings. Standard-brand packaged material with a satisfactory quality record may be inspected in this way.

3. Check brand goods occasionally for consistency of quality.

4. Check goods bought on sample, grade, and specifications for compliance with standards specified. For instance, regular laboratory tests may be needed to inspect cable; occasional tests may be necessary for rubber tape.

5. Take random samples of each lot and examine them completely. Materials of a good quality record, such as hardware or stationery, may be examined in this way.

The inspection form.—Where a report on inspection is necessary, a form for recording the results should be provided. Figure 56 shows the form used by Remington Rand, Inc.

Copies of the inspection form should be sent at least to the purchasing, requisitioning, and stores department.

Segregating rejected goods.—Rejected goods can be separated from those accepted by attaching a "defective material" tag, such as is illustrated in Figure 57. The form illustrated is used by an automobile manufacturer.

W1225

DEFECTIVE PURCHASED MATERIAL TAG

Part No.

Date

Part Name

Defect

Order No.

Rec. Report No.

Plant No.

Dept. No.

Quantity Defective

Account No.

Approved

Accept

Reject

Fix

Scrap

Charge Vendor

Insp. No.

Figure 57.—Defective Material Tag.

[Actual size 10″ x 3″]

[*Attached at the dotted line of Fig. 57*]

INSTRUCTIONS:—Made in duplicate by Receiving or Departmental Inspector by filling in all information except disposition. Reviewing Inspector punches ACCEPT, REJECT, FIX, SCRAP, or CHARGE VENDOR, detaches stub end and forwards to chart man where piece work charts are maintained for deduction on chart W1063, thence to Production Records Department; otherwise stub end forwarded to Production Records Department for recording of SCRAP or REJECT items on W565 departmental. Stub ends filed for three months, then destroyed. Wire end punched ACCEPT, remains with stock as authority for using. If punched FIX, remains attached to stock until repaired and then forwarded to time clerk as authority to pay for reprocessing. If punched REJECT, remains with the stock.

Rejection report.—When materials fail to pass inspection, a report should be made to the purchasing department. The purchasing officer must then decide whether to order the material returned or to ask for adjustment. The latter may be preferable if the material is usable but not up to specifications. Negotiations with the supplier for return of goods or deductions for substandard goods is the responsibility of the purchasing agent.

Records of rejections, if adequately prepared and retained, serve several useful purposes. They help reduce costs if they are properly studied to eliminate the cause for rejection. They act as a guide for determining suppliers' dependability and indicate whether a new source of supply should be investigated. They show the purchasing department whether greater care must be exercised in giving specifications, or whether specifications are unnecessarily rigid or impractical. If the latter is indicated, the purchasing executive should confer with the engineering or production departments to effect a remedy.

Importance of the invoice.—Receipt of an invoice is notice that the goods purchased have been shipped. It constitutes a claim against the purchasing concern. Consequently, it requires careful handling and accurate checking against the purchase order and the materials received report. Invoice checking is essentially a function of the purchasing department, often performed in conjunction with the accounting department. Sometimes this task is delegated to the accounting department, which is furnished a copy of the purchase order.

Procedure for checking invoices.—The procedure for checking and auditing invoices varies in different organizations depending on the size and the purchasing practices and policies of the company. The procedures described in the following paragraphs are representative of current practice.

1. *Single invoice checking.*—Small organizations may request but one copy of the invoice. The invoice is kept by the purchasing department only long enough to check on the receipt and condition of the goods. As invoices are checked and passed for payment, all data on the invoice are noted on the purchasing department's copy of the purchase order. The requisition and receiving record are attached to this purchase order copy. The entire record is placed in the completed order file as the order is filled and the invoice paid. Not only is an invoice file eliminated, but the purchase records themselves are simplified.

2. *Duplicate invoice checking.*—Many companies have a clause on their purchase order requiring that suppliers send invoices in duplicate. Original and duplicate are received by the purchasing department and are stamped and numbered consecutively to correspond with the vouchers. These consecutive numbers are furnished the accounting department, or the accounting department itself may do the stamping and numbering. The invoice is then approved and the original sent to the accounting department for payment. The duplicate is retained by the purchasing department, where it is filed until the goods arrive. When the purchasing department receives notice of receipt of goods and a report from the inspection department that the goods meet requirements, the duplicate copy of the invoice is forwarded to the accounting department, along with the materials received report and the inspection report as authorization for payment. The original is eventually paid and the duplicate returned to the purchasing department to be filed.

An alternative procedure is to have the invoices delivered to the accounting department, from where, after the necessary routine has been completed, they are forwarded with the copy of the purchase order attached to the purchasing department for approval.

3. *Triplicate invoice checking.*—Frequently companies require that invoices be sent in triplicate. Both the original and the duplicate may be sent to the accounting department, where the original is attached to the voucher. The duplicate is returned to the supplier in due course with a check. The purchasing department retains the triplicate for future reference.

A company with a large number of branch offices may instruct the vendor to forward invoices in duplicate to the receiving branch and a triplicate to the purchasing department in the general office. This triplicate is approved for price by the purchasing department and sent to the accounts payable department, where it is held until either a discount date is about to expire, when it is paid, or until the original, supported by the purchase order and receiving report, is received from the branch office. The triplicate copy is attached to the original and filed with the paid voucher.

Rechecking invoices.—The auditing or accounting department should recheck invoices to make sure that the following items are included: the purchase order number, the date, requisition number, terms, f.o.b. point, quantity, description, and unit price. Either all invoices can be rechecked on certain points, or an occasional spot-check or complete recheck of a single invoice or a group of invoices can be made.

10. STORES AND INVENTORY CONTROL

Responsibility for stores and inventory control.—The importance of stores and inventory control has already been mentioned on page 763 in connection with the subject of "purchasing the right amount." Stores-keeping and inventory control should be supervised by the department that has the most immediate and direct relationship with inventories. In many firms the purchasing department itself supervises stores. In many others inventory control is the responsibility of the production department. See also page 751, where the relationship of the stores department to the purchasing department is discussed.

Advantages of inventory control.—Inventory control facilitates operations by providing the type and quantity of articles needed, at the time required, with a minimum of investment. Specifically, its advantages are as follows:

1. Investment in inventory is reduced, and turnover is increased. Control of the physical size of stocks and the development of the most economical amounts and varieties to be carried result in lower taxes, insurance, storage, and handling costs.

2. Production delays are reduced because an available supply of materials is assured when and in the manner needed.

3. Savings in purchasing result when requirements can be accurately gauged on the basis of recorded experience.

4. The risk of duplicating orders or replenishments of supplies is minimized because a record exists against which all purchase requests can be checked.

5. Loss of stock through carelessness, damage, and dishonesty is reduced.

6. Less space is wasted in storing because of proper location and arrangement of materials.

7. Available stocks can be better utilized by substituting or transferring items between departments or plants.

8. Cost-accounting activities and the analysis of consumption figures, price trends, and comparisons of performance between commodities, departments, and periods are facilitated.

9. Deterioration and obsolescence of stock are minimized.

10. Inactive and obsolete stock can be more easily located and disposed of.

Location of the storeroom.—The location of the storeroom depends on the nature of and need for the materials. A large centralized storeroom, located in or near the factory, is usually best, for it permits easy control of stock. However, when quick issuance of materials and minimum storage costs are desired, shop storerooms, placed close to the centers of production, may be preferable. Regular stock items should have a permanent storeroom location. Irregular stored items should be given a location only when required, and that location must be properly indexed. Such a system avoids holding valuable storage space in reserve when it should be in active use.

Designing the storeroom.—The storeroom should be designed to protect materials against deterioration, theft, and removal by unauthorized persons. It should provide space for the actual storage of goods, for the receiving and checking of income goods, for the issuance of outgoing goods, and for filling material requisitions in advance and holding them ready for delivery to avoid delay during rush periods.

Equipping the storeroom.—The equipment of the storeroom must fit the particular needs of storage requirements. The multiple-unit plan of bin arrangements is ordinarily the most desirable because of its flexibility. Wood is cheaper for the bins, but steel provides more actual storage space, is more flexible and durable, cleaner, and fireproof. Storing in movable containers, such as tote-pans and dolly boxes, and placing piled goods on skids so that the lift trucks can be used, reduce the amount of handling. A good tiering device saves storage capacity and labor. The full height of the storeroom can be utilized by using ladders on trolleys, or a "setback" arrangement can be made with the second tier of shelves one foot shorter than the lower tier to provide a step or platform for reaching the top shelves.

Classification of stores and materials.—Classifying stores by major groups and designating items by standard terms or symbols greatly facilitate inventory control. Not only can items be located more easily, but symbols are shorter and more accurate than names. Major groups might be raw materials, material parts, supplies, in-process materials, tools, miscellaneous stores, and finished goods. These groups should then be subdivided according to the nature of the stock, and then by size and type. Frequently these classifications are by the cost-account numbers. Three methods for designation of items by symbols are recommended:

1. Assign a series of numbers to each major group. For subdivisions of a group, assign a series of numbers within the range of the major group. Then number each item in accordance with the numeration scheme.

2. Index items by their material classification. Each storeroom has a Roman numeral; each section in a storeroom has a capital letter; each row has an Arabic number; and each bin has a small letter of the alphabet.

3. Give each item a letter of the alphabet. Goods are classified according to their nature or use by the mnemonic system of sym-

bolization (omit letter I, O, and Q to avoid confusing with the numbers 1, 0, and 2). This provides twenty-three instead of ten divisions. All like articles are grouped into a main class and designated by a letter suggestive of the name of the material by its sound. Each main group is then subdivided as often as is necessary. Thus "S" would stand for all stores, "P" for iron pipes and fittings, and "B" for bushings, a form of iron fitting. The symbol "SPB" would thus refer to a bushing and be followed by a number to indicate size. All items of one group beginning with the same letter are grouped together in the storeroom with all drawers, bins, and racks arranged alphabetically. The groups themselves are then arranged alphabetically.

Bin tags.—Bin tags are commonly used to identify the contents of containers. The tags, attached to the bag, bin, rack, drawer, and so forth, are designed to work in with whatever plan is used to record receipts, issuance, and inventory of goods on hand. One form of bin tag, for example, indicates the date materials are received, the symbol or part number, the name and description of the item, the location in the storeroom, the material receipts, the amounts issued, the date of issue, the balance on hand, and the account to which issued materials should be charged. When the tag is completed, the clerk in charge of stock ledgers makes a new tag and notes on it the last balance shown on the old card. A physical count is also taken at this time.

Perpetual inventories.—The primary record of a stores-control system is the perpetual inventory form known as the "stores ledger" or the "balance of stores" record. A separate ledger card or sheet is assigned to each item of inventory to provide complete information at any time on the status of each item carried in stock. This minimizes the need for costly and burdensome physical inventory. It assures that all materials will be on hand or will be available when needed before an order goes into production. Furthermore, it permits planning of production on a definite schedule and provides a ready record of plant consumption of any article by stating the quantity on hand and the quantity on order but not delivered.

Stores ledger forms vary among companies according to the type of information to be recorded. All forms, however, normally provide for certain descriptive information that changes infrequently, plus records of current transactions. This descriptive information is shown at either the top or the bottom of the form, depending on whether a vertical- or visible-index record is used. Most forms include the following: (a) a description of the material; (b) the unit of measurement; (c) the piece or part number; (d) the name and type of material; (e) the maximum and minimum quantity; (f) the location by bin, rack, or section; (g) the stores account number; (h) the card number; and (i) annual consumption. The arrangement of the body of the ledger will depend on whether or not monetary values are included.

The stores record card used by The Atlantic Refining Co. is illustrated in Figure 58.

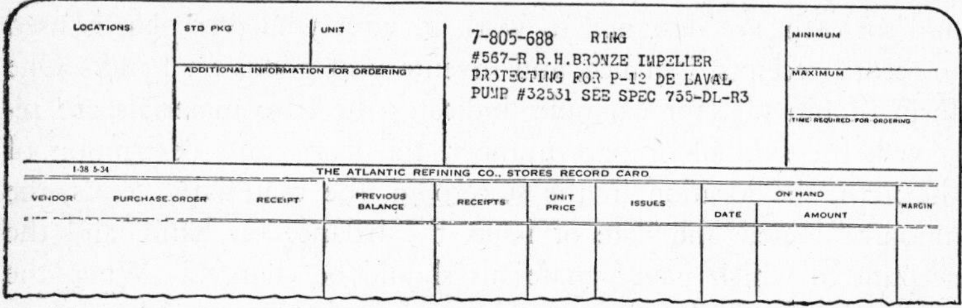

LOCATIONS

STD PKG

UNIT

ADDITIONAL INFORMATION FOR ORDERING

7-805-688 RING
#567-R R.H.BRONZE IMPELLER
PROTECTING FOR P-12 DE LAVAL
PUMP #32531 SEE SPEC 755-DL-R3

MINIMUM

MAXIMUM

TIME REQUIRED FOR ORDERING

1-38 5-34

THE ATLANTIC REFINING CO., STORES RECORD CARD

VENDOR	PURCHASE ORDER	RECEIPT	PREVIOUS BALANCE	RECEIPTS	UNIT PRICE	ISSUES	ON HAND		MARGIN
							DATE	AMOUNT	

Figure 58.—Stores Record Card.
[Actual Size 10" x 10½"]

The physical inventory.—Whether or not a perpetual inventory is kept, physical inventory of goods on hand must be made at regular intervals. If a perpetual inventory is maintained, the record is verified and adjusted on the basis of the actual physical inventory.

Some companies take complete physical inventory once or twice a year, frequently closing the plant to do so. This procedure disorganizes the plant and, because of the trouble involved, is often hurried and inaccurate. Many plants make physical inventory checking a continuous activity. Certain sections or bins are designated for checking on certain dates, and the schedule is so arranged that every item in stock will have been physically checked at least once a year. Another method of continuous inventory taking is to check the actual balance every time a requisition for a new supply is made.

Hints on taking physical inventory.—Inventory takers should normally follow the stock of material, checking each item as they come to it in the storeroom. If the count is to be entered in a stock book, the proper page of the book can be found easily if items are grouped in the book alphabetically by classification.

The accepted method of inventory taking is to start at the extreme left of a rack and continue to the right across the entire shelf or row of bins, beginning at the top and working down. Where items are placed in rack sections instead of lined up across the entire rack or row of bins, inventory should still follow stock arrangement for each section. After completing inventory of racks, the bulkier items stored on island or store platforms or on the floor should be checked from left to right, each location being completed before progressing to the next platform or floor pile. If an item is not labelled, or if there is no page in the stock book for it, a label or stock book space should be immediately provided.

Where all stock is stored in bins or racks, a double count can be taken almost simultaneously by having two counters start the checking at opposite ends of the row of bins and work toward each other. When they arrive at the other end of the row, they compare counts and have an immediate check.

Large piles should be broken down, and cases should be spot-checked or weighed. The condition of goods may be marked as slow-moving or off-grade, or classified as to market salability, style, or unit value. Material that has been unloaded from cars and not yet checked in is inventoried most easily if recorded as material due rather than as material in stock.

SECTION 8

Office Management

5. HIRING NEW EMPLOYEES

6. TRAINING EMPLOYEES

SECTION 8
Office Management

Office-management functions.—The office-management department is a staff or service department under the direction of an office manager, who is responsible to the treasurer, vice-president, president, general manager, or some other official. The functions of office management generally include direction of matters relating to the building, office appliances, furniture and equipment, stationery and forms, personnel, correspondence, stenography and typing, filing, office methods and routine, and services such as mailing, messenger, and intercommunication.

Qualifications of the office manager.—The position of office manager calls for a person with the following four fundamental qualifications: intelligence, imagination, courage, and persistence.

1. *Intelligence.*—Obviously anyone in a responsible executive position must have a keen mind that is able to grasp fundamental issues and problems and logically deduce sound conclusions.
2. *Imagination.*—An office manager must be able to visualize the merits of plans and methods in order to select the most profitable and practical ones.
3. *Courage.*—Courage to introduce, organize, and start a plan is essential if the office manager is to be successful in his work. Without courage, the best intelligence and imagination will not flower into practical results.
4. *Persistence.*—Many men having the first three qualifications fail as executives because they do not follow through with their plans. It takes constant effort to bring a plan to a successful conclusion. The general manager, president, or the board of directors must be sold on the plan; employees must be encouraged and

stimulated; co-operation from subordinates and department heads must be won.

Besides having the above fundamental qualifications, the office manager must be methodical, have an excellent knowledge of human nature, be able to get along with people, and be able to judge their capabilities and capacity. In addition, he must be resourceful, have organizing ability, and possess the attributes that make for leadership. He should come to the position of office manager equipped with previous general business experience and some accounting training.

1. PLANNING AND MAINTAINING THE OFFICE FOR EFFICIENCY

Physical factors in office planning.—Scientific office planning must take into consideration the physical factors affecting office routine. The purpose of office planning is to afford an easy and convenient flow of work and traffic. It is not enough to arrange perfect elevator service to avoid congestion and to neglect some other factor, such as location of lockers, which will offset the time saved.

The physical factors to be considered are the following:

1. Elevators.
2. Lockers.
3. Washrooms.
4. Communications.
5. Partitions, railings, doors.
6. Floor covering.
7. Lighting.
8. Air conditioning.
9. Noise reduction.

A brief discussion of the physical factors in office planning is presented in the following paragraphs.

Elevators.—It is best to have separate elevators for passengers and freight. If the organization is a large one with hundreds of employees, it is wise to stagger the working day and lunch hours so as to avoid congestion. For instance, half of the office force could start the day at 8:30, have lunch hour between 11:30 and 12:30, and leave at 4:30. The other half could come in at 9, have lunch between 12 and 1, and leave at 5.

Locate the departments using the freight elevator, such as the stock room and the mailing department, close to the elevator.

Lockers.—Lockers may be centralized in one place, or they may be placed in every department. Having lockers in every department is preferable if there is sufficient space for them, because it avoids congestion at a central point and allows the employees to be at their desks without loss of time. Metal lockers are available that accommodate the belongings of two people and take up very little space.

Washrooms.—If washrooms are to be built into the building, locate them at convenient locations on every floor. If the washrooms are already installed, make sure that the arrangement of the offices permits easy access to them for every employee.

Communications.—Messages to be conveyed may be oral or written. Oral messages are most frequently conveyed by telephone, although the use of interoffice communications systems, such as the dictograph, have become popular. Telephone service and interoffice communications are treated in another section of this book (see page 921). Buzzers, to call in stenographers and department heads, are frequently used. Oral messages to large groups of employees are sometimes conveyed by the use of loudspeakers. Most organizations reduce oral messages to a minimum, preferring written messages to oral messages. Written memos are always on record and help to fix responsibility.

Written messages may be sent by messenger (see paragraph on messenger service on page 902), or they can be sent through the central transcription department (see page 857). The use of pneumatic tubes is another method of conveying written messages, particularly in department stores and very large offices.

Partitions, railings, and doors.—Many organizations are doing away with private offices, for they take up too much space, obstruct the proper flow of work and ideas, make the problem of office planning and supervision more difficult, and give to the general public an impression of secrecy and inaccessibility. There is a marked tendency to have large open offices with partitions made of wood and glass in instances where privacy is desired.

A few suggestions are given for the use of partitions, railings, and doors.

1. Use railings in offices that are in direct contact with the public, such as employment offices, to prevent people from flocking into the office and disrupting the work.

2. Arrange all partitions and railings so that they do not obstruct the flow of traffic.

3. Have doors and swinging gates at points near the exit to street or outer office.

4. Have passages wide enough to allow traffic to travel in opposite directions.

5. Swinging doors should be partly of heavy glass to allow visibility. If clear plate glass is used, have printing on the door to make it noticeable.

Floor coverings.—Floors are made of wood, concrete, or marble. The type of covering depends not only on its decorative appeal but on a consideration of the purchase price, wearing quality, and maintenance cost. Floor coverings reduce the noise in the department and help to prevent fatigue and discomfort of employees caused by hard, cold floors. Waxed wooden floors are slippery and dangerous. Rugs and carpets are used chiefly in private offices and sometimes in foyers and hallways; linoleum, rubber, cork, or composition are used in other offices.

Lighting.—Poor lighting arrangements cause defective eyesight, increase fatigue, lower production in the office and factory, and increase the number of accidents. Any additional expense involved in improving lighting is usually more than offset by the benefits derived, and in many cases no additional expense is involved.

Lighting troubles are caused by an insufficient amount of light, or a poor quality of light. To determine whether there is sufficient light at a particular spot, measure it with a light meter (an instrument, that can be purchased or borrowed from a local power company, which measures the intensity of light in foot-candles) and compare it with the standards given below. To check the quality of light, which involves such considerations as color, glare, and shadows, follow the suggestions on page 823.

Standards for the quantity of light.—While the human eye is able to adapt itself to widely varying amounts of light, ranging all the way from 10,000 foot-candles and more on the beach on a bright summer day, to less than two foot-candles in the average poorly lighted hallway, *it works best in natural daylight.* Artificial illumination, therefore, should approach natural daylight as nearly as possible.

Many tests have been made to determine the best light for office and factory tasks. The General Electric Company summarizes these as follows:

0–5 Foot-candles: For perceiving larger objects and for casual seeing. Satisfactory for corridors and stairways.

5–10 Foot-candles: For interrupted or casual work in which seeing is important but does not involve discrimination of fine details or low contrasts. Satisfactory for conference and reception rooms, vaults, etc.

10–20 Foot-candles: For ordinary reading when not prolonged, or moderate and prolonged office and factory tasks. Suitable for filing, mail sorting, intermediate reading, and writing at a desk.

20–50 Foot-candles: For moderately critical and prolonged tasks, such as clerical work, benchwork, prolonged reading, rough drawing and sketching, bookkeeping and accounting, and stenographic work.

50–100 Foot-candles: For severe and prolonged tasks, such as proofreading, drafting, difficult reading, watch repairing, fine machine work, etc.

100 Foot-candles and over: For very severe and prolonged tasks, such as fine engraving and penwork, and discrimination of fine details of low contrast, as in inspection.

Suggestions to increase the quantity of light.—If, after testing different locations with the light meter, you find that in some places the light is insufficient, here are ways to increase that light, often at no expense:

1. Clean the lamps and reflectors. A recheck with the light meter will usually then show a higher reading. Arrange for periodic cleaning of lamps and reflectors.

2. Replace blackened bulbs with new ones; blackened bulbs are inefficient, since they do not give out so much light as new ones.

3. Make sure there are no gaps in the lighting due to burned-out bulbs or empty sockets.

4. See that bulbs of the correct voltage are being used. This will insure maximum efficiency. Lamps of too high a voltage will not burn brightly, but will last longer, while lamps of too low a voltage will burn too brightly and burn out much faster.

5. Examine the reflectors to see if the surface has deteriorated, in which case the reflecting parts should be replaced.

6. Insufficient illumination may be due to dark and dingy walls and ceilings. They are important sources of secondary light because they receive and reflect light from the lamps. Walls painted in light colors, such as buff, light-green, and gray tints, will increase illumination a great deal. Ceilings should be painted white.

7. Increase the wattage of the bulbs used. This should not be done until a check has been made to see that the circuits can stand the increase.

8. Sometimes the overhead lighting will be adequate if supplemented by Illuminating Engineering Society approved-type desk lamps. This will build up the proper amount of light on the desks.

How to improve the quality of light.—The quality of light is just as important as the quantity. Too much glare and harsh shadows make office work very tiring, even though the light may be sufficient in amount. The following suggestions are offered to improve the quality of light:

1. If bare lamps are visible, shield them.

2. If globes are objectionably bright, shade them with parchment shades, or replace with (1) oversize globes, (2) semi-indirect fixtures, or (3) indirect fixtures.

3. If illumination is spotty, provide more outlets. Often outlets can be provided by surface wiring connected to one of the outlet circuits that is not loaded to capacity. The distance between ceiling outlets should not exceed the height above the floor.

4. If sharp shadows occur, correct them by changing to fixtures of low brightness. If the shadows are caused by the fact that the light source is too small, conical parchment shades placed around the globes will help.

5. If the lamps are too dim, the reason may be a voltage drop due to inadequate wiring. In this case rewiring is necessary. To determine whether wiring is adequate, check with a voltmeter when the maximum load is on.

6. Daylight fluorescent bulbs very closely approach natural daylight and can be used to advantage where form and color must be checked closely, as in certain types of color matching and in inspection. For general office work, they supply cooler light at higher efficiencies. Special starting auxiliaries are built into the fixtures.

Air conditioning.—Various studies have been made which show that our thinking and seeing faculties vary with changes in temperature.* Air conditioning corrects the slump periods that studies indicate occur in the hot summer months by cooling the air and thereby increasing mental activity. By proper control of the air supply in an office, management can greatly reduce the time and work lost due to colds and other evidences of low resistance.

Air conditioning is the process of providing, by the use of mechanical equipment, the desired conditions of air temperature, humidity, cleanliness, and motion, and controlling these conditions to provide the atmosphere best suited for health and comfort.

The system installed may be either a permanent part of the building or it may be portable, so that the investment need not be lost if the office location is changed.

Most air-conditioning installations at the present time provide: (1) proper ventilation (air supply, air filtering, and air circulation), and (2) air cooling and dehumidification in the summer time. For winter use, air heating and humidification equipment can be added to the large units.

Among the companies manufacturing air-conditioning equipment are the Airtemp Division of Chrysler Corporation, Frigidaire Division of General Motors Corporation, Carrier Corporation, General Electric Company, and Westinghouse Electric & Manufacturing Company.

Types of air-conditioning systems available.—Several types of air-conditioning equipment are available, the choice depending upon the size of the office or building, the individual needs of the organization, and the amount of money to be spent.

1. A small compact unit can be installed in each room to serve a small area. The smallest ones are placed in the window frame

---

* Huntington, Dr. Ellsworth, *Season of Birth.* New York: John Wiley & Sons, Inc.

and serve only to ventilate the room or part of it. They keep out dust, dirt, and outside noises, since the windows are kept closed, and supply fresh air from the outdoors by means of intake fans, but do not cool and dehumidify the air. If cooling and dehumidification are desired, the unit just described must be replaced with one that ventilates and in addition cools and dehumidifies the air.

Portable air conditioners that are not connected with the windows can also be purchased. While they do not provide a fresh supply of air from the outdoors as the window units do, they will take care of a larger area.

These small units provide the maximum flexibility, for individual offices can be conditioned one at a time, and the occupant of each office has complete control over the operation. Certain disadvantages exist, however. Since each unit requires a separate motor, the combined load of several of them may necessitate extensive rewiring. The air-intake supply for the window units may be difficult to arrange. The maintenance of a large number of fans, motors, and compressors may be a serious problem.

2. Larger self-contained units to ventilate and cool can be installed to handle several rooms at once. These conditioners have a refrigerating capacity of from three to ten tons each, depending upon the size, and can be used in groups to condition an entire floor. A refrigerating capacity of three tons is the ability to melt three tons of ice in twenty-four hours. The five-ton installations will handle an area of about three thousand square feet. They can be used either without ducts to serve one large space, such as a drafting room, or with ducts to serve several small rooms. They will cool and dehumidify the air, as well as provide proper ventilation. Heating and humidifying equipment can be added for winter usage to supply warm, moistened air if desired.

3. Air conditioning can also be installed with a central station at a distance from the area to be conditioned. For example, the direct-expansion method utilizes a compressor and cooling water and air supply equipment in the basement. The cooled and filtered air is conveyed in ducts to various parts of the same floor and the floor above. It is not practical for more than two floors, since the ducts would have to be too large. Fire-code regulations in some places limit the use of this system to either the basement and first floor or the top two floors of a building.

The indirect-expansion system has the compressor and cooling water tank in the basement. The cool water is pumped to a maximum of three or four floors to air-handling equipment on each floor. Here are located the fans, air filters, and supply and return grilles to provide the cooled air. The water, after circulating through the mechanism, returns to the cooling tank to be used over again.

Smaller units are often added to these central systems to air-condition individual offices that are likely to be used at times when it is not necessary to cool the rest of the office or floor, such as an office in which a lot of overtime work is done. Such units are connected by separate water pipes to the central compressor and cooling tank. The use of such units as auxiliaries helps to reduce operating costs, since it is cheaper to operate a small unit to condition an individual office than to run the fans, and so forth, which supply the whole floor.

Equipment-cost factors in air conditioning.—No air-conditioning installation should be made, of course, without a survey to determine any special conditions that would affect the type of equipment to be used. The following factors are important in determining the needs for a particular installation:

1. *Geographical location and exposure.*—Places where hot, humid weather exists for long periods require larger equipment. Buildings more exposed to the sun's rays will require larger equipment than those that are for the most part in the shadow.

2. *Size and shape to be conditioned.*—Heat passing through the walls and windows is an important factor in the heat load of an area. Irregularly shaped offices, since they have a higher ratio of wall surface to floor area, are more expensive to condition than rectangular offices of the same area.

3. *Type of building construction.*—Porous walls or those in which windows are loosely set in the frames are more expensive to condition than others.

4. *Window area.*—Heat passes more quickly through glass than through thicker and more resistant wall construction. Therefore, the greater the ratio of window area to wall area, the greater the cost.

5. *Ventilation requirements.*—Conditioning an office where a lot

of smoking is done, or where unusual odor conditions exist, will be more expensive than otherwise.

6. *Number of people.*—A large number of people in an office will make the system more expensive to operate, since more body heat will have to be removed.

7. *Number of lights and office appliances.*—A large number of light bulbs and office machines in use will increase the amount of heat to be removed and therefore the cost.

8. *Water characteristics.*—The characteristics of the water available to remove from the equipment the heat taken from the room will affect the type of equipment to be installed.

9. *Kind of power.*—While electric motors usually drive the conditioning equipment, steam-driven equipment may in some cases be feasible. This type of equipment will affect the costs.

Operating-cost factors in air conditioning.—The hours of operation will affect the costs of running the air-conditioning system, as will protracted heat spells, type of work, amount of lighting facilities, business machines in use, and other factors. Charges for electricity and cooling water will vary with different localities. Maintenance and repairs will be necessary. The regular operating crew will be able to handle some of these, but outside organizations will occasionally have to be utilized.

The fixed charges should also be considered. Depreciation might be based on permanency of occupancy or expected life of the equipment. The usual maximum is fifteen years. Rental of the space occupied by the equipment is another element. Insurance and taxes will depend on local conditions.

Noise reduction.—Excessive noise in an office increases mental fatigue and is a disturbing factor, hampering efficient production. In some cases the ceiling and walls have to be treated with sound-absorbing materials such as felt, porous plaster, Acousti-Celotex, or Akoustolith. If the office or factory is so noisy that it is necessary to sound-proof the walls and ceilings, it is best to consult an acoustical engineer, for the job is highly technical. Usually simple precautions, such as the following, will reduce a large percentage of the noises in the average office:

1. Keep all machines, sliding drawers, doors, and so forth, in good condition and well oiled.

2. If possible, centralize all noisy machines in one department.
3. Use a floor covering of sound-absorbing quality.
4. Place sound-absorbing materials close to noisy machines.
5. Fix all noisy radiators and windows.
6. Shut off noises from hallways with doors.
7. Muffle high-pitched telephone bells or have a lower-pitched bell installed.

Office layout.—The aim of office layout is to arrange offices and equipment in such a manner that work and traffic flow in as straight a line or as continuously in one direction as possible. On the surface, such an arrangement seems simple, but the problem is complicated if space is limited, if a number of people have to use the same files, or if there are a number of windows, posts, railings, and doors limiting space available for equipment and machines. Furthermore, offices must be located in relation to other offices; for instance, the credit department should be next to the bookkeeping department, because credit men are always consulting ledger records. Offices dealing with the public should be next to passenger elevators or on the ground floor. Likewise, offices requiring the use of freight elevators should be located conveniently to them.

Steps to be taken in planning office layout.—The following steps are recommended in planning office layout:

1. Determine the amount of space needed for every employee, his desk and chair, the files, tables, machines, coat racks, and shelves.
2. Estimate the space required for future expansion, basing the estimate on past growth. The total requirements shown by steps one and two indicate the amount of space needed.
3. Study the usefulness and desirability of the existing equipment and machines and eliminate those that are not needed.
4. Make a rough sketch of the new office, showing all doors, windows, and posts and the approximate location of desks, files, and machines.
5. Cut out templates of cardboard for every piece of equipment in the office. Make them to the scale of ¼ inch to a foot. In making templates of safes, files, and cabinets, be sure to cut them large enough to allow for opening of doors and drawers.
6. Make an exact scaled drawing of the new office, showing all

the windows, doors, and posts, and using the same scale of ¼ inch to a foot.

7. Place the templates on the scaled drawing as planned on the rough sketch. The templates will give an exact picture of the new office. If the arrangement is not satisfactory, the templates can be shifted around to another position and yet be in the correct proportion to the room.

8. When the arrangement is satisfactory, take a picture of the plan as a permanent record.

Office maintenance.—A clean, well-kept office has an effect upon employee morale. It is short-sighted economy to try to save money by neglecting office maintenance.

Since the office manager is responsible for the maintenance of offices, it is up to him to establish a definite plan and schedule for the work instead of depending on haphazard methods. A simple card, filled out by the maintenance men every day, stating the date, office cleaned, work done, and the time taken provides a convenient record for the office manager and aids him in checking and controlling the work.

The following suggestions are given to aid the office manager in planning a systematic maintenance schedule:

1. Offices should be swept and dusted every night, and provision should be made for occasional washing or scrubbing of floors.
2. Windows should be cleaned at least once a month, and preferably twice a month; lighting fixtures, at least twice a month.
3. Washrooms and lavatories must be cleaned every night.
4. The condition of chairs and desks should be inspected periodically. If a desk top is badly worn, have the surface refinished or have it covered with a special desk covering of a color that does not reflect light. If chairs have splinters and are causing runs and tears in clothes, have them sanded and refinished.
5. Set aside one day a year for general office cleaning, having the entire office personnel participate.

For maintenance of office equipment, see page 849.

2. EQUIPMENT, FILES, AND APPLIANCES

Office equipment.—Office space, especially in large cities, is expensive. Consequently, the maximum utilization of space means money saved. Although economical use of space is primarily an office layout problem, the proper selection and use of office equipment are also important cost-cutting factors.

The standard equipment of an office consists of desks, tables, chairs, and filing cabinets. All of this equipment, except chairs, is made of wood or steel. Steel is preferable because of its durability and indestructibility by fire.

Desks.—The desks to be selected depend on their use. Four types are generally used in offices—the clerical desk, the typewriter desk, the secretarial desk, and the executive desk.

The clerical desk is for writing use only. The desk may be single-pedestal, 42 by 30 inches, or double-pedestal, 60 by 36 inches, with five drawers.

The typewriter desk is used for typing. It is a double-pedestal desk, 54 by 30 inches, with drawers on each side and a space directly in the center on which the typewriter is placed. When the typewriter is not in use, the center section can be closed, giving the desk a plain-topped writing surface.

The secretarial desk is designed for employees who do typing and have need for a clear writing space for clerical work. It is about the same size as the typewriter desk, but the typewriter occupies the space normally occupied by the left-hand or right-hand drawers. When not in use, the typewriter is let down and pushed into the desk under the writing space.

The executive desk is a large desk, usually about 66 by 36 inches, having five or seven drawers.

Tables.—The tables in offices vary in size depending on their use. The usual size is 60 by 36 inches, with the surface about 30 inches from the floor. If rough work is to be done on the table, it is advisable to cover the top with linoleum or some other covering.

Chairs.—Office chairs are designed primarily for correct posture, for it is recognized that the posture of an employee has a bearing on fatigue and also on the quality and quantity of his work. The four types of chairs found in offices are: (1) stenographer chairs, which are adjustable swivel chairs with posture back rests; (2) executive chairs, which are swivel chairs with arms; (3) swivel chairs without arms; and (4) straight-back non-swivel chairs. All of these chairs, except the straight-back non-swivel chairs, are set on four small, roller-bearing, swivel wheels.

Filing cabinets.—Although manufacturers make filing cabinets of various size to accommodate letters and forms of standard sizes, the standard filing cabinet is the four-drawer, 8½ by 11, wood or steel cabinet. Where space is limited, a five-drawer cabinet is available. Counter cabinets of convenient height, built to be used as counters, and having drawers in the back, are used in offices dealing with individuals who come into the office. The information pertaining to their visits is conveniently located for the clerk.

Visible-filing equipment.—Visible-record equipment has been used to great advantage by many companies to improve control over sales, receivables, inventories, and other business operations. Pertinent facts can be seen at a glance, instead of having to be rooted out of a mass of papers.

The equipment consists of record forms, movable celluloid signals to emphasize particular data, slides to hold the forms, and trays into which the slides are set. One type of arrangement is a portable tray into which the slides are set vertically. All the forms or cards in each slide are visible at once, thus making the location of a particular card almost instantaneous.

Another type of arrangement is to have panels on which small cards are fastened. The panels are placed in a vertical swinging position on a stationary or revolving rack. Both cards and panels are easily removed or replaced. On the edges of the panels the major classification tabs are fastened so that any position in the file is quickly located. The panels may also be attached together into the shape of a book and the whole book placed in a horizontal position. Some of the applications of visible-record equipment are described in the following paragraphs.

Visible records in sales management.—The cards to be used in sales management must, of course, be well planned, so that the most useful information will be readily seen. The sales-record card might be designed to indicate on the visible margin, by the use of movable colored celluloid signals: (1) the month of the last call by the salesman; (2) the month of the most recent purchase; (3) the percentage of the customer's requirements being filled; and (4) whether or not the customer bought anything in the previous year; in addition, the name and address of the customer are visible. The balance of the card would give details showing individual sales by product and amount, comparisons with other years, what the customer buys and how much and so forth.

The records are held securely in overlapping kraft pockets, which are mounted on slides to fit into various types of cabinets. The colored signals permit immediate analysis of entire groups of records without the necessity of "drawing off" figures. A positive control over salesmen is provided, making checkups easier.

The cards can be kept up to date very easily, merely by moving the signals when postings are made.

A useful procedure is to photograph each salesman's cards periodically, making the print on a piece of paper with wide margins. The salesmanager makes notations about each account on the margins and sends the photographs and notations to the salesman, who is thus provided with an up-to-date record of the status of each account, together with home-office comments.

Visible records in accounts receivable.—The application of visible records to accounts receivable is particularly useful in installment collections. Here the visible margin shows the name and address of the customer, and the celluloid signal indicates to what date he has paid. A delinquent account is easily spotted because the signal will not have been moved as far as the signals on the nondelinquent accounts.

The pocket behind the name usually contains a ledger card with credit data and details of installments paid. This card can easily be pulled out for posting and can be found very quickly with the eye because the names are visible. If desired, statements can be kept in the same pocket with the ledger cards.

The immediate visibility of the delinquency data greatly aids in keeping up collections, thus strengthening the retailer's cash position, increasing the accounts-receivable turnover rate, and reducing bad-debt losses and collection costs.

Another advantage of visibility in connection with accounts receivable is that the operator will spend a larger proportion of his time in making entries on the cards and a smaller proportion in hunting for the proper sheets, thus increasing his production.

Visible-record equipment aids purchasing.—Another application of visible-record installations is in the field of inventory control. The card used is a regular stock card containing the information on orders and requisitions. The visible edge gives the name of the item. The celluloid signal shows how many weeks' supply is on hand. As the supply is used up, the signal is moved over. Thus the stock-record clerk or purchasing agent can tell at a glance how long the supply of each item will last.

The visual signal shows when the ordering point is reached, when the supply is getting dangerously low, and when the item is overstocked. This device saves both clerical and executive time in analyzing and reduces the cost of keeping the record. The progressive signal instantly points out the items needing attention.

A schedule can be set up showing the expected turnover of each item. Assume the desired turnover is six, and that thirty days are necessary for delivery. Set the minimum "ordering point" at eight weeks' supply; then, when the signal reaches this eight weeks' line, enter a replenishment order for another eight weeks' supply at the present consumption rate. A plan will soon be in operation showing balances between a low of four weeks' supply and a high of twelve. The average will be eight, and the turnover close to six. Well-balanced stocks will be maintained at levels that eliminate both understocks and overstocks.

Visible panels in the credit department.—The panel type of visible-record equipment is extensively used in the authorizing section of the credit department in department and retail stores.

The visible cards on the panels contain the name, address, and credit limit of the customer. Different colored cards indicate whether an account is delinquent or closed. A numbered code is used to indicate various restrictions regarding the account. The panels are arranged alphabetically and have the main alphabetical divisions designated by a celluloid tab fastened to the edge of the panel.

The visible-panel filing system is also used as a master reference file in credit departments that file their accounts numerically. The cards on the panels contain the name, address, and account number of the customer. The clerk can easily find the credit record by first consulting the master file for the account number and then locating the numbered record in the visible file.

Rotary filing device.—Office-equipment companies have developed a plastic wheel for rotary filing, to which are attached metal segments holding cards. The whole is enclosed in a cabinet, the top of which is open to reveal the wheel and a section of the cards. A wheel measuring 21 inches in diameter can hold 6,500 cards. By turning the wheel, the clerk can bring the desired card into view. It is not necessary to make up a special type of card for the machine. Cards already in use can be fitted into the device.

Individual cards can be slipped out if desired. Groups of cards can also be removed, since the metal segments on which they are fastened are detachable. This feature permits easy division of the work on peak-load days, as different clerks can take segments of cards to their own desks.

The unit is portable and can be locked at night. It is desk height, thus enabling hand posting to be done more quickly and more easily and in the most natural writing position.

The device has been used by organizations with large membership lists, because it facilitates looking up the status of persons who are being registered for attendance at conferences and conventions.

Office machines and appliances.—Office machines and appliances are introduced into an office in order to save time and money and to increase the quantity and quality of work.

The types of office machines in general use are calculating machines, duplicating machines, addressing machines, time recorders, and dictating machines. These machines are being improved and modernized constantly so that the discussion given on pages 836, et seq., is limited to a description of their operation and use.

How to determine the value of an office appliance.—Modern office devices often seem expensive when the original cost is examined. A simple way of checking the economy of office appliances is to compare the estimated monthly depreciation with the operator's salary and production. If output is increased as a result of the introduction of the machine, sufficiently to offset the depreciation charge, the machine can be introduced economically.

Considerations in buying office appliances.—The following suggestions will aid in the consideration of the purchase of an office appliance:

1. Buy your office equipment from a scientific viewpoint. Standardization of equipment reduces maintenance costs, makes employee transfer easier, and allows quantity discounts. Nevertheless, standardization should not be carried so far that a $200 machine is bought for each clerk when a $50 machine would be perfectly satisfactory for some.

2. Decide whether it is necessary to perform the task that the machine is designed to do.

3. Test the machine under actual working conditions to check claims for increased production. Do not permit yourself to be biased for or against any equipment, but be sure to get supporting evidence for every claim made about it.

4. If the equipment does increase production, will you be able to utilize the spare time of the operator? If you cannot, there is not much point in getting the machine.

Calculating machines.—Adding, billing, and bookkeeping machines are the most common of the calculating machines.

Adding machines.—The simplest and most common calculating machine is the adding machine. Its use primarily is to add columns of figures. There are machines that will add, subtract, divide, and multiply, but they are not generally used in smaller offices.

The adding machine may be hand or electrically operated, list or nonlist. A list adding machine records the row of figures on a strip of paper, whereas the nonlist machine shows the accumulated total on the top or bottom of the machine.

Billing machines.—A billing machine is a combination typewriter and calculating machine. There are various types of billing machines adaptable for various uses. The machines are able to do a number of calculating jobs, such as adding, subtracting, dividing, and multiplying.

The billing machine is used in large and small organizations to prepare monthly bills. It eliminates the necessity of typing the bills with a typewriter at the end of the month.

Bookkeeping machines.—Space does not permit a detailed discussion of the various bookkeeping machines. In principle they are similar to billing machines, and both machines can be used with a little change for similar work. The bookkeeping machine is used in preparing records such as customers' statements, accounts-payable records, cash-received records, cost sheets, stores records, payroll records, and many others.

Punched-card accounting equipment.—Punched cards are used for general and cost-accounting work as well as for statistical and analytical research. The cards in many companies comprise the accounts-receivable and accounts-payable ledgers, stock records, and payrolls. In cost accounting, punched cards can be used to show the cost of direct labor, indirect material and overhead applicable to each job, thus replacing the cost sheets. Examples of statistical and analytical uses are classification of sales by salesmen, by price lines, by territories, by profit lines, and by kinds of merchandise sold. Department stores use the equipment for inventory analyses and classifications, for charge-account analyses, and the like.

Three types of machines are generally necessary to set up a punched-card-accounting process: (1) a key punch, to perforate the tabulating card with the desired holes; (2) a sorter, to separate the punched cards into the desired groups; and (3) the accounting machine, to compute, record, and print the results.

Each card is divided into "fields," in each of which are vertical columns of figures from zero to nine. The figures applicable to each field are recorded by punching out holes in the appropriate columns. The fields are arranged according to the data desired. For example, the accounts-payable card used in a retail store might have fields showing invoice data, vendor's invoice number, vendor's number, department, due date, terms, gross amount, discount, net amount, transportation, total cost, retail price, percentage markup, and posting data.

When punching has been completed, the cards are usually not in any usable order and must be arranged according to the desired classifications. This is the function of the sorter. Since the sorting is done one column at a time, the cards must be passed through the machine as many times as there are columns in the particular field being sorted. This is not a serious drawback, however, as 400 cards can be sorted per minute.

The sorted cards are then run through electric accounting machines, which are so designed as to provide complete flexibility in the arrangement of the data appearing on the forms. As much or as little information as is desired can be printed. The sorted cards can also be run through tabulating machines to give subtotals and grand totals, which are transcribed to report forms by the operator.

Advantages of punched-card accounting.—The punched holes are permanent and unalterable, so the cards, once punched and proved, eliminate errors of omission and transposition. Since the operations are entirely automatic, a uniform accuracy for all reports is assured. Reports are available much more quickly than under manual procedures, and many more reports and analyses can be made with punched cards than would be possible if costly manual preparation were necessary.

Many models of machines are available, ranging from very inexpensive to quite elaborate and expensive ones. The manufacturers of the equipment have service bureaus in leading cities that will prepare analyses and reports on a fee basis if desired, thus eliminating part of the outlay for equipment.

Proof machines to speed sorting.—Proof machines are available to list, sort, and prove bank checks, sales tickets, vouchers, and other business documents in one operation. The results, ordinarily obtained with three or more separate manual operations, are obtained with but one clerical handling. The items themselves are sorted into different desired classifications; money amounts for each classification are listed and totalled; and all amounts are listed, identified, and totalled on a single proving tape. The automatic proving eliminates the necessity for tedious, time-wasting checking and cross-checking to locate errors.

Keysort for sorting data.—Keysort is a system of sorting accounting information by the use of specially printed and punched cards and a selecting needle that resembles an ice pick. An extremely flexible system, it can be used for sales, timekeeping, and payroll records, cost distribution, personnel statistics, and other records.

Description of cards.—The information to be sorted is transcribed onto cards, different sizes and styles of which are manufactured to meet varying needs. The four margins are divided into sections according to the classifications desired. Into each section the manufacturer has punched round holes ¼ inch apart, which are used to indicate numbers within the classification. Four holes are required for each digit in the classification and are labelled, respectively, 1, 2, 4, and 7. By using combinations of these four digits, it is possible to notch out in the margin any number from 1 to 9, as indicated by the following table:

1—by notching out 1
2—by notching out 2
3—by notching out 2 and 1
4—by notching out 4
5—by notching out 4 and 1
6—by notching out 4 and 2
7—by notching out 7
8—by notching out 7 and 1
9—by notching out 7 and 2

The indication of the number is made by notching out that portion of the card between the hole and the outer edge of the card. Each group of the four holes 1, 2, 4, and 7 is termed a field. If the classification has three digits in it, three groups of four holes, or three fields, will thus be required for that section.

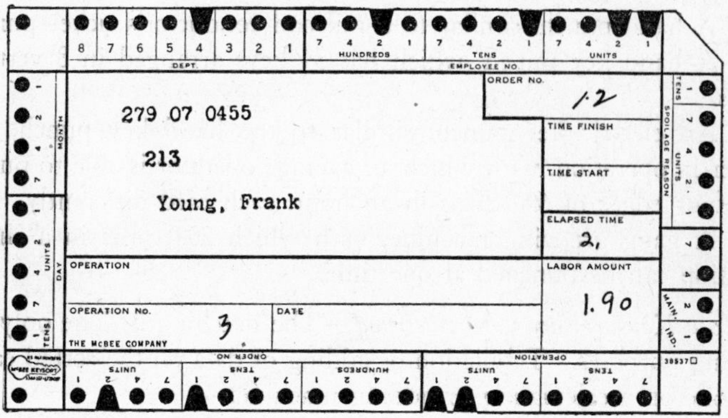

Figure 59.—Example of Keysort Card.

As an example, the Keysort card illustrated in Figure 59 is being used in connection with labor cost records, one card being used for each operation worked on by each man. The workman's name, order number, clock number, date, starting, ending, and elapsed times, amount applicable to the operation, and other necessary information appear on the body of the card. On the margin of the card appear various classifications: order number, department, employee number, operation number, and others. In this particular case, the workman's number is 213, the order number 12, the operation number 3, and the department number 4, as can be seen by an inspection of the notches made in the illustration.

Types of Keysort cards used.—The cards used may in some cases be carbon copies of invoices or other original records. They may be the original records themselves, such as the time cards just described. Again, they may be prepared from some original records as a separate operation, in which case the information to be sorted will be punched on the cards, and the amounts to be tabulated will be written on the face. In most cases only those classifications to be sorted are punched.

The most advantageous use of Keysort cards is obtained when they are used as original records, since such use does not entail transcribing data from the original records to Keysort cards, as the data are written there first.

How notching of Keysort cards is done.—Four types of punches to notch the Keysort cards are available from the manufacturer:

1. A hand punch, similar to a railroad conductor's ticket punch.
2. A hand key punch, which has 34 keys arranged in 8 vertical rows.
3. An electric key punch, similar to the hand key punch, but faster in operation, with which an average operator is able to punch the four edges of 600 cards in an hour, each card differently.
4. A gang grooving machine, with which 200 cards in a single position can be punched at one time.

How Keysort cards are classified.—The notching is done only for sorting purposes. Tabulation or adding of data on the sorted cards is done on a calculating or adding machine.

The cards to be sorted are placed edgewise on a table, face forward and right side up. One corner of each card has a diagonal cut, to make it possible to tell at a glance whether all the cards are in the right position. The selecting needle is then inserted in the hole for which classification is desired.

As an illustration, assume that from a group of time cards those pertaining to employee number 936 are to be segregated. The needle is first inserted in the 7 hole of the hundreds' field and lifted. All those cards on which the hundreds' digit is 7, 8, or 9 will fall. The needle is then inserted in the 2 hole of the hundreds' field of those cards dropping from the first sort. Cards on which the hundreds' digit is 9 will drop, since the only cards that can drop this time are those in which both 7 and 2 in the hundreds' field have been notched out. The needle is now inserted in the 2 hole of the tens' field. All cards that drop this time will begin 92-, 93-, 96-, or 99-. A sort is now made by inserting the needle in the 1 hole of the tens' classification of the dropped cards, and those cards beginning 93- will drop, since the only cards that can fall are those in which both the 2 and the 1 have been notched out of the tens' field. Two more similar sorts are necessary for the units' field, first by sorting through the 4 hole and then through the 2 hole, thus dropping all cards on which the number 936 has been punched out.

Sorters.—Filing time can be greatly reduced by the use of sorters, which run all the way from a simple bellows-shaped cardboard letter-size folder with a division for each letter of the alphabet to large sorters on tracks with several thousand divisions.

The larger sorters consist of a table for the operator, on each side of which are one to four movable trays, several feet long, each placed on a track. Each tray contains subdividing tabs the width of the papers to be sorted. The tabs are labelled according to the filing system used. The papers to be sorted are placed on the table and are inserted behind the proper subdivision by the operator, who can move the trays back and forth on the tracks by a push of the finger. The operator thus sits at her work and does not have to reach far to place a paper behind the correct tab.

With the use of sorters it is not necessary to file material daily in the filing cabinets. The tabs can be used to accumulate material for any desired period, depending upon the capacity of the sorter. Papers are as easily available as in the file cabinets, so that no time is wasted hunting for unfiled material.

Sorters have many other uses besides filing, depending, of course, on the internal organization and procedure of the company. One very practical application is in the accounts-receivable department of a department store. Here the sales slips are sorted by customers and held until the end of the month. No postings are made during the month to the customer's statement. At the end of the month, the sales checks are totalled, and only the total is entered on the statement. Copies of the sales checks comprising the total are stapled to the statement and mailed to the customer. This practice eliminates the work of posting charges daily and also avoids any chance of error. Each customer gets a copy of the original sales slip just as it was made out at the time of purchase.

Pegboard system to save time and reduce error.—The use of the pegboard system makes unnecessary the transcribing of information from several individual records to one summary record. The pegboard system consists of a steel strip, in which pegs are inserted at fixed distances apart, and forms punched across the top margin to correspond with the distance between pegs on the strip. The forms must be carefully printed so that all horizontal lines on the forms will be on the same plane.

The pegboard system used by Continental Baking Company in connection with daily orders for bread taken by the various salesmen illustrates the short cut furnished by this system. Daily each salesman turns in a "salesman's invoice." This form constitutes the order for bread to be delivered the following day. In the center section of the form, under the word "Kind," are printed the names of the different kinds of bread, and in the column headed "Trip," the quantity ordered of each. The slips turned in by all the men are then placed on the strip from left to right, as illustrated in Figure 60, so that the "Trip" section of each form is exposed. A blank sheet is then added at the extreme right of the strip, next to the last order. A comptometer operator adds the total of each variety across the sheets and enters the totals on the blank.

The procedure described renders unnecessary the copying of all individual figures from each sheet to a summary record. Time is saved, and errors in transcribing are eliminated.

Duplicating machines.—Many instances occur in an office in which several copies of a paper are needed. Among the various processes available for obtaining duplicate copies are stencil, gelatin, direct and offset printing, automatic typewriting, and photography. These processes are briefly described in the following paragraphs.

INV INV INVOICE

Name *Summary Sheet* 19—

TRIP	TRIP	TRIP	+OR–	KIND	REC'D	AMOUNT
500	800	1300		Wonder .08		
200	300	500		Wonder Sliced .08		
100	200	300		Wonder Spec. Pan Rls. .08		
50		50		Wonder Wheat .08		
50	100	150		Wonder Wheat Cut .08		
50		50		Wonder W. Pull No. 2 .18		
				Spec. Wheat Pullman .26		
	100	100		Jail Bread .06		
				Pullman No. 1 .12		
				Pullman No. 2 .16		
				Pullman No. 3 .14		
10		10		Pullman No. 4 .28		
	25	25		Pullman No. 5 .08		
				Special Pullman .29		
	20	20		Baby Buns .10		
5		5		Individual Buns .12		
	10	10		Red Bird Buns .15		
				Spec. Red Bird Buns .12		
5		5		Tavern Buns .12		
	15	15		Coneys .12		
				Small Rye .08		
				Large Rye .16		
Route No.	Route No.	Route No				

Salesman

Figure 60.—Peg Board Forms for Determining Day's Orders.

Stencil duplication by mimeograph.—Stencil duplication (mimeograph) provides exact reproduction of typewritten work. The stencil is placed in a typewriter and the ribbon is adjusted or removed, so that the letters, instead of being printed, are cut into the stencil, thus exposing the fibers through which the ink can pass when the stencil is placed on the machine. Illustrations, drawings, and other handwritten matter may also be stencilled by means of a stylus.

The stencil is placed over an ink pad that partially covers a hollow, perforated, revolving cylinder. The ink is applied to the inner surface of the cylinder and passes through the perforations to the pad and then through the letters or designs cut in the stencil, making an impression on the paper as the cylinder revolves. The paper may be fed to the machine either automatically or manually, depending upon the type of machine. With the automatic duplicator, from 1,500 to 5,000 copies can be made per hour. Removable cylinders are available, so that one can be substituted for another when two-color reproduction is desired.

Gelatin duplication.—Gelatin duplicators (Ditto) make copies by transferring ink from a typewritten or handwritten original to a gelatin duplicating composition that dissolves and holds the ink on its surface until all the copies have been run off. Hard bond paper and special duplicating ink, a duplicating typewriter ribbon, or an indelible pencil are used in preparing the original. Different colors may be combined on one original.

The duplicator consists of a flat printing bed over which is stretched a gelatin-covered roll. After one surface has been used, a fresh one may be brought into position by turning a handle.

The original is placed face down on the gelatin copying surface and smoothed with the palm of the hand or a roller. It is then lifted off, having left an impression on the gelatin. The blank sheets are placed one at a time on the gelatin surface and allowed to remain a few seconds until the imprint is made.

Direct printing (multigraph).—Direct printing may be done with a machine such as the multigraph. The type may be composed by hand or by a keyboard-operated machine that operates at the usual typing speed. In either instance, type is placed directly onto railed segments. The composed segment is then placed on the duplicating machine, and a wide typewriter ribbon is wrapped around the form, or ink is applied by an inking mechanism. As the printing drum of the machine revolves, paper is fed between the ribbon-covered type or the directly inked type and a rubber-covered platen, thus producing a facsimile typewritten letter or an ink-duplicated form at each revolution. From 2,500 to 5,000 copies can be produced per hour. Forms may be numbered consecutively with an optional numbering device.

Offset printing (multilith).—Offset printing can be done by the multilith. The matter to be reproduced is prepared on a smooth, metal or paper plate, either directly by typing, by drawing with ink or crayon, by tracing through carbon paper, or by the photo-contact process. The prepared plate is placed on a drum of the duplicating machine, and ink and a repellent are fed by rolls to the surface of the plate automatically during revolution of the drum. The drum is in rolling contact with a second drum, which has a smooth rubber blanket wrapped around it and to which the inked image is offset. The paper is fed between the offset blanket drum and impression cylinder or platen, and at each revolution of the drums a complete offset duplicated copy is made on the sheet. From 3,000 to 5,000 reproductions can be made per hour.

See page 310 for a description of the super-process—flat-bed process used in preparing letters for quantity distribution.

Automatic typewriter duplication.—Automatic typewriters are designed to produce rapidly actual typewritten letters. The machine consists of a standard typewriter operated by an electric mechanism that is controlled by a perforated strip of record paper similar to a player-piano roll. Part of the equipment consists of a perforator with a standard typewriter keyboard, with which the perforations are made.

The typist cuts the material to be produced on the perforator, each perforation representing a character in the typewriter keyboard. When the cutting of the perforations is completed, the perforated paper is cut off and the ends cemented together to form a roll, which is then placed on a drum in front of the automatic typewriter. In the drum are a number of lengthwise slots over which the perforations in the record paper rest. When the machine is started, the drum revolves, carrying the record paper forward under a set of pins. As a perforation passes under a pin, the pin drops into a slot in the drum, actuating a typewriter key as though by hand. After all the perforations have passed over the drum once, the operator removes the finished letter and repeats the process.

The machine may also be used as a standard typewriter, so that at any point the operator may stop the automatic mechanism and typewrite, by hand, information of interest only to the recipient of that particular letter.

Photographic duplication.—When several copies of a letter or other document are desired, a device known as *Portagraph* may be used. The item to be copied is placed on a plate-glass surface at the top of the machine; it is then covered with a piece of sensitized paper; a lid is closed down over the two sheets; an automatic timer is set in motion; and a few seconds later the exposed paper is ready for development. An experienced operator can produce up to 125 copies per hour, whereas a stenographer takes an hour to copy five one-page letters. It is estimated that the cost is approximately one third that of the copying cost of typing and proofreading. No photographic experience is necessary to operate it, and, since the printing paper used is not sensitive to daylight, no dark room is necessary for either printing or developing. The unit is compact, can be easily carried, and can be used wherever electric current is available. It is particularly useful where facsimiles of art work, maps, signatures, seals, trade-marks, and so forth, are desired.

Electric typewriters.—Electric typewriters have several advantages over nonelectric typewriters. The entire keyboard is electrically powered, including carriage return, backspacer, tabulator, shift and space bar. The touch is a much lighter one, and, since each character receives the same power impulse, the type impression is uniform and even. Fatigue is prevented and production greatly speeded up. As many as twenty clear carbon copies can be printed on some electric typewriters.

Addressing machines.—Much time is often lost in typing the name and address of a new customer on the various forms used in the office. This time can be saved by the use of addressing machines, which are of two types: (1) machines that use a fiber stencil cut out with a typewriter, and (2) machines that use an embossed metal plate prepared by a special machine. The plates or stencils are fed into the addressing machine in the order in which they are filed. The machine is able to print all the names, but it can be adjusted to select any group of names desired. Tabs placed in a certain position on the plates or slots cut out from the stencil guide the machine automatically to reject or select any plate. Addressing machines can be used to print the name and address of a customer on various forms. For instance, a group of Chicago insurance companies prepared an addressograph plate and printed the name and address on the following records:

1. Customer's ledger card.
2. Postal acknowledgment of application to the applicant.
3. Identification card.
4. Policy enclosure with instructions for use in case of accident.
5. Two index cards for alphabetical and numerical files.
6. File folder.

Dictating machine equipment.—The dictating machine equipment consists of a dictating unit, a transcribing unit, and a shaving machine for shaving the cylinders for reuse.

The dictating machine is a compact machine that may be set on the desk or on a small stand beside the desk. To operate the machine, the dictator removes the cylinder from its container and slips it on the mandrel, throws the dictating lever in dictating position, and removes the mouthpiece from its hanger. By pressing or releasing the button on the handle of the speaking tube, the dictator starts or stops the cylinder. A fine needle records the dictation on the revolving cylinder by etching fine threads on the wax. The needle moves from left to right at a rate of about 160 revolutions per inch. The operator may listen back to his dictation by backspacing to the desired position and setting the lever to the reproducing position. There is a marker that travels with the recording needle and indicates the exact position of the recording. A slight touch on the small indicator lever records the end of the letter or any corrections that may occur throughout the dictation. The small indicator lever thus enables the transcriber to gauge the length of the letter and warns her of errors.

A buzzer cautions the dictator if the machine is not properly set for dictation, and a bell rings to warn the dictator that he has reached the end of the cylinder.

The transcribing unit is similar to the dictating unit in principle but is used for reproducing rather than recording. The cylinder is placed on the mandrel, and the indicator slip, which comes with the cylinder from the dictator, is placed in the holder in front of the machine. A flexible tube with earpieces transmits the voice from the cylinder to the transcriber's ears. The volume of the reproduction can be regulated by turning a thumbscrew, marked "loud," "medium," or "soft." The tone quality is controlled by another thumbscrew, which regulates the speed at which the cylinder revolves. The typist starts or stops the cylinder by pressing a foot control placed on the floor or by pressing a duplex hand control, placed in front of the typewriter, with the palm of her hand. A repeat lever on the control device enables the typist to backspace to any position.

The shaving unit is a precision lathe that shaves off a thin layer of wax from the cylinder, making it smooth and ready for reuse. The knife can be easily adjusted to shave off such a small amount of wax that the cylinders may be used over again as many as a hundred times. The unit has two drawers, one for cylinder shavings and the other for cylinder storage.

Time recorders.—Small minute wastes grow very rapidly into large money losses. For example, in a factory employing 100 people at an average wage of $25 for a forty-hour week, the annual loss is over $1,000 if each employee is a minute late in the morning and after lunch and a minute early in leaving for lunch and again at the close of the day. Attendance time recorders will eliminate minute losses by revealing the sources and by promoting punctuality. Such clocks are also of particular value today because they provide the kind of record that enables management more easily to comply, and prove compliance, with the various social and labor laws that require accurate accounting for employee time.

The efficiency of any cost system depends partly upon the accuracy with which time records are kept. In the first place, workmen tend to eliminate fractions in filling out job time cards. Moreover, if they wait until the end of the day to fill out their cards, their records are likely to be inaccurate because of hazy memories.

This lack of accuracy, of course, upsets the cost determination. Job time recorders make it possible for employees to record the time at the exact moment each job is started and finished. Cost determination is thus made more reliable because there is an accurate accounting of the exact amount of time spent on each job or operation. Mechanical job time records also help management to determine man and machine efficiency and reveal the amount of time lost between jobs. See page 855 for use of time stamps.

Maintaining office appliances.—To prolong the life of office appliances, obtain the greatest amount of service, and protect the initial investment in expensive machines, the establishment of a definite maintenance policy is necessary. Most appliance manufacturers provide a maintenance service on a yearly basis and at a nominal fee. Small organizations can well afford to subscribe to this service. Large organizations may find it more economical to train and maintain their own service department.

Maintenance and repair costs can be kept down by keeping a card index of all the office machines in use. Include on the cards all purchase data, including credit allowed on an old machine, expected life, amount of depreciation to be charged off, and so forth. On

Record of ---------------- Card #-----
Carriage Length ---------- Serial #-----
Type ------

Order #------ Date Purchased -------- Guarantee Expires ------

Purchased from ----------------
List Price .... $--------
Discount ------% .... $
Credit on old machine .... $-------- $--------
Cash Difference $--------

Turned in--------------

Date *Department* *Operator*

Figure 61.—Record of Office Machines.

the reverse side enter all details of repairs. The record helps to determine whether repair is advisable, or whether the age and condition of the machine warrant replacement instead. Excessive maintenance costs are decreased by making replacements at the proper time. The American Trust Company of San Francisco uses the form illustrated in Figure 61, the reverse side of which shows details of repairs.

Typewriter care.—An instruction sheet on how to care for typewriters, distributed among those who use typewriters, will help keep the machines in good condition and will reduce repair costs. The instruction sheet shown in Figure 62 has effectively reduced costs in one organization.

KEEP YOUR TYPEWRITER IN GOOD REPAIR

1. Keep your machine covered when not in use.
2. Move the carriage to extreme right or left when erasing to prevent eraser dust from clogging segment.
3. Oil sparingly—just an occasional drop on the carriage rails is sufficient.
4. Use only light oil—preferably a 3-1 quality, that will not gum; never use Dictaphone oil or motor oil.
5. Never oil any other part of the typewriter—wait for the repairman to oil your machine generally.
6. Clean type with a good quality brush and type cleaning fluid.
7. Wipe off entire machine occasionally with soft cloth, slightly dampened with cleaning fluid; never use alcohol as this will destroy the finish on your typewriter.
8. Use properly-inked ribbons for the style of typeface.
9. Change typewriter ribbons when necessary.
10. Fasten machines to desks for best typing results.

TYPEWRITERS ARE MONEY!
TREAT THEM AS SUCH.

Figure 62.—Typewriter Care Instruction Sheet.

Typewriter ribbons.—For superior legibility, good appearance of the finished product, and most efficient use of typewriter ribbons, it is best to use special ribbons for special purposes, rather than to make one type of ribbon do all types of work. Below are outlined ribbon characteristics for various kinds of work: *

For the sharpest and cleanest typewritten impressions, as in executive correspondence, use a silk ribbon with a high thread count to the square inch and with a thickness of .003 inches.

When strength, durability, and long ink life are sought, along with a clean-cut, sharp write, use a cotton fabric with a count of 320 to 330 threads per square inch and a body thickness of .0045 inches.

For quality at a lower cost, use a cotton fabric having a count of approximately 304 threads per square inch and a thickness of .005 inches.

For interdepartmental correspondence, where economy, long ink life, durability, and legible impressions are required, rather than an extra sharp write, use a cotton fabric with a count of 260 threads per square inch and a body thickness of .0057 inches.

To meet the stress of unusual mechanical functions as in billing and accounting machines, electrical typewriters, typewriters with hard rubber or brass platens, or flat writing beds, use a reinforced cotton fabric with a count of 260 threads per square inch and a body thickness of .0061 inches.

Old machines (since they are usually more severe in action) and those with hard platens require lightly inked ribbons. Elite type requires a more lightly inked ribbon than do Pica and Gothic types.

Thinner ribbons should be used on noiseless machines than on others. Operators with a light touch also require thin ribbons. The greater the thickness of the letterhead and copy papers, the greater the need for a thin ribbon.

Carbon paper.—Carbon paper should be selected on the basis of the type of work to be done. For example, a lighter weight of carbon paper should be used to make fifteen copies than to make three copies. Also, it must be remembered that different finishes of paper will produce different results. If the print is too black, or too dense, use a harder finish carbon. If it is too light or sharp, use a softer finish. Most carbon papers will improve with age, if properly stored.

The relative durability of two pieces of carbon paper can be tested in an adding machine that has an electric repeat mechanism. Re-

---

* From *Bankers Monthly,* "There's a Ribbon for Every Job," by Norman D. Stone, October, 1940, p. 578.

move the adding machine ribbon and hold a strip of carbon paper in place in front of the tape where the keys strike it. Repeat the same number over and over again on the machine. Each time it will strike the carbon in the same place, but the adding-machine tape will move on. Run the number off as many times as a legible print results. Repeat the same process for the other piece of carbon paper. The paper that provides the greater number of legible impressions is the more durable. To make an accurate test, use papers of the same weight and finish.

Improving carbon-copy reproductions.—Poor carbon copies may be caused by mishandling the carbon paper, using the wrong grade for the results desired, by faulty carbon paper, or by the faulty condition of the typewriter.

The carbon paper should be kept carefully in the desk to avoid curling and wrinkling; keep it face down, out of the sunlight, and away from steam pipes. Poor interleaving of the carbon paper before insertion in the typewriter will also result in poor copies.

Lack of uniformity in the carbon imprint may be due to lack of rhythm on the part of the operator. It may also be due to defects in the product, such as variations in absorbency of the base paper, even though checked at the factory, and insufficient aging.

Poor carbon copies on a typewriter may be due, not to the carbon paper, but to lack of care in handling the typewriter. The type should be cleaned periodically to prevent its becoming gummy and causing poor impressions. A harder platen is needed if a great many copies are to be made, but if the platen is too hard for the number that are being made, or if it is pitted or slippery, typewriter troubles will occur. If the spools, ribbon guides, and reversing mechanism are out of order, the ribbon will cut, fray, tear, and wear quickly, thus producing streaks on the original and on the copy.

Offset of the carbon coating to the copy will result if the feed rolls are too hard or are improperly adjusted and press too hard on the platen. If the pressure rolls are out of alignment, and force the paper in two or three different directions, the carbon paper will tree and cause streaks on the copies.

Binders and saddlebacks for carbon paper.—Binders and saddlebacks facilitate the making of carbon copies. Binders are a form of carbon-paper pad that is manufactured by folding over a piece of paper (not carbon paper) about 1/2 inch from the end and inserting and stitching several sheets of carbon paper into the fold. The copy sheets are inserted between the leaves of the pad. The pad holds carbons and copy sheets together so that no jockeying or aligning is necessary after the setup has been inserted in the typewriter.

When two or three copies are desired, saddleback carbons can be used to advantage. The most common use is in billing operations, when the ledger card, the customer's statement, and a duplicate of the customer's statement are all made at once. A saddleback carbon sheet is a piece of carbon paper folded in half, forming four pages. The second and fourth sheets are carbonized. The original is placed in front of the first page; the first copy is placed between the second and third pages; and the second copy in back of the last page. Saddleback carbon sheets to make three copies are also available. In this type, an extra fold is made in the sheet, and three carbonized surfaces are provided instead of two.

3. MAKING OFFICE PROCEDURE FUNCTION SMOOTHLY

Reception and information service.—Many organizations have found it necessary and beneficial to maintain a reception and information bureau located at a central and convenient point in the building. The need for a reception and information service is twofold: (1) to greet and direct visitors, and (2) to save employees' time.

The reception office should be spacious and simply and tastefully furnished. The equipment of the office should consist of a desk for the clerk, a telephone, comfortable chairs for visitors, and a table with literature on it, preferably pertaining to the company or its business.

Duties of a reception and information clerk.—Organizations are constantly being visited by customers, other individuals who come to transact business, and persons seeking information. It is the duty of the reception clerk to intercept these people, find out what the purpose of their visit is, whom they represent or who sent them, and whom they wish to see. Individuals who come on business, such as salesmen and dealers, should be announced by telephone to the proper party. If the employee is busy, the visitor should be asked to return, or he should be seated. Personal friends of employees should be requested to be seated, and the superviser should be notified of the nature of the visit. Visitors, such as collectors, insurance salesmen, solicitors, and the like, who attempt to reach employees at their place of business should be tactfully turned away. Undesirable visitors should be reported to the supervisor or to someone capable of handling them. Applicants for employment should be directed to the employment office or told when to call back if definite interviewing hours are maintained.

A capable reception clerk not only creates goodwill for the company but saves the time of busy employees who otherwise would be annoyed and interrupted throughout the day. The reception clerk should report the visit of all important callers on a daily report sheet noting the name, the company they represent and the person they called to see.

Qualifications of a reception clerk.—The reception clerk should have the following qualifications:

1. Good appearance.
2. Ability to converse well.
3. Pleasing personality.
4. Tolerance.
5. Courtesy.
6. Ability to make people feel comfortable.
7. Ability to think and act quickly.

Value of a well-organized mail department.—A well-organized mail department can find many opportunities to be of service. As both the first and the last point of contact between the company and those of its customers with whom business is done by mail, it can expedite the prompt handling of correspondence by early delivery of incoming mail and systematic handling of outgoing mail. In addition, the mail department is in a position to handle and operate the interoffice messenger service.

Mailing-room equipment.—Most large organizations have separate mailing rooms in which both incoming and outgoing mail is sorted. Vertical racks with separate pigeonholes for each department are set up on tables. One large insurance company has a separate section in which mail that is not addressed to the attention of any particular department is sorted. Similar racks are used to sort outgoing mail.

Hand- or electrically driven letter openers are available to expedite opening the mail. When such equipment is used, letters of the same size are gathered together, and their contents jogged down to the bottom of the envelopes by striking the bottom of each envelope on a hard, flat surface. They are then run through the machine one after the other without cutting the enclosures.

In many large organizations envelope-size trays divided into compartments are used by the messenger to transport mail between the different departments and the mailroom.

Procedure for handling incoming mail.—The first morning mail as a rule is the largest. It should be placed on a table where it will not get mixed up with other matter, and, until it is sorted, no one except the sorters should have access to it. A systematic procedure for handling the mail is outlined below:

1. *Sorting.*—Separate first-class mail from all the rest and place letters addressed to individuals to one side. Do not open mail addressed to individuals unless it is the company policy to do so.

2. *Opening.*—Open special-delivery and air-mail first, then other first-class mail addressed to the firm. Slit the end as well as the flap of the envelopes to make sure that nothing of value is left in the envelope.

3. *Time-stamping.*—Time-stamp correspondence and other papers upon arrival to speed up handling by the recipients. The time of the stamp will quickly indicate any undue delay in taking care of the matter.

4. *Money enclosures.*—Attach all money enclosures to the letter accompanying each and route at once to the cashier.

5. *Routing the mail.*—Route mail to each addressee, whether an individual or department, giving precedence to officers and executives, in the order of their importance.

6. *Damaged mail.*—When a letter is received in damaged condition, note the fact on the envelope and letter and check contents.

7. *Illegible or missing return address.*—Where the sender's identification is missing from the letter, be sure to attach the envelope securely to the letter, for even if there is nothing on the envelope to identify the sender, the postmark or handwriting may give a clue to its origin.

Messenger service.—In making mail deliveries and pickups the mail department can at the same time deliver and pick up interoffice messages. The following procedure shows how the messenger service can be made to function in conjunction with the mail department:

1. Have incoming and outgoing mail trays placed on every desk.
2. Establish a definite schedule for mail and message pickups and deliveries.
3. Designate one messenger for each floor or section and have him responsible for all pickups and deliveries for that floor.
4. Maintain a central station, preferably in the mail department, and have all mail and messages delivered to the central station. Separate messages from the mail and sort them according to floors.
5. At the scheduled time, have the messengers gather all the mail and messages from the central station, routed for their floors, and make their deliveries, commencing at the same time another pickup.

Handling office supplies.—In most organizations the purchasing agent is responsible for the buying of office supplies, but the office manager is responsible for the office-supply room and its operation.

The little sums of money that dribble away in wasted paper, pencils, erasers, and the like, every week amount to a considerable figure at the end of the year if they are uncontrolled. The following suggestions are given to aid in handling and controlling the office stockroom to prevent waste:

1. Provide a central supply room that is adequately lighted and neatly arranged. Be sure that the supply room has sufficient shelf space and is provided with alleys and ladders so that the stock is accessible.
2. Appoint one person who will be held responsible for the appearance of the supply room and the issuance of all supplies.
3. Require everyone to have written stock requisitions before issuing any supplies.

4. Use bin tags (see page 813 for description of bin tags) to mark the reorder point for supplies.

5. Standardize the shape, size, and quality of forms and paper whenever possible. It will make storage easier and require less space.

6. Eliminate waste wherever possible. Old mimeograph sheets can be cut up and glued into scratch-pads.

Operating a transcription department.—Where stenographic work is decentralized or departmentalized, an impartial survey is likely to reveal waste and inefficiencies. Usually more stenographers and typists are employed than are necessary; for example, one department having too much work for one girl but not enough for two will employ two people, and neither will be occupied all the time.

Through the introduction of dictating machines, this difficulty can be eliminated. Where such machines are installed, the usual practice is to supply each dictator with a machine and concentrate the transcription work under the direction of a supervisor in a centralized transcription department.

Centralization is not applied to those in the secretarial classification, since secretaries are valuable to their employers not merely for their stenographic ability but because of their familiarity with the work and detail involved in their employer's duties.

Advantages of a centralized transcription department.—A centralized transcription department has the following advantages:

1. Distribution of work is equalized.
2. Uniform standards are promoted.
3. Time is saved.
4. Better training of employees is possible.
5. Job classification is simplified.
6. Distracting noises are reduced in other departments.
7. Greater continuity of work is effected since the absence of one worker does not mean that the work will not be done.
8. Letters are handled more speedily.
9. The quality of work is improved.
10. Equipment is more readily standardized.
11. Less space is used.

Disadvantages of a centralized transcription department.—The disadvantages of a centralized transcription department may be summarized as follows:

1. Opposition may develop during organization.
2. Department heads do not have direct control of typists and tend to be more critical of mistakes and delays.
3. Time is spent in sending back inaccurate letters.
4. Delays may result if the transcription department is rushed.
5. Rush letters may disrupt proper handling of work.
6. A supervisor must be employed.

How to make a centralized transcription department function smoothly.—A centralized transcription department must function smoothly if it is to give the most efficient service. The following ideas will help it to function smoothly:

1. Give correspondents written instructions on how to use the dictating machine. See below.
2. Have messengers collect cylinders every hour from the different machines.
3. Have a separate proofreader to check letters for style, punctuation, and errors. This will save the time of typists. Furthermore, errors are more likely to be caught by the proofreader than by the typist doing the work.
4. Use posture chairs to eliminate fatigue.
5. Supply the typists with letterheads and tissues already stuffed with carbons. It takes less time to insert carbons for a large number of letters all at once than to insert them individually for each letter as it is typed. The carbons can be taken out by the typist after the letter is finished and used over again.

Instructions to correspondents to help transcribers.—Speed and accuracy in the centralized transcription department can usually be increased by co-operation of the correspondents. Thus it is well to give instructions on the use of dictating machines and to include the following items:

1. Place a check mark on the indicator strip where any mistake occurs, so that the typist may know ahead of time where corrections have been made.

2. Spell out proper names and unusual words to make certain the typist understands them without having to listen back.

3. While commas and periods may be judged from the inflections of your voice, it is better to dictate them. Paragraphs and unusual punctuations such as parentheses should be dictated.

4. Dictate special instructions at the beginning, or else write them on the indicator strip.

5. Tag rush correspondence with a signal for immediate action.

To: .... Date ....

In order that we may serve you efficiently, your co-operation is requested as indicated below:

- ☐ Please hold mouthpiece touching the upper lip and tilted slightly away from the lower lip.
- ☐ Please dictate in a higher pitched voice.
- ☐ Please dictate in a louder tone and enunciate your words more distinctly.
- ☐ Please dictate more slowly.
- ☐ Please spell such proper names as do not appear in accompanying files; also spell technical and unusual words.
- ☐ Please indicate all instructions or corrections on indicator slip; also indicate end of each case or letter on indicator slip.
- ☐ Please preface corrections, instructions, or interpolations of any nature in your dictation with the word "OPERATOR."
- ☐ Please dictate periods and paragraphs; also dictate such other punctuation as you do not wish to leave to the judgment of the operator.
- ☐ When listening back, be sure that control lever is in the extreme upward position; also be sure that the carriage has cleared the previous dictation, i.e., that you have *heard* the last word, before you pull control lever downward to resume dictation.

☐ ....

TRANSCRIPTION DEPARTMENT

Figure 63.—Form Used by Transcription Department.

This signal can be a red tag inserted into the indicator strip pocket or the correspondence folder.

6. When possible, place correspondence in the correspondence folder. This will save time in dictating and assure accuracy in the name and address. If there is no correspondence in the folder, mark "no correspondence" on the indicator strip. In the latter case, to assure accuracy, dictate the name of the person to whom the letter is addressed and write the name and address on the indicator strip.

A company with a centralized transcription department uses the form on page 859 when letter writers do not use the dictating machines to best advantage. The form (Figure 63), appropriately checked, is sent to the dictator by the head of the transcription department.

Daily supply folios for typists.—A daily supply folio for each typist will help to cut stationery losses. From a stationery-supply center, each typist is provided with a day's supply, according to the number of letters she is supposed to write. At the end of the day she returns her folio and is credited with the material left over. Each typist is thus made aware of any waste in letterheads, for she has a fixed number, plus error allowance, to cover estimated needs.

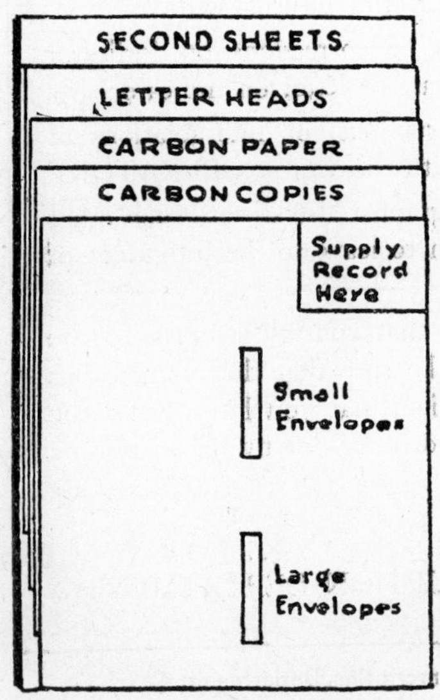

Figure 64.—Stationery Folio.

The folio is made with several manila envelopes sufficiently large to hold the size stationery being used. Seal the flaps. Slit open the top and right-hand side of each envelope, trim the under side to the size of the stationery, and the upper side two inches shorter, to allow the typist to see what is in it and to simplify taking the paper from the envelope. Next, glue the envelopes together, so that the top edge of the under side of each envelope is even with the top edge of the upper side of the one beneath it, thus forming a series of pockets, one above the other. The whole can then be mounted on heavy cardboard, and each pocket identified by printing the intended contents across the top. Finally, cut slits in the top pocket (see Figure 64) to accommodate the envelopes.

Operating a central filing system.—Filing may be centralized or decentralized. Offices with little correspondence, a small amount of filing, and little need for consulting filed material would find it simpler to file material departmentally. Offices having numerous records, voluminous correspondence, and constant need for consulting filed material would benefit from a central filing system, provided that the central files are easily accessible to all departments, and competent file clerks are available.

The following material can normally be included in the central file:

General correspondence
Interoffice and branch communications
Orders
Invoices
Shipping tickets
Bills of lading
Vouchers
Estimates and quotations for customers
Credit memoranda

Material of a confidential nature or of purely departmental interest should not be placed in the central file. The following material can ordinarily remain in the departmental files:

Payroll information
Financial statements
Tax matters
Legal correspondence
Unfilled orders
Unpaid bills
Matters of departmental interest only, such as tariffs for the traffic department, sales analyses for the sales department, quotations for the purchasing department, electrotypes and cuts for the advertising department, and blueprints and drawings for the engineering department.

Advantages of centralized filing.—A central filing system has the following advantages over a departmental filing system:

1. Filing is speedier and more accurate, and papers are located more quickly.
2. Duplicate copies for different departments can be eliminated.
3. Files can be kept in better condition.
4. Standardization of equipment is promoted.
5. Weeding and transferring can be made more systematic.
6. Greater control can be exercised over material out of the file.

Disadvantages of centralized filing.—Certain disadvantages of a central filing system must be considered before such a system is adopted.

1. Department heads often resist the idea.
2. Additional floor space is usually required, and frequently an immediate outlay is required for additional equipment.
3. Full-time file clerks may have to be employed.
4. Selection of material for the central file from the existing department files creates certain problems.

Types of filing systems.—Five basic systems of filing are in common use: alphabetical, numerical, subject, geographical, and chronological. Since each system is adapted to certain classes of work, fitness for the work in question is the test that must be met in selecting a system.

The *alphabetical* system is the simplest, oldest, and most common. Since room for expansion must be allowed in each drawer, additional equipment and more room for files are necessary.

The *numerical* filing system is an indirect filing method, since it must be used in conjunction with an auxiliary index. Under this system each new correspondent is given a number, the numbers being assigned consecutively. An index card is made out with the correspondent's number and name and is filed alphabetically in a card index. Thereafter, whenever a letter comes from a correspondent, his name is looked up in the index and his number marked on the letter to be filed. Advantages of the system are the rapidity and accuracy of refiling and the opportunity for indefinite expansion. For most companies, however, these advantages are more than offset by the disadvantage of having to maintain the auxiliary card index and to make two searches, one of the index and the second of the files, every time papers are withdrawn or new material added.

Subject filing is desirable when there are a great number of letters from different persons or concerns relating to the same subject. A common example of such a case is in connection with the letting of large contracts. Great care must be exercised in the selection of headings, in order to avoid confusion. It is advisable that one person select all the titles, because two people rarely view a subject in the same light, and each may give the same letter a different title, equally correct.

Geographical filing is used principally in sales work and in cases where the country, state, county, or community, rather than the name of a company or individual, is the chief consideration. An auxiliary alphabetical card index is ordinarily used in conjunction with this system.

In *chronological* filing, all letters are filed according to date, either in the order in which they are received, or according to the date upon which they should have attention. This system is often used in collection work. For example, a customer whose account is past due writes that the account will be paid August 6. The letter is filed in the folder for August 6, and on that date is automatically brought to the collection manager's attention. An auxiliary alphabetical index must be used if it is necessary to refer to a letter other than by date. The chronological system is often used in a "tickler" file. See page 865.

Controlling material taken out of the file.—A method should be devised for controlling papers taken from the file in order that the file clerk may be able to locate them at any moment. An essential of any method is that no one outside of the filing department be permitted to go to the files to take material.

A simple method of handling requests for filed material is to require a requisition in writing, such as that illustrated in Figure 65, for anything that is to be taken out of the files. In addition, guides of the same size as the folders used in the files should be provided. These guides should preferably be of a different color stock and should have printed on the tab the word "OUT." The guide may provide space on which an entry can be made of the material taken from the file, showing the date, what material was taken, the person requisitioning it, and the date it will be returned. This guide is then placed in the files where the extracted material was located.

Another method, which saves the work of transferring the record from the requisition to the guide, is to have a pocket on the guide into which the requisition may be placed.

A third method, which eliminates the use of guides, is to insert the requisition amid the correspondence where the letter was located. Under this method it is advisable to have a separate 3×5 inch card index identifying alphabetically all material out of the files at any time. When any requisition is made, the file clerk first looks in this index to see whether the requested material is

DATE: ....

TO FILE CLERK:
Please send to ....
Correspondence with ....
Dated .... In re............
....
....
....

Please send me order for: ....
....
(Name of customer, as billed)
....
(address)

Order Number (s) ....

Miscellaneous material: ....
....
....
....
Signature

Figure 65.—Requisition for Filed Material.

[Actual size 6″ x 9″]

already out, and thus does not waste time looking in the files for material that is not there. When any correspondence is returned to the files, the card pertaining to it in the index is destroyed, and the requisition is taken out of the place where the correspondence is inserted.

A tickler file system for correspondence wanted in the future. —The following procedure for handling material that someone in the organization wants to come up in the future has been in operation for many years in a large organization and has been found to function smoothly.

The person who will want the correspondence or material in the future fills out the form shown in Figure 66.

DATE: ....

TO FILE CLERK:
FROM ....
BRING UP THIS MATERIAL:
JANUARY: ....
FEBRUARY: ....
MARCH: ....
APRIL: ....
MAY: ....
JUNE: ....
JULY: ....
AUGUST: ....
SEPTEMBER: ....
OCTOBER: ....
NOVEMBER: ....
DECEMBER: ....
REMARKS: ....
....

Figure 66.—Form Requesting Correspondence Wanted in Future.

The form is attached to the correspondence and sent to the file clerk, who makes out a 3 × 5 inch card with the name of the company or person from whom the correspondence was received, the date it will be wanted, and the name of the person wanting it. She files this card alphabetically by name of company in a card index containing similar cards for all other correspondence that will be wanted in the future. The correspondence itself, together with the follow-up form, is filed chronologically in a separate section of the correspondence files. The separate alphabetical card index is kept to facilitate look-ups. When someone requisitions a certain letter, the file clerk first looks in the follow-up card index to see whether it is in the follow-up section.

The first thing each morning, the file clerk takes out of the chronological file all the correspondence which is wanted that day, and removes the corresponding 3×5 inch cards from the file. The correspondence is distributed by the messengers to the proper people indicated on the follow-up forms attached to the correspondence. Since this organization uses the "out" control mentioned on page 864, the 3×5 inch cards are placed in the card index used for "out" material, because the correspondence is now out of the files completely. At the same time, a memorandum is placed in the general files where the correspondence should be located.

Destruction of records and files.—In order to conserve space, a definite procedure for the destruction of accumulated records and correspondence should be established. A schedule should be worked out showing the various kinds of records that accumulate and the period during which they should be kept. In fixing the period, the statute of limitations will serve as a guide in some cases. All states have such statutes limiting the period for bringing legal action. Close following of the destruction schedule will prevent unwieldy accumulations of records, will save space, and will prevent the interruption of work that generally occurs when destruction of records is done haphazardly at long intervals.

4. ECONOMIES IN THE USE AND PRINTING OF FORMS

Designing forms.—The first consideration in designing forms is the matter of size. It is advisable to use form sizes that can be cut without waste from standard sizes used by printers. The following table shows sizes and quantities of forms that can be cut from standard-sized sheets:

Size of Form (in inches)	*Cuts Without Waste from Standard Sheet Measuring*	*Number Obtained from Single Standard-Size Sheet*
2¾ x 4¼	17 x 22	32
2¾ x 8½	17 x 22	16
3½ x 4¼	17 x 28	32
3½ x 8½	17 x 28	16
3½ x 17	17 x 28	8
4¼ x 5½	17 x 22	16
4¼ x 7	17 x 28	16
4¼ x 11	17 x 22	8
4¼ x 14	17 x 28	8
4¼ x 28	17 x 28	4
5½ x 8½	17 x 22	8
5½ x 17	17 x 22	4
7 x 8½	17 x 28	8
7 x 17	17 x 28	4
8½ x 11	17 x 22	4
8½ x 14	17 x 28	4
8½ x 22	17 x 22	2
8½ x 28	17 x 28	2
11 x 17	17 x 22	2
14 x 17	17 x 28	2

The second consideration is the quality of stock to be used. Examine the life and amount of handling of the forms used in your organization to see whether a cheaper stock of paper will serve the purpose. If a form is to be thrown away shortly after it is used, an inexpensive stock should be used. One corporation saved $4,000 in one year as the result of such a study. Its examination revealed that 75 per cent of its forms could be printed on a good grade of sulphite bond, instead of the much higher grade of paper it had been using.

A study of the stock used may also result in greater standardization of quality, which in turn may result in reduction in price through quantity orders. The degree of permanency of the form should determine the grade of paper to be used. The following table indicates the grades:

Permanency	*Grade of Paper*
1- 3 years	100% sulphite
3- 6 years	75% sulphite, 25% rag
6-10 years	50% sulphite, 50% rag
Over 10 years	100% rag

Lastly, the question of how to arrange data on the forms for practical use must be considered. The following suggestions will make the forms more useful:

1. Print the name of the form plainly at the top and provide a place for the date.
2. Give the form an identifying number.
3. Design the form to fit double typewriter spacing. This will speed up work if the typewriter is used and will provide sufficient space for handwriting.
4. Align the printed data that precedes the blank lines on the right-hand side rather than the left-hand side. This will permit the blank spaces to begin one exactly under the other, and the typist can use the tabular key when filling in the form.
5. Where possible, provide boxes in which to enter information, to encourage more economical use of words.
6. Group information by departments, so that each department which uses the form can find the information it needs in one section.
7. Confine information as much as possible to one side of the page.
8. Provide sufficient margin if the form is to be placed in a binder.
9. Make most important items prominent, and place them preferably near the top.
10. Design the form to fit a window envelope.
11. Have everybody who must use the form approve its design.

Ordering forms.—When a new form is made up, have a small quantity printed first so that waste will not result if changes have to be made. When the form has proved satisfactory, a quantity sufficient for six or eight months can be ordered.

Order forms of the same size and approximately the same quantity at the same time, to utilize full capacity of the press. This system of ordering will reduce the element of press time in the printer's bill. An additional saving is possible by arranging with the printer to print some of the forms during his slack period or at his convenience. Under this arrangement he can utilize otherwise unused press space for the forms. This policy will result in lower quotations from the printer.

Keeping large quantities of forms on hand necessitates storage space which is often expensive. Most printers will make contractual agreements whereby forms can be stored and printed on order. Have the type left standing in the case of permanent forms, to reduce composition costs.

Central control of forms.—To eliminate waste caused by unnecessary forms, facilitate standardization, and bring about greater economy in ordering forms, establish a central control of forms. The person responsible can then gather all forms together for a systematic review. The results of central control are likely to be:

1. Elimination of unnecessary forms.
2. Better dovetailing of two or more related forms.
3. A systematic plan of design, classification, and identification.
4. A procedure for introducing new forms.

All proposed forms should be reviewed by the person in control of forms before they are ordered.

5. HIRING NEW EMPLOYEES

Sources of employees.—The success of a business organization depends to a great extent on the caliber and capacity of its employees. Furthermore, when the expense of training new employees is considered, it is essential for the employer to know where to get reliable and capable personnel. The sources for new employees upon which an employer can draw are as follows:

1. *Present employees.*—Employees frequently know of friends and relatives who are either out of work or who are anxious to change jobs and who are qualified for positions in the company. It is not advisable to depend heavily on this source, for the maintenance of proper discipline is complicated when the personnel of an office is related or too friendly. Present employees, especially executives, are a good source for employees needed to fill positions such as junior executives or supervisors, for an executive usually feels responsible for his candidate and makes recommendations only after careful consideration.

2. *Applicants coming or writing to the employment department.*—A company with a good reputation and sound personnel policies

attracts a great many applicants, who either come in or write to the company for positions. The files of the employment department are an excellent source for new employees.

3. *Employment bureaus.*—Nearly all cities have private, commercial employment bureaus that are continually advertising and interviewing individuals seeking positions. Business organizations use the services of these bureaus extensively as a source of employees. These employment bureaus save the employer the time necessary to conduct preliminary interviews by weeding out the obviously unqualified applicants and sending only those who meet the employer's specifications. These bureaus operate on a fee basis, which is usually paid by the applicant. The local State employment service, an affiliate of the Federal employment service, is a free public employment bureau that should not be overlooked as a source of new employees.

4. *Trade journals, trade schools, and competitors.*—Industries that require skilled or specialized employees will find good sources by consulting the "position wanted" ads in trade journals and by contacting trade schools. Competitors or businesses that have similar trade problems will sometimes co-operate in finding new employees. Many companies that receive an application from a desirable applicant and cannot hire him at present or in the future will, in many cases, refer the applicant to a competitor.

5. *Colleges, universities, and business schools.*—A good many colleges and universities maintain employment bureaus for their undergraduates and graduates. Part-time and temporary positions can be filled by students who are seeking employment while going to school. In many cases large companies send talent scouts to colleges, prior to graduation, to interview the top ten per cent of the graduating class. Business schools are a good source for secretaries, stenographers, and typists.

6. *Appliance manufacturers.*—Office-appliance manufacturers occasionally know of, and recommend, individuals who are skilled in the operation of various office machines.

7. *Customers.*—If good customers are told of the need for new employees, they are sometimes in a position to make recommendations.

8. *Associations, welfare organizations, and fraternal societies.*—Associations such as the Y.M.C.A. and Y.M.H.A., various welfare

organizations, churches, and fraternal societies may be used as sources of new employees.

9. *Newspapers.*—Newspapers can be used in two ways as a source of employees: (1) by inserting ads in the "help-wanted" column, and (2) by watching the "situations-wanted" column. Great care must be exercised in selecting the paper in which to run the advertisement. The choice is determined by the type of personnel wanted and by the class of people reading the paper. There are disadvantages to the use of newspapers. Unless an organization has an employment office capable of handling large numbers of applicants, this method is not recommended. A single advertisement placed in a newspaper, especially during depressions, attracts not only qualified applicants but also those who think they are qualified or those who apply merely because it is another lead. To overcome this drawback, many companies insert blind advertisements in the paper requesting a written outline of the applicant's background and experience, together with a photograph, to be mailed to a post-office box.

Selection of new employees.—The call for a new employee originates in the department needing help in the form of an employment requisition. This requisition is sent to the employment department together with information about the position, such as, nature of the position, hours, working conditions, salary, the type of employee required, his duties, age, sex, physical requirement and other information useful for the interviewer. With this information available, the personnel department can make an intelligent selection of the applicants.

The steps in the selection procedure are as follows:

1. *The preliminary interview.*—Some companies require a preliminary interview, in which case a simple form, having space for name, address, and position desired, is given the applicants to fill out. A preliminary interviewer quickly interviews the applicants and eliminates those who are obviously not qualified or who do not meet the standards established by the company. An application blank is given to those who pass this preliminary interview.

2. *The application form.*—The employment application forms in common use vary in size and design. Basically, all employment applications have space for the following data.

SUGGESTED QUESTIONS FOR APPLICATION BLANKS

An analysis of a number of appliation forms used in the employment of clerical help showed that most forms cover the basic subjects mentioned on page 873. The following is a list of out-of-the-ordinary questions that companies may care to consider in preparing or revising application blanks.

PERSONAL HISTORY

1. How long at present residence? If less than a year, give previous residence and length of stay.
2. Are you a citizen? By birth or naturalization? Give naturalization and immigration details if born in another country.
3. Give birthplace and descent.
4. Do you have any friends or relatives with this company?
5. Names, occupations, and addresses of immediate family.
6. Names of near relatives now living in foreign countries.
7. If you live with parents, do they own home, rent, etc.?
8. Are you the head of a family?
9. In case of emergency, notify ....
10. Give details of any injuries and operations.
11. List accidents (driving) you have had that were reported to the police or involved personal injury.
12. How much time have you lost in illness in the past two years?
13. Have you ever worked under any name other than shown above? If so, give full particulars.
14. Do you attend church? Its address? Are you a member?
15. What are your sports and recreations?
16. To what military or fraternal organizations do you belong?
17. Give your Selective Service Local Order Number and Classification.
18. Are you sympathetic to Nazism, Fascism, or Communism?
19. Are you entirely dependent upon your salary? Other sources of income?
20. Name banks where you have had accounts.
21. Do you carry life insurance?
22. What is your total indebtedness? Give details if you wish.
23. Give any unusual details of your financial condition.

EDUCATION

24. Give titles and authors of three texts you studied in college.
25. What did you do during your college vacations?
26. What bookkeeping, accounting, economics, and mathematics courses have you taken?
27. What foreign languages do you speak, read, or write?
28. In what studies were you most interested? Which were most difficult?
29. Where did you rank in your class?
30. What are your present plans for improving your education?
31. What magazines or books have you read recently?

PREVIOUS EMPLOYMENT AND EXPERIENCE

32. Are you right or left handed?
33. Indicate type of position for which you can qualify. (List given.) Why?
34. Of which of your past positions (or what piece of work that you did in them) are you most proud?
35. Ever hired by this company before? When and where?
36. Account for all intervals of unemployment.
37. Give details if ever discharged or requested to resign.
38. If now employed, why would you prefer to work for us rather than present employer?

MISCELLANEOUS

39. For what period do you want employment?
40. Please ask any questions you would like to ask about (name of company).

(*a*) *Personal history.* Name, address, telephone number, age, sex, height, weight, lineage, religion, date born, and place born.

(*b*) *Education.* Schools, duration of attendance, degrees held.

(*c*) *Previous employment and experience.* The name, address, and line of business of previous employers, applicant's duties, date employed and date left, reasons for leaving and salary.

(*d*) *References,* both personal and business.

(*e*) *Position applied for and minimum salary expected.*

(*f*) *Interests and hobbies.*

(*g*) *Additional information.*

The application form also contains space for interviewer's remarks and rating, results of tests, and applicant's signature. Some applications contain a clause as to the conditions of employment, such as the right of the employer to terminate the employment at any time, the right to inventions, patents, and other conditions deemed necessary. A typical application blank is presented on page 874.

3. *The interview.*—The applicants who have been given an application form are next interviewed by a more experienced interviewer. The interviewer should attempt to put the applicant at ease and try to encourage him to do most of the talking, asking questions only to draw out information. Specifically, the interviewer attempts to get the following information about the applicant:

(*a*) *What is the applicant's background?*—The social and economic environment under which the applicant has lived are important factors influencing his habits, temperament, and outlook on life.

(*b*) *What does he know?*—A consideration of the applicant's education and scholastic training largely answers this question. Nevertheless, it is unwise to place too much stress on academic training. Many applicants who never had formal academic training have a well-rounded cultural background.

(*c*) *What does he want?*—A person with a clear, well-defined aim in life has a better chance of success. He is able to mobilize and concentrate all of his energies and intelligence toward his goal. Beware of the applicant who will do anything or take any position.

(*d*) *What are his interests?*—A person who is really interested in a subject usually does a better job than one who has little or no interest.

(*e*) *What is his ability?*—The answer to this question depends on the mental and physical qualities of the applicant. The results of the applicant's previous work or scholastic experience or of physical, intelligence, and aptitude tests, throw some light on this question.

APPLICATION FOR EMPLOYMENT

SOC. SEC. NO. ____________

Print Name and Address

NAME ____________ (First) ____________ (Middle) ____________ (Last) DATE ____________

ADDRESS ____________ PHONE NO. ____________

POSITION DESIRED ____________ SALARY EXPECTED ____________

DATE OF BIRTH ________ WHERE ________ NATIONALITY (DESCENT) ________ RELIGION ________

CITIZEN OF WHAT COUNTRY ________ HEIGHT ________ WEIGHT ________

SINGLE, MARRIED, DIVORCED, SEPARATED, WIDOW(ER) ________ NUMBER OF DEPENDENTS ________ RELATIONSHIP ________

LIVE WITH PARENTS, KEEP HOUSE OR BOARD ________ WHO REFERRED YOU TO US ________

NAMES OF RELATIVES OR FRIENDS EMPLOYED BY THIS COMPANY ________

EDUCATION

HIGH SCHOOL ________ DATES ________ COURSE ________

COLLEGE ________ DATES ________ MAJOR COURSE ________

OTHER SCHOOLS ________

BUSINESS EXPERIENCE
(LIST MOST RECENT EMPLOYMENT FIRST)

FIRM NAME	NAME OF POSITION	DATES OF EMPLOYMENT	SALARY	REASON FOR LEAVING

PERSONAL REFERENCES
(NOT RELATIVES OR FORMER EMPLOYERS)

NAME	BUSINESS	ADDRESS

PLACE A CHECK MARK TO THE LEFT OF EACH OF THE FOLLOWING KINDS OF WORK WITH WHICH YOU ARE FAMILIAR. IF YOU HAVE HAD MORE THAN ONE YEAR'S EXPERIENCE PLACE A DOUBLE CHECK MARK. IF YOU ARE AN EXPERT PLACE AN "X." ADD ANY NOT LISTED IN BLANK SPACES.

ACCOUNTING	ENGINEERING	STENOGRAPHY	COMPTOMETER	PHOTOSTAT
ACTUARIAL	FILING	SWITCHBOARD	DICTAPHONE	TABULATING
BILLING	MAIL ROOM	TYPING	DUPLICATOR	
CALCULATING	PAY ROLL AUDITING	UNDERWRITING	GRAPHOTYPE	
CLAIM ADJUSTING	PRINTING	ADDING MACHINE	BOOKKEEP. MACH.	
CLERICAL GENERAL	SELLING	ADDRESSOGRAPH	MIMEOGRAPH	
CORRESPONDENCE	SHIPPING	BILLING MACHINE	MULTIGRAPH	
CREDITS	STATISTICAL	CALCULATOR	KEY PUNCH	

SIGNATURE OF APPLICANT ____________

THIS SPACE FOR USE IN PERSONNEL DEPARTMENT

Figure 67.—Typical Application Blank Suitable for Positions of Average Responsibility.

During the interview the interviewer makes observations as to the applicant's appearance and characteristics. Is the applicant neatly dressed, cleanly shaved? Are his nails clean, shoes polished? Does he sit properly in his chair or does he fidget around? Does he appear excessively nervous? Does he speak well and intelligently? These observations not only give a key to the applicant's background, education, and habits but throw some light upon his temperament.

The applicant also is entitled to information about the company and the position for which he is applying. The interviewer, during the interview, should outline briefly the company's business and background, its policies, the nature of the position, duties, hours, working conditions, salary, and opportunities for promotion and advancement. The interviewer should at all times be frank and truthful. He should not be too optimistic, or encourage applicants as to the possibilities of getting a position when one is not available, or discourage youngsters in their attempt to get their first job. The interview offers an excellent opportunity to spread goodwill in the community and to establish a sound employee-employer relationship.

4. *Tests.*—Tests are tools used by employment interviewers to aid them in rating the physical and mental abilities and aptitudes of applicants. Some companies have a large variety of tests; others do not have any. It must be remembered that tests do not reveal everything, and too much reliance must not be placed on them. Tests simply give additional information. The usual tests given employment applicants may be classified as medical or physical examinations, intelligence or mental tests, and aptitude tests. A brief discussion of the tests in common use is given in the following paragraphs.

Medical or physical examinations.—The most common examination given to applicants is the medical or physical examination. Large companies have their own doctor, who tends to the medical needs of employees and examines new applicants. Small companies usually send the applicant to his own doctor. The purposes of the medical examination are: (1) to detect diseases and defects in order to have the worker correct them; (2) to prevent the spread of contagious diseases; (3) to make the proper placement of workers; (4) to reduce absenteeism; (5) to lessen accidents; and (6) to reduce the possibility of unjust claims for injuries.

Intelligence tests.—The most common intelligence test used in business and industry is the Otis Intelligence Test. This test attempts to fix the intelligence quotient (I.Q.) of the applicant. The test is designed to measure the reasoning ability of the subject, and not his education or knowledge. The test has been used on thousands of subjects and has proved to be reasonably accurate. It is easily given and is not too lengthy.

Aptitude tests.—Numerous tests have been perfected to measure aptitudes for various types of work. Stevens Institute of Technology in Hoboken, New Jersey has done a notable job in devising tests to measure dexterity required to perform certain skilled tasks. The Thurston Typing Test is used to test the speed and accuracy of typists. The Thurston Clerical Test is used in selecting clerical help. Both of these tests are available through the World Book Company of Yonkers, New York. The Benge Clerical Test, obtained from the Management Service Company, 3136 N. 24 Street, Philadelphia, Pennsylvania, is another good test for clerical applicants. A good stenographic test, which provides material to be dictated and typed and checks spelling, is the Stenogauge, also obtainable from the Management Service Company.

Introduction of new employees.—After the personnel department has interviewed, tested, and rated the applicants and checked on their references, the top three or four candidates are sent to the department head who sent in the requisition. The department head has the authority to accept one of the applicants or reject all of them and request the personnel department to send others. The applicant who is accepted is introduced to his fellow workers and is started on his training program. (See page 880 for methods of training employees.) The personnel department furnishes the applicant with an employee manual or other literature concerning the company. Most organizations hire employees on a trial basis, usually three months, and if, within that period, the new employee has proved satisfactory, he becomes a member of the regular staff of the company. In case a rush placement is necessary, the applicant is hired pending the check on his references, which usually do not come in for several days. A form sent to former employers (Fig. 68) and one sent to schools (Fig. 69), for reference are given on pages 877 and 878.

To ....

....19......

....

The person named below has applied to us for a position as.. We would consider it a favor if you will give us your appraisal. It is perhaps natural to say the best we can for a former employee. But is it not true that a frank, careful and well-weighed opinion concerning applicants for positions will help reduce turnover among employees as well as the expense incident thereto? Indeed, a complete and frank appraisal is fairer to the applicant, for with a knowledge of weaknesses, the new employer can help to overcome them and perhaps prevent failure in the new work. If you will fill out this blank in the same way you would like us to fill it out for you, we shall greatly appreciate your co-operation. We are enclosing a stamped, self-addressed envelope for your reply.

....

..............................New York, N. Y.
Personnel Director.

Name of Applicant

Address

Personal Appraisement	Better Than Average	Average	Below Average	Remarks
1. Is applicant a hard worker?				
2. " " enthusiastic?				
3. " " resourceful?				
4. " " ambitious?				
5. " " honest?				
6. " " courteous?				
7. Has " a good memory?				
8. How is applicant's health?				
9. How about applicant's habits?				

General Analysis	Yes	No	Remarks
10. How long was applicant in your employ?			
11. Were applicant's services satisfactory?			
12. Was applicant a good producer?			
13. Was applicant co-operative with your office?			
14. Was applicant co-operative with customers?			
15. What were applicant's last average yearly earnings?			
16. Would you re-employ applicant?			

17. Why did applicant leave your employ?

18. Please add other pertinent information and sum up your appraisal.

Signed..

Figure 68.—Form Sent to Employers for Reference.

Follow-up of new employees.—The personnel department makes periodic visits to the new employee for the purpose of checking his progress on the job and his attitude about his position. A simple rating form, filled out by the department head, containing the name of the new employee, the date he started to work, and a series of questions as to his progress, ability to do his work, co-operative

Sch.

Address ....
Date..........

A B C COMPANY
300 Main Street,
New York City

ATTENTION OF PERSONNEL DIRECTOR.

Gentlemen:—

In response to your request I give below, in confidence, the school record of
a former student of this school. And also our estimate of his/her general ability and future possibilities.

I am placing a cross (X) in the appropriate column below.

	Poor	Fair	Good	Exceptional
Record in studies				
Attendance and punctuality				
Conduct				
Sociability				
Estimate of general ability and possibilities				

The student made the best showing in the following subjects:..........

The following list of observations may be of service to you:..........

Yours truly,

Figure 69.—Form Sent to Schools for Reference.

spirit, faults, and prospects, provides a good method for following up the progress of a new employee. This information also provides a sound promotional record and a good check on the training program. These rating forms should be filled out, if possible, by more than one executive qualified to judge the new employee. A consensus of judgment is thus provided, and the danger of personal prejudice on the part of the department head is eliminated. A form of follow-up of new employees, addressed to department heads, is given in Fig. 70 on page 879.

Discharge of employees.—Employees may leave the services of a company voluntarily; they may be discharged; or they may be laid off because of slackened business activity. Whatever the reason for the separation of an employee from the company, it is a sound policy to allow the personnel department to interview all employees about to leave. The reasons for the "exit interview" are as follows:

1. It uncovers weaknesses in the personnel program.
2. It provides data for the study of labor turnover.
3. It suggests improvements in the training program.
4. It promotes goodwill.

CONFIDENTIAL

Name .... Began ....

The following confidential report is to be made out by you without conferring with the person about whom you are reporting. If, for any reason, any other person is better qualified than you to make the report, return the form immediately with a note to that effect, naming the person who should make out the report.

The purpose is to get a report on each new employee, once a week for four weeks, and thereafter monthly until such time as the employee can surely be trusted to do his work without supervision. Remember, the general purpose is to be as mutually helpful as possible, but at the same time, to prevent wasting time on a person who is not likely to prove satisfactory. No action will be taken on your report without personal conference with you and others who may be able to shed some light on the new employee.

(Name of executive)

1. How has he done h work during the past ....?
2. How does he measure up in respect to:

	Good	*Fair*	*Poor*
a. Grasping instructions			
b. Following instructions			
c. Initiative			
d. Industry			
e. Accuracy			
f. Clearness			
g. Speed			
h. General cooperative spirit			

3. Any other faults that should be corrected? ....
4. May he be trusted next week to do h work without further supervision? ....
5. What is the prospect that he will work out satisfactorily?
6. Other comments? (over)

Date...................... Signed...............................

Figure 70.—Record of Employee's Performance.

It should be a policy of the company never to allow a department head to have the final authority to discharge an employee without the concurrence of the personnel department. In many cases the department head or supervisor may be to blame, and a transfer to another department may save the company the valuable services of an employee.

In many companies a written record of the employee's performance is maintained to help management when faced with the problem of lay-offs. These records are reviewed by the department head and the personnel department to determine which employees are the most valuable. These records determine also the order in which laid-off employees will be called back to work.

6. TRAINING EMPLOYEES

Purpose of training employees.—Training programs are established for the following purposes:

1. To break in new employees in the cheapest and quickest manner.
2. To improve the quality and quantity of the employee's work.
3. To equip and develop employees for higher positions and more responsibility.
4. To improve employee morale.
5. To stimulate interest in the company and for the work.
6. To keep employees alert for new ideas and make them flexible for changes.

Who to train.—The common practice among a number of companies that have a training program is to train only new employees. In most cases this elementary training is very scanty. A good, sound training for all new employees is essential, but it is not by any means a complete training program. Training must be a continuous process, including old employees, supervisors, foremen, and executives, in order to obtain maximum results.

Training new employees.—The extent to which new employees are trained depends on the work for which they are assigned and the nature of the company's business. In some cases, as with industries employing highly skilled or specialized workers, the training is extensive and lengthy. In other cases, as with the training of new employees assigned to simple clerical or nonskilled work, the training is brief. The point to remember in training new employees is to show the best and quickest way to do the job. It is easier to teach a person to do the job in the right way than it is to undo the results of wrong training or of no training at all.

The following suggestions will aid in planning a training program for new employees:

1. Find the best way to do the job and establish that method as a standard. Teach all beginners the standard method of doing the job.

2. Illustrate and develop one point at a time. The average person is not capable of grasping more than one fact thoroughly.

3. Develop your training along logical lines and show the relationship between various steps in the job and between other jobs. It is much easier to follow and learn a method if the steps are presented in logical sequence and the job is presented in its proper relation with other jobs.

4. Establish the standard time to do the work and define production standards. Train the worker to develop speed and accuracy to meet standards set for speed and production.

Training old employees.—Old employees are trained for the purpose of stimulating greater activity, illustrating newer methods, reviving interest in the work, and preparing the employees for promotions and transfers. Old employees are harder to train and tend to offer more resistance to training programs than new employees. New employees realize that they do not know the business and are anxious to learn and co-operate. Old employees feel that they know all about the business and resent being treated like schoolboys. New employees may be trained in a formal manner, whereas old employees react better to informal training, where they are given an opportunity to plan and participate in the training program.

Training supervisors and foremen.—Perhaps the most common weakness of most training programs is the lack of training offered to supervisors and foremen. Supervisors and foremen have a responsible, key position in business and industry. When it is realized that most employees are in closer touch with supervisors and foremen than with any other executives, the importance of training supervisors can be appreciated. A supervisor or foreman not only guides, directs, and supervises the quality and quantity of work produced by his group, but he is also the person who actually puts into practice the personnel policies of the company. A foreman or supervisor capable of getting work done efficiently with the co-operation of the workers and with the minimum amount of friction and antagonism between groups is rapidly replacing the overlording type of foreman of the past.

Supervisors and foremen are usually old employees who thoroughly know the work and have supervisory ability. It is necessary, nevertheless, to train these men in newer and better methods. Besides this training, they should be: (1) fundamentally grounded in the psychology of handling men; (2) thoroughly familiar with the personnel policies of the company; and (3) aware of the importance of teamwork and co-operation between the various units and departments in the company.

Training executives.—Executives, more than any other group of employees, are responsible for the operation and management of a business enterprise, and it may be truthfully stated that the measure of success of a business depends to a large extent on the wisdom of the management group, if not of one individual. For this reason a training program designed to broaden the outlook of executives and to develop a reservoir for new executives is a matter of great importance. Employees will co-operate and show more interest in the training program as a whole, if they realize that the management group feels the need for training.

Suggestions of what to include in executive training, designed to broaden the outlook of executives, are as follows:

1. A study of the company policies and the aims of such policies.
2. A study of methods for evaluating and appraising the work and operations of departments, supervisors, and employees.
3. A study of business history and future social, economic, and political trends.
4. A study of the management's responsibility toward stockholders, customers, and workers.

A careful and comprehensive training program, along with promotions based on merit and along clearly defined promotional channels, creates the best reservoir of future executives. Some companies select college graduates for the purpose of training them for future executives. The candidates receive a thorough training in every department of the company. Still other companies have gone back to the plan of hiring men secretaries to important executives and promoting them to executive positions.

Methods of training.—Training may be given to employees by three basic methods: (1) on the job, (2) in a classroom, or (3) by conference.

Training on the job.—The most common method of training employees is to show them the work under actual working conditions and then have them do it. Explanations, suggestions, and corrections are made while the new employees are actually working. Care should be taken to have the work supervised by someone who knows the work thoroughly and who is in a position to watch the new employees and devote some time to them. This method requires no special equipment, is easy, and, if properly done, is the cheapest way to train new employees. The method is used extensively in training routine and nonskilled workers.

Training in a classroom.—The classroom method is advisable where large groups of employees are to be trained. This method requires the use of considerable space, classroom equipment such as desks, writing materials, blackboards, slides, books, and formal classroom procedure. The question of who is to train the employees is important. Some companies hire outside professional teachers to do the teaching. The disadvantages of this policy is that such instructors seldom know the particular problems confronting the company. Company executives who are at the same time capable teachers will sometimes devote their time to training employees. The classroom method of training must be considered as a preliminary or background training. The new employees who have successfully completed the classroom training are next placed on the job and closely observed. Those who require further classroom training are requested to attend class until their performance on the job shows a fundamental grasp of its problems.

In some cases companies will send their employees to evening school for specialized training, paying part of the tuition fee. Appliance manufacturers will co-operate in the training program by supplying lecturers and demonstrators to teach employees the use of office machines.

Training by conference method.—The conference or meeting method of training is used extensively in the training of old employees, supervisors, and executives. This method differs from the classroom method in that it is informal, depending more on the active participation of the members and less on formal lectures and guidance. The success of a conference depends on the amount of thought given to its planning and the co-operation and participation in the conference given by its members. The program of the meeting should be carefully planned and advance notice given as to the subjects to be discussed. It is advisable to allow the members to have an active part in the planning of the program, thereby stimulating interest and co-operation. Such participation is made possible by sending questionnaires to the conference members asking their suggestions and opinions, or by discussing, at the meeting, the topic to be dealt with at the next meeting. The conference chairman or group leader introduces the subject, encourages active participation, maintains order, and keeps the discussion within the scope of the subject. Various committees may be appointed to study and report on special problems. Meetings should be held regularly and on definite dates and as frequently as is thought necessary.

Company publications.—To supplement the training program and to foster interest, various publications are issued by companies. These publications are of two types, house organs and manuals.

House organs.—A house organ is an employee publication, prepared, edited, and published by employees for the purpose of stimulating interest in the company, promoting the feeling of fellowship, and building employee morale. House organs contain interesting news and timely items about the company, hints and suggestions for improving methods of performing tasks, personal news about employees (such as vacations and promotions), announcements of contest winners, and stories and jokes pertaining to the company or the employees. The house organ should receive contributions from all employees, from the president to the office boy. The design of house organs varies with each company, but in every case a house organ should be printed on good paper and in a presentable manner. It should not be too bulky, and its style should be breezy, human, and interesting.

Manuals.—Manuals are published by the company for the purpose of instructing the employees about the company, its policies and its functions. Manuals are formal in style, specific, and in some cases technical in their content; in a good many cases, they are quite lengthy. There are many kind of manuals, such as company manuals, sales manuals, and office manuals.

Company manuals usually contain information about: (1) the history and growth of the company, (2) its officers, (3) the nature of its business, and (4) its policies. These manuals are intended to present a broad picture of the company to its employees.

Sales manuals are designed to aid and instruct salesmen. The material in a sales manual usually includes product information, history of the organization, the selling policy, facts about the plant, how to sell, and company rules and regulations.

Office manuals contain standard procedures for doing office work, duties and responsibilities of employees, supervisors, and department heads, and general information of value to the employees.

Libraries.—Many companies maintain libraries for employees. These libaries contain books, magazines, and periodicals having to do with industries or lines of business in which the company is engaged. Some company libraries also contain books on all sorts of subjects, including fiction, for the purpose of stimulating the reading habits of its employees and assisting employees who have not been able to complete their education to broaden their knowledge and interests.

The library should be under the supervision of a competent librarian, who reports to the office or personnel manager. The books should be catalogued, classified, and arranged on shelves in a systematic manner. The Library of Congress system is recommended. Bulletins covering the procedure and instructions are available from the Superintendent of Documents, Government Printing Office, Washington, D. C.

Books should be purchased with money set aside for the purpose, and only after proper authorization.

SECTION 9

Telegraph, Telephone, and Postal Information

1. TELEGRAMS AND CABLEGRAMS

Kinds of Domestic Messages

Special Services of Telegraph Companies

Kinds of Cable and Radio Messages

2. TELEPHONE SERVICE

Long Distance Calls

Telephone Convenience Aids

Teletypewriter Service

Interoffice Communication

3. POSTAL GUIDE

Postal Rates and Classiffication of Mail

Air Mail

Bulk Mail

Letters

Printed Matter

Metered Mail

Printed Indicia

Precanceled Stamps, Cards, and Envelopes

Stamps

Envelopes

Government Postal Cards

Private Mailing Cards

Business-Reply Cards and Envelopes

Money Orders

Registered Mail

Insured Mail

C.O.D. Mail

Special Delivery, Special Handling, and Miscellaneous

United States Official Postal Guide

SECTION 9

Telegraph, Telephone, and Postal Information

1. TELEGRAMS AND CABLEGRAMS

How to cut telegraph costs.—Waste in the use of telegrams, cablegrams, and radiograms—a few cents here and a few cents there—is costing many business houses a considerable amount of money each year. This waste results from a lack of exact and up-to-date knowledge of the various types of services that telegraph companies offer, and of how they can be used most economically. Both Postal Telegraph and Western Union are constantly improving their services and adding new types of services to meet changing business needs. From time to time they issue circulars and advertising pieces which, in terms of dollars and cents, are well worth the few moments that it takes to read them; these circulars are obtainable from any local office of Postal Telegraph or Western Union. Western Union also publishes a monthly bulletin, "The Blazed Trail," which gives information on the latest services available, together with details of how companies in various fields are using the telegraph effectively in sales promotion, advertising, the collection of accounts, and other matters.

What to consider in trying to economize on telegrams.—In trying to make economies in the use of telegraph services, consider four things:

1. The urgency of the message. In some cases delivery on the same day may be essential; in others delivery on the morning of the following day would be satisfactory. The fastest service is, of course, the most expensive; it should therefore be used only where the utmost speed is necessary. A description of the various types

of domestic messages is given on pages 893 et seq. An outline of the various types of cable and radio messages is given on pages 907 et seq.

2. The time difference between cities and countries.

3. Terse wording of the message.

4. Special services of which you can avail yourself—such as the domestic radio service mentioned on page 907.

Consider time difference between cities.—The difference in hours between the various standard times used throughout the United States must be taken into consideration in sending telegrams. The following list shows what time it is in localities using the various standard times, when it is 12 o'clock noon in places using Eastern Standard Time.

Eastern Time	12 o'clock
Central Time	11 A.M.
Mountain Time	10 A.M.
Pacific Time	9 A.M.

The use of Daylight Saving Time must also be considered. Daylight Saving Time is one hour faster than standard time. Thus, if two cities under consideration are on Daylight Saving Time, the differences indicated above apply. If one of the cities is on Daylight Saving Time, add one hour to the normal difference indicated. For example, normally it is three hours earlier in San Francisco, which uses Pacific Time, than it is in New York City, which uses Eastern Time. However, if Daylight Saving Time were in effect in New York City, and not in San Francisco, it could be four hours earlier in San Francisco.

Saving $1.04 by considering time difference.—As an illustration of the loss of money that may result from thoughtlessness in the use of telegrams, consider the case of the Jones Company, located in San Francisco. At 3:30 in the afternoon the Jones Company decides to send to New York the following telegram:

> PRICES ADVANCING RAPIDLY YOUR IMMEDIATE DECISION NECESSARY CANNOT HOLD PRESENT OFFER BEYOND MARCH TENTH ANSWER COLLECT BY POSTAL TELEGRAPH.

If the Jones Company merely typed this message, marked it as a full-rate telegram, and despatched it, it would cost them $1.54. All that it need cost them is 50 cents.

The difference, $1.04, is accounted for as follows:

1. It is 3:30 in San Francisco. Hence it is 6:30 in New York. The people to whom the message is being sent have probably left the office for the day.

2. Since the message will, in any event, probably not be deliverable until the following morning, it should be sent as an overnight telegram. The rate for an overnight telegram from San Francisco to New York is 50 cents. This is all that the Jones Company's message need cost them.

The result of this simple piece of foresight is a saving of $1.04. If this amount can be saved on a single telegram, the amount saved in a year might be considerable.

Saving through terse wording.—While terse wording of the message should not be carried so far that the person receiving the telegram has difficulty in understanding it, considerable savings can be effected by the exercise of a little care and ingenuity. For example, notice how much more tersely the message on page 892 is expressed than the following message:

> PRICES ARE ADVANCING RAPIDLY NECESSARY YOU REACH DECISION AT ONCE CANNOT HOLD PRESENT OFFER LATER THAN MARCH TENTH WIRE REPLY COLLECT

The above message contains twenty-one words, and, if sent from San Francisco to New York City, would cost $2.14. When reduced to 14 words, as shown on page 892, it cost $1.54. Sixty cents has been saved by cutting out unnecessary words, expressing the same thought in fewer words, and using the free words "Answer Collect by Postal Telegraph." See page 900.

Kinds of Domestic Messages

Full-rate telegrams.—The full-rate telegram is given precedence over all other messages and hence is the fastest and also the most expensive type of telegraph service. The charge for a full-rate telegram is based on a minimum of ten words, an additional charge being made for each word in excess of ten. Thus the charge for a full-rate telegram sent from New York City to Detroit is 48 cents for the first ten words and 3½ cents for each additional word. Nothing is gained by condensing the message to less than ten words. The address and the signature are not counted as words. Code may be used.

Charges made for initial ten-word (or less) full-rate telegrams between principal cities are shown below.*

From / To	New York $	Chicago $	Philadelphia $	St. Louis $	Boston $	Cleveland $	Buffalo $	San Francisco $	Pittsburgh $	Cincinnati $	New Orleans $	Washington $	Minneapolis $
Albany	0.30	0.60	0.36	0.60	0.36	0.48	0.30	1.20	0.42	0.48	0.72	0.48	0.72
Atlanta	.72	.60	.72	.60	.72	.60	.72	1.20	.60	.48	.60	.60	.72
Baltimore	.36	.60	.30	.60	.48	.48	.48	1.20	.42	.48	.72	.30	.72
Boston	.36	.60	.42	.72	.20	.60	.48	1.20	.48	.60	.72	.48	.72
Buffalo	.42	.48	.42	.48	.48	.36	.20	1.20	.36	.48	.72	.48	.60
Chicago	.60	.20	.60	.42	.60	.42	.48	.90	.48	.42	.72	.60	.42
Cincinnati	.48	.42	.48	.42	.60	.30	.48	1.20	.42	.20	.60	.48	.60
Cleveland	.48	.42	.48	.48	.60	.20	.36	1.20	.30	.30	.72	.48	.60
Denver	.90	.72	.90	.72	.90	.90	.90	.90	.90	.90	.90	.90	.72
Detroit	.48	.36	.48	.48	.60	.30	.36	1.20	.36	.36	.72	.48	.60
Galveston	.90	.72	.90	.60	.90	.72	.90	.90	.72	.72	.48	.90	.90
Indianapolis	.60	.30	.60	.36	.60	.42	.48	1.20	.48	.30	.72	.60	.60
Jacksonville, Fla.	.72	.72	.72	.72	.72	.72	.72	1.20	.72	.60	.60	.60	.72
Kansas City	.72	.48	.72	.42	.72	.60	.60	.90	.60	.60	.72	.72	.60
Los Angeles	1.20	.90	1.20	.90	1.20	1.20	1.20	.48	1.20	1.20	1.20	1.20	.90
Louisville	.60	.42	.60	.36	.60	.48	.48	1.20	.48	.30	.60	.60	.60
Memphis	.60	.60	.60	.42	.72	.60	.60	1.20	.60	.48	.60	.60	.72
Milwaukee	.60	.30	.60	.48	.72	.48	.48	.90	.48	.48	.72	.60	.42
Minneapolis	.72	.42	.72	.48	.72	.60	.60	.90	.60	.60	.72	.72	.20
Mobile	.72	.72	.72	.60	.72	.72	.72	1.20	.72	.60	.30	.72	.72
Montreal	.60	.60	.60	.90	.50	.60	.60	1.20	.60	.60	.90	.60	.70
New Orleans	.72	.72	.72	.60	.72	.72	.72	1.20	.72	.60	.20	.60	.72
New York	.20	.60	.30	.60	.36	.48	.42	1.20	.42	.48	.72	.36	.72
Omaha	.72	.48	.72	.48	.72	.60	.60	.90	.60	.60	.72	.72	.60
Philadelphia	.30	.60	.20	.60	.42	.48	.42	1.20	.42	.48	.72	.30	.72
Pittsburgh	.42	.48	.42	.48	.48	.30	.36	1.20	.20	.42	.72	.42	.60
Portland, Ore.	1.20	.90	1.20	.90	1.20	1.20	1.20	.60	1.20	1.20	1.20	1.20	.90
Providence	.36	.60	.42	.72	.30	.60	.48	1.20	.48	.60	.72	.48	.72
Richmond, Va.	.48	.60	.48	.60	.60	.60	.60	1.20	.48	.60	.60	.30	.72
Rochester, N. Y.	.42	.48	.42	.60	.48	.42	.30	1.20	.36	.48	.72	.48	.72
St. Louis	.60	.42	.60	.20	.72	.48	.48	.90	.48	.42	.60	.60	.48
San Antonio	.90	.72	.90	.60	.90	.72	.90	.90	.72	.72	.60	.90	.90
San Francisco	1.20	.90	1.20	.90	1.20	1.20	1.20	.20	1.20	1.20	1.20	1.20	.90
Seattle	1.20	.90	1.20	.90	1.20	1.20	1.20	.72	1.20	1.20	1.20	1.20	.90
Springfield, Mass.	.30	.60	.36	.72	.30	.60	.48	1.20	.48	.60	.72	.48	.72
Tampa, Fla.	.72	.72	.72	.72	.72	.72	.72	1.20	.72	.60	.60	.72	.72
Toledo	.48	.36	.48	.48	.60	.30	.42	1.20	.36	.30	.72	.48	.60
Washington, D.C.	.36	.60	.30	.60	.48	.48	.48	1.20	.42	.48	.60	.20	.72

* Courtesy Western Union Telegraph Co.

Serial service.—Serial service is an expedited service providing a reduction in cost where two or more messages are sent on the same day to the same addressee at the same address. Each message sent is regarded as a section, and all sections sent the same day are charged for as one message. High speed is afforded, and rates are approximately 20 per cent higher than day-letter rates indicated on page 899.

As an illustration of the use and economy of serials, assume that the Smith Company, of New York City, has occasion to telegraph three separate ten-word messages to its representative in Detroit on the same day. Three telegrams at the rate from New York City to Detroit, 48 cents, would cost $1.44. The same three messages sent as a serial would cost only 90 cents, and a saving of 54 cents would thus be effected. Each of the sections of a serial is transmitted by the telegraph company as soon as it is received; the first message is not held pending receipt of the later messages. Code may be used.

The following regulations govern the use of serials:

1. Each message or section must be marked as a serial.
2. The messages must be sent to the same addressee, at the same address, and must be sent on the same day.
3. Serials may be set up for messages moving in one direction only, and paid and collect messages cannot be combined in the same serial. Thus, in the illustration given above, if the Detroit representative of the Smith Company wired one or more replies to the telegrams that he received from the New York office, these replies could not be counted as part of the Smith Company's serial. The Detroit representative could, however, set up his own serial.
4. A minimum of fifteen words per message or section is counted, and a charge is made for a minimum aggregate of fifty words in the course of a day.
5. If an initial message is filed marked as a serial in the anticipation that there will be other sections going to the same addressee on the same day, and, contrary to expectation, no further section is sent, the first section is charged for as a full-rate telegram for the number of words involved.

Serials are being increasingly used by business concerns in corresponding by telegraph with their branch offices and salesmen. They are also used in the collection of accounts. Some companies send two or three collection telegrams to slow customers on the same day, and, where this procedure is followed, the savings effected through serial service are substantial. In addition to being economical, serials permit greatly increased use to be made of the telegraph in everyday business, with only a slight increase in telegraph bills.

Overnight telegrams.—An overnight telegram is the least expensive message service. Delivery is made on the morning of the next day (morning of next business day in case of business messages). An overnight telegram may be filed with the telegraph company at any time up to 2 A.M. The charge is based on a minimum of twenty-five words, with an additional charge for each *group* of five words or less in excess of twenty-five. Nothing is gained by condensing the message to less than twenty-five words. The cost for a twenty-five-word overnight telegram is less than the cost of a ten-word straight telegram. Thus a straight telegram (ten words) from Detroit to New York costs 48 cents. An overnight telegram (twenty-five words) between the same cities costs 35 cents. Code may be used.

The following table may be used to compute the rate for an overnight telegram of any length:

Where the Rate for a Full-Rate Telegram of 10 Words Is	THE OVERNIGHT TELEGRAM RATE IS				
		FOR EACH ADDITIONAL GROUP OF 5 WORDS OR LESS			
	For 25 Words or Less	*From the 26th to the 50th Word*	*From the 51st to the 100th Word*	*From the 101st to the 200th Word*	*For Words Over 200*
30c	24c	1c	1c	1c	1c
36	28	1.5	1	1	1
42	30	2	1.5	1	1
48	35	2.5	2	1.5	1
60	42	3.5	3	2.5	2
72	48	4.5	4	3	2.5
90	50	7	5.5	4	3
$1.20	50	9	7.5	5	3.5

Where the full rate for a 10-word telegram is 20 cents (intra-city messages), the overnight telegram rate is 20 cents for 50 words or less and 1 cent for each additional group of 5 words or less.

Day letters.—The day letter is a deferred day service at reduced rates, the transmission being subordinated to that of full-rate messages. The charge is based on a minimum of fifty words. Nothing is gained by condensing the message to less than fifty words. The charge for a day letter is one and one-half times the initial charge for a full-rate telegram. Thus a full-rate telegram sent from New York City to Detroit costs 48 cents for ten words; a day letter of fifty words to the same city costs 72 cents. An additional charge of one fifth of the initial fifty-word rate is made for each ten words or less in excess of fifty. The address and the signature are not counted as words. Code may be used.

Timed wire messages.—Timed wire service applies only to messages transmitted over a printing telegraph machine (teleprinter) connecting the office of the sender with that of the telegraph company.

When timed wire service is used in conjunction with a printing telegraph machine, the telegraph company charges on the basis of the time that the sender takes to transmit the message over the printing telegraph machine from his office to the company's local main office (from which the telegraph company then transmits the message to its destination), instead of on the basis of the number of words in the message. The minimum charge is for a period of three minutes and is, in most cases, the same as the charge for a fifty-word day letter between the same points. The charge for each additional minute in excess of three is generally one third of the charge for the initial three-minute period.

The advantage of timed wire service is that a business concern having a printing telegraph machine in its office can make substantial economies in sending lengthy messages. Thus the cost of a fifty-word day letter sent from New York City to Detroit is 72 cents. The cost of three minutes of timed wire service for a message to the same city is also 72 cents. In three minutes, however, a highly skilled operator of a printing telegraph machine can transmit as many as one hundred eighty words.

Reservation messages.—Reservation messages are those dealing exclusively with requests for the reservation of hotel or travel accommodations, including the necessary particulars, and answers to such requests. The rate is generally 35 cents for fifteen words with a charge not exceeding 2½ cents for additional words for messages destined to places where there are Postal Telegraph or Western Union offices.

Tour-rate messages.—Tour-rate messages are those for use by travelers. They must deal exclusively with the following features of a trip: the time of arrival, the overnight stop, the health of the sender or the party, the state of the weather, a characterization of the trip, the time of departure, and the next destination or destinations. The rate is generally 35 cents for fifteen words with a charge not exceeding 2½ cents for additional words for messages destined to places where there are Postal Telegraph or Western Union offices.

Book night letters.—A special discount is available for intra-city night letters containing identical texts filed in quantities of twenty-five or more.

Greeting messages.—On special occasions such as Christmas, New Year, Easter, Valentine's Day, Jewish New Year, Thanksgiving, weddings, births, and others, Postal Telegraph and Western Union have available a number of fixed text messages that can be sent almost anywhere in the United States for as little as 25 cents. For messages of the sender's own composition, the rate is generally 35 cents for fifteen words with a charge not exceeding 2½ cents for additional words, provided such messages are destined to places where there are telegraph offices.

Although this greeting service is seemingly for the occasional user, for good business reasons concerns may find it desirable to send an appropriate greeting message to a client or a prospective customer. The greeting service provides a very economical way of doing this.

Arrangements can be made to have greeting messages sung over the telephone in certain cities at the regular full-rate telegram charges.

How the charges for a telegram are counted.—The telegraph companies apply the following rules in counting the number of chargeable words in domestic messages:

1. No charge is made for essential matter in the address and signature.

2. Names of cities, states, and countries that are made up of two or more words—such as New York, South Dakota, and United States—are counted as one word.

3. Abbreviations of single words count as one word.

4. Common abbreviations—such as OK, AM, PM, FOB, COD (note that periods are omitted)—are counted as one word.

5. Initials are counted as separate words. Personal names, such as Van der Gross, are counted as one word.

6. When used in their normal sense, groups of figures, affixes, bars, decimal points, and dashes are counted at the rate of five characters, or fraction thereof, to the word in messages between

CLASSES OF TELEGRAPH MESSAGES

Class of Message	*Basic Rate*	*Additional Charge*	*When Accepted*	*When Delivered*
Full-rate Message or "Telegram"	First 10 words, 20¢ to $1.20, according to distance	Each additional word, 1¢ to 8½¢	Any time day or night	Immediately — a matter of minutes
Day Letter	First 50 words, 30¢ to $1.80, according to distance	Each additional 10-word group, 6¢ to 36¢	Any time	Subordinated to full-rate telegrams
Overnight Telegram	First 25 words, 20¢ to 50¢, according to distance	Each additional 5-word group, 1¢ to 9¢	Up to 2 A.M. of day of delivery.	Next morning. Morning of next business day in case of business messages
Serials	A message sent in sections. No section rated at less than 15 words. For a minimum of 50 words or less, 35¢ to $2.15, according to distance	When total words exceed 50, for each additional 10-word group, 7¢ to 43¢	Any time. All sections must be filed the same day.	Immediately — a matter of minutes
Timed Wire Service	3 minutes' use of telegraph printer machine, 20¢ to $1.80, according to distance.	Each additional minute or less, 5¢ to 60¢	Any time	Immediately — a matter of minutes

points in the United States, and between points in the United States and points in Mexico. Thus "one hundred" is counted as two words, but "100" is counted as one word; "3rd" is counted as one word, the same as "third"; "44B42" (group of two figures, one letter, group of two figures) is counted as three words.

7. In messages sent to Canada, Alaska, and other points outside the United States except Mexico, figures, decimal points, affixes, bars, and dashes are counted as one word each.

8. The phrases "Answer Collect by Postal Telegraph," "Reply by Western Union," etc., are free. But "Reply Collect" counts as two words.

9. In messages between points in the United States, actual punctuation marks are not charged for, but the words "stop," "comma," etc., are counted.

Special Services of Telegraph Companies

Telegraph money orders.—Money may be telegraphed to any point in the United States and in normal times to almost any country in the world.

Gift orders.—A gift order sent by telegraph is available anywhere for the purchase of a gift of the person's own selection, or it may be cashed if preferred.

Shopping orders.—This service is designed to cover the purchase in a distant city, by the telegraph company, and delivery to the person designated, of any article available locally that can be described.

Postal telegraph money orders for mailing.—Money orders for mailing can be purchased at Postal Telegraph offices. It is a very simple, economical, and convenient way to pay rent, dues, taxes, gas, electric, and water bills and can be used for many other forms of remittances. The cost for such a money order is as low as 5 cents. Further information can be obtained at any Postal Telegraph office. American Express money orders may be obtained from Western Union.

"Will-Call" travel service.—This service is designed for travelers who have a definite itinerary and who wish to keep in touch with their home or office. The local telegraph office obtains the itinerary and the dates the traveler "will call" at the telegraph offices while en route. Those wishing to telegraph the traveler are instructed to get the next telegraph office forwarding address from the local office and send their message marked "Will Call." These messages can be forwarded to any telegraph office that is not too far removed from the regular route of the traveler without any additional charge.

Commercial news service.—Western Union furnishes ticker services that report prices and transactions on the trading floors of all principal exchanges. In addition to continuous quotations by ticker, interval quotations by telegraph from all leading exchanges in the United States and Canada are available via both Postal Telegraph and Western Union.

Tie-lines: printer; Morse; telephone.—Tie-lines are direct wires provided without charge by the telegraph companies where the volume of telegraph business justifies their installation, to connect the offices of business houses direct with the operating room of the telegraph company. There are three types of tie-lines:

1. Printer.
2. Morse.
3. Telephone.

A telegraph printer machine is operated in much the same way as a typewriter. When a key is struck on a printer located in a business office, the letter so selected is simultaneously recorded on a paper tape on that printer and on the tape of a corresponding machine in the local main operating room of the telegraph company. The message thus typed is immediately transferred to a trunk circuit for transmission to its destination. In the delivery of messages the procedure is reversed.

Morse tie-lines are similarly used for messages sent and received over them by means of the Morse code. Specially trained operators are required.

A telephone tie-line is a direct telephone connection between a business house and the local main office of the telegraph company. When the telephone is lifted, a telegraph operator is automatically signalled. The message is read to the operator, who repeats it back and then releases it for immediate transmission to its destination.

Errand service.—Telegraph messengers are available for performing all types of errands. Among the many uses of this service are the following: purchase and delivery of railroad, steamship, bus, and airplane tickets (in some cases without charge); purchase and delivery of theater tickets; delivery of packages and other rush material such as proofs, blueprints, and so forth; pick-up of packages to be sent, through the Railway Express Agency, by rail or air express (no charge); purchase and delivery of articles from stores. The uses of this errand service are almost unlimited, as is indicated by the fact that in one case a telegraph messenger was dispatched to Europe to deliver an engagement ring to a young woman. Telegraph messengers are also available to act as temporary employees and as guides for salesmen and other travelers.

Messenger distribution service.—In recent years this service has been widely used by manufacturers of automobiles, refrigerators, radios, shoes, drug supplies, food products, and so on, as well as by mail-order houses, insurance companies, retail stores, and many other business houses, in connection with sales-promotion and advertising campaigns.

In its simplest form the service consists of the delivery of a sales or advertising message, on specially designed distinctive stationery, by uniformed telegraph messengers. The messages are prepared at a central point, addressed, and sorted by cities. They are then shipped to the individual cities and delivered to addressees by uniformed telegraph messengers. A special form, different in color and detail from the usual telegraph blank, is used. The charge ranges from 5 to 20 cents, according to the quantity, the area of distribution, the method of printing, and other factors.

In addition to the above, the service also covers the distribution, by telegraph messengers, of printed sales and advertising literature of all kinds, window displays, medicinal supplies for physicians and dentists, merchandise samples, and the like. The rates for the delivery of samples and other packages, individually addressed, average from 6 to 10 cents per piece. The rates for the delivery of unaddressed printed matter and samples range from $5 to as high as $18 per thousand pieces (½ cent to 1.8 cents per piece) distributed in residential areas, and average about $3 per thousand for desk-to-desk distribution in office buildings. Street-corner and factory-entrance distributions are usually charged for on an hourly basis.

Actual examples of the use of messenger distribution service.—A number of case histories, illustrating the use that has been made of telegraph messenger distribution service are given in the following paragraphs.

1. *Messenger service announces new automobile model.*—The Hudson Motor Car Company used telegraph messenger distribution service to announce a new model just being placed on the market. The distribution consisted of over 1,000,000 copies of the following message, signed by the president of the company, and reproduced on special messenger-service telegraph blanks:

May I ask that you visit the Hudson and Terraplane display room for a preview of the latest in motor car progress stop you will find ingenuity in design, wealth of detail, character and beauty in line stop individual choice in variety of models and a completeness in equipment which justifies our frequent admonition to watch Hudson and Terraplane.

2. *Messenger distributes samples and arranges counter display.*—E. R. Squibb & Sons used telegraph messenger distribution service as a supplement to its sales campaign when Squibb's Aspirin was placed on the market. A series of newspaper advertisements was followed by a brochure mailed to druggists, directing their attention to the newspaper campaign and asking them to "Be ready for the Telegraph Messenger. His call means money to you. . . ." These steps were followed a few days later by telegraph messenger delivery of a telegraph message on special messenger-service blanks, together with a small carton of Squibb's Aspirin, which the messenger opened up and placed on display on the druggist's counter.

3. *Announcement of representative's call and distribution of folders by messenger.*—The Acacia Mutual Life Insurance Company wrote more than $1,000,000 worth of life insurance in about two months by using telegraph messenger distribution service. The

first step in the campaign was a message to all Acacia agents, offering to deliver by telegraph messenger, to twenty-five young business and professional men prospects of each agent, a message describing a new form of policy. Each of 10,000 prospects then received the messenger-service delivery; this comprised, in addition to a message containing the statement that a representative of the insurance company would call the following week, a printed folder entitled "Time Flies."

4. *Messenger service promotes Atlantic City as health and vacation resort.*—To attract people to Atlantic City as a health and vacation resort, the *Atlantic City Pictorial Magazine* utilized telegraph messenger distribution service to distribute copies of the magazine in offices of doctors and dentists throughout the country.

5. *Messenger service introduces new product.*—Telegraph messenger distribution service was used by the National Oil Products Company in introducing a new shampoo, "Admiracion." The messengers delivered sample bottles to druggists throughout the country, with a broadside addressed to the proprietor. The messengers were instructed to set up a special display disc and to paste up a window strip for the proprietor.

6. *Purchase coupons distributed by messenger.*—The Southern Cotton Oil Company utilized Western Union's extensive facilities to distribute to housewives throughout several states more than 1,250,000 coupons, which were worth 10 cents toward the purchase of a can of Wesson Oil or Snowdrift shortening at grocery stores.

7. *Catalogues weighing 1½ pounds distributed by messenger.*—On a distribution of 70,000 catalogues, weighing one pound and a half each and addressed to service managers of automobile repair shops and garages throughout the nation, Thompson Products, Inc., turned the entire job over to Western Union for complete handling from printer to individual addressees. The catalogues were delivered by the printer to Western Union's distribution center in Cleveland, where they were packed and shipped in bulk to telegraph offices in 294 larger cities for local messenger delivery at those points and also for reshipment to other near-by Western Union offices. Catalogues addressed to small towns were remailed direct to the addressee from key cities located in minimum parcel post and express zones. The cost of distribution through Western Union compared very favorably with other methods. In addition,

the company had an advantage described as follows by its advertising manager:

> There was a lot of favorable comment on the personal delivery of the catalogues by uniformed Western Union messengers, who required the signing of a receipt. This sent a "plus" value on the catalogues in the minds of the recipients.

8. *Cough drop samples handed out on busy street corners.*—F & F Laboratories have used telegraph messengers to distribute more than 30,000,000 cough drop samples every winter for several years, on busy street corners, to patrons in downtown stores, at factory and theater exits, and other locations. Smith Brothers, Ludens, and other cough drop makers also use this effective means of sampling their products.

9. *Books and booklets delivered to prospective customers.*—In a number of large cities, the publisher of a book entitled *The Bride* has a copy of the book delivered by a Western Union messenger to each woman applicant for a marriage license, under the sponsorship of prominent local merchants. Similar arrangements are also in effect for messenger delivery of suggestion booklets to mothers of new-born babies, in some instances including samples of baby foods as well as a greeting telegram from the local merchant.

10. *Initial copy of magazine delivered to new subscribers by telegraph messenger.*—A number of national magazines have made arrangements whereby the initial copy of the magazine is delivered to new subscribers by telegraph messenger. Thus the magazine *Time* announced in its radio program that listeners could place their subscriptions by merely telephoning the nearest Western Union office. The telegraph company promptly delivered a copy of the current issue, and the subscription began at once.

11. *Merchandise and samples delivered by telegraph companies.*—The telegraph companies deliver merchandise or samples by messenger in response to radio or publication advertising. For example, Western Union delivered more than 850,000 copper skillets offered as premiums by Procter and Gamble.

12. *Sample telegram calls attention to new fabrics.*—A Western Union telegram containing a sales message and three swatches of material was used by Timely Clothes, Inc., of Rochester, New York, to introduce its fall line of clothes. After attaching the swatches

to oversize telegraph blanks, the blanks were returned to the Western Union office with the names and addresses of the customers who were to receive the promotional piece. The message read:

> A preview of the Timely Clothes of the year. The worsted suit retails at 35 dollars, the summerweight coat and pants 25 dollars. May we make an appointment to show you our line which is the talk of the country. George M. Kaye, President, Timely Clothes.

Timely Clothes reported that 99 per cent of the people receiving the telegram examined the fabric swatches.

13. *Messenger service calls attention to special ads.*—When *Newsweek* signed a one-year advertising contract with *The Saturday Evening Post,* messenger service was used to call this to the attention of *Newsweek* advertisers. A copy of *Newsweek* was delivered to clients, together with a pink telegram. This type of telegram is printed, not taped, and can be secured at a lesser rate than the ordinary telegram. *Newsweek's* telegram read:

> Look at Saturday Evening Post advertisement page 9 today's Newsweek. This advertisement breaks publication advertising precedent. It's first of a series of 52 consecutive color pages. Post's expanded Newsweek schedule now one a week. Reason? Business, industrial, advertising executives, and influential people of every walk of life read Newsweek cover to cover 52 times a year. T. F. Mueller, Gen. Mgr. Newsweek.

A similar technique was used by the Eastman Kodak Co., which delivered, through messenger service, marked copies of newspapers to Kodak distributors and dealers, calling attention to special Kodak ads.

14. *Messenger service arranges displays, introduces new products.*—Messenger boys equipped with samples, folding counter displays, and pink telegrams containing a selling message helped to introduce a new product, "Jests" (a digestive aid), to 30,000 drugstores. Pink telegrams announced the features of "Jests," quoted prices, and asked for permission to have the messenger boy set up the counter display, which contained a few samples. Manufacturer of "Jests" reported considerable success with this promotional plan.

15. *Offset picture on telegram promotes train service.*—Offset pictures of a "crack" train printed on an oversize telegram containing

a selling message built goodwill and increased business for the Seaboard Air Line. Blanks were imprinted with the offset picture by Seaboard and then returned to the telegraph office, where the message was taped on, and the telegrams were addressed and delivered by messenger boys.

Merchandise surveys.—The telegraph companies will conduct fact-finding surveys of various kinds among jobbers, retailers, and consumers. For example, a food concern had a "pantry count" made from house to house in certain sections to ascertain the names of cereals kept on hand by housewives, the object being to determine how well the company's own product was represented. A shoe manufacturer had a telegraph company conduct an inspection of window displays in retail stores, to ascertain whether his brand was being displayed, and, if so, in the prescribed manner. A drug company utilized the services of a telegraph company to "clock" the number of pedestrians passing certain intersections; the results were used as the basis for determining locations for branch stores.

Kinds of Cable and Radio Messages

Domestic radio messages.—Domestic radio messages are transmitted by Mackay Radio & Telegraph Company and by R.C.A. Communications, Inc. These radio services permit full-rate messages of fifteen words to be sent for the usual price of ten available by telegraph, and the day-letter radio message permits sixty words to be sent for the price of fifty available by telegraph. The radio night letter is based on a minimum of thirty words instead of twenty-five.

Mackay Radio is available for messages between:

Baltimore, Md.
Boston, Mass.
Camden, N. J.
Chicago, Ill.
Detroit, Mich.
Long Beach, Cal.
Los Angeles, Cal.
New Orleans, La.
New York, N. Y.
Oakland, Cal.
Philadelphia, Pa.
Portland, Ore.
San Diego, Cal.
San Francisco, Cal.
Seattle, Wash.
Tacoma, Wash.
Washington, D. C.

R.C.A. is available for messages between:

Baltimore, Md.	New Orleans, La.
Boston, Mass.	New York, N. Y.
Camden, N. J.	Oakland, Cal.
Chicago, Ill.	Philadelphia, Pa.
Detroit, Mich.	San Francisco, Cal.
Los Angeles, Cal.	Seattle, Wash.
	Washington, D. C.

These services can also be used for messages to many points adjacent to and served through the above stations. For example, a message from New York to Berkeley, California, can be sent by either Mackay Radio or R.C.A., at the rate of fifteen words for the price of ten, or sixty words for the price of fifty. Messages to be sent by Mackay Radio should be filed with Postal Telegraph, marked "Via Mackay Radio." Messages to be sent by R.C.A. should be filed with either R.C.A. or Western Union, marked "Via R.C.A." Extensions of these domestic radio services are now being projected.

Foreign cable and radio messages.—The conditions brought about by World War II necessitated many changes in foreign cable and radio message services. For example, in the case of certain countries, prepayment of reply was suspended, and restrictions in the use of codes and changes in rate structure occurred from time to time. Consultation with the local telegraph office became necessary for the latest information. The information given below refers to services rendered in normal times.

How messages are sent to foreign countries.—Messages to foreign countries can be sent by either cable or radio. The following description of the kinds of messages that can be sent applies to both cable and radio messages. Messages to be sent by Mackay Radio should be filed with Postal Telegraph, marked "Via Mackay Radio." Messages to be sent by R.C.A. should be filed with either R.C.A. or Western Union, marked "Via R.C.A." Messages to be sent by Commercial Cable Company may be filed at any Postal Telegraph office.

Full-rate messages.—This is the standard service for messages in plain language. The charge per word varies according to the destination of the message. For example, the charge for a full-rate message sent from New York City to London, England, is 20 cents per word. The address and signature are counted in the charge. See page 911 for the method of counting and charging for words and figures.

CDE or code messages.—This type of service is equal in speed of transmission to the full-rate service but is designed especially for messages written in code. The charge for a CDE message is 60 per cent of the charge for a full-rate message. Thus the charge for a full-rate message sent from New York City to London, England, is 20 cents per word; the charge for a CDE message to the same city is 12 cents per word. CDE messages are subject to a minimum charge for five words. See page 911 for the method of counting and charging for words and other limitations upon CDE messages. A charge is made for the address and the signature.

Urgent messages.—The urgent service is designed for messages of extreme urgency requiring the utmost speed in transmission and delivery. A plain-language message sent by urgent service is charged double the rate per word for a full-rate message. A code message sent by urgent service is charged double the rate per word for an ordinary code message.

Deferred messages.—Deferred messages are subordinated in transmission to all other messages except night letters, discussed below. They may be written only in plain language; however, a registered code address may be used. The rule for counting is the same as for full-rate plain-language messages (see page 911), except that figure groups and commercial marks (FOB, CIF, and so forth) may not exceed one third the number of chargeable words in the text and address. The charge per word for a deferred message is one half the charge per word for a full-rate message. Thus the charge for a full-rate message sent from New York City to London, England, is 20 cents per word; the charge for a deferred message to the same city is 10 cents per word. Deferred messages are subject to a minimum charge for five words.

Night letters.—Night-letter service is designed primarily for messages of some length that are not of sufficient urgency to warrant payment under the higher-priced classifications. Night letters may be written only in plain language; however, a registered code address may be used. The rule for counting and the limitation on the use of figure groups and commercial marks are the same as for deferred messages (see above). The charge for a night letter is one third of the charge per word for a full-rate message; a charge is made for a minimum of twenty-five words. Thus the cost of a full-rate message from New York City to London, England, is 20 cents per word; the cost of a night letter to the same city is $1.67 for a minimum of twenty-five words. A charge is made for the address and the signature.

Serial service.—Serial service similar to serial telegraph service, explained on page 894, can be obtained by radio. The Mackay Radio & Telegraph Co. and the R.C.A. Communications, Inc., provide this service for those who want to send a number of messages to the same address on the same day. The rates are as follows:

Where the Rate for the Initial 15 Words Is	The Serial Service Rate Is: *60 Words*	*Each Add. 10 Words or Less*
$.30	$.55	$.09⅙
.36	.65	.10⅚
.48	.90	.15
.60	1.10	.18⅓
.72	1.30	.21⅔
1.20	2.15	.35⅚

The basis of charge for serial service is the daily cumulative word total for all sections (messages) of a series sent to one address, except that no section shall be counted at less than 15 words and no daily serial (series of sections) at less than 60 words.

The sender must indicate that he wishes this class of service by indicating "SER" on each section of a daily series (Serial).

In the event that only one section is filed, that section will be charged at the full rate.

Shore-to-ship and ship-to-shore messages.—This service permits communication to be had, by radio, with individuals aboard ships at sea. The rates are as follows:

	Per Word: *Full Rate*	** CDE Rate*
From New York		
Via Atlantic Coast Stations—		
To ships of American registry	$.21	$.13
To ships of foreign registry	.26	.16

From New York	Per Word Full Rate	Per Word * CDE Rate
Via Pacific Coast Stations—		
To ships of American registry	.29	.18
To ships of foreign registry	.34	.21

* Code rate—Five-word minimum applies.

"GTG" holiday-greeting messages and the "BDG" birthday-greeting messages † are special-rate services to and from ships at sea via Mackay Radio coastal stations. They are composed of fixed texts (which are available through the Marine Bureau, or any Postal Telegraph office) and are subject to a flat rate of $1.60 per message.

These services are available to all American and foreign ships whose controlling administrations have approved and authorized their acceptance aboard ship.

Cable and radio photo service.—This service covers the transmission of photographs by cable or radio. Its principal use is to supply American press associations and newspapers with up-to-the-minute pictures of persons or events abroad. Among the types of material suitable for transmission are: financial statements, machine drawings, production curves, fashion designs, architectural designs, typewritten matter, printed matter, affidavits, contracts, signatures, and business and legal papers of all kinds. Cable photo service is available through R.C.A. Communications, Inc.

Rules for counting charges for cable or radio messages.—The telegraph companies apply the following rules in determining the charges for messages to foreign countries:

1. In plain-language messages each plain-language word containing fifteen letters or less is counted as one word; each word containing more than fifteen letters is counted at the rate of fifteen letters to the word.

2. In code messages code words must not contain more than five letters. Plain language may be interspersed with code in code mes-

† Holiday greeting messages may be sent on the following holidays: Christmas, New Year's Day, Easter, Mother's Day; also on Thanksgiving (from ships only). Birthday greeting messages may be sent any time throughout the year.

sages and is counted at the rate of five letters to the word. Figure groups are permissible in code messages, but if such groups (counted at five figures to the word) exceed one half of the number of chargeable words in the text and signature, they are considered as cipher and subject the entire message to full rates.

3. All groups of figures of whatever length, except groups appearing in code messages in conformity with the conditions specified under 2, and all groups of letters not constituting plain-language words, containing more than five letters, are classified as cipher and are counted at the rate of five figures or letters or fraction thereof to the word. Any cipher word appearing in a message subjects the entire message to full rates. Plain-language words in a cipher message are counted as one each, up to a maximum of fifteen letters.

4. Cipher words and commercial marks, such as FOB, CIF, CAF, SVP, in plain-language messages do not affect the count of plain-language words in the same message, but the presence of code words in an otherwise plain-language message subjects all the words in the message to the five-letter code count.

5. Commercial marks composed of figures and letters are counted at the rate of one word for each five figures or letters or fraction thereof.

6. A shilling mark or stroke in a group of figures counts as a figure and not as a separate word. The same is true of fraction bar, periods, commas, and decimal points grouped with figures. Punctuation marks, hyphens, and apostrophes are not transmitted except when expressly requested, and then they are charged for as one word each. A dollar sign or a pound sterling mark counts as a separate word.

7. The names of the place of destination and of the country are counted as one word each, irrespective of how composed, but the names of streets and of persons in addresses are counted at fifteen letters or fraction thereof to a word.

8. Each word in the signature is counted.

Registered code addresses.—Registered code addresses must be arranged locally. They obviate the expense incurred in using full addresses. The fee is $1.50 for six months, or $2.50 per annum. Full information regarding the registration of code addresses may be obtained from the Central Bureau of Registered Addresses, 50 Broad Street, New York City, or from any Postal Telegraph or Western Union office.

Reversible code addresses.—Reversible code addresses represent a refinement of the code-address principle designed to save tolls that otherwise would be paid for signatures. They involve use of the same code address by the two parties to the correspondence and limitation of the use of that address to correspondence between the parties concerned.

Report of delivery.—Advices of the date and time of delivery of messages, by cable or mail, may be arranged by writing the indication "PC" for telegraphic report, or "PCP" for postal card report, immediately before the address. The charge for a telegraph report of delivery is equal to the tolls on six words at full rates between the same points.

Messages repeated back.—The repetition of a message back to the sender may be arranged at the time of filing by writing the indication "TC" immediately before the address. A charge equal to one half the full-rate tolls (in the case of a code message, one half the code tolls) is made for the repetition service.

Prepaid replies.—The sender of a message may prepay a reply. The indication "RP," followed by the amount prepaid, must be inserted immediately before the address, such indication being counted and charged for as one word. In addition to the charge for the "RP" indication, the charge for the prepaid reply is charged or collected at the time the message is accepted, since, regardless of whether or not a reply is made, the amount indicated by the "RP" instructions must be remitted by the telegraph company through the international accounts to the office of destination.

How to save money by using time-difference table.—The following table should always be consulted before a cable or radio message is sent because it enables the sender to determine whether slower transmission at the lower rates will be as effective as faster transmission at the higher rates.

For example, assume that at 2 o'clock you are sending a plain-language message from New York City to a business house in Stockholm, Sweden. By referring to the time chart, you see that

MACKAY RADIO TIME CHART

Fiji Islands	*Samoa (U. S.) Tutuila*	*Hawaii*	*San Francisco and Pacific Coast*	*Chicago New Orleans Dallas Salvador C. Rica*	*New York Detroit Boston Wash., D. C. Havana Haiti*	*Halifax Buenos Aires Chili*	*Rio De Janeiro Santos*	*British Islands Belgium France Spain Portugal*	*G.C.T.*
NOON	1:00pm	1:30pm	4:00pm	6:00pm	7:00pm	8:00pm	9:00pm	MIDNITE	0000
1:00pm	2:00pm	2:30pm	5:00pm	7:00pm	8:00pm	9:00pm	10:00pm	1:00am	0100
2:00pm	3:00pm	3:30pm	6:00pm	8:00pm	9:00pm	10:00pm	11:00pm	2:00am	0200
3:00pm	4:00pm	4:30pm	7:00pm	9:00pm	10:00pm	11:00pm	MIDNITE	3:00am	0300
4:00pm	5:00pm	5:30pm	8:00pm	10:00pm	11:00pm	MIDNITE	1:00am	4:00am	0400
5:00pm	6:00pm	6:30pm	9:00pm	11:00pm	MIDNITE	1:00am	2:00am	5:00am	0500
6:00pm	7:00pm	7:30pm	10:00pm	MIDNITE	1:00am	2:00am	3:00am	6:00am	0600
7:00pm	8:00pm	8:30pm	11:00pm	1:00am	2:00am	3:00am	4:00am	7:00am	0700
8:00pm	9:00pm	9:30pm	MIDNITE	2:00am	3:00am	4:00am	5:00am	8:00am	0800
9:00pm	10:00pm	10:30pm	1:00am	3:00am	4:00am	5:00am	6:00am	9:00am	0900
10:00pm	11:00pm	11:30pm	2:00am	4:00am	5:00am	6:00am	7:00am	10:00am	1000
11:00pm	MIDNITE	12:30am	3:00am	5:00am	6:00am	7:00am	8:00am	11:00am	1100
MIDNITE	1:00am	1:30am	4:00am	6:00am	7:00am	8:00am	9:00am	NOON	1200
1:00am	2:00am	2:30am	5:00am	7:00am	8:00am	9:00am	10:00am	1:00pm	1300
2:00am	3:00am	3:30am	6:00am	8:00am	9:00am	10:00am	11:00am	2:00pm	1400
3:00am	4:00am	4:30am	7:00am	9:00am	10:00am	11:00am	NOON	3:00pm	1500
4:00am	5:00am	5:30am	8:00am	10:00am	11:00am	NOON	1:00pm	4:00pm	1600
5:00am	6:00am	6:30am	9:00am	11:00am	NOON	1:00pm	2:00pm	5:00pm	1700
6:00am	7:00am	7:30am	10:00am	NOON	1:00pm	2:00pm	3:00pm	6:00pm	1800
7:00am	8:00am	8:30am	11:00am	1:00pm	2:00pm	3:00pm	4:00pm	7:00pm	1900
8:00am	9:00am	9:30am	NOON	2:00pm	3:00pm	4:00pm	5:00pm	8:00pm	2000
9:00am	10:00am	10:30am	1:00pm	3:00pm	4:00pm	5:00pm	6:00pm	9:00pm	2100
10:00am	11:00am	11:30am	2:00pm	4:00pm	5:00pm	6:00pm	7:00pm	10:00pm	2200
11:00am	NOON	12:30pm	3:00pm	5:00pm	6:00pm	7:00pm	8:00pm	11:00pm	2300
NOON	1:00pm	1:30pm	4:00pm	6:00pm	7:00pm	8:00pm	9:00pm	MIDNITE	2400

NOTE: PASSING THE HEAVY LINE DENOTES A CHANGE OF DATE. WHEN PASSING THE LINE GOING TO THE RIGHT ADD ONE DAY.

MACKAY RADIO TIME CHART (*Cont.*)*

Norway Sweden Denmark Lithuania Poland Germany	*Czecho-slovakia Austria Hungary Yugoslavia Italy*	*Finland Estonia Latvia Romania Bulgaria Egypt*	*Leningrad Moscow*	*India Bombay Ceylon*	*Indo-China Siam Singapore*	*Dutch E. Indies Java Borneo*	*Manila China Western Australia*	*Japan Korea*	*Eastern Australia Sydney Melbourne*	*New Zealand Auckland Wellington*
1:00am	1:00am	2:00am	3:00am	5:30am	7:00am	7:30am	8:00am	9:00am	10:00am	11:30am
2:00am	2:00am	3:00am	4:00am	6:30am	8:00am	8:30am	9:00am	10:00am	11:00am	12:30pm
3:00am	3:00am	4:00am	5:00am	7:30am	9:00am	9:30am	10:00am	11:00am	NOON	1:30pm
4:00am	4:00am	5:00am	6:00am	8:30am	10:00am	10:30am	11:00am	NOON	1:00pm	2:30pm
5:00am	5:00am	6:00am	7:00am	9:30am	11:00am	11:30am	NOON	1:00pm	2:00pm	3:30pm
6:00am	6:00am	7.00am	8:00am	10:30am	NOON	12.30pm	1.00pm	2:00pm	3:00pm	4.30pm
7:00am	7:00am	8:00am	9:00am	11:30am	1:00pm	1:30pm	2:00pm	3.00pm	4:00pm	5:30pm
8:00am	8:00am	9:00am	10:00am	12:30pm	2:00pm	2:30pm	3:00pm	4:00pm	5:00pm	6:30pm
9:00am	9:00am	10:00am	11:00am	1:30pm	3:00pm	3.30pm	4:00pm	5:00pm	6:00pm	7:30pm
10.00am	10:00am	11:00am	NOON	2:30pm	4:00pm	4:30pm	5:00pm	6:00pm	7:00pm	8.30pm
11:00am	11:00am	NOON	1:00pm	3:30pm	5:00pm	5:30pm	6:00pm	7:00pm	8:00pm	9:30pm
NOON	NOON	1.00pm	2:00pm	4:30pm	6:00pm	6:30pm	7:00pm	8.00pm	9:00pm	10:30pm
1:00pm	1:00pm	2:00pm	3:00pm	5:30pm	7:00pm	7.30pm	8.00pm	9.00pm	10:00pm	11.30pm
2:00pm	2.00pm	3:00pm	4:00pm	6:30pm	8:00pm	8.30pm	9:00pm	10:00pm	11:00pm	12:30am
3:00pm	3.00pm	4:00pm	5:00pm	7:30pm	9:00pm	9:30pm	10:00pm	11:00pm	MIDNITE	1:30am
4:00pm	4:00pm	5:00pm	6:00pm	8:30pm	10:00pm	10:30pm	11:00pm	MIDNITE	1:00am	2:30am
5:00pm	5:00pm	6:00pm	7:00pm	9:30pm	11:00pm	11:30pm	MIDNITE	1:00am	2.00am	3:30am
6:00pm	6:00pm	7:00pm	8:00pm	10:30pm	MIDNITE	12:30am	1:00am	2:00am	3:00am	4:30am
7:00pm	7.00pm	8:00pm	9:00pm	11:30pm	1:00am	1:30am	2:00am	3:00am	4:00am	5:30am
8:00pm	8:00pm	9:00pm	10:00pm	12:30am	2.00am	2:30am	3.00am	4:00am	5:00am	6:30am
9:00pm	9:00pm	10:00pm	11:00pm	1:30am	3.00am	3.30am	4.00am	5.00am	6:00am	7:30am
10:00pm	10:00pm	11:00pm	MIDNITE	2.30am	4.00am	4:30am	5:00am	6:00am	7:00am	8:30am
11:00pm	11.00pm	MIDNITE	1.00am	3:30am	5:00am	5:30am	6:00am	7:00am	8:00am	9:30am
MIDNITE	MIDNITE	1.00am	2:00am	4.30am	6:00am	6:30am	7:00am	8:00am	9:00am	10:30am
1:00am	1:00am	2:00am	3:00am	5:30am	7:00am	7:30am	8:00am	9:00am	10:00am	11:30am

WHEN PASSING THE LINE GOING TO THE LEFT SUBTRACT ONE DAY.

* *With compliments of the Mackay Radio and Tel. Co.*

at 2 o'clock in New York, it is 8 o'clock in Sweden. The probability is that there will be no one at the office to receive the message. Therefore one of the low-rate services should be used. Compare the costs of each of the services available. A full-rate message would cost 25 cents per word, and a deferred message 12½ cents per word with a minimum charge of five words. A night letter of twenty-five words or less to Stockholm would cost $2.09. Thus, on a 20-word message, the following would be the charges under the methods available:

Full rate	$4.50
Deferred message	2.50
Night letter	2.09

The message should therefore be sent as a night letter, and, if possible, advantage be taken of the five extra words. If the message were less than seventeen words, the deferred message would be cheaper than the night letter.

Daylight-saving time in the United States and in foreign countries must be taken into consideration in calculating the time differences.

2. TELEPHONE SERVICE

Long-distance Calls

Station-to-station and person-to-person calls.—A station-to-station call is made when the caller is willing to talk with anyone who answers the telephone at the called point. A person-to-person call is made when the caller must talk to some one person in particular and asks the operator to connect him with a particular person, department, or extension telephone. The rates for these calls are higher than those for station-to-station calls (in general, from 30 to 40 per cent, the percentage decreasing as the distance between the calling and called points increases).

Although a station-to-station call is cheaper, in many cases it is more economical in the long run to make a person-to-person call. If the person with whom you wish to speak at the called point is likely to be difficult to locate, use the person-to-person call, for the time spent in locating the person may run up the cost of a station-to-station call higher than the cost of a person-to-person call.

Night and Sunday rates.—Reduced rates apply daily between 7:00 P.M. and 4:30 A.M. and for the entire twenty-four hours on Sunday on calls to points in the United States, Alaska, Canada, and Cuba. These reduced rates are approximately 30 to 40 per cent lower than the day rates for calls above 35 cents in the case of station-to-station and above 50 cents in the case of person-to-person. From 5:00 P.M. to 5:00 A.M. night rates are in effect to certain foreign countries, mainly European countries. These rates also apply all day Sunday. The time at the calling point governs the application of the reduced rates. Night and Sunday rates do not apply on calls to ships at sea.

As an illustration of the saving that may be effected by night rates, assume that a businessman in New York wishes to call a company in San Francisco. The day rate for a station-to-station call from New York to San Francisco is $4.00; the night rate is $3.00. Since San Francisco time is three hours behind New York time, if the call from New York were made between 7 and 8 o'clock in the evening, it would be between 4 and 5 o'clock in San Francisco. Thus the New York caller would reach his party during business hours and save $1.00 for a three-minute call.

Messenger calls.—If it is necessary to reach someone who does not have a telephone, the operator at the called point will send a messenger for the person. If the call is not completed because the person is not available, the caller must pay for the cost of the messenger service (usually about 25 cents) plus a report charge.

Conference calls.—The conference service, a comparatively recent development, makes it possible for an executive to be connected simultaneously with a number of other telephones in any part of the country. No special equipment at the customer's station is required.

The uses of conference service are many and varied. Suppose, for example, that a manufacturer in Chicago is about to start a new sales drive. Sales managers in five cities are all waiting for the word "Go." On the morning of the new drive, each sales manager's telephone rings, and each is informed that Chicago is calling.

The voice of the president comes over the wires, giving the sales managers final directions for the new drive; or, the president and the five sales managers can discuss their plans, just as though they were grouped at a conference table.

If he so desired, the president of the company could speak to gatherings of salesmen in each of the five cities, instead of merely to the five sales managers. He could do this by having the telephone company install loud-speaker equipment. This equipment consists of a small cabinet; a control dial permits adjustment of the volume, which can be regulated for a small office or a large room.

Long-distance private wires.—Where it is necessary to make numerous calls between two points—for instance, between a headquarters office and a factory or warehouse—many business firms contract for private-line long-distance service. To establish a connection, the operator at either end of such a hookup merely plugs in and rings.

The advantages of this private-line service are:

1. The company has the exclusive use of a direct line of communication to the distant point for the entire day or for certain specified hours, depending upon the agreement.
2. Connections are very rapid.
3. A considerable saving in cost is effected where the volume of calls is heavy.

International and ship-to-shore calls.—From any telephone in the Bell System, it is now possible to call practically all important cities in Europe and many points in Africa, Asia, Australia, Central and South America, San Domingo, Japan, Iceland, Bermuda, Cuba, the Hawaiian Islands, and certain other island groups, unless the service is temporarily suspended or restricted because of war conditions. A table of rates for calls to these points is given in most alphabetical directories.

It is now possible for the businessman to transact business even when he is at sea—by means of ship-to-shore telephone service, provided that the ship is equipped for this service and can make effective radio contact with the shore station. Rates for ship-to-shore calls depend upon the location of ships at the time calls are made. Complete information on this service may be obtained directly from the long-distance operator.

Telephone Convenience Aids

Privacy key.—If an executive has merely the usual telephone equipment, it is always possible that someone else in the organization, by picking up another extension, may overhear the executive's conversation. This difficulty can be obviated by the installation of a simple device; the executive has only to operate a little privacy key on his desk, and he can then be sure that there is no chance of his conversation being overheard.

Switching device.—This device enables a secretary to receive calls intended for an executive and then to transfer them directly to his telephone. The executive, consequently, does not have to answer calls from people with whom he does not wish to speak; the secretary acts as intermediary. However, after she has taken the call and has inquired from the executive whether he wishes to speak to the caller, she does not have to flash the switchboard operator and ask her to transfer the call. The secretary uses the switching device, and the call is automatically transferred.

The plan described above is one of the simpler uses of the switching device. Almost any arrangement desired to facilitate the switching of calls can be installed.

Hold key.—This device is useful when it is necessary to make another call to secure information with which to answer the first call. A hold button enables the executive to hold the call on his line and use the same telephone (but another line) to obtain the necessary information. When he has obtained the information, the executive can switch back to the first caller, without the latter having overheard, in the meantime, the second call that was made.

Intercommunicating wiring plans.—These plans provide for direct communication between members of an organization. Thus, by merely pushing a button on his desk, one executive can communicate directly with another, without the call having to be relayed through the switchboard operator. At the same time the telephones involved in the intercommunicating wiring plan are connected with the main system, so that calls to persons who are not a part of the system can be made through the switchboard operator in the usual way. An intercommunicating wiring plan is very convenient for communication between, for example, a president and his department heads, or any other group of persons who call one another frequently. Various arrangements of intercommunicating wiring plans are possible; consult the telephone company for detailed information.

Loud-speaker equipment.—Loud-speaker equipment, which consists of a simply operated loud-speaker contained in a small cabinet, can be used with any type of telephone call—inside, local, long distance, or conference. The loud-speaker is connected directly to the telephone line but can be cut on or off at will. Hence the fact that a loud-speaker device is installed in an executive's office does not mean that every call will be received through it; the executive can receive private calls over the same telephone in the usual way. With loud-speaker equipment, the volume desired can be regulated, much as radio volume is regulated.

With a loud-speaker device attached to his telephone, an executive is enabled to call other persons into his office to hear a telephone conversation. If a loud-speaker is installed at the other end of the line, the executive can speak to a group of persons; as, for example, a group of salesmen. If a conference call is made, and loud-speakers are attached to each of the telephones, the executive can "broadcast" simultaneously to as many as five meetings in distant cities.

Teletypewriter Service

Kinds of teletypewriter service.—Teletypewriters will transmit typewritten messages to any part of the country over the facilities of the Bell System. The typewriters are specially designed electrical typewriters. Whatever is typed on one machine is simultaneously reproduced in typewritten form on one or more typewriters with which it is connected. Two kinds of teletypewriter service are available:

1. Private line.
2. Exchange.

Private-line teletypewriter service.—This kind of service involves teletypewriter machines, at two or more locations, directly connected with one another. When the machines are located within the same metropolitan area, the service is furnished on a twenty-four-hour basis. When the machines are located in different metropolitan areas, the service is furnished for twenty-four hours and usually for shorter intervals at specified times of the day.

Private-line teletypewriter service may be used not only for intra-organization communication but also for communication with other concerns. For example, two independently owned and operated companies in the same city or different cities may transact so much business with one another that constant communication facilities are necessary. The teletypewriter service, on either a full-time or part-time basis, is an excellent means of linking the two concerns closely together.

Exchange teletypewriter service.—Exchange service differs from private-line service in that a subscriber to the former may communicate with any other subscriber to the service. The connections between machines are established through a teletypewriter central office, in much the same way that telephone connections are made. If, for example, the John Doe Corporation of Pittsburgh wishes to teletype a message to the James Smith Company of Philadelphia, a John Doe employee types out the number of the Smith Company on her machine. The central-office operator immediately makes the desired connection, the teletypewriter at the Smith Company offices "answers," and the message is then written. In flexibility and speed, the whole teletypewriting process compares favorably with regular telephone service; and the permanent character of the record facilitates filing and reference work.

Connections can be established for any length of time that a subscriber wishes. Standard message charges have been developed along the same lines as have telephone toll rates, the minimum period being three minutes.

Interoffice Communication

Savings through interoffice communication.—Interior communication systems, privately owned and not connected to rented telephone facilities, can be introduced at small cost and with considerable saving of time and money in most organizations. Some of the systems are described below. Here are a few of the advantages to be gained with the proper intercommunication system:

1. The executive can speak to an associate instantly. Moreover, on some systems, the conversation can be completely secret.
2. Information can be obtained from any part of the organization while telephoning on outside lines.
3. Intermittent but important dictation can be given to secretaries over the system without waste of time.
4. Throughout the organization, better co-ordination is secured; delays are eliminated; errors are reduced; executive supervision is increased as interior communication is used to weld the organization together, to eliminate walking and visiting, to encourage instant follow-through on all work.
5. Telephone efficiency is increased by taking the load of interior communication off the city switchboard and city telephones. This improves service to the public.
6. Since every interoffice telephone call ties up two extensions, the use of intercommunication instruments reduces busy signals and annoyance caused by delays in putting through calls.
7. Telephone bills are reduced by eliminating a number of telephone extensions and by holding in check the amount of rented facilities needed at the switchboard.
8. Operating costs are reduced since the switchboard operator can, when relieved of the burden of interior traffic, give part time to clerical and other work.

Example of benefits derived from use of interoffice communication.—The Chicago Hardware Foundry Company installed a large interior telephone system with profitable results. The need for a larger outside switchboard was eliminated, and the number of outside telephones was reduced. This freed the telephone operator for some office clerical jobs. The upkeep of the phones in the interior system is estimated to be only slightly more than 10 per cent of the rent of a similar number of outside telephones. Furthermore, the number of outside personal and unnecessary calls has been reduced, since the employee has to go to his superior's desk to make the call.

Twinphone intercommunication.—The Twinphone Intercommunication Systems, a product of Executone, Inc., are available for businesses of various sizes. In its simplest form, Twinphone Intercommunication consists of a master station and one substation, each able to call and converse with the other. With the addition of a station selector, this same master station can enjoy direct two-way conversations with as many as ten widely separated offices. Should the need arise, several or all of these substations can be called simultaneously.

Several different models of Twinphone equipment, to meet the specialized needs of business and industry, have been developed. For example, there are models to eliminate background noises in the vicinity of a substation, in a press room or machine shop; to step up volume for coverage in large areas such as factory shipping floors, receiving platforms, and parking lots; to make communication possible between several master stations as well as between substation and master. The equipment also includes trumpet types for use in noisy locations or wherever the message must be heard over a large area. The trumpet substation delivers up to four times the volume output of one of the regular office types; but, for two-way conversation, it tones down the return message to the master station to the normal volume. One or more trumpet-type substations can be used in the same system with office models.

Dictograph intercommunication equipment.—The Dictograph System of Intercommunication equipment is manufactured by the Dictograph Sales Corporation. The system is purely an internal one; it has no connection with the regular telephone system. The instruments are of two types: (1) executive station; (2) staff station.

Executive station.—The little keys on the face of the instrument establish the connections. One end of the executive station contains a microphone, the other a loud-speaker. The executive's messages are transmitted through the microphone. It is not necessary that he be close to the instrument when he speaks, for the microphone is so sensitive that it will pick up a whisper in a large room. Messages from other persons come to the executive through the loud-speaker. The incoming calls are indicated by white signals.

Conference calls are easily made with the Dictograph system. Simply by pushing the keys indicating the names of the persons with whom he wishes to talk, and a conference key, the executive can establish connection with several persons and can talk to all of them at the same time. This conference device is optional.

Staff station.—This station is smaller than the executive station. It has no loud-speaker or microphone but, instead, has a handset (like a French telephone). The keys are the same, except that they are usually fewer in number. Calls can be made by simply picking up the handset and ringing with the appropriate key; calls are answered when the handset is raised from its cradle.

Dictograph makes, in addition to the standard Dictograph equipment, a special Five-Station Telematic System. This system consists of one master station and from one to four intercommunicating stations. It is recommended for doctors, lawyers, and small professional and business offices.

Idealfone intercommunication.—Automatic Electric Company's Idealfone intercommunicating system is a push-button telephone system for organizations needing any number of telephones up to ten.

The instruments are of the wall or side-of-desk type, equipped with modern, full-size molded plastic handsets. Its location on the wall or side of the desk puts it out of the way, yet the separate handset makes it just as convenient to use as a desk telephone.

The compact box on which the handset rests contains the signaling push buttons and other necessary equipment, including the bell. The system is available in four different arrangements: two-station system; code-signaling system, in which as many as ten telephones can be connected on one line, with the individual stations signaled by code; selective-signaling system, where only the bell of the wanted telephone rings; and master-station system, where it is desirable that all calls pass through a central point.

Intercommunicating equipment for more than ten connections.—Where more than ten stations are required, and it is desirable to have a system that is economically adaptable to future growth and change, privately owned automatic dial-telephone systems are often the solution. Moreover, even where less than ten stations are required initially, but standard secret telephone service and the convenience of modern "dial" operation are desired, private automatic dial-telephone systems find wide use.

These systems need only two or three wires to each telephone instead of the multiple wiring required by push-button and loud-speaker systems. Each station is connected with a central automatic switchboard, involving no operator, through which connections are automatically made with other telephones. Greater flexibility is provided and lower costs are involved since additional telephones can be installed merely by connecting them to the switchboard rather than directly to every other phone. This feature also avoids service interruptions when stations have to be moved from one location to another.

Such equipment can be provided with Automatic Electric Company's P.A.X. (Private Automatic Exchange) systems, which adapt to private use the standard commercial dial-telephone equipment made for telephone companies. Systems come in various sizes from two stations to 2,000 or more.

To make a call, it is necessary only to pick up the telephone handset or receiver and dial two or three numbers. The switchboard then automatically rings the called line, or, if it is busy, returns "busy tone" to the person calling. The calling signal ceases automatically when the called telephone is answered.

3. POSTAL GUIDE

How to save postage.—Every business organization uses mail in some form or another in transacting business. Money can be saved by knowing how and when to use the various types of mail service.

A few suggestions are offered here to reduce postage costs:

1. Use business-reply envelopes.
2. Take advantage of bulk mail wherever possible.
3. Reduce labor costs by using metered mail and printed indicia.
4. Be sure that air-mail letters will arrive at the post office in time to meet plane schedules. Unless your mail clerks are familiar with the air-mail schedules, there is a chance that air mail will not arrive any earlier than if sent by ordinary first-class rates. The difference between air-mail postage and ordinary postage (3 cents an ounce) is a dead waste unless this precaution is taken.
5. Eliminate special delivery if letters will reach destination in time for the first mail delivery.
6. Economies are possible if you know how and when various classes of mail can be used.

7. Check a day's mail now and then to see whether letters to the same person are going in separate envelopes.

8. Establish a rule that all material addressed to one branch shall be enclosed in one envelope. Saving is obvious; postage is paid on so much per ounce or fraction. Combining fractions saves ounces. Saving is also made on envelopes.

9. Have communications to branch offices written on memo paper. This reduces weight of mail going to branch offices.

10. Use lightweight paper for air mail.

11. Give thought to weight of paper and envelopes used for normal correspondence. Reduced weight need not mean sacrifice of quality.

12. Do not permit clips to go through the mail. They add to the cost of mailing. To see how much, place a box of clips on the scale.

Postal Rates and Classification of Mail

First-class matter.[1]—Included in this classification are written matter, matter sealed against inspection, postal cards (Government postal cards), post cards (private mailing cards), business-reply cards, and letters under cover of business-reply envelopes or labels. The weight limit for first-class matter is 70 pounds (with exceptions in certain places in the Philippine Islands).

First-class rate.—The rates for first-class mail vary according to the types of matter as follows:

1. Letters wholly or partly in writing (except writing authorized to be placed upon matter of other classes), 3 cents an ounce. Rate for local letters is 2 cents.
2. Matter sealed against inspection, 3 cents an ounce.
3. Postal cards and post cards, 1 cent each.
4. Drop letters or other first-class matter for local delivery, 2 cents an ounce or fraction thereof.

---

[1] Typewriting and carbon and letterpress copies thereof are the equivalent of handwriting and are classed as such in all cases. Matter of a higher class enclosed with matter of a lower class subjects the whole to the higher rate. Manuscript copy accompanying proof sheets or corrected proof sheets of the same may be mailed third class.

5. Business-reply cards and letters in business-reply envelopes, 1 cent in addition to regular postage.

How to send first-class letter mail to another post office for "local" dispatch.—If first-class letter mail in bulk is sent to another post office for "local" dispatch, follow one of these regulations:

1. If the letters are transported by a salaried employee of your own organization, they are chargeable at the local or 2 cents per ounce rate (even though they bear an out-of-city return address). The postage should be purchased at the point of mailing. When such letters are returned as undeliverable, postage due for the deficiency at the rate of 3 cents per ounce is charged.
2. Packages of letters that are addressed, sealed, and stamped may be shipped by parcel post from one post office to another, provided they bear a return address in the city from which they are to be mailed.

The postage for such letters must be purchased from the dispatching post office, and a letter should be securely attached to the package requesting the postmaster to cancel and deliver the letters.

The term "first-class letter mail" as used above distinguishes such mail from other first-class matter (postal cards, post cards, and business-reply cards) to which the letter rate does not apply.

Second-class matter.—This classification includes newspapers and periodicals bearing notice of entry as second-class matter. There is no weight limit.

Second-class rate.—The rates for second-class matter are: for newspapers and periodicals, when sent unsealed by the public (not by publisher or news agent), 1 cent for each 2 ounces or fraction thereof; or, they may be sent at fourth-class rates, if lower.

Third-class matter.—This classification includes merchandise, printed matter, and other mailable matter not in the first or second classifications, and not exceeding 8 ounces in weight. The same matter when sent in parcels exceeding 8 ounces in weight is embraced in fourth-class or parcel-post mail.

Third-class rate.—The rate for third-class matter is 1½ cents for each 2 ounces or fraction thereof, up to and including 8 ounces. (See "Bulk Mail" and "Catalogues and books," for exceptions.)

Included in the third-class group is a type of mail that is very

PARCEL POST OR FOURTH-CLASS MAIL

RATES OF POSTAGE, CLASSIFICATION, INSURANCE, AND C. O. D. FEATURES, WRAPPING, ETC.

Fourth-class Matter, known as domestic parcel-post mail, includes all parcels over 8 ounces in weight containing circulars, books, catalogues, and other matter wholly in print, together with merchandise, farm and factory products, seeds, cuttings, bulbs, roots, scions, and plants, and all other mailable matter not embraced in the first and second classes. The same matter in parcels weighing 8 ounces or less is embraced in third-class mail.

Rates of Postage on Fourth-class Matter (over 8 ounces)—To Be Fully Prepaid—are by the pound, according to distance or zone, a fraction of a pound being computed as a full pound, as shown in the following table and paragraphs (*a*), (*b*), and (*c*):

NOTE.—The rate for the first pound in each zone is shown in the table; the rates on additional pounds are: Local zone, 1 cent for each 2 pounds; first and second zones, 1.1 cents each pound; third zone, 2 cents; fourth zone, 3.5 cents; fifth zone, 5.3 cents; sixth zone, 7 cents; seventh zone, 9 cents; eighth zone, 11 cents; a fraction of a cent in the total amount of postage on any parcel being counted as a full cent.

Weight in Pounds	*Local*	Zones							
		1st, up to 50 Miles	*2d, 50 to 150 Miles*	*3d, 150 to 300 Miles*	*4th, 300 to 600 Miles*	*5th, 600 to 1,000 Miles*	*6th, 1,000 to 1,400 Miles*	*7th, 1,400 to 1,800 Miles*	*8th, over 1,800 Miles*
1	$0.07	$0.08	$0.08	$0.09	$0.10	$0.11	$0.12	$0.14	$0.15
2	.08	.10	.10	.11	.14	.17	.19	.23	.26
3	.08	.11	.11	.13	.17	.22	.26	.32	.37
4	.09	.12	.12	.15	.21	.27	.33	.41	.48
5	.09	.13	.13	.17	.24	.33	.40	.50	.59
6	.10	.14	.14	.19	.28	.38	.47	.59	.70
7	.10	.15	.15	.21	.31	.43	.54	.68	.81
8	.11	.16	.16	.23	.35	.49	.61	.77	.92
9	.11	.17	.17	.25	.38	.54	.68	.86	1.03
*10	.12	.18	.18	.27	.42	.59	.75	.95	1.14
11	.12	.19	.19	.29	.45	.64	.82	1.04	1.25
12	.13	.21	.21	.31	.49	.70	.89	1.13	1.36
13	.13	.22	.22	.33	.52	.75	.96	1.22	1.47
14	.14	.23	.23	.35	.56	.80	1.03	1.31	1.58
15	.14	.24	.24	.37	.59	.86	1.10	1.40	1.69
16	.15	.25	.25	.39	.63	.91	1.17	1.49	1.80
17	.15	.26	.26	.41	.66	.96	1.24	1.58	1.91
18	.16	.27	.27	.43	.70	1.02	1.31	1.67	2.02
19	.16	.28	.28	.45	.73	1.07	1.38	1.76	2.13
20	.17	.29	.29	.47	.77	1.12	1.45	1.85	2.24
21	.17	.30	.30	.49	.80	1.17	1.52	1.94	2.35
22	.18	.32	.32	.51	.84	1.23	1.59	2.03	2.46
23	.18	.33	.33	.53	.87	1.28	1.66	2.12	2.57
24	.19	.34	.34	.55	.91	1.33	1.73	2.21	2.68
25	.19	.35	.35	.57	.94	1.39	1.80	2.30	2.79
26	.20	.36	.36	.59	.98	1.44	1.87	2.39	2.90
27	.20	.37	.37	.61	1.01	1.49	1.94	2.48	3.01
28	.21	.38	.38	.63	1.05	1.55	2.01	2.57	3.12
29	.21	.39	.39	.65	1.08	1.60	2.08	2.66	3.23
30	.22	.40	.40	.67	1.12	1.65	2.15	2.75	3.34
31	.22	.41	.41	.69	1.15	1.70	2.22	2.84	3.45
32	.23	.43	.43	.71	1.19	1.76	2.29	2.93	3.56
33	.23	.44	.44	.73	1.22	1.81	2.36	3.02	3.67

PARCEL POST OR FOURTH-CLASS MAIL
(Continued)

RATES OF POSTAGE, CLASSIFICATION, INSURANCE, AND C. O. D. FEATURES, WRAPPING, ETC.

Weight in Pounds	*Local*	Zones							
		1st, up to 50 Miles	*2d, 50 to 150 Miles*	*3d, 150 to 300 Miles*	*4th, 300 to 600 Miles*	*5th, 600 to 1,000 Miles*	*6th, 1,000 to 1,400 Miles*	*7th, 1,400 to 1,800 Miles*	*8th, over 1,800 Miles*
34	$0.24	$0.45	$0.45	$0.75	$1.26	$1.86	$2.43	$3.11	$3.78
35	.24	.46	.46	.77	1.29	1.92	2.50	3.20	3.89
36	.25	.47	.47	.79	1.33	1.97	2.57	3.29	4.00
37	.25	.48	.48	.81	1.36	2.02	2.64	3.38	4.11
38	.26	.49	.49	.83	1.40	2.08	2.71	3.47	4.22
39	.26	.50	.50	.85	1.43	2.13	2.78	3.56	4.33
40	.27	.51	.51	.87	1.47	2.18	2.85	3.65	4.44
41	.27	.52	.52	.89	1.50	2.23	2.92	3.74	4.55
42	.28	.54	.54	.91	1.54	2.29	2.99	3.83	4.66
43	.28	.55	.55	.93	1.57	2.34	3.06	3.92	4.77
44	.29	.56	.56	.95	1.61	2.39	3.13	4.01	4.88
45	.29	.57	.57	.97	1.64	2.45	3.20	4.10	4.99
46	.30	.58	.58	.99	1.68	2.50	3.27	4.19	5.10
47	.30	.59	.59	1.01	1.71	2.55	3.34	4.28	5.21
48	.31	.60	.60	1.03	1.75	2.61	3.41	4.37	5.32
49	.31	.61	.61	1.05	1.78	2.66	3.48	4.46	5.43
50	.32	.62	.62	1.07	1.82	2.71	3.55	4.55	5.54
51	.32	.63	.63	1.09	1.85	2.76	3.62	4.64	5.65
52	.33	.65	.65	1.11	1.89	2.82	3.69	4.73	5.76
53	.33	.66	.66	1.13	1.92	2.87	3.76	4.82	5.87
54	.34	.67	.67	1.15	1.96	2.92	3.83	4.91	5.98
55	.34	.68	.68	1.17	1.99	2.98	3.90	5.00	6.09
56	.35	.69	.69	1.19	2.03	3.03	3.97	5.09	6.20
57	.35	.70	.70	1.21	2.06	3.08	4.04	5.18	6.31
58	.36	.71	.71	1.23	2.10	3.14	4.11	5.27	6.42
59	.36	.72	.72	1.25	2.13	3.19	4.18	5.36	6.53
60	.37	.73	.73	1.27	2.17	3.24	4.25	5.45	6.64
61	.37	.74	.74	1.29	2.20	3.29	4.32	5.54	6.75
62	.38	.76	.76	1.31	2.24	3.35	4.39	5.63	6.86
63	.38	.77	.77	1.33	2.27	3.40	4.46	5.72	6.97
64	.39	.78	.78	1.35	2.31	3.45	4.53	5.81	7.08
65	.39	.79	.79	1.37	2.34	3.51	4.60	5.90	7.19
66	.40	.80	.80	1.39	2.38	3.56	4.67	5.99	7.30
67	.40	.81	.81	1.41	2.41	3.61	4.74	6.08	7.41
68	.41	.82	.82	.143	2.45	3.67	4.81	6.17	7.52
69	.41	.83	.83	1.45	2.48	3.72	4.88	6.26	7.63
70	.42	.84	.84	1.47	2.52	3.77	4.95	6.35	7.74

EXCEPTIONS

(*a*) In the first or second zone, where the distance by the shortest regular practicable mail route is 300 miles or more, the rate is 9 cents for the first pound and 2 cents for each additional pound.

(*b*) On parcels collected on rural routes, the postage is 2 cents less per parcel than shown in the foregoing table when for local delivery and 3 cents less per parcel when for other than local delivery.

*(*c*) Parcels weighing less than 10 pounds measuring over 84 inches but not more than 100 inches in length and girth combined are subject to a minimum charge equal to that for a 10-pound parcel for the zone to which addressed.

important to the businessman—the form letter, or circular. See "Form letters" and "Form letters (bulk third class)."

Fourth-class matter (parcel post).—Included in this classification are merchandise, printed matter, and other mailable matter not in the first or second classifications, and exceeding 8 ounces in weight. The fourth-class weight limit is 70 pounds (with exceptions in the Philippine Islands); the size limit is 100 inches in length and girth combined. Parcels weighing less than 10 pounds and measuring over 84 inches but not more than 100 inches in length and girth combined are subject to a minimum charge equal to that for a 10-pound parcel for the zone to which addressed. The length is the distance from one end of the package to the other (not around the package), and the girth is the distance around the package at its thickest part. For example, a parcel 35 inches in length, 10 inches in width, and 5 inches in thickness, is 65 inches in length and girth combined (35″ plus 10″ plus 10″ plus 5″ plus 5″).

Air Mail

Matter mailable by air mail.—Any mailable matter except that liable to damage from freezing (cut flowers are acceptable) may be sent by air mail.

Air-mail rates and specifications.—The domestic rate for air mail is 6 cents an ounce or fraction thereof, regardless of distance. The postage fees may be supplied by the special air-mail stamps or by regular stamps; the former are better, for they are distinctive and guarantee to a great extent that the matter will be recognized by postal employees as air-mail matter and will be accorded the special attention pertaining to air-mail service.

Air-mail matter may not exceed 70 pounds in weight or 100 inches in length and girth combined.

Air mail may be registered, insured, and sent C.O.D. or special delivery if the charges for these services are paid in addition to the regular air-mail postage.

Air mail should be conspicuously marked in the space immediately below the stamps, above the address "Via Air Mail." Articles for dispatch over the trans-Pacific route destined to the

Philippine Islands and points beyond should bear the blue label "Par Avion—By Air Mail," which may be secured without expense at post offices. When it is desired that matter in the domestic mails otherwise carried by airplane shall be transported across the Pacific Ocean by steamer, the matter should be endorsed "Via Air Mail except over the Pacific." Letters bearing special-delivery air-mail stamps, as well as other air mail sent special delivery, should be conspicuously marked "Special Delivery—Air Mail." The mere fact that the matter may bear air-mail and special-delivery stamps is not sufficient.

Special-delivery air mail.—In order to obtain the fullest measure of service for the postage paid at the air-mail rate, air mail should be sent special delivery. Matter sent by airplane reaches the office of address sooner than if sent by train, but when it gets there after the last regular carrier trip of the day of its arrival, delivery is not made until the following business day, unless it is sent special delivery and the fee therefor is paid in addition to the air-mail postage.

Air-mail envelopes.—Air-mail envelopes of the distinctive designs illustrated and described below may be used. Such envelopes must be white, except when it is necessary to use envelopes of extra strength, in which case they may be of light tints of manila or kraft (see Figure 71).

The outstanding feature of the first design is a border of blue and red parallelograms with intervening white spaces, producing a distinguishing blue, white, and red border not exceeding 5/32 of an inch in width extending around the edges of both the address side and the back of the envelope. The words "Via Air Mail" must appear boldly as shown in Figure 71. The border of this envelope facilitates its identification as air mail even when in a package or distributing case with other mail, thus securing the prompt and special attention to which such letters are entitled.

The conspicuous feature of the second design consists of the blue, red, and white stripes. The stripes must not exceed ¼ inch in width and should extend entirely across the length of the envelope. The blue stripe must be not less than 1⅛ inches below the top of the envelope, in order that clear space may be left for the necessary postage stamps and postmark. The white space between the blue and red stripes should be approximately ¼ inch in

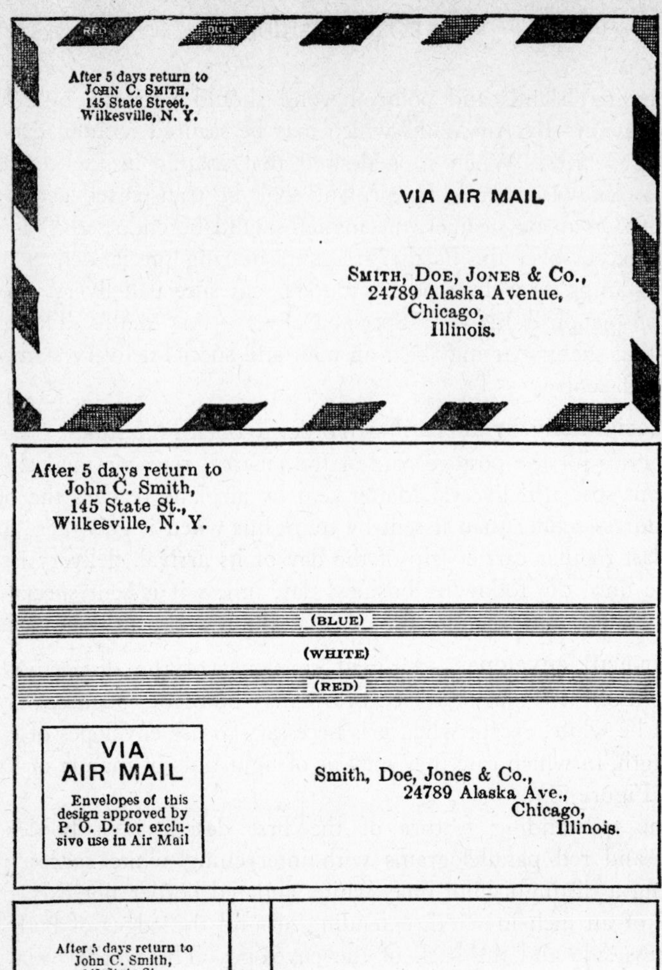

After 5 days return to
John C. Smith,
145 State St.,
Wilkesville, N. Y.

VIA AIR MAIL

Smith, Doe, Jones & Co.,
24789 Alaska Ave.,
Chicago,
Illinois.

Figure 71.—Air Mail Envelopes.

width, so that the three stripes will not cover more than approximately ¾ of an inch in all.

The two designs described apply particularly to printed envelopes. When ordinary envelopes are used for air mail, the mailer may identify the matter for transmission by airplane by placing horizontally across the envelopes two blue lines approximately ¼ inch apart, the upper line to be not less than 1⅛ inches below the top of the envelope. In such case the words "Via Air Mail" should be plainly and boldly written, hand-stamped, or printed in the upper-right portion of the envelope, preferably between the two lines. Similar lines may also be placed vertically across the envelope not less than 3½ inches from the right end. Such lines may also be placed on the backs of envelopes used for air mail. See the third design.

Air-mail envelopes cannot be used for mail not intended to be carried by airplane.

Bulk Mail

Advantages of bulk mailing.—Bulk mailing cuts down postal expense, for the rates are lower than regular rates, and the work of stamping mail is minimized; it also speeds up mail service, both at the business organization's mail department and at the post office.

Specifications for bulk mail.—A permit must be obtained from your postmaster for the use of the bulk-mailing privilege.

Bulk lots of identical pieces of third-class matter may be mailed in quantities of not less than either 20 pounds or 200 pieces at the rate of 8 cents a pound or fraction thereof for books, catalogues, seeds, plants, and so forth, and 12 cents a pound or fraction thereof for all other third-class matter—circulars, printed matter, and so forth—provided that the postage shall in no case be less than 1 cent per piece of mail.

The postage must be prepaid in money and may be supplied in the form of printed indicia, metered stamps, precancelled stamps, or Government precancelled envelopes. Uncancelled stamps must not be used on bulk third-class mail.

If there are 15 or more bulk pieces for one post office, the mailings must be tied together, and the post office must be indicated by facing end envelopes address side out; if there are less than 15 pieces for one post office, the mailings for each state must be tied together and labeled "miscellaneous," and the state must be indicated. Matter sent under the bulk-mailing privilege must be deposited at that department of the post office which is reserved for such mail. A "Statement of Mailing" must be submitted with each mailing.

For particular applications of the bulk-mailing privilege, see "Form letters (bulk third class)," "Printed matter (bulk third class)," and "Catalogues and books (bulk third class)."

Letters

Correspondence letters.—Handwritten or typewritten letters, or letters reproduced by automatic typewriter must be mailed first class. The rate is 3 cents for each ounce or fraction, except in the case of local letters, the rate for which is 2 cents. Postage may be supplied by affixing stamps, using a postage meter machine, or using printed nonmetered indicia. Envelopes should be sealed.

Form letters (regular third class).—Printed, multigraphed, and mimeographed letters and letters produced by any other mechanical process should generally be sent third class (of course, they may be sent first class). If such letters are to be subject to third-class (or bulk third-class) rates, they must be identical, with certain exceptions; they may contain a written, typewritten, hand-stamped, or printed:

1. Date.
2. Name of sender (including hand signature).
3. Name of addressee.
4. Corrections of mere typographical errors.

If changes have to be made in form letters, consult the postmaster before making them; insertions or changes other than those listed above subject the letters to the first-class rate.

Further, to be mailable at the third-class rate, form letters that are reproductions or imitations of handwriting or typewriting, whether printed, multigraphed, mimeographed, or reproduced by some other mechanical process, must be mailed in quantities of 20 or more, and deposited at a post office. If they are produced by a mechanical process but are not reproductions of handwriting or typewriting, single pieces may be mailed third class in any postal receptacle.

While printed, multigraphed, and mimeographed letters sent at third-class rates must be identical, the copy can change on every 20 pieces, as long as the physical details are identical.

The rate for form letters that meet these requirements is the regular third-class rate—1½ cents for each 2 ounces or fraction thereof.

Postage may be supplied by affixing stamps, affixing precancelled stamps, using a postage meter machine, or using printed non-metered indicia. However, the last three methods may be used only with the permission and regulation of the Postal Department.

Envelopes for regular third-class form letters must not be sealed; the back flap may be tucked in, or postage-saver envelopes may be used. Printed return cards or envelopes, order blanks, or other printed matter may be enclosed in form letters if the weight limit of 8 ounces is not exceeded.

Form letters (bulk third class).—If bulk lots of form letters (circulars) that conform to the requirements for regular third-class mail (identical in terms, no unauthorized changes or additions, and so forth) are mailed in quantities of not less than either 20 pounds or 200 pieces, they are subject to a special bulk rate. However, a permit must be obtained from the postmaster for the use of the bulk-mailing privilege.

The bulk rate is 12 cents a pound or fraction thereof, but a minimum rate of 1 cent per piece must be paid in any event. The postage must be prepaid and must be supplied in the form of printed indicia, metered stamps, precancelled stamps, or Government precancelled envelopes. Uncancelled stamps must not be used on bulk third-class mail.

If meter-machine or printed indicia are used on bulk third-class mail, the wording "Section 562 P. L. & R." must be printed above or below the stamps or printed indicia. When precancelled stamps are used, the wording must be printed or hand-stamped above or below the stamps.

Envelopes must not be sealed; the flap may be tucked in, or postage-saver envelopes may be used.

Printed Matter

This classification includes folders, printed advertising cards, broadsides, circulars, books, catalogues, and so on.

Printed matter (regular third class).—If printed matter is not of the nature of personal correspondence, it may be mailed third class. (There is a special rate for books and catalogues with over 24 pages, including the cover; see "Catalogues and books.") The pieces may be mailed singly at any mail box or post office if postage is paid with uncancelled stamps.

The rate for regular third-class printed matter is the usual third-class rate, 1½ cents for each 2 ounces or fraction thereof. Mailings exceeding 8 ounces must be mailed fourth class (parcel post).

Envelopes must not be sealed; the back flap may be tucked in, or postage-saver envelopes may be used. Also, packages of third-class printed matter must not be sealed.

Postage may be supplied by affixing stamps, affixing precancelled stamps, using a postage meter machine, or using printed non-metered indicia. Precancelled stamps may be used to seal the edges of self-mailers—booklets, folders, cards—if the matter is not sealed against inspection.

Printed matter (bulk third class).—The requirements and regulations applying to "Form letters (bulk third class)" also apply to bulk third-class printed matter.

The following is an additional requirement: If precancelled stamps are used to close the edges of self-mailers, the wording "Section 562 P. L. & R." must be printed or hand-stamped in the upper right-hand corner of the address side, if the matter is to be sent bulk third class.

Catalogues and books.—If catalogues and books have fewer than 24 pages, including the cover, all the conditions and rates set forth in connection with printed matter apply.

If printed catalogues and books have 24 or more pages, including the cover (at least 22 of these pages must be printed), and do not weigh more than 8 ounces, they may be mailed at a special rate—1 cent for each 2 ounces or fraction thereof on each individually addressed piece or package.

If printed catalogues and books have 24 or more pages (22 of which are printed), and weigh over 8 ounces and less than 10 pounds, they may be mailed at the following special rates, and must be clearly marked "Sec. 571½, P. L. & R." in order to distinguish them from other fourth-class mail. Directories, buyers' guides, calendars, agents' order books, and publications that are sold or show a sales price are not acceptable at Sec. 571½ rates.

Zone	*Local*	*1st*	*2nd*	*3rd*	*4th*	*5th*	*6th*	*7th*	*8th*
1st lb.	$.04	$.04	$.04	$.05	$.06	$.07	$.08	$.09	$.10
Each add. lb.	.005	.01	.01	.02	.03	.04	.05	.06	.07

Catalogues and books weighing over 10 pounds must be mailed at regular fourth-class parcel-post rates.

Books consisting wholly of reading matter and containing *no advertising matter,* other than incidental announcements of books, may be mailed at 1½ cents a pound.

Catalogues or books with 24 pages or more may be enclosed in sealed packages if the following words, together with the name and address of the sender, appear on the face of the envelope or wrapper: "CONTENTS, BOOK (or CATALOGUE)—Postmaster: This parcel may be opened for postal inspection if necessary." This statement must be *printed* on the label or wrapping of the package; it cannot be written or hand-stamped.

Postage may be supplied by affixing stamps, affixing precancelled stamps, using a postage meter machine, or using printed non-metered indicia.

Enclosures with books or catalogues of 24 pages or more (when mailed at the 1-cent rate) are limited as follows:

1. A single reply envelope, or post card, or both.
2. An order form.
3. A single, loose, printed circular not larger than a page of the book or catalogue. (No sales talk or extraneous matter is allowed on the circular; it is wise to submit copy to the postmaster before you print.)
4. A price list in lieu of a circular (under certain conditions).

Enclosures with books and catalogues mailed under Sec. 571½ P. L. & R. are limited as follows: While it is permissible to include with catalogues the usual loose enclosures, such as order forms, reply envelopes, circulars, and the like, provided such enclosures are incidental, this does not apply to agents' packages or salesmen's outfits containing, in addition to the catalogues, a number of identical pieces of printed advertising matter, such as blotters, illustrated display sheets, advertising posters, dealers' cards, and the like. In such cases only one blotter, one display sheet, one poster, one dealer's card, and so forth, may be enclosed with the catalogues. It is, of course, permissible to enclose more than one order form, reply envelope, or reply card.

Catalogues and books (bulk third class).—If catalogues or books that fulfill the above requirements are mailed in quantities of 200 or more, or if the total weight is 20 pounds or more, they are subject to a special bulk rate, if the following requirements are fulfilled:

1. A permit must be obtained from the postmaster for the use of the bulk-mailing privilege.
2. If there are 15 or more bulk pieces for one post office, the mailings for each must be tied together and labelled correctly. If there are fewer than 15 pieces for one post office, the mailings for each state must be tied together and labelled correctly.
3. Matter sent under the bulk-mailing privilege must be deposited at that department of the post office which is reserved for such mail.
4. A "Statement of Mailing" (supplied by the Postal Department) must be filled out and submitted with each mailing.

The bulk third-class rate for printed catalogues and books of 24 pages or more is 8 cents per pound, provided that in no case the postage is less than 1 cent a piece. Catalogues and books weighing more than 8 ounces must be mailed as fourth-class material (by parcel post).

Envelopes or wrappers for bulk third-class printed books or catalogues may be sealed if the following statement is *printed* on the face of the package "CONTENTS, BOOK (or CATALOGUE)—Postmaster: This package may be opened for postal inspection if necessary."

Postage may be supplied by affixing precancelled stamps, with a postage meter machine or printed nonmetered indicia. Uncancelled stamps must not be used on bulk third-class mail.

When meter-machine or printed indicia are used on bulk third-class mail, the wording "Section 562 P. L. & R." must be printed above or below the stamps or printed indicia. When precancelled stamps are used, this wording must be printed or hand-stamped above or below the stamps.

Manuscripts and proofs.—Manuscripts, handwritten or type-written, when accompanied by proof sheets of the same matter, may be mailed at third-class rates, or, if over 8 ounces in weight, at fourth-class rates. The proofs may contain corrections and instructions for the printer, and portions may even be rewritten if necessary.

Metered Mail

Permit required for use of meter.—If application is made to the postmaster at the mailing office, permits may, under Sections 562 and 579 of the postal laws and regulations, be issued to persons or concerns for mailing first-, second-, third-, and fourth-class matter without stamps affixed, the postage being paid in money, provided the mailings are presented in accordance with the regulations. No fee is required for a meter permit.

The person or concern that has obtained the permit takes the meter to the post office and buys a certain amount of postage. The postmaster then sets the meter in accordance with the amount of postage paid for and seals it. When the amount of postage paid for is used up, the meter locks and must be reset by the postmaster after additional money has been paid. It is possible, however, to buy additional postage before the meter locks.

Metered indicia.—The meters can be adjusted to imprint the denomination of postage desired. The amount of postage paid must appear on each meter stamp (1 cent, 1½ cents, and so forth). The indicia may be imprinted directly on the envelope, or, with the use of a meter-stamp tape attachment, the indicia may also be imprinted on a gummed strip of paper that can be affixed to bulky envelopes or packages. When used for first-class mail, metered indicia must show correct date of mailing. Insertion of the wrong date makes the mailer liable for a penalty of 10 per cent of the postage.

Type and quantity of matter that may be metered.—Metered first-, third-, and fourth-class matter, with the exception of third-class bulk matter mailed under Section 562 P. L. & R., may be

Figure 72.—Examples of Metered Indicia.

presented in any quantity and need not be identical as to contents or weight.

Metered second-class matter must be presented in quantities of not less than 300 pieces.

Metered bulk third-class matter must be mailed in quantities of not less than 20 pounds in weight or 200 identical pieces in number. When metered indicia are used on bulk third-class matter, the wording "Section 562 P. L. & R." must be printed adjacent to the indicia.

Printed Indicia

Permit required for use of printed indicia.—It is necessary to obtain a permit from the postmaster for the right to use printed indicia instead of stamps. Permits entail a charge of $10.

Printed nonmetered mail must be deposited at the post office from which the permit was obtained. The postage charges for each mailing must be paid in cash, by certified check, or as a charge against an advance deposit with the post office to cover various mailings. A form that supplies required information to the post office must be filled out for each mailing.

Form of printed indicia.—The indicia may be printed by a printing press or any other machine that has no locking device. The use of a hand stamp for placing indicia on matter is not permitted. The form for the indicia is regulated by the Postal Department and must be complied with in every case. (Consult the postmaster before printing indicia.) The indicia must appear in the upper right-hand corner of envelopes, cards, or wrappers. When the matter mailed is bulk third class, the wording "Section 562 P. L. & R." must appear on the indicia, above the words "U. S. Postage." Also, the amount of postage paid on each piece need not appear on the indicia used for bulk third-class mail. Printed indicia may be of any color that contrasts strongly with the paper on which they are printed.

Sec. 562, P. L. & R.
U. S. POSTAGE
Paid
New York, N. Y
Permit No.

Figure 73.—Printed Indicia.

Type and quantity of matter on which printed indicia may be used.—First-class matter with printed indicia must be presented in quantities of not less than 300 pieces, identical as to weight (first-class matter is rarely sent with printed indicia). Second- and third-class matter, except some bulk mail, must be presented in quantities of not less than 300 identical pieces, if it bears printed indicia. Fourth-class matter bearing printed indicia must comprise not less than 250 identical pieces, except when special authorization to do otherwise has been granted. Bulk third-class mail may bear printed indicia if the matter is presented in quantities of not less than 20 pounds or 200 identical pieces, and provided the wording "Section 562 P. L. & R." appears on the indicia, above the words "U. S. Postage."

Precancelled Stamps, Cards, and Envelopes

Precancelled stamps.—A permit for the use of such stamps must be obtained from the postmaster; no charge applies. Precancelled stamps are usable on second-class matter (subject to transient second-class rates), third-class matter (including bulk third-class), and fourth-class matter. They may not be used on containers that will be used again.

Precancelled cards.—Cards may be precancelled by the mailer if a permit is obtained.

Precancelled envelopes.—Envelopes may be precancelled by the mailer who has a permit to do so, and used to mail first-, second-, third-, and fourth-class matter, in accordance, of course, with the regulations pertaining to such matter. Bulk third-class matter may be mailed in precancelled envelopes. One-cent precancelled stamped envelopes, already imprinted with the words "Sec. 562 P. L. & R.," are sold by the post office.

Limitation.—Precancelled stamps, cards, and envelopes may be mailed only at the post office indicated in the precancellation.

Stamps

Coils of stamps.—The following quantities and denominations are available: coils of 500 and 1,000 coiled sidewise or endwise, and coils of 3,000 coiled sidewise—1 cent, 1½ cent, 2 cent, and 3 cent; coils of 500 and 1,000 coiled sidewise—4 cent, 4½ cent, 5 cent, 6 cent, and 10 cent. The 3,000 coil is designed for special types of stamp-affixing machines and cannot be used in the ordinary vending or affixing machines. For coils of 500 stamps, a charge of 3 cents, in addition to the value of the stamps, is made; for coils of 1,000, a charge of 6 cents; for coils of 3,000, a charge of 18 cents.

Redemption of stamps.—Avoid buying stamps in excess. They are not redeemable unless they are sold in damaged condition or are of the wrong denomination. If a purchaser does buy the wrong denomination by mistake, he must return the stamps for exchange to the point of purchase within two days of the date on which they were bought. Cash refunds are not made.

Envelopes

Stamped envelopes.—The Postal Department sells stamped envelopes just as it does postal cards. These envelopes are available in various sizes and in a number of colors. The postmaster will supply current prices upon request.

Printed ("special-request") stamped envelopes.—The Postal Department will print a purchaser's return card on stamped envelopes if the latter places at a post office a request for lots of 500 or a multiple of 500 of a given size, quality, and denomination. Advertisements will not be printed on the envelopes. The following are samples of return cards that follow forms prescribed by the Postal Department:

For envelopes intended to enclose letters:
After 5 days return to
JOHN DOE,
1234 5th St.,
NEW YORK, N. Y.

For envelopes intended to enclose third-class mail:
After 5 days return to
RICHARD ROE,
678 9th Ave.,
CHICAGO, ILL.
Return Postage Guaranteed.

"Office-request" stamped envelopes.—The Postal Department will also print the following form of return card on stamped envelopes:

After----days, return to

NEW ORLEANS, LA.

Privately printed stamped envelopes.—Purchasers of stamped envelopes may print their own return cards in particular styles. In using mailing envelopes approximately 6 x 10 inches or larger, it is permissible to use the entire face of the envelope for any decorative design as long as a clear (unprinted) space approximately 6 x 4 inches appears somewhere on the face of the envelope, preferably to the right or center. Smaller envelopes must have at least 3½ inches of space at the right-hand end of the envelope for address and stamps.

Window envelopes.—The Postal Department enforces special requirements for window envelopes. The transparent window must run parallel with the length of the envelope. Further, the window may not occupy any space within 1⅜ inches from the top, or ⅜ of an inch from the bottom or ends of the envelope. The sender's name and complete address must appear in the upper left-hand corner of all window envelopes—it may not appear on the back. The sender's name may be omitted only if his post-office-box number and address are given. The name of a building is not a sufficient address.

Consult the postmaster before buying or printing window envelopes. He will furnish correct specifications.

Window envelopes cost about 50 cents per 1,000 more than other envelopes, but more than four times that amount is saved by eliminating the typing of the address. For example, a typist, earning $20 a week for a 40-hour week, can address about three non-window envelopes a minute. The cost of addressing 1,000 envelopes is therefore $2.75; the saving by using window envelopes is $2.25. Furthermore, the danger of misaddressing is eliminated with window envelopes.

The claim that window envelopes create an unfavorable impression is true to a certain extent, but consideration must be taken of the fact that many business letters are delivered to the addressee's desk without the envelope.

A letter can be folded to fit a window envelope by making the first crease on a line with the first line of the body of the letter, and then folding from the top one-third the length of the sheet. If this folding is not desirable, two small marks can be printed 1 inch apart on the left edge of the sheet, as a guide for placing the address. An address typed between the marks will permit the sheet to be folded only twice to fit the window envelope.

Stamped window envelopes.—These may be purchased from the Postal Department.

Postage-saver envelopes.—This type of envelope is one of the most useful devices of modern business. One end of each envelope is left ungummed, the end flap being merely tucked in. The back flap is sealed. Consequently, postage-saver envelopes have the appearance of first-class mail but are subject to third-class rates. Postage-saver envelopes are very widely used in direct-mail selling.

Government Postal Cards

Sizes and prices of Government postal cards.—Government postal cards (not private mailing cards) in single and double form are sold at post offices for the price of the stamp on the face of the cards. The various sizes and prices follow:

No. 5—1-cent domestic single—3 x 5 inches.
No. 8—1-cent domestic single—3¼ x 5½ inches.
No. 6—1-cent domestic reply (double)—3¼ x 5½ inches (each half).
No. 7—2-cent foreign single—3¼ x 5½ inches.
No. "F"—2-cent foreign reply—3½ x 5½ inches (each half).
No. 11—3-cent foreign single—3¼ x 5½ inches.
No. 12—3-cent foreign reply—3½ x 5½ inches (each half).

Sheets of Government postal cards.—The Government also furnishes postal cards in sheets. Consequently, a business house can readily have matter printed on the cards. Sheets come in the following sizes

No. 5—1-cent single—2 cards wide—9 cards long (in cases of 4,500).
No. 6—1-cent double—4 cards wide—5 cards long (in cases of 5,000).
No. 8—1-cent single—4 cards wide—10 cards long (in cases of 10,000).

Cards in sheet form cost the same as individual cards. When the sheets are cut up, the cards must conform to the Government specifications.

Messages on Government postal cards.—The back and the left-hand third of the front of a Government postal card may contain writing, printing, illustrations, or advertising matter. The right-hand two thirds of the front must be left blank for the address. Government postal cards may not be used for dunning creditors, if the language used is offensive, defamatory, or threatening. However, cards may be used to collect payment, and so forth, if the request is a straightforward and dignified one and contains no reference to balances carried forward, previously billed, or overdue. Consult the postmaster for approval.

Redemption of Government postal cards.—If postal cards have been spoiled in the printing or addressing, but have not been cancelled, they may be exchanged for other stamped paper or stamps at the post office for 75 per cent of their face value.

Private Mailing Cards

Specifications for private mailing cards.—Post cards manufactured by business concerns must be made of an unfolded piece of cardboard similar in quality to the cardboard used in Government postal cards. The required size is as follows:

Minimum size	$2\frac{3}{4}$ x 4 inches.
Maximum size	$3\frac{9}{16}$ x $5\frac{9}{16}$ inches.

The right-hand half of the face of such cards must be left blank for the address and stamps. Post cards that meet these requirements may be mailed for 1 cent.

Double (reply) post cards.—Double post cards, each half of which meets the above requirements, may also be mailed for 1 cent. Postage need not be affixed to the reply half at the time the card is originally mailed, but when the reply half is detached and mailed, 1-cent postage must be affixed. Of course, an arrangement may be made with the post office whereby the company sending the card will pay the postage as the reply portions are returned. If this is done, the reply halves of the cards must bear printed indicia.

The address of the reply portion must be on the inside when the card is originally mailed. Stickers may be used to close cards, but this is not necessary. Metal clips may not be used to seal cards. If the reply portion is used simply to cover a message on the back of the original portion, 3-cents postage is required. Dunning cards must be sealed at the edges.

Folded advertising cards and other matter entirely in print, arranged with a detachable part for use as a post card, are mailable as third-class matter provided the initial portion is not designated as a post card and is not within the size prescribed for such cards, and provided, further, that they are so folded that the address of the reply portion is on the inside when the card is originally mailed. No inclosures may be made in double post cards.

Messages on post cards.—The entire back, and the left-hand half of the face of post cards may contain written or printed messages or advertisements and illustrations. The right-hand half of the face must be reserved for the address and stamps.

Postage on post cards.—Postage for post cards that meet the requirements set forth above may be supplied by affixing stamps or using a postage meter machine. Precancelled stamps or printed nonmetered indicia may not be used on cards that bear the words "Post Card" or "Private Mailing Card."

Cards larger than $3\frac{9}{16}$ x $5\frac{9}{16}$ inches.—If such cards are entirely in print and do not bear the words "Post Card" or "Private Mailing Card," they may be mailed at the third-class rate for printed matter. If mailed in quantities of 200 or more, they may be sent as bulk third-class printed matter. If they are not entirely in print and contain either the words "Post Card" or "Private Mailing Card," they must be mailed at the first-class rate—3 cents—whether sealed or unsealed.

Postage for these large cards, if they do not bear the words "Post Card" or "Private Mailing Card," may be supplied by affixing stamps, affixing precancelled stamps, using a postage meter machine, or using printed nonmetered indicia.

Business-Reply Cards and Envelopes

Specifications for business-reply cards and envelopes.—A permit must be obtained from the postmaster for the use of business-reply cards or envelopes, in accordance with Section 510 P. L. & R. The face of the card or envelope must agree with forms suggested by the Postal Department (consult postmaster before printing cards or envelopes). Dimensions for business-reply cards are as follows:

Minimum dimensions .... $2\frac{3}{4}$ x 4 inches.
Maximum dimensions .... $3\frac{9}{16}$ x $5\frac{9}{16}$ inches

Both cards and envelopes may be printed in one color, or two or more colors may be used.

Postage on business-reply cards and envelopes.—Business-reply cards and envelopes that meet the above specifications, and that bear the printed name and address of the distributor and the prescribed indicia (including the number of the serial permit), may be returned through the mails without the prepayment of postage. The regular postage plus 1 cent additional on each card or envelope (total of 2 cents for cards and 3 cents local and 4 cents out-of-town for one-ounce envelopes) is collected when the cards or envelopes are delivered to the original distributor.

Money Orders

Fees for domestic money orders.—The maximum amount for which a money order may be issued is $100. However, a person who wishes to transmit by money order a sum in excess of $100 may purchase more than one money order. The fees for domestic money orders are as follows:

For orders from	$ 0.01 to $ 2.50	6 cents
" " "	2.51 to 5.00	8 "
" " "	5.01 to 10.00	11 "
" " "	10.01 to 20.00	13 "
" " "	20.01 to 40.00	15 "
" " "	40.01 to 60.00	18 "
" " "	60.01 to 80.00	20 "
" " "	80.01 to 100.00	22 "

Fees for international money orders.—The fees for international money orders are as follows:

For orders from	$ 0.01 to $ 10.00	10 cents
" " "	10.01 to 20.00	20 "
" " "	20.01 to 30.00	30 "
" " "	30.01 to 40.00	40 "
" " "	40.01 to 50.00	50 "
" " "	50.01 to 60.00	60 "
" " "	60.01 to 70.00	70 "
" " "	70.01 to 80.00	80 "
" " "	80.01 to 90.00	90 "
" " "	90.01 to 100.00	$1.00

Payment of money orders.—A money order may be redeemed within one year from the last day of the month of its issue. For the convenience of travelers, the Postal Department provides that original money orders are redeemable at any money-order post office in the continental United States (except Alaska) within 30 days after date of issue. However, after 30 days have expired, an order must be redeemed at the post office designated in the order.

Anyone presenting a money order for payment must be identified if he is not known by the postmaster. Letters, bank books, calling cards, driver's licenses, and the like, are not sufficient means of identification, and the paying clerks at post offices will not accept them as such. A person may cash a money order if the postman who delivers his mail will identify him, or if someone who is known to the employees of the post office will identify him. A bank will redeem money orders for someone who has an account with that bank. The Postal Department will sanction for business firms the use of special identifying data, such as account numbers and special stamps, which must be placed on the back of money orders that are to be cashed.

Registered Mail

Mail that may be registered.—All mailable domestic first-, second-, and third-class matter, and fourth-class matter if it is sealed and first-class postage is paid, may be registered. Mailable second- and third-class matter, valued at over $100, upon which a registry fee in excess of 30 cents is paid, must be sealed and first-class postage paid thereon. Matter that should be registered is money, valuable papers, valuable goods, letters to be delivered to the addressee in person ("Deliver to Addressee only"), third- and fourth-class matter which is valuable, and so forth.

The Postal Department furnishes the sender of registered mail with a receipt. A receipt showing delivery is furnished the sender of registered mail when he so requests and pays a small additional fee, if he marks the envelope or wrapper "Return receipt requested" or "Return receipt requested showing address where delivered."

Manifold mailing records.—Manifold mailing records are furnished, without charge, to firms or individuals who frequently present three or more articles for registration at one time. Firm delivery records may be used where an addressee frequently receives an average of three or more registered articles at one time. These manifold mailing and delivery sheets furnish a convenient and compact office record of matter registered and registered mail received, and make possible the speedy acceptance of mail for registration and the receipting for registered mail received.

Limit of indemnity on registered mail.—When registered mail is lost, rifled, or damaged in transit, the Postal Department will pay an indemnity (in accordance with the value declared at the time of registry), but this indemnity may not exceed $1,000 on any one registered article, even though the lost matter was valued above $1,000 by the sender. If a sender wishes to register matter that is valued at more than $1,000, private insurance companies, in cooperation with the Postal Department, will insure the matter.

Fees for registered mail.—Registry fees, which are charged at the time of sending in addition to the regular postage, are as follows:

For registry indemnity not exceeding $5	15 cents
For registry indemnity exceeding $ 5 but not exceeding $ 25	18 "
" " " " 25 " " " 50	20 "
" " " " 50 " " " 75	25 "
" " " " 75 " " " 100	30 "
" " " " 100 " " " 200	40 "
" " " " 200 " " " 300	50 "
" " " " 300 " " " 400	60 "
" " " " 400 " " " 500	70 "
" " " " 500 " " " 600	80 "
" " " " 600 " " " 700	85 "
" " " " 700 " " " 800	90 "
" " " " 800 " " " 900	95 "
" " " " 900 " " " 1,000	$1.00

For registered mail having a declared value in excess of the maximum indemnity covered by a registry fee paid, an additional fee is charged as follows: when the declared value exceeds the maximum indemnity covered by the registry fee paid by not more than $50, 1 cent; by more than $50 but not more than $100, 2 cents; by more than $100 but not more than $200, 3 cents; by more than $200 but not more than $400, 4 cents; by more than $400 but not more than $600, 5 cents; by more than $600 but not more than $800, 6 cents; by more than $800 but less than $1,000, 7 cents; and if the excess of the declared value over the maximum indemnity covered by the registry fee is $1,000 or more, the additional fees for each $1,000 or part of $1,000 range from 8 to 13 cents according to the distance.

Mail matter without intrinsic value for which no indemnity is provided may be registered at the minimum fee of 15 cents. Air mail is accepted for registration.

Insured Mail

Mail that may be insured.—Domestic third- and fourth-class mail may be insured for an amount equal to its value. First- and second-class matter may not be insured; such matter should be registered.

Limit of indemnity on insured mail.—A single parcel may not be insured for more than $200. Packages containing articles valued at more than $200 should be registered (indemnity limit, $1,000).

Fees for insured mail.—Insurance fees and indemnity limits are as follows:

From $ 0.01 to $ 5	5	cents
" 5.01 to 25	10	"
" 25.01 to 50	15	"
" 50.01 to 100	25	"
" 100.01 to 150	30	"
" 150.01 to 200	35	"

It is absolutely necessary that the sender of any insured (or C.O.D.) piece of mail guarantee return and forwarding postage. This is understood by the Postal Department, even though the postage pledge does not appear on the wrapper. However, any concern that uses specially printed labels or wrappers is required to include on the labels or wrappers a pledge guaranteeing return and forwarding postage.

Insured packages may be sent "Special Delivery" or "Special Handling" if the fees applying to these services are paid in addition to the postage and insurance charges. The air-mail system handles insured mail if it is sent at the air-mail rate of postage.

C.O.D. Mail

Mail that may be sent C.O.D.—Domestic third- and fourth-class mail and sealed domestic unregistered matter of any class bearing postage at the first-class rate may be sent C.O.D. The price of the article and the charges thereon (including, if the sender wishes, the postage and the C.O.D. fee prepaid) will be collected from the addressee. The maximum amount that may be collected on a single C.O.D. parcel is $200. C.O.D. charges are returned to the sender in the form of a money order.

C.O.D. fees.—The amount of the C.O.D. charges determines the amount of the C.O.D. fee. Every C.O.D. parcel is *automatically insured* for an amount not exceeding the amount prescribed by the fee paid against nonreceipt of the collectible charges, and against loss, damage, and rifling in an amount equivalent to the value of the package, or the cost of repairs. The amounts of C.O.D. charges (or amounts of insurance desired) are as follows

From $ 0.01	to $	5	12	cents
" 5.01	to	25	17	"
" 25.01	to	50	22	"
" 50.01	to	100	32	"
" 100.01	to	150	40	"
" 150.01	to	200	45	"

The sender of a C.O.D. parcel must guarantee return and forwarding postage.

C.O.D. mail may be sent "Special Delivery" or "Special Handling" if the fees applying to these services are paid in addition to the postage and C.O.D. charges. The air-mail system handles C.O.D. mail if it is sent at the air-mail rate of postage.

Special Delivery, Special Handling, and Miscellaneous

Use of special delivery and special handling.—The volume of parcel post is so large that at many busy points packages and other bulky mail must be consolidated and sent out in carloads at certain times of the day—less frequently than first-class mail is sent out. Special-delivery postage on first-class mail provides immediate delivery at the office of destination. The payment of *special-delivery postage* on matter of the second, third, or fourth class gives such matter precedence over bulk matter and provides for it the same prompt handling that is accorded first-class mail—including immediate delivery at the office of destination. Payment of *special-handling post-*

age on matter of the fourth class entitles it to the same handling as is given to first-class mail—but not immediate delivery at the office of destination. Special-delivery service necessarily includes special handling, but only fourth-class mail may be sent special handling without special delivery. Special delivery and special handling do not guarantee "safety" for the matter so sent; if the matter is valuable, it should be registered or insured. Neither is special-delivery or special-handling mail delivered directly to the addressee himself.

Delivery of special-delivery and special-handling mail.—Special-delivery mail will be delivered from 7 A.M. to 11 P.M. at city delivery offices, and from 7 A.M. to 7 P.M. at all other offices (or until after the last mail, if that is not later than 9 P.M.); at all offices on all holidays; and on Sundays at offices that receive mail on that day. Special-delivery mail is delivered by messenger during the above hours to points within one mile of any post office or delivery station; points within the limits of the delivery service of cities or villages that extend their delivery service more than one mile; and points not more than one-half mile from rural routes.

Fees for special delivery and special handling.—The fees for special-delivery service, which are paid in addition to the regular postage charges, are as follows:

Weight	*1st Class Matter*	*2nd, 3rd, and 4th Class (includes special handling) Matter*
Under 2 lbs	$0.10	$0.15
2 lbs. to 10 lbs.	.20	.25
Over 10 lbs.	.25	.35

The fees for special-handling service without special delivery are as follows (applies only to fourth-class mail):

Parcels weighing not more than 2 pounds	10 cents
Parcels weighing more than 2 pounds but not more than 10 pounds	15 "
Parcels weighing more than 10 pounds	20 "

Special-delivery and special-handling matter may be sent by air mail if the fees applying to these services are paid in addition to the regular air-mail postage charges.

Sender's receipt or certificate of mailing.—Frequently it is desirable to have some proof that a letter, a package, and so forth, has been mailed. The postmaster will furnish the sender of any class of domestic ordinary mail a receipt or certificate of mailing for each article sent. The sender must pay 1 cent for each certificate. Also, the sender of domestic ordinary, registered, insured, or C.O.D. mail will be given *additional* receipts or certificates of mailing for each article sent, at the price of 1 cent per receipt—that is, receipts in addition to the *original* receipts that are given when mail is registered, insured, and so on.

Forwarding of mail.—If an addressee changes from one address to another within the same post-office district, the Postal Department does not regard the delivering of mail to the new address as forwarding, and the delivery is performed without extra charge. However, if the new address is within another post-office district, the following rules apply:

First-class mail.—All first-class matter (letters, postal cards, private mailing cards, and the like) will be forwarded from one post office to another without additional charge. First-class mail addressed locally and paid for at the 2-cent rate is forwarded collect if readdressed to a 3-cent district.

Second-, third-, and fourth-class mail.—Mail of these classes is subject to the payment of additional postage each time it is forwarded from one post office to another. When mail must be forwarded, the postmaster notifies the addressee of the amount necessary to pay for the forwarding. The addressee must return the correct amount to the postmaster before the mail will be sent. There is no charge for delivering second-, third-, or fourth-class mail to a new address in the same post-office district.

Remailing of first-class mail.—Postal regulations explicitly cover the remailing of first-class mail. Prepaid audience or fan mail sent to broadcasting stations may, if it has not been opened, be remailed to other points in bulk at the third- or fourth-class postage rate, according to the weight of the packages. This regulation applies whether such mail is remailed to the headquarters or other stations of the radio-broadcasting systems, or to advertising agencies, or the sponsors or advertisers, irrespective of whether the letters are to be opened finally by the persons or concerns to whom they are remailed in bulk. The same applies to letters prepaid at the first-class rate that were originally sent to feature writers in care of newspapers and remailed unopened in bulk by the latter to the addressees or their agents. This regulation also applies to the advertiser who prepares locally a campaign to be mailed by various dealers or branch offices throughout the country.

If the letters have been opened and are then prepared for remailing in bulk, they are subject to postage at the first-class rate.

Notice of change of address and reasons for nondelivery.—The Postal Department provides a service that is of real value to concerns doing a considerable amount of direct-mail advertising. If such concerns wish to keep their mailing lists up to date, or to make additional efforts to have mail delivered, the procedure is as follows. On the lower left-hand corner of the envelope or wrapper used to send third- or fourth-class mail, the sender must print one of the following statements, depending upon the checkup desired:

1. "Postmaster: If addressee has removed and new address is known, notify sender on form 3547, postage for which is guaranteed."
2. "Postmaster: If undeliverable as addressed FOR ANY REASON, notify sender, stating reason, on form 3547, postage for which is guaranteed."
3. "Postmaster: If undeliverable as addressed FOR ANY REASON, notify sender, stating reason, on form 3547, postage for which is guaranteed. In case of removal to another post office, do not notify the addressee, but hold the matter and state on form 3547 the amount of forwarding postage required, which sender will promptly furnish."

The postmaster will then send a card notification giving the information called for by the statement. The card costs 2 cents. However, this charge does not cover the forwarding of the mail in case the new address is in another post-office district. If the mail is to be forwarded, the extra postage must be sent to the postmaster.

Requests to postmaster for notification on form 3547 must be incidental to the general purpose of mailing and may not be made for the purpose of collecting from, or obtaining the new address of, a debtor.

Return of mail: *First-class mail.*—Undeliverable letters and other first-class matter with postage of 3 cents or over will be returned to the sender free of charge if his address appears on the face of the envelope or wrapper. Undeliverable double postal cards and double post cards on which return postage has been prepaid will be returned free of charge if the sender's address appears on the face of the cards.

Single postal cards and post cards, and double post cards that have no postage on the return card, will be returned to the sender if his address appears on the face of the card, but only when they are mailed for local delivery. If they have been mailed out of town, they will not be returned unless additional postage is paid, and then only when the words "Return Postage Guaranteed" and the name and address of the sender appear on the face of the card.

Second-class mail.—The rules governing the return of this class of mail are detailed and exacting; consult the postmaster.

Third and fourth-class mail.—Undeliverable mail of these classes will be returned to the sender only when his address appears on the upper left-hand corner of the envelope, card, or wrapper, and when a pledge guaranteeing the payment of return postage appears on the face of the envelope or wrapper ("Return Postage Guaranteed"). When these two requirements are fulfilled, the postmaster will return undeliverable mail, and the extra postage will be collected C.O.D. When the return postage pledge does not appear (but the sender's name does), and the contents of third- or fourth-class mail are obviously of considerable value, the postmaster will notify the sender that the mail is not deliverable and that return postage is required, but he will not return the matter until the sender pays the necessary amount.

United States Official Postal Guide

For companies that send out large quantities of mail—direct-mail men in particular—the *Official Postal Guide* is an invaluable reference volume. It covers in detail every aspect of postal service. The price is $1.50 (cloth); a subscription to the monthly supplements costs 75 cents a year additional. The *Guide* is for sale by the Superintendent of Documents, United States Government Printing Office, Washington, D. C.

SECTION 10

Credits and Collections

I. SOURCES OF CREDIT INFORMATION

General Mercantile Agency

Special or Trade Agencies

Credit Interchange

Agencies Reporting on Individuals and Making Special Investigations —Published Services

Salesmen as Credit Reporters

Attorneys as Credit Reporters

Banks as Credit Reporters

The Personal Interview

2. LAW OF CREDIT INSTRUMENTS

Law Relating to Checks

Law Relating to Notes

Law Relating to Drafts or Bills of Exchange

3. HOW TO WRITE CREDIT LETTERS

4. HOW TO WRITE COLLECTION LETTERS

Collection Reminders

Letters for the Early Stages of Collection

Letters for the Middle Stages of Collection

Letters for the Late Stages of Collection

Miscellaneous Collection Problems Handled by Letter

5. HOW TO USE FORM COLLECTION LETTERS

6. COLLECTION METHODS

SECTION 10

Credits and Collections

1. SOURCES OF CREDIT INFORMATION

Classification of sources of credit information.—The sources to which a credit man can turn for information concerning an applicant for credit may be classified as follows: (1) general mercantile agency; (2) special or trade agencies; (3) agencies reporting on individuals and making special investigations; (4) published services; (5) salesmen; (6) attorneys; (7) banks; (8) personal interviews. Each of these sources is discussed in the following pages.

General Mercantile Agency

Information from mercantile agencies.—Mercantile agencies have been established to ascertain the credit position of persons in business and to provide prompt and reliable information for subscribers to the agency services. Agencies ordinarily try to anticipate inquiry and provide subscribers with either a book of ratings, giving a general capital and credit estimate, or with a detailed report. Mercantile agencies are both general and special. The general agency covers a vast field and extends its services to foreign countries. The special agency limits its field to a particular branch of business and specializes within an industry.

Dun & Bradstreet, Inc.—The general mercantile agency of Dun & Bradstreet, Inc., maintains a central office in New York City and branch offices throughout the country. Its system of reporting covers the entire country by dividing it into districts, each of which is identified by a number. An attempt is made to reach every merchant, no matter how remote his location. The agency maintains a nation-wide network of trained reporters and correspondents.

The credit reporter interviews the merchant at his place of business, discusses his financial condition and sales trend, and observes his merchandising methods, his stock, his location, and competition. The investigator also calls upon local sources of credit information.

The agency provides subscribers with both rating books and special reports. Because of the peculiar character of its service, Dun & Bradstreet requires that all reports be held in strict confidence. Moreover, it does not sell its books, but lends them as property of the agency to be returned to the agency for disposal upon the issuance of a new edition.

Dun & Bradstreet ratings.—Dun & Bradstreet ratings are compiled in books and issued every two months by the agency to its subscribers. The present edition contains about two million names and covers concerns in the United States and Canada. The names of companies are arranged alphabetically under city location, and the type of outlet is identified by a symbol. The rating books contain maps of the states, lists of banks, and a compilation of State collection and bankruptcy laws. The population of each town or city is stated and its banking facilities indicated. For the convenience of salesmen and others, the agency also publishes the rating books in State pocket editions, issued twice a year.

Nature of Dun & Bradstreet ratings.—A Dun & Bradstreet rating presents condensed conclusions, in the form of a letter, to show a concern's "estimated pecuniary strength" and a number to show its "general-credit" standing. The symbol may be omitted when there are peculiar conditions or insufficient information to justify the assignment of a rating.

As indicated by the key, reproduced in Figure 74, the numerals have different significance when allied with different capital ratings. Thus the highest general-credit rating for a concern rated AA as to estimated pecuniary strength is A1, while the highest general-credit rating for a concern rated E as to estimated pecuniary strength is 2.

How to use Dun & Bradstreet ratings.—The Dun & Bradstreet ratings may be used as follows:

1. As a means of checking small rush orders that have to be passed on immediately.

Subscribers are warned to consult the detailed reports in our possession in every case involving credit. Reasonable prudence requires that they should do this. The date of this book is the month of its publication. It was compiled before that month. Changes in names and ratings are numerous each business day. Also, the work is so vast that other causes of error are not and cannot always be avoided. Hence, we assume no responsibility to subscribers for the correctness of the ratings herein.

		Left-Hand Column Estimated Pecuniary Strength	Right-Hand Column General Credit: *High*	*Good*	*Fair*	*Limited*
*1	AA	Over $1,000,000	A1	1	1½	2
	A+	Over 750,000	A1	1	1½	2
	A	$500,000 to 750,000	A1	1	1½	2
	B+	300,000 to 500,000	1	1½	2	2½
	B	200,000 to 300,000	1	1½	2	2½
	C+	125,000 to 200,000	1	1½	2	2½
*2	C	75,000 to 125,000	1½	2	2½	3
	D+	50,000 to 75,000	1½	2	2½	3
	D	35,000 to 50,000	1½	2	2½	3
	E	20,000 to 35,000	2	2½	3	3½
*3	F	10,000 to 20,000	2½	3	3½	4
	G	5,000 to 10,000		3	3½	4
	H	3,000 to 5,000		3	3½	4
	J	2,000 to 3,000		3	3½	4
*4	K	1,000 to 2,000		3	3½	4
	L	500 to 1,000			3½	4
	M	Less than 500			3½	4

**Numerical Rating* — When a numeral *only* (1, 2, 3 or 4) follows a name in the Reference Book it is an indication that the financial strength, while not definitely determined, is considered within the range of the ($) figures in the corresponding bracket, and that a condition is believed to exist which warrants credit in keeping with that assumption.

Absence of Rating — The absence of *any* rating following a name signifies circumstances which preclude forming a definite decision as to financial strength or credit standing of the individual or concern named, and should suggest to the Subscriber the advisability of reading the detailed report.

Dividend Partner Liability — Where an italic *d* in parentheses precedes a rating, it is an indication that one or more of the partners in the firm are liable in another or other firms, and the responsibility is in that sense divided. THUS: (*d*) B + 1.

Ratings of Branch Houses should always be looked up at Headquarters. The letters "N. Q." at the foot of any report mean: *not quoted* in the Reference Book.

Figure 74.—Key to Dun & Bradstreet Ratings.

2. As a preliminary sales guide to determine whether an order warrants attention.

3. As a check upon other credit information.

4. As a source of information when a periodical revision of the credit file is being made. A change in rating, either up or down, indicates that a change in the line of credit should be made upward or downward as the case may be.

5. As a guide to determine whether a credit report is necessary.

Limitations in the use of credit ratings.—Ratings by Dun & Bradstreet are intended to serve mainly as an index to the contents of the reports. The cautious credit man is seldom guided solely by the rating when he is considering a risk of any great amount. He wants to know all the details and to reach his own conclusions, which may or may not be the same as the agency's.

The credit man should recognize that a rating, while an accurate picture today, may be quite untrue a month hence because of the dynamic nature of business. Rating books are subject to constant revision in many particulars besides ratings. New names are added, old names removed, and addresses kept up to date. About 130,000 changes occur monthly. Hence, in the case of a fairly large account, the credit man will need to supplement the rating with more current information.

Dun & Bradstreet reports.—When a subscriber desires more information than is afforded by the Dun & Bradstreet rating book, he may ask the agency to give him a detailed report on the individual or firm. The subscriber may receive a full analysis of an account over the telephone by calling a special number. This analysis includes all information in the report. The subscriber's contract with the agency makes provision for a certain number of reports during the year. Inquiries in excess of the contract figure are charged for additionally.

All reports are uniform in style, and facts are presented in order of credit importance. The reports are subject to an automatic follow-up. The subscriber's number is registered to indicate that he is interested in a certain concern, and for a year all reports written on that concern are voluntarily supplied him. At the end of this time the subscriber is notified that he has been served for one year, and he is asked if he wishes further reports on the concern. This continuous service affords an automatic vigil on customers and prospects. Colors used on the right-hand border of the reports show at a glance the credit importance of the individual or firm: green indicates no change in the rating; amber warns the credit man that a change in rating, either upwards or downwards, has occurred and cautions him to read carefully; and red heralds unfavorable or important information such as change of ownership, fire, death, suits, liens, and judgments.

All the reports have the same basic characteristics, but some have been developed in special classifications to suit the sales and credit needs of subscribers. These classifications are:

1. *Commercial narrative report.*—This report is prepared on medium-sized and small concerns and comprises the bulk of Dun & Bradstreet reports and listings in the reference book. The report consists of the history of the concern, methods of operation and fire hazard, financial statement, trade reports, summary, and rating.

2. *Analytical report.*—Dun & Bradstreet, Inc., issues analytical reports on large companies having a complicated financial structure. These reports are used by credit men, banks, and investment organizations and include information similar to that included in other reports, in addition to such data as the number of subsidiaries, the extent of stock ownership, and a description of intercompany merchandise sales or loans. These reports are divided into three sections and are usually long.

3. *Registered supervised report.*—Accounts in all lines which have important news value, and which have somewhat less complicated capital structures than lines suitable for analytical reporting, are covered in the registered supervised report. This report is divided into two sections with appended balance sheets. The first section summarizes the credit position of the business for quick decisions. Section two gives the history of the business and the complete antecedents of the principals, a full description of methods of operation, type of activities, products sold, territory covered, seasonal factors, and other pertinent features of interest, in addition to the terms of sale and the number of salesmen and accounts. Reports are automatically revised within six months of the report date appearing on the first page. In addition, current developments are reported immediately.

4. *Specialized-industries report.*—The specialized-industries report is prepared principally on retailers, and occasionally on wholesalers and manufacturers of wide credit interest in any line where trade problems, sales terms, or other factors are of a specialized nature. This type of report is used particularly in the following lines: shoes, furniture, coal, men's wear, women's wear, household electrical appliances, laundry and dry cleaning, lumber and building materials, and paint and varnish.

Supplementary services.—Besides the four standard reports prepared by Dun & Bradstreet, the following supplementary service divisions and departments prepare reports and offer assistance and information of value to the credit man:

1. *Insurance division.*—This division serves fire-insurance companies and general agencies. The division issues the regular commercial report, as well as a questionnaire-style report for fire and casualty underwriters.

2. *Municipal department.*—Reports prepared by the municipal department give the economic and social factors of cities, towns, and other governmental units, their administration, debt obligation, and current operations.

3. *Foreign division.*—The foreign division serves American exporters with a Foreign Report Service and the Latin America Sales Index. The Foreign Report Service prepares and has on file reports on the leading foreign customers for American goods. The Latin America Sales Index contains a list of more than 80,000 manufacturers, wholesalers, retailers, and professional men in the twenty-nine Latin-American countries. These concerns and individuals are rated by capital code key and trade code key. The index is supplemented periodically.

4. *Mercantile-claims division.*—This division supplies a service to Dun & Bradstreet subscribers in the collection of past-due accounts.

5. *Publications and letters of introduction.*—A monthly publication, *Dun & Bradstreet Review,* reporting general financial and market conditions is provided. Many special bulletins on general credit problems are also available.

Letters of introduction will be furnished to any subscriber permitting his representative to inquire for information at any of the agency's branch offices without extra charge.

6. *Research and statistical departments.*—The results of the work of the research and statistical division are made available in special bulletins, newspapers, trade papers, and in the *Dun & Bradstreet Review*.

Occasions for use of a Dun & Bradstreet report.—Some of the situations in which it is advisable to obtain a report are when:

1. The order is from a new account.
2. The order is of considerable size.
3. A change in rating has occurred.
4. The rating indicates that unfavorable conditions exist.
5. Examination of the ledger indicates that unfavorable tendencies in the account are developing.
6. Adverse information is obtained from trade sources.
7. The credit requested is disproportionate to the usual amount.

Illustration of commercial narrative report with continuous service.—The character of the service that Dun & Bradstreet renders its subscribers is illustrated in the following series of reports. This particular series reflects the decline of a once-flourishing business. The first report resulted from an inquiry from a subscriber. The report indicated that at the time the storekeeper's condition was apparently satisfactory, prospects appeared favorable, and his creditors had no complaints to make. On the basis of these facts the store was given a rating of F3. Six months later, new facts concerning this store came to the attention of the agency. Accordingly, the agency sent to all of its subscribers who had previously manifested an interest in this account, a report having an amber border, indicating a change in rating from F3 to F3½. Another amber report sent six months after the second report reflected another drop in the credit rating. The fourth report, on red paper, warned of unfavorable news.

Service on all but the first report was voluntary on the part of the agency and illustrates the continuous service, which is a part of the original report, offered to the subscribers for a period of one year after the original request is received.

[*REPORT TO AGENCY SUBSCRIBER*]

Furniture Division

COWLES & COLVIN, Inc.	Furniture, Floor Coverings & Draperies	JAMAICA, L. I., N.Y.C. Boro of Queens 166–02 Walker Avenue

John H. Cowles, Pres.
Allen Colvin, Secty.
Frank Tobin, Treas.

DIRECTORS: The officers
CD 764 1 February 15, 19__

History

Incorporated under New York laws, September 15, 19__, with an authorized capital of $25,000, of which $9,000 is now paid in. The Tangible Net Worth as of December 31, 19__ was $13,479. Capital stock ownership is equally divided among the three officers. The business was started from a smaller store at 162–12 Jamaica Avenue, but on January 10, 19__, larger quarters were rented at the present address.

John H. Cowles, who is 36, married, and native born, started business in 19__, purchasing a curtain and drapery store at 21 Rogers Street, Brooklyn, N. Y., for $1,500. That store was sold in 19__ for $5,000. After two months, Cowles bought a financial interest in Bernstock & Conell, wholesale notions, at 1750 First Street, New York City. Following voluntary liquidation in 19__, creditors were paid in full.

Allen Colvin, 34, married, and native born, was employed as a salesman by the Smithville Drapery Co., retailers, Smithville, L. I., from 19__ until 19__. His initial investment in this business was represented by $1,000 savings and $1,500 borrowed from a relative, since repaid.

Frank Tobin, 38, married, and a native of Canada, came to this country in 19__, and is naturalized. For the next five years he was employed in the furniture department of Abrahams & March, Inc., department store, New York City. A small furniture store was opened by Tobin at 4096 Avenue A., Roselawn, L. I., in 19__ with $2,500 cash. That enterprise was sold in 19__ for $4,500. Tobin then began to sell a general line of household furnishings on a house-to-house basis, but after losing $2,000 in the next two years, discontinued and opened a dry goods store at 42 Cypress Avenue, Brooklyn, N. Y. In 19__, that store was liquidated, and $3,000 was realized from the sale. Tobin then invested $3,000 in this company.

Method of Operation—Fire Hazards

Retails medium- and low-priced curtains, draperies, floor coverings, occasional furniture, and a medium grade of custom-made living-room furniture. 25% of sales consist of draperies and curtains, 35% of floor coverings, and 40% furniture. Upholstered furniture is made by a local manufacturer against specific orders only; this company supplies the fabrics while the manufacturer furnishes all the other materials. 65% of sales are for cash, and 35% on 60- and 90-day charge-account terms. Clearance sales are held in February and August. Two floors are occupied measuring 25 x 50 feet, with two display windows. Premises are attractive. Location is in the center of the block on this main shopping street. All three officers are active, and a bookkeeper and truck driver are employed on a part-time basis. There are two stores carrying similar types of merchandise within the next three blocks. The early Spring and Fall months represent active periods, while sales in the Summer drop to a low level.

Rents this entire building comprising two floors and a basement. The basement is used for storage purposes. To the north there is a two-story building with a radio store on the ground floor and a beauty parlor overhead. To the south is a three-story motion picture theater. FIRE RECORD: No fires reported.

Statement

	Dec. 31, 19__	Dec. 31, 19__	Dec. 31, 19__
Current Assets	$ 8,421	$16,077	$15,228
Current Liabs.	1,200	4,110	3,729
Other Assets	2,729	2,516	1,980
Tangible Net Worth	9,950	14,483	13,479
Net Sales	42,320	61,976	62,191

From inventory of December 31, 19__:

Assets		Liabilities	
Cash	$ 3,422.63	Loans from Bank	$ 500.00
Accts. Rec.	4,612.72	Accts. Payable	2,970.15
Merchandise	7,192.65	Accruals	130.00
		Customers Deposits	129.00
Total current	$15,228.00	Total current	$ 3,729.15
Fixtures—net	1,065.00		
Truck	600.00		
Security Deposits	200.00	Common Stock	9,000.00
Prepaid	115.15	Surplus	4,479.00
Total assets	$17,208.15	Total	$17,208.15

Net sales, $62,191; cost of goods sold, $42,647; gross profit on sales, $19,544. Annual rent, $4,500. Other expenses and officers' salaries, $16,048. Net loss, $1,004. Fire insurance on merchandise and fixtures, $8,000. Merchandise valued at cost. Lease expires 19__. No receivables discounted or pledged for loans. No contingent liabilities. Bank loans are unsecured.

(Signed) Feb. 13, 19__ COWLES & COLVIN, Inc.
(by) John H. Cowles, President.

Based on audit by:
Robert Finchley, C. P. A., 120 Downey Street, New York City.

* * *

The net loss for 19__ is in contrast to a $1,533 profit for the preceding year, although sales for the two years were approximately the same. On the other hand, expenses in 19__ were higher, mainly because of a change in location and the addition of a furniture department. In view of the additional space needed for display, the larger store was leased at an increased rental of $500 a year. At the same time, $300 was spent for newspaper and pamphlet advertising, expenses increased $1,200 for additional help, and finally, with a third officer drawing, aggregate officers' salaries were increased $3,000 a year. While gross profit was 5% higher because the furniture markup is normally larger than that in the other departments, the inability to increase sales to the desired point, and heavier expenses brought about a moderate loss for the year.

Profitable operations of previous years and investment of $3,000 additional capital in 19__ made it possible to absorb last year's loss without changing financial condition materially. Trade liabilities, as in the past, are moderate in comparison with Tangible Net Worth and were incurred in the course of regular seasonal purchases. The bank loan, obtained on the endorsement of officers to assist seasonal buying, was paid at maturity. John H. Cowles, President, stated on February 15, 19__ that approximately 40% of the accounts receivable at December 31, 19__ had been collected and that all accounts over six months old are written off regularly. Seasonal merchandise at an approximate cost value of $500 is now being liquidated through the usual February clearance sale.

Trade Reports

(Feb. 15, 19__)

Hc	Owe	P. Due	Terms	Payments	Remarks
1500	370		2–30–60	Disc	Sold 3 yrs.
1000	173		2–30	Disc	Sold since 1933.
700	120		2–30	Disc	Selling for yrs.

Trade Reports (Cont.)

(Feb. 15, 19__)

Hc	Owe	P. Due	Terms	Payments	Remarks
500	200		2–30–60	Disc	Good account.
1000	400		2–30	Disc to Prompt	$600 on order.
800	300		4–70	Disc to Prompt	Sold two yrs. Satis.
500	100		4–70	Prompt	
300			2–30	Prompt	Will sell up to $2,000.
1200	1200		2–30–60	1st sale.	
1000	1000		2–30–60	1st sale.	

Summary

EXPENSES ARE RATHER HEAVY, BUT PRESENT FINANCIAL CONDITION IS WELL BALANCED.

[*CONTINUOUS SERVICE REPORT*]

[*This report, on amber-bordered paper, indicates a change in rating from F3 to F3½. Ed.*]

Furniture Division

COWLES & COLVIN, Inc.	Furniture, Floor Coverings & Draperies	JAMAICA, L. I., N.Y.C. Boro of Queens 166–02 Walker Avenue

John H. Cowles, Pres.
Allen Colvin, Secty.
Frank Tobin, Treas.
DIRECTORS: The officers
CD 764 1 August 15, 19__

History

[*Same as on page 968. Ed.*]

Method of Operation—Fire Hazard

[*Same as on page 969. Ed.*]

Statement

	Dec. 31, 19__	Dec. 31, 19__	June 30, 19__
Current Assets	$16,077	$15,228	$15,982
Current Liabs.	4,110	3,729	6,874
Other Assets	2,516	1,980	3,169
Tangible Net Worth	14,483	13,479	12,277
Net Sales	61,976	62,191	28,560 (6 mo.)

From inventory of June 30, 19__:

Assets		Liabilities	
Cash	$ 1,972.50	Accts. Payable	$ 5,424.37
Accts. Rec.	5,300.61	Accruals	250.62
Merchandise	8,709.20	Installment Notes on Leasehold Improvements	1,200.00
Total current	$15,982.31	Total current	$ 6,874.99
Fixtures—net	1,421.08		
Leasehold Improvements	1,200.00		
Truck	325.00	Common Stock	9,000.00
Deposits & Prepaid	223.60	Surplus	3,277.00
Total assets	$19,151.99	Total	$19,151.99

Net sales, 6 months, $28,560; cost of goods sold, $19,421; gross profit on sales, $9,139. Rent, 6 months, $2,250. Other expenses and officers' salaries, $8,091. Net loss, 6 months, $1,202. Fire insurance on merchandise and fixtures, $11,000. Merchandise valued at cost. Lease expires 19__. No receivables discounted or pledged for loans. No contingent liabilities.

(Signed) Aug. 13, 19__ COWLES & COLVIN, Inc.
(by) John H. Cowles, President.

Based on audit by:
Robert Finchley, C. P. A., 120 Downey Street, New York City.

* * *

For the six months ending June 30, 19__, sales and gross profit compared favorably with other years. On the other hand, increased expenses—principally rent, advertising, wages, and officers' salaries—brought about a net loss of $1,202. The heavier expenses resulted from the addition of a furniture department early in 19__.

As sales in the furniture department did not increase sufficiently to offset the greater expense, two new steps were taken in May, 19__, in an effort to expand volume: (1) extension of more liberal credit in the form of 9 months installment terms, and (2) addition of a line of case goods. A $3,000 stock of case goods was bought in June preparatory to the season starting in the latter part of July. In order to have adequate space, the basement was converted into a sales floor at a cost of $1,200, payment being made by six unsecured notes of $200 each, due monthly starting August 1, 19__.

Losses have reduced Tangible Net Worth and, as the result of a larger investment in inventory and expenditures for store renovations, liabilities have become heavy.

Trade Reports

(Aug. 15, 19__)

Hc	Owe	P. Due	Terms	Payments	Remarks
2100	840		90	Prompt	Sold 4 yrs.
1530	650		70	Prompt	Sold 1 yr. On order $1,700.
1000	500		60	Prompt	Selling for yrs.
1200	1200	400	2–30	Prompt to slow 30	
800	400	100	2–10–EOM	Prompt to slow 15	Now becoming a little slow.
1000	800		2–30–60	Slow 30	Slowing up.
800	300		2–30	Slow 15	Satisfactory.
500			2–30–60	Slow 30–60	No recent sale.
300	30	30	2–30–60	Slow 45	On order $800.
200			2–30	Slow 60	No recent order.

Summary

SALES COMPARE FAVORABLY WITH OTHER YEARS, BUT EXPENSES ARE HEAVY, SELLING TERMS HAVE BEEN LENGTHENED, AND AFFAIRS ARE IN A SOMEWHAT UNBALANCED CONDITION.

F 3 to F 3½

[*CONTINUOUS SERVICE REPORT*]

[*This report, on amber-bordered paper, indicates another drop in the rating. Ed.*]

Furniture Division

COWLES & COLVIN, Inc.	Furniture, Floor Coverings & Draperies	JAMAICA, L. I., N.Y.C. Boro of Queens 166-02 Walker Avenue

John H. Cowles, Pres.
Allen Colvin, Secty.
Frank Tobin, Treas.

DIRECTORS: The officers
CD 764 1 February 10, 19__

History

[*Same as on page 968. Ed.*]

Method of Operation—Fire Hazard

[*Same as on page 969, except that last sentence of first paragraph is omitted. Ed.*]

Statement

	Dec. 31, 19__	Dec. 31, 19__	Dec. 31, 19__
Current Assets	$16,077	$15,228	$29,042
Current Liabs.	4,110	3,729	17,289
Other Assets	2,516	1,980	2,526
Tangible Net Worth	14,483	13,479	14,320
Net Sales	61,976	62,191	65,329

From inventory as of December 31, 19__:

Assets		Liabilities	
Cash	$ 670.30	Accts. Payable	$ 7,289.30
Accts. Rec. Pledged	15,000.00	Notes Payable—Relative (Unsecured)	2,500.00
Accts. Rec. Unpledged	7,355.40	Due Finance Co. (Secured)	7,500.00
Merchandise	6,017.20		
Total current	$29,042.90	Total current	$17,289.30
Fixtures—net	1,126.40		
Leasehold Improvements	1,100.00		
Truck—net	200.00	Common Stock	9,000.00
Deposits & Prepaid	140.00	Surplus	5,320.00
Total assets	$31,609.30	Total	$31,609.30

Net sales, $65,329.40; cost of goods sold, $39,197.40; gross profit on sales, $26,131. Annual rent, $4,500. Other expenses, including drawings, $25,290. Net profit, $841. Merchandise valued at cost. Lease expires 19__. No contingent liabilities.

(Signed) Feb. 19, 19__ COWLES & COLVIN, Inc.
(by) John H. Cowles, President.

Based on audit by:
Robert H. Finchley, C. P. A., 120 Downey Street, New York City.

* * *

Formerly only curtains and draperies were handled, but since 19__ furniture sales have been emphasized and, largely because of changes in selling terms, a generally unbalanced condition is reflected in the latest year-end statement.

Until 19--, volume was insufficient to produce the margin needed to cover increased rent, employees' wages, and advertising, and, in order to expand sales, selling terms were liberalized. Prior to 19--, 65% of sales were on a cash basis and the balance on 60-day open-account terms. Last year, however, sales for cash constituted only 15% of the total volume, while 60% of sales were made on 9-months installment terms and 25% on 60 and 90 days' open account. Although a larger margin of profit on sales was obtained, only a small net profit was realized for 19--, and net working capital at December 31, 19-- was represented almost entirely by installment accounts receivable.

A loan of $7,500 was obtained from a finance company in October, 19--, secured by pledge of installment receivables in a ratio of 2 to 1. Also, a $2,500 loan was obtained from a relative of one of the officers on an unsecured basis. Nevertheless, trade payables have not been held to a figure where normal 60- and 70-day maturities can be met, as indicated by the trade report of February 10, 19--. Fully two thirds of the sales for the last six months of 19-- were on the books as installment or charge-account receivables at the close of the year, and liabilities at December 31, 19-- were considerably in excess of Tangible Net Worth.

Interviewed on February 10, 19--, John H. Cowles, President, stated that an additional $1,000 has been borrowed on the same basis as previously from the finance company. He also stated that sales for January, 19--, were 5% ahead of those for January, 19--.

Trade Reports

(Feb. 10, 19--)

Hc	Owe	P. Due	Terms	Payments	Remarks
3100	1840		90	Prompt	
2610	1000		70	Prompt	
1500	500	200	60	Slow 10–20	Sold 3 yrs. to date.
1200	400	240	60	Slow 30	Now limiting.
1000	359	259	30	Slow 60	Unsatisfactory.
830	570	400	2–30	Slow 30–60	PLACED FOR COLLECTION.
612	400	309	2–30	Slow 60–90	Unsatisfactory.
519			4–70	Slow 70	Closed by dated check.
325	312	112	2–30–60	Slow 90	Trend slow.
210	100	100	2–30–60	Slow 60–90	
100	50	50		Slow	

Summary

RECEIVABLES AND LIABILITIES HAVE INCREASED SUBSTANTIALLY, AND LATE FIGURES REFLECT A GENERALLY UNBALANCED POSITION.

F 3½ to --

[*SPECIAL NOTICE*]

[*This notice, with a red border, gives warning of unfavorable news. Ed.*]

Furniture Division

COWLES & COLVIN, Inc.	Furniture, Floor Coverings & Draperies	JAMAICA, L. I., N.Y.C. Boro of Queens 166-02 Walker Ave.

SN 764 1 July 30, 19__

On July 30, 19__, a petition for an Arrangement was filed under Chapter XI of the Amended Chandler Act. The petition listed liabilities of $19,465, of which $10,000 were secured; and assets of $28,-765. It was stated in the petition that accumulation of installment and charge account receivables, together with resulting heavy indebtedness, was the primary cause of present financial difficulty. A 35% settlement is proposed.

Special or Trade Agencies

Two kinds of special agencies.—Special agencies are either mutual or privately operated. The former are voluntary associations of manufacturers, jobbers, and wholesalers, organized for the purpose of gathering and disseminating credit information among the members. Credit bureaus are set up, and the members contribute to the support of the agency. The private agencies are maintained for purposes of profit to their proprietors and sell their services to subscribers. Many maintain collection departments as a regular part of the organization.

Special agencies confined to a single industry.—Special or trade agencies report only on concerns in particular industries. Among special agencies are the Credit Clearing House, Inc.; National Credit Office, Inc.; Credit Interchange Bureau of the National Association of Credit Men; Lyon's Furniture Mercantile Agency; Lumbermen's Credit Association, Inc.; Shoe and Leather Mercantile Agency; Jeweler's Board of Trade; Produce Reporter Co.; and many others. The services rendered by the special agencies mentioned are briefly described beginning on page 978.

While, from the standpoint of the agencies themselves, the general agency and the special agency consider each other as competitors, from the viewpoint of the credit man the two might well be looked upon as complementary.

Services of special agencies.—The services and methods of operation differ in the various special agencies. The more important and more usual services are as follows:

1. *Special-agency ratings.*—Most of the special agencies issue rating books, although some of the mutual agencies do not. The ratings used by special agencies are often somewhat different in form from general-agency ratings.

2. *Special-agency reports.*—The reports supplied by the special agencies follow for the most part the pattern of the general-agency reports. They are likely, however, to contain more complete ledger information, especially where the co-operation of members is active. Subscribers are permitted a certain number of reports under their contracts, and they are required to pay an additional fee if they exceed that number.

3. *Special-agency "credit-recommendation" service.*—A feature of the work of some of the special agencies is their so-called "credit-recommendation" or "credit-checking" service. Inquiry may be made either in writing, on a form supplied by the agency, or by telephone. The agency responds by making a definite recommendation as to whether or not the order in question should be shipped. The subscriber may request merely the recommendation, or may ask for a report. Where a report is obtained, a recommendation is appended to it.

4. *Special-agency weekly bulletins.*—In addition to the rating books and reports, the special agencies, in practically every instance, issue weekly bulletins. These are sent to all subscribers and indicate, usually by states, facts such as the following about merchants in the line: change in firm name; change in rating; change in location; death of an officer; incorporation; robbery; fire; loss by swindle; attachments; assignments; claims for collection; and bankruptcy. In short, anything that would be of interest to a creditor of these merchants is included.

5. *Special-agency tracers.*—Another feature of special-agency service is the so-called tracer, or clearing-house report. A creditor in doubt about a certain account may request the agency to look up the recent information received from other creditors who have had

experience with the account; the agency may also, from its own observation, deem it wise to initiate such an inquiry. The agency then circularizes its membership for information on the account in question, offering to furnish all those who supply information with a tabulation of the results. In this way there is made available to all who co-operate a complete statement of the status of the particular merchant's accounts with the trade in general. This interchange is a valuable feature of the special-agency service.

6. *Collection service.*—A collection department is operated for members by some of the special agencies.

Examples of the various types of special-agency service will be found in the descriptions of the leading special agencies given below.

Credit Clearing House, Inc.—One of the largest specialized agencies is the Credit Clearing House, whose credit-checking service covers retailers and jobbers in men's and women's ready-to-wear, dry goods, and allied industries. Subscribers are primarily manufacturers and wholesalers of wearing apparel. Located throughout the country in principal cities and marketing areas are branch offices, some of which clear credit information for industries not covered by other branches. As soon as credit information is received at a branch office, it is sent on to the New York office, where it is placed in the master-card folder. These folders thus provide a centralized record of all credit information and reflect the buyer's activities in all markets on the same day that commitments are made. Information is gathered from personal interviews and investigations, trade clearances, statements, banking data, and a continuous record of the account's buying and payment experiences, as indicated by inquiries from subscribers. Credit files are continuously revised upon the credit-manager's recommendation, usually when a negative factor appears.

How the Credit Clearing House operates.—The Credit Clearing House provides information only when a subscriber inquires about a particular account, except for a provision to notify inquiring subscribers of any change in recommendations within one year following the date of inquiry. Inquiries are answered with a recommendation (see Figure 75) that shipment be made or withheld. Both inquiry and answer are usually made by telephone, teletype, or telegraph and confirmed by mail the same day. Recommendations are made by a member of the credit staff after a review of the current inquiry and master-card data. Master cards consist of: (1) a folder containing all credit reports and general information, and (2) attached cards on which are recorded every credit inquiry.

OFFICES IN ALL PROMINENT TRADE CENTRES

CONFIDENTIAL

THE CREDIT CLEARING HOUSE

JOHN W. CAMPBELL
CHAIRMAN OF THE BOARD

EXECUTIVE OFFICES
15 VANDERBILT AVENUE,
NEW YORK, N.Y.

Answering your inquiry:

We recommend that you ship this order. Current information is satisfactory.

R-16

THIS RECOMMENDATION COVERS THIS ORDER ONLY.
INQUIRE ON ALL RE-ORDERS.

IMPORTANT—
NOTIFY US IF ACCOUNT BECOMES 30 DAYS PAST DUE.
INQUIRE IF YOU RECEIVE CHANGE OF RECOMMENDATION.

THE CREDIT CHECKING DEPARTMENT.

Figure 75.—Credit Clearing House Recommendation.

2—C.C.D.

INQUIRY TICKET

(Always use this form when inquiring regarding ALL ORDERS and PAST DUE ACCOUNTS

THE CREDIT CLEARING HOUSE Date........................

Name Street Always important

Trading as Town State

Successors to Also at

Amount of Order	Terms	Date of Shipment	Highest Credit in two years	Amount Owing	Amount Past Due	When Due	Manner of Payment	How Long Sold	Returns Goods Unfair Discounts Unfair Claims

Amount of Back orders unfilled. DO NOT WRITE IN THIS SPACE SUBSCRIPTION NO.

If you have sold before, it is essential that you give previous ledger experience above.

Figure 76.—Credit Clearing House Inquiry Ticket.

The latter thus give a cumulative credit and payment record for several years.

An inquiry (see Figure 76) must show the subscriber's code number and type of goods sold, the dollar amount and date of shipment of the order in question, the previous high credit granted, the amount owing and the due dates, and the length of the subject's account with the subscriber.

Part of the member's subscription number indicates his market area. This code, together with the key letter indicating the type of merchandise sold and the daily chronological record of inquiries from all markets in which any order has been placed, is the agency's first indication of fraudulent purchasing.

Services offered by the Credit Clearing House.—When the agency's recommendation is to be confirmed in writing, it may be done in one of the following ways:

1. A checking-service recommendation as to whether or not to ship, with the reason given where the advice is negative.
2. A digest report giving a brief review of the essential credit facts contained in the files, in addition to a financial statement and recommendation.
3. An analytical report showing in detail the trade's experience with the account, payment record, antecedents, agency comments upon methods of operation, financial statement, and recommendation.

The subscriber requests the type of report he will need to confirm each individual inquiry. Naturally, the price differs for each type of report.

The Credit Clearing House also offers to its subscribers rating books listing approximately 350,000 accounts. These books indicate with symbols the capital and credit rating as well as the agency's own opinion of the account's current trading position. This opinion is drawn from a working-capital analysis on the basis of which the working capital is rated as excellent, good, fair, restricted, and poor. A fourth symbol also appears when an important part of the total net worth is represented by real-estate equities or other assets not usually considered as working capital. Rating books are revised four times a year.

National Credit Office, Inc.—Another specialized mercantile agency is the National Credit Office, Inc. This agency is affiliated with Dun & Bradstreet, Inc., but operates as an entirely separate unit with headquarters in New York City and branches in Boston, Chicago, Cleveland, Detroit, and Philadelphia. The agency reports on almost every concern in the country that is a manufacturer, converter, or wholesaler of textiles and steel products, and a manufacturer of rubber, leather goods, furniture, and paints. No retail concerns are covered except chain stores operating in the above industries, large furniture stores, and department stores.

Credit-line suggestions made by the National Credit Office, Inc.—The agency's reports summarize the credit responsibility of the subject on the basis of a thorough personal investigation and analysis of the subject's credit position. If a concern is in a satisfactory condition, the report will make a definite suggestion regarding the average amount of credit to be extended by merchandise suppliers. If the concern is a marginal enterprise, no suggestions are made. The line of credit suggested is for an average order with source of supply well spread. When a subscriber supplies an account with the larger part of his requirements, the agency will provide the subscriber with a specialized report by telephone or personal letter and increase the suggested credit line in proportion to the subscriber's importance as a supplier.

In a typical textile report, for instance, the amount of credit is determined by dividing the normal seasonal purchase requirements of the concern by the number of its merchandise suppliers. In addition to the suggested credit line, the report will show: the firm's name and address; names of officers or principals at interest; brief synopsis of the principal's records; trend of the business; summarized current financial condition and trend; current detailed trade investigation; names of important sources of supply; and an analysis of the record and financial condition. A second page gives a more detailed record of the method of operation and principals. A photographic copy of the latest available balance sheet is also provided. Wherever unusual items require explanation, the necessary supplemental details appear.

Reports of the National Credit Office, Inc.—National Credit Office, Inc., reports are revised automatically twice a year by means of a tickler system. Further revisions are made whenever any unfavorable information concerning an account is obtained either from within the trade or from the financial statement. The agency maintains a file supply of all reports. In this way it has immediately available for subscribers information about any account for which a report has previously been made.

The agency maintains a master card for each concern. When an inquiry is made, a file copy of the report is immediately sent to the inquiring subscriber, and the number of the subscriber making the inquiry and the date are entered on the master card. This record of inquiries on the master card is used in sending out revised reports. All subscribers who have inquired about any account are furnished revised reports and current financial statements for a year following the date of inquiry. When the year is up, the subscriber is automatically recharged for the service and receives the next report on the account with a card notifying him of the renewal of the service. If the subscriber wishes the service to be discontinued, he returns the card.

Reference rating books published by National Credit Office, Inc.—The steel department is the only department in the National Credit Office for which reference books with ratings are available in addition to the specialized reports. A separate reference book is published monthly for each of the department's four divisions: manufacturers whose products are made largely of steel; manufacturers of radio sets, parts, and accessories; manufacturers of aeronautical engines, aircraft, and their distributors; and jobbers of automotive parts, radios, and radio supplies. The reference books are in loose-leaf form and contain a credit rating or classification as well as valuable supplementary data. Generally included in the supplementary data are the amount of current assets and current debts; net worth at successive dates over a period of years; names of all officers; estimated annual capacity; number of units actually produced yearly for several years; and a running monthly tabulation of the manner in which trade payments are made to primary suppliers. In reports on jobbers, mention is made of the principal products handled for trade-promotion purposes. These reference books are valuable not only for credit-reference purposes but also as leads for sales departments.

Supplementary activities of the National Credit Office, Inc.—The National Credit Office, Inc., has two additional services—the trade-group meetings and the sales service.

The agency prepares materials for and participates in the monthly discussions of fourteen credit groups in the textile, rubber and steel products, and paint and varnish industries. In most groups each member may submit for discussion up to a certain number of crucial or questionable accounts, usually five to ten. The names are given to the agency two days prior to the meeting and are immediately investigated to obtain all available current information. The agency's reports, combined with data that the members bring to the meeting, provide an adequate basis for judging the current financial condition and paying habits of these concerns.

The sales service consists of a card index on all active concerns in each industry covered by the agency. Some lines are broken down into refined-price groups. Each card shows the product manufactured or handled and the approximate amount of annual sales. Subscribers to this service receive cards automatically for the particular line of industry in which they are interested. They are used, of course, for lining up prospective customers.

Credit Interchange Bureau of the National Association of Credit Men.—The National Association of Credit Men is the professional and service organization of the commercial credit managers and financial executives of the United States. It is a nonprofit, co-operative corporation, founded in 1896, and owned and controlled by its membership, which is made up of producers, manufacturers, wholesalers, financial institutions, and other firms in the commercial field. Its membership comprises approximately 20,000 firms in the above categories, locally organized in affiliated units at the major distributing centers of the country. These local credit associations are co-ordinated to make up the national system known as the National Association of Credit Men.

The Credit Interchange Bureaus of the National Association of Credit Men are national in scope. A central clearance bureau is maintained in St. Louis, Missouri. The actual work of collecting the data and handling inquiries is done by local bureaus located throughout the country. Inquiries can be made only on current accounts and on prospective customers whose applications for credit have already been received. The system cannot be used for sales-promotion work, for it is not intended that inquiry should be made merely for the purpose of finding out, from the experiences of others, whether it would be worth while to solicit a certain account. In the case of an account already on his books, the inquirer must state on the inquiry sheet his own ledger experience.

Procedure of the Credit Interchange Bureau of the National Association of Credit Men.—The Credit Interchange Bureau's procedure for gathering and disseminating information requires that each local bureau obtain from each of its members, as a condition of membership, a complete list of customers and the names of new credit applicants as they come in. An identifying number or symbol is given to each member of the system. The key to this number is treated by some local bureaus as strictly confidential, while others make the key available in list form to all their members. The names of all customers reported by the members are filed. Each such record shows a list of all members reporting this name as an account on the books.

Members are furnished inquiry blanks (see Figure 77), which they are to use to request information and report their own experience. The member may request a preliminary or complete report, which takes more time to prepare. If the bureau has a current

MEMBER INQUIRY AND REPORTING FORM
CREDIT INTERCHANGE BUREAUS, Phone CHestnut 6177
P. O. Box 1294 Central Station, St. Louis, Mo.

VIGILANTIA — REG. U.S. PAT. OFF.

Name .... Date ....
Trade Style .... Business ....
Address (Give Street, City, State, Branches if any, etc.)

WE HAVE FIRST ORDER $........ IF ORDER WAS UNSOLICITED CHECK HERE ☐
WE HAVE REQUEST FOR SAMPLES ☐ QUOTATIONS ☐ CATALOG ☐

WE HAVE HAD THE FOLLOWING UNSATISFACTORY EXPERIENCE:
☐ Taking unearned discounts ☐ Making unjust claims ☐ Countermanded order
☐ Returning merchandise ☐ Checks returned

SEND US REPORTS AS INDICATED BY CHECK BELOW:
SINGLE REPORT ☐ AUTOMATIC REVISION REPORTS 4 MOS. ☐ 6 MOS. ☐

Our previous experience as follows: Report Dollars Only.

HOW LONG SOLD	DATE OF LAST SALE	HIGHEST CREDIT	AMOUNT OWING (INCLUDE NOTES)	AMOUNT PAST DUE	UNFILLED ORDERS	TERMS OF SALE	MANNER OF PAYMENT
							☐ Discounts ☐ Pays When Due .... Days Slow

Comments........

List references and known sources of supply below:

(Use reverse side for further references)

No.

Figure 77.—Inquiry Ticket of Credit Interchange Bureaus of National Association of Credit Men.

report, this will be supplied. Otherwise, the old report is sent, stamped by some bureaus to indicate that a revision is under way, and all members listed on the customer's card as dealing with him are notified and receive inquiry blanks. When the replies from all members solicited for information are received, a report is prepared and sent to all the members requesting it. This procedure is also used for a name that does not appear in the bureau's files to date. Information may also be secured by telephoning the bureau.

The N.A.C.M. is now prepared to supply "Automatic Revisions" on a selected list of names. These names are cleared with suppliers at intervals designated by members, and the results are forwarded to subscribers to this service. In this way a continuous and up-to-date picture of payment habits is available on doubtful accounts.

Clearing credit information through the Central Bureau.—Since the local bureau is restricted to a certain zone, and the subject concern may be trading outside of this zone, the local bureau automatically effects a clearance through the Central Bureau in St. Louis. The Central Bureau does not tabulate reports or gather and disseminate ledger experience. It merely oversees the system and records all markets interested in individual accounts. If the records of the Central Bureau indicate that the subject concern is trading in zones other than the zone in which the inquiry was originally made, the Central Bureau forwards to the other local bureaus a request for a clearance for the benefit of the inquiring bureau. Each bureau then mails its report directly to the bureau making the original inquiry.

Credit Interchange Bureau report.—The Credit Interchange report is intended to give an accurate, positive picture of all transactions, just as the debtor himself has set them down on the books of his creditors. The facts reported are the length of time the account has been sold, the highest recent credit, amount owing, amount past due, terms of sale, manner of payment, and general comments. Such information reveals the character of the account, such as the limit of credit enjoyed, the amount of indebtedness due and past due, both open account and otherwise, manner of payments, and other facts. The general-comment column may contain reports of accounts placed for collection or reveal unethical practices, such as taking unearned discounts or unauthorized returns of merchandise.

CREDIT INTERCHANGE REPORT OF THE NATIONAL ASSOCIATION OF CREDIT MEN.

REPORT ON:

Business Classification	How Long Sold	Date of Last Sale	Highest Credit	Amount Owing	Amount Past Due	Unfilled or First Orders	Terms of Sale	Manner of Payment			Comments
								Discounts	*Pays When Due*	*Days Slow*	
DETROIT 731–127											
Drug	Yrs	6–42	424	317	317	225	2–10–30				Pays on account to 12 months slow.
CHICAGO 804–1038											
Fdp	3–35	6–42	17				2–10–30		x		
Paper	1932	6–42	2000	1000	1000		2–10–30			180	
LOUISVILLE 804–315											
Paint	Yrs	9–41	484	169	169		60			6–12 mos	Claim in Adjustment Bureau, N.A.C.M.
PHILADELPHIA 804–419											
Glass	Yrs	7–41	114	85	82		30			150	
Drug	Yrs	7–41	800	522	522		2–10–30			45	

REPORT ON:

Business Classification	How Long Sold	Date of Last Sale	Highest Credit	Amount Owing	Amount Past Due	Unfilled or First Orders	Terms of Sale	Manner of Payment			Comments
								Discounts	*Pays When Due*	*Days Slow*	
CENTRAL NEW YORK											
804–949											
Inst	8–32	3–42	88				30			60–90	Collected by attorney
CINCINNATI											
806–213											
Seed	6 mos	4–42	18				30			60	
News	2 yrs	7–41	19				30			30	
TOLEDO											
804–413											
Groc	Yr	7–42	77	77	77					180	Pays on account as he can.
Mfg	Yrs	1–42	37	21	21		2–10–30			60–120	
Jwly	Yrs	7–42	124	58			2–10–30	x			
INDIANAPOLIS											
804–229											
Drug	Yrs	6–42	519	233	231		2–10–30			180	
Chem	3–30	5–42	7				2–10–30			30–90	
				2482	2419	225					

Form 93

LYON - RED BOOK CREDIT KEY.

SPECIAL CREDIT CONDITIONS Based on General Information	CAPITAL RATINGS Estimated Financial Worth	PAY RATINGS Based on Majority Reports
When only "Capital" and "Pay" Ratings are given, **Credit** is assumed to be proportionately NORMAL, and nothing unusual or irregular in record or prospects.	**A** $1,000,000 or over **B** 500,000 to $1,000,000 **C** 300,000 to 500,000 **D** 200,000 to 300,000 **E** 100,000 to 200,000 **F** Financial responsibility believed high, but cannot estimate definitely.	1 - Discount. 2—Prompt. 3 - Medium. 4—Variable, prompt to slow. 5—Slow. 6—Very slow. 7—C. O. D. or C. B. D. 8—Pay rating not established, but information favorable. 9 — Claims to buy always for cash.
11—Credit restricted to very small amounts. **12**—Recently commenced, or reputation for credit apparently not established. **13**—Inquire for report. **14**—Good character and reputation only known basis for credit. **18**—Take discount in violation of terms. **19**—Very arbitrary and exacting. **20**—Make complaints, want allowances, or troublesome. **21**—Buys small, usually pays cash. **23**—Sells on commission. **24**—Name listed for convenience only. **25**—Capital rating based solely on statement. **29**—Rating blank or undetermined. **30**—Rating in abeyance, pending later information. **31**—Financial statement declined, or repeatedly requested and not received.	**G** 75,000 to 100,000 **H** 50,000 to 75,000 **J** 40,000 to 50,000 **K** 30,000 to 40,000 **L** 20,000 to 30,000 **M** 15,000 to 20,000 **N** 10,000 to 15,000 **O** 7,000 to 10,000 **P** Financial responsibility believed moderate, but cannot estimate definitely. **Q** 5,000 to 7,000 **R** 3,000 to 5,000 **S** 2,000 to 3,000 **T** 1,000 to 2,000 **U** 500 to 1,000 **V** 100 to 500 **W** Financial responsibility believed small, but cannot estimate definitely **Y** Financial responsibility believed very limited **Z** No financial basis for credit reported.	● or 112—New in business. ✤ or 116—New statement recently received. ▲—Indicates information of unusual importance. ⊙—Sells on installment plan ?—Sells from residence or office, or catalogue. Con—Denotes continued rating. R. F. D.—Rural Free Delivery —P. O. Address. The omission of a rating is not unfavorable but indicates that sufficient information is not at hand on which to base rating.

NOTE

No system of ratings can ALWAYS convey an accurate summarization of existing conditions. Book ratings reflect conditions believed to exist when assigned, and are based upon information obtained from financial statements, from the trade, special reporters, correspondents and other sources deemed reliable, but the correctness thereof is in no way guaranteed.

Conditions are constantly changing, and changes as made are shown in the "LYON Weekly Report and Supplement", and in Credit Reports.

Should any error, or inaccuracy in rating be noted, it should be reported only to the Agency, in order that correction may be made.

Inquire for Detailed Credit Report on all new accounts, and make inquiry at least once a year on old accounts or when change in rating is indicated in the "LYON Weekly Report and Supplement".

(OVER)

Figure 78a.—Key to Ratings of the Lyon Furniture Mercantile Agency.

SPECIAL RATINGS

Key Numbers interpreting Credit Items and Business Conditions as appear in

LYON WEEKLY REPORT AND SUPPLEMENT AND LYON NATIONAL INTERCHANGE CLEARING HOUSE OF TRADE EXPERIENCE

32—First order.
33—Settles by note.
34—Usually settle with notes, which are paid at maturity.
35—Pay notes, but slow on open account.
36—Takes extra time when giving notes.
37—Hard to collect from.
38—Would now refuse to sell.
39—Check returned unpaid, or protested.
40—Note returned unpaid, or protested.
41—Settles with trade acceptance.
42—Acceptance unpaid.
43—Has failed to answer important letters.
44—Turned order down.
45—Seems to be ordering freely.
46—Draft attached to B. of L.
47—Will not accept drafts.
48—Pays drafts.
49—Dissolved.
50—Succeeded by-
51—Rating raised to-
52—Rating lowered to-
53—Should rate, or rating changed to-
54—Rating suspended.
55—Given bill of sale, or notice thereof.
56—Reported selling out, or discontinuing
57—Sold out.
58—Sold out at auction.
59—Damaged by water.
60—Damaged by flood or storm.
61—Damaged by fire.
62—Burned out.
63—Partially insured.
64—Fully insured.
65—Stock not insured
66—No insurance.
67—Will continue.
68—Deceased.
69—Estate continues.
70—Claim for collection.
71—Disputed claim.
72—Claim settled direct.
73—Claim collected.
74—Claim returned as uncollectible.
75—Suit reported.
76—Execution issued.
77—Judgment reported.
78—Reported attached.
79—Closed by Sheriff or Marshal.
80—Sold out by Sheriff or Marshal.
81—Chattel mortgage.
82—Chattel mortgage foreclosed.
83—Deed of trust for benefit of creditors.
84—Real estate mortgage.
85—Real estate mortgage foreclosed.
86—Failed.
87—Assignment for benefit of creditors.
88—Petition for Receiver filed.
89—Temporary Receiver appointed.
90—Receiver appointed.
91—In hands of Receiver.
92—Voluntary petition in bankruptcy.
93—Involuntary petition in bankruptcy.
94—Petition for arrangement, reorganization extension or composition.
95—In bankruptcy.
96—Call for important new report.
97—Late report at office.
98—Trustee appointed.
99—In liquidation.
100—First dividend paid.
101—Second dividend paid.
102—Final dividend paid.
103—Asking extension.
104—Called meeting of creditors.
105—Offering to compromise.
106—Unable to locate.
107—Discontinued or out of business.
108—Claims should be given immediate attention.
109—Settled and resumed.
110—Settlement paid.
111—Removed to-
112 or ●—New in business.
113—Capital stock increased to-
114—Name changed to-
115—Cannot report definitely as yet.
116 or ✣—New statement recently received.
117—Received discharge in bankruptcy.
118—Discharge in bankruptcy denied.
119—Not listed, business foreign to lines covered.

(OVER)

Figure 78b.—Reverse Side of Key to Ratings of the Lyon Furniture Mercantile Agency (Fig. 78a).

Conversely, reports of progress in getting out of a bad-debt situation may appear here. The date of last sale is probably the most important information on the report, as the value of the information depends on its degree of recency. The table on pages 986–987 illustrates a credit-interchange report.

Lyon Furniture Mercantile Agency.—This agency reports on manufacturers, wholesalers, and retailers of furniture, carpets, floor coverings, lamps, mirrors, baby carriages, and refrigerators, and upon undertaking establishments in the United States. Credit reports give the business record of the officers; history of the business; size of assets, liabilities, and net worth of the company; comparative financial statements; trade experience; collection information; and a summary of the report. The agency maintains headquarters in New York City and branch offices in the key cities in the furniture trades.

Lyon Furniture Mercantile Agency issues a semiannual rating book called the *Lyon-Red Book* and supplements it weekly. A pocket-size travelers' edition of the rating book is available for any state, giving names of dealers, wholesalers, and manufacturers, as well as addresses, business classification, and ratings.

Through a "tracer sheet" sent weekly to subscribers, the experience of subscribers with concerns selected for current investigation because of some unusual circumstance is obtained. The tracer sheet is arranged to enable the subscriber to report on the manner in which the subject under investigation is paying bills. Special columns and codes simplify the reporting procedure. All users of the service that supply information on the tracer sheet are sent a copy of the report prepared on the basis of the information collected.

Lumbermen's Credit Association, Inc.—This agency, with headquarters in Chicago and a branch office in New York City, has been providing a thorough credit and collection service in the lumber and woodworking industries since 1876. The agency reports on manufacturers, wholesalers, retailers, larger consumers of lumber, importers, exporters, and commission men in the lumber industry. The reports contain current trade information; the latest financial statement available; antecedent information; the names of officers, directors, partners, or proprietor; a definite summing up of the credit risk; and a rating. An elaborate rating key indicates the estimated net worth and gives a pay rating and other information for the guidance of credit men.

The agency publishes a rating book twice a year in April and October and keeps the rating book up to date with twice-a-week supplements that are replaced monthly with a cumulative supplement. The supplements give notices of all changes of ownership, removals, deaths, lawsuits, fires, failures, new concerns, and other items of current interest. Through interchange among subscribers, the agency is able to offer co-operating subscribers tabulated results of ledger experience with accounts and reports on the payment record of delinquent accounts. The ledger-experience clearances are made through the agency's tracer system, under which a list of names is sent with the supplements to all subscribers with a request for detailed ledger experience. Subscribers who answer the tracer obtain all the tabulated tracer results on those particular names on which they gave their current experience.

Each subscriber obtains the number of special reports that he has contracted to receive. Extra reports are obtainable upon payment of a reasonable charge.

Shoe and Leather Mercantile Agency.—This agency maintains headquarters in Boston with branch offices in New York, Chicago, and Philadelphia and correspondents at other shoe and leather centers. The agency gives credit reports on tanners of leather; and manufacturers, wholesalers, and retailers of shoes, luggage, handbags, leather belts, and leather novelties. The reporting service is supplemented by four reference books published quarterly, containing the name, line of credit, and ratings. The key to ratings is shown in Figure 79. These books are further supplemented by weekly bulletins, keeping the information up to date (see Figure 80).

A tracer department sends out requests to members for information on companies that are being investigated, as illustrated in Figure 80, and, in return for the information, offers a copy of the report containing the ledger experience, and so on, of all who contribute to the report.

The agency also operates a collection department for its members.

Jewelers Board of Trade.—The Jewelers Board of Trade, a mutual, nonprofit membership association, gives a highly specialized credit service to its membership, which comprises manufactur-

Capital		High (1st)	Good (2d)	Fair (3d)	Limited (4th)
		Credit			
A	$1,000,000 and over.	A 1	B 1	C 1	D 1
B	500,000 to $1,000,000	A 1	B 1	C 1	D 1
C	350,000 to 500,000	B 1	C 1	D 1	E 1
D	200,000 to 350,000	B 1	C 1	D 1	E 1
E	150,000 to 200,000	B 1	C 1	D 1	E 1
F	100,000 to 150,000	B 1	C 1	D 1	E 1
G	75,000 to 100,000	B 1	C 1	D 1	E 1
H	50,000 to 75,000	C 1	D 1	E 1	E 2
K	35,000 to 50,000	C 1	D 1	E 1	E 2
L	25,000 to 35,000	C 1	D 1	E 1	E 2
M	15,000 to 25,000	C 1	D 1	E 1	E 2
N	10,000 to 15,000	D 1	E 1	E 1½	E 2
O	5,000 to 10,000	D 1	E 1	E 1½	E 2
P	3,000 to 5,000	D 1	E 1	E 1½	E 2
Q	1,500 to 3,000	D 1	E 1	E 1½	E 2
R	1,000 to 1,500		E 1	E 1½	E 2
S	500 to 1,000		E 1	E 1½	E 2
T	300 to 500			E 1	E 2
U	0 to 300				E 2
V	No financial basis for credit.				
W	Cannot estimate.	C 1	D 1	E 1	E 2

Key to Code Numbers

4 Not recommended for credit.
6 If interested, inquire at office.
10 Recently commenced business.
11 Partnership dissolved.
12 Retired.
13 Succeeded by.
14 Left town, moved away.
15 Removed to.
16 Sold or closed out business.
18 Advertising to sell out.
19 Reported selling or sold out.
20 Called meeting of creditors.
21 Embarrassed—suspended.
22 Assigned.
23 Failed.
24 Bankruptcy petition filed.
25 Receiver appointed.
26 Offering to compromise.
27 Asking general extension.
28 Extension granted.
29 Compromise effected.
30 Sued.
31 Judgment entered.
32 Attached.
33 Have given chattel-mortgage.
34 Chattel-mortgage foreclosed.
35 Closed by sheriff or execution.
36 Real estate mortgage.
38 Have given bill of sale.
39 Have given trust deed.
50 Claim collected by our draft or on demand.
50-X Claim collected by our Expert Office Service.
51 Claim collected by attorney.
53 Paid claim after suit.
70 Burned out.
71 Loss by fire.
73 Fully insured.
74 Partially insured.
75 No insurance.
76 Loss by flood or tornado.
77 Deceased.

Figure 79.—Key to Ratings of the Shoe & Leather Mercantile Agency, Inc.

The only mercantile agency representing exclusively the shoe and leather interests

NUMBER 3,981 — **BULLETIN** — March 17, 1941

The Shoe & Leather Mercantile Agency, Inc.

Established 1879

EXECUTIVE OFFICES

183 Essex Street, Boston, Mass.

New York Office, 277 Broadway — Chicago Office, 173 W. Madison St. — Philadelphia Office, 148–151 Bourse Building

The correctness of the items contained on this sheet is not guaranteed. They have been obtained from authorities deemed thoroughly reliable and are transmitted to you in accordance with the terms of your contract; and they are not to be divulged to the parties to whom they refer. Should any Subscriber find them incorrect, kindly communicate with this Agency at once.

ALABAMA

BIRMINGHAM
Hardin George L (1810 Third Ave N)....ret clo 10

CALIFORNIA

LOS ANGELES
Klitzke Harvey A ("Hollywood Foot Comfort Shop")....ret shoes....reported 30

CONNECTICUT

BRIDGEPORT
Berger Joseph N ("Joe's Army & Navy Store") (1367 Main St)....gen mdse..........Lee B Brooks elected trustee under $500 bond

EAST PORTCHESTER
Greenwich Footwear Corp....mfrs....reported 71 (water damage)

WILLIMANTIC
Rosenthal Sadie ("Eagle Shoe Store") (786 Main St)....ret shoes....13—Benjamin Prague

FLORIDA

PUNTA GORDA
Persons Grover C ("Persons Bros") (218–20 E Marion Ave). .ret shoes & clo....reported out of business

GEORGIA

BAINBRIDGE

NEW JERSEY

BURLINGTON
Levin Louis (341 High St)....ret shoes....notice of sale in bulk for March 20th

JERSEY CITY
Restful Footwear Co Inc (31 Wilkinson Ave) mfrs....trustees filed schedules listing Liab. $168,776 and Assets $185,320. 26—at 27½%

SUMMIT
Schmuckler Meyer (27 Maple St)... ..ret shoes 13—Sarah Hess

NEW YORK

BROOKLYN
Consolidated Sportswear Co Inc... ...sportswear recently incorporated

Davis Box Toe Co Inc (3611–14th Ave)....mfrs Michael Karet Treas 77

Fishman Meyer (370 Grand St)........ret shoes 13—Meyer & David Fishman

Hockman Rose (Mrs) ("Joe's Sample Novelty Shoes") (4115 13th Ave)....ret shoes....reported 71

Rogam Sportswear Corp. ..sportswear...recently incorporated

Sterlit P C Shoe Co Inc (291 Utica Ave).. ret shoes....reported 30

FARMINGTON
Bernies Army & Navy Store Inc....gen mdse recently incorporated

MOUNT VERNON

WISCONSIN

BELOIT
Groose & Boettge (406 E Grand Ave)...ret shoes H W Boettge partner withdrawn

Tracer Department

LEDGER EXPERIENCE is a vital and timely barometer of your customer's credit position.

FREE OF CHARGE, it is a potential that you simply cannot afford to forego. Check the names listed below carefully. They represent ac-

Figure 80.—Section of a Bulletin of The Shoe & Leather Mercantile Agency.

ers and wholesalers of silverware, watches, diamonds, precious, semiprecious, and imitation stones, syndicate merchandise; importers and exporters of precious stones; banks; insurance companies; and advertising agencies and representative organizations throughout the country that cater to the jewelry trade. The organization maintains a reporting division with headquarters in New York City, Providence, Chicago, and San Francisco.

Members may draw, without charge, one hundred credit reports a year and may obtain additional reports at a low charge. Twice a year, in March and September, the board publishes a reference book, known throughout the trade as the *Red Book*. The book contains the names and addresses, arranged geographically, business designations, and capital and credit ratings of those engaged in manufacturing, importing, wholesaling, and retailing jewelry, diamonds, precious stones, imitation stones, and the like. In addition, a weekly service bulletin is issued to members supplementing the reference book with new information. The service bulletin contains a record of changed ratings, deaths, dissolutions, incorporations, financial embarrassments, establishment of new outlets, and other information of interest and immediate importance to members. A "green-slip" service, which supplements the weekly service bulletins, gives interested members immediate, day-to-day news of financial embarrassments occurring in the jewelry trade. By subscription to *Continuous Service,* members can receive all credit reports and special notices issued on all subjects of inquiry for one year from the date of the original inquiry. The organization also conducts a research department, an advisory accounting department, a collection service, and an adjustment department that assists, as far as it is legally competent, in the adjustment of financial problems and affairs of honest debtors.

Produce Reporter Co.—The Produce Reporter Co. maintains headquarters in Chicago and functions as a specialized credit agency reporting on wholesale handlers of fruit, vegetable, and allied lines throughout the country. Credit reports are prepared on brokers, exporters, importers, packers, growers, jobbers, commission merchants, and retail and wholesale grocers in the industry.

Owing to the fact that the industry is seasonal, has constant market fluctuations, and has unusual risks caused by the perishable nature of the commodities, the credit report emphasizes the moral responsibility of the person concerned.

The Produce Reporter Co. publishes a yearly book called the *Blue Book,* which prints the names, addresses, and ratings of all wholesale handlers of fruits, vegetables, and allied lines. The book rates each firm by code, as to the nature of its business, number of carlots handled, commodities handled, net financial worth, and moral responsibility. Other information in the *Blue Book* includes summary of trading rules and laws; association, state, and federal grades; at the head of each town the population, name of bank, attorney, and railroads; state maps; terminal maps of 32 principals' markets; and a supply directory.

The rating book is kept up to date by weekly credit sheets that report the changes in financial and moral ratings, names of new firms, delinquencies, bankruptcies, and other credit facts. Three supplements of the *Blue Book,* issued in August, November, and February, consolidate the changes reported by the weekly credit sheets. Confidential reports are offered, and advance sheets giving information in advance of publication, either by telegraph, phone, or mail, depending upon the importance of the information, are offered to users of the *Blue Book* Service. A "watching service" is available, covering special confidential watching of any firm with reports at frequent intervals summarizing the results of constant investigation. In addition, the Produce Reporter Co. issues weekly Exchange Bulletins containing interpretative summaries of political and economic trends affecting the fruit and vegetable industry.

The agency has an adjustment, collection, arbitration, and traffic service available for its subscribers.

Credit Interchange

The use of credit interchange.—Credit interchange is the exchange among business houses of actual ledger experience with regard to customers. It is helpful in revising accounts, in eliminating undesirable buyers, and in granting or refusing extensions. It aids in checking special accounts, keeps the credit files alive and up to the minute, tells whether a customer is overbuying or buying outside his legitimate territory, or whether he is paying his new creditor promptly and allowing others to wait. Sometimes ledger credit-interchange reports reveal that a creditor house is mistaken in its belief that it is the principal creditor.

Credit interchange is also valuable to firms selling a small house whose rating is as yet unestablished. It is also useful when a former customer requests a reopening of his account.

Credit-interchange bureaus.—To facilitate this exchange of credit information, credit-interchange bureaus have been organized. Some of the special mercantile agencies, as indicated in the preceding pages, offer interchange as one of their services. In a number of industries interchange bureaus are operated by trade associations. The best-known and most widely used system of interchange of ledger information is that of the National Association of Credit Men.

Trade-group interchange.—Another method of direct interchange of ledger experience is the group meeting. Creditors located in the same trading center, who are members of the same credit association and sell to the same line of trade, get together periodically to exchange information on their customers. For example, the credit men representing the wholesale plumbing and heating trade of a large midwestern city meet once a week to exchange information on credit conditions. Each member comes supplied with a quantity of reporting blanks, which are filled out as reports are given. Starting at one end of the table, Mr. Blank reports an order from John Doe, amount $20,000, and gives whatever information he has concerning the customer. Then the man next to him reports the experience of his firm, if any, and so on around the table. The two or three hours' time spent at the meeting each week is more than offset by the time saved during the week.

Other trade groups that have less occasion to meet regularly are "on call" for any time, the secretary of the local association calling the group together on short notice whenever any account requiring immediate attention comes up. In this way doubtful accounts concerning which there have been unfavorable experiences are generally brought to light in time to prevent serious damage.

The members of another bureau go one step further. When the monthly report which the bureau makes up shows that John Doe has bought from different members more than he should have, or that he is getting behind in his payments, he is cordially invited to a luncheon meeting of the association. There his situation is discussed in his presence, and an effort is made to reach some solution that will be agreeable to him. Oftentimes the creditor finds that the credit men have suggestions which are of practical assistance to him, and the informality of the meetings precludes any ill-feeling.

Agencies Reporting on Individuals and Making Special Investigations—Published Services

Difference between mercantile agencies and agencies reporting on individuals.—The preceding paragraphs have dealt with sources of credit information regarding companies. The problem of obtaining credit information on individuals is somewhat different. Whereas credit information on a business firm requires an investigation entailing special knowledge of the industry, ability to interpret financial statements, and the like, and covers a period of years, a report on individuals is relatively simple and extends over a much shorter period. A local investigation of the individual is usually sufficient. Banks, loan companies, and installment houses may use these agencies to advantage.

Although there are a number of agencies exclusively in the field of individual reporting, only a few of the leading ones are treated here

Hooper-Holmes Bureau.—The Hooper-Holmes Bureau maintains headquarters in New York City and branches in 78 cities in the United States and 5 cities in Canada. The agency serves mainly as a clearing house for insurance companies, although it also serves banks, finance companies, installment houses, and retail stores. The agency does not obtain credit information from its files but makes an individual, outside investigation as soon as a request for credit information is received. The reports are, consequently, up to date, and they are a great aid to credit men in large cities where individuals move about frequently. For the credit man desiring information on individuals, the agency offers two reports, the individual report and the narrative report.

The individual report is a one-page confidential form report carrying a series of questions in one column regarding: (1) the contacts made in the investigation; (2) the individual's age, lineage, race, dependents, reputation, and habits; (3) the individual's occupation; and (4) his finances. The investigator's answers are in the column to the right of the questions. A space is provided at the bottom of the report for details of any incomplete or unfavorable answers to the questions.

The narrative report is a report on an individual who has furnished credit references. The report contains the names and addresses of three references, ledger experience, and columns of questions regarding contacts made, the individual's finances, his business, and personal data. The investigator's answers are given to the right of the questions. Additional details are given at the bottom of the report.

A third form of report, called the delinquent debtor report, is a one-page form report of use to the credit man who wants to revaluate a delinquent account. It is similar to the individual report in form but is somewhat shorter. The report answers questions regarding: (1) the present and previous addresses; (2) age, marital status, and dependents; (3) place of employment; (4) worth and income; and (5) local credit reputation of the individual.

Derogatory information about an individual, coming to the attention of the agency after a report has been sent to a client, is passed on to the subscriber.

Retail Credit Company.—Retail Credit Company, established in 1899, furnishes personal information on residents of any place in the Western Hemisphere, through its headquarters at Atlanta, Georgia, its 100 branch offices, and its 737 sub-branches. It serves such firms as petroleum companies, direct-selling and mail-order houses, automobile finance companies, building and loan companies, mortgage loan companies, farm-implement corporations, property-improvement companies, and many others. Companies using the service are furnished inquiry forms for requesting the various types of reports offered by the agency. The types include:

1. Character-credit report—individual, which provides credit, financial, and character information on persons other than farmers.

2. Character-credit report—farmer, which provides credit, financial, and character information on farmers, and covers, in addition to usual data, size of farm, type of farm, crop prospects, stability, and other information.

3. Delinquent-purchaser report, which provides information to aid in judging the collectibility of past-due accounts.

4. Personal-history report, which provides general antecedent information on persons being considered for employment.

5. Special investigations, which provide information on unusual situations or transactions beyond the scope of the regular reports. These reports are made on an hourly charge basis and are the result of exhaustive investigation. Findings are presented in narrative form.

The first four types of reports mentioned are in question-and-answer form. Thus, in the individual character credit report, groups of questions are included, dealing with identity, employment, character, worth, and income. The answers are inserted in a separate column directly opposite the question. A section for "remarks" offers a paragraph on each of the following items: the individual's credit record; his business-character; his property; and, if the report covers a woman, the name and occupation of her husband (if married) or father (if single) and an estimate of his net worth and annual income.

A current investigation is made in all cases. Persons well acquainted with the subject of the report—employers, trade sources, landlords, associates, and others—are interviewed. Unfavorable facts are confirmed through records or additional informants. In addition, the agency draws upon information contained in its files, which include previous reports and other recorded data on approximately 20,000,000 persons.

The Retail Credit Company gives to the customer ordering the report any subsequent information that it is felt may be of assistance in handling the case.

Proudfoot's Commercial Agency, Inc.—The Proudfoot's Commercial Agency, Inc., is located in New York City. The agency makes confidential and comprehensive reports, in letter form, on individuals, corporations, partnerships, and associations. The files of the agency contain information and reports on more than seven million names gathered over forty years of service.

The reports on individuals cover the following data regarding the person under investigation:

1. Age, place of birth, and home life.

2. Extent of education.
3. Complete antecedent history and business activity.
4. Dates of all former connections.
5. Record of suits, judgments, and bankruptcies.
6. Criminal record.
7. Favorable or derogatory comment relative to past record.
8. Financial condition and method of paying bills.
9. Bank and other credit information.
10. Integrity, moral standing.
11. Business reputation.

The reports on partnerships and corporations have three sections: (1) the antecedent history and personal background of the principals of the enterprise; (2) a detailed financial picture, including statement analysis, trends over the past several years, as well as a digest of present activity and immediate outlook for the future; and (3) bank and trade investigations and availability of credit.

The agency also reports on professional firms such as law, accounting, engineering, investment counsel, and others.

Although the bulk of the reports serve concerns and individuals in New York City and its environs, they are available to subscribers over a wide area.

Bishop's Service, Inc.—Bishop's Service, Inc., established in 1895, is located in New York City and is engaged exclusively in the business of making investigations and credit reports, based on personal character and moral risk, with respect to individuals, firms, and corporations located throughout this country and Canada.

The credit reports are narrative in style and rather comprehensive. They emphasize the personal and business records and the habits and associations of the individuals involved, including those charged with the direction and management of firms and corporate activities. The reports do not have credit ratings, summaries, or financial statements.

Hill's Reports, Inc.—Hill's Reports, Inc., maintains offices in Chicago, New York, and New Orleans, and serves principally Chicago commercial banks and trust companies, securities houses, hotels, and insurance companies. Credit reports are prepared on individuals, partnerships, and corporations by trained reporters and correspondents. These reports are based on individual investigation of each inquiry plus available data from the files of the agency. Although the reports emphasize the character and moral responsibility of the individuals involved, their contents vary according to the requirements of the subscriber. The reports are narrative in style, with no summary or ratings.

Publications.—Besides the mercantile and specialized agencies, the credit man may consult various publications issued by publishing companies to aid him in formulating a credit decision. The most important of these services are published by Moody's Investment Service, Inc.; Poor's Publishing Company; Fitch Publishing Company, Inc.; Standard Statistics Company, Inc.; and Alfred M. Best Company, Inc.

All of these companies publish yearly manuals, available to subscribers, containing valuable information on nearly every concern in the country that has securities in the hands of the public. Data contained in these manuals cover the financial condition of the company, earnings record, names of officers and directors, and description of obligations and capital securities of the company.

The first four companies serve the investment field, while Alfred M. Best Company operates in the insurance field.

Salesmen as Credit Reporters

Value of salesmen as credit reporters.—In the case of smaller accounts, salesmen are frequently a valuable source of credit information. The advantages of using salesmen as credit reporters are the following:

1. The salesman is frequently the only representative of his house who comes in personal contact with the customer. The experienced salesman may be able to determine from observation and inquiry the presence or absence of those specific factors which make a risk acceptable to his concern.

2. Where salesmen visit customers often and the amount of each sale is small, the expense of obtaining credit data from outside sources may not be warranted. Salesmen can supply the necessary information at minimum cost to the house.

3. When a salesman's credit report accompanies the order, delivery of the goods is expedited.

4. Extravagant promises to the customer by salesmen are eliminated, such as promises of immediate delivery to customers whose accounts need investigation. Customers ordinarily expect that their credit is examined before their order is accepted.

5. Any change affecting the credit risk, financial or otherwise, can be reported immediately, permitting the company to lose little time in reducing or extending the credit limit.

6. Where the account is doubtful, the salesman can advise the customer of ways to improve his business, thereby building a future customer although the credit department will not pass on present orders. Salesmen can advise on merchandising, buying, selling, display, adjusting inventory, and so forth.

Nature of information obtainable through salesmen.—In connection with new customers, the salesman may consider the following points:

1. *Personal habits and local reputation.*—Through direct contact the salesman is in an excellent position to form an estimate of the customer's character. By discreet inquiry he can also determine the merchant's local reputation. The salesman might even, when absolutely necessary, visit the local banks or attorneys to obtain their opinions on the customer's character. However, it must be remembered that the salesman is a confirmed optimist and that his opinion will be colored accordingly.

2. *Business experience and ability.*—The salesman can quickly size up the condition of the merchant's stock. He can tell at a glance whether the stock contains any great quantity of out-of-style merchandise, which, if it ever sells, will move very slowly and at reduced prices. By observing the prices at which merchandise is marked to sell, he can judge whether the merchant is making a fair margin of profit or is cutting prices. The salesman may also note whether the merchant buys recklessly or prudently. A careless buyer is usually a careless payer. Thus the salesman knows that if his customer overbuys, paying any price for his merchandise or accepting any style or pattern, he does so probably because he does not seriously consider his obligation to pay his bills when they become due. On the other hand, a discriminating buyer usually is earnestly concerned with his duty to meet his bills promptly.

3. *Location of business.*—The customer's location in relation to

the business center of his city is an important consideration. Under this heading the salesman may note: character of the street on which the business is located, and whether the trend is toward or away from that section of the city; transportation facilities, such as trolley and bus lines; parking facilities; and nearness of competitive businesses.

4. *Local conditions.*—The salesman should inform the credit department of those purely local conditions that affect the entire community and the business of any particular merchant. For example, an important industry may shut down or move to another locality; a strike may be impending; the local crop may have failed. Any factors that are likely to affect the purchasing power of the community should be noted.

5. *Trade and bank references.*—Salesmen may obtain trade and bank references either by direct inquiry of the merchant or by indirect means. Because the merchant may be inclined to give only the names of those houses whose bills he pays promptly, and since it is usually a comparatively simple matter to keep in good standing with three or four houses, references obtained by indirect means are often more useful to the credit department. The salesman may obtain the names of the merchant's creditors by noting the nature of the merchandise displayed. Trade references should always be attached to the first order. For bank references the salesman can call in person at the local banks or merely list on his credit report the references supplied by the merchant.

6. *Financial statement.*—When he obtains a first order from a small dealer, the salesman may request a financial statement to accompany the order and to facilitate checking by the credit department. Many credit men, however, question the advisability of this procedure. The merchant may be reluctant to discuss his financial status with the salesman, and in many cases the information sought is already on file with the mercantile agencies.

7. *Credit recommendation.*—In order to place a greater degree of responsibility upon the salesman and to emphasize the importance of his report, some concerns require him to state in his report the line of credit that he believes should be extended. Such a procedure tends to make the salesman careful in answering questions, while at the same time it does not obligate the credit department to follow his suggestion. In cases where the salesman's suggestion

is entirely out of line with the amount decided upon by the credit man, a conference between the two will often disclose the fact that one possesses information about the customer of which the other has no knowledge. In fact, the credit man must always guard against a tendency on the part of salesmen not to pass along all they know because it is assumed that the credit man already possesses the information.

Objections to salesmen as credit investigators.—Many credit men feel that salesmen as a source of credit information are greatly overestimated, and that such work should be confined to salesmen dealing with small firms. The salesman, for instance, is not always able to inspect all of the merchandise. Nor can he afford to spend too much time on credit work, since his main job is selling. Besides, many prospects prefer requests for information, particularly for financial statements, to come from credit men. For these reasons many credit departments provide salesmen with forms on which to report their credit information.

A form of salesmen's reports.—The following form of report for salesmen is sent by one company to salesmen, branch offices, and brokers once a year. The company reports great diversity in the nature of the comments, for which space is provided at the bottom of the page. Some salesmen will merely note "O.K."; others write a few lines; some jot down a few paragraphs on the back of the form; and still others will attach a two- or three-page comment.

Our credit records show a credit line of ____________________ authorized for:

____________________________ of ____________________________

Will you please give us your present comments and recommendations on this line. This is to assure us that:

Your records agree with ours; and that

You believe the line is suitable and proper.

If you believe the line should be revised, either to facilitate the sale of our merchandise, or to conform with the normal requirements of the account, please let us know.

Or, if it is unnecessary that a line be continued, we want to suspend credit and make the file inactive.

Thank you for your co-operation.

Very truly yours,
Company's name
Credit manager's name
Credit Department

Please write your comments below and return this form.

How to get the salesmen to co-operate.—To what extent the salesman will furnish the information that he can obtain depends to a large degree upon the credit man himself. The credit man will soon enlist the salesman's active assistance if he is broadminded, if he does his work with the idea of business promotion, and if he treats customers considerately and thus helps the salesman to retain the goodwill of his trade. Among the specific methods used by various companies to enlist the salesman's co-operation are the following:

1. *Conferences between salesmen and credit man.*—Periodically, the credit man discusses with each salesman, individually, the accounts that he handles. This mutual exchange of information and viewpoint is invaluable to both men. The credit man becomes familiar with the salesman's problems. Personal contact also enables the credit man to judge to what extent he can rely on information given to him by salesmen. Some salesmen are keen judges of human nature, know their territory thoroughly, and can report upon a given situation with accuracy and judgment. Other salesmen, by reason of temperament, are not so reliable when it comes to forming an opinion of an account from the credit standpoint. For his part, the salesman learns from conferences with the credit man what constitutes a good credit risk, what factors have to be taken into consideration, what the credit policy of his house is, and, specifically, why some of his accounts have been turned down.

In one large chemical-manufacturing company, a member of the credit department attends all sales meetings and speaks of the credit department's functions, relationship to customers, and benefits to salesmen. He receives all complaints from salesmen and analyzes them in open discussion from the salesman's point of view.

2. *Payment on n.c.u.p. basis.*—Under the n.c.u.p. plan ("no commission until paid"), the salesman's personal account on the ledger

Form 1306 B · Litho. in U. S. A

MAIL TO ______

MAIL TO ______

MAIL TO ______

CREDIT APPROVAL WITHHELD

Firm Name ______

Proprietor ______

Address ______

Order Date & No. ______ Amount ______

Del'y Date ______ Salesman ______

REASON FOR NON-APPROVAL

Owes Us ______ $ ______ Past Due ______

Owes Us ______ $ ______ Dating ______

Total

Credit Line ______ Dun. ______ Brad. ______

New Account - Credit Investigation Started ______

REMARKS ______

Per ______ (CREDIT DEP'T) Date

Made in Triplicate · 2 Copies with Order Attached To Sales Manager, 1 for Credit Man's File

Figure 81.—Notice to Salesmen of Order Held.
[Actual Size $5\frac{1}{2}'' \times 8\frac{1}{2}''$]

is credited with the commission at the time the sale is made, but the amount is not paid to him until the customer has settled his bill. The effect is to make the salesman more discriminating in soliciting accounts.

3. *Collection contests.*—Information will be given much more freely and accurately by salesmen if they are made wholly, or even only partly, responsible for collections. A number of companies have reported successful operation of a plan by which a cash prize is awarded each month to the salesman who leads his district in collections. The salesman is less likely to recommend a doubtful account if he knows that he will be expected to assist in collecting it. See page 1103 for further discussion of collection by salesmen.

4. *Notice of refusal to grant credit.*—Salesmen will co-operate better with credit departments if they feel that the credit department does not keep them waiting for information as to the acceptance or rejection of orders. Some credit departments have therefore adopted the practice of sending out a notice to salesmen whenever extension of credit has been withheld. The salesmen, knowing that this practice is followed, do not wire or write in to the credit department long before the credit man has completed his investigation to determine whether the order has been accepted. A producer of tires and rubber goods uses the form reproduced in Fig. 81, in the case of both new and old accounts, if an order is not approved by the credit department.

Attorneys as Credit Reporters

Nature of information obtainable through attorneys.—Much of the credit information obtainable through attorneys is similar to that obtainable through salesmen; it refers to such matters as:

1. Personal habits.
2. Local reputation.
3. Business ability.
4. Location of business.
5. Local trade conditions.
6. Value of real property, and encumbrances thereon.
7. Claims and lawsuits.

Some houses restrict their use of attorneys as credit reporters to cities with a population of 15,000 or less, because they feel that it is only in such cases that the attorney has sufficient personal knowledge of and contact with the subject to render his report of value. There are, however, numerous individual attorneys and firms that make a specialty of collection work and the furnishing of credit information; these attorneys have expert staffs and maintain extensive credit records.

Attorneys' directories.—Attorneys' directories, such as those described on page 1107, may be used for locating attorneys who are willing to serve commercial houses as credit reporters, as well as collectors. Some of the publishers of attorneys' directories provide users with attorneys' credit-report forms. An example of such a form is shown in Figure 82. These forms usually produce better results than a mere general request for credit information.

Objections to attorneys' reports.—In using attorneys' reports, the credit man should bear in mind the following objections that may detract from the value of the report: (1) the attorney is unacquainted with the credit standards of the inquiring house; (2) he may be a personal friend of the credit applicant; and (3) local pride may affect his judgment. In order to be sure that the attorney gives the request for credit information proper attention, he should be compensated for his efforts. Remuneration may be in the form of placing collection work with the attorney, or it may be a fee based upon the amount of work done in furnishing the report.

Banks as Credit Reporters

Availability of credit information from banks.—In the conduct of their own business, banks maintain complete credit files of their depositors in order to be equipped with full credit information on the basis of which applications for loans can be intelligently considered. This information is for the bank's own use and is kept confidential.

Unless a bank is authorized by a customer to give credit information to a specific inquirer, or unless the inquiry comes through a correspondent bank, very little, if any, credit information can be

United States Fidelity and Guaranty Company
Attorneys List Department
Home Office, Baltimore, Md.

Report Blank

Form F

Report on.. .... of.. ....

Sent to...Correspondent at...

Date sent..Date Received...

DO NOT FORGET TO ENCLOSE PROPER POSTAGE—See Instructions on the Cover of these Blanks

RETURN REPORT BELOW TO

To the Attorney: Our Subscriber, whose name or number appears hereon, is entitled to the mercantile report herein requested prior to the date of expiration above noted. Please detach this stub and preserve for future reference, so that you can advise subscriber promptly in the event of any change in the financial condition of the party reported upon after the date of your reply to this inquiry. You must not reveal to any one the fact that you have been asked for this report.

E. ASBURY DAVIS, *President*

United States Fidelity and Guaranty Co.
Attorneys List Department
Home Office, Baltimore, Md.

Name of Party reported on.. Date.......................................

Correspondent will please detach this stub and file for future reference.

TO BE SENT TO SUBSCRIBER

City...19........

To ....at ....

Dear Sir:-Kindly mail to us in enclosed stamped envelope full information, based on your knowledge and investigation, as to the age, character, habits, capital, responsibility and promptness in meeting obligations of

Full Name..City ....

Street and No...Business ....

Your prompt reply will be greatly appreciated, as **Delayed Reports are of no Value.**

ANSWER HERE:

Supposed net worth? $ ....

Individual Names (if a firm)?...

Married or Single? ....**Age approximately?** ....

Reputation for Ability?..............................**Honesty?**.......................................Moral Character?..........................

Ever failed?...**Been sued?**..

How long in business? ....**Business seem prosperous?** ....

Value of stock on hand (estimated) ? $.. Insurance? $........................

Value of real estate above homestead and encumbrance?..

Do you know of any unsatisfied obligations, chattel mortages, judgments or claims in hands of attorneys?

....

FURTHER REMARKS

....

....

....

....

All the facts tending in anywise to a just estimate of party's credit-worth are highly desirable.
Do not under any circumstances divulge the name of the party desiring this report.

Figure 82.—Attorney's Credit Report Form, United States Fidelity and Guaranty Company.

obtained other than the fact that the customer has a deposit at the bank, and possibly the age of the account.

Banks are not particularly receptive to inquiry forms sent by nondepositors seeking information about a depositor. These are usually filled out meagerly, if at all. To discourage such promiscuous inquiries, many state bankers' associations and other organizations of bankers have adopted rules providing that requests for credit information, unless authorized by the customer, or received through a correspondent bank, must be accompanied by a fee.

Information that may be obtained from banks.—The following list enumerates items of credit information that may be obtainable from a customer's commercial bank, upon authorization, if the customer has ever borrowed from the bank. If he has not, only part of the items may be covered in the bank's report.

1. Age of the account. Frequent changing of banking connection is in itself regarded as unfavorable.
2. A general statement of the relationship with respect to loans and deposit balances, including information on how satisfactorily the account is conducted.
3. Promptness of the subject in meeting his obligations to the bank.
4. Whether many drafts are presented to the subject through the bank, and, if so, whether these drafts are honored by the subject.
5. Comment on the subject's financial statement, provided that it is authorized by the subject.
6. General local reputation of the subject and the bank's opinion of him.
7. In the case of some banks, a definite or general expression of opinion regarding the risk.
8. A short summary of the history and antecedents of the company.

Information that is not obtainable from banks.—The bank is ordinarily not in a position to furnish credit men with the following information:

1. The exact amount of the depositor's account. The bank will give the credit man a general idea of the depositor's responsibility. Such terms as small (three figures), moderate (four figures), or

large (over four figures) are frequently used to describe the amount of deposits. The bank may, however, confirm a balance reported by a customer on a balance sheet.

2. Details of loans that are outstanding. This information can be secured only on the proper authorization.

3. Information concerning the customer's financial statement.

Getting information from the credit man's bank.—When the credit man is faced with a particularly difficult decision, he may ask his own bank to obtain a credit report from the customer's bank. Banks in the same city have an accurate credit-interchange system and can quickly obtain such information. If the customer is out of town, the credit man's bank will communicate with its correspondent bank in the customer's city, which in turn will get in touch with the customer's bank.

Generally, more complete information is obtainable if this method is used than when the credit man goes direct to the customer's bank. However, the method is one that can be used only infrequently, and then only if the bank is anxious to please the depositor who makes the request.

The Personal Interview

Value of the personal interview.—Through personal interviews, or personal calls on customers, the credit man can obtain useful information as well as promote better understanding between the selling house and its customers. The properly conducted interview enables the applicant to present his own case most advantageously and to receive useful suggestions; it permits the credit man to make personal observations and to inquire carefully concerning doubtful points; and, finally, a free and frank discussion leads to a more satisfactory mutual understanding. Wherever a personal contact can be justified by the size of the order received or prospects of future business, and especially where, as a result of the call, the credit man can make necessary arrangements to hold worth-while business, the credit man should make every attempt to interview the applicant.

A friendly and human attitude on the part of the credit man accomplishes more than anything else during the personal call.

The credit man wants the customer to talk freely. This situation is best induced by pleasant and informal discussions in which the credit man asks as few direct questions as possible and permits the customer to do the talking. However, the credit man should review the case before the interview in order that he may direct the conversation along the proper channels. It is preferable to refrain from writing during the interview. As soon as it is terminated, the results of the interview should be put in writing.

Special need for a personal interview.—A personal interview or a personal call by the credit man is especially useful in the following cases:

1. When an old and valued account is becoming slow in meeting its obligations. The credit man, through his intimate and widespread knowledge of the trade, may be able to suggest to the customer means by which the progress of his business can be restored. Thus the creditor may suggest a change in the customer's location (the customer is often the last person to realize that the current trend of local business is moving away from the street or section in which he is located), clearance sales to dispose of old stock, new methods of window display, new methods of advertising, new lines of goods that might be carried to attract patronage, more complete and efficient bookkeeping methods, and so forth.
2. When a new account is under consideration offering unusual opportunity for sales, but involving greater than ordinary risk.

Traveling credit representatives.—Some credit men for larger houses spend a considerable part of their time in travel; others make a tour of their principal customers once or twice a year. Still other houses employ special credit representatives who spend their entire time visiting customers to inquire into their credit standing. The advantages of these practices are:

1. The credit man is able to visualize the personality, business circumstances, and so forth, of each customer. The credit man who remains always at his desk gains his perspective on credit risks entirely at second hand.
2. Goodwill between the customer and the selling house is cemented. A call by the credit man establishes a personal relationship between the customer and the name signed to the credit and collection letters.

3. The credit man gains insight into the problems of the sales department, and his judgment may be modified and corrected thereby.

4. By visiting references, especially banks, in person, the credit man or representative can usually obtain more definite and reliable information than can be obtained by correspondence.

2. LAW OF CREDIT INSTRUMENTS

Law Relating to Checks

Post-dated check not invalid.—A check is not invalid merely because it bears a date later than that on which it is drawn. For example, if on February 1 Tom Downey draws a check to the order of Albert Taylor dated February 20, the check is good. True, Mr. Downey's bank on which the check is drawn will not honor the instrument until the 20th of the month, but the check is not for that reason invalid. Nor is there anything to prevent the holder of the check from transferring it before the date on which it is payable. It has been held by the courts that a person who takes a check which is post-dated is not thereby put upon inquiry as to defects in the payee's right to the proceeds of the check. The Negotiable Instruments Law* specifically provides that an instrument "is not invalid for the reason only that it is ante-dated or post-dated, provided this is not done for an illegal or fraudulent purpose. The person to whom an instrument so dated is delivered acquires the title thereto as of the date of delivery."

Unsigned check received; how to handle.—It is not uncommon in the course of business to receive a check which has not been signed. Omission of the signature may and generally is merely an oversight on the part of the drawer of the check, but it has been known to be used as a time-gaining device. As in the case of other irregularities in the drawing of a check, the instrument may be returned to the drawer for correction, but a more effective and perhaps safer course is open to the holder of the check. He may

* The Negotiable Instruments Law is a codification of the principal rules of law relating to negotiable instruments as announced in numerous decisions, and was adopted by the various states in response to the general need for uniformity.

deposit it in his bank for collection with the understanding that the drawer will be requested to sign it upon receipt by the bank on which the check is drawn. Or he may deposit the check in his bank with a sight draft attached, and arrange to have the check and draft forwarded to the bank in which the drawer of the check has his account. If omission of the signature was inadvertent, the drawer of the check will be glad to sign it promptly upon request or to honor the sight draft. If it was deliberate, the use is defeated, and little if any loss of time in obtaining payment has been suffered by the payee.

Check received on which amount in writing and amount in figures disagree; how to handle.—The Negotiable Instruments Law provides that where the amount payable is expressed in words and also in figures, and there is a discrepancy between the two, the sum denoted by the words is the sum payable. While the law furnishes this rule of construction, the banks will generally refuse to accept checks where the amount in writing disagrees with the amount in figures. If a debtor, through inadvertence or in a wily effort to gain time, forwards a check with the amount thus incorrectly indicated, the creditor may, of course, return the check for correction. A much more practical plan is to place an indorsement on the check, guaranteeing it for whichever is the correct amount, and deposit the check for collection. The debtor is then forced to indicate the correct amount of the remittance, and to make immediate payment.

Effect of certification of a check.—By certifying a check, a bank undertakes the following:

1. It guarantees the drawer's signature.
2. It represents that it has in its possession funds of the drawer sufficient to meet the check.
3. It engages that the funds will not be withdrawn from it by the drawer to the prejudice of any bona fide holder of the check

Where the payee of the check has it certified, he, in effect, accepts the bank as his debtor, and he thereby releases the drawer of the check, as well as any person who has indorsed it; should the bank become insolvent before the check is paid, the loss falls on the holder of the check, not on the drawer. On the other hand, if the drawer of a check has it certified, he remains liable on the check in the event of insolvency of the bank before payment. If a bank has certified a check by mistake, it may revoke the certification provided it acts promptly and provided no right belonging to the holder of the check has been diminished or lost.

Time within which a check must be presented for payment.—The Negotiable Instruments Law provides that a check must be presented for payment within a reasonable time after its issue and that failure to do so, resulting in loss to the drawer of the check, discharges him from liability thereon to the extent of the loss caused by delay in presentation. The law does not define the period which may elapse between the giving and presenting of a check, and what is a "reasonable time" must be determined according to the circumstances of each particular case. Ordinarily, if a check is delivered at the same place where the bank is located, it must, in the absence of special circumstances, be presented to the bank on which it is drawn during the business hours of the next regular business day after it is received; if the holder fails to present it within that time and the bank on which the check is drawn becomes insolvent so that the drawer loses the amount which he had on deposit to meet the check, he is discharged from liability and the loss must be borne by the one who was lax in presenting the check for payment. The courts have held in some cases that deposit by the payee in his own bank for collection on the day following the receipt of the instrument and presentation by the collecting bank on the day thereafter is a sufficiently prompt demand. The period for presentation of a check is not extended by the fact that the payee indorses it over to a third person.

Check returned marked "insufficient funds"; how to handle.—Where a check received from a debtor is returned by the bank marked "insufficient funds," it may, of course, be sent back to the drawer. However, the creditor may thus lose entirely his evidence of the debtor's acknowledgment of his obligation, and give him the opportunity of delaying payment indefinitely. Or, if the debtor has merely been slow in making a deposit in his bank sufficient to cover the check, time will be unnecessarily lost while the check travels back and forth between the parties. Rather than return the check to the drawer, the payee may arrange with the bank on which the check has been drawn to leave the check at the bank until sufficient funds have been deposited to cover it, at which time the bank will certify the check and return it to the creditor. If the debtor's account is short by only a small amount, it may be a good plan for the holder of the check to deposit to the credit of the maker sufficient funds to raise the account to the necessary amount, and then have the check certified. It should be noted that in some states, including New York, a person who, with fraudulent intent, issues a check knowing that he has insufficient funds for its payment, may be subject to criminal prosecution.

Effect of the death of the drawer of a check.—One of the chief points of difference between a check and a bill of exchange is that the death of the drawer of the check revokes the authority of the bank to pay, while the death of the drawer of a bill of exchange does not. The reason for this is that a check is a mere order for the payment of money; it does not operate as an assignment of any part of the fund which the drawer of the check may have on deposit in the bank on which the check is drawn. At any time before the check is paid, the drawer may stop payment on it and countermand the authority of the drawee to collect the amount of the check, or the authority of the bank to pay on it. The death of the drawer of the check operates as a revocation of the order to pay. A bank is not, however, presumed to know when the drawer of a check has died. If, without knowledge of the death of the drawer of a check, the bank makes payment, it cannot be held liable therefor.

Check given in full settlement of a claim.—Ordinarily, if part of a past-due indebtedness is paid, the balance remains due and owing, and an agreement on the part of the creditor to accept part in discharge of the whole debt is not binding on the creditor unless some additional consideration is given for his acceptance. Payment of a smaller amount may, however, operate as a full discharge of a debtor's obligation and bar any further action by him on the original claim where:

1. There is a bona fide dispute concerning the claim.
2. A check is given to the creditor in settlement which recites that it is in full payment of the claim.
3. The check is accepted by the creditor or collected by him without objection.

The creditor cannot accept the check and keep alive the debtor's obligation by writing to the debtor advising him that he does not accept it in full settlement and demands further payment. Nor can a person by striking out the words "in full" written on the check avoid being bound by his acceptance of the check in full payment. Where a check is given in settlement of a disputed claim, therefore, it is important to indicate clearly on the instrument the fact that it represents payment in full of the claim. And if a check is received in settlement of a claim so marked, it should be returned at once if the amount is not acceptable.

Payment of a forged check by a bank; is the bank liable to the drawer of the check?—In disbursing the funds of a depositor, the bank can make payment only in conformity with the depositor's directions. If it pays a check on which the indorsement of the payee's name has been forged, it is not making payment according to the directions of the depositor and may be required to answer to the depositor for the payment. Similarly, the bank is bound to know the signature of its depositor and must account to him if it pays a check on which the depositor's signature has been forged. The bank is from necessity responsible for any omission to discover the original terms and conditions of a check, properly drawn upon it, because at the time of payment it is the only party interested who has the opportunity of inspection. In order to give the bank a fair opportunity to protect its own interests in recovering payment made on a forged check and prosecuting the forger, the Negotiable Instruments Law provides that no bank shall be liable to a depositor for the payment by it of a forged or raised check, unless within one year after the return to the depositor of the voucher of such payment, such depositor shall notify the bank that the check so paid was forged or raised.

Law Relating to Notes

Note accepted for an old debt.—Generally, in order to render the maker of a note liable therefor, some consideration must have been given to bind the transaction; that is, something of value in the nature of a benefit to the maker or of a detriment to the payee must have induced the execution of the note. This consideration need not have a value equal to the amount of the note; its value may, in fact, be trivial. A debt which is due and owing from the maker of a note to the payee is deemed to be a sufficient consideration for the note. The Negotiable Instruments Law specifically provides that an antecedent or preexisting debt constitutes value, whether the note is payable on demand or at a future time. If Mulligan owes Peters $100, Peters may accept a note from Mulligan which will be binding upon the latter; the old debt is a valid consideration. Similarly, if Mulligan owes Peters $100, Peters may accept Casey's note for the debt, provided Peters thereby agrees to forbear from bringing suit against Mulligan. Even if Peters has previously brought an action against Mulligan and reduced his claim to judgment, he may accept a note from Mulligan to evidence his claim, and the old debt constitutes a good consideration for the note.

Note executed on Sunday is generally invalid.—In most states, a promissory note executed on Sunday is invalid, so far as the maker and the payee are concerned, and will not be enforced by the courts. This does not mean that a note may not properly be drawn, signed, or dated on a Sunday. These are all preliminaries to "execution," with which the law does not concern itself. A note becomes effective on the date of its delivery, and it is the act of delivery which is prohibited on the Sabbath. Even if a note is executed on Sunday, if it appears on its face to have been made on a secular day and is transferred in good faith, for value, before maturity, to a person having no knowledge of the fact that it was executed on Sunday, the transferee may enforce the note. A maker of a note which has been executed on Sunday may also be held liable on the note either to the original payee or a subsequent holder if he ratified it on a secular day by a payment on the note or by any distinct recognition of his obligation.

Note executed by a minor is voidable.—A person under 21 years of age is a minor or an "infant" in the eyes of the law, and is allowed, under certain circumstances, to repudiate his obligations. A note executed by an infant is generally not void, but voidable; that is, the note is valid, but the infant may repudiate it before he becomes of age or within a reasonable time thereafter. Similarly, if an infant indorses a note, he may disaffirm his contract of indorsement within the time indicated. What constitutes a reasonable time depends upon the circumstances of the particular case. If the infant fails to repudiate or disaffirm within a reasonable time after arriving at majority, he is deemed to have affirmed his obligation and is bound thereon. A person, therefore, who takes a note from an infant does so at his peril, for the infant may decline to perform his part of the agreement.

The fact that an infant has signed or indorsed a note does not, however, prevent the holder of the note from transferring it, and no person liable on the note, other than the infant, may set up the infant's incapacity in defense of his own obligation. The Negotiable Instruments Law specifically provides that the indorsement or assignment of a note by an infant passes the property therein, notwithstanding that from want of capacity the infant may incur no liability thereon. This means that while an infant who has indorsed a note may repudiate his contract of indorsement, the indorsee has the right to enforce payment of the note from all parties who executed the instrument prior to the infant indorser, and the incapacity of the minor cannot be availed of by them.

Interest payable on a note.—Interest is not payable on the amount of a note prior to its maturity, unless provided for expressly or impliedly, or unless the governing state statute specifies that interest shall be payable. Where a note does provide for the payment of interest on the principal, without indicating when the interest is to be paid, the interest is not payable until the note matures. If a note is not paid at maturity, interest is generally recoverable on the principal of the note from the due date to the date of payment. In the case of a demand note, interest runs from the date of the note, since a note payable on demand becomes due immediately. The interest is in the nature of damages for a detention of payment; it does not constitute a distinct claim, and if payment of the principal of the note is accepted, an action cannot afterwards be maintained to recover the interest.

Note obtained fraudulently; is the maker liable thereon?—Fraud on the part of the payee of a note in the consideration for which the note was given or in procuring the note may be set up as a defense by the maker in an action brought against him by the original payee to recover the amount thereof. Where, however, a note has been transferred to an innocent holder who acquires it for value, without any notice or knowledge of the fraud, the maker cannot always avoid liability on the note even if he can prove the fraud. In some states, the rule is that such an innocent purchaser may hold the maker liable on the note regardless of the nature of the fraud practiced by the payee. In other states, a distinction is made by the courts between two kinds of fraud:

1. Ordinary fraud, such as misrepresentation as to the quality or nature of merchandise for which the note was given.
2. Fraud in inducing the signing of the note: as, for example, where the maker of the note signs the instrument thinking that it is a receipt or an order for goods.

In the first type of fraud, if there is nothing on the face of the instrument to arouse inquiry and no evidence of any suspicious circumstances attending the transfer or any proof tending to establish the fact that the purchaser had knowledge or notice of the fraud on the part of the payee, the innocent purchaser may hold the maker liable. In the second type of fraud, the maker can avoid liability even against the innocent purchaser if he proves that he was not guilty of negligence in signing the instrument. Whether or not the signer of the note was negligent depends upon the circumstances of each case. A person is expected to ascertain what an instrument contains before he signs it, either by reading it or by having it read to him. If he signs a note without reading it, when he can read and an opportunity to do so is furnished, he cannot set up his own omission as a defense to his liability. An illiterate person is generally required to ask someone other than the party seeking his signature to the instrument to read it before he signs, but in the case of one dealing with an old acquaintance and trusted friend, carelessness might not be imputed if the signer was deceived by relying on the representations of the other party. In any case, in order to avoid liability because of fraud, it must be shown:

1. That a material representation or statement was made intending that the defrauded person act upon it; the test of materiality is whether, without the representation complained of, the note would have been executed.
2. That the representation was false.
3. That the person believed it to be true.
4. That he acted thereon to his damage.

Purchase of a note which has been lost or stolen.—Ordinarily, the owner of personal property cannot be divested of his right to the property without his consent, and if the property is lost or stolen no one can acquire good title thereto as against the true owner, not even one who purchases the property in good faith and for value. There is, however, a distinct and universally recognized exception to this rule in the case of negotiable instruments, such as promissory notes, which are payable to bearer or indorsed in blank. To a large extent negotiable instruments take the place of money and in the ordinary course and transaction of business they are treated like money or cash, which passes freely from hand to hand without earmarks. Where a person receives a note before maturity, for a fair consideration, without any reason for suspecting that the title is in any way defective, he acquires a good title to the note; he can hold the note against the true owner, and may recover on it against the maker and other parties even if the note has been stolen from or lost by the former holder. The former holder retains all his original rights only against the thief or finder, or whoever received the paper from them under suspicious circumstances. A person who takes a note is not bound, at his peril, to inquire into the title of the holder, for his right to the instrument is not dependent upon that of the person from whom the note was obtained. He takes the note free from any imperfections which may attach to it in the hands of the previous holder, provided he is a "holder in due course." A holder in due course is defined in the Negotiable Instruments Law as one who has taken the instrument under the following conditions:

1. That it is complete and regular upon its face.
2. That he became the holder of it before it was overdue, and without notice that it had been previously dishonored, if such was the fact.
3. That he took it in good faith and for value.
4. That, at the time it was negotiated to him, he had no notice of any infirmity in the instrument or defect in the title of the person negotiating it.

Effect of alteration of a note.—Before the adoption of the Uniform Negotiable Instruments Law, there was some difference of opinion as to the effect of a material alteration of a note by the payee or a holder, after issuance and delivery of the paper as a completed instrument, without the knowledge or consent of the maker, where the alteration was facilitated by the form in which the instrument had been drawn. One line of decisions held that such alteration invalidated the instrument even in the hands of a holder in due course without notice. Another line of cases decided that the maker or indorser of the note was liable to a bona fide holder for the amount of the note as altered, on the theory that since the negligence of the maker or indorser induced the alteration, he and not the innocent holder should be made to suffer. Some cases held that the innocent purchaser might recover on the note according to its original tenor. This conflict was settled by the Negotiable Instruments Law. The law now provides that where a material alteration is made in a note without the assent of all the parties liable thereon, the note is avoided except as against the party who has made or authorized or assented to the alteration and subsequent indorsers; where, however, a note is in the hands of a holder in due course who is not a party to the alteration, he may enforce payment of the note according to its original tenor. A material alteration, as defined by the Negotiable Instruments Law, includes any alteration which:

1. Changes the date.
2. Changes the sum payable, either for principal or interest.
3. Changes the time or place of payment.
4. Changes the number or the relations of the parties.
5. Changes the medium or currency in which payment is to be made.
6. Adds a place of payment where no place of payment is specified.
7. Makes any other change or addition which alters the effect of the instrument in any respect.

The following changes, among others, have been held in court decisions to constitute material alterations:

1. Erasing the name of the payee and inserting a different name.
2. Adding a clause providing for interest, where the instrument made no provision for interest.
3. Changing the rate of interest.
4. Inserting the words "or order" or "or bearer" after the name of the payee.

5. Adding names of attesting witnesses subsequent to maker's signing of instrument, and without his knowledge.

Effect of signing a note, leaving blanks to be filled in.—Where a person signs his name to a blank paper and delivers it to another person in order that the paper may be converted into a note, the person to whom the paper is delivered is presumed to have authority to fill it up as a note for any amount. Similarly, where a note is blank in any material particular, the person in possession of the instrument is presumed to have authority to complete it by filling in the blanks. Even if the blanks are filled in contrary to the intent of the signer of the note, it is enforceable against him by a third person who acquires the note in good faith for value, after completion and before maturity, and without notice or knowledge of any defect in the instrument.

Forgery of signature on a note.—The Negotiable Instruments Law provides that where a signature is forged or made without authority of the person whose signature it purports to be, it is wholly inoperative, and no right to retain the instrument, or to give a discharge therefor, or to enforce payment thereof against any party thereto, can be acquired through or under such signature, unless the party against whom it is sought to enforce such right, is precluded from setting up the forgery or want of authority. This means that where the signature of the maker of a note is forged, he cannot ordinarily be held liable on the note even by one who has purchased the note in good faith and for value, without notice or knowledge of the forgery. The maker may, however, be precluded from avoiding liability although his signature has been forged, where the forgery has been made possible by his negligence. He may also be prevented from setting up the defense of forgery in a suit brought against him on the note where he has, with full knowledge of the facts affecting his rights, ratified the note after it has been negotiated. The fact that the maker's signature on a note is forged is not available as a defense to the liability of an indorser of the note, for by his signature the indorser impliedly warrants the validity and genuineness of the instrument to all subsequent holders in due course. Nor, if an indorser's signature is forged, may indorsers other than the one whose signature is forged, avoid liability on that account.

Effect of failure to make timely demand for payment of a note.—It is not necessary, in order to hold the maker of a note liable thereon, to present a note to him at maturity and to demand payment; his liability attaches automatically upon maturity of the note. To hold an indorser liable, however, the note must be presented for payment to the maker, for the indorser agrees to pay only if the maker has failed to pay after due demand has been made. Due demand means that the note is presented for payment at a proper place on the day it falls due, or in the case of demand note, within a reasonable time after issuance. If the place of payment is specified in the note, the note must be presented at that place. If no place of payment is specified, but the address of the person who is to make payment is given in the note, it should be presented there. If no place of payment is specified and no address is given, the note must be presented at the usual place of business or residence of the maker. The note must actually be exhibited to the person from whom payment is demanded. Presentment of a note to the maker, sufficient to bind the indorser, cannot be made by a telephone demand upon him at his place of business where the note is payable, although he is notified that the note is in the possession of the communicant and ready for delivery.

To the rule, as indicated above, that timely presentment for payment to the maker is necessary to hold the indorser liable, there are some exceptions. Where a note was made or accepted for the accommodation of the indorser and he has no reason to expect that the instrument will be paid if presented, presentment for payment is not required in order to charge an indorser with liability. Delay in making presentment for payment is also excused when the delay is caused by circumstances beyond the control of the holder and not imputable to his default, misconduct, or negligence. The following circumstances are generally deemed to excuse delay:

1. Inevitable accident or overwhelming calamity.

2. Prevalence of a malignant disease which suspends the ordinary operations of business.

3. The presence of political circumstances amounting to virtual interruption and obstruction of ordinary trade negotiations.

4. Breaking out of war between the country of the maker and that of the holder.

5. Occupation of the country where the parties live, or where the note is payable, by a public enemy, which suspends commercial intercourse.

6. Public and positive interdictions and prohibitions of the state, which obstruct or suspend commerce and intercourse.

7. Utter impracticability of finding the maker or ascertaining his place of residence.

When the cause of delay ceases to operate, presentment must be made with reasonable diligence. Where the holder of a note has died, and no executor or administrator has qualified to present the note for payment, presentment for payment within a reasonable time after appointment and qualification of the executor or administrator is sufficient.

Effect of failure to give timely notice of non-payment of a note.—The general rule is that if an indorser is not given notice of the fact that a note has been dishonored by non-payment, he is discharged from liability. The reason for this rule is that an indorser has a right to be put into possession of the material facts on which his liability is based, so that he may take the steps necessary for his own protection. Notice of non-payment may be given over the telephone, in personal conversation, or by writing, and may be conveyed in any terms which sufficiently identify the instrument and indicate that it has been dishonored by non-payment. An indorser may waive notice of non-payment orally or in writing, in which case his liability attaches although proper notice of non-payment is not given to him. The waiver need not be direct and positive, but may be implied from usage, understanding between the parties, or from any acts or conduct clearly calculated to mislead the holder and prevent him from treating the note as he otherwise would. To constitute an implied waiver, the acts of the indorser must be such as would warrant the holder in not taking the steps necessary to charge the indorser. As in the case of timely presentment of a note for payment, delay in giving notice of dishonor is excused when the delay is caused by circumstances beyond the control of the holder and not imputable to his default, misconduct, or negligence; but when the cause of delay ceases to operate, notice must be given with reasonable diligence.

Law Relating to Drafts or Bills of Exchange

What is a draft or bill of exchange?—The terms "draft" and "bill of exchange" are used interchangeably. The Negotiable Instruments Law defines a bill of exchange as an "unconditional order in writing addressed by one person to another, signed by the person giving it, requiring the person to whom it is addressed to pay on demand or at a fixed or determinable future time a sum certain in money, to order or bearer." The person who draws the bill of exchange is the "drawer"; the person who is to pay the bill is the "drawee." The drawer, by affixing his signature to the instrument, represents to all holders of the bill that the drawee has funds of the drawer to meet the bill.

Difference between a draft and a check.—The Negotiable Instruments Law expressly defines a check as "a bill of exchange drawn on a bank payable on demand." A check is, therefore, included in the term "bill of exchange," but it differs from the ordinary draft or bill of exchange in the following important respects:

1. A check is always drawn on a bank, and it is always payable on demand; a draft may or may not be drawn on a bank, and it is generally made payable a fixed period of time after sight. A bill of exchange, drawn on a bank and payable on demand, is a check.
2. A draft must be presented to the drawer for acceptance; a check need be presented only for payment.
3. Death of the drawer of a bill of exchange does not revoke the drawee's authority to pay the bill, but death of the drawer of a check does revoke the bank's authority to honor the instrument.
4. In the case of a draft, delay in presenting the draft to the drawee for payment may discharge the drawer; in the case of a check, failure to present promptly for payment discharges the maker of the check only if he has sustained injury by the delay.

Difference between a draft and a note.—At its inception, a note involves two parties—the maker and the payee. Upon transfer of the note by the payee to a third person, the note becomes similar to a draft. The note is then an order by the payee upon the maker, to make payment to the indorser. A bill of exchange, on the other hand, becomes, in effect, a promissory note upon acceptance; the acceptor or drawee corresponds to the maker and is primarily liable, and the drawer corresponds to the first indorser who is secondarily liable. The Negotiable Instruments Law provides that "where in a bill the drawer and drawee are the same person, or where the drawee is a fictitious person, or a person not having capacity to contract, the holder may treat the instrument, at its option, either as a bill of exchange or a promissory note."

Necessity of presenting a bill of exchange for acceptance.—Acceptance of a bill of exchange is the signification by the drawee of his assent to the order of the drawer. Where a bill of exchange is payable at a certain time or on demand, it is not necessary to present it for acceptance in order to hold the drawer or an indorser liable thereon, although it is customary to do so. Where, however, the bill is made payable a designated length of time after sight, it must be presented for acceptance, for otherwise the maturity date of the bill cannot be ascertained. Under the Negotiable Instruments Law, a drawee is allowed twenty-four hours after presentment in which to decide whether or not he will accept the bill, but if he does accept, the maturity date is reckoned from the day of presentation.

Necessity of presenting a bill of exchange for payment.—Failure to present a bill of exchange to the drawee for payment does not release the acceptor of the bill from liability. But presentment for payment is necessary in order to charge the drawer. Where the bill of exchange is not payable on demand but at a fixed or ascertainable time, it must be presented on the day it falls due. If it is payable on demand, it may be presented within a reasonable time after the last negotiation of the bill. The bill of exchange must be presented for payment at the place specified in the instrument. If not so specified, it must be presented at the address of the person by whom payment is to be made, given in the instrument, or if not so given, then at the usual place of business or residence of such person.

Necessity of protesting an inland bill of exchange, dishonored for non-acceptance or non-payment.—An inland bill of exchange is defined by the Negotiable Instruments Law as "a bill which is, or on its face purports to be, both drawn and payable within the state." Any other bill is a foreign bill. Unless the contrary appears on the face of the bill, the holder may treat it as an inland bill. It is important to distinguish between a foreign bill of exchange and an inland bill, for a foreign bill which is dishonored by non-acceptance or non-payment is required to be protested * before the drawer of the bill can be held liable, but an inland bill of exchange need not be so protested. All that is necessary in the case of an inland bill is that notice be given to the drawer of the fact of dishonor. The Negotiable Instruments Law specifically provides that where a foreign bill of exchange, appearing on its face to be such, is dishonored by non-acceptance, it must be duly protested for non-acceptance, and where such a bill which has not previously been dishonored by non-acceptance is dishonored by non-payment, it must be duly protested for non-payment. It further provides that if the bill is not so protested, the drawer and indorsers are discharged, but that protest is unnecessary where the bill does not on its face appear to be a foreign bill.

If a drawee accepts a forged bill of exchange, has he any recourse?—It is the duty of the drawee of a bill of exchange to satisfy himself that the signature of the drawer is genuine before he accepts it, for by his acceptance he is deemed to admit the genuineness of the drawer's signature. If he accepts a bill of exchange on which the drawer's signature is forged, he can neither repudiate his acceptance nor recover any money which he has paid to a bona fide holder of the instrument. The drawee of a bill of exchange is not, however, bound to know the signature of the payee, and if he pays a draft upon a bill containing a forged indorsement, he may recover the amount from the person to whom payment was made. Similarly, the drawee is not presumed to know whether or not any part of a bill of exchange, other than the drawer's signature, is genuine, and if the bill has been altered, the drawee has a right to recover the amount paid on the bill to an indorser.

3. HOW TO WRITE CREDIT LETTERS

Letters asking customers for credit information.—Letters of this type must be written with great tact, especially if they are to be sent by mercantile houses to small concerns that may not be familiar with customary credit procedure, or by retailers to persons

* "Protest" is the making of a formal certification, generally by a notary, attesting the refusal to accept or pay a bill of exchange.

who have probably had little business experience. The customer must not be given the impression that the letter is a reflection upon his standing, that his credit is considered doubtful, or that he is being singled out for special investigation. The fact should be made clear that the request for credit references or for a financial statement is merely standard business practice. The tone of the letter should not be negative or formal, but courteous and individual.

New customers.—When a letter is received from a new customer requesting credit, or a request is received with an order, or merely an order is received, the letter to the customer requesting credit information will accomplish its purpose if it is constructed as follows:

1. Welcome the customer and thank him for his inquiry or order.
2. Explain or suggest your usual credit procedure or policy.
3. Ask the customer for credit references or for a financial statement. Enclose a printed form for him to fill out and return.
4. Stimulate prompt action by showing the customer that it is to his own interest to supply the necessary information at once, and express the hope that his inquiry or order is the beginning of a friendly and mutually profitable business relationship.

Example of letter asking customer for credit information:

Gentlemen:

Thank you very much for your order of May 3. It calls for a well-selected assortment of merchandise for which you will find ready and profitable sale.

In connection with the usual credit formalities of a new account, we would appreciate your filling out and returning the enclosed property-statement blank. This is not more than any established house requires, and we feel that you will appreciate our coming directly and frankly to you for such information. For our part we would much rather place our confidence in your own statement than in any reports we might obtain through other sources. This information is for our own files only and will be regarded as strictly confidential.

As credit is largely a matter of mutual confidence, perhaps you may wish to know more about us. We refer you to any bank or business house in Boston, and to Dun & Bradstreet, Inc.

Your account can be opened just as soon as the property statement is returned to us, and shipment of your order can then be made at once.

We hope that this is only the start of a long business relationship, which we shall try to make both pleasant and profitable to you.

Very truly yours,

Example of letter from retail store asking for credit information:

Dear Mrs. Smith:

Thank you for your inquiry concerning the opening of a charge account in our store. An application form is enclosed, and on its return to us we will endeavor to open your account promptly.

We are confident that you will find it convenient and pleasant to shop with us regularly. A fully itemized bill will be rendered on the first of each month and is payable in full by the tenth.

An addressed envelope is enclosed for your convenience in returning the signed application, and we will be looking forward to opportunities to render service.

Very truly yours,
Department of Accounts

Old customers.—In connection with a periodic revision of the credit files, it may be necessary to write to old customers for an up-to-date financial statement. The following is a practical outline for a letter of this type:

1. Thank the customer for his past business.
2. State that you are revising your credit files and are asking all your customers to supply you with a new financial statement. Make it clear that this request is being made of all your customers.
3. Ask the customer to provide you with the necessary information. Enclose a printed form for him to fill out and return.
4. Assure the customer of your willingness to co-operate with him, as in the past.

Sell the idea to the customer in a persuasive, sympathetic letter with constructive ideas presented cheerfully and considerately.

Example of a letter to an old customer asking for recent financial statement:

Dear Mr. Holden:

Every time you send us an order you pay us a compliment, and we want you to know that we sincerely appreciate the business you have given us in the past few months. We value your confidence and goodwill and will always try to be deserving of it.

At the present time we are making the usual revision of our credit files, and in connection with this revision are asking all our customers to provide us with an up-to-date financial statement. This we are doing because we take a personal interest in the progress of our customers, and we feel that they appreciate our coming directly to them for credit information from time to time. It has always been our policy to place our confidence in your own statement rather than in any reports we might obtain from other sources.

We are enclosing a copy of our regular property-statement form, and would appreciate your filling it out and returning it to us within the next few days. The information is solely for the purpose of bringing our files up to date, and is kept strictly confidential.

We hope that we will continue to receive a share of your business as in the past, and assure you that we are always glad to be of service to you at any time.

Sincerely yours,

Reply to customer who refuses credit information.—Although most people are familiar with the necessity for giving credit information, a customer occasionally refuses to complete the form sent him. Following is a practical outline for a letter of reply covering this situation.

1. Thank the customer for his letter and for the opportunity it gives you to explain your credit policy. Express regret that your previous letter has given rise to misunderstanding.
2. Explain that request for credit information is merely standard business practice; that no reflection is intended; that the information is treated as strictly confidential; and that you yourself give information concerning your own financial standing to the houses from whom you buy.
3. Assure the customer that his business will be appreciated, and that you will be glad to co-operate with him in every way, and renew your request that he fill out and return the printed form.

Example of letter to customer who refuses to give credit information:

Dear Mr. Clark:

I am glad of the opportunity that your letter of June 6 gives me to explain our request of June 1. I am very sorry that you feel that our asking you to fill out a property statement casts reflection upon your credit standing. No reflection whatsoever was intended.

Our request was merely in line with our usual credit policy. It is a practice with us, as with most established business houses, to ask each new customer to fill out and return a form identical with the one sent you. That we intended no reflection upon you is indicated by the fact that we follow this procedure in opening all new accounts.

We feel that we and our customers are partners in business, and that without a friendly and frank exchange of credit information there cannot be complete co-operation between us. Furthermore, we would always much rather place our confidence in your own statement than in any reports we might obtain from other sources.

We ourselves are glad to supply our creditors with such information about our own standing as we requested from you, because we know that without their co-operation we could not do business on our present scale. We therefore feel that our creditors are entitled to know our financial condition.

Credit is very largely a matter of mutual confidence. We, as the seller, show our confidence in you by accepting your credit. You, as the buyer, show your confidence in us by your willingness to indicate a few essential facts regarding your business.

We hope that you will co-operate with us by supplying the information requested. We assure you that it is intended solely for our files, and that we regard it as strictly confidential. We shall greatly appreciate your business and shall do everything in our power to make our relationship pleasant and profitable to you.

Very truly yours,
Credit Manager

Letters of inquiry to customer's credit references.—Letters requesting credit information from references supplied by the customer may be brief and concise and should offer to reciprocate when occasion arises. If definite information is desired, ask specific questions or enclose a printed form to be filled out and returned. Letters of this type are usually form letters.

Examples of letters to credit references requesting information:

Dear Mr. Brown:

John Doe, 24 Kilburn Road, Dallas, Texas, wishes to open an account with us and requests a credit limit of $100. He has given us your name as a reference.

We shall naturally appreciate any information you can give us regarding Mr. Doe's ability to meet his obligations promptly. Any other facts which will help us in determining the amount of credit to extend will be welcome.

At any time that we can serve you in a similar way, we shall be glad to do so.

Yours very truly,

* * *

Gentlemen:

The person or firm named below wishes to open an account with us, and has given your name as a credit reference.

Mr. James S. Wilson

____

256 Maple Avenue

____

Newark, N. J.

____

Any information you may furnish us will be treated as strictly confidential.

We shall appreciate an early reply, and assure you of our willingness to reciprocate at any time. A stamped, addressed envelope is enclosed for your convenience.

Very truly yours,

* * *

Please answer the following:

Acct. opened (date) ____________ Highest recent credit __________

Owing now __________________ For month of _________________

Date last paid _________________ Pays in __________________ days

Remarks as to occupation _______________________________________

Worth (property)? ____

Character ____

* * *

Gentlemen:

We shall be grateful if you will answer the questions listed below, giving us your frank opinion of the character, habits, business ability, and financial standing of the person or firm named.

We shall appreciate a prompt reply, and hope that we may soon have the opportunity of reciprocating your kindness.

Hamilton & Smith, Inc.

Name of person or firm ________________________________

Hackensack, N. J.

Location ________________________________

Is he now a customer of yours? ________________________________

How long has he done business with you? ________________________________

What credit do you extend? ________________________________

Does he take cash discounts? ________________________________

If not, does he pay bills promptly when due? ________________________________

Give an idea of the extensions he asks for, if any ________________________________

____

If not contrary to your policy, state how much he owes you now, and what part, if any, is past due ________________________________

____

Has your experience with this customer been generally satisfactory?

____

Have you any reason to believe that he is not so good a risk at the present time as he has been in the past? ________________________________

____

Other data bearing on credit risk ________________________________

____

____

____

____

Very truly yours,

Letters granting credit.—A letter granting credit should state clearly the terms of payment, so that there may be no subsequent misunderstanding. It need not, however, be written merely in formal or routine style; it represents an opportunity to capitalize on the customer's interest in the firm and its products. Hence a good letter of this type shows appreciation of the account and ties the customer to the house by creating goodwill and emphasizing service.

Examples of letters granting credit:

Dear Mr. Whittemore:

We are very glad to extend to you, in accordance with your request of March 12, our most favorable credit terms, 2/10 net 30.

The information which we have received concerning you is so completely favorable to you personally and as a businessman that we appreciate your choosing us to supply you with merchandise. Your order is going forward today.

We want you to feel that the quality, delivery, and prices which brought us this first order are also to be found in all the other electrical supplies we carry, such as electrical devices manufactured by the Westinghouse Electric & Manufacturing Company and other substantial organizations.

And as our acquaintance ripens, and you become more familiar with our stock, the feeling will grow that for anything and everything electrical, you can depend on Hyland as a sure and constant source of supply.

Please be assured of our appreciation for this initial order. We shall strive to do everything possible to cause it to be but the first of many.

Very truly yours,

* * *

Dear Mrs. Jones:

It is our pleasure to notify you that a (name of store) charge account has been opened in your name. We will constantly endeavor to serve you courteously and to your complete satisfaction.

Arrangements have been made to place at your disposal credit amounting to $________. If it is your wish to make purchases of a larger amount, now or in the future, I would welcome an opportunity to discuss your requirements with you.

Bills will be rendered on the first of each month and are payable in full by the tenth.

An identification plate and a booklet that explains in more detail the facilities now at your disposal at (name of store) are enclosed. We are sure that you will find your account a convenience and hope that you will always consider it a pleasure to shop with us.

Very truly yours,
Director of Accounts

Dear Mr. Jones:

Your "Extended Three Months' Account" at May Brothers has been opened and is now ready for use.

Statements are rendered the first of each month. One third of your purchase is payable on or before the tenth of the first month following the date of purchase. The balance is payable in two equal payments to be made on or before the tenth of the two succeeding months. There is no interest or carrying charge whatsoever!

We are glad to extend to you this Extended Account privilege. Its purpose is to make it easy for you to enjoy quality apparel without any financial strain.

What we are really selling at May Brothers is Permanent Customer Satisfaction. Please keep this in mind and remember we are always at your service, with a sincere desire to please you and to make your shopping so pleasant that you will always want to say—"Let's go to May Brothers."

Very truly yours,

P.S. Your Extended Three Months' Account is open now. Just say "Charge It."

* * *

Dear Mr. ____________________

It is a pleasure indeed to advise you that your credit application has been approved and your name placed on our records as one of our charge customers.

Our aim is to develop this new business relation between us into a lasting friendship. To this end we shall do our best to serve you so efficiently that it will be an incentive to use the MALCOLM BROCK COMPANY as your shopping headquarters.

You will want to know our terms. All purchases made up to a few days before the end of each month will appear on the statement you will receive on the first, and are payable in full on or before the tenth of the month following.

We want you to enjoy thoroughly shopping on your account, and your suggestions for the improvement of our service are always welcome.

Cordially yours,

Letter to husband of credit applicant.—If the applicant for credit is a married woman, in addition to sending a letter to her similar to that described in the preceding paragraphs, one is also sent to the husband. While the purpose of such a letter obviously is to inform the husband that an account has been opened for his wife, the letter is given a sales slant. In the following example, the men's store is introduced to the husband. The letter takes the form of an engraved four-page announcement measuring 5½ x 7 inches. The company seal takes the place of a letterhead. On the third page is a statement of terms. On the last page is a statement of the ideals of the store and a list of addresses at which stores are located.

It is a pleasure to inform you that, as requested by your wife, a charge account has been opened for your joint use.

You will enjoy shopping for your personal needs in ____________ stores for men, where we hope to have the privilege of serving you often.

Letters refusing credit.—A letter refusing credit should be courteous and constructive. It should convince the applicant that the refusal is made with his best interests in mind and that some other form of purchase at present is to his advantage. Such a letter may be constructed as follows:

1. Cheerfully thank the applicant for providing you with credit information and acknowledge receipt of data from other sources.
2. Analyze the applicant's financial condition. Begin with the more favorable aspects and pass tactfully to the less favorable. Explain frankly, but sympathetically, the reasons for your decision not to grant credit. Do not be vague or apologetic.
3. Suggest a definite and practical means by which he can improve his credit standing in order to place himself in a position to receive credit. The suggestion may be that he try to secure additional capital, that he reduce his inventory by disposing of out-of-date merchandise, that he expand the scope of his business only with caution, and the like. Offer the firm's co-operation.
4. Try to get the customer's business on a cash basis. Retain goodwill by appealing to his sense of sound business policy and thus leave the way open for business relations in the future.

Example of letter refusing credit:

Dear Mr. Benson:

Thank you very much for your business statement of March 1 and also for the references.

We sincerely appreciate this evidence of your interest in our goods. All the references you gave us spoke very highly of you, both personally and as a businessman.

We regret, however, that we feel we are unable—for the present at least—to grant the credit accommodation you ask. From a study of your assets and liabilities it appears to us that you are, frankly, somewhat undercapitalized. In our opinion, however, it is only a matter of time until you will be able to remedy this situation. With your personal ability and a favorable location for a hardware store in Westport, there is every indication that your future prospects are excellent. As a constructive suggestion we would advise that you secure $2,500 additional capital if it is at all possible for you to do so.

In the meantime, we recommend that you cut your order to us by one-half and that you advise us to ship to you on a cash basis. You will receive a 2% discount for cash, and the balance of your order can be forwarded at a moment's notice if you find that you need it. By cutting your order in half you will lessen the risk of having your shelves overstocked.

As soon as it appears that accepting your credit will not jeopardize your prospects, we shall be glad to co-operate with you by selling to you on open account. For the present we offer you our most favorable cash terms and assure you of our desire to be of service.

We hope that the arrangement suggested will appeal to you as temporarily the most satisfactory from your own standpoint. We are ready to make immediate shipment if you will give us a favorable reply.

Sincerely yours,

Example of letter refusing credit and obtaining business on a cash basis.—The following letter was successful in obtaining a cash order. Notice how sympathetically yet frankly the firm's decision to refuse credit is stated. Analysis of the situation in this case makes it easy for the customer to feel the readiness of the firm to co-operate. A solution is offered, and action is stimulated.

Dear Mr. Jones:

I want to thank you for the order you 'phoned us the other day for a copy of the Tax Diary and Manual, now ready for distribution.

The order has been held up by our Credit Department, but as you obviously wanted a copy of the book, I felt I should write you, particularly since I know of the various reasons and situations which can result, often unjustly, in this status of an account.

Sometimes an account gets into the dubious class as a result of a practical joke—reply cards being returned with names forged by offenders who cannot be traced. In such cases, receivers of books occasionally refuse—with some justification—to return the books or to pay for them.

Possibly something like this happened in your case—either on books sent to you by us or by other publishers with whom we exchange credit information.

In any event, when good faith is shown in such instances by a willingness to send us an order with remittance enclosed, we usually mark the accounts "O.K." for future approval orders.

If, with this explanation, you wish to order a copy of the Tax Diary and Manual on our money-back guarantee basis, as offered by the special form herewith, we shall be glad indeed to count you among our good customers.

A reply envelope, requiring no postage, is enclosed. Thank you.

Yours very truly,

Letter referring unacceptable accounts to the Credit Bureau.—Frequently the credit man does not wish to undertake an analysis and constructive criticism of the applicant's credit position when his credit cannot be accepted, and prefers instead to refer him to the credit bureau. This is particularly true of retail stores. Should this be the case, the following letter may be used:

Dear Mrs. Smith:

We acknowledge with thanks your application for a charge account, but regret our inability to accommodate you at this time.

The Credit Bureau of Chicago, which is the Clearing House for credit information on individuals purchasing in Chicago, has been unable, from the material on hand, to furnish us with sufficient data to warrant our approval of your application.

May we suggest that you call personally at the office of the Bureau and supply such additional data as may be required to complete its records. The Bureau will then report to us.

Very truly yours,
Director of Accounts

Letters to insistent customers who are not desirable.—Instances occur where the credit department does not want the account of a certain customer who has insisted upon credit. The following letter may be used. Notice that it makes no mention of patronizing the store on a cash basis, the reason being that the credit manager felt it would be presumptuous to ask for cash under the circumstances.

Dear Mrs. Doe:

We appreciate your interest in opening a charge account with (name of store), but regret our inability to complete arrangements for you at this time.

It is hoped that there may be other ways in which we can be of service.

Yours very truly,
Director of Accounts

Letter where credit is refused and merchandise is delivered.—If a customer was permitted to take goods with her at the time the application for credit was made, or if the merchandise was delivered immediately, and investigation shows the account to be undesirable, a letter such as the following may be used:

Dear Mrs. Henry:

We appreciate your interest in opening a charge account with (name of store), but regret our inability to complete arrangements for you at this time.

However, as an accommodation, we delivered and charged the merchandise which you selected at the time of making the application. You will receive a bill on the first of the month which will be payable in full by the tenth.

It is hoped that there may be other ways in which we may be of service to you.

Yours very truly,
Director of Accounts

Many stores attempt to make the sale on a C.O.D. basis if for some reason the purchase cannot be charged. In such cases a printed form of explanation such as the following may be used.

Why

We Are Sending This C.O.D.

In order to deliver this package to you without delay, we are sending it C. O. D., because we are unable to locate a record of a charge account. It is possible that the name is incorrectly spelled or the account is carried under a different address. If this is properly a charge, will you kindly have our representative telephone the Credit Department, and the undersigned will be glad to release the package to you.

____

Charge Authorization

By ________________________________

Letter suspending charge privilege before credit period expires.—Frequently the credit department finds it necessary to suspend temporarily the charge privilege before the time for payment expires, because the credit limit has been exceeded. In such a case, the following letter may be used:

Dear Mrs. Smith:

All stores doing a credit business place a limit on each account up to which they will accept charges without question as long as the account is paid promptly. This is done to provide control on the amounts owed by customers.

KIRKMAN'S customers establish their own limits in the sense that the amount of each customer's average monthly payments is considered the limit on that account. We are writing you now because, in approving your recent charge, we noticed that your account exceeds your charge limit, which has been determined according to our established methods.

For this reason we should appreciate your calling at the Credit Department before making any further charges. I am sure that satisfactory arrangements can be made at that time. If we have made an error in your charge limit, we shall be glad to discuss the matter with you when you are next in the store.

Thank you for your co-operation, Mrs. Smith.

Very truly yours,

Letters of reply to credit inquiries.—In replying to credit inquiries, the credit man should satisfy himself that the inquirer will treat the information confidentially and that the information offered violates no confidence. The reply should be frank and specific and as helpful to the inquirer as possible. Replies are often so worded that no express or implied responsibility is assumed by the writer.

Because of the law of libel, caution must be exercised where the reply is unfavorable. Many firms omit any mention of the subject's name and address and make their statements as general as possible when sending derogatory information.

A standard form for reporting on ledger experience has been prepared by the National Association of Credit Men. Should the credit manager prefer to write a personal letter in reply to a credit inquiry, the following letters will serve as a guide.

Favorable replies to credit inquiries:

Gentlemen:

We are glad to answer your letter of September 6, in which you inquire about our experience with Mr. John Simpson, 874 Locust Avenue, Mobile, Alabama.

Mr. Simpson has had a credit account with us for the past three years and has always paid his bills promptly. With us he has a credit limit of $300.00.

Mr. Simpson is one of our desirable customers.

Very truly yours,

* * *

Gentlemen:

We are glad to answer your letter of April 3, in which you inquire about our experience with Hamilton & Smith, Inc., of Hackensack, N. J.

Hamilton & Smith, Inc., have had a credit account with us for the past two years and are still active on our books. Their limit with us has been $350. Although they have not discounted their bills, they have usually paid promptly. On two occasions their account ran past due, the first time forty days and the second thirty days. This, however, was thirteen months ago; their account has been satisfactory for the past year.

We regard Hamilton & Smith, Inc., as a reasonably good risk up to the amount stated.

Very truly yours,

Unfavorable replies to credit inquiries:

Gentlemen:

We regret to inform you in reference to the person mentioned in your letter of (date) that our information prevents us from endorsing his credit standing for the amount you mention.

Yours truly,

* * *

Gentlemen:

In reply to your letter of February 10, we are sorry to report that our experience with the firm mentioned has been unsatisfactory.

During the two years that we have served this firm they have failed to discount their bills and have several times caused us difficulty in collecting. At the present time they owe us a considerable amount on past-due accounts.

Very truly yours,

4. HOW TO WRITE COLLECTION LETTERS

Acknowledgment is made to John Whyte and F. R. Otte for permission to reproduce letters from "Letters That Collect" (New York: Prentice-Hall, Inc.)

Two essentials of the effective collection letter.—The effective collection letter is one that is written with two purposes in mind:

1. Getting the money.
2. Keeping the customer's goodwill and business.

To accomplish the first purpose without regard to the second is relatively easy, but to accomplish both purposes requires a high degree of skill. The letters reproduced in this section have been selected, on the basis of proved effectiveness, from actual collection correspondence; they represent a cross section of the work of trained and experienced collection men.

Classification of delinquent debtors.—From the standpoint of collections, debtors may be classified somewhat as follows:

1. Customers who overlook accounts simply because of negligence or poor business methods.

2. Customers who disregard due dates because of the smallness of the account.

3. Customers who disregard due dates because they think they can "get away with it," or (and) because it is more profitable for them to use the creditor's money than the bank's.

4. Customers who take unearned discounts because they expect to "get away with it," and because it is profitable for them to take these discounts.

5. Customers who are temporarily slow, but who usually pay on time. They pay on time when the due dates of the creditor's bills coincide with the seasonal high points in their own business, and they make the creditor wait when these periods do not coincide.

6. Customers who are chronically slow.

7. Customers who are temporarily slow because of local trade conditions.

8. Customers who are verging on insolvency or who are actually insolvent.

9. Customers who are crooked or deliberately fraudulent.

Placing the customer in one of the above classes, on the basis of information obtained from the ledger, from the salesman, and possibly from interchange reports or trade-group discussions, simplifies the collection problem and indicates the type of treatment that will be likely to prove most effective.

Stages in collection procedure.—Although the circumstances of each individual case necessarily modify the collection procedure, collection correspondence is largely based on the cumulative effect of repetition and variety of appeal. The typical unpaid account passes through the following stages of collection correspondence:

1. Reminder.
2. Inquiry.
3. Appeal.
4. Demand.

In this section letters are presented in the following groups: (1) reminders; (2) letters for the early stages of collection; (3) letters for the middle stages of collection; and (4) letters for the late stages of collection.

Suggestions for writing collection letters.—The following suggestions may be used as a guide in writing collection letters:

1. Be cheerful, optimistic, and constructive in considering the debtor's predicament.

2. Visualize and individualize the debtor, know his kind of delinquency, his business, its location and its condition. Consult the credit files, salesmen, and, if necessary, the debtor himself. If sufficient data are lacking, be helpful in guarded phrases.

3. Be specific. Express your own individuality or that of your firm. Avoid stereotyped and over-courteous phrases particularly. A human, personal appeal must be direct to be sincere.

4. Adopt the "you" attitude. This does not mean that the personal pronoun need be used constantly, but that behind every word there lies sympathetic consideration of the individual case.

5. Beware of brevity. A too-short collection letter becomes curt and gives the impression of dunning. Letters must be compact if they are to conserve the reader's time. But they must also be long enough to analyze the debtor's financial condition.

6. When writing to women, avoid the colloquial, breezy style that might be suitable for other debtors. A dignified letter of a reserved and courteous tone, correct in language, should be sent on smaller than the usual 8 x 11 inch business stationery. Because women are sensitive and generally unfamiliar with technical terms, such words as ledger, dealing, and accounts receivable should be omitted.

7. The tone of the strong collection letter should be, wherever possible, one of fairness and goodwill. There should be no hint of exasperation. There are times, however, when a forceful letter becomes necessary. Before writing one, it is well to obtain legal advice, for certain threats are punishable by law. An uncounseled letter might easily do more harm than good. Many credit men wait until the next day after a forceful letter is written before mailing it.

8. Fix a definite schedule for writing collection letters, preferably in the morning. Irritating negative words and phrases are less likely to creep into correspondence written at the beginning of the day when the writer is still fresh. Correspondents are not interrupted by rush requests for information, and the afternoon is left

free for other credit work. Furthermore, letters can be in the mail by the end of the day, which minimizes discrepancies between status of account when the letter is written and when it is mailed.

9. Omit, whenever possible, such words as "enforce," "insist," "demand," "compel," "handle," "impossible," "unable," and "annoyed." These are negative words that serve only to irritate the customer.

Collection Reminders

Forms of reminder.—In the first stage it may be assumed that the customer's failure to pay is due to forgetfulness or carelessness. It is therefore necessary to bring the status of the account to the customer's attention. For this purpose a milc and inoffensive reminder may be used; this reminder may take one or other of a number of forms.

1. *Duplicate bill or statement and reminder phrase.*—A reminder may consist of a duplicate bill or statement, on which is prominently typewritten or rubber-stamped a phrase such as:

Past due.
Please remit.
Account past due. Please remit.
Please!
A prompt remittance will be appreciated.
Please mail us a check.
May we have check, please?
Blank days past due. Please remit promptly.
Please give this your attention.

2. *Stickers.*—More forceful than a typewritten or rubber-stamped phrase is a sticker attached to a duplicate bill or statement. Examples of stickers are reproduced in Figure 83.

3. *Printed cards.*—A reminder may consist of a printed card, without salutation or signature, on which details as to the standing of the account are filled in. These cards are often preferable to letters for the first reminder since they are impersonal and customers realize that all other delinquents are receiving them under the same circumstances. They should be courteously worded to show fairness, to recall the agreed credit terms, and to impress customers

Figure 83.—Collection Stickers.

with their impersonal and impartial nature. Where temporary suspension of the charge privilege will be impartially applied, the card should warn the customer without giving offense.

Figure 84 is an example of a printed card showing a statement of account that may be sent as a first reminder.

STATEMENT OF ACCOUNT

Balance last bill.................................. $........

Payments or Merchandise Returned................ $........

Balance now due.................................. $........

An itemized statement of the above balance has been previously sent. If it is correct and in accord with your records, we would appreciate payment.

BROWN & SMITH, INC.

Please return this card with your check.

Figure 84.—Reminder in the Form of a Printed Card.

Other brief reminders that may be used on such a card are the following:

We respectfully request your immediate attention to the past-due account.

Just another friendly reminder of our terms which are ordinarily—monthly in full.

You have perhaps allowed this account to escape your notice. Please give it your attention.

This statement is sent to you for comparison and as a reminder of mutual understanding as to terms.

Another type of printed card for collection reminder is a simply worded notice enclosed with the statement. This eliminates any extra addressing and mailing expenses and ties it in immediately with the unpaid account. A different color may be used for each card to prevent sending of the wrong notice. Notices may be printed on lightweight paper, safety bond paper, or card stock of about 3x5 inches. The seal of a credit organization occasionally embellishes these cards.

An example of such a card is Figure 85.

> Your attention has already been called to the unpaid balance on the enclosed bill and we would greatly appreciate prompt payment.
>
> Since we first opened accounts and rendered bills we have specified that accounts are payable in full early in the month following purchase. If anything has occurred contrary to this understanding, we are sure that you will not hesitate to advise us.
>
> In the meantime, we shall understand that additional purchases will not be charged to your account until the overdue portion has been paid in full.
>
> THE RICHFIELD STORE

Figure 85.—Notice as Collection Reminder.

4. *Combination statement and reminder message.*—The reminder correspondence for the first stage of a series of collection letters may be combined with a statement, as illustrated in Figure 86, or may be a brief form letter as illustrated below:

Gentlemen:

If you have not already done so, won't you mail us a check to cover your due account, $256.34?

We shall be grateful for prompt attention.

Very truly yours,

The Denoyer-Geppert Company, Chicago, through whose courtesy the illustration on page 1050 is reproduced, has used a series of four combination statements and letters. A different color is used for each unit of the series. The statement-letters are folded and enclosed in window envelopes; it is thus necessary to type the customer's name only once—for letter, statement, and envelope.

5. *Aged statement and reminder.*—A statement analyzing the overdue balance according to actual monthly purchases has proved an effective way to begin the collection drive against overdue accounts. To many customers, particularly women, a statement sent,

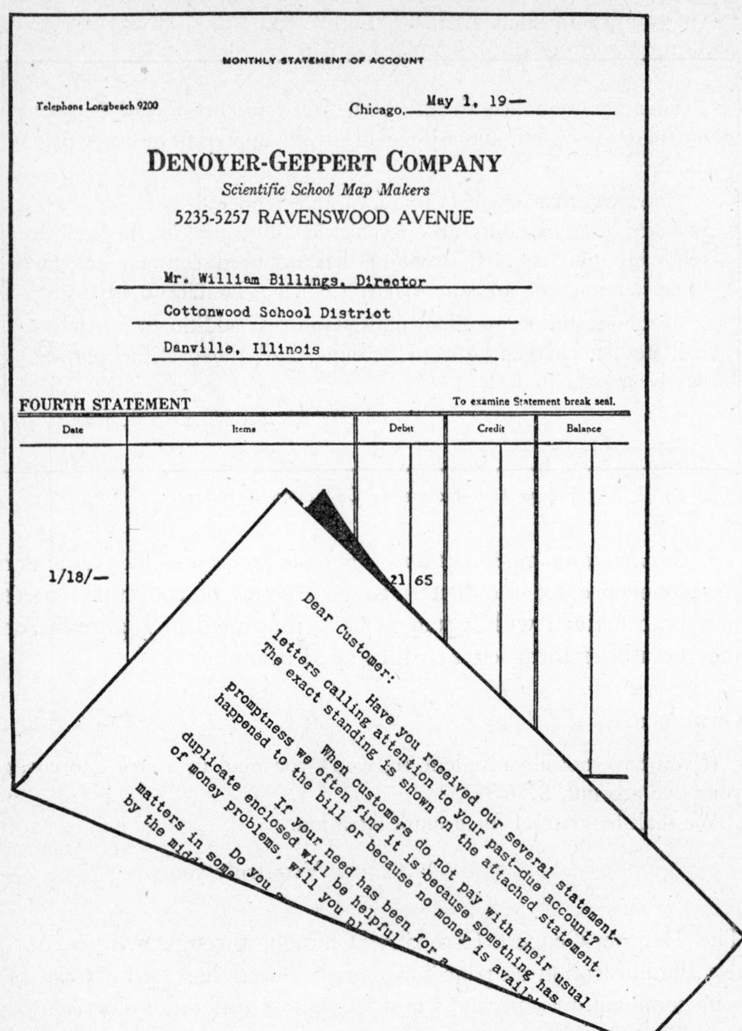

MONTHLY STATEMENT OF ACCOUNT

Telephone Longbeach 9200

Chicago, May 1, 19—

DENOYER-GEPPERT COMPANY

Scientific School Map Makers

5235-5257 RAVENSWOOD AVENUE

Mr. William Billings, Director
Cottonwood School District
Danville, Illinois

FOURTH STATEMENT

To examine Statement break seal.

Date	Items	Debit	Credit	Balance
1/18/—		21 65		

Dear Customer:

Have you received our several statement-letters calling attention to your past-due account? The exact standing is shown on the attached statement.

When customers do not pay with their usual promptness we often find it is because something has happened to the bill or because no money is availa

If your need has been for a duplicate enclosed will be helpful or money problems, will you pl

Do you

matters in some

by the midd

Figure 86.—A Combination Statement and Letter.

for example, in November showing an August balance is more startling than one showing a balance 90 days old. The statement illustrated in Figure 87 is sent 45 days after the bill and is interchanged with card reminders twice a month until the account reaches a six months' classification. At that time a series of letters stressing the urgency of payment is started.

PLEASE RETURN THIS STUB WITH YOUR REMITTANCE

STATEMENT

JOSKE BROS. CO.

SAN ANTONIO, TEXAS

M

	BALANCE OF MONTHLY PURCHASES DUE ACCORDING TO SCHEDULE ON LEFT MARGIN		
JANUARY			
FEBRUARY			
MARCH			
APRIL			
MAY	Just to Remind You-- that this account has probably been overlooked and we'll appreciate your remittance. Thank You!		
JUNE			
JULY			
AUGUST			
SEPTEMBER			
OCTOBER			
NOVEMBER			
DECEMBER			
TOTAL	ACCOUNTS ARE PAYABLE IN FULL ON 10TH. OF MONTH FOLLOWING DATE OF PURCHASE		

Figure 87.—Reminder Statement for Overdue Accounts.

6. *Envelope message.*—The collection envelope illustrated in Figure 88 has been used successfully especially by firms in the clothing industry. The name and address of the creditor is printed on the envelope, making it ready for mailing.

Another variation of the use of an envelope to hasten collections in the reminder stage is the combination of envelope with collection message. A reply envelope is enclosed with each bill. Printed on the outside of the flap is the statement "Our Story Is Inside." This

STATEMENT

DEPARTMENT OF ACCOUNTS

TO________________________________

________________________________ ____________________19____

This statement of your account is sent believing you have overlooked payment. As our terms provide for prompt settlement of accounts when due, we are calling it to your attention.

DATE	MEMO	DEBITS	CREDITS	BALANCE
	Amount in Last Column is the Balance Due			

Inclose remittance or reply here ☞ Seal, Stamp and Mail.

IN YOUR REPLY PLEASE USE THIS SELF ADDRESSED ENVELOPE

NOTICE

SPECIAL CREDIT SERVICE

To avoid the possibility of error or misunderstanding, we use a special system of Accountancy in our bookkeeping department. This system of accounting automatically protects the credit position of our customers by preventing accounts that become, *inadvertently* or *temporarily*, past due from *injustly* passing to our delinquent file. It is necessary, however, that immediate cooperation be extended by promptly acknowledging the receipt of this statement, and if payment is not made herewith the accuracy of the statement must be verified, and a time definitely stated as to settlement.

IT IS THE POLICY OF THIS COMPANY TO EXTEND EVERY POSSIBLE COURTESY TO OUR CUSTOMERS CONSISTENT WITH SOUND BUSINESS PRINCIPLES.

COPYRIGHTED 1939
MFG. ENVELOPE CO.

Figure 88.—Collection Envelope.

refers to the customer's story (enclosed check) as well as the company's story printed on the underneath side of the flap, which reads:

OUR INSIDE STORY

One of our ideas about being in business is to be as helpful as we can to our customers. We even help them pay their bills by sending them handy return envelopes like this one.

Won't you slip your check into this envelope to balance your account and help us with our collections? Thank you.

When the flap is opened, there appears a reminder printed on the body of the envelope, which is covered when the flap is sealed. The reminder reads:

MEMO STATEMENT

of Your Account

Balance Due -------- $--------

THANK YOU

7. *Oversight letter.*—Should the collection department desire to use the "oversight" approach for its reminder letter, the following letter may serve as a guide:

Dear Mr. Kirkman:

Your account with us shows a balance of $--------, which is now past due. This is possibly an oversight. We therefore call it to your attention now.

You may overlook this matter again if you put this letter aside, so why not pin a check to it right now and return it in the enclosed envelope.

Very truly yours,

8. *Other types of reminder letters.*—A type of reminder letter that has been used successfully thanks a customer for his business and at the same time subtly calls attention to the fact that his account has been checked and is past due. Without actually asking for payment, the mention of the date and amount of purchase and the signature of the credit department leave little doubt as to the intent of the letter.

The success of any business is in direct proportion to its Goodwill.

We hope we have pleased you with our products and our service. We, in turn, are grateful for your patronage and believe it only fair that we should say so.

Thank you, then, for your (month) purchases amounting to $------.

Yours very truly,
Credit Department

* * *

Time out!

We want to pause for just a moment in the daily round to tell you of our cordial appreciation of your business.

Here's the pause............

And here's a friendly "thank you" for your (month) purchases totalling $------.

Yours very truly,
Credit Department

* * *

"Hurry back!"

That familiar and delectable parting of the guest, so typical of the Sunny South, carries a wealth of warmth and friendliness.

And we want you to feel the deep sincerity of our appreciation of your business and our thanks for your (month) purchases amounting to $------.

"Hurry back!"

Yours very truly,
Credit Department

Letters for the Early Stages of Collection

Second stage: Letters of inquiry.—In the second stage of the collection series, assuming that one or two reminders have not brought a response, the creditor should make a direct inquiry as to why the bill has not been paid. Is there a legitimate reason for the delay? Or is the debtor just stalling off as long as he can? If the creditor has no traveling representative in the territory, he will have to write and ask the cause. Does it lie with the creditor's goods or services? Are the debtor's collections slow? Are local conditions strained? If the debtor replies with an explanation, the creditor should offer every assistance to help him through his difficulties.

Examples of letters in the second stage.—Following are examples of letters that can be used in the second stage in the collection series:

Dear Sir:

It's rather a novelty to have occasion to write you concerning your account for any purpose other than to thank you for a check, for an account such as yours is a boon to a business house.

However, it would appear, unless our records are wrong, that your June account, amounting to $78.50, has not met your customary prompt payment.

Have we made any mistake, or are there any special circumstances that have held up payment of this account?

Very truly yours,

* * *

Gentlemen:

You are one of our new customers, and this is our first credit relation with you. Our three statements and our letter of March 3 have as yet been unanswered. This would indicate that something is wrong.

Did we not come to a satisfactory credit understanding?

Have we made some mistake in the charge?

How do you wish us to handle your account?

By all means be frank in telling us if any mistake has been made, for you will find us more than willing to correct it.

Very truly yours,

* * *

Gentlemen:

Is there something wrong with the merchandise covered by the above sum? Do you question the correctness of the charge?

If so, you have only to tell us about it—on the back of this letter, if you wish—and we shall be glad to go into the matter thoroughly with you.

If everything is satisfactory, but you just haven't got around to sending in your check, surely you will want to forward it to us now.

Very truly yours,

Letter of inquiry with form for reply.—Many collection men include a form for reply in their second letter of a collection series. The following are examples:

Gentlemen:

Our books show your account to be $85.43 past due, but our files give no indication of the difficulty.

Will you please answer the questions listed below, and return this letter to us? A stamped envelope is enclosed for your convenience.

Your answers to these questions will help us to co-operate with you. Please reply promptly.

Very truly yours,

Enclosing check for $____

Payment will be made on (date)__________________________________

This account has not been paid because____________________________

____

____

(Signed)________________________________

* * *

Gentlemen:

It doesn't seem possible that your account is thirty days past due—but it is.

You will want to take care of it now, I know; so let's have a check—either a real check, or a check in one of the brackets below:

( ) Mailed you one on ________________________________

( ) Here's a part of it; balance will follow on _______________

____

( ) Here's all of it. Glad to send it.

( ) Can't possibly make it today. Will send it ______________

____

Cordially yours,

In some cases the following item is included in the form:

This account has not been paid because ______________________

A sharper tone for a second letter.—In certain instances, such as for the poor risk, the second letter of a collection series should assume a slightly sharper tone, as illustrated in the following letter:

Gentlemen:

We have no way of knowing, unless you tell us, why we have not received payment of our invoices of (date—amount) and (date—amount).

We know that you must have a good reason, but that neither settles the account nor enlightens us as to why we should carry it any longer. You cannot expect us to let it drift along without some explanation. It will take you only a moment to write us a letter and put the facts before us. We are sure that our attitude is understandable, for we must have some knowledge of the situation in order to know just where we stand in the matter.

Why not write us about it now?

Very truly yours,

Cards to be used with second statement.—Figure 89 is a card, recommended by the National Association of Credit Men, which might well be used instead of a letter and enclosed with a second statement, especially where an impersonal card has been enclosed, or a sticker has been used with the first statement as a reminder.

Do you know

How seriously *your credit standing is affected* by *neglect* or *indifference* to the correspondence of your creditors relating to overdue accounts?

If you cannot remit when due, don't let the creditor *guess* the reason. He may make an undesirable guess. Give him the reason straight, and thus encourage that frankness among business men that is worth dollars to all.

PUNCTUALITY IN CORRESPONDENCE IS A MOST IMPORTANT CREDIT AND BUSINESS BUILDER.

NATIONAL ASSOCIATION OF CREDIT MEN
ONE PARK AVENUE NEW YORK CITY

10M 2-36

Figure 89.—Collection Card.

Letters for the Middle Stages of Collection

Third stage: Letters of appeal.—The third letter of a collection series will depend largely upon the reply to the second. If the debtor responds with an actual grievance, or if circumstances beyond his control make payment impossible, the creditor's reply will take on an appropriate personal character. If there is no reply, however, the debtor is obviously trying to avoid payment and needs more urgent prodding. Send the poor risk either a draft or a very strong letter. Try to induce payment from the medium or good risk by appealing to such motives as pride, duty, justice and fairness, or self-interest.

An appeal to pride, addressed to a new customer.—The following letter, sent as the third letter in a collection series to a new customer, appeals to his pride in his reputation among his associates.

Dear Sir:

You will remember that, when you placed an order with us last January, you furnished us with some references to whom we wrote for the purpose of establishing an account in your name. We did not know you ourselves, never having done business with you, and depended entirely upon what these other people and you told us; and when they said you would take care of an account promptly, we trusted you without any hesitation.

However, instead of paying our accounts promptly, you have permitted them to go unattended to, so that, at this time, we find there are owing two January bills of $24.46 and $35.28, respectively, about which we have written you three times unsuccessfully. Now, of course, there may be some reason why you haven't been able to take care of these bills, but it would seem as though, under such circumstances, you would write us and not permit us to form an erroneous impression of the manner in which you take care of your obligations.

Won't you please let us have your check for $59.74 immediately, so that it will not be necessary to mark your account as slow pay?

Yours very truly,

An appeal to pride, addressed to an old customer:

Dear Mr. Hogan:

We regret very much to find that your account is gradually becoming larger and that your purchases during the current month far exceed your payments.

We have always considered your firm as one of our banner customers, and we take it for granted that there is some just reason why you are withholding payment. If that be the case, won't you let us know? Or, better still, just step into our office and go over the matter with us so that we may adjust it to the satisfaction of both.

We want you to know that we greatly appreciate your account and want you to continue on our books.

This account is now sixty days past due and we know that you do not want that condition to exist.

If it is not convenient for you to come to our office, just call the writer on the telephone, and we may be able to adjust the account.

Very truly yours,

An appeal to co-operation based on mutual interest.—A letter that appeals to co-operation based on mutual interest can be used as the third in a series of collection correspondence.

Dear Mr. Fisk:

We are going to make an extra appeal for payment of your account, because we must have your full support if our relations with each other are to be profitable to both of us.

You know that we are interested in your business, and that we are eager to be of assistance to you. But you place us in a difficult position when you do not pay our bills—you discourage by just so much our efforts to be of most service to you.

We still feel that you want to work with us, so we have hesitated to put our request for payment in the form of a demand. Yet we do think that we are not unreasonable in asking for and expecting your check at once.

Very truly yours,

Another appeal to the customer's co-operation:

Gentlemen:

The other morning I happened to be sitting in a seat ahead of two gentlemen riding to work on a streetcar, and having nothing to do but listen, I did. Their conversation ranged all the way from Haile Selassie to Mussolini and to the more personal subject of "when will I get out of the red?" One of the men—evidently the more business-like—explained that he was working on a budget and figured that by the first of the year he would be all square. The other hemmed and hawed. He couldn't see the light of day and didn't know when he would. At that point I got off the car, wondering.

Before me today I have a list of wholesalers who are past due, some quite a bit, some not so much. You are one of them, and I am wondering how many will be like the first man—all square and ready to discount by the first of the year. Will you be one of them? I hope so.

Believe it or not, this credit department is here to help you with your problems; to help you work out a plan that will make it possible for you to begin discounting by January 1, but to do so we must have some expression from you—some outline as to how things are going with you.

The delinquent balance that was due on your account November

1 amounts to $25.76. Not large, it is true, but nevertheless important to you and to us. If you need more time, write me. If you can pay, send your check today in the attached envelope. Will you co-operate?

Yours very truly,

An appeal to the customer's sense of honor.—The third letter of a collection correspondence series appealing to the customer's sense of honor is effective if the customer was fully informed of the credit terms when he received credit. Failure to pay at maturity means breaking the contract to which he bound himself by accepting the shipment. For this reason the appeal to honor usually stresses the contractual obligation. It will be effective only insofar as credit men conscientiously educate their customers to realize the sanctity of their credit obligation. The following letter makes this appeal:

Gentlemen:

We are unwilling to assume that businessmen of your standing would intentionally neglect our account or ignore the many letters received from us concerning it.

We expressed our confidence in you when we delivered, on open terms, the goods covered by our April bill of $43.90, and we are reluctant to think that that confidence was misplaced. We have been glad to serve you in the past, and undoubtedly you will want further credit accommodations in the future. If you are to preserve your standing with us, however, you must see to it that immediate provisions are made for settlement of your account.

We know that there are times when the bills seem to pile up faster than the money to pay them. If you have run across some adverse conditions, please tell us about it. If you are not in a position to remit our entire bill now, please let us have a check for half immediately and a second check for the balance post-dated a week or ten days.

We believe that you want to adjust matters in a friendly way, and we trust that you will accept our invitation to let us hear from you by return mail.

Yours very truly,

Another appeal to the customer's sense of honor.—The following letter, in stressing the justice of the creditor's position, is simple, patient, and considerate. The appeal is not obtrusive, for all its dramatic quality. Yet it avoids a morally superior tone and retains the respect for the debtor's sense of honor. Further, the very important "you" attitude prevails throughout.

Dear Mr. Young:

You, as a businessman, have often extended credit, expecting that your debtor would pay on time.

If you did not receive payment on the expected date, you sent a statement. After a week or ten days, you mailed another statement—and then another. You had full confidence in your debtor, or you would not have extended the credit. You assured yourself, after getting no response to your first statement, by thinking: "There are many reasons why a man cannot always pay promptly." And after the second statement you probably thought: "It is strange that I do not hear from Mr. Smith." After no reply to the third statement you must have thought: "Mr. Smith is not much concerned with this account, for even if he cannot pay, he can surely explain conditions."

To be convinced of Mr. Smith's good intention, you should then have had his explanation or a check balancing his account.

This is the history of our account with you, amounting to $--------. Will you not convince us of your good intentions?

Yours very truly,

An appeal to the customer's sense of fairness.—Another effective appeal in a collection letter is one to the customer's sense of fairness. Imply that he has not been treating the firm fairly; the creditor has delivered satisfactory goods and services; and the debtor should in justice pay promptly and satisfactorily.

Gentlemen:

It is necessary for us to call attention to your account for the months of September and October, which is still unpaid. The September account, under the liberal terms that we are extending to you, should have been paid on or before October 20.

When your account became due, it was not paid, and of course it was natural for you to order your supplies elsewhere. For that reason we have not received any of your orders for thirty days.

In all fairness, we want to ask whether you think it is right that the reward for carrying your account during the past thirty days should be the loss of your business for that length of time. If we had insisted on payment, would we not still be able to look upon you as an active customer?

We appeal to you to send us a check immediately to cover your account, thereby re-establishing sound business relations and putting us in a position again to receive your orders. We are sure that we will hear from you by return mail.

Very truly yours,

Another appeal to the customer's sense of fairness:

Dear Mr. Robertson:

We have written you on more than one occasion regarding your account. The balance is noted above. It is considerably overdue. We have waited patiently and cannot understand why you have not paid us by this time.

We now request your immediate attention to the matter, and we frankly ask that you send us a check without further delay.

In making this request, we feel that we are asking for nothing more than that to which you consider us fairly entitled.

Yours very truly,

Another appeal to the customer's sense of fairness:

Dear Mr. Hawkins:

When I was a boy, I was told that if I wanted anything and asked for it in a nice way, my chances of getting it were pretty good.

It would seem that this should hold true in business also.

Now, you owe my house a bill that is overdue, and I should like to have you send me a check for the amount within the next couple of days.

I am asking for it in the nicest way that I know how, and I think it's going to be pretty hard for you to refuse.

Very truly yours,

Unique appeal to fair play.—The note of sincerity in this unique "50-50" letter appeals to the customer's sense of fairness.

OUR HALF of this letter:

You will see at a glance that this is a real "50-50" letter, because exactly one-half of it belongs to you.

Being human, we can appreciate what hard work it is—and we mean just that—for most of us to sit down and write a letter. Also, we can understand how easily payment of a small bill can be unintentionally overlooked. With these things in mind, we are sending you a reply as your half to our half of this letter. All you have to do is sign your name and address in the space provided and return it to us.

We feel sure you want to pay the amount past due on your account. Please meet us on a "50-50" basis—just tear off and mail back your half, and you will have a better understanding of our earnest desire to meet you half way.

DO IT NOW!

YOUR HALF of this letter:

Dear Mr. Simmons:

Of course I will meet you half way. You have shown the right spirit—so will I.

I have overlooked forwarding my remittance for the amount due you up to this time.

Please accept the enclosed payment for $-------- as an evidence of my good intentions.

Name ----------------------

Street ----------------------

City ----------------------

State ----------------------

Mat. No. ----------------------

Course ----------------------

An appeal to the customer's self-interest.—An appeal to the customer's self-interest probably brings better results, on the whole, than any other appeal. Show the customer that it is to his own personal advantage to pay now, and that prompt payment improves his credit standing and enables the firm to sell at lower prices. Call his attention to the periodical reporting of delinquents to credit associations, without actually suggesting blacklisting. The latter not only destroys goodwill but may render the creditor liable to legal punishment.

Gentlemen:

When your account was opened with us, we had every reason to believe that you would pay it when it became due.

In making the usual credit investigation, we found that all those with whom you had done business spoke very highly of you in a personal way, and declared that you would meet your obligations promptly.

It is therefore difficult for us to understand why you have not taken care of our account amounting to $193.45.

Before investigating further your manner of making payment to others, in which investigation we should, of course, have to state what our experience has been with you, we want to give you another opportunity to pay your long past-due account with us.

It would not favorably impress those who have recommended you so highly to learn that our experience has not fully justified the unqualified recommendations which they gave to us.

Can we plan—definitely—on hearing from you by return mail?

Very truly yours,

Another appeal to the customer's self-interest:

Dear Mr. Becker:

We are enclosing a statement of your account, which shows a balance due us of $98.23, and for which remittance in accordance with our terms should have been received on a net basis last month.

Our friends in the trade very frequently call upon us for information as to the financial responsibility and habits of payment of our customers, because they too have you on their books, and they like to get the benefit of our experience.

We want to be able to tell these firms that you take care of your obligations on a discount basis, or that you pay when due.

You, on the other hand, have sufficient regard for your credit reputation to verify this by taking care of your obligations promptly.

With this in mind, we feel sure that you will not wish to allow your account to become delinquent, and we, in turn, will be gratified to report "good pay" to inquiries regarding your company. Please give us this opportunity and yourself this advantage by sending your check now.

Yours very truly,

Another appeal to the customer's self-interest:

Gentlemen:

About a year ago you referred a firm in Philadelphia to us, and we were very glad to tell this firm that our accounts had been paid promptly.

Today, this same firm informed us that you had not met their account so promptly, and asked how you stood on our books at the present time. We were forced to tell them that obligations were not being met as well as formerly. This was not pleasant to do. We never like to give unfavorable reports on any of our customers. Please don't make it necessary with your account.

Won't you send us a check at once to cover the amount as shown on the enclosed statement? We want to tell the Philadelphia firm that the account has been paid, and that we are sure your tardiness was due simply to an oversight.

Yours very truly,

Letters for the Late Stages of Collection

Fourth stage: Letters of demand.—If the debtor has not replied to the first three letters sent him, the credit man can assume that he is unduly negligent, irresponsible, or has no intention of paying. Write a fourth letter impressing him with the urgency of the situation and demand payment. Drafts are often used at this stage. If his record is bad, threaten to bring suit or to turn the account over to a collection agency. Even a demand letter can retain customer goodwill by restraint in phrasing and an attitude of fairness, and by showing the debtor that the firm has been patient and considerate. Also, caution should be exercised in threatening to resort to force, for a fifth or sixth letter often brings payment. Many solvent merchants, for instance, feel that they can take their time about paying, since the creditor knows that he will eventually get his money.

Demand letters, formal in tone.—Following are examples of demand letters, formal in tone, that may be used as the fourth letter in a collection series. Notice how the third illustration, particularly adaptable to retail collections, is firm in demanding payment, but gives the customer the benefit of the doubt.

Dear Sir:

Your neglect of your overdue account—$56.78, now four months past due—has obliged us to take measures to protect our interests.

We have therefore scheduled the claim to be placed for collection with the Mercantile Collection Agency on April 15 if it is still unpaid at that time.

This notice, however, gives you another chance to settle direct.

We trust that you will take advantage of the extension and thereby avoid mutual unpleasantness and expense.

Yours very truly,

* * *

Gentlemen:

We regret keenly that it is necessary to write again about your account.

Many lenient efforts to make an arrangement convenient for you have failed, and the time has now arrived when we must take determined steps for collection.

Unless we hear from you within ten days regarding suitable arrangements for settlement of your debt, we shall not hesitate to turn your account over to our attorney for collection without further notice to you.

Yours very truly,

* * *

Dear Miss Jones:

Thus far in our efforts to collect your account, we have proceeded on the assumption that you have the will to pay and intend to do so.

We shall not change this attitude unless you force us to do so. Although you have ignored the letters we have sent you during recent weeks, we are still not quite convinced that you do not intend to pay this bill.

It would be to your interest to call on our credit manager while we are still in this frame of mind—say, within the next three days.

Very truly yours,

* * *

Dear Mrs. Thompson:

As all ordinary means used for collecting your delinquent balance of $_______ out of court have failed to bring the desired results, we are notifying you that unless this balance is paid in full or suitable arrangements are made within seven days, it will be placed with the Adjustment Department of the Chicago Credit Bureau with instructions to bring suit at once.

Yours very truly,

A demand letter, more conciliatory in tone:

Gentlemen:

We hope that our co-operation with you, in allowing exceptional time for the payment of your past-due account, has been of help to you.

We have been very considerate in this matter and had sincerely hoped that you would willingly send us your check before this time.

If you have any reason for withholding payment, you should write us fully and frankly at once. You will find us reasonable and willing to continue our co-operation. However, when an account such as yours runs so long past the due date, and we do not hear from you, there is no alternative left for us but to place your account in the hands of our attorneys for collection.

We dislike being forced to take this action, as it is not consistent with our policies, and as it will cause you expense and inconvenience.

We hope that you will send us your remittance at once and not make this step an actual necessity.

Yours very truly,

A demand letter, firm but not unfriendly:

Dear Sir:

This is going to be our last opportunity to deal directly with each other.

We have tried in every possible way to persuade you to settle your indebtedness with us. We have written you over and over again. We have waited patiently for you to come forward with some reasonable proposition, but you have not even attempted to meet us halfway.

Further continuation on this basis would be neither good business nor good sense. If we do not hear from you in response to this letter, we shall turn the account over to an attorney in your city for collection. This statement is not intended as a threat, but simply to get all the facts before you.

Perhaps there is something to be said on your side. Perhaps you have cause for complaint against us. If so, we should like very much to hear from you, and assure you that we shall read your letter in a spirit of fairness. Are you not willing to write in the same spirit?

We are as anxious as you for a friendly settlement of this account. Such a settlement is still possible. We shall wait five days for your reply.

Yours very truly,

A demand letter, without a direct threat.—In many instances it may be wise to omit a direct threat to resort to force in the fourth letter of a collection series, in which case the following novel aspect may be stressed. Notice the veiled implication and partial assumption of the blame.

Dear Mr. Jones:

I think you will agree that I have every reason seriously to consider my next step in the collection of your account.

Possibly I have been at fault in being too lenient in my follow-up system—but, if so, then you too are at fault for having taken advantage of my leniency.

It isn't too late, however, to set matters right, and I sincerely hope that you will arrange for settlement on receipt of this letter.

Very truly yours,

Action to be taken if the fourth letter brings no response.—Should the fourth letter still bring no response, many concerns cite success in sending a letter signed by an officer of the company, such as that reproduced below. Send a fifth, sixth, or seventh letter, decreasing the intervals between them by a day. Express confidence in the debtor, yet, at the same time, point out the seriousness of neglecting bills and appeal to the saving that could have been possible through a discount had the bill been paid on time. Courtesy should be the keynote in announcing legal steps.

On the basis of replies to these letters, the creditor will know whether or not, and, if so, when, to turn the account over to an attorney or collection agency. If these letters are sent by registered mail, especially the one announcing recourse to legal action, or are accompanied by a wire, the effect on the debtor will be heightened.

Letters signed by officials of the company:

Dear Mr. Grant:

I was asked this morning to approve placing your account with our attorneys, but before approving such action, I am writing you this letter.

There is one very important reason why neither you nor I should want this action taken. If we sue you we will get our money, but lawsuits destroy the friendly relationship which we take pride in maintaining with our trade. We value your account and are exceedingly reluctant to take any steps that would interrupt our pleasant business relationship. We wish to keep your goodwill and are confident that you wish to keep ours.

In selling our line of goods, you are setting a high standard of merchandise and, without doubt, you wish to set an equally high standard of business practice. Believing this, we have tried to be fair and certainly have been patient with you. We have now reached the time when your bills must be paid; therefore, unless you show some disposition to protect your credit, I must authorize the placing of your account with our attorneys.

We trust that you will not force us to take this action by further delaying settlement. Help us to avoid drastic action, please, by mailing us your check immediately.

Very truly yours,
President

Writing for part payment before threatening suit.—Before writing a fourth or fifth letter in which immediate suit is threatened, it is often good policy to attempt to secure part payment with other payments arranged at specified intervals. This has usually been found to bring some sort of reply. Notice in the letter below that the customer has an "out" by which to save face, although there can be little doubt as to what the consequences will be if this letter, too, is ignored.

Gentlemen:

Ninety per cent of the accounts we collect through attorneys are handled that way because customers will not answer our letters.

We are forced to sue because friendly requests bring neither payment nor explanations.

Your account of $-------- is long past due. We assume that the amount is correct, for you have never questioned it.

You have disregarded our letters about it; but in spite of that, we really cannot believe that you do not care. There must be some other reason. Perhaps you cannot pay it all. But don't you think in fairness to yourself, as well as to us, that you should mail us a check for all you can and frankly say how you are situated and what you can do about the rest?

We both want to keep away from the lawyers if possible. So, before sending the account to our attorney, we will wait ten days for your letter and check.

Yours very truly,

Notifying debtor to honor a draft.—A letter that may be sent to debtors to whom you are sending a draft follows:

Gentlemen:

You have received a number of reminders from us regarding your past-due account, which is now too old to be continued. We are giving you a final opportunity to make an adjustment without the aid of more drastic measures.

We have therefore drawn upon you today a draft at five days sight, through the State National Bank.

We hope that, upon receipt of this letter, you will promptly arrange to take care of the draft when presented, and thus make unnecessary the unpleasantness and expense that will result if the account is placed out of our hands.

Yours very truly,

Stunt collection letters.—Most collection correspondents shy away from stunt letters, since they feel that these have no place in a letter dealing with a serious business matter. Occasionally, however, a stunt will prove the most effective way of collecting an account, especially with dealers. For example, the following rubber-band letter did the trick for a company in the women's garment industry. In the spot marked by asterisks was pasted a rubber band. The letter was as follows:

Dear Mr. Jones:

Here is a typical, conventional, normal, common, ordinary, everyday, familiar variety of rubber band.

* * * *

A certain amount of stretching keeps the rubber lively according to rubber manufacturers, but too much stretching will break it.

Credit terms are a lot like that, aren't they? There's a point beyond which they cannot be stretched.

I hope the rubber band will serve as a reminder. You have stretched sufficiently. Send us a check now.

Very truly yours,

A stunt letter with a timely appeal.—The Denoyer-Geppert Company, Chicago, used the following stunt letter effectively by having it prepared as a facsimile handwritten document on a irregularly cut sheet of colored paper, somewhat smaller than letterhead size. Part of the company's seal was stamped in the lower left-hand corner. Since the company, which manufactures maps, globes, charts, and models, has a special type of clientele, it was felt that a special type of approach was advisable.

Treaties? ?

If both of us were European diplomats, we probably would regard our contractual obligations as mere scraps of paper. You would then feel free to tell us to forget our account, and we would tell our suppliers of raw materials, and our employees the same thing.

But happily, that isn't the American way. We do pay our debts and our customers do admirably well in paying theirs to us.

Right now WE are faced with a large task, in providing funds to meet Fall purchase bills and repaying our bank for loans during the slack season (summer). Anything that can conveniently be done to hurry remittance on the attached statement will be greatly appreciated and will help in fulfilling our "non-aggression pacts" with bank and suppliers' Credit Departments.

And—apart from the immediate purpose of this letter—may lasting peace come to a troubled World soon.

Done at Chicago, Illinois this first day of September, in the year 19--, in the full faith of

Denoyer-Geppert Co.

Collection letter resembling legal document.—Realizing that legal-appearing documents are rarely ignored by customers who have long-outstanding debts, a firm multigraphed the following collection letter on a sheet of white paper, stapled it into a blue cover, and folded it to resemble a legal form. The tone of the letter takes the "sting" out of the presentation.

Our Accounting Department does solemnly affirm, maintain, and assert that you owe us $-------- since December 1, 19--.

We hate to get excited about so small an amount. We also dislike the usual "collection letter" that bursts into tears in the first paragraph and yells for the law in the second.

Trouble is, though, that when you and 999 other customers owe us small bills like this, the sum total is something to give our Mr. Kimball a headache. He was absent from school the day they taught arithmetic, but even he knows that you can't meet payrolls without cash.

Seriously . . . we have tried to be good-humored and patient about your account, but it HAS run for more than six months. Won't you please send it *now—by return mail?* Thank you a lot.

One-word follow-up breaks monotony of series.—A series of collection letters, no matter how well-worded or cleverly composed, may become monotonous. The following letter, injected in a series, not only breaks this monotony but usually jolts the reader into attention.

Dear Smith:
Well?

The Ohio Overcoat Co.,
E. M. Flowers, Credits

Miscellaneous Collection Problems Handled by Letter

Letters on small past-due accounts.—The following illustrate the type of letter that has proved most successful in collecting small past-due accounts.

A small-account letter, friendly and courteous:

Dear Mr. Adams:

Each time we write you about that little balance of $4.64 it costs us, everything included, 35 or 40 cents.

The profit on this item has long since been exhausted.

Won't you save us time, money, and annoyance by writing a check for us now, today, while you think of it?

Very truly yours,

Another friendly small-account letter:

Dear Mr. Benson:

When a man is puzzled over the dozen or so problems that come up in everyday business—buying, selling, advertising, and managing a store—little matters such as the enclosed account readily slip his mind.

They do with me, and I like to be reminded of them, so I feel sure that you will be glad to have this again brought to your attention.

The enclosed stamped, addressed envelope offers a quick, easy way of getting the check back to us.

Very truly yours,

A letter on a small item long past due:

Dear Mr. Breden:

The credit and collection department has called to my attention an old balance on your account, amounting to $80.20. This balance is an amount left over from purchases made by you more than a year ago.

You have been a mighty good customer of ours and, compared with the business that you have given us, the balance of $80.20 is insignificant. Still, it takes money, you know, to keep the wheels of progress properly oiled and greased, and in order to do this accounts must be collected. This particular bill that I am writing about happens to be so old that it has an accumulation of dust on it.

You have been good enough to send us several payments on account during the year, but it is now pretty close to the end of the year, and I am therefore going to ask you please to write out a check for the full amount and put it in the enclosed addressed envelope so that we may balance your account when the next mail arrives.

Your personal attention to this will be much appreciated.

Very truly yours,

Letters educating the customer in the use of discounts.—Letters such as the following, pointing out to the customer the advantages of taking the cash discount, are often productive of good results.

A persuasive letter on the taking of discounts:

Gentlemen:

In looking over your account today, we noticed that of late you have been losing some cash discounts.

As a means to profit, the cash discount is almost indispensable. Whether your net profit is 2 per cent, 4 per cent, or more, cash discount is a vital part of it. No company can lose discounts and compete successfully in these days of high overhead and narrow margins.

We know that it is your desire to make use of every means of increasing your net profit, and that, therefore, it is your plan and policy to avail yourselves of the 2 per cent whenever it is offered.

When we noticed that you had been losing some Pet Milk discounts, we decided that the cause could be nothing more than oversight, and that you would welcome having the matter brought to your attention. We are anxious to have you add to your profit every possible Pet Milk discount. It amounts to about eight and one-half cents per case.

It pleases us to have your company as one of our distributors. We appreciate your business and shall always be glad to co-operate with you.

Yours very truly,

P.S. Please note that money used for discounting, on the basis of 2 per cent ten days, will earn 36 per cent per year.

A lesson on the advantages of discounts:

Gentlemen:

A notably large percentage of our customers discount their bills, a very satisfactory procedure from every point of view—theirs and ours. We are hoping that we shall soon include you among them.

We are wondering whether you appreciate how much discounting your bills amounts to, both financially and as a foundation for credit.

Take your case as an illustration. You have been buying from us, on the average, $500 worth of goods a month. Two per cent discount would net you a saving of $10, and for a period of twelve months you would earn $120 through your policy of paying promptly. This is certainly a nice amount to save on one account alone. If you added the discounts that you could save by paying all your bills promptly, you would find that the figure amounts to a considerable sum.

May we not urge that you give this matter your consideration, and determine from now on to take advantage of every discount offered.

Yours very truly,

A reminder before the discount period expires:

Dear Mr. Swanson:

It is our policy to offer our customers a discount of 2 per cent for payment of a bill within 10 days from date; otherwise the amount is due and payable in 30 days net, as per the terms printed on our invoice.

Since the attached bill should be paid in 30 days anyway, perhaps you would prefer to save 2 per cent by sending your check by return mail.

The amount in this case being $345.60, you can effect a saving of $6.91 by remitting immediately.

Letters on the taking of unearned discounts.—The following letters illustrate methods of handling the problem of deduction of unearned discounts.

*A general letter to all dealers:**

Dear Sir:

We are convinced that a great deal of mischief results all around from taking cash discounts where they have not been earned. As you know, bills rendered by us are supposed to be paid by the 10th of the month to earn the 2 per cent discount.

We have been receiving plenty of checks dated the 10th, but something peculiar seems to happen to the envelopes containing them the minute they are turned over to Uncle Sam for delivery. Apparently they hang around the post office for days and even weeks before they reach us.

Now for a confession: We too have been careless about cash discounts due the other fellow, and those from whom we buy raw materials and supplies might well write us in the same way we are writing you. Recently, when we were urging one of our salesmen to correct this matter in his territory, he challenged our own practice. We saw the light and have changed; all our checks dated the 10th are getting in the mail that same day. That puts us in a position to expect the same prompt payment from our own customers. Our determination to take cash discounts only where they are earned will be maintained at all costs.

This letter is being sent to all of our friends because we believe this is a matter of general interest.

Yours very truly,

An unearned-discount letter requesting check for deduction:

Gentlemen:

We acknowledge your check for $75.25, which is very much appreciated and which we have applied to your account.

---

* From an article by Ray Giles, "Curing the Dealer Who Takes Unearned Cash Discounts," in *Advertising & Selling,* April 26, 1934.

With regard to the deduction of 2 per cent cash, we are sorry that we cannot consistently allow it in this instance, as our cash discount terms are 2 per cent 10 days from the date of invoice.

Serving as we do about forty thousand customers, it frequently happens that deductions of this nature are made, and were we to allow them, the aggregate sum involved in the course of a year's business would be large. You will appreciate, also, that it would not be fair for us to allow you the discount in this case when we deny it to other concerns with whom we do business. We feel that it is not fair to the trade to make special concessions to some that are contrary to our requirements from others.

We are sure that you will agree with us and that you will co-operate with us in the maintenance of our terms. We are enclosing a statement showing a balance of $10.25, and will very much appreciate receiving your check for this sum.

Very truly yours,

A letter refusing a request for longer terms:

Gentlemen:

The request in your letter of October 4, that cash discount be allowed when payment is made between the 10th and the 15th of the month following shipment, has been made to us from time to time by various customers, some of whom buy in very large quantities. We have invariably felt, however, that we were unable to grant the request, for two reasons:

First: Cash discount is a premium offered for prepayment of an invoice, and if the invoice is not paid within 10 days, the extra profit has not been earned. If we have to wait an average of 30 days, our bills are due net, and we are obliged to disallow the discount privilege.

Second: It would obviously be unfair to our many customers who pay in 10 days to permit others to remit in 30 days, as it would be giving the latter a better price than those who pay more promptly. We do not think you would expect us to discriminate in this way.

We want you to know, however, that we fully appreciate your point of view, as we ourselves, with about twenty factories, find it a difficult task to put our discount bills through for payment in 10 days.

We feel confident that, after considering the foregoing, you will agree that our attitude is the only just one to assume, when all the circumstances are taken into account.

Very truly yours,

Explaining why interest is charged on overdue accounts.—A letter explaining to the debtor the reason for interest charges on his overdue account is reproduced below.

A very complete and courteous explanation of interest charges:

Gentlemen:

Thank you very much for your check for $893.50, covering our February and March bills. Your prompt response to our C.O.D. message is greatly appreciated.

We notice that in remitting you have deducted the item of interest, amounting to $27.50, and, believing that you probably did this because you thought it was an unjust charge, we take the liberty of writing you, in order that you may understand our point of view on this subject.

In the first place, you will appreciate, by taking your own account as an instance, that in order to grant the accommodation asked by our trade, it is necessary for us to carry on our books a large amount of money which otherwise we could be using in our business.

This accommodation we are, as you know, very glad to extend, but we do not feel, and we are sure you do not wish, that we should suffer a loss by so doing. That is just what happens, however, unless we can get interest on our money, or, in other words, on outstanding past-due accounts; for, if our bills were paid promptly, we would never have to go to our bank for loans.

The bank, of course, charges us interest, and it is this interest charge that we pass on to you. We think that such an expense, incurred in accommodating our customers, should be assumed by our customers, and that you, for instance, should pay your share, especially in view of the fact that the rate we charge, and which is exactly what we pay ourselves, is considerably less than you would have to pay if you borrowed the money from your own bank in order to meet your bills as they fell due.

All we want you to do is to think this over, and if you decide that we are right, we will be pleased to receive your remittance for $27.50.

With our best wishes for a record holiday business,

Yours very truly,

Letters on time extensions.—A debtor should be granted an extension of time when he advances a good reason, or if it is actually impossible to collect anything on the account at present, although there is hope for future payment. The grant should be made graciously but should indicate that the procedure is an exception. The following letter to a retail customer is illustrative.

Dear Madam:

Thank you for your letter of August 24 explaining why you have not paid your account for June. Whenever our customers are in difficulties, we appreciate their writing to us frankly.

Since yours is an accommodation account, payable in full by the tenth of each month, we usually insist on strict adherence to the terms of credit. However, in view of your explanation, we are glad to grant your request for an extension of time on your account.

We shall, then, expect your check in full payment of your account on September first.

Very truly yours,

Another letter granting an extension of time:

Dear Mr. Johnson:

We have received your letter of May 1, requesting an extension of time on your account.

While we feel, as you no doubt can appreciate, that our usual terms of 90 days are sufficiently long to enable our customers to prepare for and arrange payment of their accounts, we are always glad, in an exceptional case such as yours, to grant reasonable accommodation.

We are, therefore, extending the due date of your account to June 1. Won't you, however, please bear this date definitely in mind, and mail your remittance promptly. We shall be looking for it not later than June 3.

Very truly yours,

A letter refusing an extension of time:

Dear Mr. Laswell:

We have your letter of November 10, containing a check for $690.00 in payment of our invoice of October 1. Please accept our thanks.

The following items remain open on our records:

October 15	$460.00
October 31	460.00
	$920.00

The first of the above bills matures tomorrow, and the other on December 1.

You ask that we grant you an additional 30 days on the account that is now due; from this we assume that you refer to the bill of October 15. We are embarrassed by your request, for, if we decline, we risk being thought unappreciative of the business which you have given us, and, if we agree, we are discriminating against others of our customers whom we require to pay promptly in 30 days.

In our opinion, extensions are in reality loans, and we do not think that we should be called upon to usurp the function of the bank in this particular. In addition, the nature of our business is such that close collections are an absolute necessity, and especially at a time when the cost of raw materials has advanced to such an abnormal degree.

We feel confident that you will understand the spirit in which this letter is written, and will withdraw your request.

Yours very truly,

Selling through collections; letters combining collections and sales.—The collection letters reproduced up to this point have had as their chief aim the obtaining of payments that are overdue; these letters are illustrative of the more standard types of collection correspondence. The collection letter, however, may also be regarded as partly a sales letter, or as a form of advertising. Many concerns in various lines of business do so regard it, and when writing to a customer with reference to his account, take advantage of the opportunity that the collection letter offers them to:

1. Request additional orders.
2. Emphasize and advertise to the customer the merits of the merchandise sold, and also to suggest to the customer methods by which sales of the merchandise through his own outlets can be increased.
3. Introduce the customer to new lines of goods being sold by the house.
4. Inform the customer of improved service now available.

Some examples of this type of collection letter follow.

A combination collection and sales letter:

Gentlemen:

We notice that your past-due account amounting to $65.43 is still open. Won't you please let us have your check by return mail. It is our policy not to ship additional orders while past-due accounts are outstanding, and at this time of the year you will certainly wish to prepare for the big holiday trade.

Our new line is now ready for your inspection and selection. It is exceptionally strong, and includes complete assortments of broadcloths, silk fibres, shadowynes, poplins, imported madras, and numerous novelty cloths.

All of our shirts are cut very full and made with the greatest care and skill.

We will pack any number per dozen or over in individual Christmas gift boxes, at no additional cost to you.

Delivery December 1 to 10.

Mail us your order now, together with your check for $65.43.

Samples submitted, if desired.

Yours very truly,

Another combination collection and sales letter:

Dear Mr. Miller:

Your account today shows an unpaid balance of $30.16.

Perhaps you had not noticed its maturity, but now that you recall it, we know that you will act promptly.

Cut silks are coming back strong, and the new patterns and shades are the finest we have had for years. If you can use some with which to brighten up, just indicate your requirements on the enclosed order blank and return it with your check for $30.16. Both will be appreciated.

Yours very truly,

A collection letter that also resells the customer:

Dear Mr. Johnson:

So far we have not received your check for the ten cases of Pet Milk delivered on June 10.

When you bought this Pet Milk, you didn't intend simply to add merchandise to your inventory. You bought it to increase your sales and your profit—and you selected the ideal brand for that purpose.

"Company Coming?" is the title of a Pet Milk advertisement that has been read by practically every woman in your neighborhood. This advertisement suggests a tempting and delicious dinner to be served to the company coming that evening. It starts in with cream of tomato soup, baked veal, sweet potatoes, and down the line to pineapple mousse, spice cake with caramel frosting, coffee, and candies.

How many women in your neighborhood have company coming to-day? How many will come into your store in a quandary as to what to serve—and what will you do to help them solve their problem?

Every one of these women is a golden opportunity for you—an opportunity to make suggestions, to make sales, to make profits. We want to help you to make these suggestions. We want to help you increase your sales not only of Pet Milk, but also of other things as well. If you are at a loss as to what to suggest, please return this letter to us and we will send you a supply of recipe leaflets that will help you do the job.

For your own good, for your own profit, we urge you to use these leaflets. It takes more than just a store with a stock of merchandise to make a successful and profitable business. Your success depends upon the salesmanship you put behind your merchandise—and salesmanship is largely suggestion.

Pet Milk plus *your* salesmanship equals profit. Try it. You will find that it works. In the meantime, won't you please send us your check to cover our invoice of June 15?

Yours very truly,

A collection letter that also advertises a new product:

Gentlemen:

It is not only because we want to see this account paid that we ask you to send a check today, but it is because we want to do more business with you, and we're afraid that the overdue account, amounting to $36.57, is keeping you away.

The popularity of our new ELECTRA model warrants your stocking this new line. A circular is enclosed. Although introduced only two months ago, the ELECTRA is already demanded in preference to all others. It is advertised in all the leading magazines.

We have not received an order from you for several months, and doubtless you are now in need of some of our line. Just add a number of ELECTRA to your next order, and, at the same time, let us have your check for $36.57 by return mail.

Thank you.

Yours very truly,

A collection letter that also advertises improved service:

Dear Mr. Gately:

Many of our customers call at the yard for their own supplies. To speed up our end of the affair we have just installed the very latest loading equipment and have also put extra men in the warehouse. Your trucks can now reduce their loading time here by from 30 to 50 per cent—a very substantial saving.

We haven't seen any of your drivers for some time. We hope, however, that you will soon give us an order and test out for yourself the efficiency and economy of our new loading system.

If you would care to stop in at our office some day next week, we would be glad to have you inspect the new equipment. At the same time we would like to talk over your account, now $73.56 past due. We feel sure that you will want to give us at least a substantial payment.

Drop in next week. We will be glad to see you.

Yours very truly,

5. HOW TO USE FORM COLLECTION LETTERS

Use of form letters.—Opinion differs among credit men as to the value of form letters. Some use them almost exclusively; others use them only in the reminder stage of the collection procedure. Many firms, especially department stores, mail-order, and installment houses, handle so many accounts by mail that form letters are the only practical solution, the expense of individually dictated letters being prohibitive. Similarly, either a small or large concern whose business does not necessitate close personal contact with customers, such as wholesalers or jobbers having many small past-due accounts, can use form letters effectively. Manufacturers, wholesalers, and small retailers with a smaller clientele find individual treatment more effective.

Form-paragraph manuals.—A number of houses have successfully compromised between the form and the individual letter by creating hundreds of form paragraphs to fit every possible contingency. Each paragraph is given a key number, and each correspondent is provided with a form-paragraph manual. The collection correspondents, by the use of dictating machines, indicate the number of the form paragraphs that are pertinent to the particular case, inserting original material only where special circumstances require it. The records are then transcribed by typists. This system enables a relatively small office staff to handle a heavy volume of collection correspondence and to have each letter individually typed and signed.

Grouping delinquents to assure applicability of collection procedure.—Identical form letters for all delinquents are inadvisable because of the great diversity in the character of the delinquents. Reasonable applicability of form letters can be secured by grouping delinquents and using a special selection of form letters for each group. Delinquents may be classified according to the following:

1. Causes of delinquency, such as illness, unemployment, dishonesty, negligence, and inability to pay. If groupings are sound and letters are applicable to the group, form letters should be almost as satisfactory as individually written ones.
2. Credit ratings. The groups may be as follows:

(*a*) Poor credit risk, or customer whose ability to pay and habits of paying justify a small credit limit and a short time for payment. Should he neglect to pay on time, the collection procedure is started immediately.

(*b*) Medium credit risk, or customer whose ability to pay and habits of paying are somewhat better than the poor risk. A longer interval of time is allowed for the operation of the collection system.

(*c*) Good credit risk, or customer who has large financial responsibility even though he may be somewhat slow in paying. Because of his high credit limit he receives the mildest and most lenient collection treatment consistent with the company's policy.

The collector using the credit-rating system must guard against keeping customers in the original classification after their rating has changed. Continual reclassification is an integral part of this grouping system.

Rules governing use of form letters.—The following general rules should be observed for an effective collection series:

1. Letters should be revised at periodic intervals, or different series should be alternated every few months. Variety is highly important if effectiveness is to be maintained.

2. The series should be carefully graduated in tone, from perfunctory reminder to threat.

3. The system should be sufficiently elastic to permit of its being adapted to the type of customer. Thus, the habitually slow risk would receive fewer reminders and reach the threat stage sooner than the good risk. Moreover, the time interval between letters may be shorter for the poor risk. Otherwise, the series should be comparatively automatic and mechanical in regard to the particular type of notice or letter to be sent on the definitive date decided upon when the system is devised.

4. Allow for dictation of individual letters when irregularities occur, or when form letters need adaptation to special classes or cases of delinquents. This is tantamount to so arranging the series that the form letters may be dropped as soon as the debtor has replied.

Multigraph letters are generally inadvisable. No debtor's attitude is improved if he gets the impression that he is not worth a personally dictated letter.

Form-letter files and manuals.—For effective and easy use, form letters should be numbered and indexed and kept in a form-letter file. When a particular form letter is sent to a debtor, the number of the letter can be marked on the collection or ledger card. This system obviates the necessity for carbon copies of form letters.

In companies where there are many correspondents, a credit and collection correspondence manual has been found a good device for improving the quality of collection letters. Such manuals not only supply the correspondents with form letters and form paragraphs, but they also serve to instruct them in the writing of collection letters that get the money and keep the customer's goodwill. A loose-leaf credit and collection correspondence manual used by the Puget Sound Power & Light Company, Seattle, Washington, covers the following subjects:

Correspondence Material

Closing sentences or paragraphs
Letter analyses
Letterheads and copy sheets
Miscellaneous paragraphs
Opening sentences or paragraphs

LETTERS

Appreciation	Merchandise transfer
Auditor's verification	Miscellaneous
Closing bill	Novelty
Deposit	Reminder
Deposit refund	Seriously past due
Discontinuance	Seasonal
Merchandise	Stockholder
Merchandise reclaim	Transfer balance

New letters and other material are added to the manual from time to time by the correspondence committee, which is responsible for the manual. Correspondents are urged to submit copies of outstanding letters to the committee so that they may be considered for inclusion in the manual. Many of the letters may be used verbatim, yet it is not the intention to develop stereotyped or form usage through this medium.

Timing collection correspondence.—The first letter of a mercantile collection series can be sent the afternoon of the day on which the account is due if the check has not arrived. Successive letters can be spaced anywhere from six to ten days apart. Writing when the bill is due is, psychologically speaking, the best time, because the debtor knows the bill is due and is, in most cases, still enjoying the goods. The longer the creditor lets the account run, the harder it is to collect without offense. Following is a suggested schedule of letters for the poor and good risk.

	Poor Risk	*Good Risk*
January 15	Purchase made	Purchase made
February 1	Statement	Bill
February 15	Formal reminder	Statement
March 1	First letter	First formal reminder
March 10	Second letter	
March 15		Second formal reminder
March 20	Third letter	
April 1	Threat letter	First letter
April 15		Second letter
May 1		Third letter
May 15		Fourth letter
June 1		Threat letter

Eight-letter sequence.—The following sequence illustrates a long series.

NO. 1

Gentlemen:

This letter is being mailed to you just as a reminder of your account with us.

Under the terms of sale, invoice of June 9, amounting to $75.98, is now due for payment.

We shall be pleased to receive your check.

Very truly yours,

NO. 2

Gentlemen:

As you have always been prompt in meeting your obligations, it would appear that our invoice of June 9, carrying terms of 3% 10 days, net 30, to the amount of $75.98, has either gone astray or been misfiled.

We are attaching a duplicate covering the charge in question, and know that you will remit promptly upon having the matter called to your attention.

Very truly yours,

NO. 3

Gentlemen:

Has the mailing of a check to cover a past-due item been overlooked by you? We are sorry not to have received a reply to our letter of July 24.

The item referred to covers merchandise invoiced under date of June 9, to the amount of $75.98.

A reply to this letter in the form of a check will indeed be appreciated.

Very truly yours,

NO. 4

Gentlemen:

Will you please refer to our letter of August 4, in which we brought to your notice an overdue item?

We have received no reply, and our records indicate that you still owe us for shipment of June 9, amounting to $75.98.

The time allowed for payment, based on the terms of sale, has long since expired, and remittance should now be made.

Please give this matter your prompt attention.

Very truly yours,

NO. 5

Gentlemen:

There have been mailed to you a number of reminders of our invoice of June 9, but to none of our letters have we received a reply.

In view of the length of time your account has been appearing as past due, we must insist that the matter of payment now have your attention without further delay.

We shall look forward to receiving, not later than August 29, your check drawn for $75.98.

Very truly yours,

NO. 6

Gentlemen:

The credit department has just called to my attention the fact that you have not responded to its letters dated July 24, August 4, 14, and 24, which were in reference to your past-due account.

You, of course, appreciate that when accounts are neither discounted nor paid promptly when due, it has a tendency to impair your credit standing, particularly so when the creditor's experience is reflected in the trade reports that are from time to time compiled by various agencies.

Perhaps you have some good reason for not responding to the letters that the credit department wrote you. An investigation of our files does not, however, disclose any letters from you complaining about the character or quality of our merchandise, or about the service rendered to you.

In view of this we feel justified in asking that you now give our account your immediate attention.

Yours very truly,
Assistant Treasurer

NO. 7

Gentlemen:

If you were a credit manager and letters written by your assistant and then a letter written by yourself were ignored, particularly when an account was long past due, what would you do?

We have several times requested the payment of your account and have yet to receive a reply telling us either why payment has not been made, or when your check may be expected.

Since we do not appear to be receiving the co-operation to which we believe we are entitled, we feel that more drastic measures will have to be taken.

When your orders were received, they were given our very best attention—and we felt confident that you would meet your bills within a reasonable time. Apparently our confidence has been misplaced.

Our files are being advanced to September 10, at which time we shall expect to receive your check. If it is not received, we shall be obliged to take other steps to protect our interests.

Yours very truly,
Assistant Treasurer

NO. 8

Gentlemen:

Since you will neither reply to the various letters that we have written you, nor remit for your past-due account, insofar as we can see there is no course for us to pursue other than to refer the matter to an attorney in your city with instructions to proceed with the collection of the account in whatever manner may be deemed necessary to protect our interests.

You will, within the next few days, receive a communication from the attorney, advising you of the action that he proposes to take.

Yours very truly,
Assistant Treasurer

Five-letter series emphasizing courtesy.*—"Collection-letter courtesy" has been a powerful collector of overdue accounts and a compelling sales argument for new business for a coal dealer. Here are some of the dealer's collection letters that have brought both payment and repeat business through the assumption that the customer really intends to pay. Notice the friendliness and sincerity in the writer's concern for the debtor, particularly as regards any jeopardy to his credit standing. The letters progress in severity from a first reminder employing the "oversight" approach to the final demand letter.

NO. 1

Oversight:

Dear Mr. Blank:

Does the date of this letter remind you of something you've forgotten? Right—it's that small amout of $______ due us by the 10th.

---

* *Coal Herald,* Nov., 1940, p. 6. "Collecting Goodwill—and Cash," by John L. King.

We know how it is—with business and social engagements keeping one busy, it's easy to overlook bills—so why not attach your check now to this note, and get it off your mind, and the money into our till?

It will help us keep our accounts with our suppliers in order, and it will free you of the necessity of thinking of this bill again.

Thank you.

NO. 2

Unexpected expenses:

Dear Mr. Blank:

Because we know you realize the value of keeping your credit good by prompt payment, we are wondering whether your failure to pay our account of $------ on the 10th is due to some unexpected demand on your budget. If so, we sympathize with you, for believe me, in this business of ours, unexpected demands are popping up all the time.

However, if you've got that situation licked, is it possible to enclose check with this letter, so that we can clear the account? We want to be able to make AAA-1 reports on your credit—your check will make that possible.

If there is to be further delay, will you please note on this letter when we may expect payment?

Thank you.

NO. 3

Delay fault of seller:

Dear Mr. Blank:

Was there something wrong with that last delivery of coal, either in quality of coal or service?

We hope not, but your delay in payment of the bill, $--------, makes us wonder. If there was, won't you phone us, and let us make it right?

And, if there wasn't, won't you please attach check to this letter, for we want to keep your credit record in good order, so that when reference is made to us we can say "Okay."

Thank you.

NO. 4

Keeping debtor's self-respect:

Dear Mr. Blank:

If someone borrowed your lawn mower, and, after you had asked him several times to return it, he failed to do so, what would you think?

Exactly.

Well, we're somewhat in the same position—on (date) we loaned you the use of $-------- belonging to us, when we extended credit for -------- tons of coal. We've asked you to return that money to us; asked you several times, and you haven't done so.

What must we think?

Won't you prove to us that we're still right in thinking we showed good judgment in giving you this credit, by sending us a check today.

Thank you.

NO. 5

The final threat:

Dear Mr. Blank:

You've made us lose confidence in our judgment; we can't help that, but that is all the loss we intend to take.

We've asked you repeatedly to pay your account of $--------, and you haven't even thought your good credit worth enough to answer our letters, to say nothing of paying the bill.

As much as we regret it, there is only one step for us, and unless the bill is paid by (date), we'll take that step. We'll turn your account over for collection on (date) unless we have your check before that date.

For your good, and our comfort, please do not make this step necessary. Your check in the mails today will prevent our taking legal action.

6. COLLECTION METHODS

Guide for collection procedure.—Remembering always that the creditor has a right to his money, the collection department should follow a technique in its collection procedure that takes into account the following advices:

1. Create a collection program that is systematic, persistent, tactful, and human. In follow-up work, let the attitude be one of friendly co-operation and mutual interest.
2. Make the debtor feel that he is paying voluntarily.
3. Take it for granted that the customer is honest until he proves otherwise.
4. Design all material sent out by the collection department to create the impression that: (a) the bill will be collected when due; (b) there is little doubt in the creditor's mind that the debtor is able to pay; (c) should there be any attempt to defer payment

against the creditor's will, all force available will be used, not so much for the recovery of the money as to uphold the principles of good business.

5. Do not accept unusual methods of payment unless unforeseen trouble has made full payment utterly impossible.

6. Use force as a last resort and generally avoid conveying threats.

Effect of statutes of limitations in collection of accounts.—Executives responsible for the collection of accounts and contractual payments must familiarize themselves with the provisions and applicability of the statute of limitations of the state wherein the company is operating.

A statute of limitations is a statute limiting the period within which legal action may be brought upon a matured debt. A debt is matured when it is due and payable. All 48 states and the District of Columbia have statutes of limitations. While the applicability of the statutes is very similar in all jurisdictions, the periods set by the statutes vary from state to state and according to the type of instrument used to evidence the debt.

How the statute of limitations operates.—When a debt or claim is matured—that is, due and owing, action for the collection of this debt or claim must be brought within the period required by the local statute, or all future legal action to enforce collection will be barred. However, it is possible to interrupt the running of the statute—that is, to lengthen the limited period—by obtaining from the debtor a payment on account or a promise to pay. For example, suppose an account is payable on October 15, 1941. Assuming it to be a New York account, if the claim is unpaid, legal action must be brought before October 15, 1947, or all legal action will thereafter be barred. However, if, some time before the expiration of the statutory period, let us assume July 7, 1943, the debtor makes a payment on account or makes an acknowledgment of the debt with a promise to pay, the statutory period is renewed and begins to run anew from the date on which the payment or promise to pay is made. Thus, in our example, the creditor would have until July 7, 1949 to begin legal action.

Alert collection managers, therefore, periodically review old delinquent accounts to check on the time remaining in which action may be brought on any particular claim.

STATUTES OF LIMITATIONS (In Number of Years)

State	*Open Accounts*	*Notes*	*Con-tracts*	*Contracts under Seal*	*State*	*Open Accounts*	*Notes*	*Con-tracts*	*Contracts under Seal*
Alabama	3	6	6	10	Nebraska	4	5	5	5
Arizona	3	6	6	6	Nevada	4	6	6	6
Arkansas	3	5	5	5	New Hampshire	6	6	6	20
California	4–2	4	4	4	New Jersey	6	6	6	16
Colorado	6	6	6	6	New Mexico	4	6	6	6
Connecticut	6	6–17	6	17	New York	6	6	6	See B
Delaware	3	6	3	No Provision	North Carolina	3	3	3	10
District of Columbia	3	3	3	12	North Dakota	6	6	6	6
Florida	3	5	5	20	Ohio	6	15	15	15
Georgia	4	6	6	20	Oklahoma	3	5	5	5
Idaho	4	5	5	5	Oregon	6	6	6	10
Illinois	5	10	10	10	Pennsylvania	6	6	6	20
Indiana	6	10	20	10–20	Rhode Island	6	6	6	20
Iowa	5	10	10	10	South Carolina	6	6	6	20
Kansas	3	5	5	5	South Dakota	6	6	6	20
Kentucky	5–6	15	5	5	Tennessee	6	6	6	6
Louisiana	1–3	5	10	10	Texas	2	4	4	4
Maine	6	6	6	20	Utah	4	6	6	6
Maryland	3	3	3	12	Vermont	6	6 See C	6	8
Massachusetts	6	6 See A	6	20	Virginia	3	5	5	10
Michigan	6	6	6	6–10	Washington	3	6	6	6
Minnesota	6	6	6	6	West Virginia	5	10	10	10
Missouri	5	10	5–10	5–10	Wisconsin	6	6	6	10–20
Montana	5	8	8	8	Wyoming	8	10	10	10

NOTES: A. Witnessed notes, 20 years.
B. 20 years, except actions on bonds of public officers or on covenants in deeds and mortgages of real estate, when 10 years.
C. Witnessed notes, 14 years.

Age analysis.—An age analysis of accounts affords a complete picture of the state of collections, helps locate accounts that are becoming habitually slow, and makes possible prompt and appropriate action.

CUSTOMER'S ACCOUNTS RECEIVABLE

NAME AND ADDRESS	CURRENT	LEDGER BALANCE	ANALYSIS				
			ONE MONTH	TWO MONTH	THREE MONTH	FOUR & OVER	REMARKS

PAST DUE LIST

DISTRICT DEPOT DATE

CUSTOMER	ADDRESS	K	CLAIMS	30 DAYS	60 DAYS	90 DAYS	TOTAL PAST DUE	SALESMAN	REMARKS

COLLECTION OFFICE

DELINQUENT ACCOUNTS RECEIVABLE

OFFICE

DATE 194

DUE DATE	CONTRACT NUMBER	NAME OF CUSTOMER	BALANCE OF ACCT.	PAYMENTS PAST DUE				LAST PAYMENT		REMARKS
				20-29 days	30-59 days	60-89 days	90 days & over	DATE	AMOUNT	

	BAL	OVER 4 Mo	JULY	AUG	SEPT	OCT
Name of account Address	44 75		13 36	5 05		26 34 ☆☆
Name of account Address	6 35					1 11 ☆☆
Name of account Address	14 05					14 05 ☆☆

Figure 90.—Age Analyses of Overdue Accounts.

Accounts should be aged periodically. A convenient time is when the monthly accounts-receivable trial balance is prepared. Figure 90 shows several examples of age-analysis lists of overdue accounts. Where the account is of questionable collectibility, bad-debt action should not be delayed. Otherwise, the account can be subjected to the regular collection methods used for the particular group in which it appears.

Follow-up from aging records.—Accounts should first be analyzed according to those which are current, less than 30 days old, 30 to 60 days, 60 to 90 days, 90 to 120 days, and older. This is done by analyzing each individual account that is in arrears, removing it from its current classification, and placing it under the proper grouping according to the length of time it is past due.

The following procedure is effective for follow-up from aging records:

1. Place age-analysis figures directly on the ledger sheet at the end of the month in a special column at the far right- or left-hand side of the sheet.

2. Have a clerk go through the analyzed ledgers and note on a memorandum, as illustrated in Figure 91, each account having a past-due balance.

3. For all accounts 60 days past due, make the memorandum in duplicate, the original for the collector and the duplicate for the collection correspondents. For accounts 30 days delinquent, make

NAME OF COMPANY

Date ....

Name ....

Address ....

BALANCE				AMOUNT
Jan.	Feb.	Mar.	Apr.	
May	Jun.	Jul.	Aug.	
Sept.	Oct.	Nov.	Dec.	

CALLED

Figure 91.—Memorandum to Collector.

only one copy of the memorandum for the correspondents, since the collectors are not called in until later.

4. Mark the word "File" on the ledger sheet when the first letter is written to the customer. This warns the correspondent to consult the file before writing again or taking any other action. Also mark the word "File" on all memoranda made of the account. This warns the collector that correspondence has begun on the account.

Informing customer of age analysis of account.—Many collection men think it effective to keep customers informed as to the age analysis of their accounts. For instance, in one company, whenever any part of a customer's balance is past due, the monthly statement, which is prepared in duplicate, shows an age analysis. The original statement is sent to the customer, and the duplicate is retained for use in connection with the collection procedure.

Another company sends its delinquent customers a collection notice on a small card showing the age analysis of the account. The notice, illustrated in Figure 92, shows immediately what portion of the balance has been past due for over four months, 120 days, 90 days, 60 days, and 30 days, the current balance and total. Notices

NAME OF COMPANY
ADDRESS

TERMS: Accounts payable in full in 30 days.

....

....

Your attention is again called to the past-due portion of your account. Prompt payment will be appreciated.

Over 4 Months Past Due	*120 Days Past Due*	*90 Days Past Due*	*60 Days Past Due*	*30 Days Past Due*	*Current*	*Total*

Figure 92.—Notice to Customer Showing Age Analysis of Account.

are sent to all accounts 60 days past due or over. After the company has sent three aging notices, the account is considered ready for the firm's outside collector.

Aging statement sent to salesmen.—Some firms follow the practice of breaking down each salesman's accounts according to age of outstanding amounts, in order to make salesmen more credit-collection-minded, and to gain their co-operation. Figure 93 illustrates an aged-account list for salesmen used by a Midwestern milling company.

ACCOUNTS RECEIVABLE

....Office

Entered by ...... Rechecked by ...... Date............ 19..

	DATE	NAME AND ADDRESS	AMOUNT OF INVOICE				
			1 to 30 days	30 to 60 days	60 to 90 days	over 90 days	Total

Figure 93.—Aged Account List for Salesmen.

Tickler systems for collection follow-up.—For a sound collection program, a method must be devised for "tickling" overdue accounts in order that the regular collection procedure can be applied efficiently. In the following paragraphs several collection tickler systems are described.

Tickler system used by a manufacturer.—At the time of invoicing, an extra copy of the invoice, called a collection copy, is typed. These copies are retained by the collection department, where they are placed in a tickler file to come up on the due date of the invoice, or after whatever period of grace is allowed. At this time invoices are compared with the ledger, and all paid ones are destroyed. A short statement or reminder is typed for those remaining unpaid, a copy of the reminder being attached to the invoice. The papers are sent to the tickler file to reappear after another waiting period, usually 10 days. Thereafter, statements are mailed weekly until the item is brought to a conclusion. After the second week, the file itself (invoice and reminders) goes to the desk of the collection manager, who decides what pressure to apply in the way of form or individual letters, phone or wire.

Tickler for dunning department-store accounts.—After accounts are thirty days delinquent, a statement is drawn off in duplicate. The originals are mailed on the day on which they are taken from the ledger, and the duplicates are kept in a binder. To understand how the system operates, assume that early in August a statement is made up in duplicate for an account showing a balance open for June. Early in September ledgers are again checked, and blank statements are inserted at accounts that are one or two months overdue. The duplicate statements in the binders are checked against those accounts at which blank statements are inserted. Where accounts are two months overdue, the duplicate statement in the binder is sent to the account with an impersonal card reminder. If there is no statement inserted at an account for which there is a duplicate statement in the binder, the account is assumed to have been paid, and the statement is removed from the binder and destroyed. If, by early in November, the account is still unpaid —that is, ninety days after the first statement was sent—the account is followed up as a collection routine, and a collection card as illustrated in Figure 94 is made up. The application for credit is used in preparing the collection card.

<table>
<tr><td colspan="8">1 2 3 4 5 6 7 8 9 10 11 12 13 14 15 16 17 18 19 20 21 22 23 24 25 26 27 28 29 30 31
LAST NAME FOLIO</td></tr>
<tr><td rowspan="3"></td><td colspan="4">Res. (1) Phone</td><td colspan="3">Pay Habits</td></tr>
<tr><td colspan="4">Res. (2)</td><td colspan="3" rowspan="2">Opened Line H. Cr. H. Cash</td></tr>
<tr><td colspan="4">Bus. Phone</td></tr>
<tr><td>Year & Month</td><td colspan="2">Dr.</td><td>Cr.</td><td>Balance</td><td colspan="3">Closed</td></tr>
<tr><td></td><td></td><td></td><td></td><td></td><td rowspan="3">Form 1</td><td rowspan="3">Form 2</td><td rowspan="3">Form 3</td></tr>
<tr><td></td><td></td><td></td><td></td><td></td></tr>
<tr><td></td><td></td><td></td><td></td><td></td></tr>
</table>

Figure 94.—Collection Follow-Up Card.

Tabbed ledger cards tickle overdue installment accounts.—Ledger cards to which colored tabs are attached are used by many of the larger credit clothing firms to check installment accounts. The cards are 5 x 8 inches and have the days of the month listed at the top. All cards are filed alphabetically, and a black tab is placed at the date payment is due. This provides an easy, visual control. Each morning the cards are reviewed, and all cards tabbed at that date are taken out of the file. If payments are not received, red tabs are substituted, and the red tab is moved ahead to the next payment date. A notice is sent to the customer at each date of default, and, if more than one payment lapses, a smaller interval is allowed for reply.

The full history of each account is kept on the ledger card so that the credit manager can tell at a glance what action to take with delinquents. The follow-up letters are numbered, and, as each letter is sent out, its number is indicated at the bottom of the ledger. Most of these firms use collectors to follow up slow-paying customers.

Tickler system through cubbyhole equipment.—The credit manager of a large installment house uses a rack of cubbyholes set at the back of his desk to "tickle" collection action. The rack contains thirty-one cubbyholes numbered in sequence, and seven additional cubbyholes numbered 1 to 7, as shown in Figure 95. When the account is set up, a follow-up slip containing only the customer's name is placed in the cubbyhole dated one day after the next payment is due. If there is any doubt regarding the exact status of an account, the slip is checked against the customer's ledger card. To illustrate, if payment is due on the 15th, the slip is placed in cubbyhole 23, since weekly payments are required. If payment is made by that date, the slip is moved up to the date after the next payment is due. If the payment is not made, a letter is sent to the customer calling his attention to the "oversight," and the slip is moved up eight days. If there are further defaults, additional follow-up letters are used. However, if, after four weeks, no payments have been received, the slip is put in the cubbyholes at five-day intervals instead of eight-day intervals.

The separate cubbyholes marked 1 to 7 are used in directing collectors. When four weekly installments or two monthly installments have been defaulted, the customer's follow-up is placed in one of the seven cubbyholes. The collectors cover a different territory each day of the week. The delinquent customer's slip is checked against the ledger for address, and then placed in the cubbyhole showing the day of the week in which the debtor's territory is covered by the collector.

If the debtor promises the collector to pay on a certain date, his slip is removed from the collector's cubbyholes and placed in the 1 to 31 series at the promised date. Some customers prefer to make their payments through collectors, and in such cases the follow-up slips are retained in the collectors' file under the date on which the customer's territory is covered.

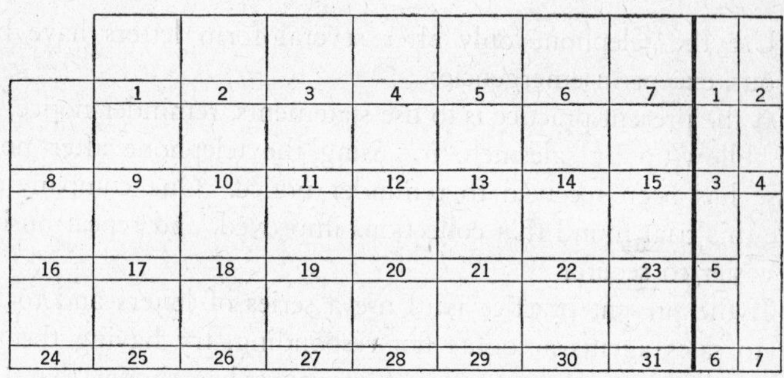

Figure 95.—Numbered Cubby Holes for Follow-Ups.

Collections by telephone.—In recent years more and more collection executives are using the telephone to speed up their collection work. It is an economical and time-saving substitute for the collection interview obtained in a personal visit.

The following advantages recommend the use of the telephone for collection purposes: (1) A telephone call is personal and direct; it usually affords ready and direct access to the person whom the collection executive wishes to reach, and it gets his attention. (2) As it is two-way, the telephone call offers an opportunity to discover reasons for nonpayment and to adapt the collection effort to circumstances disclosed in the interview. (3) The telephone call permits discussion, during which arrangements for a satisfactory settlement can be made. (4) The telephone call is flexible; it can be a gentle reminder or a forceful demand, as circumstances dictate. (5) This personal communication with customers presents opportunities to promote understanding and the goodwill of customers whose continuing patronage is desired.

Long-distance calls to speed up overdue payments have been found to be particularly effective because they emphasize the importance and the urgency of the communication.

It is a good idea to keep records of collection calls made and the results obtained just as you keep records of other methods of collection. These will be helpful in recalling conversations, reasons for nonpayment, and so forth, in connection with subsequent calls or letters.

Suggestions as to when the telephone should be used for collections are as follows:

1. Use the telephone only after several form letters have been sent out, except in emergencies.

2. If the present practice is to use statements, reminder notice, and final follow-up by salesmen, try using the telephone after no response has been received to reminder notice. One company that made this trial found that collections improved, and repeat business was easier to secure.

3. If the present practice is to use a series of letters and to turn over to sales agents accounts not responding, try having the sales agents telephone the accounts. Experience has shown that there are fewer delays if the telephone is used, because sales agents may not have time to call on accounts for several weeks.

4. Telephone large accounts before expiration of discount period.

Collections by telegraph.—Excellent results are reported from the use of telegrams for collection. A telegram has the advantage of actually reaching the person to whom it is addressed and commanding his immediate attention. It is short, and its urgency is direct. It bears a certain air of finality. A short wire following several letters to the overdue account asking for a reply is usually effective. If it brings no reply, follow it with another longer one threatening legal action, although the sender must exercise caution in regard to threats of legal action.

Another effective method is to dispatch three wires within one day or over a period of two or three days. A debtor will seldom stand up against the irritation and publicity of such a series. Collection men and telegraph companies report that telegrams do the trick from 70 to 90 per cent of the time.

Both Postal Telegraph and Western Union have tested forms of collection telegrams that can be procured at their offices. Both companies also offer a serial service that permits the sending of several wires in one day to the same addressee. Each wire is limited to a minimum charge of 15 words. At the end of the day, the total wordage is added, and the sender is charged at the day-letter rate plus a surcharge of 20 per cent. Should the first wire transmitted as a serial telegram elicit a response and obviate any further wires, the sender is charged as a straight wire for this one message.

For further information as to serial-telegram service, see page 894.

Examples of collection telegrams.—In framing a collection telegram, care should be taken to avoid threat of bankruptcy or of criminal prosecution. In some states such threats constitute the crime of extortion or attempted extortion and are, furthermore, libelous *per se*. A list of sample collection telegrams follows.

(1) Cannot understand failure to answer recent letters. Please wire collect.

(2) Closing books for audit. Please oblige with remittance today.

(3) Have you overlooked overdue account. Please mail check today.

(4) Please wire collect reply to our letter September 6.

(5) When may we expect remittance covering overdue account. Wire collect.

(6) Very important remittance reach us October 3. Ask your co-operation.

(7) Will you please send check air mail today. Thanks.

(8) Have been very patient. Won't you kindly remit. Urgent.

(9) Must have immediate payment overdue account. Please wire collect.

(10) Please settle overdue account today. Cannot wait longer.

(11) What action taken on previous wire. Reply collect.

(12) Your failure to answer letters makes it hard to co-operate.

(13) Please assist to continue friendly relationship by mailing check today.

(14) Your promise March 5 not fulfilled. Must have check immediately.

(15)* Surprised no reply to frequent letters regarding overdue account now three months in arrears. Extended you credit without hesitation on basis of favorable trade opinions and gave you best service. Please reciprocate by mailing check today. Wire reply collect.

(16) Attention overdue account imperative today. Dislike to take further action.

(17) Avoid legal action. Please pay overdue account today.

(18) Last chance make good. Wire remittance today.

(19) Make payment noon tomorrow to avoid court action.

(20) Will wait until April 3 before taking action overdue account.

(21) Unless check received tomorrow account placed with attorney.

(22) Demand full remittance covering overdue account otherwise starting suit.

(23)* Must take action if account not settled immediately. Appeal to you to co-operate and to protect credit standing. Please wire collect what we may expect so that unnecessary step will not be taken. Avoid embarrassment of litigation.

(24)* Regret to take legal action on overdue account after friendly relationship of several years. Cannot understand your evasive replies to recent letters. Have been very patient but must have definite information immediately. Please mail check or write full explanation today. Legal action scheduled April 7.

(25) Mail check today and avoid embarrassment of legal action.

Collections by personal call.—The personal call by a collector on the debtor has been used advantageously in the following circumstances:

1. When legal processes cannot be used, as in the case of:
   (*a*) Small claims.
   (*b*) State, Federal, or municipal debts.
   (*c*) The honest, but judgment-proof, debtor.

2. For general use by charge-account stores and installment houses for those slow-pay accounts on which mail and telephone have proved unsuccessful.

3. Early in delinquency when the skip risk is believed to be high.

4. For occasional delinquencies where the conditions of risk, size, misunderstanding, or other circumstances demand it.

---

* Day or night letter; the other messages each contain ten words or less.

5. For use in combination with delivery of statements, current or past due, or regular collection of installments.

6. For almost any local account after form letters have been sent out.

This method is, however, expensive. Moreover, many stores prefer to have customers come in to pay their bills, for this means contact with the merchandise. Others object to it because they are afraid of "spoiling" customers.

The outstanding objection to personal collection is the expense entailed. A good collection man should command a good salary and is expected to collect five times his weekly salary. Few concerns can really afford this. Hence, many stores have adopted the system of remunerating on neither straight-salary nor commission basis, but on a combination of both. Thus, the collector receives a small straight weekly salary and above this a commission based on the age of accounts, a higher commission being paid for the older account. This provides both security and incentive.

Where the firm does not need a full-time collector, the group plan may prove economical. The group collector divides his time among several noncompeting clients. Each client pays him a weekly or monthly fee which, in the aggregate, is enough to hold a really skilled man.

Collections by salesmen.—The sales and credit department must determine whether salesmen shall collect overdue accounts. In certain lines of business, as, for example, mercantile houses, the majority of whose customers are small retailers, salesmen can be used effectively as collectors of overdue accounts. These advantages are gained by using salesmen as collectors:

1. The salesman is in a better position to keep the customer within the credit limit.

2. He can obtain prompt action by the credit department in approving orders that might otherwise have to be held until he had corresponded with the customer and secured a check or note.

3. Small businessmen regard it as natural to pay the salesman, since to them he represents the selling house.

4. It is harder for the customer to refuse payment to the salesman than to ignore dunning letters.

5. It saves annoyance to the customer from frequent dunning letters and therefore makes it easier to get repeat orders.

The following plan for having salesmen perform collection work has been used successfully. Each salesman is sent a weekly itemized statement of the past-due accounts on his next week's itinerary, the statement being timed to reach him during the weekend before he makes the calls. (For discussion of aging statement sent to salesmen, see page 1096.) The salesman is provided with report forms and is required either to collect the amount of the bill or to send a report to the district office explaining why the customer is unable to make immediate payment. These reports supply material for follow-up letters from the district office. At the end of the month, the results are totalled, and each salesman receives a report showing him the standing of his accounts and his collection-loss record. A prize may be awarded each month to the salesman who leads his district or group in collections.

Aids for the collector.—The following ideas have been used successfully to aid in collections by personal collectors:

1. When an account is opened, include a full description of the customer on the ledger card. Give this information to the collector, together with the necessary credit information. The collector can thus "spot" the customer and address him by name. This plan prevents the customer from pretending to be someone else and saying, "Mr. ---------- is not at home." It also prevents any mistakes from being made because of similarity in names.

2. While ordinarily the debtor should be approached in a private place, in the case of the tricky, irresponsible debtor, whose account is not wanted, approach him in public and hand the bill to him in front of others. This can be at his place of employment, at home when he is entertaining, in a store where friends are present, and similar places.

3. If the debtor claims to have just sent a check, ask to see the stub so that it can be traced in the office.

4. If the debtor is always "out" when the collector arrives, leave some evidence of the attempt to collect the bill. For example, slip under the door a printed card bearing a courteous message. Then

follow up by telephone. Or, leave the bill with a note penciled thereon that the collector will return again tomorrow.

5. Learn from the debtor's wife his place of business, pay day, and amount to expect, and then await the debtor at his place of business at the right time with the right demand.

6. If the debtor cannot pay the entire amount, secure some payment on account with a promise for the remainder in the future. Make sure to call on the day specified for payment, for the debtor must not secure the impression that the collector is careless or indifferent.

7. If the debtor states that he cannot make a payment, have the collector tell him that the final decision rests with the credit manager. Persuade the debtor to telephone the credit manager to explain the circumstances and have the debtor telephone in the presence of the collector.

8. Test the debtor's attitude before taking action to repossess the merchandise sold under a conditional-sales contract with a "repossession" clause. Approach the delinquent customer with the statement, "You may lose your (object purchased) if you don't make your payment." If the customer shows little concern over the possible loss, or even suggests that the firm repossess the merchandise, proceed immediately to repossess the property, since the customer's attitude reveals that he has little interest in settling the account, or finds it impossible to do so. It might also show that he has little regard for the merchandise and that it may be damaged if left in his possession. On the other hand, if the customer shows that he is anxious to retain possession, he will usually find some means of continuing payments, and in such cases enforcement of the repossession clause may not be advisable.

Placing an account with a collection agency.—The chief advantages of placing an account with a collection agency rather than with an attorney are:

1. In many cases the agency is able to effect collection without instituting legal proceedings. This results from the fact that the average debtor realizes that if he fails to make payment when requested to do so by an agency, the entire business community will learn of his delinquency, and his credit will suffer in consequence.

The usual procedure is for the agency to write the debtor a series of strong letters, or to send an investigator to his place of business.

2. If legal proceedings are necessary, the agency's wide experience enables it to choose a reputable and conscientious attorney.

3. The agency selects the attorney from a bonded list. The creditor is thus fully protected against malfeasance.

4. The creditor is relieved of the burden of direct correspondence with the attorney and supervision of his activities.

5. The agency can be relied upon to see to it that prompt action is taken and the amount collected promptly remitted.

6. No extra expense is incurred. The agency and the attorney share the fees, which are usually those established by the Commercial Law League of America.

The creditor should thoroughly investigate an agency before utilizing its services, since from time to time various irresponsible agencies have been established. A reputable agency will furnish a bond for the amount of the claim, or for the amount of the creditor's annual collection business, if requested to do so.

Many companies have found the most satisfactory collection agency to be the collection division of a local association of the National Association of Credit Men.

House collection agencies.—Many firms have set up their own so-called "house" collection agencies, which are in reality dummy concerns. A name is chosen, stationery printed, and threat letters sent to the debtor. Every effort is made to convey the impression that the agency is independent of the creditor company. While these agencies have proved very successful, some credit men doubt the propriety of the procedure.

Placing an account with an attorney.—An account should not be placed with an attorney for collection until all other methods of collection have proved fruitless, and the creditor is prepared to sever business relations with the debtor. Many firms have found the most satisfactory time at which to present an account to an attorney to be sixty days after the maturity date. If allowed to run ninety or one hundred and twenty days, accounts usually become a dead loss. Presentation after sixty days ordinarily results in a fairly sizable recovery. A good collection attorney will acknowledge a claim as soon as he receives it and will proceed immediately to attempt to obtain payment without going to law. If this is impossible, he will advise the creditor as to whether a suit is expedient, basing his advice upon such factors as the provability of the claim and the collectibility of such judgment as may be obtained.

The creditor has, in general, two alternatives in choosing an attorney. He may select the name of an attorney in the debtor's city from a directory (see below) and send his claim to this attorney direct; or, he may place his claim in the hands of an attorney in his own city, who will in turn forward it to another attorney in the debtor's city. When this procedure is followed, no extra expense is incurred; the forwarding and the local attorney share the fee, the former usually receiving one third and the latter two thirds. The use of a forwarding attorney may be expedient where the amount of the claim is small, since a local attorney is likely to be more prompt if the claim is transmitted to him by another attorney for whom he acts or expects to act frequently, than if it is forwarded as a single request from a commercial house.

The collection fees charged by attorneys vary in different localities. The usual fees, however, are those established by the Commercial Law League of America—namely:

15 per cent on the first $500.
10 per cent on the excess of $500.
Minimum fee, $7.50 (Claims under $15, 50 per cent of amount collected).
For suit: A minimum suit fee of $7.50, added to above commissions, the total not to exceed 50 per cent of the amount of the claim. Suit fees are not contingent.

How to locate a competent collection attorney.—National attorneys' directories are published by several companies, among which are the United States Fidelity and Guaranty Company (home office, Baltimore, Maryland); the Mercantile Adjuster Publishing Company (Chicago); Commercial Law League of America (Chicago); Wilbur Law List (New York City); Columbia List (New York City); Commercial Bar (New York City); American Lawyers' Quarterly (Cleveland); The B. A. Law List (Milwaukee, Wisconsin); and Clearing House Quarterly (Minneapolis, Minnesota). Some of the publishers of these directories stand responsible for any claims collected by a listed attorney, provided the creditor notifies the publisher, on a form supplied by the latter, at the time the claim is placed. In many attorneys' directories each name is rated as to estimated net worth, character, legal ability, and promptness in paying claims collected.

The local associations of the National Association of Credit Men are privileged to suggest the names of several good attorneys who may represent the creditor firm.

Settlement by note.—When a debtor offers to pay his past-due account by note, the creditor should consider several questions before accepting the note in settlement. There are possibly three arguments in favor of the note:

1. A note serves as practically conclusive evidence of the debt and facilitates proof in the event that it subsequently becomes necessary to sue the debtor.
2. The debtor may consider a note a more solemn obligation than the open account. He realizes, for example, that a note may be discounted at a bank and presented to him at maturity by the bank. For this reason he may be more careful in preparing to meet the note than to pay the open account at any fixed date.
3. A note may be more easily transferred and realized upon by the creditor.

As against the above, the following serious objections to the note may be stated:

1. Failure to pay a note at maturity is by no means uncommon, especially among retailers. Frequently the debtor offers to pay only a part of the note on the due date, tendering another note for the balance.
2. Acceptance of a note serves as a bad precedent. As a rule, a creditor who has accepted several notes will find it very difficult to obtain from the debtor any other form of payment; and, if acceptance of notes becomes the practice in the creditor's collection effort, the debtor is buying regularly on greatly extended terms.
3. The creditor, by accepting a note, waives all right to expect or demand payment until the due date of the note, which usually lengthens rather than shortens the period of deferred payment. In the event that any immediate action, such as the bringing of a lawsuit to enforce payment, were considered desirable, the creditor

would have to postpone such action until after the maturity date of the note.

4. It gives rise to the tendency of accepting a note when a little more pressure would bring cash.

In view of these disadvantages, it is in many cases advisable tactfully to decline the debtor's offer of a note, and to suggest to him one or other of the following as an alternative:

1. Part payments on the open account. This procedure extends the time of payment. By not binding himself to a definite exten-

DRAWER'S INSTRUCTIONS TO BANK

CONFIDENTIAL—PLEASE DO NOT SHOW TO DRAWEE

If the enclosed draft is paid at maturity, remit proceeds direct to us. If dishonored, please deliver or mail to..

....Attorney,

Address..

....

Drawer

OVER

A. L. 258-A ★ 3-41

Figure 96a.—Instructions to Accompany Draft Illustrated in Figure 97.

STATEMENT

DRAWER'S INSTRUCTIONS TO ATTORNEY

Dear Sir: Payment of our annexed Draft having been refused, we, the undersigned drawers thereof, hereby authorize you to take prompt action for its collection on the terms stipulated in "The Attorneys List."

Promptly acknowledge receipt and advise what course is best to pursue. Wire, if in your opinion the circumstances warrant.

Do not make any compromise nor receipt debtor in full for any partial payment. Remit all money collected direct to the undersigned by P O Money Order, Bank Exchange or Express.

A. L. 258-A ★ 3-41

Figure 96b.—Reverse Side of Figure 96a.

sion, however, the creditor may leave himself free to take whatever action may be necessary in an emergency.

2. Immediate payment of part of the account, and one or more postdated checks for the balance.

3. In place of a note bearing only the debtor's signature, a note bearing the accommodation endorsement of a third party known by the creditor to be financially sound.

4. In place of an ordinary note, an installment note providing for the payment of small amounts from time to time, on condition, however, that the entire amount shall become due and payable in the event of a default in any installment.

When draft is acknowledged by attorney Send this to:

LETTER OF ADVICE

UNITED STATES FIDELITY AND GUARANTY COMPANY
Attorneys List Department, Baltimore, Md.

Take notice that the Draft we made on...debtor
for $...being unpaid, was, on our order, handed by
the Bank to...Attorney named in your latest
revised List at.......................................on.......................................19......
This notice is a compliance with the requirements of your bond which we hold.

Name...

Location...

Draft Drawn by a Subscriber to the Credit and Collection Service of the
United States Fidelity and Guaranty Company
Baltimore, Maryland

$.............................. 19
WITH CURRENT EXCHANGE

At..............................sight, Pay to the order of the..............................Bank
of..............................the sum of..............................Dollars
WITH CURRENT EXCHANGE

Value received and charge to account of ....
DRAWER

To.............................. DEBTOR .... NO. STREET

Address.............................. .... CITY STATE

A L Form 258 ★ REVISED EDITION COPYRIGHT 1941 BY UNITED STATES FIDELITY AND GUARANTY COMPANY

Figure 97.—Draft and Letter of Advice.

Collections by draft.—Important considerations in connection with the use of a draft are the following:

1. In most lines of business the practice of sending a draft is looked upon as a somewhat drastic, if not unfriendly, step, likely to antagonize the debtor. The drawing of a draft should therefore

be deferred until it appears that letters are productive of no good results. The draft may be regarded as the last step preliminary to the placing of the account with a collection agency or attorney.

2. Presentation of the draft through the debtor's own bank is in many cases the most effective procedure, because of the psychological effect upon the debtor. It is worth while to note in the ledger the name of each debtor's bank as ascertained from checks.

3. To insure that the bank will give careful attention to the presentation of the draft, it is advisable for the creditor to enclose a small fee of from twenty-five to fifty cents.

4. The debtor should be notified by letter that he is being drawn

DRAFT NOTICE

Dear Sir: We hand you herewith specimen of the Draft that we are drawing on you, as per ours of recent date. Prompt payment thereof, at the Bank mentioned below, will prevent further procedure.

If not paid, we have instructed the Bank to deliver this Draft to an Attorney named by us for collection.

$...is the amount you owe us.

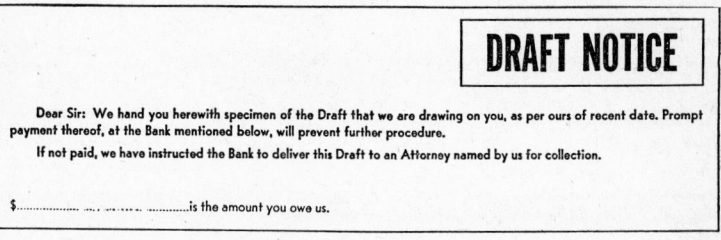

Figure 98.—Reverse Side of Creditor's Copy of Figure 97.

upon and that he will be expected to honor the draft. See page 1070 for example of letter of notification.

5. The bank should be instructed as to what to do with the draft if the debtor fails to honor it. The creditor may instruct the bank to return the draft to him with a notation of why the debtor will not pay it, or may authorize the bank to hand the draft to a certain attorney in the debtor's city after a specified number of days has elapsed. In the latter case the letter of notification to the debtor should contain a warning of the consequences of failure to honor.

Special forms of drafts are those issued to their subscribers by various law list publishers, such as the United States Fidelity and Guaranty Company. These drafts have attached to them stubs instructing the bank to hand the draft to a named attorney if payment is not made. The forms supplied to its subscribers by the United States Fidelity and Guaranty Company are illustrated in Figures 96a, 96b, 97, and 98.

SECTION 11

Dealings With Embarrassed Debtors

7. INVOLUNTARY OR VOLUNTARY CORPORATE REORGANIZATION UNDER CHAPTER X OF THE BANKRUPTCY ACT (EXTENSION OR MODIFICATION OF SECURED AND UNSECURED DEBTS)

8. VOLUNTARY WAGE EARNERS' PLANS

SECTION 11

Dealings With Embarrassed Debtors*

How should a creditor deal with an embarrassed debtor?—When a debtor fails to pay his debt at maturity, the claim against him may be turned over to an attorney and the machinery of the law set in operation against him in an effort to effect collection. While this might appear to be the simplest way of disposing of a troublesome situation, it may in fact prove to be highly ineffective.

When a debtor is insolvent, his assets are virtually a trust fund in which all creditors share alike. In proceeding independently, a creditor may find that, even though he may obtain a judgment against the debtor, other creditors may by appropriate proceedings prevent an unlawful preference. Therefore, in order to obtain the greatest amount for all creditors, some other method of dealing with the embarrassed debtor may be advisable.

To determine what method shall be used requires familiarity with debtor and creditor statutes, state insolvency laws, statutes regulating assignments for the benefit of creditors, and bankruptcy laws. Under these statutes and the decisions affecting them, which are sometimes motivated by economic and social expediencies, an embarrassed debtor's business is subject to different forms of treatment. The statutes should be considered with the idea of invoking the law that best deals with the problem at hand. The services of an attorney are usually indispensable in dealing with embarrassed debtors.

Considerations in dealing with embarrassed debtors.—Causes of failure, the relation of the debtor to the creditor, and other practical considerations will enter into the determination of how to deal with the embarrassed debtor.

---

* Acknowledgment is made to Samuel C. Duberstein, Member of New York Bar, Professor, St. John's University School of Law.

A debtor's failure may be due to large overhead expense, competition, incompetence, lack of capital, high living expenses, gambling, fraudulent schemes, or other causes. In one instance the business should be liquidated; in another efforts should be made to reorganize it. Rehabilitation is the hope of both the creditor and the debtor, but conditions may be such that it would be folly to have the debtor continue further in business and incur additional losses. The businessman who cannot realize an annual net profit is better off out of business. The constant reverberations which follow daily failures create a disturbance in the business world that results in tragedies for the honest merchant with limited capital.

Relation of the debtor to the creditor may be important in a creditor's consideration of the method of dealing with an embarrassed debtor. For example, if a debtor is an important outlet for the creditor's merchandise, and the termination of the business would adversely affect the creditor's volume, he would consider an extension agreement in an out-of-court adjustment (see page 1120), provided that he is interested in preserving the business and has confidence in the management. On the other hand, if the debtor's embarrassed condition is due to faulty management, and it is not proposed under any plan submitted to creditors in an out-of-court adjustment to substitute new management, then the creditor should endeavor to make the best composition settlement that is possible (see page 1122). If a composition settlement cannot be effected, then the creditor may well join with other creditors in precipitating the debtor into bankruptcy, provided that the debtor is insolvent and has committed an act of bankruptcy (see page 1126), on the theory that the first loss in an ill-managed enterprise will ultimately prove the least costly.

In all cases where dishonesty is one of the causes of the debtor's embarrassed position, creditors usually prefer to refuse any settlement, in order that the illegal, dishonest, or fraudulent acts may be investigated in bankruptcy proceedings (see page 1132). While administrative expenses in bankruptcy may result in a creditor receiving a smaller dividend on his claim than would have been realized in a voluntary offer of composition, it is always possible that recoveries may be made by a trustee in bankruptcy against the former management with respect to their acts of dishonesty or fraud. Furthermore, a vigorous course of action against a dishonest debtor acts as a deterrent against other debtors who might otherwise commit similar acts of dishonesty.

Methods of dealing with embarrassed debtors.—The following methods of dealing with embarrassed debtors are discussed in this section, subsequent to a brief explanation of collection of claims by suit on the unpaid obligation:

1. Agreements outside of court to give the debtor an extension of time to pay creditors' claims or to compromise with creditors.
2. Liquidation under an assignment of the debtor's assets for the benefit of creditors, preferably to a designee of the creditors.
3. Equity receivership proceedings.
4. Reorganization under Chapter X or arrangement proceedings under Chapter XI of the National Bankruptcy Act.
5. Voluntary wage-earners' plan.

1. COLLECTION OF A CLAIM BY SUIT ON THE UNPAID OBLIGATION

Suing to collect an account.—When an account has proved uncollectible in spite of a methodical collection effort, and legal action seems advisable, a *final date for payment* should be set, and, if the debtor then fails to pay, the account should be placed with a lawyer with instructions to take immediate action to protect the rights of the creditor.

The various states have enacted laws that provide not only for the maintenance of ordinary suits for the collection of debts but also for "provisional" remedies which may be invoked at the commencement of a suit or while the suit is pending. Without such remedies the creditor might find himself, at the termination of the case, with an uncollectible judgment.

The remedies are: (1) attachment; (2) arrest; (3) receivership; and (4) injunction.

1. *Attachment.*—In the legal proceeding of attachment, a levy is made on property of the debtor. The circumstances under which an attachment proceeding is allowed are fixed by the State statute. Following are the principal grounds for obtaining an attachment:

a. The debtor is a nonresident of the state or is a foreign corporation, and attachment is sought against property in the state.

b. The debtor has departed from the state with intent to defraud creditors or avoid process.

c. The debtor keeps himself concealed in the state.

d. The debtor has removed property or is about to remove property from the state with intent to defraud creditors.

e. The debtor has secured property from a creditor through fraudulent representations.

A creditor who obtains a writ of attachment is generally required to furnish a bond to cover the costs of the proceeding and to protect the debtor from any injury that may result to him if the attachment is wrongful.

2. *Arrest.*—An order of arrest may be obtained where the debtor is a nonresident, or where a resident debtor is about to leave the state, if the judgment would be ineffectual as a result of the nonresidence or departure.

3. *Receivership.*—A receiver may be appointed to take possession of and manage the property which is the subject of the action when it appears that there is danger of fraudulent transfer or removal of the property during the pendency of the action, and if the appointment of a receiver is necessary to preserve the property before final judgment is entered. While Federal equity receivership proceedings are practically obsolete today because of the provisions of Chapter X, dealing with reorganization, and Chapter XI, dealing with arrangements, of the National Bankruptcy Act, explained on pages 1132 et seq., ordinary equity receivership proceedings may be maintained in the several states. This form of action in equity may be instituted by a creditor to set aside transfers fraudulently made by a debtor in violation of state laws. Generally the creditor must first obtain a judgment and secure the appointment of a receiver who institutes the action to obtain the equitable relief. The statutes of the various states must be consulted in order to avoid objections that may be made by a debtor and his confederates who are seeking to frustrate creditors' rights and remedies by technical obstructive measures.

4. *Injunction.*—A temporary injunction is obtainable where the creditor seeks to restrain the continuance or commission of an act that would cause injury to him during the pendency of the action,

or where the debtor is doing or threatens to do an act in violation of the creditor's rights respecting the action that would render eventual judgment ineffectual; or where the debtor is about to dispose of his property with intent to defraud the creditor.

Rights after recovery of judgment—execution, supplementary proceedings, and garnishment.—If ordinary suit is instituted by service of summons and complaint on the debtor, and the debtor defaults in answering (or if the creditor wins at the trial), judgment is entered, and an *execution* is issued, which authorizes the sheriff or marshal to seize and sell the property at public auction. The amount realized upon the sale is applied to satisfy the judgment.

Should the execution be returned "unsatisfied" by the sheriff or marshal, application should be made to examine the debtor in *supplementary proceedings*. In such proceedings third parties, such as banks, and the like, may also be examined. Here assets belonging to the debtor may be uncovered and a receiver appointed to take charge. Occasionally the examination discloses that the debtor receives an income from wages, salary, earnings, trust funds, profits, or insurance disability payments, in which event an order of garnishment should be procured. To obtain the order, the creditor is usually required to file with the clerk of the court an affidavit indicating the amount due him and stating his belief that certain designated persons have property belonging to the debtor, or that such persons are indebted to the debtor, and that the process of garnishment is necessary to satisfy his claim. The order is served upon the person having possession of the property of the debtor or indebted to him (known as the garnishee), and from the time of service of such writ the garnishment becomes a continuing levy upon the property in an amount generally not exceeding ten per cent thereof, and continues as a levy until the claim is satisfied. The debtor may, in some states, secure a release of the garnished property by giving a bond in the amount prescribed by the statute.

In some states, after a judgment has been rendered against a debtor, and notwithstanding the provisions for garnishment, the courts may order the judgment debtor to pay to the judgment creditor or apply on the judgment, in installments, such portion of his income as the court may deem proper after taking into consideration the needs of the debtor and his family.

2. OUT-OF-COURT AGREEMENTS

What is an out-of-court agreement?—The out-of-court form of settlement agreement is an instrument by which a settlement can be arrived at quickly, economically, and with the least disturbance to the debtor's business. Under this type of settlement the debtor may offer a composition (part payment) in full settlement of the account, or the debtor may request an extension of time to pay the account. This method of out-of-court adjustment does not always prove effective because such a settlement agreement requires the approval of *all* creditors. Sometimes ignorant or obstinate creditors refuse to co-operate with the majority, even though the acceptance of the settlement agreement is in the interests of all creditors. Failure to obtain the necessary consents may lead to the use of one of the other methods of administration described in this section.

How to start an out-of-court adjustment.—The signs of weakness in a debtor's business are: his checks or notes are returned unpaid or protested; suits are instituted against him; a chattel mortgage is filed; he is selling merchandise below cost; he is gambling.

When any of these conditions appears, the creditor should arrange to confer with his debtor. The creditor should tell the debtor that there are rumors about his condition "on the street"; that it is generally known that suits have been instituted against him. The creditor may indicate his desire to co-operate by giving the debtor the benefit of constructive suggestions in order to facilitate his rehabilitation. He may ask to see the accountant's last report. If it appears that the debtor cannot continue normally, and if he is apparently honest, the creditor may suggest the calling of a meeting of the debtor's largest creditors. As this procedure often leads to an agreement whereby the debtor may continue in business and creditors may obtain the eventual payment of their accounts, it is advisable to consult an experienced attorney to prepare a valid and binding agreement embodying the terms and conditions.

Adjustments through credit bureaus.—If the creditors are unwieldy, it may be advisable to have a credit association of which some of the creditors are members call a meeting of all creditors, at which the debtor's affairs may be discussed.

Credit bureaus have been organized throughout the country not merely to supply credit data and to collect accounts receivable but also to supervise the administration of a debtor's business affairs. These bureaus are generally organized by credit men so as to minimize credit risks. A meeting of creditors of the debtor is usually called at the bureau either at the instance of the debtor or of the creditors. At such meeting the debtor is required to furnish a statement of his financial condition, showing his list of creditors and the amounts respectively due them, as well as an itemized statement of his assets. Creditors frequently require an audit of the debtor's books in order to ascertain whether or not the debtor has been honest or whether his failure has been due to conditions beyond his control. At the same time the debtor generally makes known his offer of settlement. After the creditors' investigation, if there should appear to be a prospect of the debtor's future success, the creditors may accept a reasonable offer for payment of their obligations. Often, where the debtor's offer is insufficient, the bureau will require the debtor to deliver to it an assignment for the benefit of creditors so that the debtor's assets may be under the direct supervision of the bureau or a creditors' committee that may have been appointed. If the debtor has committed fraud, or has made unlawful preferences, bankruptcy proceedings may be in order.

Ordinarily a committee of creditors should be chosen from the general body of creditors, a custodian placed in charge of the assets, an inventory taken, the debtor's books examined by a certified public accountant, the accounts receivable aged, and, if practicable, the debtor's checks countersigned by a member of the committee. The results of the investigation should be reported promptly to the creditors. As a general rule, it is good policy to follow the recommendations of the committee.

When creditors cannot agree.—As previously indicated, if all the creditors do not agree, some other method of dealing with embarrassed debtors must be undertaken. The making of an assignment for the benefit of creditors, explained on page 1122, may be the solution. Unfortunately this plan leads to a cumbersome and expensive means of liquidation. Another disadvantage of this procedure is that it seldom leads to rehabilitation.

If some creditors refuse to co-operate, in the proper case a bankruptcy "arrangement" proceeding, explained more fully on page 1132, will have the salutary effect of compelling the acceptance of the terms of the settlement by a recalcitrant minority group. Therefore, from the point of view of benefits, both to the debtor and the creditors, in cases where difficulty is encountered in obtaining the written consent of all creditors to an out-of-court agreement, the machinery provided by the National Bankruptcy Act, either in an "arrangement" proceeding or a "reorganization" proceeding, may be the most effective means of dealing with embarrassed debtors.

3. ASSIGNMENT FOR BENEFIT OF CREDITORS

What is an assignment for benefit of creditors?—An assignment for the benefit of creditors is a transfer by a debtor of his property to an assignee in trust, to apply the property or the proceeds thereof to the payment of his debts, and to return the surplus, if any, to the debtor. In order to operate as an assignment, there must be an absolute transfer of property without retention of any control by the debtor, and the transfer must be made to an assignee. The transfer is generally effected by the execution of a deed of trust or an assignment for the benefit of creditors by the debtor to the assignee, but no particular form is ordinarily required. The statutes in many states specifically authorize the execution of an assignment for the benefit of creditors under specified conditions; assignments executed pursuant to such statutes are known as "statutory assignments." Where these statutory conditions are not met in the execution of an assignment, the assignment may in some states operate as a common law assignment.

Statutory provisions governing assignment for benefit of creditors.—The statutes regulating assignments for the benefit of creditors vary in the different states. The following matters are those most commonly covered:

1. *Form of assignment.*—Some statutes specifically require that the assignment be in writing, signed by assignor and assignee, and duly acknowledged before a notary public.

2. *Property to be included.*—The assignment should embrace all of the assignor's property except such as is exempt from execution.

If all the property is not assigned, a dissenting creditor may set the transfer aside as fraudulent. Omissions of unimportant property do not generally invalidate the assignment; the property omitted must be of such importance as to show an intention to hinder, delay, or defraud creditors.

3. *Recording.*—Many statutes require that the assignment be filed or recorded in the office of a designated public official; in some states failure to file or record makes the assignment invalid.

4. *Filing of inventory.*—The assignee is required to file an inventory of the property and a description thereof within a fixed period.

5. *Bond of assignee.*—The assignee is required to file a bond to secure the faithful performance of his duties.

6. *Notice to creditors.*—Notice of sale and to present claims must be given to creditors either personally or by publication, as prescribed.

7. *Filing of creditors' claims.*—Verified claims of creditors must be filed within a designated period with the assignee or his attorney.

Many states have enacted laws forbidding the giving of preferences by insolvent debtors. In any event, if a transfer is made with intent to hinder creditors for the debtor's own advantage, such a conveyance is invalid, and the assignment may be declared fraudulent.

Qualifications and duties of an assignee.—The assignee must be a competent person, capable of performing his duties as assignee. Unless the statute provides otherwise, a debtor has a right to choose the assignee without the consent of the creditors, if he does so in good faith. If creditors are consulted before the assignment is made, it is advisable to suggest the designation of a major creditor to act as the assignee.

It is the duty of an assignee for the benefit of creditors to administer the trust to the best advantage and to protect it for the benefit of the creditors and of the debtor. To this end, he may employ and pay for counsel to advise and assist him in legal matters arising out of the administration of the assigned estate. The assignee may be held liable for failure to exercise good faith in his transactions; failure to use reasonable diligence in the management of the trust; willful misapplication of trust funds; and negligence, want of caution, or misconduct, such as permitting the debtor to retain possession of assigned property. Following are some of the specific duties of an assignee under an assignment for the benefit of creditors:

1. File or record the assignment; give notice of the assignment, requesting creditors of the assignor to present their claims, and requesting debtors to make payments to the assignee.
2. Execute a bond for the faithful performance of his duties.
3. Take possession of the property transferred under the assignment.
4. Collect the debts of the assignor.
5. Sell the property transferred under the assignment at public sale, upon due notice to creditors; also advertise at least once before date of sale.
6. Pay all priority claims including taxes; make distribution to creditors out of the proceeds realized upon the sale of the property, and turn over any surplus remaining after such distribution to the assignor.
7. Keep a full and accurate account of the property received and disposed of, and render an account. Generally the account of the assignee must be approved by the court before the assignee may be discharged.

Personal liability of assignee for obligations created by him.—The assignee is personally liable for contracts made by him after assumption of his representative capacity. He is also personally liable for any new debts that he creates in the administration of the assignment. The hiring of an attorney, expenses incurred for labor, gas, electricity, and the paying of rental of a house—all these are obligations created by the assignee for which he is personally liable. He may, of course, make a claim for reimbursement out of the assets of the assigned estate.

An assignee who receives as an asset of his assignor an unexpired lease has a reasonable time within which to decide whether he will accept the lease and assume the burdens of its covenants on behalf of the estate, or whether he will surrender possession of the premises to the landlord. If he does not accept the lease, but continues in possession, he is personally liable for the value of the use and occupation.

Participation of creditors in assignment.—After creditors have shared in the assets available under a general assignment, they may, unless they have received from the assignee the face amount of their claims with interest, realize on the remainder of the amount due on their claims out of any additional property that the debtor may acquire. The assignment may not provide that acceptance of the proceeds of the assignment shall operate as a release or discharge of the claims, since this is the field of the Federal Bankruptcy law, by which Congress has superseded the local statute on the subject of discharge.

Assignment as an act of bankruptcy.—Regardless of whether or not the debtor is insolvent, an assignment for the benefit of creditors is an act of bankruptcy under the Federal bankruptcy laws, if made within four months of the filing of a petition in bankruptcy. An involuntary petition in bankruptcy may not be filed by any creditor who assented in writing to the assignment. If bankruptcy follows, the assignee is required to turn over the property that came into his hands to the trustee in bankruptcy or to account therefor. The assignment need not conform to the technical requirements of the state statutes in order to constitute an act of bankruptcy; it may have been executed in the form of a deed of trust.

4. EQUITY RECEIVERSHIPS

Equity receiverships supplanted.—Until recently the equity receivership instituted by a creditor's bill was considered the best means of administering insolvent debtors. This form of liquidation, discussed under receivership in connection with provisional remedies, on page 1118, has been in effect supplanted by the methods of administration provided for under the National Bankruptcy Act.

5. ORDINARY VOLUNTARY OR INVOLUNTARY PETITION IN BANKRUPTCY (Liquidation)

Policy of the bankruptcy law.—The policy of the bankruptcy law is to give creditors control of the administration of a debtor's affairs with reasonable safeguards to creditors in the treatment of the assets and to afford creditors notice of all important steps that eventuate in the final distribution of the assets among creditors on an equitable basis.

Kinds of bankruptcy proceedings.—The National Bankruptcy Act provides for two kinds of bankruptcy proceedings—voluntary and involuntary.

Any person, partnership, or corporation (except municipal, banking, insurance, and railroad corporations and building and loan associations) may become a voluntary bankrupt on his or its own petition, regardless of the amount owed to debtors.

An involuntary proceeding may be instituted against any natural person (except a farmer or a wage earner) and against any business, commercial, or moneyed corporation (except banking, municipal, railroad, and insurance corporations and building and loan associations), and against any unincorporated company, such as a partnership, owing $1,000 or more.

What the petition in bankruptcy alleges.—The petition in bankruptcy must allege that the bankrupt's principal place of business, residence, or domicile was situated within that territorial jurisdiction for the preceding six months, or was situated within that territorial jurisdiction for a longer portion of the preceding six months than in any other jurisdiction.

In an ordinary involuntary petition, where the alleged bankrupt has twelve or more creditors, at least three creditors must sign the petition; where there are less than twelve creditors, one or more creditors must sign. In either event, the aggregate amount of the petitioning creditors' unsecured claims must be $500 or over.

An involuntary petition must allege that the debtor has committed at least one of the acts of bankruptcy as provided by Section 3 of the National Bankruptcy Act, within four months preceding the filing of the petition.

Acts of bankruptcy.—The acts of bankruptcy consist of the alleged bankrupt having:

1. Conveyed, transferred, concealed, or removed any part of his property, with intent to hinder, delay, or defraud his creditors.
2. Transferred, while insolvent, any portion of his property to a creditor, with intent to prefer such creditor over his other creditors.

3. Permitted, while insolvent, any creditor to obtain a lien upon any of his property through legal proceedings, and not having vacated or discharged such lien within thirty days from the date thereof, *or* at least five days before the date set for any sale of such property.

4. Made a general assignment for the benefit of his creditors.

5. While insolvent or unable to pay his debts as they mature, permitted, voluntarily or involuntarily, the appointment of a receiver or trustee to take charge of his property.

6. Admitted in writing his inability to pay his debts and his willingness to be adjudged a bankrupt.

Petition for appointment of receiver.—Following the filing of the petition in bankruptcy in triplicate with the Clerk of the Court, to whom is paid the filing fee of $30, the next practical step is to prepare and submit the creditors' petition for the appointment of a receiver. Unless the alleged bankrupt's consent or waiver has been obtained, the application for the appointment of a receiver must be accompanied by a petitioning creditors' bond in the sum of $250 to indemnify the alleged bankrupt for damages in the event that the petition in bankruptcy is dismissed.

The mere filing of the petition in bankruptcy is not a basis for the appointment of a receiver. To justify the appointment of a receiver, the Court must be satisfied that the appointment is necessary to preserve the estate.

Creditor's right to interpose answer to involuntary petition.—The right formerly given to a creditor to interpose an answer to an involuntary petition has been taken away in the "ordinary" bankruptcy proceeding. In a corporation reorganization proceeding under Chapter X (see page 1134), a creditor may file an answer.

Adjudication of the bankrupt.—If the alleged bankrupt defaults in interposing an answer to the involuntary petition, or if the trial of the issues results in the upholding of the petition, the Court will enter an order or decree of adjudication. This means that the alleged bankrupt has been judicially adjudged a bankrupt within the purview of the acts of Congress relating to bankruptcy. It is not necessary, however, to await the entry of such adjudication in order to enable a creditor, by petition, to examine the bankrupt and others concerning the acts, conduct, and property of the bankrupt.

The immediate and intelligent use of this examination very often forms the basis for the recovery of assets fraudulently or preferentially transferred and the prosecution of dishonest bankrupts and their confederates.

Filing of schedules by the bankrupt.—Following the entry of the order of adjudication, and within five days thereafter, the bankrupt must file schedules of his assets and liabilities (also unliquidated and contingent claims), as well as a "Statement of Affairs," on a form prescribed by the United States Supreme Court. (See page 1131.) If a debtor files a voluntary petition in bankruptcy, he should accompany it with similar schedules and a "Statement of Affairs."

The bankruptcy statute is intended to give the creditors the control and administration of a bankrupt estate. It should be recognized that, at the outset of the proceeding, the Court may, on proper petition, without ascertaining the views of the general body of creditors, appoint a receiver, but this "temporary" official must eventually give way to the permanent administrator known as the *trustee in bankruptcy*.

Sales.—Ordinarily sales must be on at least ten days' notice to creditors and must realize at least 75 per cent of the appraisal, unless specially confirmed.

Election of trustee in bankruptcy.—A majority in number and amount of creditors' claims is required to elect a trustee. Creditors who have filed their proof of debt may elect one or three trustees. Stockholders, directors, and officers of a corporation that is bankrupt may not participate in the voting for the appointment of a trustee; nor may creditors who are relatives of the bankrupt participate.

In computing the number of votes for any candidate, the Court has a right to exclude from voting all claims of $50 or less, insofar as number is concerned. However, such claims may be included in the amount. The purpose of excluding these small claims is to prevent them from creating a deadlock or from controlling an election.

Filing proofs of claims.—Creditors are entitled to receive dividends only when they have filed their proofs of claim with the referee. Proofs of claim must be filed within six months after the date set for the first meeting of creditors. The Court cannot grant any additional time. Creditors may elect a creditors' committee of not less than three members at the first meeting of creditors, to consult and advise with the trustee in the administration of the bankrupt's estate.

Assets acquired by the trustee.—The trustee acquires title to assets of the bankrupt debtor as of the date of the filing of the petition in bankruptcy, as well as title to property passing to the bankrupt by way of devise, inheritance, or bequest within six months from the date of adjudication.

Section 70a of the Bankruptcy Act enumerates the following classes of the bankrupt's property that pass to the trustee as assets of the bankrupt estate:

1. Documents relating to the bankrupt's property.
2. Patents, copyrights, and trade-marks.
3. Powers that the bankrupt might have exercised for his own benefit.
4. Property transferred by the bankrupt in fraud of creditors.
5. Property, including rights of action, which, prior to the filing of the petition, could by any means have been transferred by him or which might have been levied upon and sold under judicial process against him.
6. Rights of action arising upon contracts or the unlawful taking of or injury to the bankrupt's property.
7. Contingent remainders, executory devises, rights of entry for condition broken, rights of reverter, and like interests in real property, which were nonassignable prior to bankruptcy and which, within six months thereafter, become assignable interests or give rise to powers in the bankrupt to acquire assignable interests.
8. Property held by an assignee for the benefit of creditors.
9. Property that vests in the bankrupt within six months after adjudication by bequest, devise, or inheritance.
10. Property in which the bankrupt has at the date of bankruptcy an estate or interest by the entirety, and which within six months after adjudication becomes transferable in whole or in part solely by the bankrupt.

Duties of the trustee.—The trustee has the burden of administering a bankrupt estate. He must, by sale, reduce the assets to cash and deposit the funds in a banking institution specially designated by the Court. He is required to examine the bankrupt. He must examine proofs of claim and object to improper ones. He may, without special authorization by creditors, file specifications of objections to the bankrupt's discharge. He must pay dividends to creditors as ordered by the referee. The trustee must file, from time to time, reports showing the condition of the bankruptcy estate. It is his duty to institute appropriate proceedings, suits, and actions against the bankrupt and third parties to "turn over" or account for assets belonging to the estate. The trustee's lot is eased somewhat by the recently enacted law by which, in the absence of the bankrupt's books or records, a presumption now exists that the sales price is the cost price. Of special help to the trustee in recovering assets is Section 67 of the Bankruptcy Act, sometimes referred to as the "Uniform Fraudulent Conveyance Act."

Since the trustee has title to all the assets of the bankrupt estate he represents, he has the power and right to bring any and all such actions as are necessary in order to collect assets which legally belong to the estate, but of which he has not secured possession. Moreover, since he represents all the bankrupt's creditors, he may commence such proceedings as any of the creditors might institute to avoid fraudulent or illegal transactions. Where the trustee fails or refuses to bring such action, the creditors may then petition the court for an order compelling the trustee to bring the suit or apply for his removal.

Referee's duties.—The referee in bankruptcy, appointed by the United States judges, presides at the first meeting of creditors and at adjourned hearings, as well as at the examination of the bankrupt and other witnesses. He also has other duties related to discharge of the bankrupt and arrangement proceedings mentioned at page 1132.

Examination of the bankrupt.—The bankrupt must attend the first meeting of creditors. The statute requires that the referee shall examine the bankrupt publicly. The bankrupt must also attend the hearings on the objections to his discharge and such other hearings as the Court may direct. He may also be required to file in court in duplicate a sworn inventory giving the cost of merchandise or of other property remaining on hand as of the date of bankruptcy.

The "Statement of Affairs" referred to on page 1128, which must be filed by the bankrupt or debtor whether or not he is engaged in business, is in the nature of a questionnaire, wherein the bankrupt furnishes, in effect, a history of his business career within six years preceding the filing of the petition; a statement of his books and records showing by whom they were kept and audited; and also records of his financial statements, inventories, income tax returns, bank accounts, legal proceedings affecting his assets, transfers of property other than in the course of business, losses by fire, theft, or gambling, loans repaid, and so on. This very comprehensive review of the bankrupt's affairs must be filed within five days prior to the holding of the first meeting of creditors and is usually of inestimable help to the Court and examining creditors' counsel.

Discharge of the bankrupt.—Where an individual bankrupt, including a partnership and its members, is concerned, his adjudication in bankruptcy acts automatically as a petition for a discharge. The bankrupt corporation, however, is required to file a petition for discharge within six months of the date of adjudication.

The referee is required to mail to creditors a thirty-day notice of the date set for the filing of specifications of objections to a bankrupt's discharge. If no specifications of objections to the discharge are filed, the referee grants the bankrupt's discharge.

Reasons for denial of discharge.—The bankrupt will be denied his discharge if he has committed any one of the following acts:

1. An offense punishable by imprisonment as provided by the bankruptcy law.

2. Destroyed, mutilated, falsified, concealed, or failed to keep or preserve books of account or records from which his financial condition and business transactions might be ascertained, unless the Court deems such acts or failure to have been justified.

3. Obtained money or property on credit, or an extension or renewal of credit, by making or publishing or causing to be made or published, in any manner whatever, a materially false statement in writing respecting his financial condition.

4. At any time after the first day of the twelve months immedi-

ately preceding the filing of the petition, transferred, removed, destroyed, or concealed or permitted to be removed, destroyed, or concealed any of his property, with intent to hinder, delay, or defraud his creditors.

5. Has, within six years prior to bankruptcy, been granted a discharge, or had a composition or an arrangement by way of composition or a wage earner's plan by way of composition confirmed under the Act.

6. In the course of a proceeding under the Act, refused to obey any lawful order of, or answer any material question approved by, the Court.

7. Failed to explain satisfactorily any losses of assets or deficiency of assets to meet his liabilities.

Investigation of fraud.—Creditors may call upon the United States Court through its officers, the referee or trustee, to refer to the United States attorney the matter of inquiring into the acts, conduct, and property of the bankrupt where it is believed that a criminal offense has been committed in violation of the laws of the United States, such as concealment or fraudulent transfer of assets, using the mails to defraud (for example, mailing a false financial statement), or giving false oaths in bankruptcy proceedings. The United States Attorney will submit the facts to the Federal Grand Jury, which frequently indicts the violators of the law. If necessary in the public interest, the United States Attorney, who now receives notice of hearing on the bankrupt's application for discharge, may file specifications of objections to the bankrupt's discharge.

6. VOLUNTARY ARRANGEMENT PROCEEDINGS UNDER CHAPTER XI OF THE BANKRUPTCY ACT (Extension or Modification of Unsecured Debts)

What is an arrangement?—The newly created Chapter XI of the Bankruptcy Act is known by the title "Arrangements." In effect, this chapter supersedes the provisions of the old Bankruptcy Act for compositions and extensions of time for payment of debts. The expression "arrangement" is intended to give effect to the negotiations between a debtor and the creditors. Whether one pays one hundred cents on the dollar over a period of time or a lesser sum, the term "arrangement" covers both.

Chapter XI provides only for the treatment of several classes of unsecured creditors and permits the rejection of burdensome executory contracts.

Filing a petition.—An arrangement proceeding can be filed only as a voluntary proceeding; that is, only a debtor may file a petition under Chapter XI. It may be instituted by an individual, a partnership, or a corporation, before or after adjudication in a pending bankruptcy proceeding, but the District Court will not stay the old bankruptcy proceeding, except upon terms of indemnity.

The petition for arrangement should be accompanied by the schedules of the debtor's liabilities and assets, including a statement of executory contracts of the debtor. It is imperative that there be attached thereto a "Statement of Affairs" and the debtor's proposed plan of arrangement.

Immediately upon the filing of the arrangement petition, the matter is referred to a referee in bankruptcy, and from that time on the appointed referee exercises complete and original jurisdiction.

The Court may authorize the debtor to continue and operate the business, but the debtor will be required to indemnify the creditors for any loss resulting from the operation of the business during the time the plan of arrangement is being considered.

Creditors' meeting.—The referee calls a meeting of creditors upon at least ten days' notice to consider the plan of arrangement. Such notice to creditors is accompanied by a copy of the plan and a summary of schedules of liabilities and assets. At this meeting the debtor must be examined. A creditors' committee may be appointed, and a tentative trustee may also be nominated at this meeting, at which creditors should file their proofs of claim.

Confirmation of arrangement.—The referee will confirm the arrangement if he is satisfied that it is for the best interests of creditors; that the plan is fair and equitable; that the debtor has not been guilty of any acts which would have barred his discharge in bankruptcy; that good faith has been shown on the part of the creditors and debtor; and that written acceptances have been filed by a majority in number and amount of those creditors who have filed their claims; and that the consideration to be paid to creditors and allowances have been deposited.

Termination of proceedings.—Upon confirmation of the arrangement, the debtor is discharged from all unsecured debts provided for by the arrangement, except debts that are not dischargeable. A final decree must be entered discharging the receiver or trustee and closing the estate.

If the plan of arrangement is not acted on favorably by creditors or is abandoned by the debtor, the Court enters an order adjudging the debtor a bankrupt and directs that further proceedings be had as in the case of ordinary bankruptcy. If a bankruptcy proceeding was pending when the petition for arrangement was filed, the Court will dismiss the Chapter XI proceeding and direct that the previous bankruptcy proceeding be continued. Where the debtor has perpetrated fraud in the procurement of the confirmation of an arrangement, it will be set aside upon application made within six months of the date of confirmation.

7. INVOLUNTARY OR VOLUNTARY CORPORATE REORGANIZATION UNDER CHAPTER X OF THE BANKRUPTCY ACT

(Extension or Modification of Secured and Unsecured Debts)

Corporate reorganizations.—Chapter X of the Bankruptcy Act is known as the law pertaining to corporate reorganization. It is an outgrowth of the old Section 77 B. By this method the debtor, stockholders, and creditors seek to avoid the consequences of foreclosures, liquidations, forced sales, and other drastic deflationary effects. This law deals only with the corporate debtor and provides mainly the basis of a modification of secured debts or a change in the corporate capital structure. Chapter X should be invoked only when no adequate relief can be obtained under Chapter XI, which deals with the modification of unsecured liabilities.

The pendency of the ordinary bankruptcy, either before or after adjudication, will not prevent the filing of a Chapter X petition.

Another interesting feature is that under Chapter X the proceeding may be voluntary or involuntary, while under Chapter XI only a voluntary proceeding may be filed. The petition under Chapter

X may be filed only in the jurisdiction where the debtor has its principal assets, or its principal place of business, for the period of six months preceding the date of the filing of the petition, or for a longer portion thereof than in any other jurisdiction.

Filing petition in involuntary reorganization.—In the involuntary proceeding the petition must allege that the debtor has been adjudged bankrupt in the pending proceeding; or that a receiver in equity has been appointed because of insolvency or inability to pay debts as they mature; or that an indenture trustee is in possession by reason of a default; or that a foreclosure proceeding is pending against the debtor's property; or that the debtor corporation has committed an act of bankruptcy (see page 1126) within four months prior to the filing of the petition.

In contradistinction to the rights of a creditor in the ordinary bankruptcy proceeding, a creditor may interpose an answer to an involuntary reorganization petition. The reorganization petition must be approved by the Court and must be shown to have been filed in good faith. If it is not approved, the petition will be dismissed.

Appointment of trustee.—Where the liabilities are over $250,000 in a Chapter X reorganization proceeding, the Court must appoint a disinterested trustee. In cases where the liabilities are less than $250,000, the Court may appoint a trustee or permit the debtor to continue in possession. The trustee must be independent, but there is also provision for the appointment of a co-trustee, who may be drafted from the corporate debtor. He may be a director or an officer. The attorney for the trustee must also be disinterested. The trustee must conduct an examination into the past affairs of the debtor. He is the one who must promulgate the plan of reorganization. He calls upon the creditors, debtor, and others for information and data, but the trustee is the one in the first instance to initiate the plan of reorganization. In making his report as to the condition of the debtor's affairs as he finds it, the trustee must make that report to the judge, the creditors, the stockholders, and also to the Securities and Exchange Commission, popularly referred to as the "S.E.C."

If in a case involving less than $250,000 in liabilities, the judge declines to appoint a trustee but permits the debtor to continue in the operation of its business, the Court may appoint an examiner to conduct a disinterested examination into the affairs of the debtor corporation, for the information of the Court and others.

Plan of reorganization.—If for any reason the trustee's plan is not found satisfactory, then, and not until then, the creditors (and stockholders where the corporation debtor is solvent) may submit a plan of reorganization. The judge has the right to fix the time for filing the claims and to classify creditors.

In cases where the liabilities exceed $3,000,000, the judge must refer plans that he regards as worthy of consideration to the Securities and Exchange Commission for examination and report. In other cases no duty devolves upon the judge to refer the plan to the S.E.C., but he may do so. The S.E.C.'s report is merely advisory; it is not binding on the judge.

Acceptance of plan of reorganization.—It is necessary to obtain acceptances of two thirds in number and amount of each class of creditors whose claims have been allowed in order to present the matter of the application for confirmation of the plan to the Court. Insofar as stockholders are concerned, where the corporation is solvent, a majority in number of shares is required to modify their rights. Usually the judge will confirm any plan of reorganization that has been accepted by the requisite number and amount of the creditors and stockholders affected by the plan, but he must find, as a prerequisite, that the plan is "fair and equitable" based upon his informed and independent judgment. Creditors are entitled to priority over stockholders against all of the property of an insolvent corporation, and in such event stockholders are excluded from participation in any plan of reorganization unless they make a reasonable cash contribution.

8. VOLUNTARY WAGE EARNERS' PLANS

Dealing with embarrassed wage earners.—Frequently wage earners incur obligations through the purchase of automobiles, jewelry, and furniture on the installment plan and through borrowing from finance companies. If the debtor happens to be such a wage earner, it is advisable to point out to him that if his creditors sue and obtain judgments against him, his wages will be garnisheed, and the resulting annoyance to his employer may lead to his discharge. The debtor should be made acquainted with the provisions of Chapter XIII of the Bankruptcy Act, entitled "Wage Earners' Plans," under which he can obtain effective relief and at the same time deal honorably with his creditors on the basis of an extension or compromise of his obligations.

Procedure under Chapter XIII.—Although no involuntary petition in bankruptcy may be filed against a wage-earner debtor unless his earnings exceed $1,500, under this new important provision for relief, a wage earner who earns from all sources of income a sum not exceeding $3,600 per year may, at modest expense, invoke this form of procedure by which he can submit a plan to pay his obligations out of his future earnings. The debtor's voluntary petition indicating that he is insolvent or unable to pay his debts as they mature must be accompanied by his schedules of assets and liabilities, as well as a "Statement of Affairs." Immediately after the filing of the petition, the Court issues an order restraining all creditors from proceeding outside of the Federal Court. The referee promptly notifies the creditors to attend a creditors' first meeting, at which the debtor's plan is considered.

Creditors should file with the referee at the first meeting of creditors their proofs of claim, similar in form to those used in ordinary bankruptcy proceedings. Each creditor filing a claim must state under oath that such claim is free from usury.

Confirmation of plan.—The Court will confirm the wage-earner's plan if accepted in writing by a majority in number and amount of the claims of creditors as filed, and if satisfied that the plan is fair, equitable, and feasible. Until the provisions of the plan are complied with, the Court continues to retain jurisdiction of the debtor and his affairs.

Since by this method the debtor submits his future earnings to the control of the Court, the Court may, from time to time, after obtaining the views of the debtor and his creditors, increase or reduce any of the installment payments under the plan or extend or shorten the time for such payments as the circumstances and financial condition of the debtor warrant.

[illegible] due or to become due from his wages will be terminated [illegible] the existing [illegible] employer [illegible]. This line should be read in connection with the [illegible] Chapter XIII of the Bankruptcy Act [illegible] under which [illegible] with his creditors [illegible].

Procedure under Chapter XIII.—[illegible]

[illegible]

Confirmation of plan.—The Court [illegible] the wage earner's plan [illegible]

[illegible]

SECTION 12

Financial Statements

I. HOW FINANCIAL STATEMENTS ARE CONSTRUCTED

The Balance Sheet

Explanation of Items in the Balance Sheet

Current Assets

Fixed Assets or Fixed Capital

Tangible Fixed Assets

Intangible Fixed Assets

Investments

Analysis of Working Capital

Working Capital Ratio

Other Factors in Financial Analysis

False Financial Statements

SECTION 12

Financial Statements

1. HOW FINANCIAL STATEMENTS ARE CONSTRUCTED

Kinds of financial statements.—Statements showing the financial condition of a business are of two principal types:

1. A statement of the financial position of the business on a certain day, known generally as the *balance sheet.*
2. A statement of the origin of net income or of net loss for a definite period of time, known generally as the *income statement.*

Both these statements are frequently identified by other names, which may or may not have special significance. The variations in names are discussed on pages 1145 and 1182.

How financial statements reflect financial condition.—The balance sheet shows the financial position of a business on a certain day by listing the monetary values of all the assets and the amounts of all the liabilities. The difference between the two represents the net worth or deficit of the business on the day as of which the balance sheet is prepared. The balance sheet also shows the proprietary interests in the net worth of the business. The balance sheet amounts are based on the assumption that the company will continue in business indefinitely, and therefore the net worth shown in the statement is in no sense an indication of the amount that might be realized if the company were to be liquidated immediately. Usually the balance sheet presents the condition of the business at the beginning of the period as well as at its close. The date as of which the balance sheet is prepared is always the closing date of the period for which the income statement is drawn up.

The income statement is a summary, for a definite period, of income received from business operations, all costs and expenses involved in producing the operating income, all income from sources other than the direct operations of the business, all deductions from income, and the net results of the conduct of the business for the period covered. The income statement may be combined with a statement of surplus, in which case it will show distributions of income made during the year to the stockholders, and other changes in the surplus account. In the case of sole proprietorships and partnerships, the income, profit, and loss statement may be combined with the capital accounts to show the changes made in the capital accounts during the year.

Clarification of published financial statements.—The tendency to make all published financial statements more comprehensive and informative began as a voluntary movement on the part of forward-looking corporate executives who saw in the increase in the extent of ownership of corporate securities a need for offering to investors understandable information concerning the financial condition of the company. The movement gained impetus after the economic crisis that began in 1929. The Government's investigation of certain corporations after the collapse of the stock market, and its inquiry into the activities of the New York Stock Exchange, made it incumbent upon corporations to allay the suspicions of their security holders by offering more comprehensible information in their annual reports to stockholders. The requirements of the Securities and Exchange Commission in connection with new financing compelled the preparation of detailed statements of condition and their availability to the public.

The following excerpt from the annual report of a large public utility shows clearly the influence of the Government's control of new issues of securities upon financial statements offered to stockholders and the public:

> . . . it has been deemed desirable this year to depart from the presentation of accounts commonly adopted by this Company and others similarly situated and to present the financial statements and notes thereto and the auditor's certificate in substantially the same form as filed with the Federal Trade Commission* in the Registration State-

* The functions of the Federal Trade Commission in regard to new issues of securities were transferred to the Securities and Exchange Commission in 1934.

ment. Footnotes on the balance sheets and on the consolidated income account explain certain items in more detail than is customary.

More and more corporations are addressing annual reports to employees, and in these reports there is a marked tendency to clarify financial statements.

The Balance Sheet

Meaning of descriptive terms in the balance-sheet title.—The statement of financial condition on a certain day is most commonly called a "balance sheet." The term implies that the statement has been drawn up from the books of account and that the figures represent the balances shown in a double-entry ledger after closing. The following descriptive terms are used to show the nature of the statement:

1. *General balance sheet.*—The term "general" has no special significance. It is employed principally by the railroads in presenting their balance sheets.
2. *Condensed balance sheet.*—The word "condensed" is used to indicate that the balance sheet is a summary and that details are omitted. It implies that the balance sheet is supported by schedules, which may or may not accompany the statement. (See page 1151.)
3. *Comparative balance sheet.*—Any balance sheet so entitled will make comparisons with data for the immediately preceding closing date, or some earlier date or dates. Such statements usually contain columns showing increases or decreases in amounts during the intervening period.
4. *Consolidated balance sheet.*—The prefixing of the term "consolidated" indicates that the statement shows the financial condition of a group of companies controlled by the same interests. In other words, the assets and liabilities of the companies whose stocks are owned by the parent company are substituted for the stock of the subsidiary companies, and the financial condition of the group is presented as though the subsidiaries had no separate corporate existence. All intercompany relationships are necessarily eliminated in the preparation of the consolidated balance sheet. For example, if parent Company *A* has loaned subsidiary Company *B* $50,000 and has taken Company *B*'s note therefor, the item would not appear in the consolidated balance sheet, since the note receivable in

Company *A*'s accounts is offset by the note payable in Company *B*'s accounts. Another example is the elimination of intercompany profits from the inventories.

No fixed rule is followed by accountants in the determination of the amount of control necessary to justify the inclusion of the subsidiary accounts in the consolidated balance sheet. If the controlling interest is only 51 per cent, it is generally not regarded as sufficient to warrant combining the accounts of the subsidiary with those of the parent company in the consolidated balance sheet. Some accountants consider that a 60 per cent interest is sufficient; others do not combine the accounts of a subsidiary in the consolidated balance sheet unless a 75 or 80 per cent interest is owned by the parent company. On the other hand, some accountants take into consideration the size of the subsidiary company, and if it is so small that a 40 per cent interest is insignificant in comparison with the net worth of the parent company, they will see no objection to consolidating its accounts. Unless a note is appended to the balance sheet to show what principles have been applied in the consolidation, the term "consolidated balance sheet" conveys no accurate idea of what group of companies is covered.

If the accounts of subsidiaries that are not completely owned by the parent company are combined for balance-sheet purposes with those of the parent company, the interest of the minority stockholders must be set forth in the balance sheet as a liability, or, as some accountants call it, an "accountability." This item is further explained on page 1176. The parent company's equity in the aggregate earnings or losses of the unconsolidated subsidiaries must also appear on the balance sheet.

Combinations of titles.—Various combinations of the terms mentioned above are used in entitling balance sheets. Thus it is not uncommon to come upon a "comparative condensed general balance sheet," or a "condensed consolidated balance sheet," or any other combination of the terms.

Other titles for balance sheets.—Balance sheets are sometimes entitled as follows:

1. Statement of financial condition.
2. Financial statement.
3. Statement of condition.

4. Statement of assets and liabilities.
5. Statement of resources and liabilities.
6. Statement of assets, liabilities, and net worth.
7. Statement of worth.
8. Statement of affairs.

A statement bearing one of the above titles is not necessarily a reflection of balances appearing in the books of account on the date mentioned in the statement. The use of any of the titles in place of "balance sheet" does not attach any particular meaning to the statement except insofar as usage and practice have given them special significance. Statements rendered to banks and others for the purpose of obtaining loans are frequently called "financial statements." The term "statement of condition" is employed in the presentation of the balance sheets of banks. "Statement of affairs" identifies the financial statement of an insolvent company.

How a statement of affairs differs from other balance sheets.—A statement of affairs is prepared from the viewpoint of liquidation. Thus it contains two columns for assets, in one of which the going-concern value is given, and in the other of which the estimated realizable value is noted. It furthermore classifies accounts differently from an ordinary balance sheet in that the assets are grouped to show those which have been pledged with creditors and those against which there are no liens, while the liabilities are arranged according to priorities, as prior, fully secured, partially secured, and unsecured.

What a pro-forma balance sheet is.—A statement that carries the title

PRO-FORMA BALANCE SHEET, ------------ ------, 19--

is one that gives effect to changes that have not in fact taken place. It portrays a financial condition that does not exist, but which it is expected will exist as a result of certain contemplated transactions. Such balance sheets are prepared, for example, in connection with new financing, mergers, recapitalizations, reorganizations, and the like. They are sometimes called "giving-effect" balance sheets. The statement should indicate the transactions to which effect has been given. Thus, the title would appear as follows:

THE ________________ COMPANY
BALANCE SHEET, DECEMBER 31, 19__
(Giving effect as of that date to the subsequent issuance and sale of $8,500,000 Refunding Mortgage Bonds and the proposed application of the proceeds thereof)

How to entitle the balance sheet.—The heading of the balance sheet should contain the following three points of information:

1. The name of the person, firm, or corporation whose financial condition is portrayed.
2. What the statement purports to be.
3. The date as of which the statement is prepared.

The following illustrates a balance-sheet heading:

INTERNATIONAL HARVESTER COMPANY AND AFFILIATED COMPANIES
CONSOLIDATED BALANCE SHEET, DECEMBER 31, 19__

The date is usually the day on which the books were closed. This is generally the last day of the calendar year or of the fiscal year. The latter term generally means an accounting period of twelve months ending on the last day of any month other than December. The expression "as of" or "at" before the date is sometimes used; the usual practice, however, is to omit such expressions. If the balance sheet is a comparative one, showing amounts for the current date and for an earlier date, both dates appear in the heading as follows:

DECEMBER 31, 19__ AND DECEMBER 31, 19__

Form of the balance sheet.—Unless a form of balance sheet is prescribed by some regulating body, bank, or other outside organization calling for a statement of financial condition, the arrangement of the balance sheet need follow no particular order. The most common setup of the balance sheet presents the assets on the left-hand side of the sheet and the liabilities, capital stock, and surplus on the right-hand side. The balance sheet thus resembles an account.* It is not unusual, however, to list the assets in the upper part of the balance sheet, and to place the liabilities, capital

* In England, the practice is to use the left-hand side of the balance sheet for liabilities, capital stock, and surplus, and the right-hand side for the assets.

stock, and surplus immediately below the assets. This form is referred to as the "report" form.

The assets and liabilities that appear in the balance sheet vary with the nature of the business, the accounts maintained in the books of the company, and the purpose for which the financial statement is prepared. The items on the asset side can generally be classified into:

1. Current assets.
2. Permanent investments.
3. Sinking funds.
4. Fixed assets.
5. Deferred charges.

The liabilities side of the balance sheet can be divided into:

1. Current liabilities.
2. Fixed liabilities.
3. Deferred credits.
4. Proprietary interests.

An explanation of the groups and the items that comprise them is given on pages 1152, et seq. No fixed rule exists as to the order in which these groups shall be presented in the balance sheet. A relationship should be maintained, however, between the two sides of the balance sheet. If the current assets are presented first on the asset side, the current liabilities should head the liabilities side; if the fixed assets are listed first among the assets, the fixed liabilities or the proprietary interests should be stated first among the liabilities.

A balance sheet prepared for submission to a bank, a credit agency, or a creditor for purposes of obtaining a loan or credit generally takes the form of an account, with the current assets listed first on the left-hand side and the current liabilities first on the right-hand side.

Methods of clarifying the balance sheet.—The following methods are commonly used to simplify the reading and understanding of the balance sheet.

1. *Captions above each class of items to indicate their nature.*—The classification given above suggests the captions that may be used. Others will be mentioned as the items are discussed.

2. *Footnotes.*—Any item requiring further explanation may be marked with an asterisk or superior figure, and the star or number may be explained at the foot of the balance sheet. The following is an example:

CURRENT ASSETS:		
Cash	$58,667,466.42	*
Marketable securities, at the lower of par or market	49,282,522.00	*
* Amount required for retirement of special stock on April 15, 19__	47,866,368.65	

3. *Notes or comments.*—The tendency in recent years has been to clarify the balance sheet by appending thereto notes or comments pertaining to the balance sheet as a whole or to particular items. With regard to the balance sheet as a whole, if there has been any change as compared with the preceding period, either in accounting principles or in the manner of their application, which has had a material effect on the statement, the nature of the change should be indicated. The explanation of items in the balance sheet, beginning on page 1152, points out those that require elucidation and indicates how, by means of explanatory notes, the items can be clarified. See page 1156 for an example.

4. *Expansion of items.*—The following illustrates an expansion of the item "Property":

Real Estate and Plants, Raw Sugar Properties, Warehouses, Cooperage, Railroads, Tank Cars, Steamships, Coal Barges, Wharves and Garages, with their machinery, equipment, etc., and timber and other lands owned in fee or through ownership of the entire capital stock of constituent companies, at cost less depreciation $80,571,809.70

5. *Running comments in the body of the statement.*—The following excerpt from an actual balance sheet shows a liberal use of comments:

CURRENT ASSETS:

This group comprises cash and items which in the ordinary course of business are convertible into cash in time to meet maturing obligations.

CASH .... $ 566,483.22

This item represents money on deposit in banks, in transit, and on hand in the companies' offices.

INVESTMENTS—At Market Value:	
State, County, and Municipal Bonds	530,522.50
Railroad, Industrial, and Public Utility Bonds	104,310.00
Other	3,101.00
The three preceding items represent the temporary investment of excess current funds.	
NOTES, DRAFTS, ACCOUNTS RECEIVABLE, AND ACCRUALS	1,520,738.12
These items at September 30, 19__, represent accounts receivable from customers (after deducting reserves of $111,687.15 for items which may be uncollectible) and interest receivable from investments, $21,274.91, salesmen's advances, $7,814.68, amounts due from employees, $8,565.25, and debit balances in accounts payable and sundry accounts receivable, $55,115.83 (after deducting reserves of $17,630.98).	
DUE FROM EMPLOYEES FOR PURCHASES OF CAPITAL STOCK	6,950.92
This amount is receivable from employees on their purchases of shares of stock; the market value of such shares, which are held as collateral, was $11,250.00 at September 30, 19__.	
INVENTORIES	1,243,950.19
This represents the cost of manufactured finished goods, the lower of cost or market of goods purchased for resale, and generally the lower of cost or market of materials and supplies.	
TOTAL CURRENT ASSETS	$3,976,055.95
The sum of the preceding items. (The excess of total current assets over total current liabilities, $3,161,260.73 at September 30, 19__, constitutes "Working Capital.")	

6. *Schedules.*—Since for most purposes a condensed balance sheet is sufficient, it is frequently advisable not to make the statement bulky by including details that can be furnished in the form of schedules. Any item in the balance sheet may be expanded by means of a schedule. The following is a list of schedules commonly prepared in connection with condensed balance sheets:

(*a*) Property account.
(*b*) Securities owned.
(*c*) Investments and advances—affiliated companies.
(*d*) Funds in the hands of trustees.
(*e*) Inventories.

(*f*) Deferred charges.

(*g*) Depletion, depreciation, amortization, and current maintenance reserves.

(*h*) Funded debt.

(*i*) Capital stock.

(*j*) Contingent liabilities.

Explanation of Items in the Balance Sheet

Current Assets

What the current assets of a business are.—The current assets of a business are cash and other assets that will be converted into cash during the normal operations of the business, as well as those that can readily and quickly be converted into cash without interfering with the regular operations of the business. The items that ordinarily make up the current assets are discussed below.

Cash.—This item includes demand deposits in banks, legal tender, checks, bank drafts, and money orders. It may also include paper left at a bank for collection, if the bank has credited the depositor's account with the deposit. Cash will be overstated if the company has, for the purpose of showing a strong cash position, recorded as of the last day of the period amounts received after the close of the period.

Time and special deposits.—Time deposits may be shown separately among the current assets or may be included with the cash item. In the latter case, the sum representing time deposits should be indicated in parentheses, thus:

Cash (including $1,000,000 in time deposits) $1,635,928.00

Special deposits from which predetermined disbursements are to be made, such as dividend accounts, payroll accounts, and the like, may be included among the current assets.

Marketable securities.—This item may include only those securities with a ready marketability that are being held during a period of small cash requirements and that will be sold as soon as a need for cash develops, or it may include as well all securities that are readily marketable and that can be disposed of without undue interference with the business. It should not include marketable securities that will not be sold in the ordinary course of business. For example, securities that represent investments made to maintain trade relations are not current if by a sale of them the company would interfere with the purpose for which they were acquired. The item of marketable securities is sometimes divided into "Government securities" and "Sundry marketable securities." When listed among the current assets, marketable securities should be included at the lower of cost or market value. The valuation may be shown in the following manner:

U. S. Government securities at lower of cost or quoted market value (market value $25,419,946)	$24,937,026
Other marketable securities at lower of cost or quoted market value (market value $874,363)	864,210

Accounts receivable.—This item should represent the net amount of accounts receivable that will be converted into cash in the regular course of business, after accounts ascertained to be worthless have been eliminated. The account should show the amount of reserves for bad debts and the reserves for any other deductions, such as freight to be paid by the customer and deducted from his bills, allowances, and discounts. The following illustrates a common method of showing the reserve:

Accounts receivable (less reserves for discounts, freight, and doubtful accounts—$100,754.40)	$235,535.67

In many balance sheets, receivables that will not be converted into cash within a year, such as deferred-payment contracts to the extent to which they are not payable within the year, are not included among the current assets. They may appear as a separate item below the total of current assets, or among the "other assets." See page 1170. It is generally considered proper to classify past-due items as current receivables, unless collection will be deferred beyond a year.

Accounts receivable should be divided into "trade receivables" and "other receivables" in order that the statement may clearly reveal what portion of the receivables has resulted from trade and what portion represents current receivables resulting from other transactions. A further division should be made to indicate the amount of receivables arising from sales on regular or installment terms. In the absence of the latter division, the reader of the balance sheet may be led to believe that all of the receivables are collectible within the normal period of 30, 60, or 90 days, depending upon the terms of sale in the business. The information may be presented thus:

Customers' accounts:	
Regular retail terms	$2,274,074.70
Installment terms	734,802.51

In a consolidated statement, the amount of reciprocal intercompany receivables and payables is eliminated. (See page 1145.) Any amounts collectible currently from affiliated companies, not eliminated through reciprocal intercompany transactions, should be listed separately under the accounts receivable as "Affiliated companies' accounts" to distinguish them from customers' accounts and other accounts. The item should not be included among the current assets if the debtor company does not have a satisfactory margin of current assets over current liabilities, including such accounts. Under the latter circumstances, the affiliated companies' accounts would appear under investments or some other title, as the circumstances indicate.

Notes receivable.—Notes receivable, or bills receivable, as they are sometimes called, are frequently combined with accounts receivable. Whether so combined or entered as a separate item among the current assets, the amount of notes receivable should not include dishonored notes—that is, those that have passed their maturity without being collected. The form of balance sheet contained in the bulletin entitled "Verification of Financial Statements," issued by the Federal Reserve Board, includes past-due notes among the current assets, but the manner of presenting them, illustrated below, leaves no room for misunderstanding.

Notes and accounts receivable:	
Notes receivable, customers' (not past-due)	
Accounts receivable, customers' (not past-due)	
Notes receivable, customers' (past-due)	
Accounts receivable, customers' (past-due)	
Less:	
Reserve for bad debts	
Reserve for discounts, freight, allowances, etc.	

If the reserve for bad debts takes into account possible losses on notes receivable, it should be deducted in the balance sheet from the total of notes and accounts receivable; if not, the reserve should be deducted only from the accounts receivable.

Notes receivable that are not due within a year should be segregated from the current assets, unless trade practice warrants a different treatment. (See page 1168.) Notes arising from transactions outside of the ordinary business of the company, and notes from stockholders, directors and employees, should be separated from those arising from trade accounts. (See page 1170.)

What was said of accounts receivable of affiliated companies is equally applicable to notes receivable. Notes of affiliated companies should be listed separately from customers' notes, and should be included among the current assets only if the debtor company has a satisfactory margin of current assets over current liabilities, including such notes.

See page 1175 for the manner of noting in the balance sheet the possibility of liability on customers' discounted notes.

Inventories.—This item varies in the balance sheet with the nature of the business. A company that purchases finished goods for resale would have a merchandise inventory; one that manufactures products would have an inventory of finished goods, goods in process, raw materials, and supplies. Supplies usually denote commodities used in the operations of a business which are not ingredients of a manufactured product and which are not sold specifically. Since they represent prepaid expenses, they may be excluded from the inventory and placed among the deferred charges. Supplies, however, are frequently included among the inventories because they involve a physical inventory rather than because they constitute assets of greater currency than other deferred charges.

Containers, barrels, cartons, bottles, cans, and the like, may represent materials entering into the production of the product, supplies, or permanent assets. If they constitute materials entering into production, they may be placed among the current assets; if supplies, they may appear among the deferred charges; and if permanent assets, they may be included among the fixed properties. (See page 1160.)

Included in the inventories may be goods sent out on consignment and not sold, valued at cost of the goods plus any expenses incurred in sending the merchandise to the consignee. The inventory should not include merchandise received to be sold on consignment.

What the valuation of inventories in the balance sheet represents. —The standard rule for the valuation of inventories is "cost or market, whichever is lower." While most balance sheets generally show the basis of valuation by the inclusion of a parenthetical statement immediately after the item, indicating that the lower of cost or market has been used, that information is not sufficient for a proper understanding of the valuation. Without a fuller explanation of the basis of valuation, such questions as the following may arise:

1. Have the incidental expenditures for freight, drayage, and storage been included in calculation of cost?
2. Have cash discounts been treated as a reduction of cost or as financial income?
3. What method has been used to arrive at the cost where purchases have been made during the year at fluctuating prices and where goods have been manufactured during the year at various costs?
4. How have reductions from cost to market been treated in the accounts, and how are reduced inventories treated in the succeeding period?

In a consolidated statement, the question arises: How have intercompany profits on goods included in the inventory been handled? The intercompany profits should be eliminated, unless it is impracticable to do so, and in that event, a note in the balance sheet should explain that they have not been eliminated. A note in the balance sheet, summarizing in general terms the instructions issued by the company to those charged with the duty of preparing the actual inventories, would throw some light upon the inventory item. The following two examples of notes, taken from actual balance sheets, demonstrate how the inventory item can be clarified. Neither of the notes, to be sure, answers all the questions that arise in an analysis of the asset.

> Raw materials and bulk supplies are priced at the lower of cost or market. Miscellaneous supplies, work in process, and finished products are priced at cost or less, a large portion being covered by sales orders

at prices in excess of inventory value, the remainder being valued conservatively, in the opinion of the management, by the provision of reserves considered adequate for losses anticipated from obsolescence.

* * *

The quantities of inventories on hand at the end of the year 19__ were ascertained by employees of the Corporation, by weight, count, or measurement, except in the case of certain raw materials the taking of physical inventories of which was impracticable. As to the latter, the quantities shown by the books were used, the book balances having been adjusted from time to time during the year on the basis of estimates made by such employees.

Inventories, other than contract work in progress, were valued at the lower of cost or market. (Reference is made here to a schedule of inventories.) In valuing such inventories, interdepartment, interplant, and intercompany profits have not been included.

Contract work in progress was valued at cost, as adjusted by estimated profits or losses on certain work nearing completion or on separate units thereof. Such profits and losses have been taken or provided for, based upon estimates of probable final costs. The income account is charged with such estimated losses and is credited with such estimated profits. The unbilled portion of the cost of the contract work in progress does not include interdepartment, interplant, or intercompany profits.

Other current assets.—A number of other assets may properly be added under the caption of "current assets," or grouped under a separate heading called "other current assets." They include:

1. Agents' balances.
2. Amounts due from employees. This item may be included in "other assets." See page 1170.
3. Accrued interest and dividends receivable.
4. Bonds and other securities maturing in the near future. The names of the securities and the maturity dates should be indicated in the balance sheet.
5. Sight drafts with bills of lading attached, and C.O.D. items.
6. Advances that are returnable within a short period.
7. Good-faith deposits on United States Government contracts.

Fixed Assets or Fixed Capital

What are the fixed assets of a business?—All property of a permanent nature, whether tangible or intangible, that is used in the operation of the business and that is not intended for sale may be considered the fixed assets of an enterprise. Fixed assets appear in the balance sheet under the caption of "fixed assets," "fixed capital," or "capital assets." The use of the latter term is not recommended, since the assets properly classified as fixed assets do not include all of the assets that represent capital. The items making up this group of assets will be discussed below under the two principal headings of:

1. Tangible fixed assets.
2. Intangible fixed assets.

Tangible Fixed Assets

What the tangible fixed assets are.—Tangible fixed assets include land, buildings, machinery and tools, furniture and fixtures, patterns, delivery equipment, containers, and similar property.

How tangible fixed assets are valued.—The values of fixed assets set forth in the balance sheet may be:

1. Cost, regardless of upward or downward changes in market value.
2. Increased value on the basis of an appraisal. The latter is justified if the increase has not been credited to the surplus account and if the fact that the books show appraised value has not been overlooked in the determination of depreciation.
3. Decreased value on the basis of appraisal.

The basis of valuation should be indicated for each item, with the year of appraisal noted if appraised value is the basis. The following excerpt from a balance sheet illustrates how the basis is noted:

Land, factory sites, etc., at cost	$ 3,711,960.41
Buildings, docks, etc., at sound values as appraised in 19__, plus subsequent additions at cost	12,465,553.81
Machinery, equipment, motor trucks, etc., at sound values as appraised in 19__, plus subsequent additions at cost	14,328,714.54

If the basis of valuation is the same for all the items, it may be noted in the caption as illustrated below:

Fixed Assets, as Revalued by the Company, December 31, 19__, plus Subsequent Additions at Cost:

The reserve for depletion, depreciation, wear and tear, and obsolescence of the properties included among the fixed assets should appear as a deduction from the values of such properties.

Land.—When this item is included among the fixed assets, it should represent land used for plant purposes and not land held for speculation or for future plant use. Nor should it include land held under long-term leases. If cost is the basis, the value may include brokers' commissions, fees for examining and recording title, taxes accrued at the date of purchase, and the cost of such improvements as installing sewers and laying pavements. Interest on installment payments of assessments should not be included in the cost of the land.

The item "real estate" in the balance sheet may represent land and buildings. In the books of account, however, the two assets are ordinarily kept separate, since items of depreciation and insurance may affect one and not the other.

Buildings.—Both buildings acquired and buildings constructed are included in this item. In the case of buildings acquired, cost covers the purchase price, the cost of all alterations, improvements, and repairs made to restore depreciation that occurred before the property was purchased. In the case of buildings constructed, the cost covers material and labor, or the contract price, and many other incidental items occurring during the period of construction, such as payments for permits, architects' fees and superintendents' salaries, premiums on workmen's compensation, and taxes and insurance during the construction period.

Machinery and tools.—The valuation of machinery on the basis of cost includes the purchase price, freight, duty and installation charges, as well as a capitalization of costs of breaking in the machinery and testing it, where these are necessary. It should not include any amounts expended in rearranging the machinery after the initial installment. Such expenditures may be carried as a deferred charge. Tools and machinery are generally kept in separate accounts on the books, since they are subject to different considerations in determining depreciation.

Furniture and fixtures.—The value of furniture and fixtures in the balance sheet indicates the cost of permanent equipment; it should not include amounts expended upon rearrangements and replacements that add no value to the asset. The reserve for depreciation may be given separately or bulked with the general reserve for depreciation of property.

Patterns.—If this account is conservatively maintained, the balance will reflect the values of patterns used for regular stock work and will not include the costs of patterns made for special jobs, or patterns, lasts, and so forth, for products that are no longer manufactured. Furthermore, it will show values after substantial reductions have been made from book value.

Delivery equipment.—Motor trucks and other delivery equipment are valued at cost less depreciation in the balance sheet. The amount should not include the cost of parts requiring frequent replacements.

Containers.—Bottles, boxes, barrels, cans, and the like, that have not been charged to customers, and that are owned by the business, may be included among the fixed property at a valuation that makes liberal allowance for depreciation and for loss through failure of customers to return them. If containers have been billed to customers, the value of any in circulation will be included in the accounts receivable (unless, as in the brewery business, the intent is that the containers are charged to customers merely "on memo"), and the property account will not reflect them.

What the balance sheet does not show about the property items.—Information on the following points in regard to fixed tangible assets is generally not disclosed in a balance sheet unless a note is appended to the statement.

1. Whether the property accounts are charged only with new property or with replacements and improvements as well.
2. Whether the property accounts include any charges, in addition to direct cost, for overhead expense, interest, or other similar expenditures.
3. Whether cash discounts taken on purchases of fixed assets have been treated as a reduction in the cost of the property, or have been recorded as a financial income.
4. How provision for depreciation has been made—that is, what

classes of property have been considered, what basis has been used, and what depreciation rates have been applied.

5. What classes of expenditures, if any, are charged against reserves for depreciation.

6. Upon a sale or abandonment of property, what disposition is made in the accounts of the difference between depreciated value and realized or realizable value.

7. Upon purchasing property from a subsidiary, whether cost to the subsidiary or some other basis is used in charging the property account.

Intangible Fixed Assets

What the intangible fixed assets are.—The intangible fixed assets generally include patents, copyrights, trade-marks, formulas and processes, leaseholds, and goodwill. In many balance sheets the intangibles are not valued separately, but are presented as a combined asset and given a value of $1 or some other nominal sum. This does not mean that the intangibles have no greater value than that indicated. It merely indicates that with regard to these items the company has been conservative in not capitalizing them; it furthermore serves to remind the reader of the balance sheet that such assets exist. If the nominal valuation is presented merely for balance-sheet purposes and does not represent the value at which the intangibles are carried on the books, a note such as the following may be inserted after the item:

> Intangibles carried on the books at substantial amounts are shown at the nominal amount of $1 for the purposes of the published accounts.

In the following discussion, each of the intangible items will be discussed separately. First, the intangibles that are subject to amortization will be presented—that is, those that should be written off over a definite period of time—patents, copyrights, franchises, leaseholds, and leasehold improvements; then the intangibles that are not subject to amortization—goodwill, trade-marks, and formulas and processes.

Patents.—All patents ultimately lose their value, since they are issued for a limited period of seventeen years. They may become valueless long before the expiration of the patent because other patents have superseded them, or because the product manufactured under the patent has lost its marketability, or for other reasons. Deductions must therefore be made from the valuation of patents to allow for the disappearance of the asset. These deductions, known as *amortization,* are generally not set forth in the balance sheet; the value indicated, rather, is a net valuation after the appropriate deductions have been made. Since patents are generally either purchased or applied for, the valuation shown in the balance sheet may represent the following expenditures after deduction for amortization has been made:

1. The cost of the patent, if it was acquired by purchase.
2. The expense involved in obtaining the patent, in providing working models, and in experimenting with them, if the patent is obtained otherwise than by direct purchase.
3. The cost of conducting an experimental department for developing patentable devices. Only so much as may be applied to successful patents granted should be included.
4. The cost of successful litigation that has established the patent.

Copyrights.—This item, when more than nominal in value, may indicate that the copyright has been purchased from a previous owner. A conservative treatment of this asset, whether obtained by the company directly from the Government or acquired by purchase, would in most cases require it to be written off against the income from the first edition rather than over the life of the copyright, which is twenty-eight years with the possibility of a renewal for an additional twenty-eight years, since few publications are marketable during the entire life of the copyright. However, in certain instances less drastic treatment may be justifiable.

Franchises.—The asset franchises appears usually in the balance sheet of a public-service company and not in that of an industrial enterprise. It represents the cost of obtaining the franchise, less a deduction for amortization, if the franchise has been granted for a limited period. Franchises that are not perpetual and are not limited to a fixed number of years should be written off rapidly.

Leaseholds.—The valuation of leaseholds among the intangibles ordinarily represents the advance payment of rent made by the lessee or sublessee on a long-term lease, less the appropriate deduction for amounts written off over the life of the lease. Sometimes the account includes a capitalization of the saving in rent made possible by an advantageous lease. If so, that fact should be evident from the inclusion in the statement of a special surplus account representing the amount added by the capitalization of the saving.

Leasehold improvements.—If the lease provides that the lessee shall pay the costs of any alterations or improvements of the leased property, such as new fronts, partitions, and other changes, the improvements become the property of the owner at the expiration of the lease. During the life of the lease, however, the costs of such improvements may be carried in the balance sheet as leasehold improvements, but the cost should be written off during the life of the lease.

Goodwill.—The following enumeration of items that frequently make up the goodwill account shows the great difficulty the reader of the balance sheet encounters in understanding the significance of the account.

1. The amount paid for goodwill upon acquisition of a going concern. Many accountants justify a goodwill account only when it is created through the circumstances of a purchase of a going concern.
2. The amount expended in excess of a normal sum, for advertising with the intent of creating goodwill.
3. Valuations arising through the writing-off of the patent account to goodwill instead of to income in cases where the patent has given the owner a monopoly that is expected to continue after the expiration of the patent.
4. Amounts added to the account that in fact are deferred charges or expenses, such as organization expenses and costs of establishing a business.
5. Amounts improperly added to the account as arbitrary capitalizations of earnings in excess of a normal return on capital.

The cost of goodwill acquired upon the purchase of a going concern need not be written off, even though it has declined in value because of a falling-off of profits. Should the goodwill acquired by purchase increase in value, any writing-off would result in an understatement of the net worth and accumulated profits and the creation of secret reserves. Additions to the goodwill account arising in ways other than by purchase are generally not justified.

Trade-marks.—This item, when it appears in the balance sheet, represents the cost of trade-marks acquired by purchase. Frequently its value does not appear separately in the balance sheet but is included with goodwill. Since a trade-mark does not expire as does a patent or copyright, its value is not subject to amortization. Just as it is improper to capitalize permanently in the goodwill account amounts expended in creating goodwill through advertising and other sales-promotion outlays, so it is considered equally unjustifiable to capitalize amounts spent in advertising a trade-mark.

Formulas and processes.—Formulas and processes acquired from a going concern at a direct cost are generally included in the goodwill and are not valued as a separate item in the balance sheet. Like trade-marks, formulas and processes have an unlimited life and therefore need not be amortized. They should be written off when they are no longer used.

Investments

How investments appear in the balance sheet.—The investment group in the balance sheet embraces permanent investments, temporary investments that cannot be liquidated or that are not intended to be used for current business needs, and advances that will not be collected within the near future. This division of investments, however, is not generally made in the balance sheet. The most common method of presenting investments is to include a caption "Investments," or "Permanent investments," and to show a valuation for:

1. Investment in and advances to affiliated companies.
2. Funds.
3. Other investments.

The investments in affiliated companies may be mentioned by name, if they are not too numerous.

If any of the securities have been pledged, or hypothecated, that fact and the book value of such securities should be stated on the balance sheet. The following illustrates how the item would appear:

INVESTMENTS:	
Securities of subsidiary and affiliated companies owned (including $31,964,672.66 pledged as collateral to notes payable of this company and to guaranty of notes payable of a subsidiary company) at book value	$256,850,853
Investments in, advances for account of, and account receivable from Deep Rock Oil Corporation (in receivership)—at book value	34,149,623
Other Investment Securities (including $6,984,402.32 pledged as collateral to notes payable of this company and to guaranty of notes payable of a subsidiary company)—at book value (market value at December 31, 19__, $3,216,546.25)	7,056,176

Valuation of permanent investments.—The securities held by a company may comprise mortgages, bonds, and stocks. Mortgages may be included at their face value, unless it is known that the security behind them has declined in value below the face of the mortgage. Stocks and bonds held for permanent investment are ordinarily valued at cost. All minor market fluctuations and all increases in market value should be ignored. If the market value is considerably less than the cost, a reserve should be set up equal to the difference between the cost and the market value. The reserve is a charge against surplus rather than against profit and loss because it does not arise from operations. (See page 1177.)

In the case of bonds acquired at a premium or at a discount, the valuation reflected in the balance sheet should give effect to adjustments for amortization of premiums paid and for the accumulation of discounts. Such adjustments are made periodically for the purpose of bringing the valuation of the securities upon the books to par at maturity.

Investments in controlled subsidiary or affiliated companies.—The valuation in controlled or affiliated companies may reflect one of the following:

1. The cost of the securities plus the holding company's proportion of the subsidiary's profits (or if the subsidiary's profit and loss statement shows a loss, less the holding company's proportion of the loss), less the dividends received from the subsidiary.

2. The proportionate share of book value of net assets of controlled companies.
3. The cost of the investment to the holding company.

Unless the balance sheet indicates how the securities of controlled and affiliated companies are dealt with, there is no way of determining the true meaning of the valuation.

A consolidated balance sheet will omit from the investment item the stocks of subsidiaries owned by the parent company if the assets and liabilities of the subsidiaries are included in the consolidated accounts. However, the value of investments in controlled and affiliated companies whose accounts are not included in the consolidation will appear in the balance sheet. (See page 1145.)

Other investment securities.—This item includes securities of uncontrolled companies and holdings of nonaffiliated companies acquired to create and maintain favorable business connections. The valuation indicates the cost of the securities less any reserve that has been set up to reduce the book value from cost to market. The amount of the reserve may be mentioned in parentheses after the item, as:

Other investments, at cost (less reserve, $26,000) $136,020

or the reserve may be shown as a deduction from the value. Frequently the item is presented in the balance sheet at cost, with a parenthetical statement of the value on the basis of market quotations.

Real property.—Properties held for speculative purposes or for use in future expansion of the plant should be listed among the permanent investments at cost, irrespective of changes in market value. The carrying charges, such as taxes, may be included in the cost.

Investments in the company's own stock.—A company that has purchased its own stock with the intention of reissuing it may regard the shares it holds in the same light as it does the securities of other companies and carry it on the books at the cost or market value, whichever is lower. However, if the stock acquired is regarded as retired, but is not actually retired because retirement would involve an amendment of the certificate of incorporation, the par or stated value of the amount held should be shown as a deduction from outstanding capital stock in the capital-stock section of the balance sheet. (As to shares that are held in the treasury as a result of donations, see page 1179. Many accountants hold that treasury stock should in any event be reflected in the balance sheet as a deduction from the capital stock.)

Sinking funds.—Sinking funds are generally created to meet a contractual obligation undertaken at the time of the creation of an issue of bonds or notes. The nature of the investments purchased with the funds depends upon the terms of the indenture requiring the creation and maintenance of the fund. Frequently the investments consist of bonds of the very issue that the fund is designed to protect, and other securities of the same or different companies. The value of the sinking fund shown in the balance sheet may represent the total par value of the bonds of the same issue held in the sinking fund, the cost of other securities, uninvested cash, and accrued interest on the securities owned. If the company's own bonds have been acquired for the sinking fund and cancelled, they will not appear in the sinking fund as an asset, but will be accounted for in the reduction of outstanding obligations among the liabilities. The item may appear on the balance sheet as follows:

Cash resources held by Trustees' account Bond Sinking Funds	$437,652
(Trustees also hold $13,340,000 of redeemed bonds, not included as liabilities in this balance sheet)	

Other funds.—Other funds may include:

1. Funds for the retirement of capital stock.

2. Funds to meet some contingent liability; as, for example, a fund to pay damages that may result from an unfavorable decision under pending litigation.

3. Funds for the payment of future liabilities; as, for example, funds to pay for advertising.

4. Funds representing investments of reserves, such as endowment funds, insurance funds, pension funds, and replacement funds. (See page 1178 for an explanation of funded reserves.)

A separate classification is sometimes made in the balance sheet of funds that represent neither permanent investments nor the usual funds. Amounts held by trustees for the payment of matured and called bonds would, for example, not represent an investment or a fund.

Securities held as investments of funds are ordinarily valued as permanent investments. (See page 1165.)

Long-term notes receivable.—Notes receivable not maturing within a year from the date of the balance sheet may be included among the permanent investments, since they may not be considered current assets.

Temporary investments.—When this asset is included among the investments and not in the current assets, it represents securities that will not be sold in the ordinary course of business and should be valued in the same manner as permanent investments.

Advances.—Advances made to subsidiary companies for permanent working capital constitute, for practical purposes, investments by the parent company in the subsidiary companies, in addition to the investment represented by ownership of the securities of the subsidiary companies. The item therefore belongs with the investments. It is frequently combined with the investments in the balance sheet in the following way:

Investments in and advances to affiliated companies	$1,428,333

or included under the caption of investments, as follows:

Notes of and advances to associated companies:	
Controlled companies	$2,333,363
Noncontrolled companies	630,000

Or, the advances may be listed in the balance sheet as a separate item, without a caption.

Advances to stockholders, officers, and directors may appear under the investments, under "other assets," or under some other caption, except current accounts receivable.

Deferred Charges

What the deferred charges are.—Practically every balance sheet includes a group of items representing deferred charges, for in the operation of a business there are always certain expenses that are paid in advance. They may be designated in the balance sheet as "deferred charges," "deferred assets," "deferred charges to future operations," "prepaid and deferred charges," "deferred items," "suspense items," or by other names. The items generally include prepaid expenses, unamortized charges, and miscellaneous suspense accounts.

Prepayments.—The usual prepayments among the deferred charges are unexpired insurance, prepaid interest, taxes, rent, royalties, and advertising.

Unamortized expenditures.—The following deferred charges arise through the application of the amortization process to expenditures that will eventually be entirely charged off to profit and loss:

1. Unamortized bond discount and expense. This item in the balance sheet generally represents the difference between the face amount of bonds issued and the consideration received for them that must still be written off before the entire discount at which the bonds were issued by the corporation is wiped out.

2. Unamortized improvements to leased property. Amounts expended in erecting buildings upon leased property and in making alterations and improvements to such property must be written off over the life of the lease, for the additions, alterations, and improvements usually revert to the landlord at the expiration of the lease. (See page 1161.) The sum shown among the deferred charges as unamortized improvements to leased property reflects the expenditures that must still be written off. Improvements to leased property are sometimes not included among the deferred charges but are presented as a separate asset, without caption, immediately below the fixed assets. In that case the amortization may be shown as a reserve, in the following way:

Alterations and Improvements to Leased Properties:	
At independently appraised reproductive values at December 31, 19__, adjusted for property changes since 19__, including additions at cost	$7,131,149.63
Less Reserve for Amortization	2,875,252.44
	$4,255,897.19

3. Unamortized organization expenses. This item among the deferred charges indicates the sum expended for organization costs that must still be written off.

Miscellaneous suspense items.—A variety of items make up this category, such as questionable assets, merchandise of doubtful marketability, and expenditures that have not finally been classified as assets or expense items.

Other Assets

What is included among other assets.—Many balance sheets do not contain this title, for the assets of the company fit properly under the principal categories heretofore discussed. Items that do not fit into the standard groups may be included without caption in the balance sheet, or may be grouped under the heading of "other assets." The following accounts are frequently placed among the "other assets":

1. Stock subscriptions. When there is no immediate intention of calling upon the subscribers for the unpaid balances of their subscriptions, the unpaid subscriptions may be included in the "other assets" or may be deducted from the capital stock, as explained on page 1179. Subscriptions may appear among the current assets when the collection of the subscriptions is expected in the near future. The item should not be listed among the assets at all, but as a deduction from capital stock, if there is no probability that the stockholders will be required to pay the unpaid subscriptions.
2. Deposits as security or guaranties—for example, bonds on deposit with the State Labor Commission; lease deposits.
3. Amounts due from officers and employees.
4. Advances to salesmen and employees.
5. Miscellaneous accounts receivable.
6. Insurance policies. This item is sometimes included among the investments. The value should represent the cash-surrender value and not a capitalization of premiums paid for the policies. Although the cash-surrender value of insurance policies is immediately available, the asset is not a current asset unless there is a definite intention of surrendering the policies in the near future.

Notes and comments relating to assets.—Notes and comments of an informative character may be used freely in the balance sheet to clarify the meaning of any item not apparent from its title, to furnish information not reflected in the accounts of the company, and to supplement the accounts. The following are examples of asset items that may require notes and comments at the foot of the balance sheet.

Contingent assets.—Contingent assets do not appear in the body of the balance sheet, since they represent items that are not real assets but that may some day become assets. For example, claims in dispute are contingent until they acquire the status of a collectible item. Contingent liabilities, discussed on page 1175, are frequently offset by contingent assets. For example, if the company has endorsed the notes of another company, it has created a contingent liability; should the original maker of the note default and the company become liable as endorser, it will have a claim against the original maker of the note for reimbursement. That claim is a contingent asset. A footnote in the balance sheet may explain the nature of any contingent assets.

Sinking-fund arrears.—If the sinking fund is in arrears, a note at the foot of the balance sheet should indicate the amount of the arrears. The following is an example of such a note:

> The Company was in arrears in the amount of $10,000 on December 31, 19--, on sinking-fund contributions required by the trust indenture.

Current Liabilities

What the current liabilities are.—The current liabilities of a business set forth in the balance sheet should disclose all liabilities for goods purchased; all liabilities for services rendered; all accrued liabilities for wages, interest, taxes, bonuses, and the like; and all liabilities upon due bills, trading stamps, and merchandise coupon books.

Accountants are not in agreement as to the period which determines that a liability is current. In some balance sheets the current liabilities may represent debts that mature within ninety days; in others they may include liabilities payable within a year of the date of the balance sheet. The usual debts included among the current liabilities are discussed below.

Accounts payable.—This item generally includes obligations on open accounts due trade creditors and amounts due others for expenses. It also includes liabilities for taxes, salaries, and wages, though these items are frequently listed separately with the current liabilities. The advantage of showing separately amounts due trade creditors is that this method offers the reader of the balance sheet an opportunity to analyze the relationship of the amount due for merchandise and raw materials to purchases for the period. Liabilities to affiliated companies should be shown separately.

Notes and acceptances payable.—Sometimes notes and acceptances payable are divided into trade-notes payable and other notes payable. As in the case of accounts payable, a separation of trade-notes payable from other notes payable throws light upon the relation of debts for merchandise to goods bought. The balance sheet, or supporting schedules, should indicate whether the debts are secured or unsecured. Notes payable to affiliated companies should be shown separately.

Discounted notes, acceptances, and so forth.—The sum noted for this item indicates the extent to which the company has become indebted because of the default of customers whose notes or acceptances have been discounted.

Accounts and notes due to officers, stockholders, and employees.—This debt should appear as a separate item if the amounts are large; if small, they may be included among the accounts payable. In balance sheets that are prepared to be submitted to banks, the amount should be stated as a separate item.

Accrued liabilities.—The accrued liabilities may be separated from other current liabilities by a caption. They include amounts that are liabilities at the time the balance sheet is made up, but that are not yet due. The usual accruals are for salaries and wages, commissions, taxes, interest, rent, gas bills, dues, and other sundry expenses.

Other current liabilities.—A number of other items may be included among the current liabilities if they represent debts that must be paid within the near future; among them are:

1. Purchase obligations. This may represent payments that will be due currently or during the year on account of purchases of capital assets.

2. Customers' deposits. This debt belongs with the current liabilities whenever there is an obligation to return deposits within a

short time or to apply them against sales. Customers' deposits may be carried as a separate item when they are to be held for a long period. Public-service corporations, for example, usually list customers' deposits as a separate item.

3. Customers' credit balances.

4. Matured interest payable. This item usually refers to sums payable about the time that the balance sheet is made up. For example, interest may be due on January 1 and the balance sheet prepared as of December 31. The fund to meet the interest due may be in the hands of the interest-paying agent or in a special bank account of the company.

5. Dividends declared on certain classes of stock and payable after the date of the balance sheet.

6. Matured long-term debts unpaid. This class of debt arises through the failure of holders of matured or called bonds to present their bonds for payment.

7. Unpresented interest coupons and unclaimed dividends.

8. Long-term debts maturing in part or in whole during the year. Some accountants maintain that if the debt is to be refunded—that is, if the sum to meet the maturing obligations is to be raised by the issuance of other long-term obligations—the item should not appear in the current liabilities but should be carried among the fixed liabilities.

9. Reserves representing actual liabilities. (See page 1177 for a discussion of this class of reserves.)

Fixed Liabilities

What constitute the fixed liabilities?—The long-term liabilities, or fixed liabilities, generally include all obligations, whether secured or unsecured, maturing in more than one year from the date of the balance sheet. The items that usually make up the fixed liabilities are discussed below. They appear in the statement, usually, under the heading of "funded debt."

Mortgages.—Any mortgages upon the property of the company should be listed among the fixed liabilities and should not be presented as a deduction from the property account.

Long-term bonds, debentures, notes, and certificates of indebtedness.—While most balance sheets merely show the par value of long-term debts outstanding, the statement would be more useful for analytical purposes if it showed:

1. The name of the issue, the rate of interest, and the maturity date.
2. The par value of bonds outstanding of each issue.
3. The amount of bonds of each issue still unissued.
4. Whether any of the unissued bonds have been pledged.

A schedule of funded indebtedness may be appended to the balance sheet, giving the above data.

The difference between the par value of bonds outstanding and the price received for them should be charged to bond discount, if they have been sold for less than par, or credited to the premium on bonds account, if they have been sold at a premium. Both of these accounts are written off periodically. The amount of discount on bonds remaining to be amortized will be included among the deferred charges, as explained on page 1169. Any premium on bonds unamortized will be stated among the deferred credits.

In a consolidated balance sheet, the long-term debt may represent the net amount outstanding in the hands of the public if any of the affiliated companies whose accounts are included in the balance sheet hold bonds of a related company. In other words, the bonds held as an asset of one company may be offset against the bond liability of the other company.

Deposits.—Customers' deposits held for a long period, such as deposits held by public-utility corporations, appear as separate items among the liabilities.

Under some circumstances, installment payments received from employees under employee stock-purchase plans are treated like deposits and entered as a liability. The amount is offset by the asset cash. The usual treatment of subscription installment payments, however, is to show the amount due on subscriptions among the assets and to deduct from the capital stock on the liability side of the balance sheet the amount of uncollected subscriptions. (See page 1170.)

Deferred Credits

What deferred credits represent.—The deferred credits in a balance sheet, sometimes called "deferred income" or "miscellaneous unadjusted credits," represent the opposite of "deferred charges," explained at page 1168. They represent an item of gross income that is to be credited to Profit and Loss in a future period, and comprise advance collections of income, unamortized credits, and miscellaneous suspense accounts. The group usually consists of the following items:

1. Advance collections of interest, rent, royalties, dues.
2. Advance collections on contracts or other sales when these are not properly included among the current liabilities.
3. Unamortized premiums on funded debt.
4. Miscellaneous suspense items; that is, receipts that have not definitely been classified as liabilities or income items.

Contingent Liabilities

What are contingent liabilities?—Contingent liabilities are not ordinarily incorporated in the balance sheet proper because they do not affect the accounts while they remain contingent. No objection, however, can be found to the practice of including a caption for contingent liabilities and entering the items "short"—that is, without carrying the amounts out to the columns that reflect the actual liabilities. The more common practice is to indicate the nature and amount of contingent liabilities as footnotes below the balance-sheet totals. The following are examples of contingent liabilities and the manner in which they have been treated in actual balance sheets:

Notes receivable discounted.—"Contingent liability on notes discounted, $42,980.54."

Obligations of others guaranteed.—"The -------------------- Company was contingently liable at December 31, 19--, as guarantor and indorser of obligations of subsidiary companies, aggregating $6,379,137.61."

Contingent liability as surety.—"On December 31, 19--, the -------------------- Company was surety on a bond for $13,112,668.94 executed by the -------------------- Co., as principal, providing for the refund by that company to telephone users of sums, if any, which may be found to have been collected under rates in excess of those ultimately held legal. The -------------------- Company was surety on a similar bond of the ------------------ Company in the amount of $3,000,000."

Unsettled tax disputes.—"Federal income taxes for certain prior years are subject to final settlement with the United States Treasury Department."

Accounts assigned.—"The company was contingently liable on December 31, 19--, in the amount of $8,500 as guarantor of assigned accounts receivable."

Lawsuits.—"The item of $34,149,623.15, representing the book value of investments in, advances for account of, and account receivable from Deep Rock Oil Corporation (in receivership), includes a claim of Standard Gas and Electric Company against the Corporation for $9,342,642.37, against which a counterclaim has been asserted. In the opinion of counsel for the Company, the determination of the claim and counter-claim should result in a substantial liability from the Corporation to Standard Gas and Electric Company."

Cumulative dividends in arrears.—"No provision has been made in the above statement for cumulative undeclared dividends on the $6 preferred stock, amounting to $6,844,291.12, and on the $5 preferred stock amounting to $7,032,566.25 on September 30, 19--."

Indemnification of underwriters.—"Standard Gas and Electric Company, in connection with the solicitations of deposits of its twenty-year 6 per cent gold notes and 6 per cent convertible gold notes, both of which were originally due October 1, 19--, agreed under Extension and Deposit Agreement dated June 18, 19--, to indemnify the underwriters from all loss, liability, or expense incurred or sustained under the Securities Act of 1933, as amended, or at common law or otherwise, arising out of, or based upon, an untrue statement of a material fact, or the omission to state a material fact in the registration statements or the prospectus, subject to certain exceptions as to statements or omissions based entirely on information furnished to the Company by the underwriters."

Minority Interests

Liability to minority stockholders.—As indicated on page 1145, the interest of minority stockholders in controlled companies must be set up as a liability if the accounts of a subsidiary are taken into the consolidated balance sheet as though the companies were completely owned by the parent company. The item is generally stated simply as a liability, under no particular caption, in such terms as the following:

Capital stock and surplus of minority interests $755,143.49

The portion of surplus of subsidiary companies applicable to the minority interest may be indicated in the item as follows:

Preferred and common stocks of subsidiary companies (consolidated) in hands of public, including $118,483 surplus applicable thereto $1,928,883

In some balance sheets, the minority's interest is shown in the capital-stock section of the balance sheet instead of as a separate item among the liabilities.

Reserves

What reserves are listed among the liabilities?—In the discussion of the assets shown in a balance sheet, such reserves as the reserve for bad debts and reserve for depreciation were mentioned. These reserves appear on the assets side of the balance sheet as deductions from the valuation of the assets to which they pertain because they represent reserves against decreases in the value of the assets. All other classes of reserves appear on the liabilities side of the balance sheet. They may be classified as follows:

1. Reserves that represent actual current liabilities. A reserve for the payment of Federal and state income taxes, for example, should be listed among the current liabilities.

2. Reserves for contingencies. These may be treated in three ways:

(*a*) A reserve for a contingency that is very likely to become a reality should appear as a separate item among the liabilities. For example, a reserve for payments to be made under a pending lawsuit for which an unfavorable verdict is expected should be presented as a distinct liability. Companies with investments in Continental Europe during World War II set up contingent reserves among their liabilities as a provision for possible irrecoverable losses in connection with foreign investments.

(*b*) A reserve for a contingency that is likely to become a reality and decrease the value of an asset may be presented as a deduction from the asset. For example, a reserve for declines in the market value of investments, or a reserve for declines in the market value of merchandise, might appear as deductions from the assets to which they apply.

(*c*) A reserve for a contingency of loss that is merely possible and not definitely probable should appear under the caption of reserves. An example is a "reserve for unforeseen possibilities."

3. Reserves that represent net worth. Such reserves are either:

(*a*) Appropriations of surplus.
(*b*) Unrealized profit reserves.

A reserve that represents an appropriation of surplus may be either required by contract—as, for example, a reserve for sinking funds—or voluntarily set up—as, for example, a reserve for plant extension. Such reserves should appear under the surplus caption. An unrealized profit reserve—as, for example, a reserve for unrealized profit on appraisal of plant—may appear under the caption of reserves; but if the asset to which the reserve refers has actually increased in value, the item may be included as a separate item under surplus.

Reserves for corresponding funds.—When a reserve appears on the liabilities side of a balance sheet and a corresponding fund is included among the assets, the conclusion may be drawn that the fund shown among the assets has been created out of profits of the company to the extent indicated in the reserve for the particular fund. Such reserves are temporary appropriations of surplus and belong in the balance sheet under the general heading of surplus. They have the effect of reducing the amount of free surplus available for dividends to the extent of the reserve. When the fund is finally disbursed, the reserve will revert to surplus and be available for dividends.

Capital Stock and Surplus

What the capital stock section should show.—The capital stock section of the balance sheet should indicate the various classes of stock and as to each class the following information should be given:

1. Par value, if any, or the fact that the stock is without par value. In the case of preferred stock, redeemable at or entitled in liquidation to an amount in excess of par value, the preferred stock may be carried at its liquidation value.

2. The preferences and other special rights, if any, of each class of stock.

3. The amount authorized, issued, and outstanding, held in the treasury, and reserved for issuance upon exercise of stock purchase warrants.

If part of the purchase price of the stock is still unpaid, and there is no intention of immediately calling the unpaid subscriptions, the uncollected subscriptions should appear as a deduction from the capital stock, thus:

Capital stock—authorized, 10,000 shares of $100 par value; issued and outstanding, 800 shares	$800,000
Less uncollected subscriptions	200,000
Paid-in capital	$600,000

(For the inclusion of unpaid subscriptions among the assets, rather than as a deduction from the capital stock, see page 1170.)

The premiums on stock that has been sold above par may appear in the capital stock section as a separate item, indicated as "Premiums on Capital Stock." The amount will remain on the balance sheet indefinitely unless it is eventually transferred to "paid-in surplus" or to "surplus." It will not be transferred to surplus if under the laws of the state in which the company is organized amounts representing premiums on stock may not legally be distributed as dividends.

The discount on stock that has been sold below par may appear in the capital stock section of the balance sheet as a deduction therefrom.

Treasury stock should appear as a deduction from the capital stock outstanding to the extent of its par value, since it is not outstanding. However, at times it may appear among the assets valued at cost. (See page 1167.)

Valuing no-par stock in the capital stock section of the balance sheet.—Stock without par value is indicated by that title in the capital stock section of the balance sheet and is given a valuation. That valuation may represent:

1. The full price received for no-par stock by the corporation.

2. The minimum price that the law of the state in which the corporation is organized requires to be paid for the stock.

3. The "stated," or "declared," value placed upon the no-par stock, if the law of the state in which the corporation is organized provides that directors may place a stated or declared value upon no-par stock.

4. An amount arrived at arbitrarily by the board of directors.

Any amount received for no-par stock in excess of the minimum price or above the stated or declared value becomes surplus or "paid-in surplus." If the excess is permitted to be treated as surplus under the laws of the state in which the corporation is organized, and is so treated by the corporation, the surplus out of which dividends can be paid is augmented by an amount that has not been earned by the corporation. If the excess is carried as paid-in surplus in the balance sheet, it is clear that the corporation does not regard the amount as a part of its free surplus. However, the mere separation of the paid-in surplus from the surplus does not signify that the former will not be used for dividends.

A reader of the balance sheet cannot tell how the sum indicated for no-par stock was determined; he can merely conclude that the amount noted reflects the capital investment behind the outstanding no-par shares.

The capital-stock item in a consolidated balance sheet refers to the capital stock of the parent company. The stock of the subsidiary companies included in the consolidation has been eliminated in the preparation of the consolidated statement. To make this clear, consolidated balance sheets sometimes indicate the name of the parent company in the capital stock item, as follows:

CAPITAL STOCK:	
____________________ Corporation	
Common capital stock:	
Authorized, 2,500,000 shares of no-par value	
Issued, 1,509,556 shares	$52,539,547.11
Less held in treasury, 7,943 shares	276,453.22
Outstanding, 1,501,613 shares	$52,263,093.89

Treatment of surplus in the balance sheet.—The surplus account is not analyzed in the balance sheet. It is analyzed either in the income statement or in a separate account. If the latter method is used, the balance sheet will show the amount of surplus and will refer to the separate analysis of the surplus account. The explanation of the surplus account, given on page 1189, shows how the item included in the balance sheet is generally made up.

How capital and surplus generally appear in the balance sheet.—Various methods of presenting capital stock and surplus are followed in practice, the most common of which are identified and illustrated below.

1. A caption combining capital stock and surplus:

Capital Stock and Surplus:	
Common Stock—No-par value:	
Authorized ....250,000 shares	
Issued and outstanding ....189,538 shares......	$1,014,000.00
Surplus as per annexed statement	1,588,663.53
	$2,602,663.53

2. A caption combining Capital Stock and Paid-in Surplus, with earned surplus listed separately:

Capital Stock and Paid-in Surplus:		
6% Cumulative Preferred Stock—$100 par value:		
Authorized—	100,000 shares	
Issued—	61,657 shares.........	$ 6,165,700.00
Common Stock (No-par value):		
Authorized—	2,500,000 shares	
Issued—	2,263,150 shares	
Less in Treasury	7,229 shares	
	2,255,921 shares	
at stated value of $10.00 per share	....	22,559,210.00
Paid-in Surplus	....	28,782,600.00
		$ 57,507,510.00
Earned Surplus, as per annexed statement		$ 76,595,940.83
		$154,154,698.44

3. Separate captions for capital stock and surplus:

Preferred 7% cumulative (authorized and outstanding, 20,000 shares of $100.00 each; called for re-

demption on February 1, 19--; at redemption value as of December 31, 19--)	$ 2,500,000.00
Common—without par value (authorized, 1,000,000 shares; issued, 711,000 shares)	18,486,000.00
Total capital stock	$20,986,000.00
Surplus	3,681,301.12
Total	$25,756,976.49

The Income Statement

How to head the income statement.—The heading of the income statement should contain the following points of information:

1. The name of the person, firm, or organization whose profit and loss statement is being rendered.
2. What the statement purports to be.
3. The period of time covered by the statement.

The terms "condensed," "comparative," and "consolidated" in the title of the income statement have the same significance as they do in the title of the balance sheet. (See page ....)

The period is generally indicated as "for the year ended -------- ----, 19--"; or "------ months ended -------- ----, 19--"; or "fiscal year ended -------- ----, 19--."

Titles for the income statement.—As great a variety of terms is used for the title of the income statement as is used for the balance sheet. The most common are the following, with the prefix of such terms as "condensed," "comparative," or "consolidated," or combinations of these words:

1. Statement of income.
2. Income statement.
3. Income account.
4. Summary of consolidated income.
5. Income and profit and loss statement.
6. Statement of profit and loss.
7. Profit and loss account.
8. Profit and loss statement.
9. Income and earned surplus accounts.
10. Statement of profit and loss and earned surplus.

If the title does not include a reference to the surplus, a separate statement concerning surplus is generally rendered.

Form of the income statement.—The income statement is generally presented in "report" or "narrative" form, sometimes also called the "reducing-balance" form or the "running" form. In statements so prepared, the items are presented in logical order, one under the other. Even statements that carry the word "account" in their title do not present the items in account form—that is, as debits and credits.

Divisions of the income statement.—Every income statement is divisible into two parts:

1. Items dealing with operations of the business.
2. Items relating to nonoperating income and nonoperating charges.

Many statements of income contain a third part—namely:

3. Items showing disposition of the net income.

When this section is omitted from the income statement, it is usually found in a statement of the surplus account.

Grouping of items.—Income statements show a greater variety of items and less uniformity of grouping than balance sheets. Manufacturing concerns set up accounts to reflect cost of production; companies engaged in trading have no such accounts. Organizations that are not engaged in manufacturing or trading would employ accounts suitable for their needs. Whatever the business, and whatever the accounts, the statement is likely to be segregated into the following groups:

1. Sales.
2. Cost of goods sold.
3. Selling expenses.
4. General and administrative expenses.
5. Income other than operating income.
6. Charges other than operating charges.

No typical order of the groups can be presented. An examination of many published income statements, reflecting the practices of leading accounting firms, reveals a great difference of opinion on the subject of placement of the various deductions from and additions to income. In the explanation of items in the income statement that follows, some of the variations in practice will be indicated.

Methods of clarifying the income statement.—The income statement may be clarified in ways similar to those employed in elucidating items in the balance sheet. They are as follows:

1. By fairly full explanations of the items within the statement proper. For example, the item "Net sales billed" is clearer if presented as follows:

> Aggregate net amount billed for products shipped and other classes of business (excluding sundry sales, real estate, and certain miscellaneous services), less sales commissions, returns, and other allowances.

2. By running comments in the statement. The following is an example of this form of presentation:

GROSS PROFIT BEFORE DEDUCTING DEPRECIATION	$5,277,070.19
The amount remaining from sales income after deducting manufacturing and purchase costs exclusive of depreciation.	
ADVERTISING, SELLING, DISTRIBUTING, AND ADMINISTRATIVE EXPENSES	4,572,971.74
The cost of marketing the products and administering the business of the companies.	
PROFIT FROM OPERATIONS BEFORE DEDUCTING DEPRECIATION	$ 704,098.45
The amount remaining after deducting the above-described costs and expenses.	
OTHER INCOME	128,963.11
Includes interest on investments, discounts earned for prompt payment of bills for purchases, etc.	
GROSS INCOME BEFORE DEDUCTING DEPRECIATION ...	$ 833,061.56
The sum of the two preceding items.	
OTHER DEDUCTIONS (exclusive of depreciation, interest, and taxes on income)	123,560.13
Includes discounts allowed customers for prompt payment of bills, provision for uncollectible accounts receivable, pensions paid to former employees, net loss on sales of investment securities, etc.	

3. By notes or footnotes appended to the income statement. For example:

Gross profit on sales—See Note A	$2,206,800.28

Note A explains the item as follows:

> All profit on installment sales is taken into income at the time the sales are recorded on the books, and Federal income taxes are accrued annually thereon, even though such taxes are paid only as the installment accounts receivable are collected.

4. By the use of schedules. Published income statements are supported by few schedules, although many are prepared in connection with the income statement for the use of the business executives. The schedule most commonly made available is that showing depreciation, renewal, maintenance, nonoperating income, and other charges and credits.

Points in income statements requiring special clarification.—Income statements do not show upon their face what principles are followed in allocating charges and credits to income account and surplus account. This can be determined only from a statement prepared especially to disclose this information. As yet business enterprises have not adopted the practice of furnishing such an explanatory statement.

The nature of income from companies controlled but not consolidated is not obvious from the income statement unless the information is especially given.

The company's proportionate share of the undistributed earnings or losses of controlled companies whose accounts are not consolidated for the purposes of the income statement is not apparent from the statement unless a note concerning such income is included in the statement.

Explanation of Items in the Income Statement

Many published income statements are abbreviated or condensed to such an extent that they disclose little information. For example, they start with gross operating income or merely operating income, and present no information as to sales or operating costs. The following explanation includes items that would appear in a statement which reveals all the sources of revenue and all costs and charges.

Sales.—The sales, when set forth, are variously termed "gross receipts," "net sales and billings," "net sales billed," or "net sales." These terms generally reflect the volume of sales, less such deductions as returns, allowances, rebates, allowances made under price guaranties, freight on sales, allowances for the return of containers, and the like. Provision for doubtful accounts may be deducted from the sales or included among the operating charges. The deductions may or may not include commissions and cash discounts. Commissions allowed on sales are frequently treated as selling expenses, and cash discounts are sometimes regarded as operating expenses and included under the operating charges.

Operating charges.—The components of operating charges are not clearly defined, nor do companies in their published statements undertake to disclose the exact nature and determination of the operating charges. For purposes of this explanation the following are considered the operating charges:

1. Cost of goods sold.
2. Operating expenses.

Many of the items included in the following explanation of these two divisions of operating charges are subject to different treatment. The variations in treatment will be noted.

Cost of goods sold.—In a manufacturing concern the cost of goods sold is made up of the total of:

1. Inventory at the beginning of the period,
2. Direct labor,
3. Overhead expenses,

less the inventory at the end of the period. In a trading concern the cost of goods sold is the merchandise cost, which includes buying expenses.

The difference between the cost of goods sold and the sales is termed the "gross profit on sales," or "trading income."

Operating expenses.—The operating expenses include:

1. Selling expenses.
2. General expenses.
3. Administrative expenses.
4. Taxes. This item sometimes omits income taxes, which are treated as a deduction from income. Other classes of taxes besides income taxes are also treated as deductions from income in some income statements.

5. Provision for doubtful accounts. This item may be treated as a deduction from the sales, as indicated above.

6. Depreciation and depletion attributable to operations. This item is also sometimes found among the deductions from income.

7. Provision for possible losses. This deduction includes reserves and may be included under the heading of "reserves."

The difference between the "gross profit on sales" and the operating expenses is the "net operating revenue" or "operating income." If all of the items constituting operating expenses have not been deducted, attention may be called to the fact by labeling the difference somewhat as follows: "profit from operations before deducting depreciation"; or if the reserves are separately enumerated, the difference may be termed "operating income before deduction of reserves."

Operating income in a consolidated income statement.—In a consolidated income statement, the operating income may omit the profit on intercompany transactions of subsidiaries considered in the consolidation. Or, intercompany profits may be shown as a deduction in some other part of the income statement. The operating income may include dividends received from subsidiaries and affiliated companies not consolidated, as well as the parent company's equity in the undivided profits or losses of subsidiaries and affiliated companies whose accounts are not consolidated in the statement.

Nonoperating income.—Additions to income arising from nonoperating sources are included in this group generally under some heading such as "other income," "income from other sources," "nonoperating income," or merely under the word "additions." The following items are the usual nonoperating sources of revenue:

1. Interest on securities.
2. Interest on bank balances, notes receivable, and the like.
3. Profits realized on sale and on maturity of securities.
4. Dividends.
5. Discounts earned for prompt payment of bills. This item would not appear here if the discounts were considered in determining cost of goods sold and in the valuation of inventories.
6. Royalties.
7. Losses recovered.

When these items are added to the "net operating income," the total is generally called "total income." Frequently the addition is made on the statement without labeling the total or by merely calling the sum "total."

Nonoperating charges.—Deductions from income resulting from financial expenses are subtracted from the total income under the heading of "deductions from income," "interest and other charges," "other charges," or "deductions." The usual nonoperating charges are:

1. Interest on funded debt.
2. Other interest.
3. Discount on bonds.
4. Depreciation and depletion, not included under operating expenses.
5. Income taxes and other taxes not included among the operating expenses.

The difference between "total income" and the "deductions from income" represents the "net profit" or "net loss" for the period.

The income statement may end with the net profit or net loss and be supplemented by a statement of surplus, or it may be continued to show the changes in the surplus account during the period. In the latter case, the title of the statement will include a reference to the surplus. The presentation of the make-up of the surplus account is practically the same whether it is appended to the income statement or presented in a separate statement. In this discussion the statement of surplus is treated separately, below.

Portion of profits or losses applicable to minority interests.—A consolidated statement that is prepared as though the parent company had a 100 per cent ownership of the stock of subsidiary companies, when in fact less than 100 per cent of the stock of the subsidiary is owned, must show the proportion of the income or loss applicable to minority interests. This item usually appears after the "net profit" or "net loss" item, although in some statements it is placed ahead of the figure showing the net profit or loss for the period.

The Statement of Surplus

How to head the statement of surplus.—The heading of the statement of surplus, when presented apart from the income statement, should contain the same three points of information as the income statement—namely:

1. The name of the corporation whose surplus account is presented.
2. What the statement purports to be. If the statement analyzes earned surplus, as differentiated from capital surplus, the title should show it to be a statement of earned surplus; similarly, if the changes in the capital-surplus account are being presented, the title should convey that information. If the statement covers capital surplus and earned surplus, the general term "surplus" may be used in the title.
3. The period of time covered by the statement. The period is indicated in the same way as in the income statement.

What capital surplus is.—The term "capital surplus" has no universal significance; it is generally used to distinguish the portion of the surplus that is not ordinarily available for dividends. It may comprise:

1. Paid-in surplus.
2. Realized increments in net worth; as, for example, profits on the sale of fixed assets, or profits from transactions in treasury stock.
3. Unrealized profits from the writing up of assets. Some accountants do not consider this a proper capital-surplus item, but treat it as a component of surplus.

Usually, paid-in surplus constitutes the major capital-surplus item. It is created in the following ways:

1. By payment of a premium on par-value stock.
2. By considering part of the payments received from no-par stock as paid-in surplus.
3. By donations of stock or assets.

What the statement of surplus should show.—The statement of surplus should indicate:

1. What the surplus was at the beginning of the period.
2. Additions to profits not resulting from the operation of the business during the period covered by the income statement. These may be given under the heading of "surplus credits." The following are examples of such additions to surplus:

(*a*) Increases in the market value of marketable securities.
(*b*) Increase in dollar value of net current assets due to variations in foreign-exchange rates.
(*c*) Reinstatement of excess provision made in previous year for shrinkage in market value of investment securities.
(*d*) Adjustments of reserves where charges to depreciation in previous years proved to be excessive.
(*e*) Recovery of Federal income taxes for prior years.

3. Deduction of charges not affecting the operations for the period covered by the income statement. These may be given under the heading of "surplus charges." The following are examples of such deductions.

(*a*) Obsolete property abandoned.
(*b*) Provision for shrinkage in market value of securities.
(*c*) Taxes applicable to previous years.
(*d*) Net loss on disposal of machinery and equipment.
(*e*) Write-down of marketable securities.

4. The amount of net income added for the year or the amount of net loss deducted. This is the sum shown in the income statement for the period.
5. The deduction of dividends declared during the year, set forth as to each class of stock.
6. The balance of the surplus. This amount is shown on the liabilities side of the balance sheet. (See page 1181.) It may be divided as follows:

(*a*) Appropriations for special purposes; for example, reserves for plant extensions and other reserves representing net worth.
(*b*) Capital surplus.
(*c*) Undivided, or "earned," surplus.

2. HOW TO ANALYZE A FINANCIAL STATEMENT

How financial statements are obtained.—A statement of the financial condition of a business that is asking for credit can be secured either directly from the customer or indirectly from such sources as the credit agencies (see "Sources of Credit Information," page 961). The procedure in asking for a statement directly from a customer is generally to submit to him a printed form, such as that reproduced in Figure 99, asking for a balance sheet, a profit and loss statement, and the answers to certain questions that will throw light upon the financial strength of the credit applicant.

It is advisable to keep on file the postmarked envelope in which the financial statement is mailed, for frequently, following a debtor's bankruptcy, the statement, if false, is the basis of an indictment charging the use of the United States mails to defraud. The form reproduced on pages 1192–1193 is a self-mailing form, thus assuring preservation of the evidence of mailing.

Businessmen have become educated to the point of submitting financial information willingly. Some firms will even furnish creditors, upon request, with monthly trial balances, where the financial statements they offer are several months old.

Extent to which financial statements are used in credit work.—The policy of business houses in asking for financial statements varies. Some stress the importance of putting the customer to as little trouble as possible and call for a financial statement only when they consider it necessary. Others make it a practice to request new financial statements from all customers at regular intervals, in order to keep their files up to date. Such factors as the length of time the applicant has been in business, its record in the community, the experience of the seller with the account, the amount of credit that is sought, and similar elements, determine whether a financial statement should be required. If a newly established firm is seeking credit, a financial statement is invariably requested. In some lines of industry, most of the firms will ask for financial statements in any case where the order is in excess of $500.

What part of the balance sheet reveals credit strength?—The current assets and current liabilities sections of the balance sheet

Form 4E

Date ________ 194__

FOLD IN ON THIS LINE

FINANCIAL STATEMENT OF ________

Kind of Business ________ Address ________

At Close of Books on ________ **194**__

ISSUED TO ________ ← { Name of firm asking for statement

[THIS FORM APPROVED AND PUBLISHED BY THE NATIONAL ASSOCIATION OF CREDIT MEN]

For the purpose of obtaining merchandise from you on credit, or for the extension of credit, we make the following statement in writing, intending that you should rely thereon respecting our exact financial condition.

[PLEASE ANSWER ALL QUESTIONS. WHEN NO FIGURES ARE INSERTED, WRITE WORD "NONE"]

ASSETS	Dollars	Cents
Cash (*on Hand and in Bank*)		
Accounts Receivable		
(Amount past due $ ________)		
(Amount Sold or Pledged $ ________)		
Notes and Trade Acceptances Receivable		
(Amount Sold or Pledged $ ________)		
Merchandise not on consignment or conditional sale (How valued: at cost ☐ or "at cost or market, whichever is lower" ☐)		
—Other current assets (describe):		
TOTAL CURRENT ASSETS		
Land and buildings (present depreciated value)		
Machinery, fixtures and other equipment (present depreciated value)		
Due from partners, or others not customers		
Other assets (describe):		
TOTAL ASSETS		

LIABILITIES	Dollars	Cents
Accounts payable for merchandise, etc.		
Acceptances and notes payable for merchandise		
Owe to ________ Bank (When Due) ________ (Secured) (Unsecured)		
Taxes, interest, rental, payrolls, etc., accrued		
Unpaid city and/or state sales taxes, accrued		
Payable to partners, friends, relatives, etc.		
Other current liabilities (describe):		
TOTAL CURRENT LIABILITIES		
Mortgage on land and buildings		
Chattel mortgage or liens on mdse. and equip't		
Other liabilities not current (describe):		
TOTAL LIABILITIES		
Net Worth		
TOTAL (NET WORTH AND LIABILITIES)		

FOLD IN ON THIS LINE

STATEMENT OF PROFIT AND LOSS FOR PERIOD FROM ______ TO ______

Sales for period, cash			Detailed Expense of operation		
Credit			Salaries—owners		
TOTAL			employees		
Inventory at beginning of period					
Purchases for period			Rent		
TOTAL			Advertising		
Less Inventory close of period			Freight and Express		
Cost of goods sold			Miscellaneous		
Gross profit			TOTAL		
Less expense of operation					
Net profit for period			If incorporated, amount of dividends paid		

Title to real estate is in name of ______

If business premises are leased to you, state length of lease and annual rental ______

In whose name is title to business premises? ______

Amount of fire insurance (Building) $ ______ (Stock) $ ______ (Fixtures) $ ______

Life insurance for benefit of business $ ______ For what amount are you liable as endorser, guarantor, surety, etc.

$ ______ Name and address of your bank ______

What amount of merchandise do you hold on consignment? $ ______ Merchandise charged to you not included in assets

$ ______ What amount of machinery or equipment is under lease contract, state monthly payments $ ______

What amount of machinery or equipment is held under conditional sale? $ ______ Balance due $ ______

at $ ______ per month. What books of account do you keep? ______

When were your books last audited? ______ By whom? ______

Names BUY FROM THE FOLLOWING FIRMS:	Addresses	Amount Owing

The foregoing statement has been carefully read by the undersigned (both the printed and written matter), and is, to my knowledge, in all respects complete, accurate and truthful. It discloses to you the true state of my (our) financial condition on the ______ day of ______ 194__ Since that time there has been no material unfavorable change in my (our) financial condition, and if any such change takes place I (we) will give you notice. Until such notice is given, you are to regard this as a continuing statement. The figures submitted are not estimated. They have been taken from my (our) books and physical inventory taken as on date shown.

Name of Individual or Firm ______

If Partnership, Name Partners } ______ ______

" Corporation, " Officers } ______ ______

How long established ______ Previous business experience ______

______ Where ______

Date of Signing Statement ______ Street ______ City ______ State ______

Witness ______ Signed by ______

Residence Address of Witness ______ Title ______

Figure 99.—Statement Form Approved by National Association of Credit Men.

contain the data from which to gauge the credit strength of the customer, for the current assets show the amount of ready funds available with which to meet the current liabilities. The excess of the current assets over the current liabilities is known as the "working capital" of the business.* Since financial statements obtained from an applicant for credit are generally a "window-dressed" portrayal of the financial condition of the company, the reliability of the figures from which the working capital results must be proved. Each item in the current assets and current liabilities must therefore be examined and analyzed before judgment can be passed upon the financial standing of the credit applicant.

Place of fixed assets in credit analysis.—The fixed tangible assets and the capital liabilities through which they were secured are of secondary importance in the analysis of financial statements for the purpose of determining credit strength alone. The intangible assets, such as goodwill, patents, and the like, have no place in a credit analysis.

The attention to be given to fixed tangible assets depends upon the following factors:

1. The nature of the business of the credit applicant. The fixed assets of a retail establishment may be an inconsequential factor in the determination of credit strength, while the fixed assets of a manufacturing concern may have a direct bearing upon working capital.

2. The prosperity or lack of prosperity experienced in the immediate past. The item of fixed assets in a manufacturer's statement should be given greater attention after a period of low earnings such as is experienced during an economic depression than need be given to it during or immediately after a period of profitable activity. The reason for this is that in many industries, as a result of decreased earnings, the fixed assets are permitted to run down; they become obsolete and in order to be maintained require greater asset strength. In many cases a part of the decrease in earnings

* The term "working capital" is sometimes applied by businessmen to all the current assets, and the term "net working capital" to the excess of current assets over current liabilities. In this discussion, working capital refers to the difference between the current assets and the current liabilities.

suffered by the business is due to the fixed overhead cost that must be met while plant and machinery stand idle.

A disproportionate amount of fixed assets would indicate an investment in property beyond the strength of the organization and a need for more working capital than would be required if less were invested in plant and equipment. If a financial statement shows large investment in plant and equipment, greater attention must be given to the earning power and management of the business.

Place of prepaid expenses in credit analysis.—The prepaid expenses are not considered as current assets in an analysis of financial statements for credit purposes, in spite of the fact that the argument is sometimes raised that the practical effect of excluding prepaid expenses, such as prepaid taxes, insurance, supplies, and the like, is to show less credit strength than actually exists.

Need for comparative data.—An adequate analysis of financial statements requires comparison with previous years; it is therefore highly desirable that the financial statements for several years be available. The conclusions reached from an analysis of a single financial statement may be quite different from those drawn from an analysis of the same statement in comparison with other years, and may present a misleading picture of the applicant's affairs.

The comparative statement.—Since many business houses ask regularly for financial statements from their customers, they are in a position to have available comparative figures without asking their customers for comparative statements. Figures 100a and 100b illustrate a comparative statement taken from the files of a large chemical concern. The credit department of a large textile manufacturer uses the form shown in Figure 101. The comparative statement is made up as soon as comparative figures become available.

In transcribing to the comparative statement the balance sheet offered by the customer, no changes are made in the amounts to give effect to the findings upon an analysis of the statement. Thus, if a study of the accounts receivable reveals that many of the accounts are doubtful and that the reserve for bad debts is insufficient, no indication of this conclusion is made on the comparative state-

NAME .... ANALYZED BY ....

ADDRESS .... DATE ....

COMMENT ....

Assets	*19—*	*Per Cent*	*19—*	*Per Cent*
Cash	5,679.36	2.78	1,574.98	.89
Accounts Rec. (less Reserve)	37,963.17	18.58	31,179.16	17.65
Notes and T. A. Rec.	11,692.70	5.72	9,753.07	5.52
Mdse. Inventories	69,619.03	34.07	54,504.40	30.86
Misc. A/R (claims and agreements)	321.48	.16	2,256.50	1.28
Total Current Assets	125,275.74	61.31	99,268.11	56.20
Investments (listed)				
Stocks and Bonds			2,932.86	1.66
Real Estate	8,000.00	3.91	8,000.00	4.53
Buildings and Machinery (less Dep.)	61,686.83	30.19	56,990.01	32.26
Delivery Equipment (less Dep.)				
Fur. & Fix. (less Dep.)				
Total Fixed Assets	69,686.83	34.10	67,922.87	38.45
Goodwill and Org. Exp.	5,400.00	2.64	5,400.00	3.06
Patents, Formulae, etc.				
Prepaid Items	3,962.85	1.93	4,049.21	2.29
Total Intangible Assets	9,362.85	4.57	9,449.21	5.35
Deficit				
Total Assets	204,325.42	100.00	176,640.19	100.00
Taxes and Int. Pay.	2,594.09	1.27	2,492.36	1.41
Accounts Payable	40,870.98	20.00	34,270.26	19.41
Notes and T. A. Payable			4,000.00	2.26
Loans Payable (Bank)	6,000.00	2.94	8,000.00	4.53
Total Current Liabilities	49,465.07	24.21	48,762.62	27.61
Mortgage Payable	12,000.00	5.87	4,000.00	2.26
Bonds Payable				
Total Fixed Liabilities	12,000.00	5.87	4,000.00	2.26

Figure 100a.—Form of Comparative Statement.

Liabilities	*19—*	*Per Cent*	*19—*	*Per Cent*
Sinking Funds....................				
Special Reserves..................				
Total Reserves.............				
Capital Stock (Common)...........	183,000.00	89.56	91,500.00	51.80
Capital Stock (Preferred)...........			12,000.00	6.79
Surplus and Undivided Profits.......	40,139.65	19.64	20,377.57	11.54
Total Net Worth..................	142,860.35	69.92	123,877.57	70.13
Total Liabilities..................	204,325.42	100.00	176,640.19	100.00
Contingent Liabilities..............				

Analysis	*19—*	*Per Cent*	*19—*	*Per Cent*
Current Assets....................	125,275.74		99,268.11	
Current Liabilities.................	49,465.07		48,762.62	
Working Capital...............	75,810.67		50,505.49	
Investments......................			2,932.86	
Available Working Capital..........	75,810.67		53,438.35	
Equity in Fixed Assets.............	57,686.83		60,990.01	
Actual Net Worth.............	133,497.50		114,428.36	
Consisting of Capital Stock.........	183,000.00		103,500.00	
Surplus (Deficit).............	49,502.50		10,928.36	

Ratios	*19—*		*19—*	
Cur. Assets to Cur. Liabilities........	2.03 to 1		2.53 to 1	
Fixed Assets to Fixed Liabilities......	16.98 to 1		5.80 to 1	
Avail. Working Cap. to Cur. Liabilities	1.09 to 1		1.53 to 1	
Total Assets to Total Liabilities......				
Sales to Total Assets..............				
Net Profits to Total Assets..........				
Net Profits to Net Worth...........				
Days Sales Outstanding............				
Sales to Net Profits................				

Figure 100b.—Form of Comparative Statement (Cont.).

_________ MILLS INC.

_____ STREET

NEW YORK

CORPORATION

COMPARISON OF STATEMENTS

NAME..

ADDRESS..

BUSINESS..

ASSETS					
Cash					
Notes Receivable					
Accounts Receivable					
Merchandise, finished					
Merchandise, unfinished					
Raw Material					
Less Reserves					
NET QUICK ASSETS					
Real Estate					
Buildings					
Machinery, Fixtures and Equipment					
Goodwill, Patents, etc.					
Deferred Charges and Misc.					
Less Reserves					
NET FIXED ASSETS					
TOTAL ASSETS					

Figure 101.—Form of Comparative Statement Used by a Large Textile Manufacturer.

LIABILITIES																					
Bills Payable Merchandise																					
Bills Payable to own Bank																					
Bills Payable otherwise																					
Accounts Payable																					
Deposits																					
Accrued Liabilities																					
Reserve for Taxes																					
TOTAL CURRENT LIABILITIES																					
Bonded Debt																					
Mortgage Loans - due																					
Reserve for Depreciation																					
Other Liabilities																					
Total Liabilities and Reserves																					
Capital Account																					
Preferred Stock Issued																					
Common Stock Issued																					
Surplus and Undivided Profits																					
TOTAL LIABILITIES																					
TOTAL QUICK ASSETS																					
" CURR. LIABILITIES																					
EXCESS QUICK																					
Ratio																					
Sales																					
Net Profit																					
Dividends																					
Depreciation																					
Contingent Liabilities																					
Insurance																					

Figure 101.—Form of Comparative Statement Used by a Large Textile Manufacturer (Cont.).

ment. The working papers of a particular analysis show the results of the analysis. The comparative statement is used principally to show trends in the customer's business and is referred to whenever the most recent statement is examined.

It will be noticed that in Figure 101 columns are provided to show the percentage that each item in the balance sheet bears to the total. Such percentages are known as "analytical percentages."

	1939	1940	1941	1942	1943	1944	1945	1946
JANUARY								
FEBRUARY								
MARCH								
APRIL								
MAY								
JUNE								
JULY								
AUGUST								
SEPTEMBER								
OCTOBER								
NOVEMBER								
DECEMBER								
TOTAL								
Poslindex PAT. JAN 13 '20 SEPT. 14 '20 APR. 3, '23 FEB. 8, '27 RIVERSIDE & DAN RIVER COTTON MILLS 26-C 6740-9 P								
FIGURES								
CASH								
ACCOUNTS								
MERCHANDISE								
CURRENT ASSETS								
CURRENT LIAB.								
WORKING CAPITAL								
NET WORTH								
SALES								
MARK UP %								
EXPENSE %								
LOSS −								
GAIN +								
NCO REP. & LINE								
M & B FROM NCO								
WOODS								
DUNS REPORT								
DUNS RATING								
DTCG. CL.								
ON P/D								
TERMS								
CREDIT LINE								

ADDRESS:

NAME	BUSINESS

Figure 102.—Combination Credit Record and Comparative Financial Statement.

They are not indispensable in an examination of financial statements and are frequently omitted.

In some companies the information contained in the customer's financial statement is transferred to a combination credit record and financial statement card such as is reproduced in Figure 102. The upper half of the card is a progressive statement of the account by months for eight years, filled in on the first of each month from the regular monthly statements sent to the customer. The lower half is an eight-years' record of the account's financial standing. The several initials printed along the first column on the lower third of the form are abbreviations of the various credit bureaus. This section of the form is checked every month at the time entries are made on the upper half.

Procedure in analyzing financial statements.—A thorough analysis of financial statements cannot be made by merely scanning the statement and drawing conclusions from the impressions gathered. A procedure of analysis that will yield all the pertinent information with a minimum of effort should be adopted. No method of procedure can be offered as suitable for every examiner of credit risks. Credit men work as individuals; the practice of one efficient individual may be quite different from that of another equally efficient person. One individual may go rather far in making written notes of his analyses of the financial statements submitted; another may leave no written evidence of the analysis. The following procedure is suggested as one that will accomplish the purposes of any analysis of financial statements to determine credit strength.

1. Rearrange all data to facilitate the analysis.
2. Reduce the figures to simplify the study.
3. Analyze each current asset and each current liability.
4. Make ratio tests.

Rearrangement of the data in financial statements.—Financial statements obtained from customers may be submitted in various forms, with the items grouped in sundry ways. For purposes of analyzing the statement to determine the credit strength of the applicant, the balance-sheet items should be grouped in the order shown in Figure 101. All assets that are not current should be removed from the current group, and all liabilities that are current should be included in that classification.

The determination of what is current and what is not current depends upon:

1. A general knowledge of accounting (see page 1152 and 1182 for an explanation of current assets and current liabilities).
2. An understanding of the credit applicant's business.
3. The answers to questions that have been put to the applicant.
4. Specific inquiry in the absence of information.

Simplification of figures.—In the analysis of statements it is sometimes convenient to reduce the figures in the balance sheet to their simplest terms by omitting the minor digits. After such a reduction, the current assets would appear in the working papers as follows:

(000.00 omitted)

	19--	*19--*
Current Assets		
Cash	$150	$216
Marketable securities	69	104
Accounts and notes receivable	23	29
Inventories	97	91
	$339	$440

Or, the amounts may be set up in the working papers in round figures, without omitting the digits.

Reducing figures to ratios.—In the credit analysis of financial statements, certain ratios are helpful in throwing light upon the credit strength of the applicant. A ratio, which is the relationship that one amount bears to another, or the proportion which one amount is of another, is found by dividing the first amount by the second. Thus, to find the ratio of current assets to current liabilities, divide the current assets by the current liabilities. Suppose the result obtained is 2.73. This would mean that for each dollar of current liabilities there are $2.73 of current assets.

In noting the ratio on the financial statement or in the working papers, it may be entered as: (1) 2.73; (2) 273 per cent; or (3) $2.73.

Present-day use of ratios in determining credit strength.—Most books on the subject of credit analysis go into a detailed explanation of analysis of financial statements by means of ratios. They present perhaps a dozen ratios that may have some significance in determining the credit worth of a business organization. The authors recognize, however, that the ratios have limitations and that too great reliance cannot be placed upon their efficacy.

Much less importance is attached to ratios today than was the case several years ago. In certain trades the use of ratios in statement analysis has been entirely eliminated, while in others they are resorted to sparingly. Where the use of ratios, other than a few fundamental ones, has not been abandoned, no rigid rule is followed in the application of the ratios; in some analyses many ratios are calculated in arriving at judgment of the financial strength of the credit applicant; in others, only a few ratios are calculated. The comparative statement illustrated in Figure 101 (pages 1198–99) shows some of the ratios in use; it will be noticed that in the case presented, only three of the ratios were computed.

Among banks the same variation in the use of ratios in statement analysis exists. Some banks have so little faith in the soundness of ratio analysis that they never calculate any other than the current ratio and the ratio of quick assets to current liabilities (see page 1223); while others, in some analyses, calculate many ratios before accepting or rejecting an application for a loan. On the whole, it may be said that ratios are used more extensively by the banks than in the trade.*

---

* Prochnow and Foulke, in *Practical Bank Credit,* published by Prentice-Hall, Inc., mention the following fourteen comparisons of specific items and groups of items that should invariably be made in the internal analysis, the objective of which is to determine whether the receivables, the inventory, the fixed assets, the payables, the sales, and the profits are in satisfactory proportions.

(1) Three important capital ratios
  (a) Fixed assets to tangible net worth (Per Cent)
  (b) Current debt to tangible net worth (Per Cent)
  (c) Net working capital represented by funded debt (Per Cent)
(2) Three important inventory ratios
  (a) Net sales to inventory (Times)
  (b) Net working capital represented by inventory (Per Cent)
  (c) Inventory covered by current debt (Per Cent)
(3) Three important sales ratios
  (a) Average collection period (Days)
  (b) Turnover of tangible net worth (Times)
  (c) Turnover of net working capital (Times)
(4) Three important net profit ratios
  (a) Net profits on net sales (Per Cent)

In the following discussion only ratios that are useful in an average credit analysis are explained. They include:

Accounts Receivable to Sales (see page 1207).
Sales to Inventories (see page 1214).
Accounts Payable to Raw Material Purchases (see page 1218).
Current Assets to Current Liabilities (see page 1219).
Quick Assets to Current Liabilities (see page 1219).
Sales to Working Capital (see page 1223).
Sales to Net Worth (see page 1223).

Analysis of Working Capital

Scrutinizing the items that make up the current assets.—The items that commonly make up the current assets are: cash, accounts receivable, notes receivable, inventories, and marketable securities. Each of these requires separate analysis to determine the correctness and significance of the amounts shown. Before each item is studied, the following question must be considered, for upon its answer depends the conclusions that will be drawn in the analysis: Does the statement show the influences of seasonal activity or inactivity? The answer is available from general knowledge of conditions in the industry and from the date of the statement.

Examination of cash.—The correctness of the cash item can be checked by inquiry at the banks in which the company whose statement is under consideration keeps its funds; or, if this procedure cannot be followed, by inquiry directly of the applicant for credit to determine the following:

1. Whether any I.O.U.'s are included in the cash balance.
2. Whether the balance has been distorted by the addition of

(b) Net profits on tangible net worth (Per Cent)
(c) Net profits on net working capital (Per Cent)

(5) Two important supplementary ratios
(a) Current assets to current debt (Times)
(b) Total debt to tangible net worth (Per Cent)

Dun & Bradstreet, Inc., publish tables annually showing the above fourteen average important ratios over five-year periods for some sixty different lines of industry and commerce, including manufacturers, wholesalers, and retailers. These ratios give a fairly wide basis of comparison in analyzing statements for companies in the lines covered.

amounts received after the close of the period for which the balances are shown.

3. Whether any of the funds are deposited in banks that are closed.

The inclusion of foreign bank balances, or any suspicion that the cash includes such balances, should lead to further inquiry as to the exchange rates that have been applied in reducing the balance to dollars and the availability of the funds. Obviously, the state of the foreign-exchange market at the time that the analysis is made should be considered in checking the cash.

Since the amount of cash required by a business varies with the nature of the business and the season, no rule can be offered as to the proportion which should exist between cash and other items.

Examination of accounts receivable.—The following questions arise in the analysis of the accounts receivable:

1. Are the accounts receivable as stated all customers' accounts? If the answer is not furnished with the statement, it must be ascertained by inquiry.

2. What portion of the accounts receivable represents debts due from subsidiaries, and when are payments generally made by subsidiaries? The answer to this question must also be determined by direct questioning.

3. Have any of the accounts been pledged or assigned? This question is important because any property that is pledged to one creditor is not available to others. Furthermore, the pledging of assets may be evidence of financial weakness. If the balance sheet does not show by footnote or other indication that any of the accounts have been pledged, the information must be obtained by direct inquiry. In the absence of information in the financial statement, inquiry should also be made to ascertain whether there is included in the accounts receivable amounts that are not collectible because they have been assigned. In case any of the accounts have been assigned, inquiry should be made as to what contingent liability has been assumed through the guaranty of the accounts upon their assignment.

4. Is collection of any part of the accounts receivable likely to be adversely affected by regional or local conditions? To answer this question information must be available as to the location of

the customers of the credit applicant and as to business conditions in various parts of the country.

5. What is the quality of the accounts receivable? The purpose of looking into the quality of the accounts receivable is to determine whether adequate provision has been made for bad debts. The following methods are available for testing the quality of the accounts receivable:

(*a*) Obtain the names of the accounts receivable outstanding with amounts in excess of a certain sum. This procedure is, however, not usual.

(*b*) Ascertain the age of the accounts receivable.

Ascertaining the age of accounts receivable.—The firm that has submitted the financial statement is frequently asked for a statement showing the age of the accounts receivable outstanding. The following illustrates the form of aging schedule that may be offered in answer to such a request:

	December 31, 19__	
	Amount	*Per Cent*
Less than 30 days old—from date of invoice....	$30,000	30.93
31 to 60 days old — " " " "	24,000	24.74
61 to 90 days old — " " " "	16,000	16.50
91 to 120 days old — " " " "	12,000	12.37
Over 120 days old — " " " "	15,000	15.46
	$97,000	100.00

The valuation of the accounts receivable on the basis of their age and in relation to the usual terms of sale will show the amount that should be deducted from the accounts receivable as reported, for purposes of estimating credit strength. The percentage of value to be applied to each group of accounts depends upon:

1. The nature of the business.
2. The collection experience of the company whose statement is being analyzed.

Thus, in one business where the credit terms were thirty days, the valuation was made on the following basis: All accounts less than 30 days old (from date of invoice) were taken at their face value; those in the 31-to-60-days-old class, at 85 per cent of their face value; those in the 61-to-90-days class, at 50 per cent of their face value; and those over 90 days old, at zero.

Determining age of accounts receivable through ratio of accounts receivable to sales.—In the absence of an aging schedule of accounts receivable, the average length of time that accounts are outstanding can be estimated by applying the following formula:

$$\frac{\text{Accounts Receivable Outstanding}}{\text{Sales for the period}} \times \text{days in the year} = \text{Average collection period}$$

Assume the following facts to be shown by the financial statement and that the term of credit granted is 30 days:

Net credit sales	$1,383,866.42
Accounts Receivable—customers at end of year	129,665.14
Reserve for Bad Debts	3,780.12

The item of reserve for bad debts is omitted in the computation but is tested as to adequacy after the age of the accounts receivable has been determined. If we apply the formula as indicated above, the average age of the outstanding accounts receivable is 33.73 days, as compared with 30 days, the term of credit allowed.

$$\frac{\$129,665.14}{\$1,383,866.42} \times 360^{*} = 33.73 \text{ days}$$

The above ratio may also be read as the number of days' sales outstanding. With net credit sales for the year of $1,383,866.42, the average daily sales would be $3,844.07 ($1,383,866.42 ÷ 360), and accounts receivable outstanding of $129,665.14 would show 33.73 days' sales outstanding. If the credit terms are 30 days, the fact that 33.73 days' sales are outstanding would indicate that a very few of the accounts are overdue.

If the average age of the outstanding accounts greatly exceeds the normal credit period, the following may be the reasons:

1. The company has been too liberal in extending credit.
2. Its collection department has been too lax in following up slow customers.
3. Included in the accounts receivable are amounts due from officers, directors, salesmen, and others.
4. Collections have slowed up due to general abnormal business conditions.

---

* In practice 360 days rather than 365 days is generally used.

The comparison of average age of accounts outstanding with the average terms of credit serves as a guide in estimating the amount that should be reserved for bad debts.

Another method of applying the test of accounts receivable is to multiply the annual sales by the fraction of the year represented by the credit terms. Thus, if the annual sales were $800,000 and the terms of credit were 60 days, the sales would be multiplied by 1/6. The result, $133,333, shows the amount of accounts receivable that would be outstanding at the end of the month if collections were made on time. If the accounts receivable outstanding are far in excess of this figure, and the excess is not accounted for by seasonal conditions, the conclusion may be drawn that many of the accounts are past due.

Weaknesses in test of ratio of accounts receivable to sales.— The calculation made above assumes the following three facts, which, if nonexistent, will render the ratio misleading:

1. That there is an even flow of sales during the year. Suppose the business is a seasonal one and that a quarter of the year's sales are made during the month of December. If the ratio is calculated from the balance sheet of December 31, the ratio will show a longer period for collection of accounts receivable than is actually the case. The seasonal movements in the business and the date of the balance sheet and income statement must therefore be taken into consideration.

2. That there is uniformity of collectibility during the year. Suppose sales have an even flow during the year but that December collections are normally slower than other months. The ratio calculated from a December 31 balance sheet and income statement would show accounts to be older than they would appear if the ratio were calculated for any other twelve months' period.

3. That all sales are made on the same terms of credit. The income statement ordinarily does not divide the sales into cash sales and credit sales. If the figure for credit sales is not available and it is known that a large proportion of the sales is made for cash, the ratio calculated by the use of total sales figures will not give a reliable index of the quality of the accounts receivable.

Comparison of age of accounts shown by ratio with percentages in the industry.—Any specific information on the general subject of collections of open-credit accounts in the industry may help in the judgment of the quality of the accounts receivable in the particular company under consideration.* Some of the Federal reserve banks publish in their monthly business reviews current information on the ratio of collections during the month to accounts and notes receivable outstanding at the close of the preceding month in particular industries. This information may be used with great advantage. For example, the following is typical of the statistical data contained in the monthly business reviews of some of the Federal reserve banks:

---

* The Department of Commerce has issued annual reports on retail credit conditions that include valuable information on the average percentage collected monthly on open-credit sales and installment-credit sales and the average number of days accounts were outstanding, in various retail lines, in different sections of the country, in different months of the year, and for different-size business units. The "Retail Credit Survey," 1939, revealed, for example, that in 1939 department stores collected 46.6 per cent of their accounts, owing at the end of the month, in the following 30 days. This percentage indicated that it would take an average of 64.4 days to collect the full amount outstanding. The following table shows the percentage collected monthly and the average length of time accounts were outstanding for the kinds of stores indicated.

	Open-Credit		Installment	
	Per Cent Collected	*Days Required for Collection*	*Per Cent Collected*	*Days Required for Collection*
Automobile	83.2	36.1	13.9	215.8
Automobile tire and accessory	55.7	53.9	26.9	111.5
Coal, fuel oil, and wood	56.9	52.7	13.4	223.9
Department	46.6	64.4	16.6	180.7
Furniture	46.1	65.1	10.1	297.0
Grocery, total	73.8	40.7	----	----
With fresh meats	76.6	39.2	----	----
Without fresh meats	62.9	47.7	----	----
Hardware	51.8	57.9	13.8	217.4
Household appliance	56.1	53.5	10.2	294.1
Jewelry	47.7	62.9	13.6	220.6
Lumber and building material	48.6	61.7	15.2	197.4
Men's clothing	40.9	73.3	33.3	90.1
Milk	108.7	27.6	----	----
Plumbing and heating equipment	64.7	46.4	----	----
Shoe	45.4	66.1	----	----
Women's specialty	38.6	77.7	21.3	140.8

WHOLESALE TRADE, 201 FIRMS

LINES	Ratio July collections to accounts outstanding July 1
Automotive supplies (9)	71
Shoes (5)	54
Drugs & sundries (10)	104
Dry goods (8)	47
Electrical goods (19)	79
Groceries (56)	96
Hardware (15)	49
Industrial supplies (10)	87
Paper & products (9)	74
Tobacco & products (10)	87
Miscellaneous (50)	70
District Average (201)	73

Source: Bureau of the Census.

In the wholesale dry-goods industry of the particular Federal Reserve District covered by the monthly business review from which the above figures were taken, 47.0 per cent of the accounts owing at the end of December was collected in the following month. This percentage indicates that it would take an average of about 64 days (30 divided by .47) to collect the full amount outstanding. In other words, the average length of time open accounts receivable were outstanding is 64 days. If one were analyzing the accounts receivable of a dry-goods firm in the District referred to, from a statement bearing a date corresponding to that for which the statistics apply, and found the outstanding accounts to be much more than 64 days old, the quality of the accounts receivable would be considered unfavorable, in comparison with general conditions in the trade.

Another source of information pertaining to average collection periods in various industries is the Dun & Bradstreet, Inc., tables referred to in the footnote on page 1204. One of the ratios given in these tables is "average collection period."

Examination of notes receivable.—The item of notes receivable among the current assets raises the following questions:

1. Is the presence of notes receivable in the statement unusual? In many lines of business, sales are made on open account, and

notes are taken only to close out a past-due account. Notes receivable originating in this way represent an inferior asset and must be scrutinized carefully. Their valuation depends upon such factors as:

(*a*) Whether the notes are past due.
(*b*) Whether they have been renewed repeatedly.
(*c*) Whether interest has been defaulted even though the maturity date has not been reached.

Notes received at the time of a sale, in accordance with an established practice of accepting notes in payment for merchandise, such as exists in industries which market high-priced units, represent better assets than open accounts receivable, for the following reasons:

(*a*) The note receivable is written evidence of a promise to pay.
(*b*) It can be discounted and converted into cash at lower cost and more readily than the account receivable.
(*c*) It usually bears interest.

2. Do all the notes receivable represent customers' accounts? Notes received from officers, stockholders, employees, and others for transactions outside the regular trade should not be considered as current assets unless there is reliable information presented to the effect that the notes will be paid within a short period.

3. Are any dishonored or discounted notes included in the total? The notes receivable should not include instruments that have been discounted, assigned, or transferred.

Examination of trade acceptances.—In evaluating the asset "acceptances receivable," consideration should be given to the following points:

1. The trade acceptance, when properly used, represents an acknowledgment of a debt incurred by the purchase of a particular bill of goods.

2. Trade acceptances are sometimes misused in connection with past-due accounts, loans, or renewals and accommodations, where no transfer of goods is immediately involved.

3. It is the practice of many concerns to use the trade acceptance only in transactions with their less reliable customers; those whose

credit standing is regarded more favorably are sold on open account. Furthermore, strong customers generally prefer to buy on open account and pay their bills in time to secure the cash discount.

Before the value of the asset "acceptances receivable" can be determined, therefore, inquiry may have to be made of the company whose statement is being analyzed, to ascertain:

1. Whether the acceptances originated from current transactions that represent the purchase of goods.
2. Whether, if the first question is answered affirmatively, the company follows the procedure of selling on acceptances only to risks considered doubtful.

Trade acceptances arising through a proper use of the instrument in a business which customarily uses the trade acceptance in selling constitute an asset of ready convertibility, for the acceptances can be discounted or sold in the open market through acceptance dealers. Trade acceptances that arise in other ways may have no superiority as an asset available to meet current debts and may, in fact, be inferior to open accounts receivable.

Testing the adequacy of the reserve for bad debts.—A minimum reserve for bad debts, varying with the line of industry, and ranging usually from 5 to 10 per cent of the accounts receivable outstanding, is generally considered necessary, regardless of the condition of the receivables. The valuation of the accounts, notes, and acceptances receivable on the bases explained above will indicate whether adequate provision has been made in the balance sheet for bad debts.

Examination of inventories.—The following are the chief points to be considered in appraising the worth of inventories, determining whether too much capital is tied up in them, and detecting misrepresentations.

1. How the inventory was determined. The amount of inventories should represent a valuation of stocks on hand ascertained, where practicable, through an actual count, and not a sum arrived at from records of perpetual book inventories or an amount estimated by guesswork. Statements prepared by public accountants

generally indicate what check the accountants have made to substantiate the inventories shown in the statement. If the statement does not disclose whether a physical inventory was taken, and if there is no accountant's verification thereof, direct inquiry must be made of the applicant as to how the valuation was made.

2. How the merchandise is valued. One of the purposes of scrutinizing the method of valuing inventories is to discover whether sufficient allowance has been made for declines in value due to such causes as changes in styles, deterioration, spoilage, waste, and other losses. (See page 1155 for further discussion of this subject.)

3. What part of the inventory represents prepaid expenses that rightfully belong with the deferred charges. Supplies, for example, that will never become a part of the finished product, eventually to be sold on account and finally converted into cash, should not be included with the merchandise inventory.

4. What the nature of the inventories is. The financial statement of a manufacturer should show what portion of the inventory is raw materials, what part is goods in process, and what amount represents finished goods on hand. Each of these has different values from the standpoint of convertibility into funds for debt-paying purposes. In the event of insolvency, raw materials consisting of stable commodities may be disposed of with greater facility than other merchandise; goods in process are practically valueless in case of forced sales to raise funds; finished goods have a more limited market than raw materials. A division of the inventory into these items is furthermore required to show whether, in view of market conditions and the volume of business done, too much capital is tied up in raw materials.

5. The seasonal influences. In analyzing the inventory item of the balance sheet, the seasonal factor must not be overlooked. A balance sheet drawn up at the close of a season should show a reduction in inventories, whereas one prepared at the beginning of a season, or in the midst of it, may disclose heavier inventories.

6. Whether merchandise has been pledged as collateral. Information should be obtained relative to this question, if the balance sheet does not contain the answer.

7. What conclusions can be drawn as to the condition of the stock from information contained in the balance sheet and income

statement. Some light can be thrown upon the valuation of inventories and the probable salability of the goods by applying certain tests to the inventory.

Determining quality of inventory from ratio of sales to inventories.—An estimate of whether the inventories are out of proportion to the demand being made upon the firm for its products can be determined by applying the following formula:

$$\frac{\text{Sales}}{\text{Average Inventory (at Sales Price) of Finished Goods}} = \text{Number of times finished stock turns over.}$$

The figures shown by an application of this formula indicate how many times the finished goods on hand are turned over during the course of a year. The figure can be converted to show how much time is consumed in converting inventories to sales. Thus, if the ratio of sales to inventories is 3, indicating that inventories turn over three times in the year, it is clear that 4 months are consumed in converting inventories to sales. The normal period in which stocks should be converted into cash or receivables through sales varies with the particular industry and must be known before the significance of the merchandise turnover becomes clear. In comparison with the normal figure, the higher the turnover, the better the inventory control and the more favorable generally the condition of the firm; the lower the turnover, the poorer the control of inventory and the more costly the price of converting inventories to cash, for the longer it takes to move merchandise, the greater is the financial burden of doing so.

A slow turnover of merchandise may indicate that the inventories are overvalued and that they have not been properly depreciated; that they contain unsalable goods; or that the business has overbought. An unusually rapid turnover might indicate that all purchases of material received before the preparation of the statement had not been included in the balance sheet.

Another method of calculating merchandise turnover is given in the following formula:

$$\frac{\text{Cost of Goods Sold}}{\text{Average Inventory of Finished Goods at Cost}} = \text{Finished goods turnover.}$$

The disadvantage of employing this ratio in testing the inventory is that usually the financial statement shows the cost of goods sold, including operating expenses; in order to obtain a true turnover, the cost of goods sold before the addition of operating costs should be used.

Difficulties in applying the merchandise-turnover test.—Two difficulties are encountered in using the ratio of sales to inventories as a test of the inventories:

1. The ratio, in order to be accurate, should make use of average inventories for the year. These are generally not available to one who is analyzing a financial statement for purposes of determining credit strength. An average of the inventories at the beginning and end of the year, if both figures are available, or only the inventory at the end of the period, must of necessity be substituted.

2. The balance sheet does not present the inventories at sales price, and an estimate of the profit that will be made upon the sale of the merchandise must therefore be made to arrive at the denominator of the fraction in the formula. Thus, if the gross margin of profit in the particular line of industry is 50 per cent of cost, a markup of 50 per cent can be applied to the inventories at cost to estimate their selling price.

Possible explanations of excessive inventories and slow turnover of merchandise.—If the inventory is found to be too large, and the merchandise turnover consequently slow, certain unusual factors such as the following may account for the condition:

1. The inventory may reflect increases in purchases in anticipation of seasonal demand.

2. The trend of prices may be upward, and the large inventory may represent a deliberate stocking up in anticipation of a further rise in prices.

3. The inventory may be high because a larger volume of business is anticipated.

4. The turnover of merchandise may be slow because the firm engages in functions that lengthen the period between the acquisition of inventories and their sale. For example, one manufacturer may be engaged largely in assembling parts produced by others; another may undertake the manufacturing of parts as well as their assembling. Obviously, the second firm will have larger inventories than the first.

5. Large inventories may be required because of the distance of the firm from the market. Thus a firm located at a great distance from the source of its supplies would require larger inventories than one that can replenish its stock at short notice.

Examination of marketable securities.—In analyzing the item of marketable securities, three steps are necessary:

1. Determine whether it is the policy of the company in whose statement the item appears to treat marketable securities as available for meeting current debts. If the company does not follow this policy, the item should be removed from the current assets and placed among the investments.
2. Secure a list of the stocks and bonds that make up the marketable securities, in order that their current value may be checked against that shown in the balance sheet. Stocks and bonds that are not listed on a stock exchange are likely not to be readily convertible into cash and may, with justification, be omitted from the current assets.
3. Inquire whether any of the investments have been pledged.

Examination of current liabilities.—Examination of the current liabilities is the next step in the analysis of working capital. The review of current liabilities should be made with the following objects in view:

1. To see that all of the current debts, including accruals for salaries, wages, and interest, are included among the current liabilities. Inquiry should be made as to the following:

(*a*) Whether all bills for goods received prior to the preparation of the statement have been included as liabilities.

(*b*) The maturity date of any mortgage outstanding, in order to be certain that the debt is included among the current liabilities if the mortgage matures in the current year.

(*c*) Whether any dividends are to be paid or withdrawals to be made that will materially reduce the current assets shown on the statement; if dividends are cumulative, inquiry should be made as to the amount in arrears on the statement date. This information will indicate whether the company's dividend policy is jeopardizing the interests of creditors. Thus, if dividends are being paid while working capital is inadequate, or while profits are low, the credit applicant can be considered a poor risk.

(*d*) The nature of reserves, if that is not clearly indicated in the statement. Any reserves which represent liabilities that will mature within a short period, such as a reserve for taxes, should be included among the current debts.

2. To determine whether there are any contingent liabilities that may, upon the happening of the contingency, increase the liabilities. (See page 1175.) If the balance sheet or income statement gives no evidence of contingent liabilities, direct inquiry should be made to ascertain if there are any.

3. To discover, through a study of the nature of the liabilities, any implications reflective of the credit standing of the applicant. For example, the item of loans payable to banks, commercial paper houses, or notebrokers implies that the company's credit capacity has been tested by the bank or other institution that has extended credit.

4. To ascertain the promptness with which bills are paid.

Examination of accounts payable.—The following information should be ascertained concerning the accounts payable:

1. What amount of the accounts payable, if any, represents debts due for money borrowed from officers, stockholders, friends, and others? The answer to this question must be learned by direct inquiry.

2. Are the accounts payable unusually large or very small because of seasonal influences? Information as to the months in which the accounts payable are at their maximum and minimum, and the totals at such times, obtained by direct inquiry, will enable the analyst to make allowances for seasonal factors in analyzing the accounts payable.

3. Is the company paying its bills promptly? Information regarding this question may be obtained in the following ways:

(*a*) A schedule of the age of the accounts payable, similar to that requested for the accounts receivable (see page 1206), may be requested of the customer. If obtained, this report will show the volume of past-due accounts and the extent to which the company is failing to take advantage of cash discounts.

(*b*) An estimate of the age of the accounts payable may be made by comparing the number of days' purchases unpaid with the credit terms, as explained below.

(*c*) Credit agencies may be asked to make reports upon the payment record of the credit applicant, in which case it will be unnecessary either to ask for an aging statement of the accounts payable, or to estimate the promptness with which the company is paying its bills.

Estimating the age of accounts payable.—In the absence of definite information as to the age of outstanding debts incurred in the purchase of materials, some indication of the promptness with which the applicant for credit pays his bills may be obtained by determining, through the following formula, the number of days' purchases unpaid:

$$\frac{\text{Accounts Payable}}{\text{Raw Material Purchases}} \times 360 = \begin{array}{l}\text{Number of days'}\\\text{purchases unpaid.}\end{array}$$

A comparison of the number of days' purchases unpaid, with the average terms of credit, which are ascertained by direct inquiry if the information is not available from other sources, may reveal the promptness with which bills are paid. Suppose that the application of the formula to a particular financial statement indicates that 60 days' purchases remain unpaid and that the average credit terms are 30 days. It would appear that half of the accounts payable are past due. This conclusion would, of course, be unsound if seasonal purchases were reflected in the amount of accounts payable.

The formula should not be applied if bank loans appear in the balance sheet, for such loans may have decreased the amount of accounts payable outstanding. If the bank loans were used for the payment of purchases of merchandise, they could be added to the accounts payable in making the calculation; however, the balance sheet does not reveal to what use the bank loans were put, and direct questioning on this point is not worth while.

Examination of notes, bills, and acceptances payable.—Notes payable should be broken down into the following classifications, for various factors as to the financial standing of the credit applicant will thereby be revealed.

1. Amounts representing notes given to merchandise creditors. The following inquiries must be made in order to judge the significance of the total:

(*a*) Is it the custom in the particular line of industry for notes or acceptances to be given in the normal course of trade, or have they been given by the applicant for credit in settlement of overdue accounts? Obviously, if they have been given in settlement of past-due accounts, the credit applicant is a poor risk.

(*b*) Do the instruments carry any outside endorsement? If the notes bear outside endorsements, the applicant is undoubtedly a poor risk, since his name on the notes has not been regarded as sufficient.

(*c*) Are the obligations past due?

(*d*) Have earlier notes been partly paid when due, and do those at present outstanding represent notes tendered for the balance?

2. Amounts representing notes discounted by banks. A company that has discounted its own notes at the bank has passed the bank's test for extension of credit. This is clearly a point in favor of the credit applicant, unless the loan has had to be renewed and carried along by the bank after the borrower completed the season's business. Inquiry should therefore be made to discover the bank's experience with its loans to the credit applicant.

3. Amounts representing notes sold through notebrokers. The ability of the company to sell its notes through notebrokers is a sign of strength, for only companies of high credit standing can raise funds in this way.

4. Amounts representing notes given to friends and relatives who have loaned money to the business. The fact that the owners of the business have had to borrow from friends and relatives should be regarded as a signal to move cautiously in granting credit.

Working Capital Ratio

Ratio of current assets to current liabilities.—In estimating the ability of the applicant for credit to meet his debts promptly, it is essential to discover from the financial statement how many dollars of current assets there are for each dollar of current liabilities. This figure, which is known as the current ratio or working-capital ratio, is found by applying the following formula:

$$\frac{\text{Current Assets}}{\text{Current Liabilities}} = \text{Current ratio.}$$

A company that has the following working capital setup would have a current ratio as indicated below.

	December 31, 19--
Current Assets	
Cash on deposit and on hand	$145,141.17
Marketable securities (Less reserve, $16,105; value at market quotations, Dec. 31, 19--)	23,132.91
Accounts and notes receivable	223,996.17
Inventories of raw materials, supplies, work in process, and finished products (Less reserve, $77,334)	478,007.59
Total current assets	$870,277.84
Current Liabilities	
Notes payable	$ 18,941.87
Accounts payable	132,327.97
Accrued taxes	20,869.65
Accrued payrolls	23,694.61
Advances received on sales contracts	20,869.65
Total current liabilities	$216,703.75
Working capital	$653,574.09
Current ratio, or dollars of current assets per dollar of current liabilities	4.01

A current ratio of 2 to 1—that is, of $2 of current assets to $1 of current liabilities—is usually considered satisfactory, irrespective of the industry. Current ratios vary considerably, however, in different lines of trade. One study made for 36 different lines of business showed the current ratios to range from 1.32 for companies rendering services to 10.23 for a group of companies engaged in the cotton goods business. The current ratio does not of itself, however, furnish the criterion for judging the capacity of the customer to pay, and full reliance should not be placed upon it.

Importance of current ratio.—The importance of the current ratio, as compared with working capital, as a factor in determining credit strength is clear from the following illustration of the working capital of a company at two different periods:

First Period

Current Assets	$3,000
Current Liabilities	2,000
Working Capital	$1,000

Second Period

Current Assets	$2,000
Current Liabilities	1,000
Working Capital	$1,000

In both periods the working capital is $1,000; but in the second period the current ratio is 2 to 1, while in the first it is 1.50 to 1. The company has a better working-capital position in the second period than in the first, because in the second period it has $2,000 of shrinkable assets with which to pay non-shrinkable liabilities of $1,000, while in the first period it had $3,000 of shrinkable assets with which to meet $2,000 of non-shrinkable liabilities.

Consideration to be given to the current ratio.—The current ratio can be accepted as an indicator of the credit strength of the firm whose statement is being analyzed only after consideration is given to the following factors:

1. An analysis of the nature of the items that are reflected in the current ratio. This is clear from the preceding analysis of working capital. A strong current ratio, for example, carries little weight in favor of the credit applicant if examination of the inventories shows them to be overvalued and if an analysis of the accounts receivable reveals a large volume of doubtful accounts.
2. Seasonal influences. A statement that reflects the financial status of a company during an inactive period may show a more favorable current ratio than would a statement of the same concern a few months later when purchases have been made in anticipation of new seasonal demand and merchandise has not yet been converted into accounts receivable and cash.
3. The proportions which the various items that make up the current assets bear to the total current assets. Since some of the assets are more liquid and more stable than others, it is necessary to study the current ratio in the light of this consideration. The importance of the distribution of current assets is discussed further in the next paragraph.

4. The outlook for expansion or contraction of operations after the date of the balance sheet.

5. Significance of changes in the company's working capital. (See page 1224.)

Distribution of current assets.—A study of the distribution of the current assets is important in the analysis of working capital because certain assets are more liquid than others. A company may have maintained a current ratio of 2 to 1 for two years, and yet may be considerably weaker in the second than in the first year, and vice versa. This can be readily seen from the following comparative statements of working capital:

	December 31			
	Second Year	*Per Cent*	*First Year*	*Per Cent*
Current Assets				
Cash	$ 40,000	16⅔	$120,000	50
Receivables	80,000	33⅓	80,000	33⅓
Inventories	120,000	50	40,000	16⅔
Total Current Assets.	$240,000	100	$240,000	100
Current Liabilities	120,000		120,000	
Working capital	$120,000		$120,000	
Current ratio	2 : 1		2 : 1	

In both years the company has a current ratio of 2 to 1. In the second year, however, it is in a less liquid condition than it was in in the first year, for in place of $40,000 of inventories and $120,000 of cash, it now has $40,000 of cash and $120,000 of inventories. However, if it is expected that the inventories will be converted into sales at a profit and that the eventual value of the current assets will increase as inventories are converted into accounts receivable and ultimately into cash, the apparent weakness may be no barrier to the extension of credit. Ordinarily, the shift from assets of greater liquidity to those of lesser liquidity is regarded unfavorably in analyzing credit strength.

It is not essential in the analysis of working capital to reduce the distribution of the current assets to percentages of the total if the correct conclusions can be drawn from a study of the figures as they appear in the statement. Many credit men make their analyses directly from the figures.

The "acid-test," or "quick," ratio.—A test often applied to determine the immediate ability of the applicant to meet current liabilities is to find the ratio of cash, receivables, and marketable securities ("quick-current" assets or "dollar" assets) to current liabilities. This ratio is called the "acid-test," or "quick," ratio. Inventories are omitted on the principle that they are not liquid assets. If the marketable securities are stocks that fluctuate violently, they should be omitted from the acid-test ratio. Ordinarily a company that has its working capital temporarily invested in marketable securities purchases the highest-grade bonds; such securities may be regarded as dollar assets. One dollar of quick current assets to one dollar of current liabilities is generally regarded as favorable; that is, a ratio of 100 per cent, or 1 to 1, is the generally accepted standard.

Other Factors in Financial Analysis

Sales volume as a factor in financial analysis.—The relationship of the volume of sales to working capital and to net worth must be watched for signs of strain due to overtrading. An increasing volume of sales must be accompanied by sufficient working capital and adequate net worth.

The first ratio is determined as follows:

$$\frac{\text{Net Sales}}{\text{Working Capital}} = \text{Working Capital Turnover.}$$

The second ratio is determined as follows:

$$\frac{\text{Net Sales}}{\text{Tangible Net Worth*}} = \text{Capital Turnover}$$

The ratio tests are useful when compared with the turnovers of the same company for previous periods and with average ratios

* In a corporation, the net worth is the total of the capital stock, surplus, and reserve accounts that represent surplus. (See page 1178.) In a partnership, the net worth is the sum of the partners' capital accounts. In a single proprietorship, the net worth is represented by the proprietor's capital account. For purposes of credit analysis, however, the tangible net worth is used; this is found by subtracting from the net worth as above determined the goodwill, copyrights, trade-marks, patents, leaseholds, mailing lists, and any other intangible fixed assets.

for a group of companies in the same line of business. Average ratios for various industries are available from time to time in such publications as the *Dun & Bradstreet Monthly Review*.

When the working capital turnover and the capital turnover are much higher than the average for the same line of business, it may indicate a capital insufficient to do the volume of business; when much smaller, the capital is not active enough.

Importance of the sources of working capital.—The sources from which the credit applicant has acquired its working capital are extremely important in analyzing its credit strength, for the following reasons:

1. The sources have a direct relation to the control that the firm has over its inventories and other current assets. For example, if all the sources for borrowing have been exhausted and among the liabilities are debts representing loans in the open market that are likely to be pressed for payment at maturity, the company will find itself in an awkward position sooner than if it had not tapped all the sources of working capital and if its current debts represented only purchases on account.
2. The costs of raising working capital, which constitute a drain upon working capital, vary with the source. Borrowing through bank loans and open-market loans is more costly than long-term borrowing; however, the latter involves more permanent and rigid obligations.
3. The responsibility for payment varies. A company that has increased its working capital through additional investments by owners of the business is in a better position than one that has improved its position by borrowing in the open market, for the obvious reason that there is no obligation to repay investors, while there is a definite responsibility to repay on a certain day the loans made in the open market.
4. The shifts made from one method of raising working capital to another may reflect the difficulties of the firm in maintaining an adequate supply of working capital.

Determining the sources of the credit applicant's working capital.—The sources of working capital used by the enterprise whose statement is being analyzed can be learned from:

1. The nature of the liabilities shown in the financial statement.

2. Direct questioning of the credit applicant.

3. The changes in working capital revealed by a study of the comparative statements of the credit applicant. (See page 1195.)

By tracing any increase in working capital to the following conditions, the analyst can decide the degree of improvement in the working-capital position, for each source has obvious strength or weakness.

1. Application to working capital of new contributions of capital by the owners of the business.

2. Application to working capital of funds received upon the sale of long-term obligations.

3. Earnings that have been reinvested in the business and that are reflected in the current assets.

4. Reserves against taxes, contingencies, depreciation, maintenance, and sinking funds or amortization of debts that are reflected in the current assets.

5. Writing up of merchandise inventories and marketable securities.

Similarly, by tracing any decrease in working capital to the following causes, the analyst can weigh the seriousness of the decline.

1. Losses incurred.

2. Distribution of earnings, or withdrawal of capital.

3. Use of current funds in the acquisition of fixed and non-current assets.

4. Use of current funds to fund reserves, to use reserves for maintenance and other purposes.

5. Marking down of inventory values and marketable securities.

Information of importance in the analysis of financial statements.—Through the preceding explanation the need for making direct inquiry in judging the financial strength of a credit applicant was brought out. The following list of questions generally included in the form of financial statement sent to a firm that is seeking an extension of credit shows how the questions are framed. Some of the questions apply only to a partnership or individual, and others apply exclusively to a corporation.

Date business was established..
Under laws of what state incorporated?..
Amount of authorized capital $..
Amount of capital subscribed $..
How is bond issue secured? ....
Is there a mortgage against any of your assets?...
Are any of your merchandise creditors secured?..
If so, how?...
Names and addresses of banks..
Maximum lines of accommodations promised by............................Bank $..................
What is the nature of the security held by banks for borrowed money?..................
Are all purchase bills for goods received prior to the date of preparation of the statement included as liabilities? ....
Are loans payable to friends and relatives, or exchange check items, shown as liabilities or included as invested capital? ....
When did your liabilities reach their maximum last year?.......................$..............
When did your liabilities reach their minimum last year?.......................$..............
Have you been charged with any merchandise not included in your statement, and if so, how much? ....
On statement date, to what extent were you obligated for merchandise commitments or contracts for future delivery?..
Are there any dividends to be paid or withdrawals to be made that will materially reduce the current assets shown on the statement?...
If dividends are cumulative, give the amount in arrears on the statement date...........
Are members of the firm individually liable as endorser, guarantor, or otherwise for the obligations of others; if so, to what extent? $...
Are there any suits or judgments pending against the firm or individual members?
State amount of contingent liability. $..................How incurred?..............................
Is the merchandise inventory figure supported by any permanent stock record? ....
Does your merchandise inventory represent actual count of stocks?..........................
At what time of the year is the inventory highest?..................Lowest?...................
Do you pledge, hypothecate, or borrow upon your accounts receivable or merchandise? ....
Have you excluded all bad and doubtful accounts from the above accounts receivable? ....
Do accounts receivable as shown in the statement contain loans receivable, exchange checks, drawing accounts, loans to officers, or any other items other than amounts due customers? ....
Have you included in your accounts receivable any charges for merchandise out on memorandum, conditional bill of sale, or consignment, or merchandise charged but not delivered?..
Are selling offices, branches, or affiliated companies financed entirely by you, or independently? ....
Are their loans included in this statement?.......................Are shipments to them carried on inventory or accounts receivable?...
Explain the present connection of members of the firm with any other business ....
Fire insurance on merchandise $..
Fire insurance on machinery and fixtures $...
Fire insurance on buildings and plant $...
Amount of life insurance payable to the firm $..

Have any of your insurance policies been assigned, transferred, or pledged?...............

During the period covered by the statement, has any money been added to net worth from sources other than profits, and if so, how much? $..............................

How much is your total rent liability per year? $..

Lease(s) expires ....

Do you keep books of account? If so, state what books you keep. (Answer yes or no after each book)..

Sales ledger...........Purchase legder...........General ledger...........Private ledger........... Sales book...........

Cash book...........Stock book...........Manufacturing book...........Shipping book........... Journal...........

Day book...........Check book...........Bank deposit book...........

What books other than those enumerated above do you use?.......................................

Do you have your books regularly audited by a C.P.A.?...............When?.................. By whom?...........................

To what date has the U. S. Treasury Department audited your income tax?...............

Has any deficiency tax been assessed against you?...............How much? $...............

False Financial Statements

Laws providing punishment for false financial statements.—A person or firm that has been defrauded by one who submitted a false financial statement in an effort to obtain credit may look to the following three classes of laws under which to prosecute the wrongdoer:

1. State larceny laws providing for punishment of persons who obtain money or property by means of false pretenses or misrepresentations.
2. State "false statement laws."
3. Federal laws providing punishment for those who use the mails for fraudulent purposes.

Prosecution under larceny laws.—All of the states have laws making it a crime to obtain money or property under false pretenses. Prosecution under the larceny laws, of persons who obtain credit through the presentation of false financial statements, has proved unsatisfactory, for in order to obtain a conviction it is necessary to prove that:

1. The person accused intended to deprive or defraud the true owner of his property.
2. The accused obtained the property.
3. The statement contained fraudulent or false representations or pretenses.

4. The defrauded person relied upon the false statement.
5. The money or property was delivered to the person charged with the crime.

The difficulty of legally proving that the above elements existed has frequently resulted in the acquittal of persons who were undoubtedly recipients of goods obtained from a creditor who relied upon a false financial statement. The court decisions yield many examples of acquittal handed down because the defrauded creditor could not supply satisfactory evidence that the merchandise actually was received by the accused, or because he could not prove to the satisfaction of a jury that the purchaser did not intend to pay for the merchandise.

The inadequacy of the larceny laws as a basis for prosecuting the maker of a false statement gave rise to the passage of the false-statement laws.

Prosecution under the false-statement laws.—Thirty-five states have enacted a uniform false-statement law that overcomes the difficulties encountered in prosecuting the maker of a false statement under the larceny laws. These states are: Alabama, Arkansas, California, Connecticut, Delaware, Florida, Illinois, Indiana, Kentucky, Louisiana, Maine, Maryland, Massachusetts, Michigan, Minnesota, Missouri, Nebraska, New Hampshire, New Jersey, New Mexico, New York, Ohio, Oklahoma, Oregon, Pennsylvania, Rhode Island, Tennessee, Texas, Utah, Vermont, Virginia, Washington, West Virginia, Wisconsin, and Wyoming. The false-statement laws are alike in the states mentioned with regard to the definition of the crimes for which punishment is provided; they vary in minor particulars and in the penalties imposed.

In states which have the uniform false-statement law, all that need be proved against a defendant is:

1. That he made or caused the statement to be made.
2. That the statement is materially false.
3. That the statement was made for the purpose of securing credit.
4. That the statement was made with the intent that it should be relied upon.

Who can be punished under the false-statement laws?—The New York law, which is typical of those enacted in most of the states, and is in the form of the model law, provides for the punishment of any person who commits the following crimes:

1. Makes or causes a false statement regarding financial condition to be made in writing, for the purpose of procuring property or credit, and with the intent that it shall be relied upon.

2. Procures property or credit upon the faith of the false statement, knowing that the statement is false, regardless of whether the person procuring the property or credit made the statement.

3. Falsely represents, orally or in writing, that a financial statement theretofore made continues to be true, and procures property or credit upon the faith thereof.

Superiority of protection afforded by false-statement laws.—The superiority of the protection afforded by the false-statement laws as compared with the larceny laws may be summarized as follows:

1. It is unnecessary to prove that any property was obtained upon the strength of the statement; it is unnecessary to prove the physical delivery of the property. In Alabama, Colorado, Florida, Georgia, Idaho, Nevada, and Virginia, there are special statutory provisions for the punishment of persons who, on the strength of false reports, get possession of money, property, credit, or some other valuable thing.

2. It is unnecessary to prove any intent to defraud.

3. Whereas under the larceny laws mere extension of time in which to pay a debt cannot be made the basis of a charge of larceny, under the false-statement laws the giving of a false financial statement for the purpose of obtaining an extension of time is a crime.

4. It is not essential that the maker of the false statement and the receiver of the credit or property be the same person. Thus a partner in a firm who receives credit or property on a false statement rendered by another partner may be liable for punishment; and a director who receives credit or property for the benefit of a corporation may be liable under the statute.

Prosecution under the Federal mail-fraud statute.—The Federal laws against using the mails to defraud are a valuable weapon against a debtor who has secured merchandise on credit by mailing a false financial statement. To obtain a conviction under the Federal law, the prosecution must be prepared to prove the following:

1. That the statement is false.
2. That it was made for the purpose of securing money or property.
3. That it was made with the intention that it should be relied upon.
4. That the statement was mailed.
5. That money or property was obtained by means of the false statement.

The punishment provided under the Federal law is more severe than that imposed by the State laws. Furthermore, difficulties sometimes encountered in prosecution under the State laws are overcome by prosecution under the Federal law. For example, under the New York statute, cases must be prosecuted in the county in which the statement was made, regardless of where the statement was delivered, and proof must be furnished that the statement was made in the county in which the prosecution is sought. Under the Federal law, the action may be begun either in the district in which the statement was made, or in that in which the statement was delivered.

The National Association of Credit Men recommends the use of a self-mailing form of financial statement in order to make it easy to prosecute under the Federal mail-fraud statute. The self-mailing form is a combination statement and envelope; when folded, the financial statement is contained within the envelope, and the address of the one to whom it is being sent is on the back of the statement. See Figure 99, pages 1192–1193.

Some tests in determining whether prosecution should be undertaken.—Before deciding to prosecute on an alleged false financial statement, the firm or person contemplating such action must consider whether the statement was materially false. A test to apply is to ask the question: Would credit have been extended if the items that are believed to be false were correctly stated? If the answer is "no," the falsity is probably material.

The difficulty that will be encountered in proving the falsity of a statement must also be considered. Certain items in the balance sheet, such as inventories, machinery, furniture and fixtures, and land and buildings represent estimated values that are subject to fluctuations, different methods of appraisal, and honest differences of opinion. Great difficulty is likely to be experienced in convincing a jury that the valuations set forth in these items are false. However, the valuation of such items as cash, accounts receivable, notes and acceptances receivable, accounts payable, notes and acceptances payable, and mortgages payable are based upon ascertainable facts, and falsification of these items can be more readily proved to a jury. It is well to remember that the jury must be convinced beyond a reasonable doubt that the items alleged to be false, are in fact falsely stated.

Can an accountant be held for an incorrect statement?—A person or firm that has extended credit, relying upon a financial statement prepared by a public accountant, which later proves to have been erroneous, has no claim against the accountant if the errors are due to ordinary negligence, not fraud, on the part of the accountant or his assistant, even though the accountant is aware that the statement will be used to obtain credit, provided that no contractual relation exists between the accountant and the firm that extended credit.

If the accountant has perpetrated fraud in the preparation of the statement, he can be held liable by persons who extended credit on the strength of the statement, even though there was no contractual relation between the accountant and the third person, and even though the report was not especially prepared for such third person.

Gross negligence in failing to ascertain facts before making a statement, even when not equivalent to fraud, is none the less evidence to sustain an inference of fraud. Thus, where accountants had knowledge that a large amount of accounts receivable of a firm whose accounts they were auditing were dead and that reserves for bad debts were inadequate, and the accountants failed to note this condition on the balance sheet, the accountants were held liable to a trust company which loaned money relying upon the accountants' certified balance sheet. In this case the accountants knew that the statement would be used to obtain credit.

SECTION 13

Business Insurance

1. HOW TO REDUCE THE COST OF AMPLE INSURANCE PROTECTION

2. LAW GOVERNING INSURANCE POLICIES

3. TYPES OF INSURANCE POLICIES

4. FIRE INSURANCES

5. LIABILITY INSURANCE

6. WORKMEN'S COMPENSATION INSURANCE

7. AUTOMOBILE INSURANCE

8. BURGLARY, THEFT, AND ROBBERY INSURANCE

9. FIDELITY AND SURETY BONDS

10. CREDIT INSURANCE

11. MISCELLANEOUS INSURANCE COVERAGES

A. Fire and Allied Coverages

B. Other Property Insurance

C. Floater Policies

D. Miscellaneous Coverages

12. BUSINESS LIFE INSURANCE

13. GROUP INSURANCE

SECTION 13

Business Insurance*

1. HOW TO REDUCE THE COST OF AMPLE INSURANCE PROTECTION

Purchase the proper form of insurance.—Insurance, like all other commodities, is placed on the market in various kinds of packages; some packages contain much more protection for a given premium than others.

Purchasing the *most* suitable form of insurance for the situation can keep costs down considerably. For example, any risk may be covered by "specific fire" insurance. If the value of the property at risk, however, fluctuates sharply, it will be much cheaper to buy at least a part of the coverage as "reporting insurance" if the business qualifies for it. The saving arises from the fact that under the reporting form of policy, a premium is charged only on the actual value of the property at risk; whereas, under the specific form of policy, the premium must be paid in advance on the full face value of the policy. Since the face value of the policy must be at least equal to the maximum amount that may be at risk at any time, it is apparent that the reporting form of insurance would be cheaper in such an instance.

Select your broker or agent carefully, and keep him informed.—An insurance broker or agent who takes an interest in his client's business has been compared to a doctor of medicine. Like a qualified doctor the broker or agent can diagnose the needs of his client after a careful analysis of all the surrounding circum-

* Acknowledgment is made to Jerome S. Miller, Insurance Consultant, for his assistance in revising this section.

stances, and can prescribe the proper remedy. The agent or broker, on the other hand, who merely "writes up" something when his client informs him that he needs some "burglary insurance," is like the old country "horse doctor" who gives out "snake oil" or some similar preparation, for every ailment.

A good broker or agent who is interested in the welfare of his policyholders, and who is kept informed by his clients of changes in their circumstances, can do a great deal to point out ways and means by which the assured can keep down the cost of ample and proper insurance protection.

Many businessmen make a habit of turning over all policies and supplementary documents to their insurance broker or agent every year for examination and analysis. This habit is a good one and should be cultivated by everyone. In many instances minor changes can be made that will more nearly fit the policy to the needs of the assured, or that will facilitate the settling of a claim in case of a loss. The following example illustrates a condition that is often found when a lease and a policy of insurance taken out in accordance with its terms are examined.

Leases usually contain some provision relative to liability for rent, and so forth, following a fire. Recently a broker, in examining a lease covering the property of his client, found that although the lessee was paying fire insurance premiums, he was not protected. One provision of the lease provided that the lessee should pay over to the landlord premiums to effect insurance upon the property. The landlord then took out insurance in his own name. Yet another clause of the same lease stated that in event of a loss, the lessee would be liable therefor. As a result of the second clause, in event of a loss, the insurance company would have paid the amount thereof to the landlord, and then would have sued the lessee (who had actually paid the premiums) for the amount of the loss. Such a result was prevented in this instance by the addition to the policy of a clause whereby the insurance company agreed not to sue the lessee.

This case illustrates the importance of keeping in close touch with your insurance agent or broker and informing him of all facts that may affect the insurance carried.

Read your policy.—The importance of reading your policy before a loss is incurred cannot be overstressed. While most of the states have provided by law for so-called standard policies, the number and variety of permitted endorsements renders it very easy for the insurer to reduce his liability. Furthermore, in many comparatively new forms, practice has not been standardized, and each company issues policies conforming to its own ideas of what liability should or should not be assumed.

Despite the fact that practically every word of the older standard contracts has long since been interpreted by the courts, almost 4 per cent of all litigation involves insurance or insurance contracts. Manifestly, the proper time to cure ambiguities, to add endorsements, or to remove unwanted clauses, is before a loss is incurred. But unless the assured will take the time to read his contract (or, better still, read it in company with his broker or agent), he will never know what changes should be made to adapt the contract to his particular needs.

Some examples of the cost of failure to read a policy.—The cost of failure to read a policy before a loss occurs can probably best be illustrated by a few recent cases selected at random from among the many court decisions handed down during the past few years.

Case 1.—The Frisco Frolics Company took out a so-called Theater Floater Policy. The standard Theater Floater Policy covers against transportation hazards only while the assured's property is being transported by a common carrier. The Frolics Company, however, usually transported their property and effects in their own trucks. The Frolics Company apparently believed that they were fully protected against loss from all fire and transportation hazards. A loss was incurred while the Frolics Company's property was being transported in the theater company's trucks. Subsequently the insurance company refused to pay the claim on the ground that the risk was one which they had not assumed. The Court upheld the contention of the insurance company. Failure of the Frolics Company to have an endorsement attached to the standard policy permitting transportation of property in the company's own trucks voided the insurance when the goods were thus transported. (Insurance Company v. Frolics Company, 65 F.(2d) 928.)

Case 2.—The Walsh Construction Company procured a depositary bond protecting it against loss of deposits that were made in a designated bank. The Walsh Company believed that it was fully protected. The policy, however, contained a clause which read: "It is agreed that this bond does not cover certificates of deposit or any other indebtedness

. . . not subject at all times to immediate withdrawal by the Walsh Construction Company." The Court held that this clause restricted the coverage of the policy to demand deposits, and that, therefore, the Walsh Company could not recover any part of $200,000 which was deposited in a savings account when the bank failed. (Construction Company v. Insurance Company, 67 F.(2d) 679.)

Case 3.—The assured, a lumber dealer, purchased a fire insurance policy which contained a so-called "clear-space clause," whereby the assured agreed not to place any lumber within one hundred feet of any manufacturing establishment or dry kiln. The assured, unaware of the clear space provision contained in the contract, did not remove certain lumber from the prohibited area. A loss was incurred, and the insurance company refused to indemnify on the ground that the policy was void at the time of the fire, inasmuch as the assured had violated the clear-space provision. The Court upheld the contention of the insurance company, and stated that ignorance that the policy contained the clear-space clause did not excuse a violation thereof, even though the agent who had sold the policy knew of the violation. (Insurance Company v. Post, 62 S.W. 140.)

In each of the above cases the assured suffered a loss through failure to take the elementary precaution of reading his policy. Such cases are not infrequent and point to the fact that the time required to read your policy is time well spent.

Budgeting insurance premiums; purchase of long-term policies.—Insurance contracts, other than life, are ordinarily issued for a single year. Upon request, however, such policies may be issued for terms of two, three, four, or five years. Such a procedure results in a considerable saving in gross premiums. For example, in fire insurance, if the original premium is the amount shown in the first column of the following table, the premium for other terms will be the amount shown in the respective columns.

TERM POLICY RATES

One-year Premium	*Two-year Premium*	*Three-year Premium*	*Four-year Premium*	*Five-year Premium*
.10	.175	.25	.325	.40
.25	.438	.625	.813	1.00
.50	.875	1.25	1.625	2.00
1.00	1.75	2.50	3.25	4.00

The term that will be the most economical in any given instance can be said to depend upon the rate of interest which could be earned on the prepaid premiums if they were retained in the business.

The disadvantages of paying premiums for terms longer than one year may be largely eliminated by either of the following methods:

1. Budgeting premiums. By properly scheduling the time at which each policy is to come due, the same amount may be paid each year, yet each premium will represent a term longer than one year.

2. Finance companies will advance the portion of the premium applicable to the term beyond one year, at a charge which will still leave a worth-while saving. See your broker about this service.

Savings resulting from frequent appraisals.—Frequent appraisals of insured property may result in considerable savings in premiums. Since, in the event of a loss, only the actual amount thereof is recoverable, it is folly to carry insurance for an amount in excess of the value of the property insured. But at the same time, coinsurance clauses (see page 1257 for further explanation) generally compel the policyholder to carry insurance to at least 80 per cent of the value of the insured property, under penalty of reducing the amount recoverable in event of a partial loss. The problem is further intensified by the fact that values are constantly changing. For example, a prominent engineering concern has estimated that an average building which was worth $150,000 in April, 1932, had increased in value to $200,000 in March, 1934, but was worth only $194,000 in June, 1935. Consequently, if the assured is to be fully covered, without at the same time paying for unneeded insurance, it is advisable that expert appraisements be made each year.

Reducing the cost of insurance by means of improvements reducing the risk.—In many lines of insurance, rates are based on "schedules." From a basic rate certain sums are added for defects below the average, or subtracted for improvements above the average. A comparison of the amount which can be saved over a period of a few years with the cost of making the necessary improvements will often disclose that such improvements form a highly profitable investment.

The outstanding economic justification for agents' and brokers' commissions is the ability of these men to point out to the assured the ways and means by which he can reduce the cost of his insurance by improving the risk. The assured, therefore, should not hesitate to call upon his broker or agent for information pertaining to specific improvements which he can make, and the savings to be realized therefrom; brokers and agents are able and willing to offer this service to their clients without charge.

Savings effected by application of the deductible principle.—This principle, as indicated in the section on "self-insurance," is closely allied with assumption of risk and excess loss insurance (see page 1257 for further explanation). Inasmuch as administrative expenses in connection with minor losses are very high, and since a greater moral hazard exists where an insurance company assumes responsibility for all losses, no matter how trivial, large savings can often be effected by the application of the deductible principle without sacrifice of any essential insurance protection.

The effect of a deductible clause is to limit the liability of the insurance company to large losses, and to render the assured liable for all small losses, as well as a small part of any large loss. For example, in automobile collision insurance, in the event of a loss of $200 under a policy containing a $50 deductible clause, the company will be liable for only $150; while if the loss does not exceed $50, the assured will have to assume all liability.

Persons carrying insurance other than fire should ask their broker about the savings that they may effect by application of the deductible principle.

Savings effected by the three-fourths value clause.—Under the three-fourths value clause the policyholder cannot recover more than three-fourths of the actual value of his property at the time of a loss, regardless of the amount of insurance that may be carried. For example, if a building worth $100,000 were insured for $90,000 under a policy containing a three-fourths value clause, then, assuming that the value of the building is still $100,000 at the time of a loss, the insured would be paid the following amounts under the policy:

(1) If the building were completely destroyed........... $75,000
(2) If ¾ of the value were destroyed $75,000
(3) If ½ of the value were destroyed $50,000

Where the policyholder does not deem it practicable or desirable to insure more than three fourths of the value of his property, a three-fourths value clause may be advantageously inserted in the policy. Inquire of your broker or agent as to the possible savings that you will effect by following such a course.

Savings effected by the three-fourths loss clause.—This clause is often confused with coinsurance clauses. However, its effect is entirely different, since under a coinsurance clause, the assured can recover the full amount of every loss if a proper amount of insurance is carried, while under a three-fourths loss clause, not more than three fourths of the amount of any loss can be recovered, regardless of the amount of insurance carried. In short, the assured must pay one fourth of every loss.

A three-fourths *loss* clause differs from a three-fourths *value* clause in that the loss clause applies to all losses, partial and total, while the value clause does not affect the amount recoverable until the loss exceeds three fourths of the value of the insured property.

Where the assured wishes to practice a limited amount of self-insurance, use of a three-fourths loss clause may result in premium savings out of all proportion to the reduction in the amount of insurance protection which is sacrificed. Consult your local agent or broker as to the possible savings that may be realized through the use of a three-fourths loss clause.

When purchasing insurance under an experience rating plan, do not reveal the fact to persons covered.—This principle can be best described by illustration. In the automobile field, many employers have found that salesmen who do not know that the employer has purchased public liability and property damage insurance present fewer claims for accidents occurring while they are engaged on the business of the employer than do salesmen of other firms (or even of the same firm) who possess such knowledge. Consequently, premiums can be kept lower by not revealing to employees the fact that third parties are protected against loss through negligence of the employee while he is engaged in the business of the employer.

Points to investigate in choosing an insurance company.—Before insurance is placed with any particular company, the following points with regard to the company may be investigated.

1. *Financial stability of the company.*—If the company is a stock company, obtain its most recent financial statement. In analyzing

the financial statement, compare the income from premiums and investments with the disbursements. Also, study the kind and quality of the securities composing the assets, the ratio of the total surplus and capital to the liabilities, and the ratio of the total assets to the total outstanding insurance.

If the company is a mutual company, follow the same procedure as that given for stock companies. In addition, ascertain whether or not you will be liable for assessments; whether the company charges a redundant premium, and operates on the reserve principle; or whether it charges a premium that is barely adequate to meet its ordinary losses, and depends on assessments to meet its extraordinary losses.

2. *Record of the company for paying losses promptly.*—The amount of time required to investigate and settle a loss depends to a great extent upon the type of insurance involved, whether the loss is total or partial, and whether the assured kept adequate records. Reliable companies attempt to settle just claims as quickly as possible after presentation without quibbling over minor details.

3. *Services offered by the company that tend to reduce or eliminate the hazard.*—Prevention is just as important (and in some lines more important) as reimbursement for loss. Some companies maintain adequate, well-trained, and well-equipped inspection staffs; others do little or no prevention work. Inspection services are particularly important in compensation insurance, and in the various lines under the general titles of liability and boiler insurance.

4. *Liberality of the contract.*—Many clauses may be inserted or omitted that will change either the extent of the coverage granted by any policy, or the amount of reimbursement following any loss, or both. Such clauses naturally have a direct effect upon the cost of the insurance. Should two contracts, apparently the same, be offered at substantially different premiums, the assured should be sure to compare the contracts carefully in order to ascertain if there is any basic difference in the coverage offered.

5. *Cost of the contract.*—In property and liability insurance, only the current premium need be considered. However, if the company is a mutual, the possibility of dividends or assessments should not be overlooked.

In life insurance, the usual contract extends over a much longer period than in property insurance. Consequently, the rate of return earned by the company on its investments, the amount of surplus, and the ratio of actual deaths to the number expected may be more important than the quoted premiums for the first year, except in the case of nonparticipating contracts.

Self-insurance; its advantages and dangers.—The term "self-insurance" is used in many senses by the insuring public. Depending upon the person applying the term, it may mean:

1. No insurance.
2. An attempt to build up certain reserves, which in turn may be either segregated from, or mixed with, the ordinary assets of the business.
3. The scientific application of insurance principles, the maintenance of an adequate segregated reserve, and constant effort to reduce losses.

In all cases self-insurance is distinguished from private insurance by the fact that the assured does not *transfer* the "risk" (that is, the chance of financial loss) to a professional risk-bearer, but assumes all risks himself. The advantages of self-insurance, of course, arise from alleged savings in administration expenses and the elimination of premiums.

The temptation to use self-insurance is often so great that many persons succumb to its lures and are only awakened when a loss occurs by the realization that they possess no insurance whatever. The very nature of insurance involves the distribution of risk and the application of the law of averages; unless some basis exists upon which to distribute the risk and to apply the law of averages, there can be no insurance in the proper sense of the word, regardless of the presence or absence of reserves.

Successful self-insurance.—The only form of self-insurance that will prove successful is that of the third type; it must involve more than the mere assumption of risk. Consequently, its proper use is limited to large enterprises that have numerous units to insure. Furthermore, each unit should be located so that the respective units are not subject to the conflagration hazard (that is, loss of all units by a single occurrence of the event insured against). A third requisite of self-insurance is that all units be of approximately equal value. If self-insurance is applied where the units are not of equal value, private insurance should be obtained to cover the values in excess of the average; otherwise a single large loss may wipe out the whole insurance reserve. The fourth requirement for the successful operation of a self-insurance fund is that it be embarked upon slowly; the assured should not attempt in any one year to cover by self-insurance more than 5 per cent to 8 per cent of the total value of the risk; complete assumption of the risk should not take place, therefore, in less than twelve to twenty years.

In general, there are those who feel that a business enterprise which owns a minimum of twenty-five widely separated units of approximately equal value has the minimum requirements to self-insure against the hazards involved in the destruction of the property itself. On the other hand, it is said that no attempt should be made to self-insure the compensation hazard unless a minimum of 200 employees are regularly employed, inasmuch as a wide divergence exists between the possible minimum and maximum losses that may result from an accident.

Points to consider in deciding whether to self-insure.—In deciding whether or not to transfer any cover from private carriers to a self-insurance fund, the assured should consider the following factors:

1. The maximum possible loss as compared to the amount of loss that the company is prepared to meet readily.

2. Possible legal expenses for the defense of suits that the insurance companies promise to defend under practically all liability (and some property) insurance covers.

3. Whether or not inspection, collection, and other services that the insurance company guarantees under some forms of contracts will be curtailed, extended, or remain unchanged under the self-insurance program. The assured should remember that a curtailment of such services often results in a material increase in losses.

4. The potential cost of:

(*a*) Setting up the fund on a secure and satisfactory basis, which will probably require the services of an insurance expert.

(*b*) Administration expenses.

5. The amount that can be earned by the self-insurance fund if invested in conservative securities which are readily marketable in case of a loss.

6. The nature of the risk and the property to be insured. For example, no greater loss can occur from the collision or theft of an

automobile than is involved in the value of the motor vehicle, but the possible loss through liability to third parties for destruction of life and property by the automobile extends into at least six figures.

7. The number of losses that are likely to be incurred within a relatively short period (such as a year).

Very often a business may safely self-insure the common, ordinary losses that may be expected in the normal course of business, and purchase so-called *excess loss insurance* to protect itself against the extraordinary losses. Under such policies the insurance company does not become liable until a loss exceeds a specified amount, and then for the excess only. Application of the same principle is also made under *deductible* policies, of which the automobile deductible collision clause is probably the best example.

What types of insurance are most important.—Athough an answer to this question that will be applicable to every business cannot be given, the results of an "Insurance Buying Practices" survey conducted by the National Association of Credit Men indicate that the following lines of insurance, in the order named, are the most important to the average businessman.

INSURANCE BUYING PRACTICES

I *Coverage*	II *Per Cent of Total Businesses Which Need Coverage*	III *Per Cent of Those in Col. II Who Have Coverage*
Fire	100	96
Compensation or Employer's Liability	100	91
Automobile Public Liability and Property Damage	100	74
General Public Liability	100	71
Robbery, Burglary, or Hold-up	100	58
Auto Fire and Theft	100	52
Forgery or Check Alteration	100	50
Windstorm	100	41
Explosion	100	35
Automobile Collision	100	30
Riot, Strike, and Civil Commotion	100	29
Truck Shipment	91	18
Rail Shipment	87	12
Truck Public Liability and Property Damage	76	96
Truck Fire and Theft	76	86
Nonownership Public Liability	76	63
Parcel Post (private, not Government)	76	40

INSURANCE BUYING PRACTICES (*Cont.*)

I *Coverage*	II *Per Cent of Total Businesses Which Need Coverage*	III *Per Cent of Those in Col. II Who Have Coverage*
Truck Collision	76	35
Schedule Fidelity Bonds	75	39
Power Plant Insurance	70	66
Salesmen's Samples	63	10
Sprinkler Leakage	58	64
Use and Occupancy	55	39
Individual Fidelity Bonds	48	63
Profits and Commissions	45	25
Rent and Rental Value	45	17

2. LAW GOVERNING INSURANCE POLICIES

Conflicts between printed provisions and endorsements.—Since standard insurance policies are general contracts, endorsements are frequently added to such policies in order to adapt them to the specific needs of the assured. Very often such endorsements are in conflict with other provisions of the same policy. Where such a difference in meaning exists, the superimposed or endorsed portions of the contract (whether written in longhand, typewritten, stamped, or printed on a separate sheet and attached) control the standard provisions of the contract, and on the theory that they represent the most recent agreement between the parties, only such endorsements are considered in interpreting the policy.

Interpretation of an insurance policy where ambiguities exist.—When the wording of any clause or phrase of an insurance contract, whether such clause or phrase is contained in an endorsement or a provision of the contract, lends itself to more than one interpretation, the courts have generally tended to give the benefit of the doubt to the assured, and reject that construction which limits the liability of the insurance company. Moreover, when a literal construction will lead to manifest injustice to the assured, and a liberal but nevertheless reasonable interpretation will prevent injustice by not requiring an impossibility, the courts will adopt the latter construction because the parties are presumed, when the language used by them permits, to have intended a reasonable and not an unreasonable result. And in any event, if the language of an insurance policy is not as clear and unequivocal as it might be, and therefore fairly susceptible of two meanings, one of which is contended for by the assured, such language generally will be construed against the insurance company, and in favor of the policyholder.

If an ambiguity exists because of two clauses of an insurance policy being so repugnant that they cannot stand together (both clauses being provisions, and neither one constituting an endorsement), the courts usually interpret the policy as though the first of such clauses (that is, the one which will normally be read first by a person reading the contract from beginning to end) were the only one appearing therein, and as though the second did not exist.

Violation of a policy; is policy again valid when violation ceases?—The answer to this question depends upon the construction given to insurance contracts by the courts of the state wherein the insured property is located (or, in some cases, in the state wherein the policyholder is domiciled). In general, the courts hold that if, after a violation, the conditions of the policy are again complied with, the policy revives, and is in full force and effect, even though the insurance company never consented to the violation. Thus the courts of New York and Pennsylvania hold that if a policyholder vacates his building for a period exceeding that permitted by the policy, and without the consent of the insurance company, the policy is void during the period of vacancy, but if afterwards the building is again occupied and a loss occurs, the insurance company would be liable. In a few states, however, a policy once voided remains so until the insurance company consents to its restoration.

If any provision of an insurance policy is violated, the policyholder should consult with his broker or agent as to the advisability of obtaining appropriate endorsements from the insurance company.

Legal status of brokers.—A broker is considered the agent of the policyholder, and not of the insurance company. Consequently, knowledge on the part of the broker does not constitute knowledge on the part of the insurance company until transmitted by the broker to the company. Likewise, should the broker neglect to turn over a premium to the insurance company, the policy may be void. In many states, however, including New York, the broker is considered the representative of the company for the purpose of premium collections, particularly where credit has been extended.

Opinion of agent not binding on insurance company.—Insured persons often inquire of the agent as to the meaning of particular clauses of the insurance policy. The courts have generally held that the opinion of the agent as to the legal effect of any provision of a policy is not binding on the insurance company, on the theory that a mere opinion does not change old nor create new obligations. Consequently, the assured should consult his agent carefully when in doubt as to the meaning of any provision, and thereafter have the insurance company add a clarifying clause to the contract, if necessary.

Oral waiver of policy provisions by agent is not binding.—Notwithstanding that the standard fire contract, and many other insurance covers, specifically state that "no one shall have power to waive any provision or condition of this policy except as by the terms of this policy may be the subject of agreement added hereto, nor shall any such provision or condition be held to be waived unless such waiver shall be in writing added hereto," many courts have held that an oral waiver by the agent of the insurance company is valid and binding on the company. The courts have been particularly prone to uphold such oral waivers where the agent was more than just a soliciting or collecting agent. However, the United States Supreme Court has departed from the rulings formerly so generally accepted by the state courts, and repudiated the doctrine as fundamentally unsound. Many of the states have now repudiated the doctrine, and refuse to recognize a waiver unless endorsed on the policy in writing. Consequently, the assured should protect himself by sending the policies involved to the agent of the insurance company for proper endorsement.

Warranties and representations by the assured.—A warranty is a statement which, if subsequently proved false, will void the policy regardless of importance. On the other hand, a representation is a statement which need only be substantially correct, and to avoid the payment of a claim, the insurance company must prove that the statement was both false and material. A statement is ordinarily considered as material if, had the insurance company been aware of the facts involved, the company would not have issued the policy, or would not have issued it in the existing form or at the existing premium.

Most of the states have now enacted laws that declare warranties to be illegal in insurance policies and class all statements made by the assured as representations.

Assignment of an insurance policy.—Inasmuch as a policy of insurance is a personal contract, the courts have upheld the insurance companies in their demand that the consent of the company must be obtained to the transfer by assignment, before a loss, of a property insurance contract. Consequently, where the assured assigns his interest in a policy prior to a loss without the consent of the insurer, the policy becomes null and void. However, this does not preclude the assured from assigning his right to the proceeds of a policy of insurance *after* a loss has been incurred, since the right to such proceeds is considered as a chose in action.

Territorial limits on property insurance policies.—Practically all insurance contracts written on property which is subject to loss outside of the territorial limits of the United States and Canada contain a clause that the company is not liable, in the absence of a provision to the contrary, for a loss occurring outside of the United States and Canada. For example, the usual automobile policy does not protect the assured without special endorsement while he is driving his car in Mexico.

"Other insurance" on the same property.—The standard fire-insurance policy, and most other forms of property insurance, state that unless otherwise provided by an agreement in writing added to the policy, the insurance company will not be liable while any other insurance (that is, another policy protecting the same interest, in the same property, against the same hazard), whether or not valid, is carried on the same property and interest. This clause has been declared reasonable and valid by the courts. It is not designed to prevent the policyholder from obtaining sufficient insurance, or to prevent him from obtaining insurance with another company, but only to lessen the moral hazard by making it more difficult to obtain insurance for a greater amount than the insured property is worth.

The assured may protect himself against the operation of the "other insurance" clause by either:

1. Obtaining the consent of the insurance company each time that he wishes to take out additional insurance.

2. Securing from the insurance company an endorsement to the standard policy permitting additional insurance at will. Such endorsements are issued without extra charge.

Each policy is an independent contract.—Every policy of insurance is regarded as a new and independent contract, the construction of which is not dependent upon the terms of any policy that preceded it, unless the policyholder and the insurance company have expressly agreed to the contrary. Where a contract is "renewed," however, the general rule is that such renewal constitutes a continuation of all the terms and conditions of the original contract, unless otherwise specifically provided.

Doctrine of entirety of contract.—Frequently several items of property, such as several buildings, or the building and contents, or several automobiles, are insured under one policy, and the premium paid in one sum. In such cases the courts of a majority of the states have usually held that the contract is to be considered as one and inseparable, and therefore, if violated as to one item, the entire contract will be void. Thus, where the building and contents were covered under one policy, and a provision of the policy in regard to encumbrances was violated as to the building, the court held that the assured could recover for neither the building nor the contents, for the contract was a unit and, if violated as to one item, it was also violated as to all others. Conversely, where two buildings were insured under one policy, and the insurance on one became void because of violation of the vacancy permit, the court held that if the insurance company admitted liability as to one building, it was also liable for loss on the other.

Recently, however, the courts have tended to consider the nature of the risk in applying the doctrine of entirety of the contract. If the several items covered are widely separated and not related to one another so as to be destroyed by a single disaster, and a breach as to one part of the contract cannot affect the other parts, the courts of many of the states have usually considered the contract as divisible. Under this interpretation a breach of a condition affecting only one class of property will not void the policy as to the rest of the property.

Doctrine of insurable interest.—Under American law, to constitute a valid contract of insurance, the assured must have an "insurable interest" in the subject matter covered. Otherwise, the policy is classed as a "wagering policy," and no action can be taken under it in any court of the United States, or in any court of the several states. However, it is usually not necessary for such interest to exist at the time that the policy is issued; if an insurable interest subsists for a time during the life of the policy, and again at the time of the loss, it is sufficient. In life insurance, however, the general rule is that an insurable interest need exist only at the time that the insurance is taken out.

Briefly, a person has an insurable interest in the subject matter insured whenever he will directly suffer financial loss by damage thereto, or destruction thereof. Insurable interest in the matter of life and health exists to any amount in the assured's own life, and in the lives of others where a relationship arises by reason of monetary advancements (such as debtor-creditor), ties of marriage, blood, or affinity, and the policyholder expects some benefit from the continuance of the life of the assured.

Insurable interest may assume hundreds of forms and may exist under varying conditions. While such an interest must be neither illegal nor immoral, it may be either legal or equitable. Title to the property insured is not necessary. The interest may be either conditional or contingent; insurable interest does not imply ownership of property, or even a present or future right to its possession. The only requisite is that some expectation of profit or benefit must arise from the interest insured and be present at the time of the loss. Thus an owner or part-owner, one who is in possession of property, custodians of property entrusted to their care, creditors in the property of the debtor, debtors in property seized for debt, consignees and consignors of goods, stockholders in corporate property, and tenants for life, have an insurable interest in such property to the extent of the monetary damages which they may sustain by reason of its destruction.

Nevertheless, inasmuch as the standard fire policy, and many other forms of insurance, specify that the interest of the assured must be that of "unconditional and sole ownership," unless otherwise provided by agreement in writing added to the contract, the assured should disclose the exact nature of his interest to his broker or agent at the time that he applies for the insurance in order that such broker or agent may attach the proper endorsements to the policy contract. Similarly, if any change takes place in the nature of the policyholder's interest during the life of the policy, the broker or agent should be immediately notified.

Protection of beneficiaries of life insurance from claims of creditors.—Practically all of the states, either by statute or by court decision, exempt the proceeds of life insurance payable to a specifically named beneficiary, including the cash-surrender value of the policy, from the claims of creditors of the assured. In addition, most of the states have now enacted a provision exempting all or part of the proceeds of life insurance held by an insurance company (and in some instances by a trustee) from the claims of creditors of the beneficiary, where the assured has provided that such proceeds are not to be available to creditors of the beneficiary.

For example, the law of Pennsylvania provides as follows:

> Whenever under the terms of an annuity or policy of life insurance, or under any written agreement supplemental thereto . . . the proceeds are retained by such company at maturity or otherwise, no person entitled to any part of such proceeds, or any installment or interest due or to become due thereon, shall be permitted to commute, anticipate, encumber, alienate, or assign the same, or any part thereof, if such permission is expressly withheld by the terms of such policy or supplemental agreement; and if such policy or supplemental agreement so provides, no payments of interest or of principal shall be in any way subject to such person's debts, contracts, or engagements, nor to any judicial processes to levy upon or attach the same for payment thereof. . . .

Under such laws as that quoted above, it is possible for the assured to protect his beneficiaries from levy by their creditors against the proceeds of or income from the insurance. In short, by proper provision, the assured may insure his insurance. An attorney should be consulted as to the law of any particular jurisdiction, and as to the type of provision that will comply with the terms of the law.

3. TYPES OF INSURANCE POLICIES

Insurance division.—Generally speaking, there are two types of insurance:

1. Insurance that pays the person insured money because of some loss which the insured has suffered.

2. Insurance that prevents the person insured from suffering a financial loss because of some circumstance or event, by stepping in and paying such money for and in behalf of the insured to a third party.

The first is usually known as property insurance, and the second as liability, or third-party, insurance.

Below are discussed some general forms that property insurance may take. For a detailed discussion of liability insurance and the specific forms which it may take, see page 1266.

Adaptability of insurance.—Insurance may be adapted to the needs of any particular individual, firm, or corporation by means of:

1. Purchase of the basic policy in a *form* that is advantageous to the assured.

2. Endorsements attached to a basic policy.

Endorsements usually limit or extend the risk otherwise assumed by the insurance company. The form of the policy detracts or adds to the ease with which the assured may:

1. Secure coverage on additional property purchased after the original policy was issued.

2. Cancel insurance on property that the assured no longer owns.

3. Adjust the amount of insurance to the value of the property.

4. Transfer property from one location to another without affecting the insurance coverage.

Specific policies.—Property insured under a specific policy must be:

1. Described in the policy in such a manner as to be identifiable from all other property.

2. Located at a definite, fixed location.

3. Insured for a specified sum.

A change cannot be made in any of these three fundamental requirements without the consent of the insurance company. Furthermore, if the policy covers more than one article, each article is insured for a specified sum. For example, under a specific fire-insurance policy applying to the building, stock, and fixtures of a retail merchant, the building might be insured for $50,000, the stock for $20,000, and the fixtures for $5,000. The total insurance would therefore be $75,000. Yet, if the actual value of the stock was $30,000 at the time of a loss, and such stock was totally destroyed, if the fixtures were damaged to the extent of $3,000, and the building to $30,000 (total damage, $63,000), the assured could recover a total of only $53,000 ($30,000 on the building, $20,000 on the stock, and $3,000 on the fixtures). Furthermore, such recoverable loss might be further reduced as the result of the operation of a coinsurance clause (for explanation of coinsurance clause, see page 1257).

Blanket policies.—A blanket policy may cover either:

1. The building and its contents, without any definite amount of insurance being assigned to either kind of property. Thus, if in the example given in the preceding paragraph the assured had placed $75,000 of insurance on "building and contents, blanket" and had suffered the same loss, he could have recovered in full, or $63,000.
2. Two or more buildings at definite locations (together with the contents of such buildings), without any definite proportion of the insurance being assigned to any particular location.

General cover contract, or reporting insurance.—Essentially, a general cover contract (often called reporting insurance) is not a policy of insurance, but rather an agreement on the part of the insurance company to furnish insurance in such amounts as the assured may need on a month-to-month—sometimes week-to-week or day-to-day—basis. The contract is usually an automatic reporting interim binder and provides a convenient method for obtaining adequate protection on fluctuating stocks of goods in stores and warehouses. Ordinarily the contract is issued only to cover risks involving five or more locations. A limit is usually specified in the policy as to the maximum amount for which the insurance company will be liable at any one location.

The general cover contract is designed to prevent underinsurance or overinsurance by automatically increasing or decreasing the amount of insurance applying at any given location—within the limits specified in the policy—to correspond with fluctuations in the value of the property insured. The premium is computed at the end of each specified period by ascertaining the average amount at risk during the period and applying the standard rate to such amount. Short-rate cancellations, and a great deal of detail work that would otherwise be encountered if specific insurance were to be increased or decreased, are thus entirely avoided.

Excess loss insurance.—Ordinarily insurance is concurrent—that is, in case of other insurance on the same property, losses are prorated among the various carriers. Excess loss insurance, however, does not apply until all other insurance is exhausted, and the loss exceeds a specified sum. This form of insurance is designed to cover only unusual, catastrophic losses, and the premium per $1,000 of insurance is therefore much lower than that on the ordinary primary forms.

Coinsurance clauses.—The insurance companies have added so-called coinsurance clauses to most property-insurance contracts affecting business risks. Such clauses are also sometimes referred to as "average clauses," "reduced-rate average clauses," "percentage-value clauses," "reduced-rate coinsurance clauses," "contribution clauses," and so forth. Regardless of the name applied to it, or the exact reading of the clause, coinsurance provisions have the same general effect.

Coinsurance is a basic principle of fairness in business. Too often it is misunderstood. Without it no equitable distribution of risks and losses by the insurance companies could exist; schedule rating would be impossible; and underwriting would be guesswork. If no coinsurance existed, buyers of insurance, knowing that most losses are partial losses, would always buy only a smaller amount of insurance to take care of these and thus pay a smaller premium. This practice would result in the company paying all the small losses and taking the entire risk of any fire (or other event), small or large, while receiving a premium only for the losses that happen most frequently. The result would be either failure of the companies or tremendous increases in the cost of insurance.

Coinsurance is a mutual agreement between the insured and the insurance company that, in consideration for the company's action in assuming the risk at the premium named, the insured will secure and maintain insurance in an amount at least equal to a specified percentage of the property's total value. Assuming an 80 per cent coinsurance requirement, for instance, the coinsurance clause becomes an agreement between the company and the insured that the insured, on his $10,000 building, will secure and maintain at least $8,000 worth of insurance.

If this requirement is completed by the insured, there is no limitation within the coinsurance clause as to the amount collectible in case of loss.

If, however, the insured does not maintain enough insurance to equal the percentage of total value named in the clause, the wording of the clause expresses a penalty on the insured for this failure. The penalty is this: the insured is considered to have assumed the risk to the extent of the deficit and, in case of loss, shall bear that proportion of the loss himself.

For example, assume that a building worth $100,000 is insured under a policy bearing an 80 per cent coinsurance clause. If the owner carries at least $80,000 of insurance (under one or more policies), he has satisfied the coinsurance requirements and will be paid the full amount of any loss (up to a limit of the amount of insurance, of course). Suppose, however, that he carries only $50,000 of insurance. He has not lived up to the coinsurance requirement; he must suffer the penalty and become an insurer in effect for his portion of the deficit. The company's payment is determined as the proportion of the amount he is carrying ($50,000) to the amount he should have carried to satisfy the coinsurance requirement ($80,000) or five eighths of any loss. His deficit, then, is three eighths, and that is the proportion of every loss which he must suffer himself. The following table shows the operation of the 80 per cent coinsurance clause where less than the required insurance is carried and loss occurs.

LIABILITY OF COMPANY UNDER 80 PER CENT COINSURANCE CLAUSE

Value of Property	*Amount of Insurance Carried*	*Amount Required under Coinsurance*	*% of Any Loss Co. Will Pay*	*Loss*	*Amount Company Pays*
$100,000	$40,000	$80,000	50%	$6,000	$3,000
100,000	40,000	80,000	50	40,000	20,000
100,000	80,000	80,000	100	2,000	2,000
100,000	80,000	80,000	100	90,000	80,000*
100,000	90,000	80,000	100	90,000	90,000
100,000	60,000	80,000	75	10,000	7,500
100,000	40,000	80,000	50	80,000	40,000
100,000	40,000	80,000	50	85,000	40,000*

* Cannot be more than the amount of insurance in any case.

Floater policies.—This type of policy is designed to protect property that is frequently moved about from one location to another. The insurance applies no matter where the property described in the policy may be (except as to places that may be specifically excluded). The wide variety of such property has brought forth a correspondingly wide selection of insurance coverages in floater form.

For instance, in the commercial field, a firm may insure the samples carried by its force of salesmen against loss by burglary and theft wherever the samples may be—in the salesman's car while he is at lunch, in a customer's showroom, in a hotel room, while being shipped to the salesmen en route, and so forth.

Another example of this type of insurance is a floater policy that protects merchandise owned by a firm while it may be in the hands of a processor (and while in transit to and from that place), then while it is sent to a dyer, then while it goes to a dresser, and finally, while on the way to the owner's premises. All the possibilities of loss during the time it is being processed and worked upon are eliminated by means of the policy coverage.

4. FIRE INSURANCE

Protection afforded by the standard fire insurance policy.—The insuring clause of the standard fire insurance policy of New York (which has been adopted without substantial change by nearly all the states) reads as follows:

> The Insurance Company, in consideration of the stipulations herein named and of $-------- Dollars premium, does insure Richard Roe and legal representatives, to the extent of the actual cash value . . . of the property at the time of loss or damage, but not exceeding the amount which it would cost to repair or replace the same, . . . against all direct loss and damage by fire and by removal from premises endangered by fire, except as herein provided, . . . to the following described property while located and contained as described herein, or pro rata for five days at each proper place to which any of the property shall necessarily be removed for preservation from fire. . . .

Meaning of clauses in the standard fire insurance policy.—Practically every word of the standard fire insurance policy has, at one time or another, been before the courts for interpretation. As a result, it has obtained a definite and exact meaning.

1. *"Direct loss and damage by fire."*—The courts have given a very liberal interpretation to the phrase "direct loss and damage by fire." Practically any loss is covered where fire is the motivating or primary cause. The fire need not be the cause closest in point of time, but it must be possible to trace an unbroken connection between the fire which is alleged to be the cause of the loss, and the event which caused the loss, without the intervention of some new and independent cause. Thus, damage by water, or by the falling wall of an adjoining building, where fire caused such wall to fall, are covered, even though the fire itself never came in contact with the insured premises. Again, a midwestern lumber concern owned a small locomotive that it used to haul timber from the forest. A forest fire burned out a bridge and left the locomotive stranded in the mountains. Although the fire did not injure the locomotive, the court held that inasmuch as the cost of constructing a new bridge would be greater than the value of the locomotive, the locomotive was a total loss, the value of which had been proximately destroyed by fire.

To constitute "fire" within the meaning of the policy, there must be actual ignition and flame. Damage from mere heat and smoke without a flame is not covered. Furthermore, the fire must be a hostile fire; that is, not a friendly fire, which is defined as one that has not left the place intended for it, such as a stove or lamp. The company is liable for the smoke damage done by a hostile fire and damage caused by water or other means of extinguishing the fire.

Property "removed from premises endangered by fire" is covered "pro rata for five days" at any location to which the property is removed for preservation from fire. After the expiration of five days from the time that the property was removed from the premises described in the policy, however, it must be reinsured at its new location. Such coverage includes loss from mishandling during removal, but not from theft (the latter being specifically excluded).

Direct loss from fire is further construed to mean only the damage to the property itself. Contingent and indirect losses are not covered. Thus a slight fire may cause a business to close down, with a resulting loss in profits many times the value of the property actually destroyed. However, unless an endorsement to the contrary is entered on the policy, only the damage to the tangible property actually destroyed may be recovered. (With regard to covering loss of profits, see "Use and occupancy insurance," page 1297.)

2. *"Actual cash value of the property destroyed."*—The fire-insurance policy is a contract of indemnity; it is not intended that the assured should recover more than he has lost, but that he shall be placed, economically, in the same position as he occupied prior to the fire. To this end, the policy specifies that, regardless of the face value of the policy, and irrespective of whether the loss is total or partial, the assured may recover only to "the extent of the actual cash value (ascertained with proper deductions for depreciation) of the property at the time of loss or damage," but in any event, "not exceeding the amount which it would cost to repair or replace the same with material of like kind or quality within a reasonable time after such loss or damage, without allowance for any increased cost of repair by reason of any ordinance or law regulating construction." Furthermore, the company reserves the option to "repair, rebuild, or replace the property lost or damaged with other of like kind and quality." The assured, however, may not surrender his proprietary rights to property that has been partially destroyed, and claim a total loss, inasmuch as the policy provides that "there can be no abandonment to this company of the property described."

Since it would be impracticable for insurance companies to make accurate valuations of property at the time that a risk is assumed, and since values fluctuate from year to year, the above provisions of the policy represent a sound application of the true doctrine of insurance. Nevertheless, a number of states, particularly those in the west and south, have passed "valued-policy laws." Generally, such laws provide that in the absence of intentional fraud, the amount recoverable under the policy in case of a total loss is the face value of the policy.

The "actual cash value" of the property destroyed is a question of fact to be determined by appraisal and agreement with the insurance company. As a general rule, the actual cash value is not the cost of the property, nor the cost less depreciation, but the cost of replacement (without allowance for any increased cost by reason of any ordinance or law), less the depreciation. Thus, if a building erected in 1922 at a cost of $75,000 was completely destroyed in 1937, and if, at the time of the loss, the cost of replacing the building (the law regulating construction not having been changed) was $100,000, and the rate of depreciation was 2 per cent per year, the actual cash value of the property destroyed would be $100,000, less depreciation of $30,000 (2 per cent of $100,000 equals $2,000 per year, times 15 years), or approximately $70,000.

In the case of manufactured goods, it has been stated that the actual cash value is the "wholesale price, less unincurred expenses and unearned profits."

Fire insurance policy is a personal contract.—The fire insurance contract states that it "does insure ------------ and legal representatives." It does not "insure the property." It follows, therefore, that the fire insurance policy is a personal contract, agreeing to indemnify the assured against loss through destruction of the described property. The insurance does not follow the property in event of a change in ownership unless the company gives its consent. Such a rule is necessary since, otherwise, a given property would remain insured even though it passed from an honest and careful owner to a dishonest and careless one, although it is apparent that such a change would increase the risk tremendously. Consequently, the insurance company, in fairness to itself and other assureds, requires that its consent be obtained to any assignment of interest under the policy, or to any change of interest, title, or possession of the subject of the insurance. Violation of these requirements voids the policy. As a rule, the company's consent to any change is readily given whenever requested.

Risks excluded in fire insurance policy.—The insuring clause of the fire insurance policy states that it protects against direct loss and damage by fire, "except as herein provided." The exceptions are set out in another section of the policy as follows:

1. The company is not liable for loss or damage caused directly or indirectly by invasion, insurrection, riot, civil war or commotion, military or usurped power, theft, and neglect of the assured to use all reasonable means to save and preserve the property at and after a fire or when the property is endangered by fire in neighboring premises.

All except the last of these exceptions—neglect of the assured—can be covered by other forms of insurance. See "Riot and civil commotion insurance," page 1297.

2. Unless otherwise provided by agreement in writing added to the policy, the insurance company is not liable for loss or damage occurring under the following circumstances:

(*a*) The insurance company is not liable while the assured possesses any other insurance, whether or not valid, covering the same interest in whole or in part. This clause is not designed to prevent the assured from obtaining as much insurance as he desires in as many companies as he wishes, but to make overinsurance more difficult and to reduce the moral hazard. When the additional insurance is justified, permission to obtain additional insurance is readily granted. In other instances, where the assured is reputable, the company will endorse the policies in advance, permitting the assured to obtain other insurance at will.

In practice, where all insurance is placed through a single broker or agent, no difficulty arises from this clause. Where different brokers are employed, however, the assured must be careful to inform all parties of all other insurance covering the same interest. Otherwise, all of the insurance may be void.

(*b*) The insurance company is not liable while the hazard is increased by any means within the control or knowledge of the assured. This clause forbids the assured to change the physical structure of the insured building, or to alter the uses for which it was employed at the time that the policy was written, in any manner which would increase the hazard of fire, without securing a permit to do so from the insurance company and paying any extra premium which may be required. An increase in hazard also occurs if any tenant, within the knowledge of the assured, commences to carry on any more hazardous activity after the policy is issued than he was engaged in at the time of such issuance.

If the assured is in doubt as to whether any particular incident or activity constitutes an increase in hazard, he should consult with his broker or agent.

(*c*) The insurance company is not liable while mechanics are employed in the building, altering or repairing the described premises, beyond a period of fifteen days. If such mechanics are employed beyond a period of fifteen days, it is necessary to obtain the consent of the insurance company; otherwise the insurance will be void during the remainder of the time that the building is undergoing such repairs or alterations.

(*d*) The insurance company is not liable while gas or vapor is generated on the premises; or while there is kept, used, or allowed on the described premises fireworks, greek fire, phosphorous, explosives, benzine, gasoline, or any other petroleum product of greater inflammability than kerosene oil, gunpowder exceeding twenty-five pounds, or kerosene oil exceeding five barrels. The presence of any such substances on the premises will void the policy while they remain thereon, unless the assured notifies the insurance company thereof, and pays any extra premium required. However, the weight of authority from court decisions is to the effect that the use or presence of such an article does not void the policy if the prohibited article is a regular part of the stock of the assured, or is known to be regularly used in the business. Thus, where a policy was issued to cover "articles usually kept for sale in retail drug stores," it was held that the presence of reasonable amounts of gasoline, benzine, ether, and so forth, which were regularly kept for sale, did not void the policy, even though the policy provided otherwise.

(*e*) The insurance company is not liable, if the property insured be a manufacturing establishment, while it is operated in whole or in part between the hours of 10 P.M. and 5 A.M., or while it ceases to be operated beyond a period of ten days. Either of these conditions, in the case of manufacturing establishments, is deemed to increase the risk. Hence, if the plant is operated between the hours specified, or if the plant is closed for a period in excess of ten days, a special endorsement permitting such operation or cessation should be obtained from the insurance company.

(*f*) The insurance company is not liable while a described building is vacant or unoccupied beyond a period of ten days. Unoccupied buildings are considered poor risks. However, in some instances, an endorsement may be obtained permitting the building to remain vacant. Such endorsements are readily issued for periods of short duration.

(*g*) The insurance company is not liable for damage caused by explosion or lightning, unless fire ensue, and then for the loss or damage done by fire only. This provision, at times, presents difficult cases for adjustment, since where a fire follows an explosion, it is frequently impossible to ascertain the amount of damage caused by the explosion, as separate from the loss caused by the fire.

(*h*) The insurance company is not liable for damage to described property while such property is encumbered by a chattel mortgage. However, property not encumbered by a chattel mortgage is not affected. By special agreement with the insurance company, this restriction may be removed.

3. If a building, or any material part thereof, falls, except as the result of fire, all insurance on such building and its contents ceases at once. This provision is inserted on the theory that when the insured building has fallen in part or in whole, it is no longer the original building that burns, but simply the debris. The two most common causes of falling buildings are windstorms and earthquakes. Both of these risks may be covered by separate insurance.

Kinds of property excluded in fire insurance policy.—In addition to excluding losses due to the risks described in the preceding paragraphs, the standard fire-insurance policy excludes certain kinds of property from coverage.

1. Accounts, bills, currency, deeds, evidences of debt, money, notes, or securities are not covered. Such property is considered to be uninsurable, partly because it affords opportunity for fraud, being subject to easy concealment, and partly because the determination of the value of such articles is difficult, the company being obliged, in most cases, to depend upon the statement of the assured. See, however, "Accounts receivable insurance," page 1300.

2. Bullion, manuscripts, mechanical drawings, dies, or patterns are not covered unless an endorsement is added to the policy.

Endorsements to fire insurance policy.—The standard fire insurance policy was necessarily designed to meet a general situation. It applies to circumstances common to most property owners. However, it often fails to meet the exact needs of the individual policyholder.

Endorsements have been designed to meet practically any situation imaginable, in order to adapt the standard policy to the specific needs of each policyholder. Such endorsements may:

1. Extend the insurance coverage by providing that risks otherwise excluded are to be assumed by the insurance company.

2. Limit or distribute the indemnity otherwise provided by the contract. Practically all policies covering mercantile or manufacturing risks, in order to establish equity among the various policyholders, are endorsed with 80 per cent—sometimes 90 per cent and 100 per cent—coinsurance clauses (for explanation of coinsurance clauses, see page 1257). In other instances, in order to reduce the moral hazard, a three-fourths loss clause (see page 1243) may be endorsed on the policy. If the property is situated in different localities, a so-called "distribution" or "pro-rata" clause may be used to limit the amount of insurance applicable to any one location (see "Blanket policies," page 1256).

3. Warrant that the assured, in consideration of a reduced premium, will take certain steps to reduce the hazard. Such an endorsement might provide for the proper maintenance of fire-protective devices, or limit vacancy of a mercantile or manufacturing risk to only one third of the establishment.

4. Permit an increase in the hazard that is not contemplated by the standard policy.

5. LIABILITY INSURANCE

Purpose of liability insurance.—The law imposes upon everyone the duty of taking reasonable care and precaution to avoid damaging the property, or injuring the person, of others. When the negligence of one party is responsible for a loss suffered by another, the injured party is entitled to recover damages from the negligent person, firm, or corporation. Since such damages may amount to many thousands of dollars for a single accident, business concerns are greatly in need of some form of protection against such unforeseen financial losses. Such protection may be obtained through liability insurance (sometimes called third-party insurance).

As a general rule (the exact definition differs from state to state), negligence is the failure to do something that a reasonable and prudent man would do under like conditions, or the commission of an act that a reasonable and prudent man would not do under like circumstances. The question of "what a reasonable and prudent man would do" is usually one for the jury.

A recent case illustrates the application of the doctrine. A customer was standing at a counter in a large New York store about eight feet away from a large plate-glass window when the window crashed without warning. The customer was not struck by the flying glass, but, in the excitement, she was pushed down by the crowd and trampled on. The court held that the storekeeper was negligent in allowing a "condition to exist which caused the window to fall," and was therefore liable to the customer for damages, inasmuch as "the rush or stampede was a normal response to the fear or emotional disturbance which the defendant's [storekeeper's] negligent conduct was a substantial factor in creating."

Types of liability insurance.—Under the general title of liability insurance a variety of policies are written to protect the policyholder against direct or indirect losses arising out of claims or suits based upon the law of negligence. The most prominent forms of liability insurance are:

1. *Workmen's compensation insurance.*—Workmen's compensation insurance covers the employer's liability to his employees under workmen's compensation laws. Forty-seven states have enacted such laws. (For detailed discussion see page 1270.)

2. *Employer's liability insurance.*—Employer's liability insurance is designed to protect the employer in Mississippi, which has not adopted workmen's compensation insurance laws, and also, in those states which do have workmen's compensation laws, to cover the employer's liability to employees not covered by the law. (For further discussion, see page 1273.)

3. *Automobile public liability and automobile property damage liability insurance.*—These policies are designed to protect the owner and operator of an automobile against financial loss from claims for damages arising out of the ownership, maintenance, or operation of such automobile. (For further discussion, see page 1274.)

4. *Manufacturer's public liability insurance.*—This policy protects manufacturers against financial loss from claims for damages brought under the law of negligence, for injuries sustained by any person other than an employee as the result of the alleged negligence of either the manufacturer, his agent, or any of his employees in the conduct of the business.

5. *Contractor's public liability insurance.*—This policy is similar to that issued to manufacturers, except that it applies to contractors.

6. *Owners', landlords', and tenants' public liability insurance.*—

All persons other than manufacturers and contractors may secure protection against damages resulting from legal liability under the law of negligence by purchasing this policy. The policy is similar to that issued to manufacturers.

7. *Elevator public liability insurance.*—This policy protects the owner of a building from financial loss as the result of suits brought to obtain damages for injuries suffered in any elevator accident.

8. *Product public liability insurance.*—This policy protects manufacturers from loss as the result of their legal liability for damages suffered by the public through the use of their product.

9. *Teams public liability insurance.*—The policy protects the owner of teams from loss resulting from suits for damages caused by careless drivers, careless loading or unloading, or frightened and uncontrollable horses.

10. *Theater public liability insurance.*—This is a specialized policy for theater owners protecting against financial loss that may arise as the result of suits brought by the public for injury or alleged injury occurring in the theater.

11. *Garage public liability insurance.*—Like the theater policy, this is a specialized policy designed to meet the many needs of the public garage operator and owner. (For further discussion, see page 1281.)

Standard provisions of liability insurance policies.—The following provisions are common to all liability insurance contracts:

1. A promise on the part of the insurance company to pay all judgments assessed against the policyholder.

2. A promise by the insurance company to serve the policyholder by investigating all claims, negotiating for settlements, defending all suits within the scope of the policy and paying all expenses incurred in connection with such suits, and to reimburse the policyholder for the expense of necessary immediate surgical aid.

3. A promise by the policyholder to give immediate written notice to the company upon the occurrence of any accident covered by the policy, and to aid the company, when so requested, in securing information, evidence, attendance of witnesses, and to render to the company all the co-operation and assistance within his power.

4. A stipulation that the policyholder shall not voluntarily assume any liability and that the insurance company will not be liable for

any settlements or expenditures voluntarily made by the policyholder.

5. A limit of liability that will be assumed by the insurance company of:

(*a*) $5,000 for injuries (or death) to any one individual.

(*b*) $10,000 for injuries (or death) as the result of any one accident, regardless of the number of persons so injured.

These limits may be increased, for an additional premium, to any figure desired. Thus, limits of $10,000 and $20,000, respectively, can be secured for a premium of 12 to 15 per cent more than the basic premium.

A few forms of property insurance that are primarily intended to cover only direct losses also contain a provision making the insurance applicable to indirect losses. For example, power plant insurance of all kinds includes a provision that protects the assured against loss as the result of suits brought against him after an accident, as well as reimbursement for loss to the power plant itself.

Contingent public liability insurance.—Under certain conditions, a contractor may be liable for the negligence of his subcontractor, an owner for the negligence of a contractor employed on his premises, or a landlord for the negligence of his tenant. To protect themselves against such risks, contractors may procure contractor's protective public liability and property damage insurance; the owner of real estate may take out owner's protective liability insurance as a protection against his contingent liability for the acts of a contractor engaged on his premises, and landlord's protective liability to protect against loss arising from contingent liability for damages for which a tenant is primarily liable.

Fiduciaries' liability insurance.—The law is well settled that executors, administrators, trustees, guardians, and other fiduciaries are personally liable for negligence that results in a loss to the fiduciary's principal, or to the trust estate. In some cases fiduciaries have even been held liable for losses that occurred without fault on their part. Until recently insurance was not available to protect the fiduciary against his personal liability for loss to the trust estate, but casualty companies are now offering such protection.

Comprehensive public liability and property damage insurance.—Recently the insurance companies have introduced a form of policy that seeks to provide a new approach to the problem of insuring against financial loss through liabilities imposed by law. The previous descriptions of the various liability policies available exemplify the concept of this form of insurance as it has existed: one policy for each hazard or type of hazard, with that policy excluding coverage for all other forms of loss through legal liability.

The comprehensive liability policy, however, insures the policyholder against all liability losses that occur during the policy term, whether or not such liabilities were existent or apparent at the time the policy was issued. The premium is determined at the end of each policy year by making a charge for the determinable avenues of liability.

This form of all-inclusive insurance should be looked into seriously by every business firm. It represents the most important advance in available protection in many years and provides the first means of protecting against unknown hazards that may appear at any time.

6. WORKMEN'S COMPENSATION INSURANCE

Why workmen's compensation insurance is necessary.—Under the common law an employer is liable, subject to certain defenses, for injuries sustained by his employees through his negligence. By statute, however, every state but Mississippi has abridged or replaced the common-law rule with workmen's compensation laws. Generally these laws provide that every employee is entitled to recover from his employer certain prescribed amounts for injury sustained in the course of his employment. Since the amount of payments that an employer may be required to make within any one year is subject to wide fluctuations, most employers prefer to transfer to an insurance company the obligation to compensate injured employees. Such a transfer is effected by the purchase of workmen's compensation insurance.

Methods of meeting the liabilities imposed by workmen's compensation laws.—The methods that the employer may use to meet the liabilities imposed by the various workmen's compensation insurance laws depend upon the law of the state in which the employer conducts his business. In a majority of the states, however, the employer has a free choice from among several methods; he may choose one of the following:

1. Insurance in a State fund.
2. Insurance with a private insurance company.
3. Self-insurance.
4. Partial self-insurance.

1. *Insurance in a State fund.*—Eighteen states provide a State fund. In six of these states the fund is monopolistic; that is, it operates to the exclusion of private insurance companies. In two states, certain approved risks may be self-insured, but on condition that they contribute to the maintenance of the State-fund system. In the other ten states, insurance in the State fund is voluntary.

Where insurance in a State fund is optional, the employer should carefully investigate the economy and efficiency of such insurance in comparison with insurance with a private insurance company or self-insurance. In several states the experience of some employers has been that insurance in the State fund has not provided prompt claim service, proper treatment of injured workmen, effective accident-prevention service, or an equitable distribution of costs between different industries and the employers included therein; in short, employers insured in some of the State funds have felt that they did not receive everything for which they paid. However, the economy and efficiency of insurance in a State fund naturally varies from state to state. Accordingly, an employer who is contemplating insurance in a State fund should make inquiry among other concerns within the state as to their experience.

2. *Insurance with a private insurance company.*—In all but six states the employer may insure with a private insurance company. The standard workmen's compensation policy provides that the insurance company will:

(*a*) Pay promptly to any person entitled thereto the benefits provided by the workmen's compensation law of the state.

(*b*) Indemnify the employer for loss arising from suits for damages in instances where the employee alleges that the compensation act is not applicable.

(*c*) Protect the worker against loss of benefits resulting from the bankruptcy of the employer.

(*d*) Pay for the benefit of the injured employee the proper cost of medical, surgical, nurse or hospital services, apparatus, appliances, and medicines; and funeral expenses in case of fatal injury.

(*e*) Make necessary inspections of the places of work in order to reduce accidents.

(*f*) Investigate all reported claims.

(*g*) Defend, and pay the costs therefor, all suits brought against the employer-policyholder for damages as a result of injuries to employees, even though such suits are fraudulent.

3. *Self-insurance of the workmen's compensation risk.*—Self-insurance, on proof of solvency, is permitted in most of the states. The requirements of the law vary. In some instances the employer need only demonstrate that he is financially solvent, while in others he must put up a bond or place a specified amount of cash with the state as security to meet all losses.

In estimating the savings to be derived from adoption of a self-insurance scheme for workmen's compensation, the employer should not overlook:

(*a*) The cost of defending his own lawsuits.

(*b*) First aid, hospitalization, and other medical costs.

(*c*) The cost of investigating and adjusting claims.

(*d*) The cost involved in either maintaining, or failing to maintain, an adequate accident-prevention program.

(*e*) The stigma that will attach to him personally should he later become bankrupt and be unable to pay just compensation claims.

4. *Partial self-insurance of the workmen's compensation risk.*—Partial self-insurance is permitted, of course, in all states that permit self-insurance. Under this system the employer assumes the liability for all losses under a specified amount (the limit may be either per accident or per employee), and the excess risk is placed with a private insurance company. This system has many advantages for the financially responsible employer; it enables him to carry his own normal loss risk without becoming subject to staggering losses that would impair the financial stability of the business.

Safety devices and employee education.—Experience has demonstrated that a conscious effort to minimize the number and severity of accidents has worth-while results in the form of savings in premiums. Accident prevention may take either or both of two forms:

1. Installation of safety devices.
2. Education of the worker, including observation to discover dangerous practices or habits.

At present, the general consensus is that while safety devices are invaluable, a logical program of education will result in greater savings than are to be gained from the mere installation of safety devices.

As an outstanding example of what may be accomplished by means of efficient and scientific safety work, the record of the Western Clock Company of LaSalle, Illinois, has been cited. Not a single lost-time accident occurred between December 17, 1931, and January 1, 1935, when the record was reported. When it is considered that during this period, 10,029,681 man-hours of labor were involved, and that hazardous devices, such as power presses, screw machines, and tool-making machines, were constantly used, the record is remarkable.

Another outstanding example is illustrated in the 1940 accident safety report of General Motors Corporation. For every million hours worked, there were but 3.43 lost-time accidents among the more than 200,000 hourly rated workers during that year. In addition to this record, the Fisher Body Division plant at Janesville, Wisconsin, has gone three years without a lost-time accident, and four other of their plants have gone two years without a lost-time accident.

Most private insurance companies maintain an experienced and trained staff to make inspections of risks. The insurance company reserves the right to make inspections or investigations whenever it deems them desirable.

Employer's liability insurance.—Mississippi has not yet enacted workmen's compensation laws. In this state the common-law rule, which holds employers responsible for injury to their employees only where negligence is shown, still prevails, except as modified by statute.

Employers may protect themselves from loss arising from their legal liability to injured employees by the purchase of employer's liability insurance.

Employer's liability insurance also forms a part of every contract of workmen's compensation insurance. This provision protects the employer in the event an employee is injured while in the course of employment, but is not covered under the regular compensation contract. Such liability may arise as the result of an accident which occurs while an employee is engaged in interstate commerce, or as the result of an employee's election (in a few states in which he is permitted to choose) to forego the benefits of the compensation statute and to sue the employer under the common law.

7. AUTOMOBILE INSURANCE

Types of automobile coverage.—The term "automobile insurance" may refer to protection against:

1. Losses resulting from legal liability for injury (or death) to another person. (No coverage for injury sustained by the insured himself, since this is covered by life and accident insurance.)
2. Losses resulting from legal liability for damage to the property of another.
3. Losses resulting by reason of damage to the insured's car through collision or upset.
4. Losses caused by theft.
5. Direct damage to the insured's car caused by fire, lightning, tornado, cyclone, windstorm, hail, earthquake, explosion, and other happenings.
6. Legal liability of an employer for losses for which an employee is primarily responsible.
7. Legal liability of garage keepers, service stations, and automobile mechanics for negligence resulting in losses to customers.

The first five of the above risks may be covered under separate policies or under a single contract. Generally, the assured may freely choose which risks he desires to insure.

Automobile public liability insurance.—A business firm, as the owner of an automobile, or as the employer of a person operating an automobile, is legally liable to third parties who may be injured by reason of the operation or maintenance of such automobile. The only limit to a loss of this nature is the aggregate value of all the assets of the business.

The standard automobile public liability policy will indemnify the assured for all loss sustained by reason of legal liability for bodily injury (or death) incurred by any person other than the assured accidentally resulting from the ownership, operation, or maintenance of the described automobile within the United States and Canada. The insurance company also agrees to defend the assured in all suits for damages within the scope of the policy, and to investigate all claims. The basic minimum limit of liability assumed in the standard policy, however, is $5,000 for injury or death to one person, and $10,000 for damages arising from one accident for injury or death to any number of persons. Inasmuch as jury awards are often substantially in excess of these figures, every business should secure an endorsement increasing the limits of liability to at least $10,000 for injury to a single person, and $50,000 for loss from one accident; the cost of such increased limits is only slightly higher than the charge made for the standard limits. For example, limits of $10,000 and $20,000, respectively, cost only 15 per cent more than the basic limits of $5,000 and $10,000, while the premium for limits of $25,000 and $50,000 is only 12 per cent higher than the rates for $10,000 and $20,000.

The coverage granted by the liability policy is very broad. In a recent case the Supreme Court of Pennsylvania made the following remarks in commenting on the protection afforded by a public liability insurance policy:

> The policy of insurance was unquestionably intended to indemnify the assured against liability resulting from an accident due to the use or operation of the car. It does not matter under what circumstances the liability might arise. The assured may even be protected against the acts of the driver or his own that may involve a criminal statute; generally accidents are due to the violation of some law legislatively declared as of criminal aspect, as, for illustration, fast or reckless driving, but insurance policies have always been treated as effective and valid under those circumstances.

Automobile property damage liability insurance.—Similarly to liability for bodily injuries to third parties caused by automobile accidents, a business firm may also be financially responsible for damage to the property of third parties arising from the operation of a motor vehicle.

The protection and services offered under this policy are identical with that of the public liability contract, described above, except that the limit of liability assumed by the insurance company under the standard policy is $5,000 per accident.

Automobile collision insurance.—A business firm may incur a substantial loss as the result of accidental collision damage to its own motor vehicles. The collision contract protects against direct loss caused by contact of the insured car with another object.

The cost of full coverage collision insurance has always been high. Consequently, so-called deductible forms are widely used. Under such forms the assured agrees to assume liability for an agreed amount, such as the first $25, $50, $100, of any loss. For example, if a $100 deductible clause was inserted in a policy, and the insured car was damaged to the extent of $500, only $400 would be paid by the insurance company.

The following rates for a new Chrysler sedan in a large city territory bring out the difference in cost for the different coverages:

Full Coverage	$170
$25 deductible	68
$50 deductible	46
$100 deductible	29
$250 deductible	18

By the use of a deductible provision, a business may economically protect itself against the more serious losses; the minor losses, which to a great extent may be anticipated, can be assumed by the business by means of an accounting reserve.

The collision policy should be examined to ascertain whether or not "upset" is specifically covered. At the present time most of the companies agree to indemnify for loss caused "solely by accidental collision with another object or by upset." Whether or not "upset" is covered in the absence of a policy provision depends upon the interpretation given to the word "collision" by the courts of the particular state.

Automobile theft insurance.—Full-coverage theft insurance protects the assured against loss or damage arising from the theft, robbery, or pilferage of the described automobile. Under the standard policy, theft by an employee, however, is excluded. In addition, theft of accessories and tools is not covered unless the entire car is stolen.

Automobile fire, lightning, and transportation insurance.—The standard automobile fire policy protects against direct loss caused by damage to, or destruction of, the body, machinery, or equipment of the automobile, arising from fire or lightning, or, while the insured motor vehicle is being conveyed by another vehicle or vessel, against the perils of transportation. In general, however, the usual exclusions incident to ordinary fire policies, such as loss attributable to use of the insured car, and loss attributable to personal effects left in the car, are not covered.

Comprehensive damage coverage.—The theft and fire insurance coverages for automobiles may be combined in one policy form that provides an even broader coverage than the specified perils of theft, fire, lightning, and transportation. Called "comprehensive," this coverage protects against loss or damage to the automobile insured from any source. Collision coverage is either included or excluded from the policy, at the choice of the buyer. This policy form has become extremely popular in those states in which it is in existence.

Nonownership automobile liability insurance (contingent liability insurance).—The law of agency renders the principal responsible for the acts of his agent. Consequently, in those instances where salesmen, or other employees engaged in the business of the employer, drive their own cars, the employer may be liable to third parties for damages inflicted as a result of the operation of such cars.

While the rules established by the courts of the different states vary somewhat in their application to particular circumstances, in general, the employer is liable for the acts of his employee (provided such employee is not an "independent contractor"), if an accident occurs within the scope of, and in the course of, his employment. Whether the employer had knowledge of the use of an automobile by an employee, whether the employee had been forbidden to drive an automobile in the course of his employment, and whether the employee was paid by salary or commission, have been held, by various courts, to be unimportant.

Where the employee-owner carries ample public liability insurance containing the so-called "omnibus clause" (see below), the employer may be protected jointly with the employee. However, even where such insurance is carried by employees, the employer cannot always obtain adequate information as to its validity and sufficiency. A need, therefore, exists for a form of insurance that will protect the nonowner-employer regardless of the circumstances surrounding the use of the automobile by the employee. Such protection is offered by nonownership automobile liability insurance, sometimes called contingent liability insurance. A common form of this policy automatically covers all employees, regardless of their usual duties. Another form covers only employees who are named in the policy.

As indicated above, an employer is not liable for the acts of his employee if such employee is an "independent contractor." Advice of counsel should be obtained, however, as to whether or not a particular set of facts constitute an employee an "independent contractor."

If, after consultation with an attorney, the employer is advised that a court "would" or "might possibly" hold him liable for the acts of his employee-drivers, nonownership liability insurance should be immediately taken out. On the other hand, if in the attorney's opinion such "employee-drivers" are "independent contractors," the employer is fairly safe without nonownership liability insurance. He should remember, however, that although it is unlikely that he will be held liable for the acts of his employees, where such employees are independent contractors, he may, nevertheless, be sued for such damages, and will be liable for court costs. Many employers find that the defense services of the insurance company fully warrant the cost of the insurance.

Omnibus clause in automobile insurance.—The standard automobile policy contains a provision, known as the "omnibus clause," which in effect makes the insurance follow the car, with certain exceptions, rather than the named assured.

Under this clause, the terms of the policy are extended to cover:

1. The legal liability of any other person using the insured automobile, or riding in such automobile, with the permission of the named assured. "Permission" for a given purpose, however, does not imply permission for all purposes; the permission must have

been granted or implied for the use of the car in the manner in which it was employed at the time of the accident.

2. Any firm or corporation legally responsible for the operation of such automobile. This provision extends the protection of the policy to an employer, where an employee operates such automobile with the permission of the named assured.

Under no circumstances, however, is the protection granted by the policy available to "a public automobile garage, automobile repair shop, automobile sales agency, automobile service station and the agents or employees thereof." The Supreme Court of Pennsylvania has held that this exception extends to a mechanic or person engaged in the business of repairing automobiles, even if the repair work is done at the home of such mechanic.

Automobile fleet insurance.—Business firms owning five or more automobiles of any type may insure them under a single policy on the "fleet plan," which gives them a more flexible form of insurance than individual specific policies.

The advantages of the fleet plan are:

1. Premiums are based on the actual time each car was in use. Reports are made to the company of suspension, disposal, and acquisition of automobiles, and a proper premium is retained by the company.
2. Automatic coverage for newly acquired cars is provided.
3. Fleet discounts in the premium are available. Depending on the number of cars, the discount ranges from 5 per cent upwards.

Experience rating of large automobile fleets.—If the assured desires, he may submit his fleet for special rating, provided at least ten automobiles have been insured on a full-time basis for a minimum period of twenty-one consecutive months, or at least five automobiles involving an annual basic premium of $1,000 or more have been insured for twenty-one months immediately preceding the application for special rating.

Where the previous experience of the company with the policyholder has been satisfactory, a reduction in premium from that specified in the manual rates may be obtained from the insurance company by application for special rating. On the other hand, if the policyholder has had a large number of accidents, and if the experience of the company with the policyholder has been generally adverse, a special rating may result in rates higher than would otherwise be payable.

The policyholder should consult his broker or agent as to the advantages and disadvantages of applying for experience rating.

Which automobile coverage is most important?—A recent survey conducted in New Jersey by Yale University and the United States Department of Commerce disclosed that unsatisfied judgments arising out of automobile accidents were either a major or a contributing cause of bankruptcy in at least 4 per cent of all cases. The judgments ranged from $60 to $25,000, and averaged $5,230. In 10 per cent of the cases, practically the only liability of the business was the judgment; in 50 per cent of the cases, the judgment amounted to 75 per cent or more of all liabilities. In addition, a number of other cases were discovered in which payment of an automobile judgment had precipitated the firm into bankruptcy.

When this bankruptcy record is considered in conjunction with the fact that over twice as many persons are killed by the automobile each year as meet death through industrial accidents, the outstanding need for automobile liability insurance is self-evident. If workmen's compensation insurance is a necessity, certainly insurance against a far greater hazard should be considered as indispensable. It therefore follows that the liability lines (that is, automobile public liability, non-ownership liability, and property damage liability) are the most important automobile coverages from the standpoint of any business.

Self-insurance of automobiles.—Under no circumstances should self-insurance of the so-called liability lines (see above) be attempted. The outstanding reason for insuring such risks with a reliable company arises, of course, from the fact that no limit exists to the possible loss which may be incurred. Furthermore, insurance companies are usually better prepared to defend fraudulent suits than are small individual business concerns.

On the other hand, the collision and theft hazards offer almost an ideal situation for the application of the principles of self-insurance where a large number of units are involved. The value of each unit is almost identical; the chance of loss of all units at the same time is practically nil; the amount of any individual loss is limited to the value of the automobile or truck, representing a small part of the business assets.

Self-insurance of the fire hazard is not quite so satisfactory, inasmuch as one of the greatest risks is the conflagration hazard—the chance that all machines stored in a single or adjoining building will be destroyed by a single catastrophe.

Garage-keeper's insurance.—The ordinary automobile insurance contracts are not suitable, by reason of their exclusions, for automobile dealers, automobile manufacturers, service stations, and garage-keepers. Consequently, a number of special policies have been designed to cover the hazards encountered by such concerns.

Garage liability insurance may be obtained under any one of the following plans:

1. Payroll basis, under which the premium is based on the total garage payroll. This form is the most liberal, covering both inside and outside hazards, and extending to all automobiles owned or operated at any time by the garage-keeper or any of his employees. Experience rating is available to large risks under this plan.
2. Named-driver basis, covering only accidents occurring while any automobile is being driven by the driver named in the policy.
3. Specified-car basis, covering each automobile described in the policy. The coverage afforded by this policy is very limited.

Garage collision insurance may be purchased either under a blanket contract or on the specified car plan.

Various methods have been devised to insure the fire and theft hazards, including specified-car basis, blanket policies, and reporting policies. The most advantageous form depends upon the circumstances of each individual case, such as the number of cars owned and the volume of business transacted.

In considering the desirability of taking out insurance, garage-keepers should remember that the rule relative to proof of negligence is reversed in most jurisdictions, and that where a customer of a public garage charges negligence, the burden of proof is upon the garage-keeper to show that he was not negligent. Thus, the Supreme Court of Minnesota, in a case involving an automobile that had been stolen from a public garage where it had been stored for pay, said:

Where a loss occurs under such circumstances as are here disclosed the burden is upon the bailee [garage-keeper] to show that he was free from negligence; that is, that he exercised such care to keep the property safely as a prudent man would ordinarily exercise under such or similar circumstances.

Nor will a sign placed upon the floor disclaiming liability for fire or other losses (or such a provision placed in a storage or other contract) relieve the garage-keeper of liability where he or his employees were negligent. For example, in a suit against a warehouseman for recovery of the value of goods destroyed by fire, the court held that failure to supply sufficient hose to reach to all parts of the building constituted negligence which was the proximate cause of the destruction of goods by fire, and that the warehouseman was liable for damages, regardless of the fact that the contract under which the goods were received "expressly provided against liability for loss from such cause." Signs and clauses of such a nature are "effective to exempt from liability only in the event the loss by fire was not caused or contributed to by the negligence of the storer."

Comprehensive liability and property damage insurance.—Along with the comprehensive form of public liability and property damage insurance has been introduced a comprehensive liability policy for automobile hazards. This policy protects the insured against any and every liability loss that may occur in connection with automobiles during the policy period. It makes available a single policy by which a business firm can protect itself not only against accidents involving cars that the firm or its employees may own or hire with or without notice to the firm but also against any unknown or unthought-of possibilities of loss which may, and do, crop up unexpectedly. Every business firm should carefully discuss this all-inclusive form with its broker or agent.

8. BURGLARY, THEFT, AND ROBBERY INSURANCE

Standard definitions of burglary, theft, and robbery.—Under the general designation of burglary, theft, and robbery insurance, a variety of policies are issued.

The insurance companies have adopted, and the courts have upheld, standard definitions for the offenses against which protection is offered. The assured should carefully read all such definitions, inasmuch as they differ from both the commonly accepted meaning of the terms and sometimes from the statutory definitions. However, most policies define the crimes of burglary, theft, and robbery as follows:

Standard definition of "burglary."—Burglary losses are indemnifiable when "occasioned by any person making felonious entry into the premises by actual force or violence of which there shall be visible marks made upon the premises at the place of such entry by tools, explosives, electricity, or chemicals." Burglary, therefore, as far as insurance is concerned, does not include loss attributed to sneak thieves or persons who have access to the property.

Standard definition of "theft."—Theft and larceny are both used to denote the stealing of property of another where visible marks of illegal entry are not made upon the premises, and the assured is unaware of the theft at the time of the loss; for instance, losses caused by tradesmen, servants, and mechanics working on the premises.

Standard definition of "robbery."—Robbery is generally defined as meaning "a felonious and forcible taking of property: (a) by violence inflicted upon the person or persons in the actual care and custody of the property at the time; (b) by putting such person or persons in fear of violence; (c) by any other overt felonious act committed in the presence of such person or persons, and of which they were actually cognizant at the time; or (d) from the person or direct care of a custodian who, while conveying property insured under the policy, has been killed or rendered unconscious by injuries inflicted maliciously or sustained accidentally."

Types of burglary, theft, and robbery insurance.—The principal burglary, theft, and robbery policies commonly used by business concerns are:

1. Mercantile open-stock burglary insurance.
2. Interior robbery insurance.
3. Outside messenger robbery insurance.
4. Payroll robbery insurance.
5. Mercantile safe burglary insurance.

6. Merchants' protective bonds.
7. Safe deposit box (securities) insurance.

Mercantile open-stock burglary insurance.—Huge losses are suffered each year by retailers, wholesalers, jobbers, and manufacturers as the result of burglary of merchandise from storerooms, show windows, lofts, and warehouses. In addition, the ruthless procedure of the thieves, forcible entry to the premises and display cases, and their haste to "get away" is responsible for the infliction of much damage to goods which are not removed, to the premises, and to the fixtures. To meet these risks, the mercantile open-stock burglary policy is available.

The policy promises to indemnify the assured for direct loss or damage to furniture, equipment, merchandise, and goods usual to the business, caused by "felonious entry into such premises by actual force and violence when the premises are not open for business." The protection does not apply, however:

1. If the assured, any associate in interest, servant, or employee is implicated in the burglary.
2. Unless books of account are kept in such manner that the exact amount of loss can be accurately determined.
3. If the loss is caused, or contributed to, by fire.

Certain other less important conditions must also be complied with before the company is liable. Unless an extra premium is paid, the company is not liable for loss in "an amount in excess of $50.00 on account of any one article of jewelry," nor for the burglary of furs from within any show window after the glass therein has been broken from the outside.

Interior robbery.—Business organizations that have property (either money or merchandise) of value within their premises which is exposed during the hours the business is open are in need of protection against holdup occurring within the business premises.

The interior robbery policy covers loss of money, securities, and loss of or damage to merchandise, and damage to the furniture, fixtures, and other such property in the premises. It insures against such loss occasioned by robbery, or an attempt at robbery, committed at any time during the day or night. The insured is also protected in case any custodian, after the business has been closed, is compelled under threat: (1) to return to the premises and admit the thieves, or (2) forcibly detained and made to furnish others with information or the means of entering the premises.

The stealing of the insured property from within a show window in the premises while open for business, through the glass having been broken from the outside, is also covered.

Outside messenger robbery insurance.—Banks, hotels, investment houses, theaters, jewelry stores, furriers, and other business concerns that frequently send valuable property other than payrolls outside of the premises need suitable insurance coverage. To meet this need, the outside messenger policy has been designed. As the name implies, it is implicable only to the property of the assured that is in transit outside of the assured's premises. Robbery occurring on the premises is not covered; in this particular the policy is narrower than the payroll policy, which applies at all times while the payroll is in the hands of the paymaster.

The contract agrees to indemnify the policyholder for all loss or damage by robbery committed at any hour to any property carried by a custodian, including payrolls, provided such robbery occurs outside of the assured's premises.

Discounts from the regular premium are allowed:

1. If the custodian travels in a private car, and an additional allowance is made if such car is armored.
2. If the funds are carried in an approved safe, chest, satchel, or wallet.
3. If the custodian is accompanied by a guard at all times.

Payroll robbery insurance.—The hazard of loss of payroll by robbery may be transferred to an insurance company by means of payroll robbery insurance. This type of insurance makes good the insured's loss of payroll money or checks (and the receptacle in which the money is carried), if the loss is occasioned by robbery, or an attempted robbery, from a custodian of the payroll while engaged in any of his regular duties in connection with such payroll outside or inside the premises. Notice that this policy covers the payroll money whether it is away from or inside of the business premises, whereas the robbery insurance discussed in the two previous headings above is limited to coverage either outside or inside the premises.

The stealing of such money or checks by compelling the custodian, while outside the premises, to admit someone to the premises or furnish him with the means of entrance is also included in the policy coverage.

Mercantile safe burglary insurance.—By purchasing mercantile safe burglary insurance, merchants, manufacturers, lawyers, doctors, and private individuals may protect themselves against loss occasioned by the felonious abstraction of money, jewelry, securities, or merchandise from any vault or safe (or part thereof) described in the policy, after entry into such safe or vault has been effected by force or violence.

The company is not liable:

1. Unless books are accurately kept by the assured so that the amount of any loss can be readily determined.
2. If the assured or any employee was implicated in the burglary.
3. For the loss of negotiable securities unless the assured attempts to prevent their negotiation, payment, or retirement.
4. For loss effected by the opening of any safe or vault by the use of any key, or by the manipulation of any lock.

In addition to loss by burglary, this policy form covers the damage caused to the safe or vault itself, equipment, merchandise, and fixtures in the premises but not in the safe or vault, and damage to the building if the insured is the owner or is liable for it. Of course, this protection applies only when a burglary, or attempted burglary, is committed on the safe insured.

Discounts are allowed from the regular premium for:

1. Prepayment of a three-year premium.
2. Employment of watchmen.
3. Excluding money from coverage.
4. Use of underwriter's approved safes, locks, and alarm equipment.
5. Approved tear-gas systems.
6. Division of insurance, where the same policy covers more than one safe.

Merchants' protective bonds.—Merchants' protective bonds are a combination of burglary insurance, robbery insurance, and fidelity bonds, designed to protect for limited amounts the smaller merchant against loss arising from most of the miscellaneous hazards to which he is subject. A typical "bond" may protect against:

1. Larceny or embezzlement of property or money by any employee.

2. Loss of money or personal property through holdup during business hours.

3. Loss of money or personal property through robbery while such money is being transported within a given radius by either the owner or any employee.

4. Loss resulting from burglary of safe contents.

5. Loss through damage to doors, windows, locks, and premises caused by forcible and felonious entry.

6. Loss or damage to stock or fixtures occasioned by the use of explosives to force entry to a safe.

7. Loss resulting from forgery or alteration of checks.

8. Loss by reason of acceptance of counterfeit money.

9. Loss or damage to cash register, caused by forcible entry.

In addition, the contract agrees to pay a reward of $100 to any person giving information leading to the arrest and conviction of a person committing burglary, robbery, or murder upon the premises.

Another such grouped policy is known as the "storekeeper's burglary-and-robbery policy" and insures, up to $250 on each item, against:

1. Inside robbery.

2. Outside robbery.

3. Kidnapping custodian and forcing opening of the premises.

4. Safe burglary.

5. Burglary from the home of the custodian of funds held overnight, or from the night depository of a bank.

6. Mercantile open-stock burglary.

7. Damage to property, merchandise, and so forth, in connection with any of above.

Securities insurance.—An individual business concern that customarily keeps a large amount of valuable securities in a safe-deposit box may desire insurance for two reasons:

1. Usually a bank will not reimburse its customers for losses unless it possesses adequate insurance or is legally liable. As a general

rule, a bank is not liable for losses resulting from burglary or theft of safe-deposit boxes unless the customer can prove that the bank was negligent. The circumstances that constitute negligence vary from state to state, but ordinarily it must be shown that a lesser degree of care was used by the bank in protecting the property of its boxholders than in protecting its own property, or that the other banks located in the same city commonly exercised greater care than was exercised by the burglarized bank. Consequently, it is impossible for a boxholder to determine in advance whether or not the bank will be legally liable for any loss.

2. Even if the bank has purchased a blanket safe-deposit box burglary and robbery policy, the individual boxholder cannot be certain of the security that it grants to him, since losses sustained by the bank itself through burglary or robbery of its own securities are reimbursed first; recovery for loss arising from any one box is limited to 10 per cent of the face of the banker's blanket policy; and, as a rule, the amount of valid insurance carried by the bank cannot be ascertained.

The bank policy protects only against loss resulting from:

1. Burglary of the contents of the safe-deposit box (burglary is defined as a forcible entry by the use of tools, and so forth).

2. Robbery of the property of the assured from within:

(*a*) The vault containing such safe-deposit box.

(*b*) That part of the bank's premises reserved for the use of customers in its safe-deposit-box department.

(*c*) The banking enclosure reserved for the use of employees of the bank, while at least two such persons are regularly at work therein.

(*d*) The bank's premises while the assured or any person authorized by him is conveying the property between the said vault and the entrance to the bank's premises at any time while two or more of the bank's officers or office employees are regularly at work on the premises.

The individual policy, however, protects against *all loss* of securities except infidelity and the voluntary giving over of possession or title by the insured (whether through fraud or otherwise).

Securities in safe-deposit vaults are subject to the hazards of burglary, robbery, mysterious disappearance, explosion, fire, entry by misrepresentation, and so forth.

9. FIDELITY AND SURETY BONDS

Use of bonds.—A bond is a written promise to pay a sum of money under one or more specified conditions. In this sense it is like a contract of insurance or indemnity. But, more formally, a bond is a guaranty to the party named in it as the "obligee" (who corresponds to the "assured" named in an insurance policy) that the person or persons named in the bond as the "principal" will perform a certain duty or task, and that, if the principal fails in this, the insurance company, the "surety," will make good the money or other damages suffered by the obligee because of this failure of performance.

The bond is given to facilitate business; its purpose is to guarantee the responsibility of the principal. The premium charged for the bond, unlike an insurance premium, is not entirely a charge for the risk assumed by the company, but is for the service performed by the company in issuing its bond. In most cases, for instance, the company will not issue its bond until it is completely satisfied as to the responsibility of the principal through investigation and often through the deposit with it of collateral equal to the financial risk assumed by the company.

In practice, if the principal fails to perform as expected, the surety company immediately pays to the obligee the sum involved, and then proceeds against the principal for reimbursement.

A bond usually provides in substance that:

> John Doe __________, as Principal, and the Guaranty Company __________, as Surety, are held and firmly bound unto ____ Richard Roe ____________ as Obligee in the penal sum of ____ten thousand dollars ($10,000) the condition of the bond being that John Doe, as Principal, shall faithfully perform an obligation herein described, and that if he does perform such obligation, this bond shall be considered void and fully discharged; otherwise it shall remain in full force and effect.

Fidelity bonds.—Fidelity bonds cover employees in positions of trust, and in substance guarantee the employer against loss should the person bonded prove to be dishonest. Some bonds also cover negligence and incompetency, but such forms are rare.

Four forms of fidelity bonds are in common use:

1. Individual bonds, covering only a specified person in a specified position.
2. Position bonds, covering any employee who occupies a specified position.
3. Schedule bonds, covering all employees named in an attached schedule. New employees must be added by endorsement. Some forms, however, automatically cover new employees for a period of ninety days.
4. Blanket bonds, covering all employees at all times, including employees hired after the bond is issued.

Surety bonds.—Surety bonds differ from fidelity bonds in that under the fidelity bond the surety company guarantees that the principal will *not* do a dishonest or other specified act, while the surety bond guarantees that the principal *will* faithfully perform certain duties or obligations. Surety bonds are issued to cover only persons of excellent reputation. As a rule, they may not be cancelled, and consequently are written only after thorough investigation.

As a condition of the issuance of a surety bond, if the surety company has any doubt as to the ability of the principal to perform his obligations, the principal is usually required to place with the surety company securities or other collateral from which the surety company may reimburse itself for any loss that it may suffer under the contract.

Contract bonds.—Municipalities, states, and private concerns often require as a condition for letting a contract that the contractor be bonded for the faithful performance and completion of his contract. Bonds guaranteeing such performance are known as contract bonds. Surety companies usually issue such bonds with little delay to reliable and experienced contractors.

Court or judiciary bonds.—Litigants at law are required many times to file a bond or other security guaranteeing that they will pay to the other party, if unsuccessful in the litigation, the monetary damages awarded by the court. Such bonds are known as court or judiciary bonds. They are essentially a guaranty of financial strength, and hence surety companies often require that ample security be deposited as a condition for the issuance of the bond. Another class of court bonds are known as probate bonds. Such bonds are issued to executors, administrators, and other fiduciaries to guarantee the faithful performance of their legal duties.

Miscellaneous indemnity bonds.—Bonds are used to give "obligees" all sorts of guaranties involving proper performance of certain obligations and protection against financial loss by the obligee. Some typical bonds may be:

1. Bonds covering the issuance of a duplicate certificate of stock or other security, where the original has been lost.
2. Bonds required by railroads guaranteeing the payment of freight charges.
3. Bonds to indemnify railroads against loss for delivery of freight without first requiring the surrender of the bill of lading.

10. CREDIT INSURANCE

Need for credit insurance.—The annual credit losses exceed the annual fire losses. Too little attention has been paid by businessmen to the advantages of credit insurance.

Forms of credit insurance policies.—Credit insurance is designed to protect business enterprises from unusual credit losses (as distinguished from the "normal" credit loss common to all business), to curtail credit losses by encouraging proper investigation, and to give the assured the benefit of a scientific, efficient collection service.

Two basic forms of credit insurance policies are available:

1. *Without collection provision.*—Under this form losses are payable only when caused by insolvency of the debtor or impairment of the debtor's assets in some special way. Although the insolvency need not necessarily involve legal bankruptcy, the assured must prove his loss.

2. *With collection provision.*—This form is further subdivided into:

(*a*) *Optional collection.*—Under the optional type of credit policy, the company permits the policyholder to elect to file any overdue account (regardless of insolvency) within a fixed period specified in the policy. If an account is not filed, the company will assume any loss where the debtor actually becomes "insolvent," as defined by the policy, during the term thereof.

(*b*) *Compulsory collection.*—The compulsory collection form is similar to the optional form except that an overdue account must be filed within a specified number of days after it becomes past due. If an account is not filed within such specified time, the assured may be penalized by exclusion of the account from coverage, or by being permitted to recover only a reduced portion of the loss.

On all accounts filed for collection, the insurance company either collects the amount due from the debtor, and remits the same to the assured, less certain fees, or admits the account as a loss, and reimburses the assured therefor according to the terms of the policy. As a rule, coinsurance and normal-loss provisions of the policy preclude recovery of the full amount of any loss. ("Normal loss" may be defined as that loss which any business normally expects to incur as the result of credit transactions. The exact percentage of such loss varies with different kinds of business enterprises; until sufficient experience of the individual policyholder is obtainable, the rate for the industry as a whole, tabulated from many years of experience, will be used.)

Underwriting basis of credit insurance.—The credit insurance policy is designed primarily to cover only risks that are rated in first and second credits by a specified mercantile agency. The best-known agency of this kind is that of Dun & Bradstreet, Inc. Many other agencies have been organized, however, which specialize in particular lines of industry. (See page 976.) The assured may usually select the credit agency that he desires to be used for determining insurable risks under his contract. However, it is possible to obtain partial protection for inferior risks upon compliance with two general conditions:

1. Payment of an extra premium.
2. Assumption by the policyholder of an increased normal loss, and higher coinsurance limits. Under the regular policy, the assured is usually deemed a coinsurer or self-insurer to the extent of

10 per cent of all losses; on inferior risks this percentage may be increased to 33⅓ per cent or more.

Some policies are issued without mercantile credit ratings. Thus:

1. The *blanket* policy (issued only to firms of high standing) covers all accounts of the assured, whether or not they are rated by any agency.

2. The *approved credit risk* policy covers debtors whose credit is passed upon satisfactorily by the insurance company.

3. The *specific* policy may be issued to protect the creditor on a single large account.

Endorsements on credit insurance policy.—Any basic credit policy may be modified by riders or attachments to cover situations peculiar to the assured, or more nearly to fit the policy to the needs of the assured. Some of the more common endorsements are:

1. *Inferior rating rider.*—Attachable to an ordinary policy in order to protect the assured from loss through insolvency of concerns that are rated lower than first or second by the rating agency specified in the policy.

2. *Antedating rider.*—If the assured desires to be protected on credits extended previous to the date on which the policy was issued, an antedating rider may be added to the policy at the time that it is taken out. The policy then applies, with certain exceptions set out in the rider, as though it had been written at the earlier date.

3. *Back sales rider.*—A "conditional" back sales rider may be attached to a policy which has expired, but which has not been renewed at once, to cover losses arising during the interim between the date of expiration of the original policy and the issuance of the renewed policy.

4. *Equivalent agency rider.*—Under an equivalent agency rider, the debtor must meet certain requirements relative to the relation between his "capital" rating and his "first credit" rating, as published by the rating agency specified in the contract. If such relation is below the standard set out in the rider, the "maximum loss" for which the insurance company might otherwise be held liable under any one account is reduced by 25 per cent.

5. *Goods in process rider.*—Such a rider renders the insurance company liable for loss sustained through insolvency of a firm that

had previously placed an order for goods "entailing the purchase of special material, and the manufacture of goods not usually kept in stock," where such insolvency occurs while the goods are "in process."

6. *Freight rider.*—The credit policy does not cover freight charges. Where the freight charges appear on the customer's account, such charges may be added to the amount recoverable under the policy through addition of the "freight rider."

7. *Excluded or included sales rider.*—Certain classes of risks or types of sales, such as cash transactions, or to a specified company, may be excluded from the policy, thereby reducing the premium, by an "excluded" sales rider. Sales of a subsidiary concern, or sales made by a manufacturer who operates under several trade names, may be covered under the regular credit insurance policy by the insertion of an "included" sales rider.

8. *Interim adjustment rider.*—Generally, claims are paid only at the end of the policy year. If the assured desires more frequent settlements, an "interim adjustment rider" may be added to the credit insurance contract. An additional premium is charged for such an endorsement.

9. *Consignment rider.*—Ordinarily only completed sales are covered by the credit insurance policy. Losses arising from sales made "on consignment" may be included within the scope of the policy by the insertion of such a rider.

Collection service of the insurance company.—In addition to the protection furnished the policyholder through the indemnification for unusual credit losses, the credit insurance company renders an important service, that of investigation and collection. Such collection services are fully as important to the assured as are the reimbursement-for-loss provisions of the policy. The benefits that accrue to the policyholder as the result of such services include:

1. A lower loss ratio, and therefore, over a period of years, a lower premium charge.
2. Inexpensive and capable collection of past-due accounts.
3. Elimination of waste through duplication of effort.
4. Quick payment of collected accounts to the policyholder.

Limit of coverage in credit insurance.—Every credit insurance policy contains a maximum loss per account limit for every customer of the policyholder. The amount for which the company will be liable is governed by the credit rating of the debtor. In addition, some policies contain a maximum "aggregate-loss" limit, whereby the amount of loss for which the insurance company will be liable as a result of all failures during the policy term is definitely limited.

How to reduce the cost of adequate credit insurance.—To reduce the cost of adequate credit insurance, it is necessary for the policyholder carefully to define his needs to his insurance broker in order that the policy may conform precisely to the requirements of the assured. Premiums paid for unneeded protection are wasted. On the other hand, the policyholder should be certain that he is fully protected.

A consideration of some of the elements that are considered by the insurance company in computing the premium will disclose several points at which the cost of credit insurance may be safely reduced.

1. *Single account limits.*—The single account limits of coverage required on the different ratings are one of the principal factors entering into the computation of the premium. The limits should be high enough to cover fully all the *ordinary* sales. If an occasional account is larger than the ordinary, it might be excluded from the regular policy (see "excluded sales rider," page 1294) and insured under a "specific" credit insurance policy.

2. *Type of policy.*—To a considerable extent, the type of policy that the needs of the policyholder require controls the premium. Thus, a collection policy is more expensive than a non-collection, since the former covers both services and protection; a policy covering debtors with inferior ratings costs more than one covering only debtors rated in first and second credits. An approved credit risk policy may possibly be less expensive than a regular policy.

3. *Special endorsements.*—Special endorsements and riders may either increase or decrease the premium. Endorsements tending to decrease the premium include (see pages 1293–4 for definitions):

(*a*) Equivalent agency rider.
(*b*) Excluded sales rider.
(*c*) Guarantor rider (whereby the rating of a guarantor is substituted for that of the debtor).

4. *Normal loss.*—The credit insurance policy is designed to cover unusual, unpredictable losses. Consequently, the so-called normal loss, or predictable loss, is deducted from the gross loss. Inasmuch as the cost of the insurance constitutes total losses plus underwriting expenses, it is to the advantage of the assured to assume all loss that may be covered by an accounting reserve.

5. *Coinsurance limits.*—Under the ordinary policy, the assured is made coinsurer for 10 per cent of all losses. Where this percentage is increased, the liability of the insurance company will be decreased, and the premium consequently reduced.

6. *Past experience of applicant.*—Credit insurance makes provision for merit rating. Hence, if the policyholder carefully investigates all risks before extending credit, over a period of years he may be able substantially to reduce the cost of his insurance.

7. *Reputation and practices of the policyholder.*—Each credit insurance risk is considered on its own basis, and the premium rate computed in accordance with the individual circumstances. As a result, a conference with a reputable insurance expert may disclose other means by which total credit insurance premiums may be reduced.

11. MISCELLANEOUS INSURANCE COVERAGES

A. Fire and Allied Coverages

Supplemental contract.—The fire insurance policy may be endorsed with the "supplemental contract" at an additional premium to cover losses due to windstorm; cyclone, tornado, and hail; explosion; riot; riot attending a strike; smoke; motor vehicles; and aircraft. The cost of adding these grouped coverages is low and has been widely accepted as a step forward in broadening the protection easily and inexpensively available to business. Each of the coverages is practically self-explanatory. The "contract" becomes part of the fire policy.

Explosion.—This coverage may be purchased separately, and it is usually advisable to do so if the "supplemental coverages" must be purchased in too great an amount because of the coinsurance requirements of the fire policy. Explosion insurance written separately in a specific policy can be bought on varying coinsurances.

Riot, and riot attending a strike.—Direct loss and damage from pillage and looting is covered here, when the loss occurs during and at the place of riot or strike. This coverage can also, in conjunction with explosion insurance, be bought under a separate policy.

Business interruption (use and occupancy).—Fire—and other insurable hazards, such as lightning, sprinkler leakage, or explosion—often causes a greater indirect loss through the resulting cessation of business operations than arises from the direct loss to the property actually destroyed. To reimburse the assured for such losses, use and occupancy insurance (sometimes called business interruption insurance) has been designed. Various forms are in use, but the usual contract promises to indemnify the assured for all loss caused by the forced stoppage of business which results from destruction of, or damage to, the premises, machinery, raw materials, stock, or instruments necessary for the transaction of business. Such indemnifiable loss includes estimated net profits, fixed charges, and expenses that continue during enforced idleness (such as interest and salaries paid under contract), and expenses necessarily incurred for the purpose of reducing the loss (for example, cost of moving to a new location until the destroyed premises can be replaced or repaired).

The common items of continuing expense, which are paid under this policy, may include:

1. Rent.
2. Taxes.
3. Telephone charges.
4. Light, heat, power.
5. Advertising previously contracted.
6. Payroll of office staff, important shop employees, and others.
7. Officers' salaries.

The net profits that would have been earned if there had been no interruption in the business are also collectible. This policy is becoming recognized as a primary form of business insurance.

Contingent use and occupancy insurance.—The ordinary use and occupancy policy does not reimburse the assured for loss occasioned by a cessation of business resulting from an interruption to the continuous supply of an article that is absolutely necessary for the operation of the business. Contingent use and occupancy insurance may be purchased to cover this risk. The usual policy promises to indemnify the assured for loss of profits, and expenses incurred, arising out of damage to or destruction of another business unit upon which the assured is dependent for essential raw materials or parts. The coverage is applicable for the length of time it would take to place the damaged plant in a condition where deliveries could be resumed.

Profits and commissions insurance.—One of the indirect losses arising from fire (tornado, riot, explosion, water damage, or other hazard) that is not covered by the standard policy is deprivation of profits or commissions on stocks of finished goods where delivery is prevented through damage to such goods by the hazard against which insurance is taken. Profits and commissions insurance is available for manufacturers, jobbers, and wholesalers, and for retailers.

Rent insurance.—Owners of real property are subject to huge losses through the loss of rent or rental value as the result of the destruction of, or damage to, their property by fire, lightning, windstorm, riot, explosion, earthquake, and so forth. To cover such losses, rent and rental value insurance have been designed. In most states the coverage can be effected by merely attaching to any basic direct loss policy a rent insurance endorsement.

Generally, the rent insurance policy promises to indemnify the assured for loss of rent or rental value for the period of time that the assured's property is damaged to the extent that it becomes untenantable. The cover may be issued to owners, lessors, or sublessors receiving rental income from a residence or other type of building; to owners of such property which, although not rented, is apt to be rented at any time; to fiduciaries receiving income from rents; and to owners who occupy their own premises.

Two standard forms are available:

1. Indemnity based upon the rental income or rental value for the period estimated to be required to restore the building to a tenantable condition. This form is generally the most suitable for small buildings.

2. Indemnity based upon the annual income or rental value of

the property. This form allows a longer period for restoration and is therefore more suitable for large buildings requiring a long period for replacement.

Under either form, the entire building, whether occupied or vacant, or only the actual rented or occupied portions of the building, may be covered.

Leasehold insurance.—Leasehold insurance, as distinguished from rent insurance, is designed to cover the interest of the tenant or lessee. All rights under a lease are usually cancelled when the leased premises are destroyed or rendered unfit for use. The termination of an advantageous lease may result in loss to the holder thereof, arising from numerous circumstances, including:

1. Should the premises be leased at a figure below current full-rental value, or for less than the lessee would have to pay for other similar property, a loss amounting to such difference would follow termination of the lease.
2. If the original lessee subleased the premises at a profit, such profit would be lost.
3. A sublessee may have paid a cash bonus to purchase a valuable long-term lease from the original lessee. Cancellation of the lease would result in a loss of all or part of such bonus.
4. The lessee may have made certain improvements, the value of which he would lose by cancellation of the lease. This interest, however, is usually covered by improvements and betterments insurance, for which see page 1300.

In addition to the interest represented, leasehold insurance is distinguished from rent insurance by the manner in which the loss is calculated. Under rent insurance indemnity is paid for such period as is actually required (subject to policy limitations) to restore the building to tenantable condition. Under leasehold insurance, however, a definite calculable loss takes place immediately upon termination of the lease. For example, if a building were leased for a period of ten years on July 1, 1941, at a yearly rental of $15,000, and a fire on July 1, 1943, resulted in the termination of the lease, and forced the lessee to rent other premises at a yearly rental of $25,000, the lessee would have incurred a loss equal to the difference in the yearly rentals ($10,000), times the number of years the lease had to run (8), or $80,000. But since the whole of such loss is not incurred until the end of the lease-period, the actual loss is the present value of such sum, or in this instance, if the policy specified that the present value was to be obtained by discounting at 4 per cent, the amount payable would be approximately $58,448 (the sum which at 4 per cent compound interest will equal $80,000 in eight years; see "How to calculate the compound present value," page 46).

Rates for leasehold insurance are based upon the fire building rate, modified for the provisions of the fire-cancellation clause of the lease, or, in the absence of such a clause, the statutory provisions of the state wherein the property is located.

Leasehold insurance does not cover loss that arises through other than a specific contingency insured against, such as fire or earthquake. Loss resulting from the commission or omission of any act by the policyholder, or by exercise of an option to terminate the lease, is not covered.

Improvements and betterments insurance.—The interest of a lessee in improvements, additions, betterments, alterations, and repairs installed as a permanent part of a building, or its fixtures, by the lessee at his expense under the terms of a lease, may be protected against all direct loss or damage, arising from fire or other specified contingency, by the purchase of improvements and betterments insurance. The form is not standardized, and care should be taken to ascertain that the exact coverage desired is secured.

Accounts receivable insurance.—Reputable firms may obtain insurance to cover loss by reason of destruction by fire of books of accounts. The cover is written, however, only by a few companies, and then only under very rigid conditions. One such condition is that the accounts be stored in a fireproof safe. The basic fire policy specifically excludes losses from destruction of accounts and evidences of indebtedness.

B. Other Property Insurance

Sprinkler leakage insurance.—The installation of sprinkler systems gives rise to a new hazard arising out of the danger of accidental release of water from the pipes of the sprinkler system that are placed on the ceiling and fitted at intervals with sprinkler heads containing valves held in place by a fusible link. The valves open at a certain degree of heat whether or not such heat is caused by fire, and sometimes as the result of freezing or jarring. The ordinary fire policy covers water damage only when caused by fire; loss from water released by other causes may be covered by the sprinkler leakage policy.

Power plant insurance.—Power plant insurance refers to a number of miscellaneous covers that are designed to indemnify the policyholder for all direct damage or loss resulting from the accidental explosion or breakdown of boilers, wheels, engines, pressure vessels, steam and water turbines, electrical apparatus, and other machinery used in connection with the generation, distribution, control, or storage of energy for power purposes. In addition, endorsements may be added to cover indirect damage and consequential loss.

While the forms differ somewhat as to definitions of "explosion," "breakdown," and so forth, for the different subjects of power plant insurance, the standard policy provides indemnity for:

1. Damage to the insured boiler, engine, turbine, machinery, or other described property, caused by internal explosion, or accidental breakdown of such property.
2. Damage to other property of the assured, caused by the explosion or breakdown of the insured property.
3. Damage to property of others for which the assured is liable, caused by the hazard or hazards insured against.
4. Liability of the assured arising out of a hazard covered by the policy for loss of life or injury to members of the public.
5. Defense of suits, even though groundless or fraudulent, brought against the policyholder because of the occurrence of an accident insured against, including payment of expenses of such defense, interest on any judgment within the limits of the policy, and court costs assessed against the assured in such a case.

Among the indirect damage covers which are often added to such contracts by endorsement is that for business interruption (see page 1297).

Power plant inspection service.—An important part of all types of power plant insurance is the inspection service that is rendered with the insurance. The insurance company does not promise to make any designated number of inspections, but usually attempts to make, in the case of steam-boiler insurance, for example, two external and one internal inspection each year.

Experience of insurance companies conducting such inspections indicates that losses caused by inspected boilers and machinery are 80 to 90 per cent less than similar losses arising from uninspected boilers and machinery. As a result, rates are not only reduced, but many policyholders regard the inspection service as more valuable than the payment of a loss in the event of an explosion or breakdown.

Exclusions in power plant insurance policy.—The following are the principal exclusions under most power plant insurance:

1. Loss or damage caused by fire, or by explosion resulting from fire, is not covered, inasmuch as this is a risk assumed under the standard fire insurance policy.
2. Damage occurring while any safety device, or regulator of pressure or speed, is altered, taken out, made ineffective, or set in a manner to provide a pressure or speed in excess of that approved by the insurance company.
3. Business-interruption losses, unless covered by an endorsement.
4. The cost of any repairs necessitated by wear and tear, or depreciation.
5. Boiler insurance usually excludes damage caused by "mere cracking or fracturing of a cast iron boiler hereby insured unless standard cracking endorsement is attached to the policy."
6. Some forms of power plant insurance exclude damage for breakdown of machinery caused by riot, strike, or civil commotion.

Earthquake insurance.—Geologists have determined that no section of the United States is entirely free of the earthquake hazard. Earthquake insurance, therefore, is needed in sections other than on the Pacific Coast.

The standard earthquake policy covers against all direct loss or damage resulting from earthquake or volcanic eruption, including damage by fire where the fire insurance has been voided by the earthquake (that is, after a material part of the building has fallen). The cover may be issued either separately or in conjunction with the fire policy. Some companies, however, consider it as an accommodation line and issue earthquake policies only when an equivalent amount of fire insurance has been purchased.

Windstorm and tornado insurance.—Windstorm and tornado insurance promises to indemnify the assured for direct loss or damage resulting from the action of windstorm, cyclone, or tornado. Care should be taken to ascertain whether or not losses arising from fire after a material part of the building has fallen (thereby voiding the fire policy) are covered.

Plate glass insurance.—This form indemnifies the insured against loss by reason of breakage of glass. The cost of lettering and ornamentation on the glass involved may also be insured. The service performed by the insurance companies in this field of insurance is the prompt replacement of broken glass. A store window which is broken is of no value to the merchant. Speedy replacement so that the window may be used for its proper show purposes is important. Thus, more important than the cost of the glass many times, is the prompt replacement service of the insurance company.

C. Floater Policies

Transportation insurance.—Merchandise shipped by business concerns may suffer loss or damage from many unforeseen causes before it reaches its destination, regardless of the type of carrier used to transport the merchandise. To protect firms against loss by reason of these unforeseen events, transportation insurance has come strongly to the fore as an important insurance coverage.

Many forms of this policy are written, but all basically insure the merchandise involved from the time it leaves the premises of the owner until it arrives at and is actually delivered to the destination. Thus it is insured, for example, while in transit to the freight station, while there awaiting shipment, while en route, while at the unloading shed at the consignee's city, and while in transit to the offices of the consignee.

This insurance may be purchased to cover single shipments or on an annual basis to cover all shipments made during the year. A separate policy is available if the firm uses its own trucks to ship and carry goods. Still another form is designed to protect the independent motor truckman for loss involving damage to merchandise of his customers while in his trucks during shipment.

Parcel post insurance.—Insurance companies issue a liberal "all-risk" policy providing indemnity for loss or damage to packages or contents while in the custody of the post-office department, or for loss in case of failure to arrive at destination.

Retailers, jobbers, and manufacturers who ship 100 or more packages per year will generally find that private parcel post insurance is cheaper, more convenient, and entails less clerical detail than Government parcel post insurance.

Registered mail insurance.—Banks, trust companies, investment houses, and other concerns making numerous shipments of currency, securities, and other valuables by registered mail (including air mail), may protect themselves against loss or damage from practically all risks, except the perils of war and the hazard of theft by employees of either the assured or the addressee. Policies may be issued to cover only a single large shipment, but concerns making numerous shipments during the year will find it advantageous to procure a reporting form (see page 1256 for description), under which all shipments made during the policy period are automatically covered. This policy may also be endorsed to cover shipments by express.

Garment contractor's insurance.—A floater type of policy is used by manufacturers who do not complete all the work in their own plant that is necessary to turn out completed garments. The articles, during their manufacture, may be sent to various types of contractors who will perform some work on them and then return them to the owner. The insurance protects the owner while the goods involved are away from his plant and while they are in transit.

Bailee's customers' insurance.—Businesses that are in the position of bailee, such as public storers, dyers, cleaners, laundries, warehouses, and the like, are ordinarily responsible for the articles entrusted to their care. This form of insurance indemnifies them for damage or loss to those articles and not only gives protection to the bailee and to the owner of the goods, but also serves as a good-will policy by attracting customers to the obviously responsible bailee and, in times of loss, preventing costly and troublesome arrangements between the bailee and his customers.

Salesmen's samples insurance.—Business concerns that send out with salesmen valuable merchandise for use as samples may secure protection with salesmen's samples insurance. The policy is a liberal "all-risk" contract. However, the contract should be carefully read before purchase, inasmuch as the line is not standardized; a few companies issue contracts covering only specified hazards.

Jewelers' block insurance.—Manufacturers, wholesalers, and retailers may protect themselves against practically all types of loss or damage to jewelry stocks by purchasing a jeweler's block policy. The coverage is very broad; only a few specified risks are excluded.

D. Miscellaneous Coverages

Title insurance.—As contrasted with all other forms of insurance, title insurance does not protect against hazards occurring in the future; the policy covers only against loss arising from titles that may have been rendered defective in the past. A large part of every premium is for the service of searching. The usual policy guarantees that, except as otherwise specified, the title is perfect at the time that the assured bought or sold the property to which it attaches.

Rain insurance.—Indemnity for loss of income, or reimbursement for expenses incurred where rain, hail, snow, or sleet cause the abandonment of an enterprise, may be secured through rain insurance. Some contracts specify that 1/10 or 2/10 inches of rain must fall before the assured will be entitled to recover for any damage, while under others the company assumes liability if any rain, no matter how little, falls. The premium, of course, is higher on the latter form.

Rain insurance does not cover damage to tangible or real property.

Check alteration and forgery insurance.—Although the general principle of law holds the depositary bank responsible for forgery, it does not hold the bank responsible for alteration in the body of the check. Furthermore, many exceptions to this rule exist, and there are cases on record where the bank has not been held liable for forgery or alteration. Thus, in addition to the doubt that may exist as to the liability of the bank in any particular transaction, the depositor will have to pay the costs of a legal prosecution and may lose the interest on his money, which is tied up in the meantime. Consequently, there is a genuine need for check alteration and forgery insurance.

Two forms of check alteration and forgery insurance are in common use by business concerns other than banks:

1. *Depositors' forgery policy.*—This policy may be written to protect the checking account of any individual, firm, or corporation other than a bank. The contract promises to protect the assured, as well as any bank or banks in which he carries a checking account, from any direct loss, up to the limit of the contract, resulting from forgery or alteration of checks or other standard negotiable paper (notes, drafts, bills of exchange, trade acceptances) issued or ostensibly issued by the assured. The policy does not cover instruments drawn in lead pencil, unless indelible, or loss encountered by reason of the assured's acceptance of forged or altered checks in the course of his business.

2. *Commercial forgery policy.*—This policy may also be sold to any individual, firm, or corporation other than a bank, but it is peculiarly appropriate for retail concerns and others who daily accept checks from strangers in payment for merchandise sold.

The agreement is divided into two sections. Section "A" is identical with the coverage offered by the depositors' forgery policy.

Section "B" protects the assured against all loss resulting from alteration or forgery of incoming bank drafts and checks that the policyholder may take in good faith in the course of his business. The agreement, however, does not cover loss arising from instruments drawn in lead pencil, unless indelible, or upon checks returned and marked "no account" or "not sufficient funds." Furthermore, the policy usually contains a three-fourths loss clause (for explanation, see page 1243).

12. BUSINESS LIFE INSURANCE

Types of organizations that should be interested in business life insurance.—Business life insurance is regular life insurance applied to the needs of a business. It protects the business of the assured in the same manner that personal life insurance protects his family.

Although life insurance can be applied to the needs of virtually every form of business organization, it is of particular value to:

1. Sole proprietorships.
2. Partnerships—general and limited.
3. Close corporations.

Uses to which business life insurance can be profitably applied.—The various uses to which business life insurance may be profitably applied include:

1. To reimburse the business for loss resulting from the death of a person who has contracted to do some particular or unusual work, or who has undertaken a program of expansion, the fulfillment of which depends upon the personal performance of such person.

2. To protect the business against loss at the death of an employee by:

(*a*) Compensating for the loss of unusual services.

(*b*) Indemnifying for the loss of goodwill attached to the person of an employee or official.

(*c*) Protecting the credit of the business where the extension of credit is dependent upon the business connections or services of an employee or official.

(*d*) Providing a fund to train a successor.

3. To protect the business at the death of a sole or part-owner by:

(*a*) Providing funds for the transfer of the decedent's interest in the business to his heirs in a predetermined manner so that the business itself is not disturbed financially, business-wise, or management-wise.

(*b*) Protecting the credit of the business.

(*c*) Providing a fund to act as a "shock absorber" to tide the business over the difficult period that always follows a sudden change in management.

4. To protect the business against unusual exigencies by:

(*a*) Providing a sinking fund (the cash value of the insurance) which may be used in case of emergency.

(*b*) Hedging an ordinary sinking fund designed to retire bonds of the corporation where sale of the bonds is predicated upon the services of certain officers.

Business life insurance trusts.—A free choice may ordinarily be made as to whether the proceeds of business life insurance are to be paid to:

1. The partnership or corporation.
2. The proprietor's estate, a creditor, or a named beneficiary.
3. The surviving partners or stockholders.
4. A trustee.

Whenever any policy of business life insurance is placed with a trust company under an agreement whereby the trustee will collect and distribute the proceeds, a business life insurance trust exists.

When the services of a trustee are necessary.—Where any part of the proceeds of a policy is to be used for the purchase of the decedent's interest in a partnership, or for the retirement of stock interests in a corporation, it is desirable to arrange for payment of the proceeds to a trustee, preferably a corporate fiduciary. This is true for a number of reasons, chief among which is the difficulty of placing a fair valuation upon the interest of the decedent after his death.

When the services of a trustee are unnecessary.—In general, the services of a trustee will represent an unwarranted expense where the only purpose of the insurance is to act as a shock-absorber, to compensate for loss of goodwill, or to reimburse any party for loss suffered through the death of an employee, part-owner, or contractor.

Determining factors where use of a trustee's services is optional.—Where no part of the insurance is designed for the retirement of business interests, the advantages of having the insurance proceeds paid through a trustee should be compared with the charges made by the trustee.

The outstanding advantages of the insurance trust are:

1. If the trustee is given certain discretionary powers, a single policy may sometimes serve several purposes, thus decreasing the net cost of the business-insurance program.

2. In business-liquidation plans, the trust agreement interposes between the legal representatives of the deceased and the survivors in the disinterested services of a fiduciary whose sole aim is to

fulfill faithfully the terms of the trust for the benefit of all the parties concerned.

3. In drafting the various agreements involved, the experience of a corporate fiduciary is often invaluable in suggesting the best ways and means of carrying out the desires of the owners of the business.

4. Where insurance is taken out to strengthen or enhance the credit of the enterprise, the services of a trustee render the creditor more secure than if the proceeds were paid directly to the business (since in that event they would be available to all creditors), and protect the interests of the business to a greater extent than if the proceeds were paid to the creditor, himself, in trust.

Charges made by corporate fiduciaries.—The charges made by corporate fiduciaries vary in different parts of the country, and sometimes as between different trust companies in the same city. The fees for handling business insurance trusts are quite reasonable and depend upon the duties and responsibilities involved.

Methods used to evaluate the interests of a decedent in a stock-transfer or partnership-liquidation agreement.—The following methods are now in general use for the valuation both of stock in a close corporation and of the interest of a decedent in a partnership.

1. *Arbitrary valuation.*—A definite price may be specified by agreement between the owners of the business. Inasmuch as values are subject to substantial change within a relatively short period, however, this method, although simple, is highly unsatisfactory, and is usually unjust either to the decedent's estate or to the surviving owners.

2. *Book value.*—Another simple method is to specify by agreement that the book value of the decedent's interest as of the date of death shall be used. Although this is an improvement over the first method, injustice still results, since book value seldom represents actual fair market value.

3. *Arbitrary valuation revised at regular intervals.*—The parties may specify the value of the interest of each owner at the time that the agreement is entered into, and provide for revision from time to time to conform with changes in value of the various interests. If carefully carried out, and if revisions are made at intervals of ap-

proximately six months, this is one of the most desirable and satisfactory methods. In practice, however, the owners frequently fail to certify the proper value at the specified times, with the result that when a death occurs, the last revision in value will be either higher or lower than the fair market value of the decedent's interest in the business.

4. *Arbitration.*—Another common method of valuation is to provide by agreement for arbitration between representatives of the decedent owner and the surviving owners. Provision is also made in most cases for selection of a third, and supposedly neutral, party to represent both interests. If the agreement provides that the determination of the arbitrators is to be binding upon all parties, the only objection which can be raised is the possible delay that may be encountered, and the ill-feeling that may be engendered.

5. *Valuation supervised by the trustee.*—The trustee may be directed to conduct an audit of the books of the enterprise as soon as convenient after the death of any owner, and fully to inform all parties in interest as to the results of the audit. If the surviving owners and the decedent's estate can then agree upon a satisfactory valuation for the interest of the decedent, such value will be final. If, after a reasonable time, the parties in interest fail to agree among themselves, the trustee is directed to employ one or more experts to ascertain the fair market value of the decedent's interest. Such experts, after investigation, certify to the trustee the fair market value of the decedent's interest. The certified value is then binding on all parties. The objections to this method arise from the unwillingness of most trustees to assume the added responsibility, and the additional service charges where the responsibility is assumed.

6. *Suggested method.*—As indicated above, the third method, if correctly applied, is probably the most satisfactory. Therefore, in order to overcome the objections to this method, it is suggested that the transfer agreement provide:

(*a*) For valuation by the respective owners of their interest in the business at intervals of six months.

(*b*) That if a valuation has been certified to the trustee within seven months of the death of any owner, such valuation is to be final.

(*c*) That in case no certification of value has been made within seven months of the death of an owner, the trustee shall conduct an audit to ascertain the book value of the decedent's interest as of the date of death.

(*d*) That all parties in interest shall be fully informed by the trustee as to the results of the audit.

(*e*) That if the surviving owners and the decedent's executors are then able to agree upon a fair market value for the decedent's interest in the business, such value shall be final and binding on all parties.

(*f*) That if the parties in interest are unable to agree upon a fair value, the trustee shall designate one or more persons who are thoroughly familiar with conditions in the particular industry and locality to make an investigation, and upon the basis of such investigation, to ascertain the fair market value of the decedent's interest, and to certify the same to the trustee.

(*g*) That in such event, the price certified to the trustee shall be final and binding upon all parties.

13. GROUP INSURANCE

Nature and scope of group insurance.—Group insurance represents the insurance under one blanket or "master" policy of all the lives of an entire group of employees, without medical examination, and at a premium lower than the aggregate of premiums that would be charged for separate coverages on the same lives. Although group insurance originated with life insurance, applicability of the plan is by no means so limited; the group-insurance principle has been successfully extended to include:

1. Life insurance.
2. Accident and health insurance.
3. Retirement annuities and pensions.

Types of group insurance available.—The following are the most common forms of group insurance available:

1. *Group life insurance.*—Life insurance provides for the payment of a definite sum to the beneficiary designated by the employee, in the event of the death of the employee while the insurance is in

force. The insurance is in force for the individual employee while he is employed by the firm in whose name the group policy is written.

2. *Group accident and health insurance.*—The standard coverage under accident and health policies provides weekly indemnity for temporary or permanent disability resulting either from sickness or from accidental injury suffered while not engaged in the duties of regular occupation (that is, this insurance does not cover compensable injuries under workmen's compensation insurance laws). Generally, house confinement is not required, indemnity being paid to any employee as long as he is "wholly and continuously unable to perform the duties of his occupation," subject to the contract limit, which as a rule may not exceed 52 weeks. However, injuries or sickness that are not of sufficient severity to require treatment by a physician are not covered.

3. *Group accidental death and dismemberment insurance.*—This form of insurance provides for benefits in accordance with a schedule contained in the policy for accidental death or dismemberment resulting directly and independently of all other causes from bodily injuries effected during the term of the policy through accidental means. Such death or dismemberment must occur within ninety days of the date of the accident. The benefits usually provided are:

For Loss of	*Amount Payable*
Life	face amount of certificate
Both hands	" " " "
Both feet	" " " "
Sight of both eyes	" " " "
One hand and one foot	" " " "
One hand and sight of one eye	" " " "
One foot and sight of one eye	" " " "
One hand or one foot	½ face amount of certificate
Sight of one eye	½ " " " "

4. *Group annuities.*—While annuities are not insurance, the group plan has been applied to them in certain respects. Group annuities may be purchased by employers who wish to establish a scientific plan for the accumulation of reserves for the retirement of workers at a specified period or age.

No standard group-annuity contract is now in general use; while every plan is, in outline, similar to most others, each scheme is designed to meet the needs of the individual employer.

Three plans on which group insurance may be written.—Group insurance may be written under any one of the following plans.

1. *Non-contributory plan.*—Under a non-contributory plan, the employer pays all premiums, and the employees in the classes eligible for the insurance are automatically insured upon completion of the probationary period.

Practically all group policies specify that new employees are not to be covered until they have served a prescribed probationary period with the company. The provision is designed to protect the employer, rather than the insurance company. As a rule, the probationary period should not be shorter than thirty days nor longer than a year. However, the employer is entitled to designate any period that he desires. Retirement plans often specify a longer probationary period than other forms of group insurance.

The advantages claimed for non-contributory plans are:

(*a*) Maximum flexibility as to details of plan. The employer is in a position to modify the plan at any time.

(*b*) Certainty that all employees will come under the plan. Unless employee contributions are compulsory, 100 per cent coverage is seldom obtained except under non-contributory plans.

(*c*) Avoidance of appearance of dictation or direction by employer in regard to employee's savings. This is particularly true with respect to group annuities.

(*d*) Avoidance of administrative and clerical expense arising from payroll deductions.

2. *Contributory plan.*—Under a contributory plan, premiums are paid by the employer and employees jointly. New employees, otherwise eligible, are not covered until they have signified their intention of joining the group and have given the employer permission to make the necessary payroll deductions. The principal advantages of contributory plans are usually held to be:

(*a*) More liberal coverage is possible if the cost is shared by the employer and the employees.

(*b*) Employees are encouraged in systematic habits of thrift.

3. *Composite plan.*—A composite plan is a combination of the contributory and non-contributory plans. Under this arrangement

the employer furnishes a certain minimum of insurance to all employees and contributes jointly with the employees for the purchase of additional coverage. The more important advantages of composite plans are:

(*a*) All employees are included, at least to a limited extent.

(*b*) Employees who are interested may voluntarily increase the amount of their insurance.

Conditions with which the employer must comply.—To be eligible to take out group life insurance, an employer, under the laws of most states and the rules of most insurance companies, must comply with certain conditions and stipulations.

Where the insurance is written on the non-contributory plan, the following are the conditions that must be complied with:

1. There must be a minimum of 50 lives regularly employed, except that for a group annuity plan, there need be only 25 lives. ("Wholesale" group insurance can be arranged for as little as 10 lives, at rates slightly higher than regular group life insurance.)

2. The lives to be covered must be all the employees of one employer, or all the lives in any class or classes of employment.

3. If only the persons in a certain class or classes are to be covered, such classes must be determined by conditions pertaining to the employment itself; that is, the employer may not name certain persons who are, and others who are not, to be included in the plan, but he may specify that only the employees in a certain department or departments are to be covered.

4. The amount of insurance to be taken out on the life of any single employee must be based upon some plan which will preclude individual selection; that is, neither the employer nor the employee may designate the amount of insurance which is to be carried upon a particular employee. The same amount of insurance may be placed on all employees; otherwise, the amount of insurance must be determined by conditions such as length of service, salary, or any other conditions or combinations thereof which are not arbitrary.

5. All new employees are automatically insured upon their completing the service or probationary period set forth in the plan (usually one month to one year), while the insurance automatically ends upon the termination of employment.

6. The insurance benefits must be paid to a beneficiary named by the employee; in no case can benefits revert to the employer.

7. The policy is issued to the employer.

Where the insurance is written on the contributory plan, the following are the conditions that must be complied with:

1. At least 75 per cent of the eligible employees of one employer must agree to contribute before any insurance can become effective. Furthermore, such 75 per cent must equal at least 50 lives.

2. Conditions two, three, four, five, and six are the same as under non-contributory groups.

3. The policy is issued to the employer, to whom the insurance company will look for collection and payment to the company of the premiums required.

How the amount of insurance for each employee may be computed.—The amount of insurance for each employee may be computed in one or other of a number of ways:

1. A "flat sum" for each employee.

2. A flat sum modified for salary. For example, $1,000 insurance might be provided for those earning less than $1,500 per year; $2,000 insurance for those earning more than $1,500 per year, but less than $2,500; and so forth.

3. Amount of insurance based upon salary classifications, to be increased when salary is increased. Thus, insurance might be issued equal to one year's salary to the nearest fifty or one hundred dollars.

4. Amount of insurance based upon length of service. For example, $1,000 of insurance might be provided for each five years of continuous service.

5. Amount of insurance based upon combination of service and salary. Thus, the insurance might equal a percentage of salary multiplied by the number of years of service. This is the most popular plan for use in connection with group annuities. For example, an employee might be entitled to a pension of 3 per cent of his salary, multiplied by service. If he had served twenty years at retirement, he would be entitled to receive a pension of 60 per cent of the average salary that he had received during his term of employment.

Employer controls group-insurance policy.—A contract of group insurance is entirely between the employer and the insurance company. Except in the case of group annuities (the only group plan under which large reserves are accumulated), the employees are in no way parties to the contract, although they are furnished with individual certificates showing the benefits provided for them by the policy. Hence, unless the policy specifically provides otherwise, the employer is entitled to alter, amend, or cancel a group-insurance policy at any time without the consent of employees.

Termination of group-insurance policy.—A group-insurance contract may be terminated for the following reasons:

1. As to an individual employee, the insurance automatically ends upon the termination of employment, except that in the case of disabled, retired, temporarily laid off, or reinstated employees, by special provision in the contract, the insurance may be continued. However, an employee leaving the service while the group contract is in force is entitled, without medical examination, to a regular policy at his attained age in any amount not exceeding the amount of his protection under the group policy, provided application and payment of premium for such substitute insurance is made within thirty-one days after termination of employment.
2. Upon failure to pay premiums when due, the insurance automatically terminates, except that in the case of group annuities, benefits previously purchased will be held for the benefit of employees.
3. The insurance company may terminate the policy, for any reason, within two years from the date of issuance. After such two years, the insurance company may not cancel group life-insurance contracts except for nonpayment of premiums. Generally, accident and health-insurance policies may be cancelled at the end of any policy year.

How group insurance benefits the employer.—A group-insurance program (including group annuities) may benefit the employer in any or all of the following ways:

1. Inexpensive, favorable publicity and advertising is usually secured from a well-conceived program of group insurance.
2. Goodwill is generally created among both employees and the general public.

3. A liberal program of group insurance tends to attract efficient labor.

4. Group insurance may supply an additional stimulus for greater efficiency. This is particularly true of non-contributory life, health, and accident insurance, and of any group annuity contract under which the employer bears a fair portion of the cost, since a pension may be considered as a "deferred additional wage."

5. Group insurance of all kinds tends to reduce labor turnover, and therefore costs.

6. Assurance of an adequate pension at retirement creates a spirit of independence and accomplishment among employees, and, therefore, group annuities promote a better *esprit de corps*.

7. Group insurance creates better morale by alleviating distress among employees and their families, and consequently eliminating the necessity for "passing the hat" when an employee dies or is injured.

8. Contributory features of group annuity plans encourage thrift.

9. Group annuities eliminate "hidden pensions" and enable the employer to amortize the cost of retiring an employee over the useful life of the worker.

SECTION 14

Directors, Officers, Stockholders

I. LAW RELATING TO DIRECTORS

2. LAW RELATING TO OFFICERS

3. LAW RELATING TO STOCKHOLDERS

4. DOING BUSINESS IN OTHER STATES

SECTION 14

Directors, Officers, Stockholders

1. LAW RELATING TO DIRECTORS

Who are qualified to act as directors.—The statutes in most states require either that a director be a stockholder of the corporation or that he be a stockholder, if the articles of incorporation do not provide otherwise. Reasonable qualifications for its directors may also be included in the by-laws of the corporation. In the absence of any provision in the statute, charter, or by-laws prohibiting some person or class of persons from acting as a director, or requiring certain qualifications for directors, any person may be a director who is legally competent to contract. In some states one or more directors are required to be residents of the state of incorporation or are required to be citizens of the United States. Even though some of the members of the board may not have the required qualifications, the acts of the board in behalf of the corporation are binding so far as the public is concerned.

Number of directors that a corporation is required to have.—The statute of the state of incorporation generally fixes the minimum number of directors that a corporation must have—usually three—and the maximum number of directors that a corporation may have. The actual number that a corporation decides to have, within the statutory limitations, is fixed in the charter or in the by-laws. This number may be increased or decreased in the manner provided by statute. If the number of directors is fixed by the charter, an amendment of the charter is generally required to change the number. If the number is fixed in the by-laws, those who had power in the first instance to enact the by-law fixing the number of directors may amend the by-law to change the number.

Term of office of directors.—The by-laws usually fix the period for which directors are to hold office, but even if that period has expired, they continue to hold office until their successors are elected. In some states the statutes provide that directors may be divided into two or more classes whose terms expire at different times. These statutes generally indicate the number of directors who must be elected annually and the maximum period for which any class or directors may hold office. Even in the absence of such statutes, a corporation may classify its directors, unless its charter or by-laws require that all directors be elected annually. The chief advantage of classifying directors is that there are always some members of the board who are experienced as directors. For example, suppose a corporation is authorized to have nine directors and is permitted to classify them. At its organization, nine directors are elected, three directors to serve for a term of one year, three for a term of two years, and three for a term of three years. At the expiration of the first year, three new directors are elected for a period of three years, to take the place of those three directors whose term has expired; at the expiration of the second year, three new directors are again elected for a term of three years, to take the place of the second group whose term has now expired. At the end of the third year after organization, the third group of directors is replaced by three new ones elected for a period of three years. Each year thereafter, three new directors are elected to fill the vacancies caused by the expiration of the term of one group of directors; the board will always consist of six old directors and three new ones.

Removal of a director with or without cause.—A corporation has an inherent right to remove a director for cause. It may remove a director even without cause:

1. If the director was not elected for a fixed term and removal for cause is not expressly required by statute, charter, or by-laws.
2. If removal without cause is expressly permitted by statute, charter, or by-laws.

A director who is elected for a fixed term can be removed only for cause unless removal without cause is expressly authorized by statute or charter. The power to remove a director rests with the stockholders unless otherwise provided under the laws of the state in which the corporation is organized; directors cannot remove a director unless expressly authorized to do so. The statutes in most states give the right of removal to the stockholders in express terms and specify not only what vote is necessary to effect the removal, but also the notice that must be given to the director proposed to be removed and to the stockholders. The corporation's by-laws often contain a provision regulating the removal of directors by the stockholders in accordance with statutory requirements. A director who is to be removed for cause must be given reasonable notice of the intention to remove him, sufficient time to prepare his defense, and a fair hearing.

Resignation of a director.—A director may resign at any time, even if he is elected for a fixed period, unless restricted by the corporation's charter or by-laws or by the laws of the state in which the corporation is organized. If a director has entered into a contract with the corporation to act as director for a fixed period, his resignation before the expiration of the period will make him liable to the corporation for damages caused bv the breach of his contract.

Where the resignation states that it is to take effect on acceptance, acceptance is necessary to end the tenure of office. Where it states that it is to take effect immediately, no acceptance is necessary unless the statute, charter, or by-laws make it necessary. Any form of resignation, whether written or oral, is sufficient, provided the intention to resign is clear. It is advisable that the resignation be in writing, in order that a record may be made for future use in case of controversy, and that it indicate when the resignation is to take effect. In the absence of such a statement, a resignation takes effect immediately.

Filling of vacancies in the board of directors.—The by-laws provide how vacancies in the board of directors shall be filled. These by-laws must be consistent with any provision contained in the charter of the corporation or in the statutes of the state in which the corporation is organized. A usual provision is that a vacancy in the board shall be filled by the board and that the directors so appointed shall hold office until the next annual election. In the absence of any provision in the by-laws, charter, or statute, the power to fill vacancies in the board rests with the stockholders. The board of directors may continue to transact business even though a vacancy has occurred in the board, and even though the remaining number is less than the number of directors required by statute or by the charter, but it cannot transact business if the remaining number of directors does not constitute a quorum.

How to fill vacancies in board where several directors tender resignations at same meeting.—The resignations of several directors should not be accepted at one time where the number of directors remaining will constitute less than a quorum, for, in the absence of a quorum, the directors will be unable to fill the vacancies caused by the resignations or transact any business. Each resignation should be accepted separately, and, immediately after each acceptance, the place of the resigned director should be filled. The director filling the vacancy should then assume his duties as director and participate in the acceptance of the resignation of the next director and the election of his successor. The secretary of the meeting should make certain that the directors who are to be elected to fill the vacancies will be present at the meeting so that they can participate in the elections immediately upon their taking office. The necessity for separate acceptance of resignations and separate elections is eliminated where the statute permits resignations to take effect at a future date and vacancies to be filled by the board immediately but to take effect when the resignations take effect.

Are directors entitled to compensation for their services?—Directors are not entitled to compensation for services rendered within the scope of their duties as directors, unless compensation is authorized in one of the following ways:

1. By charter.
2. By by-law.
3. By resolution of the stockholders.
4. By resolution of the directors before the services were rendered, where the directors have authority to fix their own compensation.
5. By express contract between the director and the corporation.

Nor are directors entitled to compensation for attending meetings, unless payment is expressly authorized. In some jurisdictions, however, directors are entitled to compensation for services rendered outside of their ordinary duties as directors, provided the services are performed at the instance of the corporation and with an understanding that compensation is to be paid. Where, for example, a director devoted practically all of his time to the corporation and acted as its manager and superintendent, it was held that he was entitled to be compensated.

Directors cannot, ordinarily, vote themselves compensation unless authorized to do so. Such vote must come from the stockholders. Directors may, however, fix the salary of a corporate officer, who is also a director, for services performed as such officer and outside of his duties as a director, unless expressly prohibited from doing so. If, however, the resolution authorizing payment of compensation is carried only by including the vote of the director who is to receive the compensation, the resolution may be held not to be binding on the corporation. As a general rule, interested directors cannot even be counted in determining whether a quorum is present to vote upon the question of their own salaries. Where the directors fill all or most of the offices of the corporation and it is desired to vote them compensation for their services, the only solution is to have the stockholders either vote the salaries or ratify the action of the directors in voting the salaries. The votes of interested directors who are also stockholders may be counted.

Power of directors to manage the corporation.—The directors, acting as a board, have the power to manage the business of the corporation, to exercise the corporation's powers, and to control its property. This power is exclusive with the directors unless the governing statute, charter, or by-laws provide otherwise. In most states the statutes, in express terms, give to the board of directors entire control over the corporate affairs. In the absence of such statutes, management of the corporate affairs is expressly vested in the board of directors by provision in the charter or by-laws. Stockholders have no right to interfere with the management of the corporation by the directors, except insofar as the consent of stockholders is required by statute, charter, or by-laws, to effect certain transactions, such as an increase in the capital stock, transfer of all the corporate assets, dissolution, and so forth. The fact that the stockholders are holders of substantially all of the outstanding stock, while the directors hold only a few shares necessary to qualify them for office, does not change the general rule. The management is nevertheless vested in the board of directors.

When the courts will interfere with management of the corporation by the directors.—The courts will not interfere with the management of the corporation by the board of directors merely because of errors of judgment on its part. Where, for example, the directors honestly and in the exercise of their judgment overexpand the business activities of the corporation to such an extent that the corporation suffers heavy losses, the courts will refuse to oust them from office. Similarly, the courts will not substitute their own judgment for that of the directors who have entered into a lease, in behalf of the corporation, which the directors deem fair and advantageous. Where, however, the directors have acted fraudulently, illegally, oppressively, or beyond their powers, the courts will interfere in order to protect the corporation. If, for example, the directors authorize payment to themselves of large sums of money as compensation for special services which, in fact, they never render to the corporation, stockholders may obtain the aid of a court of equity to protect the corporation from such diversion of the corporate funds.

A director cannot agree to relinquish his duty to manage the corporation.—The stockholders have a right to expect from every director good faith, reasonable care, and prudence in the consideration of every question that is presented to the board of directors in managing the corporate affairs. A director cannot relieve himself of this obligation by contract. He cannot agree with the stockholders, with his codirectors, or with the corporation that he will act merely as a nominal or "dummy" director. So far as the law is concerned, a director's function is to direct, and no such thing as a "dummy" director exists.

Limitation on power of directors to effect fundamental changes in the corporation.—The power of the board of directors to manage the corporate affairs includes the transaction of the ordinary business of the corporation. It does not include the making of fundamental and vital changes in the corporation, such as an increase or reduction in its authorized capital stock, a change in the purposes for which the corporation was organized, a transfer of all the assets of the corporation by sale or lease, a voluntary dissolution of the corporation, and so forth. In most states the statutes contain specific provisions requiring the approval of a certain percentage of the stockholders to enable the directors to effect such basic changes.

What powers may directors delegate to others?—The board of directors may delegate to others the performance of ministerial acts and the transaction of the ordinary routine business of the corporation. For example, the board may engage an individual to manage one of its branch stores, with power to hire and fire any and all employees necessary in running the store. It may authorize officers to prepare, execute, and deliver certain documents; to enter into contracts of employment; and to sell securities for the corporation. The directors cannot, however, unless the articles of incorporation specifically authorize them to do so, transfer to others any duties imposed upon them that involve the exercise of judgment and discretion. For example, the board of directors cannot give an employee general power to lease property of the corporation; it cannot delegate to officers the power to determine when calls shall be made for the payment of subscriptions to stock. Nor can the directors delegate powers given to them by the stockholders, which powers they would not otherwise have had. If the stockholders should adopt a resolution granting to the board of directors power to make and adopt all by-laws for the corporation, the board would have no power, in its turn, to adopt a resolution granting to the president the power to make and adopt by-laws.

Is a resolution necessary to effect a delegation of powers by directors?—In delegating any of its powers to others, it is advisable that the board of directors, formally, at a duly called meeting, adopt a resolution setting forth clearly the nature and extent of the authority given. A resolution is, however, not essential. The board of directors, by its acquiescence in a course of dealing by the person to whom it has delegated authority informally, is bound by that person's acts performed pursuant to such delegation of authority. The election of a person to an executive office may in itself imply that that person has the usual powers accompanying the office. Even if a resolution delegating authority is adopted, and that resolution specifies the powers granted thereby, the corporation will be bound by the exercise of additional powers not mentioned in the resolution if the board of directors acquiesces therein.

Power of directors to appoint committees.—The board of directors may appoint committees to perform various functions for it, the members of which may be directors or others. The power to appoint committees is expressly granted to the board by statute in some states and is confirmed in the by-laws of many corporations. The committee most commonly appointed by the board of directors is the executive committee, which exercises the powers of the board in accordance with the policy of the corporation and under the direction of the board during intervals between directors' meetings. The powers of the executive committee include the transaction of the ordinary business of the corporation; it may be authorized to make loans, to endorse notes in the corporate name, to make purchases for the corporation, to collect debts owing to the corporation. An executive committee that has powers of the board when the board is not in session may not assume sole control of the corporation for an indefinite period, amend by-laws that only the directors are by statute permitted to amend, change the number of members of the committee, remove a member by a majority vote, or appoint or remove officers and fix their salaries. Nor may such an executive committee execute a contract upon which the corporation is about to act. The calling of a meeting of the board may suspend the power of the executive committee to act in place of the board.

Power of directors to employ, compensate, and remove agents and servants.—As an incident to its power to manage the corporation, the board of directors has the power to determine who shall carry out its orders, and to appoint such agents and servants for the corporation as it sees fit. This power is generally confirmed by the charter or by-laws of the corporation. In the absence of fraud, the courts will not interfere with the board of directors in its appointments. It is also within the discretion of the board of directors to fix the amount of compensation of agents and servants appointed by it, and the terms of their employment. The board may provide for payment of compensation in advance; it may authorize payment of commissions in addition to salaries; it may give bonuses to employees.

The power of the board of directors to remove agents and servants follows the power to appoint them. If the length of employment is not fixed by contract, the employee may be removed by the board of directors at any time. If the contract does fix a definite term of employment, a discharge by the directors before the expiration of the time fixed, without proper cause, may subject the corporation to liability in an action by the employee for breach of contract.

May directors appoint agents for a term beyond their own term of office?—The board of directors may contract with agents to perform services for the corporation beyond the board's own term of office, provided the contract is reasonable in the light of the surrounding circumstances. The following test of reasonableness has been laid down: Does the power given to the agents appointed beyond the directors' term of office deprive the stockholders of their right to change the management of the corporation at subsequent annual elections? If it does, it is not reasonable, and the contract of employment is invalid. A contract employing an officer for a period as long as the corporation continued in existence was held unreasonable. On the other hand, a contract employing a general manager for a period of ten years was held valid.

May directors ratify unauthorized acts performed by others in behalf of the corporation?—The board of directors may ratify unauthorized acts of others only if it could in the first instance have granted authority to perform those acts. For example, the general manager of the corporation, who has no authority to make purchases in behalf of the corporation, buys a carload of merchandise. The board of directors may ratify the purchase, since it could have authorized the general manager to make the purchase in the first place. In order that ratification may be effective, however, it must be made with full knowledge of all the facts. If, for example, the general manager had made a secret profit in the purchase of the merchandise, and the board of directors, unaware of his personal interest in the transaction, had ratified the contract of purchase, the ratification would not be binding upon the corporation, and the directors could subsequently, upon learning the facts, repudiate the transaction.

Is a resolution necessary in order that directors may be deemed to have ratified an unauthorized act?—The directors may ratify an agent's unauthorized act by resolution, but such resolution is not essential. Ratification may be implied from acquiescence by the board of directors in the unauthorized act, with full knowledge of the facts. Mere silence on the part of the board of directors does not always mean that the directors have acquiesced. For example, an individual, falsely representing that he is employed by the corporation, contracts with a third person to purchase a truck for the corporation. The individual is a total stranger to the corporation, was never employed by it nor appointed an agent for it. The board of directors hears of the matter, but says nothing about it, and, upon delivery of the truck, refuses to accept it. The corporation is not bound by the contract of purchase, for the board has not ratified the unauthorized act. If, however, the corporation had previously held out the individual to the public as having authority to make purchases in its behalf, silence on the part of the directors in the face of his purchase might be deemed to constitute ratification.

Power of directors to make contracts for the corporation.—As an incident of their power to manage the corporation, the directors have the power to make any contracts in behalf of the corporation necessary, suitable, and proper in carrying out the corporate purposes. In the absence of fraud, their contracts are binding upon the corporation, although they may prove to have been unwise.

The directors may and often do delegate to officers and others their power to contract. Contracts entered into in behalf of the corporation by officers and others without authorization from the board of directors have also been held binding upon the corporation where such unauthorized persons were held out as having had the authority to contract for the corporation, and where the rights of innocent third persons were involved. The directors are not required to sign contracts that they have authorized. Authority to sign in the name of the corporation is generally given to designated officers by statute, charter, by-law, or resolution of the board of directors.

May a director or officer contract with the corporation?—A director or officer may enter into a contract with the corporation, provided that he deals openly with the corporation and that the contract is properly authorized. If a director is personally interested in a matter that is being authorized by the board he should not vote upon the question.

Contracts with interested directors are not void merely by reason of the relationship between the parties. A corporation may, however, avoid the contract under the following circumstances:

1. If the interested director or officer participated in authorizing the corporation to enter into the contract, and his vote was necessary to bind the corporation. It is generally held that such a contract may be set aside even if it was fair to the corporation and even if the interested director or officer acted in good faith.

2. If the interested director or officer participated in authorizing the contract, but his vote was *not* necessary to bind the corporation, the courts are in conflict as to the right of the corporation to set aside the contract. Two rules exist:

(*a*) The Federal courts and those of a majority of the American jurisdictions hold that a contract with an interested director or officer who participated in authorizing the contract, but whose vote was not essential to such authorization, is voidable only if unfair to the corporation. These courts examine the contract closely for fraud, and place the burden of proof of fairness upon the officer or director.

(*b*) Some jurisdictions, including New York, hold that a contract with a director or officer may be set aside where the interested director or officer participated in authorizing it, irrespective of whether or not the contract was a fair one, and without any showing that the influence of the interested director or officer determined the action of the corporation. The theory on which this view is based is that a director or officer stands in the relation of a trustee to the corporation, and all contracts made by a trustee or fiduciary in which he is personally interested may be set aside at the election of the party he represents.

3. Whether or not the interested director or officer participated in authorizing the contract, it may always be set aside if it is shown that the contract was not fair to the corporation or that it was not entered into in good faith by the officer or director.

Power of directors to borrow money for the corporation.— The power to borrow money rests with the board of directors as an incident of its power to manage the corporation. The directors may, however, delegate the power to borrow to an officer or agent of the corporation expressly by resolution of the board, impliedly by permitting it to appear that the officer or agent has authority to borrow, or by acquiescing in his acts. For example, the board of directors delegates to the vice-president the management of the business. In the course of his duties as manager, the vice-president from time to time borrows money from the bank in order to finance the purchase of merchandise necessary in carrying on the business. The corporation in this case is bound by the loan to the corporation, for the directors have, by entrusting management of the corporate affairs to the vice-president and permitting him to make loans, clothed him with authority to borrow in behalf of the corporation. Even if the vice-president had had no authority to borrow, either express or implied, the directors could not retain the benefits of the loan for the corporation and at the same time disown the acts of its vice-president.

The directors' power to borrow in behalf of the corporation is coextensive with the power of the corporation to borrow. Where the statute or charter limits the amount of indebtedness that the corporation is authorized to incur, the directors are, of course, bound by that limitation. Some statutes impose personal liability upon directors who permit the corporation to incur debts beyond the amount limited by statute.

May the directors give security for loans to the corporation? —As an incident of its power to borrow money for the corporation, the board of directors may issue evidences of the corporation's indebtedness in the form of promissory notes, bonds, and so forth, and may give security for the loans to the corporation. This security may be in the form of a mortgage or pledge of specific personal property, a mortgage of specific real property, or a mortgage of all the property owned by the corporation at the time of execution of the mortgage and to be acquired by it in the future. The board of directors may give a mortgage to secure future advances, the mortgage becoming operative when the advances are actually made. It may also give security for a debt that already exists against the corporation, provided the debt is a bona fide one, and the security is given in good faith. The fact that the creditor happens to be a director or stockholder of the corporation does not prevent the giving of security for an antecedent debt, but the courts will scrutinize such transactions closely to determine whether or not they were effected in good faith.

Must the directors obtain the stockholders' consent to mortgage corporate property?—The general rule is that the power to mortgage property of the corporation rests with the board of directors as an incident of its power to borrow, subject to contrary provisions in the statute, charter, or by-laws. Officers have no power to mortgage the corporate property unless authorized to do so by the board of directors expressly by resolution, or impliedly by holding out the officer to the public as possessing the power to mortgage. In some states the statutes specifically require the consent of a fixed proportion of the stockholders to the mortgaging of property, and, as a protection to the stockholders, specify the formalities to be followed in obtaining such consent. In New York, for example, upon a mortgage of corporate property, a certificate showing that the consent of the holders of not less than two thirds of the total number of shares outstanding has been given is required to be executed by an officer of the corporation and recorded in a designated public office in the same manner as the mortgage. In determining, therefore, whether or not the directors must obtain the consent of stockholders to mortgage corporate property, the statutes of the state of incorporation must be examined and followed, for a mortgage made by the directors without the required consent is invalid. However, although the statutes may require the consent of stockholders, the stockholders themselves cannot mortgage the corporate property without action on the part of the directors.

May a director or officer lend money to the corporation?—A corporation needing funds to carry on its business may borrow them from a director or officer, unless it is specifically prohibited from doing so by statute of the state of its incorporation, or by the provisions of its charter or by-laws. Loans by directors or officers may be made in the form of direct advances of funds or by endorsement of paper executed and negotiated by the corporation. The director or officer may accept interest on the loan at the legal rate, and he may take security for repayment. The entire transaction must, however, be entered into in the utmost good faith, and the courts will subject it to rigid scrutiny. Where a corporation does not need funds, a loan by a director or officer to the corporation is improper, and the director or officer may be compelled to account for any interest received on his loan and to return any security given.

May a director or officer borrow money from the corporation?—The statutes in many states prohibit loans by the corporation to directors, officers, or stockholders, and impose upon those authorizing the loan a liability to the corporation for the amount advanced. In other states such loans are permitted provided interest is paid and security given. In the absence of any restrictive statutes, loans may be made to directors, officers, and stockholders provided the transaction is entered into in the utmost good faith. It may be advisable not to lend any funds of the corporation to directors, officers, or stockholders, for such transactions are always regarded by the courts with great suspicion.

Power of directors to make guaranties in the corporate name.—In some states the statutes expressly grant to a corporation the power to bind itself as a guarantor; in others the power is expressly forbidden. In the absence of such statutes the general rule is that a corporation has the power to guarantee the obligations of others only where such an act is reasonable and necessary to enable the corporation to carry out the purposes for which it was organized. Where a corporation has power to guarantee the obligations of others, the power to make the guaranty rests with the board of directors. Thus the board of directors of a corporation having power to bind itself as a guarantor may endorse the note of, or guarantee payment of interest and principal on bonds of, a subsidiary corporation. The board of directors may ratify the unauthorized guaranty made by an officer in the corporate name if the corporation has the power to make the guaranty.

Power of directors to purchase and sell property in behalf of the corporation.—The power of a corporation to purchase property is exercised by the board of directors. If the directors act in good faith, and the corporation has the power under its charter to acquire the property, the judgment of the directors in acquiring property for the corporation cannot be questioned.

The directors also have power to make sales of property in the course of the corporation's business, and to fix the terms of sale. In the absence of fraud, stockholders cannot object to sales made by the directors on the ground that the price is inadequate. If the directors, for example, in the exercise of their judgment, believe that it is advisable to sell merchandise below market price or below cost, they have a right to do so. Directors may not, however, without the consent of stockholders, sell all the assets of the corporation or so substantial a portion of them that the business of the corporation cannot be continued. The test in determining whether or not the directors may sell property of the corporation without the consent of stockholders may be said to be this: Is the property sought to be sold essentially necessary to enable the corporation to transact its ordinary business? If it is, the property cannot be sold without the consent of stockholders; if it is not, the directors have power in their own discretion to sell it. For example, a corporation engaged in the business of buying and selling real estate and having numerous real estate holdings may have authority to sell any or all of the real estate holdings of the corporation upon the authorization of the directors alone and without action on the part of stockholders. Another corporation organized to own and operate one particular building may not sell that building without the consent of stockholders, for the sale would terminate the business for which the corporation was organized.

Power of directors to lease corporate property.—Where a corporation has power to lease its property, that power may be exercised by the board of directors. A lease of corporate property by an officer of the corporation is not binding upon it unless authorized or ratified by the board. Consent of stockholders is not necessary to authorize a lease of property made in carrying on the ordinary business of the corporation unless required by statute, charter, or by-laws. Where, however, it is desired to lease all the property of the corporation, the directors have no power to lease it without the approval of stockholders. The statutes in the various states generally indicate the proportion of stockholders whose consent is necessary to the leasing of all the property of the corporation, and in many instances the statutes define the rights of stockholders who object to the lease. The same authority is necessary to effect a surrender of a lease as was required to make the lease in the first instance.

Corporate property may be leased to directors or stockholders of the corporation, provided the lease is made:

1. In good faith.
2. For the best interests of the corporation.
3. For an adequate consideration.

Power of directors to make gifts of corporate property.—Ordinarily the board of directors has no power to give away any property of the corporation. It may, however, donate property in the course of the corporation's business where some benefit accrues to the corporation. For example, the directors may dedicate for public purposes a parcel of the corporation's real estate in order to enhance the value of other parcels of property owned by it and to stimulate their sale. Bonuses may be paid to employees to foster increased effort and efficiency. Donations to charities may be upheld where they are made to further the goodwill of the business. Endowments may be made to a university to carry on research that may benefit the corporation's future productive activities.

May a director buy from and sell stock of the corporation to stockholders for his own account?—The rule in most jurisdictions is that directors may deal with stockholders provided they do so at arm's length. A director may for his own account buy stock of the corporation from, and sell such stock to, a stockholder freely, provided he acts in good faith and without misrepresentation or fraudulent concealment. The director is not bound to give information regarding the value of the stock, for the stockholder could obtain this information for himself by an examination of the corporate books. The director must, however, answer honestly all questions that the stockholder asks of him regarding the stock, and, if he has knowledge of any special facts affecting its value, he is bound to disclose them.

Some jurisdictions hold that a director occupies a fiduciary relationship to stockholders which requires him to disclose to a stockholder all the information that the director has regarding the value of the stock to be sold to or bought from the stockholder.

Both the Securities Exchange Act of 1934 and the Public Utility Holding Company Act of 1935 contain a provision that permits recovery of any profits realized by officers and directors of companies subject to the acts from transactions in securities of such companies within a period of six months, unless the securities were acquired in good faith in connection with a debt previously contracted. Another important check against the use of inside information by directors and officers for personal gains is the requirement in the Stock Exchange Act of 1934 that officers and directors of any corporation whose stock is registered on a national securities exchange, and holders of more than 10 per cent of any class of registered equity security, must file reports for any month in which there has been a change in ownership. A similar requirement, relating to directors and officers, is contained in the Public Utility Holding Company Act of 1935, and in the Investment Company Act of 1940.

Power of directors to elect officers.—The officers of the corporation, required by statute, charter, or by-laws, are generally elected annually by the board of directors. In addition to the power to elect these required officers, the by-laws often give to the board of directors the power to appoint such additional officers as it deems necessary in the interests of the corporation. Where the board creates an additional office pursuant to this power, it has the right to abolish that office.

Removal of officers by directors with or without cause.—Directors may generally remove an officer for cause, and the courts will not interfere with their action unless it appears that the removal was entirely unwarranted. An officer may be removed without cause only under the following circumstances:

1. If the officer was not appointed for a definite term, and removal for cause is not required by statute, charter, or by-laws.
2. If the statute, charter, or by-laws expressly provide that an officer may be removed without cause.

An officer who is being removed for cause must be given notice of the proposed removal and an opportunity to defend himself.

Power of directors to issue stock.—The amount of capital stock that a corporation is authorized to issue is fixed in the articles of incorporation. However, not all of the amount so authorized need be issued at one time. The power to issue stock from time to time rests with the board of directors. Ordinarily action with regard to the issuance of stock must be taken by the board of directors at a meeting, properly called. An issuance of stock is not, however, necessarily invalid because formal action was not taken. If all the stockholders and all the directors are present and concur in the authorization of an issue of stock, the board of directors is presumed to have ratified the issuance even though it did not adopt any formal resolution of issuance. The kind of stock to be issued, the consideration to be received for the stock, and the manner and terms of issuing it, are determined by the board of directors, subject to provisions contained in the laws of the state in which the corporation is organized, its charter, and its by-laws. Directors have no power to issue stock without consideration. As a corollary of the directors' power to issue stock, the by-laws generally give the directors power to issue options to purchase stock.

Directors may incur liability for improper issuance of stock, as, for example, where they issue stock to themselves in order to gain control of the corporation, or where they issue stock to themselves without paying value therefor. For other liabilities of directors in connection with stock issuance, see page 1351.

Power of directors to make calls on stock subscriptions.—A call is an official declaration that the whole or a part of the subscription price of stock is due and payable. The power to make calls for payment on unpaid subscriptions rests with the board of directors and is generally conferred specifically upon the board by statute, charter, or by-laws. If the call is made in good faith, for corporate purposes, and not in violation of any agreement with the subscribers, it is valid, and the stockholders will not be permitted to question it. A call should be made by resolution at a duly called meeting of the board, but a call made at a meeting at which all the directors participated is valid even though proper notice of the meeting was not given. The amount of the call must be uniform as to all stockholders and in ratable amounts; that is, each stockholder must be called upon to pay the same amount on each share of stock that he holds. However, if some stockholders have paid less on their stock than others, the board of directors may call for an amount from the former sufficient to equalize the payments. The resolution should contain the following information:

1. The stockholders to whom the call applies.
2. The amount or percentage of the subscription required to be paid.
3. The time when payment is due.
4. The person to whom payment should be made.

5. The place at which payment is to be made.
6. Directions that notice of the call be given by the proper officer of the corporation.

Notice of the call is generally required to be given to the subscribers in order that the corporation may bring an action for nonpayment of the amount of the call. The length of notice to be given is determined by the requirements of the statute, charter, by-laws, or subscription contract; in the absence of such requirements, reasonable notice is sufficient. The statute, charter, by-laws, or subscription contract may also indicate what information must be set forth in the notice of call.

Power of directors to declare dividends.—The power to declare dividends and to determine the manner in which they shall be paid rests with the board of directors. This rule is, however, subject to the following limitations: (1) the directors must act in good faith; (2) a statute may limit or control the action of the board of directors; (3) the charter or by-laws of the corporation or some other governing instrument or contract may place an obligation on the directors to declare a dividend, or may limit its power to do so.

The courts will not interfere with the discretion of the directors in determining whether or not a dividend should be declared unless it appears that the directors have acted fraudulently, oppressively, or unreasonably. Dividends may, however, be declared only out of profits or surplus of the corporation and not out of capital. It is the duty of directors to determine not only whether it is expedient from a business standpoint to distribute profits or surplus to the stockholders but also whether a surplus or profit exists according to the law of the state in which the corporation is organized. These laws vary from state to state.

In some states a legal surplus is said to exist where there is an excess in the aggregate value of all assets of the corporation over the sum of its entire liabilities, including capital stock at its par value. In other words, dividends may be paid out of net profits only, or, conversely stated, when the payment does not impair the capital stock of the corporation. Thus, if a corporation's balance sheet shows assets accurately valued at $200,000, a capital stock outstanding having a par value of $150,000, and liabilities of $40,000, the corporation has a surplus of $10,000, which, in the discretion of the directors, may be distributed to the stockholders as dividends.

In other states, a legal surplus is said to exist when there is an excess in the aggregate assets of the corporation over the sum of its entire liabilities, including capital stock, not at its par value, but at the actual value received from the sale of the stock. Thus, if a corporation has issued and outstanding $3,000,000 par value of its stock, through the sale of which it has realized an actual value of $1,700,000,* and its assets amount to $2,500,000 and its liabilities to $300,000, the corporation has a surplus of $500,000 available for dividends.

The by-laws generally give the directors power to close the stock-transfer books of the corporation a certain number of days before a dividend date or to fix a record date to determine which stockholders are entitled to dividends.

Are formalities required in the declaration of dividends by directors?—While no formalities are required in declaring a dividend, it is advisable in all instances for the board of directors to adopt a resolution at a duly convened meeting, declaring the dividend and indicating the following:

1. The rate or amount of the dividend.
2. The class of stockholders to whom the dividend is payable.
3. The date set for determination of who is entitled to the dividend.
4. The date when the dividend will be paid.
5. The medium in which the dividend is to be paid.

The minutes of the directors' meeting at which the resolution is adopted should also show the names of those present at the meeting and of those who voted against passage of the resolution declaring the dividend.

May directors revoke a dividend?—Ordinarily directors cannot, without the consent of stockholders, revoke a dividend once

* While ordinarily stock is required to be sold at not less than its par value, the statutes of some states permit the sale of par-value stock at less than par value. It has also been held that, in the absence of an express statutory, constitutional, or charter provision calling for payment of stock at par value, a corporation may make a valid agreement with subscribers for sale of stock at less than par, provided the rights of other stockholders are not violated, and no fraud is practiced against creditors.

it has been declared, for a declaration of a dividend creates a debt from the corporation to the stockholders. Revocation of dividends has, however, been upheld by the courts in the following instances:

1. Where the directors illegally declared a dividend that would impair the capital of the corporation, acting under a mistaken belief that there were profits legally available for dividends.

2. Where the action of the board in declaring the dividend had not been made public, and no funds had been set apart for payment.

3. Where, after declaration of the dividend, some event occurred making it inadvisable to pay the dividend; as, for example, where a fire destroyed property of the corporation after declaration of a dividend, and the directors honestly believed it advisable to use the money to restore the property rather than to pay the dividend; or, where war broke out after declaration of a dividend, seriously affecting the corporation's business and making payment of the dividend highly inadvisable.

4. Where the dividend was declared payable in stock, and the stock out of which the dividend was to be paid had not yet been issued. Where, however, the stock dividend was declared payable out of treasury stock, it was held that the dividend could not be revoked.

Liability of directors for illegal dividends.—In most states the statutes specifically provide that directors who declare illegal dividends are liable personally to the corporation and to its creditors. The extent of the liability is determined by the governing statute. The liability may be limited to the amount of debts outstanding when the dividend is declared; it may be extended to debts incurred at any time during continuance of the directors in office; or it may apply to the amount withdrawn from capital, with interest. Penalties in the forms of fines and imprisonment are also imposed in some states. Directors who dissent from the declaration of the illegal dividend or were absent from the meeting at which the illegal dividend was declared may be relieved of liability by statute. The statutes may, however, specify the manner in which such dissent or absence should be indicated or noted in the minutes of the meeting, and these instructions must be followed in order to obtain the exemption from liability. Directors cannot avoid liability for illegal dividends on the ground that they did not know the dividend was illegal, where the facts could have been ascertained with reasonable diligence.

A director who dissents from the declaration of a dividend should, in any event, note his dissent on the minutes of the meeting. A director who was absent from the meeting at which an illegal dividend was declared should, immediately upon learning of the declaration of the dividend, inform the board of directors of his dissent, in order to avoid liability for the acts of his codirectors. See page 1350 for further discussion of director's responsibility for wrongful acts of his associates.

The corporation may recover the illegally paid dividends from stockholders. The fact that the stockholder who received an illegal dividend has transferred his shares does not relieve him of liability for repayment of the dividend.

Power of directors to prosecute and defend suits and to employ counsel.—The board of directors has the power to determine whether or not suit should be brought in behalf of the corporation, and, in the absence of fraud, the courts will not interfere with the exercise of the board's discretion. The directors also have the power to employ counsel to protect the interests of the corporation in instituting, prosecuting, or defending actions, and to incur incidental expenses in the conduct of litigation for the corporation. The litigation must, however, involve the corporation, not the directors personally. Where, for example, stockholders bring suit against the directors personally for mismanagement of the corporation, the directors have no right to engage counsel to defend them at the corporation's expense. They may, however, employ counsel at the corporation's expense where minority stockholders bring action against the corporation itself, even though such action is based upon alleged misconduct on the part of the directors or their agents.

Actions to enforce the liability of a director to the corporation are also instituted by the board of directors.

Power of directors to compromise claims.—The board of directors has the power to compromise claims against the corporation if, in the honest exercise of their judgment, the directors believe such compromise to be for the best interests of the corporation.

In the absence of fraud, the courts will not interfere with their action, even though it appears that better terms could have been secured. Even if the directors have acted fraudulently, the courts may refuse to interfere if the rights of an innocent third person are involved, and the corporation may be relegated to its remedies against the directors themselves.

May a director engage in a competing business?—A director may engage or have an interest in a business that competes with the corporation of which he is a director, provided he acts in good faith. Where, however, his interest in the competing business is harmful to the corporation, and where he uses his double connection to injure the corporation, he may be held liable for damages. For example, a director learns at a meeting of the board that oil has been discovered on a tract of land adjoining that owned by the corporation; if the oil is extracted, the output of the corporation's own oil fields will be diminished. He secretly purchases the tract and organizes a corporation to operate it. The director can be held liable for damages, and the corporation may be permitted to appropriate the tract of land for its own use.

A director who has severed his connection with the corporation may engage in a competing business provided he does not violate any contractual obligation toward the corporation or disclose any of its trade secrets.

Liability of directors for negligence and neglect of duty.—Directors are personally liable for losses to the corporation resulting from their negligence in the conduct of the corporation's affairs. This liability exists regardless of whether or not the statutes of the state of incorporation impose liability for acts constituting negligence. They are not liable for mistakes or mere errors of judgment, but they are required to use reasonable care, skill, and prudence in the performance of their duties. Whether or not a director has used reasonable care and diligence is a question of fact, to be determined from the circumstances surrounding each particular case. Gross inattention to the business of the corporation that results in loss to the corporation constitutes negligence for which the directors are liable. A director must devote his time and attention to the affairs of the corporation. The fact that the directors have delegated their powers to others does not relieve them of liability. So far as the law is concerned, no such thing as a "dummy" director exists. The director's duty is to direct.

Are directors liable for failure to attend board meetings?—It is the duty of every director to attend meetings of the board with a fair degree of regularity. If a director fails to do so, he may be held liable for losses that the corporation may sustain because of his negligence in attending. For example, if one director is continually absent from board meetings, and his codirectors during his absence dissipate the assets of the corporation by voting themselves enormous salaries, the absent director may be held liable as well as his codirectors, even if he knew nothing of their action. Had he been present at board meetings, he might have been able to prevent the wrongful action of the other directors. A director is presumed to know everything concerning the corporate affairs that he could have ascertained had he used reasonable diligence in performing his functions. Absence of a director from a particular board meeting because of pressing business or illness, however, does not constitute actionable negligence.

If no directors' meetings are held, the whole board may be liable for losses sustained by the corporation by reason of its failure to manage the corporate affairs. For example, if the president, in the absence of directors' meetings, has assumed entire management of the corporation, using the corporate property for his own purposes, the directors may be held liable to the corporation for the value of the property diverted.

Liability of directors for misapplication of assets.—Directors hold the property of the corporation in trust for the corporation, its stockholders, and its creditors. They must account for all assets that come into their hands, in the form of cash or otherwise, and are liable for misapplication of any of the assets, whether the misapplication is innocent or fraudulent. For example, a director may be forced to account for a loan made to him in violation of a State statute; he may be required to return the amount of a gift voted to him by his codirectors; he may be held liable for an amount paid by the corporation as compensation for counsel employed to defend the director personally; he may be compelled to reimburse the corporation for the use of corporate assets to pay his personal debts.

The liability of directors for misapplication or misappropriation of corporate assets applies whether or not a State statute imposing a liability exists. The statutes in many states specifically make the directors liable for excessive and improper loans to directors or stockholders and for improper issuance of stock.

The directors will not be held liable if no rights of creditors are affected by their improper acts, and all the stockholders have consented thereto.

Liability of directors for acts beyond the corporate powers.—Acts that are outside the corporation's powers are known as *ultra vires* acts. A director who participates in such acts is liable for any loss resulting therefrom. For example: A corporation is organized to manufacture pianos. The directors decide that it would be profitable for the corporation to manufacture and sell sporting goods and contract to purchase a complete line of bicycles. The purchase and sale of bicycles is clearly not within the scope of the corporation's powers. The directors may be prevented from carrying out the transaction, or they may be held personally accountable for the full amount expended by the corporation in the *ultra vires* transaction, together with interest. Of course, if the stockholders acquiesce in the unlawful transaction, they cannot afterwards hold the directors liable for having entered into it.

Liability of directors for secret profits.—Directors are required to act in the utmost good faith in all transactions affecting the corporation. If they secretly profit personally by any transaction either with the corporation or affecting the corporation, without full disclosure of the facts, the corporation may recover such profits. For example, where the corporation purchases a parcel of real estate and the seller secretly pays a commission on the sale to one of the directors of the purchasing corporation who was instrumental in bringing about the sale, the director can be compelled to account for the secret commission that he has received. Even if he has given part of the commission to others, he must account for all of it. The corporation may also, upon discovery of the facts, rescind the contract, even though the purchase price may have been a fair one and the purchase advantageous to the corporation. A director who enters into a direct transaction with the corporation in which he has an interest must account for any profits made by him in the transaction if he fails to disclose his interest. For example, a director sells to his corporation at a fair price some merchandise that he owns. He fails to disclose that he has bought the merchandise at a very low price with the express purpose of reselling it to the corporation. The corporation, on learning the facts, may either rescind the sale or hold the director liable for the profit that he made on the transaction. On the other hand, had he disclosed the facts, he would not be compelled to surrender his profits, for a director may deal with the corporation provided he does so fairly.

Liability of directors for fraudulent statements and acts.—A director is personally liable for his fraudulent statements and acts to anyone who was damaged by relying upon them. It is not necessary that the fraudulent statements shall have been made directly to the person injured. For example, a director sends to a credit agency a statement of the corporation's affairs that he knows to be false. The credit agency submits the statement to one of its subscribers who has applied for information concerning the financial strength of the corporation. Acting upon the false statement, the subscriber extends credit to the corporation, which, as a matter of fact, is hopelessly insolvent. The subscriber may hold the director personally liable. The fact that the director was acting for the corporation and not in his own behalf does not relieve him of liability.

Liability of a director for preferring himself over other creditors.—While a director may properly be a creditor of the corporation, he cannot use his power as a member of the board to obtain an unfair preference over other corporate creditors. For example, if a director who has loaned a sum of money to the corporation, discovering that the corporation is on the verge of bankruptcy, has the corporation pay him the full amount due, he may be held liable to other creditors of the corporation for the amount by which the sum repaid to him exceeds the proportionate amount that he would have received as a general creditor of the corporation. While his claim against the corporation is a just one, and he has received no more than the corporation owed him, he has violated his duty to the creditors as trustee of an insolvent corporation—that is, the duty to distribute the insolvent corporation's assets pro rata among all the creditors.

May a director prefer one creditor over others?—While a director to whom a corporation is indebted may not obtain an advantage over other creditors of the corporation by paying off his own debt in the face of the corporation's insolvency, he incurs no personal liability if he gives a preference to some other creditor in whose claim he has no interest. The preference itself may be illegal, and the creditor who receives it may be held accountable, but the director himself will incur no personal liability to other creditors.

Are directors liable to creditors and stockholders or only to the corporation?—Ordinarily directors are liable primarily to the corporation for their acts of malfeasance, misfeasance, and nonfeasance in the management of the corporate affairs, and neither the creditors nor the stockholders may sue to enforce such liability except in a representative capacity on behalf of the corporation. Where, however, the misconduct of a director toward an individual creditor or stockholder has resulted in loss to him, he may hold the director liable in an individual action. The statutes in some states also make directors liable to creditors under specified circumstances; as, for example, where directors assent to the creation of a debt beyond the amount of indebtedness permitted by statute, or where directors authorize the declaration of an illegal dividend.

Acts for which directors may incur criminal liability under State laws.—The following are some of the offenses for which directors are made liable by statute in the various states:

1. Doing business before receiving proper authorization therefor; doing business as a foreign corporation without a license.
2. Conducting the business of a corporation for an unlawful purpose.
3. Issuance of stock certificates before payment of franchise tax.
4. Signing or issuing improper certificates of stock.
5. Exhibiting false records to public officers examining the corporation's affairs.
6. Fraudulent reissuance of cancelled stock certificates.
7. Refusal to exhibit list of stockholders entitled to vote.
8. Signing, issuance, sale, or assignment of notes, bonds, stock, and so forth, fraudulently and without authority.
9. Receiving gratuities for making contracts or transacting business.

10. Sale of position of director of certain classes of corporations, or receipt of consideration for resigning.

11. Failure to notify other directors or officers of service upon director of application for injunction affecting the property or business of the corporation.

12. Refusal or failure to make proper entries in corporate books and records; making of false entries in books, statements, and reports.

13. Failure or refusal to make reports.

14. Illegal authorization of dividends.

15. Misuse of corporate funds.

16. Illegal loans.

17. Making of false statements in advertising for corporation.

18. Engaging in agreements and practices in violation of laws against trusts and monopolies.

19. Violation of laws against political contributions by corporation.

Some of these statutes refer expressly to both directors and officers; others merely impose a liability upon officers or upon offenders in general, and directors are liable thereunder by implication. In a few instances, penal statutes refer only to directors and not to officers; as, for example, a New Jersey statute making it a crime to fail to display the corporate name as required by law.

How a director can avoid liability for action taken by his codirectors.—The general rule is that, in the absence of a statutory provision, a director is responsible for the wrongful acts of his associates where they have come to his knowledge, and where he acquiesces therein and takes no steps to avert the injurious consequences of the acts when, by due diligence, he might have prevented them from being done. An absent director will not be held liable for acts of his associates if he has not connived at or participated in the acts, or if he was not negligent in failing to act. (See also page 1345.) If he is present at a meeting at which action that he believes to be against the best interests of the corporation is taken, he should have his disapproval noted on the records. A director who fails to do so may be deemed to have concurred in the action taken by the board. The following notation may be made in the minutes of the meeting:

Mr. ____________________, director of this corporation, opposed the motion made at this meeting to *(here insert nature of motion)* on the ground that *(here insert reason for opposition)*, and, upon passage of the said motion without his vote, demanded that his dissent from the action thereby taken be entered upon the minutes of this meeting of the board of directors. This entry is made to satisfy the demand of Mr. ____________________.

Some statutes specifically require that a director's dissent be noted on the records of the meeting in order that he may avoid liability for action taken at the meeting.

Directors' liabilities under Federal laws.—Most of the Federal laws that affect the conduct of business, such as tax laws, antitrust statutes, fair-trade acts, and laws regulating wages and hours, impose civil or criminal liabilities, or both, for violations of the law. While all of these statutes do not expressly apply the civil or criminal penalties against directors and officers, there is always the possibility that under interpretations of the penalty provisions directors and officers of corporations that have violated the law will be subject to the penalties. Under certain Federal laws, however, civil and criminal liabilities are imposed directly upon directors and officers for failure to comply with the provisions of the laws. Three such acts are mentioned below.

1. The Securities Act of 1933, which requires the filing of a registration statement with the Securities and Exchange Commission and the use of prescribed prospectuses, in connection with new offerings of securities to the public through the mails and through the channels of interstate commerce, imposes civil and criminal liabilities upon directors, officers, and others responsible for the issuance of the securities for failure to comply with these and other requirements of the law, as well as for the sale of securities by means of fraud or misrepresentation.

2. The Securities Exchange Act of 1934 imposes civil or criminal liabilities, or both, upon directors, officers, and others in connection with: (a) applications, reports, or documents filed or required to be filed by the corporation; (b) statements as to ownership of stock in the corporation and transactions in such stock; (c) manipulation of security prices; (d) use of manipulative and deceptive devices; (e) solicitation of proxies; and (f) unlawful representations.

3. The Public Utilities Holding Company Act of 1935 imposes civil or criminal penalties, or both, upon directors and officers of corporations that are subject to the law for false and misleading statements with respect to a material fact in any application, report, registration statement, or document filed under the act.

The imposition of heavy penalties against directors and officers by Federal and State laws has tended to make individuals more cautious about accepting corporate office. A number of corporations have reduced the membership of their boards; many directors have resigned from boards on which they were inactive; and an increasing number of boards are made up exclusively of staff executives. Some companies are adopting a by-law which provides that each director and officer (and his heirs, executors, and administrators) shall be indemnified by the corporation against reasonable expenses incurred by him in connection with any suit to which he may be made a party by reason of his being a director or officer of the corporation. Of course, such indemnity does not apply if the director or officer was negligent or if in the suit he was adjudged to have been derelict in the performance of his duty.

2. LAW RELATING TO OFFICERS

What officers is a corporation required to have?—The statutes in most states specify what officers a corporation must have and leave the creation of additional offices to the discretion of the board of directors or of the stockholders. The officers specifically required by statute generally include a president, a secretary, a treasurer, and a resident agent for service of process upon the corporation. In the absence of any statutory requirement as to the number of officers, the charter or by-laws may fix the number to meet the needs of the particular corporation. The following are the most usual officers of a corporation:

1. Chairman of the board of directors.
2. President.
3. Assistant to the president.
4. One or more vice-presidents.
5. Secretary.
6. Assistant secretary.

7. Treasurer.
8. Assistant treasurer.
9. Controller.
10. General manager.

Who are qualified to act as officers?—The statutes in some states prescribe certain qualifications for officers; as, for example, that the president must be a director of the corporation or that some or all of the officers must be stockholders. More frequently, however, the charter or the by-laws specify the qualifications of officers. One person often holds two offices in the same corporation, and the power to do so is confirmed by statute in some states. Two corporations may have the same officers, without impairing transactions between the corporations that have been entered into in good faith. However, in certain classes of corporations that are subject to special legislation, such as banks, public utilities, holding companies, and investment companies, statutory restrictions may prevent an officer or director of one company from holding office in another corporation at the same time.

How officers are chosen.—The statutes in most states vest in the board of directors the power to elect or appoint officers. The by-laws also generally contain a provision, consistent with any statutory requirements, for the election of officers. It is sometimes provided that the officers shall be elected by the board of directors after its election by the stockholders and that a meeting may be held without notice for this purpose immediately after the annual meeting of stockholders and at the same place. Formal acceptance of office is not required, but an individual cannot be forced into an office against his will. The power to fill vacancies in office rests with those who originally had the power to elect or appoint the officers, unless the statute or by-laws give to others the power to fill vacancies in office.

Effect of failure to elect officers.—If new officers are not elected, the old officers continue to hold their offices, regardless of whether or not they were elected for a fixed term, until they are removed, until they resign, or until the new officers are elected and qualify. The failure to elect required officers does not ordinarily cause a dissolution of the corporation. Some statutes do, however, provide that a corporation may be dissolved upon a petition to the courts by a creditor, where the corporation has not elected officers or done business within a fixed time.

Term of office of an officer.—The term of office is usually fixed by the statute of the state in which the corporation is organized, or by the corporation's charter or by-laws. The term may be:

1. One or more years.
2. At the pleasure of the board of directors, in which case the board may not have power to enter into a contract for a definite period of time.
3. For such time as the board of directors may by contract or resolution determine.
4. Until the next annual meeting of directors and until their successors are elected.

If the term of office is not fixed, an officer holds his office at the pleasure of the corporation or until he resigns and his successor is elected. An officer's term of office does not expire merely because the term of the directors who appointed him has expired.

Resignation of an officer.—An officer may resign at any time, although elected for a fixed period, unless he is restricted by the corporation's charter or by-laws, by the laws of the state in which the corporation is organized, or by the terms of his contract with the corporation. He may resign even if it is provided that officers of the corporation shall hold office until their successors are elected or appointed. A resignation must be tendered in good faith. Where, for example, all the officers resign at one time in order that the corporation may be placed in a receiver's hands, the resignation will not be recognized by the courts, for it will be deemed to be fraudulent.

If a resignation is tendered to take effect on acceptance, it must be accepted before it is effective. If it is tendered to take effect at once, acceptance is not necessary unless made so by statute, charter, or by-laws. The resignation may be written or oral, and no particular form is required.

Removal of an officer with or without cause.—A corporation may remove an officer for cause, even if his term of office is fixed. An officer may be removed without cause if his term of office is not fixed, and removal for cause is not required. An officer may also be removed without cause even though his term of office is fixed, if the statute, charter, or by-laws expressly authorize removal without cause. The power to remove an officer rests with the person or persons authorized to elect or appoint him. Generally, this power is given to the board of directors. An officer who is removable at the pleasure of the board need not be given notice of removal or a hearing. Where, however, an officer is being removed for cause, reasonable notice of intention to remove, adequate time to prepare his defense, and a fair hearing are required. An officer who has been removed unlawfully may apply to the courts for reinstatement.

Can the officers bind the corporation by their acts?—The officers of a corporation are its agents. They can bind the corporation by their acts only when such acts are within the scope of the authority granted to them. Authority to act may be given to an officer by statute, by the corporation's charter, by its by-laws, and by express resolution of the stockholders or directors granting him authority to act. An officer also has implied authority to do acts that are reasonably necessary to carry into effect the express powers granted. For example, if a corporation gives an officer power to borrow money in its behalf, the officer also has power to arrange the terms of the loan and to agree to give security therefor.

In addition to express and implied powers, officers have so-called "apparent" powers by which they can bind the corporation. For example, where a corporation permits an officer to assume certain powers or holds him out as possessing those powers, the corporation cannot afterwards deny, as against an innocent person who relied upon the officers' apparent authority, that the officer had authority to act. Similarly, if a corporation ratifies an unauthorized act of its officer, that act will be binding upon it. The corporation may not, however, ratify an act of the officer in its behalf that is beyond the powers of the corporation itself. Those who deal with an officer of the corporation are deemed to know the limitations on his authority. Where, however, a limitation is contained in a by-law, an innocent person who knew nothing of the limitation is not bound by it.

Duties performed by officers.—Officers have very few inherent powers; that is, powers that exist merely by virtue of their holding a particular office. Such powers as they do have are derived from the State corporation laws, from the corporation's charter and by-laws, and from resolutions of the board of directors and of the committees appointed by the board. The duties performed by persons holding the same office vary widely from one corporation to another. The following lists indicate the detailed duties generally assigned to the chief officers of the corporation. The table on pages 1361–64, compiled from information furnished by several hundred corporations, indicates in percentages the number of corporations in which certain administrative functions are supervised by certain officers.

Duties of chairman of the board of directors.—The following are the usual duties of the chairman of the board.

1. Acts as senior officer of the corporation.
2. Presides at meetings of the board and of the stockholders.
3. Directs the policy of the corporation.
4. Has primary control over methods and amounts of capital financing.
5. Delegates powers to the president.
6. Acts as ex officio member of all standing committees.
7. Appoints members of all committees not otherwise ordered by the by-laws.

In some corporations, the chairman of the board is not the senior officer, but ranks immediately below the president.

Duties of the president.—The following are the usual duties of the president.

1. Calls meetings of stockholders.
2. Signs statements and reports required to be filed with State officials.
3. Makes acknowledgments of instruments.
4. Acts as executive officer and has general management and direction of business.
5. Performs all duties of chairman of board in his absence or in case of his inability to act.
6. Signs certificates of stock with secretary or assistant secretary.
7. Signs and executes in corporate name all deeds, mortgages, bonds, contracts, and so forth.

8. Executes stockholders' consents, and attends and votes at stockholders' meetings of corporations in which the company owns stock.

9. Acts as ex officio member of all committees.

10. Prescribes duties for officers and employees not otherwise defined.

11. Countersigns checks, drafts, and orders for payment of moneys.

12. Appoints officers and employees, except those selected by the board of directors; removes such officers and fills vacancies.

13. Employs and discharges all employees and fixes their salaries.

14. Compensates directors for special services.

15. Appoints his assistants.

16. Sees that all orders and resolutions of the board are carried into effect.

17. Reports to the chairman of the board and consults with him.

See also table on pages 1361–64, indicating that the president often handles real-estate matters, leases, investments, loans, patents, reports to stockholders, budgets, and publicity.

Duties of assistant to the president.—The following are the usual duties of the assistant to the president:

1. Relieves a busy president of some of his duties, such as representing him at conferences and meetings.

2. Directs administration of a distinct department of the business, such as production, engineering, sales promotion, merchandising, office management, and so forth.

3. Co-ordinates activities between individual executives or department heads.

4. Serves as member of committees, such as executive committee, management advisory committee, workers' council, pension board, and employee stock-purchase committee.

Duties of the vice-president.—The following are the usual duties of a vice-president:

1. Performs the duties of the president in his absence or in case of his inability to act.

2. Acts as assistant to the president and under his direction.

3. Performs such duties as are assigned to him by the board of directors or by the president.

4. Signs certificates of stock with the secretary.
5. Signs bonds, debentures, and dividend checks.

See also table on pages 1361–64, indicating that the vice-president is sometimes charged with budgeting, leases, loans, patents, and real-estate matters.

Duties of the secretary.—The following are the usual duties of the secretary:

1. Prepares schedules of meetings and gives notices of meetings.
2. Drafts resolutions, attends and records proceedings of meetings of stockholders and directors; acts as secretary at meetings of executives, branch managers, and department heads.
3. Signs or attests statements and reports filed with State officials, published, or submitted to stockholders.
4. Signs acknowledgments of instruments.
5. Maintains the register of stockholders and other stock books and allows inspection by stockholders; prepares stock list and keeps it open for inspection.
6. Executes proxies or powers of attorney to vote stock owned by the corporation.
7. Signs certificates of stock with some other designated officer.
8. Gives notice of sale of stock forfeited for nonpayment of assessments.
9. Keeps the records and seal of the corporation, and affixes the seal where necessary.
10. Sees that books, reports, and documents are properly prepared, kept, and filed; guides other officers in matters pertaining to corporate procedure and issuance of corporate reports.
11. Maintains a calendar or follow-up record of dates on which various departments are required to take action, and notifies them in advance of the action to be taken.
12. Advises officers and directors of their election.
13. Prepares abstracts of papers belonging to the corporation, and records them.
14. Publishes action in respect to dividends.
15. Registers bonds of the corporation.
16. Transmits to auditor, for recording, copies of contracts providing for payment of money to or by the corporation.
17. Looks after physical care of buildings, real estate, and so forth.

18. Maintains insurance on corporate property.

19. Has charge of correspondence and personal relations with security holders. See also table on page ...., indicating various administrative functions supervised by secretary.

Duties of assistant secretary.—The following are the usual duties of an assistant secretary.

1. Acts in place of the secretary in his absence or in case of his disability.

2. Performs secretarial duties where the corporation has principal offices in several cities.

3. Where assistant secretary acts for subsidiary, he keeps in communication with secretary of holding company, and sends copies of resolutions, records, documents, and so forth, for filing in main office.

Duties of the treasurer.—The following are the usual duties of the treasurer.

1. Files reports of financial condition and tax reports with officials of the State.

2. Prepares reports upon demand of stockholders.

3. Has charge and custody of and is responsible for all funds and securities of the corporation.

4. Deposits funds and maintains bank accounts in banks designated by the board of directors.

5. Keeps books of account of moneys received and paid out in behalf of the corporation.

6. Exhibits books and records to directors during business hours.

7. Receives and gives receipts for moneys due the corporation.

8. Renders a statement of condition of finances at regular meetings of directors and renders full annual report at stockholders' annual meeting.

9. Signs certificates of stock with a designated officer.

10. Arranges for listing of corporation's securities on stock exchange.

11. Signs checks, bills of exchange, and promissory notes.

12. Advises the corporation in regard to financial matters.

13. Handles surety bonds.

Duties of assistant treasurer.—The following are the usual duties of an assistant treasurer:

1. Performs all the duties of the treasurer in his absence or in case of his inability to act.

2. Assists treasurer and performs duties assigned to him by the treasurer or by the board of directors.

Duties of the controller.—The following are the usual duties of a controller:

1. Acts as principal accounting officer in charge of accounting books and records.

2. Audits payrolls and vouchers and causes them to be properly certified.

3. Initiates, prepares, and issues standard practices relating to all accounting matters and procedures and co-ordinates systems throughout the corporation, including clerical and office methods, records, reports, and procedures.

4. Obtains from agents and from departments of the corporation reports for recording general operations or for directing accounts.

5. Maintains and enforces classification and other accounting rules prescribed by regulating bodies.

6. Causes to be prepared and filed reports and statistics required by law or prescribed by the president.

7. Prepares balance sheets, income accounts, financial statements, and reports.

8. Prepares, as budget director, in conjunction with other officers and department heads, an annual budget covering all activities of the corporation, for submission to the board of directors prior to the beginning of the fiscal year.

9. Approves for payment vouchers, drafts, and other accounts payable, when properly authorized by the president or others designated by the president.

10. Endorses checks, notes, and obligations for collection, deposit, or transfer.

11. Countersigns warrants drawn by the treasurer for depositing securities in safe-deposit boxes or for withdrawing the same.

12. Countersigns checks drawn by the treasurer against funds of the corporation, except as otherwise provided by resolution of the directors.

13. Appoints an auditor and subordinate employees and fixes their compensation.

14. Has charge of records and clerical and office procedure throughout the departments of the corporation and its subsidiaries.

See also table below, indicating that the controller often handles dividend payments, insurance, leases, and tax matters.

Duties of the general manager.—"General manager" is the title given to one who has general direction and control of the corporate affairs. While an officer of the corporation, such as the president, vice-president, secretary, or treasurer, may also hold the office of general manager, the latter is ordinarily not an officer of the corporation. He is an agent with power to bind the corporation by contracts necessary in the prosecution of the corporate business. His powers vary with the nature of the business, but usually include the following:

1. Directing and supervising the ordinary details relating to manufacturing, sales, and transportation.
2. Keeping complete records showing all business transacted by him, and all contracts and trade commitments made.
3. Reporting to the president the exact nature, extent, terms, and conditions of all business transacted by him, and contracts and commitments made.
4. Performing such other duties as are prescribed by the board of directors.

TABLE SHOWING DIVISION OF ADMINISTRATIVE FUNCTIONS AMONG OFFICERS*

Duty	*Officers Responsible*	*Percentage of Total Inquiries*
Accounting: supervision of department	Controller	53
	Treasurer	21
	Secretary	15
	Miscellaneous (including C. P. A., auditor, etc.)	11

* Duties performed by one who holds the office of both secretary and treasurer have been accredited in the table to the secretary; duties assigned to one who holds the position of vice-president, as well as that of secretary or treasurer, have been accredited to the secretary or treasurer.

TABLE SHOWING DIVISION OF ADMINISTRATIVE FUNCTIONS AMONG OFFICERS (*Cont.*)

Duty	*Officers Responsible*	*Percentage of Total Inquiries*
Annual report: preparation	Controller	27
	Secretary	25
	Treasurer	17
	President	15
	General officers	15
	Auditor	1
Bonds: registration, interest and coupon payments (aside from trustee or interest paying agent)	Treasurer	63
	Secretary	37
Budgeting	Controller	33
	Treasurer	22
	President	14
	Secretary	7
	Vice-president	4
	Miscellaneous (including finance committee, budget manager, office manager, etc.)	20
Dividend payments (aside from dividend disbursing agent)	Treasurer	55
	Secretary	32
	Controller	10
	Miscellaneous (including accounting department, etc.)	3
Documents and records: custody of same	Secretary	61
	Treasurer	30
	Controller	4
	Miscellaneous (including corporation counsel, divided control, etc.)	5
Filing: supervision of general system	Secretary	25
	Treasurer	15
	Controller	11
	Office manager	10
	Heads of individual departments	9
	Miscellaneous (including office manager, planning department, chief accountant, public relations division, etc.)	30
Insurance	Secretary	34
	Treasurer	34
	Controller	8
	Miscellaneous (including insurance committee, insurance department, auditor, real estate agent, etc.)	24

Duty	Officers Responsible	Percentage of Total Inquiries
Investments	Treasurer	57
	President	15
	Secretary	9
	Miscellaneous (including principal officers and economist, chairman of the board, executive officers, finance committee, etc.)	19
Leases	Secretary	25
	Treasurer	19
	Vice-president	12
	Real estate department	8
	Controller	4
	President	4
	Miscellaneous (including land agent, general manager, legal department, purchasing agent, sales department, etc.)	28
Loans	Treasurer	57
	President	25
	Vice-president	4
	Secretary	3
	Miscellaneous (including finance committee, all officers, etc.)	11
Notices of stockholders' and directors' meetings: preparation	Secretary	92
	Miscellaneous (including corporation's counsel, stockholders' relations division, etc.)	8
Patents	President	34
	Legal department	14
	Secretary	15
	Vice-president	10
	Patent division	7
	Miscellaneous (including head of research department, chief engineer, corporation's counsel, etc.)	20
Proxies: preparation	Secretary	95
	Miscellaneous (including corporation's counsel, etc.)	5
Proxies: review after return	Secretary	83
	Miscellaneous (including proxy committee, assistants, etc.)	17

TABLE SHOWING DIVISION OF ADMINISTRATIVE FUNCTIONS AMONG OFFICERS (*Cont.*)

Duty	*Officers Responsible*	*Percentage of Total Inquiries*
Publicity or public relations	President	36
	Public relations division	12
	Vice-president	10
	Secretary	8
	Miscellaneous (including assistant to president, advertising department, all officers, etc.)	35
Real estate matters	Secretary	23
	Treasurer	23
	Vice-president	12
	Real estate department	10
	President	6
	Miscellaneous (including land agent, purchasing agent, finance committee, general manager, legal department)	26
Tax matters	Controller	30
	Secretary	29
	Treasurer	17
	Legal department	10
	Miscellaneous (including tax committee, auditor, manager of tax division, real-estate agent, etc.)	14
Transfer of stock (aside from transfer agent)	Secretary	80
	Treasurer	20

Are officers entitled to compensation for their services?—Officers of the corporation who have discretionary control over the management of the corporation's business are not entitled to compensation for services rendered as an incident of their office unless authorized:

1. By charter.
2. By by-law.
3. By resolution of the board of directors or the stockholders.
4. By agreement between the officer and the corporation, express or implied.

Like directors, however (see page 1327), they may be entitled to compensation for services rendered outside of the ordinary duties of their office. Ministerial officers who are neither directors nor stockholders are entitled to be paid a reasonable amount for their services, unless it was mutually intended that no compensation was to be paid. A ministerial officer may include a secretary, assistant secretary, manager, secretary, cashier, treasurer, and other officer, depending upon the nature of the officer's duties.

An officer who is guilty of gross misconduct or fraud in management of the corporation's affairs forfeits his right to compensation. He is not, however, deprived of compensation because of absence on account of illness, particularly where he had some other officer perform his duties, and the corporation suffered no loss through his absence.

May an officer lend money to or borrow from the corporation?—The principles set forth on pages 1335–36, covering the right of a director to lend money to or borrow money from the corporation, are equally applicable to an officer.

Liability of an officer for mismanagement.—An officer occupies a fiduciary relation toward the corporation. By accepting office, he impliedly undertakes to give the corporation the benefit of his best care and judgment and is bound to exercise the utmost good faith in transactions touching his duties to the corporation and its property. He may not profit as an individual by his official position; he is liable for secret profits, even though the corporation suffered no damage. An officer is not, however, personally liable for depletion of the corporate assets unless he was grossly negligent in managing the business entrusted to his care or was guilty of willful destruction. In the absence of positive misfeasance, the courts are reluctant to hold an officer liable for losses suffered by the corporation because of the manner in which the officer discharged his duties. An officer is not chargeable with losses to the corporation caused by mere mistakes or errors in judgment. He is, however, bound by restrictions in the corporation's charter and by-laws and is liable for loss resulting from his failure to observe such restrictions.

As to statutory restrictions against profiting from transactions in the company's securities, see page 1339.

Acts for which officers may incur criminal liability.—The liabilities listed on pages 1349 et seq. for directors are also applicable to officers.

3. LAW RELATING TO STOCKHOLDERS

Have stockholders a right to participate in management of the corporation?—Stockholders have no right to participate in the conduct of the ordinary affairs of the corporation. Management of the corporation is entrusted by the corporation laws of the various states to the board of directors. However, since the board of directors is elected by the stockholders, the stockholders have some measure of control over the conduct of the corporation's affairs. Further, the State statutes or the articles of incorporation may require that the consent of all or of a proportion of the stockholders be obtained before certain action is taken. The following matters are generally subject to approval of the stockholders:

1. Acceptance of the corporate charter.
2. Amendment of the corporate charter.
3. Adoption of by-laws, unless the power is expressly given to the board of directors by the State laws or by the articles of incorporation.
4. Amendment of the by-laws, if the power to amend is not expressly given to the board of directors.
5. Removal of directors.
6. Merger or consolidation of the corporation with another company.
7. Transfer of all the assets of the corporation by sale or lease.
8. Voluntary dissolution and liquidation of the corporation.
9. Assessments on fully paid stock.

The fact that the consent of stockholders is required for certain action does not mean that the stockholders can take such action without action by the board of directors. Action taken by stockholders without the board of directors will, however, be binding on the corporation if the board of directors ratifies it, or if the corporation acquiesces in the stockholders' action and receives the benefits of the transaction.

Right of stockholders to adopt and amend by-laws.—By-laws are simply rules adopted by the corporation for the regulation of its affairs. Since the stockholders constitute the corporation, the power to adopt by-laws rests with them. The board of directors may, however, be authorized to adopt by-laws either by the State statutes or by the provisions of the corporation's articles of incorporation, or the stockholders themselves may by resolution delegate the power to adopt by-laws to the board of directors.

The power to amend by-laws also rests primarily with the stockholders, but the directors may be given the right to effect changes in the by-laws by State statute, by the articles of incorporation, by resolution of the stockholders, or by the by-laws themselves. Directors who are given power to adopt by-laws have no power to amend by-laws adopted by the stockholders, unless the power to amend as well as the power to adopt is expressly given to the directors. Where both stockholders and directors have the power to make and amend by-laws, the by-laws of the directors are subject to the by-laws of the stockholders.

The manner in which the by-laws are amended is prescribed by statute in some states. In the absence of statutory provision therefor, the by-laws themselves may specify the notice and vote necessary to effect an amendment.

Power of stockholders to elect directors.—The right to elect directors annually is generally given to the stockholders by statute. The manner in which the election is to be conducted is also regulated in some states. Many statutes require that election shall be by ballot and that it shall be conducted by inspectors or judges of election, appointed as provided in the by-laws. By-laws cannot modify any statutory requirement as to election. If the statute, for example, provides that directors may be chosen by a plurality of votes, a by-law cannot require a majority vote for election. The right to fill vacancies in the board for an unexpired term may be taken away from the stockholders by statute and given to the directors. Even under such statutes, however, the stockholders and not the directors generally have the right to elect newly created directors where the number of directors has been increased.

Liability of stockholders to corporation for payment of stock.—The stockholder is liable to the corporation for the amount that he has agreed to pay for his stock. This is true even though the certificate of stock issued to him is marked "fully paid and non-assessable." If the stock has a par value, he must generally pay a price not less than the par value. If it is without par value, the price is usually fixed by the directors, under authority granted by the stockholders or the charter.

The time when and the manner in which payment must be made depends upon the terms of the contract between the stockholder and the corporation. If the contract of purchase does not indicate when payments are due, it is implied that they are payable upon call of the directors, made pursuant to statutory provisions. A call is an official declaration that a sum is required to be paid upon a stock subscription. The length of notice of the call that must be given to the stockholders depends upon the provisions of the statute, charter, by-laws, or contract. Failure to respond to a call for payment gives the corporation the right to sue for the amount called for. In addition, the statutes of the various states give other remedies, including the right to sell the shares and apply the proceeds to the payment of the installment, or to forfeit the shares and all previous payments made thereon.

Is a stockholder who transfers his stock relieved of liability for a call on an unpaid subscription?—The general rule is that a stockholder who transfers his stock is relieved of liability for calls made after the transfer, provided:

1. He acts in good faith.
2. The transfer is recorded on the corporate books.

The transferee is liable for calls made after such transfer, but not for those made before the transfer. The date of the call, not the date when payment is due, fixes the liability as between the transferor and the transferee. For example: A call for payment of the balance due on *A*'s stock is made on April 5, payable April 15. *A* transfers his stock to *B* on April 10, and the transfer is recorded on the corporate books on that date. *A* remains liable for the call, since it was made before the date of transfer. Note, however, that while this is the general rule, in some states the statutes make other provision for liability of stockholders upon transfer of their shares. In some states, for example, both the transferor and the transferee are liable for the full amount remaining unpaid on the shares, whether a call is made before or after transfer.

It is generally held that if a corporation is insolvent at the time stock is transferred, a transferor is not relieved of liability for calls unless the transfer is made to a person who is financially responsible, or at least apparently so.

Is interest payable upon the amount that a stockholder owes on his stock?—In addition to his liability to pay the full amount of the purchase price of his stock, a stockholder is liable to the corporation for interest on the unpaid balance thereon, at the legal rate, from the date when payment is due to the date when payment is made. The purchase price may, under the terms of the subscription contract, be payable immediately, or it may be payable at some future date fixed in the contract.

Liability of stockholders to creditors.—The extent of the liability of stockholders to creditors depends upon whether or not the stock has been fully paid. Where a stockholder has paid the full amount due on the stock, the following rules prevail with respect to his liability to creditors:

1. The general rule is that the stockholder is not personally liable for the debts of the corporation beyond the amount paid on his stock, unless the statute of the state where the corporation is organized imposes an additional liability.
2. In some states an additional liability is imposed upon stockholders of certain classes of corporations, as, for example, in the case of banking corporations, where a double liability is imposed; that is, in addition to the amount due on the purchase price of the stock, the stockholder is liable for an additional amount equal to the amount of the stock held by him.
3. In some states stockholders of insolvent corporations are made liable for debts due laborers, servants, and other classes of labor, although they have fully paid for their stock. Whether or not a stockholder is relieved of liability for labor debts by a transfer of his shares depends upon the law of the particular state. Generally, the stockholder is not liable for debts contracted after he has made a valid transfer. Some states make both the transferor and the transferee liable for debts contracted prior to the transfer.

Where a stockholder has not fully paid for his stock, the following rules prevail with respect to his liability to creditors:

1. The liability of stockholders to creditors to pay the amount due on their subscriptions arises generally only upon insolvency of

the corporation and is governed by constitutional or statutory provisions of the state in which the corporation is organized.

2. The stockholders' liability is limited to the amount which remains unpaid on his stock, unless the statute imposes an additional liability.

3. The stockholders are generally liable to pay to creditors only so much of the amount due on the stock as is necessary to satisfy creditors' claims.

4. Each stockholder is required to bear only his proportionate share of the amount necessary to pay the debts. While each stockholder may be compelled to pay the entire sum remaining unpaid on his shares, if the amount that he has been compelled to pay is more than his proportionate share of the debts, measured by the proportion which his stock bears to the whole stock, he is entitled to contribution from the other stockholders who have not borne their proportionate share of the debts of the corporation.

Liability of stockholders for assessments on fully paid stock.—An assessment is a demand upon stockholders for payment of an amount above the par value or contract price of the stock held by them. A stockholder who has paid for his stock in full cannot be required to pay any additional amount unless an assessment on fully paid stock is authorized by statute or by charter, or unless the stockholder has consented to the making of the assessment. Such consent may be implied, as, for example, where the corporation has adopted a by-law providing for assessment, and the stockholder has purchased his stock with full knowledge of and acquiescence in the by-law. In some states, the immunity of a holder of fully paid stock from liability for further assessments is confirmed by statute. Other states permit assessments for limited amounts and for specified purposes, such as payment of expenses, payment of debts, conducting of business.

Authority to levy the assessment is given to the stockholders under some statutes or charters, to the directors under others. Notice of the assessment must be given to the stockholders in strict compliance with statutory or charter requirements. If the stockholders fail to pay, the corporation may bring an action against them. The shares of defaulting stockholders may also be subject to sale and forfeiture if the statute or charter so provides.

Issuance of a duplicate certificate of stock upon loss, theft, or destruction of a certificate.—A stockholder has a right to the issuance of a duplicate certificate of stock in the event of loss, destruction, or theft of his old certificate. The statutes in most states confirm this right and indicate the conditions under which the new certificate may be issued. Generally these conditions are also outlined in the corporation's by-laws. The following are the usual requirements:

1. An order from the stockholder upon the corporation, instructing and authorizing the corporation to stop any transfer of the lost certificate.
2. An affidavit from the stockholder, setting forth the facts surrounding the loss of the certificate of stock.
3. Advertisement by the stockholder of the loss of the certificate of stock, and furnishing of evidence of the advertisement to the corporation.
4. A bond of indemnity furnished to the corporation by the stockholder, with surety approved by the board of directors, in the amount required by statute, or by the board of directors if the amount is not fixed by statute. The amount of the bond is usually double the current value of the stock.
5. The lapse of a specified period of time, usually from three to six months, after the stockholder has complied with the requirements, before issuance of the new certificate of stock.

The board of directors may pass a resolution authorizing the issuance of a new certificate of stock in each instance, or it may pass a blanket resolution authorizing a designated officer or its transfer agent and registrar to issue duplicate certificates of stock upon compliance with the required conditions.

The corporation must issue a duplicate certificate of stock when the required conditions have been met; otherwise it will subject itself to liability for damages, and may be compelled to issue the new certificate by court procedure. The corporation may be compelled to recognize not only a bona fide holder of the new certificate of stock but also a bona fide holder of the old certificate, for the reasons mentioned below. In that event, it is protected by the indemnity bond which it requires the stockholder to furnish as a condition precedent to issuance of the duplicate certificate of stock.

The rights of a purchaser of the old certificate of stock may have to be recognized even though he purchased from a person who found or stole the lost certificate. Under the Uniform Stock Transfer Act, which has been adopted in many states, a bona fide purchaser of a stock certificate that has been properly endorsed acquires a good title to the stock although he has purchased from a finder or a thief. If, however, the endorsement was forged, the rights of the purchaser, even though he purchased in good faith, may be defeated by the superior claim of the true owner of the certificate. Under the common-law rule, which is generally applicable in states that have not adopted the Uniform Stock Transfer Act, where certificates of stock endorsed in blank are stolen before delivery, the thief cannot ordinarily pass good title even to a bona fide purchaser. If, however, the owner of the stock made the theft possible through his negligence, the right of the bona fide purchaser is deemed superior to that of the owner.

In some states a corporation is not required to issue a duplicate certificate of stock unless a court order has been obtained. A corporation may, nevertheless, voluntarily issue a new certificate without a court order.

Power of stockholders to increase stock.—The power to increase the amount of capital stock that the corporation is authorized to issue rests with the stockholders. It may, however, be conferred upon the directors by express resolution of the stockholders or by charter, unless a statute expressly prohibits such delegation of power. The laws of the state in which the corporation is organized usually indicate the manner in which the increase is to be effected. An amendment of the charter, effected in the following manner, is generally required:

1. The board of directors adopts a resolution, at a meeting properly called and held, recommending an amendment of the charter to increase the amount of the authorized capital stock and calling a meeting of stockholders to pass upon the amendment.

2. The stockholders, at a meeting duly called and held, adopt a resolution authorizing an amendment of the charter to increase the authorized capital stock and instructing the proper officers of the corporation to file the necessary papers required by law to carry out the amendment.

3. The officers execute and file with the State official designated by statute a certificate of amendment or other documents required by law.

In some states, an amendment of the charter is not required to effect an increase in the authorized capital stock. The steps required to be taken to effect an increase are, however, similar to those outlined above; instead of a certificate of amendment of the charter, a certificate of increase is required to be filed.

Stockholders' pre-emptive rights upon issuance of additional stock.—The pre-emptive right is the right of each stockholder, upon the issuance of additional shares of stock, to purchase his proportion of the new stock in order to maintain his relative control and interest in the corporation. For example, if *A* owns $10,000 of the $100,000 worth of stock issued and outstanding, and the corporation increases its authorized capital stock to $200,000, *A* will have a right to purchase 1/10 of the new issue, or an additional $10,000 worth of stock, before the stock may be offered to outsiders. The stockholder has a right to purchase the stock at the price fixed by the corporation, and, if he fails to take it, it cannot be offered to anyone else upon more favorable terms. He must be given reasonable notice of his right to subscribe, and a reasonable opportunity to exercise the right. Stockholders who are not in a position to take and pay for the stock to which they are entitled may sell the rights to anyone who can.

The pre-emptive right of stockholders is governed by statute in many states. These statutes indicate the kind of issues to which the pre-emptive right attaches and in some instances provide that the certificate of incorporation may deny the pre-emptive right to any issue or to any class of stock. Thus statutes may show whether the pre-emptive right applies to issuance of additional stock out of an amount previously authorized; whether it applies only upon an increase in the authorized capital stock; whether it applies upon the issuance of stock for property or for cash; and whether it applies upon the issuance of treasury stock. Frequently the certificate of incorporation will regulate the pre-emptive rights of stockholders pursuant to the governing statute. In the absence of regulating statutes and charter provisions, the court decisions in the particular jurisdiction must be examined to determine under what circumstances the pre-emptive right exists. These decisions, it must be admitted, are in many instances conflicting and confused.

A stockholder may waive his pre-emptive right by agreement with the corporation.

Right of stockholders to reduce capital stock.—The right to reduce capital stock rests with the stockholders, as does the right to increase it. The directors have no power to effect a reduction without the approval of the stockholders, unless expressly authorized by statute, by the corporate charter, or by the stockholders themselves. An amendment of the charter is generally required to authorize a reduction in the amount of authorized capital stock. The amendment is effected in the same manner as an amendment to increase the capital stock; that is, by resolution of the directors recommending the amendment and calling a meeting of stockholders, and by resolution of the stockholders approving the amendment. The vote of a majority or two thirds of the stockholders, given at a meeting duly called, is usually required. In addition to the filing of a certificate of amendment with some designated official, some states also require the filing of a statement signed by officers and directors to the effect that the proposed reduction will not reduce the actual value of the assets of the corporation to an amount less than the total amount of its debts and liabilities, plus the amount, as reduced, of its capital stock.

Stockholders' right to inspect corporate books and records.—Stockholders have a right to protect their interest in the corporation by keeping themselves informed as to whether the directors, officers, and agents of the corporation are attending to their duties properly. They may, at reasonable times and for a proper purpose, inspect the books and records of the corporation, including:

1. The corporation's record of its by-laws.
2. Minutes of its meetings.
3. The stock book or register.
4. Account books, ledgers, etc.
5. Minutes of directors' meetings.

A demand for inspection must be made at the office of the corporation in which the books and records are kept or at the principal place of business of the corporation. The inspection need not be made by the stockholder personally; his agent or attorney may inspect and make copies and abstracts of the records. The right of stockholders to inspect the books and to examine the corporate records is confirmed by statute in many states. In some instances, these statutes restrict the right of inspection and examination to designated books and records, such as the list of stockholders, the stock-transfer books, the books of account and financial records, and reports required by law to be filed in some public office. Where the right to inspect is given by statute, it may generally be exercised irrespective of the motive of the stockholder in seeking an inspection. The statutes sometimes impose upon the corporation and its officers or directors penalties for refusing to permit inspection upon proper demand.

4. DOING BUSINESS IN OTHER STATES

May a corporation do business in any state?—A corporation is an artificial entity created by the state in which it is organized, and as such has no inherent right to compel any other state to recognize its existence. In a state other than that in which it was organized, it is known as a foreign corporation. As a matter of comity, the states permit corporations to do business within their borders provided the corporations comply with special terms and conditions imposed. These conditions generally include:

1. Registration of the presence of the foreign corporation in the state by the filing of certain documents with State officials.
2. Designation of a person in the state to act as agent for the service of process upon the foreign corporation.
3. Payment of certain fees and taxes.

The right of states to regulate the activities of foreign corporations within their borders is subject to various limitations contained in the Federal Constitution. One of these limitations, and by far the most important, is that a state cannot unwarrantably interfere with business carried on by a foreign corporation which is interstate commerce as distinguished from intrastate business. Interstate commerce means shipment from state to state; intrastate business means business done within the state.

What constitutes "doing business" in another state.—It is not always easy to determine whether a corporation is engaged in interstate commerce, and is thus free from State regulation, or whether it is doing business within a state. What constitutes "doing business" within a state is determined by the wording of the various State statutes, the interpretation of these statutes by the courts, and the facts and circumstances surrounding each particular case. The following rules are generally accepted in deciding whether or not a foreign corporation is doing business within a state:

1. *Isolated transactions.*—Occasional and isolated transactions that do not indicate an intention on the part of the corporation regularly to conduct a substantial part of its business in a state do not constitute doing business in that state. Doing business means a continued activity in carrying out the purposes for which the corporation was organized. For example, a corporation is organized in New York, where it carries on all of its business. A friend of the corporation's president, who lives in Michigan, orders a bill of goods while on a visit to New York. The goods are delivered to the friend in Michigan. The corporation is not doing business in Michigan and need not qualify as a foreign corporation in Michigan. Even where several transactions are effected in the state, the corporation is not necessarily doing business in the state if the transactions are incidental and not in the exercise of the purposes for which the corporation was organized.

2. *Solicitation of business.*—A foreign corporation is generally held to be engaged in interstate commerce and not to be doing business in the state when it merely employs salesmen to solicit orders in the state without closing the sale in the state or making shipments from the state. Nor is a corporation engaged in doing business in the state if it merely receives or solicits orders by mail by means of circulars, catalogues, and so forth, but accepts the orders and fills them outside the state. Where, however, the foreign corporation's agent solicits orders from local retailers and turns the orders over to local wholesalers who fill them and receive payment from the retailers, the corporation is doing business in the state. Some courts hold that while a foreign corporation that merely solicits business in the state may not be required to qualify as a foreign corporation, it may, however, be subject to service of process.

3. *Appointment of agents.*—The appointment of an agent in a state does not, in itself, constitute doing business in that state. Whether or not a foreign corporation which has an agent in another state is doing business in that state depends upon the nature of the agent's acts. For example, if all the agent does is solicit orders for goods that are to be shipped into the state, the corporation is not required to qualify as a foreign corporation in the state or to pay taxes on the business solicited. If, however, the agent has the power to bind the corporation by contract, or if he sells goods in the state and makes deliveries from stock on hand, the corporation is deemed to be doing business in the state.

4. *Purchases of goods.*—Where a foreign corporation purchases goods in the state through its agents or through the mails, which goods are to be sent to the corporation outside the state in the same condition in which the goods were purchased, the corporation is not doing business in the state. This is the general rule applicable where the question involved is whether or not the corporation is required to qualify as a foreign corporation in the state. Some courts have held, however, that where the question involved is whether or not service of process may be effected upon the foreign corporation, the corporation is doing business in the state if it makes its purchases with regularity and employs agents for the purchase of goods in the state as part of its regular business.

5. *Sales of goods.*—A foreign corporation that sells to a resident of another state goods which at the time of sale are outside the state in which the purchaser lives, and which are to be shipped to the purchaser, is not doing business in the state in which the purchaser resides. Even if the goods sold are already in the state in which the purchaser resides, the corporation is not doing business in that state if the transaction is an isolated one.

6. *Ownership of property.*—The mere passive ownership of either personal or real property by a foreign corporation in the state does not constitute doing business in that state, and the corporation is not required to qualify as a foreign corporation.

7. *Maintenance of an office.*—A foreign corporation is not deemed to be doing business in a state merely because it maintains an office in the state. The maintenance of any office, however, may be a strong factor in determining the question, and the conclusion drawn depends upon the purpose for which the office is used. For

example, where the foreign corporation directs its internal affairs from the office in the state, holds directors' and stockholders' meetings there, keeps its books and records there, it is generally deemed to be doing business in the state. On the other hand, where the corporation maintains an office in the state for the convenience of its salesmen, and the business conducted through the office is entirely in the nature of interstate commerce, the corporation is generally held not to be doing business in the state.

How a foreign corporation qualifies to do business in a state.—Each state has its own requirements as to the method of qualification. In most states qualification is effected by the payment of an entrance fee and the filing of the following documents:

1. Application for permission to do business in the state.
2. Copy of the articles of incorporation and all amendments thereto, properly certified.
3. Copy of the by-laws of the corporation, and all amendments thereto, properly attested.
4. Certificate designating a place of business in the state and appointment of an agent for the service of process in the state.
5. Statement of financial condition of the corporation, its capitalization, and the amount of capital and assets to be employed in the state.

Some states also require the filing of a tax report, a certificate of the names and addresses of officers and directors, and an acceptance of the provisions of the state constitution.

In some states, permission to do business is granted for a limited period only and must be renewed upon expiration.

After qualification, is a foreign corporation required to pay any additional taxes or to file any additional reports?—Some states require foreign corporations to pay annual taxes based upon the amount of capital employed in the state, and to file the following documents after qualification:

1. Annual tax or information reports.
2. Statement of change in place of business in the state or change in resident agent appointed for service of process on the corporation in the state.

3. A copy of any amendment to the corporation's articles of incorporation.

Penalties that may be incurred by a foreign corporation which does business in a state without qualifying.—The statutes of the various states generally impose one or more of the following penalties for failure of a foreign corporation doing business in a state to comply with the requirements imposed by the state as a condition of doing business:

1. A fine on the corporation.
2. A fine on officers, agents, or employees of the corporation.
3. Imprisonment of officers, agents, or employees of the corporation.
4. Liability of officers, directors, or stockholders for corporate debts or liabilities arising out of transactions within the state.
5. Voiding of contracts entered into by the corporation, or making such contracts unenforceable until compliance with statutory requirements for qualification.
6. Prohibition of the corporation's instituting, maintaining, or defending suits in any State court until compliance with the state's requirements for qualification.
7. Restriction against holding by the corporation of real property in the state, and voiding of conveyances to the corporation.

SECTION 15

Corporate Meetings, Minutes, and Resolutions

1. PREPARATIONS FOR MEETINGS

2. STOCKHOLDERS' MEETINGS

3. DIRECTORS' MEETINGS AND COMMITTEE MEETINGS

4. HOW TO KEEP MINUTES OF MEETINGS

5. PARLIAMENTARY PROCEDURE

SECTION 15

Corporate Meetings, Minutes, and Resolutions

1. PREPARATIONS FOR MEETINGS

Kinds of corporate meetings.—In the conduct of business by a corporation, the following classes of meetings are held:

1. Stockholders' meetings. These are sometimes called "corporate" meetings. They may be regular or special. Regular meetings—which are sometimes called "general" meetings, "stated" meetings, or "annual" meetings—are usually required to be held once a year, for the election of directors. Special meetings—which are sometimes termed "called" meetings or "extraordinary" meetings—are held as the need for them arises.

2. Directors' meetings. Meetings of directors are also regular or special. The regular meetings are those held at regular intervals, as fixed by the by-laws, usually monthly; all other meetings of the board are special meetings.

3. Committee meetings. These meetings are held, for example, by the executive committee, which in large corporations is appointed by the board of directors to exercise during intervals between board meetings all the powers of the board in accordance with the policy of the corporation. The meetings of the executive committee are also usually regular and special.

Who makes preparations for corporate meetings.—Preparations for stockholders' meetings are made by the following people, depending upon the division of responsibility in the organization:

1. The secretary.
2. The secretary and the attorney for the corporation.
3. The secretary, the attorney for the corporation, and an organ-

ization employed by the attorney to attend to the holding of meetings.

Preparations for directors' meetings and for executive committee meetings are generally made by the secretary of the corporation.

Employment of a service organization to hold annual corporate meetings.—The services of an outside organization are employed principally where the holding of meetings is merely a perfunctory matter, and where it is inconvenient for anyone interested in the corporation to attend the meeting. For example, a corporation is organized under the laws of the state of Delaware by a parent corporation, incorporated under the laws of New York and located in New York, to hold title to certain patents. The only stockholder of the Delaware corporation is the New York corporation. The principal office of the Delaware corporation, in Delaware, is in the charge of a resident agent, generally supplied by the service organization. Under the charter of the Delaware corporation, a meeting of stockholders must be held annually for the election of directors. The directors of the New York corporation, who are also the directors of the Delaware corporation, do not want to hold the meeting of the Delaware corporation in New York, for they do not want to do anything that might indicate that the Delaware corporation is doing business in New York. Nor do the directors want to journey to Delaware to hold the meeting. The officers of the Delaware corporation, therefore, direct their attorney to advise the service organization, which maintains the principal office of the corporation in Delaware, to hold the annual meeting of the stockholders in Delaware by proxy. The directors of the Delaware corporation will appoint as proxies those who are actually to be present in Delaware at the meeting. The meeting is held by the proxies, and the necessary election takes place. Ordinarily the minutes for such a meeting are prepared by the service organization and examined and approved by the corporation's attorney.

One of the principal companies offering the type of service described above is Prentice-Hall, Inc., 70 Fifth Avenue, New York City; the service is available only to attorneys.

Preparations for a stockholders' meeting where responsibility rests with the secretary.—A secretary's preparations for a stockholders' meeting can be divided into two parts:

1. Permanent preparations for all meetings.
2. Preparations for a particular meeting.

Permanent preparations for all stockholders' meetings.—A permanent-meeting file in which is kept the following material (to be taken by the secretary to every meeting of stockholders) must be maintained:

1. A pamphlet copy of the corporation laws of the state in which the corporation is organized.
2. A copy of the corporation's charter and by-laws and the amendments thereto.
3. A form of check list of preparations for stockholders' meetings (see page 1391).
4. A sheet showing the order of business as usually followed.

Preparations for a particular stockholders' meeting.—The following are the steps to be taken in preparing for a particular stockholders' meeting (some of the items refer only to an annual meeting and will, of course, be omitted when preparations are being made for a special meeting):

1. *Send notice of the meeting and proxies to stockholders.*—The notice of the meeting may be:

(*a*) A post card, in which case the proxy will be attached to the notice in the form of a business-reply card.

(*b*) An announcement sent in a sealed envelope. The announcement may be accompanied by a "proxy statement" required of corporations that are subject to the Securities Exchange Act of 1934.* The proxy in this case may be on a separate business-reply

---

* The Securities Exchange Act of 1934 prohibits the solicitation of proxies in respect of registered securities (other than exempted securities) in contravention of rules and regulations of the Securities and Exchange Commission. The regulations require that a written "proxy statement" be furnished concurrently with or before the solicitation of the proxy, containing the items of information set forth in the regulations. The proxy statement need not be contained in a single document. Every proxy statement must state whether or not the proxy is revocable and, if revocable subject to conditions, what the conditions are. The required information also includes a statement of the names of the persons by whom, directly or indirectly, the cost of the solicitation is to be borne, the method of solicitation used, the names and interest of the person soliciting the proxy, and a concise description of the substance of each of the various matters which, at the time of solicitation, are intended for consideration by the meeting at which the proxy is to be exercised.

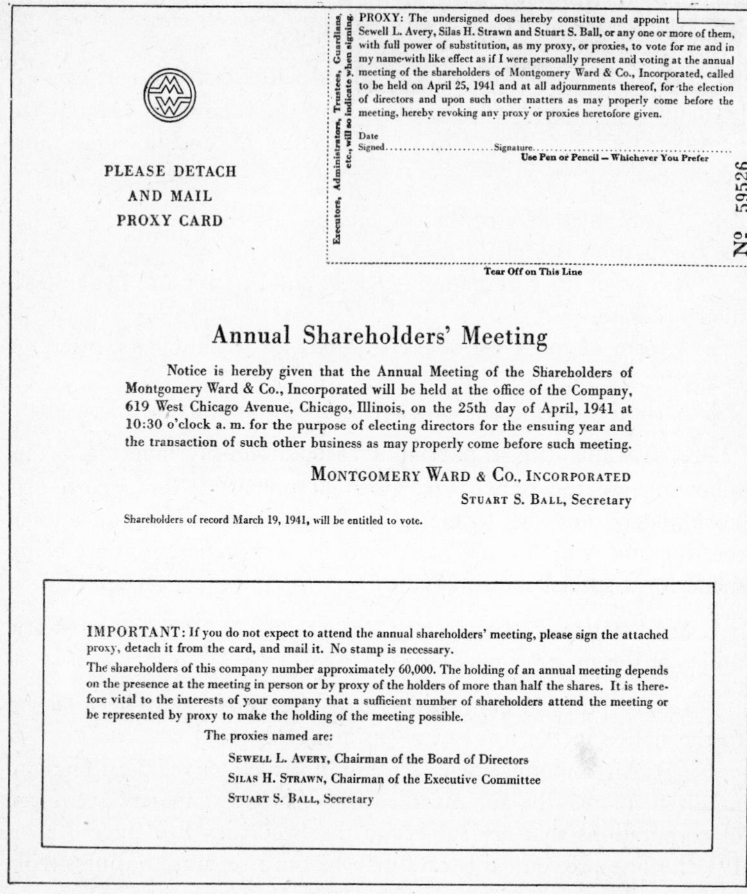

PLEASE DETACH
AND MAIL
PROXY CARD

Executors, Administrators, Trustees, Guardians, etc., will so indicate when signing.

PROXY: The undersigned does hereby constitute and appoint Sewell L. Avery, Silas H. Strawn and Stuart S. Ball, or any one or more of them, with full power of substitution, as my proxy, or proxies, to vote for me and in my name with like effect as if I were personally present and voting at the annual meeting of the shareholders of Montgomery Ward & Co., Incorporated, called to be held on April 25, 1941 and at all adjournments thereof, for the election of directors and upon such other matters as may properly come before the meeting, hereby revoking any proxy or proxies heretofore given.

Date
Signed........................Signature..

Use Pen or Pencil – Whichever You Prefer

№ 59526

Tear Off on This Line

Annual Shareholders' Meeting

Notice is hereby given that the Annual Meeting of the Shareholders of Montgomery Ward & Co., Incorporated will be held at the office of the Company, 619 West Chicago Avenue, Chicago, Illinois, on the 25th day of April, 1941 at 10:30 o'clock a. m. for the purpose of electing directors for the ensuing year and the transaction of such other business as may properly come before such meeting.

MONTGOMERY WARD & CO., INCORPORATED
STUART S. BALL, Secretary

Shareholders of record March 19, 1941, will be entitled to vote.

IMPORTANT: If you do not expect to attend the annual shareholders' meeting, please sign the attached proxy, detach it from the card, and mail it. No stamp is necessary.

The shareholders of this company number approximately 60,000. The holding of an annual meeting depends on the presence at the meeting in person or by proxy of the holders of more than half the shares. It is therefore vital to the interests of your company that a sufficient number of shareholders attend the meeting or be represented by proxy to make the holding of the meeting possible.

The proxies named are:

SEWELL L. AVERY, Chairman of the Board of Directors
SILAS H. STRAWN, Chairman of the Executive Committee
STUART S. BALL, Secretary

Figure 103a.—Notice of Annual Meeting and Detachable Proxy.

card enclosed with the announcement, or it may be attached to the notice, to be detached and returned in a stamped and self-addressed envelope or in a business-reply envelope that is enclosed with the notice and proxy.

The selection of the style of notice and proxy to be used depends upon such factors as:

(*a*) Cost.
(*b*) The necessity for receiving a large number of proxies.

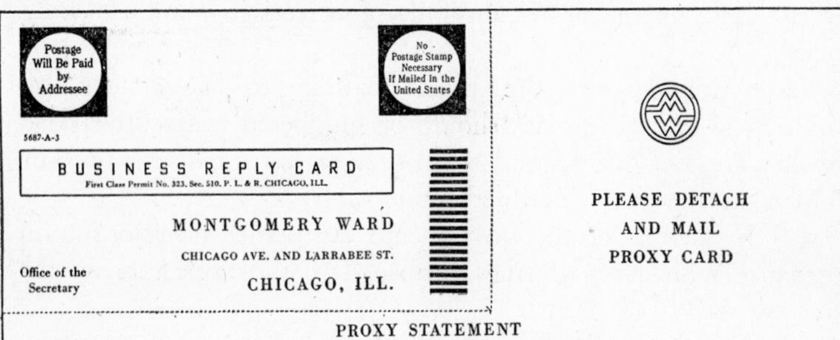

Postage Will Be Paid by Addressee

No Postage Stamp Necessary If Mailed in the United States

5687-A-3

BUSINESS REPLY CARD

First Class Permit No. 323, Sec. 510, P. L. & R. CHICAGO, ILL.

MONTGOMERY WARD

CHICAGO AVE. AND LARRABEE ST.

Office of the Secretary

CHICAGO, ILL.

PLEASE DETACH AND MAIL PROXY CARD

PROXY STATEMENT

ANNUAL MEETING OF SHAREHOLDERS, APRIL 25, 1941

The following information is given in connection with this solicitation of proxies pursuant to the rules of the Securities and Exchange Commission.

The attached proxy is solicited on behalf of the management for use at the Annual Meeting of Shareholders to be held at the office of the Company, 619 West Chicago Avenue, Chicago, Illinois, on April 25, 1941. Except for possible personal solicitation of brokers, fiduciaries or nominees and some of the larger shareholders personally or by telephone by officers or employees (who will receive no remuneration therefor in addition to their regular compensation), all solicitation of proxies on behalf of the management will be by mail. The cost of preparing, assembling and mailing this proxy statement, proxy and other enclosed material and the cost of such incidental personal solicitation, will be paid by the Company. We estimate the cost of such solicitation otherwise than by mail at not over $1,000.

A shareholder returning a proxy will have power to revoke it at any time prior to its exercise.

The purpose of the meeting will be the election of a Board of eleven Directors and the transaction of such other business as may properly come before the meeting. The individuals for whom it is intended that a vote will be cast pursuant to the proxies in the election of directors are hereinafter named, and, according to information received by the Company, such individuals are directly or indirectly the beneficial owners of the approximate number of shares of each class of the Company's stock stated after their respective names:

Name	Class "A"	Common	Name	Class "A"	Common	Name	Class "A"	Common
Sewell L. Avery	200	68,681	Charles F. Glore	None	None	Silas H. Strawn	None	255
David A. Crawford	None	629	Donald R. McLennan, Jr.	None	100	James W. Thorne	1,638	5,746
Harry P. Davison	None	1,345	Harold L. Pearson	None	250	Eugene R. Wimmer	None	300
Percy B. Eckhart	None	507	Clement D. Ryan	None	100			

If at the time of the meeting circumstances now unforeseen by the management require the omission from said list of nominees of any of the above persons, discretion is reserved by the persons named in the attached form of proxy to vote said proxy in accordance with their judgment for some other person or persons in lieu of the persons whose names are omitted from the list.

The above nominees are, with two exceptions hereinafter noted, men who have constituted the Board of Directors during the past year. Mr. Donald R. McLennan, Jr., who has not heretofore been a Director, is Vice-President of Marsh & McLennan, Incorporated, and will be nominated to fill a vacancy caused by the retirement from the Board of his father, D. R. McLennan, who had been a Director of the Company for many years. Mr. Clement D. Ryan, the other exception, is a Vice-President and is General Merchandise Manager of the Company. Both Mr. McLennan and Mr. Glore are officers and directors of corporations which own substantial blocks of the Company's common stock.

The aggregate amounts of remuneration received during the last fiscal year by Sewell L. Avery, Chairman of the Board of Directors and President, Clement D. Ryan, Vice-President, and Eugene R. Wimmer, Vice-President, who are the persons receiving the three highest amounts of remuneration from the Company during its last fiscal year, were: Sewell L. Avery $100,450.00, Clement D. Ryan $55,833.30, Eugene R. Wimmer $47,733.31. The aggregate amount of remuneration paid during the last fiscal year to persons acting as directors and officers of the Company, as a group, for services in all capacities, was $580,440.08. In addition, the law firm of Winston, Strawn & Shaw, of which Mr. Silas H. Strawn is a partner, received during the year $4,000.00 for legal services.

The management does not know of any matters to be brought before the meeting for a vote of the shareholders other than the election of Directors and certain routine matters such as election of tellers, approval of minutes of the last annual meeting of shareholders, etc. The action taken with respect to such minutes is not intended to constitute approval or disapproval of any of the matters referred to in such minutes. Should any matters properly come before the meeting other than the election of Directors, the persons named in the attached form of proxy intend to vote it in accordance with their judgment.

Figure 103b.—Proxy Statement and Reverse Side of Proxy.

Experience has proved that a greater number of proxies are returned if the notice and proxy are forwarded by first-class mail than if the post-card method is employed.

Figures 103a and 103b, on pages 1386 and 1387, show a single-sheet arrangement of the notice of meeting, the proxy, and the proxy statement.

2. *Prepare for handling proxies as they are received by the corporation.*—A plan for handling the proxies upon their return should be worked out in advance and should make provision for:

(*a*) Assignment of responsibility for receiving and checking proxies.

(*b*) Arrangement of the proxies according to class of stock and in numerical order. Proxies should be numbered consecutively before they are sent out, so that when they are returned, they will be in alphabetical order when filed numerically.

(*c*) Inspection of the proxies and acceptance or rejection in accordance with a set of rules furnished to the inspectors by the secretary. See page 1408.

(*d*) Tabulation daily of the number of shares represented by proxies returned, and report to the secretary.

(*e*) Examination of questionable proxies by the secretary or the attorney of the corporation.

3. *Decide, if possible, who shall be nominated as directors.*—In most cases the selection of directors depends upon ownership of the controlling interests, relationships with financial institutions, and other factors that make it possible to know in advance who will be the directors for the forthcoming period.

4. *Compile the list of stockholders.*—The statutes or by-laws generally require that the corporation prepare a complete alphabetical list of the stockholders a certain number of days before each annual election. In some states it is necessary to file the list for a certain number of days before the meeting at the place where the meeting is to be held. The secretary usually prepares the list as of the date required and has it ready for use at the annual meeting. Where the corporation has an independent transfer agent, the latter prepares the list.

5. *Prepare the ballots.*—The preparation of ballots depends upon the method of voting to be employed at the meeting. No particular form of ballot need be used even where a ballot is required, but the ballot for the election of directors should show the name or names of the person or persons voted for, the number of votes cast for each person, and the name of the person casting the vote, with provision for indicating that several stockholders are being represented by one person acting as proxy. The forms on page 1389 illustrate a ballot suitable for straight voting—that is, where each share of stock is entitled to one vote—for cumulative voting (explained on page 1412), and for voting on a particular question.

BALLOT FOR STRAIGHT VOTING

THE ____________________ CORPORATION

ANNUAL MEETING, ________________ __, 19__.

I, the undersigned, hereby vote __________ shares of stock for the following named persons to serve as directors for the ensuing year:

____

____

____

____
(*Stockholder signs here*)

By ________________
Proxy

BALLOT FOR CUMULATIVE VOTING

ANNUAL ELECTION OF DIRECTORS OF THE

______________________ CORPORATION

Name of Stockholder ____

Name of Proxy ____

Number of Shares ____

Directors to be Elected ______________________________________

Number of votes entitled to _____________ (multiply the number of directors to be elected by the number of shares).

BALLOT FOR DIRECTORS

Names	*Votes*
____________________	__________
____________________	__________
____________________	__________
____________________	__________
____________________	__________

____
(*Stockholder signs here*)

By ________________
Proxy

BALLOT FOR VOTE ON RESOLUTION

SPECIAL MEETING OF PREFERRED STOCKHOLDERS

OF

__________________ COMPANY

Held ____________ ___, 19___.

In favor of:
Against:
the resolution with respect to the creation and issuance by the Company of its Ten-Year 5% Sinking Fund Debentures in the principal amount of ________ ($______) Dollars with Common Stock Purchase Warrants attached.

Holding ________ shares of Preferred Stock

Represented by proxy ________ shares of Preferred Stock

Dated at __________ (City) _______ (State) __________ __, 19__.

____
(Stockholder or proxy signs here)

6. *Schedule the order of business.*—The business to be transacted at the meeting need not follow any particular order, even though one is prescribed in the by-laws. A logical order of business, however, expedites the business of the meeting. The following is the order generally pursued at an annual meeting of stockholders:

(*a*) Call to order.
(*b*) Election of chairman and appointment of secretary, if necessary.
(*c*) Presentation of proofs of the due calling of the meeting.
(*d*) Presentation and examination of proxies.
(*e*) Announcement of a quorum present.
(*f*) Reading and settlement of minutes of previous meeting.
(*g*) Presentation of list of stockholders.
(*h*) Reports of officers and committees.

(*i*) Appointment of inspectors of election.
(*j*) Opening of polls.
(*k*) Election of directors.
(*l*) Closing of polls.
(*m*) Report of inspectors.
(*n*) Declaration of election of directors.
(*o*) New business.
(*p*) Adjournment.

7. *Decide who shall be nominated as inspectors of election.*—See page 1414 for the necessity of this step.

8. *Prepare a tentative draft of the minutes of the meeting and of any resolutions to be presented at the meeting.*—This may take any number of forms, including:

(*a*) A synopsis of the minutes.
(*b*) A digest of the topics to be discussed.
(*c*) A skeleton of the minutes, with spaces to be filled in with the missing details as they develop in the meeting.
(*d*) Prepared resolutions.

The form of minutes of meetings given on page 1433 may be used as a guide in preparing tentative minutes.

Check list of preparations for a stockholders' meeting.—The following is a form of check list that will aid the secretary in:

1. Preparing for the meeting.
2. Making notes of essential data at the meeting.
3. Writing up the minutes of the meeting.

The check list is filled in as the various matters are attended to and is retained permanently by the secretary, who keeps the list in the file pertaining to a particular meeting.

CHECK LIST OF PREPARATIONS FOR STOCKHOLDERS' MEETING

STOCKHOLDERS' MEETING
OF
(NAME OF COMPANY)

Date	To be held____________________as	Regular______ Special______
Adjournments	Adjourned to ______________________________	

Notices Prepared (date) Mailed (date)
Published (date) Waiver (to be procured: date __________)
Special purposes to be contained in notice __________

____

____

____

Quorum Shares required for quorum ____________________

Present (If a small meeting is held, names may be inserted here; if many attend, the roll may be made up on separate sheets. If these sheets are preserved, they may be "incorporated by reference" into the minutes, and thus space may be saved in the minute book.)

Official Lists Lists of those entitled to be present:
To be prepared by__________(check when in hand)
As of (date)______________________________
To be available_____________(check when in hand)

Proxies Name of proxy committee____________________

____

Substitute proxies to be given to__________________
(Check when substitute proxy is given, or check names of committee, first when they have been notified to be present, and again when they have given their word that they will be present. Check proxies; list names of persons to do this, and indicate date when their report is available. Ordinarily a preliminary report will be available a day or two before the meeting, and final checking of proxies tendered by persons at the meeting will have to be done while the meeting is in progress. This, of course, applies only to large meetings and not to those of small companies, or of subsidiaries. Reference should be made to the rules and regulations of the Securities and Exchange Commission regarding restrictions against solicitation and use of proxies.)

Chairman Chairman: Notified to be present (date)
(If regular chairman has indicated inability to be present, arrange for substitute and for proper selection at the meeting.)

Reports	(List officers responsible for reports; indicate dates reports are to be ready in manuscript, and if to be printed, dates for submission to printer; indicate date reports are to be available for meeting. Check off dates as each step is taken.)
Action	(List action to be taken. If any matters require resolutions that can be prepared in advance, list them by number, and correspondingly number sheets on which resolutions appear. Prepare resolutions in sufficient number to facilitate discussion and amendment; for latter purpose, it is well to triple-space the typewritten copies of resolutions.) (The following should follow title of each proposed action: Proposed by____________Seconded by___________ For:___________shares Against:_________shares) (Note: It may be well to omit the action at this place, but to have separate sheets therefor in order that as many items and as many "proposed action sheets" as are necessary may be included.)
Inspectors	Inspectors: (Name them if selected in advance, and check if present; otherwise, write in names as selected, and note how selected.)
Nominations	(Leave space for names of persons nominated.)
Opening and Closing of Polls	How opened _________________________________ How closed _________________________________
Results	(List names of those elected here; above, under nominations, set opposite each nominee's name the number of votes received.)
Certificate Received	(Put down time for receipt of formal certificate of judges or inspectors of election, and note later time when received.)
Publication	(Note any requirements as to publication or filing of reports; this note can be made before the meeting.)
Memoranda of Follow-Up	(A space should be left to note action that must be taken to follow up resolutions that have been passed.)

Adjournment Hour of adjournment______________
(If the meeting is adjourned, a new checkup sheet should be prepared for the adjourned meeting and attached to that for the original meeting.)

Preparations for a stockholders' meeting where secretary and attorney are responsible for meeting.—Where the responsibility for holding the stockholders' meeting is delegated to the attorney of the corporation, the secretary has little if any preparation to make. Whatever action he takes will be at the request of the attorney, who will ask the secretary for information needed in making his preparations. Proxies are ordinarily returnable to the corporation, even in instances where the attorney is responsible for the preparation and conduct of the meeting, and the secretary makes all arrangements for handling the proxies as they are returned. Also, the corporation secretary may have to prepare the stock list.

Preparations for a directors' meeting.—The steps in the preparation for a directors' meeting, regular or special, include the following:

1. *Send notice of the meeting to directors.*—The notice may be:

(*a*) A printed card with blanks to be filled in by the secretary as to the place, date, and hour.

(*b*) A typewritten notice.

(*c*) A notice with space for the recipient to indicate whether or not he will be present at the meeting.

The last-named form of notice is essential if directors are not actively engaged in the conduct of the business. The secretary can tell from the replies received whether a quorum of directors will be present, and if replies indicate that there will not be a quorum present, he can notify the directors that the meeting will not be held as scheduled. The following is a form of notice of a directors' meeting, illustrating the last type of notice.

NOTICE OF DIRECTORS' MEETING

____________________CORPORATION

You are requested to attend a regular meeting of the Board of Directors at the office of the Corporation, No. _______ __________, New York, on Tuesday, ______________ __, at three o'clock P.M.

Please notify me whether or not you will be present.

Respectfully,

Secretary

I will / will not be present

----

2. *Gather data to be presented at the meeting.*—Secretaries usually devise their own systems for accumulating the papers and documents likely to be required at the meeting, for conferring with officers in advance of the meeting, and for notifying officers of reports that are to be ready for the meeting.

3. *Write up the agenda.*—The agenda (or "docket," or "order of business," as it is sometimes called) is the outline of action to be taken at the meeting. It is prepared several days in advance of the meeting and has attached to it the papers, reports, and documents that will be required at the meeting as each item of business is taken up. The following order of business may be observed in the agenda:

(*a*) Call to order (by chairman of board, or president, if there is no chairman or if he be absent).

(*b*) Announcement of quorum present.

(*c*) Reading and approval of minutes of previous meeting.

(*d*) Reports of officers and committees.

(*e*) Unfinished business.

(*f*) Election of officers (if there is to be an election).

(*g*) Declaration of dividends (if there is to be such).

(*h*) Other new business.

(*i*) Adjournment.

4. *Prepare material for use of directors at the meeting.*—To facilitate the conduct of a meeting, secretaries sometimes furnish the directors, at the time of the meeting, with:

(*a*) Copies of the agenda and reports to which the agenda refers.

(*b*) Copies of the minutes of the previous meeting.

(*c*) Copies of resolutions to be voted upon at the current meeting.

If this practice is followed, the secretary must see that the proper number of copies is made ready.

5. *Arrange for the payment of fees.*—Directors are frequently paid fees for attendance at meetings in cases where the directors are not employed by the corporation and are not receiving a salary. Where the distribution of fees is delegated to the secretary, he usually requisitions from the treasurer the sum required, in the correct denominations, and makes whatever preparations are necessary for the distribution either at the meeting or by mail after the meeting.

6. *Make preparations for recording minutes.*—These preparations are the same as for meetings of stockholders. See page 1391.

2. STOCKHOLDERS' MEETINGS

Necessity for holding stockholders' meetings.—Meetings of stockholders are necessary for the following reasons:

1. The courts generally hold that the stockholders must act concurrently; that is, they cannot bind the corporation if they act individually, even though a majority of them concur and express their consent in writing, unless, however, consent in writing is sufficient under a governing statute.

2. The laws of the state in which the corporation is organized, the charter, and the by-laws give the stockholders certain rights and powers that must, under the law, be exercised at a meeting. Sometimes these powers can be exercised, under the statute, by consent in writing, and a meeting may not be necessary; however, as a matter of expediency, it is wise even in such cases to hold a meeting to obtain the written consents.

3. The corporation is an entity and is entitled to the joint action of its owners, each one of whom has a right to be enlightened by the views of the others. Without a meeting, such interchange of views is impossible.

However, according to the decisions of the courts, the validity of a corporate act does not always depend upon whether or not a meeting of the corporate body has been held in a formal way, even if the act is one of major importance. Irregularities in the holding of the meeting do not necessarily invalidate the proceedings of the meeting; before an objecting stockholder can succeed in nullifying the proceedings at a meeting, he must show that, by the irregularity in the meeting, his rights have been affected.

Calling stockholders' meetings.—Stockholders' meetings are called as follows:

1. By the officers empowered by the by-laws of the corporation to call regular and special meetings of the stockholders. Occasionally the certificate of incorporation, and in some instances the statute, designates who shall call meetings of stockholders. A statutory provision on the subject must be observed, and if the by-laws conflict with the statute, the latter governs.
2. By the board of directors, in the absence of statutory or by-law provision as to who shall call the meeting.
3. By a certain number of the stockholders, if that power is given to the stockholders by statute, charter, or by-laws. Many of the statutes specifically provide that if an election of directors is not held on the day designated in the by-laws, a meeting for the election of directors may be called by a certain number of the stockholders, if notice has been given as prescribed by the statute. Stockholders may also obtain the power to call a meeting by bringing a suit for mandamus to compel the corporate officers to call a meeting, if they have wrongfully refused to do so.

Necessity for notice of stockholders' meetings.—The necessity for notice of stockholders' meetings depends upon the kind of meeting that is to be held, as indicated below:

Regular meetings.—If the statute, charter, or by-laws do not require notice of regular meetings to be given, and the charter or by-laws fix the time and place at which regular meetings are to be held, the charter or by-laws themselves are sufficient notice to all stockholders, and no further notice is necessary. In all other cases, notice of regular meetings is necessary.

Special meetings.—Notice of special meetings must be given to the stockholders in the manner provided in the statute, charter, or by-laws.

Adjourned meetings.—Unless otherwise prescribed by the by-laws, notice of an adjourned meeting is unnecessary if the notice of the original meeting was given as prescribed. In order that the notice of the prior meeting shall extend to the adjourned meeting, however, the latter must be held for the same purpose as the original meeting and must be virtually a continuation of it.

Notice need be given only to those stockholders who are entitled to vote, unless the statute expressly provides otherwise. Where the statute does not specifically require the publication of notice, newspaper notices may be omitted.

Length of notice.—Great care should be exercised to give the notice in due time. The by-laws or statutes usually indicate how many days before the meeting notice must be given, and such requirements must be strictly observed. Thus, where the by-laws require thirty days' notice, a meeting will be invalid if only twelve days' notice is given. If the statute requires publication of the notice for ten days, it means that the notice is to continue in the publication for a period of ten days. In a daily paper this would require ten different inserts; in a weekly paper, two inserts.

Stockholders' meetings that are valid without required notice.—If notice has not been given as required, action taken at a stockholders' meeting will be valid under the following circumstances:

1. If notice is waived by participation in the meeting. A person who is present in person or by proxy, and who participates without dissent in a meeting, thereby waives defects in the notice.

2. If the stockholders waive notice in writing. The signature of a stockholder to a waiver of notice of a meeting should be obtained either before or at the meeting, although waivers signed after the meeting have been held to be effective. The following is a form of waiver of notice of meeting that may be used for any meeting of stockholders.

WAIVER OF NOTICE OF STOCKHOLDERS' MEETING

The undersigned, being all the stockholders of the ______________ Corporation, a corporation created and organized under the laws of the State of ______________, do hereby waive any and all notice as provided by the statutes of ______________, or by the Articles of Incorporation or By-laws of the said Corporation, and do hereby consent to the holding of a ________________ meeting of the stockholders of the said Corporation, to be held on the -- day of -----------, 19--, at ------- o'clock in the -------noon, or any adjournment or adjournments thereof, at the office of the Corporation, Room -------, No. ------- -----------, City of -----------, State of -----------, for the following purposes [*insert purposes of meeting*], and do hereby consent to the transaction of any other business that may come before the meeting.

Dated at -----------, ---------, this -- day of ---------, 19--.

--------------------------------, holding ---------- shares

--------------------------------, " ---------- "

--------------------------------, " ---------- "

(*Signatures of stockholders*)

Contents of notice of stockholders' meeting.—The notice of the meeting should contain information as to the following:

1. Time of the meeting, including the hour. The general rule is that a meeting must take place at the time designated in the by-laws or the charter. Generally, where an annual meeting is not held at the time specified in the by-laws, the directors may call a meeting within a reasonable time thereafter.

2. Place of the meeting. Some statutes require meetings to be held within the state; others provide that they may be held either within or without the state. Statutory provisions as to the place of meeting must be followed. If the statute prohibits corporations from meeting outside the state, the proceedings at meetings held without the state will be void, and the board of directors elected at such meetings will have no more power than if no election had been held.

As a matter of practice, if the governing statute requires stockholders' meetings to be held within the state, and a meeting at such place is inconvenient at the time, the meeting may be held at the most convenient place, and all transactions concluded at the meeting may be ratified at a meeting held within the state by dummies acting on stockholders' proxies. If no provision is made in the statute, charter, or by-laws, the stockholders' meetings must be held within the state. However, where all the stockholders participate, a stockholders' meeting held without the state will be valid. Furthermore, if the stockholders waive the invalidity of a meeting convened without the state, or ratify the acts done at the meeting, they cannot later claim that the meeting was invalid.

3. The purpose of the meeting. It is not absolutely essential that the notice of a regular meeting include the purpose of the meeting, unless so required by statute or by-laws. However, if some unusual business is to be transacted at a regular meeting, such as a sale of the corporate property or the amendment of the corporate charter, notice of such unusual business should be given. In the case of special meetings, the notice should include a statement of the matters to be discussed at the meeting.

4. The officer or others who are calling the meeting. This is necessary to indicate that the meeting is called by competent authority.

Time at which stockholders' meeting should start.—A meeting is not legal if it is held before the exact time specified in the notice of the meeting, unless all the stockholders are present. It is not essential that the meeting start on the stroke of the hour for which it is called; it is sufficient if it is convened within a reasonable time after the hour fixed in the notice.

Getting a stockholders' meeting started.—Several clerks should be appointed to act as ushers, if a large number of stockholders is expected to attend the meeting. The clerks may conduct the stockholders to seats, or they may permit the stockholders to take any seat they wish. Usually the stockholders are permitted to sit where they please. As each person arrives, the clerk asks his name and address, whether he is a stockholder, and whether he has been appointed proxy for a stockholder. The stock records or a list of the stockholders, as well as the filed proxies, should be in the meeting room. The clerk immediately checks the information. If the stockholder has not filed a proxy, he may be asked whether he wishes to do so. If he has filed a proxy, the clerk may inquire whether the stockholder wishes to revoke the proxy or to let it stand. Some corporations discard the proxy if the stockholder is present in person at the meeting.

It is generally advisable to have some executive officer present at the meeting of stockholders, although there is no requirement that the directors or officers attend. In large corporations, general counsel is usually present at the stockholders' meeting to act as adviser to the chairman.

Who presides at a stockholders' meeting.—The person who is to preside at the meeting of stockholders is determined in the following ways:

1. The by-laws may designate the officer who is to preside at all stockholders' meetings. By-laws generally give the president or some other officer this right. Occasionally the provision appears in the corporate charter. Provision in the charter or in the by-laws as to who shall preside at the meeting of stockholders must be observed.
2. The stockholders present at the meeting may elect a chairman, if no provision is made in the charter or by-laws as to who shall preside. In making the selection the stockholders may vote by a show of hands, a stock vote not being required to give validity to the meeting, in the absence of a statute or by-law providing otherwise. Where the by-law states that "at stockholders' meetings each stockholder shall cast one vote for each share of stock owned by him," the by-law applies to the election of a chairman as well as to the proceedings carried on after the meeting has been regularly organized. Similarly, where the by-law provides that upon demand of a stockholder the vote on any question shall be by stock vote, a stockholder has the right to demand a stock vote for the election of the chairman, and in the absence of such a demand the chairman may be elected by a viva-voce vote.

Who may call stockholders' meeting to order in absence of presiding officer.—If no provision is made in either the charter or by-laws, anyone has the right to call a meeting of stockholders to order and to proceed until a chairman is elected. To avoid any unnecessary disturbance in getting the meeting started, or if several persons attempt to call the meeting to order, the order of precedence should be as follows: chairman of the board; president; vice-presidents in order of nominal designation of authority (first vice-president, second, and so forth), or, if no designation has been made, then in order of seniority of service, or, where coequal in that regard, then in order of seniority of age; secretary; treasurer; assistant secretary; member of executive committee; directors (executive committeemen and directors are to be preferred in the order of seniority of service in the committee or on the board, or, when coequal in that regard, then in order of seniority of age); stockholders, in the order of the amount of their stockholdings, or, if coequal in that regard, then in the order of seniority of age.

Selection of a secretary.—When a secretary must be selected because the person designated by the by-laws to act as secretary at the stockholders' meetings is not present, the chairman may appoint a secretary. Any stockholder, however, may require an election of a secretary to be held immediately.

Necessity for a quorum to be present at stockholders' meeting.—A valid meeting of stockholders cannot be held unless a quorum is present, and if the amount of stock necessary to constitute a quorum is not represented, in person or by proxy, the meeting must adjourn to another time. A quorum, as specified in the statute, charter, or by-laws, must be present not only to begin a meeting but to transact business. Thus, if during the meeting a number of stockholders depart, leaving less than a quorum present, the meeting must be disbanded by adjournment. However, if a meeting is once organized and all the parties have participated, no person or faction can then, by withdrawing capriciously and for the sole purpose of breaking a quorum, render the subsequent proceedings invalid. If stockholders have withdrawn for the purpose of breaking a quorum, because of whim, caprice, or chagrin, the law will consider the action as unavailing and will permit the meeting to proceed.

A quorum is always presumed unless it is questioned at the meeting, or unless the record shows that a quorum in fact is not present.

What constitutes a quorum.—The person conducting the meeting should at the outset determine whether or not a quorum is present. The number necessary to constitute a quorum is determined as follows:

1. The by-laws, statute, or charter may fix the amount of stock required to be represented at a meeting. If the by-laws conflict with the statute, the statute must be followed, since the by-law is then void. Thus, if a provision in the by-laws fixes the amount of stock necessary to constitute a quorum at stockholders' meetings, and a

provision of the statute specifies that directors shall be elected at an annual meeting of such stockholders as shall attend for that purpose, the directors may be elected by those present, even if the shares represented at the meeting do not constitute a quorum in accordance with the by-law provision.

2. If the statute, charter, or by-laws do not indicate what proportion in interest of the stock outstanding shall constitute a quorum, the persons present at the stockholders' meeting constitute a quorum, no matter how few they are, although there is authority to the effect that at least two persons must be present.

In determining whether or not a quorum is present, only issued stock is counted; stock that has been subscribed and not paid for is not included, unless there is a provision to the contrary in the law or in the certificate of incorporation. Stock that cannot be voted cannot be counted for quorum purposes.

Meaning of terms relating to quorum.—If the by-laws or statute do not explicitly define what constitutes a quorum, the following definitions arrived at by the courts may be helpful:

1. *Majority.*—The term "majority" used in defining a quorum means more than one half.

2. *Three fifths of the stockholders.*—A provision in the by-laws that "three fifths of the stockholders shall constitute a quorum" applies to stockholders per capita, and not to stockholders in interest.

3. *Majority of stock issued and outstanding.*—A by-law provision stating that "a majority of the stock issued and outstanding shall constitute a quorum, and all questions shall be decided by a majority of the votes cast" means that quorum members must be voting members.

Who has the right to be present at a stockholders' meeting.—Every stockholder who has a right to vote at a meeting has the right to be present at the meeting. Stockholders who have no voting power are not entitled to be present at the meeting. As a matter of policy, however, it may be advisable to permit nonvoting stockholders to attend, unless it is anticipated that nonvoting stockholders will object to action in which they have no voice. An outsider may be permitted to attend a meeting of stockholders even though he has no legal right to do so, but if objection is made to his presence, the matter of whether the outsider is to remain may have to be put to a vote and decided in the same way that other questions are settled.

Conducting a stockholders' meeting.—In the absence of express regulation by statute or by-laws, stockholders' meetings, including those for the election of directors, are controlled largely by accepted usage and custom. The fundamental rule is that all who are entitled to take part will be treated with fairness and good faith. While a stockholders' meeting is not of such a formal nature that the rules of parliamentary law must be observed, the ordinary parliamentary usages apply to it.

If the by-laws provide that stockholders' meetings shall be conducted according to the rules prescribed by a manual of parliamentary procedure, the requirement must be enforced. On pages 1442 et seq. a complete explanation of parliamentary rules that may be followed in the conduct of stockholders' meetings is given; see especially, "Conduct of the meeting," on page 1442.

Who may vote at a stockholders' meeting.—Every owner of capital stock has, as an incident of the ownership of shares, the right to vote the stock at all meetings of stockholders, unless such right is denied by some statutory or charter provision, or by an agreement under which he holds his shares. Whoever has the legal title to the stock has the right to vote. Since the officers of a corporation would be placed in an embarrassing position if they had to determine who was the owner of the legal title to stock, it is generally provided in the by-laws that the right to vote rests with the person who appears as the registered owner of the stock on the books of the corporation. In some instances the statute or charter makes this provision.

Holders of record on a certain day to vote.—Unless there is some provision to the contrary, a stockholder's right to vote at a meeting is to be determined as of the time when the meeting is held. It is clear that if only the true owners of stock at the time when the meeting is held were permitted to vote stock, just prior to the meeting the corporation would be inundated with demands for transfers of stock in order that the true owner might be present and vote at the meeting. This would mean that until the last minute before the meeting, the corporation could not prepare a list of the stockholders entitled to vote. To avoid this difficulty, there developed the practice, sanctioned by statute, of closing the transfer books a certain number of days before the meeting in order to provide ample time for compiling the necessary list of stockholders. During the period that the books are closed, no transfers can be effected. This expedient, however, proved unsatisfactory and another practice, now used more than that of closing the books, was instituted—namely, that of preparing a list of the stockholders of record on a certain day before the meeting. The list is prima-facie evidence of ownership of the stock and is used to determine who has the right to vote at a stockholders' meeting. The advantage of using the stock list, as against closing the transfer books, is that transfers of stock are not interrupted, but are merely disregarded for purposes of determining the rights of stockholders to vote at a meeting.

In determining who may vote at an adjourned meeting, the chairman may disregard the fact that the meeting is a continuation meeting. Thus new stockholders of record, and stockholders who were not present or represented at the original meeting, but who are present or represented at the adjourned meeting, are permitted to vote.

Disputes as to who may vote.—When a dispute arises as to who has the right to vote, the meeting must be guided by the corporate records or the list of corporate stockholders prepared for the meeting. The officers need not look behind the books to ascertain who are the real owners of the shares, although a court of equity will do so in a dispute in which it is seeking to settle the rights between the claimants as such. If one of the stockholders claims that the record is incorrect, he may apply to a court of equity for a writ compelling the acceptance of his vote. This writ must be obtained before the meeting and must be presented to the chairman; in the absence of such writ, the stockholder of record on the books of the corporation should be given the right to vote. The courts have frequently held that a duly qualified stockholder does not lose his right to vote if his name fails to appear on the proper stock-record book or on the list of stockholders because of the negligence, contrivance, or ignorance of the corporation in maintaining its records.

Some instances in which questions as to who may vote arise.—Most of the difficult problems as to who has the right to vote arise through the following circumstances:

1. *Sale of stock by the registered holder without transfer on books.*—If a stockholder has sold his shares to another, and the transfer has not been registered before the day fixed for determining who has the right to vote at the meeting, the transferee may not vote. The purchaser, however, although not registered as a stockholder, may secure a proxy from the seller and thus obtain the right to vote. If there is no provision in the statute, charter, or by-laws requiring transfer to be made on the books, the purchaser of the stock is entitled to vote if he produces evidence that the stock has been transferred to him.

2. *Pledge of shares by the registered holder.*—As between the pledgor and pledgee, the pledgor has the right to vote, since he retains legal title to the stock pledged. If, however, the pledgor permits the pledgee to register the pledgee's name on the books of the corporation as the owner of stock without reservation, the corporation will be justified in recognizing the pledgee as having the right to vote. It has been held that if the pledgor fails to appear at a meeting in person or by proxy, the pledgee has the right to be represented at the meeting.

3. *Stock not fully paid for.*—If there is no provision to the contrary, the subscribers to the capital stock of a corporation who are in fact stockholders are entitled to vote at a meeting of stockholders, even if no certificates of stock have been issued. If the subscription to the stock is such that it does not make the subscriber a stockholder, as, for example, where the subscription is merely a contract with the corporation to purchase stock, the subscriber is not entitled to vote.

4. *Stock held by a minor.*—Where there are no statutory provisions on the subject, the rule seems to be that minors cannot personally vote their shares. The guardian of the minor, or the trustee who holds the shares for a minor, has the voting power.

5. *Death of a registered holder.*—When an owner of stock dies, title to the stock passes immediately to the deceased owner's legal representatives. When a representative is able to establish his appointment as administrator or executor, he may vote the stock with-

out even causing a change in the corporate records. When the legal title is vested in several executors, they can vote only as co-owners. (See 7, below.) Letters testamentary that are issued by competent authority to an executor are conclusive proof of title to the shares of stock of the corporation and of the right to vote in respect thereof. After delivery of the stock to the heirs, the administrator does not have the right to vote the stock in defiance of the transferees' wishes, even though the transferees fail to transfer the stock out of the name of the administrator to themselves.

6. *Stock registered in the name of a trustee.*—The trustee, not the beneficiary, has the voting power. Even if the statute gives to the beneficiary the right to vote, his right will not accrue unless his name appears on the company's records.

7. *Stock owned in the name of two or more people.*—Co-owners of stock must unanimously agree as to the manner in which the stock shall be voted; otherwise their vote will not count. As a matter of practice, one co-owner may present proxies from the other co-owners and exercise the right to vote on that basis. Where stock stands in the name of a partnership, and one partner alone attends the meeting, he may vote the stock in behalf of his partners. If one of the partners dies, any surviving partner may vote the stock standing in the name of the partnership.

8. *Stock registered in the name of a corporation.*—Where stock is registered in the name of a corporation, it is voted by proxy properly authorized by the corporation owning the stock. A corporation that has acquired its own stock cannot vote the stock. Nor can the directors of a corporation vote stock of the company held by one of the corporation's subsidiaries.

Voting by proxy.—Absent stockholders are generally given the right by statute, charter, or by-laws to vote at a meeting by written proxy. The provisions of the statute, charter, or by-laws must be strictly observed, and proxies that do not meet the requirements should be thrown out. Ordinarily the presiding officer at the meeting is the person who decides whether or not a proxy is acceptable, but in large corporations the power to pass on the validity of proxies is frequently delegated to a special committee of inspectors. These inspectors may be furnished with a set of rules, drawn in the light of the statutory, charter, and by-law requirements of the particular corporation, and with knowledge of the general principles of law relating to proxies. From the following principles relating to various parts of the proxy, a set of rules can be drawn up that will be suitable for a particular corporation.

Acceptance of proxies.—The following are the principles forming the basis of rules as to acceptance of proxies.

1. *Compliance with statutory provisions.*—While the statutory provisions vary from state to state, the following are the usual provisions:

(*a*) The proxy must be in writing.

(*b*) It is revocable at the pleasure of the person making it.

(*c*) It will expire a certain number of months or years from the date of its execution unless the stockholder signing the proxy indicates the length of time it is to continue in force.

(*d*) The term of the proxy is limited to a definite period.

2. *Form of proxy.*—Proxies need not be drawn in any particular form, unless otherwise provided by the statute, charter, or by-laws. Thus, even if a corporation has sent out its own form of proxy with the notice of the meeting, it cannot throw out a proxy simply because some other form has been substituted.

The Securities and Exchange Commission's regulations governing the solicitation of proxies by companies subject to the Securities Exchange Act of 1934 set forth certain requirements as to the form of the proxy. These should be strictly followed. For example, the proxy must contain a space wherein the person solicited may specify how his vote shall be cast on each matter or group of matters described in the proxy statement.

3. *Date.*—The proxy need not be dated; hence it should not be thrown out because no date appears on it. The secretary may instruct the examiners of proxies to fill in a date approximating the date of mailing. He may also instruct them that if a proxy is dated prior to the time when it was sent to the stockholder, it may be accepted, provided the stockholder who sends the proxy is actually a stockholder on the date shown on the proxy.

4. *Witnesses.*—A witness to the signature of a proxy is not necessary unless the statute, charter, or by-laws provide otherwise. However, witnessing is advisable, for in case the signature is questioned, the witness can assist in proving the signature.

5. *Seal.*—The proxy need not be sealed.

6. *Name of person appointed as proxy.*—Unless the statute or by-laws otherwise provide, it is not essential that the person to whom the proxy is given should himself be a stockholder. The proxy may be designated as, for example, "any member of the firm of A-B & Co.," without the individual being specifically named. In some of the larger corporations, a proxy committee is selected at the annual meeting of stockholders, which committee, in effect, represents those who control the corporation. The names of members of the proxy committee are placed on what is known as the official proxy, which is sent out with notices of meetings during the course of the year.

7. *Number of shares filled in.*—It is not essential that the space provided for the number of shares be filled in. Nor does the filling in of an incorrect amount by the stockholder invalidate the proxy. The inspectors of the proxies may be instructed to insert the correct number of shares owned by the stockholder.

8. *Name of the corporation.*—A proxy is not invalid merely because the name of the corporation is incorrectly given, if the name agrees with the name given in the notice of the meeting.

9. *Legibility.*—A proxy that is illegible should not be accepted.

10. *Signature of the stockholder.*—The most important part of the proxy, with regard to its acceptability, is the signature. The following is a suggested set of rules to be observed by inspectors of proxies in examining signatures:

(*a*) A proxy in which the name of the stockholder is written in the body, but not at the close of the proxy, is void and should not be accepted.

(*b*) The name signed to the proxy should be the same as that in which the certificate is issued. Proxies may be accepted, however, if the initial of the given name, rather than the full name, is given, even though the full name appears in the certificate. If the name is different from that of the registered name, authority for such different signature should accompany the proxy.

(*c*) If the certificate is issued in the name of two or more persons as trustees, the signatures of all the trustees must appear on the proxy, unless the certificate, as issued, specifically empowers one or certain of the trustees to sign.

(*d*) If the certificate is issued to a corporation, authority from the board of directors authorizing the officers to sign the proxy should accompany the proxy. As a matter of practice, however, many corporations accept proxies without the filing of the authority, if the proxy is not challenged.

(*e*) If the certificate is issued to a company that has been succeeded by another corporation, and the proxy is signed and sealed by the successor company, proof of the successorship should be obtained, although the proxy may be accepted if not challenged.

(*f*) If a certificate is signed as an attorney, executor, administrator, or guardian, papers showing the authority should accompany the proxy.

Powers of proxies.—The word *proxy* is applied both to the document evidencing the authority of one person to vote for a stockholder and to the person acting as representative. The relationship created by a proxy is governed by the general rules of principal and agent. Proxies may be either general or limited. A general proxy, like a general agent, can represent his principal in all ordinary business, but not in extraordinary business, such as voting on the question of dissolution. Where a proxy is given limited power, or is given instructions as to how to vote, he must act within the limitation and according to instructions. Consequently the secretary should accept a vote only if it is cast in accordance with the instructions; if a proxy attempts to vote otherwise, he acts outside of the scope of his authority, and his vote is not valid. It would seem that the secretary cannot alter the proxy's vote to make it conform to the instructions contained in the proxy, for the vote is given not by the written authorization but by the person. If the administration desires that the vote be in accordance with the instructions, the correct practice would be to adjourn the meeting, notify the stockholder to revoke the proxy, send a new proxy, and get the vote at the adjourned meeting. To save the time of the other stockholders, their proxies could be taken immediately, so that they might be voted at the adjourned meeting in accordance with the administration's desires.

Where a proxy votes for his own personal interests and contrary to the interests of his principal, and the latter promptly repudiates the vote, the action of the proxy may be set aside, unless the interests of third parties would be adversely affected. A proxy may act on questions subsidiary to the principal question on which he is authorized to act; thus he may waive irregularities in a meeting at which he represents a stockholder as proxy, such as a defect in the notice.

Under the regulations issued by the Securities and Exchange Commission, and applicable to a corporation subject to the Securities Exchange Act of 1934, the person to whom the proxy is given may have conferred upon him discretionary authority with respect to matters as to which no specification has been made by the person solicited, with respect to matters not known or determined at the time of the solicitation, and with respect to the election of directors or other officers.

Where several persons are named to act as proxies, and they are not named in the alternative, all those named must agree as to the vote; otherwise their vote will not be received.

Methods of taking the vote at a stockholders' meeting.—A vote in an election or upon any question may be taken in the following ways, depending upon the statutory and by-law requirements:

1. By ballot. A ballot must be used if the statute or by-laws so require; otherwise its use is optional.
2. By a show of hands, or by a viva-voce vote; that is, a call for "ayes" and "noes." This method is impractical in stockholders' meetings if there is any dissent, for it shows the per-capita desires of the stockholders and not the per-share determination of the question.
3. By reading the roll of stockholders. Since the roll indicates the number of shares owned by each stockholder, a count of the per-share votes is thus obtained.
4. By written consent of the stockholders. Where written consent to any action is required, a document setting forth the consent should be prepared and signed by the stockholders, with an indication of the shares held by each stockholder.

How many votes is each stockholder entitled to?—At common law each member of an incorporated body was entitled to one vote.

Today, however, the general rule is that each stockholder is entitled to one vote for each share of stock that he owns, unless the statute, charter, or by-laws provide otherwise.

Sometimes the statutes make special provision regarding the right to vote, as, for example, that stockholders who are in arrears or who are in debt to the corporation may not vote, or that stockholders whose stock has been attached may vote until title is divested. Furthermore, the certificate of incorporation may provide some other method of voting. For example, the holders of a certain class of stock may be given ten votes for the first ten shares and one vote for each ten shares thereafter until a maximum of one hundred shares is reached, whereupon voting rights in respect to shares cease.

Cumulative voting; how conducted.—Under the system of cumulative voting each shareholder is entitled to a number of votes equal to the number of shares he owns multiplied by the number of directors to be elected. He may cumulate the votes—that is, cast all the votes for one candidate—or he may distribute his votes among the candidates in any way he sees fit. The majority under this method is always certain to obtain control of the board of directors, and the minority is certain to be represented on the board, if the votes are cast properly.

The corporation laws of some of the states prescribe that directors shall be elected by cumulative voting. In other states, cumulative voting is permitted when the certificate of incorporation or the by-laws so provide. The right to cumulative voting cannot be claimed unless that method of voting is provided for as follows:

1. By statute.
2. By the corporation's charter or by-laws.
3. By contract among all the stockholders, provided the agreement is not otherwise illegal.

To illustrate how cumulative voting operates to give the minority the opportunity to be represented on the board of directors, take as an example the following situation: The corporation has outstanding 100 shares; the majority controls 51 shares and the minority 49 shares. The faction strength is nearly equal. If 5 directors are to be elected, the majority is entitled to 255 votes (51×5) and the minority to 245 votes (49×5). If the majority contents itself with casting this cumulative vote for three out of five directors, it can secure their election by giving each director 85 votes. The minority can elect only 2 directors by giving one of the directors 122 votes and another 123 votes. In this case, if the majority frittered away its strength among the five directors, while the minority concentrated its strength upon four, the minority would gain control of the board.

Determination of shares necessary to control an election under cumulative voting.—Often it becomes necessary to determine how many shares one should hold or control under the system of cumulative voting, to insure the election of a certain number of directors. The following method may be used:

1. Multiply the total number of shares entitled to vote by the number of directors it is desired to elect.
2. Divide the figure found in (1) by one more than the total number of directors to be elected.
3. Add one to the figure obtained in (2); the result will be the least number of shares that it will be necessary to hold or control in order to elect the desired number of directors.

Thus, if a company has outstanding 1,000 voting shares, 5 directors are to be elected, and it is desired to elect 2 out of the 5, the least number of shares that it will be necessary to hold or control in order to accomplish this result will be found as follows:

$$\frac{1{,}000 \times 2}{5+1} + 1 = 334\,1/3$$

The desired result, therefore, can be accomplished only if 335 shares are held or controlled (where there is a fraction, it is to be counted as an extra share).

Elections of directors.—It is not necessary to elect all of the required number of directors at one meeting. In the election of directors, nominations need not be seconded. A motion to close the nominations may be made and put to a vote at any time. No person has the right thereafter to make nominations, but the closing of the nominations will not prevent the casting of ballots for other persons. Where the election is unanimous, the secretary may cast a ballot for the slate; the ballot is deemed a vote from all voting stock represented at the meeting, and the election is recorded accordingly.

The polls may be kept open for a prescribed period during which votes will be taken. After the polls are closed and the vote is announced, they cannot be reopened to receive additional votes. The election is not vitiated, however, if after the polls are closed additional votes are received, provided, of course, that the election results have not been announced. The final results of an election may not be announced until the time has arrived for the closing of the polls, unless a majority of the voting stock has been voted in favor of a slate. Any stockholder may change his vote at any time before the results of the election are announced.

Conduct of election of directors by inspectors.—A common regulatory provision of the statutes concerning the election of directors is that the election shall be conducted by inspectors or judges of election appointed in the manner prescribed by the by-laws. It would seem that, in the absence of a statutory requirement, inspectors are not essential. In large corporations it is advisable that inspectors of election be appointed, regardless of whether or not they are required. The function of the inspectors is to distribute and collect the ballots, count the vote, and report, under oath, the result of the election. The inspectors are ministerial officers with some discretionary powers in passing upon the eligibility of the voters. Their decisions, however, are subject to review by the courts. The inspectors may reject votes and may keep the polls open for a reasonable time after the closing hour in order to give stockholders who are ready to vote the opportunity to do so.

Vote necessary to decide an election of directors.—The vote necessary to decide an election is determined by:

1. The provisions of the statute, charter, or by-laws.
2. In the absence of any provision, a majority of the votes cast, as distinguished from a majority of those present, will decide the result of an election.

This latter rule applies even if those voting do not constitute a majority of the stockholders, or do not represent a majority of the stock. A majority of the votes actually cast will determine the election, even if stockholders present who had an opportunity to vote refrained from doing so.

Rules governing tie vote in election of directors.—The following illustration explains the effects of a tie vote in an election of directors. Five directors are to be elected by cumulative voting. Six candidates have been nominated. Four hundred votes have been cast. The ballots are tabulated, and the following is shown to be the result of the voting:

A	80	votes
B	80	"
C	60	"
D	60	"
E	60	"
F	60	"

The chairman of the meeting may not declare that no board has been elected and that the old board shall continue in office. *A* and *B* will be considered elected, and the chairman must permit the stockholders to vote again and again, if necessary, until it is demonstrated that further balloting is futile.

The above rule applies also in the following situation, where straight voting is in effect. 100 shares of stock are to be voted. The shares are divided among four stockholders as follows: Jones, 2 shares; Smith, 25 shares; Brown, 40 shares; and Grey, 33 shares. The by-laws require that directors must be elected by a majority of the votes cast. Three directors are to be elected, and there are six candidates. Each stockholder would have as many votes for each of three directors as he has shares. The votes cannot be split among the six candidates. The votes are cast as follows:

A	100	votes
B	100	"
C	2	"
D	25	"
E	40	"
F	33	"

A and *B* are considered elected and the balloting continues for the election of a third director.

Where the votes are divided between two factions, it is inadvisable for either faction to remain silent or to refuse to vote while the other faction votes, for by so doing the voting group is enabled to carry the election.

Results of failure to elect a board of directors.—If a majority of the board has been elected, the number is sufficient to constitute a new board of directors, provided the election is valid. The entire old board steps out; the elected majority assumes the duties of the board; and the places of directors not filled at the election are considered vacant. The vacancies are filled in the manner in which vacancies due to causes such as resignation and removal are filled. This procedure has been explained on page 1325.

If less than a majority of the board is elected, those elected cannot be inducted into office, and the old board of directors holds over until its successors are elected.

A similar rule applies in case no election of directors whatever is held on the day designated for the election of directors. The old directors continue to hold office and may discharge their duties until their successors are elected. The statutes generally direct that another meeting for the election of directors be held as soon after the day fixed by the by-laws for the election of directors as may be convenient, or within a certain number of days thereafter.

Vote necessary to decide questions other than election.—The vote necessary to decide questions other than an election is determined as follows:

1. By the requirements of the statute, charter, or by-laws.
2. By a majority of the stock represented at the meeting, in the absence of statutory, charter, or by-law requirements. This rule holds even though the majority is less than a majority of the number of stockholders, and less than a majority of the total amount of stock outstanding.

Determining whether vote required by statute is obtained.—Where the consent of stockholders is being obtained in accordance with a statutory requirement, care should be exercised to determine just what proportion of the corporate stock is necessary to carry the proposal. Ordinarily the statute specifically states what percentage of the outstanding stock is required. Sometimes the statute is ambiguous and does not state whether the proportion required applies to the individual stockholders or to the number of shares outstanding, irrespective of the number of holders thereof. A provision in the statute or by-laws requiring the approval of "a majority of the stockholders" upon a particular question has been held to mean a majority in interest of the stockholders, and not a majority in number only. But the more general view is that the term "majority of the stockholders," as ordinarily used, means a per-capita majority when the right to vote is per capita, and a stock majority when each share of stock is entitled to vote.

In some cases the statute is so worded that the percentage of consent required is a percentage of the total amount of stock outstanding, irrespective of the classes into which the stock is divided. In other cases certain percentages of each of the several classes of stock are required. Sometimes the statutes require that the consent be obtained from stockholders having the right to vote. In still other cases the statutes provide that the consent be obtained from the stockholders, and the question as to whether stock that is ordinarily nonvoting has the right to participate in the action is left open. It would seem that nonvoting stock should have the right to vote in any matter specifically affecting the rights of the holders thereof, unless the statute is very clear in indicating that their consent is not required.

Revocation and reconsideration of action by stockholders.—The stockholders, while they are still in session, may alter or change any resolution or motion adopted by them at the meeting. They may also reconsider and repeal any vote or resolution after the meeting, unless such action will disturb rights that have become vested as a result of the vote or resolution. Thus, if the stockholders had by resolution authorized the offer of certain shares of stock to an individual at a certain price per share, and the offer was accepted by such individual, the stockholders could not revoke the resolution or alter its terms, without the consent of the individual, for by doing so they would disturb rights that had become fixed under the first resolution.

Adjournment of meeting.—In the absence of a provision in the statute, charter, or by-laws to the contrary, a meeting that is regularly convened is not legally adjourned unless the motion to adjourn has been passed by a majority of the stock represented at the meeting, even though it has been passed by a majority of those present at the meeting. The adjournment may take the following forms:

1. To a day certain.
2. *Sine die;* that is, without naming a date. In this case, the adjournment is final.
3. Subject to call of the chair.

If the motion to adjourn indicates no special form, the adjournment is final.

Adjourned meeting; business that can be transacted.—At any adjourned meeting at which a quorum is present, unless all the stockholders are present and consent to the transaction of other business, only such business may be transacted as might have come before the original meeting, since an adjourned meeting is only a continuation of the original meeting. In regard to voting at an adjourned meeting, see page 1405. In regard to notice of adjourned meetings, see page 1397.

3. DIRECTORS' MEETINGS AND COMMITTEE MEETINGS

Necessity for holding directors' meetings.—As a general rule, the directors can bind the corporation by their acts only when they are fully assembled at a meeting. The reason for this rule is that the stockholders have the right to expect the directors to give conscientious consideration to all questions through the interchange of ideas at a formal meeting duly called and noticed, at which all the directors may be heard and their opinions deliberated upon by the other members of the board.

The above rule has the following important exceptions that make it possible for the directors to bind the corporation even though they have not consulted together as a board:

1. If the statute authorizes specific acts to be done by the directors separately, no meeting is necessary.
2. If by usage or custom the directors have managed the affairs of the corporation without formal meetings, and the corporation and its stockholders have by long practice acquiesced in an informal manner of doing business, the acts of the directors, if they are within the scope of their power, are valid; otherwise, great injury may be done to third persons relying on this course of conduct.
3. If the stockholders waive the necessity for directors' meetings, transactions consummated without any meeting can be attacked only by the state. This right of waiver is based on the fact that the directors derive all their power from the stockholders.
4. Where the directors own all the stock, acts done outside of a

formal meeting by all the directors, even though done separately, are valid.

5. If the stockholders, or directors, with knowledge of the facts, acquiesce in informal action by the directors, they are bound thereby, if the acts done or authorized are within the power of the board in the first place. However, it has been held that where the law authorizes an act to be done by the board of directors only at a meeting, validity cannot be given to the acts done by the directors acting severally at different times and places through the signing, by all of the members, of a paper falsely reciting that they were present at a meeting of the board and consented to the acts.

6. Unanimous consent of the directors, even though the consent of each is given separately, may obviate the necessity for a board meeting. However, in some cases, acts of directors have been held invalid even though all of the directors consented thereto.

Calling directors' meetings.—Directors' meetings are called as follows:

1. By the officers empowered by the statute or by-laws to call meetings of directors. If the by-laws give the president the power to call special meetings of directors, and provide that, in his absence, the vice-president shall take his place and perform his duties, the vice-president may call any special meeting that the president could have called had he been present.

2. By a certain number of the directors, if provision is made therefor in the by-laws. Where the by-laws provide that special meetings of the directors shall be called by the president or, at his request, by the secretary, the secretary and another member of the board, even though they constitute a majority of the board, have no authority to call a special meeting.

In the absence of other provisions in the statute or by-laws, the meeting need not be called in any particular manner.

Directors' meetings falling on a Sunday or holiday.—If the day set for a regular meeting of directors falls upon a Sunday or a holiday, the following should be done:

1. Follow the by-laws, if provision is made for such a contingency.

2. If no provision is made for holding meetings that fall upon a Sunday or holiday on some other day, give the directors ample

notice that the meeting will be held at some other time. The directors should not hold the meeting on the day following the regular day set by the by-laws without notice, for action taken at such a meeting may be invalid. In one instance, a sale of stock sold for failure to pay an assessment levied by directors at a meeting held on the day following the regular day, because the regular day fell on a holiday, was declared invalid.

A statutory provision holding that if the day on which an act of a secular nature, appointed by law or contract to be performed on a particular day, falls on a holiday it may be performed on the next business day, does not apply to meetings of directors, since meetings are held according to by-law regulations, and a by-law is not a contract within the meaning of such statutes. While it would seem, therefore, that directors' meetings can be held on a Sunday or holiday, if proper notice is given where necessary, and if there is no prohibiting statute, attention should be given to the laws prohibiting the transacting of business on a Sunday or holiday, if the transactions to be authorized at the meeting are to include the making of contracts. A meeting of directors held on a Sunday is valid if affirmed at a subsequent weekday meeting.

Necessity for notice of directors' meetings.—The rules as to the necessity for giving notice of directors' meetings vary, as shown below, with the kind of meeting to be held.

Regular meetings.—Unless expressly required by statute, no notice of regular meetings need be given where the by-laws, charter, or resolution of the board of directors specifies the time of the regular meeting.

Special meetings.—Notice of a special meeting must be given to every director, unless:

1. There is some express provision in the charter or by-laws, or established usage, to the contrary.

2. It is impractical or impossible to give the notice to each director. For example, failure to give notice is excused where an emergency demands immediate action, and the directors who are not given notice cannot be notified in time to enable them to attend the meeting.

Where the exceptions are not present, a special meeting held in the absence of some of the directors and without any notice is illegal, and the action of such a meeting, even though affirmed by a majority of the directors, is invalid.

Adjourned meetings.—If notice of the original meeting was given, notice of an adjourned meeting need not be given either to directors who were present at the original meeting or to those who were absent, unless otherwise required by the by-laws. An adjournment of a regular meeting at which some directors were absent, without a statement of the hour at which the adjourned meeting will be held, requires notice to be given to the absentees.

When directors' meetings are valid without the required notice.—If notice has not been given as required, action taken at the meeting will not be invalid under the following circumstances:

1. If all the directors attend the meeting and do not object to the lack of notice. In many cases the courts have held valid action by the directors in instances where some of the directors did not receive proper notice of the meeting, but where a meeting had been held with a sufficient number of directors present to constitute a quorum, and where the absent directors did not complain or find any fault with what the majority did. In explanation of this leniency, one court has said:

> To hold that in all instances technical conformity to the requirements of the law of corporations is a condition to a valid action by the directors would be to lay down a rule of law which could be used as a trap for the unwary who deal with the corporations, and to permit corporations sometimes to escape liability to which an individual in the same circumstances would be subjected.

2. If the action is ratified at a subsequent meeting. Action taken by the directors at a meeting for which proper notice has not been given may be ratified at a subsequent meeting at which all the directors are present. If the subsequent meeting is called upon proper notice, the business transacted at the improperly called previous meeting may be ratified, even if all the members of the board do not attend the subsequent meeting.

3. If the directors sign a waiver of notice prior to the meeting. Directors who were absent from a meeting, the time and place of which were not fixed, cannot waive the required notice after the meeting has been held. The following is a form of waiver of notice of a directors' meeting.

WAIVER OF NOTICE OF SPECIAL MEETING OF DIRECTORS

We, the undersigned, being all the directors of the ______________ Corporation, a corporation organized and existing under the laws of the State of __________, do hereby waive any and all notice as provided by the statutes of __________, or by the Articles of Incorporation or By-laws of the said Corporation, and do hereby consent to the holding of a special meeting of the Board of Directors of the said Corporation, to be held on the __ day of __________, 19__, at ______ o'clock in the ______noon, or any adjournment or adjournments thereof, at the office of the Corporation, Room ____, No. ______ ______________, City of ____________, State of __________, for the following purposes [*insert purposes of meeting*].

We hereby also consent to the transaction of any other business that may come before the meeting.

Dated at __________, __________, this __ day of __________, 19__.

____

____

____

(*Signatures of directors*)

Form of notice of directors' meeting.—Unless a statute, the charter, or a by-law prescribes a particular form of notice of directors' meetings, any form will be satisfactory. If written notice is prescribed, oral notice is not sufficient unless all the directors attend the meeting. The requirement that the notice be in writing does not mean that it must be signed by the person calling the meeting.

If the notice is received by a director or if he attends the meeting, it is immaterial by what means notice was conveyed to him. The manner of serving notice becomes important only when a director is absent from the meeting and a question arises as to whether notice was properly served upon him. If the by-laws are silent regarding the manner in which written notice shall be served, the best practice is to mail notices to directors. There are some cases, however, which hold that when no method of giving notice of directors' meetings is provided for in the by-laws or regulations of a corporation, personal notice must be given to each director.

Contents of notice of directors' meeting.—Notice of a meeting of directors should disclose the following information:

1. *Time of the meeting.*—In the absence of any statute, by-law provision, or practice of the corporation fixing the time or method of calling meetings of the board of directors, a reasonable notice is necessary for the validity of the meeting. What is reasonable notice depends upon the circumstances. One day's notice of a meeting that is to be held at a place 24 hours by rail from the place at which notice is served on a director is insufficient.

2. *Place of the meeting.*—The statutes of most of the states authorize the holding of directors' meetings, as provided in the by-laws, either within or without the state. If the statute specifies that meetings shall be held within the state, a meeting held outside the state will not be legal, and the action taken by the directors at such a meeting will not be binding. In the absence of any express provision naming a particular place, the directors may designate any reasonably convenient place within the state. The courts generally agree that the directors may meet outside the state, in the absence of a provision restricting the place of meeting to the state of incorporation, to transact any business in which they act as mere agents of the company or as superintendents of the business. A difference of opinion exists concerning the power of directors to meet outside the state to act upon such matters as the election of officers and the levying of assessments; in other words, to act in a purely corporate capacity. Thus, in one case it was held that the directors may not meet outside the state to make calls upon stock, while in another it was held that a meeting for this purpose may be held outside the state of incorporation.

3. *Purpose of the meeting.*—The purpose of a directors' meeting need not necessarily be mentioned in the notice of the meeting, although if the meeting is extraordinary, it is best to state the purpose. The general rule is that at a special meeting called by a general notice any business whatever may be transacted. If the notice of a special meeting states the purpose, the courts are likely to hold that any extraordinary business outside of that stated in the notice cannot be transacted unless all the directors are present.

Quorum at directors' meeting.—A quorum of directors must be present at a meeting to enable the directors to transact business.

If there is less than a quorum present, the meeting must necessarily adjourn. A quorum is presumed to be present unless the presumption is questioned, or unless the record discloses that one is not present. A director who is disqualified from voting because of a personal interest in the transaction cannot be included in determining whether or not a quorum is present. A director cannot be tricked into attendance at a meeting against his will in order that a quorum be obtained.

Where there is no provision in the statute, charter, or by-laws, a majority of the required number of directors is the minimum requirement for a quorum, even where there are vacancies in the board. If, by reason of vacancies in the board, the number is reduced to less than the number required for a quorum, the board cannot transact any business until the vacancies are filled. But if the number of directors is reduced below the minimum required by law, business may still be transacted by the board if a quorum still exists and is present.

Vote necessary to authorize action at directors' meeting.—Unless expressly provided otherwise in the statute, charter, or by-laws, a majority vote of the directors present at a meeting, as distinguished from a majority of the full board, is sufficient to authorize action. Any director present at a meeting may vote on any subject in which he is not pecuniarily interested. Directors cannot vote by proxy.

Conduct of directors' meeting.—In the case of smaller corporations, meetings of the board of directors are usually conducted in an informal manner. Larger corporations, however, generally conduct their directors' meetings with considerable formality.

The chairman of the board sits at the head of the directors' table. The president sits at the right of the chairman, or, if the office of chairman of the board does not exist, the president sits at the head of the table. Usually the secretary sits next to the chairman, often at his left, so that he can be consulted conveniently on any matter in the order of business and hand documents and records to him with a minimum of disturbance. The president generally presides at meetings of directors, unless some other provision is made by the by-laws. Votes are usually taken in an informal way at directors' meetings, generally by a call for "yes" or "no" answers. (For the conduct of directors' meetings at which vacancies are to be filled, see page 1326. For preparation for a directors' meeting, see page 1394.)

Right of directors to rescind action taken at former meeting.—The directors have the right to repeal any resolution passed at a previous meeting, or to rescind any previous action, provided the repeal or rescission does not involve a breach of contract or disturb a vested right. (For right of directors to revoke declared dividends, see page 1342.)

Executive and finance committee meetings.—The executive and finance committees are the most active bodies in many large corporations. They are generally created in accordance with the provisions of the by-laws, or by resolution of the board of directors. The by-laws usually prescribe the manner of calling committee meetings, the number of persons necessary to constitute a quorum, the method of filling vacancies, the number of votes necessary to take action, and similar regulations. The by-laws or the resolution creating the committees may provide that the committees shall set up their own rules of procedure. In the absence of special rules governing the conduct of committee meetings, the rules governing meetings of directors apply. Thus the executive or other committee must act as a whole. In the absence of specific requirements, a majority of the committee will constitute a quorum, and a majority of those present at any meeting will have the power to decide questions that come before the meeting. Committee meetings are ordinarily not conducted with so much formality as are meetings of the board.

4. HOW TO KEEP MINUTES OF MEETINGS

Necessity for keeping minutes of meetings.—Minutes of stockholders', directors', and committee meetings are necessary for the following reasons:

1. The statute, charter, or by-laws may require minutes.
2. A written record of the proceedings eliminates misunderstanding and guides the directors in carrying out their own decisions and those of the stockholders.

3. Minutes are useful if the corporation brings a legal action or is sued upon a matter that was taken up at a meeting. Ordinarily the minutes are prima-facie evidence of what they purport to show as to the corporate business transacted at the meeting; frequently they are the best evidence. The minutes, however, are subject to contradiction by oral evidence to show what the actual proceedings were, if the minutes do not correctly record them.

From a legal standpoint it is not essential to the validity or binding effect of acts done or authority given by the directors or the stockholders that their votes or decisions be recorded, unless a record is required by the statute, charter, or by-laws. In fact, failure to keep minutes, even when they are expressly required, will not invalidate an act of the board or of the stockholders, if the act is admittedly that of the corporation or if invalidation would injuriously affect the rights of third parties.

Necessity for adopting resolutions.—Since, from a legal standpoint, it is not necessary that minutes be kept, it follows that it is not essential that a formal resolution be adopted in order either to bind the corporation or to confer authority to bind the corporation. However, the rule does not diminish the necessity for resolutions from the standpoint of expediency. Resolutions minimize misunderstandings, form a permanent and accurate record of the action agreed upon, and are invaluable as proof of proceedings at a meeting.

When action should be taken by resolution.—No hard and fast rules specifying when action should be authorized in the form of a resolution can be drawn. Under the following circumstances resolutions are either required or appropriate:

1. If the matter is one that the statute, charter, or by-laws require to be covered by resolution.

2. If a certificate showing that the authority granted by stockholders or directors to perform a certain act is required to be filed, or likely to be required at some future time.

3. If the matter regulates the management of the corporation and is meant as a permanent rule until changed.

4. If the matter is one of importance.

5. If the matter is one that is likely to be referred to from time to time.

6. If the matter consists of amendments to the charter or by-laws.

Motions and resolutions.—Most matters of business that come before a meeting are introduced by a motion recommending that the body assembled express an opinion, take certain action, or order something to be done. A motion, in other words, is a proposal, and the expression "I move" is equivalent to "I propose." A resolution is adopted by a motion, made and seconded, that the resolution be adopted. Every motion need not be followed by a resolution. For example, someone may move that the meeting be adjourned, that a particular discussion be postponed, or that the report of a committee be accepted. Action frequently takes place with neither motion nor resolution. For example, the report of the inspectors of election may be unanimously approved and the secretary directed to file a duplicate in the office of the county court in the state and to attach another to the minutes of the meeting.

When action should be embodied in a by-law rather than made a resolution.—In some instances either a resolution or a by-law will accomplish the object desired, and it is a matter of discretion with the directors as to which shall be used. It should be remembered that the by-laws are permanent and continuing rules adopted to govern the corporation, its officers, directors, and stockholders, and that by-laws are less easily changed than is a resolution. It is advisable to embody action in a by-law, rather than in a simple resolution, in the following circumstances:

1. If the subject is to become a fixed policy of the corporation.

2. If notice of the action is to be conveyed to all of the directors and stockholders.

Drafting resolutions.—The drafting of resolutions is generally done by the secretary. Frequently resolutions are drafted in advance of a meeting in order to clarify the subject matter and to facilitate discussions. The secretary may submit the draft of the resolution to the officer or department which originated the proposition to make sure that the resolution expresses the wishes of those sponsoring the matter.

The necessity for simple, unambiguous language in recording the minutes of meetings and in drafting resolutions cannot be too strongly emphasized. The courts have repeatedly held that a resolution of the directors or stockholders may constitute a contract. In writing up the minutes, the secretary should use words in their ordinary and general sense. When taking action pursuant to a statute, it is a good plan, in framing the necessary resolution, to follow as nearly as possible the wording of the statute.

Resolutions involving routine matters are usually drafted by the secretary without the aid of counsel. Resolutions relating to matters that involve legal technicalities are generally drafted by counsel. However, the secretary sometimes prepares the initial draft of a resolution requiring legal knowledge, and then refers it to the legal department, with appropriate oral or written explanations. In some organizations the resolutions are submitted to the president for his approval after they have been examined by counsel.

Certain action may require the passage of a resolution in a form satisfactory to some outside person or organization. For example, a resolution to amend the charter may have to be in a form prescribed by the secretary of state; in such case, of course, counsel for the corporation, or the secretary, need only obtain the form and complete it as required. Other resolutions may be prescribed by other outside institutions, as, for example, by the trustee, if the action relates to cancellation of a mortgage; by the transfer agent, if the resolution refers to the appointment of a certain bank or trust company to act as transfer agent; by the bank in which the company is authorizing its officers to deposit funds of the corporation.

Where new topics are brought up unexpectedly at a corporate meeting for discussion, and the secretary has had no opportunity before the meeting to draft a resolution, he may immediately write out the resolution in full and have it approved by the chairman, or he may follow the practice of writing out the resolution after the meeting. The resolution, under the second plan, is accurately worded in the typewritten minutes but is not read until the succeeding meeting. This practice is more suitable for directors' than for stockholders' meetings. At stockholders' meetings it is advisable that adequate time be taken to frame an exact resolution to be voted upon at the meeting.

Recording discussions in the minutes.—Generally the argument on particular questions and the discussion that take place at a meeting are not made part of the record, unless some member present specifically requests that his views be made a matter of record. Frequently it is advisable to include an explanatory statement of the resolution or motion in order to clarify the proposal. Where this is necessary, the statement may well become a part of the resolution by being included in the preamble, under the "whereas" clause. The secretary should not hesitate to record in his minutes full details of the transaction; too many secretaries err on the side of brevity.

How to record motions, resolutions, and votes taken.—The names of proposers and seconders of motions are generally omitted, although in some cases it may be advisable to show by whom the proposal was introduced. In most cases it is not necessary that the names of those voting for or against a proposition be recorded, unless the statute, charter, or by-laws require this information to be shown. In the case of stockholders' meetings, it is generally sufficient to show the number of shares voting for and against a proposition. Furthermore, by recording the vote in this way, the minutes show that a quorum was present when the business was authorized. Where a special request is made for the recording of dissenting votes by a minority, the entries should be so made by the secretary. It is advisable to indicate in the minutes that a director personally interested in a particular transaction did not vote, or that he left the room.

If no vote is taken on a certain question, and the chairman obtains the consensus of the directors in an informal manner, it is sufficient to note in the minutes that "it was the consensus that," or that "each director present expressed his approval of," or that "doubt was expressed as to," followed by a statement of the facts. This puts on record some evidence of the points covered and the general reaction.

All important written proposals, contracts, or other papers brought before the meeting may be ordered "spread upon the minutes"—that is, written out in full in the minute book.

In certain actions dissenting directors should be particularly careful to have their opposition noted. For example, where the statute places a personal liability upon directors who consent to the issuance of stock for property in excess of the actual value of the property, the minutes should show the names of the directors concurring in the judgment of the value of the property. In connection with the declaration of dividends, recording of dissent may be necessary to save the directors from personal liability for dividends illegally declared.

Arrangement of minutes.—The secretary is not required to write the minutes out in his own handwriting. While the minutes can be written in any form, the most usual arrangement is the following:

1. Heading designating whether it is a stockholders', directors', or committee meeting.
2. Time and place of the meeting.
3. Presiding officer and secretary.
4. Proof that notice was given or waived.
5. Statement of amount of stock represented in person or by proxy, with a notation that a quorum was present.
6. Approval of minutes of previous meeting.
7. Report of all business transacted, usually arranged in accordance with the established order of business.
8. Adjourned.

Rules for typewriting minutes of meeting.—The following is a suggested set of rules relating to the form to be followed by those who typewrite the minutes in the minute book:

1. The heading designating the meeting should be capitalized and centered.
2. Paragraphs should be indented ten spaces.
3. Names of attending directors and absentees, or similar lists, should be indented fifteen spaces.
4. The text of the minutes should be double-spaced.
5. Double space should be left between paragraphs, and triple space between items in the order of business.
6. Resolutions should be indented fifteen spaces and single-spaced.
7. The words "Board of Directors" and the word "Corporation," when reference is being made to the corporation whose minutes are being written, should be capitalized.
8. Captions in margins should be in capitals or in red type.

9. A margin of an inch and a half or two inches should be left on the left-hand or right-hand side of the page, depending upon whether it is a left-hand or right-hand page, for captions and indexing.

10. The minutes should be summarized in marginal headings.

182	
REGULAR DIRECTORS MEETING	THE .... CORPORATION DIRECTORS' MEETING APRIL 30, 19 .. ---oOo---
APRIL 30, 19 ..	A regular meeting of the Board of Directors of The .... Corporation was held at the office of the Corporation in ...., Chicago, Illinois, on Thursday, April 30th, at ten thirty o'clock in the forenoon.
PRESENT	There were present: F.S. .... Chairman presiding. C.L. .... A.R. .... M.R. .... P.S. .... J.M. .... A.B. .... M.F. .... comprising a quorum of the board; also A.G. .... Secretary.
ABSENT	Absent: W.I. .... H.F. .... A.C. .... P.H. .... I.H. .... H.H. .... F.B. ....
MINUTES APPROVED	The minutes of the annual directors' meeting held on April 7,19 .., were read and approved. On motion duly made, seconded, and carried, the minutes of the Finance Committee meetings of February 12, March 10 and 30, April 16 and 24, 19 .., were approved.
PRESIDENT'S REPORT	The president reported that results this year slightly exceeded those of last year, both in the number of ...... sold and in the amount of the net profits, which were $1.84 per share on the common stock. Plant operations, which were under curtailment in January and February, were increased to capacity in March. ...... in dealers' stocks and in transit to them, including demonstrators, on April 1st were 46% less than on the same date in 19 .., and 25% less than in 19 ... The regular dividends on the preferred and common stocks were paid March 1st, which action in the case of the latter stock completed the tenth consecutive year of dividends. The balance sheet shows substantial increases in cash and decreases in inventories, plant investments, and liabilities. Eleven plants are now operating at capacity, and production for the second quarter will exceed 4,000 ..... Demand greatly exceeds output, and ... are therefore being distributed among dealers on a pro rata basis. April collections will be about $ .... Generally speaking, conditions with us were never better.

Figure 104a.—Minutes of Directors' Meeting, Page 1.

11. The words "Whereas" and "Resolved" should be capitalized and followed by a comma, and the word "That" after resolved should be capitalized.

12. Sums of money, when mentioned in a resolution, should be written first in words and then in figures in parentheses, as follows: Ten Thousand ($10,000) Dollars.

The treasurer submitted a general profit and loss statement for the first three months of the year 19 .., showing a net profit for that period, after deduction of all interest charges and reserves, of $ .... He also submitted a general balance sheet as of March 31, 19 .., showing a surplus on that date (exclusive of Special Surplus Account) available for dividends of $ .... These reports were ordered placed on file. 183

On motion duly made and seconded, the following resolution was unanimously adopted:

WHEREAS, it appears from the report of the treasurer that the net profits of this Corporation for the three months' period ending March 31, 19 .., after deduction of interest charges and reserves, amounted to the sum of .... ($ ....) Dollars, and 611

WHEREAS, it appears from the report of the treasurer that the surplus (exclusive of Special Surplus Account) available for dividends on March 31, 19 .., was .... ($ ....) Dollars, and the treasurer has reported that the same has not been diminished since that date, it is therefore

PREFERRED STOCK DIVIDEND

RESOLVED, That for the purpose of paying the regular June quarterly dividend of one and three-quarters (1¾%) per cent on ...... Million Two Hundred Thirty-five Thousand ($ ....) Dollars preferred stock of the .... Corporation, there is hereby set apart, out of the surplus, net profits arising from the business of the sum of .... ($ ....) Dollars, and from such sum so set apart, the treasurer is hereby authorized and directed to pay, or cause to be paid, the said regular June quarterly dividend of one and three-quarters (1¾%) per cent on June 1st, 19 .. to the preferred stockholders of record at the close of business on May 9th, 19 ...

The treasurer further reported that the present condition of the Special Surplus Account complied in all respects with the conditions required by the Certificate of Incorporation to exist for the payment of dividends on the common stock, and that the surplus available for dividends on the common stock on March 31st, 19 .., after deduction of the sum of $ .... heretofore at this meeting set apart for the payment of the June quarterly dividend on the preferred stock, is $ 612

On motion duly made and seconded, it was unanimously

COMMON STOCK DIVIDEND

RESOLVED, That for the purpose of paying a quarterly dividend of One ($1.00) Dollar per share on .... (..........) shares of the common stock of The .... Corporation now outstanding, there is hereby set apart, out of the surplus net profits arising from the business of the Corporation, the sum of .... ($ ....) Dollars, and from such sum so set apart the treasurer is authorized and directed to pay, or cause to be paid, the said quarterly dividend of One ($1.00) Dollar per share on June 1st, 19 .. to the common stockholders of record at the close of business on May 9th, 19 ... 613

REPORT OF V.P. IN CHARGE OF MFG

The vice-president in charge of manufacturing read a written report on manufacturing conditions in the plants, which was ordered received and placed on file.

REPORT ON SALES

In the absence of the vice-president in charge of sales, the president made a report in which he stated that dealers' stocks are very low, and that the demand for ..... is greater than it has ever been. Mechanically the ...... are excellent, and practically no complaints are received in this regard. Report ordered received and placed on file.

On motion duly made and seconded, the meeting adjourned.

.... Secretary

.... President

Figure 104b.—Minutes of Directors' Meeting, Page 2.

Examples of minutes.—The reproduction of minutes of a regular directors' meeting shown in Figure 104a-b indicates the large-size minute page (13 x 8½ inches) adopted by many corporations. Oblong holes are punched in the sheets so that they may be inserted in the locking binder. The left-hand margin is 1½ inches wide; thus ample room is provided for the use of convenient index captions. Each sheet must be accounted for by its number in the upper outside corner.

A set of minutes that may be used as a model for an annual stockholders' meeting is given below. A set of minutes for an annual meeting of directors is given on pages 1436 et seq.

MINUTES OF ANNUAL MEETING OF STOCKHOLDERS HELD PURSUANT TO WRITTEN NOTICE OF MEETING

[*Note—The headings in italics ordinarily appear in the minute book as marginal captions.*]

[*Time and place of meeting*] The regular annual meeting of the stockholders of the ______________ Corporation, a [*give state of incorporation*] corporation, was held at the office of the Corporation, ______ __________ Street, in the City of __________, State of __________, on the __ day of __________, 19__, at ______ o'clock __M., pursuant to a call made by the President, and written notice given by the Secretary.

[*Presiding officer; Secretary*] Mr. ____________, President of the Corporation, presided at the meeting, and Mr. __________________, Secretary of the Corporation, was secretary of the meeting, as provided by the By-laws.

The Secretary presented and read the following notice of the meeting:

[*Insert notice of meeting*]

[*Proof of notice*] The Secretary presented an affidavit, duly signed and sworn to by himself, showing that notice of the meeting had been mailed to each stockholder, addressed to such stockholder at the address given by him to the Corporation, postage prepaid, as required by the By-laws of the Corporation. The affidavit was approved and ordered attached to these minutes.

[*List of stockholders; quorum*] A certified alphabetical list of the stockholders of the Corporation was presented, and upon a call of the list and an inspection of proxies, it was found that there were present in person stockholders of the Corporation holding ________ shares of stock and represented by proxy, stockholders of the Corporation holding _______ shares of stock, being more than a majority of the total number of shares outstanding and entitled to vote.

The proxies were filed with the Secretary.

Thereupon the President announced that legal notice of the meeting had been given, that a quorum was present, and that the meeting was now regularly and lawfully convened and ready to transact business.

[*Inspectors of election*] Upon motion duly made and seconded, ________________ and ________________ were unanimously elected Inspectors of Election to count the votes presented to the meeting in person or by proxy. The Inspectors of Election thereupon submitted their oaths as such Inspectors, duly subscribed by them, and the Secretary was directed to attach the same to these minutes.

[*Approval of minutes*] The Secretary then presented the minutes of the annual meeting of stockholders held on ____________, 19__, which were read and approved.

[*Approval of acts of directors and annual report*] Thereupon the President presented to the meeting the following papers and documents, all of which were laid upon the table and were publicly declared by the President to be open for inspection by any stockholder:

1. The minutes of the Board of Directors, covering all purchases, contracts, contributions, compensations, acts, proceedings, elections, and appointments by the Board of Directors since the annual meeting held on ____________ __, 19__.

2. The ________ (insert number) annual report, a copy of which has been mailed to every stockholder of record.

Upon motion duly made and seconded, it was unanimously

RESOLVED, That all purchases, contracts, contributions, compensations, acts, proceedings, elections, and appointments by the Board of Directors since the Annual Meeting of Stockholders of the Corporation on ____________ __, 19__, and all matters referred to in the Annual Report to Stockholders for the fiscal year ending ____________ __, 19__, be and the same hereby are approved and ratified.

The meeting then proceeded to the election of five directors as successors to the directors whose terms expire with this annual meeting, to hold office for the term of ______ year(s), and until their successors shall be elected and shall qualify.

[*Nomination of directors*] The following were nominated and seconded to be directors:

A	________________________	*F*	________________________
B	________________________	*G*	________________________
C	________________________	*H*	________________________
D	________________________	*I*	________________________
E	________________________	*J*	________________________

There were no other nominations.

Upon motion duly made, seconded, and unanimously carried, the nominations were closed.

Upon motion duly made and seconded, it was unanimously

[*Voting*] RESOLVED, That the polls remain open for one hour, commencing at ______ o'clock __M., and closing at ______ o'clock __M.

The President stated that the polls were now open, and would remain open as stated, and that the Inspectors of Election were prepared to receive the votes of the stockholders.

At ______ o'clock, the polls having been kept open for one hour, and no others desiring to vote, it was, on motion duly made and seconded, unanimously

RESOLVED, That the polls be closed.

The Inspectors of Election thereupon inspected the proxies and counted the ballots, and submitted their report in writing.

[*Report of Inspectors of Election*] Upon motion duly made and seconded, the report of the Inspectors of Election was unanimously approved, and the Secretary was directed to file the original report and to attach a copy to the minutes of this meeting.

The report of the Inspectors of Election is as follows:

[*Insert report of Inspectors of Election*]

[*Declaration of election*] The Chairman thereupon declared that the five persons receiving the highest number of votes, namely [*insert names*], had been duly elected directors of the Corporation, to serve for the term of ______ year(s), and until their successors shall be elected and shall qualify.

[*Adjournment*] No other business having come before the meeting, it was, on motion duly made and seconded, adjourned.

________________________	________________________
President	*Secretary*

MINUTES OF ANNUAL MEETING OF DIRECTORS

[*Note—The headings in italics ordinarily appear in the minute book as marginal captions.*]

[*Time and place of meeting*] The __________ annual meeting of the Board of Directors of the ______________ Corporation was held at the office of the Corporation, ______ __________, in the City of __________, State of __________, on the __ day of ______, 19__, at ______ o'clock in the ______ noon, immediately following the adjournment of the annual meeting of the stockholders.

[*Attendance*] The following directors, being all the directors of the said Corporation, were present:

____

____

____

____

____

[*Chairman; Secretary*] Mr. ________________________, President of the Corporation, presided, and Mr. ________________________ acted as secretary of the meeting.

[*Quorum*] The Chairman announced that a quorum of the directors was present, and that the meeting, having been duly convened, was ready to proceed with its business.

[*Notice of meeting*] The Secretary presented the notice of the meeting pursuant to which the meeting was held. The same was ordered to be entered in the minutes and is as follows:

[*Insert notice of meeting*]

[*Presentation of minutes of annual stockholders' meeting*] The Chairman laid before the meeting the minutes of the annual meeting of the stockholders of the Corporation, held on the __ day of __________, 19__, showing the election of the following persons as directors of the Corporation, to hold office for the term of ______ year(s), and until their successors shall be elected and shall qualify.

____

____

____

____

____

[*Election of officers*] On motion duly made, seconded, and unanimously carried, the Board of Directors thereupon proceeded to elect the following officers of the Corporation—to wit: President, Vice-President, Secretary, and Treasurer.

Mr. ____________________ was nominated for the office of President of the Corporation. No other nominations being made, upon motion duly made, seconded, and unanimously carried, Mr. ____________________ was elected President of the Corporation, and was declared duly elected to the said office.

Mr. ____________________ was nominated for the office of Vice-President of the Corporation. No other nominations being made, upon motion duly made, seconded, and unanimously carried, Mr. ____________________ was elected Vice-President of the Corporation, and was declared duly elected to the said office.

Mr. ____________________ was nominated for the office of Secretary of the Corporation. No other nominations being made, upon motion duly made, seconded, and unanimously carried, Mr. ____________________ was elected Secretary of the Corporation, and was declared duly elected to the said office.

Mr. ____________________ was nominated for the office of Treasurer of the Corporation. No other nominations being made, upon motion duly made, seconded, and unanimously carried, Mr. ____________________ was elected Treasurer of the Corporation, and was declared duly elected to the said office.

Each of the officers so elected was present and thereupon accepted the office to which he was elected.

Upon motion duly made, seconded, and unanimously carried, the Board of Directors proceeded to fix the salaries to be paid to the President, Vice-President, Secretary, and Treasurer for the year 19__.

[*Compensation of officers*] The Chairman announced that the salary of each officer would be voted upon separately, and that the officer whose salary was under consideration would not participate in the vote.

Mr. ____________________, President, thereupon left the room.

On motion duly made, seconded, and affirmatively voted upon by all the directors then present, it was

[*Salary of President*] RESOLVED, That the salary of Mr. ____________________, President of the Corporation, be fixed at $______ for the year beginning __________ __, 19__, and ending

__________ __, 19__, payable in semimonthly installments on the fifteenth day and the last day of each calendar month.

The vote having been taken, Mr. ___________________ was recalled to the meeting.

The Vice-President then left the room.

(*Repeat the minutes given above for each officer.*)

[*Adjournment*] There being no further business to come before the meeting, the same was, upon motion, adjourned.

____
President

____
Secretary

How to correct errors in minutes.—One of the purposes of reading the minutes of a previous meeting is to offer an opportunity to make corrections of any misstatements or errors that may have crept into the record. The fact that corrections are made after the minutes are prepared is comparatively unimportant, from a legal standpoint, if the entry faithfully shows what was done.

The manner of correcting errors depends upon the importance of the matter to be changed. The chairman may informally direct correction of simple errors such as mistakes in the spelling of names. If a dispute arises as to the correctness of a statement, motion, or resolution reported in the minutes, it may be necessary to put the matter to a vote to determine how the minutes shall read. If the error can be corrected immediately, the correction may be made at the meeting, and the minutes, as changed, offered for approval. If, however, the correction involves a revision of the minutes, the minutes of the current meeting will report the corrections of the minutes of the previous meeting.

Manner of revising minutes.—Either of the following methods may be used for revising minutes:

1. Strike out the erroneous matter by drawing a red line through each line of the incorrect material and write in between the red lines the correct minutes. Make a reference in the margin of the minutes to the minutes of the following meeting, showing when the correction was ordered.

2. Strike out the erroneous material in red, and put a note in the margin showing where the revised minutes appear; insert the correct minutes at the end of the original minutes.

Where loose-leaf books are used, it is inadvisable to throw away the pages that were incorrectly written. The better practice is to retain the original pages, to indicate that the minutes are obsolete by reference to the minutes of the meeting at which the errors were discussed, and to insert the corrected minutes in a subsequent page.

If the effect of a resolution adopted at a meeting is to create a contract between the corporation and some other party, the resolution cannot be changed by a memorandum entered on the records after the adjournment of the meeting, without the knowledge or consent of the parties to the agreement. Clerical errors in the writing of minutes are immaterial where the proof is clear that the entry is erroneous. Thus, where it is evident that the directors met on the same day as the stockholders, immediately after the stockholders' meeting adjourned, and that both meetings were held on a certain day, a different date at the head of the minutes of the directors' meeting is simply a clerical error and is immaterial. The fact that corrections are made after the minutes are prepared is comparatively unimportant, from a legal standpoint, if the entry faithfully shows what was done.

Rexall, A. G.

Secretary: 411, 463, 536, 667, 735, 767, 805, 843, 884, 922.

Ex Comm.: 412.

Asst. Treas.: 679, 736, 806, 844, 885, 922.

Figure 105.—Index Card Used for Indexing Minutes.

Indexing of minutes.—Large corporations usually have their minutes carefully indexed so that any business which has been passed upon at a formal meeting, however remote in time, may be referred to and reviewed easily and quickly. Card indexes, loose-leaf binder indexes, or bound books may be used for the purpose.

The making of the index is facilitated by the use of captions in the minutes, as illustrated in Figure 104a-b. The index card contains the subject matter taken from the captions and a reference to the page on which the caption appears. The samples of index cards shown in Figures 105 and 106 illustrate how subjects of resolutions are cross-indexed. If a more detailed index is desired, the captions appearing on the page may bear a number, and the reference on the card may be made to the number rather than to the page. The numbers, of course, should run consecutively through the minute book.

Secretary.

Elections: 42, 58, 228, 296, 411, 463, 536, 576, 615, 667,
735, 767, 805, 843, 884, 922.

Resignations: 58.

Figure 106.—Index Card Showing Cross-Index of Certain Items in Figure 103.

Arrangement of minute books.—As a rule, the minutes of the stockholders' meetings and those of the directors' meetings are kept in separate books. Small companies, however, sometimes use one book for both stockholders' and directors' meetings, dividing the book into two distinct parts. Naturally, there are many more pages devoted to directors' meetings than to stockholders' meetings, since the latter usually occur only once a year. An illustration of a standardized type of minute book is shown in Figure 107.

The minute book of stockholders' meetings (or the single minute book if only one is used) may be arranged as follows: Bind or paste a certified copy of the corporation's charter in the first pages of the book, or merely copy the charter into the book. Leave several blank pages to provide for insertion of amendments. Then, beginning at the top of a right-hand page, copy the by-laws of the

Figure 107.—Typical Minute Book.

corporation, leaving a few blank pages for new by-laws or amendments. After the by-laws, insert the minutes of the first meeting of the stockholders. Continue the minutes of stockholders' meetings after the minutes of the first meeting of stockholders, beginning each set of minutes at the top of a new page.

Resolutions book.—Some companies follow the practice of keeping a copy of all resolutions in a separate book, properly indexed. This system avoids the inconvenience of having to leaf through pages of minutes of unrelated matter when reference is made to a particular action authorized by resolution. Furthermore, by keeping the resolutions in a separate place, the minute book is preserved, and perusal of confidential matters contained in the minute book by someone interested only in a particular resolution is prevented.

In some companies the set of resolutions is preceded by a copy of the by-laws, and the resolutions and by-laws are kept up-to-date in the following way. Ample margin is provided at the left of each page, in which subsequent actions affecting a section or subsection of a by-law or a resolution can be indicated by cross-referencing to the minutes where the actions are recorded. A more convenient way is to enter a copy of the actions on numbered supplementary sheets to which reference is made in the margin of the affected by-law provision or resolution. The marginal note may read "Repealed. Sup. p. 7" or "Changed to 15 days. Sup. p. 10." The latter note shows immediately what the change is and refers to supplementary page 10. At supplementary page 10, the minutes which changed the notice, for example, required to be given for a certain purpose from 20 days to 15 days will be found, as well as a cross reference to the minutes of the meeting from which the excerpt is taken. The purpose of the supplementary sheets, of course, is to avoid the necessity of hunting through the series of books in which minutes are recorded; the by-laws and resolutions book forms a single complete record.

5. PARLIAMENTARY PROCEDURE

Necessity for parliamentary procedure.—Parliamentary procedure is ordinarily not necessary at stockholders' meetings, but some adherence to its elementary principles is always to be recommended. If the by-laws provide that a certain manual of procedure is to be followed, the requirements must be enforced. Action at meetings must always be taken in such a definite way that the rights of stockholders to be heard will be preserved, and the true intent and will of the assemblage will be given effect in the announced result of a division on any subject.

Conduct of the meeting.—The chair is taken when a quorum for business is present—not before. If, after waiting a reasonable time for a quorum to appear, a quorum does not arrive, the chair may be taken, and the meeting adjourned. Any member may call for a count of those present, and if it is found that no quorum is present, business is suspended. If a quorum is present, the chairman explains the purpose of the meeting and then takes up the order of business. If reports are first in order, they will be read and discussed, and a motion may be made to "receive," to "receive and file," to "accept," or to "adopt" (in which case the recommendations of the report become the action of the meeting).

When the business of the meeting is brought up by the chairman, he may make some brief explanation of it. He should not argue on the question, but it is quite proper for him to state the problem involved and the possible solutions; he may even go so far as to indicate the implications of each solution. A motion is then made, and, when seconded, it is "open to debate," or, as is sometimes said, it is "before the house." The motion results in a "question": Shall the motion be "carried" or "defeated"? When the debate has come to an end, the "question is put"—that is to say, "the chair puts the question"—and the vote is taken, whereupon the chairman announces the result of the vote and calls up the next order of business. The chairman may often expedite business by considering a motion and announcing the result in this way: "If there is no objection, the motion is deemed carried." If there is an objection, it should be made promptly, and then the motion should be put formally.

Quorum.—A "quorum" that is properly noted at the beginning of a meeting is always presumed to continue throughout the meeting, unless some objection is raised by a member privileged to vote, at which time the question must be determined and the result recorded and acted upon. An objection that no quorum is present need not be made by motion and does not require recognition by the chairman. (For a discussion as to what constitutes a quorum, see page 1402.)

Authority of chairman.—If disorder should arise, the chairman, acting in his discretion, as a matter of right, can quit the chair and announce the adjournment of a meeting; and upon his so doing, the meeting is immediately adjourned.

Silence should ensue whenever the chairman rises to speak, in order that he may be heard without interruption; and deference should be paid to his authority.

Getting the floor.—A person desiring to speak at a meeting should rise in his place and address himself to the chair; no interruption of his speech should be permitted, except as shown in the following paragraph.

When two or more persons rise to speak, the chairman calls upon the person who first rose in his place; and order is best maintained by acquiescence in the chairman's decision.

A motion may be made that a person who has risen to speak "be now heard."

Any person may rise to speak upon a matter of "order" suddenly arising; but the objection must be taken as soon as possible after the provocation has occurred. (See points of order, page 1445.)

Holding the floor; stockholders' right to address the meeting.—The only business that may interrupt a speaker while he has the floor is the following:

1. A point of order (see page 1445).
2. An inquiry pertinent to business before the meeting.
3. A question of privilege requiring immediate action (see page 1448).
4. A call for the order of the day (see page 1449).
5. An objection to consideration of the question (see page 1457).
6. A proposal to have entered on the minutes a motion to reconsider (see page 1459).

No person may make a speech without the consent of the chairman, except where a distinct motion has already been submitted to the meeting as a question for deliberation, or is to be submitted by the person making the speech. Where a point of order is raised, no speech may be made even with the consent of the chairman, since a point of order takes precedence over other procedure (see page 1445).

Each person who rises to speak must direct his speech to the motion under discussion, to a motion or amendment to be proposed by himself, or to a question of order.

No person may speak twice on a question except in explanation or reply.

A person who has spoken may be heard again to clear up some misunderstanding in regard to some material part of his speech, but he is not to introduce new matter; nor is he to interrupt for that purpose a person who is speaking.

A reply is allowed to the mover of a substantive motion, but not to the mover of an amendment, of a motion for adjournment, or the previous question.

After a question has been fully put—that is to say, when a question has been put from the chair, and the votes have been given thereon, both in the affirmative and the negative—no person may speak thereon.

Points of order.—A "point of order" is a call for a ruling as to the relevancy of debate, the decorum in debate, or any other irregularity in proceedings or violation of rules. The chairman may decide a point of order immediately, subject to appeal with right of rebate thereon, or he may submit the question to the assembly. Points of order, by suspending all business until they have been decided, take precedence over all other procedure. The form of addressing the chairman on a point of order is: "Mr. Chairman, I rise to a point of order." Upon being asked by the chairman what his point is, he states it.

Inquiries.—Inquiries, if pertinent, may be made without first getting recognition from the chair. If reasonable, they have the same right of precedence as points of order. If they involve questions of interpretation as to the meaning of a proposal, they should be decided at once. The form for an "inquiry" is: "Mr. Chairman, I rise for information," or "for a point of information," or "to inquire." The inquiry is not usually stated until the chairman asks the speaker for his question.

Motions.—Except in the case of formal motions, such as motions to adjourn, motions should be given to the chairman in writing if the chairman or secretary so requests. No motion may be proposed that is the same, in substance, as a motion which has already been resolved in the affirmative or in the negative. (For the order of priority of motions, see page 1447.)

Motions are generally seconded before being discussed. (For motions not requiring seconding, see the table on pages 1462–3.) The seconder must indicate that he is seconding by rising or raising his hand, although he need not wait for recognition from the chair.

Getting recognition from the chair simply means that the speaker arises and addresses the chairman, thus: "Mr. Chairman," whereupon the chairman may give him recognition either by addressing him or otherwise indicating that he has the floor. Where a speaker arises "without getting recognition," he addresses the chairman and immediately states his business, by which action the chairman will know whether or not he is entitled to be heard.

Although under parliamentary procedure motions are generally seconded before being discussed, it may be wise to omit this rule at stockholders' meetings, since in stockholders' meetings every stockholder, except the holder of but one share, has more than one vote, and therefore has the right to second his own motion. Furthermore, in certain situations the seconding of a motion may serve no purpose. The seconding of a motion was adopted as a device for saving time by avoiding unnecessary discussion. For example, if a motion seemed to be giving rise to discussion, the chairman would call for a second in order to avoid discussion on a motion to which everyone, except the person who introduced it, was opposed. It would seem logical, then, to omit the seconding of a motion that calls for no discussion and that is unanimously acceptable to the assemblage. In that case, the minutes might read: "Upon motion duly made, the following resolution was unanimously adopted."

Should the chairman refuse to entertain a motion, the correct procedure is to appeal from the chairman's decision. It would be a violation of parliamentary law for the member to put the motion and take a vote thereon. However, should the chairman refuse to put to a vote a motion that is properly before the body, a temporary chairman may be selected immediately, and a vote may be taken on the motion.

Amendments.—Amendments to motions, like the motions themselves, should be given to the chairman in writing, if requested. Every amendment should be so framed as to indicate clearly how the motion as amended will read. As in the case of an original motion, no amendment may be proposed that is the same, in substance, as an amendment already resolved either in the affirmative or in the negative. (In regard to when motions "to amend" may be made, see "Order of priority of motions," on page 1447.)

Division of the house on questions.—A "division of the house" means that instead of a viva-voce, or standing vote, or a vote by a show of hands, the vote must be ascertained on a per-share basis, either by ballot or by roll call. Without first obtaining recognition, any member may call for a division of the house, but this motion should be seconded, unless the person calling for a decision clearly controls a minority of the voting stock.

Order of priority of motions.—The following order of priority of motions may be adopted, although, in the absence of objection, any action taken by the stockholders under the guidance of the chairman—that is, the action and will of the stockholders, fairly ascertained on the basis of voting rights—will be binding on the stockholders:

1. Motion to fix the time to which to adjourn.
2. Motion to adjourn.
3. Questions of privilege.
4. Orders of the day.
5. Motion to lay on the table.
6. Previous question.
7. Motion to postpone to a certain time.
8. Motion to commit or to recommit.
9. Motion to amend.
10. Motion to postpone indefinitely.
11. Appeals.
12. Objection to reconsideration.
13. Withdrawal of a motion.
14. Division of a question.
15. Suspension of rules.
16. Motion to fill blanks.
17. Motion to read papers.
18. Motion to reconsider.
19. Motion to rescind.
20. Motion to substitute.
21. Main, or principal, motion.

Each of the above motions is discussed below in the order given, and summarized in a chart on pages 1462–3. The first four motions are sometimes called *privileged* motions. Motions 5 to 10 are called *subsidiary* motions because they are intended as a means of disposing of principal questions to which they apply. The next group of motions, from 11 to 15, are called *incidental* motions; their purpose is to affect the procedure in some way.

Motion to fix time to which to adjourn.—A motion "to fix the time to which to adjourn" cannot be debated when it interrupts another motion.

Motion to adjourn.—A motion "to adjourn" cannot be debated or amended.

Questions of privilege.—These questions may affect the rights and privileges of the whole body of stockholders, and, if so, should be disposed of before those questions affecting the privileges of a single stockholder. When rising for a "question of privilege," and before receiving recognition, the stockholder should say: "I rise to a question of privilege." Refusal to recognize the question is subject to appeal. If the question is recognized either by the chair or on appeal, it must be disposed of at once.

Procedure on a question of privilege.—The following is an illustration of the correct procedure on a question of privilege:

In the midst of the debate on a motion ratifying gifts to charities made by directors, one member rises:

A: Mr. Chairman, I rise to a point of privilege.

Chairman: Will Mr. *A* state his point of privilege?

A: I do not think this corporation should make gifts to religious or political bodies, because—

Chairman: I am sorry, but the speaker is debating the main question, and is not talking to a point of privilege. He must obtain the floor in the usual way.

B: I rise to a point of privilege.

Chairman: Will the gentleman state his point of privilege?

B: I notice that some of the stockholders have copies of a list of the contributions made. I should like a copy so that I might follow the discussion more intelligently.

C: Mr. Chairman, I rise to a point of privilege.

Chairman: Will the gentleman state his point?

C: A number of persons are in this room who are neither stockholders with the right to be present, nor proxies representing stockholders, nor employees of the company assisting the officers in the conduct of this meeting. They should be asked to withdraw.

Chairman: The point is in order, and we must first settle the question of privilege affecting the whole meeting. Will all the gentlemen who are not voting stockholders or employees withdraw immediately?

D: Mr. Chairman, I rise to a point of privilege.

Chairman: Will the gentleman state his point of privilege?

D: I move that all stockholders, whether voting stockholders or not, be privileged to remain.

Chairman: This is not a privileged question, and the motion is out of order. After I have decided the question of personal privilege raised by Mr. *B,* a motion to postpone the main question until this question of the presence of nonvoting stockholders is decided, will be in order. I will ask that as soon as all nonvoting members have withdrawn, each stockholder be supplied with a copy of the list of contributions.

[The nonvoting members should then be required to withdraw. The meeting does not need to be held up until the copies are distributed, but may proceed while the distribution is being made. It would then be proper to postpone by a motion the main question on ratification of contributions until a motion is made admitting stockholders who had no right to vote. Upon the conclusion of that business, the meeting will resume where it left off on the discussion of the motion to ratify contributions.]

Call for the order of the day.—A call for the "order of the day" is a means of deciding by vote that all business currently pending shall give way to the business previously agreed upon to be taken up at that time. This motion need not be seconded, and it cannot be amended or debated. (For an illustration of a call for the order of the day, see page 1450.)

Motion to lay on the table.—This is a motion to defer action, if, for example, it would be impolitic to get an expression of opinion at the time, or if a different result is likely to be procured and is desired at another time. The opposite motion to this is a motion "to take from the table," which in priority comes at the foot of the list, coequal with a main or principal motion. The motion "to lay on the table" can be neither amended nor debated.

Moving the previous question.—A proposal "to move the previous question" requires a two-thirds vote, and can be neither amended nor debated. The requirement of a two-thirds vote is made because the effect of the motion is to close debate and discussion, and since the motion itself is not debatable, the rights of the minority to be heard are seriously affected.

Procedure on moving the previous question and calling for order of the day.—The purpose in moving a "previous question" and calling for the order of the day may be illustrated as follows. Let us suppose that a motion has been made and seconded at an adjourned meeting to pay a salary of $15,000 to the secretary, but that the hour has arrived when, according to a motion carried on the previous day (the original notice date of meeting, when the proceedings were dragging), the question of the removal of the principal office of the company to another location was to be considered. After much debate on the salary question, the following discussion ensued:

A (a stockholder): Mr. Chairman.

Chairman: Mr. *A.*

A: I move the previous question.

Chairman: Any second?

B: I second.

C (without first getting recognition, rises and says): Mr. Chairman, I call for the order of the day—that is, to consider the removal of the office, as already agreed upon.

Chairman: There is a call for the order of the day. This motion does not need to be seconded, and takes precedence over the motion for the previous question. All those who are in favor of abandoning the subject under discussion to consider the removal of the office say "aye"; all contrary-minded say "no." [This is a viva-voce vote that may leave some doubt as to the per-share decision. If there is any doubt, there should be a roll call. If, instead of assuming, as is done below, that the "noes" have it, it were assumed that the "ayes" have it, then the question of removal of the office would be considered immediately, and when it was finished, the motion for the previous question would be resumed. The chairman need not put the question on a motion for the order of the day, and may even declare the order of the day himself to interrupt business, unless there is a dissenting voice, for the reason that the assembly, in having carried a motion to consider a certain question at a certain time, has already expressed its desire, and the chairman is merely giving effect to that desire. In passing, it may be said that the opposite of the call for the order of the day is the motion to take up a question "out of order," which question ordinarily is neither debatable nor amendable and requires a two-thirds vote, since it in effect overrules the will of the assembly previously expressed.]

The "noes" have it, and I now put the previous question. Ladies and gentlemen, let me explain that the previous question was moved and seconded before the call for order. The previous question is not debatable. All in—

F (arising, and without getting the recognition of the chair): Mr. Chairman, I rise for information. Would it not be better—

G (arising, and without getting the recognition of the chair): I rise to a point of order. The very form in which Mr. *F* asks for his information shows that he is engaging in discussion on the previous question.

Chairman: The point of order is sustained. Mr. *F*, you are out of order.

K (arising, and without getting the recognition of the chair): Mr. Chairman, if we vote "aye," what is the result of our vote?

Chairman: The inquiry or point of information is in order, and I am glad it was asked. If the "ayes" carry this vote, then, without further debate, we must vote on the question of the salary.

K: Could not a motion be first made to reduce the amount of the salary from $15,000 to $12,000?

Chairman: No. [It will be noted that the chairman's answer coincides with the order of motions as indicated in the list given on page 1447; the previous question is No. 6 and the motion to amend is No. 9.]

Chairman: All in favor say "aye." All contrary say "no." The "ayes" have it, with the dissent of two stockholders whom I recognize as owning less than one third of the stock represented at the meeting. We are ready for the vote on the question of the salary. Will the secretary read the motion?

K: How can we decide that we are in favor of $12,000 instead of $15,000? [It certainly is proper, if parliamentary rules are being as closely followed as indicated in this material, that questions of information be ruled "in order," and that the chairman help the assemblage to express its exact will.]

Chairman: Since the previous question has been affirmed, I must put the question on the $15,000 salary without amendment. If you are in favor of a salary for the secretary of either more or less than $15,000, vote against the motion, and I will entertain a new motion with another amount stated instead of $15,000. All in favor say "aye"; all opposed, "no." The "ayes" have it.

K: Mr. Chairman.

Chairman: Mr. *K.*

K: I move that the secretary be paid a salary of $12,000 a year.

Chairman: That question was decided by the motion carried to pay $15,000. Your motion is out of order.

Motion to postpone to a certain time.—A motion "to postpone to a certain time" applies only to substantive questions—not to motions relating to procedure—and is amendable only to the extent that the time stipulated in the motion may be changed. The motion is debatable, but the debate should not include any discussion of the merits of the principal question to which the motion relates. When the time arrives to which a question has been postponed, it becomes an order of the day.

Motion to commit or to recommit.—Suppose a motion had been made to amend by substituting for the words "Fifteen Thousand Dollars" in a motion to pay a salary of $15,000 to the secretary, the words "Twelve Thousand Dollars." A motion is then made to refer the whole question to a committee of three stockholders who are to inquire into the salaries paid other secretaries in similar corporations. This latter motion is known as a "motion to commit." The motion to commit would have to be put before the amendment is put, and, if it is carried, the whole question is deferred until the committee reports. The motion to commit may be amended thus; "that the committee shall consist of three persons to be immediately balloted for by the meeting." This amendment, if not accepted by the persons who made and seconded the motion to commit, would have to be voted on first. If it were lost and the motion to commit were carried, the committee would be announced at once by the chairman, who could be overruled on a motion that the committee be appointed in some other way. If, after the committee has made its report, the assemblage finds that the matter requires further investigation by the committee, a motion to recommit may be made. The debate on a question "to commit" or "to recommit" should be confined to the motion, and should not involve the merits of the question that it is sought to commit.

Motion to amend.—Probably no problem of parliamentary conduct requires more careful and clear thinking than an involved problem of amendments to amendments. The general rule is that an amendment cannot be offered to change the meaning of a motion, for example, to place a "not" in a proposal, since the mere effect is to reverse the meaning of the votes to be taken. If the motion is not clear, it is always best for the chairman to assist in getting the motion into its simplest, clearest form, and then to ask the mover and seconder to accept the motion in the revised form. The next general rule is that motions "to amend an amendment," and a motion "to amend the amendment to an amendment," and so on, should always be put in the reverse order of their submission, in order that the last shall be put first. To prevent confusion, a good rule to follow is that a vote must always be taken on an amendment to an amendment; no other amendments can be offered until a vote replaces the first amendment as the question before the assemblage. The chairman may always announce such a rule, since it does not cut off amendments indefinitely but merely keeps the "atmosphere clear."

The mover of the original motion may always avoid a vote on an amendment by accepting the amendment, if there is no dissent to it, in which event the original motion is deemed offered in the form in which it has been amended.

No motion to amend may be offered to another part of the original question when a motion to amend is pending; all that can be considered is a motion to amend the amendment. In other words, the first amendment with its amendments must be disposed of before the original question can again be considered in whole or in part. However, while a motion to amend is pending, a member may always give notice of his intention to offer another amendment, since this notice may affect the result of the vote on the amendment under consideration.

When a meeting is considering the adoption of a set of by-laws for the corporation, it is proper to read the whole of the by-laws first, then to consider each section for the purpose of getting amendments, and, when all sections have been passed in finally amended form, to adopt the by-laws as a whole.

Procedure on motion to amend previous motions.—The following illustrates an amendment problem. The motion on the floor is: "The secretary shall receive a salary of $15,000 a year."

A: Mr. Chairman.

Chairman: Mr. *A.*

A: I move to amend by striking out $15,000 and substituting $18,000.

B: I second.

C: Mr. Chairman.

Chairman: Mr. *C.*

C: I move to amend the amendment by adding at the end of the motion the words: "but the secretary is to receive only half pay during all absence in excess of three weeks in any calendar year for any causes." [This amendment might be ruled out as an amendment to the original motion instead of an amendment to an amendment. But in all matters of parliamentary procedure, the chairman should go by the spirit and not by the letter. The amendment to $18,000 might be satisfactory as against $15,000 if it were coupled with the qualification of no pay during absence, and from that viewpoint, the qualification in *C*'s amendment may be accepted as an amendment to the amendment.]

B: I second.

D: Mr. Chairman.

Chairman: Mr. *D.*

D: I move to amend by adding the words "and the treasurer each" after the word "secretary."

Chairman: Your motion is out of order until we dispose of the problem of the amount of salary to be paid. After we dispose of the two amendments now before us, we may take up your motion.

D: Mr. Chairman.

Chairman: Mr. *D.*

D: I move to amend the amendment to the amendment by changing the words "three weeks" to "four weeks."

Chairman: I must rule, in order that we may not become too involved, that we cannot take more than one amendment to an amendment. Perhaps Mr. *C* will accept your amendment?

C: I do not.

Chairman: Then we must vote on Mr. C's amendment, and, when it is disposed of, since there will be only one amendment before us, I will entertain another amendment to the original amendment.

E: Mr. Chairman, I want to give notice that when this amendment to the amendment is disposed of, I shall offer an amendment to the original amendment by adding to it: "but the secretary is to receive only half pay during all absence for any causes, except illness certified to by a physician, in excess of three weeks in any calendar year."

Chairman: I must put the amendment to the amendment. Please notice the intention of Mr. *E.* If you favor his idea or any idea modifying the restriction on the payment of salary to the secretary during absence, vote "no" on this amendment. All in favor of the amendment to the amendment say "aye"; all contrary-minded, "no." The "noes" have it.

Chairman: I will recognize Mr. *E.*

E: I move to amend the original amendment as I indicated before.

Chairman: Ladies and gentlemen, you are now to vote on the question of whether the payment of the salary to the secretary, if $18,000, shall be qualified by one-half payment during absence in any year in excess of three weeks unless for sickness certified by a physician. All in favor of the amendment say "aye"; all contrary-minded, "no." The "ayes" have it. [If, before this vote was taken, *F* offered an amendment to change three weeks to four weeks, the chair would rule him out of order, since there can be no more than one amendment to an amendment.]

Chairman: Ladies and gentlemen, the question now before you is: Shall the original motion, which is to pay the secretary $15,000, be amended to pay him $18,000, with the proviso that the payment shall be at half rate during absence in excess of three weeks except for sickness?

X: Mr. Chairman, are we voting on the salary to the secretary?

Chairman: No, we are voting now on an amendment. The question before you is: If any salary is to be voted on—and that question you will decide when you have decided this amendment—I repeat, if any salary is to be paid, shall that salary be $18,000 with half pay during absence in excess of three weeks except for illness? All in favor say "aye"; all contrary-minded, "no." The "ayes" have it. I am now ready to put the original question.

D: Mr. Chairman.

Chairman: Mr. *D.*

D: I now move to insert after the word "secretary" in the first part of the motion, the words "and the treasurer each," and to change the words "the secretary" as they appear for the second time, to the word "each."

G: I second.

Chairman (after listening to debate): All in favor of the amendment to include the treasurer in the payment of an $18,000 salary with half pay during absence in excess of three weeks except for illness, say "aye"; contrary, "no"; the "ayes" have it. Will the secretary now read the motion?

Secretary: "Moved, that the secretary and the treasurer each shall receive a salary of $18,000 a year, but each to receive only half pay during all absence in excess of three weeks in any calendar year, for any cause except illness certified to by a physician."

Chairman: All in favor say "aye"; contrary-minded, "no." The "ayes" have it, and the salaries of the secretary and of the treasurer will be $18,000 a year with the restriction indicated in the motion as finally carried.

Motion to postpone indefinitely.—The purpose of this motion is to remove from consideration some pending motion and all subsidiary motions. It is similar to some extent to the motion to lay on the table, but differs in the important respect that while the latter is not debatable, the motion "to postpone indefinitely" is debatable, and gives an opportunity for an expression of opinion on the appropriateness of passing upon or delaying the whole proposition. A motion to postpone indefinitely cannot be amended, committed, tabled, or postponed, but having been passed, it may be reconsidered.

Appeals.—Appeals from the ruling of the chair do not require recognition from the chair. They must, however, be promptly taken; otherwise they are out of order. An "appeal" is debatable unless it applies to a question of priority of business or to a violation of the rules. The motion is always put as follows: "Shall the chair be sustained?"

Objection to consideration.—The purpose of this motion is to get quick action on a question that is of little interest. Hence it is not debatable and should be carried by a two-thirds vote. Failure to carry the motion by a two-thirds vote indicates that the interest in the subject which the motion suppresses is sufficiently great to warrant some consideration. An "objection to consideration" cannot be amended or debated and requires no seconding.

Withdrawal of a motion.—In the absence of objection, and with the consent of the seconder, the proposal "to withdraw a motion" need not be put to a vote. The following is an illustration of the procedure. A motion has been made by *A* and seconded by *B* to pay the secretary a salary of $5,000. Upon debate it transpires that the secretary, in the capacity of assistant treasurer, is also doing most of the work of the treasurer. There seems to be a general feeling that the $5,000 salary proposed is inadequate.

A: Mr. Chairman.

Chairman: Mr. *A*.

A: With the consent of the seconder, I withdraw the motion and substitute the following: "That the secretary be paid a salary of $8,000 a year for his work as secretary and assistant treasurer."

B: I consent.

C: I object. [If there had been no objection, the debate on the $8,000 salary would have continued just as though that were the motion under discussion, and as though the original motion had not been made. At this point the chairman, without a motion, may put a motion as follows: "Ladies and gentlemen, do you give Mr. *A* leave to withdraw his motion?" Or the procedure may continue as indicated.]

D: Mr. Chairman.

Chairman: Mr. *D*.

D: I move that Mr. *A* be given leave to withdraw his motion.

E: I second.

[At this point, the chairman puts the question.]

Division of a question.—This motion furnishes a means of breaking up a motion in order that each part may be considered separately. When made, it should include a very definite statement of how the motion is to be divided for consideration. If the motion fails, a motion to amend by substitution or by striking out may be tried as a means of simplifying the question before the assemblage, or of accomplishing what the mover of the motion "to divide" seeks to accomplish.

Suspension of rules.—The purpose of this motion is to do what a motion to postpone accomplishes (see page 1452), and, in addition, to bring up another question. It is always appropriate for the mover to bring his question before the assemblage in somewhat the following form: "I move to suspend the rules in order that we may consider, before Mr. Jones leaves, the proposal in which he is interested—namely, the question of ratifying the charitable contributions made by the directors during the past year." Very often this motion is put by the chairman in this way: "If there is no objection, we will consider the rules suspended, and I will entertain a motion to ratify charitable contributions made by the directors." A motion "to suspend the rules" cannot be amended or debated or made subject to any other motion. It requires a two-thirds vote; the two-thirds vote is proper because the rules basically represent the will of the assemblage.

Motion to fill blanks.—A motion "to fill the blanks" need not be seconded. The chair may entertain various motions for the same purpose and may put that motion that he thinks is likely to pass. Upon the defeat of one motion, others may be put by the chairman seriatim. As an illustration, let us suppose that *A* has proposed that the secretary shall receive a salary of blank dollars, and that *B* has seconded it.

C: Mr. Chairman, I suggest $12,000.

D: Mr. Chairman, I suggest a larger sum, $20,000.

E: Mr. Chairman, I think that $12,000 is too small and $20,000 too large. I suggest $15,000.

Chairman: In order to facilitate our procedure, I am going to put the motion that we fill in the blank with $15,000.

F: Mr. Chairman, a point of information. If we vote for $15,000, does that mean that we vote the salary?

E: Mr. Chairman.

Chairman: Mr. *E.*

E: Of course, we do not vote for the salary if we vote to fill the blank with $15,000. I move the previous question.

Chairman: I think we all understand that we are not voting for the salary and are voting merely to fill the blank in order to make the original motion more definite. I will not put the previous question, if there is no objection, for I think we can pass on the motion to fill the blank now without further debate. [Strictly speaking, the chairman should have put the previous question, by saying, "All in favor of the previous question say 'aye'; contrary, 'no.'" But since the chairman has sensed that the assemblage was ready to vote on filling the blanks, he merely saved time by ignoring that motion and practically considering that it had been passed. Notice that the previous question here was not applied to the question of paying a salary of blank dollars, but to that of filling the blank with the sum of $15,000. If the motion to fill the blank with $15,000 were lost, the president could accept other suggestions or could take a vote on either of the two suggestions already made—viz., $12,000 or $20,000.]

Motion to read papers.—Leave "to read a paper" may be directed or denied by the chairman and will be put to a vote only upon objection to the chair's ruling. It will be seen that in effect the motion is at first a request and will be put to a vote really as an appeal from the chair. The chairman may put the question as an appeal, or he may ask if leave to read is seconded and then put the motion as a means of granting a privilege by the assemblage whose time is being requested for the purpose of reading a paper.

Motion to reconsider.—This motion may be made even at a meeting subsequent to the one at which the question that it is sought to reconsider was passed, if no action has been taken on the motion to be reconsidered, or if the rights of no persons have in the meantime been crystallized. It is debatable or nondebatable, depending upon whether or not the original question was debatable. It must always be made by a person who voted on the prevailing side in the determination of the original question, although this latter rule may be waived by a two-thirds vote on a motion to suspend the rules.

The same vote is necessary for the reconsideration of a resolution as was required by statute for its original passage, where no rule has been adopted regulating the practice on motions for reconsideration.

The motion "to reconsider," if passed, does not change the vote but simply brings the matter again on the floor for consideration and determination. Reconsideration should not be allowed, not only where a change would result in a breach of contract, but on motions to adjourn, suspension of rules, an affirmative vote to lay on the table (the procedure here is a motion to take from the table after other business has been transacted), and on the motion to reconsider. Nor should a question that has already been reconsidered be again reconsidered, except, of course, under suspension of the rule that requires a two-thirds vote.

The motion "to reconsider" is an important one in the affairs of corporations. When a motion is passed, it becomes or may become a contract binding on the corporation, but because of the right to reconsider, the action is never conclusive while the same session is being held. For this purpose, it would seem that an adjourned meeting is not the same session, and therefore, when a meeting adjourns to a day, instead of *sine die,* if the action taken at the first meeting amounts to an acceptance of an offer, or to an offer which is unilateral in its nature and is to be accepted by a change of position on the part of somebody else, and that person changes his position, the action taken is final, and cannot be reconsidered or rescinded at the adjourned meeting. However, if no rights intervene, there is no reason why any parliamentary rule should prevent reconsideration (see page 1417).

In parliamentary law generally, a motion to reconsider an election is ordinarily not in order, but the courts have held otherwise in corporate elections.

Motion to rescind.—A motion "to rescind" is subject to debate if the motion to which it applies is debatable. It should be used only when the motion to reconsider would be out of order on account of the lapse of time. The action taken on this motion differs from that taken on the motion to reconsider in that it immediately negatives or affirms the previous action and does not merely bring up the original question for renewed consideration.

Notice that a motion "to rescind" in effect is likely to involve a breach of contract. There may be a reason for breaking a contract, either because it would be less fatal for the corporation to face the penalty of breach than to go ahead with the contract, or because the breach of the contract is justified by the conduct of the other party.

Motion to substitute.—This motion is akin to an amendment, but instead of altering the original motion in part, it provides something new. The new matter, however, must relate to the same subject matter as the original question; otherwise, it brings up a new subject when a question is on the floor. Where an original motion and a motion "to substitute" are both subjected to motions to amend, the amendments to the original motion should first be brought before the assemblage; then the amendments to the substitute motion; and, when both are in submittable form, the motion to substitute should first be submitted. If it is carried, then, of course, the original motion is disposed of, and all discussion and action are on the substituted motion, which may be treated as a new proposition subject to amendment. If, however, the motion to substitute is applied to a by-law or to a resolution that was already adopted, after it has been passed it takes the place of the standing by-law or resolution, and no further action, except to reconsider, is available.

Main or principal motion.—The "main," or "principal," question is the problem of the corporation that is up for discussion, presented in the form of a motion or resolution, and is distinguished from all of the above motions (1-20), listed on page 1447, in that the latter deal with procedure at the meeting, whereas the main question looks to action or statement of policy on the part of the stockholders. A main or principal motion has precedence on the floor only over other main or principal questions.

Table of motions.—The table on pages 1462–3 is complementary to the foregoing rules and is to be regarded as a part of them. The information is placed in this form for ready reference for participants in meetings as well as for chairmen. The motions down to and including the main motions are arranged in the order of their priority.

TABLE OF MOTIONS

(Y = Yes; N = No; ? = Depends upon circumstance or necessity; † = If put to vote; M = Majority)

	Recognition of Chair Required	*In Order if Another Has the Floor*	*Second Required*[1]	*Requires Immediate Decision*	*Debatable*[2]	*Debate May Extend to Main Question*	*Amendable*	*Two-Thirds Vote Required*[5]	*May Be Reconsidered*
To fix the time to which to adjourn..	Y	N	Y	N	N[3]	..	Y	M	N
To adjourn....................	Y	N	Y	Y	N	..	N	M	N
Questions of privilege..............	N	?	N	Y	N	..	N	..	..[9]
Order of the day..................	N	Y	N	Y	N	..	N	Y	Y
To lay on the table................	Y	N	Y	Y	N	..	N	M	N
Previous question..................	Y	N	Y	N	N	..	N	Y	Y
To postpone to a certain time.......	Y	N	Y	N	Y	N	Y	M	Y
To commit......................	Y	N	Y	N	Y	N	Y	M	Y
To amend......................	Y	N	Y	N	Y	N	Y	M	Y
To postpone indefinitely...........	Y	N	Y	N	Y	Y	N	M	N[6]
Appeals.......................	N	N	Y	N	Y	N	N	M	Y
Objection to consideration..........	N	Y	N	Y	N	..	N	Y	Y
Withdrawal of a motion...........	N	N	Y	Y	N	..	N	M	N[6]
Division of a question.............	Y	N	Y	N	Y[4]	N	Y	M	N
Suspension of the rules............	Y	N	Y	Y	N	..	N	Y	N
To fill blanks....................	Y	N	Y	N	Y	N	Y	M	N
To read papers..................	Y	N	Y	Y	N	..	N	M	Y
To reconsider..................	Y	N	Y	N	Y[4]	Y[4]	N	M	N
To rescind.....................	Y	N	Y	N	Y	Y	Y	M[7]	N[8]
To substitute...................	Y	N	Y	N	Y	N	Y	M	Y
Main, or principal, motion.........	Y	N	Y	N	Y	N	Y	M	Y
Point of order..................	N	Y	Y†	Y	N	..	N	M†	N†
Inquiry.......................	N	?	Y†	Y†	N	..	N	M†	Y†
Division of house................	N	Y	Y	Y	N	..	N	M	N

[1] It may be advisable in stockholders' meetings to eliminate entirely requirements for a seconding of motions, since practically every stockholder, except a holder of a single share, has more than one vote, and in effect, therefore, has the right to second his own motion.

[2] Even where a question is not debatable, the chairman may desire debate or tolerate it to facilitate business or to preserve unity, but he is always justified in terminating debate; and he should terminate it if a point of order is raised as to the propriety of debate. Under parliamentary procedure, the minority has the right to deliberate and, if possible, to convince those not in agreement; this right the majority cannot take away. It would seem, however, that this applies only to questions that are debatable.

[3] If no other question is on the floor, it is debatable.

[4] This motion is debatable only if all or any part of the original question is debatable.

[5] In spite of what may be said in the table as to a majority being sufficient, special rules of the corporation or of the statutes may require a two-thirds or any other vote. Unless otherwise stated in a rule or in a statute, a percentage required to carry a question means a percentage of the voting strength present.

[6] The answer applies to negative vote on the question only.

[7] If previous notice of intent to rescind has not been given, a two-thirds vote is required.

[8] A negative vote may be reconsidered.

[9] A question of privilege is decided by the chair, but the decision is subject to appeal.

SECTION 16

Partnerships

SECTION 16

Partnerships

Who may become a partner.—Any person who is competent to enter into a contract may become a partner.

Alien.—An alien may become a partner, provided the nation of which he is a citizen is not at war with the United States. If, after the partnership is organized, war does break out between this country and that of the alien partner, the partnership is suspended and is, in practical effect, dissolved.

Infant.—An infant—that is, a person under the age of 21—may enter into a contract of partnership, but he may set aside the agreement if he chooses. During the infant's minority, he may avoid personal liability on partnership transactions. He may also avoid liability after attaining his majority, provided he disaffirms the obligation within a reasonable time after he becomes of age. Neither the adult partner nor third parties may, however, avoid any liabilities on the ground of the infancy of the partner. Nor can the infant prevent the application of the partnership assets to the partnership debts, or recover his original capital contribution to the business.

Incompetent person.—An incompetent person who has been adjudicated insane cannot, generally, become a partner; if no judicial declaration of insanity has been made, a partnership agreement although valid may be set aside. If a partner becomes insane during the life of the partnership, the partnership is not thereby dissolved, but the insanity may furnish a ground for dissolution by a court of equity. Until such dissolution, the insane partner's rights and liabilities as a partner continue.

Married woman.—A married woman may now generally be a partner, for the statutes in most states have removed the disability to contract imposed upon married women by the common law. In most jurisdictions, a married woman may even become a partner with her husband.

Corporation.—A corporation cannot be a partner unless expressly authorized to do so by its charter. It may, however, enter into agreements with others for the purpose of co-operation and joint service.

Partnership.—Two or more partnerships may enter into a partnership agreement with each other.

What a partnership agreement should contain.—The provisions of the partnership agreement will vary with the needs of the particular enterprise. Every partnership agreement, however, should contain the following:

1. The name under which the partnership is to be conducted.
2. The kind of business to be conducted by the partnership.
3. The principal place of business.
4. The amount of capital to be invested by each partner; a statement of whether the amount is to be paid in cash or in property; if any part is in property, a full description thereof, and the amount at which it is to be valued.
5. The amount of interest, if any, which is to be allowed on capital.
6. The amount that each partner is to receive as salary or any other form of compensation or drawing.
7. The amount of interest, if any, that is to be charged against drawings.
8. The manner in which the profits and losses of the business are to be divided among the partners.
9. The powers and duties of each partner.
10. The duration of the partnership.
11. The manner in which the partnership is to be terminated; division of partnership assets among the respective partners.

The partnership agreement may also provide for the keeping of partnership books; the time or times for accounting; the method of settling disputes; the continuation of the partnership business in the event of withdrawal, death, or incompetency of any partner.

Form of agreement of partnership.—The following is a typical form of partnership agreement.*

* Reproduced from *Gordon's Standard Annotated Forms of Agreement,* page 871. New York: Prentice-Hall, Inc.

Agreement, made in the City of ----------, State of ----------, on the ------day of ------------, 19--, between --------------, residing at No.------ ----------Street, City of----------, State of ----------, herein called the "First Party," and --------------, residing at No.------ -----------Street, City of----------, State of ----------, herein called the "Second Party,"

Wherein It Is Mutually Agreed, as Follows:

1. That the parties hereto shall, as partners, engage in and conduct the business of buying, selling and dealing in dry goods, at wholesale and retail.

2. That the name of the partnership shall be ---------------- & Co.

3. That the term of the partnership shall begin on October 1, 19--, and shall end on September 30, 19--.

4. That the place of business of the partnership shall be located at No.------ --------Street, City of----------, State of----------.

5. (a) That the capital of the partnership shall be the sum of ten thousand ($10,000) dollars; and each party shall contribute thereto, contemporaneously with the execution of this agreement, the sum of five thousand ($5,000) dollars in cash.

(b) That neither party's contribution to the capital of the partnership shall bear interest in his favor.

6. That the capital of the partnership, and all other moneys of, as well as all instruments for the payment of moneys, to the partnership, shall be deposited in the name of the partnership, in the ----------- Bank, in the City of----------, State of----------; and all moneys credited therein to the partnership shall be subject to withdrawal only by check, made in the name of the partnership, and signed jointly by the parties hereto.

7. (a) That neither party shall, without the written consent of the other, advance any moneys to the partnership, in excess of the amount of his aforesaid contribution to the capital thereof; but any advance that shall be made by either party, with the written consent of the other, shall bear interest, at the rate of six per cent (6%) per annum.

(b) That if either party shall, with the consent of the other, become indebted to the partnership, such indebtedness shall bear interest, at the rate of six (6%) per cent per annum.

8. That each party shall devote all of his time and attention to the business of the partnership, and shall not, during the term of this partnership, either directly or indirectly, engage in any other business.

9. (a) That full and accurate accounts of the transactions of the partnership shall be kept in proper books; and each party shall cause to be entered in the said partnership books a full and accurate account of all of his transactions in behalf of the partnership.

(b) That the books of the partnership shall be kept at the place of business of the partnership, and each party shall, at all times, have access to, and may inspect and copy, any of them.

10. That each party shall be entitled to draw one hundred ($100) dollars a week from the funds of the partnership.

11. That neither party shall, without the written consent of the other party, make, execute, deliver, endorse, or guarantee, any commercial paper, nor agree to answer for, or indemnify against, any act, debt, default, or miscarriage, of any person, or partnership (other than that of the parties hereto), or corporation.

12. (a) That, at the end of each calendar year, a full and accurate inventory shall be prepared, and the assets, liabilities and income, both gross and net, shall be ascertained, and the net profits, or net loss, of the partnership, shall be fixed and determined.

(b) That the net profits, or net loss, shall be divided equally between the parties hereto, and the account of each shall be credited, or debited, as the case may be, with his proportionate share thereof.

13. That, at the termination of this partnership, by the expiration of its term, or by reason of any other cause, a full and accurate inventory shall be prepared, and the assets, liabilities and income, both gross and net, shall be ascertained; the debts of the partnership shall be discharged; and all moneys and other assets of the partnership, then remaining, shall be divided in specie between the parties, share and share alike.

14. That if any disagreement shall arise between the parties, in respect of the conduct of the partnership business, or of its dissolution, or in respect of any other matter, cause, or thing, whatsoever, not herein otherwise provided for, the same shall be decided and determined by arbitrators; and each party shall select one of such arbitrators, and both of such arbitrators shall select a third arbitrator, and the decision of two of such arbitrators, when made in writing, shall be conclusive upon the parties hereto.

In Witness Whereof, the parties hereto have hereunto set their hands and seals, the day and year first above written.

In the presence of

-------------------- -------------------- (L. S.).

-------------------- -------------------- (L. S.).

Changes in partnership agreement.—A partnership agreement may be changed at any time with the consent of all the partners. Changes relating to business practices that are not fundamental to the enterprise may even be effected by a majority of the partners. Any provision of the partnership agreement may be waived by any partner, and habitual assent to a violation of a provision in the partnership agreement may be deemed to be a waiver thereof. In order to avoid future disputes, it is well to reduce to writing any changes in the partnership agreement. If the agreement is to undergo substantial change, it is best to have an entirely new agreement drawn.

Division of profits and losses among the partners.*—The partnership agreement often provides for other than an equal distribution of profits and losses. Some of the most common methods of distribution are:

1. On the basis of the ratio of capital invested at organization of the business.
2. On the basis of arbitrary ratios.
3. On the basis of the ratio of the capital accounts at the beginning or at the end of each period.
4. On the basis of the ratio of average investments.
5. Part of the profits may be distributed as salaries or as interest on capital invested, and the remainder in some other ratio.
6. If the investment is less than the amount agreed upon, interest is charged on the shortage; and if the investment is more than the amount agreed upon, interest is credited on the excess; the resulting profit or loss is then distributed in an agreed-upon ratio.

Division of profits on basis of arbitrary ratios.—The method is indicated in the following example.

EXAMPLE

A and *B* are partners. *A* has $3,000.00 invested, while *B* has $2,500.00 invested. *A* is to receive ⅔ of the profits, and *B* is to receive ⅓. The profits for the year are $2,400.00. What is each partner's share?

---

* The material on division of profits is from Curtis and Cooper, *Mathematics of Accounting*. New York: Prentice-Hall, Inc.

Solution

Net Profits	$2,400.00
A's share, ⅔ of $2,400.00	1,600.00
B's share, ⅓ of $2,400.00	800.00

Division of profits on basis of ratio of capital accounts at beginning or end of each period.—The method is indicated in the following example.

EXAMPLE

January 1, *A*'s investment	$10,000.00
January 1, *B*'s investment	6,000.00
January 1, *C*'s investment	4,000.00
Total	$20,000.00
December 31, Profits	$ 4,000.00

Profits are to be shared in the ratio of investments at the beginning of the year.

Solution

	Investment	*Ratio*	*Profits*	*Shares*
A	$10,000.00	10/20	$4,000.00	$2,000.00
B	6,000.00	6/20	4,000.00	1,200.00
C	4,000.00	4/20	4,000.00	800.00
	$20,000.00	20/20		$4,000.00

Division of profits on basis of ratio of average investments.—The procedure under this method is as follows:

1. Multiply each investment by the number of months from the date made until the end of the period; find the sum of the products obtained.

2. Multiply each withdrawal by the number of months from the date withdrawn until the end of the period; find the sum of the products obtained.

3. Deduct the sum of the withdrawal products from the sum of the investment products; the result for each partner is his average investment expressed in month-dollars.

The above three steps are performed for each of the partners' accounts. Then:

4. Add the month-dollars of each of the partners.

5. Multiply the profits by the ratio of each partner's month-dollars to the total month-dollars.

EXAMPLE

A

Debit		*Credit*	
Feb. 1	$1,000.00	Jan. 1	$10,000.00
June 1	1,500.00	May 1	4,000.00
Nov. 1	500.00	July 1	1,000.00

B

Debit		*Credit*	
July 1	$1,000.00	Jan. 1	$ 6,000.00
Dec. 1	1,000.00	Aug. 1	4,000.00
		Oct. 1	2,000.00

Solution

A

Investments Date	*Amount*	*Time to End of Year*	*Month-Dollars*	
Jan. 1	$10,000 ×	12 months =	$120,000	
May 1	4,000 ×	8 months =	32,000	
July 1	1,000 ×	6 months =	6,000	
				$158,000
Withdrawals				
Feb. 1	$ 1,000 ×	11 months =	$ 11,000	
June 1	1,500 ×	7 months =	10,500	
Nov. 1	500 ×	2 months =	1,000	
				22,500
A's month-dollars				$135,500

B

Investments				
Jan. 1	$ 6,000 ×	12 months =	$ 72,000	
Aug. 1	4,000 ×	5 months =	20,000	
Oct. 1	2,000 ×	3 months =	6,000	
				$ 98,000

Withdrawals

July 1	\$ 1,000 × 6 months = \$ 6,000	
Dec. 1	1,000 × 1 month = 1,000	
		7,000
B's month-dollars		\$ 91,000

Net profits of the business for the year were \$4,530.00. The distribution is as follows:

A's month-dollars	\$135,500.00	
B's month-dollars	91,000.00	
Total month-dollars	\$226,500.00	
A's share of profits, $\frac{135,500}{226,500}$ of \$4,530.00..........		\$2,710.00
B's share of profits, $\frac{91,000}{226,500}$ of \$4,530.00..........		1,820.00
		\$4,530.00

Division of profits after first deducting interest on capital.— The procedure under this method is indicated in the following example:

EXAMPLE

January 1, *A*'s investment.....................	\$10,000
January 1, *B*'s investment.....................	6,000
January 1, *C*'s investment.....................	4,000
December 31, Net profits	4,000

By agreement, each partner is to receive 5% interest on his investment (this interest to be deducted from total profits), and the balance of the profits is to be distributed equally.

Solution

A's investment, \$10,000 × .05................	\$ 500 interest
B's investment, 6,000 × .05................	300 interest
C's investment, 4,000 × .05................	200 interest
Total	\$1,000

Net profits, \$4,000 — \$1,000 = \$3,000, to be divided equally. \$3,000 ÷ 3 = \$1,000, each partner's share after interest is deducted.

	Interest	*Profit*	*Total Credit*
A	\$500	\$1,000	\$1,500
B	300	1,000	1,300
C	200	1,000	1,200
Total			\$4,000

Procedure where profits are insufficient to cover interest on investments.—If it is agreed that each partner is to be credited with interest on his investment, the interest must be credited to each partner, even though the total profits are not large enough to cover the credit. A loss incurred by the distribution of the interest should be divided among the partners in accordance with the agreement as to the division of profits. The same rule holds good where there is a loss before interest is credited.

EXAMPLE

January 1, *A*'s investment	$10,000
January 1, *B*'s investment	6,000
January 1, *C*'s investment	4,000
December 31, Business profits	700

By agreement, each partner is to receive 5% interest on his investment, and the profits are to be shared equally.

Solution

A's investment, $10,000 × .05	$ 500	interest
B's investment, 6,000 × .05	300	interest
C's investment, 4,000 × .05	200	interest
Total interest to be credited	$1,000	
Profits earned	700	
Net loss	$ 300	

Since the loss is to be shared equally, each partner's loss is $100.

	Credit Interest	*Debit Loss*	*Net Credit*
A	$500	$100	$400
B	300	100	200
C	200	100	100
Total			$700

Adjustments of capital contribution.—If the partners do not invest the agreed amounts, adjustments may be made, provided the contract so states. Partners may be charged with interest on the amount of the shortage of their investment from the agreed amount and may be credited with interest on the excess of their investment over the agreed amount. These adjustments should be made before the profits for the period are prorated. If interest adjustments result in a net loss, the loss is divided in the ratio of the division of profits, unless otherwise agreed upon.

EXAMPLE

	Agreed to Invest	*Invested*
January 1, *A*	$10,000	$12,000
January 1, *B*	6,000	5,000
January 1, *C*	4,000	2,000
December 31, Profits for the year..		3,100

By agreement, *A* is to be allowed 5% interest on his excess investment, and *B* and *C* are to be charged 5% interest on their shortages. After these adjustments have been made, profits are to be divided equally.

Solution

A's excess, $2,000 × .05....................	$100 interest	
B's shortage, $1,000 × .05....................	50 interest	
C's shortage, $2,000 × .05....................	100 interest	
Charge to *B*'s account....................	$ 50	
Charge to *C*'s account....................	100	$150
Credit to *A*'s account....................		100
Net amount of interest		$ 50

The net amount of interest, $50, is added to net profits.
Profits before distribution:

Net profits	$3,100
Add net interest	50
Total	$3,150

$3,150 ÷ 3 = $1,050, each partner's share after interest adjustment.

A's ⅓ profits.............	$1,050	
Add interest.............	100	$1,150, total credit of *A*
B's ⅓ profits.............	$1,050	
Less interest.............	50	1,000, net credit of *B*
C's ⅓ profits.............	$1,050	
Less interest.............	100	950, net credit of *C*
Total profits.........		$3,100

Division of profits in absence of express agreement.—If the partners have failed to include in their articles of copartnership an agreement as to the method by which profits are to be distributed, the law provides that the profits shall be divided equally, regardless of the ratio of the partners' respective investments.

Division of losses in absence of express agreement.—If losses are incurred and no provision has been made for their distribution, the profit-sharing ratio governs.

States which have adopted the Uniform Partnership Act.—The Uniform Partnership Act has been adopted in the nineteen states listed below:

State	*Year Adopted*	*State*	*Year Adopted*
Alaska	1917	New Jersey	1919
California	1929	New York	1919
Colorado	1931	Pennsylvania	1915
Idaho	1919	South Dakota	1923
Illinois	1917	Tennessee	1917
Maryland	1916	Utah	1921
Massachusetts	1922	Virginia	1918
Michigan	1917	Wisconsin	1915
Minnesota	1921	Wyoming	1917
Nevada	1931		

The act in many of its provisions merely codifies general common-law principles governing the relations of partners to persons dealing with the partnership, the relations of the partners to one another, and the rights, duties, and obligations arising out of the partnership relation. In some instances, however, as is indicated in the succeeding paragraphs on partnership problems, the law under the Uniform Partnership Act is different from the common law.

Right of partner to receive interest on capital.—The partners may agree among themselves whether or not any interest is to be paid on capital contributed by the respective partners to the partnership. In the absence of such an agreement, the partners are not entitled to interest on capital.

Right of partner to receive interest on loans.—A partner is entitled to interest on any loans made by him to the partnership, unless it is agreed that he shall receive no interest. The Uniform Partnership Act provides that a partner who, in aid of the partnership, makes any payment or advance beyond the amount of capital that he agreed to contribute shall be paid interest from the date of the payment or advance.

Right of partner to indemnity and contribution.—A partner who fails to conform to the partnership agreement or to use the proper skill and diligence in the conduct of the partnership affairs must indemnify his copartners for any losses sustained thereby. Further, if a partner pays more than his just proportion of the firm's debts, he may compel his copartners to contribute their relative shares, unless the partners have agreed among themselves that there shall be no right of contribution or that the amount of contribution shall be limited to a specified amount. The Uniform Partnership Act provides that the partnership must indemnify every partner in respect of payments made and personal liabilities reasonably incurred by him in the ordinary and proper conduct of its business, or for the preservation of its business or property.

A partner is entitled neither to indemnity nor to contribution for payments or losses occasioned by the partner's own negligence, bad faith, or breach of duty.

Difference between partnership property and partnership capital.—Partnership property consists of all the assets of the partnership, real and personal, that the partners intended to devote to the partnership business, including property originally brought into the partnership and property subsequently acquired on account of the partnership by purchase or otherwise. The partners may own property individually or jointly exclusive of the partnership, and whether certain property is partnership property or whether it belongs to the partners outside of the partnership depends upon the partners' intention as determined by the manner in which the property was acquired and is used.

Partnership capital is the aggregate of the amounts contributed by the partners, pursuant to their agreement, to carry on the partnership business. Capital contributions are not necessarily money; they may be paid in the form of securities, patents, goodwill, or any other property convertible into money.

The partnership property varies from day to day; partnership capital remains fixed and cannot be increased or diminished without the agreement of all the partners.

Property purchased with partnership funds; is it necessarily partnership property?—It is presumed that property acquired with partnership funds is partnership property. The Uniform Partnership Act, which in this respect merely codifies the common law, provides that, unless the contrary intention appears, property acquired with partnership funds is partnership property. The intention of the parties, however, governs. If, at the time the property was purchased with partnership funds, the parties intended that it should belong to the partnership, and the partnership used the property for its business and paid all operating expenses, the property belongs to the partnership and not to the partners individually. However, where property is purchased with partnership funds, but is not used for the business of the partnership, it is not partnership property. The mere fact that property is used by the partnership does not make it partnership property.

Liability of a general partner to creditors of the partnership.—Each partner is personally liable to creditors for all the debts of the partnership. If the assets of the partnership are insufficient to satisfy the claims of its creditors, the creditors may resort to the personal assets of any one or more of the partners. A partner who is compelled to pay a creditor out of his personal assets is entitled to contribution from each of the other partners. The partners may agree among themselves as to the division of liability among them for partnership debts, but creditors are not bound by such agreements; they may look to any or all of the partners for payment. As between themselves, and in the absence of any contrary arrangement in the partnership agreement, the partners are liable for debts of the partnership in the same proportion that they share in its profits. For liability of an incoming partner, see page 1492. For liability of a limited partner, see page 1507.

Liability of a secret partner; of a dormant, or silent, partner.—A secret partner is one who is active in the business, but whose interest in the partnership is not generally known to the public. A dormant or silent partner is one who is neither known to the public as a partner nor engaged actively in the partnership affairs. Both the secret partner and the dormant or silent partner are liable to creditors of the partnership in the same manner as any other partner, regardless of whether or not the creditors knew of their interest in the partnership. In the event of their withdrawal from the partnership, however, no notice need be given creditors to avoid liability for obligations thereafter incurred; since the public did not know of their connection with the partnership, it cannot be misled by lack of notice of termination of the connection. The dormant or silent partner has no voice in the management of the partnership affairs.

Liability of an individual as a partner although he has not entered into a partnership agreement.—A partnership relation may be implied from the acts of parties although no agreement of partnership, either written or oral, has been entered into. For example, where two people contribute capital to a joint enterprise and share in the profits and losses of the business, they may be deemed to be partners and subjected to a partner's liability to creditors. Similarly, if one person represents to the public that another person is his partner, and that other person makes no denial of the representation, the second person will not be permitted later to deny that the partnership relation existed, and he may be held liable by creditors as a partner of the business. The rule is that where a person leads others to believe that he is a partner and to act on that belief, he subjects himself to a partner's liability.

The Uniform Partnership Act provides that the receipt by a person of a share of the profits of a business is prima-facie evidence that he is a partner in the business, but no such inference shall be drawn if such profits were received in payment:

1. As a debt by installments or otherwise.
2. As wages of an employee or rent to a landlord.
3. As an annuity to a widow or representative of a deceased partner.
4. As interest on a loan, though the amount of payment vary with the profits of the business.
5. As the consideration for the sale of the goodwill of a business or other property by installments or otherwise.

Liability of the members of a partnership for the tort of one partner.—A tort is an injury inflicted otherwise than by a mere breach of contract. The members of a partnership are liable for injuries inflicted upon outsiders by one of the partners only where the partner has caused such injury in the course of the partnership affairs. For example, copartners have been held liable in the following situations:

1. Where a member of a firm of attorneys gave negligent advice to a client.
2. Where a partner, while driving his car on partnership business, collided with another automobile.
3. Where a partner made false statements with respect to the financial responsibility of a competitor of the partnership.
4. Where a partner borrowed money for the partnership upon false representations as to the financial ability of the partnership.
5. Where a member of a publishing firm printed a libel in the partnership paper as news.
6. Where a partner in a butcher firm negligently left bad meat about, and a dog that ate it died therefrom.

Copartners have been held *not* liable for damages caused by a partner under the following circumstances:

1. Where a partner maliciously told about a third person untruths which constituted libel, but which were not told in furtherance of the partnership business.
2. Where a partner converted property to his own use.
3. Where a partner, without the consent of his copartners, instituted malicious prosecution against a third person for theft of partnership property.

The Uniform Partnership Act provides that where, by any wrongful act or omission of any partner acting in the ordinary course of the business of the partnership or with the authority of his copartners, loss or injury is caused to any person not a partner in the partnership, or any penalty is incurred, the partnership is liable therefor to the same extent as the partner so acting or omitting to act.

Management of the partnership affairs.—In the absence of any contrary arrangement, each partner has an equal right to participate in the management of the partnership affairs, regardless of his proportionate interest in the partnership. The Uniform Partnership Act specifically provides that all partners have equal rights in the management and conduct of the partnership business.

Each partner has inherent power to act as agent for the partnership and to bind it with respect to matters relating to the partnership business. This power, however, may be limited by the terms of the partnership agreement or by any other agreement between the partners, but the limitation is not binding on outsiders who have no knowledge of it. The Uniform Partnership Act provides that an act of a partner that is not apparently for the carrying on of the business of the partnership in the usual way does not bind the partnership unless authorized by the other partners.

Where partners disagree as to how the ordinary affairs of the partnership should be conducted, the opinion of a majority of the partners is generally controlling, provided the majority acts in good faith and for the best interests of the partnership. If a dissenting partner is dissatisfied, he may withdraw from the partnership, or, if the action of the majority is improper, he may apply to the courts for an injunction. The Uniform Partnership Act provides that any difference arising as to ordinary matters connected with the partnership business may be decided by a majority of the partners; but no act in contravention of any agreement between the partners may be done rightfully without the consent of all the partners. It also provides that, unless authorized by the other partners, or unless they have abandoned the business, one or more, but less than all, of the partners have no authority to:

1. Assign the partnership property in trust for creditors or on the assignee's promise to pay the debts of the partnership.
2. Dispose of the goodwill of the business.
3. Do any other act that would make it impossible to carry on the ordinary business of a partnership.
4. Confess a judgment.
5. Submit a partnership claim or liability to arbitration or reference.

The partners may, of course, agree among themselves that certain decisions may be made by one or more of the partners. The partnership agreement may also provide a method for arriving at decisions in case of dissension. If the vote is equally divided and the division of opinion prevents the operation of the partnership business, a dissolution of the partnership becomes necessary.

May one of two partners prevent his copartner from binding him by his acts?—Each partner is an agent of the other in effecting transactions within the scope of the partnership business. If, however, one partner objects to certain action taken by his copartner, he may, by giving notice to a third person, prevent his copartner from binding him to any new obligation. For example, each partner has power to issue negotiable paper in behalf of the partnership; but if one of two partners refuses to assent to the issuance of a promissory note and has notified the payee, the payee who accepts the note after such notification cannot enforce the note against the partnership. However, partners cannot impose additional burdens on third persons by objecting to acts of their copartners performed in the course of their implied powers as partners. For example, a partner has implied power to accept payment for partnership debts. A debtor may make payment to a partner even in the face of a notice from his copartner not to pay any sums to him.

Has a partner power to borrow money or to execute negotiable instruments?—In considering the power of a partner to borrow money for the partnership, a distinction must be made between trading and nontrading partnerships. A trading partnership is a commercial enterprise in the conduct of which merchandise is bought and sold periodically and continuously. A nontrading partnership is one in the conduct of which buying and selling is not involved, incidentally or otherwise; the business of such a partnership generally relates to some employment or occupation. A partner of a trading partnership has implied power to borrow money to carry on the partnership affairs, and even if he appropriates borrowed funds to his own use, all the partners are liable therefor. As a corollary of the power to borrow, a partner of a trading partnership may make, accept, and endorse negotiable instruments for the partnership, and may pledge partnership property as security for loans and give chattel mortgages thereof. A partner of a nontrading partnership, however, has no implied power to borrow money for the partnership, nor has he implied power to execute negotiable instruments or give security for loans. If such a partner borrows money in behalf of the partnership, his copartners are liable only if they authorized the partner to negotiate the loan or if they ratified it.

Power of a partner to collect partnership debts.—A partner has implied power to collect partnership debts and to give receipts for payment. Cash and negotiable paper may be accepted, and if it is customary to do so, goods may also be accepted in payment. A partner may compromise debts of the partnership if he acts in good faith and with reasonable care. A corollary of the power to collect debts is the power to resort to ordinary legal proceedings for their collection. The Uniform Partnership Act, however, provides that, unless authorized by the other partners, or unless they have abandoned the business, one or more, but less than all, of the partners have no authority to confess a judgment or to submit a partnership claim or liability to arbitration or reference.

Power of a partner to lease partnership property.—A partner has implied power to lease both real and personal property in behalf of the partnership, provided the lease is reasonably necessary to carry on the partnership business in the ordinary course of its affairs.

Power of a partner to employ assistants.—Each partner has implied power to employ such assistants and to appoint such agents as are reasonably necessary to carry on the partnership business in the ordinary course of its affairs, and to discharge such assistants or agents. A partner may employ counsel to act in behalf of the partnership.

Power of a partner to purchase and sell personal property.—A partner has implied power to make purchases for the partnership, on the credit of the firm, of such goods as are reasonably necessary to carry on the partnership business in the ordinary course of affairs. This is true whether the firm is a trading or a nontrading partnership,* as long as the goods purchased are necessary for the transaction of business in the ordinary way. For example, a partner in a grocery business may purchase a crate of canned goods; a partner of a law firm may purchase law books for the partnership. The partnership is liable for payment even if the partner misappropriates the goods to his own use. A partner also has implied authority in the regular course of business to sell or otherwise dispose of personal property of the partnership, including merchandise, negotiable paper, patents, trade-marks, accounts receivable, and, as an incident of the power of sale, to make warranties as to quality and soundness. The extent of a partner's power of sale depends upon the general

---

* For difference between a trading and nontrading partnership, see page 1483.

nature of the partnership business. A partner has no authority, however, to use partnership property in payment of his individual debts.

Power of a partner to convey real property belonging to the partnership.—Except in the case of partnerships whose business is the purchase and sale of real estate, a partner has no implied power, under the common law, to convey real estate of the partnership. The Uniform Partnership Act provides, however, that where title to real property stands in the partnership name, a conveyance of real property by any partner is binding as against an innocent holder for value, although the partner had no authority to make the conveyance. Where title to the real property stands in the name of one or more of the partners, but not all of them, a conveyance by the partners in whose name the title stands is valid as against an innocent holder for value, although the partners had no authority to convey. Where title is in the name of all the partners, a conveyance executed by all of them passes all their rights in such property.

At common law, title to real property could not be taken in the firm name, nor could real property be conveyed by the partnership. Under the Uniform Partnership Act, however, any estate in real property may be acquired or conveyed in the partnership name.

May a partner engage in any other business?—A partner may not, without the consent of his copartners, engage in any business, either openly or secretly, which competes with the partnership. If he does so, he may be enjoined by a court of equity, and may be required to account to the partnership for profits made in the competing business. A partner may, however, engage in a noncompetitive business, subject to any provision in the partnership agreement requiring him to devote all of his time and energy to the business of the partnership. In the absence of any express provision, a partner impliedly agrees to devote his time, efforts, and ability to the success of the partnership, within reasonable limits. A partner may avail himself of information obtained by him in the course of the partnership affairs for a purpose outside the scope of the partnership business and not competitive with it.

Is a partner entitled to compensation for his services?—It is an implied duty of every partner to devote all his time, skill, and energy for the best interests of the partnership. He is not entitled to be paid for his services in carrying on the partnership affairs. The contract of partnership may, however, provide for the compensation of one or more of the partners for services rendered. This compensation may take the form of a fixed salary or of an additional share in the partnership profits. Contracts of partnership often specify an amount that partners may draw at regular intervals out of the business; generally, this is not by way of compensation for services rendered, but a division of the profits to which the partners are entitled. The Uniform Partnership Act provides that no partner is entitled to remuneration for acting in the partnership business, except that a surviving partner is entitled to reasonable compensation for his services in winding up the partnership affairs. At common law, when a partner dies, the surviving partner is held not to be entitled to reasonable compensation for his services in winding up the partnership affairs.

Does a partner have a lien on partnership assets?—Every partner has a right to have the partnership property applied to the payment of the partnership debts in order that he may be relieved of liability for such debts. Further, before the surplus assets of the partnership are divided, he has a right to have any indebtedness due from his copartners to the partnership deducted from any amount payable to them. This right has been termed an equitable lien on the partnership property and on its surplus assets. A partner also has a lien on partnership property to this extent—that his copartners may not without his consent convert the partnership property to their own use.

Power of a partner to execute instruments in the firm name.—Under the common law, the power of a partner to bind his copartners by executing instruments in the firm name is subject to the following rules:

1. As to contracts not under seal, a partner has implied power to sign the partnership name, but only to contracts within the scope of the partnership business; the partnership will not be bound where a partner signs the firm name to evidence obligations outside of the partnership business.

2. As to instruments under seal, a partner has no implied authority, by virtue of the partnership relation alone, to bind the firm or other partners by instruments under seal; hence a sealed instru-

ment, executed in the name of a firm by one of its members, without proper authority, where a seal was necessary, is the deed of such member only, and he alone is bound by it.

3. If a partner executes an instrument, which is not by law or by the custom of trade required to be under seal, and which would bind the partners if it were executed as a simple contract, it will bind them, although there may have been an unnecessary seal attached, and the seal is regarded as surplusage.

4. An instrument under seal executed by a partner is valid although the partner was not authorized to execute instruments under seal, where the instrument was executed in the presence of the copartners and with their knowledge; it is also valid if it appears that the copartners subsequently ratified the unauthorized act.

5. As an incident of the partner's implied power to collect and compromise firm debts, it has been held that a partner may execute a general release under seal releasing the firm obligation.

The Uniform Partnership Act makes no distinction between sealed and unsealed instruments. Under the Act, every partner is an agent of the partnership for the purpose of its business, and the act of every partner, including the execution in the partnership name of any instrument, for apparently carrying on in the usual way the business of the partnership of which he is a member, binds the partnership unless the partner so acting has in fact no authority to act for the partnership in the particular matter, and the person with whom he is dealing has knowledge of the fact that he has no such authority.

Instruments executed in a partner's individual name; may a partnership be bound thereby?—Where a partner signs his own individual name without signing the partnership name, the partnership may nevertheless be bound if it is shown that the instrument was intended as a partnership obligation and that the transaction was one entered into for the partnership. The partnership may even be held liable where the other party to the contract was unaware of the existence of the partnership when the contract was made. The presumption is, however, that where a partner signs his individual name, it was intended to bind him individually. One partner has no authority to sign the individual name of another partner without his consent.

Partner's right to information and inspection of books.—Every partner has the right to full information as to the partnership affairs. In furtherance of this right he may at any time inspect any and all partnership books and records and may make extracts therefrom. The books and records must be kept at the firm's place of business, and no partner may remove them from that place without the consent of the other partners. The right to inspect the books and to make extracts therefrom may, of course, not be used by a partner for a fraudulent purpose.

Under the Uniform Partnership Act, a duty is imposed upon partners to render on demand true and full information of all things affecting the partnership to any partner or the legal representative of any deceased partner or partner under disability. The act also requires that the partnership books be kept, subject to any agreement between the partners, at the principal place of business of the partnership, and that every partner shall at all times have access to the books and be permitted to inspect and copy any of them.

When has a partner a right to an accounting?—A partner is always entitled to an accounting upon dissolution of the firm. An accounting without dissolution will also generally be granted under the following circumstances:

1. If the partner is wrongfully excluded by his copartners from the partnership business or from possession of partnership property.
2. Where a partner breaches his fiduciary relation and wrongfully derives profits for himself from the business or by use of its property.
3. Where the partners have agreed to a periodical accounting and to settlement of distinct transactions upon their completion, without a dissolution.
4. Where the interest of a partner in the partnership has been attached by his individual creditor.

The Uniform Partnership Act provides that any partner shall have the right to a formal account as to partnership affairs:

1. If he is wrongfully excluded from the partnership business or possession of its property by his copartners.
2. If the right exists under the terms of any agreement.
3. Where a partner is accountable as a fiduciary.
4. Whenever other circumstances render it just and reasonable.

Ordinarily partners can determine their respective interests in the partnership by an examination of the books, without a formal accounting, and may settle the firm's affairs in a private accounting without resort to the courts if there is no disagreement between them and if the rights of creditors are protected.

Duty of a partner to account for personal benefits.—Partners are required to observe the utmost good faith toward one another. If one partner secures any private advantage from a transaction that concerns the partnership or through any wrongful use of partnership property, he is required to account to his copartners for the profits which he derives therefrom. For example, a partner who secretly and without knowledge of his copartners obtains for himself a renewal of a lease previously held by the partnership violates his duty toward his copartners. Even if the term of the lease to the partner individually is to begin upon the termination of the partnership existence, the benefits of the lease belong to the partnership, and the partner must account to the partnership therefor. The Uniform Partnership Act provides that every partner must account to the partnership for any benefit, and hold as trustee for it any profits derived by him without the consent of the other partners from any transaction connected with the formation, conduct, or liquidation of the partnership or from any use by him of its property. This provision also applies to the representatives of a deceased partner engaged in the liquidation of the affairs of the partnership as personal representatives of the last surviving partner.

May one partner sue another partner?—Ordinarily one partner cannot bring an action at law against another partner on a partnership claim or liability. Until the affairs of the partnership are wound up, what one partner may owe the partnership is not a debt due to his copartners, but to the partnership. Similarly, if the partnership owes a sum of money to one of the partners, it is not a debt due to him from his copartners, and he cannot bring an action against his copartners on his claim against the partnership. While a partner cannot sue at law to enforce the obligations of his copartners, he may, however, do so by applying to a court of equity for an accounting and settlement of the partnership affairs.

Where there is but a single partnership transaction that is fully closed, one partner may maintain an action at law against the others for his share of the profits of that single transaction without a formal accounting. Similarly, where the partnership accounts have been settled, a balance struck, and an agreement made to pay the balance due, an action at law may be maintained to recover the balance.

Expulsion of a partner from the business.—When one or more of the partners ceases to be a member of the firm, the partnership is dissolved; that is, the partnership agreement is terminated, and if the business is to continue, a new agreement must be entered into. Accordingly, a partner cannot be expelled from the business without dissolution of the partnership. This does not mean that the dissolution must be decreed by a court of equity. The partners may be able to arrive at a friendly accounting and determine their respective interests in the business. If, however, an amicable adjustment is impossible, resort must be had to the courts to compel an accounting and to decree a dissolution of the partnership. The remaining partners can then form a new partnership to carry on their enterprise. Partnership agreements sometimes provide for the expulsion of a member under certain circumstances and indicate the manner in which the capital contribution of the expelled partner is to be repaid. The expulsion of a partner under such a provision in the contract of partnership does not prevent the dissolution of the partnership; a new partnership must nevertheless be organized by the remaining partners.

May a partner transfer his entire interest in the partnership?—The general rule is that the partnership is dissolved if a partner sells his interest in the partnership. Partners may agree in advance under their partnership contract to accept as a partner an assignee of a partner's interest in the firm, but the partnership is nevertheless technically dissolved upon admission of the assignee and a new partnership is created.

Under the Uniform Partnership Act, a conveyance by a partner of his interest in the partnership does not of itself dissolve the partnership. The assignee is not entitled to interfere in the management of the partnership affairs, nor may he require any information or account of partnership transactions, or inspection of the partnership books; the assignee is merely entitled to receive the profits to which the partner who has assigned his interest would have been entitled.

Withdrawal of a partner.—Where no time is fixed in the partnership agreement for the duration of the partnership, a partner may withdraw at any time, provided he does so in good faith and without injury to his copartners. Even if the term of duration of the partnership is fixed by the contract of partnership, a partner may withdraw from the partnership before the expiration of the period; he may, however, subject himself to liability to the other partners if the latter are injured by his withdrawal.

The withdrawal of a partner results in dissolution of the partnership. If the remaining partners desire to continue the business of the partnership, they must pay the retiring partner the value of his interest in the partnership, less any damages caused by his premature withdrawal. The goodwill of the business is not included in arriving at the withdrawing partner's interest. The remaining partners may agree to assume the liabilities of the partnership, but such an agreement will not relieve the withdrawing partner from liability to any creditor of the old partnership who has not consented to release him. The withdrawing, or outgoing, partner may also be liable to new creditors of the old partnership who extend credit to it without knowledge of his withdrawal. To avoid such liability, the withdrawing partner must advertise his withdrawal in a newspaper of general circulation in the place where the business of the partnership is conducted. Further protection against liability to creditors may be afforded the withdrawing partner by an agreement of indemnification by the remaining partners.

Admission of a new partner into the business.—A new partner cannot be brought into the business without the consent of every one of the partners. Further, although all the partners may agree to admit the new member, the old contract of partnership is terminated, and a new partnership agreement must be entered into. However, the transaction of the partnership business may continue without interruption.

The Uniform Partnership Act specifically provides that no person can become a member of a partnership without the consent of all the partners.

Liability of an incoming partner.—Where a person is admitted as a partner into an existing partnership, he is not liable, under the common law rule, for partnership debts incurred before he became a partner, unless he has assumed such liability.

The Uniform Partnership Act provides that a person admitted as a partner into an existing partnership is liable for all the obligations of the partnership arising before his admission as though he had been a partner when such obligations were incurred, except that this liability shall be satisfied only out of partnership property.

Effect of death of a partner.—A partnership is dissolved upon the death of a partner. Even if the contract of partnership provides for the continued existence of the partnership after the death of any partner, the legal representatives of the deceased partner cannot be compelled to continue the existence of the partnership. The surviving partners become the representatives of the partnership, and it is their duty to pay the firm debts and to distribute the remaining assets among the surviving partners and the representatives of the deceased partners. They have a right to wind up the affairs of the partnership without interference by the legal representatives of the deceased partner. The surviving partners cannot, however, bind the estate of the deceased partner by new contracts. They must render an accounting to the legal representatives of the deceased partner and pay them in cash the value of the deceased partner's interest, including goodwill as a partnership asset. The surviving partners are entitled to a reasonable sum as compensation for winding up the partnership affairs.

Surviving partners and all outsiders are, at common law, deemed to have knowledge of the death of a partner and of the resulting dissolution of the partnership; the power of the partners to act for the partnership automatically ceases upon death of a partner except insofar as it may be necessary to wind up the affairs of the partnership. Under the Uniform Partnership Act, however, no such knowledge of death and notice of the termination of the partner's authority is imputed. Where a partner, having no knowledge or notice of the death of a partner, acts for the partnership and creates a liability, each partner is liable to his copartners for his share of the liability so created as if the partnership had not been dissolved. Further, under the provisions of the Act, the partnership may be bound by the acts of the partner after dissolution as to outsiders who had no knowledge or notice of the dissolution. Notice of dissolution should be advertised in a newspaper of general circulation in the place where the partnership business is regularly conducted.

Effect of bankruptcy of a partner.—If any partner becomes bankrupt, the partnership is immediately dissolved, for the bankrupt loses his right to exercise control over his property, and his interest in the partnership passes to the trustee in bankruptcy. The Uniform Partnership Act expressly states that dissolution is caused by the bankruptcy of any partner or of the partnership.

Continuance of a partnership beyond its fixed term.—Where the partnership agreement fixes a definite period for the duration of the partnership, but the business is continued after expiration of the period without any new agreement, the partners are, in effect, doing business as a partnership pursuant to an oral agreement. Whether or not their rights and duties are the same as under the original partnership agreement will depend upon the intention of the parties. It may be assumed, in the absence of any evidence to the contrary, that the partners intended to continue the same relationship that existed prior to the expiration of the original agreement.

The Uniform Partnership Act provides that when a partnership for a fixed term or particular undertaking is continued after the termination of such term or particular undertaking without any express agreement, the rights and duties of the partners remain the same as they were at such termination, as far as is consistent with a partnership at will. It further provides that a continuation of the business by the partners or such of them as habitually acted therein during the term, without any settlement or liquidation of the partnership affairs, is prima-facie evidence of a continuation of the partnership.

Difference between dissolution and liquidation of a partnership.—A dissolution of a partnership is merely a termination of the original partnership agreement, which may be brought about by death of a partner, admission of a new partner, withdrawal of an old partner, adjudication of a partner as an incompetent person, or bankruptcy of a partner. The remaining partners may continue the business without interruption despite the dissolution, and proceed to organize a new partnership. A liquidation, on the other hand, involves not only a dissolution of the partnership, but also a sale of the partnership assets, payment of partnership liabilities, and distribution of the balance among the partners in the proportions to which they are entitled.

The Uniform Partnership Act defines dissolution of a partnership as the change in the relation of the partners caused by any partner ceasing to be associated in the carrying on, as distinguished from the winding up, of the business. It further provides that on dissolution the partnership is not terminated, but continues until the winding up of partnership affairs is completed.

Incapacity of a partner as ground for dissolution.—Where a partner is temporarily incapacitated from performing his partnership duties, such incapacity does not furnish ground for dissolution. If, however, his incapacity is permanent, dissolution will be allowed by the courts, since the partner is unable to fulfill one of the essentials of his agreement—that is, to devote his time, effort, and ability to the success of the partnership enterprise.

Failure to make profits as ground for dissolution.—Dissolution of a partnership will be allowed by the courts on the ground that it is reasonably certain that the business cannot be carried on at a profit. This is true whether the failure to make profits is the result of misconduct on the part of one of the partners or whether it is due to the business itself.

Powers of partners after dissolution.—Upon dissolution of the partnership, the power of the partners to bind one another generally by their acts ceases. A partner does, however, have power to bind his copartners and the partnership property by such acts as are reasonably necessary to wind up the partnership affairs. In the absence of any agreement to the contrary, each partner has implied power to take possession of the firm property and to sell, pledge, or otherwise dispose of it in order to wind up the business; to collect debts and settle claims; and to complete existing obligations. The partners have no power, however, to incur new obligations by the execution of new contracts, or to make acceptances or renewals of negotiable paper, or to make endorsements of negotiable paper other than endorsements without recourse.

The Uniform Partnership Act provides that, except so far as may be necessary to wind up partnership affairs or to complete transactions begun but not then finished, dissolution terminates all authority of any partner to act for the partnership.

Who has power to liquidate the business upon voluntary dissolution?—When dissolution is brought about by the acts of the partners themselves, each partner has, in the absence of any contrary agreement, an equal right upon dissolution of the partnership to the possession of its assets, and is under an equal obligation to apply the assets to the discharge of the partnership debts. Each partner may collect debts due and may pay off liabilities until the assets are exhausted.

The Uniform Partnership Act provides that, unless otherwise agreed, the partners who have not wrongfully dissolved the partnership, or the legal representative of the last surviving partner, not bankrupt, have the right to wind up the partnership affairs; provided, however, that any partner, his legal representative, or his assignee, upon cause shown, may obtain winding up by the court.

Division of profits and losses upon liquidation.—If, upon complete liquidation of the partnership affairs, there are profits or losses, they must first be divided in the profit-or-loss ratio—that is, in the proportion in which the partners share profits and losses under the terms of the partnership agreement—and the remaining capital should then be shared by the partners in the capital ratio—that is, in the proportion in which they are entitled under the terms of the partnership agreement to a return of the capital which they have invested in the business. Where the partnership is insolvent, the sharing by the partners of losses in the profit-and-loss ratio may result in a deficit in capital for some one or more of the partners. Each partner with a deficit should contribute to the firm the amount of his deficit. If he is unable to pay into the firm any portion of his deficit, the remaining partners must pay in, in the profit-and-loss ratio, an amount sufficient to cover this deficit. A partner who has paid in more than his share of the firm's liability has a right to enforce contribution from the other partners to the extent of the excess.

Distribution of capital upon liquidation.*—Liquidation may be accomplished in two ways:

1. All the assets may be converted, all the liabilities paid, the profits or losses distributed, and all the capital divided at one time.

2. A periodic distribution of the capital may be made before all the assets are converted.

Total distribution.—The first method of liquidation does not involve any very difficult calculations.

EXAMPLE

From the following figures, show the amount of capital distributed to each partner at dissolution:

	A	*B*	*C*
Capital balances before conversion of assets	$10,000	$6,000	$4,000
Profit ratio	40%	40%	20%
Assets converted into cash	$30,000		
Liabilities to be paid	14,000		

Solution

Assets		Liabilities		Net Assets
$30,000	—	$14,000	=	$16,000

Total Investment, $20,000, less Net Assets, $16,000 = Loss, $4,000

	A (40%)	*B* (40%)	*C* (20%)	*Total* (100%)
Capital balances before conversion of assets..	$10,000	$6,000	$4,000	$20,000
Distribution of loss	1,600	1,600	800	4,000
Balances	$ 8,400	$4,400	$3,200	$16,000
Cash distributed	8,400	4,400	3,200	16,000

Periodic distribution.—Periodic distribution may result from either of two causes:

1. The desire of the partners to reduce the capital of the firm, or completely to dissolve the firm, even though it is still solvent.

2. Forced liquidation.

Usually, in either case, unless the partnership is insolvent, the assets are converted into cash, and after the debts are paid, the balance

* The examples of methods of distribution are from Curtis and Cooper, *Mathematics of Accounting*. New York: Prentice-Hall, Inc.

is distributed periodically to the partners. If this is done, it should be done in such a way as to reduce the accounts to the profit-and-loss ratio existing among the partners. The distribution is made on the assumption that all book assets are a total loss until converted into cash.

The following example illustrates the adjustment of capital ratios to profit-and-loss ratios.

EXAMPLE

From the following data, show the periodic distribution of the cash collected:

	A	*B*	*C*	
Capital balances before conversion of assets	$10,000	$6,000	$4,000	
Profit ratio	40%	40%	20%	
First period:				
Net loss				$ 1,000
Cash collected				9,000
Assets unrealized				10,000
Second period:				
Net loss				1,000
Cash collected				5,000
Assets unrealized				4,000
Third period:				
Cash collected				2,000
All other assets uncollectible.				

Solution

	A	*B*	*C*	*Total*
Capital balances before conversion of assets	$10,000	$6,000	$4,000	$20,000
Distribution of loss	400	400	200	1,000
Balance after distribution of loss	$ 9,600	$5,600	$3,800	$19,000
For the purpose of making a test, it will be assumed that the unrealized assets will never be realized.				
Test loss in profit-and-loss ratio	(4,000)	(4,000)	(2,000)	(10,000)
After the test loss has been deducted, the remaining amounts will show the proper distribution of the cash balance	5,600	1,600	1,800	9,000
Balance at the end of the first period	$ 4,000	$4,000	$2,000	$10,000
Net loss for period	400	400	200	1,000
Balance after distribution of loss	$ 3,600	$3,600	$1,800	$ 9,000

The balances of the accounts are now in the profit and loss ratio.				
Distribution of cash	2,000	2,000	1,000	5,000
Balance at end of second period	$ 1,600	$1,600	$ 800	$ 4,000
Net loss for third period	800	800	400	2,000
Balance after distribution of loss	$ 800	$ 800	$ 400	$ 2,000
Cash distribution	800	800	400	2,000

The following example illustrates the adjustment of capital to the profit-and-loss ratio, where a deficiency of one partner is involved.

EXAMPLE

Show how each period's cash should be distributed in the following:

	A	*B*	*C*	
Capital balances before conversion of assets	$10,000	$8,000	$2,000	
Profits to be shared equally.				
First period:				
Net loss				$1,500
Cash to be distributed				8,000
Second period:				
Net loss				1,500
Cash to be distributed				3,000
Third period:				
Remaining assets sold for				4,000

Solution

	A	*B*	*C*	*Total*
Capital balances before conversion of assets	$10,000	$8,000	$2,000	$20,000
First period's loss distributed	500	500	500	1,500
Balance after distribution of loss	$ 9,500	$7,500	$1,500	$18,500
Test loss of amount of the remaining assets	(3,500)	(3,500)	(3,500)	(10,500)
It will be observed from the test loss that *C*'s possible loss is $2,000 greater than his capital. If the test loss should become an actual loss, *C* will owe the firm $2,000, and if *C* should be unable to pay in this $2,000, *A* and *B* would be required to bear this additional loss. To provide against this contingency, a further test loss charge of $2,000 is made against *A* and *B*	(1,000)	(1,000)	2,000	

When the sum of the two test losses, $4,500 ($3,500 + $1,000), is deducted from *A's* investment of $9,500, it can be seen that *A* should receive $5,000; it can also be seen that the sum of *B's* test losses deducted from his investment gives the amount of cash which is payable to him.

Cash distribution	$ 5,000	$3,000		$ 8,000
Balance of capital undistributed	$ 4,500	$4,500	$1,500	$10,500
Second period's loss distributed	500	500	500	1,500
Balance after distribution of loss	$ 4,000	$4,000	$1,000	$ 9,000
Test loss of unrealized assets	(2,000)	(2,000)	(2,000)	(6,000)

What applied above applies again here. *C's* account shows that he owes the firm. The amount that he owes must be distributed as an additional loss to be taken up by the other partners.

Test loss for *C's* account	(500)	(500)	1,000	
Cash distribution	1,500	1,500		3,000
Balance undistributed	$ 2,500	$2,500	$1,000	$ 6,000
Third period's net loss	667	667	666	2,000
Cash on hand	$ 1,833	$1,833	$ 334	$ 4,000
Cash distributed	1,833	1,833	334	4,000

Changing a partnership to a corporation.—A business that operates under a partnership form of organization may be converted into a corporate form only if all the partners consent. The following steps are generally taken to effect the change:

1. The partners re-evaluate the assets of the partnership in the light of current market conditions, goodwill being entered as an asset on the books.

2. If the value of the assets is thereby increased, the increased value is credited to the partners in the proportion in which they are entitled to share in the profits of the partnership.

3. The partnership sells all its assets to a corporation formed to carry on the business, the corporation undertaking to accept all the liabilities of the partnership. Many states have enacted statutes known as the Bulk Sales Act for the protection of creditors upon sale, transfer, or assignment in bulk of any part or the whole of a stock of merchandise pertaining to the conduct of the business, otherwise than in the ordinary course of trade. These laws differ

in the various states, but in general they require that a certain number of days before such sale in bulk, notice thereof be given to creditors. Strict compliance with Bulk Sales laws may be necessary upon transfer of the partnership assets; otherwise the sale may be deemed fraudulent or void.

4. The corporation issues stock to the partners in payment of the assets so transferred to it. The amount of stock issued by the new corporation to each partner is generally determined by the amount of capital that he has contributed to the partnership. It should be remembered, however, that while each partner has, in the absence of a contrary agreement, an equal voice in the management of the partnership affairs and shares equally in its profits, a stockholder is ordinarily entitled to one vote for each share of stock that he holds in the corporation, and dividends are payable to him on each share. In order that the individuals may have the same relative interest in the corporation that they had in the partnership, some special arrangement may be required either in the nature or characteristics of the securities issued by the corporation to represent the respective interests, or through the payment of salaries to the individuals. In this respect, the partnership form of organization has greater simplicity than the corporation, for the contract of partnership may easily provide for any desired division of profits.

SECTION 17

Types of Business Organizations

SECTION 17

Types of Business Organizations

Choosing a form of organization for a business.—In starting a new business or in reorganizing an old one, the first problem to be considered is the form in which the enterprise will be conducted. The choice generally lies among:

1. A single proprietorship.
2. A general partnership.
3. A corporation.

The individual who expects to conduct a business as sole proprietor will ordinarily choose between the single-proprietorship form and the corporate form. Two or more individuals who propose to enter into a business enterprise together will generally choose between the partnership and the corporation. These forms of business organization are, however, not exclusive. Two or more individuals may carry on an enterprise as:

1. A limited partnership.
2. A joint adventure.
3. A joint-stock company.
4. A Massachusetts or business trust.

Factors affecting choice of form of organization.—Which form of organization shall be chosen in any case will depend upon the relative advantages and disadvantages of each kind of organization to the particular business. The factors as to which advantages and disadvantages should be carefully weighed are:

1. Manner of organization.

2. Stability of enterprise; that is, whether or not the organization may be easily disrupted.

3. Extent of risk; that is, extent of liability to creditors of those who have contributed capital to the business.

4. Flexibility of management and control.
5. Raising of additional capital.
6. Power to do business in any state.
7. Definiteness of governing law.

Manner of organization.—The *single proprietorship* is the simplest form of organization. Formalities are unnecessary to establish it. All that the individual need do is to ascertain whether a license is required to conduct the particular business, and whether a license fee or tax must be paid to State or local authorities.

A *general partnership* is also organized with comparative ease. It is usually formed by having the parties interested in the enterprise sign a partnership agreement. A written agreement is not, however, essential to the existence of a partnership. Not only may an oral partnership agreement be effective in establishing the partnership relation, but a partnership may even be implied from the acts and representations of the parties engaged in an enterprise, although no agreement, oral or written, has been made.

When a *limited partnership* is organized, the laws of the state of organization must be complied with strictly; otherwise the enterprise will be deemed to be a general partnership. Organization is effected by filing with some designated State official a contract drawn in accordance with legal requirements.

The chief difference between a general partnership and a limited partnership is that in the latter the liability of one or more of the partners may be limited to the amount agreed to be invested in the business. The limited partnership may have one or more general partners and one or more limited partners. A limited partner must contribute capital to the partnership, and, under the Uniform Limited Partnership Act, the contributions may be cash or other property, but not services. The surname of a limited partner may not appear in the partnership name unless it is also the surname of a general partner or unless the partnership had been carried on, before the time the limited partner entered the business, under a name in which his surname appeared.

The limited partnership should not be confused with the *limited-partnership association,* the organization of which is permitted by a few states. In the state of its organization, the limited-partnership association is treated as a corporation; in other states it is usually treated as a general partnership. Organization of the association is effected by the filing of a certificate of association with the secretary of state and the county clerk and the payment of an organization tax. Interests in the business are represented by shares which resemble the shares of stock of a corporation but differ from them in that a purchaser can acquire no rights in the shares until he is elected to membership in the association.

The organization of a *corporation* is not so simple as that of a single proprietorship or a general partnership. It may be accomplished only by complying strictly with the laws of the particular state in which the corporation is being organized. These laws provide that a certain number of persons, generally three or more, may form a corporation by filing in the office of a designated State official a statement, known as the articles of incorporation or the certification of incorporation, giving certain specified information, and by paying initial taxes and filing fees. Further, in order to carry out the purposes for which the corporation is organized, it is necessary to hold various organization meetings at which specified details of organization must be handled.

The *joint adventure* (or *"syndicate,"* as it is sometimes called) is very much like the partnership and may be organized with equal ease. It is formed merely by agreement between the parties interested in the enterprise. It differs from the partnership in certain technical respects, and in the fact that it is organized for a particular purpose, upon the accomplishment of which its duration terminates.

The *joint-stock company* resembles both the partnership and the corporation. Like the partnership, it is organized under a contract, known as the articles of association, between the parties in interest. Like the corporation, however, it is subject to State laws regulating its organization and the manner of conducting its business, and its capital is divided into transferable shares evidenced by certificates.

The *Massachusetts trust* is created by the execution of a deed of trust—an instrument in the nature of a contract between the creator of the trust, certain persons designated as trustees, and one or more beneficiaries. Under the terms of this deed of trust, property is turned over by the creator of the trust to the trustees, to be managed by them for the beneficiaries who are parties to the agreement and any other beneficiaries who may become interested in the trust.

Interests in the trust are evidenced by certificates resembling the certificates of stock issued by corporations. In some states the statutes specifically authorize the creation of Massachusetts trusts and regulate the conduct of their business. In others, such trusts may be organized without express statutory authorization. In a few states the organization of a Massachusetts trust is not permitted.

Stability of enterprise.—By stability is meant not the length of time for which the organization may continue but whether or not it may be easily disrupted.

A *single proprietorship* is not limited in its duration by law. It is not, however, a stable form of organization, for illness of the owner may interrupt it, and his death terminates it. A *partnership* is unstable—although it may be organized for a long period of time —for it is terminated by death or withdrawal of any one of the partners. A *corporation,* even though its duration may not always be perpetual, is a stable form of organization, in that it has continuous succession. Death, disability, or bankruptcy of a party interested in the corporation does not terminate it, and the certificates of stock that represent the interests in the enterprise may be transferred from one person to another without interrupting the business. The *joint adventure,* or syndicate, continues only until the specific purpose for which it was organized is accomplished. The *joint-stock company* is stable, for not only may it have unlimited duration but also it issues transferable certificates of interest. The life of a *Massachusetts trust* is limited in most states, for the law does not generally permit a trust to continue for an unlimited time; the trust is nevertheless a comparatively stable form of organization, for, as is true of the corporation, the interests in the enterprise are represented by transferable certificates that give the trust continuous succession.

Extent of liability.—The extent to which those who have contributed capital to an enterprise are liable to creditors of the business is a very important factor in the choice of a form of organization. Regardless of the form in which an enterprise is organized, creditors are entitled to be paid out of the assets of the business before capital contributed to the enterprise may be withdrawn. Where, however, those assets are insufficient to satisfy creditors' claims, to what extent may the owners of the business be compelled to pay out of their own property?

An individual who acts under a *single-proprietorship* form of organization is personally liable for all the debts of his business to the full extent of the property that he owns; he cannot limit his liability to creditors to the amount that he puts into the business. Each member of a *general partnership* is fully liable personally for all debts incurred by the partnership, regardless of the amount of his investment in the partnership business. In a *limited partnership*, the limited partners, like stockholders of a corporation, risk only the amount that they have invested in the business. The general partners in a limited partnership, however, are each personally liable for all debts incurred by the enterprise. There must be one or more general partners in any limited partnership.

The *corporation* has a decided advantage over the other types of organizations, in that the creditors of the corporation are limited in the collection of their claims to the assets of the corporation, and if a stockholder has paid for his stock, he cannot ordinarily be compelled to pay creditors out of his own property, even though the corporate assets may be insufficient to pay the creditors' claims.

While the interests of members of a *joint-stock company* are evidenced by certificates of stock, members are personally liable for the company's debts; the statutes of some states, however, permit limitation of liability by inclusion of a provision therefor in the articles of association.

Trustees of a *Massachusetts trust* are liable to creditors for debts of the trust, unless they obtain exemption from liability by contract with creditors. They may also be liable to the beneficiaries for gross negligence or fraud in the management of the trust property.

Flexibility of management and control.—In the *single proprietorship*, management and control are concentrated in one individual. This may operate both as an advantage and as a disadvantage. On the one hand, concentration of control avoids the difficulties often caused under other forms of organization by opposing factions and divided responsibilities, and the fact that the person who runs the business has a direct and full interest in its success is conducive to careful management of the enterprise. On the other hand, one individual may not be personally well equipped to perform all the functions of management, and the exclusive management that ties the owner down to his business may become highly burdensome. True, the owner may, without formalities, employ assistants and delegate various powers to them, but he will nevertheless have to bear ultimate responsibility for their acts.

In a *general partnership,* each partner usually has an equal right to participate in management, and control is divided among the partners. The fact that the ability and experience of several individuals is thus combined in the furtherance of one enterprise may give the partnership an advantage over the single proprietorship. The division of control among the various partners may, however, generate disagreement as to business policies and administration. As compared with the corporate form of organization, the partnership has this advantage—decisions may be arrived at and changes may be effected simply by agreement among the partners, without the formalities necessary under a corporate form of organization.

In a *limited partnership,* a limited partner may not participate in management of the business; if he does, he may be held liable as a general partner. The limited partner is, however, entitled to inspect the books of the partnership and to obtain full information regarding the partnership affairs.

In the *corporation,* those who have contributed to the capital of the business do not necessarily participate in conducting its affairs. Management may be concentrated in the hands of a group of experts who may own but a small portion of the stock of the corporation. The corporation thus avoids the difficulty of the single proprietorship, the business of which may be hampered by the limited ability or experience of one individual. On the other hand, it runs the risk of inefficient management where those who control the business do not have a direct financial interest in it. The corporation also has this advantage over the partnership, that whereas in the partnership each partner has power to act as general agent for the partnership, stockholders cannot bind the corporation by their acts merely because they are stockholders.

From the point of view of management, the *joint adventure* or syndicate resembles the single proprietorship; the syndicate is generally operated by one individual who acts as manager, with the assistance of agents appointed by him. The manager is, of course, answerable to the participants in the syndicate.

The *joint-stock company* resembles the corporation from the point of view of management and control. The articles of association under which the joint-stock company is formed generally provide that management shall be vested in a board of directors or governors elected periodically by the shareholders. These shareholders, like stockholders in a corporation, cannot bind the company by their individual acts, and they participate in the management of the company only by electing the board of governors and by acting at their meetings on matters brought before them by the board.

The *Massachusetts* or *common-law trust* is managed and controlled by the trustees, whose appointment may be permanent. The powers and duties of the trustees are indicated in the trust agreement. The shareholders or holders of certificates of interest in the trust may not exercise any control; otherwise they will be liable as partners. They cannot elect trustees periodically in the same way that stockholders of a corporation may elect new directors, and they may be given power to elect a new trustee only in the event of death, withdrawal, or removal of the trustee for dishonesty or neglect of duty.

Raising of additional capital.—Every business enterprise, regardless of the form in which it is organized, may require additional capital from time to time in the furtherance of its business. Inability to obtain adequate working capital is often the cause of failure of an enterprise. It is important, therefore, before deciding upon the form of organization for a business, to consider what means for raising capital will be available under the various forms of organization.

In a *single proprietorship,* the proprietor may raise additional capital needed for his business by borrowing from banks, by purchasing goods on credit, and by himself investing additional amounts in the enterprise. Since he is personally liable for the debts of his business beyond the amount that he has invested in it, banks may be ready to advance funds and merchants may be willing to extend credit to an extent commensurate with the single proprietor's personal means. The amount thus made available will nevertheless always be limited, and a business requiring a large amount of capital to operate successfully should not be organized as a single proprietorship.

A *partnership* may be able to raise capital with greater ease than a single proprietorship, for the resources of several individuals are combined in one enterprise. As in the case of the single proprietor, the partners assume full personal responsibility for partnership debts, and not only may the partnership be able to borrow on better terms than a corporation, but outsiders may be more willing to extend credit to it because of the security afforded by the partners' full liability.

The *corporation* is generally in a better position to raise large sums of money than are other forms of organizations. It may sell stock and other securities to the public in small amounts that attract many widely scattered investors, for participation in the corporation and ownership of an interest therein will not subject them to any financial risk beyond the amount of their investment.

Power to do business in any state.—An individual who resides in one state may carry on business in any other state without paying any greater taxes and without incurring any obligations other than those imposed on residents of the state, whether he operates alone as a *single proprietorship* or with others as a *partnership* or a *joint adventure*. His right to do so is guaranteed by the United States Constitution, which provides that the citizens of each state shall be entitled to all the privileges and immunities of citizens of the several states. The state may require the obtaining of a license and the payment of a license fee for carrying on a particular kind of business in the state, but the license will be available to the citizen of any state who meets the uniform conditions imposed, and no greater license fee will be required than is fixed for residents.

Forms of organization that do not create an artificial entity enjoy a freedom of movement in any state which is denied to the *corporation*. The corporation owes its existence to the state in which it is organized, and no other state need recognize its existence. The various states do permit corporations created under the laws of other states to do business within their borders, but only if such corporations comply with certain special State requirements (see discussion on page 1375).

In states that do not recognize the *joint-stock company* as a distinct legal entity, such a company may conduct business in the state without being subject to restrictions imposed upon corporations. However, the statutes of many states governing the right of foreign corporations to do business include joint-stock companies in the definition of foreign corporation.

In doing business outside of the state in which it was organized, the *Massachusetts trust* is now generally subjected to the same restrictions and regulations as a corporation. It was formerly the general rule that trustees of a Massachusetts trust could carry on business in any state on the same terms as local trustees; the trustees were, however, always subject to local rules governing their relationship to the beneficiaries of the trust and to third persons.

Definiteness of governing law.—The legal status of a *single proprietorship* is well established, and little doubt, if any, exists as to the relationships between the owner, his agents, his creditors, and any other outsider with whom he may come in contact in the course of his business. The same may generally be said of a *partnership,* the laws governing which are fairly uniform and have been codified in many states by the Uniform Partnership Law. *Corporations,* on the other hand, are governed by State statutes that vary from state to state and which, even when similar in wording, are differently interpreted. In the conduct of the corporation's affairs, a familiarity with the corporation laws of several states may be indispensable, for questions may arise in the course of the corporation's business which are governed by the laws of a state other than that in which the corporation was organized. Despite the uncertainty as to the legal effect of corporate acts, however, the corporation is universally recognized as a form of organization, and its essential characteristic, that of granting limited liability to the stockholders who contribute capital to the enterprise, is uniform in every state. In this respect the corporation has an advantage over the *joint-stock company* and the *Massachusetts trust,* the legal status of which is not definitely conceded in every state. The Massachusetts trust is, perhaps, confronted with the greatest difficulties, for not only do the laws vary considerably from state to state, but the law relating to the trust has not been fully established. A business that is to be carried on in various states may well hesitate to organize as a Massachusetts trust, for the legal effect of many of its acts will be far from certain. For example, the courts present a great diversity of opinion as to whether the holders of certificates of interest in the trust may appoint and remove trustees, whether a certificate holder has a right to inspect the stock records, and whether he can compel the declaration of a dividend out of surplus profits.

Summary of advantages and disadvantages: *Single proprietorship.*—Following are some of the advantages of a single proprietorship:

1. Organization is easy, for formalities are unnecessary.
2. Business may be conducted freely in any state without Government interference or regulation.
3. Control is concentrated in one individual; thus the danger of opposing factions and division of responsibility is avoided.
4. Careful management is assured by directness of interest.
5. Assistants may be employed without formalities, may be given limited powers, and their connection may similarly be ended with ease.
6. Termination of the business is simple and may be effected at any time.

Following are some of the disadvantages of a single proprietorship:

1. The single proprietor is personally liable for all the debts of the business.
2. The burden of management falls entirely upon the one individual, who may not be personally well-equipped to perform all the functions of management.
3. The raising of capital may not only be difficult, but the single proprietor must assume personal responsibility therefor.
4. Termination of the business upon death of the owner makes for instability of the enterprise.

General partnership.—Following are some of the advantages of a partnership:

1. Organization is comparatively easy; as a rule, a partnership may be organized simply by the partners' entering into a partnership agreement, either oral or written.
2. Business may be conducted freely in any state, without Government interference or regulation.
3. A greater amount of capital may be available for a partnership enterprise than for a single proprietorship, because the resources of several individuals are combined.
4. Decisions may be arrived at in the management of the business, and changes in the enterprise may be effected, simply by agree-

ment among the partners, without the formalities necessary under a corporate form of organization.

5. The direct responsibility placed upon each partner is conducive to use of the partner's best efforts in behalf of the enterprise.

6. The ability and experience of several individuals are combined in furtherance of one enterprise.

7. Credit may be readily available because the partners are personally liable for partnership debts.

Following are some of the disadvantages of a partnership:

1. Each partner is personally liable for the partnership debts.

2. Control of the business is divided among several individuals, involving the danger of disagreement in policy and administration.

3. Each partner may bind the partnership by his acts with respect to partnership matters.

4. Large amounts of capital cannot be raised from public sources through the sale of securities, as is possible under a corporate form of organization.

5. Because death, disability, or withdrawal of a partner terminates the partnership, the business is unstable.

Corporation.—Following are some of the advantages of a corporation:

1. Those who have contributed capital are not personally liable to creditors of the corporation beyond the amount of their stock.

2. The corporation is stable, for its existence is not interrupted or terminated by the death, withdrawal, or transfer of interest of any person who has contributed capital.

3. Capital may be obtained from widely scattered sources through the issuance of stock and other securities.

4. Management may be concentrated in the hands of a group of experts.

Following are some of the disadvantages of a corporation:

1. Legal formalities of organization, prescribed by the statutes of the state in which the corporation is being organized, must be complied with strictly.

2. Legal formalities in connection with the holding of meetings, authorizing the taking of action, and otherwise managing the cor-

poration's administrative affairs, prescribed by the State laws, must be complied with substantially.

3. Changes in the powers of the corporation, in its capital structure, and other changes in its charter may be effected only by strict observance of legal formalities prescribed by State statutes.

4. The corporation may do business in a state other than that in which it is organized only by complying with regulations prescribed by that other state.

5. One who has contributed capital to the enterprise may have little or no voice in its management. The fact that ownership may be separated from management may lead to decreased efficiency in the operation of the enterprise.

Joint-stock company.—Following are some of the advantages of a joint-stock company:

1. Organization is simple and is accomplished merely by the drawing up of a contract, known as the articles of association, between the parties in interest.

2. The business is stable, for death or withdrawal of a member does not terminate its existence, and the articles of association may provide for unlimited duration.

3. The business may be managed by experts who are not necessarily its owners.

Following are some of the disadvantages of a joint-stock company:

1. Members are personally liable for the company's debts, unless the State statutes permit limitation of liability by provision in the articles of association.

2. As in the corporation, the fact that management may be separated from ownership may lead to decreased efficiency in the operation of the enterprise.

Massachusetts trust.—Following are some of the advantages of a Massachusetts trust:

1. Creation of the trust is simple, for as a rule no formalities other than the drawing up of the trust agreement, are required.

2. The trust is stable, for not only is its existence unaffected by a change in membership, but its management is permanent.

3. The trustees and beneficiaries may obtain limited liability by contract with creditors.

4. The trust is free from extensive State regulation; the amount of securities that the trust may issue and the classification of such securities are not regulated; any number of persons may act as trustees; trustees are not required to be residents of the state or to hold meetings in the state.

Following are some of the disadvantages of a Massachusetts trust:

1. The governing law varies from state to state and has not been fully developed.

2. The trust is generally subjected to restrictions and regulations in doing business outside the state in which it was organized.

Combined forms of business organizations.—Subject to legal restrictions against combinations and competitive practices, a business enterprise may be carried on in combination with other enterprises in the form of:

1. A gentlemen's agreement.
2. A pool.
3. A holding company.
4. A trade association.
5. A co-operative.

The *gentlemen's agreement* is an oral agreement between companies in the same line of business to limit competition for a prescribed period by restricting the amount of production, the price of commodities, or the scope of the markets. A party to the agreement may withdraw at any time without incurring legal liability or any other penalty, for such agreements are generally deemed illegal under Federal antitrust laws.

A *pool* is an agreement between various companies engaged in the same industry, for the purpose of restricting competition by maintenance of prices, reduction of output, and division of markets. The pool differs from the gentlemen's agreement in that the pool agreement is usually in writing, and penalties are provided for its violation. Like the gentlemen's agreement, however, it is not generally enforceable because of the Federal antitrust laws which render such pools illegal. Agreements between various companies for the interchange of patent rights are also in the nature of pools, but many such agreements may be legal, for they do not necessarily restrict competition between owners of the pooled patents.

The *holding company* is organized to control the business of one or more other companies through ownership of stock of such other companies. Generally the holding company is organized as a corporation; it may, however, be a joint-stock company or a Massachusetts trust. Holding companies sometimes engage in independent business activities in addition to controlling other organizations. The holding company differs from the investment trust in that it is concerned not only with the income from the securities which it holds but also with the management and control of the companies issuing such securities, and in that its ownership of the securities of such other companies is permanent. The holding company is often formed for the purpose of combining various organizations engaged in the same line of business in order to limit competition. While the holding company is sanctioned by law, it is nevertheless subject to Federal restrictions prohibiting combinations in restraint of trade.

The *trade association* is organized to promote the interests of those engaged in a similar industry, by voluntary action to end abuses and to foster fair competitive opportunities, regulating relations with employees, disseminating credit information and statistical information with respect to their products, and co-operating in advertising. It may and often is organized as a nonprofit corporation under State statutes and is managed by a board of directors or trustees elected annually by the members of the association.

A *co-operative* may be in the form of an unincorporated nonprofit association or it may be organized as a profit-making corporation. Examples of nonprofit co-operatives are stock exchanges, chambers of commerce, trade unions and others. Examples of co-operatives organized to carry on business are agricultural marketing associations, chain food stores, taxicab associations, and others.

Choosing a name under which to do business.—Single proprietorships are generally conducted under the name of the individual who owns and operates the business. The name of at least one of the partners is also often included in the name under which a partnership operates. Both single proprietorships and partnerships, however, sometimes find it desirable to carry on business under an assumed or fictitious name. Before using such a name, it is important to ascertain whether or not an assumed or fictitious name must be registered with a State official under the laws of that state. Many states require that every person transacting business under an assumed name, or under any designation, name, or style other than the real name of the individual conducting the business, must file in the office of a designated Government official a certificate setting forth the true name and address of the person transacting such business. Penalties are imposed for failure to file such certificates. In some states no suits may be maintained on contracts by individuals who have failed to comply with the statute. Unless the statute refers exclusively to partnerships, regulations governing the use of fictitious names by individuals would also apply to joint adventures and to joint-stock companies, for such organizations are not considered legal entities but are deemed to be conducted by the individuals interested in the enterprise.

Some states impose other restrictions upon the use of fictitious names, as, for example, New York, where the designation "and Company" or "and Co." must represent an actual partner. As far as corporations are concerned, the law in many states requires that the name of the corporation indicate the form of its organization; in some, the use of the word "Company" or "Corporation," followed by "Inc.," is mandatory.

In selecting a name for a business, it is important to choose one that is not already in use by some other organization, for otherwise liability may be incurred for infringement of the goodwill of the older company.

Similarity in corporate names.—In most of the states, the secretary of state is directed by statute not to file a certificate of incorporation if the name of the proposed corporation so closely resembles that of an existing corporation that deception or confusion might result. In the absence of statutory provisions, it has been held that the secretary of state is justified in refusing to file a certificate of incorporation where the name selected bears too great a likeness to an existing name. When the state grants a charter to a corporation, it merely authorizes the use of the name selected by the corporation in a legal manner. The state does not adjudge the name to be legal, nor does it decree that its use throughout the state will be lawful.

The corporation's name is an element of its existence. It belongs exclusively to the corporation and will be protected from imitation that constitutes unfair competition. Priority in adoption and use usually confers the superior right to the name. Even aside from statutory provisions, the corporation's right to its name will be protected by an equity court so far as may be necessary to safeguard property rights developed under it and to protect the corporation against fraud, actual or constructive.

Where it is found that there is a similarity in names, the court does not at once grant relief, but proceeds to ascertain whether the facts are such that deception and injury are likely to result. The law will not interfere to restrain a corporation in the use of its name where there exists no conscious intent to injure, no effort to secure for itself the benefit of another's industry, business capacity, and capital outlay, and no harm to the public from imposition through probable confusion. A change of name or the use of an explanatory phrase will be required where deception and injury result from similarity in names.

GLOSSARY OF ABBREVIATIONS

A

@ ...... at (referring to price)
a. ...... acre(s)
a.a. ...... always afloat (shipping)
A. & C.P. ...... anchors and chains proved
A. & F. ...... August and February
A. & O. ...... April and October
a.a.r. ...... against all risks
A.B. ...... Bachelor of Arts; able-bodied seaman
A.B.C. ...... Audit Bureau of Circulation
abt. ...... about
A/C ...... account current
a/c ...... account
acc. ...... acceptance; accepted
acct. ...... account
A/cs Pay. ...... accounts payable
A/cs Rec. ...... accounts receivable
A/d ...... after date
ad lib. *or* ad libit. ...... at one's pleasure, freely, to the quantity or amount desired
ad loc. ...... to, *or* at, the place
admr. *or* adms. *or* admstr. ...... administrator
admrx. *or* admx. ...... administratrix
Ad. val. ...... ad valorem (according to value)
afft. ...... affidavit
A.F. of L. ...... American Federation of Labor
a. g. b. ...... a good brand
A.G.F.A. ...... Assistant General Freight Agent
agst. ...... against
agt. ...... agent; against; agreement
a.h. ...... after hatch; ampere-hour(s)
A.J.O.J. ...... April, July, October, January
A.M. ...... Master of Arts
amp. ...... ampere(s)
amt. ...... amount
a.n. ...... arrival notice (shipping)
A.N.F.M. ...... August, November, February, May
anon. ...... anonymous
ans. ...... answer; answered
a/o ...... account of
A/or ...... and or
A/P ...... additional premium; authority to pay
Apd. ...... assessment paid
approx. ...... approximately
A/R ...... all risks; against all risks (marine ins.)
Ar. M. ...... Master of Architecture
art. ...... article
A/S ...... after sight; account sales; alongside (chartering)
a. s. ...... at sight
assd. ...... assigned
assigt. ...... assignment
assmt. ...... assessment
assn. ...... association
A.S.S.R. ...... Autonomous Socialist Soviet Republic
Asst. ...... assistant

A/T ...... American terms (grain trade)
at. no. ...... atomic number
A. to O.C. ...... attached to other correspondence
ats. ...... at suit of (law)
atty. ...... attorney
at. vol. ...... atomic volume
at. wt. ...... atomic weight
A/V ...... ad valorem (according to value)
av. ...... average
A/W ...... actual weight; all water (transp.)
A.W.G. ...... American wire gauge

B

b/- ...... bag(s); bale(s)
B.A. ...... Bachelor of Arts
B. Acc. ...... Bachelor of Accounting
B.Ag. *or* B.Agr. ...... Bachelor of Agriculture
B. Ag. Sc. ...... Bachelor of Agricultural Science
bal. ...... balance
B.A.O. ...... Bachelor of Obstetrics
B. Ar. *or* B. Arch. ...... Bachelor of Architecture
B.A.S. *or* B.A.Sc. ...... Bachelor of Applied Science
b.b. ...... bail bond; bill book; break bulk
B.B.A. ...... Bachelor of Business Administration
bbl. ...... barrel(s)
B/C ...... bill of collection
B.C.E. ...... Bachelor of Chemical Engineering; Bachelor of Civil Engineering
B.Ch. *or* B.Chir. ...... Bachelor of Surgery
B.Ch.D. ...... Bachelor of Dental Surgery
B.C.L. ...... Bachelor of Civil Law
B.Com. *or* B.Comm. ...... Bachelor of Commerce
B. Com. Sc. ...... Bachelor of Commercial Science
B.C.S. ...... Bachelor of Chemical Science
B.D. ...... Bachelor of Divinity
B/D ...... bank draft; bar draft (grain trade)
bd. ft. ...... board feet
B.D.S. ...... Bachelor of Dental Surgery
B.D.Sc. ...... Bachelor of Dental Science
B.E. ...... Bachelor of Education
B/E ...... bill of exchange; bill of entry
B.E.E. ...... Bachelor of Electrical Engineering
B.Eng. ...... Bachelor of Engineering
B.Eng.A. ...... Bachelor of Agricultural Engineering
B.F. ...... Bachelor of Finance; Bachelor of Forestry
B/F ...... brought forward (bookkeeping)
B.F.A. ...... Bachelor of Fine Arts
B/G ...... bonded goods
B/H ...... bill of health
b.h.p. ...... brake horsepower
B.Hy. ...... Bachelor of Hygiene
B.I.S. ...... Bank for International Settlements
B.J. ...... Bachelor of Journalism
bk. ...... bank; backwardation; book
bkpt. ...... bankrupt
bkt. ...... basket(s)
B/L ...... bill of lading

bl. ...... bale(s)
B.L.E. ...... Brotherhood of Locomotive Engineers
B.Lit(t). ...... Bachelor of Literature, *or* Letters
B.LL. ...... Bachelor of Laws
B.L.S. ...... Bachelor of Library Science
B.M. ...... Bachelor of Medicine
b.m. ...... board measure (timber)
B.M.E. ...... Bachelor of Mining Engineering
B.Mech.E. ...... Bachelor of Mechanical Engineering
B.Met. ...... Bachelor of Metallurgy
B.Mus. ...... Bachelor of Music
b.o. ...... buyer's option; branch office
b/o ...... brought over
B.P. ...... Bachelor of Pharmacy
B/P ...... bills payable; bill of parcels
B.Pay. ...... bills payable
b.p.b. ...... bank post bill
B.P.E. ...... Bachelor of Physical Education
B.Phil. ...... Bachelor of Philosophy
B/R ...... bills receivable; builders' risks
B.Rec. ...... bills receivable
brl. ...... barrel(s)
B/S ...... bill of sale; bill of store
B/s ...... bags; bales
B.S. ...... Bachelor of Science; balance sheet; boiler survey
B. Sc. ...... Bachelor of Science
B.Sc.Agr. ...... Bachelor of Science in Agriculture
B.S.(Cer.E.) ...... Bachelor of Science in Ceramic Engineering
B.Sc.F. *or* B.Sc.For. ...... Bachelor of Science in Forestry
B.Sc.Tech. ...... Bachelor of Technical Science
B.S.Ed. ...... Bachelor of Science in Education
Bs/L ...... bills of lading
B.S.M.E. *or* B.S.(Min.E.) ...... Bachelor of Science in Mining Engineering
B.S.P. ...... Bachelor of Science in Pharmacy
B/St ...... bill of sight
B.T. *or* B.Th. ...... Bachelor of Theology
b.t. ...... berth terms
B.T.C. ...... Bachelor of Textile Chemistry
b.t.u. ...... British thermal unit(s)
bu. ...... bushel(s)
B.U.J. ...... Bachelor of Both Laws, i.e., the Canon and Civil Law
B/v ...... book value
B.V.Sc. ...... Bachelor of Veterinary Science
B.W.G. ...... Birmingham wire gauge

C

c. ft. ...... cubic feet
cg. ...... centigram(s)
C.G.A. ...... cargo's proportion of general average
cge. pd. ...... carriage paid
cgm. ...... centigram(s)
Ch.B. ...... Bachelor of Surgery
Ch.D. ...... Doctor of Chemistry
Ch.E. ...... Chemical Engineer
Chir.Doct. ...... Doctor of Surgery
Ch.J. ...... Chief Justice
Ch.M. ...... Master of Surgery
C.I. ...... consular invoice

C/I ...... certificate of insurance
c. ...... cent(s)
c/- ...... case(s)
C.A. ...... Chartered Accountant
C/A ...... capital account; credit account; current account; commercial agent; close annealed
ca. ...... centare(s)
C a/c ...... current account
c.a.f. ...... cost, assurance, and freight
c. & d. ...... collection and delivery
c. & f. ...... cost and freight
c. & i. ...... cost and insurance
Cantab. ...... of Cambridge
cart. ...... cartage
C/B ...... cash book
C.B.D. ...... cash before delivery
C.C. ...... continuation clause (marine ins.)
C.C.A. ...... Circuit Court of Appeals
ccm. ...... centimeter(s)
c/d ...... carried down (bookkeeping)
C/D ...... commercial dock; consular declaration; certificate of deposit
cf. ...... compare
c/f ...... carried forward (bookkeeping)
c.f.i. ...... cost, freight, and insurance
C.f.o. ...... coast for orders
C.I.D. ...... Criminal Investigation Department
C.I.E. ...... captain's imperfect entry (Customs)
c.i.f. ...... cost, insurance, and freight
c.i.f. & c. ...... cost, insurance, freight, and charges
c.i.f. & e. ...... cost, insurance, freight, and exchange
c.i.f. & i. ...... cost, insurance, freight, and interest
c.i.f.c. & i. ...... cost, insurance, freight, commission, and interest
c.i.f.i. & e. ...... cost, insurance, freight, interest, and exchange
c.i.f.L.t. ...... cost, insurance, and freight, London terms
C.I.O. ...... Committee on Industrial Organization
ck. ...... cask(s)
C/L ...... cash letter
cl. ...... centiliter(s)
c.l. ...... carload
c/l ...... craft loss
C.L.D. ...... Doctor of Civil Law
cld. ...... cleared
C.M. ...... Master in Surgery
cm. ...... centimeter(s)
C/N ...... credit note; consignment note; circular note
C/O ...... cash order; certificate of origin; case oil
Co. ...... company; county
c/o ...... carried over (bookkeeping); in care of
c.o.d. ...... cash on delivery
com. ...... commission
consgt. ...... consignment
c.o.s. ...... cash on shipment
C/P ...... charter party; custom of port (grain trade)
C.P.A. ...... Certified Public Accountant
C.P.D. ...... charterers pay dues
C.R. ...... class rate; current rate; company's risk; carrier's risk
Cr. ...... credit; creditor
C/S ...... colliery screened (coal trade)

c/s ...... cases
CSC ...... Civil Service Commission
C/T ...... cable transfer; California terms (grain trade)
ct. ...... cent(s)
ctge. ...... cartage
c.t.l. ...... constructive total loss (marine ins.)
c.t.l.o. ...... constructive total loss only (marine ins.)
c. to s. ...... carting to shipside
cu. cm. ...... cubic centimeter(s)
cu. in. ...... cubic inch(es)
cu. mi. ...... cubic mile(s)
cum. ...... with; cumulative
cur. *or* curt. ...... current
c.v. ...... chief value
C.W. ...... commercial weight
c.w.o. ...... cash with order
cwt. ...... hundredweight(s)

D

d. ...... pence
D/A ...... deposit account; documents against acceptance; discharge afloat
d/a ...... days after acceptance
D.Agr. ...... Doctor of Agriculture
dal. ...... decaliter(s)
D. & J. ...... December and June
d. & w.t.f. ...... daily and weekly till forbidden
D.Arch. ...... Doctor of Architecture
D.B. ...... day book; deals and battens (timber trade)
D.B.B. ...... deals, battens, and boards (timber trade)
d.b.h. ...... diameter at breast height
dbk. ...... drawback
D/C ...... deviation clause
D.C.L. ...... Doctor of Civil Law
D.Cn.L. ...... Doctor of Canon Law
D.C.T. ...... Doctor of Christian Theology
D.D. ...... Doctor of Divinity
D/D ...... demand draft; delivered at docks; delivered at destination; dock dues
D/d ...... days after date
dd. ...... delivered
dd/s ...... delivered sound (grain trade)
D.D.S. ...... Doctor of Dental Surgery
D.D.Sc. ...... Doctor of Dental Science
D.E. ...... Doctor of Entomology
decim. ...... decimeter(s)
deld. *or* deldr. ...... delivered
D.Eng. ...... Doctor of Engineering
depr. ...... depreciation
d.f. ...... dead freight
D.F.A. ...... Division Freight Agent
dft. ...... draft
dg. ...... decigram(s)
D.Hy. ...... Doctor of Hygiene
dis. ...... discount
D.J. ...... Doctor of Law
D.J.S. ...... Doctor of Juridical Science
dkg. ...... dekagram(s)
dkl. ...... dekaliter(s)
dkm. ...... dekameter(s)
dks. ...... decastere(s)
D/L ...... demand loan
dl. ...... decileter(s)
D.Lit(t). ...... Doctor of Literature, *or* Letters
D.L.O. ...... Dead Letter Office
d.l.o. ...... dispatch loading only

D.L.S. ...... Doctor of Library Science
D.M.D. ...... Doctor of Dental Medicine
D.Met. ...... Doctor of Metallurgy
D.M.J.S. ...... December, March, June, September
D.M.S. ...... Doctor of Medical Sciences
D.Mus. ...... Doctor of Music
D/N ...... debit note
D/O ...... delivery order
D.Oec. ...... Doctor of Economics
D.O.S. ...... Doctor of Optical Science
D/P ...... documents against payment
d.p. ...... direct port
D.P.H. ...... Doctor of Public Health
D.Phil. ...... Doctor of Philosophy
D/R ...... deposit receipt
Dr. ...... debit; debtor; drawer
dr. ap. ...... apothecaries' dram(s)
dr. av. ...... dram(s) avoirdupois
D/s ...... days after sight
ds. ...... decistere(s)
D.Sc. ...... Doctor of Science
D.S.S. ...... Doctor of Holy Scripture
D.S.T. ...... Doctor of Sacred Theology
D.T. *or* D.Th. ...... Doctor of Theology
D.T.M. ...... Doctor of Tropical Medicine
D.V.M. ...... Doctor of Veterinary Medicine
D.V.M.S. ...... Doctor of Veterinary Medicine and Surgery
D.V.M. ...... Doctor of Veterinary Science
D/W ...... dock warrant
d.w. ...... dead weight
d.w.c. ...... dead weight capacity
dwt. ...... pennyweight(s)
D/y ...... delivery
D.Z. ...... Doctor of Zoölogy
dz. ...... dozen

E

ea. ...... each
E. & O.E. ...... errors and omissions excepted
E.A.O.N. ...... except as otherwise noted
Ed.B. ...... Bachelor of Education
Ed.D. ...... Doctor of Education
Ed.M. ...... Master of Education
e.e. ...... errors excepted
e.g. ...... for example
Eng.D. ...... Doctor of Engineering
e.o. ...... exofficio
e.o.h.p. ...... except as otherwise herein provided
e.o.m. ...... end of month (payments)
est. ...... estimated
et al. ...... and others
etc. ...... et cetera
et seq. ...... and the following
et sqq. ...... and those following
Ex.B.L. ...... exchange bill of lading
ex.cp. *or* x/cp ...... ex coupon
ex d. *or* ex div. ...... ex dividend
exd. ...... examined
ex int. ...... ex interest
ex n. ...... ex new
ex r. ...... ex rights
ex ship ...... delivered out of ship

F

f.a. ...... free alongside
f.a.a. ...... free of all average (marine ins.)
fac. ...... facsimile
f.a.c. ...... fast as can
F. & A. ...... February and August
f. & d. ...... freight and demurrage
f.a.q. ...... fair average quality; free at quay
f.a.q.s. ...... fair average quality of season
f.a.s. ...... free alongside ship; firsts and seconds (lumber)
f.b. ...... freight bill
fbm. ...... feet board measure
f.c.&s. ...... free of capture and seizure (transp.)
f.c.s.r.c.c. ...... free of capture, seizure, riots, and civil commotions
f.d. ...... free discharge; free delivery; free dispatch; free docks
ff. ...... following
f.f.a. ...... free from alongside; free foreign agency
F.G.A. ...... foreign general average (marine ins.)
f.h. ...... fore hatch
f.i.a. ...... full interest admitted
f.i.b. ...... free into bunkers; free into barge
f.i.o. ...... free in and out
f.i.t. ...... free of income tax; free in truck
f.i.w. ...... free in wagon
F.L.N. ...... following landing numbers
fl. oz. ...... fluid ounce(s)
fm. ...... fathom(s)
F.M.A.N. ...... February, May, August, November
F.O. ...... firm offer; free overside
f.o. ...... for orders; firm offer; full out terms (grain trade)
f.o.b. ...... free on board
f.o.c. ...... free on car; free of charge
f.o.d. ...... free of damage
f.o.q. ...... free on quay
f.o.r. ...... free on rail
f.o.r.t. ...... free out rye terms (grain trade)
f.o.s. ...... free on steamer
f.o.t. ...... free on truck
f.o.w. ...... free on wagon; first open water
F.P. ...... floating (or open) policy; fully paid
F.P.A. ...... free of particular average (marine ins.)
F.P.A.A.C. ...... free of particular average, American Conditions (marine ins.)
F.P.A.E.C. ...... free of particular average, English Conditions (marine ins.)
f.p.m. ...... feet per minute
f.p.s. ...... feet per second
F/R ...... freight release
fr. ...... franc(s)
f.r.o.f. ...... fire risk on freight
frt. ...... freight
f.t. ...... full terms
F.T.W. ...... free trade wharf
fwd. ...... forward
f.w.d. ...... fresh water damage

G

G/A ...... general average (marine ins.)
G/A con. ...... general average contribution (marine ins.)

G/A dep. ...... general average deposit (marine ins.)
gal. *or* gall. ...... gallon(s)
G.A.R. ...... Grand Army of the Republic
G.F.A. ...... General Freight Agent
g.f.a. ...... good fair average
g.gr. ...... great gross
gi. ...... gill(s)
gm. ...... gram(s)
G.P.A. ...... General Passenger Agent
g.p.m. ...... gallons per minute
gr. ...... gram(s); gross
gro. ...... gross
gr. wt. ...... gross weight
G.T.C. ...... good till canceled, *or* countermanded
G.T.M. ...... good this month
G.T.W. ...... good this week, becomes void on Saturday
guar. ...... guaranteed

H

ha. ...... hectare(s)
H.C. ...... held covered (insurance)
H.F.M. ...... hold for money
hg. ...... hectogram(s)
hhd. ...... hogshead(s)
hl. ...... hectoliter(s)
hm. ...... hectometer(s)
H.P. *or* hp. ...... horsepower
H.P.N. ...... horsepower nominal
H.W. ...... high water
H.W.M. ...... high-water mark
H.W.O.S.T. ...... high-water ordinary spring tide

I

I.B. ...... invoice book; in bond
I.B.I. ...... invoice book, inwards
ibid. ...... in the same place
I.B.O. ...... invoice book, outwards
I.C. & C. ...... invoice cost and charges
id. ...... the same
i.e. ...... that is
I.F.T.U. ...... International Federation of Trade Unions
I.H.P. ...... indicated horsepower
I.L.O. ...... International Labor Organization
I.L.P. ...... Independent Labour Party (*Brit.*)
imp. gal. ...... imperial gallon(s)
in. ...... inches
int. ...... interest
I.P.A. ...... including particular average
i.v. ...... invoice value; increased value
I.W.W. ...... Industrial Workers of the World

J

J/A ...... joint account
J.A.J.O. ...... January, April, July, October
J. & D. ...... June and December
J. & J. ...... January and July
j. & w.o. ...... jettison and washing overboard
J.B. ...... Bachelor of Laws
J.C.B. ...... Bachelor of Canon Law; Bachelor of Civil Law
J.C.D. ...... Doctor of Civil Law
J.D. ...... Doctor of Laws
J.O.J.A. ...... July, October, January, April
J.P. ...... Justice of the Peace
J.S.D. ...... Doctor of Juristic Science

J.S.D.M. ...... June, September, December, March
J.U.D. ...... Doctor of Both Laws, i.e., the Canon and the Civil Law

K

kc. ...... kilocycle(s)
K.D. ...... knocked down
K.D.C.L. ...... knocked down, in carloads
K.D.L.C.L. ...... knocked down, in less than carloads
kg. *or* kgm. ...... kilogram(s)
kilo. ...... kilometer(s)
K.K.K. ...... Ku Klux Klan
kl. ...... kiloliter(s)
km. ...... kilometer(s)
kn. ...... kronen
kv. ...... kilovolts
kw. ...... kilowatt(s)
kw.-hr. ...... kilowatt-hour(s)

L

l. ...... liter(s)
L/A ...... letter of authority; landing account; Lloyd's agent
L.A.M. ...... Master of Liberal Arts
lat. ...... latitude
L.B. ...... Bachelor of Letters
lb. ...... pound(s)
lb. ap. ...... apothecaries' pound(s)
L/C ...... letter of credit
l.c.l. ...... less than carload lot
ldg. ...... loading
ldg. & dely. ...... landing and delivery
lds. ...... loads
lg. tn. ...... long ton(s)
L.I.P. ...... life insurance policy
Lit(t).B. ...... Bachelor of Literature, *or* Letters
Lit(t).D. ...... Doctor of Literature, *or* Letters
lkg. & bkg. ...... leakage and breakage
LL.B. ...... Bachelor of Laws
Ll. & Co.'s ...... Lloyd's and Companies
LL.D. ...... Doctor of Laws
LL.M. ...... Master of Laws
L.M.C. ...... Lloyd's machinery certificate
l.m.c. ...... low middling clause (cotton trade)
L.M.S.C. ...... let me see correspondence
loc.cit. ...... in the place cited
log. ...... logarithm
long. ...... longitude
lr. ...... lire
L.R.M.C. ...... Lloyd's refrigerating machinery certificate
L.S. ...... place of the seal
l.t. ...... long ton
Ltd. ...... limited
ltge. ...... lighterage
Lt.-V. ...... light vessel
L.W. ...... low water
L.W.M. ...... low-water mark
£E. ...... pound Egyptian
£T. ...... pound Turkish

M

M. ...... thousand
m. ...... meter(s)
M.A. ...... Master of Arts
m/a ...... my account
Ma.E. ...... Master of Engineering

M.Agr. ...... Master of Agriculture
M.Agr.Sc. ...... Master of Agricultural Science
M.A.I. ...... Master of Engineering
M. & N. ...... May and November
M.A.N.F. ...... May, August, November, February
M. & S. ...... March and September
M.A.O. ...... Master of Obstetric Art
M.Arch. ...... Master of Architecture
M.A.S. ...... Master of Applied Science
max. cap. ...... maximum capacity
M.B. ...... Bachelor of Medicine
M.B.A. ...... Master in, *or* of, Business Administration
M.B.C.M. ...... Bachelor of Medicine and Master of Surgery
M.B.M. ...... thousands (of feet) board measure
M.B.Sc. ...... Master of Business Science
M.C. ...... Master of Surgery
M/C ...... metalling clause (marine ins.); marginal credit
m.c. ...... marked capacity (freight cars)
M.C.D. ...... Doctor of Comparative Medicine
M.C.E. ...... Master of Civil Engineering
M.Ch. ...... Master of Surgery
M.C.L. ...... Master of Civil Law
M.Com(m). ...... Master of Commerce
M.D. ...... Doctor of Medicine
M/D ...... memorandum of deposit
m/d ...... months after date
M.D.S. ...... Master of Dental Surgery
M.D.Sc. ...... Master of Dental Science
M.E.C. ...... Master of Engineering Chemistry
Mech.E. ...... Mechanical Engineer
M.Ed. ...... Master of Education
M.Eng. ...... Master of Engineering
m.e.p. ...... mean effective pressure
M.F.A. ...... Master of Fine Arts
mg. *or* mgm. ...... milligram(s)
M.H. ...... main hatch
M.Hy. ...... Master of Hygiene
mi. ...... mile(s)
min. B/L ...... minimum bill of lading
M.I.P. ...... marine insurance policy
m.i.t. ...... milled in transit
M.J.S.D. ...... March, June, September, December
ml. ...... milliliter(s)
M.Lit(t). ...... Master of Letters
M.L.S. ...... Master of Library Science
mm. ...... millimeter(s)
M.M.E. ...... Master of Mining Engineering
M.Mech.E. ...... Master of Mechanical Engineering
mo. ...... month(s)
M.O.H. ...... medical officer of health
M.P.E. ...... Master of Physical Education
M.Ph. ...... Master of Philosophy
M.P.H. ...... Master of Public Health
m.p.h. ...... miles per hour
M.P.L. ...... Master of Patent Law
M.R.E. ...... Master of Religious Education

M.S. ...... motor ship
M/s ...... months after sight
M.S.Agr. ...... Master of Scientific Agriculture
M.Sc. ...... Master of Science
M.S.(Cer.E.) ...... Master of Science in Ceramic Engineering
M.Sc.Tech. ...... Master of Technical Science
M.S.F. ...... Master of Science in Forestry
M.S. in C.E. ...... Master of Science in Civil Engineering
M.S. in Ch.E. ...... Master of Science in Chemical Engineering
M.S. in E.E. ...... Master of Science in Electrical Engineering
M.S. in M.E. ...... Master of Science in Mechanical Engineering
ms(s). ...... manuscript(s)
mst. ...... measurement
M.T. ...... metric ton
mtg. ...... mortgage
M.Th. ...... Master of Theology
M.V.Sc. ...... Master of Veterinary Science
mt. ...... empty
M.V. ...... motor vessel

N

N/A ...... no advice (banking)
n/a ...... no account (banking)
n.a.a. ...... not always afloat (shipping)
N. & M. ...... November and May
N.B. ...... note well
N/C ...... new charter; new crop
n.c.u.p. ...... no commission until paid
N.C.V. ...... no commercial value
N/E ...... no effects (banking)
n.e. ...... not exceeding
N.E.P. ...... New Economic Policy (Russia)
n.e.s. ...... not elsewhere specified
n/f ...... no funds (banking)
N.F.M.A. ...... November, February, May, August
N.H.P. ...... nominal horsepower
n/m ...... no mark
No. ...... number
N/O ...... no orders (banking)
N.O.E. ...... not otherwise enumerated
N.O.H.P. ...... not otherwise herein provided
nom. std. ...... nominal standard
N.O.S. ...... not otherwise specified
N.P. ...... no protest (banking)
n/p ...... net proceeds
N.P.L. ...... non-personal liability
n.r. ...... no risk; net register
n.r.a.d. ...... no risk after discharge
N/S *or* N.S.F. ...... not sufficient funds (banking)
n.s.p.f. ...... not specially provided for
n.t. ...... net ton; new terms (grain trade)
nt. wt. ...... net weight

O

o/a ...... on account of
O. & A. ...... October and April
o. & r. ...... ocean and rail (transp.)
obs. ...... obsolete
o/c ...... open charter; old charter; old crop; open cover; overcharge
o/d ...... on demand
o.e. ...... omissions excepted
O.J.A.J. ...... October, January, April, July
O/o ...... order of

O.P. ...... open, *or* floating, policy
op. cit. ...... in the work cited
Opt.D. ...... Doctor of Optometry
o.r. ...... owner's risk (transportation)
o.r.b. ...... owner's risk of breakage (transp.)
o.r.c. ...... owner's risk of chafing (transp.)
o.r.d. ...... owner's risk of damage (transp.)
o.r.det. ...... owner's risk of deterioration (transp.)
o.r.f. ...... owner's risk of fire, *or* freezing (transp.)
o.r.l. ...... owner's risk of leakage (transp.)
o.r.s. ...... owner's risk of shifting (transp.)
o.r.w. ...... owner's risk of becoming wet (transp.)
O/S ...... on sample; out of stock; on sale or return
o.s. & d. ...... over, short, and damaged (transp.)
o/t ...... old terms (grain trade); on truck
Oxon. ...... of Oxford
oz. ...... ounce(s)

P

P/A ...... particular average; power of attorney; private account; Purchasing Agent
p. & i. ...... protection and indemnity
P. & L. ...... profit and loss
P/Av. ...... particular average
P.B. ...... permanent bunkers
P/C ...... price current; petty cash; per cent
P.D. ...... port dues
pd. ...... passed; paid
Pe.B. ...... Bachelor of Pediatrics
pf. *or* pfg. ...... pfennig
pfd. ...... preferred
Phar.B. ...... Bachelor of Pharmacy
Phar.D. ...... Doctor of Pharmacy
Phar.M. ...... Master of Pharmacy
Ph.B. ...... Bachelor of Philosophy; Bachelor of Pharmacy; Bachelor of Physical Education
Ph.C. ...... Pharmaceutical Chemist
Ph.D. ...... Doctor of Philosophy
Ph.G. ...... Graduate in Pharmacy
Pi. ...... piaster(s)
pk. ...... peck(s)
pkg. ...... package
p.l. ...... partial loss
plf. *or* plff. ...... plaintiff
P/M ...... Put of More (stock exch.)
pm. ...... premium
P/N ...... promissory note
P.O.D. ...... pay on delivery
P.O.R. ...... payable on receipt
p.p. ...... picked ports; per procurationem (on behalf of)
ppd. ...... prepaid
p.p.i. ...... policy proof of interest (marine ins.)
ppt. ...... prompt loading
pro tem. ...... for the time being
P/S ...... public sale
pt. ...... pint(s)
p.t. ...... private terms (grain trade)
p.w. ...... packed weight (transp.)
pwt. ...... pennyweight
P.X. ...... please exchange

Q

q.d.a. ...... quantity discount agreement

qlty. ...... quality
qn. ...... quotation
qt. ...... quart(s)

R

R/A ...... refer to acceptor
r. & c. ...... rail and canal (transp.)
r. & l. ...... rail and lake (transp.)
r. & o. ...... rail and ocean (transp.)
r. & w. ...... rail and water (transp.)
R/C ...... reconsigned
r.c. & l. ...... rail, canal, and lake (transp.)
rcd. ...... received
R/D ...... refer to drawer
r.d. ...... running days
r.d.c. ...... running down clause (marine ins.)
recd. ...... received
res. ...... residue
rev. A/C ...... revenue account
R.F.D. ...... Rural Free Delivery
rfg. ...... refunding
R.I. ...... re-insurance
R.I.L.U. ...... Red International of Labor Unions
r.l. & r. ...... rail, lake, and rail (transp.)
RM ...... reichsmark(s)
rm. ...... ream (paper)
R.O.G. ...... receipt of goods
r.o.m. ...... run of mine (coal)
rotn. no. ...... rotation number
R.P. ...... return premium
R/p ...... return of post for orders
R.P.D. ...... Doctor of Political Science
r.p.m. ...... revolutions per minute
r.p.s. ...... revolutions per second
Rs ...... rupees
R.S. ...... Revised Statutes
R.S.F.S.R. ...... Russian Socialist Federal Soviet Republic
R.S.V.P. ...... please reply
R.V.S.V.P. ...... please reply at once

S

s. ...... shillings
s/a ...... subject to approval; safe arrival
s. & c. ...... shipper and carrier
S. & F.A. ...... shipping and forwarding agent
S. & M. ...... September and March
s.a.n.r. ...... subject to approval no risk (no risk until insurance is confirmed)
S.B. ...... short bill
S/B ...... statement of billing (transp.)
S.C. ...... salvage charges
s.c. & s. ...... strapped, corded, and sealed (transp.)
Sc.B. ...... Bachelor of Science
Sc.D. ...... Doctor of Science
S.C.D. ...... Doctor of Commercial Science
Sc.M. ...... Master of Science
S/D ...... sea-damaged (grain trade); sight draft
S.D.B.L. ...... sight draft, bill of lading attached
S.D.M.J. ...... September, December, March, June
S.E.C. ...... Supreme Economic Council (Russia)
S.F. ...... sinking fund
S.F.S.R. ...... Socialist Federation of Soviet Republics
s.h.p. ...... shaft horsepower

sh.tn. ...... short ton
s.i.t. ...... stopping in transit (transp.)
S.J.D. ...... Doctor of Juridical Science
sk. ...... sack(s)
s.l. ...... salvage loss
S/N ...... shipping note
S.O. ...... seller's option; shipping order; ship's option
S.O.L. ...... shipowner's liability
S.P. ...... supra protest
s.p.a. ...... subject to partial average (marine ins.)
s.p.d. ...... steamer pays dues
sq. ch. ...... square chain(s)
sq. ft. ...... square feet
sq. in. ...... square inch(es)
sq. mi. ...... square mile(s)
sq. rd. ...... square rod(s)
sq. yd. ...... square yard(s)
S.S. ...... steamship; screw steamer
S.S.B. ...... Bachelor of Sacred Scripture
S.S.D. ...... Doctor of Sacred Scripture
S.T.B. ...... Bachelor of Sacred Theology
S.T.D. ...... Doctor of Sacred Theology
std. ...... standard (timber trade)
stg. ...... sterling
stk. ...... stock
str. ...... steamer
S.T.M. ...... Master of Sacred Theology
S. to S. ...... station to station
S.U.C.L. ...... set up in carloads (transp.)
S.U.L.C.L. ...... set up in less than carloads (transp.)
s.v. ...... sailing vessel
S.W. ...... shipper's weights
S.W.G. ...... Standard Wire Gauge

T

t. ...... ton(s)
T.A. ...... Traffic Agent
T. & G. ...... tongued and grooved (timber trade)
t.b. ...... trial balance
T/C ...... until countermanded
T/D ...... time deposit
T.E. ...... trade expenses
tf. *or* t.f. ...... till forbidden (advtg.)
T.G.B. ...... tongued, grooved, and beaded
Th.B. ...... Bachelor of Theology
Th.D. ...... Doctor of Theology
Th.M. ...... Master of Theology
T/L ...... time loan
t.l.o. ...... total loss only (marine ins.)
T/O ...... transfer order
T/R ...... trust receipt
T.R. ...... tons registered (shipping)
T.T. ...... telegraphic transfer

U

U/A ...... underwriting account (marine ins.)
U.J.D. ...... Doctor of Either Law, i.e., Canon Law or Civil Law
ult. ...... of the last month
u.p. ...... under proof
U.S.S.R. ...... Union of Socialist Soviet Republics
U/w ...... underwriter

V

V.C. ...... valuation clause
vide ...... see
V.M.D. ...... Doctor of Veterinary Medicine
v.o.p. ...... value as in original policy

W

W.A. ...... with average (marine ins.)
w. & r. ...... water and rail (transp.)
W.B. ...... water ballast; warehouse book; way bill
w.b.s. ...... without benefit of salvage (marine ins.)
w/d ...... warranted
w.g. ...... weight guaranteed
w.i. ...... when issued (stock exch.)
W.I.I.U. ...... Workers' International Industrial Union
W/M ...... weight and/or measurement
W.O.L. ...... wharfowners' liability
w.p. ...... without prejudice; weather permitting
W.P.A. ...... with particular average (marine ins.)
w.p.p. ...... waterproof paper packing
W.R. ...... warehouse receipt
w.r.o. ...... war risk only
wt. ...... weight
W/W ...... warehouse warrant

X

x-c. *or* x-cp. ...... ex coupon
x-d. *or* x-div. ...... ex dividend
x-i. *or* x-int. ...... ex interest
x-n. ...... ex new
x-rts. ...... ex rights

Index

A

C

D

E

F

H

M

N

O

P

Q

R

S

T

U

V

W

Y

Z